THE MIDDLE EAST UNDER ROME

THE MIDDLE EAST
UNDER ROME

Maurice Sartre

TRANSLATED BY

Catherine Porter and Elizabeth Rawlings

with Jeannine Routier-Pucci

The Belknap Press of Harvard University Press
Cambridge, Massachusetts
London, England
2005

An abridged edition of *D'Alexandre à Zénobie*
by Maurice Sartre, copyright © 2001
Librairie Arthème Fayard.

ISBN 0-674-01683-1 (alk. paper)

Designed by Gwen Nefsky Frankfeldt

CONTENTS

ILLUSTRATIONS

Mithraic relief from Hauran. National Museum, Damascus, Syria. Scala / Art Resource, NY. 305

Votive relief from Palmyra. National Museum, Damascus, Syria. Reproduced from *Syrie: Mémoire et Civilisation* (Flammarion / Institut du Monde Arabe, 1993). 306

Relief from Palmyra showing Tyche and unidentified goddess. National Museum, Damascus, Syria. Erich Lessing / Art Resource, NY. 307

Statue of the goddess Allat in Palmyra. Palmyra Museum. Reproduced from *Städte in der Wüste: Petra, Palmyra und Hatra* by Henri Stierlin (Belser, 1987). 307

Statue of Heliopolitan Jupiter from Baalbek. Réunion des Musées Nationaux / Art Resource, NY. 308

Stele from the Temple of the Winged Lions at Petra. Photograph by Jane Taylor. 308

Small temple at Baalbek. Scala / Art Resource, NY. 311

Plan of the sacred area at Baalbek. From *Religionsgeschichte Syriens: Von der Frühzeit bis zur Gegenwart* by Peter W. Haider, Manfred Hutter, and Siegfried Kreuzer (W. Kohlhammer, 1996; Editions Gallimard). 312

Model of the sanctuary of Bel in Palmyra. Palmyra Museum. Reproduced from *Städte in der Wüste: Petra, Palmyra und Hatra* by Henri Stierlin (Belser, 1987). 313

Plan of the temple of Bel in Palmyra. Reproduced from *D'Alexandre à Zénobie* by Maurice Sartre (Fayard, 2001), p. 915. 314

Fresco from the synagogue at Dura-Europos: Samuel anointing David. Art Resource, NY. 326

Marble head of Philip the Arab (M. Iulius Philippus). Museum in Shahba, Syria. Erich Lessing / Art Resource, NY. 348

PREFACE TO THE
ENGLISH-LANGUAGE EDITION

GLEN BOWERSOCK'S friendship and the attention he has given to my work for many years provided the basis for this English-language edition of my book, which was published in France under the title *D'Alexandre à Zénobie: Histoire du Levant antique, IVe siècle av. J.-C.–IIIe siècle apr. J.-C.* That work (1,196 pages long, in the revised edition published in September 2003) would have been difficult to produce in translation, and we agreed that it should be condensed for publication in the United States. Rather than abridge the whole in order to produce a more accessible volume—which might reduce the appeal it seems to have had for its original readers—I have willingly adopted Glen Bowersock's wise suggestion that I excerpt the Roman sections without cuts. All of the "Roman" chapters of the French edition, with illustrations, are found here intact, except for some revisions to avoid reference to developments described in the original edition but missing from this one. Moreover, I wanted to include in this text certain historical information that is indispensable to a full understanding of the whole. Chapter 1 is entirely new; it offers a summary of the earlier events that seemed crucial to the understanding of the stakes and the problems facing the Roman administrative authority. Lastly, although the additions to our knowledge since the French edition was first published (May 2001) have not been revolutionary, I have tried to enrich this edition with the most recently published information and to correct various errors or lapses that had previously escaped me. The book that is offered here to English readers, although taken directly from the French edition, is in part a new work, more limited in chronological scope but revised and brought up to date. This difference between the two editions accounts for the occasional references to the French edition regarding developments related to the Hellenistic era.

This American edition has benefited from significant improvements. Not only has it been enriched by all the corrections suggested for the second French edition—in particular, by Julien Aliquot, Pierre-Louis Gatier, Annie Sartre-Fauriat, and Jean-Baptiste Yon—but Catherine Porter's attentive reading and patient research has made it possible to complete or correct a large number of references. In the course of our meetings and exchanges, I was able to appreciate the pertinence of her observations and the quality of her work. If this book is less imperfect than its original model, it is in large part thanks to her and her colleagues, and I want to express my full gratitude here. Finally, I must single out Glen Bowersock as the alpha and omega of this adventure. His thorough rereading has allowed me to avoid those errors that only a specialist in the period can spot, and to make sure that the translation is in compliance with Anglo-American conventions. I would like him to know, once again, how deeply grateful I am.

Maurice Sartre

ACKNOWLEDGMENTS

WRITING A BOOK is always a personal undertaking. In the present case it has been a long and drawn-out process, because some chapters were first drafted more than ten years ago. As an author who set out to traverse arid stretches of erudition, I know very well how much I owe to those who made it possible to stay the course, who provided missing resources at just the right time, who more than once removed methodological or documentary obstacles, and who offered encouragement at every stage of the process. For a long time, I doubted that I would ever reach my goal; I kept deferring an end point that seemed to recede with every step I took. Was I like every other author for whom "tomorrow," like the Arabic word *boukra,* means "someday," or even "never"? I needed to reach that end point. In the process, many people helped, whether they knew it or not.

I think first of the students in Tours, who contributed more than they realized, chapter by chapter, to the development and maturation of this book. The final result is quite different from the early discussions they heard, and the material has been continually enriched over time; still, thanks to them, their questions and sometimes their incomprehension, I knew whenever I was on the wrong track. Whatever this book has gained in clarity and readability, it owes to them—and this is not an empty phrase.

The material for this book comes from innumerable publications devoted to ancient Syria, but I cannot express how much I have learned from contact with colleagues working in the field. I would have to acknowledge the abundant correspondence, the conversations, and the exchanges of publications that have kept me in constant touch with a great many remarkable scholars around the world. I do not dare attempt to name them all, for fear of omitting many. I must, however, express my gratitude here to Glen W. Bowersock, whose friendship enabled me to spend two months in the spring of 2002 as a visitor at the Institute for Advanced Study at Princeton. His encouragement and his own work, always stimulating, have been of immeasurable benefit. My undertaking has also been nourished throughout by Jean-Charles and Janine Balty, Edward Dąbrowa, David Graf, Benjamin Isaac, David Kennedy, Michael Macdonald, Thomas Parker, Andreas Schmidt-Colinet, and Thomas Weber, to name just a few of those who have assiduously kept me informed about their own work.

My colleagues and friends in France are too numerous to count. I will mention only those who worked in some capacity at the Institut français d'archéologie du Proche-Orient, its successive directors Georges Tate, François Villeneuve, Jean-Marie Dentzer, and Jean-Louis Huot, who were always welcoming, and also those colleagues who offered intellectual assistance at one time or another: Frédéric Alpi, Catherine Aubert, Pierre-Marie Blanc, Marc Griesheimer, Mikaël Kalos, and Jacques Seigne. I must also express my gratitude to my friends at the Maison de l'Orient Méditeranéen-Jean-Pouilloux, particularly Marie-Françoise Boussac, Georges Rougement, Jean-François Salles, and Pierre-Louis Gatier. I would be remiss if I did not add my friends Françoise Briquel-Chatonnet, Denis Feissel, Pierre Leriche, Leila Nehmé, and Javier Teixidor, whose works have been immensely valuable. Finally, I must not neglect my friends and colleagues at Tours who have endured, particularly during these past few months, my near-monomania for Syria: Nancy Gauthier, Brigitte Beaujard, Frédéric Hurlet, and Christophe Hugoniot have given me more than they know. Among my Tours colleagues I am particularly indebted to Patrice Brun, who graciously agreed to reread the entire manuscript and did so in record time, allowing me to avoid a great many errors while at the same time pointing out publications I had overlooked.

Finally, I am grateful to my wife, Annie Sartre-Fauriat, for her many useful suggestions, important corrections, and necessary changes, not to mention our frequent and always profitable discussions about Syria—and for a great deal more, of course, as goes without saying for someone who has been a traveling companion throughout Syria for so many years. Some debts can never be repaid.

My thanks go to all, though I alone am responsible for the omissions and mistakes that diligent censors will not fail to point out. I accept their reproofs in advance, knowing that six centuries of history as fertile as the period outlined here, enriched by two centuries of scholarship, cannot be summarized with impunity.

Maurice Sartre

TRANSLATORS' NOTE

FOR THEIR HELP in making the English translation as accurate and complete as possible, we would like to thank Glen Bowersock, Ross Brann, Culver Mowers, Philip Lewis, Pietro Pucci, Hunter Rawlings, Jeffrey Rusten, and Karin Schlapbach. We owe special thanks to our manuscript editor, Wendy Nelson, for her patience and persistence in bringing consistency to an exceptionally complex scholarly apparatus. Above all, we wish to thank the author himself for his willingness to review our work, his prompt answers to our queries, and his invaluable help in preparing the comprehensive list of works cited.

Catherine Porter
Elizabeth Rawlings
Jeannine Routier-Pucci

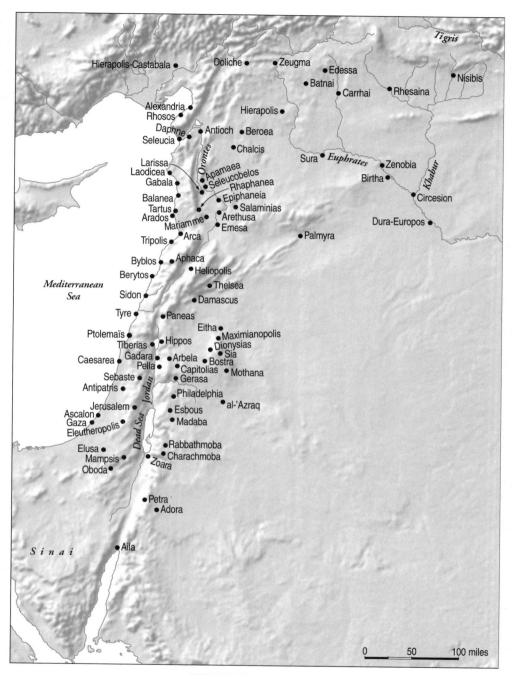

Tigris

Hierapolis-Castabala •   Doliche •   • Zeugma
    • Edessa   • Nisibis
• Batnai
• Carrhai   • Rhesaina

Alexandria •   Hierapolis •
Rhosos •
Daphne •   • Antioch   • Beroea
Seleucia •

• Chalcis

Sura •   *Euphrates*   • Zenobia

Larissa •   *Orontes*
Laodicea •   • Apamaea   • Birtha
Gabala •   • Seleucobelos
     • Rhaphanea   *Khabur*
Balanea •   • Epiphaneia   • Circesion
Tartus •   • Salaminias
Arados •   Mariamme •   • Arethusa
     • Emesa   • Dura-Europos
Tripolis •   • Arca
     • Palmyra
Byblos •   • Aphaca
Berytos •   • Heliopolis

Mediterranean
Sea
Sidon •   • Thelsea
     • Damascus
Tyre •   • Paneas
     Eitha •
Ptolemaïs •   • Maximianopolis
Tiberias •   Hippos •   Dionysias •
Caesarea •   Gadara •   Arbela •   • Sia
    Pella •   • Bostra
Sebaste •   • Capitolias   • Mothana
Antipatris •   • Gerasa
Jerusalem •   • Philadelphia
Ascalon •   • Esbous   • al-'Azraq
Gaza •   • Madaba
Eleutheropolis •
    Jordan
Elusa •   • Rabbathmoba
Mampsis •   • Charachmoba
Oboda •   *Zoara*
    Dead Sea
    • Petra
    • Adora

Sinai   • Aila

0   50   100 miles

THE ROMAN MIDDLE EAST

I N T R O D U C T I O N

THE Near East? The Middle East? Today's terminology hesitates to define spaces with imprecise limits, even though current events place them at the heart of our preoccupations every day. Should I have gone back to the ancient terms? The uncertainty would probably be just as great, and, as we shall see, the ambiguity would not have disappeared. So I have had to choose, and to explain. The term *Middle East* designates, in this book, not the vast set of countries that are often included, from Turkey to Iran and Yemen; rather, it refers to what is roughly the central part of the Near East, a region ancient authors would doubtless have designated by the umbrella term *Syria*. But this term, too, is ambiguous and has always designated a space with shifting borders.

Today, in the narrowest sense it has ever known, the word *Syria* designates a country of about 180,000 square kilometers, occupying the northeast part of the Fertile Crescent, from the Mediterranean Sea to the Middle Euphrates. If we were to go back a little more than half a century, we would have to add contemporary Lebanon and the Turkish vilayet of Hatay—that is, the Antioch region.[1] If we are speaking of ancient Syria, the term covers a larger but no less ambiguous space; indeed, it has at least two common meanings. On the one hand, *Syria* refers to the entire inner portion of the land bordered by the northeastern fringe of the Mediterranean. It is land that was populated by the Aramaeans, land that has been called at least since the beginning of the first millennium *kol Aram*, "all Aram," a term that the Greeks later Hellenized, without understanding it, as *Koile*

Syria (Coele Syria), translated as "Hollow Syria."[2] In this restricted sense, Syria is distinguished from coastal Phoenicia and from Palestine, which prolongs it to the south. On the other hand, the word *Syria* can also be used to designate the whole of the western Semitic Near East between the Mediterranean and the Euphrates or the Syro-Arabian desert, including Phoenicia and the southern Levant: the territory of the Achaemenid satrapy of Eber Nahr, "beyond-the-river," or the Transeuphrates, for an observer located in Babylon or in Susa. It is in this broader sense that I am using the term here, unless there is explicit mention to the contrary (for example, when I am discussing the Roman province of Syria). The territory has sometimes been extended to Commagene, and even (although less often) to Cilicia, regions whose history has been linked at least at certain times with that of their more southerly neighbors.

Why choose the Middle East, or rather—since it is the term that will be used from here on throughout the book, in order to avoid a terminological anachronism—ancient Syria, in the definition of what I have just presented as the object of study? By focusing on this region, I am not seeking to deny the interest of the other regions opened up to the Greeks by Alexander's conquests, or to affirm the primacy of Syria. But one of the reasons that can be put forward, perhaps the main one, is the disdain manifested toward Syria—consciously or not—by historians. Hellenistic Syria has never been the object of a real synthesis, has never been at the center of a comprehensive study. Among the few attempts that come close, that of Félix-Marie Abel covers only the provinces of ancient Israel and part of the Transjordan,[3] and that of John D. Grainger is limited to Hellenistic Phoenicia.[4] Most of the time, Hellenistic Syria has been studied only in passing, in a general history of the Seleucids or the Ptolemies, or even of the Roman Empire. Much the same was true for the imperial era, until Fergus Millar devoted a vast synthesis to the Roman Near East, a synthesis in which Syria as I am viewing it here obviously holds a highly prominent place.[5] The disingenuous claim that our information is limited and inherently inadequate cannot be used indefinitely as an alibi.[6]

In any event, one cannot neglect the Hellenistic antecedents in which the history of Roman Syria is rooted, certainly not the crucial phenomenon of "Hellenization." How did Phoenicians, Jews, Aramaeans, and Arabs react to the conquest? How did they take in the new way of life, the new language, the new forms of political organization introduced by the Greeks? How did the Greeks settle in, and what upheavals did they provoke as they appropriated and exploited the land? What was their policy toward the natives, and how successful was it? Three centuries of Greek presence in Syria profoundly marked the political, economic, social, cultural, and even religious structures of the country. A synthetic summary of these changes is provided in Chapter 1, focusing in particular on those developments that were destined to endure into the Roman era.[7]

Naturally, the arrival of the Roman *imperatores* raises new questions. How did Rome organize the Roman province of Syria and then the provinces created later? What role did it assign to the indigenous elites emerging from the Hellenistic colonization, and how did it integrate them into the governing classes of the empire? How did a western power whose culture and language were Latin take over the Hellenistic cultural heritage? How was Syrian Hellenism transformed and perpetuated up to the dawn of the Christian empire?

But the questions are not limited to the seemingly colonial phenomenon of the spread of Hellenism. For the integration of Syria first into the Greek world and then more broadly into the Roman Empire offered the opportunity for cults and customs originating in Syria or Arabia to spread well beyond their starting point. Thus we need to pay attention to the diffusion of Syrian and Arabian cults outside of Syria; we need to analyze the syncretisms to which they were subjected, and measure the attraction they exercised over newcomers and the transformations they underwent owing to the Hellenization of some of their adherents. Similarly, we shall try to see to what extent there was a properly Syrian contribution to Greek civilization, or rather try to discern a "Syrian" version of Hellenism. Finally, we shall have to take into account all the resistances, passive and active, to the imported modes, resistances that were asserted with violence in certain Jewish milieus but that were no less real in other sectors of the population, Aramaean or Arab.

I have chosen to present here just one period in the long history of Greek Syria. Of the thousand years of the presence of Hellenism in the Near East, between Alexander's conquest and the defeat of the Byzantine armies on the banks of the Yarmuk in 636, this book deals only with the three and a half centuries between Pompey's annexation of Syria in 64 B.C.E. and the fall of Palmyra in 272 C.E. A brief history, perhaps, but one in which Syria was profoundly transformed. Moreover, we cannot forget that this period does not constitute a uniform era. The creation of the Pompeian province probably brought some security to an area where brigands were at large, but it also threw all of Syria into the convulsions of the Roman civil war. Peace and security did not return until the 30s B.C.E., although Augustus's reign did not mark a radical break with the former period in terms of the organization and management of Roman Syria, where client states and principalities proliferated—a situation that ended with the annexation of the client state of Nabataea under Trajan, in 106, and the creation of the province of Arabia. The conquest did not end there (Lucius Verus and, after him, Septimius Severus extended the empire beyond the Euphrates), nor did the history of the client states (two survived: Osrhoene and Hatra), but by annexing the Nabataean kingdom, Trajan truly marked the liquidation of the situation that had been created by the emergence of indigenous states in Syr,ia starting in the middle of the second century B.C.E. The whole of Syria was finally provincialized, thus regaining a unified administrative management (by way of three provinces) that it had scarcely known since the Achaemenid period.

A period of great prosperity opened up at this point for Syria, although we cannot establish a direct link between this phenomenon and the political decision to provincialize. The second and third centuries probably marked a sort of apogee for Greco-Roman Syria: a flourishing economy to which Palmyra and the Phoenician ports bear witness; an intense civic life in a grandiose monumental framework; prosperous villages even in regions the least well suited to harbor them, on the fringes of the steppes and the desert. This did not prevent crises (the Bar Kokhba revolt) or foreign invasions (Ardashir's invasion around 230), but broadly speaking the Syrian provinces enjoyed a prosperity that seemed to be maintained well beyond the era of the Severi.

The decision to conclude this presentation with the fall of Palmyra is more symbolic than historically pertinent. To be sure, the seizure of the city and the capture of Queen Zenobia took place after a long period of troubles that had weakened Syria. But the effects do not lend themselves to analysis, and we have to wait for Diocletian's reign to draw all of their military and administrative consequences. I could just as well have extended this study up to the reforms of the tetrarchy, or to Constantine's death (337),[8] or even to Julian's (363), the latter marking the return of peace with the Persians. But it seemed to me that by stopping on the eve of Diocletian's reforms, I could maintain a certain unity in the subject I am addressing, and that to go further I would have had to take into account two new developments that established the originality of Byzantine Syria: the reform of the defense system, involving recourse to neighboring nomadic tribes, and Christianization, which was well under way before the end of the third century and became an essential factor starting with the Edict of Milan in 313.

THE HELLENISTIC LEGACY

IN NOVEMBER 333, on the Issos plain, Alexander the Great won an unexpected victory over the Persian army led by Darius III Codomanos. The outcome of this single battle opened all of Syria to Alexander, because the Macedonian had chosen to move in the direction of Mesopotamia to rebuild his troops. After some local difficulties in Tyre and later in Gaza, Syria had a new master.

Having become a satrapy of Alexander's empire (except for Phoenicia, which, although subjugated, kept its own kings), Syria was the object of heated struggles among Alexander's generals and successors after his death in Babylonia in June 323. For Syria unquestionably represented a strategic stake of the first order. Ptolemy, who held Egypt, saw it as the traditional rampart of the Delta and a means for preventing any invader coming out of the north from approaching the Nile Valley. Those who, like Perdiccas and then Antigonos Monophthalmos, tried to take over Alexander's entire legacy viewed Syria as the indispensable link in the long chain of communication that tied the Mediterranean world to Mesopotamia, Iran, and Central Asia. And for those who were opposed to seeing a single man in command of the entire empire, the conquest of Syria was to endanger Antigonos's overall authority.[1]

The long and complex conflicts that followed entered an initial phase of stabilization after the defeat and death of Antigonos Monophthalmos at Ipsos in 301.[2] While Ptolemy I took control of the entire southern region of Syria, including Phoenicia[3] up to the frontier of Eleutheros (nahr al-

Kebir), Seleucos I was granted full possession of the country by his allies (except Ptolemy), although he was actually able to take control only of what would henceforth be known as "Seleukis," along with just one Phoenician city-state, Arados. But this solution could only be provisional, as Seleucos I did not give up his rights to the entire country; he refrained from waging war against Ptolemy I only because of the long-standing bonds of friendship between them. Indeed, after Ptolemy I died in 283 and Seleucos I in 281, their successors fought a series of wars—about which we know very little—for control of the country. Only in 200–198 did Antiochos III succeed in driving the Ptolemies out of their Syrian territories for good, and in recapturing all that Seleucos I had been granted after the battle of Ipsos.[4]

But even this situation did not last. Although the Ptolemies were unable to reestablish an enduring foothold in Syria, other powers emerged and contributed to shrinking the Seleucids' Syrian holdings. The existence of a Nabataean kingdom in the southern Transjordan region by the late fourth century had probably prevented the Ptolemies from exercising their authority in that area. During the second century, the Nabataean state was continually expanding toward the north (it eventually covered most of contemporary Jordan and part of southern Syria), while it was also progressing toward the sea, in Idumaea (the Negev), up to the outskirts of Gaza. Other states soon appeared on the scene. The most important was that of the Hasmonaeans, created in Judaea around Jerusalem in 150–140, as a result of the extremely violent revolt carried out by traditional Jews under Judas Maccabaeus and his brothers against the Hellenized Jews and their Seleucid supporters; the Hasmonaean state rapidly spread beyond its point of origin.

We are less well informed about the regions located farther north, but there, too, new states, some of considerable scope (Commagene, a kingdom in the Amanus region) and some extremely small, profited from the internal conflicts among members of the Seleucid royal family to acquire de facto independence. Commagene, centered around Samosata, was probably already organized in the third century, but it became autonomous during the second century. Around 132 B.C.E., the Greek city of Edessa fell under the control of an Arab dynasty.[5] Other micro-states were constituted in the mountains, in particular in central Lebanon, where they remained up to the Roman era.

But despite the difficulties encountered by the Seleucids beginning around 150 B.C.E., the Hellenistic period marked a profound change in the history of Syria. The Greeks were hardly unknown to the Phoenicians,[6] who had been doing business with them for more than half a millennium.

For a century, relations had been intensifying, for two reasons: Phoenician merchants traded in Piraeus and probably also in the other major Greek ports, and, starting in the late fifth century, numerous Greeks enlisted in the Achaemenid armies stationed in Syria and Phoenicia. It is difficult to measure the reciprocal influences with any precision, but one thing is clear: by the end of the fifth century, some inhabitants of Phoenicia had adopted various Greek customs and objects. For example, by the fifth century several city-states had begun to mint coins following the Greek example, and the practice became widespread during the fourth century. A pronounced taste for Greek art became apparent, as attested by the lavish sarcophagi of the royal Sidonian necropolis, and even by the anthropoid sarcophagi of the same region. It would be going too far to speak of "Hellenization," but it is at least legitimate to assume that Syria enjoyed a certain familiarity with things Greek.[7]

Though some features of Syria remained unchanged, Alexander's conquest and the creation of Hellenistic kingdoms brought about deeper and more rapid transformations.[8] In the first place, modifications were introduced into existing political structures. Starting with the fall of the Aramaean kingdoms in the eighth century, then the fall of Israel and Judaea, Syria had become accustomed to being controlled by a state whose political center was far away: Assur, Nineveh, Persepolis. After the conquest, Syria became the heart of the Seleucid kingdom, with its capital at Antioch. For the Syria of the Ptolemaic south, in the third century, Alexandria was close by. Far from being a remote province in a great empire, Syria was now at the very center of power.

Moreover, fairly rapidly, large numbers of colonizers from Greece and the wider Aegean basin settled in Syria. The movement began shortly after Alexander's conquest, and it continued until at least the middle of the third century. To be sure, there were significant regional disparities, but the fact remains that tens of thousands of Greeks populated Syria and put new customs and practices on display. Not that they sought to be models, or wanted to persuade the indigenous populations to behave as they did. Contrary to a widespread opinion, the Greek and Macedonian conquerors did not feel that they had to carry out a civilizing mission, and they did not seek to "Hellenize" anyone at all. Unlike many colonial enterprises of more recent periods, the Macedonian conquest left everyone free to accept acculturation or not. As Isocrates declared as early as the middle of the fourth century, Athens "has brought it about that the name 'Hellenes' suggests no longer a race but an intelligence, and that the title 'Hellenes' is applied rather to those who share our culture than to those who share a common blood."[9] Thus to be "Greek" no longer meant simply that one was born Greek; it meant that one identified with Greek culture, or with some fundamental aspects of that culture—in particular, the use of the Greek language. This is, moreover, the first meaning of the verb *hellenizein*, "to speak Greek." To this we can add the choice of clothing, the practice of sports (and athletic nudity), the consumption of wine and olive oil, participation in Greek competitions, and devotion to the Greek gods. But none of these practices was obligatory, and there must have been a great variety of "Greeks" in Hellenistic Syria, depending on how many features of Hellenism each individual adopted.[10]

A second essential aspect of Hellenistic Syria, one whose effect continued to be felt up to the Islamic conquest and beyond, was the foundation of many Greek city-states *(poleis),* by either the creation of new cities or the transformation of existing ones.[11] Among the new cities, we need only think of Antioch, Seleucia in Pieria, Apamaea, and Laodicea, the four "sister cities" of the Syrian Tetrapolis, or Dura-Europos in the Euphrates Valley. All were well positioned to welcome the new Greek and Macedonian colonizers, who needed a familiar framework in order to feel at home in the foreign environment. Several dozen new (or practically new) cities thus arose, chiefly in "Seleucid" Syria and in the Euphrates Valley. But the model they provided was soon imitated elsewhere, particularly in the native cities that had received from their kings the right to set themselves up as poleis. This happened very early on with Phoenician cities that got rid of their kings and simply gave Greek names to their ancient civic institutions. They were imitated by virtually all the indigenous cities, such as Damascus, Rabbath Ammon (Amman), Ascalon, Gaza, and even, briefly, Jerusalem.[12]

This urbanization effort (in northern Syria) and the transformation of urban institutions profoundly modified Syria's political, social, and cultural organization. By the third century, countless members of the indigenous population who had acquired some of the distinctive features of the Greeks were considered Greek. Inhabitants of Tyre, Sidon, and Byblos, for example, were accepted as competitors at the great Panhellenic games at Olympia and Delphi;[13] there is hardly a better way to demonstrate that Syria was now part of the Greek world. From then on, when the Syrian Greeks are mentioned, the term applies not only to the descendants of the former Greek and Macedonian colonizers, but especially to the numerous indigenous Phoenician, Aramaean, Jewish, and Arab families who spoke Greek and who had espoused some features of Greek culture and the Greek way of life.

Despite the undeniable success of Greek culture in Syria, as attested by numerous philosophers, orators, and poets,[14] it would be a mistake to think that Syria as a whole had suddenly been transformed into a "New Hellas."

For outside the cities, and even within them, there were still large numbers of people who had conserved intact their culture and ancestral traditions—their language first and foremost. In Phoenicia, to be sure, the Phoenician language steadily lost ground; both written and spoken forms had disappeared almost completely by the beginning of the Christian era. It was gradually replaced by Greek, but also by Aramaic, as has recently been demonstrated.[15] Everywhere else, Aramaic continued to be the principal language of communication. We have too little information about the countryside of Hellenistic Syria to say whether Hellenism penetrated deep into the rural populations, but a few scattered indications point to the almost complete maintenance of native traditions where religious life and naming patterns were concerned. Not that there was any deliberate rejection of foreign customs; there was simply indifference on the part of populations from whom royal power expected nothing more than the payment of taxes and the absence of conflict.

Most of the time, the confrontation between cultures did not lead to major uprisings. But there was one exception, involving the Jews.[16] The Jews were no more subject than the other inhabitants of Hellenistic Syria to pressure from their new masters to adopt Greek culture. But, as happened elsewhere, some community leaders adopted a few elements of that culture, including the language. One can argue ad infinitum about the underlying reasons for the choices made by these leaders: a sincere espousal of a seductive culture, an interest in modernizing ancient practices, a desire to wipe out Jewish particularism, or mere political opportunism with the goal of holding on to power. The underlying cause is of little significance here; moreover, it undoubtedly varied from one person to another. In any case, there were enough Hellenized Jews in the governing classes—led by the high priest Jason himself—to propose the transformation of Jerusalem into a *polis*, an Antioch-Jerusalem, in 175. This extreme measure, which did not challenge the Jewish character of the city (the accusations of its adversaries notwithstanding) and did not directly threaten Judaism itself, met with total incomprehension on the part of the majority, and soon unleashed a popular uprising fueled by the extravagant cost of this decision. The revolt of "the Maccabees" came as a considerable shock for Hellenistic Judaism. It obliged everyone to choose sides unambiguously, and, as in any civil war, it led early on to a radicalization of the extremists on both sides. But in the long run it obliged the Jews to take a stand with respect to Greek culture, and to consider whether or not it would be possible to preserve the Judaism of Nehemiah and Esdras intact in a world that had changed and in which Hellenism enjoyed prestige as the culture of the governing elites.[17]

Once the weight of the stringent measures taken against Judaism in 168 was lifted, the Jews succeeded in expelling first the most extreme "Hellenists"[18] and then the Seleucid occupying troops. Thus a new and independent Jewish state, something that had not been seen since the fall of Jerusalem to the Babylonians in 587, gradually emerged. The imperialism of this state became quickly apparent as it sought to expand throughout the southern Levant and adopted some of the features of the Hellenistic states: the high priest assumed the royal title *(basileus)* in 104–103 B.C.E. Leaving aside the fundamental innovations that were introduced into Judaism around this time (Messianism, anticipation of the end-time, and belief in the resurrection of the dead), it should be noted that, out of the violent confrontation arising from its resistance to Hellenization, Judaism emerged highly Hellenized.

The history of Hellenistic Syria cannot be reduced to a clash of cultures, or to a more or less fertile coexistence.[19] The settling of Greek and Macedonian colonists also resulted in a partial redistribution of land, traces of which are found in recently excavated fossil records. Farming practices were not disturbed, and the newcomers clearly had a great deal to learn from the indigenous inhabitants about agricultural techniques, irrigation in particular. But the needs of the Greeks, whether colonists or Hellenized natives, nevertheless encouraged the cultivation of particular crops such as grapes and olives. Similarly, certain things considered indispensable to the Greek lifestyle had to be imported: the flow of trade between all the settlements of the eastern Mediterranean expanded and intensified. Thanks to the Zeno archive,[20] we have a greater understanding of the essential role of the Phoenician ports that received goods from throughout the Aegean world or the North Sea, and shipped them on to Egypt and probably to the interior of Syria and Mesopotamia. In fact, Alexander's conquest contributed to the creation of a more homogeneous economic region comprising all the settlements of the eastern Mediterranean, despite the continuation of distinct states and separate monetary systems.[21] At the same time, Syria became (in competition with Alexandria) the crossroads for trade in luxury goods from Arabia Felix, India, and China, such as incense, myrrh, perfumes, spices, and silk. This contributed to its growing wealth, but also gave it its reputation as a mythical land: how could a country that produced the most expensive items (such as Tyrian purple) not be fabulously rich?

And yet, at the time when this story begins, Syria had been through several decades of countless political problems, with consequences for the populations involved that are difficult to assess.

We must go back to the death of Antiochos IV to understand the causes. Three mutually exacerbating factors combined to permanently weaken the authority of the Seleucid kings. The first was a dynastic crisis: a crisis of legitimacy that led to usurpations and hence to fratricidal conflicts in Syria itself. The second was a rise in local autonomy: in Judaea, but also in Syria, in the coastal cities as well as among the Arab tribes of the interior, local populations took advantage of the dynastic crisis to distance themselves from royal authority and to wangle their "freedom" in exchange for promising support to various competitors; in some cases, they simply filled the vacuum left by the disappearance of the royal administration. Finally, external pressures and interventions increased. Beginning with Ptolemy VI, the Ptolemies intentionally kindled dynastic quarrels, often through convenient marriages of Ptolemean princesses to Seleucids. The Parthian advance paralyzed the most energetic leaders (Demetrios II, Antiochos VII) and threatened Syria itself at the beginning of the first century. The Nabataeans advanced toward the north, approaching Damascus. Rome, which had followed the events in Syria ever since the time of the treaty of Apamaea in 188, intervened more and more directly in Syrian affairs.

To appreciate the situation the Romans encountered at the time of Syria's annexation, we must consider certain prior events that had a lasting impact on the history of Roman Syria.

We need not be concerned here with the origins and multiple vicissitudes of the dynastic crisis, because it was already coming to an end: the two powerless minor kings who were competing for power in Syria had no bearing on the history of the country. Nevertheless, we should remember that the war between the Seleucid claimants constituted an almost permanent background for all the events that figure in this final episode of Hellenistic Syrian history, and this background explains in large part why the kings were powerless to deal with the difficulties facing them.[22]

However, we need to highlight the emergence of the surrounding states, which were Hellenistic although ruled by local dynasties: the Hasmonaean state, the Nabataean kingdom, and Commagene, not to mention other secondary states encountered during the first century of the Roman presence. Although in some ways the Hasmonaean state concerns us the least (politically, in any case), it is nevertheless useful to look at its broad outlines, because it achieved the unification of a vast part of southern Syria that retained a degree of originality.

We shall then turn our attention to the pressures brought to bear on Syria from distant but still influential powers, in particular Parthia and Rome, in order to focus on the origins of the presence of each in the eastern Mediterranean region and to see the first contacts between them take shape. We shall also try to understand how they came to be there.

Finally, we must conclude with an episode that marks the first time the

Seleucids lost control of Syria: the Armenian conquest. A brief summary of the problems that existed on the eve of the Roman intervention will be helpful.

THE CREATION OF NEW STATES

The Hasmonaean State

The new Jewish state, built upon the ruins left following the Maccabaean revolt, won its independence slowly. Not only was it constantly challenged by the Seleucids, it also had to deal with hostility from some of its neighbors and with opposition from within. Nevertheless, it ultimately achieved de facto, if not de jure, independence, despite the fact that the process was interrupted by harsh setbacks and resounding defeats. In addition, the Hasmonaean state was expanding even before its independence was entirely assured. When independence finally seemed to have been achieved, the state covered nearly all of the southern Levant. Was it a national Jewish state in the tradition of King David, or was it instead a Hellenistic kingdom that brought diverse populations together under its authority? It is impossible to keep entirely separate these two aspects of the creation of the Hasmonaean state.[23]

The primary stages in the territorial development of the Hasmonaean state can be summarized briefly. When Jonathan, Judas Maccabaeus's brother, first came to power in Jerusalem in 152, his authority scarcely extended beyond the narrowest boundaries of Judaea—that is, the region around Jerusalem (including Azotus, Joppa, and perhaps Ascalon).[24] This was the situation for the most part until 142, when King Demetrios II ceded to Jonathan the three Samaritan districts of Aphairema, Lydda, and Ramathain, to which the Jews laid claim by virtue of an ancient concession made by Alexander the Great.[25] These fragile acquisitions appeared to be seriously compromised when an energetic Seleucid king, Antiochos VII, besieged Jerusalem. The city fell in 131, but the king's disappearance during an expedition against the Parthians allowed John Hyrcanos to resume his expansionist policy, first in Samaria, where he seized Shechem and destroyed the Mount Gerizim temple in 128,[26] then on the coast, where he succeeded in occupying all the coastal cities with the exception of Gaza, Ascalon, and Ptolemais. At the same time, he waged war in Idumaea, where, after sacking Marisa (in 112–111) and Adora,[27] he seized numerous villages, taking some, such as Beersheba, from the Nabataeans (by 104 at the latest), and forcibly converted the inhabitants to Judaism.[28] Between 111 and the beginning of 108, he razed Samaria, then seized Scythopolis.[29]

Only a short while later, Rome recognized the Jewish possession of the conquered lands for the first time.[30] This was a continuation of a long-standing policy of alliance that had not lapsed despite the Hasmonaeans' growing power. Starting in 165 or 164, Roman legates passing through Syria had offered their good offices and support for the Jews who were in revolt against the Seleucids, and in 161 Judas sent an ambassador to Rome. Jonathan had renewed the friendship and alliance in 146. His brother Simon later was confirmed as high priest, general, and ethnarch of the Jews by a popular assembly in 140, and shortly afterward sent his own ambassador, who obtained a *senatus consultum,* a decree of the Roman Senate, guaranteeing the Jews possession of their territory;[31] all the independent cities and states of the Orient were notified. Hyrcanos in turn had his title of "friend and ally" renewed around 127–125. It is clear that every new ruler of Judaea had to obtain recognition from Rome, which seemed to provide security against a new Seleucid offensive.

Jewish independence asserted itself increasingly during this period. The appearance of an independent Jewish coinage minted around 110 provides additional evidence.[32] According to Aramaic legend, this first coinage was issued in the name of "Yehohanan the High Priest and the council [or community][33] of the Jews," with a cornucopia. It was a tangible sign of the birth of a new state, the very symbol of sovereignty. When John Hyrcanos died at the beginning of 104, after a thirty-one-year reign, the Hasmonaean state seemed firmly established.

Following the very brief reign of his brother Aristobulos (104–103), Alexander Jannaeus resumed the expansionist policies of his predecessors.[34] He occupied the entire coast from Carmel to Gaza, and took over Gadara in the Transjordan.[35] In the same year, Jannaeus set off to campaign in the opposite direction, seizing Raphia and Anthedon and defeating Gaza, which was forced to surrender after a yearlong siege, despite assistance from the Nabataeans, for whom it was the natural outlet to the sea.[36] Jannaeus attacked the Nabataeans once more, seeking control of Moab and Galaad, the western sectors of the Transjordan. But the war with Obodas I ended in disaster for the Hasmonaeans on the Golan (the battle of Garada).[37]

In 88 or 87, Jannaeus faced yet another Seleucid army, headed this time by Antiochos XII Dionysos, who planned to conquer the Nabataeans. Jannaeus tried in vain to build a fortified wall (of wood) from Kapharsaba to Joppa, but he was unable to stop Antiochos XII, who passed through but was defeated and killed by the Nabataeans in the battle of Cana.[38] Aretas III attacked Judaea in turn, around 84–83, and handed Jannaeus one more defeat in the battle of Adida.[39] However, this did not prevent

Jannaeus from expanding his empire across the Jordan River in subsequent years as he conquered Pella, Dion, Esbous, Seleucia-Hippos, and Gamala. By the time he died in 76, almost all of the southern Levant, the western Golan, and a large swath in the Transjordan from Mount Hermon to the east of the Dead Sea—the area of the country that had the greatest rainfall and therefore was the most fertile—were under his control. Only Ascalon had eluded him.

With the death of Alexander Jannaeus, the kingdom experienced a period of internal strife that halted further expansion. Jannaeus's widow, Salome Alexandra, ruled as queen while her oldest son, Hyrcanos II, quite overshadowed, had to be content with the title of high priest. A woman assuming royal power alone while there were adult male heirs was something entirely new. Alexandra had no incentive to engage in a war abroad; the presence of Tigranes, a powerful new leader in Syria, was an inducement to lie low. The most she could do was send an expedition to protect Damascus from the maneuvers of Ptolemy, son of the Ituraean chief Mennaios, after Aretas III had evacuated the city. When she died, in 67, the quarrel that had been simmering between her two sons finally broke out.

Hyrcanos II had probably assumed the title of king before his mother's death, but his brother challenged his right to govern. After several battles, a peace was concluded in which Hyrcanos agreed to cede royal power to his brother Aristobulos (II) in exchange for a guarantee protecting his property.[40] Josephus says nothing about it, but it is most likely that Hyrcanos retained the office of high priest. That did not suit the Idumaean Antipatros, a former member of the inner circle around Jannaeus and Alexandra, who managed to persuade Hyrcanos that his life was in danger and that he should seek refuge among the Nabataeans, with whom Antipatros enjoyed privileged relations (he had married a Nabataean). Hyrcanos hesitated briefly, but finally agreed to call on Aretas III for help. The latter, who hoped to regain the Transjordan villages he had had to give up to Jannaeus, did not hesitate to come in and crush Aristobulos II, who took refuge in the temple. This is how things stood when the Roman legates reached Damascus. As soon as he arrived, Pompey had to arbitrate the dispute. We shall return to this point.

Hasmonaean imperialism can be explained in part by the presence of Jews living in most of the areas surrounding Judaea, but this explanation alone does not suffice, because some of their endeavors had no such justification: there were no Jews in the Greek coastal cities or in Ituraean territory. Thus it is fair to say that the expansion involved a search for new lands where Jews who had none could settle. And indeed, Jewish conquests for the most part were accompanied by a program of rural colonization, such as we see particularly around the Greek coastal cities, in Galilee, or on the Golan. But the policy of forced Judaization adopted by Hyrcanos, Aristobulos I, and Jannaeus would seem to run counter to this objective, because by offering the conquered peoples a choice between expulsion or conversion, rulers left them the option of retaining their land and thus avoiding confiscation.

It seems likely, therefore, that the Hasmonaean program of territorial expansion was also dictated by a concern for rebuilding a kingdom that would coincide with the Promised Land. A reading of ancient and recent[41] prophets could have helped leaders see events of the time as signs sent from Yahweh, and many conquests had a basis in scripture. Thus, when Demetrios II fell into the hands of the Parthians, was this not a fulfillment of a number of prophecies (Isaiah 13:17–14:27; Jeremiah 51:11; Daniel 2:41–44)? When the Median king seized the king of Assyria and Babylon, was this not a sign that the Chosen People would soon seize empires? Goldstein has shown that the expansionist policy of John Hyrcanos and his successors was based to a great extent on the prophecies of Isaiah, Ezechiel, Jeremiah, and Amos.[42] Out of respect for scripture, certain people who settled in the Promised Land (for example, the Edomites and the Ituraeans) were forced to convert, while others (such as the Moabites, outsiders whose conversion is explicitly forbidden in Deuteronomy 23:3) were not. Descendants of David and of Solomon, the Hasmonaeans could extend their claims very far indeed if they intended to repossess all the land their ancestors had held: it is no accident that they could be found campaigning as far away as the central and northern Beqaa (Hamath).[43] Generally speaking, Judaization was effective. Gérald Finkielsztejn notes that finds of Rhodian amphorae became rare or even nonexistent in sites that were gradually taken over by the Hasmonaeans, as in Jerusalem itself after the 140s. This absence is evidence of a scrupulous respect for the rules of ritual purification.[44]

Although the process of Judaization was unquestionably successful, the vast territory under the control of the Hasmonaeans at the time of Alexander Jannaeus's death was by no means populated exclusively by Jews. Jews annexed the Greek coastal cities (Gaza, Raphia, Azotus, Strato's Tower, Dor, Joppa, Iamnia) and the cities of the Decapolis (Gerasa, Gadara, Scythopolis, Dion, Pella), which they sought to Judaize by force; they razed Pella when its inhabitants refused to convert.[45] This policy was no doubt responsible for the exile of certain prominent Greeks from the cities Jannaeus had threatened. It was during the same period that Meleagros of Gadara settled in Campania and his compatriot, Philodemos, in Cos. Demetrios of Gadara, who was sold on the Roman slave market following the wars, according to Pliny,[46] might have been expelled under the same conditions: he was emancipated by Pompey, who later rebuilt the city to please him.[47] Other possible exiles, of lower standing, have been identified in Athens and Delos.[48] In the south, in Idumaea, we can probably link the departure of some Idumaeans for Egypt to Hyrcanos's expansionist policy in the last quarter of the second century: Idumaean colonies appeared in various Egyptian sites during that time.[49] Generally speaking, we can discern a systematic policy of establishing Jewish villages around the Greek coastal cities, from Gaza to Dor; we know that when Herod wanted to establish a Greek city on the site of Strato's Tower (which had been a Greek city in the first place), he had to expel the Jews, who had probably settled there after the Hasmonaean conquest.

Perhaps we should also relate the imperialist Hasmonaean policy to the abandonment, by the middle of the second century, of a number of Palestinian sites, such as Gezer,[50] Bethzur, Shechem, Bethshan, Lachish, possibly Bethel, Dothan, Shiloh, Tell Zakariyeh, and other less important sites,[51] or, at the beginning of the first century, sites such as Tel Anafa[52]—not to mention cities whose destruction is well known, such as Samaria, Marisa, Adora, and Beersheba. All these factors helped make the Hasmonaean kingdom a Jewish nation-state populated predominantly by Jews, even though the Hasmonaeans did not manage to eliminate the significant pagan, Greek, and indigenous minorities.

The Hasmonaean state must have seemed strong enough to discourage Tigranes of Armenia from touching it when he seized Syria in 83. In eighty years the Hasmonaeans had managed to create a kingdom occupying all of ancient Israel, reaching all the way to the borders of Phoenicia (with the exception of a few cities such as Gaza and Ascalon) and encompassing part of the Transjordan (Peraea) and Idumaea. All this territory had been taken from the Seleucid empire. We can more fully assess the decline in the influence of the last Seleucids after examining the encroachment of other neighbors—the Nabataeans and the Commagenes.

The Expansion of the Nabataean Kingdom

We know little of the history of the Nabataeans in the time between the expedition against Petra in 312 under the command of Antigonos Monophthalmos and the era of Alexander Jannaeus. What knowledge we have is conjecture, not yet supported by archaeological evidence. Nevertheless, it will be useful to survey the extent of our knowledge of the time when the Nabataeans were emerging from the shadows and beginning to play a decisive role in the southern Levant. For a long time the Nabataean kingdom had spanned the desert regions from south of the Dead Sea to the Hejaz, although Nabataeans traveled far beyond that region, sometimes settling, trading, or pasturing their herds in lands as far away as the Hauran. A Nabataean state was established during the third century at the latest, and may have existed even earlier. By the end of the third century, we find a Greek from Asia Minor, Moschion of Priene, indicating that he was in regular contact with the Nabataeans.[53] The oldest Nabataean inscription, found in Elusa in the Negev, mentions "Aretas, king of the Nabataeans."[54] The writing suggests an early date, perhaps in the third century,[55] which would clearly distinguish this Aretas from a contemporary of the Maccabees by the same name.[56]

Are we to conclude, then, that the Nabataeans were already dominant in the central Negev during the third century? This is not impossible, because the Negev was a traditional axis of Arab trade and may well have been one of the preferred directions for Nabataean expansion. It is known that by the second century the Nabataeans were present farther to the west, where they successfully launched a campaign to conquer the territory north of the Sinai.[57] However, they did not succeed in taking Gaza (100), the natural port for merchandise brought by caravan from the southern half of the kingdom; thus Rhinocolura, situated farther west, came to serve as their port. In the struggle for control of a Mediterranean outlet, they were competing not so much with the Seleucids as with the Hasmonaeans.

It is difficult to trace the Nabataeans' progress to the north. A mention of Aretas (I), "tyrant of the Arabs," in 169, may show that the Amman region was under their sway by that time, but the region around the Hauran was not; there the Nabataeans, met by the armies of Judas Maccabaeus, clearly set themselves apart from the people of the neighboring towns who were pursuing the Jews.[58] It was the Nabataeans who informed Judas of the misfortunes that had befallen the Jews of Galaad (north of the Transjordan) and the cities of the Hauran. This suggests that they were herding in the region rather than settling there, which might indicate a northward movement in their migrations but not an expansion of their kingdom.

The expansion must have occurred during the years 160–150, perhaps owing to the quarrels that had weakened the Seleucid dynasty. In any event, at the end of the second century and at the very beginning of the first, the Nabataeans were unquestionably dominant in the northwestern Transjordan (with the exception of Greek cities such as Gerasa and Philadelphia) as well as in the region south of the Hauran, and they were attempting to move into the Golan, where they skirmished with Hasmonaean troops.[59] The fighting became most intense during the time of Alexander Jannaeus, on the Moab plateau and the Golan, and in Idumaea. Although the Nabataeans were partially successful, they were not able to prevent the destruction of Beersheba (before 104) or the capture of Gaza. In any case, the battles for control of the Golan during the reign of Obodas I show that from that point on the Nabataeans were masters of the Hauran. We see this confirmed by the Damascenes' appeal to Aretas III in 84 B.C.E.: these people would not have asked for help from a king who was far away.

We know little about the succession of the Nabataean rulers. Although the ordinal numbers that have been assigned them have been widely accepted, these should be considered only provisional, as the list of rulers is incomplete. After the first Aretas of the third century—who has not been ranked—and the Aretas I who was a contemporary of Jason and of Jonathan (he is thought to have ruled at least from 169 to 160–159), scholars generally place Rabbel I, whose statue was restored during the era of Aretas III.[60] That would put Rabbel I toward the end of the second century, the period when the Nabataeans are thought to have engaged in maritime piracy, profiting from the revival of activity in the Red Sea.[61]

Aretas II, whose existence is attested by Flavius Josephus, is usually believed to have ruled around 100. When Alexander Jannaeus besieged Gaza, the residents called upon "Aretas, King of the Arabs" as one might expect from the city that was the Nabataeans' principal *emporion,* or warehouse.[62] Was this Aretas the first to adopt the royal title? We cannot know for sure, but the fact that Nabataean currency was introduced during his reign might be evidence of this; moreover, he was a contemporary of the Hasmonaean Aristobulos, who took the title of king. However, it is not at all certain that he should be identified with the Arab Erotimus described by Justinus as having raided Egypt and Syria.[63]

During the 90s, Obodas I ruled in Petra, probably beginning in 96. He was the son of Aretas I, if the dedication of the Siq dating from "the first year of Obodat, king of Nabatu, son of Haretat, king of Nabatu" actually refers to him.[64] It was he who defeated Alexander Jannaeus on the Golan around 93[65] and founded the city of Obodat in the Negev, where he was honored as Obodas the God.[66] This was probably a means of consolidating the Nabataean presence in the central Negev after the Hasmonaeans took control of the northern territories, from the Dead Sea to Gaza, by way of Beersheba and Elusa.[67]

Worried about the new strength of the Nabataeans, Antiochos XII led two successive expeditions, one in 88–87 and another in late 85. During the second campaign he followed the coast, fought off Arabs who tried to stop him near Joppa, and kept going despite opposition by Jannaeus. He was finally defeated in the battle of Cana by an Arab king whose name we do not know.[68] Given the fact that Antiochos XII had crossed Judaea in order to surprise this king, it is clear that he was a Nabataean. Was Obodas I still king, or had Aretas III already succeeded him? The answer cannot be determined;[69] the issue is further clouded by a reference in Stephanus of Byzantion citing Uranius's *Arabica*. Uranius identifies "Motho" as "an Arabian village where Antigonos the Macedonian was killed by Rabbel king of the Arabs."[70] Motho is a village on the Moab plateau, well placed to be the scene of a battle between Antiochos XII, attacking from Judaea, and a Nabataean king. Hence the name of Antigonos (Monophthalmos) has frequently been replaced by that of Antiochos (XII). Should we then change the name of the Nabataean king? If we accept Uranius's attribution, the king was Rabbel, probably the same one whose statue was restored by Aretas III; this would situate him in the early 80s and not in the second century. The question might have been resolved if the inscription on the statue had not been damaged just at the point where Rabbel's patronymic appears. Only the last letter remains, and it could indicate either "Aretas" or "Obodas."

In sum, we can establish two different patterns of succession: the sequence Aretas II (100), Obodas I (93), Rabbel I (85), and Aretas III (84) rests on the (amended) citation in Uranius but presents the troubling necessity of placing two reigns between the (fixed) dates of the siege of Gaza and Aretas III's coronation in Damascus; the same sequence without Rabbel I allows more room for Obodas I and, more importantly, does not require us to amend Uranius, who could be alluding to actual events of 312.[71] We cannot be certain until new discoveries are made that provide more precise genealogical evidence.

This Nabataean victory may have played a role in the Damascenes' decision when, threatened by the Ituraeans from the Beqaa in 84, they went looking for a protector. They appealed to the king of the Nabataeans—no longer Obodas I, who had not survived long after his victory over Antiochos XII, but Aretas III, who had just defeated Alexander Jannaeus in the battle of Adida.[72] Thus, for twelve years Aretas III had control of a city that had been the capital of the last Seleucids from time to time. Aretas seems to have remained in Damascus until 72, when he was overthrown by Tigranes, who in turn abandoned Syria in 69.[73] There is no evidence that Aretas III took advantage of the circumstances to return to Damascus. When Pompey arrived in Syria, Aretas III was involved in Jewish affairs along with Hyrcanos II and Antipatros, and that is what led Pompey to take an interest in him.

We are a long way from understanding the internal development of the Nabataean state, for we have to settle for scant information that is difficult to interpret. The dynastic principle appears to have been respected on the whole. For the early period, inscriptions are not sufficient to establish a clear genealogy, but sovereignty seems to have passed from father to son. Strabo, who had the advantage of firsthand information from his friends Aelius Gallus and Athenodoros,[74] explains that the king's chief minister had the title "brother," while the queen was traditionally called "sister." We may see this as an imitation of the hierarchy of the Hellenistic courts,[75] but it may actually have been a combination of local traditions that led to sharing power within an extended family and a Greek vocabulary that in the last analysis was able to express local customs reasonably well. It would be very difficult to describe the structure of the state and its administrative workings in greater detail. We should point out the various titles borrowed from Greek, however: the Nabataeans probably borrowed from the Ptolemaic or Seleucid kingdoms the titles *strategos*,[76] *hyparch*,[77] and *stratopedarch* (chief of camp),[78] terms that are documented in the final century of the Nabataean kingdom.

One other feature betrays the influence of the Hellenistic kingdoms: this was the Nabataeans' introduction of a currency.[79] The oldest coins were struck in the era of Aretas II (and perhaps even a little earlier, around 129–128),[80] as a series depicting a helmeted Athena on one side and Nike on the other, a type modeled on Alexander the Great's gold *stateres*.[81] It is interesting to observe that the first Nabataean currency is thus contemporary with the first Hasmonaean currency, because the latter dates unquestionably to Hyrcanos I.[82] The contemporaneous introduction of the two currencies is not an accident; rather, it reflects the competition between two rival kingdoms.

In the field of archaeology, it is difficult to follow the development of the Nabataean cities before the reign of Aretas IV. The earliest substantiation of the site of Petra goes back to the eighth century B.C.E., on the Umm al-Biyyara summit, where a dig has found Edomite constructions.[83] The presence of Nabataeans goes back at least as far as the end of the fourth century, because Petra appears to have been their principal center already and as such the target of attacks by Antigonos Monophthalmos.[84] But there is no datable archaeological evidence going back that far, and little is known about how the space at Petra came to be occupied during the Hellenistic period.[85]

What kept the Nabataeans in that location was probably its natural protection. Not only could the Siq be easily defended, but the neighboring peaks were virtually impregnable citadels. In fact, neither Antigonos Monophthalmos in 312 nor Aemilius Scaurus in 62 ever managed to seize Umm al-Biyyara, which was equipped as an ultimate refuge. On the summit of the plateau, cisterns hollowed out of the soft sandstone were filled by an ingenious system of channels etched into the bare rock; the only path leading from the foot of the mountain began by traversing a gorge configured in such a way that a handful of people could cut off passage. Then it climbed straight up, blocking any frontal attack by assailants who by some miracle might have broken through the outer wall.

Moreover, the site was not lacking in natural resources. At the eastern entrance to the city, the 'Ayn Musa springs provided an abundance of water (540 cubic meters per day), and in the city itself there were wells that never ran dry. In addition, despite the desert conditions (less than 150 millimeters of annual rainfall in the best years), there were numerous possibilities for cultivation in surrounding areas toward the north in the region of Beida and Wadi Sleysel, to the south around Wadi Sabra, and on the slopes of Jebel Harun.[86] Terraces were built to retain soil and water, and the discovery of presses attests to the presence of vineyards. So far, no one has been able to find a permanent settlement from earlier than the first century B.C.E.; however, this does not rule out the existence of a much earlier sedentary or quasi-sedentary population.

In any case, it was during the first century B.C.E. that the prime features of urbanization were established in Petra. The location of the principal sanctuaries was probably determined very early, but we do not know the architectural style in which they were built. Rows of terraces for tents at the site of az-Zantur have recently been excavated: the same occupants must have returned year after year to that location, just as could be seen recently when Bedouins were living amid the ruins of Petra. During the course of the first century B.C.E., one crude house was nevertheless built in this sector, offering evidence that some nomads were beginning to adopt a sedentary existence.[87] This does not mean that nothing permanent was built at Petra before this late date. It may be that housing retained its nomadic character longest, for some of the monumental tombs date from the late second or early first century B.C.E.[88] Moreover, public installations, meeting halls, baths, and cult sites could all date from this period: the "bath" paintings belong to the late Hellenistic era, or even to the second century B.C.E.[89] Still, the most important monuments do not appear to have been constructed earlier than the reign of Aretas IV (roughly 9 B.C.E. to 41 C.E.).[90]

Despite Petra's importance and the quite justifiable fascination inspired by the exceptional character of its location, we should not forget that the Nabataeans were also responsible for founding cities in the central Negev: Avdat, Mampsis, and Elusa. Elusa almost certainly existed quite early: the oldest extant Nabataean inscription was found there. Its importance led Alexander Jannaeus to capture it[91] and the Nabataeans to retake it as quickly as they could.[92] But how important were these cities before

Pompey's time? Only Obodat (modern Avdat) is known for its early Hellenistic and Roman layers. A temple to Aphrodite with a triple *cella*, following a model known elsewhere (including in Petra), dates from the Nabataean period and occupies the site of the future Roman-Byzantine fortress.[93] The Wadi 'Arabah, a dry and torrid depression connecting the Dead Sea and the Red Sea, links the region around Petra and the Negev; Nabataeans appear to have occupied this area in growing numbers. In fact, although few Hellenistic sites have been found in this depression (Moyet Awad),[94] numerous sites in the southeastern sector, recently excavated, have turned up Nabataean pottery comparable to Roman pottery from the beginning of the early empire, suggesting continuous occupation from the first century B.C.E. to the second century C.E.; surveillance towers and farms have been located as well.[95] It is known that the Nabataeans succeeded in taking Beersheba before Hyrcanos I brutally drove them out around 104, shortly before his death.[96]

Ongoing digs have provided precious information on the development of Aila (modern Aqaba), at the bottom of the gulf of Aqaba. The site of the Iron Age town (Tell al-Khalayfeh) was inhabited until the beginning of the Hellenistic period and perhaps a little later. At a time difficult to determine, a new settlement was founded at a point situated about two kilometers southwest of the old city. Can this settlement be related to the founding of the Ptolemaic Berenice in the third century? The importation of a great many Eastern Sigillata A, mixed in with Nabataean sigillata, suggests a later date, in the second half of the second century, which would mean that the Nabataeans could be credited with founding the new town. In any case, the settlement was flourishing in the first century B.C.E., with wine imported from the west and glass from Sidon, but we shall probably have to wait for new discoveries to date the beginnings of the settlement with certainty[97] and to measure its importance in long-distance trade.[98]

Although the more southern regions of the Nabataean kingdom were never part of any of the kingdoms that emerged following Alexander's conquest, it is obvious that when the Romans arrived in Syria, the Nabataean kingdom had been greatly enriched by the Seleucid spoils, from Moab to Damascus and from the Ammonite region to the eastern Golan. With less brilliance than the Hasmonaeans, but no less effectively, the kings of Petra were able to spread their influence as far as the borders of the Greek cities of the Decapolis and, briefly, as far as Damascus. Created and dominated by a largely nomadic people, the Nabataean kingdom came to include large tracts inhabited by sedentary farmers in the Transjordan, on the Golan, and in the Hauran. Antiochos XII's failed attempt to bring an end to this expansionist policy, if it was not simply driven by the lure of easily acquired booty, might point to a growing uneasiness in Damascus and in Antioch about this northward movement that no one seemed able to halt.

The Emergence of the Commagene Kingdom

Strabo begins his description of Syria with Commagene, which he views as the northern part of the country.[99] We might suspect that he was influenced by the administrative geography imposed by Rome, but Commagene was not annexed before 72 C.E., except for a brief period during Caligula's time, about which Strabo could have known nothing. And yet he states that Commagene "has now become a province" (eparchia). It is a small error, and it makes little difference in terms of the status of the country in Augustus's time; we should simply remember that the geographer saw Commagene as belonging to Syria, not to eastern Anatolia.

This small district situated on the upper reaches of the Euphrates,[100] just before the river leaves the high mountains, remained largely independent of its large neighbor to the south. Commagene was part of the regions of eastern Anatolia that were never conquered, either by Alexander or by his immediate successors. The Commagene kings claimed to be descended from the Orontids, a powerful Iranian family that had ruled the area during the Achaemenid period. They were related to the Achaemenids who had built a kingdom in Armenia. In fact, until the beginning of the second century the history of Hellenistic Commagene is totally unknown, and it is useless to speculate about the accuracy of these ancient claims. More precisely, although we cannot be certain of their relationship to the Seleucids, it is likely that Samos I and his son Arsames, known from coins, inscriptions from Nemrut Dag, and a few rare literary allusions, ruled both Sophene and Commagene in the middle of the third century.[101]

Seleucid domination of Commagene began at the latest under Antiochos III.[102] This fact appears to be confirmed by a reference in Diodoros to the first sovereign's attempt to reestablish Commagene's independence shortly after the death of Antiochos IV. Diodoros indicates that Ptolemaios was the "epistate" of Commagene but was not very concerned about its Seleucid masters;[103] thus we can infer that the Seleucids officially controlled Commagene and that their local representative enjoyed a high degree of autonomy.

For reasons we do not know, Ptolemaios declared independence in 163–162.[104] He profited from the Seleucids' preoccupation with internal affairs and apparently provoked very little response from them. Thanks to the support of his Armenian allies, Ptolemaios even attempted to enlarge his nascent state at the expense of Cappadocia by seizing Melitene, but a strong counteroffensive by Ariarathes V forced him to withdraw to Commagene.[105] Despite this failure, as a way of reaffirming his independence he proclaimed himself king; this, at least, is the title given him by his great-grandson Antiochos I in an inscription setting forth his genealogy.[106]

His successor, Samos, is little more than a name on a few inscriptions and coins, but Samos's independence was even less an issue for the Seleucids after Antiochos VIII Grypos gave his daughter Laodice Thea Philadelphia in marriage to Samos's son Mithradates Callinicos. From then on, the dynasty was integrated into the vast system of matrimonial alliances that ultimately united all the royal families of the Near East.

By marriage, Mithradates I Callinicos became the brother-in-law of five future Seleucid kings.[107] He does not seem to have become embroiled in the fratricidal quarrels that were drawing the attention of the kings of Antioch away from Commagene. Moreover, he arranged alliances with the Parthians as well as with the Armenians. Although we have little chronological information, he seems to have reigned roughly between 96 and 69; we do not know how he got through the Mithradatic War. Commagene may have survived the passage of Tigranes' armies, but it is impossible that Tigranes would have allowed a sovereign of Samosata who had not sworn allegiance to remain in power. Perhaps the coins issued by Antiochos I should be seen as a sign of submission, for they show him wearing the Armenian crown, an image validated by sculpted portraits of the king.[108]

Although we see the Commagene dynasty taking hold, it is much more difficult to analyze its external and internal politics, owing to a lack of precise information. Externally, it is clear that the Commagenes were attempting to establish balanced relations among the larger neighbors surrounding them, not only Seleucids and Parthians but also Armenia and Cappadocia. But what is most remarkable is surely the establishment, by the reign of Mithradates I at the latest, of a royal Commagenian religious identity that combined Greek and Iranian traditions. It is true that the greatest achievements in this area, the royal tombs of Arsameia at Nymphaios and at Nemrut Dag, date from a later period, but experts agree on an earlier date for this syncretism, before the reign of Antiochos I. The Commagene kings had presumably found in this highly original expression of power a means of forging a national identity for a dynasty that may have been quite recent, even though it claimed to be directly descended from the Achaemenids by way of the Orontids.[109]

By contrast, we know nothing about the development of Commagene under the first three kings. Their capital, Samosata, bears the name of the second known independent king, but it was already known by that name to Eratosthenes in the third century B.C.E.;[110] Samosata may thus date back to Samos I.[111] In the same way, at least two other settlements may be attributed to a third-century Arsames: Arsameia of Nymphaios, the city where the dynastic *hierothesia,* sacred monuments, were erected, and its neighbor Arsameia near the Euphrates. Still, the evolution of these cities before the middle of the first century B.C.E. remains completely unknown.[112]

Shortly before Pompey's arrival in Syria, Commagene had gotten a new king. Mithradates I Callinicos was succeeded by his son Antiochos I before 69. We do not know the precise date, but it was very probably before the defeat of Tigranes, because it would seem curious for him to have adopted the Armenian crown as the symbol of royalty right after Tigranes' defeat. In any case, he must have quickly made a show of allegiance, and he was undoubtedly among the dynasts confirmed first by Lucullus and then by Pompey. The choice of official epithets constitutes a political and diplomatic project in itself: the king's official title, the one that figures on numerous inscriptions, is nothing less than "the Great King Antiochos, Just and Manifest God, Friend of the Romans and Friend of the Greeks."[113] The order of the last two phrases is certainly not accidental.

SYRIA BETWEEN PARTHIANS, ROMANS, AND ARMENIANS

The benefits of internal anarchy were not limited to the city-states, the Hasmonaeans, the Nabataeans, or bandits. Pressure from the large empires grew, further aggravating the internal situation. The Parthians to the east, who had settled on the Iranian plateau in the middle of the third century B.C.E., had been advancing ever since: by the end of the second century they were at the gates of Syria. To the west, weighing heavily on the affairs of the Seleucid kingdom, was one foreign power from outside the region that had asserted itself in the affairs of the eastern Mediterranean starting in the early second century: namely, Rome. Although their interests were contradictory and they were almost certainly not acting in concert, Romans and Parthians both worked continually to weaken what remained of the Seleucid empire. But the first to benefit from this was Tigranes of Armenia.

The Parthians

The Parthians had been in Mesopotamia since the middle of the second century: Babylon fell in July 141 at the latest,[114] and following the death of Mithradates I (139–138) the border of the kingdom was fixed west of the Tigris. Antiochos VII's victorious campaign was cut short by the king's death, and although Babylon did not immediately fall under Parthian control, owing to the Parthians' ongoing problems to the east, the Seleucids gained nothing from the Parthians' difficulties. However, all of Mesopotamia was Parthian by about 122, and Dura (also called Dura-Europos) appears to have fallen in 113.[115] The Parthian advance continued to the north, possibly toward Commagene, around 92.[116] Only serious internal turmoil could temporarily halt the Parthian advance west, but the pressure continued to be felt. Tigranes' invasion of Armenia cannot be entirely separated from this context, but it followed a series of conflicts in which Rome was heavily involved: we cannot take it up without first giving an overview of Roman-Seleucid relations.

Rome

Rome emerged as an inevitable partner in Seleucid diplomacy[117] following the Antiochene war (193–189) and the peace of Apamaea (188). In Syria itself,[118] Rome maintained a quite discreet role: it observed more than it intervened. However, Rome was able to exert a great deal of pressure through the credit it extended to the Seleucids and the royal hostages it held. When necessary, it could intervene diplomatically: a single day in Eleusis produced one of the sharpest diplomatic reversals ever suffered by the Seleucids.

In the campaign against Egypt in 168, Antiochos IV had set up camp at Eleusis, outside Alexandria, where he seemed to be poised to capture the city.[119] Then a Roman envoy, G. Popillius Laenas, on orders from the Senate, commanded Antiochos to immediately abandon Cyprus—which he had just conquered—and Egypt. As if to further humiliate him, Popillius Laenas forbade him to meet with his council and, in a symbolic gesture, drew a circle in the sand around him in which he was kept prisoner until he gave an answer.[120] The king, who had just learned about Perseus's defeat at Pydna and the collapse of the Macedonian kingdom, had no alternative but to obey Rome. His military victory thus ended in a diplomatic fiasco. The grandiose feasts of Daphne organized in 166 (or 165) B.C.E. therefore looked like a response to the Roman ultimatum and to the triumph of Aemilius Paulus over Perseus of Macedonia, celebrated at Amphipolis in Thrace in 167. Because he was forbidden by Rome to move his army either west or toward Egypt, Antiochos IV prepared a major expedition to Iran. On the eve of his departure, he organized a triumphal parade of elite units, particularly the new units outfitted in the Roman style.[121] This was also a way of challenging the increasingly entrenched Roman ideology of the time, *imperium orbis terrarum*,[122] a claim to universal domination. Because

Rome lacked the means to institutionalize its aspiration to create a province, the policy was carried out instead through vigorous diplomatic intervention, signifying to all peoples and their rulers that all their affairs were Rome's concern.[123]

After the death of Antiochos IV, Rome played a discreet but effective role. In dynastic quarrels, for example, every claimant sought Rome's diplomatic support in order to be recognized by the Senate as the legitimate ruler: Alexander Balas and Demetrios II both sent delegates to Rome, with varying degrees of success. Roman delegations regularly crisscrossed the Hellenic east and Syria in particular (there was a delegation in 164,[124] one in 163–162 when Gnaius Octavius was assassinated in Laodicea,[125] and another around 130 involving Scipio Aemilianus), but embassies to Rome from the Near East were even more numerous. When Rome decided to intervene militarily in Syria, there was little it did not know about local problems. We shall return to this point later, when Pompey's delegations appear, but it is not too soon to note that even at this date Roman interventions were solely diplomatic; no Roman soldier set foot in Syria before 65–64 B.C.E. It is safe to say that, apart from its consistent desire to weaken the Seleucid empire,[126] Rome's objectives remained vague. But its strategy of maintaining a permanent presence in the region becomes clearer when we recognize that, above all, Rome wanted to demonstrate that everything that happened in the lands around the Mediterranean was its business. To this end it created multiple opportunities to intervene militarily if necessary, wherever its interests were involved.

The immediate objective of weakening the Seleucid empire was amply achieved, not by Rome alone, but by all of the Seleucids' adversaries working together. By the 90s, Syria seems to have been exhausted by internal strife. If the Parthians had not been engaged in the east at the time, and then in the grip of a lengthy succession crisis during the 80s, there is no doubt that they could easily have occupied all of Seleucid Syria. Faced with the vacuum created by the absence of heirs, the cities worried about outbreaks of anarchy and crime. Finally, after considering all the possible protectors, the Antiochenes called upon Tigranes of Armenia in 84–83 B.C.E. It was an excellent choice a priori, but it involved Syria in the crisis that gripped the entire Orient, a crisis initiated by Mithradates VI Eupator, king of Pontus, when he invaded the Roman territories of Asia Minor.[127]

Syria under Tigranes

Chosen by the Parthians and allied with his father-in-law Mithradates VI, king of Pontus, Tigranes ruled Armenia beginning in 95 B.C.E. In ten short years, he created a vast kingdom that reached as far as Cappadocia in the west and Mesopotamia in the south, thus drawing Armenia out of its narrow Caucasian world. At a time when the Parthians were dealing with serious internal problems involving the succession of Mithradates II, Tigranes appeared without question to be one of the most powerful kings in the Near East. The Antiochenes first considered turning to Mithradates VI, who had the misfortune of having been defeated by Rome and of still being viewed by them with suspicion; they also considered Ptolemy IX, but they deemed him too weak and all too eager to reclaim the southern part of Syria. In 84–83 B.C.E. they finally turned to Tigranes as the only king capable of taking command who was not known to have ambitions in that region. Rome does not seem to have reacted to the choice.

The occupation of Syria and the Cilician plain took place without major difficulty in 83 B.C.E., despite a few pockets of resistance: Seleucia Pieria closed its gates and held out during the entire Armenian occupation. Strabo describes the operation as a campaign of conquest,[128] to be sure, but in a kingdom where every community had a habit of playing its own part, it would have been surprising to find unanimous support for the Antiochenes' choice. As for Tigranes, invited or not, he did not hesitate to play the role of conqueror, a ruler from a foreign kingdom. He surely did not accept the Antiochenes' invitation just to please them; the opportunity almost certainly coincided with objectives of his own. The problem lies in knowing just what those objectives were. If we judge by the geography of the conquest, the question remains open. Tigranes took control of all of northern Syria (excluding Seleucia), but he seems to have had only limited, or belated, ambitions in the south. Not only was there never any question of challenging Hasmonaean independence, but for a long time Tigranes had to put up with both the Nabataean presence in Damascus and the presence of Cleopatra Selene, the mother of a potential Seleucid heir, in Ptolemais. Damascus did not fall until 72, and Ptolemais not until 69, on the eve of Tigranes' evacuation from Syria. Moreover, Tigranes' era seems to correspond generally with the rise of the Ituraean principality of Lebanon, which asserted its autonomy in the entire region from Chalcis of Lebanon to Arca by way of Baalbek.

We cannot assess the consequences of the Armenian occupation with any precision. Tigranes, who came in response to the invitation of one city-state, does not appear to have been concerned with asserting his royal authority over all the others: Apamaea gained the right to coin money,[129] and Laodicea introduced an era of freedom in 82 or 81, as did Berytos in 81–80.[130] Seleucia's resistance did oblige Tigranes to make do with alternative ports. Moreover, although Tigranes and his army had traversed the Aradian region, there is no indication that they occupied the island.[131] According to Pompeius Trogus, the era of Armenian rule was a felicitous one in Syrian history.[132] This may have been a clear reflection of the city-states' satisfaction with their increased autonomy, but it may also have resulted from a period of peace such as the country had not known in years. We must observe, however, that Tigranes does not seem to have solved the problems of piracy and banditry, plagues that remained unchecked in 69 B.C.E. when the Armenians withdrew from Syria. The truth was that he had no navy, so he was obliged to cede control of the seas to pirates.

In the absence of archaeological evidence for the chronology of this brief period, the circulation of coins remains an essential resource, but coins alone do not give us a very clear idea of the situation. For one thing, several city-states that had previously minted coins ceased their production at the time when Tigranes appeared: this was the case in Seleucia, which may have experienced a shortage of metal on account of the blockade imposed by the Armenians or may have found that declining use made further production unnecessary. It was also true, however, of city-states such as Byblos and Tripolis, which must have yielded quickly to Tigranes' domination. In contrast, Apamaea inaugurated a very stable currency, while Laodicea turned out an abundant and stable series of tetradrachms; it was perhaps necessary throughout northern Syria to compensate for the end of Seleucian minting. But does this reflect the needs of the economy or those of the king? Indeed, while there was an abundance of civic currency, Tigranes also went ahead with the overstriking of bronzes in ten Syrian and Phoenician mints, with Arados accounting for two-thirds of the production.[133] These were older coins (some had been in circulation for around forty years); their weight did not meet Attic standards, and they were good for little but paying Tigranes' Armenian soldiers. When he had to resort to Greek mercenaries, Tigranes introduced a currency of stable tetradrachms.[134]

By occupying Syria, Tigranes in no way harmed Rome's interests, and Rome, having little sympathy for the last remnants of the Seleucids, was all the more willing to look the other way. However, in Rome's eyes, Tigranes was guilty of two major offenses: he did nothing to control the pirates and bandits who were allied with Mithradates VI Eupator, a fact best explained by his lack of a navy, and he offered the same Mithradates refuge in his mountainous kingdom in the Caucasus. For this reason, Tigranes' adventure in Syria cannot be separated from the Mithradatic War. Thus when Lucullus undertook to drive Mithradates VI out of Asia entirely, he fought in eastern Anatolia, wintered in the Caucasus, and penetrated into Armenia.[135] Faced with this occupation of what was the heart of his kingdom, Tigranes withdrew from Syria as of 69 B.C.E., when he had just taken

Ptolemais and was perhaps preparing to do the same to the southern part of the country. He left some troops, however, under the command of Magadates.

The disappearance of the largest and most powerful kingdom to come out of Alexander's empire took place, this first time, in an atmosphere of general indifference, with none of the existing powers showing any inclination to react. Rome was obsessed at the time with the consequences of the Mithradatic War and was most concerned with reestablishing its authority in Asia Minor. In addition, rivalries between the Roman *imperatores* who were responsible for resolving the crisis interfered with the effectiveness of the armed forces and Roman diplomacy. What was to become of a Syria newly liberated from the Armenians? Would it see the return of the Seleucids, who had demonstrated their own ineffectiveness? And if so, which Seleucid?

THE END OF SELEUCID SYRIA AND
THE FIRST ROMAN RULE

(69–31 B.C.E.)

Tigranes' withdrawal from Syria threw the country into a situation even worse than the one it had known in 84. The region does seem to have been freed from incessant conflicts among petty kings who were incapable of governing but rich enough to produce constant mischief. Would the states that had gradually absorbed vast stretches of the Seleucid empire now seize the territories that Tigranes had abandoned? The Hasmonaeans could claim land all the way to the Euphrates if they wanted to follow the example of David and Solomon. The Nabataeans had shown that they were not averse to taking Damascus. The Parthians had reached Dura, and it appeared that the only thing that might stop them from pushing westward was their constant infighting. In addition, a host of Arab emirs were eager to ransom lands held by sedentary tribes.

To Lucullus, allowing the return of the Seleucids had seemed the lesser evil. Pompey, however, lost no time in reversing his rival's work: after a century of more or less discreet supervision, Rome intervened directly in the Hellenized Near East. For some thirty years, against a backdrop of civil wars and foreign invasions, Syria experimented with a new form of government. "Experiment" is indeed the right word, for Rome employed diverse and novel means of exercising authority. Besides the classic *provincia*, it set up client kingdoms, increased the number of indigenous chiefdoms, and prodded or penalized cities; in short, it tried to make good use of the multiple forms of authority it found in Syria in order to manage and exploit a province whose resources appeared substantial.

Piracy and the ambition of Mithradates VI Eupator, king of Pontus, were the principal reasons, or pretexts, behind Rome's increasingly direct involvement in the east: in the first half of the first century B.C.E., Rome added four provinces, including Syria, to Asia, which had been its only eastern province since 129. Moreover, some neighboring states of varying dimensions were placed under Roman supervision and became virtual client states. Without going into great detail, it is important to describe in its broad outlines the political context that allowed the Seleucid kingdom to disappear for good.

Pirates, Bandits, and Tyrants

The increase in crime, in the absence of any defensive strategy for dealing with bandits operating in and around the Seleucid kingdom, had led to the creation of what the Greeks called "tyrannies," authorities operating outside the traditional norms of city-states and kingdoms. These might be Greek chiefs imposing their rule within city-states, or Arab emirs assuming power in areas abandoned by the Seleucids. There are also indications that common thievery added to the crime rate. Peasants constructed crude defenses in response. Hence, in the Hauran, we find guard towers clearly designed to protect villages and harvests, dating from the end of the second century B.C.E. up to the first century C.E. They may be even older, but they seem to have been in use during the late Hellenistic period.[1]

On the eve of the Romans' arrival, tyrants and marauders of every sort swarmed far and wide. Thus Silas the Jew retreated to the fortress of Lysias, somewhere in the Apamene region.[2] In Transjordan Philadelphia, as in Gerasa, the local "tyrant-thieves" appear to have been either Greeks or members of one of the Hellenized indigenous families, as was the case with Zeno Cotylas and his son Theodoros.[3] Strabo also mentions a certain Dionysios, son of Heraklion, a tyrant simultaneously ruling Beroea, Bambyke, and Heraclea on the Euphrates, even before Pompey's arrival;[4] we know, too, that somewhat earlier Beroea (Aleppo) had been in the hands of a man named Strato, an ally of Philip II.[5] On the coast, Zoilos controlled Dora and Strato's Tower during Alexander Jannaeus's rule,[6] but marauders were also well established in Tripolis (Dionysios) and Byblos. As for pirates, some presumably settled in Joppa, but it is not clear exactly when.[7] Many cities in the region must have cooperated with pirates, willingly or not, either by building ships in their shipyards or by tolerating the flow of stolen goods, and especially slaves, through their markets.[8] This attitude toward pirates appears to have been common, for Strabo emphasizes that the Aradians "would not even once take part with them in a business of that kind,"[9] which strikes him as exceptional on the Syrian coast.

Before the Armenian occupation, Arab emirs wielded authority in northern Syria and in the central valley of the Orontes River, in the interior of Lebanon. Ituraean Arabs in Lebanon made the central Beqaa a true principality. The local authorities considered them a band of thieves because the Ituraeans eluded their authority and because they were capable of ransoming Berytos (modern Beirut), Byblos, and Damascus simultaneously.[10] Their leader Ptolemy, son of Mennaios, minted money and built a true principality in the region of Chalcis of Lebanon, though the exact location has not been established;[11] his authority may well have extended to include the Ituraeans in the Trachonitis.[12]

In northern Syria, close to the Euphrates Valley, other Arab chiefdoms held sway. Azizos, an Arab phylarch, was active during the final throes of the Seleucid dynasty; he forced Demetrios III to end his siege of Aleppo,[13] then took Philip II hostage, though the latter managed to escape.[14] Azizos was not alone, however, and Strabo indicates that the entire country from the Euphrates to Massyas (in other words, the southern Beqaa) belonged to the Scenitae Arabs, and he cites several chieftains or tribes, such as those of Gambaros, Themellas,[15] and even the Rhambaeans along the Euphrates.[16] Farther east, Arab emirs, who, despite the ancient authors' low opinion of them, could not be considered outlaws, had long been in control at Edessa (Abgaros II).[17] These Arab chiefs settled in Greek city-states that apparently had not been abandoned by their Greek inhabitants or even by the Seleucid king's officials; the Seleucid mint at Edessa continued to operate.

The most important of these groups—the one destined to retain real independence the longest—was that of Sampsigeramos. Members of this tribe may have come down from the borders of upper Mesopotamia and from eastern Anatolia and settled quite early in the region of the future Emesa in central Syria.[18] In 151 Alexander Balas actually entrusted his son to a certain Iamblichos (Yamlikel), chief of the Emesenoi, a tribe of nomads located in the region of Apamaea at the time.[19] This suggests that the tribe gave its name to the homonymous city rather than the reverse. This was presumably the origin of the powerful Emesene dynasty (whose dynastic name alternated between *Iamblichos* and *Sampsigeramos*); this group had demonstrated its importance very early on when the Seleucid king entrusted his son to its care. We do not know when the tribe settled in the region, but we do know that it moved, at the beginning of the first century B.C.E., from Apamaea southwest to a somewhat drier zone around Arethusa and Emesa. We know nothing about this city-state before the first century B.C.E., but the fact that it never had a Seleucid dynastic name attests either to its mediocrity or to its establishment at a later date. It may have been founded relatively late, once the Emesenoi had decided to become partially sedentary. Among the fortresses in the area around Apamaea, Strabo includes "Arethusa, belonging to Sampsiceramus and his son Iamblichus, chieftains of the tribe of the Emeseni" but he never mentions the city of Emesa itself.[20]

Syria was not alone in suffering from the plague of lawlessness.[21] The entire Mediterranean and Pontus Euxeinos were teeming with pirates from the second century on. These pirates had substantial inland bases, moreover, notably in Cilicia Tracheia, in Lycia, and in Crete, as well as on various islands and coastal areas throughout the Mediterranean.

The reasons for this lie in the weakening of states that, in the third and second centuries B.C.E., had been responsible for policing both land and sea. Following the peace of Apamaea in 188, the Seleucids were no longer free to send a fleet beyond Cape Sarpedon. Rhodes, which had long possessed the most powerful navy in the Aegean and eastern Mediterranean, was ruined economically by Rome, for political reasons, in 167–166 (when the rival free port at Delos was built) and was no longer playing an important role in the region. Similarly, after 133, when the kingdom of Pergamon vanished, that kingdom's army and navy were never replaced. Finally, anarchy in Syria, especially after 125–120, encouraged pillaging there and in Cilicia, and some of the kings (such as Diodotos Tryphon and Alexander Jannaeus) did not hesitate to appeal to bands of brigands for support.

The dangers were so great that even the profitable commerce between Rome, Greece, and the east maintained by Roman *negotiatores* was threatened. Rome reacted under pressure from its merchants, many of whom had political connections; their interests were beginning to suffer from the hands-off policy they had long found beneficial. In 102–101, the praetor Mark Antony campaigned in Cilicia, Pamphylia, Lycia, and Lycaonia, and along the entire southern coast of Anatolia.[22] Apart from one success celebrated officially in 100, the results were modest. A law against piracy was passed the same year (fragments of the text have been found in Cnidos and Delphi in particular),[23] urging all eastern kings to collaborate with Rome. The command of a *provincia Cilicia* was established for the purpose of fighting piracy (it was assigned to Sulla in 96); however, it lacked a territorial base and had no lasting success.

When the Pontic troops invaded Asia, crossing the Aegean and routing the Roman armies, the situation grew significantly worse, all the more so because Mithradates VI did not hesitate to ally himself with bands of pirates in order to scour the Aegean and prevent the Roman troops from sailing back into Asia. After the signing of a fragile peace at Dardanos in 85, Rome attempted to resume the fight against this scourge. Murena, the governor of Asia, assembled a fleet in 84 under A. Terentius Varro, but the effort failed. Finally, in 77–75, P. Servilius Vatia campaigned in Lycia, Pamphylia, and Isauria, attacking the roots of the problem in the interior— in other words, on *terra firma*. Vatia earned the nickname *Isauricus* during the campaign, but his results were nevertheless mediocre.

All these limited campaigns had proven ineffective. In 74 the Senate adopted a new strategy and gave M. Antonius (Creticus), the son of the man who was praetor in 102, an *imperium infinitum* (extraordinary command) to deal with piracy in the east on all fronts at once. Such a decision manifested an awareness of the extent of the problem, but a substantial outlay of resources for the operation and the appointment of a capable military leader would have been necessary to deal with it. Neither of these requirements was met, and M. Antonius was defeated. This was the situation (aggravated by the resumption of the Mithradatic War at the same time) that confronted Pompey in 67 when he was given an imperium infinitum as well as ample resources authorized by the *Lex Gabinia,* or Gabinian Law.

Hence the situation was particularly serious. The Armenian occupation of 83–69 had prevented a solution to the problem, if indeed it did not actually make things worse.[24] Tigranes' withdrawal from Syria in 69 had in any case left the field open to adventurers from all sides, in the absence of any authority capable of restoring order. It was not the gravity of the situation in Syria that persuaded Rome to intervene, however, since the Romans seem to have had only minor economic and financial interests in the region. It was once again the demands of the war against Mithradates VI Eupator that brought the Roman armies back to the east.

Mithradates, Lucullus, and the Seleucid Restoration

Ever since he had become king of Pontus in 120, and increasingly after he seized full power around 112 when he reached his majority, Mithradates VI had sought to make his kingdom a vast state extending from the Crimea across the Caucasus to the Aegean. Following a string of successes, he quickly acquired significant power and launched an assault first on the province of Asia in 88, then on Greece (taking Delos, Athens, and other city-states); in all these places, Romans were massacred. The reconquest, achieved in part by Sulla, ended in 85 with a hasty peace (the Peace of Dardanos) that the Roman Senate never ratified.

A second war erupted in 74. After the second Pontic invasion of the kingdom of Bithynia, Lucullus led the offensive. Thanks to a strenuous and rather punishing campaign (the Roman troups spent the winter of 70–69 in the mountains of the eastern Anatolia), Lucullus seized Pontus itself and forced Mithradates to flee into Armenia in the summer of 71. By the end of 70, the entire Pontic kingdom was in Roman hands. But Tigranes, who until then had refused to anger Rome by assisting his father-in-law Mithradates VI, provided the means for a counteroffensive: with that the crisis quickly became intertwined with Syrian affairs, because by that time Tigranes had been ruler of Syria for thirteen years. What until then had been of little concern to Rome took on major importance: Syria, with its access to the Mediterranean, became a strategic pawn that could not be allowed to fall into the hands of Mithradates and his main ally.

Lucullus spent all of 69 in Armenia and in Mesopotamia. His efforts were rewarded: even before the conquest of Tigranocerta, his ephemeral (and Mesopotamian) capital, on October 6, 69,[25] Tigranes recalled the troops he had left behind in Syria under the command of Magadates.[26] Not knowing what to do with his conquest, Lucullus allowed an heir of the former dynasty, Antiochos XIII, the last descendant of Antiochos VII, to claim the throne (although he did not personally install the new king).[27]

Thus, effortlessly, the Seleucids found themselves back in Antioch, albeit as a vassal state of Rome. Stripped of all resources, the new king was condemned to impotence.[28] In the meantime, Lucullus's victory had brought him the support of several local chiefs, including Alchaudonios, the emir of the Rhambaeans on the Euphrates, and Antiochos of Commagene.[29]

Nevertheless, internal problems in Rome quickly undermined the results of Lucullus's eastern campaign.[30] First, there was a revolt in the army; the soldiers were exhausted from the harsh winter and no doubt manipulated by their leader's political adversaries, and Lucullus was forced to give up the war with Tigranes. Moreover, demonstrations by the *populares* in Rome gradually stripped him of his command: in 68, Cilicia was given to Q. Marcius Rex, while Asia was reserved for another governor who had yet to be appointed.[31] Lucullus was to be governor solely of Bithynia-Pontus, while Pontus still remained to be reorganized. In 67, Lucullus was stripped of his command and his legions were demobilized. When the Roman commissioners, sent to organize the province of Pontus, arrived in Asia Minor, there was no Roman Pontus: Mithradates VI had reoccupied his kingdom. Overall, the only result of Lucullus's campaign had been the return of the Seleucids to Syria. Cilicia escaped them, however: the date for the founding of this province is disputed,[32] but Cilicia Campestris (Cilicia-on-the-Plain) could not have been incorporated before 69. Throughout this entire incident, it is obvious that Syria mattered little, and that it was of only peripheral concern to Lucullus.

This is not the place to examine the reasons for the elimination of Lucullus, but in 67 there arrived in the east a new Roman imperator: Pompey. He had not come specifically to initiate a change of policy, but, besides representing other financial interests, he had the advantage of substantial resources that would enable him to handle both the war on piracy and the Mithradatic crisis.

POMPEY AND SYRIA[33]

The Struggle against Piracy

Piracy was not unrelated to the Mithradatic War: in order to disrupt Roman transports, Mithradates had encouraged pirates. Throughout Lucullus's war, communications with Rome had been threatened, and pirates reached as far as Ostia: the Senate thus decided to renew the effort launched in 74 by creating an imperium infinitum throughout the Mediterranean and coastal regions. The Lex Gabinia gave this command to Pompey, who quickly mounted a campaign.[34]

By taking control of the entire sea at once and systematically chasing down the pirates in their bases on land, Pompey managed for the most part to secure the Mediterranean. In the end, the last pockets of resistance were in Cilicia Tracheia: wielding force and diplomacy simultaneously, Pompey rid even Cilicia of its bandits.[35] At the end of 67, the piracy problem was more or less solved. That left only the problem of bandits in inland Syria, a less immediate threat to Rome.

Pompey in Syria: The Liquidation of the Seleucid Kingdom and the Struggle against Banditry

During the winter of 67–66, the *Lex Manilia* gave Pompey full power to move decisively against Mithradates.[36] Beginning in the spring of 66, he invaded Pontus, forced Mithradates to flee east into Colchis, then invaded Armenia and marched into the Caucasus. After Tigranes' defeat and the organization of Anatolia,[37] unable to capture Mithradates (who was hiding in the Crimea), Pompey went down into Syria in the summer of 64 to begin a necessary reorganization.[38]

Starting in 66–65, Pompey's legates in Syria took on the struggle against pirates and bandits. Lucius Lollius joined Metellus Nepos, the legate given responsibility in 67 for the coast from Lycia to Phoenicia, while Afranius eliminated the thieves who had been infesting the Amanus passes.[39] In 65, these two men were in Damascus, though we do not know exactly what they were doing, and Aemilius Scaurus joined them there;[40] in 69, Tigranes had withdrawn from the city, and it appears to have been free after that date. There is no indication that the Roman legates had troops at their disposal, and it is surprising to find them there at a time when Antioch officially had a Seleucid king whose authority should have included Damascus. In any case, we know they did little against the bandits in central or southern Syria because Pompey had to rid the country of them as soon as he arrived.

Pompey arrived by way of Cilicia in the middle of 64 and began by going to Antioch to settle the fate of the Seleucids. Lucullus had allowed Antiochos XIII to return in 69. However, part of the Antioch population rose up against this king who had been defeated by the Armenians. Antiochos XIII managed to put down the rebellion; its leaders fled to Cilicia, where they proclaimed as king Philip II, son of Philip I and grandson of Antiochos VIII Grypos.[41] Both kings were supported by Arab chiefs more powerful than they: Antiochos XIII by Sampsigeramos of Emesa, Philip II by an emir of northern Syria, Azizos, who had been the one to crown him.[42] According to Diodoros, the two emirs had agreed to share power in Syria and to eliminate their protégés. But Philip II, getting wind of Azizos's intentions in 67, fled to Antioch, where he may have perished in a riot in 66–65.[43] Meanwhile Antiochos, who was closely controlled by Sampsigeramos, had time to make an official request to Pompey that he be recognized as king, which the imperator refused to do: the king then fled to Sampsigeramos, who, not eager to displease his new master, promptly had him killed.[44]

Pompey had in fact decided to end the Seleucid dynasty and annex Syria. There are several reasons for his decision, the principal one probably being a desire to break with Lucullus's policy. "[S]ince this country had no legi[ti]mate kings," as Plutarch wrote,[45] faithfully echoing Pompey's propaganda, Pompey decided to annex the kingdom. But the claim that Syria had no legitimate kings is patently false, because there were Seleucid heirs, and it contradicted decisions that Lucullus had made in Rome in 69.[46] Another reason was Pompey's desire to reap the maximum benefit from his defeat of Tigranes: "Pompey claimed that the Seleucids, who were overthrown by Tigranes, were not the legitimate rulers of Syria, but rather Rome, which had captured it from Tigranes."[47] By invoking the laws of war, Pompey gave his actions a firmer justification and could foreground his own effectiveness. In reality, Antiochos XIII was nothing but a puppet. According to Pompeius Trogus, Pompey refused to give the throne to a king

who, during Tigranes' eighteen-year reign in Syria, had stayed hidden in a corner of Cilicia and then, seeing that Tigranes was defeated by the Romans, tried to claim the fruits of their labor; and, as a result, Pompey would not give the scepter to someone who had been unable to defend the throne and unable to get it back after losing it to Tigranes; he feared that doing so would once again leave Syria open to marauding Arabs and Jews.[48]

A very nice analysis of a political realism that was difficult to counter.

In contrast, it is difficult to assess the role Parthia played in Pompey's decision to reduce Syria to the status of a Roman province. Josef Dobiáš, and numerous writers after him, saw no Parthian involvement in the annexation.[49] However, other voices have been raised against this assumption,[50] by those who argue that the conflicts in Roman-Parthian relations during the years 70–63 had to have affected Pompey's actions in Syria. In fact, Pompey continued to challenge the Parthians in his interventions in Armenia and Anatolia without much response, inasmuch as the authority of the Parthian king was often very shaky. Still, the Parthians were not as inactive as some have claimed; although we have no evidence that they were ready to throw themselves on the ruins of the Seleucid kingdom, they had still not given up the idea of expanding to the west. Demetrios III Eukairos, for example, who had been defeated by Philip I, had taken refuge with the Parthians.[51]

Pompey's decision to annex Seleucid Syria meant giving Rome everything that was left of the once-prestigious kingdom of Antiochos III and preventing Syria from becoming a hotbed of banditry once more, after all the efforts to restore freedom of movement in the Mediterranean. Even if we assume that his action was governed by internal politics, we cannot rule out certain diplomatic and military ambitions involving the Parthian Empire. Still, it is important to be wary of the economic explanations that were advanced at one time,[52] because although Roman merchants may have traded in Syria before Pompey's arrival, we have no traces at all of their presence. There is evidence that certain Roman business interests were already in contact with Syria, but we can hardly claim to know what influence they had on Pompey. Nevertheless, there was one new factor that could have prompted Roman merchants to come to Syria to trade directly: the quasi destruction of Delos. Ever since 167–166, the Italians had been accustomed to doing business with Syrian merchants in Delos. But the island had suffered enormously during the Mithradatic War; not only were Romans massacred there in 88, but Delos was devastated by Mithradates at the end of that year. Liberated by Sulla in 87, it rebounded somewhat, but another raid by pirates allied with Mithradates in 69 reduced it to bare survival, and the city, though it was not abandoned, ceased to be the great marketplace it had once been.[53] In the absence of this intermediary, it might have been tempting to go directly to the source of the trade. Still, the fact that the Romans might have harbored such hopes does not mean that

Pompey was acting under pressure from them. Saying that Roman merchants profited from the conquest does not prove that they were the driving force behind it.[54]

The task of restoring law and order still remained. Afranius had already fought in Amanus, and Scaurus had rejoined Lollius and Nepos at Damascus, where there is no evidence that Aretas III had regained power after the Armenian troops left in 69.[55] Pompey left Antioch at the beginning of 63 and headed for Damascus; on the way, he leveled the hideouts of bandits who were threatening the cities of the region, including that of Silas the Jew in Lysias,[56] and he executed local tyrants such as Dionysios of Tripolis. But he allowed the most powerful to surrender and pay ransom: for example, Ptolemy of Chalcis, who was taxed a thousand talents,[57] and the Emesene Sampsigeramos in his capital, Arethusa.[58] Similarly, the Arab Abgaros II, ruler of Edessa, owed his life to the fact that he had helped Afranius in his battles in the Amanus region,[59] while Antiochos I of Commagene had also earned Pompey's gratitude.[60] In regions where Rome's interest was only marginal, Pompey assessed the actual power of each chief and decided to recognize the local authority of the ones who had succeeded in taking control, giving them a quasi-official status, rather than waste time in battles where the outcome would be uncertain. Thus some indigenous principalities that had been erected on the ruins of the Seleucid kingdom were strengthened.

When he reached Damascus, Pompey joined his legates just as they confronted a quarrel between the last two heirs of the Hasmonaean dynasty. Before he could organize the new province permanently, Pompey had to fight one more battle near Jerusalem.

Pompey and the Jews

The dissolution of the Hasmonaean state occurred between 65 and 41 in complex circumstances. At the time when Pompey was finishing off the Seleucid kingdom and reducing Syria to the status of a Roman province, the Jews were powerless and infuriated witnesses to a dispute between Hyrcanos II, the weak but legitimate high priest, and his brother Aristobulos II, who was demanding power and seemed ready to do anything to get it. (We last encountered the two brothers at the point when the settlement they had reached was challenged once more by the efforts of Hyrcanos's adviser, Antipatros, who was not happy to see power pass into Aristobulos's hands.)

The weak Hyrcanos II,[61] who was driven out of Jerusalem and supported by the Idumaean Antipatros, called on Aretas III of Petra to help reclaim his throne. On the opposing side, Aristobulos II held Jerusalem and its treasury. While Hyrcanos and Aretas were besieging Aristobulos in the Temple, both brothers, Hyrcanos and Aristobulos, made tempting offers to Pompey's legate Aemilius Scaurus as soon as he arrived in Jerusalem.[62] Without regard for the legitimacy of the eldest brother, but judging that whoever held Jerusalem and the Temple would be more solvent, Scaurus decided to support Aristobulos and ordered Aretas to lift the siege of Jerusalem, whereupon the latter retreated toward Philadelphia. Hoping to be rid of his brother once and for all, Aristobulos set off in pursuit and defeated the Nabataean troops "at a place called Papyron."[63]

When he arrived in Damascus in 63, Pompey once again found three Jewish delegations: Hyrcanos II, Aristobulos II, and ambassadors from the people, Pharisees who opposed both brothers. Pompey put off resolving the conflict until later and announced his intention to march on Petra.[64] However, faced with Aristobulos's provocation, he temporarily abandoned his Nabataean expedition and marched on Jerusalem, via Dion, Pella, and Scythopolis. Aristobulos yielded quickly, but his troops, who were holding the Temple and the surrounding area, refused to surrender. Pompey occupied the city and began a siege on the Temple that lasted three months, until the autumn of 63. The Temple was taken by force and part of it desecrated: Pompey entered the Holy of Holies and came out to declare it empty! A century after the first encounter between Jews and the Roman legates Quintus Memmius, Titus Manlius, and Manius Sergius, the friendship between Rome and former rebels seemed to be over. The principal enemy, the Seleucids, had disappeared, and the Jews, allied objectively with Rome as long as it was necessary to weaken the kings of Antioch, were no more than a destabilizing element in Romanized Syria.[65]

Pompey thus settled the fate of the Jewish state in hope of ending the unrest. Aristobulos II and his family, viewed as rebels, were imprisoned and held as trophies for the triumphal celebration Pompey was planning in Rome; they would lead the convoy of Jewish captives taken during the siege of Jerusalem.[66] Hyrcanos II was confirmed as high priest but was denied a royal title; the Pharisees, who had long viewed the illegitimate concentration of titles with hostility, were thus appeased. Still, the Hasmonaean state had been seriously diminished: it now included only Judaea, Samaria (except for the city of Samaria itself), southern Galilee, and eastern Idumaea. Lands that had been appropriated were awarded to other kingdoms, and many city-states were added to the province of Syria in particular. These included not only all the cities situated beyond the Jordan and Lake Tiberias (Hippos, Gadara, Pella, Gerasa, Dion), but also cities of the southern Levant, along the coast as well as inland (Scythopolis, Samaria, Iamnia, Gaza, Joppa, Dora).[67] With this reorganization, Pompey inaugurated a policy of client states in Judaea like the one already in place in much of Anatolia.

The Organization of Pompey's Provincia

When he was deciding the future of Syria, Pompey was pressured on two fronts, neither of which could be easily overlooked. First, Rome realized that it could not install an efficient administration in the newly conquered territory through the efforts of its agents alone. The province of Asia, created in 129, had remained notoriously under-administered, and the creation of Bithynia, Cilicia, Pontus, and now Syria, within just a few years, worsened the problems of governance. Moreover, Rome's custom was not to increase the number of its representatives, but rather to depend upon local communities, in particular the Greek city-states—assuming there were any. Second, many of the practices adopted in Syria during the long decline of the Seleucid monarchy could not be easily changed from one day to the next: dynasties, city-states, and emirs had all grown accustomed to an autonomy that might prove advantageous to Rome in the long run. In a sense, the second difficulty could be used to alleviate the first.

Indeed, the city-states of Syria formed the very backbone of the province; these were located in the former Seleukis and Phoenicia, plus there were a few groups of more or less isolated city-states in the Transjordan region or on the Palestinian coast. All the others remained in the hands of client kings. In the province itself (which, owing to this dispersion, did not constitute a single geographic unit), Pompey nurtured the development of the region's real infrastructure, the city-states, to fill the gap left by the almost nonexistent provincial administration. We have seen that many cities were emancipated during the long crisis in the Seleucid kingdom. Pompey did not reverse this situation, and it may have been during this period that some city-states saw their territory increase (Arados, for example, may have grown at the expense of Baitokaike).[68] Many city-states had suffered from the Seleucid wars, from banditry, or from the Hasmonaean expansion, or even from all three at once. It was important to help them rebuild.

Pompey restored damaged and destroyed cities everywhere. Above all, he guaranteed the independence of cities formerly occupied by Hasmonaeans, on the coast (Gaza, Anthedon), in Idumaea and Samaria (Samaria itself, Adora, Marisa), as well as in the Transjordan region, where Gadara, Pella, Gerasa, and Dion in particular were liberated and integrated into a district originally comprising ten cities that seem to have been linked geographically and administratively rather than politically. It would be helpful to know more precisely what Pompey did for the city-states, for presumably he did not limit himself to making promises. We know only about the example of Gadara (and even here we know very little), where Pompey's freed slave Demetrios was born. Living in Rome, having been enslaved in the aftermath of Alexander Jannaeus's wars, Demetrios nurtured a fierce hatred of the Hasmonaeans. It has been suggested that Pompey reconstructed Gadara after liberating it from Hasmonaean occupation in order to make Demetrios happy.[69] Demetrios, who grew rich and powerful through his master's largesse,[70] had been active in construction in Rome itself,[71] and he soon saw to it that his liberated city benefited from his own experience, influence, and resources.[72] It is likely that Pompey relied upon city-state leaders wherever he went, and by providing various advantages, particularly financial ones, he was able to help them rebound. In any case, between 64 and 62,[73] all these cities, independently of one another, entered a new era known as "Pompeian," an indication that the city-states considered Pompey's achievements, extended by some of his successors, as amounting to a rebirth. These eras, also recognized in Phoenicia, are proof of the importance of Pompey's activity in this regard throughout Syria.

Pompey understood that among all the inhabitants of Syria only the Greeks, meaning Hellenized natives as well as descendants of the colonists, were committed to the new order, and would therefore be Rome's strongest supporters in Syria. Neither the Jews, jealous of their independence, nor the barely Hellenized Arabs could look favorably on Rome's presence in the east. Hence it was worthwhile for Rome to rely on the city-states, where the majority of the Greeks were clustered. This policy was not without drawbacks, however; in fragmenting power, Pompey made it more difficult to achieve a sense of unity in the face of a potential threat, whether from neighboring Parthia (as in 41–40) or from the meddling of a Roman imperator. Nevertheless, the policy adopted was probably the only, or at least the best, possible choice in 63.

Apart from the city-states, Pompey also recognized the power of client states, which were more or less firmly confined to the margins. We have seen what had become of the Hasmonaean state, which was greatly reduced in size. Pompey also had to acknowledge the most powerful of the Arab chiefs. Ptolemy, son of Mennaios of the Ituraean dynasty, was granted a principality covering the central Beqaa and north of Mount Lebanon, though not before he had paid a fine of one thousand talents[74] in compensation. Similarly, Sampsigeramos received confirmation of his dynastic power over Emesa and Arethusa slightly farther north. At the edge of the desert, the emirs were also recognized as allies; step by step, Rome established a network of client states it expected to rely upon. In contrast,

Palmyra retained its independence: the first time its name appeared in connection with Syrian affairs was in 41 B.C.E. when Antony led his troops against it, which means that it could not have been part of the Roman alliance at the time.

SYRIA AT THE TIME OF THE ROMAN CIVIL WAR

The First Legates

When Pompey left Syria near the end of 63, upon learning of Mithradates' death,[75] he left as governor one of his closest friends, his legate Aemilius Scaurus, who had preceded him to Damascus when he himself was busy in Armenia.[76] The province, created on Pompey's own initiative, apparently had not been visited by a senatorial commission charged with establishing new institutions. Hence Scaurus was acting as Pompey's legate rather than as a promagistrate reporting to the Senate. It was not until 59 that the first regular governor was appointed, the propraetor Lucius Marcius Philippus,[77] who was followed in 58 by Gn. Cornelius Lentulus Marcellinus.[78] Beginning in 57, a proconsul was assigned to the province, no doubt owing as much to its wealth as to its strategic location. Aulus Gabinius was the first proconsul, serving from 57 to 55, but he was recalled for misconduct[79] and replaced by the triumvir M. Licinius Crassus—proof of the importance Rome attached to the province. Furthermore, Licinius Crassus was appointed for a five-year term. After his death in battle, the province was governed until the end of his mandate by his quaestor, G. Cassius Longinus, until M. Calpurnius Bibulus succeeded him in 51, arriving in the middle of the Parthian invasion. When Bibulus left in October 50, he left the province in the hands of his legate Veiento.[80]

The first provincial governors did little to leave their mark on provincial organization, with the exception of Gabinius, who proposed a reorganization of Judaea. This may be just an illusion owing to the fact that the reorganizations carried out later, by Antony and then Augustus, overshadowed the work of their predecessors. However, the information available does not support such a hypothesis. The few confirmed facts can be stated briefly.

In monetary affairs, the new authorities began issuing provincial coinage only under Gabinius, and even then they simply countermarked coins made under Philip I, or minted new ones with a Roman counterseal. This was the policy followed until 17–16 B.C.E., when the last Roman "philips" were issued; the only innovation was introduced in 47 by Caesar, who had his coins dated from the first Caesarian era in Antioch. At the same time, the Seleucid coins and those of Tigranes, without Roman countermarks, continued to circulate freely until Augustus's reign, proof of the absence of any truly provincial currency before that date. However, one short-lived attempt to issue a Roman coinage in Syria, probably in 38–37, should be mentioned. Lucius Calpurnius Bibulus, one of the prefects of Antony's fleet, had new bronze coins minted on the Syrian coast between Tripolis and Seleucia; these included the *as*, the *dupondii*, the *tressis*, and bronze *sesterces* (an innovation). To facilitate the identification of each coin by the local populations for whom they were intended, the coins bore the indications *A*, *B*, *G*, or *D*, specifying their ratio to the base unit (1, 2, 3 or 4). Bibulus's initiative was not an isolated one, as it coincided with coinages issued by Atratinus and by Capito in Greece. Not many such coins were minted, and the experiment ended quickly, but this early initiative is worth noting.[81]

In terms of fiscal policy, Rome quickly established a system for collecting tribute, customs duties, and other taxes. As elsewhere, the system depended on *publicani* (tax collectors), and as elsewhere it led to abuses.[82] Roman financial societies leased the rights to collect taxes and sold them at auction in Rome, where their agents skimmed off enough on the spot to cover the initial capital investment plus a considerable profit. Nothing like the extensive documentation that we have about Asia is available for Syria, but some references indicate that the systems were very similar. Perhaps the presence in Antioch of an important colony of Roman *negotiatores* in 48 B.C.E. can be understood in relation to these activities of the publicani.[83]

In addition to the revenues skimmed off by the tax collectors, there were also the governors' profits. Gabinius, whom Cicero accused on several occasions,[84] may have allowed the indigenous communities to buy him off, taking one hundred million sesterces from his province while the publicani were paralyzed by his legal decisions or prevented from doing their work by the lawlessness that raged in the province, where bandits and Arab marauders were left unchecked.[85] Crassus is said to have behaved in a similar fashion and, according to Plutarch, prior to the expedition against Parthia he spent his time assessing the wealth of the cities and collecting a substantial part of it for his own benefit.[86] We must be cautious, however, about accepting information distorted by propaganda or, as in Plutarch's case, filtered through a moralizing lens. As for Gabinius, all our information comes from Cicero, who was aware that Gabinius had obtained his governorship of Syria from the tribune Clodius,[87] who had forced Cicero into exile in 59;[88] Cicero cannot find words harsh enough for Gabinius, whom he describes as effeminate and debauched.[89] Actually, by putting a brake on the tax collectors' extortionary practices, Gabinius may have prevented a general revolt in the province, or at least may have tried to help the cities rebuild by granting them some fiscal relief.[90] But it is possible that Gabinius was pursuing the more ambitious goal of entirely eliminating tax collecting by the publicani, in order to begin his own direct collection.[91] Whether it was a genuine effort to lighten the burden on the provinces or a scheme to increase his own profits is beside the point: the confrontation between Gabinius and the Syrian publicani is undisputed.

The governors' achievements on behalf of the province appear more limited. However, it is likely that the early governors carried on Pompey's work of rebuilding the Greek city-states. If not, it would be hard to understand why some of the city-states adopted epithets derived from governors' names. For example, Pella of the Decapolis was proud to bear the name Pella Philippiana,[92] Canatha that of Gabinia;[93] we can infer that such names must have been linked to the receipt of certain important privileges, or some assistance that amounted to an authentic refounding. Archaeology is of little help in determining the extent of the phenomenon, because it is rarely possible to identify with any precision the levels corresponding to the specific phase of urban history in question; however, there seems to be evidence of a fresh start at Anthedon, where major constructions from the beginning of the Roman occupation have been identified near the sea,[94] and we know that Gaza also experienced a true renewal, no doubt under Scaurus since the local era began in 61.[95]

As a province bordering Parthia, surrounded by rather bold client states, and harboring micro-states whose loyalty was questionable, Syria required particular attention in the military sphere. It was a place where ambitious governors found a platform for accumulating honors in war and enriching themselves at the same time. But some of the dangers threatening the province were very real, even if some expeditions were undertaken for booty and glory alone.

The expedition Aemilius Scaurus undertook in 62 against Petra and the Nabataeans was of the latter sort. It seems to have been Pompey's idea, but he was distracted by the difficulties being caused by the Jews. Scaurus's expedition was not justified by any Nabataean aggression or threat, despite statements to the contrary by ancient authors. Aretas III had actually evacuated Damascus when Tigranes seized the city, and there is no evidence that he ever returned. The Romans could not even accuse him of supporting Hyrcanos II, because Rome itself supported the high priest in his fight with his brother. In fact, if we look closely at the expedition, we are forced to conclude that Scaurus was simply after booty, tempted by the image of rich merchants that prevailed in Rome based on a few merchants' firsthand reports. Having put himself in a difficult situation by burning the harvests,

Scaurus agreed to leave the area voluntarily in exchange for an indemnity of three hundred talents. After that, the Nabataeans behaved like faithful allies, lending aid and support to the Romans on every occasion, even though they nurtured certain prejudices against other Roman allies in the region, allies whose interests might conflict with those of the kings of Petra; this was the origin of the skirmishes with Cleopatra and—especially—with Herod.[96]

Scaurus's successors are reputed to have fought against the Arabs as well, but it is not clear whether these were Nabataeans, and the later governors might have been fighting Ituraean or Trachonite Arab bandits (who are mentioned right up to Augustus's time) or still others along the Euphrates. The data are too vague to allow us to draw conclusions, except to note that Pompey's pacification program lasted for some ten years following the arrival of his legates in Damascus in 65–64.

Gabinius's governorship shows the strategic importance of Syria in a striking way. During his two years there, Gabinius not only had to administer the province and intervene in Syria's own client states (notably in Judaea), but also had to lead Roman armies simultaneously into eastern Anatolia, against Parthia and into Egypt. This was not simply from a desire for glory and riches, as Cicero, who was particularly hostile toward Gabinius, would have us believe;[97] it was also to fulfill the duties assigned to him.

Within Syria itself, we have just seen the role that Gabinius had to play vis-à-vis the tax collectors. Apart from these internal affairs, he had to intervene primarily in Judaea. Faced with Hyrcanos's inability to maintain peace in Judaea, Gabinius divided the Jewish state into five districts administered separately; Hyrcanos II kept the position of high priest, but he had no political responsibilities.[98] In fact, the most powerful person in Judaea, in dealings with the Romans, was the Idumaean Antipatros, who had only recently converted to Judaism under Jannaeus; wealthy and adept, a friend of the kings of Petra, he quickly proved himself an indispensable ally of the Roman administrators.

Gabinius also had to take steps to deal with the Parthian threat on the Euphrates, a threat that has been underestimated until recently.[99] Cicero, of course, accused him of "waging war upon quiet peoples, that he may pour into the bottomless whirlpool of his lusts their ancient and untouched wealth."[100] Although Cicero never mentions the Parthians by name, the allusion in this passage, taken together with another, is quite clear.[101] The facts are quite different. Gabinius arrived in the province in the spring of 57 and was very probably ordered by the Senate to wage war on Parthia—a decision made, if not before he had left Rome, certainly by the summer of

57 at the latest. For one thing, the choice of a proconsul as governor (previously, former praetors had always been named) leads us to suppose that war was already in the air. Moreover, Strabo says that Gabinius rejected the assistance of Archelaos, high priest of Comana, for this campaign, after consulting with the Senate, which did not want to rely on the services of a man who claimed to be the son of Mithradates VI.[102] After this rebuff, Archelaos turned on Egypt and seized the throne left vacant when Ptolemy XII Auletes fled in 56. Gabinius's Parthian war, far from being an illegal individual initiative, was planned with the Senate's approval. When Cicero alluded to it at the end of September 57,[103] it was a thoroughly official project despite his disapproval. The campaign did not begin before 55, because in the interim Gabinius had to settle affairs in Judaea.

So it was not until 55 that Gabinius crossed the Euphrates, and we do not know his precise motives. They may well have included factors relating to the succession of Phraates III, who had been assassinated by his sons Mithradates and Orodes. When Gabinius started the campaign early in 55, the older son, Mithradates III, who had already been removed from the throne by his younger brother, was at his side.[104] If Gabinius intended to reestablish Mithradates at Ctesiphon, he was never able to do so, because he soon had to abandon this campaign and go to Egypt, where Rome had more pressing needs: restore Ptolemy XII (Auletes) to the throne.[105] The Parthian plans were thus deferred.

Crassus had Syria assigned to himself when the provinces were divided in 55, with the ambition of acquiring what he most lacked in his competition with Caesar and Pompey: military glory.[106] The Parthians' reputation for weakness and laziness seemed to make them a manageable adversary.[107] It has long been thought that Crassus's attack was not based on any real threat from the Parthians, and that he was simply looking for an easy win in a project begun by Gabinius.[108] In fact, this view is based on a number of misperceptions. First, contrary to accepted opinion, there is no evidence that there was common agreement about the border on the Euphrates set by Pompey:[109] it is hard to believe that the Parthians willingly allowed limits to be placed on their territorial ambitions without putting up a fight against the Romans. Secondly, there are several indications that the Parthians were not inactive during the years following Pompey's departure: the expedition planned by Gabinius must have been in response to a perceived threat, real or not. Moreover, Crassus had the means to conduct such an expedition, and the Senate certainly would not have provided the resources for it simply to satisfy his desire for glory.[110] Moreover, he began to organize a Parthian expedition as soon as he arrived in Syria, and, despite Plutarch's claim that the law of 55 attributing provinces for five years included no such plan,[111] it is likely that everyone knew that Crassus would have to resume Gabinius's aborted expedition.

He invaded Parthia in 54. He must have been targeting Seleucia on the Tigris, where Mithradates III was presumably still hiding,[112] but for unknown reasons he began the campaign in Upper Mesopotamia.[113] He occupied the regions lying between the Euphrates and the Balikh, one after another, and the Greeks in the area welcomed him warmly—only the city of Zenodotia, under the tyrant Apollonios, was closed to him. He then realized just how much it would take to pursue Orodes II in Armenia and settled for controlling the head of the Pontus before turning back to spend the winter in his own province. Ancient authors have reproached him for that, but he probably needed to polish the training of his troops and find additional funds.[114] When the operation resumed in 53, he was dealt a defeat at Carrhai in Osrhoene that ended in complete disaster: Crassus was killed, more than twenty thousand Romans died or were taken prisoner, and the ensigns of the Roman legions were carried off to Ctesiphon.[115] Only Crassus's legate Cassius managed to escape; he hid in Antioch with a small number of followers.[116]

A political disaster compounded this humiliating defeat. Until then, the Parthians had allowed the Romans to settle in Syria without incident; but in late August 51 they crossed the Euphrates[117] and reached the region of Antioch. Pacoros, son of king Orodes II, attacked Cassius in Antioch,[118] where he occupied the lower part of the town.[119] However, lacking the equipment and even the technical skills to undertake a siege, the Parthians proved incapable of taking the city.[120] Withdrawing to the vicinity of Antigoneia, they were plagued by Cassius, who pulled off a striking victory over them on October 7, 51.[121] The Parthians subsequently abandoned the Antioch region, but they nevertheless spent the winter in northern Syria.[122] The threat seemed to be temporarily removed, and most ancient authors give Cassius credit for permanently chasing the Parthians out of Syria.[123]

However, Bibulus, who took his post at the end of 51, was forced to withstand a new siege at Antioch in the winter of 51–50;[124] through a variety of maneuvers he managed to sow chaos in the enemy camp, and the Parthians finally left Syria in the second half of 50.[125] Perhaps as an expression of their gratitude, the people of Antioch are said to have offered Bibulus the statues of Athena and Zeus Keraunios that had been erected in Antioch by Seleucos I, as a gift to the Roman people.[126] It was a surprising gesture, and we are too familiar with the pillaging of works of art, including the most venerated of cult statues, not to be suspicious of such an offer, when the people of Antioch were strongly encouraged to give away what would have been seized from them in any event.[127] The fact that at least one of the statues was later returned argues in favor of it being a theft rather than a gift.[128]

Bibulus was not content simply with chasing off the Parthians. Despite Cicero's malicious statements (Cicero himself sought to take all the credit for the expeditions against bandits in the eastern half of the province of Cilicia),[129] Bibulus had his heart set on fighting the marauders from the Amanus region, who had grown rich from Gabinius's supposed carelessness and profited from the disorder brought about by the Parthian invasion.

Syria during the Civil War

During the distribution of provinces for 49, Syria went to Metellus Scipio, Pompey's father-in-law;[130] Pompey sent him to equip a fleet in anticipation of the resumption of war against Caesar, which appeared inevitable. With unusual harshness, Metellus demanded huge sums from the people and city-states of Syria, seized the assets of the publicani, and forced them to advance the following year's taxes, following a practice that has been well documented in Asia Minor.[131] He levied new taxes on slaves, on colonies, and at tollgates; he also began drafting cavalrymen, infantrymen, and oarsmen, demanded supplies of wheat, arms, and war machines, and requisitioned animals and men to transport all the equipment to Greece. Like the rest of the eastern part of the empire, Syria was thus an active participant in the civil war between Pompey and Caesar. Pompey's defeat at Pharsalus on June 6, 48, threatened to bring Caesar's justifiable revenge upon the Syrians: as soon as the news reached Antioch, the Roman residents and the local population pursued Pompey's supporters, preventing Pompey from taking refuge in Syria.[132]

The first thing Caesar had to do was deal with the Egyptian question (in the winter of 48–47). In this he was assisted by numerous Syrian dynasts and kings: the Idumaean Antipatros, Malichos I of Nabataea, Iamblichos of Emesa, and Ptolemy (son of Sohaimos) of northern Lebanon all gave considerable support to Caesar, who was trapped in Alexandria in 47.[133] Although he confirmed Hyrcanos II as high priest, Caesar gave responsibility for administering the region to Antipatros, who named his two sons as aides: Phasael as governor of Jerusalem and Herod in Galilee.

Caesar then crossed Syria on a route that would lead him to Pontus, where Pharnaces II, the son of Mithradates VI, had taken up arms against Rome. Caesar arrived in Antioch on April 13, 47, preceded by a friendly letter announcing the liberation of the city, inaugurating a Caesarian era of freedom. He also agreed to the construction of several new buildings, among them a basilica known as Kaisareion, the apse of which held a statue of Caesar himself and of the Roman Tyche; this was the first instance in which Caesar and Rome were cast in roles that previously had been reserved for Greek rulers. The extent of the works undertaken elsewhere (reconstruction of the Pantheon, construction of a new theater, an amphitheater, an aqueduct, and public baths) attests both to the importance Caesar accorded Syria and to the prestige still attached to the ancient royal capital, whose approval he was anxious to win.

Syria, however, soon found itself once more in the thick of the Roman civil war. The new governor sent in 47, Sextus Julius Caesar, a relative of Caesar, was soon assassinated by mutinous troops at the urging of Q. Caecilius Bassus, one of Pompey's allies.[134] His successor, Lucius Antistius Vetus, was never able to take control, and civil war raged for several years between those who supported Caesar and those who opposed him. The arrival of G. Cassius, one of the leaders of the conspiracy against Caesar, complicated the issue, because this meant that a third faction was in effect added to the earlier two. Cassius managed to remove Q. Caecilius Bassus, to build himself a large army of twelve legions, and to confront the new pro-Caesar governor, Cornelius Dolabella, who was unable to remove Cassius from Antioch.[135] Dolabella retreated to Laodicea, tried unsuccessfully to get help from Arados, and soon found himself trapped in Laodicea by Cassius.[136] Once he had obtained the support of Tyre and Arados, Cassius appeared to be the true master of Syria,[137] but he was defeated, along with Brutus, at the battle of Philippi in Macedonia in 42. Once again, Syria found itself on the side of the vanquished.

Antony's Syria

Antony, one of the two leaders who had defeated Caesar's assassins, hastened to Syria in search of funds, and his presence there seems to have stirred up a number of problems. To begin with, Arados refused to free one of the Ptolemys who claimed to be Cleopatra's brother,[138] and he executed Antony's envoys, who had been sent to demand money.[139] But Antony was only passing through: he ended up settling in Egypt, and from there he gradually began to determine Syria's future. Before leaving Syria, however, he struck against Palmyra, simply to allow his army, which had received nothing from the peaceful occupation of Syria, to collect booty. Once this objective had been met, Antony went to Alexandria, but not before installing Decidius Saxa as governor.[140] Almost immediately, Syria was confronted with an unexpected consequence of the Roman civil war.

Brutus had sent a Roman, Q. Labienus, to enlist the aid of the Parthians. Despite the defeat and death of the two "liberators," the Parthians had not abandoned their enterprise, and a Parthian army, led jointly by Labienus and Pacoros, invaded Syria in 41. The Roman armies were defeated, Apamaea and Antioch taken, and the whole country occupied except for a few pockets of resistance (including Tyre). It was not until 39 that P. Ventidius Bassus was able to mount a systematic reconquest, pushing Labienus's army back from Asia Minor, where it had made inroads. In 38, the country was finally liberated, after Ventidius had defeated Pacoros in Cyrrhestica. However, Antiochos's Commagene had resisted, as had Arados, which feared possible reprisals both for the murder of Antony's envoys and for its potential support of the Parthians.[141] Consequently, Antony attacked Arados in 38: the famished and disease-ridden city surrendered after several months, in 37.[142] The Phoenician city-state, which had already lost its northern sector along with Gabala after Caesar's march, now lost Balanea as well; the latter issued an independent currency in 37.[143] Coins engraved with portraits of Antony and Fulvia or Antony and Cleopatra, issued in Arados in 38–37, in a sense mark the end of Aradian independence.[144]

Syria enjoyed a number of years of peace under Antony's government. However, the new ruler of the east pursued policies that led to profound territorial changes throughout the Near East.

Antony apparently sought to retain as much of the system of indirect administration as he could, by means of a network of client princes that had proved itself in Anatolia and Asia Minor as well as in Syria. Not only did he leave in place existing principalities, such as those of Malichos I of Nabataea, Sampsigeramos of Emesa and Arethusa, Tarcondimotos in the Amanus region, and Ptolemy's son Lysanias in the Anti-Lebanon, but he contributed to further partitioning as well. On the one hand, with Octavian's approval, in 41 he had restored a kingdom in Judaea that benefited Herod, Antipatros's son and a faithful ally of Rome since 63, to the detriment of the last Hasmonaean, Mattathias Antigonos, who had made the mistake of helping the Parthians.[145] Herod had conveniently married a Hasmonaean, Mariamme, and had become a grandson by marriage of Hyrcanos II and of Aristobulos II; he was thus guaranteed a certain legitimacy, at least in the eyes of the Romans. In fact, he had to reconquer his entire kingdom, because he had been made king of a country entirely occupied by Parthians. Moreover, Cleopatra VII, the Egyptian queen and Antony's mistress since 41, used her liaison with the imperator to try to regain part of her ancestors' kingdom. In 37–36, in a major redistribution project that included anticipated conquests as well as the lands in the east that were already his, Antony gave Phoenicia, Coele Syria, and part of Cilicia back to Cleopatra. However, owing to Herod's persuasive influence there, he refused to let her have Judaea as she had demanded, except for the balsam woods of Jericho.

Ultimately, Syria ought to have disappeared as a Roman province, because on the eve of his Parthian expedition, Antony had planned to give Syria, Phoenicia, and Cilicia to Ptolemy Helios, one of the two sons he had had with the queen.[146] Such a project would not have compromised Rome's control of the region, but its domination would have taken a different form. Antony probably imagined a series of subject kingdoms under his own governance, while his sons and representatives would bear royal titles and would direct day-to-day affairs in the territories under Rome. The defeat at Actium in September 31 and the deaths of Antony and Cleopatra the following summer put an end to all those plans.

Pompey's conquest had profoundly changed political conditions, but some thirty years later the balance sheet was decidedly mixed. On the one hand, Rome had fought off marauders and had subdued or destroyed many local tyrants who had terrorized the populace, both in the cities and in the country. Here, however, Pompey proved to have been selective: in the last analysis, once they had achieved a certain power, outlaw leaders became respectable princes with whom he had to deal (for example, Sampsigeramos and Ptolemy the Ituraean). On the other hand, the Romans had put an end to the Seleucid dynasty, with its interminable and petty quarrels. As a result, Syria found itself thrown instead into the vortex of the Roman civil war. Whereas the cities had effectively resisted the armies of the minor principalities, they could not possibly stand up to the power of the Roman army. The pillaging under Metellus and Antony revealed that the city-states had gained nothing in the change of regimes. And finally, the Parthian advance had not been halted—indeed, far from it. Something that had never happened before now happened twice: in 51 and again in 41, Syria was invaded by Parthian armies. It is true that the Romans pursued them and ultimately drove them back, but the country had suffered once again.

This first period of Roman domination was not entirely negative, however. Rome consolidated the city-states, strengthened the role of local leaders, and reinforced the power of the most important client princes. All of these were stabilizing factors, so long as peace prevailed.

FROM AUGUSTUS TO TRAJAN:
CREATING A PROVINCE

ALTHOUGH the battle of Actium marks a decisive turning point in the history of the Roman civil wars as well as in the history of Roman institutions, it had only minimal consequences for the province of Syria and the client states that revolved around it. It is true that Octavian had to make some quick decisions about the fate of a few disloyal or inept clients; still, Antony's friends did not suffer much overall as a result of his defeat. As Herod had understood very well, what ultimately mattered was loyalty to Rome, rather than to whoever happened to represent Rome's authority in the east at a given moment. Moreover, Octavian could not afford to depose Antony's clients, because he had no trustworthy replacements available.[1] Local leaders who had demonstrated their commitment and loyalty could hope to have their services quickly called upon. As Herod loftily directed upon meeting Octavian in Rhodes: "Don't think about whom I befriended, but what a friend I was!"[2] Octavian, who had been so critical of Antony's policy toward client princes, adopted the same policy himself, and he preserved Antony's organization in Syria almost intact. In this respect, Octavian's victory at Actium resulted in little change, apart from some subtleties that we shall note in due course. In fact, very few local leaders suffered from the change of imperator, and some of the kings friendly to Rome must have rejoiced at Cleopatra's demise. Herod and the kings of Petra had had to resist the territorial aspirations of the last Ptolemaic queen on several occasions; at least they were relieved of this concern.

The principal issue facing Octavian in Syria was presumably arranging for its defense: he needed both to secure the region against the threat of a Parthian invasion and to deploy troops that could be sent off on campaigns beyond Syria's borders. Once peace was assured, the temptation to expand the conquest was considerable. But the failure of the expedition into Arabia Felix ended any such hopes, especially as it was well known in Rome that the main threat came not from the south but from the east and the northeast, from Parthia and the Caucasus.

THE PROVINCIA AND ITS GOVERNORS

Since its creation by Pompey, the province of Syria had undergone only a few minor changes, resulting from Antony's gifts to some of his clients; for example, two cities of the Decapolis, Gadara and Hippos, were given to Herod.[3] For the most part, however, all of the former Seleukis, as well as Phoenicia from Arados to Dora, Damascus, and the Transjordan cities of the Decapolis,[4] continued to be part of the province. Its territories were fragmented because a few minor client states remained, some in close proximity to the most urbanized sectors, and they governed populations that were only slightly Hellenized, if at all, and not very urban.

Apart from a few modifications, some of which were short-lived, Octavian—who had virtually no support in Syria—retained the basic organization set up by Pompey and later by Antony. In 30 B.C.E. he annexed the kingdom of Tarcondimotos I in the Amanus region, in eastern Cilicia, and also the principality of Iamblichos of Emesa. Tarcondimotos had been one of Antony's most faithful allies: on coins he is called Philantonios,[5] and he perished in the service of the triumvir at Actium.[6] His son Tarcondimotos II immediately succeeded him but made the mistake of allowing groups of gladiators trying to rejoin Antony in Egypt to pass through unopposed. As for Iamblichos of Emesa, he had been executed by Antony, who suspected him of treason, and his brother Alexander (or Alexas) had replaced him; we do not know exactly what Alexander did to displease Augustus, but he was deposed, displayed in Augustus's triumphal procession, and later executed.[7] Ultimately, all these annexations proved premature. Given Rome's inability to administer the outlying regions, Octavian (who had become Augustus in the interim) gave the two states back to members of local dynasties in 20 B.C.E. Tarcondimotos II Philopator regained his kingdom, and Iamblichos, the son of the homonymous dynast who had been executed in 31, replaced his uncle Alexander at Emesa. The only annexed territory the province of Syria retained was Cilicia Campestris (Cilicia-on-the-Plain, which had been annexed in 30 B.C.E.). This was the eastern part of Cilicia, the richest and most urbanized sector, where Sulla and Cicero distinguished themselves:[8] it was the sector Antony had given to Cleopatra. Deciding not to make it a separate province, Octavian annexed it to Syria, thus joining together two regions that formed a single unit geographically and were linked by strong cultural ties.[9] Other minor annexations were carried out as well, such as those of Seleucia on the Euphrates (Zeugma), and also perhaps Doliche; these were removed from the kingdom of Commagene for strategic reasons,[10] and at the time of Herod's death in 4 B.C.E., Gaza, Gadara, and Hippos were also annexed.[11] Herod's kingdom, by contrast, was divided among his surviving sons. It was not until 6 C.E. that Archelaos's Judaea was confiscated and finally reunited with Syria, even though it was actually separated from the rest of the province by the principates of Herod Antipas and of Philip in Galilee, on the Golan and in the Hauran; it touched Phoenicia only on the coast near Dora and Ptolemais.

The geographic fragmentation of the province—aggravated by the difficulty of traversing it, due to the topography and the fact that the Roman possessions stretched across a thousand kilometers (from Tarsos to Gaza)—obviously posed problems. To address these, the governor of Syria administered certain districts through delegated prefects: this was the case in Judaea beginning in 6 C.E.,[12] and in the Decapolis possibly during Augustus's time and certainly under the Flavians.[13] The prefects enjoyed broad powers, both military and judicial, but in one way or another they were placed under the authority of the Syrian governor, even though the latter did not personally select them. This situation was not unusual in the empire; Hannah Cotton has established a judicious parallel between these prefects and the *praefecti gentium* in northwestern Spain who were assigned to administer specific city-states or populations.[14] Despite appearances, and despite Josephus's ambiguous testimony, Judaea did not constitute a fully functioning province governed by a procurator; it was simply a component of the province of Syria, run by a prefect.[15]

When the provinces were divided up between Augustus and the Senate in 27 B.C.E., Syria, a new province and one abundantly supplied with troops, was given to Augustus, who assigned a legate with consular rank. The legate continued to reside in Antioch, as had been the case since the province was constituted, despite its remoteness from the "capital."[16] From then on, Syria remained an imperial consular province (according to the misleading terminology of modern scholars).[17] Owing to the presence of numerous legions, it was often entrusted to a very high ranking official.[18] Augustus's legates in Syria included P. Quinctilius Varus (7–4 B.C.E.), previously the proconsul of Africa; L. Calpurnius Piso Pontifex (4 B.C.E.–1 C.E.),

Augustus's relative by his aunt Calpurnia (Caesar's wife); L. Volusius Saturninus (4–6 C.E.), who belonged to one of the richest senatorial families of the time; and P. Sulpicius Quirinius (6–7 C.E.), a newcomer, but covered in glory from his victories over the Marmaridae and the Garamantes in Libya and the Homonadaeans in Pisidia.[19] Given the number of troops stationed in Syria and the wealth of the province, only the most loyal men could be trusted to run it. Thus throughout the first century we find men of the highest rank and with vast experience named as heads of Syria, often fifteen or twenty years after their service as consul; only one, Gn. Calpurnius Piso (17–19), was brought to trial, as a result of some obscure maneuvers. Ordered by Tiberius to keep Germanicus under control during his tour in the east, he must have displeased the latter, who removed him from office. After Germanicus's premature death (Piso was accused of poisoning him), Piso attempted to seize control of the province, failed, and returned to Rome, counting on Tiberius's indulgence. But he could not escape trial, and he chose to commit suicide rather than wait for the inevitable verdict.[20]

By contrast, we know very little about the people around these early governors. We know that they could employ legates; some of these were used simply to control the legions, but others helped administer the province: when Herod's sons were tried, G. Sentius Saturninus was supported by two legates, who voted as he did.[21] However, there is no evidence that the legates were responsible for specific districts (*conventus*) in Syria, like those we know of in Asia.[22] We have seen that two prefects were in charge of Judaea and of the Decapolis. We should probably add to the list the prefect of Commagene, who was appointed during the period of annexation between 18 and 37 C.E., even though there is no evidence that he was dependent on the governor of Syria[23]—and we could interpret Strabo as saying just the opposite, for he referred to Commagene as if it were a Roman province.[24] There is a complete list of the prefects of Judaea, and later of the procurators who replaced them after the interruption of Agrippa I's reign (41–44), but we have no such information for the eparchy of the Decapolis, for want of a local Flavius Josephus.

Naturally, the province was also home to imperial procurators responsible for managing the provincial finances and, where such already existed, the imperial domains. The financial procurator in charge of the provincial accounts belonged to the highest echelon of his profession, that of the *ducenarii.*[25] We find several of these at work, first of all in Judaea: Volumnius, whom Josephus calls sometimes a tribune, sometimes a procurator,[26] looked after Rome's interests at Herod's court.[27] Sabinus, however, was sent to Jerusalem after Herod's death to secure his assets, which were potentially Rome's property as long as Augustus did not decide to recognize the dead king's sons' authority over their father's kingdom:[28] this was a normal responsibility for a provincial procurator. For the first century, we know of at least five other procurators: Q. Octavius Sagitta at the beginning of the era,[29] G. Clodius Priscus between 14 and 66,[30] M. Mettius Modestus around 45–50,[31] Ti. Claudius [—] around 72–75,[32] and Claudius Athenodoros, who received a letter from Domitian instructing him to resist excessive requisitions;[33] however, Athenodoros may simply have been a procurator charged with administering the imperial domains.[34] The function was important enough that on occasion (or regularly) an adjunct was named *adiutor procuratoris Syriae* or *subprocurator;* the names of three men who held this position in the first century are known to us.[35] For specific duties, a special procurator such as Q. Aemilius Secundus could be called on; Secundus was in charge of the census at Apamaea in 6–7 C.E.[36] There were also procurators charged with managing the imperial domains.

We know that Augustus supported, or at least permitted, the establishment of a cult in his honor around 29 C.E. in Bithynia-Pontus and in Asia. For a long time scholars doubted that an imperial cult was organized early on in Syria. We now know with certainty that a provincial imperial cult was begun early in the Augustan era, and that the first high priest was a certain Dexandros, a Greek from Apamaea who was also a tetrarch, "friend and ally of the Roman people"—in other words, the ruler of some local principate in central Syria.[37] The imperial cult, celebrated in Antioch, had regional ramifications at the level of what the texts call the "eparchies."[38] During the Julio-Claudian era, there were three of these districts: a northern one with its seat in Antioch, a southern one whose delegates met in Tyre, and a third that brought together the city-states of Cilicia.[39] That was the situation just before the reign of Vespasian, at any rate, and there is a good chance that it goes back to the beginning. In 72, a Commagenian eparchy must have been added following the suppression of the kingdom of Antiochos IV, whereas Cilicia was split off during the course of the 80s, after which it became a province in its own right.[40] Finally, Hadrian created a fourth eparchy, that of Coele Syria, by taking several cities from the Phoenician eparchy along the Palestinian coast and in the Decapolis.[41] Every eparchy had its imperial sanctuaries and its high priest, but in Antioch there was a "high priest of the four eparchies" who was the supreme head of the imperial cult in Syria.[42]

In itself this organization is not original; it is found in virtually the same form in the Anatolian provinces. We have no evidence to suggest that there was a provincial assembly *(koinon)* in Syria that brought together delegates from the cities and other member communities in the province.[43] There must have been such an assembly, at least for the celebration of the provincial imperial cult, but no trace of its political activity has been found. Similarly, the division into four eparchies is the only one of its kind, or at least the only one to which this terminology is applied. The word *eparchy* usually designated a province, not a conventus as seems to have been the case in Syria.[44] This is all the more peculiar in that eparchies, which at first corresponded to provincial boundaries, were not modified to reflect subsequent administrative changes. We may wonder, then, whether the eparchies had any purpose other than this celebratory one, and whether they were thus not markedly different from the Asian conventus, which provided both the setting for the administrative functions of the proconsul (who named the legates) and the seat of the courts.

The question then arises as to whether an organized conventus system existed, parallel to the organization of the imperial cult itself.[45] The way the province was designated suggests a composite structure, as was often the case in Asia Minor: a senator of the Augustan era was *legatus pro praetore diui Augusti iterum Syriam et Phoenicen obtinuit*,[46] which would imply a two-headed province, along the lines of Bithynia-Pontus or of Crete-Cyrenaica. But it is surprising that Cilicia is not mentioned: this suggests that it did not have its own koinon. At the beginning of Trajan's reign, C. Antius A. Iulius Quadratus bore the title of imperial legate of Syria, Phoenicia, and Commagene,[47] and so did C. Iulius Quadratus Bassus at the end of the same reign,[48] as we would expect after the final annexation of Commagene under the Flavians. But this observation invites several comments. In the first place, we notice that provincial modifications were not immediately followed by reorganizations in the regional structure of the imperial cult. To be sure, from Augustus to Vespasian, the three component regions—Syria, Phoenicia, and Cilicia—formed three districts of the imperial cult. But Cilicia continued to celebrate the imperial cult in Antioch after 70–72, when Commagene was added. After Cilicia had instituted its own cult organization, during the 80s, the two systems were once again in conformity, but the creation of the eparchy of Coele Syria under Hadrian again disrupted their organization: after 106, certain cities that had belonged to Coele Syria (Gerasa, Dion, Philadelphia) found themselves in the province of Arabia, and others (Scythopolis, Hippos, Gadara, Pella) belonged as before to Judaea-Syria Palestine, although this did not stop them from celebrating the imperial cult in a structure falling under the jurisdiction of the province of Syria.

In the second place, there is not the slightest trace of any regional *koina*, with delegates who might have met regularly for nonreligious purposes.[49] But the mention of a Phenikarch,[50] a Syriarch[51] or a Kilikarch[52] does not mean we should view the province of Syria as an exception, even if we can find no hard evidence of the koinon functioning there. However, the organization of common games allows us to suppose that there was a koinon for the entire province[53] (a municipal bronze from Antioch during Trajan's reign provides some evidence for this). Finally, there may have been cities that the governor visited on a regular basis for the purpose of dispensing justice—which was the particular function of the capital of a conventus—although these were not limited to Antioch, Tyre, and Samosata, the "capitals" of the province's three sectors.[54] It would be surprising if the governor did not hold court at least in Apamaea, Berytos, and Damascus. We noted earlier that during Herod's reign C. Sentius Saturninus had had at least two legates: they may have been responsible for a particular district, a subdivision whose name has been lost.

As new provinces—such as Judaea in 44 or 70 (it became Syria-Palestine in 134), then Arabia in 106—came into being, one would expect to find similar arrangements. In Judaea, however, there is no trace either of the imperial cult or of a koinon.[55] We do not know when the provincial cult in Arabia was organized, and there is no real evidence of it before the middle of the third century; if it was instituted earlier, we do not know whether it was celebrated in Bostra, the capital of the province, or in Petra, the ancient royal capital, honored with the label *metropolis* under Trajan.[56] By contrast, Philip the Arab had a vast municipal sanctuary dedicated to the imperial cult built in his native village, which became the city of Philippopolis.[57] But this was an exceptional case, linked to emperor's personal origins, and we still have practically no useful clues concerning the imperial cult in Arabia before the middle of the third century.[58] As for Judaea, no trace of the organization of a provincial imperial cult remains, although municipal cults did exist in Caesarea, Jerusalem, Samaria, and probably a number of other cities in the province.

THE DEFENSES OF IMPERIAL SYRIA IN THE FIRST CENTURY

Legions, Auxiliaries, and Military Camps

An inventory of the legions and their camps is easy to construct, despite a few gaps in our knowledge. There were four legions in Syria under the first Julio-Claudians: Legio III Gallica was probably stationed in northern Syria, although we cannot say exactly where, or when it was sent there.[59] VI Ferrata was first posted near Laodicea before it left to replace XII Fulminata in Raphanaea in central Syria,[60] X Fretensis was located in Cyrrhos,[61] and XII Fulminata in Raphanaea until 70.[62] Around 56, IV

Scythica was posted in Zeugma in northern Syria, close to the Commagene border, at a crossing point on the Euphrates.[63] That brought the number of Syrian legions to five; each was headed by its own legate, as was customary in provinces housing numerous legions, where the governor could not fulfill the duties of commander to them all.[64]

After 70 c.e., X Fretensis remained garrisoned in Jerusalem, where it had been dispatched during the Jewish revolt,[65] while XII Fulminata was ordered by Cestius Gallus to move to Melitene in Cappadocia, a move that was seen as punishment for its failure at the beginning of the war.[66] Shortly after 75,[67] XVI Flavia Firma set up camp in Samosata, in the former capital of the recently annexed Commagene.[68] Perhaps this final reorganization of the legions was related to the "Parthian war" of 75–76,[69] as an allusion in Pliny the Younger suggests, but it may have been in relation to the invasion of the Alans into Media Atropatene and Armenia, for which Vologases requested Rome's assistance.[70] Thus, under the Flavians, Syria proper retained its four legions, while Judaea was home to only one permanent legion. The arrangement was completed by the possibility of Roman squadrons using the port of Seleucia of Pieria, where Vespasian ordered work done to prevent silting; however, there is no proof that a permanent squadron, the *classis Syriaca*, existed during this period, and there is no reference to such a unit during the first century.[71]

In addition to the legions, numerous auxiliary units were present. The exact details are not well known, but the works of several military diplomas (individual records of soldiers' privileges), taken together, provide a fairly precise picture of the auxiliary units stationed in Syria in 88 and 91.[72] We can then compare this picture with one produced by information possibly pertaining to the Syrian army that was provided by a military diploma from the very end of Claudius's reign (54);[73] we can also draw on accounts provided by Josephus during the 60s, and on various documents dating from the middle of the second century c.e., including a list of the units stationed in Syria and placed under the sole command of M. Valerius Lollianus during a campaign that may have taken place during Hadrian's reign.[74] The comparison suggests the following conclusions, according to Edward Dąbrowa: around 60, Syria had seven cavalry wings (*alae*) and seven cohorts representing a minimum of 7,000 men, if we estimate that each one consisted of 500 men (however, we might have to add 2,000 men if some wings were as large as 1,000). In 88–91, there were twelve wings (at least one of which consisted of 1,000 men) and twenty-two cohorts (at least two of which were 1,000 strong), for a total of 18,500 men. These numbers remained more or less stable, for in the middle of the second century Syria contained six wings (with 1,000 troops in at least two of them) and twenty-two cohorts (three of which numbered 1,000) for a total of 16,500 men. The sharp increase that was seen after the Jewish revolt probably had nothing to do with the revolt itself, but it illustrates the risk to the eastern frontier posed by a certain Terentius Maximus in 80, when he tried to pass himself off as Nero and forged an alliance with the Parthians.[75]

During the early empire, then, among the provinces that made up the eastern frontier of the empire, Syria was the one with the greatest number of troops.[76] This can probably be explained by the relatively open landscape, which offered a large number of possible routes between the Parthian Empire and the Roman Empire. Whereas in the high valleys of the Tigris and Euphrates, controlling a small number of passes was enough to provide security,[77] at the point where the Euphrates leaves the mountains the entire riverbank had to be defended. This explanation may be inadequate, however. In fact, the legions were not deployed in any numbers along the border; they seem rather to have spread out within the province itself. The placement of camps[78] near Laodicea, in Raphanaea, and in Cyrrhos hardly suggests an army protecting Syria against an invasion from the east. This has led Benjamin Isaac to argue that in the Near Eastern provinces the Roman army constituted an occupying force more concerned with the job of maintaining internal order than with defending the empire against Parthian incursions.[79] While this may be the case, it is probably a slight exaggeration. Syria's very shape called for a specific organization. Some troops were stationed in immediate proximity to the border, in nondesert zones: in Samosata and in Zeugma, for example. But farther south, troops were stationed in regions that could support them, not in the steppe, where patrols roamed. This may explain the choice of Cyrrhos, situated in the rear, but still in proximity to the border along the Euphrates. These logistical considerations do not explain everything, however, for the fact that a legion was located near Laodicea, far from the frontier and in a city with poor communication with the interior, leads us to believe that the legion in question was intended more for north–south than for east–west movement. Similarly, while Raphanaea, without being on an important axis, had the advantage of being equidistant from Apamaea and the Homs pass (from which point troops could quickly intervene on the northern coast of Phoenicia as well as in Emesa), it was still quite far from the Euphrates front, and indeed from any border. Conversely, it is somewhat surprising that no legion was stationed in the south of the province—in Ptolemais or Damascus, for example—near Judaea, which became a hotbed of agitation after Herod's death.

The mission of the Syrian legions cannot in fact be reduced to a single purpose. Protecting the frontier no doubt remained a priority, but this may have become a secondary consideration once the Parthian threat abated. Surveillance of the Syrian cities undoubtedly constituted a second objective, but here again there does not seem to have been significant unrest, despite some problems in the Phoenician cities under Augustus. According to Tacitus,[80] this would explain the apathy allegedly manifested by the soldiers in the Syrian legion on the eve of the expedition to Armenia.[81] Ultimately, the primary function of the legions in the province was to provide an initial expeditionary force in case of Roman intervention in the east, in the Parthian kingdom, or in Armenia, conjointly with the Cappadocian troops following the reduction of the provincial kingdom of Archelaos to a province in 17 C.E. But these campaigns were widely separated in time: after a long period of unrest from 65 to 36 B.C.E., it was not until 52–63 C.E., and then Trajan's Parthian expedition in 112–117, that the legions were mobilized against the Parthians. That left long periods of virtual inactivity—in other words, of routine.

The Creation of a Road System

What we know about Rome's establishment of a road system in the first century remains largely conjectural at present.[82] No thorough on-site study of any road has been undertaken; we have to rely on a set of fortuitous discoveries. An initial study of Syrian milestones, published in 1917, has never really been replaced.[83] It needs to be corrected and completed if we are to attempt even a rough outline, however partial.

Moreover, we need to agree on what we mean by a road system. A number of texts give us the impression that, apart from a few strategic routes dubbed "royal roads,"[84] no one had thought about communications across kingdoms before the Romans came, and one wonders how trade was possible in a country so badly neglected. It is true that Hellenistic kings were not in the habit of writing their names on milestones placed at regular intervals, thus depriving us of valuable information. Nevertheless, whatever may eventually be discovered, there was surely a dense network of roads across Syria before the Romans appeared, and the inhabitants of Syria did not wait for the Romans in order to travel from one city to another.

What did Rome add, then, in this domain? Its most obvious contribution was clearly the construction of hard-surface roads—raised roadways paved with stone. Although near Tell Aqibrin, in northern Syria, we still find impressive (but perhaps late) remains of the Roman road that connected Chalcis and Beroea with Antioch, it would be a mistake to think that this type of construction was widespread. Other ruins have been found in Arabia and in Mesopotamia, dating from the end of the second or the beginning of the third century. There is no evidence that the entire route was built this extravagantly; such expensive roads may have been limited to areas that were muddy in winter or especially rocky. Elsewhere, Rome generally settled for maintaining the dirt roads that were already in use or those that were roughly paved with stones. Nothing rules out the possibility that these roads, too, were lined with milestones like the ones M. Ulpius Traianus, the father of the future emperor, set up some fifteen kilometers east of Palmyra.[85] We are heavily dependent on such milestones: in a way, our assessment of Roman road-building activity is based on an individual governor's decision to engage in propaganda work along the roadway. We must be cautious when it comes to a line of argument *a silentio*.

Rome was clearly concerned with bridge building, although most bridges in Syria appear to belong primarily, here again, to the second and third centuries. The bridge over the Chabinas between Samosata and Melitene is an exception: this one, although it was repaired under the Severi, may have been constructed as early as Vespasian's time.[86] What was undoubtedly most important was the more or less regular placement of guard posts that ensured the safety of travelers, especially in areas exposed to Bedouin raids. In this area also, however, in first-century Syria, a great deal of work remains to be done, because the groundbreaking accounts of Antoine Poidebard and René Mouterde do not allow even approximate dating, given the lack of milestones or dated inscriptions directly relating to marked roadways.[87] Without denying the importance of the Roman presence in the Syrian steppe, we are probably safe in assuming that it was fairly light in the first century, and that the oldest of the permanent small forts spotted by airborne archaeologists most likely date from the second and third centuries, as is the case in Arabia. We shall come back to this topic in a later chapter.

To return to the question of roads, the only one we know a little about is the one along the coast that leads, according to a milestone found south of Beirut, "from Antioch to the new colony of Ptolemais."[88] This means that the first reference to the building of this road is no earlier than the foundation of the colony of Ptolemais in 54. The oldest milestone we know of dates in fact from 56;[89] for the next three centuries, we have only twenty-five milestones from twenty sites, at least half of which come from the Berytos-Sidon section. So we cannot draw any conclusions about the significance of this route, but we may observe that, for the period that interests us here, the milestones that have been found belong to the reigns of Vespasian and Domitian. This is not surprising, considering the importance of easy communication between Syria and Ptolemais, the gateway to Judaea.

Judaea does not appear to have been provided with a road system superior to that of the rest of Syria, at least not during this period. In 69, a milestone in the name of M. Ulpius Traianus, commander of Legio X Fretensis, was located on the Caesarea–Scythopolis road, which may have continued as far as Pella and Gerasa;[90] this is the only milestone that predates Hadrian's reign. However, during the 70s there were milestones showing the construction or improvement of certain axes that had military importance. One such milestone stood on the Apamaea–Raphanaea road in 72,[91] and another, dating from 75, shows that there was a marked route across the desert between Palmyra and Sura on the Euphrates at that time;[92] this makes sense only if there were also good routes between Palmyra and Emesa or Palmyra and Damascus. A third milestone, from 75–76, stood near the intersection where the route going from Palmyra to Apamaea crossed the one going from Chalcis of Belos to Emesa.[93] This gives us reason to believe that an effort was made to control central Syria, including the steppes, during the time of Ulpius Traianus's government.

External Threats, Real or Imagined

The Euphrates border, while never the object of any treaty, was preserved despite various Parthian incursions into Syria. There is no indication that Augustus ever seriously considered pushing it farther back: rather, he thought he was protecting this flank of the empire by placing a client of Rome on the Armenian throne, and thus we see no attempt at conquest in that direction. That did not prevent Rome from having to wage war there. But it was to the south that Rome directed its armies, first and foremost, for reasons having nothing to do with security.

AELIUS GALLUS IN ARABIA FELIX

The legendary riches of the Nabataeans had captured the imagination of Antigonos the One-Eyed, Pompey, and Aemilius Scaurus. Each of them had attempted to take the Nabataean capital, where they expected to find gold, silver, perfumes, and aromatics in abundance:[94] people who traded in such costly products had to be fabulously wealthy! Moreover, in Rome as in the Greek world, an image of power was associated with the possession of perfumes and aromatics, an image that in some sense provided the basis for the legitimacy of authority,[95] according to a standard dating back to the time of Alexander the Great.[96] Augustus, who now controlled the Mediterranean trade outlets in Arabia Felix, either directly, as in Egypt, or through the intermediary of the Nabataean kingdom, seems to have wanted even more; he wanted to get his hands on the means of production themselves. That is the only explanation we can reasonably invoke to justify the expedition launched in 26–25 B.C.E.[97] by the Egyptian prefect Aelius Gallus.[98] Indeed, the small southern Arabian kingdoms[99] did not pose any sort of threat and could not be accused of meddling in Rome's affairs.

Aelius Gallus took charge of a large expedition in which some 11,500 men were mobilized and transported to the Arabian coast on the Red Sea after a difficult crossing.[100] We do not know exactly where the expedition landed: probably somewhere in the far north, in the region of 'Aynunah rather than in the south near al-Wajh, because the troops still had to traverse a lengthy land route. As a guide, Aelius Gallus counted on Syllaios, the Nabataean minister whose assistance as a go-between was essential: not only did the Roman army have to cross territory belonging to the kingdom, but only the Nabataeans knew the roads and watering holes and could negotiate with local tribes encountered on the way and obtain provisions. The Romans probably had not expected the route to be as long as it was; despite its successes, the army was exhausted when it reached its final destination. Although it won its battle beneath the walls of Marsiaba (according to Strabo) or perhaps Mariba,[101] the expeditionary force had to do an about-face. If Strabo's Marsiaba turns out to be al-'Abr and not Marib, as some have recently and convincingly argued,[102] the Roman army would have been only two days' march from Shabwa, the heart of incense production at Hadramaout.

Historiographical tradition has long held that the Aelius Gallus expedition was a failure.[103] This mistaken view comes principally from Strabo's account; Syllaios's execution by the Romans, on the pretext that the Nabataean had betrayed, or at least misled, Aelius Gallus, is described in an epilogue. In fact, there is reason to doubt that Syllaios's execution was directly related to the expedition of 26–25, or at least that the expedition was its sole cause, because the execution did not take place until 6 C.E., after a delay that is hard to explain; it thus appears to be much more connected with the terms of the succession of Obodas III, who died in 9 B.C.E. and was replaced under difficult circumstances. Moreover, Strabo's account notwithstanding, the Romans do not seem to have regarded the expedition as a failure. The undertaking produced a series of military successes achieved without great cost: according to Strabo, Rome lost only seven soldiers in combat, among them the cavalryman P. Cornelius, whose Latin epitaph has been discovered at Baraqish.[104] There were thus good reasons why Augustus could count the Arabs among the peoples he had conquered; their names and faces figure among other defeated peoples on the northern portico of the Sebasteion of Aphrodisias, constructed under the

Julio-Claudians, in a series that probably repeats the list of those whose effigies had adorned Augustus's funeral procession.[105] Moreover, in the middle of the first century, the *Periplus Maris Erythraei*[106] mentions Karib'il, king of the Himyarites and the Sabaeans, as the "friend of emperors": this may be the sign of some degree of allegiance on the part of the princes of southern Arabia after Gallus's campaign. Moreover, Glen Bowersock dates the minting of the "class B" coins at Sanaa to the immediate aftermath of the Roman expedition; one of these bears an unmistakable portrait of Augustus, yet another sign of allegiance.[107] Finally, the Indian embassies sent to Augustus[108] may have responded to a need to assess the changes that had occurred on the peninsula and to take into account the new role that Rome intended to play there.

One further sign of the importance of the expedition for both parties is more difficult to interpret. A new era, called the *nbt* era, was introduced between 49 and 21 B.C.E. Its name most probably comes from the Nabataeans rather than from some other unknown namesake. A number of different origins have been suggested, such as Actium[109] or the Julian reform,[110] but neither of these events had the slightest connection to the Nabataeans. However, Aelius Gallus's expedition may well have been perceived by the inhabitants of southern Arabia as undertaken by their Nabataean neighbors. Defeating this foe would have justified the proclamation of a new era.[111] There are problems with this theory, however. First, the very name of the era is problematic: we could understand an "era of the victory over the Nabataeans," not an "era of the Nabataeans" if indeed the latter were defeated. In addition, the celebration of victory would seem to be in contradiction with the signs, noted earlier, of at least formal submission to Rome. Alternatively, of course, we might grant that the peoples of southern Arabia satisfied Rome with inconsequential tokens (coins with the effigy of Augustus), thus allowing Rome to claim victory (the Aphrodisias monument) while they themselves celebrated the defeat of Rome's allies.

Rome had now led its armies to the southern part of the Arabian Peninsula. The results were disappointing, but at least the Romans had measured the vastness of the deserts that stretched south of the Nabataean kingdom. Conquest appeared to be impossible, and indeed, after Aelius Gallus no one ever made the attempt again.[112]

THE EUPHRATES FRONT[113]

The fact that there were almost no flare-ups on the Euphrates front for almost a century and a half does not mean that the Roman army in Syria was inactive. During the expeditions against Armenia organized in Augustus's time, Syria served as a rear base. The details, objectives, and outcomes need not concern us here, except where Syria itself is directly involved.[114]

Gaius Caesar's mission to the east obviously depended on Syria. The meeting between Gaius Caesar and the Parthian king Phraates V, an encounter that prevented war between the two empires, took place on an island in the Euphrates in the year 1 C.E.[115] In 3 C.E., from Syria, Gaius attacked the usurper Addon, who had managed to draw him into Armenia, but we do not know which troops he took with him on the ill-fated operation during which he received the wound from which he died soon afterward.[116]

Interventions were not always armed, and the governor of Syria sometimes only followed what was going on from the other side of the Euphrates. For example, in 15–16 C.E. the governor Creticus Silanus was instructed to place the Parthian Vonones—the eldest son of Phraates IV, who was greedily eyeing Armenia—under guard at Antioch (although with full royal honors).[117] Shortly afterward, Gn. Calpurnius Piso was asked to make himself available to Germanicus, who was in charge of a mission to the east, while the governor of Syria was responsible for moving Vonones from Antioch to Pompeiopolis in Cilicia.[118] In 35, Vitellius, then governor of Syria, had to support pro-Roman candidates for the thrones of Armenia and the Parthian Empire,[119] as well as to negotiate with Artaban II after the military failure of his protégés: once again, the meeting took place on the Euphrates, symbolically reinforcing the idea that the river constituted the border between the two empires.[120] In 51, the Syrian governor Ummidius Quadratus convened his council to decide whether it was time to intervene in Armenia,[121] and after the unfortunate intervention of Iulius Paelignus, the procurator of Cappadocia, another Syrian legate, Helvidius Priscus, had to restore order in Armenia, taking with him one of the legions transferred from the Syrian garrison.[122]

Just as the young Nero was rising to power in Rome, a new expedition against Armenia to expel the Parthians appeared necessary.[123] Troops of the client princes were called together in Syria while bridges were being built across the Euphrates. Some of Syria's client princes were even given responsibility for administering the areas bordering on Armenia: Herod's grandson, Aristobulos, had Lesser Armenia, and Sohaimos of Emesa had Sophene. The general responsible for the campaign, Gn. Domitius Corbulo, was put in charge of half of the troops in Syria: III Gallica, VI Ferrata, a *vexillatio* (detachment) from X Fretensis, and quite probably some auxiliary units as well.[124] But it did not take him long to realize that these troops, lacking training and sometimes even weapons, were incapable of carrying out the campaign. He had to restore order in the Syrian army before it could be made operational.[125]

Throughout the long campaign begun in late 57, the details of which are not important here,[126] all the Syrian legions were called upon to contribute, both during the early part of the campaign under the command of Corbulo himself as well as later under his successor, L. Caesennius Paetus (who used IV Scythica and XII Fulminata), and during Corbulo's return to take command of the troops again after the defeat at Rhandeia.[127] We may infer, then, that Rome had little fear of unrest in Syria itself, despite the ongoing problems that plagued Judaea.

ROME AND THE NOMADS

Nomads—frequently confused with Arabs—had an unfortunate reputation among ancient authors for banditry. However, there is no indication that Rome ever had to combat them on the Syrian borders. Pompey's immediate successors at the head of the province may have had to do so: we are told that they had to fight "the Arabs," although that does not necessarily mean the Nabataeans. Our information on this point is sparse. Nevertheless, we cannot ignore the fact that Arab groups had been settling in the area surrounding the Syrian steppe since Hellenistic times. Certain groups, such as those known collectively as Safaites, were already there (we shall look more closely at them later on). Did Rome attempt to intervene in tribal wars? Did provincial cities require Rome's protection against nomad raids? Nothing in the available documentation allows us to answer. The regions where ongoing raiding is documented lay in states governed by client princes, notably in the kingdom of Judaea, and the raiders in question were not necessarily nomads.[128]

The only information that may eventually be linked to the control of the desert concerns relations between Rome and Palmyra. We have seen that Antony did not hesitate to send his troops against the city in 41 B.C.E. for the sole purpose of acquiring booty. The record of more than half a century of the city's history is missing, but in 19 C.E. at the latest,[129] and probably during that very year,[130] Palmyra was incorporated into the Roman Empire. It would be easier to explain Germanicus's presence in the city in 19 if the city was already under Rome's control. From that time on, perhaps under Claudius's reign, and certainly under the Flavians, the "community of the Palmyrenes" (*gbl tdmr* in Aramaic)[131] increasingly acquired civic institutions on the Greek model, which implies that the city was part of the empire. The same can be said of the project to install milestones undertaken by M. Ulpius Traianus, governor of Syria under Vespasian; such projects underline Rome's interest in taking effective control of the roads and trails that crossed the desert.[132] Until that time, Palmyra had preserved its status as a free city outside the empire, without being subject to the Parthians, either: its independence may have been one of the sources of its fortune, but its wealth also made it desirable. The incorporation of Palmyra into the Roman Empire did not interfere with the development of commerce in any way: as we shall see, the apogee of Palmyrene commerce was reached in the early empire.

Whatever problems the nomad groups may have posed for Rome, we have no way of knowing how Rome dealt with them. In fact, although we know with some precision the number (and names) of the auxiliary units stationed in the province, we are unable to establish their distribution on the ground; that alone would enable us to know whether these troops were positioned to confront the nomads, the Parthians, the city-states, or all three at once. The archaeological record does not fill in these gaps, because we have not been able to identify any small forts constructed on the edge of the desert before the second century.

THE CLIENT STATES IN THE FIRST CENTURY C.E.

Tetrarchs,[133] Dynasts, and Principates: From Rex Socius to Rex Datus

We have seen how a network of client states was gradually built up, beginning under Pompey, and how Antony maintained and expanded upon this system, as he had done in Anatolia, in order to govern the less Hellenized areas of Syria.[134] After Antony's final land grants, the province of Syria proper found itself surrounded on all sides by client states that separated it from the other Roman provinces: the principate of Cilicia Tracheia to the northwest, the sacerdotal state of the Teucrids around the sanctuary of Olba a little farther east, the kingdom of Amanus in the high Pyramos valley, the kingdom of Commagene, the principate of Emesa, the kingdom of Herod covering almost all of Palestine but extending quite far into the interior of Lebanon and the south of Syria, the Nabataean kingdom in the Transjordan and finally in the Negev. Augustan Syria had virtually no common border with any other Roman province.

Besides these kingdoms and principates that surrounded the provincia on all sides, there remained within the province itself indigenous principates, entrusted to tetrarchs who were "friends and allies of the Roman people"—for example, the tetrarchy of Dexandros,[135] an Apamaean Greek who was fortunate enough to have a principate carved out for him in the vicinity of his native city. The principates of Lebanon and the Anti-Lebanon (Chalcis of Lebanon, Arca, Abila of Lysanias) were among the largest, but there were others in the mountain and steppe regions. Pliny names several in the Alouite mountains (Jebel Ansarie), such as the tetrarchy of the Nazareni, separated from Apamaea by the Orontes, the two tetrarchies of the Granucometai, and that of Mammisea; and he reports that there were seventeen other "tetrarchies divided into kingdoms and bearing barbarian names,"[136] probably in the mountainous regions of northern and central Syria. A more precise geography of the principates would probably enable us to understand better why these kingdoms were maintained, but Pliny does not see fit to name them or to situate them, even roughly.

The chiefs of these principates normally had the title *tetrarch,* a term found not only in Pliny's list, in the Gospels, and in Josephus, but also in a quite official inscription in Apamaea: L. Iulius Agrippa claims to descend from tetrarchs who were "friends and allies of the Roman people" on both his mother's and his father's side.[137] The term *tetrarch* is the only title known for these leaders besides that of king. In stressing the fact that tetrarchies were viewed as kingdoms, Pliny no doubt sought to emphasize their standing as independent states even though they were friends and allies of Rome. We also know, however, that Rome reserved the royal title for its most loyal and most capable allies: in 4 B.C.E., Augustus refused to give the title to Herod's three sons and successors, remarking that time would tell whether or not they were worthy of it.

The fact that Rome maintained these client states is usually attributed to the specific characteristics of rural and mountainous regions; Rome no doubt believed it had more to lose than to gain by administering these regions directly. This same situation turns up again in northern Syria, since tetrarchies continued to exist not far from Apamaea or Antioch. It appears, then, that the proximity of the large Greek cities did not suffice, after three centuries of uninterrupted presence, to integrate enough indigenous leaders for them to be able to act as relays for the Roman government. However, we must acknowledge that our ignorance is too great at present to be able to argue that there was a single rationale for the creation or continuation of all these principates. There may also have been a complex interplay of personal relations, balances of power, and even financial interests: we can recall that even Pompey himself preferred to recognize the Ituraean brigand chieftain Ptolemy, son of Mennaios, in exchange for one thousand talents, rather than annex his territory. How many local leaders, installed on their own initiative during the time of the last Seleucids, bought their political survival in the same way? We shall probably never know.

Although we cannot fully account for the decision, we know that Rome opted for indirect rule, through the intermediary of these loyal clients who were also probably better suited than Roman officials for maintaining order and for pacifying sometimes inaccessible regions. Moreover, it was a less costly way to govern, and Rome knew that in times of serious trouble it could always dispatch Roman troops stationed in the provincia proper.

Rome's expectations of the client princes never varied, whether they descended from ancient indigenous royal families or owed their recent fortune entirely to Rome. In Commagene, as in Palestine, these client rulers were the ones who propagated a policy of urbanization that resulted in the founding of several cities. Other princes were associated with a policy of beautification that seems to have been encouraged by the Roman authorities, if not developed by them. Thus the Herodians covered the cities of Phoenicia with lavish monuments.[138] Under the Flavians, Palmyra and Bostra benefited from simultaneous urban development projects;[139] but while the governor of Syria had to act as Rome's agent in carrying out the imperial policy in Palmyra (which was integrated into the province in 19 c.e.), in Bostra the policy was carried out by King Rabbel II (71–106), who had made the city a sort of capital of the northern part of his kingdom.[140] Thus, within his own realm a king played the same role as the governor in a province. What better proof is there that the client state was simply one way of governing what amounted, in any event, to Rome's empire?

It may seem excessive to consider all these tetrarchs or Roman client kings as equals. Obviously, they differed in terms of their power; one cannot compare Dexandros of Apamaea with Herod or Aretas IV. Yet they had at least one thing in common: the conditions under which they were appointed. To be sure, the Herodians appear to have been the most dependent on Rome: their royalty had no legitimate basis, deriving simply from a decision made by Antony. For the others (at least those about whom we have some information), the situation was quite different. In Emesa, the dynasty of Sampsigeramos did not derive its power from Rome, since it was already in place when Pompey arrived. However, when Augustus removed Alexander (Jannaeus) from his principate of Emesa in 30 B.C.E. and restored the principate to Iamblichos ten years later, he was clearly signaling that he had the power to make and unmake kings.[141] In the case of the Nabataeans, whose dynasty went back at least to the beginning of the second (if not to the third) century B.C.E., we might expect that their own rules of succession were applied without Roman interference. Yet the legitimate heir could not accede to the throne without Rome's consent: when Aretas IV succeeded Obodas III without asking for Augustus's approval (in 9 B.C.E.), Augustus was so angry about it[142] that he may have briefly confiscated the kingdom.[143] If that is indeed what happened, Augustus was sharply underlining the fact that Aretas derived his power from Rome, not from an independent Nabataean dynastic tradition. Similarly, by confiscating Commagene in 17 B.C.E., prior to reinstating Antiochos IV in 37, then removing Antiochos again before restoring his kingdom to him in 41, Rome made it obvious that Caesar alone could make a king, in Samosata as in Jerusalem, in Emesa as in Petra.

Government by way of a client intermediary allowed Rome to rule at less cost, but it deprived the imperial treasury of fiscal resources because revenues were shared with the client prince, who maintained an army[144] and paid administrative costs. Moreover, the increasing number of dynasts, and the power some of them held, could be a political threat. There was always the possibility that princes who ruled important states might be tempted to try to regain greater independence. The Roman government was concerned that they might form alliances; for example, the governor of Syria broke up a meeting of six client princes that had been called in Tiberias at the initiative of Agrippa I.[145] Finally, the client princes were not always as effective as the Roman government expected, and on several occasions Rome had to come to the aid of incompetent princes, particularly in Judaea. Roman officers and officials played roles in certain client states, and although we do not know their precise responsibilities, we can easily imagine that their job included support and oversight. For example, a certain Volumnius, whom Josephus identifies sometimes as a tribune, sometimes as a procurator, was part of Herod's entourage.[146] Under Agrippa II, a Roman officer, L. Obulnius, directed a wing called the Augusta, which, despite its name, must have belonged to Agrippa's army, not Rome's.[147]

This system certainly did not constitute a panacea, and it soon showed its limitations. Thus, for reasons that varied from state to state, a gradual integration of client states began under Augustus's reign (starting with Judas of Archelaos in 6 C.E.). But this policy also reflected the differing approaches of successive emperors. Although Tiberius tended to favor annexation, Caligula and Claudius in contrast were inclined to reconstitute the annexed principates, remaining faithful in the main to the model created by Antony and continued by Augustus. The personal ties that linked these emperors to certain clients (Caligula had been raised with Agrippa I and with Thracian and Pontic princes), and their sense of a dynastic continuity from which they themselves benefited, may explain the survival of a form of government whose rationale gradually faded over time.[148] The ascent to power of Vespasian, a new figure who had no dynastic or personal ties to Syrian clients, changed the situation quickly.

We shall return below to the conditions under which the most important of these client kingdoms disappeared. As for the small tetrarchies of the Syrian mountains, we have no precise information, but they were probably annexed one by one as their tetrarchs died during the course of the first century, although we cannot reconstruct the chronology. By 115, the tetrarchy of Dexandros of Apamaea had long since disappeared, and its descendants are described only as former tetrarchs. It would be rather surprising if the interior principates had managed to endure even after all the great kingdoms had disappeared.

The Kingdom of Commagene and Its Vicissitudes

We last looked at Commagene just after Antiochos I had shown his good will toward Lucullus following the defeat of Tigranes of Armenia. Antiochos was presumably one of the twelve barbarian kings who came to honor Pompey in 66;[149] Pompey immediately confirmed his authority. Antiochos had good reasons to proclaim himself *philorhomaios,* "a friend of the Romans." Moreover, according to the scanty information available, he did not disappoint Rome in the perilous days to come. For Rome, Commagene was a significant ally because it controlled some of the Euphrates crossings and thus access both to Syria and to Asia Minor. Yet despite the friendship and even familial ties forged between the kings of Commagene and the Parthians, the former remained loyal to Rome. Thus envoys of Antiochos I were the ones who announced to Cicero, then governor of Cilicia, that the Parthians had crossed the Euphrates in the autumn of 51. The Commagenians were at Pompey's side at Pharsalus, as promised,[150] even if there were only two hundred of them,[151] but after Pompey's defeat Antiochos I transferred his friendship for Rome to Caesar. There was only one false note: after the Parthian invasion of 40–37, Ventidius, the new governor of Syria, accused Antiochos I of Commagene of having helped the Parthians; this provoked a Roman expedition in 37, led by Antony himself, with the aid of several client princes. However, Samosata proved impregnable under siege, and Antony had to withdraw virtually empty-handed, without even enough booty to justify the trip.[152] Antiochos I probably died a short time later, but this is not certain.

His successor, Mithradates II, first appears on record at the time of the battle of Actium, where he fought beside Antony, like all the princes of the Near East.[153] We do not know whether Antiochos I was already dead, for Mithradates seems to have been associated with his father at the end of his reign. After Actium, Octavian made no changes in the kingdom of Commagene, but in 29, when Mithradates got involved in a fight with his brother Antiochos (II), Octavian quickly put a stop to it and had Antiochos condemned by the Senate and executed.[154] The stated motive for the condemnation was Antiochos's murder of his brother's ambassador, but Octavian's speedy and unequivocal reaction no doubt reflected his unwillingness to let a dynastic crisis develop in Commagene—for such a crisis, by weakening the kingdom, would have encouraged Parthian operations. Mithradates himself died in 20.

Mithradates was probably succeeded by a nephew whose father he had had executed,[155] a young man about whom we know almost nothing, except that the kings who followed were his direct descendants. We do not know when he died; we can state with certainty only that his eldest son, Antiochos III, reigned for a time and died in 17 C.E. We know nothing about this latter Antiochos, apart from an inscription dedicated to him in Athens.[156]

Our information is obviously scanty, but we know at least that the kings of Commagene appeared strong enough to keep Rome from annexing their kingdom, and effective enough that Rome trusted them to protect the Euphrates crossings between Arsameia and Zeugma. Their power is doubtless reflected in part in the splendor of the royal tombs, the *hierothesia* erected by Antiochos I at the top of Nemrut Dag[157] and by Mithradates II at Arsameia of Nymphaios.[158] This is not the place for an analysis of the religious and dynastic significance of these tombs, but it is clear that such constructions displayed the glory of the dynasty for all to see and symbolized its desire for permanence.

Nevertheless, in 17 C.E. Commagene[159] was annexed at the same time as the kingdom of Amanus, the high valley of Pyramos around Hierapolis-Castabala and Anazarbe. The reasons for the annexation are not clear, but in the case of Commagene, Josephus refers to a request by the nobility of the kingdom, whereas the ordinary people remained loyal to the traditional monarchy.[160] The two kingdoms were incorporated into the province of Syria, and Q. Servaeus, one of Germanicus's companions, was named prefect of Commagene,[161] in keeping with the practice attested in Judaea. As early as 37 or 38, however, Caligula restored Antiochos IV, son of Antiochos III, only to remove him shortly afterward.[162] The kingdom, augmented in the west by the territory that was established at the time in honor of Caligula or Claudius and later became Germanicia, was given back to Antiochos IV by Claudius after 41, along with part of Cilicia Tracheia.

In 72 Commagene was permanently annexed to Syria on the pretext that Antiochos IV was plotting with the Parthians. At the same time, the king lost Cilicia Tracheia (Rough Cilicia), which had belonged to him since 41;[163] this territory was reattached to Cilicia Pedias (Plain Cilicia) in order to create a new praetorian imperial province entrusted to a legate living in Tarsos. Syria was thus amputated in the north and northwest, losing a vast, rich, and populous territory, and Antioch once again found itself practically on the northern boundary of the province. The loss of Cilicia was offset, at least in terms of size, by the annexation of Commagene, which lengthened to the north the part of the Euphrates that was controlled by the Syrian governor.

Emesa, Arethusa, and Arca of Lebanon

Established toward the end of the Hellenistic period, the principate of the Sampsigeramids extended around Emesa and its neighbor Arethusa, both situated on the Orontes. Just before the battle of Actium, Antony had Iamblichos, the client prince in power, executed; Iamblichos was a son of the Sampsigeramos who had become involved in the latest jockeying for power among the Seleucid kings. Suspecting Iamblichos of treason, Antony had replaced him with his brother Alexander.[164] After his victory, Octavian removed Alexander and confiscated his principate,[165] but ultimately returned it in 20 B.C.E. to another Iamblichos, son of the one executed in 31.[166]

The golden age of the principate began with Iamblichos II (20 B.C.E.–14 C.E.) and continued under his successor Sampsigeramos II (14–48).[167] These long reigns, like those of the Nabataean sovereigns of the same period, contributed both to political stability in the principate and to the principate's gradual cultural integration, at least on the surface, into the Greco-Roman world. At the same time, the principate grew rich, owing no doubt to the commercial growth of Palmyra, for which Emesa was the obligatory gateway to the sea. Moreover, the princes of Emesa maintained close ties with Palmyra, where Sampsigeramos II came to be designated in one inscription as "supreme king."[168] The principate's wealth is not visible today in monumental architecture, as Emesa is perhaps the most thoroughly destroyed ancient city in Syria. Two superb gold funeral masks survive as the only remains of a royal necropolis that must have been sumptuous.[169]

Not long after Sampsigeramos II participated in the meeting in Tiberias,[170] he was replaced by his son Azizos. The latter, who died about 53 or 54, left few traces, but he married Agrippa II's sister Drusilla, a Jewish woman, and even agreed to be circumcised.[171] Drusilla soon left him for the procurator Felix, and Azizos died shortly thereafter. He was replaced by his brother Sohaimos, whom Nero also named head of Sophene to replace Cotyx IX.[172] This double function is evidence not only of the emperor's confidence but also of the integration of the Emesene princes into the Roman system of government. During this time, Emesa seems to have been a regional power: although it had been stripped of the principate of Chalcis (despite the fact that the two families were linked), the Emesene family presumably remained close to the dynasty in Arca and exerted its influence, in religion at least, in Baalbek-Heliopolis—which, despite its status as a Roman colony, honored "Sohaimos, son of the great king Sampsigeramos."[173] This association may be explained by the kinship between the Emesene gods and those of Baalbek.[174]

We do not know just when Emesa was annexed in turn. Although the earliest solid documentation does not appear until the reign of Antoninus Pius,[175] I believe that the annexation very probably occurred between 72 and 78. Indeed, as king of Emesa, Sohaimos took part in the campaign against Commagene in 72, with the Syrian governor Caesennius Paetus.[176] However, in 78, an Emesene epitaph, dated according to the Seleucid era, bore the name of one G. Iulius Sampsigeramos, son of G. Iulius Alexion; the fact that he was a Roman citizen, as his *tria nomina* attests, strongly suggests that he belonged to the royal family.[177] There is no reference to any royal relationship, however: this could be explained most readily if the dynasty had only recently lost its kingdom. We can assume, then, that Emesa was in turn integrated into the province of Syria, thus restoring continuity between the territory of Palmyra and the western part of the province; the various milestones from around 75 C.E. mentioned earlier may well have been connected to the annexation of the Emesene principate. The dynasty was not eliminated, however; some members continued to play an influential role in Emesa itself, if only in the worship of the great local god Elagabalus.[178]

Along with Emesa, we should also mention the principate of Arca, in northern Lebanon, northeast of Tripolis, which had a direct relationship with the Sampsigeramos dynasty. This Ituraean principate was granted to a certain Sohaimos, who died in 48 or 49;[179] his very name would lead us to believe that he was related to the Emesene dynasty, even without confirmation from Josephus.[180] Upon his death, the principate was annexed to Syria, except for a section left to Sohaimos's son Ouaros (or Noaros).[181] However, the region changed hands again quickly, for in 53 the principate was given to Agrippa II and Noaros/Ouaros entered his service; we find him again at the beginning of the Jewish revolt, charged with running Agrippa II's kingdom while Agrippa was on a trip to Antioch.[182] We do not know which of the dynasts took the initiative to reestablish Arca under the name of Caesarea of Lebanon.[183] Excavations of the past twenty years at Tell Arqa have so far shed no light on this period of the history of the city.

Herod's Lineage in Southern Syria and in Lebanon[184]

When it was established in 41–37 B.C.E., Herod's kingdom included only a few territories across the Jordan, in the area known as Peraea. According to Hasmonaean tradition, there had been attempts to seize the Golan, but Alexander Jannaeus had never succeeded in going much farther east, and the Nabataeans remained in control of most of the Hauran. After Antony's death, Octavian tried to cure the paramount scourge of the region, banditry. He thought he had found an ideal solution in transferring the Trachon plateau, the main stronghold of the Ituraean bandits, to Zenodoros, an Ituraean who had seized the property of Lysanias, a tetrarch and high priest in the central Beqaa.[185] However, the cure was worse than the disease: his new status as client prince convinced Zenodoros that he could steal with impunity. Sometime between 27 and 32 B.C.E.,[186] Augustus seized the plateau and gave the Trachonitis, as well as Batanaea and Auranitis, to Herod the Great,[187] with the clear intention of bringing order and security to the area. We shall see below what means he used, although it is difficult to distinguish his own achievements from the work of his successors. In 20 B.C.E.,[188] when Zenodoros died, Augustus again enlarged Herod's territory by giving him "Zenodorus's rather large inheritance, including the lands between the Trachonitis and Galilee, Oulatha, the canton of Panion and all the surrounding area."[189] The text is not without ambiguity, since the lands between the Trachonitis and Galilee include Batanaea (which had already been given to Herod around 27–23) and the Golan.

Following Herod's death, the principates of Lebanon and southern Syria passed from hand to hand.[190] The most important possessions of Lebanon and Syria were given to Philip, whose capital at Panias became his Caesarea. Thus he controlled not only the three Hauran districts (Batanaea, the Trachonitis, and Auranitis), but also the region of Panias and Lake Oulatha. The ancient kingdom of Chalcis in the central Beqaa may have also been included, even though there is no evidence that Herod ever held it. The kingdom may have shared the fate of the tetrarchy of Abila (Souq Wadi Barada), held by an Ituraean tetrarch, a certain Lysanias (probably a grandson of the Lysanias who died in 37–36 B.C.E.), who inherited Abila in 20 B.C.E. when Zenodoros died. He must have been very young then, for he was still in power half a century later, in 29–30 C.E.

After Philip died in 34 C.E.,[191] his lands were first briefly annexed to the province of Syria, then given to one of his nephews, Agrippa I, in 37, along with the royal title. Agrippa simultaneously received the tetrarchy of Lysanias; thus we know that the latter had died between 29–30 and 37. In 39, Agrippa I reacquired the states of Herod Antipas in Galilee and Peraea; in 41, thanks to Claudius, he reestablished his grandfather's kingdom of Judaea. He then let his brother Herod have the kingdom of Chalcis, which had been given to him by either Philip or Lysanias.[192] Agrippa died prematurely in 44, and his kingdom was annexed to Syria.

Beginning in 50–51, Claudius gradually reestablished a vast state on behalf of Agrippa II. It consisted of southern Syria and Lebanon, extending from the Anti-Lebanon and Galilee to Jebel Druze.[193] Probably around 50, Agrippa II inherited the kingdom of Chalcis from his uncle, Herod of Chalcis, who had died in 48. However, near the end of 53, Agrippa returned Chalcis to Rome[194] in exchange for the three large districts of the Hauran—Batanaea, the Trachonitis, and Auranitis—plus the tetrarchies of Lysanias and Ouaros/Noaros. To these territories Nero[195] soon added part of Galilee around Tiberias and Tarichaea, and part of Peraea around Abila[196] and Livias-Iulias.[197] Agrippa II ruled over this seemingly heterogeneous realm until the final years of the first century.

Judaea cannot be regarded as typical, because it presented too many exceptional characteristics in comparison to other client kingdoms. Nevertheless, the policies Herod's descendants implemented in their possessions in southern Syria—policies celebrated perhaps in the monumental statuary group placed in the courtyard of the indigenous sanctuary of Sahr, on the Trachon[198]—help us understand what Rome expected of its client princes, at least the most powerful ones.[199] We have seen how the gradual weakening of Seleucid royal authority by the end of the second century B.C.E. gave rise to the development of local autonomy as well as banditry. The efforts of Pompey and his successors certainly brought an end to some of the worst abuses, but not all the interior regions of Syria benefited.[200] In fact, during Augustus's time we see that banditry had by no means disappeared. The basalt plateau of the Trachon provided an impregnable refuge (its contemporary Arabic name, Leja, means "refuge") for the outlaws who held up caravans on their way to Damascus and razed the surrounding villages.[201] Strabo gives a very precise and accurate description of the huge caves where the bandits hid with their booty, their herds, and their riches;[202] his account is confirmed by Josephus.[203]

As ruler of these lands, Herod immediately began to create military colonies at Bathyra,[204] Saura,[205] and Danaba, on the western front or near the Trachon, settling there the Jews who had come from Idumaea and Babylon, and perhaps some Greek colonists brought in for the purpose;[206] he also used Arab officers from the region as colonists.[207] In this respect, Herod was following the custom of the Hellenistic kings who distributed land to the cleruchs whose task was to maintain law and order. The arrangement was reinforced and perfected by his successors, Agrippa I (37–44) and Agrippa II (53–ca. 93–95), although we cannot specify exactly who did what. We see, however, that the son of Zamaris, leader of the troops from Babylon, inherited his command from his father, and Herod's troops were present in the region right up to the annexation.[208] Herod did not succeed in wiping out banditry, however; later on, one of the Agrippas issued yet another edict that mentioned people hiding in caves.[209]

The military occupation probably coincided with agricultural colonization; this would be one explanation for the increase in the number of Jewish colonists in the villages of Batanaea.[210] The details and exact chronology of the Herodian policies are not known, but banditry reportedly had disappeared by the end of the first century C.E. Some villages in the Trachonitis were reoccupied and quickly prospered: they provide the oldest Greek inscriptions in the region. The work of pacification and development had, in any case, advanced enough for Rome itself to take over the administration of the region. The civic and village infrastructure had created a fairly large class of Hellenized leaders, and Rome entrusted local administration to them while ensuring security in the region itself. Annexation confirmed the success of the Herodian policies.

The conditions under which Agrippa's states were annexed, however, are for the most part unknown. The annexation has long been thought to have taken place following the death of the king, around 92–93. This chronology has recently been challenged, however, on the basis of a weight from Tiberias dating from the forty-third year of King Agrippa's reign. According to the chronology used in Tiberias, in which the era of Agrippa II began in 55, the date of his death would shift to 97–98 at the earliest, confirming Justinus of Tiberias's report that Agrippa II died in 100.[211] The later date of death would also explain why a former officer in his army could state that he had served King Agrippa for eighteen years and then Emperor Trajan for ten, without mentioning either Domitian or Nerva.[212] Agrippa's states were brought into the province of Syria in two stages: first Batanaea, the Trachonitis, and Auranitis were taken from him between 92 and 96,[213] for reasons we do not know, and the rest (Oulatha, Panias, the western Golan, and various parts of eastern Galilee and Peraea) were absorbed into Syria upon his death in 100.[214] It was in 92 at the latest that the Chalcidian kingdom, which had remained intact around Chalcis in Lebanon, also disappeared.[215]

The Apogee of the Nabataean Kingdom

Although the Herodians may have owed everything to Rome, this was not the case for certain peripheral kingdoms that dated from Hellenistic times and were latecomers to the Roman sphere, such as Nabataea and Commagene. As we have already seen, these two kingdoms adopted all the characteristics of the Hellenistic states when they were established in the second century B.C.E. Never defeated by Rome (Scaurus was paid to leave

Petra),[216] the kings of Petra did not owe their power to Rome, as Herod did. After Pompey, however, they were indistinguishable from other client princes.[217]

Contrary to what Pompey's propaganda would have us believe, there seems to have been no basis for the suspicion in which these kings were held when the province of Syria was created. Pompey decided on an expedition against Commagene, however, and after he left for Rome, Scaurus carried out his plan. The motive behind this punitive expedition seems to me to have been pure banditry, but, despite Rome's failure in this effort, the Petraean kings subsequently proved to be loyal allies.[218]

For the successor to Aretas III, scholars now point to a certain Obodas II. His reign was very brief, for Aretas was still living at the time of Scaurus's raid in 62, and Malichos I began his reign in 59–58, as proved by an Egyptian inscription equating Malichos I's year 26 with Cleopatra's year 18.[219] One might suppose that the succession passed directly from Aretas III to Malichos I, except that we have coins representing an Obodas that are very different from the ones representing Malichos I's successor (also called Obodas) and that are dated only with the years 1, 2 and 3; thus we can conclude that an Obodas II came between the death of Aretas III and the advent of Malichos I. Avraham Negev has hypothesized that it was this Obodas—who died young, possibly during an attempt to reconquer Idumaea (which had been taken by Jannaeus)—who was deified in Oboda of the Negev,[220] but the Obodas in question was more likely to have been Obodas I.

Malichos I reigned for at least twenty-eight years and was a generally faithful ally of Rome. He sent troops to Caesar during the war in Alexandria,[221] just as he later sent troops to Antony on the eve of the battle of Actium.[222] However, he was accused of sympathizing with the Parthians during the invasion in 40, and that is doubtless what justified the imposition of a heavy fine by Ventidius[223] at the same time as the gift of part of his kingdom to Cleopatra.[224] Moreover, a permanent rivalry pitted him against Herod; Josephus identified some short-term causes for this, but this rivalry was most likely a manifestation of the continuing struggle for power between Jews and Arabs over the zones lying east of the Jordan. Malichos is said to have refused to take Herod in when the latter fled in 41,[225] and just before Actium the two kings were at war with each other. It is thought that Herod had been ordered by Antony to force Malichos to pay the tribute he owed Cleopatra. After an early Jewish victory near Dion, in Batanaea, then a brilliant Nabataean victory near Canatha that forced Herod to go back across the Jordan, a counteroffensive by Herod's troops ended with two successive Jewish victories.[226] It is certain that Malichos did not accept defeat; his plot with Hyrcanos II to overthrow Herod and replace him with a descendant of the Hasmonaeans was just one more episode in the rivalry between these two kings.[227] If Malichos had been counting on the defeat of Antony and Cleopatra to get rid of his rival, he hoped in vain, for Herod's power was quickly confirmed.

Obodas III replaced Malichos in 28 at the latest, but probably by 30 B.C.E., and he was king at the time of Aelius Gallus's expedition. We have already seen the important role the Nabataeans played in Aelius Gallus's expedition into Arabia Felix. The Romans were convinced that they had been betrayed by Syllaios. Was it betrayal or a simple misunderstanding? It is quite surprising that the Romans did not retaliate, either against Syllaios (his execution in about 6 B.C.E. was unconnected with this event) or against Obodas, who continued to rule until 9 B.C.E.

As king, Obodas III must have remained in the background, for although acts of his minister Syllaios are recorded, those of the king himself are not mentioned. Given these circumstances, it would be very surprising if he were the person deified as Obodas the God, honored particularly in the eponymous city of the Negev, Oboda (modern Avdat).[228] Still, neither a king's power nor his acts had much to do with his divinization, and if the city had been founded or reestablished under his reign,[229] he would naturally have become its *archegetes,* or founder, and worshipped as a god, even if his minister had done all the work. It actually seems more likely to me that "Obodas the God" refers to one of the other two kings of the same name, probably the first. However, it was probably Obodas III who was honored with a statue at Delos.[230]

Syllaios was in Rome in 9 B.C.E. when Obodas died. He had come to defend his recent behavior in a raid in southern Syria, and he seems to have charmed Augustus and convinced him of his good faith. Then came the news that Obodas III had died and had been replaced, according to Josephus, by someone called Aineas, who took the dynastic name Aretas IV. This Aineas was clearly not born to power, for the name seems unknown in the royal family. Was there some irregularity? Be that as it may, Augustus expressed anger that this self-proclaimed king had not first sought his approval; he may even have considered giving Herod all the Nabataean states. But he ultimately changed his mind and confirmed Aretas IV.[231] Syllaios, who may have been hoping to be given the office himself, returned to Petra, where he sought revenge by launching violent attacks on all the most prominent people in the city, without Aretas's approval, and he plotted with an imperial slave to overthrow Herod himself.[232] This was going too far: the Syrian governor Saturninus shipped him off with his accomplices to Rome,[233] where he was condemned and executed, probably in 6 B.C.E.[234]

Glen Bowersock brings subtle arguments to bear in support of his thesis that the Nabataean kingdom was briefly annexed between the years 3 and 1 B.C.E.[235] In Bowersock's view, the annexation did not occur in connection with Aretas IV's unauthorized rise to power (why the six-year delay?) but has to be seen as part of a vast reorganization of the southern regions of Syria following Herod's death. However, the basis for this assumption is not very sound, resting as it does on a rather ambiguous phrase in Strabo ("the Nabataeans who today obey our laws")[236] and a brief interruption in the coinage of Aretas IV (between 3 and 1 B.C.E.), which may simply be an accidental gap in our records.[237] If there was an annexation, it must have been very brief, and Aretas must have gotten his throne back quite quickly, perhaps under the aegis of Gaius Caesar around 1 C.E.,[238] the year he resumed minting coins. Even if we do not accept Bowersock's hypothesis, it is obvious that some confusion surrounded Obodas's succession. Aretas IV did not have unanimous support, and the conditions of his nomination are not clear. It is possible that Syllaios was a rival, and he must have relied on the support of tribal chiefs, whereas Aretas enjoyed the support of the Petraean aristocracy. In any case, the kingdom went through a turbulent period between 9 and 5 B.C.E., possibly up to 1 C.E. if we accept the idea of a temporary annexation.

Despite his early difficulties, Aretas managed to gain control, and his long reign (9 B.C.E. to 41 C.E.) marks the apogee of the Nabataean kingdom. In terms of territory, there was certainly no question of recuperating the northern parts of the Hauran, and still less of regaining the Damascus region, both of which Aretas III had controlled.[239] However, the Nabataeans do not seem to have given up hope of expanding their kingdom to the north or northeast, and the battles that took place shortly before Actium may have had such an objective. Herod avoided taking part in the war against Octavius in 31 on the pretext of an Arab threat. And the conflict did not end with Octavian's rise to power. We may wonder whether Josephus's allusion to the "Arabs" who had purchased Zenodoros's realm does not refer to Nabataeans from the Hauran, who may have been trying to control the route to Damascus. When the natives of Leja revolted against Herod in 12 B.C.E., they sought refuge with Obodas after their defeat, and they were warmly welcomed by Syllaios, who encouraged them to launch raids against Herod's kingdom. Herod complained to the governor of Syria even as he was launching a ruthless punitive expedition (Syllaios refers to twenty-five hundred deaths). Syllaios decided to go to

THE KHAZNEH (OFTEN CALLED THE TREASURY) IN PETRA,
ASSUMED TO BE THE TOMB OF ARETAS IV.

PORTAL OF ONE OF THE RECENTLY DISCOVERED TOMBS BELOW GROUND LEVEL
AT THE ENTRANCE TO THE KHAZNEH. THE RELATIONSHIP BETWEEN THESE TOMBS
AND THE KHAZNEH HAS NOT YET BEEN ESTABLISHED.

Rome and defend himself in person.[240] It is clear, then, that two "friends and allies" of the Roman people could remain mortal enemies.

The reign of Aretas IV is noteworthy for the indisputable prosperity of the kingdom, represented by the magnificent Petraean architecture. However, recent scholars are inclined to move back the dates of some of the buildings attributed to Aretas, which suggests that the prosperity of the kingdom and the cultivated elites predated his reign. For example, the building assumed to be Aretas's own tomb, the celebrated Khazneh Fira'un ("Pharaoh's Treasure," as the Bedouins call it), may date from the middle of the first century B.C.E., if not earlier, according to stylistic analyses undertaken by Judith McKenzie.[241] The recent excavation of the so-called Great Temple, a large building to the south of the main street in the lower city, revealed the existence of a huge structure dating back to the time of Malichos I or Obodas III, adjacent to a charming "paradise"-style pleasure garden with an island on which a pavilion had stood.[242] The building underwent major transformations during the reign of Aretas IV at the earliest, more probably under Malichos II or even under Rabbel II: the main room, perhaps an audience hall, was transformed at that time in order to house a performance space (theatron), a cavea consisting of about twenty terraced rows seating between 565 and 620 people that clearly served as the city's bouleuterion, the meeting place of its council.[243] Aretas IV's role in the beautification of Petra was therefore somewhat limited, but he probably deserves credit for the theater, a Greek structure par excellence, at a time when the taste for the Greek aesthetic had spread even to private homes decorated with Pompeian-style paintings. The spread of Greek names, transliterated into Aramaic, among the ruling class,[244] and the adoption of Greek or Roman terminology (stratopedarch, eparch, centurions) to designate officers in the Nabataean army also demonstrate the extent to which Nabataean society and the government adapted to contemporary standards.[245] This pattern may explain the ease with which Nabataean troops were integrated into the Roman army at the time of the annexation in 106. Other customs should probably be added, such as the consumption of wine imported from the Aegean world, as evidenced by the discovery of Rhodian amphorae dating from as far back as the second century B.C.E. and by Strabo's account of Nabataean banquets in which the number of cups is limited to eleven per guest.[246]

The adherence of the Nabataean elite to Greek taste continued under two of Aretas IV's successors, Malichos II (41–70) and Rabbel II (70–106). During their reigns, the central regions of the kingdom, the agricultural zones, were developed. We should not infer from this that the caravan trade deserted Petra: competition from Palmyra and from Egypt had an impact, but the kings of Petra must have realized how profitable the Hauran could be as long as raiders did not prevent villagers from cultivating their lands. Bostra experienced the beginning of tremendous growth under the reign of Rabbel II as a result of royal support and this new wealth.[247] At the same time, at the other end of the kingdom, Hegra also flourished throughout the entire first century, probably owing to the presence of a military aristocracy whose Hellenistic tastes were no less apparent than at Petra, both in the decoration of the monumental tombs they had built and in the sense of "staging" observed in the overall arrangement of necropolises.[248]

In 106, probably when Rabbel II died, the kingdom of Nabataea was annexed and became a new province.[249] The move was justified by the kingdom's vast size, for it covered an immense area not only in the Transjordan and the Negev, but also in northwestern Arabia; more than nine hundred kilometers separated the new capital, Bostra, from the farthest outposts in the Jawf (Dumata) and the Hejaz (Hegra) regions.[250] We do not have to look far for the reasons for this annexation, which followed the logic that Rome had pursued as far back as the Flavians. Rome presumably believed that the region included enough Hellenized leaders to serve as a local arm of the Roman administration and could govern itself directly. Although troops were sent in from Egypt (there is evidence of detachments of Legio III Cyrenaica in Petra) and from Syria (IV Ferrata was stationed in Bostra), there is no sign of fighting or of any Nabataean resistance whatsoever;[251] Roman coins struck on this occasion suggest the acquisition of a kingdom, not its capture.[252]

Following the annexation of the Nabataean kingdom, no more Syrian or Cilician client states remained beyond the Euphrates, and four provinces, including Cilicia, shared the spoils. In more than a century and a half, Rome had never tried to annex territories situated beyond the de facto limit that had been established by Sulla, Lucullus, and Pompey, and the Euphrates had come to mark the border between Rome and the Parthians.[253] All the annexations had involved regions situated to the west of the river[254] and states that had come into Rome's orbit long before. First Trajan's Parthian campaigns and later those of Lucius Verus and Septimius Severus brought this tradition to an end and carried the limits of the empire east of the river.[255] But before we come to these new undertakings, we must return to the unique situation in Judaea that had constituted a center of strife and unrest in Roman Syria for more than a century and a half.

THE CRISES IN JUDAEA FROM
HEROD TO BAR KOKHBA

JUDAEA had numerous economic, social, and cultural features in common with the rest of Syria. However, the Jews constituted a religious minority whose conduct and aspirations helped make Judaea the principal center of unrest in the Near East, especially during the uprisings that occurred in 66–74 and again in 132–135.

We have an unparalleled amount of documentation about the Jews from intertestamentary and New Testament literature, from the writings of Flavius Josephus and Philo of Alexandria, and from the Dead Sea Scrolls and the Talmuds. Many of these sources help clarify the status of Judaism and the Jews in the first to third centuries. Constituting a Jewish literature about Jews, these texts are unusual in revealing the attitudes, not solely of the groups in power, whether Greek or Roman, but of ordinary people in the province.

In addition, we cannot ignore the group from which early Christianity gradually emerged. The new religion developed out of, and defined itself in terms of, Hellenistic Judaism. Moreover, following the failed rebellions and the destruction of the Temple, Judaism itself was transformed as hope of recreating a Jewish homeland faded. The synagogue replaced the Temple; learning replaced sacrifice. For the historian attempting to describe the province of Syria as a whole, the real challenge is to avoid devoting a disproportionate amount of space to Judaea and the Jews, an imbalance that the sheer quantity of primary and secondary sources alone would seem to justify.

However, as unusual as Judaea may have been in the sociocultural landscape of Syria as a whole, there is no question that its distinctiveness faded with time, and especially following the disasters of 70 and 135. The Jews did not disappear, but Judaea (renamed Syria-Palestine) became more and more like other provinces and, despite strong Jewish communities, its inhabitants were mostly pagan. Thus I shall conclude the present history of Judaea in 135; in subsequent chapters, I shall show how the Jews were integrated into greater Syria, and how, after the defeat at Bar Kokhba, Judaea merged into a Roman Palestine that for the most part looked just like any other Roman province. In the long run, the exacerbation of Jewish "particularism" led, if not to integration, at least to normalization.

HEROD THE GREAT

During the Hellenistic period, the Jews enjoyed a distinctive state organization unknown to other Syrians (apart from the Nabataeans). Ever since Pompey's conquest of Jerusalem in 63 B.C.E., they had, of course, lived under the administrative supervision of the Romans, but after several attempts by the Jews to splinter Rome's authority, Rome handed over to Herod a kingdom that included all of Palestine and various territories beyond the Jordan. This kingdom was not at all what the proponents of Jewish independence wanted,[1] however, because Herod could not be the long-awaited restorer of the independent Jewish state promised by Yahweh. His family's Idumaean origins made him ineligible to be a high priest: he was a recent convert to Judaism; his mother, Kypros, was Nabataean; and his marriage to the Hasmonaean Mariamme was not enough to establish his legitimacy. Herod had been made king by Rome acting on its own, at a time when the Hasmonaeans, despite the criticisms to which they were subjected, had come to embody a kind of Jewish "nationalism."[2] Herod certainly knew this; just as he sought to benefit from their legitimacy by marrying the granddaughter of Hyrcanos II, he would kill Hasmonaeans when they threatened to enlist the support of his adversaries.[3] His reign marks the beginning of Israel's observation that earthly kingdoms were powerless to satisfy its people's political and spiritual aspirations, and its conceptualization of a Kingdom of David whose appearance on earth could scarcely be anticipated any longer.[4]

Despite a tradition that is unanimous in its hostility, Herod appears to have been an effective ruler who took his responsibilities seriously.[5] Named by Antony and Octavius in 41 B.C.E., at the time when all of Syria was in reality in the hands of the Parthians, Herod set out at once to reconquer his kingdom. Although the Parthians were driven out of Syria after 40, a Hasmonaean descendant, Mattathias-Antigonos, remained in power in Jerusalem. Herod arrived in Ptolemais at the beginning of 39 and began a systematic reconquest. The opposition he faced was both political (the Jews had welcomed the Parthian presence) and (especially) religious: as we have noted, as a recently converted Jew and one not descended from a royal family, he could not hold the office of high priest. The Pharisees were thus suspicious, if not hostile, from the outset. Despite these obstacles, in the spring of 37 Herod was essentially in control of his entire kingdom, despite the opposition of the majority of his subjects. For seven years, he worked to strengthen his authority by making himself the defender of the Jews and Antony's closest ally in the Orient. Despite Cleopatra's pronounced hostility (she claimed to have reestablished the ancient Ptolemaic Syria), Herod became indispensable to Antony by maintaining order in Palestine and protecting Roman Syria against the Arabs.[6]

Herod had sent troops to support Antony at Actium, but after Antony's defeat he rallied to the side of Octavian and helped him seize control of Egypt. Not only did Octavian not penalize him for having supported Antony, but he also gave Herod the lands that had been ceded to Cleopatra, including a few Greek cities adjacent to his kingdom (Gadara, Hippos, Samaria, Gaza, Anthedon, Joppa, and Strato's Tower).[7] The restructuring of the empire in 27 B.C.E. did not affect Judaea: Herod's kingdom remained intact, under the management of a *rex socius,* and between 27 and 20 it even benefited from a territorial expansion in southern Syria, where Herod received lands held until then by Zenodoros. Thus secure in his kingdom, Herod began to beautify and modernize it while at the same time honoring his new master. The reconstruction of Samaria (renamed Sebaste) in about 25,[8] the building of a new capital and a convenient port in central Palestine (Strato's Tower became Caesarea on the Sea),[9] and numerous improvements in Jerusalem (including the Temple) might well have earned him the appreciation of his compatriots, while the dynastic names given to the new cities demonstrated his support of, and loyalty to, Caesar Augustus.[10]

Herod's attitude toward Judaism was complex. As an Idumaean Jew and the son of a Nabataean mother, he had to prove his zeal in order to be accepted as king. He undertook a thoroughgoing reconstruction of the Temple of Zerubbabel in 20 B.C.E.[11] to give it the grandeur it lacked: the royal palaces were far more sumptuous than the Temple.[12] During construction, he was scrupulous about respecting the purity laws, and the scope of the work led people to speak of Herod's temple as the third in a series of great Temples, after those of Solomon and Zerubbabel. He managed to maintain satisfactory relations with the Pharisees, who seemed satisfied both to have a Jewish leader (rather than a Roman) in Judaea and to see that the new king was not claiming to play the role of high priest. Nevertheless, in 7 or 6 B.C.E. Herod did not hesitate to execute Pharisees who refused to take the oath of loyalty that had just been required of all citizens,[13] and shortly before his death, his suppression of an uprising by young Jews outraged about the installation of a golden eagle over a door of the Temple became a bloodbath.[14]

Herod's Judaism appears to have been very superficial. Apart from his polygamy and the brutality that scandalized his people, he demonstrated a profound attachment to Hellenism. The king's children were educated in Rome, he invited Greek writers (such as Nicolaos of Damascus) to court, and he behaved like any other Greek ruler. In addition to constructing new cities (Caesarea on the Sea and Samaria-Sebaste), he introduced both a theater and an amphitheater in Jerusalem, where he celebrated Greek contests (the Actiac games of 27 B.C.E.),[15] shocking as they must have been to Jews, with their nude athletes, pagan cults associated with the contests, and literary and musical themes developed by the contestants. He even underwrote the Olympic games in Olympia itself.[16] (The time when rabbis themselves

MODEL OF THE TEMPLE OF JERUSALEM AT THE TIME OF HEROD.

would visit gymnasiums and draw images of pedagogic value from them was still a long way off.)[17] Finally, outside of Judaea and Galilee, Herod was not afraid to build pagan sanctuaries, in particular to honor Augustus, in Caesarea, Samaria, and Panias.

The religious authorities in Jerusalem had no way of opposing such a policy: the high priests were merely Herod's puppets, and we do not even know all their names.[18] One was an unknown old Babylonian or Egyptian Jew (Hananel) who was dismissed (something unheard of: high priests were appointed for life) and replaced by the last—and very young—descendant of the Hasmonaeans, Aristobulos III; he was seventeen years old when Herod had him drowned less than a year after appointing him.[19] Herod also appointed his father-in-law, Boethos (or Simon son of Boethos), and four unknowns. As a result, the high priesthood was subject to ridicule and lacking in real power. In such a context, one can understand why many Jews sought refuge in eager anticipation of a Messiah who would come to deliver the nation both from its Roman occupiers and from the impious Jews who were running the country.

In contrast, Herod appeared eager to please the pagans, as evidenced by his many benefactions in Phoenicia and Syria. At the same time, he dedi-

AERIAL VIEW OF MASADA, WITH REMAINS OF HEROD'S PALACE.

cated Caesarea to the Greeks from the start, and this was later reaffirmed by Nero. German, Gallic, and Thracian mercenaries were installed in Samaria-Sebaste. In the two cities, a Kaisareion in honor of Augustus officially introduced the imperial cult. King by the grace of Rome and detested by the Jews, Herod depended upon barbarian mercenaries and built a system of fortresses designed to protect him from his subjects rather than his neighbors: Masada,[20] Herodion,[21] Machaerus, and Kypros joined the restored Hasmonaean fortresses and palaces of Jerusalem and Jericho.[22] The king's brutality in dealing with unrest as well as with his own relatives (at the time of his death only three of his numerous sons still survived), his many marriages (he had ten wives, many of them apparently at the same time), the real or imaginary depravities that transpired in those closed and often remote palaces—all these factors combined to lend credibility to the image of Herod as a bloody tyrant that was handed down without qualification by the Evangelists. It is true that he led an opulent life, upon which the discoveries at Masada have thrown some light; the finds there include amphorae of wine duly designated as containing Italian vintages (*massicum, amineum, tarentinum*), apples from Cumae, and *garum* (fish sauce) from Spain, but nothing that would have been out of the ordinary for a man in his position.[23]

Herod did establish stability in Palestine, however, by combating the Jewish and Arab bandits from Galilee and Peraea.[24] Although the costs of his building program were indeed burdensome, and although his harshness in collecting taxes was meant to crush popular resistance, he did not hesitate to lower taxes by one-third in 20 B.C.E.[25] and later, in 14, by one-quarter, in order to relieve the suffering of the people.[26] He worked to ensure an adequate food supply, and during the famine of 25 he melted down gold and silver objects from his own palace to purchase wheat from Egypt.[27] Such benefactions meant nothing in the eyes of devout Jews, however, and the Christian tradition has echoed their view of Herod.

HEROD'S HEIRS[28]

Herod had so often settled disputes among his heirs with bloodshed that he was forced to alter his will many times. Thus, when he died—possibly in 5 B.C.E., but more likely in the spring of 4[29]—several wills were found, and the various beneficiaries each angled for a favorable settlement. After violently repressing a riot in Jerusalem, Archelaos, Herod's oldest son, and his half brother Antipas hastened to Rome hoping to secure the succession. Other members of the family, in contrast, argued for direct administration from Rome. Augustus personally listened to the lawyers for all sides (Archelaos was defended in particular by Nicolaos of Damascus) but made no decision. In the meantime, a third brother, Philip,[30] intervened in turn, as did an embassy from the Jews; according to Josephus, the latter demanded to be allowed to live according to their ancestral laws, which doubtless meant that they were hostile to the Herodian monarchy. After another hearing and additional arguments, Augustus ratified the overall terms of Herod's final will. Philip received the Syrian possessions with the title *tetrarch,* and Herod Antipas was given Galilee and Peraea. Archelaos was awarded the title *ethnarch,* which acknowledged a certain preeminence, but Augustus denied him the royal title while allowing him to hope for it in the future provided he proved himself worthy; he was to administer the heart of the ancient kingdom—Judaea, Samaria, Idumaea, and a few coastal cities (including Joppa). The income that each might hope to draw from his land established a clear hierarchy of powers: six hundred talents for Archelaos, two hundred talents for Antipas, one hundred talents for Philip. Herod's sister Salome received a dowry that included Iamnia, Azotos, Phasaelis, a palace in Ascalon, and five hundred thousand pieces of silver.[31] Some of the Greek cities in Herod's kingdom (Gaza, Gadara, and Hippos) escaped the authority of his successors and were annexed to the province of Syria.[32] Augustus undoubtedly believed that he had settled the question for good, but in fact Archelaos's incompetence would force the emperor to deal with the issue again sooner than he expected.[33]

According to Josephus, Archelaos's reign lasted nine or ten years, and his dismissal and exile to Vienna, in Gaul, is usually said to have occurred around 6 C.E.; this is confirmed by an explicit reference to a census that took place thirty-seven years after the battle of Actium. His dismissal resulted from a multitude of citizen complaints; he had not even been able to maintain public order.[34] One difficulty, however, arises from a passage in Luke (2.1–5), where several elements are in direct conflict with Josephus's text. Without presenting all the theories that have been advanced, it is important to lay out the known facts.

Archelaos was removed and exiled in the ninth or tenth year of his reign, according to Josephus. The governor of Syria, P. Sulpicius Quirinius, was dispatched to liquidate Archelaos's holdings, while the equestrian Coponius was installed as prefect, responsible for the *eparchia* of Judaea, which Josephus recognized as an offshoot *(prostheke)* of Syria.[35] At the same time, Quirinius was asked to conduct a census in Syria. This is confirmed in part by a phrase in Luke 2.1–5, and, more importantly, by an inscription pertaining to the work done on that occasion at Apamaea by Q. Aemilius Secundus.[36] There is no independent confirmation in Josephus of

6 C.E. as the date of this census, for most of the stages of Quirinius's career are incorrectly dated.[37] The passage in Luke is troubling, however, because it suggests that the census occurred at the time of Jesus's birth: it implies that Joseph and Mary left for Bethlehem specifically in order to be counted in the census, and that Jesus was born there. This could not have taken place very long after Herod's death, because John the Baptist, several months older than Jesus, was born or had been conceived during Herod's rule.[38] A great deal has been written about this piece of information from Luke, but no means of confirming it has been found. Even apart from the problem of the date, none of Luke's information on this topic seems to withstand scrutiny. Not only was there never a general census in the empire (except one involving Roman citizens alone), but even if the census in question was limited to the Roman province of Syria, there is no reason for it to have involved the subjects of Antipas's client state. And even if they were included, everything we know about Roman census procedures runs counter to the idea that people might have registered anywhere but in their place of permanent residence. Finally, even if Joseph had to be counted in Bethlehem, for reasons unknown to us, there would have been no reason for him to take his wife with him, because the head of the family always had to register all the members of his household. In short, Luke's information about Joseph's trip to Bethlehem simply does not square with the historical record.[39]

Nevertheless, Quirinius did conduct a census in Syria (confirmed by the inscription of Q. Aemilius Secundus) and it may have involved Judaea. Was it this venture that coincided with the liquidation of Archelaos's holdings? And how is it possible that Luke could have erred so badly in connecting this census—if it occurred in 6 C.E.—with the birth of Jesus, when Matthew 2.1 says Jesus was born at the end of Herod's reign, which we know to have been 6 or 5 B.C.E.? There are so many unanswered questions that we must accept at least the possibility that Luke's phrase is a very early interpolation by a copyist seeking to find a rational explanation for Jesus's birth in Bethlehem when, according to tradition, he came from Galilee.[40]

In an effort to salvage Luke's testimony, some scholars have tried to adjust the chronology by eliminating the only concrete date we have—specifically, Josephus's reference to the length of Archelaos's reign. Josephus, it is true, had little to say about this ten-year reign,[41] and his various allusions to the beginnings of direct administration in Judaea are somewhat contradictory or obscure.[42] The reign of Archelaos has thus been reduced to a few months and the annexation of Judaea dated from about 4 or 3 B.C.E., coincident with Quirinius's government (his first?) in Syria. According to this view, Quirinius was sent out to conduct a census, as if for the first time (which would be curious in a province that had existed for more than fifty years). His arrival would thus have coincided with the annexation of Judaea, where establishing an inventory was undoubtedly necessary for fiscal reasons, and he would have been charged at the same time with liquidating Archelaos's holdings, most of which were to become part of Augustus's patrimony. (The job would have been better suited to an equestrian procurator, but Josephus attributes this mission to Quirinius and not to Coponius.)[43]

This early dating of Quirinius's government rests on no reliable documentation, especially because the Syrian chronology for the period reveals virtually no gaps in the series of public commemorations, despite unproven claims by those inclined to shorten Archelaos's reign. After the departure of P. Quinctilius Varus, who had been governor since 7 B.C.E. and was still in office when Herod died (it was he who quelled the rebellion in Jerusalem), L. Calpurnius Piso Pontifex was appointed and remained in office until 1 B.C.E.[44] There was thus no gap during which Quirinius could have held an earlier assignment, and a term of three to four years was the rule among imperial legates. Moreover, a hypothetical legation of Quirinius in 3–2 B.C.E. would contradict two explicit chronological indicators in Josephus: Archelaos's exile in the ninth or tenth year of his reign, and the holding of a census thirty-seven years after the battle of Actium. It seems to me that these references, which are not at all necessary to justify any aspect of Josephus's account, are much more credible than a detail in Luke that we have seen to be probably accurate on one point (census taking in Syria) but used by the Evangelist (or a commentator) in a completely unreliable way. Moreover, we would have to prolong the length of Coponius's mission to ten years if we were to maintain terms of normal length for his two successors; that is not an impossibility, but it would be exceptional. Without some new and independent evidence making it possible to date Quirinius's legation or Coponius's prefecture, I find it preferable to retain Josephus's chronology and acknowledge that Archelaos kept his states until 6 C.E., the date of Syria's annexation of Judaea.

As ethnarch of Judaea-Samaria, Archelaos accomplished very little, and he seems to have adopted his father's most scandalous habits while lacking his competence. For example, he divorced his wife in order to marry Glaphyra, who was the daughter of King Archelaos of Cappadocia, the widow of Archelaos's half brother Alexander, and the divorced wife of Juba of Mauretania; Jewish law absolutely forbade a man to marry his sister-in-law if she had had children by his brother. None of Archelaos's projects, from the decoration of the palace in Jericho to the construction of an aqueduct that would irrigate a new palm garden (probably close to an

Archelais built at his direction in the Jordan valley),[45] did anything to improve the lives of his people, and Augustus finally exiled him to Vienna after Jews and Samaritans constantly complained about his brutality.[46]

\ Philip and Antipas held on much longer and were more active politically. Philip appears to have been a moderate man;[47] his half brother Archelaos trusted him with the protection of Jerusalem during his absence when he had to rush off to Rome after Herod's death. When Philip became master of the more northern regions of the kingdom, he enlarged and improved Panias, renaming it Caesarea (called Caesarea-Philippi to distinguish it from the one founded by his father), and he reestablished Bethsaida, situated where the Jordan enters into Lake Genesareth, renaming it Iulias, in honor of Augustus's daughter Iulia.[48] Evidence of his reign is found in southern Syria in a small number of inscriptions,[49] and he appears to have caused no problems for his Roman masters. When Philip died in the winter of 33–34, Josephus spoke very highly of him: he had been a conscientious administrator of justice and spent all of his time in his states.[50] He died in Iulias; having had no children from his marriage to his niece Salome,[51] he had no heirs, and Tiberius thus annexed his kingdom to Syria.[52]

\ Herod Antipas was more like his brother Archelaos.[53] After marrying one of the daughters of Aretas IV of Nabataea, he divorced her under scandalous circumstances to marry the wife of his half brother Herod Philip,[54] which not only made him guilty of incest in the eyes of devout Jews but also provoked a war with Aretas IV in which Antipas was roundly defeated.[55] Tiberius ordered a punitive expedition led by Vitellius, governor of Syria; it was halted when the emperor died, proof that the governor had not seen the necessity of such an expedition. Ancient sources deplored the matrimonial episode but otherwise generally approved of Antipas's dealings in religious matters. Aside from the Herodias episode, Luke describes Antipas as present at the time of Jesus's trial: Pontius Pilatus, knowing that Antipas was in Jerusalem during the Passover festival, sent Jesus to him, as a Galilean and thus one of his subjects; Antipas simply ridiculed him and did not pass judgment. But the fact that Herod Antipas was in Jerusalem for the holidays (Luke 23.7) is interesting in itself. And even earlier, in connection with the death of John the Baptist, Matthew described him, if not as a devout Jew, at least as one who was respectful and fearful of such divinely inspired prophets; although responsible for John's arrest, he was saddened by Salome's demand (Matthew 14:9). On another occasion, he complained to Pilatus about bringing into Jerusalem a votive shield that offended Jewish law.[56]

Antipas also promoted the urbanization of his states. He refounded Sepphoris, which had recently been burned and pillaged by Varus and

Aretas IV (it had been the center of Judas the Galilean's revolt) and named it Autocratoris.[57] He fortified the village of Betharamphtha (or Betharamatha) and renamed it Livias or Iulias, apparently just before Augustus's death;[58] more importantly, he built a new capital, Tiberias, on the shores of Lake Genesareth. He had chosen a site that seemed propitious, close to the hot springs at Emmaus, but it proved to have been the site of an ancient necropolis, which drove off devout Jewish colonists. Antipas was thus forced to populate his new capital with foreigners and speculators. He built a stadium (demonstrating the city's Hellenic character) and a royal palace, but also a synagogue. Tiberias adopted a Greek-style constitution, with a six-hundred-member *boule* (city council), magistrates (*archontes, agoranomoi*), and a council of *dekaprotoi*, the ten leading citizens.[59] Even so, this did not diminish the Jewish character of Galilee, where Jews undoubtedly constituted a large majority of the population.

But in 39 C.E. Antipas had to be exiled, for he was clamoring too loudly for the royal title that his nephew Agrippa I had received from Caligula in 37 along with the tetrarchy of Philip (who had died during the winter of 33–34), and that of Lysanias in the upper valley of the Barada.[60] Antipas's clumsiness in his dealings with Aretas IV, his failure in the war that followed, and no doubt other blunders committed when he accompanied Vitellius during an encounter with the Parthians on the Euphrates[61] all contributed to his downfall. His audacity in going to Rome to demand the royal title from the emperor himself seems to have persuaded Caligula that Antipas had simply added fuel to the fire in Judaea; Antipas was arrested and sent far away, either to Lugdunum (modern Lyon) or to Saint Bertrand de Comminges, in the Pyrenees.[62]

Agrippa I, grandson of Herod, son of Aristobulos, and brother of the scandalous Herodias, seems to have been a less than admirable character in many respects.[63] His survival as a youth can perhaps be attributed to the fact that he was a student in Rome when his father was executed. He spent most of his time in Rome, where he lived extravagantly and was deeply in debt. Nevertheless, he seems to have enjoyed the esteem of the Pharisees and of Josephus. Using his friendship with Caligula for the benefit of his compatriots, he tried to block the decision to have Caligula's statue erected in the Temple in Jerusalem,[64] and he later intervened on behalf of the Jews of Alexandria.[65] Once he became king, he fortified Jerusalem (against the wishes of the governor of Syria)[66] and attempted to establish its independence by bringing the client kings together in Tiberias.[67] These gestures were presumably appreciated by devout Jews and nationalist elements alike.

The relationship with Caligula benefited Agrippa personally as well: in

41, along with the royal title, he possessed lands granted him by the emperor in 37 (the tetrarchies of Philip and Lysanias) and in 39 (the tetrarchy of Antipas)—that is, a kingdom bordering much of Herod's former realm. Agrippa, a Jew, was heir to both the Herodians and the Hasmonaeans (his grandmother Mariamme was a granddaughter of Hyrcanos II), and because he had been raised in Rome he was attached to the Julio-Claudians by bonds of personal friendship.[68] Claudius no doubt saw in him the ideal candidate to reestablish a single kingdom, relieve Rome of the burden of

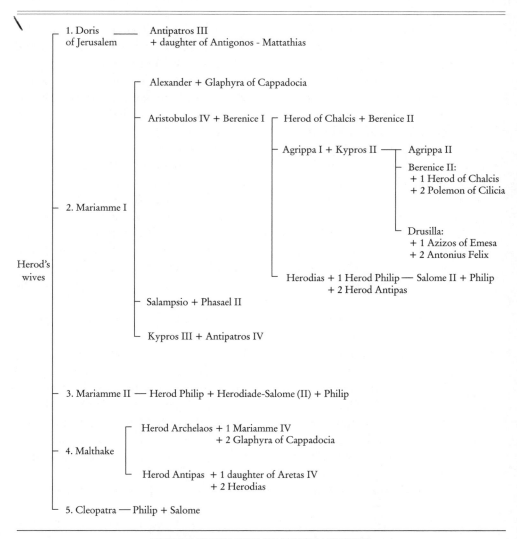

HEROD'S FAMILY TREE (SIMPLIFIED VERSION)

day-to-day management, and restore peace in Judaea. Taking away nothing that Agrippa already held, Claudius added Judaea, Samaria, and Idumaea, very nearly re-creating the kingdom as it had been under Herod (without the Greek cities).

Agrippa's reign began with acts of mercy and generosity that impressed devout Jews; Josephus relates many anecdotes attesting to his piety, his respect for Jewish traditions and Jewish law in its strictest forms. Given this pattern, it was logical that he would pursue those individuals, not yet called Christians, who appeared to him to be corrupt Jews—as he did, for example, in executing James.

In addition, he followed the same external policy of good works as his grandfather. Like Herod, he lavished gifts on the cities of Phoenicia and Syria, particularly Berytos (modern Beirut), which probably owed its preferential treatment to its status as a Roman colony. He did not hesitate to finance projects or spectacles that were completely contrary to Jewish law, including a theater, an amphitheater, baths, statues of his own daughters, gladiator fights, and Greek games in Caesarea.

If we separate his external policies from the strictly internal ones, close examination suggests that he did at least restore order within his kingdom. It was a short-lived peace, however, as the king died at the end of 43 or very early in 44.[69] Claudius could either transfer the late king's states to the latter's son, Agrippa II, or annex them to Rome; for reasons that are not entirely clear, he chose annexation. The "conclave" in Tiberias may have demonstrated the threat such an enterprising king represented for Rome, and fear that Judaea might go too far toward emancipation, with the support of a population whose nationalism had become widespread over the last half century, may have led him to choose this solution.[70] The disappointment of the nationalist elements must have been great, and it may explain the renewed unrest in the years that followed.[71]

It was undoubtedly around this time that a procurator was named, rather than a prefect, as had been the case before 41. But was Judaea really a procuratorial province? In other words, did it really have all the functions of a province? That is unlikely, because the governor of Syria retained military responsibilities. Evidence provided by contemporary sources is ambiguous, for Tacitus says that when Agrippa I died his kingdom was added to the province of Syria.[72] In any case, the fact that a procurator was named instead of a prefect unquestionably indicates a change in policy. The annexation of the kingdom might appear to mark the end of the Herodian enterprise. However, this was not to be the case.

First of all, a brother of Agrippa I, Herod, known as Herod of Chalcis, retained his kingdom in the central Beqaa, a situation that lasted until his death in 48.[73] When Agrippa I died, Herod assumed authority for the Temple as well as control of the treasury and power to appoint the high priests.[74] And then Agrippa II, the first Agrippa's son, received piecemeal a kingdom that stretched from the eastern Galilee to the Hauran; he held part of it until 92–93 and the remainder until his death in 100.[75] But the history of Agrippa II's states has more to do with the history of Syria than with that of Palestine, even though Agrippa II was deeply involved in the events that shook Judaea. His capital was not Tiberias but Caesarea-Philippi, renamed Neronias, where traces of his palace may have been found. We have seen the role he played in southern Syria. In Palestine, Agrippa II did not have the same reputation for piety among the Jews that his father had enjoyed. In fact, he seemed largely indifferent to religious questions, although he occasionally held firm on certain issues. He forced Azizos of Emesa and Polemon of Cilicia to be circumcised before they married his sisters, Drusilla and Berenice, respectively. Similarly, he decorated the Temple and finished the works begun during Herod's time. However, he was rumored to have had an incestuous relationship with his sister Berenice.[76] Above all, he was faithful to Rome in all circumstances, even during the Jewish War. He tried to dissuade his fellow citizens from revolting, but he was unable to prevent the cities of eastern Galilee under his authority (Tiberias, Tarichaea, and Gamala) from joining the rebellion. He provided auxiliary troops to Cestius Gallus,[77] participated in the siege of Gamala (where he was wounded), and received in grand style in his capital both Vespasian, in 67,[78] and Titus, who celebrated the defeat of Jerusalem with major games in 70.[79] It is easy to see why the Jews never viewed as one of their own a king who so faithfully upheld Roman control.

We can also see how, over time, the shortcomings of the client princes forced Rome to administer the country directly despite the problems that that entailed. It is worthwhile to reflect on the reasons for the Herodians' failure. For what we seem to find is a massive rejection of their authority despite their many efforts on behalf of the Temple (even Antipas came to Jerusalem for Passover), and the fact that all of them paid for improvements to make it the equal of Solomon's Temple. Moreover, compared to other clients, they were neither more nor less effective: they did not plunder their subjects and on occasion were even able to protect them from some of Rome's excesses. For their part, the Romans could certainly complain about the excessive ambition of some of their clients, such as Archelaos and Antipas, but these clients' claims to royalty were not entirely unexpected from kings' sons. Why, then, were the Herodians so despised by their subjects and abandoned by Rome?

The main reason, most probably, was that, like most of the ruling class (particularly the Temple leaders) and despite their own good intentions, the Herodians cut themselves off from their people by adopting Greco-Roman standards and customs and scorning traditional practices.[80] After two hundred years, we find the same situation we saw at the time of the revolt of the Maccabees: how could devout Jews accept as Jewish, as one of their own, someone who consistently frequented Greeks and Romans, dined with them, visited their palaces, welcomed them to court, built temples for their (false) gods and monuments for foreign spectacles, and frequented baths presided over by images of Hermes, Heracles, and other idols? Not to mention direct violations of Jewish law: for example, Antipas built a necropolis in Tiberias, married his brother's wife (even though she had borne his brother's child), and decorated his palace with animal images.[81]

In the eyes of many of their subjects, the Herodians appeared more Roman than Jewish, owing to their close ties to the Roman ruling class. We must remember that two of Herod's sons, Alexander and Aristobulos, spent five years in Rome, from 22 to 17 B.C.E., in the home of Asinius Pollio, one of the most prominent Roman senators. Herod himself maintained ties with Augustus and Agrippa that went far beyond conventional relations between heads of state. Josephus recalls that Herod was first in the affection of Augustus after Agrippa and first in the affection of Agrippa after Augustus.[82] Herod welcomed Agrippa to Jerusalem lavishly and showed him around his kingdom in 15 B.C.E.; when Agrippa died prematurely in 12, Herod named his first grandson (the future Agrippa I, born in 10 B.C.E.) after him. Moreover, this child was sent to Rome to be educated, in 4 B.C.E., and was raised, with other princes of the imperial family, in the home of Antonia Minor, Mark Antony's daughter; he remained a close friend of the younger Drusus, son of Tiberius, and was influential in Claudius's decision to accept the imperial power in 41 C.E. The toponymy of Herod's kingdom was filled with Julio-Claudian references, not only in urban projects such as Caesarea and Samaria-Sebaste but also in Anthedon (renamed Agrippias in 12 B.C.E.), a fortress in Jerusalem named Antonia, and the strongest defensive tower in the port of Caesarea, called Drusion after Antonia Minor's husband. The establishment of Autocratoris, Tiberias, Livias, Iulias, and Neronias under his successors reinforced the imperial family's presence in the toponymy of Palestine. Matrimonial arrangements were numerous as well: Herodian princesses married into all the princely families of the Near East (from Pontus, Cappadocia, Emesa, Nabataea, and Cilicia) and even into Roman circles— for example, Agrippa I's daughter Drusilla married the emancipated imperial slave Felix, and Berenice became Titus's mistress.[83]

Still, despite these exceptionally close ties, the Herodians never failed to emphasize their Judaism or to conform to the expectations others had of them. As we have seen, they frequented the Temple and contributed significantly to its embellishment. Antipas and Philip intervened vigorously with Pontius Pilatus during the affair of the shields. According to Philo's testimony, Agrippa I urged Caligula to yield on the issue of the statue the latter sought to erect in the Temple of Jerusalem.[84] Agrippa II tried to dissuade the Zealots from rising up against Rome in 66.[85] Even Herod sometimes proved to be a scrupulous Jew: the proposed marriage of his sister Salome to Syllaios the Nabataean failed because the future husband refused to be circumcised.[86] The arranged marriage between Drusilla, Agrippa I's daughter, and Antiochos IV of Commagene failed for the same reason.[87] But none of this counted at all in the eyes of the people, as measured against bonds of friendship that appeared intolerably compromising.

THE ERA OF PREFECTS AND PROCURATORS

Indications of the Roman Presence

Roman administration in Judaea was established in stages, and there were numerous setbacks. In 6 C.E. Judaea-Samaria was annexed to the province of Syria and was subsequently administered by a prefect based in Caesarea.[88] This prefect, of the equestrian class, was named by the emperor himself, and his title emphasized the military nature of his function: he was commander of the Roman troops stationed in Caesarea. Josephus—who erroneously called him a procurator[89]—states that he was also given judicial authority, including the right to assign the death penalty;[90] this is confirmed in the story of Jesus's trial.

After the short-lived reign of Agrippa I, Judaea, Samaria, and Idumaea were once again annexed to Rome and probably put in the hands of a procurator. It may be appropriate at this point to speak of an autonomous "procuratorial province" of Judaea: Tacitus credits Claudius with the creation of a province of Judaea ruled by an equestrian,[91] although in another passage he clearly says that Judaea had been annexed to Syria. This did not prevent the governor of Syria from intervening militarily in Judaea when necessary, as the number of troops stationed in Judaea itself was low, probably including no more than one cavalry wing and five infantry cohorts, stationed chiefly in Caesarea.[92]

The move to direct administration involved modifications in the fiscal system, but it is difficult to gauge with any precision their impact on the population. A royal system of taxation was replaced by a Roman system, but we do not know whether that meant an increased tax burden. Rome must have imposed its own system founded upon the *tributum soli* (tribute assessed on cultivated land) and the *capitatio* (head tax) as well as tolls and *portoria* (shipping taxes). There may well have been other specific taxes inherited from the royal system about which we know nothing.

In any case, a revolt against Roman taxation began brewing quickly. Under the very first prefect, Coponius, Judas of Galilee led a revolt against the capitatio.[93] The most serious concern was no doubt that the tributum soli and the capitatio were to be determined on the basis of periodic censuses, beginning with the one Quirinius ordered in 6 C.E., and they were superimposed on numerous taxes and interior duties, tolls, and levies that strained commerce.[94] Despite the justifications given by Jewish leaders, refusal to submit to this form of Roman domination seemed to be a prelude to total liberation. The Talmud preserves a cynical comment to the effect that the Romans built bridges only in order to collect tolls, and in another passage a peasant whose ass has been requisitioned is advised to consider it lost.[95]

The Privileged Status and Failure of the Leadership

Treated like all other inhabitants of the empire in fiscal matters, Jews also enjoyed comparable juridical autonomy, an implicit recognition of Jewish law as the law of the land. It would be misleading to claim that Judaism had obtained the status of *religio licita,* a legal concept unknown to the Romans, but it is true that because the Romans respected local laws for all travelers throughout the empire, the Torah was recognized as law. Consequently, all its religious aspects were upheld. Thus Jews were exempted from military service out of respect for the religious prohibitions (regarding food, ritual purity, and participation in other cults) that made it impossible for them to mingle with pagans in the army. In the same spirit, Augustus and Claudius reminded Romans that they were to respect the Temple, Jerusalem, sacred texts, and synagogues, as required by recognition of the Torah as the indigenous law of the Jews.

This recognition meant that the emperors had created a difficult situation for Roman administrators, because the Torah governed both civil and religious life in such a way that they were inextricably linked. Uninformed Romans may well have thought that the Jews sought to set themselves apart from others. The most fundamental institutions, such as celebration of the imperial cult, parading of military recruits, and the practice of nudity in athletics, were all forbidden in Jerusalem; in addition, Jews could not be called before the tribunal on the Sabbath. Angered by this special treatment, the Romans were often tempted to provoke a group who seemed to look down on non-Jews in all circumstances of daily life. Between the heightened susceptibility of one group and the overreactions of the other, friction and even violence were inevitable. All this combined with even deeper problems that aggravated tensions and led from rampant crime to open rebellion and civil war.

Above all, the new regime multiplied opportunities for contamination, whereas the Jews were strict about respecting the rules of ritual purity, which symbolized their fidelity to the Torah. Successive prefects showed little concern for respecting the special features of Jewish life, despite their official instructions: although these were renewed several times, from Augustus to Claudius,[96] they never amounted to a legal "charter" for the Jews.[97] Everything became a cause for confrontation: the presence of recruits in Jerusalem, the admission of pagans into the Temple, the protection of the high priests' vestments. For this reason, Rome's representatives and Jewish authorities were almost constantly in conflict. Even leaders who were most inclined to compromise with the Roman presence found themselves in an awkward position: on the one hand, they were forced to come to terms with the sitting official who guaranteed their own privileged position; on the other hand, they were being pressured by their own people to demonstrate greater resistance or lose all credibility. The situation quickly became untenable.

In fact, in Judaea as elsewhere, Rome needed to rely on existing institutions. At the highest level, the community was under the joint authority of the high priest and the Sanhedrin. Even though he was no longer chosen systematically from among the descendants of Aaron, the high priest almost always belonged to one of the same few priestly families. His charge, which was no longer a lifetime appointment, was to administer the Temple and to exercise, conjointly with the Sanhedrin, a judicial and regulatory power that brought him considerable authority in religious matters, particularly in the Diaspora. Beginning in Herod's reign, however, the high priest became an instrument of civil authority. Herod had named high priests according to his own criteria; many of those selected were without high status, and some were unworthy. The prefect Valerius Gratus (15–26 C.E.) named three different high priests in three years before selecting Caiaphas, who held the post from 18 to 37. High priests became instruments of the Romans as they had once been instruments of Herod, a status that deprived them of any prestige in the eyes of the people.[98]

The Sanhedrin[99] was a council with numerous functions, particularly in judicial matters; it held authority only in Judaea. It represented the "democratic" voice of the Jewish government in the eyes of the Pharisees, more and more of whom were members of the council. But the high priest and the Sanhedrin were kept out of policy decisions, confined to religious and judicial functions, although the Pharisees protested these limits on their power. Under the circumstances, at the city and town levels, local councils made up of "elders" and *hoi protoi* (the "firsts") never acquired responsibility for more than everyday legal matters and the interpretation of the Torah, two activities that were necessarily intertwined.

A Closer Look At the Social Crisis[100]

Greco-Roman and Talmudic sources describe Palestine as a prosperous region well suited to traditional Mediterranean agriculture. Wheat harvests yielded five to fifteen times the amount sown and in good years were exported by way of Tyre and Sidon. Vineyards were widespread throughout the region, and the wines of Sharon, Carmel, Gaza, Ascalon, and Lydda were famous enough to be sold outside Palestine. Olive oil was abundant in Judaea, although the oil of Galilee was considered of better quality. Added to these three essential resources were balsam and papyrus from the Jordan River Valley (Jericho), livestock farming in the Negev, Peraea, and Samaria, and fruits, vegetables, and fishing both in the Mediterranean and in Lake Genesareth (the Sea of Galilee).

Overall prosperity was thus not an issue;[101] however, the system of land tenure was a source of inequality. Ever since the return from exile, Judaea had been a country of free peasants with small holdings, and Jewish colonization in Galilee, which was very active starting in the third century B.C.E., was established on the same basis. But beginning around the first century B.C.E. the situation changed, and it only worsened under Herod's rule. First, the relative overpopulation of Palestine prompted a fragmentation of land ownership that was noticeable in Judaea and Samaria from the first century B.C.E. through the first century C.E. Rules of succession in Jewish law divided property among all brothers, although the eldest had the right to a double portion. In the best of cases, his brothers sold their shares and he was able to live alone on the land. But sometimes all the heirs were left with parcels too small to be profitable; they quickly went into debt and had to sell. Prosperous landowners profited from such situations to increase their holdings. The peasants who lost their land were hired for wages or, at best, as tenant farmers or sharecroppers. Farming put the peasant in a condition of complete dependency, because the landowner chose the crops, provided the seed, and pocketed the profit. A tenant farmer had to settle for a smaller share that kept him from ever getting out of debt.

Apart from the royal holdings or those of the king's own family and friends (Salome's estate in Iamnia, Herod's lands in Idumaea and Galilee), there were few examples of large landholdings. But these few may well have included large amounts of land. Shimon Applebaum ascribes a vast domain to Antipas in the area of Bir al-'Abid, Qaqun, and Hurvat Migdal, in the former Narbatene (Plain of Sharon),[102] as well as other royal holdings in the Qarawat Bene Hassan region in western Samaria,[103] around the village of Arous,[104] and others close to the Herodians probably also received such *doreai* (gifts).

However, there was also a class of well-to-do owners of medium-size properties who employed either tenant farmers (Matthew 21.33) or hourly workers (Matthew 21.1–7). We must not be misled by the Evangelists, who were quick to contrast rich and poor for instructional purposes. Even in Galilee, where there were large properties belonging to Herod's friends or to powerful people favorably disposed toward the Romans (especially around Sepphoris),[105] many property owners had medium-size holdings. But small Jewish properties were often eliminated in the wealthiest areas. Herod distributed lots to his veterans in fertile zones (six thousand in the area around Samaria), and large landowners bought up property in regions where the profits were best.

Peasant debt, made worse by a harsh tax code,[106] seems to have been intolerable. Josephus stresses the looting of the rich by "brigands,"[107] and in 66 one of the first signs of the revolt was the burning of the registration offices in Jerusalem. The problem was that debt could lead to forced servitude: although it lasted only six years and slaves could not be sold abroad, the possibility of servitude symbolized social injustice. When Simon bar Giora left Masada for Jerusalem at the beginning of the revolt, he freed his slaves; the gesture was an effective symbol for the liberation of all Jews. But this state of heightened social tension was not unique to Judaea. Complicating and aggravating the local situation was the fact that in Judaea an internal, ideological debate about the legitimacy of Roman taxation was combined with a spontaneous revolt against taxes considered excessive in terms of the actual wealth of the country. According to Tacitus, in 17 C.E. Syria and Judaea both called on Tiberius to lower the tribute owed Rome, proof that Jews were not alone in finding Roman taxes burdensome.[108]

An Identity Crisis and a Refusal to Assimilate

In general, the Roman Empire functioned better as an agent of integration than as an agent of exclusion. It is true that the emperors' policy of integration or imposing uniformity was no stronger than that of the Hellenic kings, including Antiochos IV. However, anyone willing to adopt Greek or Roman ways, language, dress, gods, diet, leisure pursuits, and so on was free to do so and could expect full acceptance in the ruling classes of the empire, provided he had the necessary means. In short, anyone who wanted to could become as "Roman" as old-line Romans, or as Greek as an inhabitant of Athens or Ephesos.

Yet while prominent citizens in every province in the empire were willing participants in the process of integration, and often brought along with them a fair number of their compatriots, in Judaea we find, on the contrary, an emphatic adherence to anything that would distinguish the Jews from all other nations. Everything in the code of ritual purity and in the interpretation of its rules was aimed at reinforcing exclusivity. Already different from the other peoples by virtue of their monotheism and their refusal to accept other gods, Jews never stopped asserting their identity, and they imposed unheard-of restrictions on everyone who lived in Judaea. There were sanctions against imagery (including even the insignia of the legions) in Jerusalem, against the practice of pagan cults, against the imperial cult, and so on. No Jew in Judaea, even among high-level dignitaries, was willing to compromise on these sanctions. Strict adherence to a Jewish identity seemed to be the sine qua non of the nation's survival in the face of a seductive Hellenism. It may be that one of the main reasons for Jesus's condemnation, which resulted more from the Jewish authorities' hatred than from the Romans' concern for order, was his refusal to exclude pagans and his uncompromisingly inclusive discourse.

Still, the overt rejection of assimilation did not stop it from happening. This rejection may even have been a desperate response to the success of integration. For Hellenism was gaining ground, owing as much to the presence of numerous non-Jews throughout Palestine as to the temptations that Greek life held for the ruling classes. We saw earlier how the Herodians, surrounded by Greeks, were profoundly Hellenized. But everywhere, except perhaps in Jerusalem and the adjacent countryside (and integration made inroads even there), Jews lived side by side with pagans and were often a minority. We see the extent of this Hellenization first of all in the widespread presence of Greek as the language of inscriptions, even on Jewish funeral urns.

The cultural situation in Palestine in the first century has been the object of lively debate along the lines of the discussion sparked by Martin Hengel's book about the period preceding the era of the Maccabees. Hengel puts the essential question bluntly: "What effects of 'Hellenistic' civilization, or more exactly the 'Greek' language, Greek life-style, in the economy, technology, education, philosophy and religion can be demonstrated in Jewish Palestine in the first century after Christ?"[109] Hengel notes that everyone uses the words *Hellenism* and *Hellenistic* without attempting to define them. It is true that for many authors the terms seem interchangeable and are used to designate anything that had a tinge of Greek culture. In Hengel's view, Hellenism had made deep inroads into Jewish milieus. He notes, for example, that there were no pronounced differences between the Judeo-Hellenistic literature of the Diaspora and the "original" Jewish literature of Palestine.[110] Herod's Jerusalem seems to him profoundly Hellenized,[111] and he agrees with James L. Kelso and D. C. Baramki that Jericho was like a slice of Rome transported by flying carpet to the banks of the Jordan River![112] As he sees it, the rebellion of 66–70 brought an end to a prosperous and original Judaeo-Hellenic culture[113] from which the Jews had both learned and profited; the notion of religious modification to meet individual needs[114] is just one example of this.

There is considerable truth in such an analysis, but it is risky to extend conclusions that are valid for the cultivated elements. Later Talmudic literature leaves no doubt that Greek modes of thought and expression had gained ground among educated Jews. Moreover, the Greek way of life and a taste for decorating in the Greek manner had spread widely. At least until the revolt of 66, however, there was a good deal of wariness about this borrowing as well as a certain number of restrictions on it, including rejection of imagery and avoidance of the company of Gentiles. Many people no doubt rejected such extreme attitudes (Jesus, for example, mixed easily with pagans), but few dared yet to defy the norm openly. Thus Hellenism must have remained superficial and limited to areas where it did not appear to threaten respect for the Torah.

Political and Religious Aspirations

For many years Palestinian Judaism had been a crossroads of widely disparate views, and Josephus surmises that, beginning in the middle of the second century, three great "philosophies," which modern scholars have come to call sects, were in place. I do not propose to discuss the religious situation in first-century Judaea systematically, or even to present these "sects" in detail; I shall focus only on aspects that shed light on their political activities. Nevertheless, it will be useful to briefly review the distinguishing characteristics of each.

The most important and probably the most influential group consisted of the Pharisees,[115] descendants of the Hasidim of the Maccabaean era. Their difficulties, first with the Hasmonaeans and later with Herod, have been mentioned above. Although they were not indifferent to the political and social conditions in Judaea, their primary concern was the Torah, the study of which was for them the central focus of every life. The Pharisees believed that God had given Moses a complete and perfect Torah during an encounter that lasted forty days and forty nights; Moses copied down only part of it, however. The entire oral tradition was simply the unwritten Law of Yahweh, and its authenticity was guaranteed by the chain of teachers who transmitted this oral law "by word of mouth" as faithfully as if it were a written text. The chain passed through Joshua to the elders from the period before the kingdom, then to the pre-exile prophets and to those that came after (Haggai, Zacharios, Malachi); from them it went on to Esdras, the final promulgator of the written Law, to Simon the Just (late third century, the last survivor of Esdras's Great Council), then to Antigonos of Socho, and finally to several pairs of rabbis: Yose ben Yoeser and Yose ben Yohanan, Juda ben Tabbai and Simeon ben Shatah, Shemaya and Abtalyon, ending with Shammai and Hillel,[116] the two masters from whom all the Pharisee rabbis claimed to descend. It is customary to contrast the two broad trends represented by Shammai and Hillel as quite rigid and somewhat more "lax," respectively. This is largely an artificial distinction, however, and the facts often present the opposite picture. What the distinction does indicate is that the Pharisee movement was not monolithic; it included tendencies that embraced divergent points of view toward important elements in the interpretation of scripture.[117] Moreover, the exegetical work of Pharisee scholars was an attempt to adapt the Law to changing circumstances and to develop a jurisprudence that could lighten the burden by taking into account the evolution of Jewish society, on the one hand, while developing the notion, on the other hand, that scrupulous respect for the Torah was simply the reflection of the soul's purity and of absolute devotion to God.

The Essenes were much less numerous and probably less influential,[118] even though most of them had not followed the Qumran sect into exile in the Judaean desert.[119] Members of this sect, whose lives seem to have been devoted entirely to study,[120] were not totally removed from contemporary reality, as the Romans proved in 68 by destroying their settlement. Those who lived among other Jews were more numerous, and they took part in the war: a man known as John the Essene was named military leader of the Lydda and Joppa sectors at the beginning of the revolt and was killed during an attack on Ascalon.[121] According to Josephus, the Essenes showed admirable courage when they were tortured by the Romans, an indication that the Romans considered them to be especially dangerous adversaries.[122] Philo describes them as pacifists, barred from bearing arms,[123] and so for Essenes to have fought in the war that started in 66 is an indication of how serious the issue was to them. They may have recognized it as what a text from Qumran called "the war of the Children of Light against the Children of Darkness," predicting the destruction of their enemies and the triumph of their sect; this was an eschatological encounter not to be missed.

The last group, the Sadducees, developed in reaction to the others[124] and brought together conservative scribes who rejected the Pharisees' and Essenes' interpretations of the Torah. They adhered to the written text of the Law. They did acknowledge the necessity of interpreting obscure or unexplained passages, but they did so through a purely legalistic lens, rejecting all moral and esoteric speculation about the text of the Law. For them, the Torah had to be applied scrupulously, but without exaggeration, and anything that was not forbidden by the Torah was considered permissible. This attitude no doubt stemmed from the desire of the aristocratic priesthood not to see its power, the right to perform sacrifices, denied by Pharisee scribes and scholars whose scriptural interpretations led to innovations the Sadducee priests considered dangerous. The priests' reactionary attitude can be understood as a concern about seeing their practices dictated by men whose zealous rigidity was not always based on the Pentateuch itself.

These three major groups did not represent all of Judaism; Pietists, Baptists, and others also have to be taken into account.[125] Of these, the Zealots deserve special mention for closely combining religious life and political action.[126] Although Josephus characterizes them as a "fourth philosophy," their doctrinal positions do not seem to differ very much from those of the Pharisees. What made them different was their impatience in political matters. For them, it was important to hasten the end-time and the coming of the heavenly kingdom through constant resistance to the Romans and their allies. Zealots could thus be found at the center of every political battle and of all the messianic and eschatological pronouncements of the first two-thirds of the first century. On the margins of the mainstream group, some radical activists, the Sicarii,[127] stood out. This group, which took its name from the small knife (sica) with which its members armed themselves, advocated acts of violence and terror against the Romans and their allies and accomplices. The assassinations they carried out did not weaken the enemy but instead led to greater repression, a response they hoped would radicalize the situation and swing a majority to their side.

Except for the Sadducees, who were ready to compromise with any authority, most Jews dreamt of a state where they would not be subject either to pressure from the Greeks or to exploitation by Roman emissaries. Even a return to the status of an autonomous tributary *ethnos,* ruled by the high priest and the Sanhedrin, was acceptable, because the Roman presence could be useful in maintaining order in some areas disturbed by "bandits" and in protecting the Jews of neighboring Greek cities from violence. However, this limited objective to which the most moderate groups rallied was considered outdated by the majority of Jews, who had long been influenced both by an apocalyptic eschatological literature and by a growing impatience for the coming of the Messiah.[128] These two longings should not be confused and were not on the same level, but they could easily coexist in the same individuals. Whereas the wait for the end-time and the triumph of the Jews focused on a more or less distant future, messianism took the form of a concrete, quasi-immediate earthly political claim.

From the time of the Babylonian exile (sixth century B.C.E.), Jews awaited the "Day of Yahweh" when a new covenant would be initiated, marking the triumph of the righteous. This eschatological view, rooted in the prophets of exile and the return from exile, was revived by scholarly exegesis. Starting in the second century B.C.E., apocalypses (revelations) proclaimed the imminence of the new covenant and gave the people new cause for hope in the depths of despair. At a time when everyone considered Israel's suffering to be endless and feared that Yahweh had abandoned them, the notion of an apocalypse with its announcement of coming salvation was encouraging, because the accumulated suffering was interpreted as a sign of the coming triumph of the Jews. Thus the genre flourished up to the Bar Kokhba revolt (132–134 C.E.), then disappeared as hope for restoration of a Jewish state receded.[129]

These speculations were shared by a great many Jews, most of them probably outside the circle of prominent priests. However, attitudes varied from synagogue to synagogue and from rabbi to rabbi as to what signs would foretell the "Day," what would actually happen (resurrection of all? of Jews alone? of the righteous alone?), and what the aftermath would look like. Despite these subtleties, by the second and especially the first century B.C.E., most Jews had come to include in their vision of the end-time the dual notion of the re-creation of an earthly kingdom and the advance coming of a Messiah.

The longed-for kingdom had been haunting the Jews since the exile. Many of them expected the end-time to coincide with the restoration of David's kingdom, a purely terrestrial event. This may have been the belief of some of Jesus's followers, who wanted to emphasize their master's descent from David's line, but many other Jews were awaiting a kingdom without reference to David.[130] In the kingdom to come, the Temple, purified and entrusted to a worthy high priest, would be restored to the highest rank, freed from the enslavement it had suffered for the past two hundred years.

Moreover, some circles believed that "the Day of the Lord" would be prepared by an emissary, someone "anointed" by God *(meschiya, christos)* who would serve as an intermediary.[131] For most Jews, this was a man, born like others (his birth perhaps unremarked) but all-powerful. Others believed that his coming would be preceded by dreadful signs or the return of Elijah. Opposing him, a coalition of evildoers led by the Antichrist would rise up and cause even greater suffering. In the end, Yahweh would triumph and the Messiah would reign in Jerusalem. The Diaspora would be reversed, Jerusalem would be purified and rebuilt, and the golden age would begin. After its thousand-year reign would come the end-time, when the dead (or the righteous) would be resurrected, and each one would be rewarded or punished.

This summary would have to be nuanced ad infinitum to account for all the diversity of views between sects and within particular sects.[132] But their basis remained the same: each anticipated an extraordinary event that would announce the liberation of the Jews. And public restlessness was acute. For although the dream of a state and the expectation of the Messiah's coming had been present for a long time, the notion that the realization was imminent was something new. Impatience for the coming of a Messiah had been growing ever since the middle of the first century B.C.E. Some speculative scholars set the date of salvation in the 30s C.E., although many others refused to propose an exact date. Not everyone prepared for it with as much care as the Essenes who had withdrawn to Qumran,[133] but it was definitely one of the main preoccupations of the Jews at the dawn of the new era, as well as evidence of the rebellious spirit that was shaking Palestine before the outbreak, in 66, of a general uprising.

From "Banditry" to the General Uprising of 66

Following Herod's reign, Palestine found itself under the control of a system of fortified posts, watchtowers, and strategic developments that were meant to repress dissent more than to defend against an external enemy. The banditry against which Pompey had struggled persisted, as a consequence of economic difficulties, the indebtedness of the peasantry, and unemployment.[134] But Josephus's narratives show that the "bandits" were also spurred into action by eschatological and messianic anticipation.

Galilee was the principal center of unrest.[135] At the beginning of his reign, Herod had fought against Ezechias the Galilean, who was plaguing Tyre. Ezechias's son Judas was one of the three messiahs who emerged at the time of the king's death. Defeated, he led a new revolt in 6–7 C.E. against the prefect Coponius. Josephus called him a "philosopher," the founder of a sect "unrelated to the others."[136] In reality, he was one of the leaders of the Zealots, a group that shared the Pharisees' viewpoints in religious matters but advocated violence against the Romans in order to hasten the coming of the Messiah.[137] This goal legitimized stealing from the rich, who were allies of the occupiers. Though Josephus does not use the term *Zealot* to describe him, the connection between Judas the Galilean and the Zealots is indisputable.[138]

Unrest was almost constant between 4 B.C.E. and the explosion of 66 C.E., with a variety of pretexts, but Nicole Belayche is right to emphasize that the situation intensified whenever a change in status led to hope for improvement or made things worse.[139] She distinguishes four critical periods: the time after Herod's death and the violence that ensued; the period of Pilatus's government; the death of Agrippa I, which removed all hope for restoration of a Jewish state; and, finally, the governments of Felix and his successors, which entailed ongoing bungling, pillaging, and repression.

Herod's death left the field free for "kings" who burned and bloodied Judaea:[140] the royal slave Simon, who impressed the mobs by his handsome bearing and great size, ravaged Peraea, burning the royal palace in Jericho and all the lavish homes in the region, thus highlighting the social accusations of the rebellion, while other insurgents burned the palace of Betharamatha in the same region.[141] Athronges, a shepherd of exceptional strength, proclaimed himself king and, with the help of his four brothers,[142] plagued royal and Roman troops for quite a long time.[143] Judas the Galilean seized the royal arsenals at Sepphoris,[144] while Herod's veterans from Idumaea attacked the royal troops.[145] The governor of Syria restored order by crucifying two thousand Jews.

In 26, a new revolt was provoked when the prefect Pontius Pilatus attempted to bring gilded imperial shields into Jerusalem.[146] This might simply be viewed as an instance of bungling or an excess of zeal, but it can also be seen as a deliberate measure, just as Pilatus's coinage can be seen as a provocation; indeed, some of his coins bore an image of a *simpulum* and others a *lituus*, both objects used in pagan sacrifices.[147] Somewhat later, he provoked a new furor when he wanted to levy a large tax on the Temple's treasury in order to build an aqueduct to bring water to Jerusalem.[148]

A long series of preachers and agitators of every stripe fed the popular outrage.[149] Around 30 C.E. Antipas had John the Baptist arrested and executed; John was a widely revered preacher who proclaimed the Messiah's coming and called on people to prepare for it by purification.[150] In 33,[151] Jesus of Nazareth, who seemed to have close ties with his predecessor John, also fell victim to the authorities' mistrust of preachers like him. Although his message was limited to the promise of a better day in an indeterminate future, his followers proclaimed him king, making him just another messiah-agitator in the eyes of the authorities.[152] Barabbas may have been in the same category (Luke 23.17–25); his popularity could be explained by a messianic message that was more exciting than Jesus's because it was more immediate. In Samaria a man aroused a mob by claiming to show them sacred urns buried by Moses himself on Mount Gerizim: he was arrested and executed.[153] In the same district, Dositheos proclaimed himself the Messiah prophesied by Moses.[154]

Throughout this time, popular uprisings alternated with provocations by the authorities.[155] In 40–41, Caligula decided to erect his own statue in the Temple. Agitation by the Jews forced the governor of Syria to delay before ultimately revoking the measure when the emperor died.[156] Following Agrippa's death and the return of direct administration for part of the country, the protests resumed in earnest, nourished by specific historical references, as noted by Nicole Belayche.[157] Around 45, a man named Theudas performed miracles before vast throngs and called for a new exodus; the procurator Cuspius Fadus had the crowd dispersed and Theudas executed,[158] which did not stop other prophets from issuing the same call for flight into the desert.[159] The sons of Judas of Galilee were charged with banditry and crucified under Tiberius Julius Alexander's government, around 46–48. Around 48–52, a riot that began in response to the insults of a drunkard led to a violent repression and some twenty thousand deaths, according to Josephus.[160] Around 51–52, Zealots avenged the assassination of Jewish Galileans in Samaria; Cumanus repressed their action with such ferocity that Quadratus, the governor of Syria, decided to send him to Rome along with the agitators. Under Felix, one of Claudius's favorites, rioting was constant. After the arrest of Eleazar, the Zealot leader who had plagued Galilee for twenty years,[161] Sicarii extremists took over, assassinating Romans and moderate Jews in order to radicalize the conflict.[162] Preachers inflamed the masses: an Egyptian Jew proclaimed the end of Roman domination and, like a new Joshua, led thousands of believers to consider bringing down the walls of Jerusalem. Felix quickly massacred them beneath the walls of the city while the Egyptian disappeared into the countryside.[163] The situation only worsened under Festus (60–64), Albinus (62–64), and Gessius Florus (64–66). The last two of these seem to have been especially inflammatory in their manner of governing. Josephus describes Albinus not only as a looter and a thief but also as an accomplice of the bandit leaders who were ravaging the countryside in the guise of resisting the occupiers:

Many of those who were in prison for brigandage were freed to return to their families after paying a ransom, and only those who could not pay were considered criminals and left in prison. As a result, the revolutionary party in Jerusalem grew even more daring: its leaders made a deal with Albinus and paid a sum of money to be guaranteed immunity in their seditious activities—and all these rogues, surrounded by their personal followers, paraded around at the head of a battalion like bandit chiefs or tyrant and used bodyguards to pillage the goods of moderates.[164]

This description aptly characterizes the atmosphere of a country at war, where corrupt leaders left the field free for the most unsavory elements, who made a legitimate cause their pretext for sheer pillaging. It was enough to infuriate many people. According to Josephus, Albinus's successor was even worse. "Gessius Florus by comparison made [Albinus] look like a perfectly decent man."[165]

Impatience for the Messiah grew as Jews encountered increasing hostility from Gentiles. In response to a new Jewish delegation, Nero established Caesarea as a Greek city where Jews had no rights.[166] Later on, in the middle of the war, as the Temple and the city were burning, messiahs appeared and persuaded the crowds to die as martyrs in the flames.[167]

All these events helped exacerbate the tensions; Palestine could be seen as being in a state of latent revolt starting around 60. Between prophets and "brigands" (listim), "charlatans" (as Josephus called them), and messiahs, there were shared hopes that inspired the populace.[168] Men such as John the Baptist and Jesus, prophets of the apocalypse and of messianism, nourished the hopes of the crowds even though neither of them personally preached a message of revolt. It was not surprising to see Jesus crucified between two thieves, because in the eyes of the authorities he was as much a troublemaker as the others.[169]

Violent movements such as these were the most visible aspect of the opposition to Rome's authority, but there was another, more hidden aspect whose real effect on public opinion is hard to measure: apocalyptic literature. The apocalypses published during the second and first centuries B.C.E.[170] doubtless continued to be read, as did writings of a messianic nature such as the famous Psalm 17 of the Psalms of Solomon, announcing a king of David's line sent by Yahweh to destroy the impious occupiers and purify Jerusalem.[171] However, new works appeared during this time as well. The Testament of Moses seems to have been published between 7 to 30 C.E. by an Essene; among other things, it proclaimed the Kingdom of God and the annihilation of the devil, along with a messenger who would dispense justice (chapter 10), and it included a bitter polemic against the Sadducees (chapter 7).[172] Similarly, the third book of the Sibylline Oracles, certainly of Jewish origin, dates from the first century C.E., around the year

70.[173] Although it was published in Alexandria, it was probably widely read in all the Jewish communities. It jubilantly announced the destruction of the Roman Empire and its replacement by the great realm of an immortal king.[174] One can understand to what extent works like these must have fostered hope and rebellion among a population infuriated by Roman demands.

Beyond the repetitive and seemingly incidental nature of the various uprisings and movements, time itself did its work. It is striking to observe how often Josephus stresses the efforts of local leaders to intervene with incompetent or greedy procurators. Although he shows no tolerance for "brigands," Josephus is well aware of the incessant provocations of the Roman authorities and of the mediating role of the Jewish ruling class—sometimes including Herodian princes. But a new element was added during the decade of the 60s: under pressure from the street, but also owing to the recognition that they had nothing to lose, the Jewish elites broke openly with the Roman authorities.[175] The arrogant attitude displayed by Felix, Cumanus, and especially Festus showed that none of them could be expected to deal evenhandedly with Jews and Greeks (as, for example, in Caesarea) or to respect Jewish law. By placing itself at the head of the uprising, the Jewish ruling class could hope to regain what it had lost in its collaboration with Rome: power and prestige.

THE REVOLT OF 66–70 AND ITS CONSEQUENCES

The revolt that broke out in 66 is the best known of all the rebellions because of its immediate and long-term consequences: the destruction of the Temple, the end of cult sacrifice, and the abolition of Jewish institutions as fundamental as the high priesthood. Without denying the importance of these facts, the historian should not fail to consider the revolt on its own terms and should not allow its ultimate defeat to influence the analysis. This, however, is exactly what Flavius Josephus—who is virtually our only source—does in order to justify his dramatic change of sides.

Setting aside the immediate and long-term consequences, I believe that the rebellion of 66 and the conduct of the war until 70 (and less crucially until 74) allow us to assess more accurately the social, political, and religious situation in Palestine in the middle of the first century, and to modify some of the misperceptions to which the various kinds of texts examined so far may have given rise. First, the rebellion demonstrated the lack of understanding between the Jewish masses, sensitive to the teaching of the Pharisee masters, and the activist minorities (Zealots and Sicarii): the momentary conjunction of interests or aims uniting leaders and Zealots at the beginning of the revolt did not withstand the test of war. Additionally, it underlined the desperation of minorities to obtain by terror what they could not win by persuasion, and highlighted the dissension that prevailed among them: the most important aspect of the war in Jerusalem is that it was a civil war among Jewish factions. Under these circumstances, it may seem surprising that Rome did not put down the revolt quickly. Other events, however, had captured the attention of the rulers, from Nero's assassination to the usurpations of Galba, Otho, and Vitellius and the conflicts they provoked. It was not until Vespasian was proclaimed emperor in Judaea that the situation stabilized and Titus was able to wage war more energetically.

From the Popular Uprising to the War of Liberation

THE PRETEXT

The revolt began as an ordinary riot, like so many others in Jerusalem, with a familiar sequence of events: provocation, agitation, repression. In the spring of 66, the procurator Gessius Florus decided to impose a tax of seventeen talents on the Temple,[176] to punish the Jews who had long wrangled with him over Caesarea.[177] The decision prompted unrest, but the amount was so trivial that a public campaign was organized for "poor Florus." Florus, who was in Jerusalem at the time with his two cohorts, refused to tolerate the mockery; he repressed the demonstration brutally, despite the intervention of a number of Jewish leaders, including Berenice herself (April–May 66). He provoked a real bloodbath (Josephus reported thirty-six hundred dead),[178] and he crucified many Jews, including Roman citizens and equestrians.[179] To humiliate the leaders who had intervened, he obliged them to hold a reception in honor of the troops who had just put down the revolt. This was too much: the people rebelled again, which led to new massacres. However, the mutineers sought refuge in the Temple and began isolating it from the Antonia fortress by destroying the porticos that linked them. Florus evacuated the city to seek reinforcements, leaving only one cohort behind.[180]

At that point, Agrippa II arrived from Alexandria and exhorted the populace not to let things get out of hand. He pleaded for loyalty to the emperor and recommended reconstructing the passage between the Temple and the Antonia fortress and even collecting back taxes, which was done.[181] However, the people refused to submit to Florus, and open war ensued. While the rebels occupied Masada, where the Roman garrison was murdered, Eleazar, son of the high priest Ananias, suspended the daily sacrifice

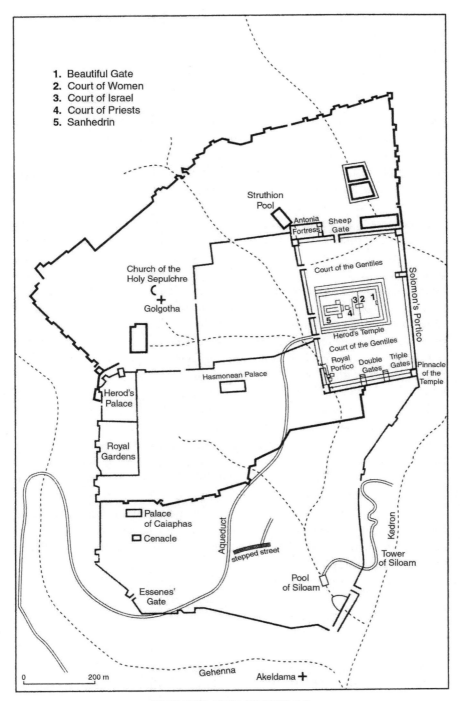

1. Beautiful Gate
2. Court of Women
3. Court of Israel
4. Court of Priests
5. Sanhedrin

Struthion Pool

Antonia Fortress

Sheep Gate

Church of the Holy Sepulchre

Golgotha

Court of the Gentiles

Solomon's Portico

Herod's Temple

Court of the Gentiles

Royal Portico

Double Gates

Triple Gates

Pinnacle of the Temple

Hasmonean Palace

Herod's Palace

Royal Gardens

Palace of Caiaphas

Cenacle

Aqueduct

stepped street

Kedron

Tower of Siloam

Pool of Siloam

Essenes' Gate

0   200 m

Gehenna   Akeldama ✝

JERUSALEM, FIRST CENTURY C.E.

offered for the emperor's health.[182] It was no longer Florus alone who was held accountable, but Roman domination itself. How had the situation reached this point?

One might imagine that the latest riot in Jerusalem was just one more example of the troubles besetting Judaea. Although there is certainly some truth in this view, it does not provide a complete explanation. Obviously, we can find in it the familiar pattern of demonstration followed by repression. But how do we explain the fact that, this time, a local riot became a general uprising involving the entire Judaean population?

A new factor accounts for this shift to all-out war: the Jewish leaders had moved to the side of "bandits," "charlatans," and other "false messiahs." It was the chief of the Temple police himself, Eleazar ben Ananias, who suspended imperial sacrifices in the Temple. What is more, after Cestius Gallus's failure against Jerusalem in November 66, Jewish leaders sent delegates to assume responsibility for operations everywhere, in the Judaean toparchies as well as in distant Galilee: Joseph ben Gurion and the high priest Ananos[183] in Jerusalem, Eleazar ben Ananias and Jesus ben Sapphia in Idumaea, Joseph ben Matthias (that is, Flavius Josephus) in Galilee. Thus from the outset they put themselves at the forefront of a movement of which they had once been only followers.

The leaders had swung to the anti-Roman side. There are several explanations for this, and all of them probably contain some truth. First of all, the effects of Jewish terrorism by the Sicarii had finally begun to be felt. Josephus asserts that the prefect Felix ordered the Sicarii's assassination of the high priest Jonathan. This is implausible, but the very suggestion may indicate the hatred that the Jewish priestly aristocracy had come to feel toward Rome. The prospect of falling victim to attack by the Sicarii may have discouraged the leaders from continuing to compromise with Rome in acts of repression from which they had nothing to gain. Florus's last move was just the latest example.

In addition, it is obvious that the Jewish aristocracy could expect nothing more from Rome. A succession of high priests had not been able to bring about any improvement in the Jews' material situation or legal status: the struggle against the "provocations" of prefects and procurators was unending. In the incident at Caesarea on the Sea that led to the war, the leaders had been stripped before being humiliated by Florus. Threatened by the Sicarii, humiliated by the Romans, these Jewish leaders had nothing to lose by throwing themselves into the revolt that had just broken out. Their best chance for regaining the power for which all sides were contending was to emerge victorious from the widely anticipated conflict with Rome.

However, regaining power was not the only objective of the Jewish leaders. It must be remembered that in some circles they, too, nourished fundamental religious aspirations that could not find expression in the current situation. Recent digs in the upper-class neighborhood at the foot of the Temple plaza have revealed luxurious homes where must have lived very wealthy people, people accustomed to imported goods (sigillata, marble, and the like) and thus open to the outside world. At the same time, baths have also been found in perfect conformity with the norms established by rabbis for ritual purification. Wealth did not preclude strict respect for the law. Nevertheless, living according to the Torah had become impossible for everyone.

Finally, we must not forget the pressure exerted by the Greeks on Jews in all sectors where the two lived side by side: the coast of Palestine, Galilee, the neighboring regions of the Golan and Phoenicia. The issue of *isopoliteia* (equality of citizenship) in Caesarea ended in an affront to the Jews.[184] Similarly, at the beginning of the revolt, an armed expedition of Tyrians, Gadarenes, and other neighbors destroyed the Jewish city of Gischala in Galilee, sending a local chief sympathetic to Rome, John ben Levi, into the armed struggle against Rome.[185]

The convergence of so much hatred and rancor, the accumulation of so many misunderstandings, put a barrier between Rome and its subjects, especially in Judaea proper. For there were regional differences that we shall examine shortly: the apparent unanimity among the Jewish rebels was only a façade.

The Reconquest of Palestine

EARLY JEWISH VICTORIES

Everything seemed to start out well for the Jews. After burning the palaces belonging to the high priest Agrippa II and Berenice in Jerusalem and the archives where debt records were stored, the rebels managed to seize the Antonia fortress (July–August 66), and then laid siege to Herod's palace.[186] The former high priest Ananias, viewed as a subversive from Rome, was assassinated by a group led by Menahem, son of Judas the Galilean (July–August 66); Menahem himself was soon eliminated by a more extremist group. The Roman troops left behind by Florus were forced to negotiate their own evacuation of the city, but the Jews, disregarding past treaties, wiped them all out: the campaign appeared to be a total success, and the break with Rome final.[187] At the same time, the Caesareans massacred twenty thousand Jews,[188] whereupon the Jews of the Decapolis responded by mounting concerted attacks against Philadelphia, Pella, Gerasa, Esbous, Scythopolis, Gadara, and Hippos, while others sacked Gaba, Ptolemais, Sebaste, Ascalon, Anthedon, and Gaza: the war was spreading throughout Palestine.[189]

Cestius Gallus, the governor of Syria, prepared to respond by putting together a large military force consisting of some eleven thousand legionnaires, including the entire Legio XII Fulminata, and two thousand men raised from each of the three other Syrian legions, four cavalry *alae* and six auxiliary cohorts as well as allied contingents furnished by both cities and client princes: Antiochos IV of Commagene (two thousand cavalry and three thousand infantry), Agrippa II (three thousand infantry and just under two thousand cavalry), Sohaimos of Emesa (four thousand men, a third of them cavalry and the rest archers).[190] All together, the army included over thirty thousand men.[191]

Gallus's troops seem to have made easy progress at first, looting without resistance as they went. Thus they regained control of Sepphoris, Caesarea, Antipatris, Lydda, and Beth Horon and reached the outskirts of Jerusalem. However, although the Jews of Gibeon (modern Gabao) were defeated in their first attack, Gallus failed to achieve significant success in Jerusalem itself. Even though he was camped on Mount Scopus and held a position in the districts north of Jerusalem, he had to give up the effort to take the Temple, and for unknown reasons he chose to withdraw. During the retreat, his troops were decimated as they marched near Beth Horon (November 25, 66). The rebellious Jews had reason to believe in a decisive victory: the leaders who had rallied to the revolt began to put the state on a defensive footing.

The revolt needed to be coordinated, and the early successes probably prompted some previously uncommitted moderates to get involved. The leaders in Jerusalem sent delegates who had been elected by a popular assembly to take control of the area.[192] Joseph ben Gurion and the former high priest Ananos had full control in Jerusalem, Jesus son of Sappha and Eleazar ben Ananias in Idumaea, John the Essene in Lydda, Joppa, Emmaus, and the toparchy of Thamna north of Jerusalem, and Joseph, son of Matthias (the future Flavius Josephus), in Galilee.[193] During this time, as part of an effort to build a unanimous movement, terror reigned in Jerusalem against anyone who was lukewarm or undecided. This united front seemed particularly necessary because the Roman counteroffensive was already taking shape under the leadership of Flavius Vespasian, named by Nero as commander of an expeditionary force in Judaea that had yet to be constituted.[194]

In fact, the collaboration between the moderate elements that had seized control of the situation and the more radical groups that had thrown the country into war was only superficial. Josephus learned this quickly in Galilee. Knowing perfectly well that that was where the Roman counteroffensive would begin, Josephus fortified vulnerable locations and the largest cities, while also raising troops (he claims to have had one hundred thousand men) equipped with confiscated weapons.[195] He was forced to leave the people of Sepphoris to do as they chose,[196] while John of Gischala single-handedly prepared his city to defend itself and showed extreme distrust of Josephus, whom he suspected of being lukewarm and a traitor helping the Romans.[197] Even before the appearance of the Roman army, Galilee was divided between supporters of these two men. Josephus worked tirelessly to regain Tiberias, Sepphoris, and other less important locales. Similar conditions arose in other regions: the high priest Ananos sent troops against Simon bar Giora, who was sacking the toparchy of Acrabata.[198]

The ensuing battles have been described many times elsewhere;[199] I shall mention only the most important details here. Vespasian, seconded by his son Titus, began to assemble a large army made up of three legions and twenty-three cohorts, in addition to the reinforcements furnished by Antiochos IV of Commagene, Sohaimos of Emesa, Malichos II of Petra, and Agrippa II, for a total of close to sixty thousand men. Vespasian spent the summer of 67 retaking control of Galilee, where Iotapata (defended by Josephus),[200] Tiberias, and Tarichaea fell one after the other, provoking a chain of defections in towns and cities that had not yet fallen. The subsequent repression was indeed often brutal, entailing massacres, deportations, and slavery. At the end of 67, with the capture of Gamala, across Lake Tiberias, followed by that of Gischala and of Mount Tabor in Galilee, the last Galilean strongholds passed into the hands of the Romans, who introduced more and more garrisons to hold the country.

At the same time or shortly afterward, the Roman troops adopted a policy of isolating Jerusalem; they were beginning to regain control of the coast little by little (for example, they held Iamnia and Azotos). In the spring of 68, Vespasian campaigned beyond the Jordan, attacked Gadora (Salt), and left his tribune Placidus to retake Abila and Livias and to rid the countryside of the gangs who were pillaging the region. He himself pursued the campaign in Judaea, going down into Idumaea, where he captured Betogabris; he established a permanent camp in Emmaus, west of Jerusalem, and another shortly afterward in Jericho in the Jordan Valley. In this way, the noose tightened around Jerusalem without the Roman army having to come very close. Knowing that civil war was raging in Jerusalem, and preoccupied by Vindex's revolt against Nero in Gaul and by the successive usurpations of Galba and Otho, Vespasian preferred to ensure his control of reconquered territory rather than risk a drawn-out siege of Jerusalem. So he sent L. Annius against Gerasa, where the Jews had been protected by the local population, but which was the birthplace of Simon bar Giora, one of the most prominent Jewish commanders. The objective everywhere appears to have been to terrorize local populations in order to cut them off from the rebels in Jerusalem. At the time, the country seemed to be full of refugees forced out as much by the insurgents (the moderates having fled Jerusalem as soon as the war broke out) as by the Romans: Vespasian settled some of them in Lydda and Iamnia, but hunted down those who had regrouped in Joppa and depended on piracy to survive.[201]

In the summer of 68, it seemed the time had finally come to march on Jerusalem. During that same period, Vespasian learned of Nero's death (June 9, 68) and the proclamation of Galba as emperor. Titus, who had been sent by his father with Agrippa II to greet the new emperor and request orders, had not yet reached Rome when Galba died (January 15, 69); the latter was replaced by Otho, while Vitellius had proclaimed himself emperor on January 2. Although the crisis at the highest levels of the empire gave Vespasian more freedom of movement, it also complicated his task. He resumed the campaign nevertheless, approaching Jerusalem, and in the late spring of 69 he seized the districts around Jerusalem that Simon bar Giora had recently held, Hebron and northern Idumaea.

During this time, civil war had broken out in Jerusalem. After the evacuation of Cestius Gallus's troops in November 66, the inhabitants of Jerusalem prepared for war in earnest, reinforcing ramparts, completing Agrippa I's wall north of the city, and stockpiling arms. A government was formed and began minting coins in the spring of 67. With the Roman victories of 67 and 68, however, a flood of refugees and soldiers who had been driven out of Galilee, Peraea, and Idumaea rushed toward Jerusalem. From the start there were two opposing factions: moderates led by the former high priest Ananos, and Zealots commanded by Eleazar bar Simon. A third faction was added in 68; it consisted of followers of John of Gischala, who tried in vain to reunite all the groups under a single authority, his own. The Zealots unleashed a reign of terror by assassinating those they considered lukewarm, and then, to escape a counteroffensive by the moderates, took refuge in the Temple and designated a new high priest, Phanni bar Samuel, as a replacement for one they deemed insufficiently radical, Matthias bar Theophilos. Under Ananos's command, the mob attacked the Zealots in the Temple: the city was split in two.

To restore their advantage, Eleazar's Zealots appealed to the Idumaean gangs that had entered the city under false pretenses. The two groups together regained the upper hand and unleashed a massacre of moderate leaders (Ananos) and aristocrats, after mock trials. When they withdrew from Jerusalem, the Idumaeans freed two thousand prisoners, most of whom rushed off to help Simon bar Giora's troops fight the war in the hills of Judaea. The Zealots, rid of their bothersome allies, increased their atrocities, while the movement was splitting into rival camps, with John of Gischala's emerging as the winner. Simon bar Giora was gaining power, controlling both the northern and the southern areas around Jerusalem. Although his attempts to force his way into Jerusalem had failed, he ultimately succeeded with the help of moderates who were looking for someone capable of putting a stop to John of Gischala's atrocities. Simon bar Giora entered Jerusalem in the spring of 69, just before the Roman troops themselves invaded Judaea.

The siege must have appeared imminent: apart from the fortresses held by the Sicarii (Machaerus, the Herodion, and Masada), only Jerusalem had withstood Rome. However, the power crisis that had developed in Rome delayed the attack. Otho, whom Vespasian supported, was defeated and committed suicide in March 69. To all appearances, Vitellius was in charge. However, on July 1, 69, following numerous consultations, the prefect of Egypt, Tiberius Julius Alexander, had his troops swear allegiance to Vespasian, who had been proclaimed emperor. The troops in Judaea and Syria immediately followed suit, as did the client princes. Vespasian then left for Egypt, where he followed the unfolding crisis in the west.

Titus became responsible for carrying out the mission, but it was not until the spring of 70, when the situation in the west had stabilized, that the operation resumed. In the meanwhile, the situation in Jerusalem had worsened. Simon bar Giora held the upper city and a large part of the lower city, and John of Gischala had been blocked at the courtyard of the Temple by Eleazar bar Simon, who constructed an impregnable garrison for himself in the interior courtyards and the sanctuary itself. Fighting between the three factions was constant, because Simon controlled the food supply. Thus the city that Titus came to attack in the spring of 70 with around sixty thousand men was a city exhausted by civil war.[202]

After just two weeks, Agrippa's wall was taken and the Romans occupied the northern district of Bezetha. A few days later, the second wall was breached and Roman troops controlled the outskirts of the Temple to the west. The most difficult task remained, because the Temple fortifications, the Antonia fortress, and the first wall presented enormous obstacles. The Romans brought in siege equipment and dug trenches around the walls; the Jews dug counter-trenches, and their vigilance repelled every assault. Fam-

RELIEF FROM THE ARCH OF TITUS, ROME: ROMAN SOLDIERS CARRYING
THE TEMPLE'S HOLY OBJECTS IN A VICTORY PARADE.

ine spread in the city, but the commanders would not give up their struggle, and the siege dragged on. It was not until the end of July that the situation came to a head: on July 24, the Antonia fortress was taken by surprise during the night. The Temple seemed to be within the attackers' grasp. However, it took another month of furious fighting for the Romans finally to capture the Temple, which they burned (August 29, 70). Still to be taken was the lower city, where various official buildings and the palace of the kings of Adiabene were torched, and finally the upper city, where the remaining resisters had fled (late September 70).[203]

The war was essentially over. The Sicarii fortresses remained, but Titus did not wait to celebrate his victory in Caesarea on the Sea and then in Caesarea of Philippi, in Berytos and in Antioch, while legates forced Herodion and Machaerus to surrender. Only Masada resisted, under the command of Eleazar bar Yair (son of Yair). Despite the significance that Masada has taken on in the Jewish imagination, the fact remains that its capture in 73 or 74[204] by Flavius Silva was no more than an epiphenomenon on the military level.[205] The fall of Jerusalem more than three years earlier had ensured the Jewish defeat.

FROM THE FALL OF THE TEMPLE TO BAR KOKHBA

The Reorganization of Palestine

The Zealots' brutality and the rebels' lack of preparedness had impelled many cities and towns to surrender without resistance at the outset of the Roman offensive. Similarly, many people had fled the besieged cities and sought refuge behind Roman lines, perhaps giving the Romans the impression that the revolt involved only an extremist minority. Once that element was defeated, Vespasian was willing to show leniency.[206]

As early as 70 (or 74), Vespasian had made Judaea an independent "imperial" province of Syria. The governor was to be a senator of praetorian rank, as well as the commander of Legio X Fretensis, which remained garrisoned in Jerusalem.[207] Auxiliary troops completed the garrison, six *alae* and cohorts, according to a military diploma from 86, probably fewer than five thousand men.[208] Beyond this, Vespasian took only one measure with a broad-based impact: the didrachm tax—a duty imposed on all Jews for the maintenance of the Temple, and whose collection had been the symbol of Jewish privilege throughout the empire—became a humiliating tax (although a light one) paid by Jews in honor of Jupiter Capitolinus. Instead of confiscating all of Palestine for his own profit as the right of conquest authorized him to do, Vespasian seized the property of the commanders and the most prominent combatants, but sold back their lands to those who wanted them, except for certain tracts given to veterans (eight hundred in Emmaus-Nicopolis) or to his friends (Josephus).[209] In reality, many Jews continued to own land in Galilee and in Judaea at the end of the first century and in the second.[210]

The ensuing calm was only relative, however. Some later texts indicate that there were anti-Jewish persecutions in Palestine before the uprising led by Bar Kokhba,[211] but none is confirmed before the end of the 120s, because the Jewish revolts of 115–117 in Cyrene, Egypt, and Cypros did not extend to Palestine. The apathy in Palestine may be explained by the scope of the disaster of 66–70, as well as by the fact that the number of dead (Josephus's claim of one million is exaggerated) and exiles had reduced the extreme social tension that existed before 66. However, discontent lingered. Confiscation of lands in Judaea and their redistribution to soldiers or other foreign owners meant that pagans hired Jews as paid laborers or tenant farmers, which for a society of landowning peasants was an intolerable humiliation. The persistent banditry described in Talmudic texts may be an indication of this latent unrest,[212] and it is significant that most of the troops in the Bar Kokhba revolt were peasants.

In other contexts, too, opposition to Rome continued. Descendants of the Zealots were influential even among rabbis, and the Messiah was still anxiously awaited. Texts such as books 4 and 5 of the Sibylline Oracles attest to the persistence of eschatological belief at the end of the first century (book 4) and during Hadrian's reign (book 5),[213] as do the Greek Apocalypse of Baruch (III Baruch) before 115–117[214] and the Syriac Apocalypse of Baruch (II Baruch) during Trajan's reign.[215] The echoes of the events in Egypt, Cyrene, and Cyprus during the years 115–117 could not have left Palestinian Jews unmoved. An unmistakable unrest prevailed in Palestine, and the selection of Lucius Quietus, who had just repressed a revolt in the Diaspora, as governor of Judaea in 117–118 may have reflected this fact.[216] From then on, the Judaean governor was chosen from among the consuls; this was justified by an increase in the number of legions.[217] A second legion was stationed in Palestine, in fact—first Legio II Traiana Fortis, around 117–120, and later, in 123, VI Ferrata, transferred from Arabia to Caparcotna (Lower Galilee), from where it could move quickly into the principal population centers.[218] We do not know if the number of auxiliaries was increased proportionately, for the first edict we have dates from 139—after the Bar Kokhba revolt[219]—and the very large increase that it shows may have been a consequence of the war. Similarly, Judaea's road system received particular attention from the authorities. Benjamin Isaac has noted that no fewer than a dozen routes were marked under Hadrian's reign between 120 and 129.[220] Although the milestones from 129 may have been directly related to the imperial visit of 129–130, it is clear that another explanation for this exceptional effort, unmatched even in Syria,[221] was the fear of a new revolt; and the construction marked the last step in the effort to substantially increase the province's permanent garrison. The Roman authorities seemed genuinely wary, but one would like to know the circumstances that justified these measures; our understanding of the causes of the Bar Kokhba revolt is seriously hampered by our lack of information.

Bar Kokhba's Revolt (132–135)[222]

It has long been thought that the revolt was the result of two decisions Hadrian made in the early 130s. First, he outlawed circumcision, perhaps around 132 (the exact date is not known). The ban was presumably not aimed specifically at the Jews, but it expanded the edicts of Domitian and Nerva against castration, a practice both the Romans and the Greeks considered barbaric, to include circumcision. However, Jews considered circumcision to be symbolic of their covenant with Yahweh. The ban not only imposed a serious religious limitation, but seemed to the Jews further proof, reminiscent of Antiochos IV's edict of persecution, that Rome wanted to destroy Judaism. In fact, the existence of this edict from Hadrian has been deduced from a reference in a somewhat unreliable source, *Historia Augusta*,[223] to a measure by Antoninus Pius authorizing Jews to circumcise their own sons and them alone; it is thus not clear that whether the second edict annulled a more restrictive measure of the first.[224]

Moreover, around 130, Hadrian decided to rebuild Jerusalem, probably to restore the former splendor of a city that had once shone brilliantly. Did it never occur to him that the ruins were sacred to the Jews, and that any pagan edifice would be further sacrilege? He decided to have a new colony built there, *colonia* Aelia Capitolina, around a temple of Jupiter Capitolinus, built not on the site of the ancient Temple, which remained abandoned, but in the heart of a new city, on the site of Golgotha. The building was finished between 131 and 132, as attested by coins issued in the name of the new colony.[225]

For many, this was the decision that lit the powder keg. Still, both Pausanias and Eusebius of Caesarea[226] attribute the Jewish revolt to the Jews' rebellious spirit and their refusal to submit to Rome. Moreover, unrest, or the fear of it, are clearly attested during the mid-120s. It has thus been possible to argue that Hadrian's decrees (including the one on circumcision, if it actually existed) represented repressive measures and should be considered in connection with others that are known to have followed the Bar Kokhba revolt.

The situation was actually far from monolithic. There were unquestionably some Jews (primarily among the priests) who were sustained by the hope that the Temple would be restored. However, there were also many Hellenized Jews on whom the Roman administration depended, and these may have given the Romans a sense of widespread Jewish support. During the 120s, Hadrian built a Hadrianeion in Sepphoris and another in Tiberias: he transformed Sepphoris into a Diocaesarea, and he knew that, although Jews constituted a majority of the population, the government of Tiberias was Greek. None of these undertakings resulted in Jewish violence; moreover, the rabbis disagreed as to the attitude to adopt toward Jews who abandoned circumcision or reversed it surgically by *epispasmos*,[227] evidence that the practice was becoming common. Was the situation once again like the one that had prevailed under Antiochos IV?[228] Far from being a provocation, the decision to build Aelia Capitolina may have been intended as an act of good management and a gesture of support for the elite Hellenized Jews who continued to live in the city.

Was the revolt the inevitable result of a long period of latent tension, or was it the unexpected and localized explosion of an oft-neglected minority? There is no way to separate the two, and we know too little about the course of the war to determine the root causes and pretexts of the rebellion. Its principal leader was Simon bar Kokhba, "Prince (*nasi*) of Israel." The messianic characterization of the movement may have been a subsequent rabbinical interpretation, a later attribution like the name *Bar Kokhba* (son of the star), because neither contemporary texts nor coins support that characterization. Inscriptions on coins announced the Jews' desire to rebuild the Temple and to liberate Israel ("year 1 of the redemption of Israel," "year 2 of the liberation of Israel," "for the liberation of Jerusalem"), but we have no idea how much of this project was carried out. Despite Leo Mildenberg's conclusions, based on the absence of revolutionary coins in Jerusalem,[229] it is possible that the rebels held Jerusalem long enough to restore the sacrificial altar and lay the foundation of a fourth Temple.[230]

A few rabbis joined the cause, among them Rabbi Aqiba, the most prominent spiritual authority in Palestinian Judaism,[231] but most of the insurgents were Judaean peasants. The movement was unquestionably well entrenched in the hills of Judaea, where the many caves offered refuge. A network of tunnels and hideouts discovered there contained a rebel archive, indicating that the operation's military and administrative organization was highly centralized. But it is not clear whether the uprising extended beyond Judaea. Rebels were certainly powerful in the regions south of Jerusalem, and there is little doubt about their sporadic presence north of the city.[232] It is also difficult to assess the extent of the damage caused by the rebels themselves.[233]

The war dragged on for at least three full years, until September 135, and, the limited extent of the battles notwithstanding, the situation was taken very seriously in Rome. The alarmist text by Cassius Dio[234] has been substantiated by a whole chain of evidence, such as the recall of Iulius Severus from Brittany, the participation of standard bearers from seven legions, a return to mandatory conscription, and probably the loss of an entire legion, XXII Deioteriana.[235] Draconian measures must have been taken to prevent the revolt from spreading, thus pressuring Arabian Jews to flee to Judaea. However, it is doubtful that Jerusalem was ever firmly in the hands of the rebels. The Romans triumphed in the end; according to tradition, they crushed the Jews near Jerusalem at Bethar, where Simon was killed. The remaining commanders were quickly arrested and executed, among them Rabbi Aqiba. The repression was harsh, even if we reject Dio's account:[236] he claimed that 985 villages were destroyed, that 580,000 Jews were killed in combat, and that an even greater number died of starvation. But many prisoners were sold as slaves in foreign markets and many Jews fled of their own accord.[237] The reward for the victors was commensurate with the terror the revolt had spawned: not only are there countless epigraphical affirmations by soldiers who received compensation during the *bellum judaicum,* but Hadrian received a second imperial salute, conferred the *ornementa triumphalia* on three legates who had participated in the war (including the governor of Arabia, Haterius Nepos), and a triumphal arch was dedicated to him by the Senate and people of Rome some twelve kilometers south of Scythopolis.[238]

Colonia Aelia Capitolina was founded and populated with veterans of Legio V Macedonica. A monumental arch, built during Hadrian's reign, marked the northern limit of the city on the site of the present gate of Damascus, while another arch, constructed slightly later during the second half of the second century, formed the monumental entrance to the space reserved for Legio X Fretensis.[239] To guarantee Jerusalem's pagan character, Jews were forbidden to enter the city on pain of death, except on 9 Ab, the anniversary of the fall of the Temple.[240] Pagan sanctuaries to Jupiter Capitolinus, Venus, Asclepius, Serapis, and the emperors were put up in a few years' time. Jerusalem became not only a pagan city like the others, but the only one forbidden to Jews! The Jewish character of the region was officially denied at the height of the revolt, probably in 133–134, and even the name of the province was changed: suppressing all reference to its Jewish population, the Romans transformed Judaea into "Syria-Palestine."[241]

Despite the fact that the battles were not extensive, the destruction was enormous. A great many villages of Judaea and Samaria seem to have been abandoned during this time rather than after the war of 70, and they were often not reoccupied, by either pagans or Samaritans, for many years:[242] what had for a long time constituted the heart of the Promised Land belonged to others or, at best, had been abandoned. Henceforth, there was no hope of rebuilding the Temple or even of Jews returning to Jerusalem, a city without Jews. A clandestine Zealot opposition lasted for a while, but by the middle of the second century that too had disappeared. Messianism faded out around the same time as apocalyptic predictions, which had become suspect: "Anyone who calculates the end (of time) will have no part in the world to come," proclaimed a rabbi soon after 135. Hope endured, but its satisfaction was deferred to a distant future. Palestine appeared destined to merge ultimately into the overall set of Roman possessions in the eastern Mediterranean—to become, finally, just another province.

FROM TRAJAN TO THE SEVERI:
CONQUESTS AND REORGANIZATIONS

A FRONTIER land bordering Parthia, with the Syro-Mesopotamian desert at its back, Syria was the most heavily armed province in the eastern Mediterranean. Its military might accounted for its status as an imperial consular province, always governed by someone of high rank. The creation of the province of Judaea in 70 and later the annexation of Arabia in 106 called for some strengthening of defenses, but despite a widespread belief to the contrary, Syria never had a true network of fortifications, at least not before the end of the third century.[1] In fact, the relative tranquility of the neighboring Parthians, the admission of new client states (Edessa, Hatra) as the Romans advanced across the Euphrates, and then the conquest of Osrhoene and Mesopotamia at the end of the second century seemed to put the rich province of Syria out of harm's way.

As Rome's key province in the eastern Mediterranean, Syria was visited by numerous emperors. Whereas only Augustus and Vespasian (under duress) had visited the province in the first century, during the second and third centuries most emperors traveled to Syria: Trajan, Hadrian, Marcus Aurelius, Septimius Severus, Caracalla, Macrinus, Gordian III, Iulius Philippus (Philip the Arab), Valerian, and Aurelian, not to mention local usurpers, all visited, often for military purposes, but they took the opportunity to honor the cities, especially Antioch.[2] The most noteworthy of these trips, and the only one that had no military objective, was probably Hadrian's, from Asia to Egypt, in 129–130. We do not know his itinerary in great detail; he may have remained primarily in Antioch, touring northern Syria from there. We know, however, that he visited Palmyra[3] (which took the title *Hadriana Palmyra* in honor of the occasion), Caesarea, and Gerasa,[4] where a monumental arch outside the city gate commemorated his arrival—before going on to Egypt via Gaza.[5] Such visits had certain advantages for the provinces that offset the expenses they could incur. Hadrian probably gave the title *metropolis* to Samosata and Damascus, both new provincial centers of the imperial cult;[6] he rebuilt Jerusalem, and granted various favors to several other cities.[7] Septimius Severus and his successors awarded the title of colony many times over. An imperial visit always demonstrated the importance that the supreme imperial authority attached to a province.

NEW PROVINCES, NEW DIVISIONS

Provincia Arabia

The removal of Rabbel II of Nabataea in 105 or 106 was undoubtedly the occasion for the annexation of his kingdom.[8] The realm was too large to be annexed to an existing province, so Rome established it as a provincia Arabia. The governor of Syria, A. Cornelius Palma Frontonianus,[9] was put in charge,[10] but he was quickly replaced by C. Claudius Severus, who had recently risen from the equestrian rank. In fact, Severus's name appears on milestones between 111 and 115, which might suggest that the province was not actually organized before that date. However, a soldier testifies in a letter dated March 26, 107,[11] that Claudius Severus was already in Arabia by then. We do not know what his precise title was at the time, but he would have to be regarded as the organizer of the province; this would account for his having spent a minimum of four years there, from 111 to 115, and even longer if we determine that he was already governing the province in 107.

In recent years, scholars have been reconsidering the details of the way Roman provinces were set up,[12] and Arabia, as a case in point, appears to bolster the argument that the process was lengthy and spread out over time, as opposed to an organizing effort that could be accomplished all at once. It seems to me that there is considerable naïveté in this misguided debate, as it fails to distinguish between the political decision that created the province of Arabia and its implementation. I do not believe that one can describe, as Philip Freeman does, the creation of Roman Arabia as tentative.[13] In fact, the decision to create a province of Arabia must have been made at the very moment when it was decided to annex the kingdom of Nabataea; hence the province existed legally as soon as Rome took possession of the kingdom, and this was indicated unequivocally by immediate references to a new era. The fact that there was subsequent hesitation over the rank of governor, and perhaps over the location of the capital or of certain offices (those of procurators, for example), and over the importance of the garrison, would seem to be of minor importance. In addition, it took some time to organize a census, and it might not have been necessary to do so immediately if the Nabataean administration had kept its own registers current. Attempting to push back the creation of the province to 111[14] is thus pointless. Similarly, it may have taken some time to integrate the Nabataean army into an auxiliary unit, the *Petraeorum cohortes*.[15]

Scholars have long wondered whether the provincial capital was located in Bostra or Petra. In fact, the presence of the early governors in Petra is amply attested. For example, besides Claudius Severus in 107, Ti. Iulius Alexander held court in Petra on October 11 or 12, 125,[16] and T. Aninius Sextius Florentinus was buried there somewhat later, which suggests that he died there.[17] However, these arguments do not seem solid enough to justify identifying Petra as the first capital. Other governors of the period are attested in Bostra (for example, Q. Coredius Gallus Gargilius Antiquus around 115–120),[18] in Gerasa (Ti. Iulius Iulianus Alexander in 125,[19] T. Haterius Nepos in 130,[20] L. Aemilius Carus in 141–142, L. Attidius Cornelianus in 150, Q. Lollius Mamercianus),[21] and in Philadelphia (L. Aemilius Carus), yet no one would argue that the capital was in Gerasa, where evidence of the presence of governors is greatest. Moreover, the legion was installed in Bostra, which may be a telling indicator. Most important, however (and for me this seems decisive), the new provincial era was known indifferently as the "era of the province" or the "era of Bostra" from the time the province was first established.[22] This does not mean that the governor could not have moved from one city to another to hold court or to confer with his administrators, in keeping with long-established practice:[23] Babatha was called to appear "before Haterius Nepos, legatus pro praetore, in Petra or elsewhere in his province."[24]

Nevertheless, there was unquestionably a concentration of inscriptions concerning procurators in Gerasa.[25] That ought to suggest that the financial administration of the province was located there, but it seems difficult to separate the financial function from the governor's seat. In any event, we must be cautious, as only a few procurators were involved.

Certain documents from the end of Hadrian's reign refer to "the new province of Arabia," from which we might conclude either that the province was created later than is generally assumed (a conclusion contradicted by the presence of legates as early as the end of Trajan's reign) or that it was reorganized or altered substantially enough to merit calling it "new."

However, it has been shown that this term—found only on papyri from Nahal Hever—was probably borrowed by scribes from Hadrian's edict of December 127 ordering a census in "the new province."[26] This does not mean that the first census had occurred only twenty-one years after the creation of the province; the text that indicates that Florentinus was responsible for carrying it out[27] does not specifically say that it was the first one. Thus it is possible to imagine that there had been another census much earlier, fourteen or fifteen years before: in other words, around 112–113, during the time of C. Claudius Severus. This seems highly likely, because the Roman treasury had to know very quickly what it could expect from the new province. Moreover, the assets of the Petraean kings had to be inventoried—as the assets of Archelaos of Judaea had been in 6 B.C.E.—before being absorbed into the *patrimonium* or sold, whether these were goods or real estate. We do not know their extent, but we know at least that there were royal lands in the region situated south of the Dead Sea.

Reorganizations and New Developments under the Severi

The usurpation of power by Pescennius Niger, the governor of Syria who was proclaimed emperor in 193,[28] had repercussions for the organization of the province of Syria. Basically, that event showed Septimius Severus just how much authority the presence of four legions, not to mention the wealth of a vast province at his disposal, gave to Syria's governor. Thus, after defeating his rival, Severus divided the overly wealthy and powerful Syria into two provinces: in the northern part, with Laodicea and later Antioch (after 200) as the capital,[29] Syria-Coele reunited Commagene with a large part of the former "Seleukis," although it did not extend beyond Apamaea; in the south, Tyre became the capital of Syria-Phoenice, which included the southern part of the former province of Syria. However, the restructuring was accompanied by an adjustment of the boundaries around the new Syria-Phoenice and Arabia. We still do not know when this change took place. There is proof that at least the northern part of the Trachonitis remained in Syria-Phoenicia at the time of the 194 division, because milestones bearing the name of the first legate, Manilius Fuscus, have been identified up to fourteen miles south of Phaina.[30] However, from an inscription in Ahireh-Ariqah (formerly Aerita) in the southern part of the plateau dated according to the Arabian era,[31] we know that definitely before 225, and possibly even before 214, the southern boundary of Syria-Phoenice was moved north, to Arabia's benefit. It has long been thought that the northern Trachonitis was not incorporated into Arabia until much later, perhaps late in the third century. A new inscription from Phaina, at the northern end of the Trachon plateau, refutes that view and proves that the entire region belonged to Arabia by 238–239 at the latest.[32] It is therefore clear that a single restructuring was undertaken before 225, in which all of the Trachonitis, northern Batanaea, and Auranitis was awarded to Arabia: in other words, all the Herodian states annexed in 92–93. This action restored administrative unity to an area whose regions were culturally linked and whose divisions could be traced back to the distribution of territories among the Herods and the kings of Petra at the end of the first century B.C.E.

The Severan era is also marked by the creation of new provinces beyond the Euphrates. As early as 195, at the time of Septimius Severus's first expedition, a province of Osrhoene, without a legion and assigned to a procurator of modest rank, was established beyond the Euphrates. It was thought that this province replaced the former principality of Edessa, even though Abgaros VIII the Great (177–211) retained his authority over the city of Edessa itself and its immediate vicinity.[33] In fact, it would have been inconsistent to allow Abgaros VIII to reign at all if anyone had wanted to punish him; he very probably retained his entire principality. In contrast, other client principalities of the region were integrated into the new province of Osrhoene, including Anthemusia (Batnai, some forty kilometers southwest of Edessa) and Carrhai (fifty kilometers south).[34] In addition, after Septimius Severus's second campaign in Mesopotamia, in 198, Abgaros retained his privileged status as client prince, and Severus gave him the honorary title "king of kings." A splendid reception in Rome crowned this reconciliation, which would make no sense if Abgaros had been reduced to the rank of tyrant of a single city.[35] At around the same time, a province of Mesopotamia was created to the east of Osrhoene, beyond the Khabur and north of the Euphrates. Two legions, I and III Parthica, stationed in Singara and Nisibis, were responsible for its defense and placed under the authority of a high-ranking prefect, identified with the prefect of Egypt, who lived in Nisibis.[36]

DEFENSE OF THE COUNTRY AND ROMAN CAMPAIGNS

Legions and Auxiliaries

Syrian provinces continued to see large numbers of troops, including both legionnaires and auxiliaries, throughout the second and third centuries. Expansion to the south (Arabia) and later across the Euphrates (Osrhoene, Mesopotamia) led to a redeployment of the forces. In fact, permanent adjustments were made to address the needs of the times. Thus, in 106, Legio

VI Ferrata entered Syria (its camp had been near Raphanaea since 70–72) and participated in the occupation of the Nabataean kingdom; it then set up camp in Bostra, while parts of III Cyrenaica, arriving from Egypt, encamped in the southern part of the new province.[37] In 123, III Cyrenaica was moved to Bostra,[38] where it replaced VI Ferrata; the latter was transferred to Caparcotna, in Galilee.[39] The turmoil that had prevailed in Judaea beginning in about 110 had already caused at least a part of II Traiana to be sent there from Egypt, and it had probably returned to its quarters in Nicopolis after 123. Hence, under Hadrian, the Syrian provinces counted six legions, three in Syria proper (III Gallica at Raphanaea where it had replaced VI Ferrata, IV Scythica at Zeugma, XVI Flavia Firma in Samosata),[40] two in Judaea (X Fretensis in Jerusalem and VI Ferrata in Caparcotna-Legio), and one in Arabia (III Cyrenaica in Bostra). This situation remained unchanged until Septimius Severus created the three Parthica legions, two of which, I Parthica and III Parthica, were stationed in the new province of Mesopotamia,[41] the first in Singara,[42] and the second in Nisibis rather than Rhesaina.[43]

This distribution of troops was complemented, as it was everywhere, by the deployment of numerous auxiliary troops. For Syria, we have no evidence as precise as that provided by the diplomas of 88–91, and, unless we turn to the *Notitia Dignitatum,* a text that seems to have been written quite late (at the end of the fourth century or the beginning of the fifth), we are forced to rely on fortuitous epigraphical discoveries.[44] The expansion of the empire along the Euphrates after Lucius Verus's campaign in 165 called for a reconsideration of the military defense structures. Dura (Dura-Europos) became an advance post facing the Parthians, and a garrison of major importance. After 168 and again in 170–171, a unit of archers from Palmyra was stationed there, and, under Commodus, Cohors II Ulpia Equitata was also found there.[45] Under Caracalla, there were also *vexillationes* from three legions (IV Scythica and XVI Flavia Firma from Syria, and III Cyrenaica from Arabia). This may be attributable to the exceptional circumstances involved in preparing an expedition against the Parthians, but David L. Kennedy has commented that under the Severi there was a shifting of legions toward the east, a trend that reached its apogee under the tetrarchy.[46] The presence of standard-bearers on the Euphrates may have been part of this trend. The unit in Dura for which there is the most evidence is Cohors XX Palmyrenorum.[47] If the accepted interpretation of the figure *XX* is correct, it provides a valuable indication of the number of auxiliary cohorts stationed in Syria. According to Kennedy, this figure can be explained by the fact that when the cohort was created, it became the twentieth to be stationed in Syria.[48] Since we know it existed in 192 and was perhaps created during Marcus Aurelius's visit in 175–176, there must have been at least ten thousand auxiliary soldiers in the cohorts in Syria, not including the *alae* and not counting the fact that certain units may have numbered one thousand.

The growing importance of Dura in military affairs is underscored by the alterations in its layout. Sometime between 209 and 216 the northern part of the city was cut off by a brick wall and transformed into a military camp. A palace was built beside the river for the commander of the military region, the *dux ripae.* This was a new position, and we do not know the precise extent of its authority.[49] Dura's military character became quite apparent, not only because one entire section of the city was occupied by the army, but also because some of the soldiers were quartered among the populace.[50] Certain sanctuaries, such as those of the Palmyrene gods, were largely reserved for soldiers, because those of Cohors XX were primarily worshippers of Iarhibol and Malakbel.[51] The same could be said of the sanctuary erected in the camp in honor of Jupiter Dolichenus, a military god par excellence, and that of Mithra, whose earliest sanctuary dates from 168.[52] Thanks to the abundance of papyri and parchments preserved at Dura, we can see the life of the garrison in considerable detail right up to the eve of the city's capture by the Parthians.[53]

For Arabia, the sources belong to different eras, but from inscriptions carved into the rocks by soldiers we know that an equestrian *ala* and another of Arabian camel-mounted troops (originally from Numidia), an *ala dromedariorum,* were stationed south of Hegra, at the extreme southern part of the province.[54] Cohorts were garrisoned in the Negev, on the Moab plateaus and in posts on the edges of the desert (al-Azraq, Umm al-Quttein, Mothana), and even in the Harra and in Nemara,[55] or on the border of the steppe, as in Dmeir (Thelsea) and along the direct route between Damascus and Palmyra,[56] while others patrolled in the wadi Sirhan as far as Dumat al-Jawf, formerly a Nabataean military site.[57] We have no military diplomas from this province, but if the auxiliaries were almost equal in number to the legionnaires, as was usually the case, we should expect to find a dozen units. For the second century, we know the names of two alae and six cohorts. The number of auxiliaries seems to have grown during the course of the third century, and we know the names of five alae of equestrian or camel-mounted troops there, and of eight cohorts that may have resided there, either permanently or for a limited period of time.[58]

In Judaea and then in Syria-Palestine several auxiliaries were added to the two legions of Jerusalem and Caparcotna, and these were relatively stable after the Bar Kokhba revolt: five or possibly six military diplomas[59] spell out the state of the auxiliary garrison. The most complete diplomas, those of 136–137 and 160, indicate exactly the same list of units, three alae and twelve cohorts (including two cohorts of one thousand), for a total of about eight thousand men. In contrast, in 186 there were only two alae and seven cohorts (including two of one thousand), for a total of about five thousand men.

Finally, the *classis syriaca* was created at the latest during the course of the second century, and it was attached to the port of Seleucia in Pieria, as we learn from the sailors' cemetery found on the outskirts of the city.[60] The port of Seleucia in Pieria had seen improvements since the reign of Vespasian: a canal thirteen hundred meters long made it possible to divert floodwaters that had inundated the port and caused silting. The port itself was not very successful initially, but an inner port was dug, linked to the sea by a narrow channel, to shelter ships from storms. The classis syriaca patrolled the coasts of Syria, Cilicia, and Pamphylia, and when necessary used several Syrian ports: Sidon, Tyre, Laodicea, Tripolis, and Dora, ports given the honorary title *navarchis,* must all have stored equipment needed by the battle fleet during its crossings, although we cannot deduce from this that the units of the fleet were ever a permanent presence.[61]

The Road Network

Although milestones were rare in the first century and we know little about the network of roads built during that time, there are many contemporaneous sources in the second and third centuries, at least for Arabia and Syria-Palestine. It was probably at the end of the second century or during the Severan era that most of the bridges were built, such as those that spanned the Afrin and the Sabun Suyu near Cyrrhos.[62] Others have been identified near Byblos, and in Berytos (on the nahr Beirut), Sidon (nahr az-Zaini), Tyre (nahr Abu al-Assouad), Damascus (east of the city, near Bab Sharqi), Jmerin, and also in Taiyybeh near Bostra, on the wadi Mujib in the Moab; but the most spectacular is unquestionably the one preserved near Kahta in Commagene, on the former Nymphaios.[63] I hasten to add, however, that the problem of bridges was not essential in Syria, where the rivers either were dry during most of the year or (like the Euphrates) were too wide to be crossed except by ferry. In some cases, improvements could be carried out by Roman troops at the expense of the local communities: a bridge over the Barada, upstream from Abila of Lysanias, had been swept away by floodwaters and was rebuilt around 163–165 by a detachment from Legio XVI Flavia Firma "at the expense of the Abilenes."[64]

The most significant project involved the *via nova* undertaken shortly after the annexation of the Nabataean kingdom; it ran "from the borders of

Syria to the Red Sea," as the inscriptions on the milestones themselves indicate.[65] This was a new road from Bostra to Aila (a distance of about 430 kilometers), no doubt incorporating old routes for the most part, especially on the Moab and Edom plateaus, where it followed the old Royal Road, spanning the deep canyons of wadi Wala, wadi Mujib, and wadi al-Hasa. This road was built to the west of Petra, and secondary roads connected it to the city. All the milestones date from 111–115, during the reign of C. Claudius Severus, although the road work may have begun somewhat earlier, judging by the letter of a soldier who wrote to his father in 107 that his comrades were breaking up rocks.[66] The paving of this old road according to Roman standards should not lead us to underestimate the scope of the development of a secondary system: a paved road, bordered with anepigraphical milestones, has been detected south of Gharandal, in the wadi Arabah.[67]

The presence of a ring road farther east, designated the *via militaris,* is less well understood. Some scholars have tried to trace a route linking several small forts east of the Royal Road, in the belief that only such a road would have had strategic importance against the threat of nomads—the only threat that could have arisen in Arabia.[68] However, such a threat seems to have been unlikely;[69] moreover, closer archaeological examination shows that the few posts found to the east do not constitute a continuous line, and that they were probably intended to protect the imperial fields cultivated in the steppe region for livestock to supply the army: we have evidence of this having been done—somewhat later, to be sure—in the Gaza region and in Africa. In fact, such posts are often found near the ruins of *qanawat* (underground irrigation channels), reservoirs, and other agricultural improvements.[70] In any case, these posts appeared later, at the earliest during the tetrarchy, and many were probably installed even later than that.

The road system in Palestine, where milestones were rare until Trajan's time, underwent a remarkable development starting in Hadrian's reign. No fewer than twelve roads had been marked by then, but, as we have seen, these projects should be considered in light of the renewed tension the province had known prior to the Bar Kokhba revolt. After the uprising had been put down, roads received regular maintenance, but with no particular zeal: we know of no milestone dating from Antoninus's reign. The only notable peak in milestone production occurred in 162, on the eve of Lucius Verus's expedition against the Parthians.[71] But that raises a question about the connection between the placement of milestones and the needs of the army. With the prospect of a new war in the east, it was natural to mobilize legions and auxiliaries and to turn attention to maintaining the roads necessary for supplying the army. However, whatever strategy was adopted by the emperors and their advisors, it is unlikely that Judaea was called upon to play a role in the coming war, except to furnish troops. Hence there would have been no need to rebuild roads or renovate forts and roadside shelters, especially because during peacetime that work would normally have fallen to Roman troops. Given the circumstances, the placing of a large number of milestones in 162 strongly suggests a propaganda campaign to mark the visit of one of the two emperors, just as the absence of milestones between 129 and 162 does not indicate a total lack of maintenance over a thirty-year period. We see from this example how risky it is to write a history of the road system on the basis of milestones.

In the provinces of Syria,[72] two strictly military projects should be mentioned. In the south, a direct road ran between Damascus and Bostra, passing just outside of Dionysias; this was a straight road laid out across the Leja plateau, where it entered Phaina from the north and continued toward Sijn in the south. Considering the very desolate character of the Leja, the road could have been intended for only one purpose: to allow the army to move quickly into the sector that had been the principal refuge of bandits during the Herodian era. The Romans constructed an almost completely straight road, one that for the most part it did not need to be paved: it followed long stretches of bedrock, which offered a perfect road surface. At regular intervals, but roughly every mile, a tower was built that could be used to send optical signals; these were sometimes placed scores of meters off the road, on an elevation, and some had cisterns. The oldest milestones date to Commodus's reign, and the road must have been built under Marcus Aurelius and Lucius Verus, as indicated by the presence of a small shrine along the road bearing the name of the governor L. Attidius Cornelianus, legate of Syria in 161–162.[73] The road does not show up in the Peutinger Table; however, there is convincing evidence that the prototype of this work probably gave the status of the road system between 120 and 160.[74] This road had the advantage of providing the shortest connection between Damascus and Bostra; it doubtless met the needs of merchants and travelers, who must have feared those vast desolate expanses, as much as it met those of the Roman administration and army.[75] Soldiers and Roman officials were careful not to let nightfall overtake them there, which explains the letter from the residents of Phaina, at the northern end of the road, to the governor of Syria, in which they complained of that soldiers and other officials demanded lodging in private homes even though a public inn existed for their use.[76]

In addition, we have seen that Syria's governors marked the road leading from Palmyra to Sura on the Euphrates as early as 75.[77] The struggle for control of the Syrian steppe went on throughout the second century: the only milestone known from Antoninus Pius's reign comes from the road between Hama and Palmyra.[78] Under the Severi, other milestones appeared along the same route from Palmyra toward Hama and Apamaea. There was a substantial Severi military presence farther south in the area of al-Azraq, and a milestone has been identified from that area,[79] as well as along the via nova, which must have been completely rebuilt in 214, given the number of Caracalla's milestones from north to south. All of this was part of a vast construction project to create a military supply route along the Syrian steppe. This was certainly not yet the Strata Diocletiana that it would become by the end of the third century (although that name was legitimate), but the various stretches that would constitute that road were gradually being put in place.[80] Still, the density of the network shows that it was not intended to ensure rapid troop movement along the border for defensive purposes as much as to improve communications between villages and cities during a period of rapid growth. Kennedy has shown quite clearly that routes linked Bostra to Philadelphia, Gerasa, Qasr al-Hallabat, and al-Azraq, and linked the latter to Deir al-Kahf and Mothana, Deir al-Kahf to Umm al-Jimal, al-Fedein and, even further, to Gerasa, not to mention the route from Philadelphia to Gerasa that was being explored.[81] Such a complex system would naturally have been useful for troops, but why would these have been crossing the region if there were not already a large number of population centers of considerable size in this sector, situated in the northeast of contemporary Jordan?[82] I am thus strongly inclined to link the development of the road system to the expansion of inhabited and cultivated areas, rather than to a potential threat from outside.

Elsewhere, we find rebuilding and maintenance projects as well as propaganda campaigns on numerous roads, and this gives us at least some idea of the course of the major routes. One of these projects included work on the Esbous–Livias road in the third century (Caracalla, Elagabalus, Maximinus, Pupienus, Balbinus).[83] In Syria, care was taken to maintain the coast road from Antioch to Ptolemais around 198 and again in 216–217,[84] and also between Heliopolis and Berytos in 194.[85] When we consider all this activity over time, it is probably no accident that, among the few milestones that have come to light along the coast road, we find some dating from Trajan's expedition against the Parthians, another dated precisely 129, the year of Hadrian's visit, four others from 198, corresponding to the second Parthian expedition of Septimius Severus, still another from the reign of Valerian and Gallienus just before the expedition in which Valerian died, and, finally, the inscription at nahr al-Kelb from 216–217. All of these correspond to periods of intense military activity. Similarly, the rebuilding of the via nova in Arabia in 213–214 probably was undertaken in anticipation of a visit from Caracalla in connection with his campaign against the Parthians. But we will probably never know whether the milestones commemorated the actual rebuilding of the road, were placed in anticipation or hope of a visit from the emperor, or were simply intended as commemorative propaganda for the benefit of the people. Personally, I am inclined to think that they served more for propaganda during an imperial visit than for any strategic purposes. It seems to me that this would explain the relatively large number of milestones that bear the name *Vaballathus* despite the brevity of that ruler's reign.

Finally, as the empire gradually extended westward, new routes were created or improved. During the short period when Trajan occupied the Jebel Sinjar, he managed to lay out a road from which just one milestone has been found.[86] After the Severan conquest, paved roads linked key points of Upper Mesopotamia, running from Nisibis to Bezabde, from Bezabde to Singara, and from Rhesaina to Singara via Thallaba in particular;[87] there was also a road between Batnai and Hierapolis-Bambyke as early as 197.[88]

Establishment of a Defense System

An occupying force[89] as well as a defensive force responsible for meeting the threat of enemy incursions, the Roman army in the east, up to the Severan era, depended on a fairly thin distribution of troops that probably varied significantly according to time and place. In spite of the pioneering work of Father Antoine Poidebard[90] and Sir Aurel Stein,[91] who were the first to make systematic use of aerial photography to explore vast expanses of desert, we cannot really talk about a deep, coherent defensive network of the type too often mistakenly called a *limes,* or fortified boundary.[92] Indeed, attempts at globalizing analyses have inevitably failed, for it is impossible to view as a uniform whole the boundary regions of the Euphrates, the Hauran, the fringe of the Moab and Edom steppe plateau, and the desert zones of the Hejaz. Whereas a Parthian or Persian invasion, or even barbarian raids out of the Caucasus, might reach northern Syria, there was no chance that the Romans could have organized the Hauran, Transjordan, and Hejaz regions to address that threat. These issues must therefore be dealt with separately.

Regarding Syria itself, Poidebard's studies, innovative for their time, are of little relevance today, owing to the lack of systematic verification on the ground,[93] although the studies do give Victor Chapot's even earlier work an archaeological dimension that it had lacked.[94] While it is true that they reveal an intense military (and agricultural) occupation of the Syrian steppe, they do not allow us to confirm the existence, starting in the early empire, of a completely unified, fortified network to answer a hypothetical threat from the east. The few digs that accompanied the aerial exploration, such as that of the *castellum* of Tell Brak in Upper Jezireh (some forty kilometers south of Nisibis), argue in favor of a later date for most of the paved constructions, the fourth century in particular. Moreover, many of the structures perceived from the sky were impossible to find on the ground: this no doubt makes aerial photographs valuable, but it limits their historical usefulness quite significantly.[95]

For the Transjordan, S. Thomas Parker has shown that the defense system was very fragmentary up until the Severi, and even as late as the tetrarchy.[96] As no serious threat was anticipated, a screen of troops with no serious potential usefulness sufficed. Parker notes that all the forts in Jordan date from the third and fourth centuries, with the exception of Jumaymah, which dates from the end of the second century.[97] This assertion should be qualified, however, for in the wadi Arabah, small forts have recently been found to be from the second century, notably the one at Qaa' as-Sa'idiyyeh.[98] Few of these small forts have actually been found in the Transjordan, and the fact that many of them are known to have undergone considerable reconstruction and occupation during the fourth century does not exclude their having been in use much earlier, perhaps during the Nabataean era or at the beginning of the annexation. In the southern part of Jordan where inscriptions are almost entirely absent, many dates are based on ceramics found on the surface, and these favor later periods. Moreover, ordinary ceramics are inaccurately dated and are not of much value for establishing a chronology. Lastly, there is now some doubt about the claim that Nabataean painted ceramics ceased to be made after the second century; they may have continued to be produced well past that time,[99] and this throws off the accepted chronology even further. When we look at other indices, we are obliged to move back the date of occupation. For example, we know from the *Notitia Dignitatum* that a cavalry unit was stationed in Mothana, on the boundary between the campaigns on the Hauran and the steppe, in the fourth century. Inscriptions found in the village allow us to confidently move the military occupation of the site back to the third century, and possibly even to the second century.[100] Another question arises about which posts housed permanent garrisons and which were simply temporary quarters for patrols. Moreover, there may have been encampments that left almost no traces other than soldiers' graffiti: this was the case at the southernmost post of the Roman army, at Jebel Ithlib, south of Hegra, the source of signatures from the cavalry of the

Getules wing stationed there, although there is no vestige of its garrison post.[101]

Given these circumstances, perhaps we should adopt the relatively pessimistic view of Zbigniew T. Fiema, according to which we are looking at a collection of forts and improvements that may have been used off and on for civil or military purposes, but we remain unable to establish a reliable list for each era.[102] In any case, Fiema is surely right to insist that we cannot understand the development of a defense network in southern Jordan by trying to analyze it in light of broad-scale strategic needs. The use or non-use of any particular fort undoubtedly depended simply on local needs for maintaining order, for the protection of caravans and travelers. This view is consistent with the opinion of Benjamin H. Isaac, who says—not necessarily pejoratively—that the Roman army in the east was in many respects an occupying army.[103] Under the circumstances, the exceptional density of occupied military posts beginning at the end of the third century and into the fourth century would not indicate rising insecurity as much as population growth and renewed prosperity necessitating a heightened military presence for security reasons.

From the Parthian Front to the Persian Front

The underlying reasons for the Parthian wars that led Roman armies beyond the eastern borders of the empire are not of direct concern here; they involve the diplomatic and military history of Rome.[104] We must, however, examine the consequences of these wars on the organization of Syrian territory and look at the alliances Rome cemented or developed with states beyond the Euphrates during this time.

When Trajan's Parthian expedition was launched in 114–117, Syria was used primarily as a rear base. The emperor himself was staying in Antioch (he almost perished there during an earthquake in January 115),[105] and he took advantage of a route running the length of the Antitaurus to reach Upper Mesopotamia. The Roman armies first marched toward Armenia and the neighboring regions (particularly Gordyene), then turned toward the south once the north had fallen. This was an opportunity for Trajan to confirm the loyalty of the princes of Edessa (where Abgaros VII [109–117] had just bought the royal prerogatives of the Parthian king Pacoros),[106] of the Phylarchs of Arabia (that is, of Sumatar Harabesi) and of Anthemusia (Batnai), and possibly those of Hatra as well, near the Tigris, although he had failed to capture their city.[107] Following the capture of Ctesiphon, Trajan annexed the newly conquered territories and organized them as provinces.[108] The creation of the provinces of Mesopotamia (in Upper Mesopotamia), Armenia, and less probably Assyria, was ephemeral: the latter, if it ever really existed, was abandoned even before Trajan left Babylon.[109] Trajan personally restored a Parthian king who was considered a client because Rome had given him his kingdom;[110] in reality, as soon as Trajan turned his back, this king was overthrown and replaced by Chosroes, and Mesopotamia and Armenia were evacuated once Hadrian came to power.[111]

Rome's successes, such as they were, came farther west. Abgaros VII of Edessa, who first stalled but later lavishly received Trajan when he had no other choice, had taken part in the general revolt against Rome in 116. Thus he was treated as an enemy: after laying siege, Lusius Quietus seized Edessa and burned it,[112] and Abgaros was overthrown. Hadrian replaced him with a client, Parthamaspates, the king whom the Romans had failed to install at Ctesiphon; Parthamaspates ruled almost four years, along with Yalud (or Yalur). But after 122, an Abgarid, Ma'nu VII bar Izates, regained the throne of Edessa.[113] In keeping with tradition, a meeting between Hadrian and the Parthian king on an island in the Euphrates in June 123 demonstrated that peace was assured.

In contrast, the principality of Mesene (Characene),[114] which had been established in Lower Mesopotamia on the Persian Gulf and whose friendship had been rekindled by Trajan's visit to King Athambelos V in 115, did not remain on friendly terms with Rome for long, although the principality survived until 151. As Paul Bernard has shown, the dynasty to which Athambelos V belonged had been overthrown by the Parthians, probably on account of their overly warm welcome of Trajan, and replaced by a younger son of Pacoros II, Mithradates.[115] Shortly before 150–151, Vologases IV invaded Mesene without provoking Rome's intervention; not only did Rome lack the means to act, but the affair had become an internal Parthian one in which Roman interests were not at stake.[116]

The second major Parthian expedition was launched at the beginning of the joint reign of Marcus Aurelius and Lucius Verus. Benefiting from the change in sovereigns in Rome, Vologases IV installed a Parthian prince, Pacoros, in Armenia. The immediate retaliation of M. Sedatius Severinus, the legate in Cappadocia, ended in disaster at Elegeia.[117] Northern Syria was invaded and the governor forced to flee, but the occupation did not last.[118] Lucius Verus, ordered to lead the expedition against the Parthians, chose to assemble his troops in Antioch, where he arrived in 162 or 163. However, in 162 a pro-Parthian prince, Wa'el b. Sahru, overthrew the king of Edessa, Ma'nu VIII (139–177), who had presumably shown too much sympathy for the Romans and was forced to seek refuge in the empire. It is difficult to know precisely what relations between Rome and Edessa were like after the return of Ma'nu VII bar Izates in 122, but it is clear that a crisis between Rome and Ctesiphon had once again extended as far as Edessa, the pretext for a confrontation between clans or members of the same family who supported either Rome or Ctesiphon. What happened in Edessa seems to have reproduced what had so often happened in Armenia in the first century, when two empires with universal aspirations were competing for mastery of a state that was really quite secondary but that, nevertheless, neither side wished to see in the hands of its rival.

Despite the relatively modest size of Ma'nu's kingdom, the stakes seemed high to Rome because control of Edessa opened the way to northern Syria. The dynasty controlled not only the city and villages but also the Bedouins of the region under the authority of the Arabarch.[119] It appears that for many years, sensitive areas of the kingdom were in the hands of members of the royal family. In the earliest Syriac inscriptions, the region of Birtha (modern Birecik) had come under the rule of a person of great importance, probably one of the king's relatives.[120] The practice became even more systematic during the second century in the region of Sumatar Harabesi, southeast of Edessa, where on several occasions the crown prince himself was in charge of the district. In 162 Wa'el was governor of Sumatar when he overthrew Ma'nu VIII and named his own son and heir Tiridates to replace him at Sumatar.[121]

Lucius Verus's success enabled Rome to move the frontier of Syria after 165 as far as Dura-Europos, which not only was the scene of a battle between Romans and Parthians[122] but also was besieged by Rome, as attested by the discovery of a Roman trench.[123] In the Euphrates Valley, Rome also gained control of the outlet of one of the great caravan routes linking Palmyra and Mesopotamia. After the victory, ties with the kingdom of Edessa were strengthened. Ma'nu VIII was reinstated over his rival Wa'el b. Sahru; as a sign of his gratitude and allegiance, he issued a coin bearing the effigy of the Roman imperial family, with the Greek legend *basileus Mannos philorhomaios*, "King Mannos, friend of the Romans."[124] To secure control of the entire kingdom, his son Abgaros (the future Abgaros VIII the Great) was named governor of Sumatar Harabesi, in keeping with tradition. For Rome, the territorial gain was minimal, although strategically important, but the acquisition reassured the network of clients along the Euphrates. It is unlikely that the dynasts who reigned during this period in Batnai (Anthemusia) and Carrhai were able to avoid alliances with Rome. However, the Roman armies came back from their expedition across the Euphrates with the plague, which soon spread throughout the empire, causing enormous losses.

During Lucius Verus's campaign, the legate from Legio III Gallica, Avidius Cassius, distinguished himself. Originally from Cyrrhos, he belonged to one of the few elite Syrian families that had risen very early to the highest ranks; his father had been Hadrian's *ab epistulis* (official in charge of the emperor's correspondence, probably *graecis*) and later prefect of Egypt at the beginning of the reign of Antoninus Pius.[125] Possibly a descendant of Antiochos IV of Commagene,[126] Avidius Cassius was admitted into the senatorial order. After the campaign against the Parthians, for reasons unknown he seems to have received exceptional authority, somewhat vague in nature, from Marcus Aurelius; Dio suggests that he was put in charge of all Asia,[127] while Philostratos indicates that he had the entire Orient.[128] Avidius was thus governor of Syria, probably from 167 to 175. What was the threat that justified his additional power? The granting of exceptional authority was not surprising in itself, as there are many other examples in both the east and the west,[129] but we do not know how far Avidius's extended (he campaigned in Egypt against the *boukoloi* [cowherds] of the Delta around 172)[130] or exactly why he received it.

In any case, flush with the prestige he had won fighting against the Parthians and the Egyptians, Avidius Cassius declared himself emperor as soon as he heard the (false) report of Marcus Aurelius's death, and provoked immediate retaliation. This time, however, Syria avoided civil war, because Avidius Cassius was killed three months later, even before the imperial army arrived.

The proclamation whereby Syria's governor, Pescennius Niger, declared himself emperor in 193 led to new expeditions beyond the Euphrates. Several client kings, notably those of Edessa and Hatra, had promised to help Niger against Septimius Severus, who had been proclaimed emperor by the legions of Germania and Pannonia. Syria was in the same situation it had been in during the republican civil wars: the clients pledged allegiance to Rome's representative in situ. After Niger's defeat and the settling of Syrian affairs, Severus crossed the Euphrates to punish those whom he chose to treat as traitors. His two campaigns of 195 and 198–199 resulted in substantial territorial gains beyond the Euphrates and the creation of the provinces of Osrhoene (195) and Mesopotamia (198).

But Pescennius Niger's usurpation had echoes farther to the east, as far as Hatra. This small kingdom in the Mesopotamian desert, between the Khabur and the Tigris, first encountered the Romans during Trajan's Parthian expedition, when Trajan had to give up the siege. However, amicable relations were established during the second century, perhaps during Lucius Verus's campaign, and when a new emperor was proclaimed in 193, the king of Hatra, Barsemias, sent him a corps of archers. This support for a rival prompted Septimius Severus to attack the city in 198, and it has long been thought that Barsemias was replaced at that time by Abdsamya,[131] who was first identified in some undated inscriptions and known to be the father of Sanatruq II.[132] However, a more recent discovery proves that Abdsamya was already king of Hatra in 192/193 and that Abdsamya and Barsemias were one and the same.

There is no evidence of a dynastic link with the family of Sanatruq I, the first nobleman of Hatra to use the royal title, around 175–177, but the reappearance of the name *Sanatruq* for Abdsamya's heir could indicate kinship; however, Abdsamya never used his father's name, and this might indicate a rupture in the legitimate line of succession. Meanwhile, the sons of Sanatruq I, Nyhr' and Nsryhb, and a grandson also called Sanatruq,[133] had no titles. If there was a change of dynasty, it was nonviolent: the statues honoring the members of the former ruling family were left in place. Moreover, the dynastic change is unrelated to any Roman intervention, because it occurred first.

Although the king of Hatra had actually helped Niger, while others had settled for making vague promises, Severus did not consider Hatra to be his principal objective. Ancient historians offer conflicting accounts. According to Herodian,[134] Severus attacked Hatra after the king of Armenia surrendered and before marching against Ctesiphon. Dio, on the other hand, says that the siege of Hatra occurred after the capture of Ctesiphon,[135] which fell on January 28, 198, according to the *Feriale Duranum*, the calendar of public holidays in Dura;[136] it was followed by a second siege sometime later,[137] but before Severus's arrival in Egypt at the beginning of 199. There is no way to reconcile these accounts. They do agree on one point— the siege or sieges failed. Nevertheless, Severus counted these events among the successes of his reign: the fourth panel of the arch of Septimius Severus in Rome depicts the siege of Hatra.[138] The military failure reported by Herodian and Cassius Dio was thus offset by a political and diplomatic success about which they are silent, Hatra's new alliance with Rome.

The results of Caracalla's second campaign, in 215–217, principally in Adiabene and Babylon, were less than spectacular. The only significant result had been achieved even before the campaign began: in 213 King Abgaros IX of Edessa, invited to Rome, had been overthrown and his city transformed into a Roman colony. However, during the campaign, the Roman armies had desecrated and pillaged the royal Parthian tombs in the city of Arbeles, in Adiabene. Whether for this reason or another, the Parthians launched a vigorous counteroffensive in Mesopotamia, which Macrinus, the new emperor, had to confront. He suffered a bloody defeat outside the walls of Nisibis in 217. Nevertheless, in exchange for a payment of fifty million deniers, the Parthians agreed to withdraw from Mesopotamia entirely. For the first time, Rome had paid to preserve a shred of the empire.[139]

From a single rather small province, one that was fragmented by client principalities at the time of Augustus's death, Syria was gradually transformed into seven provinces administered directly by Rome's agents. Only Edessa (until 212–213) and Hatra (until 242)[140] kept their status as client states in the heart of the new provinces. In roughly three centuries, Rome had profoundly altered the administrative and political landscape of Syria. Not only had it managed to integrate the disparate components acquired during Pompey's reign into a uniform system of direct administration, but it had also forced the Parthians back beyond the Euphrates and retaken control of the territories that the Seleucids had lost during the second century B.C.E.

CIVIC LIFE AND URBAN DEVELOPMENT
DURING THE EARLY EMPIRE

(Augustus . . .) who enlarged Greece with many
other Greek lands, and who Hellenized the most
important parts of the barbarian world.

PHILO, *LEGATIO AD GAIUM*, 147

It HAS been said, and not only by those who delight in paradox, that
the Roman Empire marked the apogee of the Greek city. In a strictly
quantifiable sense, this is undeniably true, for at no other time were there
as many cities, or more precisely, as many cities spread over so vast an area,
as during the empire.[1] In this, Syria was no exception, and during the empire new cities were established throughout the region, particularly in Arabia and in Palestine, in addition to those that had been created during the
Hellenistic period. The blossoming of cities in Syria is not nearly as extensive as what we find in, for example, the interior regions of western Asia
Minor, but the urban phenomenon, which had been limited to the northern
and coastal regions of the country during the Hellenistic period, spread
south into Arabia and the interior of Palestine.

The establishment of an institutional framework did not, by itself, guarantee the development of activities and attitudes characteristic of civic life.[2]
The public monuments typical of city-states and even smaller towns were
developed in all the new cities; these included theaters, gates, baths, walls,
sanctuaries in the "Greek" or "Roman" style, an agora, sometimes a stadium, and amphitheaters. Municipal activities appear to have been quite
limited at times, however; we do not find in Syria and Arabia, as we do in
Asia Minor, a large number of decrees attesting to a vigorous municipal tradition. But should the presence of decrees be our sole criterion? Can we
not evaluate the integration of Syrian and Arabian urban societies into the
value system of the *poleis* on other grounds? For example, when we look at

the effort that went into obtaining titles and privileges from the emperor, we see little difference between the cities of Syria and those of the Aegean world.

THE SPREAD OF THE POLIS AND THE CREATION OF COLONIES

The regions that made up the Syrian provinces benefited from the urbanizing efforts of the Hellenistic period,[3] but unevenly, and numerous noncivic communities continued to exist.[4] At the beginning of the early empire, three zones appear to have been favored in terms of urbanization. The first, northern Syria, located north of the Eleutheros river (nahr al-Kebir), embraced all of the Seleucid settlements in the region. Some of these, particularly the ones that constituted the Syrian tetrapolis (such as Antioch on the Orontes, Seleucia in Pieria, Apamaea on the Orontes, and Laodicea on the Sea) emerged as the most important cities of Hellenistic Syria. Other, more modest cities, such as Seleucia-Zeugma, Cyrrhos, Epiphanaea, Beroea (Aleppo), Chalcis of Belos, and Rhosos, played key roles within their regions. Still others presumably disappeared or languished, like those that are now only names on a list and for which we have neither archaeological evidence nor inscriptions nor coins. A second group comprises the ancient Phoenician cities of the coast, from Arados to Ptolemais: as we noted earlier, these quickly adapted to the Greek civic model. Lastly, a third category includes a diverse group of cities that may have been founded some time between the end of the fourth century B.C.E. and Pompey's day, and these are widely dispersed in Palestine (Gaza, Scythopolis), the Transjordan (Gadara, Gerasa, Pella, Philadelphia) and southern Syria (Damascus, Panias, Canatha). Some of them (such as Gerasa and Gaza) may have been settled by Greeks or Macedonians—although this claim may have only served to establish roots dating back to the Alexandrian era—but the indigenous element was undoubtedly predominant in Damascus and in most of the new cities.[5]

Despite the diverse circumstances of their founding, at the time of the Roman conquest all these cities seem to have been equally Greek, since there was no longer any real way to distinguish populations that were originally Greek from Hellenized Syrians. Many of them had endowed themselves with a fabulous, mythic past and had developed foundation stories rooted in Greek antiquity, while others looked by default to history, from Alexander to Pompey, for ancient titles that would contribute the most to their glory.[6]

Central Syria, southern Syria, the Transjordan, and Palestine had been

THE GODDESS TYCHE, SHOWN ON A BOWL CRAFTED IN SILVER, BRONZE, COPPER, NIELLO, AND GOLD, WITH SCENES REPRESENTING THE FOUNDATION OF THE CITY OF CAESAREA; FOURTH CENTURY C.E.

least affected by the creation of poleis: Epiphaneia and its neighbors in the middle Orontes valley, Damascus, the cities of the Decapolis that had been refounded (or founded?) by Pompey, a few isolated cities like Philadelphia in the Transjordan or Philoteria south of Lake Tiberias, constituted a fairly sparse network. Thus in the early empire, most of the urbanization effort was concentrated primarily in this region. As elsewhere in the Orient, Rome did not seek to impose its own models (colonial and municipal) but used—with a few minor exceptions—a structure familiar to the entire Hellenized east, the polis.

During the first century, the founding of cities in this region was principally the achievement of client princes. Herod the Great was responsible for the construction of Caesarea on the Sea, Samaria-Sebaste,[7] and Antipatris.[8] Built on the coast, in an area where the Jewish population was in the minority, Caesarea was destined to become Herod's capital.[9] It was not created ex nihilo, as it was already the site of an ancient city, Strato's Tower, renamed Demetrias by the Sea by Demetrios I.[10] Pompey had taken the city from the Hasmonaean kingdom in 63,[11] but Octavian returned it to Herod in 29.[12] Around 20 B.C.E. Herod decided to install his capital here, naming it Caesarea in honor of Augustus.[13] Like the Greek cities in Syria, it soon acquired a protective goddess, Tyche of Caesarea, portrayed as a young woman standing upright, wearing a short dress and the traditional tower-shaped crown as headdress; her right breast is uncovered in the Amazon style and she has one foot placed on the prow of a ship, with a sea spirit rising from the water below.[14] Quite enough to discourage any pious Jew from identifying himself as a Caesarean! The same can be said of Samaria, renamed Sebaste in honor of Augustus, a city settled by Greeks and veterans from all parts. Evidence of the city's Greek origins was seen in the cults: Kore in particular had a place of honor, and the Augusteum dominated the city.[15]

The same policy was followed by Herod's successors. Herod Antipas founded Tiberias on the shores of Lake Genesareth (the Sea of Galilee),[16] and Livias-Iulias in Peraea.[17] Philip founded a Iulias on the other side of Lake Tiberias[18] and also reestablished Caesarea Philippi-Panias near Mount Hermon,[19] which later became Neronias by order of Agrippa II.[20] Perhaps Arca Caesarea of Lebanon should be attributed to a Herodian prince as well, although its founding may have been the work of an Ituraean or Emesene prince. In either case, the very name *Caesarea* tells us that it was founded by a client prince.[21]

Beginning in the second century, the founding of new cities occurred principally in the Hauran and the Transjordan and in Palestine. Soon after the annexation of the Nabataean kingdom, municipal institutions were established in Bostra and Petra, for which evidence is found in inscriptions and papyri.[22] The same thing occurred later in Madaba (ancient Medaba),[23] Rabbathmoba (Rabbathmoba-Areopolis),[24] Charachmoba,[25] Hesban (Esbous),[26] Der'a (Adraha),[27] Suweida, where the village of Soada was separated from Canatha and established as an autonomous city, called Dionysias, around 185 at the latest,[28] and lastly Shahba, the birthplace of Philip the Arab, which was probably inaugurated as a Philippopolis at the beginning of his reign.[29] Thus an urban network along the Hauran and the high Transjordan plateau, from Damascus to the Gulf of Aila, was established along the foothills bordering Arabia.

In Palestine, Neapolis was founded by Vespasian in 72 at the site of Mabartha[30] or Mamortha.[31] Within Palestine's borders, in the Transjordan region, a Capitolias was founded at Beit Ras by either Nerva or Trajan, probably in 97–98.[32] In Galilee, Sepphoris acquired the status of a city, probably in 67–68 when the first coins were issued;[33] it was given the ephemeral name Irenopolis in recognition of the populace, which had supported the Romans very early in the war of 66–70. The seat of a *synedrion* (council) during Gabinius's time, the city had been the capital of northern Galilee;[34] fortified by Herod,[35] it had been attacked and burned by Varus in the battles following the king's death.[36] Herod Antipas rebuilt it under the name of Autocratoris,[37] and it became Diocaesarea—a name with pagan connotations—under Hadrian, who sought to mark a break with the city's

Jewish past, despite the fact that most of its inhabitants were undoubtedly Jewish.[38]

The Severi built a Lucia Septimia Seuera Eleutheropolis in 199–200 at Bet Guvrin, formerly Betogabris, on the Shephelah plain in southern Judaea, near the ruined city of Marisa.[39] Lydda-Diospolis acquired the rank of city before 201,[40] Emmaus-Nicopolis became an Antoninopolis under Elagabalus in 221, thanks to an embassy headed by Iulius Africanus, who was originally from Aelia Capitolina but who lived in Emmaus.[41] Although Septimius Severus and Caracalla had opened the municipal *curia* to Jews, who could become magistrates and priests without offending the Torah, urbanization reinforced the country's return to paganism, because in many cities a large majority of the population was non-Jewish.

Finally, we should note a few other, isolated instances of urban development. The former Batnai of Anthemusia was established as a city called Marcopolis, probably under the Severi.[42] In another example, a small town called Appadana, on the middle Euphrates, was promoted to the rank of a Neapolis around 254–255, or slightly earlier.[43]

Colonies were also established during this period. No earlier than 27 B.C.E., and probably as late as 15–14 B.C.E.,[44] Augustus founded a colony at Berytos that encompassed a vast territory, including the great sanctuary of Heliopolis-Baalbek.[45] Similarly, Claudius transformed Ptolemais into a colony between 52 and 54,[46] no doubt in order to provide a secure base close to Judaea. This too was a true creation, as veterans of four legions were installed there.[47] However, we have no way of knowing whether the city was actually refounded at this time, because we know practically nothing about what it had been before. Finally, under the heading of colony-building with *deductio* (in which part of the territory was divided into lots and distributed to colonists), we must include Aelia Capitolina, founded on the ruins of Jerusalem at the very beginning of the Bar Kokhba revolt.[48]

It is curious that Aelia Capitolina has attracted little notice for so long, as if nothing happened between the destruction of Jewish Jerusalem, first in 70 and again in 135, and the proclamation of the Christian city following St. Helena's discovery of the relic of the true cross and the site of the Church of the Holy Sepulcher. In fact, Hadrian's colony was quite successful, even though the city never grew as large as the former Jerusalem. Its population, estimated at ten thousand to fifteen thousand inhabitants, consisted primarily of pagans, Roman colonists who were army veterans, since Aelia was a colony with deductio. The city quickly took on the appearance of an ordinary Roman city, wholly dedicated to pagan cults. We should not attach too much importance to denunciations by rabbis who considered it the center of production of idols flooding the entire world:[49] this was their way of pointing out the abominable depths to which the holy city had fallen. However, it is true that during this period workshops producing lead coffins were very active, and they reproduced decorative pagan themes that would have been unthinkable before 70.[50] Similarly, the decoration of homes reflected very common Roman tastes: as elsewhere, the mosaics of suburban villas portrayed Ge, Tyche, and the seasons.[51]

There were other colonial foundations, notably those of the Severi,[52] but for the most part they did not involve refounding a destroyed city. We shall come back to these when we examine the honors bestowed on the cities. Here I shall mention only the promotion of Caesarea on the Sea to the rank of a colony sometime after Vespasian's rule, not through the introduction of Roman colonists but through a general promotion of the entire indigenous population to the rank of Roman citizens.[53] In addition, we should note the rather unusual case of Dura-Europos. This city, which had long remained under Parthian domination,[54] had ceased to be governed by magistrates; instead, during the entire Parthian era and even after the conquest by Lucius Verus, we find a "*strategos* and *epistatos* of the city"; apparently, from the first century B.C.E. up to the time of the Severi, this person was always a member of the same family. The *bouleuterion* located in the sanctuary of Artemis-Azzanathkona was restored around 200, and it housed the statue of a "strategos and epistatos" who had probably obtained certain advantages for the city;[55] however, it was still a city at that time and not a colony, as the inscription makes explicit. The colony must not have been created until later, although we cannot connect the change in the city's status with the transformations of the bouleuterion, because the latter was renovated a little later, after it collapsed, sometime during the first half of the third century; moreover, there is no proof that it continued to have any civic function.[56]

THE STRUCTURE AND ORGANIZATION OF MUNICIPAL LIFE

Institutions and Municipal Life

The provincial cities of Syria have not left for posterity the hundreds of decrees and honorific dedications that demonstrate the vigor of civic institutions in the Aegean world. As a result, it has sometimes seemed that civic status was not accompanied by established civic practices attesting to active participation by citizens in municipal affairs. Several indicators contradict this pessimistic view, however, leading us to acknowledge that the patterns of civic life in Syria were not so different from those found in other areas, even if the external manifestations are less obvious.

AERIAL VIEW OF PALMYRA, SHOWING THE COLONNADED MAIN STREET WITH, AT THE BOTTOM, THE GREAT ARCH AND, ABOVE, THE TETRAPYLION. TO THE LEFT OF THE STREET, FROM BOTTOM TO TOP, ARE THE SANCTUARY OF NABU (TRAPEZOIDAL), THE THEATER, AND THE SO-CALLED "AGORA." ON THE RIGHT SIDE ARE THE PUBLIC BATHS.

In terms of institutions, there are enough honorific inscriptions to prove that municipal institutions were indeed functioning: when a city honored a particular individual, whether the emperor, an important Roman official, or a local leader (inscriptions of this sort have been found at Rhosos, Apamaea, Palmyra, Bostra, and elsewhere), the occasion arose from a collective decision that took the form of a decree: as elsewhere, the typical tribute on the base of a statue was simply a summary of the initial decree. Sometimes the entire decree, or a long form of it, survived (as in Rhosos, Apamaea, and Palmyra). But apart from these pedestals and their summary decrees, a number of texts refer to the *demos*, "the people" (in Antioch, Apamaea, Arados, Balanea, Bostra, Damascus, Gerasa, Hierapolis, Laodicea, Mariamme, Nicopolis, Palmyra, Philadelphia, Seleucia of Pieraea, Seleucia on the Euphrates, and Tyre), sometimes including civic tribes (as in Bostra, Dionysias, Gerasa, Palmyra, Seleucia of Pieria, Edessa, and Neapolis),[57] the *gerousia* or council of elders (at Arados), the *boule* (council) or the *bouleutes* (councilors) (in more than twenty cities). In certain cases texts allow us to identify those whose names appeared at the head of the town registers (as in Bostra and Gerasa) or civic magistrates, whose titles are quite uniform: *grammateus, proedros, agoranomos, sitones, archon, astynomos,* not to mention liturgists, *agonothetes* (magistrates responsible for organizing a contest), gymnasiarchs,[58] and ambassadors: indeed, everything one would expect to find in a polis. Even in a city like Palmyra, rightly famous for remaining faithful to indigenous traditions, the vocabulary of institutions is entirely Greek, and in Aramaic versions of the texts the terms have usually been transliterated directly from the Greek.[59]

However, even though the vocabulary used in the poleis of Syria is familiar, the words tell us little about how civic institutions actually worked. Should we envision popular assemblies voting on decrees, as we know to have been the case under the empire in Asia Minor? Perhaps so, but then how was a popular assembly in a Syrian city constituted? We may suppose that it differed very little from assemblies in Aegean city-states with large numbers of citizens—in Antioch or Apamaea, for example. But what about Palmyra, Bostra, and Petra, not to mention Madaba or Adraha? The absence of any systematic posting of decisions made by the demos or the boule—beyond the summaries found on honorific pedestals—leads us to think that these were of interest only to a minority of the city's residents, those who had means of getting information other than public postings. Of course, we must be cautious on this point, because it is clear that the people of Greco-Roman Syria, and especially those who entered the empire later, such as the inhabitants of the Hauran and Palmyra, did adopt the Greco-Roman custom of architectural inscription. Usually, however, this remained linked to honors and public buildings, at least for texts outside the category of private epigraphy.

Moreover, the Syrian and Arabian cities were not exempt from the kind of factional infighting observed in Tyre and Sidon during the Augustan age:[60] Augustus "reduced them to slavery," according to Cassius Dio, which probably means that he deprived them of *libertas* (a direct relation between a city and the emperor, making the city free from provincial governance and regulations) as punishment for the agitation caused by factions, although we do not know what issues lay behind this unrest. Moreover, Jacques Seigne has argued very convincingly that in Gerasa, during the second century, the sanctuary of Artemis became more important than that of Zeus in the wake of rivalry among civic factions, and the city plan was modified accordingly.[61] The same was probably true in Palmyra as well, as Jean-Baptiste Yon has recently shown.[62] The Elahbel family appears to have been closely linked with the sanctuary at Nabu that stood north of the Hellenistic city and open to the south by beautiful *propylaea* (monumental gates). Following the addition of a major new axis north of the sanctuary (this was the main street during the Roman period), the Elahbel family sought to remodel the entire site. The rear façade of the temple was richly decorated, and inscriptions were added that would not normally have been found there, and in addition the leaders, no doubt very powerful figures and well informed of the plans, undertook to rebuild the north wall of the peribolus, facing it with propylaea even grander than those that adorned the southern wall. These propylaea were almost immediately demolished: the north wall was razed and replaced by an oblique portico that cut into a large area of the sanctuary courtyard. In place of the sumptuous entry they had envisioned, the owners of these sites had to settle for buying land for a future shop at the northwest corner of the portico and building an improvised entrance.[63] The Elahbel family, which disappeared for unknown reasons around 150, was replaced by a family that was unable to defend Nabu's interests and was forced to accept a new city plan that disfigured the traditional sanctuary.

Naturally, we rarely know the issues that were at stake in these conflicts between leaders, and perhaps between wealthy families, except that they were important to the people involved. Did they entail attempts to attract the attention of provincial authorities? And if so, for what purpose? A promotion to one of the higher ranks? The granting of exemptions? We have no way of knowing, but the fact that there were real conflicts indicates that civic life was robust, at least in some cities, at certain times, and within the limited group of those who could claim to be the city's leaders. The situation was at the very least paradoxical, for recent studies show that these same leaders did not much value their civic activities, at least in Palmyra and the Hauran.[64] Nowhere in Syria do we find, either in inscriptions honoring leaders or in their epitaphs, an enumeration of magistracies or liturgies held by themselves or their ancestors, such as are found in the Aegean world. This discretion, however, did not prevent violent conflicts between clans intent on taking and holding power.

The same intercity rivalries that characterized civic life in Asia Minor flourished in Syria as well. These quarrels, nourished by the ambition for glorious promotions that signified imperial favor, could lead to prominence or to ruin: Laodicea in competition with Antioch, and Tyre out of hatred of Berytos, joined with Septimius Severus against Pescennius Niger.[65] Many people would pay dearly: Herodian recalls that Moorish troops unleashed by Niger destroyed Laodicea and Tyre,[66] and Sidon seems to have suffered for the same reasons.[67] Antioch, reduced to the level of a village, was compelled to cede to Laodicea its function as capital of Syria.

Numerous other phenomena indicate that civic attitudes had taken root in imperial Syria. There as elsewhere, benefactions were one of the means of financing communal life, and many examples are found, even though they are often less spectacular than in Asia Minor or in Greece itself. There were also gifts from the emperor, of course, or from client princes. However, private donations were also made, even in modest cities like Balanea or Canatha, and those gifts resemble the ones found elsewhere: public buildings,[68] oil for gymnasia,[69] perfumes,[70] land for development, public buildings, or statues;[71] there were also many instances of unspecified contributions.

However, the cities also had to finance part of their expenses from public funds, and these costs should not be underestimated.[72] It would be difficult, otherwise, to understand why the cities' debts grew to such an extent that Hadrian designated *curatores* (or *logistai*) responsible for auditing civic accounts throughout Syria.[73] Antoninus Pius assigned the same task to a procurator.[74] Under both Marcus Aurelius and Commodus, a *logistes* operated in Seleucia of Pieria, in Alexandria near Issos, and in Rhosos;[75] we know of at least one in Canatha, probably in the second or third century,[76] and another was assigned to Palmyra.[77] The fact that these missions all took place during a period of great prosperity in Syria indicates that only public finances were involved, these being insufficient to support the costs of an extravagant civic life, particularly the maintenance and beautification of an urban sector that had to be as sumptuous as possible. Still, resources were not scarce, for all the cities would have received income from fines and the collection of tolls. The municipal toll of Palmyra is the only one we know well, owing to a famous bilingual source text called the "Palmyra Tariff";

this did not involve imperial fiscal policy but the finances of the city of Palmyra itself.[78] It is a complex document that required lengthy negotiations before it was adopted by the Roman authorities;[79] it must have brought significant income to the city.

We know of very few examples of loans or subscriptions like the ones Léopold Migeotte studied in the Aegean world.[80] However, some information on the financing of public buildings can be found in texts. Apart from the ordinary cases of benefactions, in which the generosity of the benefactor is made known, there are more subtle cases. For example, at Canatha the names of various people appear on pedestals in the Temple of Theandrios: these are probably donors, but the temple could not have been built column by column while awaiting the generosity of Canathians. There must have been either a system of advance subscription or an advance from the city to be reimbursed later by individual gifts. In Damascus, donors paid for the walls surrounding the sanctuary of Zeus Damascene one layer at a time, but this did not preclude parallel financing out of the god's treasury.[81] In Gerasa, the Temple of Zeus was paid for by the city, but it was reimbursed by successive gymnasiarchs, each of whom spent fifteen hundred to twenty-five hundred deniers as the *summa honoraria* reserved for this reimbursement.[82]

We must also take into account foundation stories that betray the efforts of municipal leaders to trace their city's origins back to earliest Greek history. We know that Antioch built the legend of its origins around Io's erratic wanderings.[83] Beginning in the third century B.C.E., Apamaea adopted a creation myth based on the story of Pella in Macedonia that enabled the city to boast of being as old as any city in the Aegean basin.[84] Residents of Joppa cherished the legend of Andromeda, who was said to have been offered to the sea monster there.[85] Cities like Tyre or Sidon in Phoenicia had only to delve into Greek mythology to find proof of their antiquity. In every case, scholars, mythographers, and philologists were put to work to elaborate a civic legend that would glorify the city's ancient Greek past. Echoes of this may sometimes be found in the far-fetched etymologies that blossomed in lexicons like those of Hesychios or Stephanus of Byzantium. The name *Bostra* was deemed to derive from the gadfly that pursued the heifer Io;[86] Damascus was said to be named for the skin of Askos the Giant, flayed by Hercules, or for Damascus, the son of Hermes and the nymph Alimeda, who had come to Syria from Arcadia.[87] It would be ill-advised to see these legends simply as the fantasies of scholars, for explanations that appear baseless to us are grounded in a long tradition of relationships among peoples built up since Hellenistic times[88] and are a vital part of the earliest history of the cities. Such are the sorts of stories that people loved to recount, but there is no way of knowing who really believed them. These legends are just as important as the accounts that link the Christian-ization of some town in Gaul to an imaginary bishop, or, in the east, to an apostle, not to mention tales (some of which endured into the eighteenth century) of the Trojan origins of certain cities in Gaul.

Finally, we should point out the varying degrees to which Syrian city of-ficials were integrated into the Roman urban hierarchy. A fairly precise in-ventory has already been attempted elsewhere, and here it will suffice to re-call a few essential points.[89] With very few exceptions, such as the navarch Seleucos of Rhosos,[90] almost no inhabitants of Syria became Roman citi-zens before the empire. Of course, some Roman citizens of Syrian ancestry may have had family names that went as far back as the republic, but these may just as well have been descendants of Roman immigrants, since we know that such people existed.[91] Client princes were the first to receive Ro-man citizenship: these Iulii included the Herodians, the Sampsigeramids, the kings of Commagene, and the modest tetrarchs of Apamaea. There were doubtless other beneficiaries as well, for Iulii were quite numerous in all the cities of northern Syria and in Phoenicia. During the Claudian era, a great many local leaders received citizenship, not only in Syria itself, but also in certain sectors of southern Syria (such as Canatha) that were only very fleetingly Roman under Claudius. In the cities of the Decapolis, the advent of Flavii can be viewed in connection with the role these cities played during the Jewish War. In Bostra and Palmyra, however, indigenous families were not given citizenship until Trajan's time: for Palmyra, which had been Roman for nearly a century, this may have come somewhat late, but for Bostra, which had just been annexed to the empire, it was early. The trend continued in Palmyra under Hadrian with several families of Publii Aelii, and under Antony with some Titi Aelii. Initially, only indigenous leaders received citizenship; later, army veterans were included among the new citizens. However, only a handful of leaders, such as the Septimii of Palmyra, were still obtaining citizenship on the eve of the extension of the privilege to everyone in the empire.

When we exclude the colonists at Berytos, Ptolemais, and Caesarea, along with soldiers and transitory officials, the total number of inhabitants of Roman Syria who were granted Roman citizenship before 212 was very low, considering the number of inscriptions found in Syria. This is very different from Asia Minor, where a large proportion of city magistrates carried the *tria nomina,* even in Phoenicia and the large cities of northern Syria. Unless we suppose that those who received this distinction mini-mized its importance, in which case there would be no need for further ex-amination of the subject!

ARCH AND COLONNADE AT PALMYRA.

Monumental Construction

The cities in Syrian provinces saw a significant expansion of monumental architecture, at least until the middle of the third century. The remains of cities like Apamaea,[92] Palmyra,[93] Gerasa,[94] and Bostra,[95] not to mention the sanctuary at Heliopolis, afford an excellent idea of the richness of the buildings, the size of the constructions that must have been undertaken everywhere, even in cities where uninterrupted occupation since ancient times has erased all vestiges, such as Antioch, Laodicea, Damascus, and Berytos.

The emperors' activities are particularly noticeable in Antioch, where we are fortunate to have a local historian, John Malalas, as a source. Caesar had already built a basilica (the Kaisareion),[96] a theater,[97] an aqueduct, and baths.[98] Numerous emperors or members of their courts followed suit: Marcus Agrippa added a new quarter,[99] Tiberius contributed a tetrapylon, a large gateway on the road to Beroea, a temple of Jupiter Capitolinus and another in honor of Dionysos, as well as baths;[100] Caligula rebuilt an aqueduct and baths in Daphne after the earthquake of 37;[101] Titus built a theater in Daphne,[102] Domitian a temple of Asclepios and baths (the Dometianon),[103] Trajan the architectural arch called Mese Pyle, or Middle Gate, as well as an aqueduct, baths, and a new stadium.[104] Hadrian made a great effort to reconstruct the city after the earthquake in 115, and he is responsible for a sanctuary devoted to Artemis and another to a deified Trajan.[105] Reconstruction was not completed under Marcus Aurelius, although he not only offered a nymphaeum but also rebuilt the baths damaged in 115.[106] Commodus built the covered stadium called Xystos, a sanctuary dedicated to the Olympic Zeus and another to Athena, and baths later converted to a courtroom.[107] We could add Septimius Severus and his baths to the list, as well as Probus, who contributed a mosaic portraying the Ocean.[108] We know the emperors were supported in this activity by client princes, judging from the generous contributions of Herodians in Syrian cities, carefully listed by Josephus: Herod paid for gymnasia at Tripolis, Damascus, and Ptolemais; a rampart in Byblos; exedra, gates, temples, and public squares in Berytos and Tyre; theaters in Sidon and Damascus; an aqueduct in Laodicea; and baths, fountains, and colonnades in Ascalon.[109] In Antioch itself, Herod was thought to have financed the paving of the main street. Agrippa I and Agrippa II were not to be outdone: the former gave a theater, an amphitheater, baths, and gates in Berytos, and the latter offered a theater and statuary in the same city.[110]

Not everything was the work of emperors and client princes, however, and many buildings were financed by local leaders. In Apamaea, a rich citizen donated land and rebuilt the northern baths destroyed by the 115 earthquake.[111] In Gerasa, the northern gate was paid for by Gerasenes themselves while Hadrian's Arch was paid for by Gerasenes through a bequest made by Flavius Agrippa, a leader about whom we know nothing.[112] In Palmyra, the grand colonnade was financed piecemeal, one column at a time.[113] In the Hauran, local leaders procured funding to construct a number of public buildings, but the record is ambiguous; many dedications on public buildings never mention the funding source, which may have been perfectly conventional (namely, the public treasury). By singling out texts that feature leaders or other clearly identified financial backers, we probably overemphasize certain exceptional kinds of financing to the detriment of the general rule.[114]

The growth in urban construction, which increased during the second century, continued under the Severi and does not appear to have declined until the middle of the third century—especially in regions where many buildings continued to be built throughout this period, but also in cities such as Antipatros or Samaria, which were restored under the Severi after being destroyed during the revolt of 66–70.[115] Indeed, Antioch, which was both the capital of Syria and the ancient royal capital, enjoyed imperial largesse beyond comparison to what was bestowed on more modest cities, but it is likely that as a window on the empire it must have served more than once as a model for urban elites who were short on imagination.

For many years scholars have argued that urbanization in the imperial age did not mark a clean break with the Hellenistic era. This may well be true in certain cases, but with some qualification and prudent elaboration. For example, we now know with certainty that the Roman city of Palmyra was built north of the Hellenistic city, remains of which have recently been identified south of the wadi.[116] It is risky, though, to attach an exact chronology to the urban center's move northward. During reconstruction of the temple of Bel, the earliest evidence of which goes back to 17 C.E.,[117] the Hellenistic city center must still have been very lively, because the sanctuary retains an orientation consistent with the old quarter. But a major new axis was developed north of the Hellenistic city, around what we call today the grand colonnade. The colonnade was not built all at once: while the two ends seem to be the oldest parts, the completion of the other sections stretched from the 130s to Zenobia's reign and even beyond.[118] The project required a complete reorganization of the sanctuary at Nabu, which had to conform to new traffic patterns involving remodeling that was damaging in certain respects. From this point on, the main axis of the city was shifted northward. This did not mean that the new area was developed on empty land; a temple of Allat existed there as early as 50 B.C.E.[119] and probably a Baalshamin sanctuary as well. Moreover, the orientation of the segments making up the new main street changed at a number of points, especially where the street passed the great central tetrapylon (proving that a preexisting axis, one that respected buildings already in place, was re-used). Nonetheless, the development of this section of the city does mark an important break with the preceding period.

In Berytos, excavations in the center of the city have shown that part of the Roman city was located slightly northeast of the Achaemenid-Hellenistic city, closer to the sea, even though the Hellenistic sections were not abandoned and were even rebuilt. A great many new buildings arose in the first century B.C.E. and the first century C.E. in conformity with the earlier orientations.[120] The Hellenistic city thus seems to have been the object of extensive reconstruction in the Augustan period, reconstruction that involved residential areas no less than public buildings. For example, where there had been a modest bathing facility, large thermal baths were constructed during the first century.[121] It is not clear that the layout of the ancient quarters themselves was affected, though, and archaeologists today are inclined to think that these quarters manifested an overlapping of narrow, discontinuous streets from diverse periods.[122] In a small community like Soada-Dionysias, research now in progress tends to separate the Hellenistic settlement from the early empire settlement built to the southwest according to a unified plan; the rigid alignments and the axis running between the theater and the bouleuterion confirm this.[123] At Seleucia-Zeugma on the Euphrates, evidence has emerged of a complete remodeling of one quarter (site 9) at the end of the Hellenistic period or the beginning of Roman times, with the creation of a main sewer and a lovely terraced park above the river.[124] These examples remain somewhat isolated, to be sure, but they suffice to warn us against any idea of systematic continuity. Many cities suffered from wars at the end of the Hellenistic period, and reconstruction may have been more widespread than one might suppose a priori.

We cannot overlook the rebuilding carried out during the imperial period, either, as this may have led to substantial changes in a city's layout. As we have seen in Palmyra, what is called the Roman city was not built all at once in the early days of the empire, but developed gradually, during the first and second centuries. Gerasa also must have changed in the second century. Its layout quite clearly shows the juxtaposition of two major orientations, not counting the very oldest parts that were shaped by other limitations. For example, although a regular orthogonal layout along the broad north–south street was developing, parts of which (including the temple of Artemis) were built no earlier than the mid-second century, and may be as late as 170 (for example, the southern *decumanus,* an east–west axis),[125] Hadrian's arch follows a different orientation, forming a twenty-degree angle with the preceding one, an orientation that is repeated in areas east of the wadi.[126] The placement of the arch was chosen precisely to offer a view of the sanctuary of Artemis—not the one that is seen today, but its more modest predecessor. The new areas developed gradually between 130 and 290, when the southern part of the city was destroyed.[127]

In a special category are what we might call the new cities of the imperial era, foundations or refoundations almost ex nihilo. Caesarea is such a case, where traces of Strato's Tower, which it replaced, are found a little to the north and are not very widespread.[128] Similarly, Sebaste stands on the ruins of Samaria, which was razed in 107 B.C.E. (vestiges have been found under the new city);[129] the town was so empty that Herod settled six thousand colonists there, virtually creating a new city from scratch.[130] Aelia Capitolina, another example, consisted of little more than two-fifths of ancient Jerusalem, northwest of the Temple Mount, which had been abandoned. The site offers a rare example of a legionnaires' camp juxtaposed to a city, a pattern repeated at Bostra after 106 and possibly at Rhesaina under the Severi.[131] The city, divided into seven sections *(amphodoi)*,[132] had a uniform layout but was not strictly orthogonal: the principal north–south axis opened to the north onto the Damascus Gate via an oval connecting it to another oblique secondary axis. We do not know the details of the plan, but it seems likely that the heart of the colony was the Capitol, erected on Golgotha, where a sanctuary with a triple *cella* has been identified.[133] According to literary sources, we know that at the time of its founding by Hadrian the city had two thermal baths, a theater, a nymphaeum with four porticos, and an amphitheater. The forum has been found under the Russian hospice, and we also know that there was once a sanctuary dedicated to Asclepios (it was destroyed under Constantine) as well as a temple of Serapis.[134]

Lastly, we need to look at the small cities where urbanization owes little or nothing to Greco-Roman traditions. We know too little about the plan of Canatha to use it as an example; however, without wishing to prejudice future findings, I have the impression that we will encounter the same disorder there that is apparent in neighboring villages. We do have the example of Mampsis in the Negev, which has been the object of an extensive dig documented in an attractive catalog. There, the plan provided by archaeologists conforms exactly to the characteristics of an indigenous city, where traffic patterns were not determined by axes set out in advance by a central authority, but instead followed paths established by individual users.[135]

Cities varied considerably in size, so much so that we may wonder about the urban character of certain sites. Some of the Syrian cities are among the largest in the Roman world, at least in terms of the space enclosed within their ramparts. At Antioch, where walls encircled a large part of the mountain, the size of the city is estimated at 450 hectares, although this is almost certainly an exaggeration, for it includes inaccessible areas on the slopes of Mount Silpios. Apamaea covered approximately 255 hectares, as did Laodicea, but about 50 of these included the basin around the port. Other areas were smaller, but the cities were more significant: Aelia Capitolina and Scythopolis each covered 120 hectares,[136] Caesarea Palestine 95, Gerasa 85, Bostra 80, Dura 75, Samaria and Philippopolis about 64 each.

So far we have considered only large cities, but Syria encompassed a warren of small towns that constituted its essential urban framework. These could be extremely small: Mampsis covered 4 hectares, Sobota 8, Obodas 8.5, Rehovot 10, Nessana 17, and Elusa (the only true city in the Negev) 39. And these numbers refer to an entire archaeological site that was occupied over many different epochs; they do not reflect the reality of any given moment in time.[137] Moreover, not all of the urban area was fully utilized: in Gerasa, the eastern zone, beyond Wadi Jerash, was occupied by gardens. Or an area may have developed only gradually: at Dura, most of the large houses situated along the western wall were built in the first half of the third century C.E., whereas traces of the wall itself date from the second century B.C.E.

Ramparts surrounded many Syrian cities in the early empire. But when were they built? In Apamaea, most of the wall has been found to date from the Hellenistic period, although towers were added in the middle of the third century to reinforce it.[138] We have seen that the wall in Dura was built in the second century B.C.E., but additions were made in the city itself, with the installation of an interior camp and the palace of the *dux ripai*. In Byblos, the ramparts are undoubtedly very old, but they were repaired and reinforced owing to the generosity of the Herodians during Augustus's reign: this was when the city was threatened by Ituraeans from Lebanon.[139] In contrast, Jerusalem did not have a wall until Legio X Fretensis set up camp in Aila, during the tetrarchy.[140] In Damascus, the almost rectangular enclosure included seven gates dedicated to the planets.[141] In Tiberias, the enclosure ran more than two kilometers from north to south along the lake, while the shorter sides were only a few hundred meters long.[142] However, a great deal of research remains to be done on Roman city walls, especially in Bostra, Philippopolis, Philadelphia, Gadara, and Canatha. Large, unfortified cities seem to have been rare. Palmyra was clearly one of these: its wall (which unfortunately is found on all maps regardless of the period) was not built before Diocletian's time or perhaps even Justinian's. The city was surrounded by a wall, indeed, and fragments of it have been found south of the oasis, but this wall marked a fiscal boundary, not a line of defense; in the southern part of the city, it was known for a long time as the "customs wall."[143] Similarly, in Caesarea the surrounding wall was probably not built earlier than the very end of the third century,[144] while in Gerasa at least the southern rampart has been shown to date from the turn of the fourth century at the earliest, replacing a wall that was probably among the weakest.[145]

Within the walls, as well as in the outlying areas, urban decor changed everywhere, becoming more lavish and grandiose. Syrian cities seem to have been the first to be embellished by long avenues bordered by colonnades, probably around the beginning of the second century;[146] at any rate, the oldest of gated streets in Antioch and Apamaea date from this period, probably following the earthquake of 115. According to Josephus and Malalas, the main gated street in Antioch can be dated to the time of Tiberius. Archaeological research confirms that the level preceding the reconstruction of 115 was no doubt Tiberian, but almost no vestige of the colonnade has been found. Josephus's testimony cannot be too far off the mark:[147] Malalas may have confused the works of the early first century with those of the early second, but that cannot have been the case for Josephus. If we add that the same main street in Antioch was paved thanks to the generosity of Herod the Great, it would seem that the city had an opulent axis that must have impressed visitors and aroused envy, leading to imitations.[148]

There were in fact gated roads throughout Syria, even in smaller cities. A city like Bostra had at least six, and in Gerasa and Apamaea these gated avenues were exceptionally monumental in appearance: almost 2 kilometers long and forty meters wide in Apamaea, with alternating ribbed, smooth and spiral columns,[149] 1.5 kilometers in Damascus, 1.2 kilometers from north to south in Gerasa, no less than 1 kilometer in Palmyra.[150] In Antioch, the view was interrupted or closed off by tetrapylons that Tiberius is said to have built;[151] there were similar constructions in Laodicea,[152] Palmyra, Gerasa, Bostra, and Cyrrhos as well. Arches were erected either above the main street or where secondary roads branched out, often in the same cities (such as Bostra, Palmyra, Gerasa, Petra, Jerusalem,[153] Damascus,[154] Gadara, Tyre, and Apamaea).

COLONNADE AT APAMAEA.

It is remarkable that the plans of Syrian cities under the empire seem to continue to favor a single axis, and not two as we find in the west.[155] In Gerasa, Bostra, Palmyra, Apamaea, Antioch, and Damascus, for example, to take only the best-known cases, it would be hard to distinguish between *cardo* (the principal north–south axis) and decumanus, although in every case there was a major axis, always very wide, with a variable orientation that was probably determined by an ancient road or highway; the width of forty meters found in Apamaea was exceptional, but the main street in Damascus was twenty-six meters wide, with a fourteen-meter-wide paved section. The existence of an older road whose orientation had to be respected probably explains the irregularities that are often found: in Bostra, the main east–west street changes direction three times, only slightly, but enough to break the perspective; the same was true in Jerusalem, Gerasa, and Palmyra. To conceal these irregularities, Roman architects and city planners adopted elegant solutions, sometimes breaking the perspective with an arch or tetrapylon, sometimes adding an oval park to compensate for the lack of symmetry (as in Gerasa, Bostra, Jerusalem,[156] and even Cyrrhos). In Samaria, the single main street, about eight hundred meters long, makes a sharp angle to go around the promontory where the Augusteum stood.[157]

One wonders whether the same pattern could be found in the colony in Berytos, where questions have recently been raised about Jean Lauffray's hypothetical reconstruction: Lauffray made Weygand Street a *cardo maximus*, broken by a north–south decumanus. Recent excavations would suggest instead a single, very wide street (seventeen meters) oriented east–west between the old Place des Canons and Riyadh Solh[158] Street. Still, we are looking at a part of the city that was occupied in the Hellenistic period and that cannot tell us anything about the organization of the new Roman settlements some hundred meters to the northeast.

These colonnade-bordered avenues—*plateiai*, or "broad marketplaces," as some texts call them[159]—were not merely decorative; they housed many fixtures of urban life. Shops and storehouses stood under the porticos, while intersections of small streets might be sites of daily or weekly markets, depending on the size of the city. In the same areas, some people spent the entire day drinking in taverns, some of which served as bordellos, according to the Talmuds.[160] Archaeologists have confirmed the descriptions found in texts by showing a row of shops behind a portico in most of the excavated cities. However, the main purpose of these colonnades was probably to connect all the different parts of the city, and to shield from view certain residential areas whose organization may not have conformed to "western" norms.[161]

These cities adopted not only buildings typical of Greek cities of the eastern Mediterranean, but also many structures of western origin, such as amphitheaters and hippodromes as well as features typical of the Roman urban landscape, such as arches. It can no longer be claimed, as Félix-Marie Abel did half a century ago, that

> imperial art here is nothing but Hellenistic art adapted by the Seleucids in Syria and adopted by Rome, which had itself been schooled by Greece . . . When we speak of Roman architecture in the Hauran and Arabia, we are talking not about art imported from overseas and transplanted into new soil, but about bringing the art of Hellenized Syria to Semitic Syria, an organized process methodically pursued by the genius of Roman authority, which was adept at blending the talents and creative faculties of the most brilliant people in the empire.[162]

In the first place, I do not believe that Rome followed a conscious policy of "Romanizing" the urban landscape: influential Syrians, like the leaders of other provinces, would have adopted the styles of the capital on their own readily enough. In the second place, a considerable number of buildings owe little or nothing structurally to Hellenistic traditions and show direct borrowings from Rome or from other western traditions.

Let us take the example of amphitheaters, long thought to have been nonexistent, or virtually so, in the Greek and Hellenized world. It is thought that Eleutheropolis, the new name of a settlement active well before being elevated to the level of a city, Betogabris (today, Bet Guvrin), built a thirty-five-hundred-seat amphitheater at the end of the second century or the beginning of the third, possibly even before its own promotion to the rank of city, if the dedication to Jupiter Heliopolitan in honor of Commodus that has been found in the amphitheater is in the right place.[163] An amphitheater also seems to have existed in Bostra,[164] and another very small one (one thousand seats) has been found in the heart of the military quarter of Dura.[165] Another was discovered at Scythopolis,[166] and one was added to the hippodrome in Gerasa when the rounded end was broken up with a lighter construction.[167] Texts document the existence of amphitheaters in Caesarea on the Sea,[168] Berytos,[169] Jerusalem,[170] and in Antioch after Caesar.[171] Another traditional Roman structure was the hippodrome, or circus, examples of which are found in Antioch dating from 68–67 B.C.E.,[172] as well as in Scythopolis,[173] Neapolis-Naplouse,[174] Jericho,[175] Caesarea on the Sea (where there were two),[176] Gerasa,[177] Bostra,[178] Laodicea,[179] Berytos,[180] Gadara,[181] and finally Tyre, where the largest hippodrome in the Roman world is said to have stood.[182]

In addition, we must note the thermal baths, which were exceptionally widespread. We saw above how numerous they were in Antioch, and in Apamaea an inscription describes even the sculptures that adorned the baths given by L. Iulius Agrippa after 115. Thermal baths have been found in all the cities of Syria, often in large numbers: one need only walk through the ruins to see those of Berytos,[183] Tyre, Philippopolis, Gerasa, Gadara, and so on. In Bostra, two immense thermal installations filled the entire center city; the southern one was connected to a palestra.[184] Palestinian Jews frequented the baths in the second and third centuries, and rabbinical texts reveal that they were a common feature of cities in Palestine.[185] It cannot be said that Syrians used these facilities more than others, but we know that Posidonios of Apamaea complained as early as the late Hellenistic age about Syrians who abandoned gymnasia in favor of relaxing baths.[186] Under the empire, baths became one of the principal centers of social life in Syrian cities.

A corollary to this was the development of aqueducts, which can still be seen at Berytos, Philippopolis, Tyre, Bostra, Apamaea, Antioch, and elsewhere, in addition to the traditional system of reservoirs, both covered and uncovered.[187] A set of inscriptions describes with precision the water basins that were in use in Jebel Druze in 105 to supply the new nymphaeum at Suweida and probably the entire city.[188] An aqueduct exists today in the Hauran plain, probably to supply Adraha; it comes from the north, but the location of the catchment is not known.[189] Elsewhere, aqueducts were not raised conduits but tunnels: German excavations have revealed a twenty-three-kilometer network of tunnels at Gadara; tunnel A, with a flow of 124 liters per second, seems to date from the end of the Hellenistic period or from the beginning of the Roman occupation (might it have been the work of Demetrios in Gadara?), and tunnel B, begun in the third century, was never completed.[190] Similarly, in Capitolias the huge cistern with a capacity of many-thousand cubic meters was supplied by a tunnel, while in Abila of Decapolis tunnels from diverse periods were used, some possibly from as early as the Achaemenid period.[191]

Although Greek cities were proud of the public fountains that distinguished them from simple villages, fountains were not found in Syria until the imperial age. Nymphaea were constructed at that time not only at Soada (now Suweida) but at Gerasa as well, in an impressive "baroque" style. At Gerasa the monument had a two-story façade twenty-two meters high; the first story was entirely decorated with marble columns while the second was stuccoed.[192] Still others have been studied in Bostra,[193] Byblos,[194] Palmyra, Pella in the Decapolis, and Apamaea; these all stand next to another feature of urban comfort introduced by the Romans, public latrines.[195] In Petra a monumental fountain, representing a most impres-

NYMPHAEUM AT PETRA.

sive lion,[196] was added on the road from Wadi Farasa to High Place, and two of the nymphaea mentioned above were built on the north and south sides of the main road.[197] Sometimes houses were furnished with running water by the public aqueduct, as they were at Daphne.[198]

A *macellum* or enclosed marketplace in the Roman style was erected on the edge of the forum in Bostra,[199] just east of the cryptoportico, another feature of the urban landscape unknown in the Hellenistic world.[200] Other macella existed in Apamaea[201] and in Gerasa, along the main north–south street—in other words, as in Bostra, along the primary route. This was a beautiful structure covered in marble, with a quadruple apse constructed, according to the excavators, in the first half of the second century.[202] Cryptoporticos have been spotted not only in Bostra, but also in Berytos,[203] Dora,[204] and Samaria.[205] We must also note the basilicas in Antioch,[206]

Byblos,[207] Ascalon,[208] Beth Shearim,[209] Tiberias,[210] Scythopolis,[211] Samaria-Sebaste,[212] Abila of the Decapolis,[213] and Canatha;[214] one must have existed at Berytos, too, although the one Lauffray thought he had found was later shown to be a palestra or portico.[215]

Other types of buildings that were well known in the Greek world were built or rebuilt according to Roman tastes during the empire. Hence we see temples on raised podia, such as the Temple of Artemis in Gerasa, or the Tycheion in Apamaea dominating the agora,[216] the two sanctuaries in Canatha in honor of Zeus Megistos and Theandrios,[217] and the small village temple of Sleim north of Dionysias. Coins show several examples of such temples in Damascus,[218] Gadara,[219] and Pella.[220]

Even theaters have been shown to bear the stamp of an Italo-Occidental tradition as opposed to a purely Hellenistic one. Theaters flourished in Syria under the empire (more than fifty are mentioned in texts or have been identified on site, most of them at least partially excavated),[221] and several cities had two.[222] None of these replaced a Hellenistic theater. The oldest ones date back to Herodian times (as at Caesarea, Samaria-Sebaste, and Petra), others to the Flavians (the southern theater in Gerasa),[223] still others to the second century or the Severan period.[224] All, however, are markedly different from the theaters of Asia Minor. In the first place, the architects did not mind building on flat ground (as in Bostra, Gabala, Dora, Palmyra, and the Odeon in Philadelphia) or on land not steep enough to back up completely against a hill (as in Adraha, Philippopolis, Dionysias, and Gerasa); this was rare in Asia Minor. Secondly, in the Greek tradition the *cavea* was never exceeded, but was strictly limited to a semicircle. Most importantly, the proscenium, low and wide, had a number of niches facing the orchestra, like the stage wall, richly decorated with several rows of stacked columns (as in Bostra). The annexes were generally developed, as in Bostra, with porticoed courtyards on each side of the proscenium.[225]

This was far from a simple adaptation of traditional Syrian Hellenistic-style buildings to suit contemporary tastes. A complete alteration of the urban landscape occurred in Antioch beginning in the first century, and elsewhere in the second century. The phenomenon was not limited to large cities, but also reached many small cities and even towns and villages. The beauty and ornamentation of podium-mounted temples in the Lebanese mountains popularized Greco-Roman taste all the way to the top of Mount Lebanon, even though these temples were structurally foreign to Roman art.[226] As we saw in Galilee, stadiums, temples, and baths all attested to the Roman presence and reminded the populace who was in charge in a milieu where Jews were a powerful minority and sometimes even a majority. In reaction, the Jews increased the number of ritual baths and synagogues.[227] It is rare to find this feature, typical of Galilee and perhaps of other areas where Jews were a significant presence (as in the Golan and Batanaea), in areas where the native people did not offer the same resistance to Roman innovations.

Another reason we cannot speak in terms of a sharp break with the preceding era is that we know too little about architectural developments; moreover, apart from earthquakes and raging fires, there were few opportunities to significantly modify the urban landscape or layout, because whatever was already in place always had to be taken into account.[228] However, gradual as it was, change became apparent in the long run, and it is clear that Syrian provincial cities reflected the taste of the times and used their prosperity to improve and beautify themselves. The "petrification" of wealth aptly described by Pierre Gros in relation to the cities of Bithynia in the second century[229] did not spare Syria, which set the example in some respects, such as portico-lined streets. While Hellenistic cities had done little to develop a monumental architectural style,[230] in cities of the imperial era the number of prestigious buildings greatly increased, or rather, what was once reserved for the most important buildings came to be seen as ordinary in even medium-size towns.

Unlike their counterparts in Asia Minor, these cities did not begin using the most expensive materials, such as marble, for decoration until rather late. Marble always had to be imported, as Syria had no quarries of either marble or colored stone.[231] In Palestine itself, many marble architectural elements have been uncovered, especially in Caesarea, Ascalon, and Scythopolis, and we know that a little more than half of the marble used came from Proconnesos.[232] In Syrian cities, by contrast, marble was rarer: it was often completely absent in architecture, although it appeared in decorative sculpture.[233] Nevertheless, we should not overgeneralize: marble was used in Bostra for capitals, bases, and pedestals of the *frons scaenae* (back wall) of the theater,[234] in Petra it appeared in wall plaques and later on capitals,[235] and in Palmyra it was was used for veneer.[236] In a partial but very illuminating survey, Patrizio Pensabene shows that monumental construction in Syrian and Arabian urban centers, while sometimes quite late (the second half of the second century and the Severan era), was nevertheless quite substantial and called for huge imports of marble (Dokimeion, Pentelicon) and colored stone (breccia from Skyros, cipolin from Euboea, granite from Troad and Aswan).[237]

Of course the importation of large blocks like monolithic column shafts was less common in the interior cities (though there are some in Palmyra, Bostra, and Gerasa); these were reserved for the most visible elements of urban decoration such as the tetrapylons or columns of frons scaenae in theaters, but architectural use of imported stone was abundant in the coastal cities from Laodicea to Ascalon. In particular, Pensabene has shown that numerous architectural elements, Corinthian capitals, and pieces of molding were imported after being sculpted or were finished on site by teams of hired itinerant artisans from Asia Minor. This would explain not only the close stylistic similarities between the architectural decor of various cities in Syria and Arabia, but also the diffusion into these provinces of the tastes that prevailed throughout the Aegean basin beginning in the second half of the second century. Should we hold public and private sponsors responsible for these artistic choices? Probably, but it must be said that despite its marked taste for decorative excess, Syria was just one province among others in the history of imperial art under the Severi. The importa-

MOSAIC PAVEMENT FROM THE ATRIUM HOUSE IN ANTIOCH, REPRESENTING HERACLES AND DIONYSUS IN A DRINKING CONTEST.

tion of sarcophagi from Attica, Docimium, and Proconnesus for private use suffices to confirm the elite class's taste for anything Aegean.[238]

We know little about urban dwellings in Syrian cities under the empire.[239] However, past and recent discoveries shed light on this area. In Antioch during the 1930s, at a time when the site was still occupied only by a small village that did not forbid excavation,[240] some forty homes turned out to contain superb mosaics, many of which came from the second and third centuries and a small number from the first. At the time, there was greater interest in the floor decoration than in the buildings themselves. However, the handful of diagrams provided by Doro Levi give us some idea of the richness of these dwellings.[241] Some were built on the terraced slopes of Mount Silpios (the Calendar House,[242] the House of the Drunken Dionysos,[243] and the House of the Bacchic Thiasos);[244] others were found between Antioch and Daphne (the House of Polyphemos and Galataea)[245] or in the vicinity of Daphne (the House of Menander,[246] the House of the Red Pavement,[247] the House of Dionysos Triumphant,[248] the House of the Man of Letters,[249] and others). None of these sites has been exhaustively excavated, but we can ascertain enough about common features to form an idea of their overall organization. The heart of the house consists of a large room encompassing a *triclinium,* a dining room with benches on three sides. This room, sometimes quite large, is usually preceded by a columned portico opening onto a courtyard or an apse,[250] where a basin has been dug to give guests a refreshing view. Most of the houses must have been very large, even though we know only parts of them: at least twenty rooms or courtyards have been found in the House of Menander, for example. These houses could be separate from one another, but in Daphne they were usually adjoining.[251]

Some of these houses may date back to the Hellenistic period, but none of the mosaics that adorn the reception rooms is older than the first century C.E.; mosaics have been found in the Atrium House,[252] the House of Polyphemos and Galataea, and the House of the Evil Eye.[253] Other houses, among the oldest, were not reoccupied after the earthquake of 115 (Atrium, Polyphemos and Galataea, the House of Trajan's Aqueduct),[254] or much later (such as the House of the Evil Eye, reoccupied after the fifth century). Given the scale of the damage done, it is understandable that most of the remains that have come to light are of houses from the second and third centuries.

In addition to the houses in Antioch and Daphne, a few beautiful houses have been found in Seleucia of Pieria, excavated by the same team and reported along with those of Antioch. All were built on the slopes of Musa Dag with excellent views down to the sea. This advantageous location

MOSAIC FROM PALMYRA: AN IMAGE OF CASSIOPEIA.
FOUND NEAR THE TEMPLE OF BEL.

was apparently not enough for wealthy landowners, since the House of Dionysos and Ariana, also built on a hillside, is in an area that appears to have been abandoned during the third century, as if the inhabitants had chosen to be nearer the port for greater security.[255] The same overall layout is observed in these houses, but because the excavators were primarily interested in saving the mosaics, we know only the rooms where mosaics were found—in other words, chiefly the triclinium and the porticos that led to it. This is true also of the Cilician House,[256] the House of Porticos, a very large house with several porticos,[257] and the House of the Drinking Contest.[258] The somewhat smaller House of Dionysos and Ariana has a long exterior portico running along the edge of the road,[259] a feature also found in the House of Psyche's Boat in Daphne.[260]

A number of large, beautiful homes with peristyles were identified long ago in Palmyra in the northern quadrant of the city,[261] and recent surveys have located others in the northeastern quadrant.[262] Luxurious homes on the edge of the oasis southeast of the ancient city have yielded beautiful mosaics, known since the middle of the twentieth century, that date from the middle of the third century.[263] Some of the houses were built in the second century and remained in use until the beginning of the ninth, as we know from second-century stucco fragments that fell during an episode of rooftop looting and were found on the top layer of soil during the excavation of one of the houses.[264] Still, this cannot be called a "fashionable" neighborhood, because these large homes stood next to warehouses. Moreover, at five hundred to twelve hundred square meters, they were somewhat smaller than the great houses of Apamaea and Antioch; Apamaea's measured two thousand to forty-five hundred square meters.[265] Most importantly, as far as we can tell from published reports, the floor plans varied greatly. Thus a large structure like the House of Achilles, near the temple of Bel, organized its seventeen rooms not around a central peristyle, but around three courtyards, two with peristyles,[266] providing more adequate lighting. By contrast, the house to the southeast of the theater offered a more classic floor plan, closer to that of houses in Antioch or Apamaea, with rooms arranged around a central peristyle.[267]

Urban dwellings in Apamaea have been studied with particular care, and our information about them is quite reliable.[268] The eight excavated houses are spread throughout the city and most of them have common features. The greatest difficulty in studying them stems from their having been occupied over many centuries: until the seventh century at least, and sometimes up to the tenth.[269] Successive remodelings, and especially the improvements made from the fourth century to the sixth, frequently erased the earlier decor, but excavators have at least confirmed the original floor plans and certain modifications.[270] Each had a courtyard with a peristyle, often a very large one, and in several cases there was a peristyle in the Rhodian style, with an upper gallery on one side (as in the House of Consoles, the House of Pilasters, the Stag House, and the House of Capitals with Consoles). The surface area varied, but these homes were always very large: the House of Consoles occupied the entire width of the *insula,* 52 meters, and a third of its depth (32.5 meters);[271] the House of Capitals with Consoles was the largest, 50 meters by 90; it covered three-quarters of an insula, or 4,500 square meters, of which the peristyle alone measured 1,350 square meters.[272] The interior construction was monotonously uniform: a large reception hall (13.30 meters by 9.85 meters in the Stag House)[273] was sometimes used as a dining room, but there was usually another, smaller dining room that sometimes had an apse (as in the Stag House). These houses also had a second story, at least over part of the building. All the layouts have been modified, but the core dates to the time of the reconstruction of the city following the earthquake in 115 C.E.[274] It is much more difficult to form a picture of the decor of the second and third centuries, for the floor mosaics were often renovated between the fourth and sixth centuries. Still, a geometric mosaic from the end of the third century has been found in the House of Consoles,[275] another from the second half of the third century in the House with Bilobate Columns,[276] as well as colored marble veneers (in rose, white, black, and yellow) in the House with Trilobate Columns.[277] We get an idea of the richness of the furnishings from the tables made of green or white marble (in the Stag House).[278]

In Petra, houses do not seem to have been laid out according to a preexisting Hellenistic plan: instead, they are spread out randomly, wherever possible, along the wadi and on the hillsides—like a "petrified nomad camp," in the words of Rolf Stucky.[279] Some quarters were reserved almost exclusively for dwellings, such as the western wall of al-Habis, Wadi Siyyagh, the two banks of Wadi ad-Deir; others included both homes and public buildings; in still others homes and tombs were mixed (Bab as-Siq, at-Tughra); moreover, there were outlying settlements in Bayda and Ba'ja to the north, Ras Sulayman and Sabra to the south. Hellenistic houses that had occupied the lower city until the first century B.C.E. were replaced by public buildings, which must constitute the first attempt at zoning and urban planning by civic authorities.[280] However, these were primarily cave houses, carved out of the rock. But we know, contrary to what was long thought to be the case, that some houses were unquestionably built of solid materials; Strabo notes that these were of stone, and often very costly.[281] Despite their modest appearance, the oldest excavated homes, which date from the reign of Aretas IV, used a layout not unlike the houses of Delos or Pergamon at the end of the Hellenistic period, with a peristyle and a system of small canals and cisterns, essential in the arid climate.[282] In addition, the most luxurious houses had painted ornamental murals to a height of one and a half meters (House EZ IV), using a decorative architectural technique of trompe-l'oeil found in both Alexandria and Pompeii.[283] The taste for painted walls is found even in the stone houses that were so characteristic of urban dwellings in Petra.[284] In 1996 the first house with a mosaic floor was found in Wadi Musa, just east of Petra; this confirmed, if any doubt remained, the spread of Greco-Roman taste to elite Nabataeans.[285]

Unfortunately, the present has intruded on Zeugma, where the urban residences are destined for immediate destruction with the building of a new dam on the Euphrates. However, digs from the late 1990s have already yielded evidence of luxurious homes dating from the first century on the banks of the Euphrates.[286] We now know that there were many of them there, richly decorated with mosaic floors, and that this particular collection is one of the most important, in the eyes of specialists, along with that of Antioch. Homes in Zeugma also contained a great deal of decorative painting, and some of these houses, built at a fairly high elevation, have been preserved and are currently in the process of being salvaged. I can do no more than mention them here, as they have not been described in any scientific publications to date.

This sampling of a few large cities provides a reasonably accurate picture of a prosperous urban dwelling, one that was imitated by all leading citizens in, for example, Philippopolis, where a lovely home has been excavated with its mosaics partially preserved in place,[287] and in Samaria-

Sebaste, where we have already noted the beautiful Atrium House.[288] These were all houses of the very wealthy; as is almost always the case, we know nothing about the homes of ordinary people.

Moreover, all generalizations, whether about houses or urban development, can be misleading, and local tradition was very important in this realm. Not all Syrian cities had the same sort of clustered Aegean-style houses. There were numerous local variations, such as those found in Dura. The oldest houses there date from the Parthian period and are clearly evocative of the beautiful homes of the Aegean world from that period, arranged around a courtyard. But closer inspection finds an important difference—the absence of a true peristyle: the court is bordered at most on one side by a portico with two or three columns. This local adaptation of the Hellenistic model continued without much change throughout the entire imperial epoch until the city was destroyed, and it was repeated even in some of the sanctuaries built in private homes.[289]

In the Negev, in Mampsis, a large village rather than a city, the central courtyard is seen again in a design that may suggest an atrium. However,

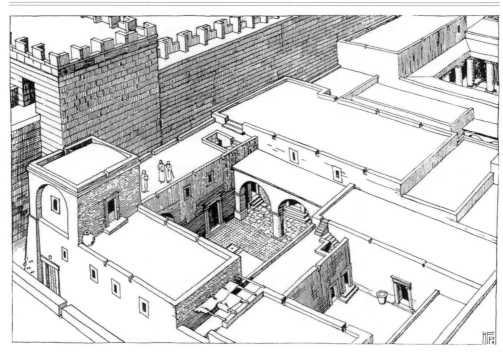

RECONSTRUCTION OF A HOUSE AT DURA-EUROPOS.

here we find neither colonnade nor pool. Surrounding the court were vaulted rooms—where would they have found the wood for framing?—which the wealthiest owners decorated with paintings.[290] As the area was still semi-rural, stables were integrated into the dwellings.[291] We may suppose that the houses of Bostra and Canatha could not have been very different, with their stone roofing shingles, their stables on the ground floor, and the residential quarters on the floor above.[292] To conceal the raw stone, the builders must have applied some kind of plaster or mortar that was later painted.[293]

At the other end of Syria, Dura provides a different example of faithfulness to local customs. To be sure, the beautiful homes respected the traditional layout of houses with *atria*. However, porticos were rare, since the local building materials, gypsum or unfired brick (stone was expensive), did not lend themselves well to this type of construction. Large reception halls were also traditional; known as the *diwan* or *medafeh* today, these are in a sense the local version of the wealthy Antiochene's triclinium. As in Mampsis, those who sought to distinguish themselves and flaunt their wealth employed painters who came to decorate their walls and ceilings.[294]

I have left for last an unanswerable question, but one that must be asked: how large were these cities, in terms of population?[295] We have an official figure for Apamaea: at the time of the census of 6 c.e., it included 117,000 citizens within the urban area, which leads to an estimate of half a million inhabitants, including slaves and rural noncitizens, for all of Apamene.[296] In Aelia, the population is estimated to have been around 10,000 to 15,000 inhabitants by the third century, a century after the colony was established. In Antioch, the population is thought to have been at least 150,000,[297] but Ernest Will believes that 200,000 to 250,000 "would hardly be surprising."[298] Dora P. Crouch has estimated the population of Palmyra and its surrounding area to have been between 150,000 and 200,000, but that number is clearly too high: it is hard to imagine that there would have been enough food and water for so many.[299] In Dura, there were between 450 and 650 houses inside the walls, eight houses to a section measuring 70 meters by 35 meters, giving a population of no more than 5,000 inhabitants.[300] This seems to have been the standard in Bostra, as well, where we should not be misled by the nine-thousand-seat theater. Not only was it built to accommodate the garrison of legionnaires, but rural people also attended regularly; thus we should not draw conclusions based on the number of seats in such structures, particularly since the absence of individual seats meant that the capacity was expandable.

Although we cannot give a precise figure for the urban population in Roman Syria, we can nevertheless conclude that the region was highly urbanized. We can make this claim not because there were very large cities (apart from Antioch) but because a significant segment of the population lived within a dense urban network.

Generally speaking, Syrian cities had changed profoundly in appearance, compared to the preceding period. Although we know very little about the cities in Hellenistic Syria, there were certain changes during the imperial epoch that could not have failed to alter their overall appearance. Colonnaded streets tended to mask the public buildings behind them and to standardize the urban landscape. The fact that the street network followed the tracks of earlier ones was not important: a quasi-uniform pattern of street layout existed throughout Syria. Some features seem to have been borrowed directly from Italy, such as the construction of imposing temples that dominated the urban landscape, as in Praeneste.[301] The tradition of building on heights and an imported architectural style combined to give the city an imposing new architectural framework that reflected its power and wealth.

The Competition for Honors

In the area of urban improvements, cities competed with zeal, if not ferocity, in a race for titles and status. As we have already seen,[302] and as everyone now agrees, none of these titles or privileges was frivolous, for each brought prestige to match the claims of rival cities. Material advantages were not always measurable, but the fact remains that cities spent a great deal of energy seeking from emperors the gifts they deemed necessary for their glorification.

First of all, imperial epithets, displayed by only a few Syrian cities, were in a class by themselves. Ordinarily these titles corresponded to the granting of favors so important that the city considered itself to have been "refounded." Hence Apamaea renamed itself Claudia Apamaea as a consequence of some exceptional imperial assistance (possibly an exemption from tribute payment) following the earthquake of 47 C.E.,[303] and the same was probably true for its neighbor on the coast, Claudia Leucas (another name for Balanea). We should keep in mind that an earthquake could necessitate the complete rebuilding of a city: Apamaea experienced two of these, one in 47 and another in 115. Adopting such an epithet was based on the same principle as that of a colony using the imperial *gentilicium* (family name) of its founder: hence we find, under Claudius, Colonia Claudia Stabilis Germanica Felix Ptolemais. Esbous bore the epithet *Aurelia* on its coins, possibly because it owed its founding as a polis to Caracalla or to Elagabalus.[304] For the same reasons, some cities adopted—often after a long delay—an epithet recalling Pompey or one of his legates, such as Gabinia Canatha, and so on. In my opinion, this suggests substantial material assistance, and sometimes perhaps confirmation of a civic status that had been at risk, but nothing more than this from a legal standpoint. Hence, I do not believe we can argue that because Palmyra adopted the name Hadriane Palmyra it must have been given its freedom during Hadrian's visit in 130.[305] Similarly, the epithets *Nea Traiane Bostra*[306] and *Augustocolonia Antoniana Metrocolonia Hadriane Petra Metropolis*[307] underline high points in the history of the cities, even though we cannot always identify precisely which emperor conferred each favor; for Bostra, Trajan probably simply conferred the status of a polis, but for Petra, the reference to Hadrian is unclear, because we know that Petra had the rank of metropolis as early as the time of Trajan.[308] Its epithet *Hadriana* may have stemmed from the imperial visit of 130, as was the case in Palmyra. Beginning with the Severi, we find an increasing number of imperial epithets that changed from ruler to ruler, and we cannot be certain that each one corresponded to an imperial gift.[309]

As for titles and privileges, cities sought, like cities elsewhere, to be granted freedom, *asylia* (exemption from reprisals or legal pursuit), autonomy (the right to live according to its own laws), the title *hiera* (holy), and the rank of metropolis or even colony, a rank that could be counted as an honor once the provincials themselves began claiming it.[310] According to Pliny the Elder, Antioch, Laodicea, and Seleucia were free cities,[311] but the same title appeared on coins of Scythopolis under Marcus Aurelius and Lucius Verus.[312] Cities that continued to mint their own silver coins may have enjoyed the same privilege: Seleucia until 6 C.E. and Antioch until 38; Sidon until 44, Tyre until 58,[313] and Laodicea until 124. However, most Syrian cities did not produce coins until later; hence we can deduce nothing from the coins regarding the cities' eventual freedom.

The term *asylia* raises complex issues, but it has recently been considerably clarified.[314] What mattered most to Syrian cities was to be acknowledged as having been granted asylia in the past rather than to acquire the title, for Kent Rigsby emphasizes that the review of asylia privileges by Tiberius and the Roman Senate in 22[315] probably ended the granting of this privilege, particularly as the Romans' understanding of asylia was different from the Greeks'.[316] The Greeks saw it as an honor for the god and the city, with a promise (rarely kept) to protect city-dwellers from looting. The Romans understood it as an unrestricted right to shelter persecuted people who came seeking refuge. Rigsby emphasizes, however, that emperors like Hadrian, nostalgic for Hellenism, may have made later grants of asylia to Syrian towns. This may have been the case for Capitolias[317] and Dura-

Europos. A single parchment, dated 254 C.E., exists as evidence of the title in Dura.[318] Because Dura had escaped the Seleucids before the title *asylia* had spread throughout their kingdom, and because it did not become Roman until well after the Senate and Tiberius had withdrawn this recognition, we must assume either that the title had been granted by a Parthian king or Tigranes, or that it was granted very late, possibly by Valerian after the first siege of the city in 253.[319] Actually, numerous Syrian towns enjoyed this title, some starting in Hellenistic times (Seleucia of Pieria around 150, Ptolemais from 132, Tyre in 126, Epiphanaea on the Orontes during the second century, Demetrias around 90, Larissa on the Orontes in 85, Sidon in 82–81, Apamaea in 75, Laodicea around 60, Rhosos around 50, Antioch in 46, Ascalon in 45), and the title continued to be granted under the empire: in Dora in 111–112, Diocaesarea in 138, Gadara and Panias in 160–161, Abila in the Decapolis in 162–163, Capitolias in 164–165, Scythopolis in 182–183, Nicopolis in northern Syria in 197, Gaza in 235.[320]

The designation *autonomia* was given to Seleucia around 150, then to Tripolis (108 B.C.E.), Laodicea (60 B.C.E.), Antioch (46 B.C.E.), Dora (111–112 C.E.), Diocaesarea (138 C.E.), Abila, Gadara, and Capitolias at the beginning of Marcus Aurelius's reign,[321] but it is hard to find any real substance in the label. Moreover, we see that the titles *autonomy, holiness,* and *asylia* usually went together, and were often—but not always—granted together. By contrast, the title *navarchis* given to Sidon, Dora, Tripolis, Tyre, and Laodicea was probably more a sign of the important role of these ports as a harbor for the Roman fleet than an indication of privilege.[322]

The reasons for granting the title *metropolis* have been much debated, without any conclusive results. Glen Bowersock has challenged the notion that its use was limited to provincial centers of the imperial cult;[323] such a limitation may have been imposed beginning with the Severi, but probably not before then. Tyre obtained the title during the reign of Domitian, Petra under Trajan,[324] Damascus and Samosata under Hadrian at the latest; we know that Tyre, Damascus, and Samosata were capitals of "eparchies" of the imperial cult (we have no evidence for Petra). Later, the title became quite common: Laodicea was a metropolis in 194 (after Antioch had lost its titles for having supported Pescennius Niger against Septimius Severus),[325] Carrhai in 212,[326] Sidon, Emesa, and Edessa in 218,[327] Caesarea on the Sea in 222, Tripolis in 235, Nisibis under Alexander Severus,[328] Philippopolis and Bostra under Philip the Arab.[329]

Colonial status sometimes resulted from true foundings, as we have seen, with deductio in the first century, and under Hadrian in Jerusalem. Far from being an honor for the local populations, these creations resulted in the expropriation of their lands and the loss of their civic status. However, beginning with the granting of colonial status to Caesarea, the measure lost its punitive nature and was transformed into an honor, because all Caesareans were granted the status of colonist. Whereas Greeks in the Aegean world had no desire for this exclusively "Roman" honor,[330] in the time of the Severi the right to colonial status—and it came to be seen as a right—had become widespread in Syria,[331] even though the resettlement of veterans continued in Tyre and Sidon (as Edward Dąbrowa has very convincingly shown),[332] and probably also in Rhesaina. Laodicea[333] and Tyre presumably received the title *colony* at the same time, in 198, since the two cities had taken the Severan side in the civil war of 193.[334] In contrast, Septimius Severus took Heliopolis away from Berytos to punish the latter for having supported Pescennius Niger.[335] Samaria-Sebaste[336] and Nisibis in Mesopotamia[337] were promoted under the same regime at some time, but we know only that in the case of Nisibis this could not have been before 198. Carrhai, in Osrhoene, and Rhesaina and Singara, in Mesopotamia, also became colonies under Septimius Severus.[338] To these foundings we must add Dura: the oldest attestation we have of its colonial status dates from 254.[339] It may have been a colony as early as the Severan era, but we have no way to know for certain.[340]

Caracalla continued this policy of promotions and conferred colonial status on his mother's native city Emesa,[341] on Antioch (which was finally forgiven for supporting Niger and reestablished as the capital of Coele Syria),[342] on Palmyra around 212,[343] and on Edessa in 213.[344] Elagabalus was probably responsible for the promotion of Sidon,[345] Caesarea-Arca in Lebanon,[346] and Petra in 221–222,[347] while Alexander Severus honored Bostra in the same way.[348] No promotions are attributed to the reigns of Maximinus or Gordian III, but Philip the Arab was probably behind the promotion of Damascus,[349] Flavia Neapolis in Palestine,[350] and of course his own native city, the Sabaoi village that became Philippopolis.[351] Finally, Scythopolis also received colonial status, although we do not know when.[352] Other cases are more difficult. According to Fergus Millar, neither Ascalon nor Gerasa obtained colonial status,[353] but a papyrus from 359 mentions the former as "Colonia Ascalon, Loyal and Free."[354] Even murkier is the situation in Gaza, Tiberias, and Gadara. In Gaza, a weight from the third century reads *kolonia Gaza*.[355] There is some doubt about Gadara, for an inscription produced after the Islamic conquest is dated from the year 726 of the colony and 42 of the Hegira;[356] however, this last, very late reference is not confirmed by any earlier evidence, making it somewhat dubious.[357] Finally, Rabbi Juda ha-nasi is said to have asked "Antoninus" (presumably Caracalla) to confer colonial status on Tiberias;[358] a coin dating from the reign of Elagabal includes the notation *col[onia]*,[359] and a *ketouba* (marriage contract) from 347 calls it a colony.[360]

At least two cities, Petra and Palmyra, were even dignified with the title *metrocolonia*,[361] a title that is unknown anywhere else but that was probably applied to Emesa and Antioch as well: it is a logical name for a polis that had been honored by the title *metropolis* and had just received the designation of colony.[362] Thus we see an accumulation of titles and honors spread indulgently around on official headings: Petra was still sporting the title *Augustocolonia Antoniana Metrocolonia Hadriana Petra Metropolis* on papyri as late as the middle of the sixth century.[363] The first title, a new one, has recently turned up in Bostra as well:[364] each of the two principal cities of Roman Arabia must have taken pains to avoid being outdone by the other in the race for honors.

The competition for honors was also played out in the historical arena. Beginning in the Hellenistic period, new foundations endowed themselves with legendary origins that would guarantee their prestige and antiquity.[365] For some, these stories were invented or perfected only rather late, when the need arose. Episodes from the distant past involving Alexander and his generals, nostalgia for the Seleucid kings, and even for Pompey and his legates: such was the material of a lively competition. We do not always understand what was at stake, but occasionally we can guess with a fair degree of confidence.

For example, Canatha—which minted coins only sporadically and in small numbers during the first century, except for a significant series right after Rome's annexation of the states of Agrippa II—suddenly trumpeted its antiquity by giving itself the epithet *Gabinia* in 190–191, while advertising its attachment to Dionysos in the iconography on its coins: all this suggests that the city was reacting to the promotion of the village of Soada—over which it had authority—to the rank of city, now called Dionysias.[366] We should note that Gabinius's benefactions must have been substantial to cause a city, after more than two centuries, to exhume a legate who did not have the best reputation in Roman historiography. The same is true for Pella and Gadara, cities that made much of the epithets *Philippeia* and *Pompeia*, respectively.

Similarly, we notice that the cities of the Decapolis showed little inclination to establish their antiquity until the second century: it was then that Gerasa honored Perdiccas and began including on coinage the phrase *Alexander the Great, Founder of Gerasa*.[367] Under Trajan, Gerasa also took back its Hellenistic name, Antioch on the Chrysorrhoas; no earlier use of this name has been found, but the absence of written documents from Hellenistic times may account for the lack of evidence; in any case, no coins prior to Trajan's reign mention the name.[368] We do not know exactly why the city chose to revert to its ancient name at this time, but it must have been a "Hellenizing" fashion that can be explained in a broader context. I had thought of linking this phenomenon with the array of imperial epithets that the upstart cities of Bostra and Petra exhibited, but Gerasa seems to have reverted to its Greek name even before the creation of the province of Arabia, so that explanation does not hold up.[369]

The participation of Syrian cities in this civic competition, or *agon*, shows to what extent they had adopted the values of Greek city-states. However, there are some major differences between the cities of northern Syria and the coast, on the one hand, and those of the south and the Transjordan, on the other. Almost all civic leaders in the old cities had Greek names, for example, and had quite often acquired Roman citizenship. By contrast, magistrates and bouleutes in the new cities in the province of Arabia usually retained their indigenous names, which were either Aramaic or Arabic, and Roman citizenship seems to have been quite rare.[370] Thus these recent cities operated with leaders who were only superficially Hellenized and whose attachment to indigenous traditions seemed quite strong. This also explains why there were no senators from Arabia or Mesopotamia, whereas northern Syria produced several.[371] The dividing line between these two types of cities followed the boundary line between the Seleucid kingdom and the indigenous states of the Hellenistic period: Emesa, like the cities of Nabataea or the interior of Palestine, had only a veneer of Hellenism, a few superficial features such as the use of Greek for monumental inscriptions or a Greek, Latin, or Hellenized name. This is indirectly confirmed by the absence of Greek contests in Palmyra, Petra,[372] and Emesa, and their delayed appearance in Bostra and perhaps Adraha. Three centuries of occupation by Seleucids (or Ptolemies) had not influenced the countryside, but it had left a mark on the cities; those areas that had not experienced this pervasive influence before the early empire never managed to overcome the "deficit of Hellenism." Whether by chance or not, this dividing line also corresponded to the one separating the most Arabized regions from the others. The vigor of Arab cultural traditions combined with a quasi lack of Hellenizing influence before the imperial epoch suffices to explain their profound originality.

CITY PROFILES

The temptation to synthesize data drawn from a wide body of documentation may well lead to an overly uniform and seriously incomplete portrayal of Syrian cities. Uniform to the extent that the effort tends to highlight common features more than differences and may imply that civic life was the same in Antioch and Dura, Tyre, and Gadara. Incomplete, because if one is looking for common characteristics, one ends up neglecting distinctive features and ignoring anything original. Consequently, although I do not claim to be offering an exhaustive study, it seems helpful to sketch a picture of a few cities, not in terms of architecture and urbanization, but in terms of the lifestyle of the inhabitants; I should like to evoke, as it were, the smells and colors of these places. Such portraits are necessarily in part subjective, because they require interpretation of a whole body of documentation, including such minor elements as epitaphs and simple dedications. These portraits are also quite incomplete because they are often strictly limited in time, corresponding to the brief period about which some documentation exists. It seems feasible to attempt to immerse oneself in the atmosphere of Antioch, Apamaea, Dura, Bostra, Tyre, Caesarea, and Gerasa. Palmyra could be added as well, but since it will be treated at length later on, I have not included it here; the same is true for Edessa, which will be discussed at length in connection with the spread of Christianity.

Third-Century Antioch

A royal capital and an imperial capital, Antioch stood out as the unrivaled metropolis of Asia for a thousand years, despite its geographical distance from the center of Syria. It very early became the residence of the Seleucid kings, and as such might appear to have been relegated to the mere rank of provincial capital by Pompey's annexation of Syria. Such was not the case, however, and the early imperatores and the emperors that followed never failed to show their solicitude for a city that, in its way, stood as a showcase for Roman power: what emperor failed to shower it with sumptuous buildings, sanctuaries, baths, theaters, gated roads, aqueducts, and more? Unrivaled in Syria, Antioch was among the rare Mediterranean "megalopolises"; it was one of the three largest cities in the empire, along with Rome and Alexandria.

To be sure, with a wall only 11.85 kilometers long, Antioch was far behind Rome (21 kilometers) or Alexandria (23 kilometers).[373] However, its size did not matter so much as the variety of its urban functions. In this respect, Antioch played all the important roles. The center of provincial administration for Syria, it housed the offices of the imperial legate, one of the most powerful in the empire, the master of four legions spread across the entire province. The city harbored only a small number of troops, just the legate's guard plus enough military personnel to maintain security in the city. Troops were stationed far away, and the expeditionary corps headed east or south were kept at a distance, more out of concern for supplies than for fear of looting or violence. Following the provincial reform of Septimius Severus in 194, Syria was cut in two, and Antioch became the capital of Coele Syria alone, but neither the city's prestige nor its actual importance was diminished as a result.

Antioch was where the Syrian *koinon* met, and it was the seat of the "priest of the four eparchies," the high priest of the imperial cult who presided over the joint games. A religious metropolis where the Greek and Macedonian cults of the first colonists mingled with those of the Syrian gods, not to mention the Jewish community that developed over time (it was already a significant element in the Hellenistic era),[374] Antioch very early began to see some of its population drawn to a new faith being preached by Jews coming from Palestine. Indeed, it was in Antioch that the followers of "Chrestos"[375] were first called "Christians." The Christian community continued to grow, and by the beginning of the third century the persecutions of the past, even Trajan's deportation of Bishop Ignatius to Rome for execution, seemed forgotten.[376] Indeed, the community prospered, and the bishop of Antioch was able to preach openly in the city.

A center of intellectual life, Antioch stood out even more for the wide range of pleasures it offered. Its holidays were famous. The calends of January brought an annual three-day holiday; the Olympic Games, begun under Augustus and renewed under Commodus, were held every four years and lasted forty-five days in July and August; other holidays honoring Artemis and Calliope drew artists and athletes. In addition to these Greek holidays, there was the *maiouma,* the May holiday in celebration of water, which in Antioch combined ceremonies honoring Dionysos and Aphrodite[377] that lasted thirty days, while the Adoneia (honoring Adonis) took place from the seventeenth to the nineteenth of July. The Jewish holidays, which attracted audiences with their resounding trumpets, were equally lavish. Christian holidays developed significantly after the Edict of Milan; until that time they remained modest. To visitors, however, Antioch seemed to live in an atmosphere of perpetual holiday, as Julian observed in 362.[378] A number of its festivals gave the public a chance to yield to excesses that only such an unbridled atmosphere could permit. Many people attended, and they came more for the beauty of the ceremony or the eloquence of the speaker than out of a deep commitment to one cult or another.[379] Moreover, people did not hesitate to switch from cult to cult: indeed, a law was passed in 315 prohibiting Jews from abusing other Jews who had converted to Christianity, while it was forbidden for Christians to convert to Judaism.

The city lent itself perfectly to the movement of large crowds at these proliferating events. Some festivals took place in Daphne, on the plateau overlooking the city to the southwest, but most of them used the streets of Antioch, its theaters, its Hellenistic agora, and its innumerable porticos, including the large, two-story ones that extended the length of the main street and beyond for nearly five kilometers. In his famous encomium to his city in the second half of the fourth century, the orator Libanios emphasized the social function of its porticos as places for promenades, meetings, and interminable discussions. The main street was not meant nearly as much for the circulation of horsemen and carts as for the pleasure of pedestrians: the paved central roadways were nine meters wide, and the porticos were just as wide on each side.[380] The activity did not end with nightfall, for the city was brilliantly lit. Dancing, singing, and processions went on endlessly, a fact that would scandalize later pagans such as the prudish and austere Julian. There were also countless taverns, bathing establishments, and bordellos, as well as private parties that took place in the luxurious terraced homes on the slopes of Mount Silpios or in the elite neighborhood of Daphne. The themes found in mosaics give a good idea of the importance of wining and dining in Antioch's social life.

In all their celebrating, the citizens of Antioch never lost their cynical attitude toward men in power. We recall that they rejected certain incompetent and ineffectual kings at the end of the Hellenistic period, preferring to submit to the Armenian Tigranes. It would seem that the holidays often became occasions for mocking local leaders, bouleutes, and magistrates, but not even imperial authority was always exempt, as Julian may have learned to his dismay in 362. Nevertheless, the city was not rebellious, and there is no indication that it ever really rose up against its leaders. It is true that in 193 it supported Pescennius Niger enthusiastically against Septimius Severus; but how could it have done otherwise when the usurper was the governor of Syria and in control of the city? Antioch paid dearly for this, as it was forced to give up its civic status and was reduced to the rank of a simple *kome,* a village with no autonomy. However, it soon regained its rank and was once again receiving imperial visits.

These visits were made necessary, in fact, by the war in the east. Caracalla came through in 215, Macrinus in 217, Severus Alexander in 230–231,[381] Gordian III in 242. Although the frontier of the empire had been pushed back as far as Nisibis and Dura-Europos, Antioch remained a likely target for Persian armies. Exceptional measures were taken and, under Philip, Antioch became the base of a *rector orientis* (governor of the Orient), none other than the emperor's own brother, Iulius Priscus. The city was sacked twice, once in 252[382] and again in 260.[383] At the time of the usurpation of Vaballathos and Zenobia, the city was taken over by Palmyrenes from 269 to 272, and retaken by Aurelius after his victory at

Immae. The city does not seem to have suffered from these battles, but the passage of the armies on the Antioch plain could not have been without consequences, if only in terms of supplies. However, neither Antioch's prestige nor its prosperity seems to have been affected, and it was only natural that Asia's metropolis should later become the capital of the eastern diocese, regaining its authority over all the Syrian provinces, which had been broken apart by Diocletian's reforms. Antioch, having become a major pillar in Christianity, entered a new stage in its history.

Apamaea, Second and Third Centuries

Perhaps it was the "New World" feeling there, but everything in Apamaea seemed larger than anywhere else. On the plateau overlooking the Orontes plain, Seleucos had built a city specifically designed to operate as a stud farm, primarily for the elephants that accounted for the superiority of his army. Whether because of its long exposure to these pachyderms or for some other reason, Apamaea retained its taste for vastness and monumentality long after the last elephant was gone.[384]

We know little about the Hellenistic city, beyond the area around the north gate; the earthquakes in 47 and 115 helped clear the terrain for new construction. The 115 earthquake was so destructive that the ruins were leveled; virtually all traces of the earlier buildings were wiped out in the process.[385] Reconstruction began right away, and on a grand scale. Apamenes could boast of having the largest theater in Syria (139 meters in diameter) and probably one of the largest in the Roman world, but also the largest colonnaded street, almost 40 meters from one wall to the other, over 20 meters just for the pavement, and more than two kilometers long. The first parts to be rebuilt, such as the Agrippan baths, were in place beginning around 116–117, but the reconstruction of the avenue with porticos took longer. The northern sector near the baths dates from this period, but the central part was not built until around 165; we know this from its ostentatiously "baroque" style as well as from dedications to Antoninus, Marcus Aurelius, and Lucius Verus.[386]

Although many Syrian cities were modeled on earlier ones, Apamaea looked new and spacious. Designed as a settlement for Greeks, the city quickly became home as well to indigenous people in the region who came there to trade. At the beginning of the first century, it already had the feel of a very large city, with 117,000 "citizens" according to the census, a number representing the free male inhabitants of the city's territory. How many native Greeks and Macedonians were among them? No one can give a precise answer, but we do know that they played an important role. As far as we can tell, Apamaea was ruled by an urban Greek or Macedonian aristocracy that included the same Dexandros who, under Augustus, became the first high priest of the imperial cult for all of Syria. The members of this group were large landholders who managed to carve out for themselves, from the declining Seleucid kingdom, principalities that Rome quickly recognized as client states before it consolidated administrative power over all of the newly conquered country. At the beginning of the second century the descendants of these tetrarchs continued to possess wealth and prestige, as documented by L. Iulius Agrippa in 115. When the destruction of the city obliged them to rebuild their houses, they thought big: they did not hesitate to build houses of two thousand to forty-five hundred square meters, and the peristyle of a single one was the size of the forum in many a small African city.[387]

Apamaea's military role may have faded over time, but it never disappeared, and as early as the Severan era the presence of the army in the city was beginning to be felt. Because of the availability of water, food, and provisions of every sort, Apamaea was frequently visited by troops who camped under its walls on their way to the Orient. The vast military cemetery just outside the city shows traces of Macrinus's army in 217–218 (Legio II Parthica and some auxiliary units), of Severus Alexander's army during the winter of 231–232, and, in the summer of 233, of the Second Parthica again. The city was so vulnerable that its wall was hastily reinforced, probably during Shapur's invasion in 256, with a series of towers built out of any material at hand. There was no one to protect the tombs of soldiers buried decades before, and their steles were used to build Tower XV.[388] These fortifications were effective, however, for although the city was taken by the Persians in 256, it broke away in 260.

Apamaea was Greek in its civic life, its culture, its artistic and architectural environment. The home of Posidonios in the second century B.C.E., it also was the birthplace of Numenios in the second century C.E., and its neo-Platonist school prospered in the third century around Aemelius Gentilianus, who moved there in 269, before Iamblichos and Sopatros brought the city renown in the fourth century.[389] The mosaics decorating private homes attest to the taste for Platonic themes as well as for Greek myths during the third century and later, and the culture transmitted by these means was not confined to the limited circle of members of the school; it spread throughout the prosperous and presumably cultivated classes of the city.[390] Groups of sculptures installed in public places recalled well-known or popular myths: Apollo, Olympos, Marsyas and the Scythian slave in the baths that were rebuilt in 116–117, Dionysos and Lycurgos along one street, gods of the Greek Pantheon in the niches of the nymphaeum, the *atlantes*—huge statues of the giant Atlas—on the walls of the Tycheion, to name only those that are known with certainty. Under the Severi, Apamaea was also home to a poet, Oppianus (or Pseudo-Oppianus), author of the *Cynegetica* in four books, dedicated—probably in 215—to Caracalla, who was visiting Antioch.[391]

All this evidence of Hellenism should not lead us to believe that indigenous peoples were absent. There was probably a Jewish community here very early, as there was in every large Syrian city, even though no inscriptions identify the synagogue before the end of the fourth century. Situated in the middle of a rich agricultural region, Apamaea must have attracted many farmers, artisans, and native shopkeepers, and, as elsewhere, Aramaic must have been spoken as well as Arabic. So far, however, excavations have mainly provided information about the Greek and Hellenized sectors of the city and about soldiers passing through—all of which the historian must record.

Dura-Europos from the Severi to Its Destruction in 256

Dura (Dura-Europos), founded by Seleucos I, had a singular destiny: a Seleucid garrison in the third century B.C.E., it took off as a city during the second century just prior to its conquest by the Parthians.[392] In this respect, it had more in common with cities in Mesopotamia than with Syrian cities. Having escaped conquest by Pompey, it remained for nearly three centuries—from 113 B.C.E. to 165 C.E.—as a frontier outpost on the western edge of the Parthian Empire. However, during those three hundred years the Greek elements of the city endured. The native Macedonian aristocracy still ruled the city, and its members' names are the ones that appear on official documents.[393]

As a border city, Dura always maintained relations with Greek and later Roman Syria. The first century C.E. seems to have been a period of prosperity, as if the benefits of the *pax romana* in Syria were felt in adjacent Parthia. Numerous buildings were erected,[394] undoubtedly paid for by funds raised through the city's foreign trade. As early as 33 B.C.E., some Palmyrenes made a dedication in Dura: is it an accident that this is also the oldest inscription we have from Dura?[395] The marked increase in bronze coins from Antioch observed after Claudius's reign,[396] as well as the presence of imported glass from the same city,[397] offer further evidence of trade. Dura was much more than just a stopping place between Palmyra and lower Mesopotamia, a more or less obligatory transfer point for caravans.

What is most striking is the city's cosmopolitan character: it was a kaleidoscope of languages, cults, and costumes. Among the texts found in Dura, most are in Greek, but there are also examples in Latin, Aramaic (from Palmyra, Edessa, and Hatra), Hebrew, Middle Persian, and Arabic (Safaitic).[398] Individuals identified as Greek are portrayed on temple walls; some have Greek names, others are dressed in the long folded trousers of the Parthians or display the high coiffures of Syrian priests; some are even in Roman military uniform. The Pantheon testifies to the same diversity. While certain gods belonged to the Greco-Macedonian tradition of the earliest colonists (Zeus, Artemis, Apollo), others came from Palmyra (Bel, Iarhibol, Malakbel, Arsu, the Gads), some from western Syria (Atargatis, Baalshamin, and Adonis), and others from neighboring areas such as Aphlad from Anath, and possibly Azzanathkona.[399] To these we may add the gods worshipped by the soldiers, such as Jupiter Dolichenus and Mithras; there was also the cult of the rulers, whose celebrations by the garrison appear on the official list in the *Feriale Duranum*.[400] And we would be

THE GODDESS ATARGATIS OF HIERAPOLIS WITH HER CONSORT HADAD, AND BETWEEN THEM A CULT OBJECT MODELED ON A ROMAN MILITARY STANDARD. A RELIEF FROM DURA-EUROPOS.

remiss to omit either the Jewish community, whose richly ornate synagogues must have rivaled the wealthiest sanctuaries in the city (those devoted to Bel, Zeus Theos, and Mithras all contained innumerable paintings),[401] or the Christian community, whose meetinghouse has been identified.[402] Apparently, the fact that each group had its own gods, spaces, and rituals was not a problem. Was there interaction and mixing? The answer is not clear: however, it has recently been noted that the worship of Palmyrene gods in Dura by Palmyrenes helped reinforce the group's sense of communal cohesiveness and solidarity.[403]

Beginning early in the third century, the most prominent feature of Dura was the omnipresence of soldiers.[404] Right after the conquest of 165, auxiliary troops were stationed in the city or in the immediate vicinity, but beginning around 208–209 the northeast part of the city was cleared of its inhabitants, and detachments of legionnaires were settled there, separated from the rest of the city by a wall—the only instance in which the camp was located inside the city itself. Around 218 the palace of the *dux ripae* occupied a site along the river, on the edge of the cliff. However, soldiers could be found everywhere in the city, as many of them were billeted with local residents, a situation that must have been an onerous burden on the population. Was it in compensation for these services that Septimius Severus gave the city the status of colony? We cannot say, because the date of this promotion is unknown. The city had retained its civic institutions during the Parthian era, for the oldest state of the bouleuterion dates from that period, and we do not know precisely under what circumstances it was renovated around 200. In any event, it is striking to observe that the Greek and Macedonian names that were those of the colonial aristocracy are almost completely absent from the record from that time forward.[405] From then on, except for a few of the most common Roman names whose origins we cannot identify, it was the Semites from abroad, particularly from the army, who were most prominent. This is not surprising, since a large number of soldiers, both legionnaires and auxiliaries, came from within Syria itself. Judging from the archives on papyrus or parchment, many were Arabs.

In addition, soldiers came to dominate the urban economy. As they

DRAWING OF A PAINTED SCENE IN THE TEMPLE OF ZEUS SOTER
AT DURA-EUROPOS SHOWING MILITARY FIGURES.

prospered, they acquired land.[406] Once they became veterans they stayed in the region, bought and sold property, and served as sponsors for their former comrades. The city remained active; unlike Alfred Raymond Bellinger,[407] I am not so sure that commerce shrank in comparison to what it had been during the second and third centuries. The fact that bronzes from Edessa and Carrhai replaced those of Antioch could be explained simply by the opening of new workshops at the beginning of the third century. The collection of texts recently published by Denis Feissel and Jean Gascou, added to the single contract published many years ago,[408] confirms trade with Edessa and Carrhai as well as with villages and towns of the Middle Euphrates. The archives of the merchant Nebuchelos, from around 235–240, reveal an active man whose business remained local.[409] He appears to have been more interested in small trading enterprises in Dura than in the long-distance export-import business. To analyze the commercial activity in Dura on the eve of its destruction on the basis of a single example would be highly misleading.

Bostra

How might an officer or a high-level official have felt when he learned he was being posted in far-off Arabia? The very word *Arabia* would have evoked a world of nomads and outlaws in an inhospitable landscape, scorched by the sun during the day and freezing at night. These images were no doubt based on reality, but they said little about the capital of Roman Arabia. A newcomer in the middle of the third century would have discovered a very different city.

Bostra stood on volcanic land, and basalt gave the ancient capital of Rabbel II an austere appearance. For anyone who knew how to use it, this grey rock, almost black when freshly cut, produced a multicolored effect when combined with the white or light-pink limestone found in the northern Transjordan. City planners and architects in Bostra used a lot of it in building the enormous stage wall in the theater and in the colonnades that lined the street leading to it. Still, the cheerfulness of the city's neighborhoods was probably not the first thing to strike a new arrival.

If he was coming from Tyre, as was most often the case, the visitor would approach the city from the west, after going through Caesarea Panias and Adraha. From afar he would have seen the city ramparts, which had just been restored and reinforced at the same time as those of Adraha, presumably for fear of a Persian attack.[410] Once he had entered the city, a beautiful street, almost perfectly straight and lined with porticos, would lead him to a central intersection where stood a monumental archway, possibly erected during the time of the Severi to celebrate the city's elevation to the rank of colony.[411] Nearby was the beautiful central area, with a cryptoportico opening onto the forum, a macellum, two enormous baths, and, to the south, the theater, rising out of the ground unsupported by the slightest hill or elevation. Proceeding further, the visitor would find sanctuaries, reservoirs, and a great many other amenities.

The scale of the baths was surprising for a relatively small city of barely ten thousand inhabitants. No less surprising was the size of the theater, with some nine thousand seats. This was because Bostra was not an ordinary city but a provincial capital and, more importantly, a garrison city. When we examine the urban population, we find that soldiers were the single largest group. As sometimes happened in the east, the legionnaires' camp was set up very close to the city, just to the north. The northern gate of the city served as the camp's southern gate. Even though the five to six thousand legionnaires were not permanently stationed in Bostra (some detachments were still patrolling outposts as far away as Hegra and Dumata, more than nine hundred kilometers away), the legion constituted a sizable group, and a prosperous one, judging from the number and quality of epitaphs. The legionnaires' need for relaxation and entertainment had to be satisfied, hence the immense baths in the city center (in addition to the baths inside the camp itself), the presence of a theater, an amphitheater, and a hippodrome. Moreover, beginning in the middle of the third century the city organized at least two Greek-style competitions: the Dousaria Actia, in honor of the city's principal god, Dousares,[412] and, starting at the end of Valerian's reign or the beginning of Gallienus's, a sacred Olympic competition.[413]

In addition to the soldiers, there were municipal leaders, for the most part wealthy landholders of the region. They owned beautiful homes in the villages and were eventually buried there, but they showed little interest in displaying their titles as bouleutes, their magistratures and liturgies, as if such things could be taken for granted. It may be significant that an abbreviation for "bouleute of Bostra" (BB) appears most often on very simple funeral steles, as if only rather modest people who had risen to the status considered it a source of pride. Relatively few seem to have acquired Roman citizenship before 212, apart from veterans, of course, from whom citizenship could be inherited; and some colonial families who had settled there during the second century and benefited from land distributions are noted in a registry that has recently been found in the plains region. For the most part, the city leaders had Aramaic or even Arabic names; they did not try to appear more "Greek" than they were. They were large landholders rather than merchants; there is no evidence to suggest that Bostra had a significant caravan trade. Although it was the first major city in Syria that anyone arriving from central or eastern Arabia by way of Wadi Sirhan would encounter, this was not the main caravan route; caravans usually came from Arabia Felix via Hegra. They certainly stopped in Bostra, as in every large city: this may explain the prosperity of goatskin-bag makers, who held reserved seats in the theater, but theirs must have been a marginal activity compared to trade in the region's agricultural products.

Nor was there any reason for Bostra to emerge as an intellectual city. The Jewish community (Rabbi Simon b. Yotzadak came from there, in the third century) was so substantial that many Palestinian teachers, such as Rabbi Abbahu of Caesarea, came to visit Bostra.[414] A Christian community must have developed quite early. At the beginning of the third century, Origen refuted its bishop, Beryllos of Bostra. A small ecumenical council was held, the record of which has been found in Egypt.[415] The council itself was not particularly significant, but it showed that this city of soldiers and landowners was not without an intellectual life.

Tyre

"Tyre . . . , formerly famous as the mother-city from which sprang the cities of Leptis, Utica and the great rival of Rome's Empire in coveting world-sovereignty, Carthage, and also Cadiz, which she founded outside the confines of the world . . . but the entire renown of Tyre now consists in a shell-fish and a purple dye!" This is the way Pliny described the city in his *Natural History* in the middle of the first century:[416] the striking contrast between what it was in antiquity and what it had become might give the impression of a profound decline or lead to the belief that the prestigious city of old had fallen to the modest level of an ordinary provincial city. Tyre had long before lost its dominance in trade, but the impact of the city in Roman Syria was still considerable, both economically and intellectually.

Tyre had ultimately emerged victorious from its centuries-long rivalry with Sidon. It was chosen as the center of the Phoenician eparchy for the imperial cult, and then as the capital of Syria-Phoenicia. Moreover, its chief competitor was no longer Sidon but Berytos, a city aglow with the prestige of a Roman colony. This became quite apparent when cities had to come out for or against Pescennius Niger in 193: Tyre did the opposite of Berytos without worrying about Sidon (which took the same side). This victory, consecrated by an accumulation of titles (Tyre was designated a metropolis at the beginning of the second century), had been long in the making. After all, Tyre was the first city in the Seleucid kingdom to be given its liberty, in 126 B.C.E. Its coinage dominated not only southern

Phoenicia but also all of Galilee and the Hauran; from there it spread far and wide. The economic power Tyre had acquired as a center of industry, and especially as a port city importing and exporting a multitude of goods, enabled it to build a vast network of relations that helped support its industries and commerce.

For Tyre was a hive of activity. Long confined to its tiny island, it now extended from the mainland to the ends of the ancient island, along the length of the artificial isthmus created by the long embankments built into the sea by Alexander. Tyrians took advantage of this by constructing an immense hippodrome just outside the walls, by the city gates, before the road crossed the rich necropolis that stretched onto the continent. Not many artisanal workshops have been found, but blocks of unused glass-making material provide evidence of the activity of glassworkers. The purple dye industry produced great wealth. Murices (purple-fish) were abundant in local waters, but the demand was so great that they were also imported from as far south as Ptolemais. Above all, Tyre benefited from its close relations with Galilee, a producer of linen, and Judaea, rich in wool. For it was not enough to possess the dye: Tyre also needed quality fabric for dyeing. There was silk, too, imported at great cost from distant lands but intended for only a limited clientele.

For the visitor, the most impressive sights were unquestionably the two ports, the most important ones on the Syrian coast, from which boats sailed all over the Mediterranean. The large southern port, open wide to the sea, contained the dry docks, while the northern port, narrower but better protected, provided a good harbor for overwintering. Tyre profited fully from its long maritime tradition and from its old relationships throughout the Mediterranean region, where its citizens had emigrated freely ever since Hellenistic times. But it also relied on the strength of its industry and the produce of a vast region that, from the southern Beqaa to the Hauran, provided it with wheat, wines, olive oil, and fabrics. All of these were exported to the rest of the Mediterranean world, sometimes after undergoing transformations at Tyre that made them even more valuable.

But Tyre was not simply a great industrial and commercial city; it also produced a galaxy of rhetoricians, philosophers, and jurists. The best known were Marinus, Maximus, and Domitius Ulpianus (Ulpian); although these three did little work in Tyre itself, they nevertheless contributed to its glorious reputation. For Tyre, like most Syrian cities, did turn out "intellectuals"—but most of them hastened abroad to find students and followers in the old intellectual centers of Greece, Asia Minor, and even Rome.

Caesarea

Since its founding by Herod in 20 B.C.E., Caesarea had continued to proclaim its position as a Greek city situated near Judaea. A royal capital and later the seat of the Roman administration, it had the unique privilege of being the first Greek city in all the Orient to be called a Roman colony—not as a result of retaliation involving confiscation and settlement of colonists, but as an honor from which all citizens benefited. As the first city so honored, it took pride in seeing its "Greek" population become "Roman," thanks to Vespasian.

Although it was a "pagan" city, Caesarea remained an object of envy. We shall not go back over the bloody confrontations that took place under Nero between the Jewish community and the Caesareans who refused to grant Jews any legitimacy whatsoever in their city. Following the war of 66–70, Jews mistrusted this city that had given such effective support to Rome (the granting of colonial status was its repayment), and it was Iamnia that drew fugitives, from Rabbi Yohanan b. Zakkai to refugees of every sort who had escaped massacre or sale as slaves.

After the suppression of the Bar Kokhba revolt, Caesarea lost its pivotal role in the control of Judaea, which had almost disappeared from history. Moreover, its fortunes declined because its port became dangerous after the breakwater sank; Ptolemais, in Galilee, and Ascalon and Gaza, in lands to the south, captured most of the traffic. Caesarea did remain the center of Roman administration for Syria-Palestine, but a handful of officials and soldiers did not suffice to maintain the glory of the ancient royal capital. We should not read too much into this relative decline, however; there were still enough rich and cultured people to support the importation of sumptuous Asian or Attic marble sarcophagi—some beautifully decorated in Dionysian or other themes[417]—and to support the construction of public monuments with very fine statuary.[418]

In addition, during the second century and especially the third century, the city seems to have been an intellectual center of some importance. Even though Caesarea was less prominent than Antioch or Edessa, it would be a mistake to underestimate its role. We do not know when the Christian community developed there, but it claimed to have its roots in apostolic times. In retroactive moves, Zacchaeus, the repentant publican, and the centurion Cornelius, the first pagan to convert to Christianity, were named the first two bishops of the city! Historically speaking, however, the first bishop did not appear in Caesarea until 189. This was Theophilos, who engaged in a debate with Narcissus of Jerusalem over the date of Easter; behind this rather technical discussion, we may surmise that the real issue involved Christian supremacy in Palestine. Origen visited a little later, in 215, and when he was exiled from Alexandria in 231 he returned there, remaining until his death in 253 or 254. The authority of this great man, his love of debate and controversy, no doubt helped animate the intellectual life of the area. It is clear that he had a number of opportunities to engage in discussions with the local rabbis.[419]

For Caesarea had gradually become a center of Jewish life once more. Rabbi Bar Kappara may even have opened a school there in the middle of the third century.[420] In any case, around 260, Rabbi Yose b. Hanina was the leader of a prosperous and influential school, frequented by the highly celebrated Rabbi Abbahu of Caesarea, one of the best-known masters of rabbinic Judaism in the late third and early fourth centuries, famous for many things and renowned for his perfect mastery of Greek.[421] The oldest parts of the Palestinian Talmud—the treatises *Baba Kamma, Baba Mezia,* and *Baba Bathra*—may have been written in Caesarea.[422] It was here, where the intellectual atmosphere was open to controversy, that the great historian of the Church, Eusebius of Caesarea, was born around 270.

Gerasa

Gerasa of the Decapolis was certainly a curious city. Along with Scythopolis, it was undoubtedly one of the most important cities on our list, definitely the one that has left the most impressive vestiges, and yet its identity eludes us.[423] Obviously successful, it was a city of paradoxes. It boasted that it had been founded very early, in Alexander's time,[424] but the earliest Hellenistic ruins date back to the end of the second century B.C.E. or later. It must be older than that, however, because the name Antioch on the Chrysorrhoas is found as early as 142 B.C.E.[425] and could hardly have been given later than the time of Antiochos IV; however, up to the second century C.E. the city used its Semitic name, Gerasa, almost exclusively, and the citizens called themselves Gerasenes rather than Antiochenes. Josephus consistently refers to it by its Semitic name.[426] We could easily understand this attitude if the urban agglomeration had replaced some powerful or well-known indigenous city whose name would have been hard to forget. This was not the case, however, and the site bears no trace of substantial prior occupation; still, the Semitic toponym in itself proves the existence of an indigenous settlement of some renown even before the Hellenistic city was founded. The city considered itself Greek, and in fact during the imperial era, from which texts are numerous enough to permit a significant onomastic study of its population, we find a much higher proportion of Greek names than in other cities such as Bostra or Adraha.[427] The tyrants who ruled the city during a troubled period in the first century B.C.E., Zeno Cotylas and his son Theodoros, were Greek.[428] And Greek identity was still clearly apparent in the cults of the chief gods, Zeus and Artemis, who towered over the Pantheon and the public square, as it was apparent in the presence of rhetors and philosophers.[429]

Yet Gerasa developed in an environment that was undeniably Semitic, and even Arabic, with the advance of the Nabataeans to the north in the second century B.C.E. The city did not extend very far to the east; its size undoubtedly was limited by the presence of the Nabataean kingdom at its gates.[430] The Greek tyrants may well have been mere puppets of the Petraean kings; at the very least, they needed the kings' consent to remain in power.[431] Some of the leaders betray their indigenous roots by their very names, such as the gymnasiarchs Zabdion, son of Aristomachos, Theodoros, son of Barnanaios, Marion, son of Phallion,[432] or a priest of the imperial cult during Trajan's reign, Malchos, son of Demetrios.[433] An Arabic god tentatively identified as the sacred god Paqeidas, "the protector, the guardian," was worshiped in Gerasa as well.[434] So it may well be that, despite the paucity of sources about the Semitic population, the city was not as different from its neighbors to the east and north as it claimed.[435]

But Gerasa presented yet another paradox. Thought to have been founded as a garrison, a bridgehead in the Transjordan, the city occupied a site that was challenging to defend, for it was surrounded on almost all sides by mountains. Its ramparts (the current ones were built much later) defined a vast perimeter (3,450 kilometers long) enclosing a space that was probably never fully occupied, especially in the eastern sector, beyond Wadi Jerash (the Chrysorrhoas), but they never ensured an effective defense. For, in a somewhat unusual situation, a river crossed the city from north to south, complicating communications between the two almost equal sectors that it created; the eastern part of the city seems to have been sparsely populated, and the two bridges that have been found may have sufficed to carry the traffic.

As a Greek city, Gerasa saw its share of political unrest. The Jewish community was by virtue of the proximity of both Judaea and Galilee, and it functioned peacefully for a time, even during the war of 66–70, because Gerasa was one of the rare cities that refused to massacre Jews.[436] One of the rebel leaders, Simon bar Giora, apparently came from the city, but we have no way of knowing whether the population was divided in its loyalty. Conflicts occurred in the second century, but we do not know what was at stake. Around 125–126, the governor Tiberius Iulius Iulianus Alexander was honored by the Gerasenes for having restored peace in the city, which suggests that the city was emerging from a period of unrest.[437] The names of several civic tribes that had been inscribed in the stands of the northern theater, which served as bouleuterion, were later defaced with hammers; this suggests that factional fighting may have raged through the city. Finally, Jacques Seigne very convincingly links the removal of the religious center away from the temple of Zeus to the south, near the sanctuary of Artemis (recently magnificently reconstructed and restored), to a similar situation of conflict between clans, civic tribes, or leading families. Without explicit texts, it is difficult to grasp the underlying issues behind the fighting, but the fact remains that this distant Arabian city led a vibrant civic life under the eyes of the resident Roman procurators.

Gerasa was also in competition with its neighbors. We need a better understanding of these nearby cities to be able to judge the extent to which changes in the urban landscape of one or another were determined by the desire to surpass neighboring rivals. We are beginning to acquire basic information about Gadara, Scythopolis, Pella, and to some extent Philadelphia. Little by little, we are coming to see parallels that cannot be accidental, but we still do not know which city took the initiative. For example, Gadara, like Gerasa, had two theaters, one smaller than the other; in Gerasa, the southern theater had three thousand seats, while the northern theater, with sixteen hundred, was not only a bouleuterion, but also a concert hall. Both cities had a hippodrome or circus; the one in Gadara, 293 meters long, was larger than Gerasa's, which suggests to me that it was also newer. At 244 meters, Gerasa's stadium was the smallest in the Roman world, and all the evidence suggests that the hippodrome served as both amphitheater and stadium. We find the same feature again in Scythopolis and in Caesarea on the Sea. They had another feature in common that could hardly have been accidental: while Gerasa built an immense monumental arch for Hadrian's visit, Gadara built a similar structure on Tiberius's route, 350 meters west of the walls.[438] Thus, despite profound differences imposed by location, materials, and the general environment, there can be little doubt that competition among cities of the Decapolis pushed them to adopt an architectural style that was increasingly impressive, but also contributed to a uniform appearance.

These sample city portraits cannot convey the full richness and diversity of Syrian cities. They may help us understand, however, that a relatively uniform monumental surface masked profound differences in history, population, tradition, and industry. There were differences, too, in climatic conditions, the color of the rock, and the general geographical landscape. It is here that the historian's narrative reaches its limits; the talents of a novelist or storyteller, combined with the photographer's art, would be required for us truly to "feel" the variety of this multifaceted world.

RURAL LIFE IN THE EARLY EMPIRE

AVAILABLE documentation about rural life in Syria toward the end of the Hellenistic period is exceptionally good, especially from the second century C.E. up to the Islamic conquest and beyond. However, the evidence is unevenly distributed: it is abundant in two regions where natural conditions are very different, at opposite ends of the country. One of these is the "Limestone Massif" in northern Syria, a combination of mountains (today quite barren) and narrow, enclosed plains located within the rough triangle formed by Aleppo, Antioch, and Apamaea; the other is the Hauran, all the basaltic lands situated south and southeast of Damascus, between the Golan to the west and the desert to the east and south. In these two regions, ruins of hundreds of ancient villages (the term *dead cities* is used only for the Limestone Massif, since the villages of the Hauran are almost all occupied) still offer the visitor impressive remains of ancient rural life: stables, houses, tombs, and cisterns, accompanied by thousands of Greek inscriptions (particularly in the south). The historian of the early empire must use all this documentation judiciously, for a significant portion of it comes from the fourth through seventh centuries, as attested by churches, monasteries, and pilgrims' inns, or, more simply, by crosses and Christian invocations found in private homes. There is thus a significant risk of interpolating on the basis of the most abundant indications and predating to the first and second centuries events for which there is no evidence before the fourth century. Enough dated monuments have been identified, however, to give a fairly accurate picture of the essential realities of the early empire.

Moreover, the documentation available today extends beyond the strict boundaries of these two regions. Besides the evidence provided in the New Testament and in the Talmuds, evidence that has been used (and sometimes overused) for a very long time, other factors are helping to refine our knowledge and provide data for a large part of ancient Syria: these factors include advances in rural archaeology in Palestine and Syria, the discovery and occasional excavation of rural houses, the fossil record in several regions (around Antioch, Laodicea, Emesa, Damascus, and the Hauran), and the discovery and study of the papyri of Nahal Hever (from the beginning of the second century) and from the Middle Euphrates (middle of the third century).

The most difficult task is to establish a reasonably accurate inventory of agricultural production in Syria. To be sure, the natural conditions suggest that the three Mediterranean crops par excellence—grains, grapes, and olives—were of primary importance. However, it would be helpful if we could rank these products, judge their quality (neither Syria's wines nor its oils seem to have had a very good reputation), and assess their distribution abroad. We may suppose in addition that animal husbandry played a role in certain districts (and not only among nomads) and that orchards and palm groves had a place in the rural economy. But all this is difficult to evaluate, as literary sources are much more likely to emphasize the exceptions than the rule. Nevertheless, certain indicators give us some idea of the probable facts.

LAND TENURE AND LAND USE

Imperial Estates

Conquered by force, Syria must have been transformed into state land, *ager publicus,* at least in part. Unfortunately, we do not know what remained of the Seleucid royal lands at the time of Pompey's conquest; without that knowledge, we have no means of determining how much was confiscated and added to Rome's treasury. Similarly, with the gradual annexation of the client states later on, the personal assets of kings and dynasts were presumably confiscated by the emperor, whether he chose to keep them as personal property or sold them for personal profit. We know that when Archelaos of Judaea was stripped of his property, Rome sent Quirinius off right away to make an inventory of his assets and sell them,[1] a move that precluded, a priori, their conversion to imperial estates. However, only part of his fortune was in land. Only recently, thanks to some unpublished documents, have we succeeded in measuring the extent of imperial estates in Syria, and these appear to have been quite significant in size at a late date. But we have yet to date the creation of these imperial holdings.

The best-known and most acclaimed of the imperial properties in Syria was the Lebanese forest, which was already heavily exploited by Hadrian's time at least.[2] The emperor did not own the soil itself, but instead owned four species of trees, certainly including cedar and juniper *excelsa,* and probably Cilician oak and pine.[3] The boundaries marked under Hadrian must have reflected a reorganization related to the management of his *patrimonium* and an interest in agricultural development, rather than indicating a new acquisition. Moreover, we know that the Lebanese forest had long been coveted by every ruler in turn. Without going as far back as the Assyrians, we need only recall that in 200 B.C.E. Antiochos III granted Jews the right to harvest cedars of Lebanon, which suggests that he had some form of ownership. It would not be surprising for the emperors to have inherited these rights from the Seleucid kings. If this is so, Hadrian was not necessarily doing something new; he was simply improving the management of the property in order to increase its value.

There were other imperial estates in Syria, for we know that one procurator was given responsibility for administering the *regio syriatica;*[4] another, a freed slave, directed a *regio parhalia* on the coast;[5] a third managed a *regio Myrsen*[—] in the Hauran. Imperial lands consisted primarily of bequests or confiscated property. Thus it is worthwhile to look at what happened after wars, uprisings, usurpations, or annexations. According to Josephus, after the defeat of 70, "all Jewish territory" was leased (with the exception of parcels given to eight hundred veterans of Emmaus),[6] and Vespasian retained the whole as his personal property.[7] However, this is probably not accurate, for most of the lands were sold or given to partisans, and we have proof that there was a good deal of property in private hands.[8] Moreover, we know that a *conductor,* the manager of an imperial estate, lived at Lydda during the first half of the second century, in the heart of what was called *hor ha-Melekh,* "the king's mountain," and that this was most probably a royal Hasmonaean estate inherited from the Seleucids, the Ptolemies, or even Alexander himself.[9] Was the imperial estate recorded in the second century C.E. inherited from the Hasmonaeans via the Herodians? Or was it a new property? The first hypothesis is the most likely, but we do not know for sure that the entire region that bore this name under the empire actually belonged to the emperors, for some unquestionable cases of private ownership have been documented.[10] However, there is reason for skepticism about imperial estates in the Plain of Sharon and in western Samaria, lands inherited from the Herodians; for the time being, Shimon Applebaum's arguments for viewing these as imperial estates seem inadequate.[11]

Jean-Paul Rey-Coquais, whose arguments have merit but are inconclusive,[12] maintains that the Herodian principates of Southern Syria became imperial lands in 92–93, when the kingdom of Agrippa II was annexed. This is not impossible a priori, and it might explain the presence of a large number of veterans who had received individual lots (this is one of Rey-Coquais's arguments, moreover).[13] The recent discovery of a Batanaean inscription in Sanamein-Aire may prove him right. This inscription from the era of the Emperor Julian (358–360) in honor of a praetorian prefect whose name has utterly disappeared, was offered by "Batanaea," which was regarded as a separate entity, and we can date it by the name of a *ducenarii*, an administrator of the domain (*saltus*).[14] This inscription should be linked with another, later, reference to a certain *saltus Bataneos*,[15] which may have existed by the middle of the fourth century. Can we go back even further and connect it to the rule of the last of the Herods? There is no proof, but I note that the same settlement of Sanamein-Aire has yielded two inscriptions, which can be dated to the second and third centuries, honoring procurators who must have had the job of administering the imperial estates in the region. Another text from the same village, in Latin (thus necessarily referring to a Roman administration), mentions the *regio Myrsen*: this term, cited above but unknown in any other context, also alludes to the presence of imperial estates.[16] I have shown elsewhere that the founding of *metrokomiai*, mother-villages, instead of cities in this particular region of Syria (in contrast to what was done elsewhere) can best be explained if the entire region constituted one vast imperial estate: the imperial status would allow for elevating some settlements above mere villages without giving them the autonomy of a *polis*, thus maintaining the full extent of the emperor's rights.[17]

For now, this conclusion appears to apply only to Batanaea—the westernmost (and richest) part of the states belonging to Agrippa II. However, we cannot rule out the possibility that it also pertained in other districts, especially the Trachonitis, which also contained metrokomiai. It seems more doubtful for Auranitis, where we see nothing of this kind and where there was at least one city, Canatha, even before the Herodian period. Yet toward the end of the second century or at the very beginning of the third, the Jewish patriarch Rabbi Juda I seems to have been farming land in the Golan that belonged to Caracalla. Other imperial holdings could have been located there as well, domains that could have begun like those in Batanaea, because Agrippa II's states also included this area.[18] Perhaps we ought to bring into the picture George of Cyprus's reference to the *Gaulanes klima*

(Gaulanes' domain) in Second Palestine.[19] We are much less well informed about the Seleucid heritage. The dynasty's slow demise may have coincided with the monopolization of royal lands by private interests, and as a result we do not know what was left of them in 64. We do not know much about Herodian estates in Judaea itself or about those of the Nabataeans. However, we do know that in a dowry for Salome, Herod bequeathed estates on the coast, specifically the palm groves of Archelais,[20] which later reverted to Livia[21] and probably ended up in the patrimonium. The balsam groves of the Jordan Valley would have become imperial property in the same way, according to Pliny, who indicates that the two ancient royal gardens had become the property of the treasury.[22] "Imperial villages" to the south[23] and west of the Dead Sea[24] are mentioned elsewhere during the reigns of Trajan and Hadrian; these seem to have been part of the royal Nabataean inheritance[25] (a document from the Babatha archive mentions a royal grove).[26] However, Hannah Cotton has shown how difficult it is to be specific about the status of lands, even when we have documentation as precise as that provided by the archives of Nahal Hever, because we do not know whether the receipts are for payment of a tax—which could tell us that the property was privately held—or for payment of rent due the emperor as landlord.[27] Cotton may be overly pessimistic, however, for a reference in the same documents to a "royal grove," an "imperial village," a "*moschantic*[28] estate of our Lord Caesar" seems to me to argue in favor of a distinction between lands that were ceded (thus justifying payments to the treasury by Babatha and Salome Komaise) and imperial estates strictly speaking. However, we must concede that the precise legal status of what we broadly and imprecisely term "imperial estates" could vary with the conditions of inheritance: Rome had to have taken over the rental agreements of tenants that were in force under the Seleucids, the Nabataeans, or the Hasmonaeans, and these were not necessarily the same everywhere.

In the Middle Euphrates region in 245,[29] an "imperial village of Beth Phouraia, attached to Appadana," is again mentioned, but it is unclear whether the village was acquired through inheritance from earlier kingdoms or in some other way later on. We should also reconsider the status of everything that may have been acquired by the emperors when the tetrarchies of central Syria, the states of Emesa and Commagene, and various Lebanese principalities were suppressed. Regarding the latter, Jean-Paul Rey-Coquais estimates that some portions must have been transformed into imperial estates and that other portions were distributed to cities in the region. That would explain why the territory of Caesarea-Arca in Lebanon (which was a client state) was splintered by imperial estates even though it extended quite far south; thus Qal'at Faqra, which belonged to

Agrippa II, would have been within an imperial property.[30] Finally, there must have been some later acquisitions, because we know that after Avidius Cassius seized power in 175, his estates in Cyrrhestica were confiscated and added to the patrimonium; according to Theodoretos, a native of the region, Avidius Cassius had owned more than one-sixth of the territory of Cyrrhos.[31]

In light of recent discoveries in Sanamein-Aire, we cannot completely overlook later references in which a saltus is mentioned. A *saltus hieratikon* was found in Third Palestine,[32] although we do not know exactly where, but we may note that its name comes immediately after a settlement called Metrokomia.[33] There are indications of a *saltus geraitikon* in the vicinity of Gaza.[34] A survey of the geographical lists established in the ninth century by George of Cyprus still refers to a saltus in coastal Phoenicia, north of Balanea-Banyas,[35] and another in the Lebanese part of Phoenicia between Palmyra and Salaminias.[36] In all these cases, however, it is impossible to fix the date of founding. Perhaps we shall need to go still further and find traces of imperial lands in references to a *klima* (domain) or a *regio*, two terms that seem to be synonymous. In this regard, there are such references in First Palestine in the Jordan Valley (Jericho) and on the western boundary of the Transjordan plateau (Livias, Gadara),[37] but also north of the Damascene in Iabroud and Ma'lula,[38] possibly in northwestern Palmyrene if the *klima anatolikon* has to be situated in Jebel Bilas.[39]

However, all of this is still very poorly understood insofar as we are unable to determine either the extent of the imperial holdings or, in most cases, their chronology.[40] The political history of the region certainly gives a priori support to the hypothesis of the early founding of a large imperial estate, if the creation of such estates came soon after the confiscation of client states. But the evidence comes later (not before Hadrian, often in the third or even the fourth century) and we should refrain from drawing conclusions. Let us recall that when Vespasian confiscated Judaea after the revolt of 70, he did not create a single huge imperial domain but instead settled veterans there and resold the land to private interests. Similarly, we cannot assert that the properties confiscated by Hadrian after the Bar Kokhba revolt were set up as imperial estates.[41]

Sacred Property

Roman Syria has not yielded a single example of vast properties belonging to a sanctuary comparable to what has been found in Asia Minor or in Anatolia; still, we cannot rule out the possibility that such properties existed. During the Hellenistic period, the sanctuary of Atargatis of Bambyke probably possessed extensive holdings that were secularized when the priestly state was transformed into a city. On the northern coast of Phoenicia, the sanctuary of Zeus in Baitokaike had some rights over the village, but we do not know which ones.[42] Georges Tchalenko assumes that the villages of the Limestone Massif belonged to a neighboring sanctuary,[43] but the documents show only that some village sanctuaries in northern Syria owned property and, as a result, acted as centers of economic development. One cannot assume that an entire village belonged to them—that these were, properly speaking, "sacred" villages—although there may have been one or two exceptions (Khirbet Sheikh Barakat, Kafr Nabu).[44] Generally speaking, the sanctuaries must have possessed some property, because we frequently find references to their treasuries, or to the god's treasury.[45] Unless we are willing to say that these are the same as the village assets (which would not change the nature of the problem), we should assume that most of the sanctuaries were also property owners.

Some sanctuaries may even have had their own dependent farmers, if the term *hierodouloi*, which we encounter occasionally (in Anatolia, for example), refers to a peasant who works the sanctuary's lands or who lives on land controlled by the cult; an example has recently been discovered in the Trachonitis[46] and another has been attested in Sia.[47] However, the term may designate other categories of people consecrated to the god; it may have no connection to land use.

Private Property

Seuleucid colonial foundations involved a huge transfer of property to Greeks and Macedonians and a new system of land tenure, according to Hellenistic cadastres from Laodicea, Antioch, Damascus, Emesa, and Aleppo.[48] Under the early empire, indigenous Hellenes joined forces with former colonists; as a result, most civic leaders continued to be landowners. Moreover, the known centuriation (division of a territory into regular parcels for distribution to colonists—probably dating from Augustus's reign) of part of the territory of Damascus[49] and of Emesa (possibly somewhat later)[50] corresponds to a reorganization of land tenure that may have followed the installation of new owners. Were these veterans? Were they given colonial-style allotments without a colony, following a model familiar in Asia Minor?[51] For now, we cannot say. Other traces of cadastres have been recovered around Antioch,[52] Laodicea,[53] and Canatha,[54] in the region east and north of Bostra,[55] near Salkhad and Imtan farther east,[56] and across the Syro-Jordanian frontier near Umm el-Quttein.[57] Similar quartering appears on old aerial photos near the Dead Sea, at at-Telah (formerly

Toloha).[58] Installation of veterans as colonists in Samaria, Gaba, and Bathyra by Herod and at Emmaus by Vespasian must have led to a considerable amount of land redistribution in those areas as well, even though we have as yet no on-site evidence of this. For now, we have two models, one very well documented in the Occident of twenty *actus,* or about 700 meters, on a side (in Emesa, Damascus, Laodicea), and the other, less common but also well documented in the Occident, of fifteen actus, about 530 meters, in Bostra.

Apart from the urban territories, two notable sectors have been studied in depth: the Limestone Massif in northern Syria[59] and the Hauran in southern Syria;[60] however, the knowledge gained from them should not be indiscriminately applied to all of Syria. Numerous discoveries made in Palestine over the last thirty years have also provided good information about rural habitation and agricultural practices.

Tchalenko believes that the Limestone Massif was abandoned at the end of the Hellenistic era. In his view, only poor villages practicing subsistence farming of grains might have survived. Thus, for him the Roman conquest brought two innovations: the cultivation of olives and the emergence of large estates that would not be broken up before the fourth century. The large landowners presumably received uncultivated imperial holdings (inherited from the royal Seleucid lands) and put the villagers to work as laborers, even though the peasantry continued to hold on to its old lands. Thus the landowners' income was based on forced labor, and the cultivation of olives was the preserve of the very rich, those who could afford to wait five to seven years for their first harvest. However, this situation would not necessarily have led to the kind of tense social relations that are thought to have resulted in Cilicia.

Tchalenko bases his hypothesis on the presence of beautiful village homes, sometimes clustered together, that existed alongside modest houses of an older type. A "large estate" of this sort would have been on an entirely different scale from the Italian *latifundia,* because in the first to third centuries the density of prosperous village houses did not allow for very extensive land holdings. However, as Tchalenko sees it, the village as a whole constituted an agricultural unit, organized around the villa of a wealthy landowner.

This view has been seriously challenged on a number of critical points.[61] In the second century, to be sure, we begin to see architectural funeral monuments linked to the wealthy, "Romanized" village leaders, and the fine homes Tchalenko described are still clearly evident. "Large" (wealthy) landowners lived in the village, were buried there, established foundations there, and made offerings in local sanctuaries. We know that some of them were Roman citizens, but were they veterans, or former officials installed by Rome, as Tchalenko suggests? Some appear to have been foreigners, and veterans were numerous, but there undoubtedly were prosperous indigenous landowners as well. Olive cultivation was still problematic during this time, and olives certainly did not constitute a monoculture.[62] Significant traces of surveying *(scamnatio-strigatio)* found in the region[63] make it clear that the Roman presence coincided with the flourishing of that sector; however, we do not know the precise period to assign to each operation because this type of field, in narrow strips up to 3.5 kilometers long and just a few meters wide, is foreign to the Roman tradition and cannot be dated. It seems inevitable that some agrarian reforms were introduced as early as the Pompeian and Augustan eras, but others must go back to the Flavians, to the first Antonini, and then to the Severi.[64] One cannot help thinking that Hadrian's agrarian policy *(lex Hadriana de rudibus agris)* would have suited this area well and may have been preceded here, as it was in Africa, by local regulations such as the *lex Manciana.* This implies that agricultural development of the Massif is not perceptible before the second century (which matches the archaeological record) and that it coincided with the significant population increase that has been observed throughout the region between the first century and the middle of the third.[65] Hence, it was only owing to the pressure of a rapidly growing population that this heavy soil, in an area difficult to access through mountainous terrain, began to be cultivated, once all the fertile plains of the interior were settled. In any case, we may note that numerous landowners living there as early as Hadrian's reign had Roman names, although they were not Romanized natives, for there were some families with names (such as *Gaius Marius*) that were unknown in other parts of Syria.[66] They must have been colonists who had come from elsewhere, from other regions of Syria or even from the west; they must have settled there under favorable conditions, for they quickly became part of the governing class, if we are to judge by the quality of their tombs and the size of their donations to nearby sanctuaries.

In southern Syria, city leaders who were substantial property owners maintained close ties to their native villages, where they tended to live (as evidenced by the presence of family tombs and sanctuary gifts). These leaders, many of whom were veterans, seem to have been mostly native born, which rules out a large-scale settlement of colonists from abroad. However, we shall have to wait for a systematic study of fossil traces of cadastres to determine the scope and dates of property redistributions that occurred between the end of the Hellenistic era and the early empire. Projects currently under way reveal the existence of regular, traditional Roman cadastres, not only in the Bostra plain (where at least one of them, consisting of square plots measuring 705 meters on a side, is from the Roman period)[67] but also in the more mountainous zones of the west side of Jebel Druze, around Canatha, and around Dionysias.[68]

Yet closer observation reveals important differences between the plain of Bostra and the Leja-Jebel Druze sector, both in village structure[69] and in funeral customs,[70] from which we could legitimately deduce differences in the system of land tenure. In the mountains and on the Trachonitis plateau there were autonomous villages possessing institutions more or less modeled on those of cities, which suggests the existence of a village community formed of fairly prosperous small and medium landowners, who are reflected in their well-built and sometimes very large homes, clustered in villages. We also find numerous family tombs, built by several members of the same family. In contrast, on the Bostra plain, village institutions are nowhere to be found, suggesting some degree of dependence on the city or on a major landowner; the villages appear to have sprung up around one or two large houses, which would make sense if we were to find that the plain was divided, no earlier than the second century, between large estates granted to foreigners (hence the signs of centuriation discovered in the plain of Bostra) who took advantage of a dependent village population. The necropolises include many small individual tombs, recognizable from steles, whereas we find only a few isolated large tombs, belonging to a single landowner.

This general impression needs to be further verified, however, chiefly through better knowledge of the chronology. A comparison of village structures (whether or not there was a large tenant farm)[71] and close analysis of village houses[72] and of the way the land was laid out would provide specific details and above all could establish the chronology of the changes that took place over time.

We are less well informed about other regions of Syria, and for some we have no information at all. However, details provided in the New Testament and the Talmuds, along with recent archaeological discoveries, shed some light on Palestine, at least.[73] The Evangelists acknowledge the growing importance in first-century Palestine of large landowners who hired permanent or temporary salaried laborers;[74] this practice inevitably betrays a decline in traditional small properties. Three prominent merchants of Jerusalem—Nakdimon bar Gurion, Kalba Sabbua, and Ben Zizit Hakeset—are said to have been capable of supplying the city for ten years: this may be explained, at least partially, by surpluses that had accumulated in the granaries of their estates.[75] The size of the fields of small landowners, when we know enough to assess them, seems quite modest: in Samaria, only about 2.5 hectares.[76] In comparison, the new pagan colonists—such as the veterans of Herod's armies (in Gaba, Samaria, and Idumaea), or colonists of any sort in search of land—seem to have been quite well off. It would be interesting to know how lands were allocated to the Herodian colonists from southern Syria (Bathyra, Danaba, and Saura) and to the residents of new cities like Neapolis of Samaria or Caesarea. The former group unquestionably included cleruchs, settled upon lands that may have belonged to the Herodians; at least this is one of the conclusions that may be drawn from the fact that imperial holdings were found in their states after annexation. A few of these military colonists from Batanaea appear to have founded new villages, whereas others settled in existing villages. Thus Josephus remarks that Babylonian Jews led by Zamaris inhabited a spot called "Ecbatana," a name that may indicate that they came from Media rather than Babylonia, assuming the name was not a corruption.[77] By contrast, Greek colonists lived in the village of Danaba, an indigenous name, which rules out a foundation ex nihilo for their benefit alone.[78]

The foundation of colonies with deductio in the first century would have entailed some land redistribution, because settlement of colonists was always carried out at the expense of the previous inhabitants. Few such modifications have been identified. In Ptolemais, however, one inscription mentions the village of Nea Kome, which may have been newly created for dispossessed natives,[79] and a subdivision marker[80] may have been found from a centuriation that appears to have been limited to the coastal plain north and south of the city. In any case, the foundation of a colony did not entail centuriation of the entire colonial territory, but only of zones close to the urban center where colonists were granted lots.[81] On-site research remains to be done in Berytos as well as in Aelia Capitolina, insofar as the excessive contemporary development in these two sectors permits; such research should be possible in the Beqaa plain around Heliopolis-Baalbek.

Land Use and Labor

There is almost no information on the way land was used in Roman Syria, outside of Palestine. The rich epigraphical records of rural northern Syria, the Emesa region, or southern Syria are often from later periods, and they tell us essentially nothing on this subject. As we have seen, the records include a few references to hierodouloi, who may have been peasants attached to cult land; we do not know for sure. Slaves are almost entirely absent from the epigraphy, of course, although this does not mean that they were absent from everyday life; for instance, rabbis addressed the case of a Jew who bought an estate with non-Jewish slaves working on it.[82] A few documents granting freedom confirm the existence of slaves, but were there many in the countryside? To believe the descriptions found in the

Talmuds, almost all wealthy landowners possessed at least a few, but this does not mean that cultivation of land depended fundamentally on slave labor.

Only in Palestine can the situation be analyzed in detail, owing to the records of the Evangelists and especially the Talmuds. The Gospels have sometimes been overinterpreted in order to demonstrate the existence of a bloc of seasonal or year-round agricultural workers, hired for a specific job.[83] The Talmuds paint a more subtle picture: they reveal several categories of landholders, with a varied nomenclature that probably corresponds to differences in status. *'Aris* appeared in the second century; they were tenant farmers who owed a portion of the harvest—usually half—to the landlord. They were typically bound by a short-term contract (one or two years), although some may have been permanent tenants whose heirs inherited their right to keep the position. Some may have been former landowners dispossessed for various reasons (including the wars of 66–70 and 132–135) and kept on their old lands, but as tenant farmers of the new owners. The *hokher* differed only in that he paid a fixed rate, not a percentage. The *sokher* rented property, paying a fixed price, for a short term. The *shattal* was hired specifically to prepare abandoned land for cultivation; he gave the landowner half the harvest, but when he left he also recovered half the value added to the land by his labor. The *sakhir* was a hired hand who received room and board and was paid only when he left his employer; the length of employment varied from one week to seven years, but the average seems to have been about three years. Finally, the *po'el*, who also received room and board, was a common day laborer, hired for a specific job when it was time to harvest grains, olives, or other crops.[84]

It is much more difficult to assess the situation in other parts of Syria. A tenant-farming contract originating in the Middle Euphrates in 242 B.C.E. shows that one could rent unseeded land plus farm buildings for one year, with the tenant obliged to pay all taxes; the landowner received a quarter of the harvest. Although such a contract seems restrictive, there is no indication that the terms were not extended from one year to the next.[85] More examples must be found before we can make any generalizations about conditions of land use in Roman Syria.

AGRICULTURAL PRACTICES AND PRODUCTION

The Issue of Water

Much of Syria, about two-fifths of the country, enjoys sufficient rainfall to permit a good yield from non-irrigated crops.[86] This is the case for the entire Mediterranean coast, especially the coastal plain and the mountains immediately to the east. The arable zone extends even farther east (to Jezireh and the Hauran) where the mountains are low, as in Palestine or in northern Syria, and rain clouds can cross them. However, non-irrigated agriculture soon reaches its limit: the Euphrates Valley, the eastern side of the Anti-Lebanon, and the Transjordan plateaus shift from one category to another, depending on annual rainfall. Other regions as well, such as the environs of Petra, the lands bordering the Dead Sea, the Negev, the Jordan Valley, and Palmyra, cannot be productive without constant irrigation.

Signs of hydrological works have been found in several regions, but dating them has proved very difficult.[87] In both the Limestone Massif and the Hauran, numerous cisterns, dug out of rock or constructed, are found in villages and cities alike (Bostra had two enormous ones that unfortunately have not been properly dated);[88] during winter, when rain and snow fell in abundance, the cisterns stored enough water for the long dry season from the end of April to the beginning of November, a period with no rainfall. It does not appear that these cisterns supplied an irrigation system, however: they were intended for human and animal use, not for crops. Similarly, storage basins and aqueducts found around Canatha and in Suweida, Berytos, Apamaea, Bostra, and Philippopolis were intended to provide water to the cities, not to irrigate fields. In Petra, a six-kilometer canal that brought water from the spring at ʿAyn Musa to the city was intended for use by the inhabitants, not for agriculture.[89] However, even the cities engaged in some rural activities that required water, whether for gardens, groves, or livestock. Thus we cannot say for certain that some part of the water collected in cities, especially in cisterns, was not used for agriculture. Moreover, with later improvements, some of the water brought to the cisterns by canals and aqueducts could be diverted along the way to irrigate fields. Even in a sector that could forego irrigation a priori, we sometimes see village fields that combined dry and irrigated agriculture, as Frank Braemer has found at Umm az-Zeitun, Breikeh, in the vicinity of Qanawat and near Bostra.[90] Similarly, in Samaria, rainwater collected in cisterns was used to irrigate groves and gardens.[91]

Still, agricultural irrigation is documented only in the large valleys and in oases. In the Euphrates and Orontes valleys, water was simply drawn from the river by means of a *chadouf* (an instrument for drawing water) or, as in Egypt, an Archimedes' screw, a technology that was not widespread before the imperial era.[92] In the Damascus oasis, a complex system of channels from the Chrysorrhoas (Barada) before it left the last buttresses of the Anti-Lebanon made it possible to distribute water over a vast area; some of the water was collected at different altitudes, providing water at varying distances within the oasis. By contrast, in Jericho the Hasmonaeans (and later the Herodians) collected water from several sources in the mountains to the north ('Ayn Auga) and east to irrigate the palm groves and royal gardens around their palaces.[93] In Palmyra, the canal system that distributed water in the oasis was covered, like the *foggara* or *qanat* systems of underground channels, but it is difficult to date it despite popular references to *qanawat romani*.[94] Even more complex arrangements have been found in the Negev. In their very arid environment, the Nabataeans had perfected a system of dams and small dikes that enabled them to collect rainwater over several hundred hectares in order to irrigate a portion of the land. This system was still in use in the imperial era, but its effectiveness was limited because rain was intermittent, and in its absence no cultivation was possible.[95] These systems were actually suited to small rural communities like the one that has been studied at Humaymah, the former Auara, northwest of Hisma. Founded by Aretas III,[96] it was situated in a very harsh, almost desert-like environment. Two cisterns have been discovered there, fed by a small aqueduct (with a flow of 150 cubic meters per day); these cisterns were initially uncovered, which must have resulted in huge losses through evaporation. John Peter Oleson estimates that there would have been enough water for 250 people, or 100 people plus eleven hundred goats, an estimate supported by the presence of some thirty houses at most. It was probably not long before cisterns were supplied with arched covers, following a design borrowed from the Greco-Roman world. Moreover, some of the water was used for irrigation, as there were fields of grain around the village,[97] but it is likely that there was no planting during years of low rainfall, whereas in a rainy year even the bottom of the wadi could be cultivated without irrigation, as is still the case today in the desert between Palmyra and Dura-Europos.

Irregular rainfall is a general problem throughout the region. Coastal Syria is somewhat protected from extreme variations, but the rest of the interior of Syria pays dearly when precipitation drops. For the most part, annual precipitation is two hundred to five hundred millimeters, but there are huge variations from one year to the next. We know that there were some years when rainfall was less than half or even a quarter of the ten-year average;[98] when that low level of precipitation continued over several years, villages on the edge of the desert were abandoned. Thus we have been able to identify cycles of long periods of habitation followed by abandonment across vast regions, including the Edom and Moab plateaus, the Hauran, and the Limestone Massif. However, there are two important points to keep in mind. First, these long cycles are not easy to identify during the three centuries covered by this study, although over the long term it would probably be possible to verify an increasing rural population in Syria, with the creation of villages extending even into lands that were a priori not conducive to agriculture. In addition, it would be foolish to analyze these cycles simply as a function of hydrology: it is clear that demographic issues are just as important, and that the constant pressure of population growth observed in the following period accounts for the gradual conquest of the lands on the edge of the steppes.

Cultivation Cycles and Yields

In Syria, as elsewhere in the Mediterranean world, agriculture depended upon a biennial crop rotation that compensated for the shortage of fertilizer, although on the local level animal herds could provide some resources in this respect. As for crops, here as elsewhere we find the well-known trio of grains, olives, and grapes. There is even a reference in the Talmud to a fortunate man who had divided his land into three parts: one-third grains, one-third olives, and one-third vines.[99]

As a staple of the diet, grains were grown everywhere: bread soaked in olive oil or accompanied by vegetables, plus figs, constituted the normal diet for a great many people. Successful farmers were honored in Syria as they were everywhere (L. Iulius Agrippa in Apamaea),[100] which tells us that supplying the cities with grain was as constant a preoccupation, and just as difficult, as anywhere else. Wheat and barley were the principal crops, but the Talmud identifies eight different kinds of grain,[101] and these were probably not limited to Judaea. On the whole, all parts of Syria were suitable for growing grain, even such semi-arid zones as Humaymah or the Palmyra area. Although one-half to two-thirds of the arable land everywhere was devoted to grains and accompanying legumes (lentils, chickpeas, and fava beans),[102] the ideal of self-sufficiency was never achieved, for at least two reasons: one was the irregular climate referred to above that could lead to the loss of crops, and the other was the development of more speculative crops like grapes and olives. In addition, in Palestine there was the obligatory sabbatical period that called for leaving a large part of the fields fallow every seven years.

Treatises in the Talmud testify to the need for interregional trade, given these conditions, but it is difficult to measure the extent of such exchanges. Highly regarded grain markets existed in Beth Shean and Sepphoris in Palestine, as well as in Susita in the Golan, where wheat from the Hauran was sold.[103] There must have been imports from Egypt at times,[104] and we know that rabbis traveled from Tiberias to purchase wheat at Iamnia at the beginning of the third century.[105] Is Daniel Sperber correct in his hypothesis that there was a general decline in agriculture in Palestine between 235 and

284[106] that might explain the frequent trips to markets? Perhaps not, since the sources he cites are sometimes ambiguous and seem to me to arise from generalizations about "the good old days" or to reflect speculative rabbinical hypotheses. Even if Sperber is right about Palestine, the claim cannot be extended to all of Syria, which seems to have enjoyed sustained growth in agriculture in the second to sixth centuries, based on the duration of building activity in villages.[107]

I hesitate to claim, on the basis of the few references to shortages or food crises, that Syria achieved a balance between supply and demand more often than other provinces; there is far too little documentation from Syria to permit as detailed an analysis of the situation as in Asia Minor. We know of one famine during Herod's reign;[108] it affected not only Herod's kingdom but also neighboring Syria.[109] We also know that, under Claudius, Queen Helena of Adiabene contributed to the purchase of wheat from Egypt during a period of scarcity.[110] But there is no indication of other local or general crises. In any case, production must barely have surpassed needs, and there is no mention of wheat being exported to other provinces, although we cannot rule out the possibility.[111] During times of famine, grains were probably replaced by legumes, especially lentils, which were widely grown, and possibly rice, which is mentioned for the first time in Palestine between 90 and 132. The precise origin of the rice is not certain; it may have come from the plain of Antioch rather than the region of Lake Houleh in Upper Galilee.[112]

Olive production is usually thought to have originated in the Roman era. This speculative crop was initially intended for Syrian city markets, and there is little evidence that it was exported abroad.[113] Olive production accounts for the exploitation of an arid mountain where grains were unprofitable. However, olive groves could be found everywhere throughout Mediterranean Syria and even beyond, in areas like Khirbet Dharih in the Nabataea,[114] because with the gradual acculturation of the native populations, the use of olive oil increased and the demand for it grew. Indeed, almost every farm that has been excavated in Palestine has yielded an olive press, and Tchalenko notes that there were countless oil presses in Northern Syria, often dozens in a single village.[115] Josephus relates an anecdote that provides interesting information about olive production and trade. He accuses his adversary John of Gischala of having made a fortune trading in olive oil. John is thought to have made his money thanks to Gischala's location in the interior of Galilee and Syria—in other words, at the frontier between Eretz Israel (an area whose products had a reputation for purity) and the pagan countries. He took advantage of an excellent harvest in Galilee to trade on the border and resold the surplus at eight or ten times the purchase price to Jews in Syria and Palestine, who were thus able to purchase oil produced by other Jews.[116] We can learn a great deal from this anecdote. First, we learn that Jews in Syria and Palestine were large consumers of olive oil, and they spared no expense to procure oil of a particular quality (in their case, for religious reasons). We also learn that it was a product that must not have been exported very widely, which probably explains why prices varied greatly from place to place. Lastly, we learn that the olive oil yield in Galilee surpassed the needs of the local population, and it was therefore produced primarily on speculation. The yields calculated by Ze'ev Safrai confirm this, and show that, with the possible exception of Judaea, the olive crop—consumed for the most part as oil—far surpassed the needs of the producers. It assured them a cash income that allowed them to buy part of their food as well as numerous items crafted elsewhere, and also to improve their own lands.[117]

Olives were clearly one of the sources of wealth for landowners, in Galilee or in Samaria as well as in northern Syria, and one of the crops that lead us to say that the rural economy in Syria, far from being closed, in fact belonged to an open economy based on trade with markets both near and far. The fiscal equivalence established during Diocletian's time between properties of different sizes is eloquent testimony to the high profitability of fields planted in olives, even in mountainous regions. The *jugum* was a fiscal unit that was worth about 5 hectares of good tillable land, 10 hectares of moderately good land, and 15 hectares of arable land of poor quality; it was worth 5 hectares of land planted in vines, or 220 productive olive trees in the plain, or 450 olive trees in the mountains. Because about 200 olive trees were planted per hectare, that meant that 1.1 hectares of olive trees equaled 1.25 hectares of vines or 5 hectares of very good wheat fields; even in the dry mountain regions, 2.25 hectares of pressed olives equaled 15 hectares of arable land in the same region, or 5 hectares in a well-watered plain.[118]

The same holds true for the grapevines that were widely cultivated during the Hellenistic period. The consumption of wine was low among indigenous peoples and the poor, and Safrai has calculated that an area of two hundred square kilometers planted in vines would have met local demand.[119] However, vineyards covered a much larger area. It has been estimated that, on two farms in Samaria, 20 to 22 percent of the land was planted in vines.[120] Obviously, not every region offered equally favorable conditions, but we know that grapes were grown throughout Judaea, around Lydda, on the Shephelah plain, and in the area around Carmel, whose vintages, like those of the plains of Sharon and Ammon, were especially well known.[121] The toponymy has occasionally preserved traces of these products, as in the village called Chalybon, meaning "vineyards," around Damascus, where grapevines seem to have been cultivated well before Alexander's conquest.[122] Thus vines were widely grown in the Damascene and the Anti-Lebanon (the Talmud mentions wine from Baalbek),[123] and judging from frequent uses of the twisting-vine theme and especially from the discovery of grape presses such as those in the plain of Sia above Canatha,[124] vines were presumably grown in Jebel Druze as well. In the Golan, in contrast, grape growing was only a marginal activity, either because the product was mediocre or because the cultivation of olives was so much more profitable.[125] On the coast, the vineyard of Laodicea on the Sea produced famous wines that were exported to the entire Mediterranean world, and we know that at a later date (from the sixth to the early seventh century) the wines of the Hauran were exported to the Arabian Peninsula;[126] we cannot rule out the possibility that the phenomenon began much earlier, given that other cases of distant exports—to India and Ceylon—have been documented. In northern Syria, grapevines were less developed than olive groves, and they were confined to the eastern zone of the Limestone Massif.[127]

Alongside these traditional pillars of Mediterranean agriculture—grains, olives, and grapes—livestock breeding seems to have been another sector that was well suited to Syria. We can assume that raising sheep and goats, both traditional in Mediterranean cultures, was also quite common, and shepherds are frequently mentioned in the New Testament and elsewhere. Nomads bred not only horses and smaller animals but also camels. Recent exploration has revealed that sedentary peoples in the Hauran and the Golan frequently raised large animals (horses and cattle).[128] Many rural houses included a stable on the ground floor equipped with individual mangers placed too high to have been meant for sheep or goats.[129] Raising livestock in a semi-arid land was no mean task. Similar observations have been made in the Golan, where extensive livestock farming seems to have developed in the third century.[130]

What we have seen so far constitutes only the most immediately obvious aspects of Syrian agricultural output, those that ensured the subsistence of the bulk of the rural population. However, a number of other crops, often limited to a particular region of the country, contributed to the country's wealth and to its trade with others. Food crops included figs (grown everywhere) and dates (grown along the Dead Sea and in the Palmyra region), which were a welcome addition to the diet.[131] Certain fruits and vegetables were especially appreciated, such as pistachio nuts,[132] Damascus plums,[133] and the interesting little onions from Ascalon that we call shallots, after their place of origin.[134] Besides rice, a few new products were apparently introduced during the Roman era, possibly including peaches and apricots, which migrated from the Orient to Greece and then to Rome during the Hellenistic period and were introduced into Syria under the early empire; similarly, around the beginning of the second century, cotton and woad (the source of a blue dye) appear in rabbinic texts for the first time.[135] In addition, Syria furnished a number of products used in manufacturing cosmetics, perfumes, and medicines. Pliny gives us an impressive list of these products—some of them appear to be unique to Syria, while those produced in Syria were of especially high quality. Some of Pliny's items should clearly be removed from the list, because even though Romans could buy them in Syrian markets they could not have been grown in Syria.[136] Nevertheless, a large number of products did come from Syria, including balsam from Jericho,[137] styrax from the vicinity of Arados and inland Laodicea,[138] ladanum from the Nabataean countries,[139] myrobalanum (behen-nut) from the Sinai and from Arabia Petraea,[140] scented reeds from Lebanon,[141] cyprus henna from Ascalon,[142] galbanum from Mount Amanus,[143] male sumac (used in pharmaceuticals),[144] and possibly also panax, or all-heal,[145] malobathrum,[146] extracted from a variety of palm used in perfumes,[147] and Arabian crocus.[148] A cosmetics and pharmaceuticals factory has been located in En Boqeq, twenty-five kilometers from En Geddi, on the west bank of the Dead Sea, near a fort that was first Nabataean and then Roman. Destroyed during the great uprising of 66–73 and later reoccupied, it clearly benefited from the variety of essences produced in the region and from the minerals of the Dead Sea.[149] Papyrus was grown in the Jordan Valley, but its production was still very limited.[150] Although the variety of products and their quality are not at issue, it is difficult to measure the importance of this output in economic terms. In some cases, all the profits went into the treasury, as with balsa wood and forestry products from Mount Lebanon. In other cases, independent producers must have increased their income by means of these products. As I see it, the only firm conclusion to be drawn from all of this is the close connection between the rural economy of Roman Syria and the flow of trade both inside and outside the empire.

VILLAGES AND VILLAGE COMMUNITIES

Greater Syria is rich in documentation, both archaeological and epigraphical, about its rural sectors. Drawing on this information, it is possible to draw a picture of Syrian villages: their layout, their architecture, and their institutions. Still, here more than elsewhere, it is important to avoid extrapolation and to remain mindful of both the dates and the geographical sources of our information.

Rural Houses

A lively debate has taken place for some time among archaeologists of rural life, especially in Palestine, over the status of the *villa* (rural estate) in the Roman Near East.[151] It could well seem surprising that this model, so frequently encountered and so characteristic of the countryside of the Roman west, has not been encountered in the provinces of the eastern Mediterranean. In reality, it is all a matter of definition, and scholars have sometimes been a little too quick to put farms and villas into a single category. If we reserve the term *villa* to designate rather luxurious dwellings, furnished in the Roman style, accompanied by separate but linked agricultural buildings, it is true that there are almost no examples of villas in Syria. It is too early to set forth a typology of rural houses, especially those from the first to third centuries, but several examples are well enough known for purposes of comparison.

The first thing that can be said is that individual farms existed in Palestine, at least from the end of the Hellenistic era and throughout the entire period preceding the Jewish War.[152] For instance, we note that a Hellenistic farm at Umm Rihan (Qsar e-Lejja) in northwestern Samaria seems to conform to older examples of farms, with agricultural buildings arranged around an open courtyard and the house located in a tower on the edge of the cluster; it appears to have been occupied without interruption from the third century B.C.E. to the revolt of 70 C.E., but it may have been built as early as the Persian period.[153] The farm at Tirat Yehuda, near Lydda, also from the Achaeminid era, shows a similar layout.[154] Another farm excavated about five kilometers northeast of Caesarea, in use between 50 B.C.E. and the revolt of 70 C.E., has several features in common with the preceding examples: a tower refuge, scattered agricultural buildings (a stable and a granary), olive and wine presses, a cistern, a dwelling equipped with a ritual bath *(miqveh)*, with all of these spread about in a disorganized way; the cluster is surrounded by a wall in the form of an L enclosing an area of twenty-eight hundred square meters, which attests to an increased sense of danger.[155] This was a village in itself, belonging to a prosperous Jewish family. The farm of Qalandiya, north of Jerusalem, occupied from the second century B.C.E. to around 70 C.E., follows the same pattern.[156]

Gradually, however, some improvements borrowed from Roman traditions began to appear. For example, on the Khirbet Muraq farm southeast of Judaea, which belonged to a Jewish family, the house has a colonnade on its façade.[157] Another Roman characteristic seems to be the appearance of a rectilinear arrangement of the buildings; this appears in the Umm Dimineh farm, near Hebron, which was occupied after 70 and until the middle of the fourth century: in keeping with local tradition, the dwelling and the farm buildings are clustered around a single courtyard, but the building techniques and the rectilinear plan are Roman. The same characteristics are found not far away at Khirbet al-Mutiyaneh, and they are similar enough to suggest a concerted effort at colonization following the Jewish War.[158] Only the presence of ritual baths *(miqva'ot)* indicates that the house belonged to a Jewish or Samaritan family.[159]

There may be one example of a true villa at Ramat Rahel, a vast rural dwelling in use in the second to fourth centuries, with a courtyard and peristyle in the style of urban houses, and connected to baths, one of the luxurious features that we expect to find in such a residence.[160] The house at Ein Yael, southwest of Aelia Capitolina on the way to Eleutheropolis, dating from the end of the second century to the middle of the third, is somehow connected with the legion of Aelia (the legion's name is stamped on a number of bricks that have been found there). It combines farm buildings with a luxurious private home possessing the usual amenities: baths and mosaic floors decorated with mythological scenes.[161] In addition, there are villas in the coastal plain, near Eleutheropolis (for example, Maqarqash),[162] and in the hills north of Jerusalem.[163] However, I do not think the details furnished by Shimon Dar for the Khirbet Basatin farmstead in western Samaria suffice to justify categorizing it as a villa.[164]

In northern Syria, rural dwellings were remarkably consistent over at least five centuries, clearly reflecting continuity in the local building style.[165] The central feature is always the courtyard—the only means of communication with the outside and the sole passageway. Does this reflect a concern for security? Possibly, but it more probably reveals a social custom that was intended to protect the privacy of the occupants. In relation to the size of the structure and thus to the wealth of its owners, we begin to see the development of an elongated house at the rear of the courtyard, sometimes preceded by a portico, or we may find the house on one side of the courtyard and the farm buildings on the other, each side covered by a roof with a two-way slope. The styles may vary, the decor may be more or less elaborate, but in all events these houses owed nothing to the influence of urban homes such as the ones found in Antioch or Apamaea. Tchalenko believes that this style represents the development of an old local model during the imperial and Byzantine periods.[166]

As a general rule, houses were modest in size, not at all like the expansive villas in Gaul, Britain, or Germany. Landowners usually lived in town, and only managers, whether free or slave, resided permanently on the land. This was the case with the rich rabbis who lived in Lydda, Iamnia, and Tiberias, and who owned one or more farms in the surrounding countryside.[167] Similarly, in a remote house at Bamuqqa in the Limestone Massif, which Tchalenko dates from the first century C.E., we see a sharp contrast between the high quality of its construction and décor, on the one hand, and its relatively small size, on the other. It is difficult to imagine a landowner living there permanently; it was more likely meant for short stays or possibly for the manager's use.[168]

Moreover, it is probably not by accident that researchers have frequently come across this type of isolated house in the Judaean hills, in Samaria (notably around Lydda), and on the coastal plain of the Shephelah, but almost never in Galilee, and rarely on the Golan, where we find a prevalence of villages.[169] Isolated farms also existed in northern Syria (Bamuqqa), but the significant increase in villages during a somewhat later period, in the fourth to seventh centuries, makes it difficult to know whether this was exceptional. In the Hauran, it would be necessary to take a closer look at the large houses that have been identified in a number of villages (Inkhil, Kafr Shams, Najran, Ezr'a, Kerak, and so on), most of which are not dated, in order to find out whether they are only the most visible parts of a village of free peasants or whether the simpler peasant houses found nearby were for their own laborers. The same can be said about Hermon, where the farm of Qal'at Bustra, attached to a temple, may have been the starting point for a hamlet that later became a village.[170]

Rural houses grouped together in a village were not structurally different from isolated houses. A village like Refade, in northern Syria, consisted of some ten very attractive houses that could have been found alone.[171] However, what made it a village was that more modest houses were included, and these have not been studied outside the Hauran. In that region, the base unit was a more or less square, two-story structure, each room of which was divided unevenly by an arch on a low base intended to support the stone ceiling beams—for the lack of trees in the region meant that houses had to be covered with stone slabs, and these slabs, necessarily limited in reach, were supported by brackets projecting from the walls or resting on the middle arch. A stable was often found on the ground floor, with mangers on one or both sides, or occasionally in a U shape around three sides: the family lived on the first floor. An exterior staircase provided access from one floor to the next. When the house was enlarged, similar units were juxtaposed one after another; almost all room-to-room communication came from the outside. Access was sometimes through a courtyard; adjoining houses might belong to different owners.[172]

Village Layouts

It has often been said, quite rightly, that Syrian villages included buildings that we typically expect to find in cities.[173] Excavators have uncovered baths, meeting halls (*androns* in northern Syria), public inns (in Phaina), and communal buildings—sometimes called *kamara* in the Hauran, for these must have been meeting rooms that were open to the outside, each with a vaulted apse, like the *iwan* of a later style. In view of all these elements, one might wonder if there was really any difference between Syrian villages and cities in terms of urban planning; certain publications unfailingly identify as cities what were probably just villages.[174] In fact, it takes only a glance at the way villages and cities were laid out to understand that they had nothing in common. For example, refounded indigenous cities like Bostra or Soada-Dionysias (Suweida) were subject to rational planning that may have taken local tradition into account but was nevertheless aimed at giving urban spaces a pronounced Greco-Roman appearance, including rectilinear streets, many with porticos, and monuments sited along a specific axis.

So far, nothing like this has been found in villages anywhere in Syria. With few exceptions, surveys undertaken at Umm al-Jimal and Sha'arah in southern Syria,[175] at Qatura[176] and Refade[177] in northern Syria, and at Khirbet Shema' and Khirbet Usha in Upper Galilee[178] all show the same type of random organization, without a primary axis orienting traffic. It is as though village street networks were defined as any areas not occupied by private houses, with no authority imposing respect for public space. Even communal buildings, where they existed and have been identified as such, enjoyed no privileged location, no particular prominence. This alone constitutes a radical distinction between villages and cities.

Some villages (in Bostra for example) did serve as real focal points, balancing the influence of the main city: Mothana-Imtan, Umm al-Jimal, and Salkhad were all the size of small cities, and at least some of them functioned like cities. Mothana and Umm al-Jimal contained garrisons. The partially excavated and well-surveyed Umm al-Jimal offers a particularly good example.[179] Here, an indigenous village, which was probably destroyed during the Palmyrene invasion in the third century, was established close to an army base where part of the population must have already settled in order to benefit from the protection of the walls. In fact, fortifications were under construction around this site by 177–180,[180] and the process continued under the Severi, as it did throughout the region.[181] After the destruction of the old village, only the sector around a small fortress remained, and this grew substantially. The resulting village is remarkable for its complete lack of directional axes in the layout and indeed for the absence of any features characteristic of Greco-Roman urban planning. We should doubtless not generalize on the basis of a single example, but for the time being nothing has been found to contradict this pattern in the numerous ancient villages of the region, either in northern Syria or in Palestine, where similar inquiries have been conducted. In Samaria, for example, we have found some villages that are significantly larger than others, for they include a network of hamlets that are linked to the central village but not to one another; these have some communal facilities—such as public cisterns, a surveillance tower, a ritual bath, and even a synagogue—yet their layout appears no more regular than elsewhere.[182]

Even the presence of a rural sanctuary had little effect on village layout. In some cases, social hierarchies may have been the key to the way a village was organized. Tchalenko describes a neighborhood in Qatura consisting of "modest dwellings squeezed against one another at the foot of the hill, built in a small, poorly connected polygonal arrangement, while in other areas, slightly higher up, a group of villas is arranged in a tidy polygonal pattern."[183] These two groupings parallel two types of eternal resting places: stone necropolises decorated with crude reliefs where the deceased had Semitic names, and rich mausoleums placed in much more prominent locations. In Refade, however, almost all the land is taken up by beautiful houses arranged around vast courtyards, and modest housing is tucked in between these islets of opulence.[184] The village of Khirbet an-Najar, in Samaria, enclosed by a wall with four doors, also looks more or less unplanned, but there, too, a house that is clearly more luxurious than the others stands out prominently on the highest point in the village.[185]

The variety of village models is probably an expression of the diversity of social hierarchies themselves, and the ongoing research, which is limited for the time being to a few favored regions, needs to be expanded to include all parts of Syria. The three large regions mentioned above (the Limestone Massif, the Hauran, and Samaria) are evidence enough that there is no single model, even if the regions are found to have certain features in common.

Village Institutions

The continuation of the tetrarchies in the first century shows us that not all Syria was divided into cities, even in the north. Some indigenous communities preserved a village structure that was independent of the neighboring cities. These can be difficult to identify, however, because even villages that had their own magistrates could be subordinate to cities.

We know almost nothing about village institutions in the early empire, apart from southern Syria.[186] Even in that limited region, we should recognize some subtle distinctions. In Jebel Druze and on the Leja, numerous inscriptions, sometimes from the second century and very often from the third and fourth, reveal a vigorous village organization. Every community had its magistrates, whose titles indicated either fiscal or supervisory functions (*pistoi, pronoetai, episkopoi, dioiketai, strategoi*) and who appear to have acted independently of any urban authority. Each village was responsible for its own treasury and sanctuaries, and each added enhancements such as public buildings (a communal house, an inn, baths, a theater, temples) at its own expense or with financial help from benefactors.[187] In contrast, policing fell under the direct control of the Roman administration and not the cities, which seems to confirm that the space under city control in southern Syria was limited, and that village autonomy remained the norm. This has not been conclusively determined, however. Indeed, we know that centurions were assigned to the territorial administration in rural areas that may have been independent of cities, in the Apamene[188] or on the Euphrates,[189] as well as in urban areas such as Bostra.[190] I shall therefore be cautious, particularly when dealing with the territory around Bostra, and note that certain villages possessed very active village institutions, whereas others did not.[191] This did not stop Rome, in the vicinity of either Bostra or Petra, from relying on the previous administrative organization in districts where villages were clustered around a larger town and where there was a resident police officer.[192]

Generally speaking, there seems to have been a territorial organization that varied from one region to the next. In Judaea, the system of toparchies, in evidence before the revolt of 66–70, continued beyond that time. It may have come down from the period of the Ptolemies' domination (judging from the name, which appears nowhere else except in Egypt); the centers of the toparchies functioned in some respects like the metropolises in Egypt, substituting for cities in a world with little urban development.[193] In Arabia, we can make out certain districts inside city territories, around Petra (Maoza, belonging to the Zoarene, which was itself on Petraean land) and Bostra (the village of Azzeiea, in the district of Aianitis, on Bostra's territory).[194]

For want of evidence from the Hellenistic period, we cannot know what part local traditions had in village structures. The institutions known under the empire, whether inherited directly from ancestral structures or modified at the time of annexation, were unquestionably recognized and encouraged by provincial authorities, and they look like ersatz forms of civic institutions. It is difficult to know just what they offered that was of interest to the provincial administration. In an earlier work I suggested that this form of organization in part of the Hauran was both a substitute for and a preliminary stage in actual urbanization.[195] We know that urbanization and Hellenization went hand in hand, the latter giving rise to the former: at least a minimal Hellenization of leaders was essential for the creation of a city. In the Hauran, Hellenization was still quite weak at the beginning of the early empire. Thus it could be argued that, instead of undertaking to "urbanize" prematurely, Rome chose to develop village autonomy as a step on the road to urbanization. A few villages were in fact gradually promoted to city status: Soada became a Dionysias, Shahba a Philippopolis, and Shaqqa a Maximianopolis, to mention only those that have been identified conclusively. Others, honored with the title *metrokomia*, "mother-village," played the role of an urban center for the surrounding villages and occupied a status midway between village and city under the early empire (Phaina and Zorava are examples) before becoming full-fledged cities during the fourth century.[196] But without retracting my earlier explanation, I need to complete the interpretation, because it now appears that the metrokomiai in southern Syria were created as substitutes for cities in a vast imperial domain: this meant that the imperial treasury need not be deprived of the income anticipated from these regions.

This type of organization seems natural for southern Syria, where village communities appear to have been just as vigorous as cities. A similar phenomenon may be discernible in the Golan and in the Anti-Lebanon, but the documentation is far less substantial. In the Mount Hermon region, we see *epimeletes* (officials) serving in Hammarah,[197] and *episkopoi* (overseers) in Segeira;[198] there are references to a village treasury in Hermon and in the Anti-Lebanon.[199] Other references in Syria are much rarer,[200] or difficult to interpret. By contrast, we know of nothing comparable in the Antioch region, in Cyrrhestica, or in Chalcedon before the fourth century: must we assume that we are victims of inadequate documentation? Perhaps, but we cannot be certain. Pierre-Louis Gatier has rightly observed another fundamental difference between northern and southern Syria: whereas village sanctuaries are abundant in the south, as evidenced either by architectural ruins (those of Sleim, 'Atil, Breikeh, Mushennef, Hebran, Rimet Hazem, Dhakir, Mouta'iyyeh, and so on)[201] or by explicit inscriptions, they are extremely rare in the north (Me'ez, and perhaps Brad); several sanctuaries have been found on northern hilltops, but these are of a very different kind, in that they are less specifically connected to a village community. Gatier relates this difference to the existence of powerful collective structures marked by autonomous village institutions in the south but not in the north.[202] It is difficult to draw firm conclusions on this point, but it is certainly one element to add to the account of regional differences in village organizations in Syria.

It is easier to understand the absence of any reference to village magistrates on the Phoenician coast because the cities shared all the land. However, we can expect to find autonomous institutions in Palestine and the Transjordan, wherever cities were scarce. We know about councils of elders in Palestinian villages, and rabbinic texts vouch for the leadership role played within Jewish communities by old or wealthy men (often both) who settled conflicts and verified adherence to the rules (protecting private property, for example, or setting the boundaries of cemeteries). But the key role seems to have involved control of village finances: this was the responsibility of the *parnasim* and the *gabbaim,* who also had the job of administering the funds collected for the poor.[203] The only difference between magistrates in the Jewish communities in Galilee and those in villages in the Hauran is that the authority of the former did not extend beyond the Jewish community, insofar as they followed the principles of the Torah in their administration. Nevertheless, it is not unreasonable to establish a fairly close correspondence between the Hauranese magistrates and their Galilean counterparts.[204]

Whether or not they were self-governing, not all villages were equivalent. As we saw earlier, several communities in the Hauran had been officially designated as "mother-villages" in the early empire. We have to assume that these villages took responsibility for specific tasks such as harboring a garrison or housing imperial officers (in this instance, administrators of imperial lands). This must have meant that these villages had specific economic functions (regular markets, specialized craftsmen, money changers, and so on), and they might even undertake a significant building program: the metrokomia in Zorava financed a public bath during Caracalla's reign,[205] and the one in Phaina provided an inn. The situation is clearer in Galilee, owing to the abundant rabbinic literature that enables us to reconstitute village life. Of course, this literature emphasizes everything that may have been a source of conflict, which explains why there are so many allusions to markets and what they contained. But there can be no doubt that certain villages played a key role as centers of trade and handicrafts.[206]

We know that in Asia Minor the more highly developed villages spared no expense to obtain city status.[207] This was not at all the case in Syria. But this does not mean that no villages were promoted. We can set aside the exceptional case of the Sabaoi village, the birthplace of Philip the Arab, that was made a city and a colony in 244–245. But in the same region, Soada, a village belonging to the territory of Canatha, received a promotion under Commodus (at the latest) and took the name of Dionysias, while the Sakkaioi village in turn became Maximianopolis in 286–287, under circumstances that are unclear. We should add a Constantine, established under the reign of Constantine or his son,[208] at an unknown location, and all of the metrokomiai that became episcopal seats as early as the fourth century. Outside of the Hauran, there was also the town of Appadana, on the Middle Euphrates, promoted to the rank of a Neapolis around 254–255 or slightly earlier.[209] In Palestine, villages that had begun to look like urban centers of some importance obtained this promotion under the Severi: Lydda-Diospolis, Betogabris-Eleutheropolis,[210] Emmaus-Nicopolis. The elevation to city status probably confirmed the economic success of a village.

NOMADS

The ancient sources made little distinction between nomadism and banditry, at the risk of contradicting themselves. Strabo explains that caravans had stopped using the Euphrates Valley because of raiders and preferred to follow a more northerly route equipped with relay points and water supplies;[211] however, the nomads themselves were probably the ones who provided these facilities. While a certain amount of pillaging may have been a source of income for nomadic tribes, it was just as likely to harm other nomads as sedentary peoples, and it was just one aspect of their way of life. The relation among Arabs, nomads, and brigands, whom many classical sources appear to equate, is a topic that deserves to be addressed in a more nuanced fashion.

There is no question that banditry occurred, and it is well attested long after Pompey was supposed to have ended it in several regions, including Arabia, Judaea, and interior Lebanon.[212] However, its precise extent in time and space needs to be analyzed. The fight against it met with some success. Ever since Pompey's time, the Ituraeans in southern Syria and in the Anti-Lebanon had been raiding caravans and holding travelers for ransom, but there are no more references to this practice after Herod's reign. On the whole, despite a few exceptions that do not suffice to support the thesis of a nomad menace,[213] from the middle of the first century nomads no longer constituted a threat to settled populations in Syria and Arabia.[214] Between the Euphrates and the Hejaz, military protection was slight, as if there were nothing to fear in that area: there is no mention of raiding before the middle of the third century.

We can identify at least three main groups among these nomads: Arabs, usually lumped together as "Safaites," roamed between the Damascus region and the northern Transjordan;[215] Nabataeans, most of whom had probably settled down to sedentary lives in the old kingdom of Edom, the Negev, and the Sinai, were both caravan merchants and herders; finally, "Thamudaeans," groups of nomads in the northern Hejaz who left numerous graffiti in alphabets of southern Arabian origin, widely recognized today as different dialects. (The name *Thamudaean* should be dropped without hesitation as entirely unjustified; the only people who called themselves Thamudaeans under the early empire did so while using both the Greek and Nabataean languages.) But this list is hardly exhaustive. At the beginning of the empire, authors such as Strabo and Pliny believed that the border lands of the steppe, extending from the Damascene to the Euphrates, were inhabited by Arab nomads, and there is a good deal of evidence for this at the end of the Hellenistic period. Yet we know almost nothing about the nomadic tribes circulating between central Syria and the Euphrates, who were more or less under the Palmyra's control. In Upper Mesopotamia, nomadic or partially sedentary Arabs occupied the eastern part of the kingdom of Edessa around Sumatar Harabesi,[216] and other groups roamed the area between Hatra and the Anti-Taurus. Let me try to summarize what is known on these various points.

The Tribes of the Harra

It has been customary for a long time to group together under the name *Safaites*[217] the members of a large number of tribes who left several thousand inscriptions on rocks (more than twenty thousand have been catalogued to date) in a large area of the desert called the Harra, from the region around Damascus to the oasis of Dumat al-Jandal, but with the greatest concentration found to the east of Jebel Druze.[218] Their name refers to the Safa, a very small part of this huge area, northeast of Jebel Druze, so the label does not appear to be justified today.[219] These people never called themselves Safaites; rather, they used the names of their various tribes. Nothing demonstrates that the tribes were organized collectively in any way, but they nevertheless shared at least two features of great importance: their lifestyle and their language and writing system. Tribe members spoke (or at least wrote) Arabic, using a writing system derived from southern Arabic alphabets; this leads us to believe that they were more recent arrivals in the area than the Nabataeans. They probably learned to write from southern Arabs in the oasis on the peninsula, but we do not know when or where.[220]

In summer, they pastured their herds on the eastern Jebel Druze or in the

GRAFFITI WITH SAFAITIC INSCRIPTIONS: TWO EXAMPLES FROM THE
FOURTH CENTURY B.C.E.

northeastern steppe region of Jordan,[221] and, Michael C. A. MacDonald's view notwithstanding, I believe that certain groups ultimately settled there.[222] Proof lies in the rare architectural-style inscriptions discovered in the villages, as on the lintel of a tomb at Rushayde (unpublished) and on a few lintels in Umm al-Jimal.[223] After the rains, they pastured their herds of sheep, horses, and, above all, camels[224] on the steppe to the east. In particular, they took advantage of the depressions (*rahaba*, sing. *rihab*) where winter and spring waters collected, forming large lakes in the heart of the desert, as in Ruhbe, the length of the wadi Miqat, near Burku' or around al-'Azraq.[225] Some of these lakes held water all year long, occasionally making it possible to raise cattle.[226] The nomads sold meat in the regional markets and supplied the Roman army with essential pack and saddle animals. The most powerful tribal chiefs were recognized by the Roman authorities as "nomad generals" or "ethnarchs," and they maintained order under the control of Roman officers.[227] A Roman military post controlled Namara in Safa, in the heart of the area the nomads traversed.[228] These Arabs had no organization other than the tribe, a unit that probably consisted of relatively few individuals, for we know that there were a great many different tribes; some ('Awidh, Daif) seem to have been more dominant than others. The inscriptions provide a clear picture of life in the desert: the brawling, the search for water and pasture, the fear of cattle thieves, prayers to the gods to escape animal disease, homesickness, and profound solitude— a condition that the pleasure of finding an older text, written by some known or unknown ancestor, could hardly relieve. For these inscriptions are mindful of genealogy: some list as many as ten generations (and even up to fifteen), doubtless as proof of the nobility of the lineage and the glory of the latest generation.

These texts present a variety of problems, however. For example, they supply almost no chronological markers, because allusions to facts outside the desert world are difficult to interpret. Macdonald has taken research a major step forward, however, by identifying with near certainty allusions to five events that occurred between the first century B.C.E. and the first century C.E.: first, a vague mention of the migration of Jews (exile or deportation) that may have been connected with the revolt of 66; next, three dates noted in turn as "the year Herod died mad" (probably Herod the Great), "the year Caesar's son died, and he heard that Philip had been killed" (a reference to Germanicus and to a rumor about Philip the Tetrarch), and "the year when the people of the Hawran complained to Caesar about Philippus" (a reference either to the tetrarch or to Philip, Zamaris's grandson); finally an invocation of the goddess Lat in a prayer for deliverance from chains of someone who "rebelled against king Agrippa."[229] Another text was dated "the year the troops of Germanicus were at *nq t.*"[230] This conclusively ends the debate over the date of the Safaitic inscriptions, which some scholars have sought to push ahead to the fifth or sixth century. The absence of any Christian symbolism argues against such a theory and in favor of a disappearance of Safaitic inscriptions long before the Islamic conquest in 634. These writings may possibly have spanned several centuries, but probably not more than two or three, for they certainly manifest nothing like the evolution of writing found among, for example, the Nabataeans. And no writing system endures unchanged over a long period of time.

We have very few details regarding the nomads' way of life, and archaeology in this area is in its infancy. The groups I am referring to here were true nomads who lived chiefly in the desert, not migrant peoples, as I was once inclined to view them as being. We are now able to identify campsites used[231] and zones traversed by particular groups, thanks to numerous inscriptions left by members of a single family from generation to generation. For these nomadic shepherds knew how to write. They were not alone in this, but the number of their graffiti exceeds anything known anywhere else. Were they literate people? Probably not, as Macdonald has rightly observed.[232] The inscriptions are extremely repetitive, with long genealogies followed by an invocation to some divinity begging for protection or relief. The shepherds generally wrote simple texts to pass the time, not out of any practical necessity and certainly not in an effort to be literary. Indeed, the two listings of the letters of the alphabet that have been found show that the writers did not know how to order them: to amuse themselves, two shepherds must have tried to recall all the letters they knew, without following any order. Only a few, probably the most talented in understanding all the possibilities of writing, used it to make notes about phenomena that had marked them or breaks in the monotony of daily life (an attack by neighbors, snow, the appearance of a panther), or, much less often, to record the muffled echo of something that had happened far away, in the empire.[233] For, all things considered, these nomads were neither entirely outside the empire nor entirely within it.[234]

The Nabataeans and Related Groups

Despite the abundance of inscriptions and writings found all along the caravan routes and in the lands traversed by herders, we do not have a great deal of data about the Nabataeans and the pseudo-Thamudaeans. Nevertheless, some of their gathering places are known. For example, in Wadi Ramm,[235] east of Aila, fairs were held near the busy sanctuary of Allat, which boasted both a rock sanctuary clinging to the mountain near a spring and a Greco-Roman style temple with a colonnade. A Roman outpost had been set up there; soldiers, too few in number to play an effective military role, observed the movement of tribes and the condition of pastures, and settled quarrels. At Ruwwafa,[236] several hundred kilometers to the south in the Hejaz, a sanctuary devoted to the imperial cult had been dedicated under the reigns of Marcus Aurelius and Lucius Verus, between 165 and 169, by an auxiliary branch of nomads recruited from the Thamudaeans, following some difficulties that remain unknown in part.[237] These Thamudaeans had the dedication of the sanctuary inscribed in Nabataean, confirming the generally accepted view that it is quite inaccurate to designate as "Thamudaean" the large number of writings in the hills north of the Hejaz and as far as the Hauran, even in certain cities of the area that seem to have no connection to the Thamudaeans.[238] The real Thamudaeans appear under the empire as a Nabataean group, or a group closely related to the Nabataeans: the dedication of the oldest Nabataean sanctuary at Ramm, a recent discovery, is in "Thamudaean."[239] Another name must be found for the Arab nomads who carved the "Thamudaean" texts in the northern Hejaz right up to the edge of wadi Ramm (the graffiti of Risqeh), texts dating from the Hellenistic era.[240]

It is very likely that a large number of Nabataeans settled either on the plateaus of Edom and Moab, in the Negev, or in the Transjordan and the Hauran. Evidence for this lies in the characteristically Arab proper names that are found throughout the region in Nabataean inscriptions. There is not enough documentation to know precisely whether these people were peasant farmers or breeders. However, some Nabataeans undoubtedly continued to live as nomads, including those who lived in the desert regions of the province, the Sinai, the Hejaz, and the Jordanian desert between the steppe and the oasis of the Jawf. Curiously, unlike the "Safaites," they left no traces of writing, unless we can attribute to shepherds some of the Nabataean rock inscriptions that have been discovered in great numbers along the principal caravan lines.[241] A few stations that developed around a sanctuary must have served as stopping places for these nomads. Thus, at Wadi Ramm, on a secondary slope between Aila and the Hejaz, the rock sanctuary of Allat attracted Nabataeans from an early date. During the Roman era, not only was there a Roman outpost,[242] which will probably be found to be linked to the recently discovered house with a bath,[243] but a heavy concentration of rock inscriptions has been discovered in the region.[244] The caravan drivers who crossed northwestern Arabia, the Sinai, and even the eastern Egyptian desert, were recruited from this group. Still, at least some of the caravan drivers may have also been shepherds, since the trade with Yemen was seasonal, linked to the autumn and spring incense harvests.[245] In any case, we have no explicit inscriptions referring to Nabataean caravan activity, and we must make do with some references by ancient authors, or the rare representations of camel caravans found in Petra.[246]

Nomads of the Euphrates and the Jezireh

Nomads lived in all the deserts bordering Syria, and so were also found around Palmyra, in the Euphrates Valley, and in the desert around Hatra and Singara.[247] Documentary evidence is very scarce, however, and we begin to discern the role nomads played only at the point when the Roman armies arrived in Osrhoene and Mesopotamia to confront the Persians. We shall come back to them in that context, but first it will be useful to note a number of phenomena observed in the first and second centuries.

In the Palmyrene, there were nomad camel drivers around the oasis, particularly to the northwest.[248] They supplied merchant caravans with the means of transportation. But there were other, more distant groups, whose relations with the Palmyrenes were less friendly. Not only was Palmyra obliged to provide troops to protect the routes, particularly in the area of Ana, near the Euphrates, where there is a record of a *strategos* in charge of security,[249] but it was also obliged at times to pay tolls for the caravans passing through.[250] The largest such group probably consisted of native

Arabs, animal breeders who contributed greatly to the Arabization of the oasis. Their gods, depicted as desert warriors, were designated as *gennaye,* or djinns.[251]

Pliny the Elder identifies several tribes in the Euphrates Valley and in the Jezireh region in the first century. Opposite Commagene were the Osroenian Aroei or Orroei;[252] around Singara, there were the Praetavi,[253] and opposite Syria on the other side of the Euphrates, the Scenitae.[254] The term *Scenitae* is not a tribal name, but designates a way of life. Strabo also mentions the Arab Scenitae, who lived in desert encampments between the Tigris and the Euphrates, explaining that they lived off tolls paid by travelers in exchange for guaranteeing safe passage.[255]

A great deal of work remains to be done before we can accurately depict rural life in Roman Syria. We know nothing of whole geographical sectors, especially the Syrian coast. Past and recent investigations, undertaken in such varied regions as northern Syria, the Hauran, and Judaea-Samaria, at least call attention to the great variety of local conditions. The differences in climate, water supply, and soils all lead to the same conclusion. However, natural conditions alone, as powerful as they are, cannot explain everything, and the influence of culture must also be considered. Thus it is all the more regrettable that we have no knowledge of Hellenistic conditions in northern Syria or in the Hauran. But we are able to discern at least a few general trends that should stand unchallenged for a long time. First of all, a greater transformation in land tenure occurred during the imperial era than had been supposed—not only around those few towns that were made colonies (on the contrary, for those sites we have no evidence at all of such transformations), but also around most of the large cities. Thus we know that there were quite significant changes in the distribution of property, and that there was probably a large-scale importation of new colonists. Furthermore, we see a constant expansion of cultivated land and a multiplication of villages, even in the marginal steppe areas. This unmistakable reflection of Syrian prosperity seems not to have declined over time; it persisted well beyond the fourth century. Finally, we still have a long way to go before we can understand the precise role of the nomads, but under the early empire they never appear as threatening presences after Augustus's reign; to the contrary, as animal breeders and caravan drivers they contributed to the general prosperity. These activities were all elements of a highly original rural life of which the Hauranese style of village organization is simply one of the best-known aspects.

THE URBAN ECONOMY IN ROMAN SYRIA

THE basis of Syria's prosperity was its robust agricultural productivity, the diversity of its artisans, and its extensive trade network. Each of these components contributed to the vitality of the others. Peasants provided raw materials such as wool, linen, and wood to artisans who transformed them; artisans in turn furnished handcrafted items from their workshops to merchants who sold them along with a variety of agricultural products and imported luxury goods (which were sometimes modified after reaching Syria); the luxury goods earned the highest profits. Too often we forget that Syria was not only a center of trade and transportation but above all a major manufacturing center of a wide variety of products. Leaving aside for the moment all the agricultural products discussed in Chapter 7, we turn now to consider the productions of craftsmen, while remaining aware that our knowledge is limited to the most outstanding examples: the items that struck the imaginations of ancient authors, the ones they viewed as most typical of Syria, were not necessarily the most important in terms of trade. We must also keep in mind that Syria was not merely an exporter: a rich and densely populated land, it also imported a variety of products from other parts of the Mediterranean world. One valuable indicator of this two-way trade can be seen in discoveries made within Syria of ceramics from outside the country, and of Syrian ceramics in other places. Although further study is needed, we already have a great deal of information to draw on, and more can be expected.

We must also consider how the Roman presence might have facilitated this trade, stimulating production and increasing overall prosperity. Romans everywhere are credited with improving roads: was this the case in Syria, and were roads an economic factor? As for currencies, we have already seen the progressive monetization of the Syrian economy during Hellenistic times, amid a profusion of monetary instruments that seems never to have been a significant obstacle to trade.[1] Did political unification eventually lead to monetary unification? Lastly, we shall try to understand how the region's coastal ports and its oases or desert "ports"[2] helped place Syria and Arabia at the heart of a vast communications network that gave Syria a fundamental place in the commercial history of the Roman Empire. In these long-distance exchanges, particularly to the east and south, nomads played a key role. Our task now is to examine the various forms of trade and establish a chronology.

ARTISANS

In antiquity, Syria was highly regarded as a center of skilled labor. Its reputation appears justified as much by the variety of goods produced as by the quantity and quality of those goods. Nevertheless, as we have seen, ancient authors often mentioned only the products that stood out because they were luxury items or in some way unusual, and these were not necessarily the most important in economic terms.

Among luxury goods, the production of royal purple dye was concentrated in Tyre and Sidon in particular (and secondarily in Ashdod[3] and elsewhere). In these areas, in others further inland (Laodicea) and along the coast (Gerasa), and probably in some villages as well, the presence of the dye-producing shellfish murex in these areas was combined with the availability of high-quality textiles. Purple dye was thus produced not only in Tyre and Sidon but also throughout the entire coastal portion of their territory and beyond, as far as Ptolemais. Given the cost of the dye, royal purple was a luxury. The dye was extracted from murex, each one providing only a tiny amount. Large numbers of the shellfish were thus needed to supply a small amount of dye: we can still see evidence of this today at Sidon, where a hill of murex shells still rises south of the ancient city. Dyeing added considerably to the value of textiles that would otherwise have faced stiff competition from the textiles of Egypt and Asia Minor. Although the purple dye industry was not exclusively Phoenician (we know of some workshops on Delos and in the southern Peloponnesos), Phoenician purple was especially prestigious;[4] the shops of Tyre and Sidon provided dyed material for the imperial court and for those members of the higher orders who were entitled to wear it.

In terms of production, however, textile manufacturing was probably more important than purple dye. Ancient sources give Syria little credit for fine textiles, except for its silk, but this is somewhat misleading. It was actually not until the sixth century C.E., when silkworms were imported clandestinely from China, that Phoenicia produced true silk. Procopios, who would have known about this innovation in his day, attributed to Phoenicia a long tradition of silk fabric production and trade; his claim can be accounted for in several ways.[5] First, there seems to have been some silk manufacturing in Galilee (in Gischala), as there had been in Cos during the Hellenistic period, using species other than the ordinary silkworm (bombyx).[6] Moreover, Phoenician artisans made substantial transformations in the raw silk fabric that reached their shops. Some was dyed, either purple or another color, as tailors used it to make clothing, while the roughest fabrics appear to have been rewoven. A passage in Lucan provides evidence of this practice under Nero's reign. Lucan says that Cleopatra's "white breasts were revealed by the fabric of Sidon, which, close-woven by the shuttle of the Seres, the Egyptian needle-worker pulls out, and loosens the thread by stretching the stuff."[7] The silk fabric had been woven in China and dyed purple in Sidon, then reworked in Egypt to make it more reminiscent of spiderwebs. Phoenician artisans themselves probably knew how to do this work, which increased the price of the cloth.

We know far less about more common fabrics. Judaea produced woolens,[8] but linen production in Galilee seems to have been more significant. In a reference to flax from Palestine, Pausanius implies that it represented the highest standard of quality.[9] Flax from Scythopolis was right at the top of Diocletian's Price Edict in terms of cost,[10] but the term *Scythopolitan* should not mislead us: the flax sold in Scythopolis came from throughout Galilee and even beyond, for some linen was made in the Damascus region.[11] Linen production did not develop significantly until the second third of the second century, but it became quite successful at that time and remained so throughout late antiquity. Workshops for treating flax, dating from the beginning of the third century, have been excavated at Gaba (Tel Shash);[12] too extensive to have been owned by a single producer, the complex must have belonged to a trade union association. Although the association with Scythopolis has endured, flax has also been found around Tiberias, in the Kinneret region south of the lake, and in the Jezreel valley, where dozens of similar workshops have been recovered; the oldest clearly date from the third century.[13] Because flax exhausts the soil, fields were supposed to be planted only every four to six years; even so, its cultivation was profitable, and fields could be planted in wheat during the interval.[14] Linen weavers were numerous and powerful; evidence that they formed associations has been found in Gerasa,[15] Tiberias,[16] and Beth Shearim.[17] These weavers were called *tarsim* (derived from *Tarsian*, in reference to the city of Tarsos, whose economic life was dominated by the linen industry);[18] they had their own synagogue in Jerusalem and in Tiberias.[19] Numerous smaller workshops that grew up around this industry specialized in preparing the fibers, weaving, manufacturing, or dyeing.[20]

Later sources refer to textile production in Sarepta[21] as well as in Scythopolis, Tyre, Beirut, Byblos, and Laodicea, without giving any details.[22] There was a maker of "Babylonian" fabric in Caesarea on the Sea,[23] and small rugs from Tiberias and Kusha in Galilee were highly valued.[24]

It will be useful to take a closer look at the textile business in Palmyra. Thanks to the dry climate that prevailed there, graves in the tower tombs have yielded numerous fragments of ancient fabrics. As expected, these include some imported Chinese fabrics, including stamped silks that we can identify as being from Hunan Province;[25] there is also cashmere from Afghanistan. As Annemarie Stauffer's highly technical analyses have shown, however, some of these fabrics were manufactured in Palmyra itself on horizontal "Syrian" looms rather than on vertical "Chinese" looms. Furthermore, studies of the way threads were twisted and of their pigmentation clearly show that Palmyra benefited from its location on the caravan route and became an important center of textile manufacturing. Production included fine silk made from rewoven raw silk, sometimes blended with local wool, as well as woolen, cotton, and linen fabric with embroidered designs that were faithful copies of decorative architectural motifs.[26] In one instance, the tapestry cartoon of works produced in China has been traced to Palmyra: a fabric has been found whose design could not have originated in China (it features kneeling camels and vineyards), yet it had to have been woven on a "Chinese" loom.[27]

We must note, in addition to weaving and reweaving, the related activities of fullers. These craftsmen were numerous enough in Antioch during the first century to justify the digging of a canal in 73–74.[28] In 207 C.E., fullers in Gerasa were organized in a corporation under the protection of Artemis, the city's principal goddess.[29] A fuller is also mentioned in an inscription from Joppa,[30] and the presence of dyers has been noted at Mariamin;[31] a master dyer was buried at Beth Shearim, though he was not necessarily a native.[32]

Leatherworking could be included with the other textile-related crafts, although it is not well represented in the records. Still, the presence of a powerful corporation of goatskin-sack makers prominent enough to have had reserved seats in the theater draws attention to a craft linked to the caravan trade and seasonal livestock herding.[33] Goatskin-sack makers seem to have been even more specialized in Palmyra, for the hides were used there to make rafts;[34] indeed, we know that merchandise went down the Euphrates on rafts that were dismantled for the return journey upstream. But this practice must have been much more widespread, as a great many products could be transported in goatskin sacks; this may explain the relative scarcity of amphorae in the interior. The Palmyra Tariff Law mentions goatskin sacks intended for transporting oil and animal fat;[35] camel or donkey transport would not permit the use of heavy containers such as amphorae. In any case, the production must have met a substantial demand, for the Tariff Law also provided for a tax on imported hides.[36] Phoenician skins are mentioned in Diocletian's Price Edict.[37]

Metalworking, too, was dispersed among a number of different centers. Sidon made a name for itself in bronze, and Antioch in gold and silver; other cities, including Damascus, Jerusalem, Bostra, Berytos, and Palmyra, were known for the production of weapons, tools, and various implements. At the beginning of the second century, Jews seem to have been experts in making weapons; some even worked for the Roman army.[38] Aila seems to have developed this activity in conjunction with the exploitation of mines in Wadi Arabah,[39] although probably not before the third century, when mining resumed.[40] Lead sarcophagi were a specialty of Jerusalem, but some probably came from workshops in other locations.[41]

The principal centers of glassmaking were located in Phoenicia, in Tyre and Sidon,[42] but there were also major workshops in Galilee.[43] The transition from molded to blown glass, which occurred toward the middle of the first century B.C.E., as discoveries in Jerusalem have shown,[44] led to a greater diversity of goods: glass of finer quality was produced in many more varied and more graceful shapes. Although molded glass production continued throughout the first century B.C.E., blown glass began to supersede it, and spread far and wide: glassware became commonplace, and was found in home furnishings as well as in tombs.[45] This trend did not preclude the production of luxury items: pieces decorated with complex reliefs, inlaid motifs, or multicolored designs, and signed by well-known craftsmen such as Ennion of Sidon. Other artisans also signed their goods: Artas, Philippos, and Neikon, for example, all of whom specified their Sidonian roots as an assurance of quality. The shapes were infinitely varied, but Phoenicia specialized in small vases for perfumes, ointments, and cosmetics, all made in regional workshops. Although the coast near Mount Carmel had the reputation of providing the best sand, which it exported to

Sidon,[46] production seems to have been quite widespread, and it was so abundant in Palestine itself that rabbis declared it illegal for Jews to use imported glass—a measure presumably designed to protect the local production, which was spread among many small workshops.[47]

Syria must have had numerous ceramic workshops to meet everyday needs as well as the demands of trade (amphorae for wine and oil). However, we know very little about this sector. As for fine porcelain, Eastern Sigillata A (ESA) continued to be produced in large quantities until the middle of the second century; production declined toward that century's end, and disappeared altogether during the third century. Although we do not know the precise location of the workshops, their products would have been a primary source of income for the artisans, who may have been concentrated around Alexandria, near Issos, although the diversity of clays argues in favor of a fairly large production zone between Antioch or even Laodicea and eastern Cilicia.[48] However, certain physical analyses indicate a single center of production in a rather limited geographical region.[49] Once again, though, no kilns or dumps have been found that would allow for more precise identifications. Only one thing is certain: the production was large, judging from the number of sherds of sigillata A found at most of the sites not only in Syria but throughout the entire Near East[50] and beyond, even if some of these sherds have not always been recognized as such. Perhaps the best evidence of the popularity of these fine ceramics is the fact that they were widely imitated. Fine porcelain copies of sigillata A have turned up in Gerasa, for example. These ceramics, characteristic both in the clay used and in their shapes, appeared around 75 B.C.E. and were produced until the end of the century, perhaps even somewhat later.[51] Catherine Abadie-Raynal has also identified a fine sigillata produced locally in Zeugma during the first century and possibly the beginning of the second, distributed only in the territory controlled by the city,[52] and she has correctly observed that a more careful study of the material found at other sites would undoubtedly reveal a number of additional local workshops like this one.

Nabataean ceramics were also quite recognizable handcrafted products,[53] with delicate surfaces and plant motifs. Following an early stage, a stylistic change occurred around the middle of the first century B.C.E.: the decoration became more formalized and the color changed from orange or bright red to reddish purple. These ceramics were not widely exported, and production may have ended during the second century C.E.,[54] although some scholars are inclined to extend the date of production to the end of the third century.[55] Scholars believed for a long time that production was limited to Petra and the cities of the Negev; however, discoveries made over

NABATAEAN POTTERY.

the last fifteen years in the northern Transjordan and the Hauran suggest that that production probably extended beyond the south. Still, the only known pottery kilns are in the south, in Petra, where a potters' quarter has recently been identified near the center of the city, behind the Qasr al-Bint,[56] and especially in Oboda/Avdat in the Negev, where a pottery workshop began operating around 25 B.C.E. at the latest, and perhaps as early as 30.[57] It ceased production around 50 C.E., when the city was sacked by nomadic tribes, and then resumed, at least partially, toward the end of the first century and the beginning of the second. Moreover, a very similar product seems to have been made in Jerusalem during the Herodian period.[58]

When Eastern Sigillata A disappeared, Syrian ceramic production seems to have stopped altogether; local fine ceramics were replaced by imported ware. Small quantities of Italian and Gallic sigillata appeared, as did some from Asia Minor. In Antioch, for example, under the Julio-Claudians, imports of western sigillata were quite small (of the known pieces, more like one in a thousand than one in a hundred), and these were probably limited to the personal property of travelers from the west. However, the number grew after 80, with pieces from workshops in southern Gaul (Banassac), then from Lezoux and central Gaul.[59] In Apamaea, a single marbled sherd from La Graufesenque (contemporary Millau) in Gaul is not enough to suggest commercial trading, and no examples of sigillata B, C, or D from Asia Minor have ever been found there.[60] In contrast, imported goods including African and Mediterranean sigillata, dating from the beginning of the third century, have been found both in cities and in rural areas.[61]

It is clear that everyday pottery was produced in workshops in every city and community of any size, and it should be possible to distinguish regional styles.[62] From archaeology and rabbinic texts, we know about centers of production in Beth Shean, Nahaf, Lydda, Bethlehem, and elsewhere. However, site-specific studies undertaken sometimes decades apart have created confusion that is difficult to unravel, and the overall picture we have of ordinary ceramics keeps changing with every new discovery. According to Stanislao Loffreda, for example, common ceramics produced locally in Capharnaum on the shores of Lake Tiberias were very similar to those of the Golan and Galilee but differed significantly from those produced farther south.[63] In the light of subsequent studies of other Galilean workshops, we may wonder whether ceramics from the Golan did not originate in Galilee. Rabbinic sources[64] do in fact mention two great pottery centers in Galilee, one at Kefar Hananya (modern Kafr 'Inan, northwest of Tiberias) and the other at Kefar Shihin, which has not been located with precision but must have been in the Netufa valley, west of Tiberias. No other allusion to possible centers of production has been found in the rabbinic literature, even in texts dealing with the great cities of the region.[65] Each of these two centers produced a particular style (cooking pots at Kefar Hananya, earthenware jars at Kefar Shihin).[66] The spread of products from Kefar Hananya indicates that this center supplied all of Galilee and part of the Golan. Cities such as Tiberias or Sepphoris depended exclusively on Kefar Hananya for ceramic tableware, and the ethnic composition of the cities played no role in this matter. By contrast, we find almost no exports south of Scythopolis.[67] There we have an example of a highly concentrated production destined for an entire region, but its success is difficult to explain. Production seems to have begun during the first century B.C.E. and to have grown rapidly until the second century, corresponding to a period of considerable population growth in Galilee. The village presumably took advantage of the excellent clay deposits, the availability of an abundant supply of water and fuel (including olive pulp), the great east–west road from Tiberias to Ptolemais, and skilled potters. The latter must have been Jews who scrupulously observed the laws governing production; their wares would not otherwise have met with the success they enjoyed among all sectors of the population in Galilee.[68]

Our understanding of amphora production is still in its infancy, although excavations in Beirut have led to some progress in this area. We have known for some time about the "Gaza" amphorae produced continuously in workshops spread throughout a large coastal area from Gaza to

Pelusa from the first to the seventh century c.e.[69] Beirut, another center of amphora production, began operating around the middle of the first century b.c.e. and produced a large quantity during the first century c.e. (several amphorae stamped col[onia] Ber[ytus] have been found), before beginning to turn out an abundance of long, thin, carrot-shaped amphorae during the second and third centuries.[70] These have turned up in excavations of the city, as well as on Cyprus, in Egypt, and as far away as the Rhone valley.[71] In addition, Tyre seems to have produced a style of amphora (FAM 10 and 43) that spread from Beirut to Galilee, as well as to Laodicea by the Sea and the Palestinian coast.[72] In any case, given the importance of oil and wine production in most of the regions of Syria, amphorae had to have been produced in large quantities everywhere.

Jerusalem specialized in the production of stone vessels. These were particularly valued for religious uses in the temples because, according to the rabbis' exegeses, stone is less susceptible to impurities than pottery. A great many workshops have been identified in Jerusalem itself and in the surrounding areas, although at this time we know of only one in Galilee, located in Reina, six kilometers from Nazareth. Stoneware production seems to have begun fairly late, in the second half of the first century b.c.e., and it disappeared with the destruction of the Temple in 70.[73]

As for the way crafts were organized, we know less about Syria than we do about Asia Minor.[74] The existence of professional associations has been attested in passing in several cities, but the list is not long: goatskin-sack makers in Bostra[75] and Palmyra,[76] tanners in Palmyra,[77] goldsmiths and silversmiths in Bostra[78] and Palmyra,[79] coppersmiths in Bostra[80] and Heliopolis,[81] cutlers[82] and carpenters in Sidon,[83] linen weavers,[84] potters,[85] fullers,[86] and agoraioi (vendors)[87] in Gerasa, basket weavers[88] (?) and stucco workers[89] in Palmyra, construction supervisors (oikodomoi) in Gadara,[90] fullers[91] and bakers in Antioch, and sea traders (naucleres) in Ascalon.[92] In several cases we have only a collective designation, for want of a specific term referring to association, but the use of the plural in such cases seems to designate a group functioning as such: for instance, at least one column in the nymphaeum in Gerasa was offered by "the potters,"[93] just as reserved seats in the theater in Bostra simply bore the name of a trade, in the plural. We should note that the term most frequently encountered, syntechnia, alludes unmistakably to the professional character of the trade associations, an allusion that is not always found when the term occurs in Asia Minor; but a rather vague term, systema, is also used. Overall this is not very much, and we note that three-fourths of the references have been found in Palmyra, Bostra, and Gerasa. Can this concentration be attributed to accidents of discovery, or does it reflect local tradition? The evidence is too tenuous to support a conclusion.

It is worth noting that names of occupations sometimes appear in inscriptions, attesting to a certain pride on the part of the artisans. In addition to the occupations examined above, we must note, above all, the frequency of references to construction supervisors, architects, and carpenters,[94] and to all building trades in general, including stonecutters.[95] Also mentioned frequently are sculptors, especially those responsible for the stone tombs at Hegra, where there were veritable artistic dynasties.[96] But the owners of rich tombs were careful not to indicate their occupations, if indeed they had any: in Hegra, there are many such identifications, but most were of high dignitaries of the Nabataean kingdom, whereas in Palmyra only 2 texts out of 137 mention an occupation by name: one refers to a tax collector and the other to the descendants of a doctor.[97] This seems to demonstrate that members of the more prosperous classes of Syrian society were no more inclined to emphasize the origins of their fortunes than were wealthy Greeks of the same period.

MONEY AND CUSTOMS DUTIES

Rome permitted several systems of monetary denomination to remain in use, even though only imperial currency was redeemable from the point of view of the treasury. Until money minted by cities disappeared in the middle of the third century, however, imperial and municipal coins coexisted, while in the client states royal or tetrarchic coins survived until the states themselves disappeared. It is quite clear that no money could have been issued without the agreement of the Roman authorities, but we do not know at what point the Romans intervened in the actual minting of coins.[98] Cities seem to have remained in sole control of the timing of issues, and of standards, denominations, and emblems. Although Syria had no gold[99] or silver mines, the supply of metal does not appear to have concerned the authorities; there must be other explanations for the sporadic nature of municipal issues.

Imperial Coinages[100]

Two particular coinages are usually considered part of a single development even though they have no a priori connections; the tight control exercised by the authorities over the issuing of these coins seems to me to justify treating them together. The first were imperial issues, including a number of Roman denominations such as the bronze *as, dupondius, quadrans,* and *semis,* the silver *denarius,* and the gold *aureus;* the second were provincial tetradrachms, coins in Greek denominations but issued by Roman authority and often in the same workshops as Roman coinage.

Coins in Roman denominations often cannot be readily attributed to specific workshops, even though we know that in Syria they were minted more or less continuously in Antioch,[101] Laodicea, Tyre, and Caesarea on the Sea. Issues were sporadic, possibly more frequent around the end of the first century and the beginning of the second. However, very large volumes of silver *denarii* and of *aurei* were issued between 69 and 73, undoubtedly in direct correlation with the demands of the Jewish War.[102] It was only then that denarii really began to circulate in Syria, for before that time references to these coins are found nowhere except in the Gospels; however, denarii were found in the treasury of Mount Carmel, which was buried in 70. We know of one large later issue of *orichalcum,* in the form of as and semis, in 115–116, for a commemorative issue of Trajan's *Vicennalia* destined to circulate widely throughout the empire.[103] Pescennius Niger produced very large issues of silver denarii to finance the war, a practice continued by the Severi, and Gordian III minted *antoniniani* in Antioch.

Alongside these Roman coinages, others were minted in Greek denominations. After the final issue of *philippi* from the Antioch mint in 17–16 B.C.E., Augustus issued silver tetradrachms in the name of the Roman Empire, finally replacing the coins bearing the head of the last Seleucid sovereign recognized by Rome as legitimate. It was not until 5 B.C.E. that these provincial tetradrachms bore the image of Augustus and began to be issued on a regular basis. Several times, the value of these tetradrachms was set to equal four silver denarii, a policy that resulted in a significant overvaluation of provincial coins when weight and values were taken into account. This happened between 5 and 12 C.E., then again starting in 60, although Nero once more increased the Roman coins' weight and value; the overvaluation came to around 25 percent, given the fine metal content of the Antioch coins. Trajan maintained this useful parity, but ended the overvaluation of the Antioch tetradrachm by increasing its weight and worth.[104] Most of these were produced in Antioch, but some came from mints in Tyre[105] and Laodicea under Augustus and Tiberius, from Apamaea and Seleucia under the Julio-Claudians, possibly from Seleucia in Pieria under Vespasian,[106] and from Tyre again starting in Trajan's reign. Production of these tetradrachms was interrupted between Hadrian and Pescennius Niger, except for some small issues during the time of the association between Marcus Aurelius and Commodus. However, after Niger, Septimius Severus continued to produce tetradrachms, and these were issued in very large quantities up to the time of Gordian III and Trajan Dacicus.

In addition to silver coins, the imperial mint in Antioch issued very large series of bronzes marked SC, for *senatus consulto,* recalling the senatorial privilege of striking bronzes. The first issues of the as were probably introduced by P. Quinctilius Varus in 5 b.c.e. and did not vary until the beginning of the third century: the weight of the coins declined notably under Caracalla, then collapsed under Macrinus and Elagabalus, while at the same time the volume of coins issued grew.[107] The stability of the weight of these issues over more than two centuries probably accounts in large part for their success, which is apparent in the wide circulation of the Antioch imperial bronzes throughout Syria. Although the denominations were Roman in principle (as, dupondius), these coins have little in common with the as or dupondii issued in the west.[108] The sole innovation was the move from Latin to Greek for the imperial titles starting in Trajan's time: titles on imperial coins corresponded to those on civic bronzes.[109] It was rather unusual for coins intended for Greek speakers to bear Latin legends; this phenomenon was virtually unknown in the east outside the Roman colonies.[110]

Antioch was not alone, however, in issuing imperial bronzes. Workshops operated sporadically as needed—for example, in Caesarea in Palestine immediately following the Jewish War,[111] in Seleucia, in Apamaea, and in Tyre and Laodicea in 198–194.[112] Finally, following the annexation of Arabia, tetradrachms were issued in the province, probably minted in Bostra (though for a long time they were mistakenly believed to be from Caesarea in Cappadocia),[113] and drachms were produced in Petra during Caracalla's rule.[114]

Alongside these provincial imperial coins, others were occasionally issued in the name of the legions, probably by the provincial authority. We must distinguish, however, between these "legionnaire bronzes" with Latin titles (such as those associated with III Cyrenaica in Bostra, which must have been issued in the provincial mint in Arabia by authority of the governor)[115] and civic coins honoring one or more legions stationed in or passing through a city; on one side these coins had the imperial portrait (with a Greek title), and on the other a symbol or even the name of the legion itself, but with an indication of the city as the issuing authority.[116]

Royal and Tetrarchic Coinage

Numerous client states produced coins: Herod and his successors, the Nabataeans, Commagene. Conditions varied from one state to another, however. As we have seen, the Nabataeans and the Hasmonaeans introduced their own currencies at about the same time. The Nabataeans continued to mint coins without any significant interruption until the end of the kingdom. They issued a series of beautiful silver coins, dated and thus easily classified, as well as more rudimentary little bronze coins; large quantities of the latter have been found even outside the kingdom—which is surprising, to say the least.[117] Coinage reached a sort of apogee under Aretas IV; during the early part of his reign (associated with Queen Huldu), Aretas alternated between silver and bronze coinages and then, during the second part of his reign (identified with Queen Shuqailat), struck silver and bronze coins simultaneously. His silver coins alone seem to have been almost as abundant as all the issues from the Petra mint combined. Certain interruptions in currency production remain a mystery. The first occurred under Malichos I, who does not seem to have issued any coins between 58 and 36 B.C.E.: was that a consequence of his having submitted to Rome? It is hard to see why the Romans would have shut down production of Nabataean currency when they themselves were minting no money in Syria. Glen Bowersock has explained the second gap, between 4–3 B.C.E. and 1 C.E., as resulting from a temporary annexation of the kingdom.[118] Lastly, and rather curiously, we have no coins from the last years of the reigns of Malichos II (between 65 and 70) and Rabbel II (after 101–102). Is this the result of a drop in metal reserves? Does it simply reflect a random gap in discoveries? We do not know.[119] It may be related to the very steep drop in silver content of Nabataean money in the first century C.E. The silver standard was maintained at 87 to 96 percent until 7 B.C.E., but it declined rapidly at that time to around 41 to 54 percent, then gradually dropped to below 20 percent around 50 C.E. It stayed at this weak level until 72, when it climbed to 42 percent; it fell again to 20 percent in 80 and stayed there until Nabataean minting came to a halt in 100. Was there a silver shortage? Was the king seeking to enrich himself at little cost? The decrease in the level of silver content probably betrays difficulties, although we cannot say exactly what they were.

Unlike the Nabataeans, the Herodians struck only bronze coins, at least in their own name.[120] Herod in particular issued large series of bronzes in small denominations, probably intended for local circulation.[121] The same was true for Archelaos, whose coinage is indistinguishable from that of his father except in the replacement of the royal title by *ethnarch*, and for Herod Antipas, whose currency lapsed between 20–21 and 29–30; this currency did not circulate outside the boundaries of his tetrarchy. The coins issued in Jerusalem observed the Jewish laws forbidding the representation of living beings and were thus strictly non-iconic, as were those issued by prefects and procurators in their turn up to the Jewish War. In Galilee and in the Herodians' territories outside of Palestine, the tetrarchies of Philip, Antipas, Herod of Chalcis, and the kingdom of Agrippa II—all areas in which Jews were mostly minorities—these rules did not apply. Philip issued a coin bearing the portrait of the emperor, or with his own image on the front, and the Augusteum of Caesarea of Philippi-Panias on the back. Similarly, Herod of Chalcis issued some coins depicting Claudius, others bearing his own image.[122] A royal currency reappeared with Agrippa I; it imitated Roman coins and presented Roman images and Roman portraits (a quadriga, Germanicus, the letters *SC*).[123] As for Agrippa II, his coinages bore a series of imperial portraits, particularly under the Flavians.[124]

The complete absence of silver coin production in a wealthy kingdom that needed silver coins for religious reasons (the half-shekel payment required for the Temple) is intriguing. Ya'akov Meshorer suggests that the Jerusalem mint was the source of the second issue of Tyrian shekels. In the long series of silver shekels bearing the name of Tyre, which continued without interruption from the year 1 (126–125 B.C.E.) to the year 191 (65–66 C.E.), an issue was introduced in 18–17 B.C.E. that was clearly less carefully crafted than the preceding ones; it bore the Greek letters KP in addition to the date. A great many of the coins in this series have been found in Israel; the oldest ones come largely from Syria and Lebanon. Meshorer has concluded that these coins were issued, with Rome's approval (the Greek P could have been the initial for Rhomaion), by the Herodians to make up for a loss of production at the mint in Tyre. That mint might have ceased issuing the silver coins with a high metal content that had depreciated in value against the provincial issues from the Antioch mint; the Herodians might have resumed minting in their own name, since Tyrian silver shekels were essential for payment of the Temple tax.[125] There is a further possible explanation for the cessation of Tyrian coin production: around 20 B.C.E., according to Cassius Dio, Augustus suppressed Tyre's liberty as punishment for the political unrest that was rampant in the city; in the absence of *libertas,* it is hard to imagine how Tyre could have retained the right to mint silver coins.[126] Meshorer notes that the disappearance of "Tyrian" shekels in 65–66 can be explained in the Jewish context, not in the context of local history. It is well known that insurgent Jews indeed produced coins in their own name beginning in 66, which meant that they no longer needed to resort to Tyrian coinage. This hypothesis, as tempting as it is, has been challenged by a number of specialists and has not yet been proven.[127]

Other client princes minted coins, including the tetrarchs of Chalcis: Lysanias and, later, Zenodoros issued occasional series.[128] In Commagene, coins were issued continuously from Mithradates I at the beginning of the first century B.C.E. up to the dynasty's disappearance in 72.[129] But other dynasts, such as those of Emesa and the minor tetrarchs of the Syrian mountains, did without their own coinages.

Locally produced coins circulated routinely in the states where they were issued, but they were seldom found elsewhere. There is one unexplained exception: so many Nabataean bronze coins circulated throughout Syria that their presence cannot be understood as accidental. They have been found in Antioch, in a number of excavations on the Syrian coast, and in Cyprus.

We must not fail to mention coins issued by Jewish rebels who on two occasions were able to use minting as an instrument of propaganda as well as an economic tool. Beginning in 66, bronze coins, particularly the tiny *prutah,* were issued with legends in ancient Hebrew. At the time of Simon Bar Kokhba's revolt, coins dating from four different years announced the rebels' objectives: liberty for Israel and the liberation of Jerusalem. Large quantities of these coins were produced, but their circulation was restricted to Judaea during the rebellion.[130]

Local Coinages

As in all the provinces of the eastern Mediterranean,[131] cities retained the right to issue their own coins with the consent of the emperor; these have been called "imperial Greeks" since the publication of a seminal article by T. B. Jones,[132] but more recent scholars correctly prefer the title *provincial coins,* placing them on the same level as coins issued by the provincial *koina* and other groups.[133] These were generally bronze, rarely silver. Most of the issues were sporadic, sometimes in quite small quantities, and they peaked under the Severi in the sense that a record number of mints is attested during that period.[134]

Only the largest cities on the Syrian coast were able to continue minting silver coins as late as the middle of the first century C.E.: Seleucia until 6 C.E., Antioch until 38, Sidon to 43–44 (but only in small numbers), Tyre until 66 (if in fact the issues attributed to that city up to the first century C.E. actually came from Tyre and not from Jerusalem),[135] and Laodicea until 124. Once silver minting ceased in these workshops, there were only occasional issues, notably during the reigns of Caracalla and Macrinus.[136] In northern Syria, these civic issues, which existed only by imperial privilege, began to display portraits of emperors quite late—starting only in 4–3 B.C.E. in Apamaea, in 6 C.E. in Seleucia, and during the reign of Caligula in Laodicea. By contrast, imperial images were featured regularly on the coins issued in the cities of the Decapolis.[137] These differences call for further study: they show the strong attachment of central and southern cities, with a long tradition of municipal coinages, to their own autonomy and identity. The continuation of Phoenician lettering on the coins of Tyre, when that language had completely ceased to be spoken, can also be interpreted as a reminder of the city's origins and thus of its inhabitants' identity.[138]

COIN FROM BYBLOS.

As for bronzes, very small issues came from mints in the first century, in Tyre, Sidon, and also from cities in the interior such as Canatha,[139] Damascus,[140] and Gadara.[141] It was not until Trajan's reign in northern Syria (Cyrrhos, Beroea, Hierapolis, Zeugma, Chalcis), and that of Hadrian and Antony in southern Syria and Arabia (Abila, Capitolias, Pella, and so on) that civic coins became numerous in Syria. This must reflect the prosperity of the country and the growing need for metal coins. But although mints were numerous, their production was relatively limited. Most mints produced coins for two or three years at the most, at intervals of ten or twenty years or more. It was only under exceptional circumstances that almost all the mints would suddenly start producing at the same time, as, for example, when Marcus Aurelius paid an imperial visit in 175.[142] Under the Severi, mints increased in number but not necessarily in economic importance. In Arabia and in Palestine, only Gadara and Scythopolis, and Aelia Capitolina from its foundation,[143] issued coins on a regular basis after the first century, whereas most were active only occasionally, or even one time only, as was the case for Esbous and Charachmoba under Elagabal. Many were closed well before the abandonment of civic mints during the years 260 to 270: Madaba stopped minting under Severus Alexander, Gadara and Scythopolis under Gordian III, Bostra under Decius, Adraha in 256–257. Of the thirty-seven cities in Palestine and Arabia that minted coins under the Severi, twenty-three ceased all production after Elagabalus's reign. Only one Arabian mint, the one in Bostra, appears to have supplied coinage to meet economic needs. Elsewhere, coins were produced for circumstantial reasons: to celebrate important imperial events or to highlight some aspect of local life, to celebrate a contest, to publicize titles, or to further some political interest.[144] In fact, most inhabitants of the region depended on the provincial currency, tetradrachms minted in Antioch;[145] infrequently issued, these coins flowed unproblematically into the mass of currency in circulation. As was the case everywhere, these municipal issues ceased in the middle of the third century, to be replaced exclusively by imperial issues.[146]

It would be a mistake to think that the inhabitants of Roman Syria carried around three separate purses in which they kept currencies from different mints. Quasi-official exchange rates among all these currencies facilitated their circulation regardless of the actual metal value of each one. In fact, the value of coinages acquired a partially fiduciary aspect as rules of exchange were established and weights varied from one coin to another. Moreover, the diversity of issuing authorities, which interests us because of its political implications, mattered little to those who used the money, all the more so because imperial and civic issues, produced in the same mint, could have had identical reverse dies.[147] One city-state, Canatha, launched into large-scale production in 94–95 and 95–96 (the coins have been found as far away as Antioch); the reasons for this sudden zeal are not clear, but Canatha was probably making up for the issues that were no longer produced in Caesarea Panias after the death of Agrippa II (in 92–93).[148] Imperial, provincial, royal, and civic currencies constituted a single money supply in terms of circulation and the satisfaction of economic needs.

It is nevertheless very difficult to get a clear picture of the degree to which the economy was monetized. The presence of a great many currencies from excavations at Arabian sites has led Christian Augé to speak of intense monetization, even in daily life, because many of these currencies were in small denominations.[149] But we can see that this applied particularly to urban sites, and these tell us little about the countryside. In contrast, the village of Dehes in northern Syria has produced only a single currency from the early empire.[150] Can this be explained as evidence of the weak development of a village that flourished mainly during the Byzantine era, or as a result weak monetization in the countryside? The question points to an important area of future research.

Customs Collection Posts

Roman customs officers located on the borders of the empire in Syria levied a uniform tax of 25 percent on all merchandise crossing in either direction. We know little about the customs posts, but the one in Palmyra is attested by references to *publicani* in several inscriptions.[151] Siegfried de Laet interprets references to tax collectors in Dura (Dura-Europos) as proof of a *portorium*, or customs collection post, but the officials in question may have been collecting local taxes.[152] It would have been logical for a Roman customs office to have operated in the city after 165, although in that case the Palmyra post would have been partially useless, unless the customs post in Dura taxed only merchandise that was on its way along the Euphrates. There was also a post in Zeugma, at the Euphrates crossing mentioned by Philostrates.[153] There must have been other posts at points of access of the main routes (such as al-'Azraq, at the exit of Wadi Sirhan, or at Hegra), but no trace of these has been found. Customs offices are attested in certain Mediterranean ports such as Gaza, Seleucia of Pieria, Berytos, Tyre, Caesarea on the Sea, and Joppa, where duties were lower than those levied on the border because they affected only merchandise circulating within the empire.[154]

Another troubling question concerns the royal Nabataean customs taxes and whether or not they were controlled by Rome. A tax collector is known to have operated in the port of Leuke Kome at the time of the *Periplus Maris Erythraei;*[155] he collected a 25 percent duty on all merchandise.[156] As this agent had the title *centurion,* some scholars argue that he must have been a Roman official,[157] while others, judging that the Nabataean kingdom was still independent during this period (mid-first century C.E.), hold that he was a Nabataean official;[158] his Roman title may have been a mistake by the editor of the *Periplus,* or it may be another example of linguistic borrowing by Nabataeans.[159] Others remain unconvinced.[160] Gary K. Young has recently argued forcefully that the tax collector had to be a Roman official, given that the amount in question was precisely what the Romans charged, and that if Nabataeans had imposed a 25 percent tax on merchandise crossing their territory on the way to Mediterranean ports or Syrian cities, where travelers would have to pay Rome an additional 25 percent *vectigal* tax, such a self-defeating policy would have led merchants to head at once for Egyptian ports on the Red Sea instead. He concludes that the *tetarte* (a duty of one-quarter) levied in Leuke Kome was for Rome; in his view, Rome established this forward outpost in order to prevent merchandise from reaching Gaza without paying any duty.[161] Young's position assumes, a priori, that in the middle of the first century, a time when Gaza belonged to Rome, there were no Roman customs posts in its vicinity. However, the passage in Pliny that Young cites as proof does not support this conclusion. Pliny does not mention the tetarte explicitly, but his reference to publicani leaves the possibility open.[162] Nothing prevents us from supposing that there was a Nabataean customs house in Leuke Kome before the arrival of the Romans, and that the Romans took it over only after the annexation of the kingdom in 106.

There were also internal customs, or rather tolls, which tenant farmers were responsible for collecting from travelers. This explains in part the presence of numerous publicani, who are widely attested in Palestine at the time both in the Gospels and the Talmuds. One rabbi even asserts that the Romans built bridges only in order to collect tolls! Local communities also levied municipal duties, however; we know most about the ones in Palmyra, thanks to the Palmyra Tariff Law.[163]

ROADS AND PORTS

Let us begin by looking at the various means of transportation and their role in facilitating trade. The Roman period does not seem to have brought any significant changes in this area. Traditionally, pack animals—donkeys, mules, horses, and camels—handled almost all traffic. Wheel ruts from carts are found on paved roads, such as the one crossing the Trachonitis, for example, but there is no evidence that the carts in question were commercial rather than military. Given what we know to date, it seems to me impossible to weigh the respective significance of transport by carriage and pack animal (donkeys, mules, and camels). The Palmyra Tariff Law assesses merchandise in terms of animal loads (donkeys and camels), but this is a very special case, hardly representative of all Syria. The Talmuds refer primarily to transport by donkey, occasionally by horse; wagons appear to have been used only for heavy materials such as stone, and over short distances; camels were used primarily, but not exclusively, in the desert.[164]

From Gaza to Seleucia, Syrian ports offered merchants the services of many skilled shipowners. But Syrian merchants themselves, many of whom traded in Italian and western ports, were the primary clientele. Tyre maintained close ties with the Tyrian community in Puteoli (Pozzuoli), as we know from frequent mentions in the first century;[165] but this is not the place for an inventory of all the Syrian communities established in the west,[166] beginning with Rome itself,[167] which probably served at least in part as a relay station for these merchants. Cities on the coast took advantage of the flow of merchandise from the east to add significantly to the value of these products: cloth was dyed royal purple, silk was rewoven to obtain finer fibers or elaborate designs, cosmetics and other products were manufactured using imported and local spices and aromatics. A thorough history of Syrian ports has yet to be written, and it is surprising to realize the extent to which the fame of Tyre and Sidon rests on literary sources rather than on realia. Despite a number of ancient accounts, we know little about the old ports of these cities.

The city of Tyre has been partially excavated, but scholars have not proceeded beyond identifying its two ports.[168] Tyre stands on a former island, now reattached to the mainland by a sandy isthmus; Strabo describes its two ports well,[169] and Arrian provides additional details in his account of Alexander's siege of Tyre.[170] The northern or "Sidonian" port, smaller and better protected, is surrounded by a wall; the southern or "Egyptian" port, much larger, is also more exposed and lies outside the ramparts. The southern port is defined by long jetties resting on rocky islets and on high spots in the seabed itself; it forms a vast rectangle with a pass through the middle of the southern jetty. Probably the most original of Antoine Poidebard's discoveries is the system of breakwaters in front of each port, north and south; these were built from isolated rocks (they can hardly be called islands!) that blocked the area around the two ports and constituted a risk for anyone approaching.

Sidon also had two ports that Achille Tatius describes at the beginning of his novel: "Sidon is a city on the sea. . . . In the folds of a bay lies a twin harbour, broad and gently enclosing the sea: where the bay bellies out down the flank of the coast on the right, another mouth has been carved out, an alternative channel for the influx of the tide. Thus a second harbour is born from the first, so that trading vessels can winter there in the calm, while they can pass the summer in the outer part of the bay."[171] Unlike Tyre's two ports, Sidon's were not located on opposite sides of the city;[172] rather, they were both north of the city, one prolonging the other, although south of the city there were anchorages that could be used by small boats, especially at the round cove near the artificial murex hill. To the north, taking advantage of two rocky strips that could support jetties, a port was built that was protected from the basin by a long dike. Jean Lauffray's detailed observations have shown that, in addition to their legitimate concern with military defense and their efforts to protect boats from tidal surges from the open sea, engineers perfected a system of sluice gates to prevent sand from filling the harbor, a well-known Roman technique.[173] There is nothing left of the quays; they were pointed out by Ernest Renan, who implicitly dated them from the Roman era by identifying the adjacent mosaics.[174] Beyond this quasi-closed port, sheltered from the open sea by a long island, the basin constituted a fore-port, where boats were sheltered during the summer, rather than an actual second port. However, Lauffray's analyses have been called into question to some extent following a new examination of the island by Honor Frost, who has shown that the basin not only provided a means of protection, but was an actual port, with a jetty, moorings, and storehouses. Frost concludes that in its own way Sidon, like Tyre and Arados, had a main port located on an island.[175] The facility was in operation between the second century B.C.E. and the second century C.E. or the beginning of the third, thanks to a rise in sea level of about a meter.[176]

The port at Caesarea on the Sea has been explored systematically with surprising results. Archaeologists hypothesize that the port experienced a peak of activity between the city's founding and the end of the first century, but that it later declined abruptly. This may have resulted from a weakening of the breakwaters, which would have made the port vulnerable. Repairs in the third and fourth centuries may have resulted in a slight increase in activity, but it is clear that Caesarea had to remain a secondary port on the Palestinian coast.[177]

Information about other ports is incomplete. The port at Laodicea was protected by a wall and open through a narrow inlet; it encompassed about 50 of the 230 hectares surrounded by ramparts,[178] and it had the advantage of paved marble quays. Arados had a double basin opposite the coast, divided by a natural jetty that was artificially reinforced.[179] None of this, however, can be dated with certainty, and it is impossible to know whether alterations in medieval times substantially changed the ancient ports.[180] In Seleucia,[181] an artificial circular port encompassed by a wall of the lower city has been found; it is probably the port established when Seleucos I founded the city. The port was completely filled with sand as a result of the alluvial runoff carried by floodwaters from the upper city. Vespasian built a canal of about 1.2 kilometers to divert the main channel. The effort was largely ineffective, however, for the port appears to have been almost entirely filled in with silt in Diocletian's time; it had to be restored again under Constantine. In any case, Seleucia seems to have drawn more attention from the emperors for its military usefulness than for its commercial advantages,[182] even though Rome had to have had some interest in a port that handled part of the goods headed for Antioch.

A number of small secondary ports, involved in both local and foreign trade, also warrant mention. On old aerial photos the ancient port of Gabala can be clearly seen south of Laodicea, artificially dug in a semicircle open to the sea through a narrow inlet. In Sarepta, between Tyre and Sidon, excavations have revealed improvements made around the end of the first century B.C.E. to a port with quays, fresh-water bays, and fish tanks.[183] The port in Byblos was rebuilt by Hadrian.[184] Ports yet to be discovered include the one at Berytos and others in southern Palestine; they are known to have been active, but they remain essentially unknown in archaeological terms.

LOCAL AND FOREIGN TRADE

In looking at the Hellenistic period, we saw how complex local trade could be, and how important it was to our understanding of the economic activity of the region as a whole. This observation naturally holds true under the empire as well, and although we may lack archives such as those of Zeno for tracing the principal trade routes, Talmudic texts provide an inexhaustible source of examples of daily commerce. Their testimony is limited to Palestine (and principally to Galilee), however, and it would be risky to try to extrapolate from them and draw conclusions about the rest of Syria. For most of Syria we know more about long-distance trade in goods coming from Yemen, India, and China, crossing Syria and continuing across the Mediterranean to Rome and the Roman west. On both of these subjects, new information allows us to get beyond the traditional pattern linking silk, purple dye, and glass in a luxury trade once thought to have enriched only Phoenician ports and the major caravan oases.

Local Trading Networks

One of the locations mentioned most often in rabbinic literature, probably because it was a locus of contact between Jews and Gentiles, was the marketplace. Every village and every city had a regular market, held with varying frequency, that drew customers from near and far. Besides the small local markets where peasants and artisans sold their products to their neighbors, some more important markets appear to have specialized in, or been best known for, specific products, such as Beth Shean's grain market.[185] The market at Ramat al-Khalil, called Botnah in the Talmuds, was located three kilometers north of Hebron; enclosed by a wall during the time of Herod, it was rebuilt under Hadrian after being destroyed by the Bar Kokhba rebels.[186] There is no need to inventory all the markets, but we can draw at least one conclusion: the economy of Roman Palestine depended upon intensive trade in the most diverse commodities, locally produced as well as imported. The autarchic ideal conceived by rabbis concerned with obedience to ritual purity laws was out of reach everywhere, even in rural areas, where people obtained many manufactured goods from elsewhere. It is likely that the image the Talmuds give of Galilee holds good for the rest of Syria as well, with slight local variations.

We have already seen how the output of the two pottery centers in Galilee met the needs of the entire region. We would like to have a better understanding of the way transactions were handled, but it seems that the potter who went off to sell his goods from the back of a pack animal was the exception, not the rule. More commonly, ceramics from these centers were purchased in specialized city markets; potters regularly supplied goods that had to be transported by the owner of a mule, a donkey, or a camel.[187] At any rate, we can see that it is dangerous to generalize about local trade by attributing the supply of agricultural products to the country-side and that of handmade products to the city: here we have a fine example of rural centers becoming rich by supplying the cities with most common artisanal items. Sepphoris, for example, an urban center, seems quite clearly to have depended on rural centers of manufactured goods, at least when it came to ceramics.[188]

We have already seen to what extent grapes and olives stand out as highly speculative crops. This suggests huge sales of surpluses in the cities of the region or beyond. In Galilee around the middle of the first century, John of Gischala is said to have amassed a fortune selling surplus oil to Syrian Jews. We are essentially certain that in northern Syria the Limestone Massif supplied oil to all the cities of the region, beginning with Antioch. We lack the tangible evidence that the discovery of containers would supply, but as we have seen, our knowledge of amphorae from the Roman era is still full of gaps. Still, for other regions there are some indicators. For example, the presence of amphorae from Tyre, Gaza, and the Palestinian coast as well as from northern Syria in the digs in Roman Beirut[189] attests to the existence of regional exchanges of products like oil, wine, and even grains.

In addition, Eastern Sigillata A spread from the northwest throughout Syria as far as the shores of the Red Sea. At Aila, of the 373 sigillata sherds, most belong to the ESA variety, which means that they were imported into the city as early as the Nabataean era.[190] In Hama, sigillata of the ESA type were the most significant group of fine ceramics from the second half of the second century B.C.E. until around 100 C.E., when they disappeared.[191] In Beirut, these were the only fine ceramics found from 60 to 150 C.E.[192] A few sherds have been found in Bostra.[193] And there are many more examples: the phenomenon was not in fact a new one, as these ceramics had spread far and wide by the end of the Hellenistic period.[194]

It is much more difficult to trace the local trade in glass, even though Phoenician glass dating from the first to the second centuries C.E., possibly intended for export to the Indian Ocean, has been found in Aila.[195] Glass-makers in Sidon were probably able to supply luxury goods for the local markets, but the numerous local workshops could ensure the production of everyday items, although the conditions of production were harder to satisfy than for ceramics, because high-quality sand was required. However, it is unlikely that glassmakers maintained production by processing discarded, defective glass.

Other products, such as basalt millstones, also warrant mention. Basalt is both hard and rough; those qualities make it an especially suitable tool. Indeed, basalt millstones are found in several regions, including those where the stone does not occur naturally. Nineteenth-century travelers reported that millstones made in Ezra', southwest of Leja, were exported as far as Jerusalem. This might very well have been the case in antiquity.

We should also note the role of the Arab nomads in supplying meat to butchers. This had been their traditional function since ancient times;[196] it is unlikely that the shepherds of the Harra were raising large flocks of sheep and goats solely for their own consumption. Similarly, they could provide horses and camels for the caravan merchants as well as the Roman army.

The circulation of money ought be able to provide some information about the flow of trade. However, this does not seem to be the case, as several examples will show. First of all, starting in the late Hellenistic period, at least, coins from Tyre far outnumber any others in most sites in Galilee, which seems to indicate the direction of the trade axes. In addition, inscriptions from Gerasa describe payment in Tyrian silver.[197] But does this really reflect a heavy flow of trade, or does it simply result from the fact that until 65–66 Tyre was the only mint in the region producing silver coins, thus furnishing most of the currency necessary for commerce? This coinage with a high silver content (96 percent) and a heavy, fixed weight was highly valued.[198] When Tyre ceased issuing its own coins, the halt in production was only temporary, as an imperial mint struck provincial silver tetradrachms there beginning in Vespasian's reign.[199]

Dura-Europos provides an equally good example, because that city never minted coins (except for a few issues under Seleucos I and possibly one during the time of the Parthian occupation). Throughout the Hellenistic period, Dura apparently depended entirely on coins issued in Antioch; these represent 95 percent of the finds from the third to the second century B.C.E. Parthians never produced their own coinages, so Seleucid coins continued to furnish the necessary cash supply until the first century C.E. After Rome's annexation of Syria, however, Parthian silver coins spread widely throughout the region, and the silver coins issued by the Romans in Antioch rarely reached Dura, at least until the time of Claudius. On the other hand, bronze coins appeared regularly, in limited quantities. After Claudius, bronzes increased significantly, then silver reappeared under Titus; up to the time of the Severi we can say that coins from the Antioch mint were the principal currency in circulation in Dura.[200] The situation changed abruptly, however, under the Severi: coins from Antioch almost disappeared, replaced by coinages minted in Edessa and Carrhai. Does this mean that Dura's economic prospects had shrunk and its trade had changed direction? I do not think so, for the shift was simply the result of the opening, under the Severi, of two new mints, in Edessa and Carrhai, closer to Dura, and their production reached the city more easily.[201] Moreover, the lower weight and value of Antioch bronzes from the reigns of Caracalla and Macrinus on meant that these were no longer an obligatory standard.

We should keep in mind that the production of imperial currency was essentially monopolized by two particular mints in Syria, those of Antioch and Tyre: each of these cities provided coinage for the adjacent region. Moreover, their coins were highly valued because of their stability: the Antioch SC bronzes were so desirable that, when the city began issuing its own coins as a Roman colony, it continued to feature the SC mark.[202] Still, civic coins were issued too sporadically to be a threat to the imperial coinage. Not that they were not valued: coins from the second century have been found in Dura from all parts of Syria and Arabia;[203] however, the volume of production was limited, far too small to meet the demand. Overall, it seems to me that very little can be learned about commercial trade from the circulation of money, because there was no real competition among currencies.

Long-Distance Trade

SYRIA AND THE MEDITERRANEAN

We have already noted the variety and quality of Syrian production in agriculture and crafts. We are only beginning to understand the extent of the long-distance trade that this productivity sustained alongside the export of luxury goods coming from beyond the empire, which we shall examine later.

Syria seems never to have been a significant source of food supply for Rome. Egypt, Africa, and Sicily are well-known sources of wheat, but Syria is never mentioned as an exporter of wheat to other regions of the empire. There may have been some exports, of course, but on too small a scale to be recorded. Moreover, the presence of numerous legions in the country would suffice to explain why all military appropriations made from the public supply (annona) were entirely consumed inside Syria.

The same was true for oil and wine. A few Syrian vintages of good quality may have been found on tables in Rome and in the largest cities of the empire, but it is impossible to estimate how much was exported. Syria was not known for its oil, so it is unsurprising that its oil production served primarily for local consumption. Moreover, the large urban populations in Syria might explain why there was little surplus available for export.

Exports did occur, however, even if only in small quantities. Evidence comes from amphorae found in the Rhone valley and farther north, along the routes from Lyon to the Rhine. Séverine Lemaître has managed to identify certain types of amphorae made in Syria, either in northern Syria or in

Phoenicia (possibly around Beirut), indicating some exchange of goods. This does not mean that only products from the coast were exported; some goods could have been carried by pack animals from the interior, in lightweight goatskin bags,[204] before being repacked for export in a port. We cannot know exactly what these Syrian amphorae contained. Lemaître has noted the presence of dates, but there is no evidence of imported wine before the fourth century, when wine from Gaza appeared.[205]

In addition, Syria was an exporter of fine ceramics, the famous Eastern Sigillata A. Large quantities have been found in Cyprus on the coast facing Syria, but far fewer have appeared in the western part of the island; this distribution probably reflects the preferred commercial trade routes.[206] A high-quality Cypriot sigillata seems to have been produced in the region of Paphos; it competed with the Syrian sigillata in Palestine and even in the Nabataean kingdom, between the middle of the first century B.C.E. and the beginning of the second century C.E.[207] Elsewhere, conditions varied enormously. In a small town such as Assos in the Troad, during the first half of the first century C.E. alone, ESA represented 2.8 percent of all sigillata.[208] In Porsuk, a site in the interior of Cilicia that could be reached only by peddlers and where ceramic finds indicate a degree of reliance on local crafts, the only imports were of ESA, in small quantities to be sure.[209] However, ESA is the most representative fine imported ceramic in Argos in the first century C.E., and it is found in significant quantities in Corinth as well as in Crete.[210] The subject thus merits careful study.

Commercial activity in Syria was not limited to exports; significant traces have been found of goods imported to Syria. The best known, because they are the easiest to identify, are products that traveled in amphorae, indestructible containers. Excavations in Masada have revealed that the Herodians imported both fine wine from Italy and *garum* from southern Spain.[211] We might consider this an exceptional situation involving a princely family accustomed to luxuries, but other garum containers have been found in Petra.[212] In Aila, in the levels of the city dating from the early empire, numerous remains of amphorae containing wine from the western Mediterranean have been found,[213] but we do not know whether the wines were intended for local consumption or for export to Arabia Felix or India. However, Egyptian-made glass has also been found in Aila. Excavations in Panias on Mount Hermon have produced Italian jars from the first century C.E.; these are rare in the Near East,[214] but we should keep in mind that the city was the capital first under Philip and later under Agrippa II. Such finds are not limited to princely capitals, however. In Berytos, imported Spanish amphorae were also quite common,[215] while a large number of "Knossos 26" amphorae, perhaps originally from Sinope, appeared beginning in the late second century.[216] We must remember, too, the Roman colony of Berytos, which had a substantial core population of Westerners whose tastes differed from those of the indigenous population and who presumably appreciated oils from Baetica as well as salt fish or garum from Pontus; the large number of imported casseroles and other cooking vessels confirms this.[217] As elsewhere, however, amphorae from Rhodes and Cos were common until the end of the second century; the first African examples appeared during the same period or at the beginning of the third century.[218]

In another sphere of commercial activity, Syria imported sarcophagi. Some ten of these from Rome have been found in Berytos, Sidon, Tyre, Caesarea, Jerusalem, and Ascalon,[219] along with a few from Phrygia (Dokimeion, Sidimara) made between 140 and 260.[220] There are more than a hundred examples of beautiful Attic sarcophagi from Syria, in addition to a number of local imitations,[221] many of which have been found in Tyre.[222] Other examples have been found in cities such as Arethusa, Bostra, Philadelphia, and Gadara, sites that were difficult for such heavy and fragile objects to reach. About 250 examples of more original ceramic sarcophagi have been found in Galilee, used by both Jews and pagans (and probably Christians as well) roughly between 150 and 350; analysis of the clay confirms that these were certainly imported. They must have been imported through Ptolemais, considering the limited number found in Galilee, for these objects weighed an average of one hundred kilos and could not have been transported very far.[223]

We have also noted that Syria imported a large quantity of different kinds of marble, as well as colored stone from a variety of sources: cipoline from Eubea, gray Troad marble, Egyptian pink granite, and still other types of stone used for building and decoration. The scarcity of beautiful stones in Syria itself meant that these materials had to be imported.

Despite the large-scale domestic production, all parts of Syria imported ceramics. We must not overgeneralize, but imports have been found at most of the sites. A few examples will suffice: Capharnaum, which was a center of production of ordinary pottery, imported numerous ceramics from the Mediterranean, from the Hellenistic period to the second century C.E. Imports were interrupted in the third century and resumed in the fourth.[224] In Hama,[225] Apamaea,[226] and Zeugma,[227] some first-century Italian sigillata have been found, but only a single sherd from Gaul in Hama and Apamaea,[228] whereas Gallic sigillata are fairly common in Antioch, and Zeugma may have supplied the easternmost sherd of Lezoux pottery.[229] But in Hama the greatest number of finds are still African sigillata, from several workshops, found in huge quantities from the beginning of the second century to the fourth, which marks the high point of their production.[230] These light-colored sigillata are also present in Antioch, Zeugma, and even Dura, beginning in the years 230–250.[231]

These examples are limited, but they suffice to show how deeply involved Syria was in both local and long-distance trade around the Mediterranean, how diverse were the products traded, and the extent to which Syria was both exporter and importer. Syria probably represented one of the most active centers of commerce in the Roman Empire, and its own manufactured goods were a significant element in the balance of trade.

TRADE BEYOND THE EMPIRE

Syrian merchants were among those who profited most from commerce between the empire and the countries to the east and south. When they gave up direct control of the sources of supplies from Arabia Felix (despite the relative success of Aelius Gallus's expedition in 27 B.C.E.),[232] the Romans traded with Syrian merchants to procure silk from the Seres,[233] aromatic herbs and spices from India (pepper) and from southern Arabia and its African annexes (cassia, cinnamon, myrrh, incense).[234] These products, which were not expensive in their home markets, underwent a steep rise in price owing in part to the taxes (portoria) imposed by Rome,[235] and in part to charges added by middlemen: these included fees for caravan escorts, the cost of land or sea transportation, and payment for caravan drivers. Of the fifty to a hundred million sesterces that India and Arabia "extorted" from Rome every year, according to Pliny,[236] most were profits earned by subjects of the empire.[237]

Chief among these were the Nabataeans, traditional conveyers of products from Arabia Felix to Petra and later to Gaza and Rhinocolura. During Augustus's era, however, this commerce was mostly diverted to Egypt:[238] Myos Hormos, Coptos, and Alexandria were stops on the new spice route, a route that was still frequented by many Nabataean merchants. Although some caravans continued to supply the Syrian market, Petra's wealth belonged to an earlier age. Recent discoveries, such as the so-called Great Temple, which help to date some of Petra's most important monuments back to the reigns of Malichos I and Obodas III, confirm the early prosperity of the city. However, the picture is somewhat complicated, as Petra shows no indications of irreversible decline, and the shrinking of its commerce may have had only minor consequences.[239] This is hardly surprising, given that Petra itself was not a favorite stop for the caravans: it was located at a dead end on the routes leading east, access required a steep descent of the cliff separating the Edom mountains from Wadi Arabah, and caravans probably took other routes further south or else stopped somewhere in the greater Petra area, avoiding the city itself.[240] Still, Petra may have attracted caravans bearing incense and other aromatics, goods whose values increased in the hands of artisans who used them to make perfumes and cosmetics.[241] Moreover, it is conceivable that the drift to the north noted during the reign of Rabbel II was related to the Nabataeans' effort to hold on to their dominant role in commerce. Perhaps the Nabataeans were present in the great sanctuary of Baalshamin in Sia simply for religious reasons,[242] but the existence in 94 c.e. of a small Nabataean colony of Dmeir, northeast of Damascus on the Palmyra road, may betray an effort to move closer to the new commercial caravan routes.[243]

It is more interesting to try to understand the precise role of the Nabataeans in this trade. We know that in Strabo's time, numerous Roman merchants frequented Petra, probably not to trade there directly but rather to conclude transportation contracts. In any case, the Nabataeans turn up in the record as caravan drivers: when part of the traffic was diverted to Egypt, they appeared riding camels on the long stretches of Arabian desert between the Red Sea and the Nile,[244] and sometimes as far away as the Delta.[245] On the Arabian Peninsula, they unquestionably played a leading role in the northwest, in the entire sector that belonged to the Nabataean kingdom, north of Hegra. Elsewhere, evidence of their presence is scant. It is striking to note that the Meda'in Saleh plain constitutes a dividing line: Nabataean graffiti abound in the northern sector, where Hegra is located, as well as along all the major routes leading north, but they become extremely rare and indeed are most often absent in al-'Ula, in the southern part of the oasis. This observation is reinforced by the scarcity of finds farther south. There are some remains of Nabataean products in Arabia, an inscription dating from 87–88 c.e. in Sha'ib Samma in southern Arabia,[246] one graffito and some Nabataean sherds in Qaryat al-Faw,[247] scattered sherds and a coin in Thaj and Qatif along the coast of the Persian Gulf,[248] a few ceramic fragments and inscriptions in Tayma.[249] But all this is very minor; it does not attest to a continuous presence of Nabataean caravans throughout the peninsula, and not even along the route to Arabia Felix south of Hegra. We cannot say that Nabataean merchants or caravans never used the southern routes, but I doubt that the dividing line for incense was located as far south as the area of Sha'ib Samma, as Michael Macdonald cautiously suggests.[250] To accept this conclusion, we would have to concede that Nabataeans did not start writing things down until they were inside the kingdom!

This should not lead us to assume that trade between Syria and Arabia

Felix was weak, however. The Nabataeans occupied a limited geographical territory, but trade with them did take place, as well as with others, and the influences were reciprocal. Evidence of any direct Nabataean influence, in art in particular, is scarce, but it was no doubt through the intervention of the Nabataeans, who themselves had been imbued with Greek artistic influences, that Greek decorative motifs and techniques spread throughout central and southern Arabia. For example, we are familiar with the famous statues of King Dhamar 'Ali Yuhabirr and his son Tha'ran, kings of Saba and of dhu-Rhaydan between the second half of the second century and the second half of the third. These monumental works were not only inspired by Greek art (heroic nudity) but were created in the Greek style, reflecting a type that goes back to Lysippos and the work of a particular Greek artist (whose name, Phokas, is engraved on the thigh) with the help of an indigenous founder (Lahay amm).[251] Syria, however, may not have figured in this case. By contrast, Ernest Will has shown how the style of the Nike of Paionios, transposed to the Hauran with great success, may have been carried by the Nabataeans as far as Yemen, with the Greek influence seen in the drapery of the statue known as "Lady Bar'at."[252] The spread of the style by way of the Hauran seems inevitable. Nabataean caravans must have linked the two. In Qaryat al-Faw, the capital of the kingdom of Kinda, a fresco on a palace wall shows a figure whose Arab name cannot erase its obvious Dionysian inspiration, crowned as it is with leaves and vines.[253] Of course, Greek influences could be felt as far as Egypt (indicated by the discovery of a Harpocrates and a bronze ibex), but this does not rule out the north–south route used by the Nabataeans.

Palmyra,[254] already a wealthy city when Marc Antony invaded it in 41 B.C.E., enjoyed exceptional prosperity beginning with the first century, as evidenced by the dedication of an enormous Temple of Baal on April 6, 32 C.E. Although located in a poor region,[255] its exceptional position allowed it to control, with mounted troops, all of the Syrian desert between Emesa and the Euphrates, and to guarantee the security of its routes. Moreover, its elite camel corps provided an abundant and indispensable means of transportation across the desert.[256] In addition, Palmyra's merchants established permanent trading facilities in Babylonia (Ctesiphon, Vologesias)[257] and on the Persian Gulf (Spasinou Charax, Phorath, Bahrein);[258] some of them followed this route as far as India.[259] This phenomenon is illustrated by a boat on a funerary relief in Palmyra,[260] as well as by an explicit reference to the chartering of a boat for "Scythia."[261] There is no proof, however, that Palmyrene merchants ever went as far as China, at least on a regular basis,[262] nor can we assert that any merchants arrived from the Far East. Although Chinese sources seemed to know the names of some Near Eastern cities[263] and Roman embassies may have reached China, we have no information about the means of trade.

In any case, merchants from the Mediterranean—including camel drivers, soldiers,[264] and bankers[265]—found the necessary infrastructure in Palmyra for their undertakings beyond the borders of the empire. For the most part, Palmyra's profits came from services rendered; it did not tax merchandise in transit. Goods in transit never entered the city; they were stored in caravan stops built some distance away.[266] The great wall that has been excavated all around the oasis, except on the eastern side where it has disappeared,[267] seems not to have had a major strategic purpose. It probably marked Palmyra's fiscal boundary: it is still called the "customs wall" on the south side even today. This municipal privilege was leased, as was the privilege of collecting Roman customs duties, and we have learned from a text predating the Roman annexation that the leaseholder, a native of the city, demanded a little more than was owed the city in order to make a profit.[268]

A number of large caravan inscriptions illustrate the traffic between Palmyra and Mesopotamia between 19 and 260 C.E.[269] They are especially numerous between 130 and 161, unquestionably marking the peak of caravan traffic in Palmyra, but we know of at least three more dating from the Severan era. The noticeable decline in trade in the third century (no caravan inscriptions between 211 and 247 have been found, possibly owing to the insecurity created by the arrival of the Sassanids after 224) probably did not lead to the closing of the routes, for it seems that merchants continued to visit Palmyra, even though the loans they contracted there were made at high rates, in view of the risks—as high as 30 or 32 percent.[270] As in other areas, we should not assume from the absence of any reference to caravans in monumental inscriptions that all commerce had ceased.

However, Palmyra and the Nabataeans were not the only intermediaries,[271] and it would be interesting to know the role played by the border cities in the Euphrates Valley or the Anti-Taurus piedmont, Edessa and Nisibis in particular. Recent excavations shed some light on the other end of Syria, on the Red Sea. The port of Aila seems to have facilitated trade relations between Syria, Arabia, and the Indian Ocean. Products imported from Syria arrived there (decorated glass from Sidon after the first century C.E.), as did products from much farther west: wine amphorae from the first century B.C.E. to the first century C.E., and, later, grade 47 amphorae,[272] while light-colored African sigillata were present in large numbers beginning in the third century.[273] Thomas Parker points out an increase in the level of imports during the second century.[274] The question is whether imported goods were meant for the local markets or for re-exportation. We cannot know for sure, but in either case, if Aila had a wealthy population large enough to justify the imports, the city must have provided opportunities for making profits, and it is hard to see what besides commerce could have flourished there. Only the discovery of products from the Indian Ocean would confirm such trade, however, and to date none have been found.

Though emphasis is usually placed on Roman imports from India or Arabia Felix, we should not forget that the empire also exported goods, and Syrian artisans provided most of the merchandise sold in Arabia and India in exchange for silk. In fact, imported glassware in India and the development of art in Gandhara provide evidence that in northern India and Arabia Felix there were regular customers for these Hellenizing products.

In the middle of the first century, the *Periplus Maris Erythraei*[275] confirmed that Egyptian artisans were producing goods in part to satisfy the taste of such clientele. Syrian workshops were doing the same in glass, textiles, ceramics (sigillata A and B were copied in India), ingots, and processed metal work, and agricultural products such as wines and wheat were exported as well. Commerce increased as traders learned to take the monsoon phenomenon into account,[276] and direct trading relations were established with Ceylon under Claudius's reign, although such trade was sporadic.[277] Egypt, with its extensive coastline on the Red Sea, probably profited more than Syria from this, but the port of Aila may have benefited as well.

By way of conclusion, I should like to be able to chart trade developments by historical period, as a means of answering a question that has never ceased to intrigue scholars: did Syria experience the effects of a crisis, a recession, a drop in production and trade and, if so, when? Understandably, this question is not easy to answer, and the answer cannot be based on economic factors alone. To judge from both inscriptions and archaeological discoveries, the construction, reconstruction, and beautification of buildings, both public and private, reached a sort of apogee under the Severi. If there was ever a "crisis," then, it had to have come after this period. However, we continue to find evidence of new building, especially in the towns and cities of the Hauran, throughout the third century, and such discoveries undermine any prognosis based solely on this criterion.[278] Evidence has been found of an unprecedented level of activity in building and renovation in Dura shortly before the destruction of the city: the synagogue and the House of the Christians were redecorated just before the middle of the third century. In Palmyra, the mosaics of the Achilles and Cassiopeia houses belong to the third quarter of the third century, as do those of

Philoppopolis. In Antioch itself, many of the mosaics were created during the third century: even if public funds were short, there were still prosperous families. In Mampsis, Nessana, and Oboda of the Negev, archaeologists have observed no decline in commercial activity or prosperity between the second century and the third.[279] Using these criteria, which are based on modern notions ("when the building trades are thriving, everything thrives"), no crisis in third-century Syria can be discerned.

Can we draw conclusions from the manufacturing sector? Some activities ceased, such as the production of fine Nabataean ceramics in the second century, and Eastern Sigillata A, and there was no equivalent local production to take their place. But these were phenomena from the beginning or middle of the second century, involving commodities competing with similar goods that could be acquired more cheaply. The end of both these lines of production probably spelled the ruin of some artisans (unless they managed to convert their output to less refined goods), but not of the Syrian provinces as a whole. We find no decline in the productions of Kefar Hananya until the beginning of the fifth century, and this was the case for many ordinary ceramics. We should not, therefore, base our conclusions on ceramic production alone.

What other indications are there? There appear to have been fewer caravans from Palmyra after the Severi. Or more precisely, inscriptions mentioning caravans are rarer. But may we not explain that by the randomness of archaeological finds? After all, for the period widely recognized as showing heavy caravan activity, we have far fewer than a single inscription per year. Should we not consider the possibility of a change in habits? We might think about what occurred in the area of funerary epigraphy: simple epitaphs seem to be rarer in the Hauran, at least beginning in the fifth and sixth centuries, whereas previously they had been plentiful. Would anyone dare conclude that people had stopped dying? In my opinion, it is rather risky to deduce a drop in traffic between Syria and lower Mesopotamia from the fact that one type of documentation has disappeared. Merchants' records showing an increase in lending rates attest to hard times, not to a break in relations. And we can count on people with commercial interests to make the best of a situation that had probably become more dangerous. The increase in risks could only be translated by an increase in profits.

For, despite the enduring prosperity, there are unmistakable signs of increasing insecurity. Reinforcement of the fortifications in Bostra and Adraha began around 249–250, at the latest, and continued after the fall of Zenobia and Vaballathos.[280] We should also recall the abrupt reinforcement of ramparts at Apamaea, hastily built in the middle of the third century. The same thing happened in the villages: a small fort was built in the middle of the village of Ramthaniyyeh on the Golan in the third century.[281] War had come; there is no room for doubt: war with the Persians, whose aggression never ceased during the third century, and war brought on by more or less powerful usurpers, from Pescennius Niger in 193, through Uranius Antoninus, Macrinus, and Ballista, to Zenobia and Vaballathos in 260–272. But what real, long-term impact did these wars have on life in Syria?

HELLENIZATION AND
INDIGENOUS CULTURES

S YRIA and Syrians were not held in high repute during the empire, notwithstanding the critical role the country and its people played in the intellectual, cultural, artistic, and religious history of the era.[1] Livy believed that the Macedonians had lost their ancestral virtues through contact with Syria and had come to resemble barbarians.[2] The contradiction between perception and reality should not surprise us: the same people who hurried off to ceremonies honoring Adonis or Atargatis also denounced the licentious rituals of those cults, and while we know that synagogues drew worshippers seeking a high moral standard, ancient authors whom we are prepared to consider highly credible on many topics did not hesitate to slander Jews. As they saw it, the "charms of the Orient"[3] could lead only to perversions of body and mind. It is no accident that Juvenal, denouncing the Greek Rome of his day, expressed dismay that the Achaean Greek model had given way to a more oriental Hellenism: "The Syrian Orontes has long since poured into the Tiber, bringing with it its lingo and its manners, its flutes and its slanting harp-strings; bringing too the timbrels of the breed, and the trulls who are bidden ply their trade at the Circus . . . foreign strumpets with painted head-dresses."[4] To be sure, we may see this as the reaction any conservative Roman might have had to the spread of Syrian cults in Rome and Italy, to the popularity that was perhaps enhanced by the presence of a sizable Syrian colony.[5] However, we should not overlook the disdain for barbarians that continued to find expression within an empire that generally respected the most diverse customs. It was not difficult to be considered barbarian: Iulia Soaemias begged her son Elagabalus to re-place the barbarian dress of a Syrian priest[6] with the toga of a Roman citi-zen before he entered Rome;[7] it was quite enough that he carry out rites "with all the wailing and frenzy of the Syrian cult."[8] Similar passages in the works of ancient authors overtly hostile to Syrians could be cited ad in-finitum. It would be pointless to analyze the causes of this phenomenon here; I prefer to attempt to portray as accurately as possible the realities countering the excesses of what we should surely call "ordinary racism" if the expression were not an obvious anachronism.

Moreover, as a land with a blended population, Syria was a melting pot not only of Greeks and Semites, but of peoples with very different customs and languages within the Semitic world itself, making any generalization about who was "Syrian" highly suspect. Alongside the old Phoenician stock limited to the central coastal region, a group whose language had been lost at the beginning of the early empire but whose culture still per-meated attitudes and behavior, particularly in religious matters, most of the part of Syria with sedentary populations was inhabited by Aramaeans or peoples who had long since adopted Aramaean ways. However, the Arab groups who appeared at various times during the course of the Achaemenid period and then in the Hellenistic era influenced the develop-ment of certain cults and introduced a new language, one that competed with Aramaic as well as Greek and kept alive a written tradition in a non-Greek language.[9]

SYRIAN HELLENISM

Greek Culture and Daily Life: Signs of Acculturation

Who spoke Greek? Who spoke Latin?[10] And why? As simple as these questions may appear, they are difficult to answer with precision. As far as Latin is concerned, we know that it was the official language of the govern-ment and the army, and we can reasonably expect to find it in widespread use in these communities. Indeed, the vast majority of epitaphs for sol-diers from every background were in Latin, as has been seen in Bostra, Apamaea, and Seleucia of Pierea, to take just three examples.[11] Similarly, dedications in honor of emperors, governors, officers, and other individu-als of high rank were also most frequently in Latin. Moreover, written Latin was by far the most widely used language in the Roman colonies of Berytos and Heliopolis until the fourth century. Latin continued to appear in certain official documents, such as the account of a case brought before the emperor Caracalla in person by the residents of Goharia, northeast of

Damascus, during his visit to Antioch in 216. These tenant farmers, who were protesting both the usurpation of the priesthood and the unjustified theft or removal of cult statues, won their case and had the minutes of the trial posted on the Temple of Dmeir. The heading is in Latin, the language of imperial justice, but the charges and the emperor's statements are reported in Greek.[12]

Despite the predictable status of written Latin, its use in speech may not have been equally widespread. Clearly, westerners who had settled in Syria, whether temporarily or permanently, continued to speak Latin. Similarly, jurists in Berytos expressed themselves fluently in Latin, particularly because many of them were originally from the west, but it seems that Greek may have been used in the schools, which were primarily intended for Greek-speaking students.[13] We do not know whether Latin spread much beyond these relatively narrow circles. Even though natives adopted exclusively Roman names, both first names (Marcus, Lucius, Publius) and surnames, *cognomina* (Severus, Antoninus, Hadrianus, and so on), they always wrote their names in Greek, not Latin. Similarly, although soldiers' epitaphs were usually engraved in Latin, some were in Greek, and veterans almost always preferred Greek.

There can be no doubt about the linguistic predominance of Greek, and not only at the expense of Latin. We shall see below that indigenous languages survived under a variety of conditions, but the fact that Aramaic, which was spoken by the largest number, practically disappeared from inscriptions on monuments outside a few marginal communities, such as Edessa, Palmyra, and Petra, shows that writing in Greek seemed natural to most people. We should not carry this inference too far, however, and I am wary of claiming that the entire Hauranese population was Hellenized and fluent in Greek just because almost all the nearly two thousand epitaphs in the Hauran are in Greek. Numerous mistakes in spelling and syntax prove that mastery of Greek was far from perfect; still, the preference accorded to Greek in private usage, as in all the epigraphy of the region, is evidence that most people in this community were assumed to have some knowledge of Greek.

In fact, Greek was able to surpass Latin to a surprising degree. For example, it may come as a surprise that, under Trajan, Greek replaced Latin on the legends of coins in Antioch. In the Roman colonies of Ptolemais and Caesarea by the Sea, no official inscriptions issued in the colonies are in Latin. The same was true in the Severan period and in the third century, when many colonies did not even bother to use Latin on coins, although that was the standard practice: some colonies, such as Carrhai or Arca of Lebanon, issued coins alternately in Latin and Greek, while others, such as

Nisibis, Rhesaina, Singara, Emesa, Antioch, and Edessa, used Greek for the legends on all coins.[14] In the other direction, Latin left its mark on Greek, in that Greek adopted certain words—such as *colonist* and *colony*—and administrative titles without translating them, but such borrowings were relatively few in number.

In any event, written language is just one aspect of acculturation. While it may be the most visible aspect, it may also be the most superficial; we need to look to the decorative arts, architecture, and tomb design for other, less tenuous signs of the acculturation of the elites.

No collective study has been made of the storytelling sarcophagi from Roman Syria, but a few partial studies give us some idea of what they were like. Numerous sarcophagi have been found, even in rural areas, that reproduce the simplest decorative themes (lion heads, garlands, and so forth),[15] simple elements borrowed from the Helleno-Roman tradition demonstrating the strong appeal that the decorative arts held at the time.[16] More relevant to the history of taste, and clearer indicators of acculturation, however, are the storytelling sarcophagi, imported at great cost, particularly from Attica.[17] Two of these, containing the story of Meleagros, have been studied in some depth; one comes from Antioch and the other, more surprisingly perhaps, is from the Jewish necropolis at Beth Shearim.[18]

Sarcophagi represent one aspect of Greek imagery in Syria; discoveries of numerous mosaics, many of the highest quality, reveal several other perspectives. Antioch, Apamaea, Seleucia of Pierea, Palmyra, Philippopolis, Gerasa, Caesarea, Edessa, and Zeugma have all provided a number of more or less sumptuous floor coverings; by contrast, only a few cities follow Dura's pattern and offer none at all.[19] Curiously (but it may simply be a matter of chance), there are no known Hellenistic mosaics,[20] although the oldest mosaics, like the geometric stone ones of the Herodian palaces (for example, the western palace of Masada), derive from the Hellenistic tradition. By far the greatest number belong to a Roman tradition that remained virtually unchanged until the end of the third century. Stylistically, as Janine Balty has noted, this art remained untouched by local influences in its overall conception; in all mosaics, relatively complex patterns of geometric squares were juxtaposed around a central theme or motif.[21] The themes themselves show the local leaders' strong attachment to Greco-Roman mythological tradition: never do we find the slightest indigenous motif in any of the works in the "western" style. In Palmyra, for instance, the mosaics in the houses of Achilles and Cassiopeia are the work of itinerant Antiochene artists and have nothing to do with local painting or sculpture.[22] An inventory of the mosaics discovered throughout greater Syria suffices to make the point: Dionysian motifs, Aphrodite and Ares, the judgment of Paris, the seasons, the Phoenix, Meleagros, Iphigenia, Orpheus, are all themes found in a variety of sites, in mosaics as well as in paintings and sarcophagi, from the first to the third century and even beyond, with little variation.[23]

A distinction must be made between style—which may be highly refined, as in Antioch and Palmyra, or quite individualized, created as was the case in Edessa by a local artisan working in his own way from patterns that originated elsewhere—on the one hand, and themes that reflected popular taste for the same mythological or heroic legends, on the other. Let us take the example of the only two mosaics of Orpheus found in Syria during the period that concerns us. One, from Philippopolis of Arabia, probably created in the second half of the third century,[24] is in a very classical style; it presumably adorned the house of a wealthy colonist in the new colony. The other, from Edessa, is in a much simpler, graphically spare style bearing a dedication in Syriac from 227–228.[25] These reflect the same shared culture and draw from the same repertoire of images, yet no one could say that they do so to the same purpose. Orpheus, in the tomb from Edessa, may be the symbol of the afterlife or even the hope of resurrection, but there is no way to know whether the owner of the tomb was Christian, Jewish, or pagan.[26]

Two mosaics found in Sepphoris, one of Dionysos and one of Orpheus, enable us to assess how much these cultures intermingled without any dilution of their cultural and religious identities.[27] Sepphoris had a large Jewish population, and Jews living in pagan communities, whether cities or villages, and even where they were a majority, were inevitably surrounded by images. Those associated with Dionysos were certainly among the most popular and thus among the most widespread. There was of course a Jewish tradition linking grapevines with various Biblical events, including the story of Noah; vine branches decorated Jewish coins beginning in the fourth century B.C.E.—such as those of Mattathias Antigonos in the first century B.C.E.—and we may recall that the entrance to Herod's temple was decorated with a golden vine.[28] The Jewish rebels of 132 adopted figures of vines, grape leaves, and amphorae for their own purposes. We can see why pagans recognized in Yahweh a double of Dionysos. In the Mambre sanctuary, near Hebron, at the site of an ancient cult of a wine god, Jews, Christians, and pagans gathered for officially different reasons, but undoubtedly in memory of a cult where wine was part of the celebration. Of course, pious Jews would never have acknowledged an identification of Yahweh with any other god whatsoever, but their own God had nevertheless eventually appropriated the functions, attributes, and rituals of this ancient god of wine, and thus could be associated with Dionysos. It seemed natural to look to Dionysian iconography for motifs that could illustrate a traditional Yahwist theme without any implicit reference to some Dionysian cult.[29] In no way does this common imagery suggest a loss of belief; it simply reflects a shared taste for the same type of decoration.

In addition to sarcophagi and mosaics, Syria also offers a wealth of ancient paintings. Beginning in the Hellenistic period, paintings decorated tombs in Marisa, houses in Berytos, and houses and public buildings in Petra.[30] Lavish tomb decorations from Roman times have been discovered in Palmyra (the underground vault of the Three Brothers, for example), in Abila of the Decapolis (the Qweilbeh necropolis), and in Phoenicia. In Sidon, recently revealed vault paintings from the archives of William John Bankes represent servers at a great earthly banquet, with descriptive names ("the wine lover," the "sweetie"); they clearly belong to a style that was well known in the Near East in the second and third centuries C.E., and at the same time they show unparalleled originality in representation.[31]

The most beautiful collection that has been studied systematically comes from Abila in the Decapolis,[32] where twenty-two tombs from a stone necropolis located northeast of the city, bordering Wadi Qweilbeh, have yielded paintings. These paintings, like the monuments themselves, date from the end of the first century (tomb Q4) to the middle of the third century C.E. Four other tombs with paintings from the same region (Capitolias, Som, Marwa, and Gerasa)[33] illustrate the diffusion of shared tastes in iconography. The same motifs have been shown to appear over and over again in many of these tomb paintings: garlands, crowns of leaves, and soaring eagles, for example, were all treated in much the same way, not only in the Decapolis but in Dura, Palmyra, and Tyre as well.[34] Dionysian themes abound; mythological themes from Homer, which are found in Beit Ras (Capitolias)[35] and Tyre,[36] are entirely absent. This painted decor generally signals the presence of a prosperous social class, although its members were not as wealthy as the aristocrats of Palmyra or Tyre, who could afford ambitious and complex iconographic designs. In Abila, the use of architectural and geometric designs (inspired by Egypt) was developed along with leaf patterns and portraits of the deceased. Alix Barbet has noted that blue, a difficult color to obtain and therefore expensive, appears only in the most opulent tomb in this group (Q13, the tomb "of the veiled women"); nevertheless, it is used in the most beautiful tomb in Syria, the Three Brothers tomb in Palmyra,[37] and in a sumptuous painted vault in Masyaf depicting scenes of the abduction of Persephone and scenes with Hermes, Jason and Medea, and Narcissus.[38] There are some stylistic differences between the

WINGED VICTORY IN A FRESCO FROM THE
PARTHIAN BATH IN DURA-EUROPOS,
SECOND CENTURY C.E.

southern Levant, the Decapolis, Palmyra, and the Euphrates region, just as there are detectable differences in quality. However, it is remarkable that the iconographic repertoire of the tomb paintings is drawn entirely from the Greco-Roman tradition. There is no indigenous tradition for these paintings, even though people of modest means settled for simple designs while the wealthy indulged in huge iconographic displays with mythological or Homeric themes. We should note that, although the same tombs remained in use for a very long time, from the middle or end of the first century B.C.E. until the fifth or sixth century, the taste for painted walls developed only during a very brief period, between the end of the first century and the middle of the third. Moreover, only one-third to two-thirds of the tombs in a necropolis, such as the one in Abila, were painted.

Paintings have also been found in a number of Syrian sanctuaries. Dura has turned out to be one of the largest centers of painting in Syria, and paintings have been found in pagan sanctuaries (notably the *mithraeum,* a sanctuary dedicated to Mithra, and the temple of the Gadde), synagogues,[39] and the House of the Christians.[40] In each case, the images chosen conformed to particular needs—scenes of offerings among the pagans, illustrations of biblical events in the synagogue, figures from the Gospels such as the Good Shepherd, the women at the tomb, or Jesus walking on water for the Christians—but the techniques and decorative styles are identical throughout.

Finally, paintings were also present in private homes. In Petra, the large Az-Zantur IV House was decorated with trompe-l'oeil murals and decorative plasters in the first century C.E., imitating Hellenistic and Roman styles of the preceding century.[41] Paintings in the second Pompeian style, however, have long been identified in stone houses at Wadi Siyyagh.[42] It is also a style that seems to have been especially popular in Judaea, where artists carefully avoided representing the human figure. Such paintings are found both in private homes in Jerusalem during the Herodian period and in royal residences, as for example in Jericho.[43] Generally speaking, despite a great deal of variation in the quality of workmanship, these decorative

TWO SYRIAN STATUES OF VICTORY, WITH AN ATHENA,
LATE SECOND OR EARLY THIRD CENTURY C.E.

painted motifs belong in all respects to the Greco-Roman tradition that
was frequently brought into Syria via Egypt.

Very different trends are found in sculpture. To be sure, there are a few
works in the Helleno-Roman tradition, such as the statue of Athena-Allat
in Palmyra, which is simply a copy of Phidias's Athena Parthenos. But
alongside the rare works of this sort, an indigenous sculpture reworked
classical iconographic themes in a provincial style. Examples include the
numerous Victories found in the Hauran, which borrow heavily from the
Nike of Paionios of Mende. Similarly, a lintel depicting the judgment of
Paris and Athena and another depicting Aphrodite with the lion, both
from Suweida, attest to the spread of Greek mythological themes in the

STATUE OF APHRODITE FROM
DURA-EUROPOS.

Hauran and are treated in a relatively classical manner.[44] Even more indicative are the moving funerary reliefs from the tomb of the priest Rapsones in Babulin in northern Syria, depicting purely Greek mythological scenes (Bellerophon and the chimaera, the chariots of the moon and the sun, the labors of Hercules, Greek-style reclining banquets, and sacrificial processions). These are treated in a very distinctive indigenous style, as is the setting: thus two girls bear the names Antoneina and Hygia, two men are called Antoneinos and Claudius, but the tomb's owner and a woman are identified as Rapsones and Martha, both Semitic names.[45] The clothing also reflects a milieu attached to ancestral ways, with wide embroidered dresses for the women; Rapsones himself seems to be wearing a toga with a fold draped across his chest, but he has a curious pleated bonnet on his head, shaped in a way completely foreign to the Greco-Roman tradition.

Dress might constitute an additional criterion, moreover, for analyzing the degree of Hellenization or acculturation. Generally speaking, in both sculpture and mosaics, artists throughout Roman Syria had adopted an iconography in which men and women alike were dressed in Greek or Roman clothes—which were indistinguishable at the time. However, in Edessa, Palmyra, and Dura we find a combination of Roman tunics and Parthian caftans and pants. On the very beautiful sarcophagi of the Palmyra necropolis, the figure laid out on the *kline,* the lid that serves as a resting place, always wears the long pleated pants topped by an embroidered tunic that were typical of Parthian dress. But the others—servants and family members who adorn the sides of the container—have bare legs and are dressed in Mediterranean-style tunics.[46] Conversely, indigenous customs remained strong among priests and frequently among women, who in Palmyra, for instance, wore a great deal of jewelry.[47] The same can be said of the Hauran, where women seem to have been more traditional in their dress than men.[48] In some cases, the Greek style seems to be linked to a particular social status: Salome Komaise specified in her marriage contract that her husband would provide for her and her children "in accordance with Greek customs and manners . . . on peril of all his possessions."[49]

Greek-style games were another indication of acculturation. As early as the Hellenistic period, games were held in Tyre and Sidon, and others were founded at various times throughout the early empire. A list of winners in Laodicea under Elagabalus probably provides a fairly complete picture of the contests as they were practiced at the time, and shows that games were held in all the large cities of Syria (Antioch, Tyre, Caesarea, Scythopolis, Ascalon, Laodicea), as well as in more modest places such as Beroea-Aleppo, Balanea-Leucas, Zeugma, Chalcis, Hierapolis, and Tripolis.[50] We know from various sources that there were other

HERACLES AND LION
FROM SUWEIDA.

contests in Damascus, and during the third century games took place in Bostra and possibly Adraha.[51] However, neither Palmyra nor Petra ever organized games; this may well indicate that the Hellenization of the elites in these two cities was limited.

There is abundant evidence of a Greek lifestyle throughout Syria, and

PORTRAIT OF A COUPLE, RELIEF FROM A TOMB IN PALMYRA.

PORTRAIT OF A WOMAN, RELIEF
FROM A TOMB IN PALMYRA.

PORTRAIT OF A WOMAN, RELIEF FROM A
TOMB IN PALMYRA.

particularly in the cities. During the imperial period we can fully measure the consequences of the Seleucids' policy of colonization and urbanization. Does this mean that there were no longer any differences at all between the descendants of the original Greek and Macedonian colonists, on the one hand, and the Hellenized Syrians, on the other? One might think so, but the claim is probably only partly true. After two generations, the colonists had indeed lost their sentimental attachments to a land, Greece or Macedonia, that they had never known; Syria was their only homeland. But the feeling of belonging to an elite did not fade away, as we have seen from the retention of characteristic names quite unlike those of the Hellenized Syrians. And the latter for their part did not always try to conceal their indigenous origins, as we have seen in the retention of an extensive Semitic nomenclature, even among cultivated classes. Was it not the writer Iamblichos of Emesa who announced proudly that he was "not a Greek from Syria, but a native, speaking their language and sharing their customs?"[52]

Greek Literature in Syria

Some of the most brilliant representatives of Hellenistic Greek culture came from Syria, spanning a wide variety of fields.[53] The tradition continued more or less throughout the imperial period, and we often find the same intellectual centers as in the preceding era, along with a few others. Gadara of the Decapolis, for example, had enjoyed great fame, and the orator Theodoros of Gadara upheld that city's intellectual tradition during Augustus's reign;[54] he was followed by the cynical philosopher Oinomaos at the beginning of the second century, and then by Apsines under Maximinus Thrax.[55] The various philosophical schools were well represented, on the whole. Aristotelianism found an ardent defender in Boethos of Sidon (second century), who had studied under Andronicos of Rhodes and became his successor as head of the peripatetic school in Athens; Boethos's work, centered around a commentary on Aristotle, has been lost, but it was widely used by his successors.[56] Alexander of Damascus was the first holder of the peripatetic chair in Athens.[57]

Oinomaos of Gadara, who was prominent for a decade starting around 120, represented cynicism with brilliance: his treatise *Against the Oracles* was preserved for the most part by Eusebius of Caesarea, but he was famous for his work in a number of different fields; his name even appears in the Talmuds, where he is identified as Abnimos, a pagan philosopher, although he may actually have been a Hellenized Jew. He was a major influence on Lucian of Samosata, on the fourth-century Cynics, and even on Christians, who were able to use his arguments against the pagans.[58] A Epicurean current also continued to flourish, especially in Apamaea, where it took an organized form.[59] In cultivated milieus, the Platonic and Neoplatonic schools were by far the most popular and influential, thanks to such men as Maximus of Tyre (ca. 125–185). Maximus was more rhetorician than philosopher, and his skill as a speaker (he left forty-one *dialexeis,* or "lectures") was a major reason for the popularity of Neoplatonism, although he never stopped defending the unity of philosophy against the schools.[60] In this arena, Apamaea and central Syria were a center of primary importance, owing to men such as Noumenios of Apamaea (second century), who is described as both a Platonist and a Pythagorean. His treatise *On the Good* survives, as does a *History of the Academy,* in which he seeks to show to what extent his master's teaching was corrupted by his successors. An eclectic, he identified with the Pythagoreans, the Magi, the Egyptians, and the Jews, and he offered an allegorical interpretation of the Jews' sacred texts. He was a decisive influence on Plotinus (who was accused of plagiarizing him), and also on Origen, Porphyry, and all the later Neoplatonists.[61] His work brought Amelius Gentilianus of Etruria,[62] the author of a one-hundred-volume exegesis of his writings, to Apamaea.

Noumenios's teaching was continued by Longinus of Emesa (c. 205–273), Porphyry of Tyre, and Iamblichus of Chalcis. The first was the nephew of the rhetorician Fronton of Emesa, who was a rival of both

Apsines of Gadara and Philostratus of Athens under the Severi; two of his epigrams may have been preserved.[63] Longinus himself, born Cassius Longinus around 205, was both a philosopher and a philologist; he was highly erudite, although Plotinus considered him a mediocre philosopher. Only fragments of his work remain. He died tragically: allied with Zenobia, he had taken up the cause of Vaballathos and was executed by Aurelian in late 272 or early 273.[64] Porphyry of Tyre, in the next generation (234–c. 305), originally called Malchus, was very learned, a philosopher and a scholar of religions. A student of Longinus and a disciple of Plotinus, he was the author of at least sixty-nine works. He wrote commentaries on the works of Aristotle and Plato, edited Plotinus's *Enneads,* worked on the history of philosophy and its links to religion, and even studied Homer. Using historical criticism alone, in his work *Against the Christians* he established a late date for the book of Daniel and deemed the book of Zoroaster a fake.[65] Finally, Iamblichos (c. 245–c. 325), originally from Chalcis of Belos,[66] set himself the task of summarizing the Aristotelian doctrine; he had a school in Apamaea and had considerable influence on late Neoplatonism.[67] This Platonist taste is manifested in a series of mosaics completed between the Severan era and the mid-fourth century or even later, in Emesa (the mosaic of Hercules under the Severi), in Shahba-Philippopolis in the middle of the third century, in Restan-Arethusa, in Palmyra,[68] and, naturally, in Apamaea.[69] These mosaics reveal the adherence of city leaders to the Neoplatonist culture of the time, despite some decorative adaptations in conformity with local tastes.

Similarly, a number of rhetoricians played a part in the development of the second sophistic, from Isaeus the Syrian (late first century)[70] to Genethlios of Petra, the third-century author of a commentary on Demosthenes,[71] and his fellow Petraean Callinicos, who taught rhetoric in Athens under Diocletian.[72] This group also included Hadrian the Phoenician (or Tyrian), a student of Herod Atticus, the rhetorician and poet who was one of the first holders of a chair in rhetoric in Athens.[73] Others are little more than names, but they attest to the continuity and intensity of intellectual life in the region: Euthydemos of Phoenicia, who was the teacher of Apollonios of Tyana in Tarsus,[74] Apasios of Byblos (mid-second century), Hermippos of Berytos, a grammarian in Hadrian's time, Ulpian of Tyre, a teacher of Attic rhetoric (and possibly the nephew of the jurist of the same name), the Syrian Pausanias, and Maior of Arabia.[75] In literature there was Iamblichus of Syria, author of *Babyloniaca* around 170, Heliodoros of Emesa, author of *Ethiopics* or *The Story of Theagenes and Charicleia,* possibly from the third century,[76] and, most brilliant of all, Lucian of Samosata, author of many stories and romances.[77]

Syrians contributed ably to the development of the exact sciences, law, and history. The cartographer, mathematician, and geographer Marin of Tyre (first to second century)[78] produced a description of the earth with measurements that were used by Claudius Ptolemy in the middle of the second century.[79] Nicomachos of Gerasa, a Pythagorean musician of the mid-second century, is best known as a mathematician, the founder of an algebraic arithmetic that departed from the geometric arithmetic of his predecessors.[80] On the fringes of mathematics, halfway between mathematics and philosophy, astrologers had considerable prestige. Although only fragments remain of the *Pentateuch* of Dorotheos of Sidon, a poet-astrologer of the first half of the second century,[81] the *Anthologies* of Vettius Valens of Antioch have been preserved: written during the time of Hadrian, these nine books combine astrology, mathematics, morals, and mysticism.[82] Working in a similar vein, the Jerusalem native Iulius Africanus, born around 180, was a Jewish writer who converted to Christianity; his *Chronography* established a genre that was to enjoy great success,[83] and his *Cesti*,[84] written during the reign of Alexander Severus, brought together military arts, medicine, veterinary arts, weights and measures, and numerous other topics on which only scattered citations remain.

Turning lastly to history, well represented as early as the end of the first century B.C. by Nicolaos of Damascus,[85] we note among Syria's most famous historians Flavius Josephus[86] and his rival, Justus of Tiberias.[87] Nicolaos, not a native Greek but a Hellenized Syrian, came from a prominent Damascus family; he was born about 64 B.C.E., just when the Romans were annexing Syria. A peripatetic philosopher, he studied in Rome, Alexandria, and Rhodes, where he must have met many of the best-known philosophers and rhetoricians. Cleopatra chose him as tutor to her twins, and he lived for a time in Alexandria, perhaps even after the queen's death. He entered the court of Herod the Great sometime between 29 and 20 B.C.E., though we do not know the exact date or specific circumstances. Almost all of his work in philosophy would have been lost had not a few extracts survived in Syriac translation. Furthermore, his historical and historiographical work is very fragmentary.[88] His works include a *Life of Augustus* published around 25 B.C.E., *Manners, Laws, and Customs of all Nations* (around 20), *Histories* in 144 books (between 14 and 4 B.C.E.), and finally an *Autobiography*. Working closely with Herod, he was deeply involved in affairs of state and in relations with Rome; had his work on contemporary events survived, Nicolaos could have provided us with a point of view quite different from that of Josephus. The fragments of his *Histories* that we do have relate to the earliest periods in the history of the Greek world, Asia Minor, Iran, and Babylon, as well as the history of the Jews.

Josephus, by contrast, is first of all the historians of the Jewish War (*De bello judaico* is the title of his earliest work); he went on to deal with all of Jewish history in *De antiquitate judaico*. His work is of capital importance, even if his own political choices dictated a certain point of view regarding the war: he came from a milieu of moderate Pharisees and joined the side of the victor before the war ended, two facts that color the explanations he offers for the inevitable failure of the revolt.[89] It would be interesting to have the work of Justus of Tiberias, his political rival: secretary and historiographer to Agrippa II after the Jewish War, Justus—although equally moderate—opposed Josephus during the efforts in Galilee in 66–67. His version of the episode of the siege of Iotapata and of the entire conduct of the military operations was undoubtedly quite different from that of Josephus.[90]

Occupying a place apart is Philo of Byblos, the author of a work in Greek on the Phoenician gods, titled *Phoinikika*, which he presents as a mere translation of a much earlier writer (predating the Trojan War!), Sanchuniathon of Berytos. In reality, this is quite probably an original work from the beginning of the second century C.E. that combines ancient Phoenician legends with contemporary beliefs. We know it only from fragments preserved in the *Praeparatio Evangelica* of Eusebius of Caesarea, not nearly enough to re-create the original work.[91] Philo's other works include *Concerning the Acquisition and Selection of Books, Concerning Cities and the Illustrious Men Each of Them Produced,* and *Concerning the Reign of Hadrian.*[92] He introduced his student Hermippos of Berytos, the author of a work on dreams, to his friend Senator Herennius Severus, who was himself acquainted with Pliny.[93] History, however, is doubtless not the Syrians' strongest field, and the work of the few known historians has not been passed down: the Tyrians Callicrates and Nicomachos are little more than names for us.[94]

We must not fail to note the Christian literature that flourished after the second century, with Justin Martyr, around 100–165 C.E., a native of Neapolis in Palestine and author of a *Dialogue with Tryphon* and *Apologies;* his works rank him among the most brilliant Christian apologists of the second century.[95] His student, Tatian of Assyria,[96] a contemporary of Lucian, devoted an entire book, *Discourse to the Greeks* (169–171), to a denunciation of pagan practices, rather curiously echoing the accusations made by Apollonios of Tyana in the first century. A virulent polemicist, he boasted of his barbarian origins and proclaimed the superiority of his fellow Christians to pagan Greeks.[97] In a somewhat different vein, Theophilos of Antioch, bishop of that city from 169 to 180 and possibly longer, produced a systematic but nonpolemical account of the Christian doctrine in *Ad Autolycum.*[98] Somewhat later, at the beginning of the third century, Bishop Beryllos of Bostra wrote works that were refuted by

WOMAN (THE MUSE MELPOMENE?) WITH MASK
FROM PETRA, FIRST CENTURY C.E.

Origen.[99] Paul of Samosata, bishop of Antioch beginning in 261, has left the impression that he was a heretic and more attached to the goods of this world than to intellectual preoccupations; at least this is the picture that emerges from the synodal letter preserved by Eusebius.[100] Although the first synod of bishops in 264 did not manage to prove the heretical nature of Paul's teaching, a second trial in 268 ordered his deposition. Owing to his ties to people in power, however, he was able to remain in place until 272, when Aurelian ruled in favor of his designated successor, Domnos.[101] Finally, Lucian of Antioch was highly influential during the last third of the third century owing to his teaching, before he died a martyr in 312.[102]

Law is brilliantly represented by Paul during the time of Hadrian,[103] then by the great jurist Ulpian of Tyre, who died in the summer of 223,[104] and later by Papinian of Emesa. Berytos, a beacon of Latin tradition, was home to a law school celebrated throughout antiquity that lasted until the sixth century.[105] In fact, in as multicultural an empire as Rome's, every community and every town preserved its traditions and in particular its own laws. Only Roman citizens were subject to Roman law in its entirety. This was especially the case for citizens residing in Roman colonies: they constituted a dense Roman core in the midst of populations where Greek and Aramaic were spoken; thus Roman law was applied in Berytos. The growth of law schools made it possible to compare Roman and local laws and helped disseminate imperial law throughout the Greek-speaking provinces.

Berytos is first mentioned as a distinguished center of legal studies in 239 C.E. in the work of Gregory Thaumaturgus. There was probably not a law school as such, at the time, but rather a constellation of study centers organized around competent teachers. These professional jurists had been increasingly drawn to Berytos since the Augustan era, because the Roman colony of Berytos was the center from which imperial edicts, published in Latin and translated into Greek, were disseminated throughout the Orient. Translation went beyond the linguistic dimension alone, for it involved comprehension and interpretation. A group of jurists schooled in the various Greek and indigenous systems of law as well as in Roman law had thus become indispensable. This was the original core of what would not be called a school of law, strictly speaking, until the late third century. From then on, students came from everywhere for the best legal training in the empire. Indeed, two of the great jurists, Paul and Ulpian, were originally from Tyre, which only added to Berytos's prestige as a center of legal studies, and the greatest scholars (Gaius, Scaevola, Marcian, Tryphonios) may have taught there. The school reached its peak in the fourth and fifth centu-

THEATER AT BOSTRA.

ries, and disappeared when the city was destroyed by a violent earthquake and tidal wave on July 9, 551. In the aftermath, the school moved to Sidon, but the best teachers left for Constantinople. Archaeologists are searching for remains of the school around the Greek Orthodox church of St. George, but it is also possible that the school was located north of the Place de l'Etoile.

Law was the only field in which Latin supplanted Greek; in no other field did native Syrian authors write in Latin. This seems self-evident, since most of the population used Greek as the language of communication. But it is worth noting that as early as the fourth century the greatest writer in the Latin language was an Antiochene, Ammianus Marcellinus.

Despite the nearly total destruction of the literature from this period, its existence attests to the strength of Greek culture in Syria. To the extent that the places of origin of the authors whose names have come down to us are telling, we find that no city of some importance is entirely without an intellectual life. We are not surprised to find that cities such as Tyre, Sidon, and Apamaea were traditional centers of learning (Antioch, by contrast, is rarely cited), as were even cities of the Decapolis such as Gadara and Gerasa.[106] But cities that were Hellenized later, such as Samosata, Chalcis of Belos, Emesa, Bostra, and Petra also contributed to the development of Greek culture in the imperial period, which probably explains why Syria played such an important role in its survival in late antiquity.[107]

INDIGENOUS CULTURES

We should not allow the successes of Greek culture to obscure the fact that Syria's rural areas offered virtually total resistance to Hellenization, apart from some superficial aspects that affected only the elites. Even the cities were far from being completely Hellenized, especially in the south; but in Antioch in the fourth century, John Chrysostom was aware that one group of converts who were attending the churches of Antioch did not understand Greek, either because they were of rural origin or because they had originally come from beyond the Euphrates;[108] as early as the end of the third century, in Scythopolis, an interpreter translated Greek into Aramaic in one church.[109] We find evidence of the strength of local traditions as well as the advance of Arabization in proper names and in the use of indigenous languages.

Onomastic studies in Roman Syria reveals some pronounced regional differences.[110] For instance, in the coastal cities of Phoenicia, proper names appear to have been almost exclusively Greek at the beginning of the imperial era.[111] The reappearance of Semitic names in Greek epigraphy under the early empire should not be taken as evidence that indigenous traditions were progressing or resurfacing, but as proof that the use of written Greek had spread into communities where people had not previously written at all, people whose indigenous names had been preserved. But even though a significant number of Phoenician names have been found, most of those mentioned in the necropolis of Tyre or Arados are Aramaic,[112] which proves that, during the Hellenistic period and perhaps as early as the Achaemenid era, Phoenicians experienced not only the effects of acculturation owing to Hellenism but also a rampant Aramaization in proper names. As a result, Phoenician was moribund in the first centuries of our era, in both its written and spoken forms; it survived only as lettering on coins.[113]

In the cities of northern Syria and the Decapolis, Greco-Roman proper names prevailed. This is quite clear in Antioch, Apamaea, and Gerasa,[114] although in Gerasa's case the statement must be modified somewhat in light of recent discoveries, many of them as yet unpublished. It seems in fact that a significant portion of the elite used Semitic, Arabic, or Aramaic names, either alone or in combination with Greek ones.[115] Consequently, when we happen to come across indigenous names in Apamaea or Gerasa, it is unclear whether the phenomenon resulted from a recent infiltration of indigenous elements or whether, as in Tyre, we are seeing a part of the population that had not produced written texts before but was now writing in Greek.

When we begin to look at Greek inscriptions in villages, the preponderance of Semitic proper names is obvious, even in the omnipresent Greek epigraphy, which is often all that remains.[116] In northern and central Syria, a strong Greco-Roman element persisted, but texts from the early empire are rare: only members of the wealthy Hellenized minority were able to write at that time. The appearance of a great many Semitic names in later texts (from the fourth to the seventh centuries) proves that Hellenism had remained marginal, at least in this respect. In southern Syria as in Arabia, except for the cities of the Decapolis, no difference has been found between urban and rural practices in this sphere: the Semitic onomastic prevailed everywhere. We find only slightly more Hellenization of proper names in Bostra, the provincial capital, and in the former Herodian lands, where Semitic and Greco-Roman names are found to be equally divided. By contrast, in an indigenous community such as Umm al-Jimal, the proportion of Semitic names rises to 85 percent.[117] Overall, the use of Greek names remained on a superficial level in Syria as a whole, since it was significant only among the fraction of the population that wrote Greek or had texts written for them in Greek. Which brings us back to questions raised earlier: In what language did people write? What language did they speak? As we have seen, writing was primarily in Greek, at least in texts intended for public announcements, by which I mean those that were carved in stone. The situation was no doubt quite different with respect to the spoken language, and to some extent with respect to texts written on perishable materials.

While Phoenician began to disappear as a written language at the beginning of the early empire, apart from symbols on coins, Aramaic, by contrast, took hold as the spoken language of the majority and, to a lesser extent, as the written language. To be sure, among the communities situated near Syria's borders, such as Palmyra and Edessa, Aramaic was written, and from all appearances it was spoken even more widely. Palmyrene, a variant of Aramaic, was still being written until the end of the third century and was fairly dominant in Palmyrene epigraphy, where Greek was a secondary language. Nabataean continued to be written in Petra and throughout the former Nabataean empire, but the situation was the inverse of Palmyra's. In Petra, the indigenous language was overshadowed by Greek; only in desert graffiti, especially around the Sinai, did Nabataean Aramaic maintain its clear dominance. Actually, it was in its Syriac (more properly speaking, Edessenian) form that Aramaic experienced a literary "renaissance" in the second century, a phenomenon that can only be explained by the support of a strong popular culture.[118] The earliest evidence of this literary renaissance is thought to be the letter of Mara bar Sarapion of Samosata, which can be dated sometime between the annexation of Samosata in 72 and the third century.[119] But Edessa emerges as the principal center of Syriac culture, in particular with Bardesanes (154–222), a philosopher, the author of Christian hymns, and the true founder of Syriac poetry.[120] His large body of work has mostly been lost, with the exception of *Book of the Laws of the Countries.* This text was probably written by a student, but it offers a faithful reflection of the teacher's thought.[121]

We must not undervalue this renaissance, for it determined in large part the history of Syrian Christianity. Neither should it appear too much like a form of "resistance" to Hellenism, because Edessa was just as much a center of Greek culture as of Syriac culture, to the extent that those involved were concerned with such categorizations. Bardesanes knew both languages and sent his son Harmonios to study in Athens; Harmonios eventually returned to Edessa and composed hymns in Syriac. In many respects, the philosophy and theology that developed in Edessa in the second and third centuries were just an offshoot of the work being done during the same period in Antioch, and Edessa, the "Athens of the East," could boast of being the center of Greek culture in Syriac dress.[122] The linguistic domination of Aramaic in Edessa naturally carried over in inscriptions, especially on mosaics, which are primarily in Edessenian rather than Greek.

We should not overlook the fact that little was written in Aramaic either in Palestine or in the rest of Syria. On this point, however, we must make a more nuanced judgment. On the one hand, it is undeniable that monumental inscriptions—honorific, commemorative, or funerary texts, carved in stone—were almost never in Aramaic, except on the fringes noted above, from Edessa to Petra and including Palmyra. We should note that in the entire empire only Palmyra carved the city's official texts in the indigenous language, either in bilingual Greco-Aramaic inscriptions or in Aramaic alone. However, as Han J. W. Drijvers has observed, Greek provided the original text and Palmyrene appears in literal translation, bringing some new expressions into the language.[123]

In contrast, private writing, intended for personal record keeping, is found both in Greek and in Aramaic, as we know from the Babatha archives as well as from papyri and parchments from Dura and the middle Euphrates in the next century. Further study will of course be needed, but I believe that this is a situation of true bilingualism in which the languages in use ultimately took on specialized functions, at least in part. In Roman Syria (excluding the more Arabized border areas), burials were not conducted in Aramaic, but contracts were signed both in Greek and in the indigenous language.

The situation was somewhat clearer in the Arab communities, which were not significantly influenced by Aramaic during the Hellenistic period.[124] Arab tribes had their own widely used writing system, borrowed from the alphabets of southern Arabia: the twenty thousand "Safaitic" graffiti demonstrate that writing was not a privilege reserved to scribes. However, the formulaic nature of these texts—the near absence of any variation in the types of texts produced—also shows that those who wrote did not regard writing as a means of expressing or transmitting just anything; they used writing almost exclusively for genealogies, invocations to the gods, or ritual expressions of hope and prosperity, and displayed very little capacity for innovation or expression of complex ideas. Still, there were a few departures from the model, suggesting that at least a few individuals saw writing as a means of transcribing something other than the customary formulas. These writing systems were abandoned in the third and fourth centuries, and Arabic may have adapted the Nabataean script—which until then had been a transcription of Aramaic with a strong Arab influence—for its own use.[125] For a long time, the epitaph of Imru' al-Qays in Nemara from the year 328 was viewed by scholars as the ancestor of contemporary Arabic writing, but Avraham Negev has proposed an example dating from the second century that appears in a text from Avdat (Obodas) in the Negev. This text cannot be dated earlier than 268, but there is also a text from Hegra dating from 267 that seems already to be in Arabic; thus the oldest known Arabic texts in traditional Aramaic writing were produced more than half a century earlier than previously supposed.[126]

Unlike the situation in Anatolia, where indigenous people wrote in Greek or not at all, in Syria Greek was only one form of writing. It was doubtless the most fashionable form, the one preferred by the wealthy and by those wishing to appear cultivated, but the continuing presence of indigenous languages, including their written forms, shows the limits of Hellenization in the linguistic realm.[127] This persistence of local languages helps explain the rapid disappearance of the veneer of Greek culture when new masters whose language was no longer Greek but Arabic took control of the country.

Language and onomastics, often the most immediately visible aspects of indigenous cultures, are nevertheless not the only ones to consider. For additional evidence of the vigor of local traditions, we must look at the durability of religious cults and gods, without trying to view them as means of active resistance to external influences. Moreover, three or four centuries after Alexander's conquest, it is not likely that Hellenism was seen as a foreign culture; it was one of the cultures of Roman Syria. Even the Jews, who had so violently opposed Hellenism in the time of the Maccabees, borrowed a great deal from it quite readily and adopted habits and behaviors that would have scandalized their forebears, such as frequenting the baths. Rather than seeing the cultures that coexisted in Roman Syria as rivals, it would be more helpful to recognize the extent to which their interpenetration helped give each social or ethnic group, and sometimes each individual, a composite appearance; all were more or less marked by Hellenism or by some variant of the Semitic cultures, and no group or individual could be considered free of the influence of the others. The complexity of the play of influences, the borrowings, conscious rejections, and unconscious acquisitions probably come across most clearly in religious life, which will be considered in the next chapter.

To return to what concerns us here—the interpenetration of cultures—a particularly fine example is found in the Hauran, in funerary epigraphy.[128] The members of the elite, whether rural or urban (and many were probably both at once), who had beautiful tombs built for themselves next to their country homes or on the edge of the city, tended to have long epitaphs in verse carved on these tombs, with imagery borrowed from Homer, Hesiod, and the Hellenistic poets. The density of these epitaphs grew in the fourth century, to such an extent that Louis Robert was prepared to speak of a veritable school of Hauranese epigrammists, testimony to a vibrant culture. Yet at the same time, a number of these leaders kept their indigenous names, laid little stress on their civic functions, and preferred to emphasize the origin of their resources (land, the army, or the administration), an attitude that contrasts with that found in, for example, the Aegean world. Most of the documentation appears to be somewhat posterior to the period studied here, but the movement began in the middle of the third century at the latest, as we know from the funeral tower of Celestinus at Rimet al-Lohf, adjacent to the Leja. In it we see an original manifestation of Greek culture, springing out of a community that remained profoundly attached to indigenous traditions, although we are unable to say whether those involved were pagans or Christians. In terms of culture, it may well make no difference; it suffices to observe that this mixed culture, profoundly Greek while remaining rooted in Semitic traditions, developed in the northern part of the Arabian province during the prosperous centuries of the early empire and endured until the Islamic conquest. Although the available documentation may favor the Hauran, Edessa, and Osrhoene,[129] the pattern was actually much more widespread, and there are numerous signs of this mutual enrichment and transformation of cultures in Galilee, in Phoenicia, and in Antioch.

PAGANS, JEWS, AND CHRISTIANS IN ROMAN SYRIA IN THE SECOND AND THIRD CENTURIES

THE birthplace of the two major monotheistic religions of antiquity, Judaism and Christianity, Syria nevertheless remained a land of multiple gods and innumerable cults (even if individual gods were sometimes known under several different names) until the fourth century at least. Phoenician, Aramaic, Arab, Greek, and Roman gods coexisted, intermingling to such an extent that it is not always possible to identify them with certainty. The names, attributes, and organization of cults and sanctuaries allow us to discern religious practices of various origins, although the practitioners themselves may not have been aware of this diversity as such. Moreover, the various gods gradually came to influence one another, while at the same time a trend toward increasing abstraction emerged. This represented not so much a movement toward henotheism as a desire on the part of believers for a guarantee of salvation, a desire that led over time to a modification of earlier conceptions of the divine. The immutable and transcendent aspects of the gods took on more importance than their terrestrial activities, and the omnipotence of divinity was more highly exalted than any particular god; we observe this in the popularity of *theos hupsistos*, "the god most high," who usually remained nameless. Similarly, the development of solar aspects within certain cults,[1] the popularity of the cult of Nemesis,[2] and the growth of magic and astrology all reflect a widely shared obsession with salvation. Philosophical speculations, particularly those of the Platonists, were probably not entirely foreign to these changes in religious life, even though we cannot say exactly what effect they had on believers. This new, more spiritual religiosity clearly prepared believers to be more receptive to forms of monotheism that proclaimed themselves as religions of salvation par excellence. Judaism and Christianity thus came to join the spiritual alternatives, and many pagans were willing to participate in the ceremonies of both faiths without any intention of abandoning their own practices and rituals—for one thing, neither Judaism nor Christianity (especially not the latter) could provide spectacles and holidays comparable to those of the pagan cults. Although we cannot speak of syncretism here, it is nevertheless obvious that many Syrians saw religious life as a whole made up of several parts, and that they were unwilling to select or to exclude any one of them.

The destruction of the Temple was only one aspect of the transformation of Jewish life after 70 C.E. From that point on, the province of Judaea—later Syria-Palestine—had no special status: in the eyes of the Romans it became just one province among others, one in which Jews were a minority (except perhaps in certain zones of Galilee). Under these circumstances, Jews had to reorganize themselves in what appears to have been another experience of exile, albeit exile in their own land. At the same time, the Greek cities along the coast (Gaza, Ascalon, Caesarea), like those in the interior (Samaria-Sebaste, Neapolis, Scythopolis) and in Galilee (Sepphoris, Tiberias), were prospering, and they helped make Palestine a typical—and affluent—province. The creation of the colony of Aelia Capitolina erased the last traces of Jewish influence in the symbolic heartland. Nevertheless, although, properly speaking, Judaea had lost many of its Jewish inhabitants, Jewish communities, both rural and urban, were numerous throughout Syria, from Antioch to Dura-Europos, from Apamaea to Bostra.

The small Jewish community that followed Jesus around the year 30 survived the death of its leader and seems even to have made new converts quite rapidly. Although they came to be called Christians around the year 40 (the name is thought to have been used for the first time in Antioch), they nonetheless remained closely tied to Judaism until the revolt of 66. To be sure, pagans adopted the new faith as early as the apostolic period, but it was especially after the migration of Christians from Jerusalem to Pella in the Decapolis in 70 that the rupture between this community and traditional Judaism appeared definitive, at least for most of its members, although some Judeo-Christians persisted in Syria until quite late. But after 70, small Christian communities recruited among pagans sprang up in a number of cities without any particular difficulty: until the general persecution under Decius in the third century, there is no evidence that Christians were subject to harassment or oppression. If we can judge from the establishment of episcopal hierarchies, Christians rapidly appeared almost everywhere. I shall attempt to give a rough outline of the geography of the spreading Christian mission in Syria and to identify some specific characteristics of Syrian Christianity. But is it possible to measure the influence of these Christians? Did they have any effect on social or religious behavior? Can any social, civic, or even political changes at the level of the state be attributed to them? These subtleties are often difficult to untangle, but we cannot avoid raising the questions in a region of the Roman world where Christians were probably more numerous than in most of the other provinces.

GODS AND PAGAN SANCTUARIES

Although it is important to keep in mind that the term *pagan* was simply a Christian invention, it is nevertheless useful for describing all those who practiced polytheism, or who at least accepted its rules even when they worshipped a favorite ethnic or familial god. The gods were infinitely diverse, and there is no need to list them all here, but it will be useful to present their various groupings, in which indigenous gods coexisted with gods imported by Greek colonists and later by the Romans. We find local gods alongside gods seen as universal, gods who protected a place alongside gods who offered salvation, and yet these diverse categories do not seem to have been mutually exclusive. There was undoubtedly some syncretism and some assimilation among the various gods, but we must be careful not to confuse them: each one retained a distinct personality that must have been quite unmistakable to believers.[3]

Pantheons and Gods

Religious life in Roman Syria included the same components as that of other provinces in the eastern Mediterranean: civic cults,[4] gods of salvation (including indigenous ones such as Atargatis and Adonis), indigenous topical and ethnic gods,[5] and of course the imperial cult. Syria was little affected by external influences, however, and indigenous gods, fairly diverse from region to region, were preeminent. Although an infinite number of local pantheons might be identified, three major characteristic groupings can be distinguished among the indigenous cults.

In Phoenicia, each city had its own pantheon, often governed by a triad consisting of a father-god, a mother-goddess, and a son-god, the latter being the active god par excellence. However this ancient organization was sometimes overshadowed by the development of more popular cults. Thus,

BAALSHAMIN, GOD OF
THE SKY AND RULER OF
THE HARVESTS, FROM
TELL GHARIYYEH
(HAURAN).

in Sidon, the healing god Eschmoun-Asclepios became paramount in relation to the others. In Tyre, Melqart, "the lord of the city," enjoyed absolute supremacy. In Byblos, it was the goddess Baalat, "the Mistress," who held the highest rank. Everywhere these cults had a strongly agrarian or naturist cast; the local Baal, master of rain and vegetation, is associated with the goddess Ashtarte, a goddess of love and fertility. However, in the back country around Arados, Zeus of Baitokaike may also have had some aspects of a healing god.[6]

In the interior of Syria, among the sedentary Aramaeans, local gods were called "Baal," meaning "lord"; this name quite often disguised (as was the case in Damascus) Hadad, the storm and rain god associated with Atargatis. Baal could also be Baalshamin, god of the sky and ruler of the harvests; Baalshamin was worshipped as a supreme god and is difficult to distinguish from Hadad, who, like him, "spread wealth." The regional epithet that differentiated among multiple Hadads—those of Damascus, Bambyke, Baalbek,[7] and Gaza (Zeus Marnas)—is highly significant.[8] Baalshamin seems to have been universally venerated in the Syrian interior and even beyond; he was apparently honored with a sanctuary at the very gates of Petra, at Gaia.[9] Atargatis was honored throughout Syria, either under her own name, as "Dea Syria,"[10] the Syrian goddess, as Derceto in Palestine, or even through assimilation with the Greek goddess Leucothea. She undoubtedly underwent many transformations that, without erasing her Semitic origins, led her to be seen as a major deity, one who could be identified with Artemis, Hera, Aphrodite, Nemesis, Demeter, Cybele, and Isis. She was a composite goddess from the outset, combining elements of the western Semitic gods Asherah, Ashtarte, and Anath; she possessed such a wealth of possibilities and attributes that Greeks in Syria and elsewhere could easily transform and adopt her.[11]

In addition to these supreme gods, there were numerous local deities associated with peaks, mountains, and other natural phenomena: Baal-Marqod above Berytos,[12] Elagabalus, whose very name means "mountain-god," in Emesa,[13] Jupiter Turmasgadus or Mithra-Turmasgades in Commagene,[14] a Baal Madbachos (Zeus Bomos, "altar") in Jebel Sheikh Barakat in northern Syria,[15] Zeus Kasios,[16] Zeus Carmel,[17] "Zeus who is in Beelphegor," a god near Mount Nebo,[18] and also Zeus Beelgalasos, recently identified at Qal'at Faqra[19]—to name only a few among a great many examples.

Finally, the Arab gods took root throughout the province of Arabia and as far as Palmyra; they vary by tribe and people. Among the Nabataeans, the supreme triad links a mountain god in Petra, Dushara (Dousares) "the lord of Shara," who had become a dynastic god, with a warrior goddess, Allat, and a heavenly goddess, al-Uzza.[20] After the royal dynasty disappeared, the gods remained the objects of popular cults as city or village deities: one representation of a traditional sanctuary in Bostra under the Severi shows a platform with three sacred stones, evoking the ancestral Nabataean triad. Dushara-Dousares also continued to be widely honored throughout the former kingdom.[21] Allat is found in Palmyra as well as among the Safaites (Lat). But many other gods—such as Azizos, Monimos, Ruda, Shai al-Qawm, the Edomite god Qos—were the objects of very popular cults.[22] Even in the Hauran, characteristic local gods have been found who were still worshipped under their Greek names, such as Lycurgos[23] and Theandrios, the ancestral god of Canatha.[24] Lastly, we must note the curious category of quasi-anonymous gods, designated as "god of . . .":

TRIAD OF GODS ON A RELIEF FROM PALMYRA: BEL, IARHIBOL, AND AGLIBOL.
FROM THE TEMPLE OF BEL; FIRST CENTURY B.C.E.

"god of Aumos," "god of Maleichatos," "god of Loaithemos," "god of Rabbos." This category occurs primarily in the Hauran, although a "god of Arcesilaos" has also been identified in the Apamene.[25] This way of identifying a deity is probably used for gods known under other names, as has been shown recently for the "god of Rabbos" in Canatha, who was actually called Theandrios. So far, the others remain anonymous.

Although categorizing gods by their various origins may be useful for the purpose of discussion, it could nevertheless be misleading: in reality, the distinctions are not as clear as they appear, insofar as coexistence of cults was the rule. Palmyra,[26] for instance, presents a blend that reflects its position at the crossroads of Syria, Mesopotamia, and the desert. To the local god, Bol, who became Bel by assimilation with the Babylonian god rather than under Babylon's direct influence, we can add indigenous gods (Iarhibol, Aglibol, Malakbel), Aramaic gods (Baalshamin, Hadad), Mesopotamian gods (Nabu, Arsu), and some Arab gods (Allat, Azizos). More than sixty deities were the object of public or private cults in Palmyra. In Edessa, we find a similar variety of gods from all regions: Babylonian gods with Nabu and Bel, gods from nearby Hierapolis-Bambyke with Hadad and Atargatis, gods of Harran such as the moon god Sin (whose cult in Sumatar Harabesi lasted until the second century C.E., unchanged from the time of Nabonide, a thousand years earlier),[27] Arab gods with Azizos, Monimos, or al-Uzza.[28] Palmyra's cosmopolitanism may have been exceptional, but I do not believe it was unique. Even in a traditional Greek city such as Apamaea, we find an oracular sanctuary devoted to Zeus Belos that is in no way Greek.[29] As for Abila of Lysanias, its pantheon was dominated by Zeus and Apis, designated as ancestral gods; the second of these comes as quite a surprise, since the cult is Egyptian and no one knows when it might have been established in this valley in the Anti-Lebanon.[30]

Some of these gods were immensely successful in specific contexts outside of Syria. Jupiter Heliopolitanus, for example, became one of the favorite gods of soldiers, along with the local Baal of Doliche, under the name Jupiter Dolichenus.[31]

Several of these gods had well-known oracular sanctuaries—for example, Bel of Apamaea, Jupiter of Heliopolis, Zeus of Carmel,[32] Zeus of Nikephorion[33] or the god of Qadesh.[34] Youssef Hajjar has identified some forty gods rendering oracles, but that may be the result of a rather broad definition of an oracle. In fact, he views any god who gives orders to believers as oracular.[35] While people may indeed have received orders during consultations of the oracular type, the same result may also have arisen from a direct relation between the god and the believer without any actual consultation. For instance, when the virgin and prophetess Hocmea noted in an inscription from Niha that the god had forbidden her to eat bread for twenty years, there is no way to know whether this was the result of a mystical vision or the answer to a question raised by the believer.[36] The same ambiguity characterizes inscriptions stating that a given person was acting "on orders from the god."

Alongside the indigenous gods, there were also Greek gods, whose importance seems clear from the Hellenistic period on:[37] although for many of them we have no evidence before the Roman period, it is likely that they were introduced into the pantheons of the Greek cities in Syria when the cities were founded, or shortly thereafter. With the arrival of the Romans, however, new gods came to Syria. This is particularly true for the colonies. In Berytos, the inscriptions honoring the gods—except for those of the indigenous peri-urban sanctuary devoted to Baal-Marqod at Deir al-Qal'a—make virtually no mention of Roman gods even when the name seems to point to one, although one bilingual inscription confirms the equivalency between the Heliopolitan Venus and Atargatis and between Diana and Artemis.[38] Several Latin dedications honor the gods of Baalbek: the Heliopolitan Jupiter, Venus, and Mercury. However, inscriptions honoring Juno Regina[39] and Mater Matuta[40] refer to a context that is clearly imported. Moreover, the Venus or the Mercury of Heliopolis need not always be equated with the homonymous deities honored in Berytos,[41] especially when the latter are associated with Apollo, Diana, Mars, Proserpine, *Fatum,* and the *Genius* of the colony.[42]

As for Aelia Capitolina, the very name of the colony is placed under the double invocation of the supreme deity in the Roman pantheon, the Capitoline Jupiter, and Hadrian as its founder. A military colony, the city was home to the gods of the legion and the cults of its officers, but other gods were ensconced in temples. The Capitoline triad was enthroned in the Capitol, standing not on the Temple Mount, but to the west, in the heart of the new colony.[43] A statue of Venus was erected nearby. However, it is much more difficult to know whether the gods whose images are found on coins (Tyche, Nemesis, Helios-Apollo) or on precious stones (Athena-Minerva, Mercury) were actually the objects of a public cult. Thus we have a very incomplete picture of religious life in Aelia Capitolina, where Serapis was also worshipped.[44]

Imported foreign cults, by contrast, were long considered to be of little importance. This was probably accurate in part, but recent discoveries oblige us to introduce some nuances. As noted above, the cult of Apis was established rather early in Abila of Lysanias, so that by the second and third centuries Apis looked like an "ancestral" god, along with Zeus.[45] This was not the only Egyptian cult found in Syria, however. A dedication to

Serapis that dates from the second century B.C.E., for example, has been found in Samaria.[46] A bust of that god has been identified in Petra;[47] he appears on coins from Bostra,[48] and a new dedication has recently been found in Humaymah.[49] In Aelia Capitolina, Serapis was the object of a cult even before the colony was founded, and he is often depicted on coins after that;[50] as a healing god he was also the object of a cult at the sanctuary located near the pool used for ritual purification.[51] In Gerasa, he was jointly honored with Isis and Neotera in 143.[52] In Laodicea, the *peliganes,* or council of elders, passed a law as early as 175–174 B.C.E. concerning a private sanctuary devoted to the cults of Serapis and Isis.[53] The cult of Isis appears to have been more widespread in Syria than was previously believed; numerous traces have been found in Petra, for example. An inscription on a bust dedicated to her dates from 25 B.C.E.[54] Her image appears on the façade of Khazneh, which is probably even older.[55] Another relief representing Isis has been found at the site,[56] and, in the Siq pass, a votive inscription includes what may be a reference to a priest of Isis.[57] In the forum in Ascalon, there is a bust of Isis dating from the third century. In the Hauran, Isis was honored in Phaina of Trachon by a soldier; this does not tell us much about how well established the goddess was in the region,[58] but Jósef Tadeusz Milik believes that she might have been introduced at the great sanctuary of Sia, near Canatha, as early as the end of the second century C.E.[59]

Clear evidence of Mithra exists in several places in Syria.[60] There was a *mithraeum* in a section of the secularized *horrea* (storage facilities) in Caesarea, near the port, around 100 C.E.[61] In Sidon, nothing is known of the mithraeum itself, apart from nine marble statues that were offered to the god around the end of the fourth century,[62] but evidence of a priest of Mithra dating from 139–140 has been found in the city.[63] The mithraeum in Dura was located near the western city wall, in the sector that was turned into a Roman encampment after 165. Like the synagogue, it was exceptionally well preserved, and for the same reason (it was filled and covered with earth to reinforce the ramparts against which it had been built); its ritual reliefs were dedicated in 168 and 170,[64] and the monument was rebuilt twice before the city was destroyed.[65] There are two mithraic reliefs from Sia, near Canatha, that are preserved in the Damascus Museum, and the French mission in southern Syria has determined that the building Howard C. Butler called the "temple of Dushara" was probably a mithraeum.[66] Not far from there, in Sha'arah, on the edge of the Trachon, Mikaël Kalos has unmistakably identified a mithraeum that included a furnished grotto connected to a building.[67] To the north, a mithraeum in Huarte has recently been discovered, about fifteen kilometers north of Apamaea, under a church; it has retained an extraordinary painted surface from the end of the fourth or the beginning of the fifth century in its final state, but excavators have found at least restorations of the paintings, and it is highly likely that the mithraeum itself existed much earlier.[68] Farther north, to the south of Cyrrhos, evidence of the cult of Mithra has been found in Arsha wa-Kibar,[69] and German archeologists have just discovered two new rural mithraea in Doliche.[70]

MITHRAIC RELIEF FROM HAURAN.

It is striking to note the extent to which the evidence of Mithra's presence is attested in places that have very little in common.[71] The mithraeum in Dura is located in what was an army camp, whereas in Caesarea it is in the port area, even though the city housed a military unit protecting the governor of Syria. Other mithraea are located in villages where there is no proof of a permanent military presence,[72] and in Sidon, where no trace of any permanent military presence has been found. Even when we take into account the number of veterans who had settled in the Syrian countryside, particularly in the Hauran, it is very likely that the cult of Mithra extended well beyond the military.

The classification of the gods on the basis of their ethnic or geographic origins, while legitimate from the point of view of the historian who seeks to trace their individual backgrounds, was probably not considered important by their followers. The gods were seen as a whole from which individuals could draw as they liked. Combinations of gods have been found on individual sites, and sometimes even in the same sanctuary. For example, the immediate surroundings of the great sanctuary in Caesarea-Philippi devoted to the god Pan have yielded remnants of numerous statues of deities; erected between the reigns of Augustus and Hadrian, these statues included figures of Athena, Zeus, possibly the Capitoline Triad, Artemis, and of course Pan himself.[73] Just as the origin of the Capitoline Triad is clearly foreign, other gods may also have been Greek deities imported during the Hellenistic period, or Greek interpretations of indigenous gods. There is almost no way to know, and the question was probably of no importance to believers.

Assimilations and Syncretism

In Phoenicia, the process of identifying indigenous gods with Greek deities appears very early: the Greeks of Herodotus's time had already recognized

VOTIVE RELIEF FROM PALMYRA REPRESENTING HERACLES (AT LEFT) WITH THE GODDESS ASHTARTE AND THE LOCAL PALMYRANEAN GODS AGLIBOL AND MALAKBEL.

Melqart as Heracles, even though his specific features earned him the designation "Tyrian."[74] Ashtarte had been adopted much earlier by the Greeks as the Aphrodite of Phoenicia or of Cyprus (or Paphos). We should note that the process of assimilation was the work of Greeks who sought their own deities in the portrayals of foreign gods wherever they went; there is no evidence that indigenous Syrians were inclined to share this attitude. It was much later, after such assimilations had become routine, that the representations of indigenous gods were modified and enriched under the influence of their Greco-Roman equivalents.

The use of Greek names to designate Syrian or Arab gods spread throughout Syria during the Hellenistic period and the early empire. The name *Zeus* tended to designate rulers of local pantheons, and thus Zeus replaced any god with a local epithet: he was Hadad in Damascus,[75] Bel,[76] Baalshamin,[77] and Dushara,[78] and was probably equated with other local gods who have not been clearly identified.[79] Other assimilations came to be based on more or less close resemblances or vague homonyms: Allat with Athena,[80] Arsu with Ares,[81] El with Kronos, Nergal with Heracles (in Palmyra), Ashtarte with Hera, al-Uzza with Aphrodite,[82] Aktab-Kutbay with Hermes and Mercury.[83] The assimilation was sometimes based on similarities among myths; thus Atargatis could be compared with the minor Greek

RELIEF FROM PALMYRA, THIRD CENTURY C.E.,
SHOWING TYCHE (AT RIGHT) WITH A MURAL
CROWN. THE GODDESS AT LEFT, WITH A FOOT
POISED ON A CLOTHED SWIMMING MALE
FIGURE, HAS NOT BEEN IDENTIFIED; SHE
MIGHT BE ALLAT OR ASHTARTE OR
BABYLONIAN HERTA.

STATUE OF THE GODDESS ALLAT IN PALMYRA
WITH THE FEATURES OF A CLASSIC
ATTIC ATHENA.

deity Leucothea, which explains the presence of this marine goddess in the mountainous area of Mount Hermon as well as in Tyre and Galilee.[84]

The phenomenon of identification sometimes extended to the way gods were represented. From the Zeus of Mount Olympus local Zeus figures borrowed the throne, the lightning bolt, and the eagle, all of which are present on numerous reliefs and coins. But the most spectacular example comes from Palmyra, where Allat is depicted in a temple with the features of Phidias's Athena Parthenos.[85] In the Arab tradition gods were not represented at all, which left the field open for the adoption of foreign models—in this instance, the most famous of all representations of the Greek goddess. When the Bedouins of the desert between Palmyra and Dura-Europos began to portray their god-protectors, they imagined them

HELIOPOLITAN JUPITER (IDENTIFIED
WITH THE LOCAL GOD BAAL) FROM
BAALBEK. STATUE IN BRONZE AND
COPPER; SECOND TO THIRD
CENTURY C.E.

more simply, in their own image, outfitted as camel drivers or horsemen, with arms borrowed from Rome.[86]

The Hellenization of representations remained limited, however. The Heliopolitan Jupiter of Baalbek belongs to a series of gods depicted in tight sheaths,[87] the best illustration of which is probably the small bronze in the Sursock collection in the Louvre, where the beardless young god is portrayed flanked by two bulls. He is mounted on a pedestal, his headdress an immense *calathos* flared widely at the top; he is wearing a clinging robe decorated with several torsos.[88] Other regional *ba'alim*, portrayed in a similar fashion, probably disguise Hadad, Zeus Hadad of Damascus, Jupiter of Akko-Ptolemais, Zeus of Aleppo, Zeus of Dion,[89] Jupiter of Niha, Jupiter of Rhosos, and an Apollo (?) of Hierapolis-Bambyke.[90] Hermes of Baalbek is entirely swathed; he stands on a pedestal flanked by two rams and he bears a calathos on his head.[91] Fidelity to tradition is still more obvious in Palmyra, even though the habit of dressing the gods as Roman soldiers was new.[92] In Petra, Atargatis of Bambyke was represented on a stylized stele with eyes, but this is probably more indicative of Nabataean sacred iconography in general than of features associated with this goddess at Bambyke itself.[93]

An absence of any representation of the gods had long been the rule among the Nabataeans: it was enough to establish a sacred stone, either rounded or rectangular; at most, an occasional stone with stylized eyes and nose has been found.[94] Many such examples have been found, not only in Petra but also in Bostra and Adraha. In Petra, for example, sacred stones accompany numerous dedications bordering the access route to the city, the Siq.[95] On coins from Adraha,[96] Bostra,[97] Charachmoba,[98] and Madaba,[99] there are representations of sacred stones where other Greek cities would place images of their gods. A very beautiful "stele with eyes," its two eyes and nose stylized and crowned with foliage, was dedicated in the al-Uzza temple of the "winged lions."[100] The appearance of these very traditional symbols on municipal coins shows the attachment of Hellenized communities to images of gods. Yet it did not prevent these communities from moving, during the same period, to anthropomorphic representations in the Greco-Roman style, such as the one of a goddess in the Siq,[101] the medallion portrait in which we can identify either a fertility goddess, a Dionysos,[102] or even the Atargatis-Derceto of the Nabataean sanctuary in Khirbet Tannur.[103] As Glen Bowersock has observed with reference to Dousares, an iconic representation of the god, a Greek image, and even a celebration of a Greek-style competition (Dousaria Actia) could very well coexist.[104]

STELE WITH EYES, FROM THE TEMPLE OF THE WINGED LIONS AT PETRA.

We should consider the furnishings of sanctuaries as well, for this reveals cultic practices foreign to Greco-Roman customs. To be sure, in Syria as elsewhere, the sacrificial altar is always outside the temple, located in front of the entrance. In several sanctuaries, however, such as that of the Heliopolitan Jupiter, the altar is very high, with an interior stairway; in Heliopolis, there are even two tower-altars. Other sanctuaries in the Lebanese mountains, while less than colossal, also had two tower-altars, sometimes surrounded by a colonnade (Qal'at Faqra, Mashnaqa).[105] A number of altars have likewise been found with small cups presumably used to hold oil for burning, as well as altars where incense was burned.[106] Even more interesting is Jean-Marie Dentzer's very relevant suggestion that the numerous *naiskoi*, the little niches with half-cupolas for holding either a simple sacred stone or an image of the god, both of which were characteristic offerings in Syrian sanctuaries, were probably fixtures copied, in more durable form, from the Arab *qubbah*, a portable sanctuary made of a light material (like the Hebrews' primitive tabernacles). Three similar monuments, all located in neighboring villages in the Hauran, seem to embody a monumental translation of these naiskoi; one of the structures in Umm az-

Zeitun is characterized in a local inscription as a *kalybe;* the Greek word designates a light construction made of twigs or fabric, just like the Arab qubbah.[107]

In writing about holidays, all the authors emphasized both their lavishness and their excesses. Of course, much of our information comes from the church fathers or other Christian authors who readily attributed a pronounced orgiastic quality to pagan holidays. Antioch's famous *maiouma,* celebrated every two years, included banquets, theatrical presentations, and brilliantly lit nocturnal processions. Many authors, however, saw it as an occasion for debauchery, and there were maioumas in other cities.[108] The importance of banquets in all the festivals (and on this point the Greek tradition and indigenous customs converge) is highlighted by the number of sanctuaries with banquet halls—including the largest ones, such as that of Bel in Palmyra, as well as the more modest *triclinia* (gathering places) in Petra. Few festivals, however, have been the object of study, and a great deal of research remains to be done.[109] In addition, the persistence of traditional rituals does not mean that Greek customs had no influence: Dushara, in addition to being the municipal god of Bostra and Adraha, was the patron of Greek competitions until the third century, at least in the largest cities.

Sanctuaries

Respect for tradition can also be seen in the sanctuaries. Some borrowed layout and design from Greco-Roman art; others remained faithful to the ancient styles.[110]

The sanctuary of Jupiter Heliopolitanus (the Latin name for the local Baal, Hadad) in Baalbek,[111] which was built over more than two and a half centuries, is an excellent example of the first type. In this structure whose construction was begun under Augustus, a peripteral temple mounted on a podium was entered through a large courtyard with a portico (from the second century), a hexagonal outer court (244–249), and monumental propylaea (added under Caracalla); below it stood a smaller sanctuary called "Bacchus's," although we do not know what god it was actually intended to honor. In style and decoration it was unquestionably Greco-Roman; it had columns, friezes, and sculpted pediments and buildings with rich interior and exterior architectural detail, and the temple was even built on a raised podium, a purely Roman feature. However, numerous indigenous features indicate cultic practices that were foreign to the Greek world: the size of the courtyard, which housed a small altar for burnt offerings and a

SMALL TEMPLE AT BAALBEK, FIRST CENTURY C.E.; SOMETIMES (INCORRECTLY) SAID TO HAVE BEEN DEDICATED TO BACCHUS.

large tower-altar where banquets were held; the presence of two wash basins recalling the importance of purification rituals; the erection of isolated columns in the place of sacred stones. These courtyards, intended to receive the faithful (like the plaza of the Temple in Jerusalem), are found in all sanctuaries of any size: in Palmyra, where the sanctuary of Bel is surrounded by a wall two hundred meters wide marking the *peribolos* (limits of the enclosure),[112] in Byblos, where the sacred stone of Adonis is clearly seen in the center of the court adjacent to the sanctuary,[113] in Sia at the sanctuary of Baalshamin (Hauran),[114] as well as in Khirbet Tannur in Nabataea,[115] and in most of the sanctuaries in the Lebanese mountains. Sometimes clustered in groups of two or three (Sfire, Qal'at Faqra, Niha),

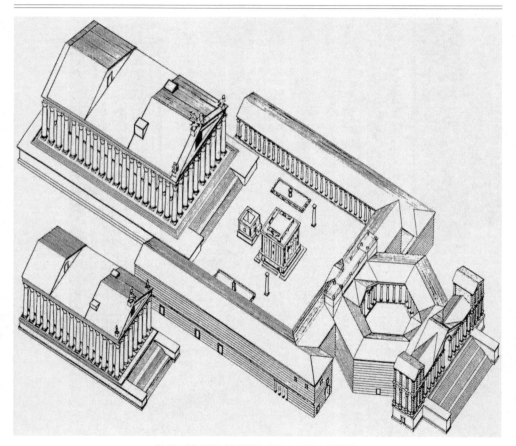

PLAN OF THE SACRED AREA AT BAALBEK.

each of these sanctuaries had a vast peribolos marked by simple stone walls. Similarly, in Hosn as-Suleiman, the sanctuary of the Most High Zeus Baitokaike stands at the center of a huge peribolos (131 meters by 70 meters) with doorways on every side and a monumental entrance on the main (north) wall.[116]

Inside, the organization of these temples owes nothing to Greco-Roman traditions. In Baalbek, "Bacchus's" temple looks from the outside like a classic peripteral temple on a platform, but the *cella* is divided into two parts, of which the higher back half must have been closed: it is the *adyton*, the inner sanctum of the temple, the "holy of holies." This pattern is found in a number of temples in the Lebanese mountains[117] and in the Hauran.[118] Most of the time, stairways built into the thick walls provided access to the roof for the celebration of certain sacrifices.[119]

The sanctuary of Bel in Palmyra,[120] consecrated on April 6, 32, is one of the most magnificent found anywhere in the Orient; it symbolizes perfectly the blending of indigenous traditions with Greco-Roman borrowings. It appears as a vast entity of two hundred meters on each side, surrounded by porticos completed under Hadrian. The use of a Corinthian colonnade might suggest that the building was Greco-Roman in style; in fact, however, the entire temple building contradicts that supposition. The temple, situated more or less in the center of the peribolos, was constructed

MODEL OF THE SANCTUARY OF BEL IN PALMYRA.

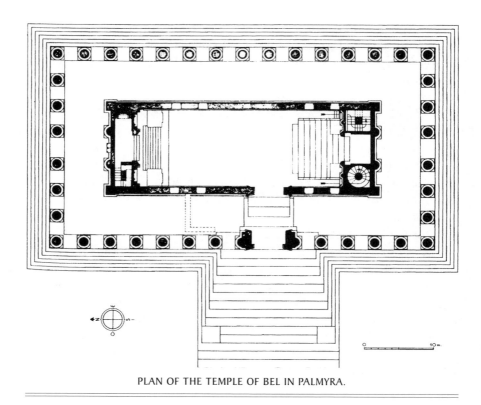

PLAN OF THE TEMPLE OF BEL IN PALMYRA.

as a rectangle on a north–south axis, surrounded by a very high colonnade topped by an entablature that was decorated by a row of crenellated triangular merlons reminiscent of Mesopotamian styles. The cella opens out on one long side. At either end there are two *thalamoi*,[121] elevated rooms facing each other, where sacred statues and symbols of the god must have once stood. Stairs provide access to the roof terrace. The sanctuary has obviously undergone modifications, and the exceptional side opening, which is not even in the center, must have been an afterthought; it is likely that the original entrance was located on the smaller south side and later closed off for reasons we do not know. Except for some elements that, taken by themselves, belong to the Greco-Roman decorative style, the sanctuary is unquestionably an original design, strongly marked by the Syro-Mesopotamian tradition; the merlons, the roof terrace, the enormous peribolos, the banquet hall erected in the interior of the peribolos,[122] and the basins for ritual ablutions are functional elements that in no way reflect the Greco-Roman Mediterranean world.

The sanctuary of Bel is by no means an isolated example in Palmyra. The sanctuary of Nabu reveals the same features.[123] Without going into detail, we may simply note that behind the "Greco-Roman" pediments, the architects created flat roofs as terraces. Moreover, two small towers adorned with merlons stand at the rear of the temple, accentuating characteristics that are quite foreign to Greco-Roman architecture. Even in those sanctuaries that appear to conform more fully to Occidental customs (for example, those dedicated to Baalshamin and Allat), the interiors are laid out in entirely new ways. The sanctuary of Allat includes the ancient, first-century B.C.E. sanctuary, the sacred niche that is essential to a traditional holy place;[124] in the same way, the modest temple in antis of Baalshamin has adopted the interior pattern of an arc-shaped cella intended to serve as the case for the traditional image of the god,[125] while a group of courtyards probably constitutes the equivalent of the periboloi found elsewhere.[126]

We can identify many other sanctuaries that are even more foreign to the Greco-Roman architectural traditions despite all their stylistic borrowings. In Arabia, in the wadi Ramm, near the stone sanctuary of Allat, a much-transformed small native temple came to resemble the exterior of a prostyle temple including a cella surrounded by a corridor allowing for processions.[127] Neither its layout nor its (almost nonexistent) decoration is in the Greco-Roman style: only the use of columns was borrowed from Greco-Roman art. In Petra, the temple known by its "winged lions" looks like a prostyle temple, but in the center of the cella, a squared colonnade outlines a vast plaza, the equivalent of the podium (motab) of the open-air sanctuaries where sacred stones were placed during ceremonies.[128] In reality, such sanctuaries, like the one in Qasrawet in northern Sinai,[129] were originally only courtyards surrounding a motab, in the tradition of open-air "high places." It was only gradually that people strove to give them the look of a Greco-Roman sanctuary, while preserving the underlying structure. In some of these Nabataean sanctuaries we recognize a layout found in certain small Egyptian sanctuaries: the initial state of the temple of Ramm clearly referred to the small Serapeion in Luxor, whereas its second state is very reminiscent of the temple of Deir Chelouit.[130] Considering the many close ties between Egypt and the Nabataeans, such borrowings are not particularly surprising.

For similar reasons, we presume that there was a comparable adaptation of indigenous decoration to the new taste and style in Lebanon. Small temples on podia, found throughout the Lebanese mountains as well as in the Anti-Lebanon,[131] also resemble the temple of Zeus Baitokaike, which appears rather modest in size (49.5 meters by 13.5 meters) in the center of its peribolos: a simple cella behind a prostyle porch with four columns stood on a high podium, necessitating a large stairway on the façade; the altar stood a little farther forward. There are many such examples in northern Syria, with uncountable variations: for example, the sanctuary of Zeus Madbachos and Selamanes in Jebel Sheikh Barakat takes the form of a prostyle temple in the middle of a porticoed peribolos; the temple of Zeus Tourbarachos in Jebel Srir follows roughly the same pattern, but it is preceded by a lopsided vestibule, and the peribolos was defined only by a simple wall, like those of Zeus Seimos, Symbetylos and "Lion" in Qal'at Kalota, two small temples grouped in the same *temenos* (sacred enclosure).[132] These principal features have been found even in the middle of the Syrian desert, although the peribolos has not been found, and two crenellated towers recall the sanctuaries of Palmyra: northwest of Palmyra on the Aleppo road, the sanctuary of Isriyeh (Seriane), dedicated during the Severan period to a divine couple of the Palmyrene type, had the external appearance of a Roman temple, and excavations have turned up a beautiful Greco-Roman statuette of Apollo.[133]

Such sanctuaries were quite numerous even in the countryside, and they attest to the popularity of this architectural style in areas that were otherwise not particularly Hellenized. It is clear, however, that only the decoration was Greco-Roman, with a tendency to excess,[134] whereas the underlying structure, the cultic furnishings, and sometimes even the choice of location were dictated by tradition.

In this respect, they are thus like many other indigenous sanctuaries, including those built in the open air. Some of these were simple rough-hewn structures put up in connection with a particular rock, a spring, a noteworthy plant, or some other natural curiosity. In Panias, we now know more about the physical appearance of the Panion, the semi-stone sanctuary devoted to Pan. A four-column façade was built at the beginning of the second century, in front of a cave with a niche above it (which can be seen on coins),[135] giving the whole a Greco-Roman appearance.[136] In the wadi Ramm, not far from Aila,[137] the location of a stone sanctuary honoring Allat was dictated by the bubbling of a spring in a desert and was marked off only by rudimentary furnishings such as a bench. The steepest summits were favored in Petra, where "high places" of worship were erected.[138] The most famous of these, Jebel al-Madhbah, consists of a vast rectangular esplanade hollowed out in such a way that the sides formed benches; in the middle of one long side, a natural podium (motab) was set aside for placing the gods' sacred stones. Another section was reserved for the altar. Cisterns, fed by rainwater, were used for ablutions and cleaning. Beneath this, two gigantic obelisks, carved out of the rocky mass, appear as sacred stones.[139] To the north, not far from Petra, on an isolated peak in the middle of the deep valley of the wadi al-Hasa, rose the Nabataean sanctuary of Khirbet Tannur; it was built toward the end of the first century B.C.E. and repeatedly modified for use, probably right up to the eve of the Roman annexation. Two interconnected parvis led to the sanctuary itself, but the sanctuary built there probably replaced an earlier Edomite sanctuary of the god Qos (the only one to be designated in texts from the site) that was reoccupied and appropriated by the Nabataeans.[140] In Bostra, under the Severi, a coin portrayed a sanctuary that had kept this traditional arrangement: on a wooden platform reachable by a ladder stood three sacred stones, presumably representing the Nabataean triad Dushara, Allat, and al-Uzza.[141] This traditional arrangement may have been encompassed by the more modern structure of a Greek-style edifice, but it is revealing that the platform and the sacred stones, rather than the Roman-style sanctuary, were chosen to symbolize the city on coins. Generally speaking, these open sanctuaries could take many different forms, and only a few examples of the most startling designs are highlighted here. In fact, in an urban area such as Petra, sites of worship were abundant, often taking the form of simple cultic niches that may or may not have been related to a gathering place (a triclinium); a systematic study of cultic spaces shows that sanctuaries and other sites of worship were distributed throughout the entire urban area.[142]

In northern Syria, a number of elevated sites have been identified and studied.[143] The sanctuary of Zeus Madbachos and Selamanes occupies the entire summit of a very characteristic mountain peak, Jebel Sheikh Barakat, and is laid out as a terrace measuring about 68 meters on a side. The temple peribolos is entirely surrounded by four porticos, while a small temple (about 20 meters by 11 meters) stands in the center. These constructions date from the first century, for the most part (an inscription marks their completion in 143 "at the god's expense"). Three other sanctuaries located on summits overlooking plains present similar features, with the exception of the peribolos: that of Zeus Tourbarachos in Jebel Srir, that of Zeus Bomos (the Greek *Bomos* means the same thing as *Madbachos,* "altar") in Burj Baqirha, and that of Seimios and Symbetylos in Qal'at Kalota. All three date from the second century, but each probably replaced an older cultic site whose shape and layout have disappeared. The sanctuary of Zeus Olympios built during Hadrian's reign at the top of Mount Garizim overlooking Neapolis of Samaria is a close equivalent that was depicted clearly on coins: a small temple surrounded by a vast enclosure at the top of a hill, reached by a long staircase.[144]

Other traditions appeared in the Euphrates Valley and particularly in Dura-Europos, where twelve sanctuaries have been identified, not including the House of the Christians or the synagogue.[145] An original feature that began to be incorporated in the common era was the presence of terraced halls (some bearing the names of the occupants)[146] where the cult of the god or goddess was celebrated. Other sanctuaries found in the network of isolated communities differ only in the details of their interior organization.[147] As Pierre Leriche has noted, however, the proliferation of sanctuaries in Dura-Europos reflected its cosmopolitan character: each community wanted its own sanctuary,[148] which led to a diversity of styles.

Did the borrowings from Mediterranean art amount simply to a superficial veneer, intended to give the Syrian gods and sanctuaries a Greco-Roman look? Had people merely yielded to a sort of passing snobbery? Certainly fashion had some effect, but I do not believe that we can treat lightly such a widespread phenomenon on which believers were willing to spend so much money. This "Greek" style of temple decoration contributed to the assimilation between "Hellenism" and "paganism" that took place over time following the triumph of Christianity—at least among extremists, both Christian and pagan. Despite the persistence of numerous indigenous aspects of the cults practiced in Roman Syria, Hellenism seems to have penetrated sufficiently for us to view all pagan cults as "Greek."

Neither the nature of the gods nor the celebration of their cults was really affected by these modifications, however. The attachment to traditional cults may explain why foreign gods from Anatolia or the Balkans never found many devotees in Syria, except for some passing foreigners. Unquestionably, too, this loyalty was one of the foundations of the strong resistance in Syria to a Hellenization that might be considered destructive of traditional values.[149] But the ability of Hellenism to adapt to a variety of local religious conditions, to espouse deeply rooted systems while giving them a new look, also helps explain its success in Syria, among Phoenicians as well as Aramaeans, pagans as well as Christians. It is true that among some of them we find similar behaviors that go well beyond their formal aspects. Thus the doctrine of absolute *enkrateia*—the refusal of all carnal relations, developed by Tatian of Assyria—corresponded in a way to the violent and bloody rites of the Syrian goddess, whose followers castrated themselves; we find a similar correspondence in the extremist doctrines of some Syrian monks later on.[150] Sometimes, when we have no evidence of the religious preferences of the individuals involved, it is difficult to make an attribution. For instance, the Orpheus and Phoenix mosaics that decorated Edessene tombs at the beginning of the third century provide a clear expression of hope in life after death, even of coming back to life. But whose tombs were they? Perhaps they belonged to pagans; still, Jews and Christians could claim them just as well.[151]

RABBINICAL JUDAISM

The New Organization of Palestinian Judaism

The destruction of the Temple in 70 had interrupted the ritual sacrifices for the first time since 586 B.C.E., and the high priest and the Sanhedrin had disappeared amid the tumult. However, the Diaspora (dispersal) had paved the way for things to come, since many Jews had never frequented the Temple, nor had they attended sacrifices, and yet their Judaism was never in question. The Torah, as much as the Temple, had served as a rallying point for Jews who came to pray in synagogues.[152] Its exegetes, Pharisee rabbis[153] who had long been the true spiritual guides of the Jewish people, quite naturally became the leaders of the new community. Although many of them had adopted moderate positions during the rebellion, no one questioned their authority over the Palestinian community after 70.

During the siege, Rabbi Yohanan b. Zakkai[154] had secretly fled Jerusalem, hidden in a coffin, and had founded a school for the study of the Torah[155] in Iamnia, with the Romans' consent. In the wake of the defeat, he issued essential decrees concerning the observance of holidays and auspicious dates for certain events (for example, marriage); in effect, he transferred the duties and privileges of the high priest and the Sanhedrin to his own circle. The president of the assembly—the *nasi,* or patriarch—took the place of the high priest as spiritual leader of the Jews and as interlocutor with the Romans. This new authority was quickly recognized by all Jews and also by the Roman officials; they needed its assistance in order to understand the indigenous legal code, which was still in use.

These leading Pharisees very quickly proposed an interpretation of recent history that was meant to restore hope. According to Rabbi Yohanan, Israel could regain Yahweh's approval only by freeing itself of its sin, which alone was responsible for its misery. Henceforth, pious Jews would make respect for the Torah the centerpiece of their religious practices. Rabbi Yohanan thus gave legitimacy to a spiritual life that was separate from the system of sacrifice. On this key point as on others, the scholars proved their ability to adapt their explanation of the Torah to circumstances. The people found in them the advice they needed in their daily lives. Moreover, the doctrines of the afterlife that the rabbis professed— survival and resurrection—were a new source of hope for a people in the depths of despair.

The greatest work of these rabbis (known as *Tannaim,* "teachers") was to put in writing the commentaries that had been transmitted orally for generations (for the chain of Pharisee rabbis reached back as far as Moses himself) and that were in danger of being forgotten. Several schools flourished simultaneously, and scholars offered divergent opinions on many points. Gradually, a compilation (the *Mishna*) was developed in which the role of Rabbi Aqiba was most influential. Promulgated around 200 under the authority of the nasi Juda I, it was quickly adopted by all the schools (or academies) in Palestine and communicated to Babylon. On the basis of this work, the second generation of rabbis (the Amoraim) in the third and fourth centuries began to publish detailed commentaries *(Guemara)* that, taken together with the Mishna, constitute the Talmuds of Jerusalem and Babylon.[156] It was an enormous undertaking, and it engaged Judaism for a very long time along a new path, which warrants our attention. But first it is important to clarify the new conditions that prevailed for the Jews in Palestine.

The Bar Kokhba revolt, despite its limited reach, had jeopardized the reorganization of Judaism under the close supervision of the Romans. Repressive measures were applied to everyone: the prohibition against circumcision was upheld (or adopted), and it was also forbidden to observe the Sabbath, ordain rabbis, and study law. Antoninus was more conciliatory, however, and he reauthorized the circumcision of Jewish infants. Judaism returned to one of its essential practices, but the imperial edict strictly forbade conversion.

Judaism reorganized itself rather quickly in a way to which the Roman authorities gave de facto recognition. Even before the end of the Bar Kokhba rebellion, rabbis had reestablished a Sanhedrin. A meeting took place in Usha, in Galilee, around 140, that brought together the survivors of the pre-revolt Sanhedrin and the rabbis who had been ordained secretly by Rabbi Juda b. Baba, despite the Roman ban. Rome had no way of forcing Jews to live under any law other than their own, and Jewish institutions had to settle disputes in areas where imperial justice had no control—disagreements over purity rites or the validity of a marriage, for example. Courts of justice began to function once again. To crown it all, the position of nasi, prince or patriarch, which had been vacant since the death of Gamaliel II during the war, was conferred on Gamaliel's son, Rabbi Simeon II ha-nasi: from then on the position was hereditary, which gave it additional weight because the head of the community avoided the hazards of competition. The nasi became the privileged intercessor with the Romans, and his authority was recognized everywhere, including in the Diaspora, as we saw when Rabbi Juda I promulgated the Mishna.

Once again, Jewish institutions recognized by the Roman authorities provided de facto leadership of the community. Moreover, in a clear sign that peace was being restored, the Jewish leaders quickly established excellent relations with the imperial power, as illustrated by certain traditions concerning the relationships between Jews and the Severi. Juda I is believed to have been friendly with Caracalla,[157] and the nasis received grants of land in the valley of Jezreel, in the Golan and near Lydda, and hired Goth and German bodyguards, a practice that would surely have required Roman approval. On the institutional level, the dangerous situation created by the war of 132–135 thus quickly improved and stabilized.

The Jews' economic and social conditions changed radically between the beginning of the second century and the middle of the third. From here on, it is necessary to distinguish between Judaea and Galilee, for the latter overtook the former as the center of Jewish life in Palestine. Indeed, after 135, Jews were a minority in southern Palestine and on the coast, forming only small isolated pockets in Hebron, Iamnia, Lydda, and Jericho, between Livias and Beth Nimra in Peraea, and around Narbata on the Sharon plain. Grants of land to non-Jews and the disappearance of a significant number of Jewish tenant farmers in the region helped turn Judaea-Samaria, like Idumaea, into areas with predominantly pagan populations. Thus they were no longer any different from other Syrian provinces, except that a large number of landowners were newcomers, many of them westerners and for the most part veterans.

Jerusalem had become a pagan city par excellence, a Roman colony symbolizing the oppression and defeat of the Jews, who were theoretically forbidden to live there after 135; still, despite this ban, a small community was soon reestablished. Jews made their reappearance in the third century, when there is evidence of a "holy congregation" *(kehilah kadichah)*.[158] Initially, only a few rabbis ventured to Jerusalem to pray, but soon there was established a community that included some rabbis,[159] a very strict community reminiscent in certain respects of the ancient Essenes. This development may have come about thanks to Rabbi Juda *ha-nasi,* whose good relations with the Severi probably contributed to the lifting of the ban, or at least to an easing of its application. In any case, two of the leaders of the Jerusalem community, Rabbi Simeon b. Menassia and Rabbi Jose b. Hameshullam, were very close to Juda I.[160]

Nevertheless, the center of gravity of the Jewish population in Palestine shifted to Galilee, whose agricultural and artisanal prosperity went back as far as the Hellenistic period and did not decline during the early empire. The area became a Jewish territory par excellence, seat of the nasi and the Sanhedrin. Here, too, however, the decline in the Jewish population was significant enough to worry the community's leaders. Many Jews, even rabbis, had fled during the repression. There were of course some communities with a Jewish majority, but these became increasingly rare; most often, Jews were only a significant minority. At the beginning of the fourth century, Eusebius of Caesarea could identify only a handful of villages as "Jewish" or "Christian," a finding confirmed by rabbis who pointed out a few examples of paired villages, one Jewish, one pagan. Mixed villages, often predominantly pagan, were thus the norm; some undoubtedly had a Jewish majority, but they were so rarely homogeneous that Eusebius, like the rabbis, could list the exceptions.[161]

In response, Palestinian rabbis undertook an intense propaganda campaign on behalf of the Holy Land, claiming that living in Palestine was henceforth "equal to observing all the laws of the Torah taken together."[162] Propaganda urging a return to the land of the ancestors thus began right after the defeats that had accelerated the dispersion, at the very moment when loss of Jewish lives had placed the community in a critical situation.

Whether in Judaea or in Galilee, in Idumaea, or on the coast, from then on living in Palestine meant living among pagans: the goyim were everywhere. For example, between the revolt of 70 and the Bar Kokhba rebellion, Jewish priests fleeing Jerusalem settled in Sepphoris, which had enjoyed city status since around 67–68. However, Hadrian made the city a Diocaesarea; he erected a capitol and a temple of Tyche there and established a classic municipal administration, as a way of confirming the city's pagan character. Several temples existed during Antoninus's reign.[163] Nevertheless, Sepphoris became the customary residence of Rabbi Juda hanasi, who compiled the Mishna there. And so, even in Galilee, which remained the fallback zone of the Jewish communities, the non-Jewish population grew, as soldiers and other groups settled there.[164] Tiberias, founded by Antipas as a Greek city, remained primarily non-Jewish until the Jewish War and perhaps until the middle of the second century. Even the southern district of Hammath, inhabited by Jews, included a palestra and baths until around 130; we do not know what caused their destruction (an earthquake is one possibility). It was not until the beginning of the third century that we see a Jewish renewal in the city, as evidenced by the construction of the first synagogue.[165] Broadly speaking, even though Jews were more numerous in Galilee than elsewhere, there was no longer a Jewish territory in Palestine. Moreover, the advance of urbanization reinforced the trend toward Hellenization, even among rabbis: it is striking to note that whereas in the second century rabbis usually lived in small communities such as Iamnia, Usha, or Beth She'arim, the third century found them living in Tiberias, Sepphoris, Caesarea, and Lydda-Diospolis.[166]

The Jewish Diaspora in Syria

Roman Palestine was becoming increasingly integrated into its Syrian environment, so there should be no need to consider the Jews of Palestine in a different light from those of the Diaspora. All were living among pagans. However, in the realms of law and religion, rabbis continued to distinguish between Eretz Israel, the land promised by Yahweh during the flight out of Egypt, to which certain privileges involving ritual purity were connected, and the land of the Gentiles, where Jews could not travel without taking certain precautions. One may even wonder whether the rabbis' frequent interrogations on this subject in the third and fourth centuries did not reveal a degree of uncertainty, or, more precisely, whether it did not reflect the threat of a gradual elimination, in the minds of the people, of any limits whatsoever. In an Eretz Israel where goyim (non-Jews) constituted a significant majority, it was useful to recall the rules and to establish the boundaries of the ancestral land, not only for immediate religious reasons but also with a view toward the day when a state could be reestablished, if that time were ever to come. The rabbis' responses are sometimes vague or awkward, revealing that they themselves tended to set the boundaries of Eretz Israel in relation to the recent Jewish colonization, although they sought support for their decisions in the ancient scriptural tradition. For example, the territory of Bostra was clearly outside the boundaries of the Holy Land,[167] but in one of his opinions, Rabbi Yohanan (who died in 279 c.e.) refers to the opinion of a local rabbi, Rabbi Hunya of Barat Hauran,[168] on the matter of that very region: "Priests usually travel as far as Darai [Adraha] and continue on that road [from Nawa, in the north] toward Bostra as far as Pardeisa."[169] Pardeisa is not identified,[170] but we must assume that the rabbis considered all of Batanaea to be included in Eretz Israel—not only Nawa, where there was a large Jewish community,[171] but also the land of the city-state of Adraha, the biblical Edrei, capital of the country of Bashan (Batanaea).[172]

The Diaspora thus began at the gates of the Holy Land, whose boundaries were even further blurred by the Romans. Eretz Israel did not actually coincide with any administrative structure, such as Herod's kingdom or that of his successors, nor did it coincide with the province of Judaea or Syria-Palestine. When traveling, pious Jews could never count on the existing boundaries; everywhere they went they encountered pagans, who were as numerous inside Eretz Israel as outside. As Josephus notes as early as the first century, this proximity meant that there were many Jews living "densely interspersed" in Syria;[173] thus one could find oneself living among Jews even after leaving the Holy Land.

The largest communities were located either in the immediate vicinity— on the Golan, in the Hauran—or in large Syrian cities. On the Golan, recent investigations have identified many sites as Jewish owing to the presence of synagogues or ritual baths.[174] In these rural establishments, Jews lived side by side with pagans and Judeo-Christians. The same phenomenon can be seen—although these regions have been less thoroughly explored than the western Golan—in the eastern part of the Golan and in Batanaea, where Jewish communities existed in Nawa (the birthplace of a certain number of rabbis),[175] Tafas,[176] Ezra',[177] Sheikh Meskin,[178] Philippopolis,[179] and presumably other cities as well. In the Hauran itself, hardly any trace remains of the groups that had flourished during the period of the Maccabees; these groups had been repatriated by force by Jonathan in 163 B.C.E.[180] There were Jews in Bostra, however, and rabbis who visited them;[181] in addition, evidence of some scattered Jews has been found in the Greek epigraphy of the area[182]—for example, in Phaina in the Trachon area.[183] With the exception of some Jewish tenant farmers identified in the Antiochene in the fourth century,[184] and a Jew from Yahmur[185] (east of Sidon) who was buried in Beth Shearim, most Syrian Jews were city dwellers. Despite the massacres that ravaged these communities during the war of 66–74, most of them survived and prospered in the second and third centuries.

Jews had lived in Antioch for a long time, although Josephus is mistaken when, making his habitual effort to justify their claims of citizenship, he says that Jews had been present in the city since its foundation.[186] It is likely that there were Jews living in the Syrian capital at an early date, but we cannot associate their arrival with a specific event such as Jonathan's Jewish troops coming to the aid of Demetrios II against the rebellious city.[187] Many were probably there before that date, for why else would the high priest Onias III have taken refuge in Daphne? To be sure, he may have had no choice: he seems to have been under house arrest. Some Jews probably did gain citizenship in Antioch, which would explain why Josephus says that in that city, when the gymnasiarch was distributing free supplies, Jews did not receive a ration of oil but instead received a sum of money with which to purchase purified oil.[188] This information, if accurate, would prove that Jews were citizens, because they benefited from the free distributions. The intervention of Jonathan's troops and the burning of the city, for which they were held responsible, could not have helped the situation of the Jewish community in Antioch.[189]

Additional groups have been identified in Apamaea,[190] where an epigraphic record refers to a synagogue covered with mosaics at the end of the fourth century, but we cannot date the first Jewish presence there;[191] we may recall, however, that a Jew was terrorizing the region when Pompey arrived. Jewish communities have been attested in Damascus, Gerasa, and Ptolemais during the period of the great revolt. Jews from Tyre,[192] Sidon,[193] Berytos,[194] Byblos,[195] Palmyra,[196] Antioch,[197] and Aila[198] were buried in the necropolis of Beth Shearim in Galilee in the second and third centuries.

Others have been found in Jerusalem: a Jew from Apamaea, Ariston, was buried there under an epitaph carved in Greek,[199] while yet another, from Berytos, bore the traditional Jewish name Eleazar.[200] It is more difficult to prove the presence of Jews in these cities from field discoveries, but there is occasionally some evidence: one Jew in Palmyra, Iulius Aurelius Samuel, yielded part of a tomb to a Palmyrene pagan, seemingly without difficulty.[201]

Generally speaking, Jewish military campaigns in the late Hellenistic period provoked deep hostility toward the Jews in neighboring cities, and Josephus tends to see this as the origin of the conflicts that he describes in the first century—in Ascalon,[202] Tyre,[203] Caesarea,[204] and Iamnia[205]—although the latter two may have had more immediate causes. Nevertheless, it would doubtless be an exaggeration to describe all Jewish–pagan relationships in terms of hatred and confrontation. There had indeed been massacres during the great revolt: Antiochians usually tried to banish Jewish citizens;[206] in Damascus 10,500 Jews gathered in the gymnasium were massacred,[207] and similar massacres took place in Caesarea,[208] Ptolemais, Ascalon, Hippos, and Gadara.[209] However, Judaism clearly had some appeal, for in Damascus the assailants acted without the knowledge of their wives, most of whom, according to Josephus, had converted to Judaism;[210] many pagans in Antioch were drawn to Judaism as well.[211] Jewish converts are attested in both Antioch[212] and Caesarea.[213] In Gerasa, where there was a synagogue until quite late, Jews were well treated in 70,[214] as they were in Sidon and Apamaea.[215] A Jewish community probably existed in Edessa as early as the beginning of the common era. According to a rapid and no doubt somewhat exaggerated calculation based on epitaphs, Han J. W. Drijvers estimates that Jews constituted about 12 percent of the total population.[216]

The Jews in Dura became quite justifiably famous after the discovery of their synagogue in 1932.[217] Their presence in the city may go back to its foundation, but scarcely any evidence has been found prior to the end of the first century C.E. Indeed, Hasmonaean coins from the reigns of John Hyrcanos and Alexander Jannaeus attest more surely to the movement of Jews between Palestine and Mesopotamia than to the existence of a Jewish community in Dura itself.[218] Yet a private house that was built along the western rampart and later became a synagogue dates at the earliest from the end of the first century or the beginning of the second; we do not know when it shifted from private to religious use—perhaps not until the beginning of the Roman occupation, some time in the last third of the second century.[219] In any event, the rather small community (there was room for only about forty people on the benches of this first synagogue) lived

PAINTING FROM THE SYNAGOGUE AT DURA-EUROPOS: SAMUEL ANOINTING DAVID.

nearby: inscriptions and graffiti suggest that several neighboring houses may have been occupied by Jews. This does not imply that there was any intent to create the forerunner of a ghetto; rather, it reflects a desire to respect the rules of the Sabbath governing the distance one could travel to reach the synagogue. Though the congregation was small, it was nevertheless organized with the advice of the elders and of its archon.[220]

The Jewish population increased at the beginning of the third century, possibly owing to Dura's important role as a garrison city. In any case, the reconstruction of the synagogue was begun; magnificent paintings covered all the walls and roof tiles, attesting to the wealth of the group. The new building was completed in 244–245, as indicated by a dedication inscribed in Aramaic. There was now room for 65 people, but the ground level was soon redesigned to double the number of benches and reach a capacity of 124. Just before the destruction of the city, the Jewish community in Dura was thriving and prosperous.

From Sacrifice to Exegesis: Rabbinical Judaism

Paradoxically, the destruction of the Second Temple was both a central drama in the history of Judaism and a marginal event. It was a central drama in that the interruption of the sacrificial cult marked a break in the history of Judaism. Its consequences were not as significant as one might think, however, because the groundwork for future developments had been in preparation for a long time, and there is every reason to believe that the changes would have occurred under any circumstances.

THE SACRIFICIAL CULT AND THE TEMPLE BEFORE 70

Even before its disappearance, the Temple as an institution had grown weak. Ever since the Hasmonaeans' time, the high priests were at best challenged by an influential group of pious Jews and at worst ignored and scorned. By combining their religious and political functions in defiance of the traditional rules, the Hasmonaeans drew the wrath of the Hasidim; the persecution of the most determined group (the Essenes) was not enough to silence them or to lessen their influence among the people. Under the Herodians and direct Roman administration, moreover, the high priests were reduced to mere puppets lacking in prestige whose only power lay in the legal authority conferred by the Torah. Apart from the sacrificial cult, they had virtually no influence. Both the moral and the spiritual authority of those responsible for the Temple had thus been weakened. This was bound to have had certain consequences, not for the Temple itself, but for the cult that was celebrated there.

A few community members had gradually begun to question the legitimacy of the sacrificial cult. We know that members of the Qumran community challenged the liturgical calendar used in Jerusalem and refused to frequent the Temple. Yet they considered themselves good Jews, which shows that there were factions of pious Jews who considered the Temple superfluous. Moreover, it is likely that members of this sect were not avoiding the Temple for strictly formal reasons. In the fourth Sibylline Oracle, Essene in origin, the author denounces "altars ... defiled by the blood of animate creatures."[221] This may sound like a conventional and unoriginal attack on pagan sacrifices, but such a reading would hardly make sense, since the Essenes never paid any particular attention to pagans. The statement thus had to have been a denunciation of the Jerusalemite holocausts, a practice that was shocking to followers of a more spiritual cult.

This trend toward the spiritual may also have found adherents among supporters of a type of allegorical exegesis prevalent in Alexandria. By giving symbolic or allegorical explanations for all the ritual restrictions, Philo of Alexandria had tended to relax the obligations of the Torah, including those that led to blood sacrifices. He too worked toward a more spiritual religion, one that could easily forego the sacrifices that related it to the pagan cults—and this during a time when the Temple was still standing.

Other forces were moving in the same direction. In Alexandria, the translation of the Bible into Greek, the Septuagint, helped give the scriptures a more spiritual, less material character: Greek could more easily express abstract notions than Hebrew or Aramaic, which tended to be more concrete. Abraham's sacrifice, for example, became more a symbolic gesture than an actual historical drama. Finally, and most importantly, we must take into account the reality of a long-standing constraint: most Jews could no longer frequent the Temple regularly, and there were many who had never done so. Sacrifice, offered in the name of all, was for many only a distant reality.

All this could only serve to reinforce the lesson that had been taught since the time of the prophets and reiterated by the scribes and rabbis: it does no good to offer sacrifices without purity of heart. Yahweh rejects sacrifices offered by unclean hands, for nothing can replace virtuous living. Thus many Jews were prepared to accept the abolition of sacrificial offerings, or rather to maintain that the disappearance of these offerings was less important than the priests cared to admit.

THE VICTORY OF THE RABBIS

The growth of synagogues reflected the new situation. The destruction of the Temple did not leave Jews without spiritual guides or places of worship. We may recall how Rabbi Yohanan b. Zakkai had fled Jerusalem during the war in order to open a rabbinical school in Iamnia: he was simply preparing for the aftermath of defeat. His authority was established at once and without apparent objection; everyone had long recognized the role of scribes and teachers as spiritual leaders. The fall of the Temple simply guaranteed the triumph of Pharisees, who were no longer bothered by their rivals, the Sadduceans and the Essenes.[222] They could then complete the construction of what might be called a "Third Temple," a colossal exegetical work that was based on all prior teachings but that took its definitive form after the fall of the Temple, in Palestine and Babylon simultaneously.

As long as the Jews had been a majority in the land they considered their own and had remained confident of their coming victory, interpreters of the Torah had sought to reinforce the group's identity by creating more barriers to their integration with the pagan world around them. But after being defeated, humiliated, and dispersed, and seeing all hope for the restoration of their state fade, Jews had to put off the end-time and come to terms with a world in which they could not live entirely among themselves. The job of the Pharisee rabbis was precisely to interpret the Torah in a way that reconciled two necessities previously seen as contradictory: they had to reinforce the Jews' cohesion by solidifying it around respect for Jewish law, yet they had to allow the group to live from day to day in a wholly pagan world. It was an enormous task, accomplished largely in Palestine beginning in the second century. It was made easier by the fact that the rabbis were henceforth living at the heart of Jewish communities that were often in the minority: scorn for ordinary people *(ammei ha-haretz)* faded during the course of the third century and rabbis became more attentive to the daily needs of ordinary Jews, for whom respect for ancestral prohibitions often became impossible.[223]

It will be useful to describe the rabbis' work and to explain some of the terms used to designate its various components. To begin with, two series of commentaries and exegeses were brought together: the first, strictly juridical in nature, is known as the *Halakha,* while the second series, consisting of historical and doctrinal texts, constitutes the *Haggada.* The Halakha clarifies legal obligations in every detail; these obligations may come from the restrictions spelled out in the Pentateuch or from unwritten customs for which the scribes ultimately achieved recognition as part of the Torah. The work was endless, since every detail, every word, was subject to interpretation. Moreover, each obligation had to be made compatible with all the others. As for the Haggada, it consisted in enriching and spelling out the doctrinal, moral, and historical content of the scriptures. The author of a Haggadic *midrash* (commentary) relied upon scripture or history to explicate whatever seemed incomplete or unclear but was useful for people's lives. For example, because the Temple fell twice, once on 17 Tammuz and again on 9 Ab, it was clear that these two days were dangerous for Jews; the author of a historical midrash would logically conclude that it was a 17 Tammuz when the Tablets of the Law were broken and a 9 Ab when Moses learned that he would not reach the Holy Land.

The Halakha and the Haggada are constantly mixed in Talmudic works that focus more or less on the one or the other.[224] The Mishna was essentially Halakhic in nature, while the Babylonian Talmud contained a large number of Haggadic writings. The totality of rabbinic commentaries, with the text of the Torah itself, constituted *midrashim.*

The texts that we group together as Talmudic include four works that overlap to a significant extent: the Mishna, the Tosefta, the Palestinian Talmud, and the Babylonian Talmud.

The Mishna (Repetition) consists of the entire set of written laws (the Torah) and transcriptions of the laws passed down through the oral tradition; it was thus the most complete legal code in existence. Promulgated by Rabbi (Prince) Juda I around 200, it is based upon even older collations prepared for the most part by Rabbi Aqiba around 120–130 and Rabbi

Meir somewhat later. It thus includes, organized by theme, both the text of the Pentateuch and the rabbinical exegeses accepted by all. The sixty treatises (sixty-three, in fact, in the published editions) were classified according to six "orders" or subjects: Seeds, Holidays, Women, Damages, Sacred Things, and Purity. Each of the Mosaic precepts is explicated and discussed. In cases where authorities disagree, the Mishna offers divergent opinions as well as the majority view (which prevails over the others). The rabbis whose contributions are included were those who ran the rabbinical schools between 70 and 200. Approximately 150 of them are mentioned, some more frequently than others. Eight of them appear more than a hundred times: Rabbi Juda b. Elai (609 times), Rabbi Yose b. Halafta (335), Rabbi Meir (331), Rabbi Simeon b. Yohai (325), Rabbi Eliezer b. Hyrcanos (324), Rabbi Aqiba (278), Rabbi Joshua b. Hananiah (146), Rabban Simeon b. Gamaliel II (103).[225] All these scholars worked in Palestine before 160 C.E. The Mishna was accepted everywhere and served as a basis for all subsequent works. The three additional Talmudic works thus incorporated it, at least to some extent.

The *Tosefta* (Supplement) is presented as a supplement to the Mishna. As such, it generally followed the order of the Mishna (with the exception of four treatises) and provided rabbinical commentaries that had been written prior to the Mishna but not included in it, or that had been included in the Mishna but only in condensed form, or that had been written after the Mishna. Although it was presented as a compilation made by Rabbi Hiyya b. Abba, a student of Rabbi Juda ha-nasi, it must have been produced by fusing previously existing compilations during the third century.

The Jerusalemite (or, more precisely, the Palestinian) Talmud is based on the Mishna, which had become the legal foundation par excellence of the Jewish community, and it brought together the commentaries of the masters in Tiberias and those of the other rabbinical academies in Palestine. First published in its present form around 400, it was a compilation of commentaries dating for the most part from the third century and the first half of the fourth. It follows the Mishna step by step, and for every paragraph it offers commentaries *(Guemara)* by Amoraim—rabbis who came after the Mishna (although it also introduces some pre-Mishnaic commentaries, known as *baraytoth*). The only parts that have survived are the first four "orders" of the Mishna and the beginning of a treatise from the sixth.

The Babylonian Talmud was produced in the same spirit as that of Palestine. It, too, offers a detailed commentary on the Mishna, which had been brought to Babylon as early as the era of Juda ha-nasi by one of the latter's students, Abba Areka. However, the Babylonian Talmud, produced later than its counterpart in Jerusalem (in the sixth century), differs from the latter in that it is more concerned with doctrine than with law—it focuses much more on Haggadic than on Halakhic considerations. Although four times as long, the Babylonian Talmud is even less complete than the Palestinian version, containing only thirty-six and a half treatises as opposed to thirty-nine.

The importance of this exegetical work has helped create an image of rabbinical Judaism as mired in ritualism, in a legalistic rigor verging on the absurd. Inevitably, such a propensity for endless commentary on the Law led to absurd consequences in some instances, and to esoteric results in others. Rules could be multiplied to the point where ordinary life became impossible. But limiting the richness and creativity of rabbinical Judaism to the development of a legal code would be a serious misconstruction.

We have already had occasion to consider how the Pharisees' schools made fidelity to the Torah the symbol of the Jews' alliance with Yahweh. Moreover, the most meticulous rabbis repeatedly insisted that respect for the Law was nothing without the practice of brotherly love and charity. In this respect, the beautiful *Pirqe Avot* (Lessons of the Fathers) offers a perfect antidote to anyone inclined to reduce rabbinical Judaism to mere Talmudic commentary. Numerous formulations by the best-known rabbis of the Mishna era (essentially from the late first century through the second) remind their followers of the importance of the Torah and place even greater emphasis on morality. They reframe the study of the Torah within a spiritual perspective that transcends its purely ritual aspects. The treatise known as the *Avot of Rabbi Nathan* repeats and amplifies these themes, commenting on them systematically. Taken as a whole, this treatise constitutes the "ethical summation of the Talmud,"[226] and curious resemblances to the teachings of Jesus are unmistakable, even though the Torah is always exalted and remains the primary concern of the faithful.

Rabbis did not limit their writings to legal texts, however. In addition to the Talmudic corpus, we must take into account the many midrashim that consisted of closely argued commentaries on the books of the Pentateuch, with no concern for the careful thematic classification adopted in the Mishna. Furthermore, the midrashim focused much more on the Haggadic aspects of the scriptures than on the Halakhic aspects, and this emphasis ensured their popularity. We must also note the nonscholarly *targumim*, free translations of the books of the Jewish Bible into Aramaic. The targum of the proselytizer Onkelos at the beginning of the second century became very popular quite early, as did Jonathan's work on the books of the prophets. Both offer simplified and popular versions of the most current scholarly commentaries. All these writings gave ordinary Jews tools they could use in their daily lives, and helped them deal with the many difficulties they were confronting.

ADAPTING TO THE WORLD

Most Jews found themselves living among pagans. It had become more difficult than ever to respect all the demands of the Torah. To live piously without cutting themselves off from their neighbors, they had to compromise with the world around them. In an environment that was changing for everyone, but especially for the Jews, the rabbis' ongoing work of interpreting the Torah turned out to be an essential tool enabling the Jews to adapt to the new conditions. For the rabbis managed to give an appropriate response to each new situation. Nothing was less rigid than the Talmudic corpus: a living entity, it was constantly being reworked. In this enterprise, the scholars of the Jewish community in Babylon played a primary part, and their influence was felt in Syria and as far away as Palestine.

The Jewish community in Mesopotamia was one of the oldest and most influential in the Diaspora. Originally consisting primarily of Jews deported by the Assyrians in the eighth century B.C.E. and then, at the beginning of the sixth, by the Babylonians, it grew steadily larger. Its principal centers were in Nehardea, on the Euphrates north of Babylon, in Seleucia on the Tigris, and in Ctesiphon, but there were also communities in the north, in Edessa, Nisibis, Nikephorion, and especially Dura-Europos. The conversion of Queen Helen of Adiabene and her son King Izates helped strengthen a community that was thoroughly embedded in Mesopotamian culture. In addition, many Jews fled to Babylon after the failure of the uprisings of 66–70 and 132–135, in order to escape Roman domination.

These communities were organized no differently from the others, but from the Achaemenid period on there may have been a central authority, the exilarch, who represented Jewish concerns at court. Under Parthian domination, the communities maintained excellent relations with the Parthian kings, who even permitted the creation of a kind of Jewish principality near Nehardea (around 20–40 C.E.). As the fourth-ranking figure in the kingdom, living in luxury and enjoying wide authority over the Jews in matters of justice and taxes, the exilarch seems to have had a very official role. Despite the difficult position they were in during the period of conflict between Rome and the Parthians, the Babylonian Jews never failed to send their financial contribution to Jerusalem; indeed, they delivered it themselves, in a well-guarded convoy. In other words, the solidarity between that part of the Diaspora and Jerusalem remained in force. When the Sassanid Persians overthrew the Parthians, however, the Jews underwent a great many trials. Mazdeism became the official state religion, and other cults were systematically persecuted. Jews were the first to suffer: some were executed, synagogues were destroyed, and the observance of feast days was outlawed, among other hardships. The situation improved gradually toward the end of the third century, but for only a short time. The community would never again experience the tranquility of the Parthian era.

Among scholars, Babylonian Judaism has long been regarded as excessively legalistic and rigid, tending to take the teachings of the Palestinian rabbis to extremes. The community's isolation reinforced this tendency, or so it has been argued. However, more recent studies, and in particular the work of Jacob Neusner,[227] show that this was not at all the case, at least not during the period that concerns us. The very official roles held by Jews in the Parthian kingdom would hardly support such an interpretation: how could Jews have scrupulously observed the requirements of the Torah while living in the Parthian court or serving in the royal army? This does not mean that the Babylonian Jews ignored the rules, but it is unlikely that they were heavily influenced by the teachings of the Palestinian schools before the third century.

The first Palestinian rabbis did not even arrive in Babylon until after 135, and only then, at the earliest, could the Halakhic teachings have acquired any significance in Babylon. In particular, it was only after 200 that the rabbis began to assert themselves, when Rab brought the Mishna to Mesopotamia and encouraged the creation of rabbinical schools there (the school in Soura, south of Babylon, was built in 219). The Babylonian scholars demanded strict respect for the laws of the Torah and were no less strict in their own practice. Accustomed to living among pagans, however, they sized up what was possible and what was not. Thus, at the start of the third century, the scholar Samuel, a physician and an astronomer as well as a teacher, taught that everyone must respect the laws of the state: the Law of Moses applied only to religious matters. This distinction between the civil and the religious spheres was of great importance, for it allowed Jews to prove themselves loyal while remaining faithful to Jewish religious laws. It introduced a principle for distinguishing between essential and inessential matters. Generally speaking, the strictly legalistic (Halakhic) commentary became less important than moral, doctrinal, or historical considerations. This is clearly reflected in the Babylonian Talmud, a later compilation that summarizes the work done in Babylonian schools from the third century on.

The synagogue paintings in Dura-Europos provide still another indication of the originality of Mesopotamian Judaism.[228] Neusner has brilliantly shown the close connection of this synagogue to a culture unique to the Jews of Mesopotamia. The discovery of the synagogue in Dura-Europos in November 1932 shed an entirely new light on an artistic evolution that had not yet flourished elsewhere in the Jewish world. It is of course well known that Judaism banned all human and animal representations; we need only recall the outcry provoked by the installation of a golden eagle over the Temple door in Herod's day. Representations of animals remained very rare in Jewish monuments during the first century, and those that existed were virtually hidden (as in 'Iraq al-Amir, Masada, and Herodion). Subsequently, however, the situation began to evolve; as early as the second century we find isolated representations of animals or human figures in Jewish homes, tombs, and other places frequented by Jews. The only explanation that had ever been given for these infractions was the influence of an atmosphere of syncretism. The discovery at Dura has obliged us to consider the question in different terms, for this was an official monument that could hardly be suspected of condoning practices forbidden by the rabbis. The walls of the synagogue in Dura are covered with paintings illustrating various episodes in the history of the Jewish people, and they include numerous human and animal figures. We are thus obliged to acknowledge that the rules established by rabbis who saw the representation of human beings or animals as an idolatrous practice had fallen by the wayside before the middle of the third century. Moreover, the Dura painter had to have borrowed from pagan artists, since Judaism could not have provided any traditional models. Thus Edwin Goodenough has shown that several scenes were drawn from themes in Greek mythology: David taking on features of Orpheus, Pharaoh's daughter those of Aphrodite, Eros conflated with Moses, Moses and his friends with the banquet of the seven sages, and so on.

The effort to explain the set of scenes as a whole and to determine their deeper significance has led to numerous controversies. Although most of the scenes have been more or less positively identified, many questions remain. It seems clear to me that most of the theses argued by Goodenough and supported by Neusner can be accepted today. Carl Hermann Kraeling, the first to describe the site, saw a very rabbinical interpretation of biblical history in the paintings; unlike Kraeling, Goodenough shows that the paintings reflect a very allegorical, messianic, and even mystical interpretation of history, if only in the choice of episodes portrayed. Moreover, Ezekiel occupies a place entirely out of proportion with respect to his role in the history of Judaism. Jacob Neusner reminds us that the figure of Ezekiel nourished a whole mystical strain in Mesopotamian Judaism, a strain that reappeared with great regularity until the middle of the third century at least, when the influence of the rabbinical schools coming out of

Palestinian Judaism began to be felt. From this standpoint, the Dura synagogue offers an excellent example of the freedom of expression and the mystical tendencies of Mesopotamian Judaism.

Finally, the Dura paintings set forth a historical, doctrinal, and messianic program in an apparent attempt to illustrate and defend Judaism. As Neusner has noted, the period when these frescoes were painted corresponds to a period of intense spiritual activity, especially in Mesopotamia. This was not only a period in which Christianity flourished as never before (some members of the Severan court were sympathetic, and Philip the Arab is said to have been a Christian), but it was also the time when Mazdeism triumphed officially, and when Mani brought about a religious syncretism that was very popular in Mesopotamia. It was therefore urgent to remind Jews (and others), by any means possible, of the greatness of Judaism and its superiority over the other monotheistic sects.

The communities of this time had come a long way from the time when pious Jews were offended to see athletes racing nude beneath the Temple walls. Now, Jews frequented baths and gyms, and rabbis (whose imagery drew upon the Greek world of gymnasia and competitive games) were willing to say that the presence of statues of pagan gods did not mean that Jews must not frequent public baths. Even this simple example is an eloquent demonstration of the way Judaism managed to adapt to changes in the ancient world without renouncing its own beliefs. The small community living in the area around Jerusalem had spread throughout the Mediterranean world and beyond. Carried along by its messianic and eschatological faith, it had tried to transcend the limitations of the present in order to ensure its future. Its failure led to a postponement of the day when its hopes would be realized, but for a long time in the synagogues people held onto their dream of meeting "next year in Jerusalem."

THE BEGINNINGS OF CHRISTIANIZATION

It is hardly possible to ignore the spread of Christianity, both because Syria was the cradle of early Christianity and because Christians must have constituted a significant element in Syrian society, at least by the early third century.[229] While I would not hazard a guess as to numbers, or even an order of magnitude, it is quite clear that Christians were highly visible. From the outset, however, historians have to bring to light the seeming contradiction that emerges from the available sources: whereas a number of texts indicate that Christianization was progressing and that Christians were participating in the "intellectual" debates of the times, the archaeological record is practically mute until the dawn of the fourth century. We know that there was a House of Christians in Dura-Europos, and there may be traces of another house that served as a church in Aila. But whereas the Jews left many identifiable traces, it is by and large impossible to distinguish Christians from non-Christians solely on the basis of the physical evidence. This situation persisted throughout the early empire and even in the fourth century.[230] Given these circumstances, it seems difficult to determine what impact Christians had during that period on the development of society, customs, and culture. Works on early Christianity paint a striking picture of a very active Christian community with a dynamic intellectual life but without any real influence on society as a whole. It is not until the third century that we see Christians identifying themselves as such, and bishops appearing among the ranks of local dignitaries. Even then, the bishops did not stand out among the leadership; they did not seem to play a determining role in any respect.

The Cradle of Christianity: The Early Church

We may recall that among the numerous prophets preaching in the half century preceding the revolt of 66, a certain Jesus of Nazareth stood out, in that his message was less political in the near term and more striking in its long-term vision. Nevertheless, he was pursued like the others and executed upon orders from Temple leaders in the spring of 33. The apparent failure of their leader did not discourage his disciples, a few of whom joined together and, proclaiming Jesus's resurrection, began to develop a doctrine of individual salvation that the resurrection itself seemed to prove. We have no written documents from before the last third of the first century, so it is futile to attempt to reconstitute the doctrine of this early community, to the extent that there may have been one. We know that a core group of followers managed to keep the memory of their master alive, portraying him in appealing terms as a bearer of hope, and attracted new followers, both Jew (Saul of Tarsus) and pagan (the centurion Cornelius).

We already have good histories of the beginnings of Christianity that describe both the successes and the failures of the Christian mission; we need not linger over that story here.[231] Within the framework of a history of Roman Syria, however, we must not overlook certain geographical facts: the first Christian congregation was established in Jerusalem; the name "Christian" was first used for the disciples of Jesus in Antioch,[232] and the first Christian communities outside of Jerusalem were established in Syrian cities (Caesarea, Antioch, and Damascus).

Until the Jewish revolt in 70, the church in Jerusalem stagnated, and the gradual disappearance of the leaders who had been at Jesus's side threatened to weaken it further (Peter was executed in 64).[233] This was all the more true because its members were quite reluctant to admit into their ranks former pagans, who, by virtue of an agreement in 49 between Peter and Paul, were exempt from most of the obligations dictated by the Torah. Jews by birth, most of the members of the Jerusalem church intended to remain Jews. The revolt in 66, followed by the anti-Jewish repression, prompted the flight of the small group of Christians to Pella in the Decapolis,[234] and spurred a certain de facto break with a Judaism that was itself undergoing changes. To be sure, Judeo-Christian communities persisted for a long time in Palestine, especially in the Transjordan, and in northeastern Syria.[235] They are known primarily through literary texts, especially that of Epiphanius of Salamis (fourth century), which devotes long notes to the best-known groups: the orthodox Nazoraeans,[236] the heterodox Ebionites,[237] and the Elcesaites.[238] They seem to have been numerous in cities (the Elcesaites in Apamaea, for example), particularly in northeastern Syria and in Arabia. But the archaeological evidence indicates that there were Christians in villages as well. For example, in the village of Ramthaniyyeh on the Golan, which had a large, mainly Jewish, population in the first and second centuries, the Judeo-Christian community combined Jewish and Christian symbols (candelabras and crosses).[239] Subsequently, however, the Christian mission focused steadfastly on pagans, and for a long time most converts in Greece, Asia Minor, and Rome came from this group.

The Spread of Christianity in Syria

Several churches in Syria boast that they were founded by the Apostles. In a few rare cases, this can be proven (as in Jerusalem and Antioch), and in others it seems quite plausible (as in Caesarea), but most often the claim is unverifiable (for example, in Edessa). It appears likely that the Christian mission began by appealing, as it did elsewhere, to Jewish communities in Syrian cities such as Damascus and Antioch.[240] But we have no way of knowing how successful this mission was in apostolic times, even if we take into account the efforts of the seventy disciples sent to preach throughout the world.

It is not until the beginning of the second century that we begin to see an episcopal hierarchy for which there is evidence other than legend.[241] Ignatius of Antioch, under Trajan, seems to have been the city's second bishop. In Jerusalem, although Eusebius was in a position to provide a continuous list starting with James (Jesus's brother and the first leader of Jerusalem's Christian community), it was not until after the Bar Kokhba revolt that the list appears to be historically accurate, when the first bishop of pagan origin appears. In several large provincial cities, it is not until the end of the second century that there is solid evidence of a first bishop (Caesarea, Tyre, Ptolemais, Tripolis); in other cases, we have to wait until the beginning of the third century (Bostra), or the middle of that century (Berytos). Despite the early presence of a Christian community and of a church in Edessa,[242] Quna, the first bishop there, probably did not serve before the very beginning of the fourth century.[243] The list of the Nicaean Fathers in 325 provides the first somewhat complete picture: it lists eighteen bishops in Palestine, nine in Phoenicia, twenty-two in Coele Syria, five in Arabia, and five in Mesopotamia. Most cities probably had a bishop well before 325, if it is true that, of the seventy or eighty bishops who met in Antioch to judge Paul of Samosata in 268–269, most were from the region;[244] "region" is a vague notion, however, and could designate Syria, Cilicia, and Cappadocia together. It is more interesting to note that the sixty bishops present or represented in Nicaea came from cities throughout Syria, even though many important cities—including Beroea, Gerasa, Tiberias, and Heliopolis—were apparently still without an episcopal hierarchy at the beginning of the fourth century.

This does not necessarily mean that only urban areas were affected by Christianity. Eusebius identifies a few scattered villages in Palestine and Arabia as Christian,[245] but these probably drew his attention only because they were entirely Christian. We have seen, however, that in Nicaea there were *chorepiskopoi,* bishops whose territory was rural; similarly, in addition to the bishop of Sebaste (in Samaria), there was a bishop of the Sebastene region. Although Christians remained a small minority in the countryside, we cannot rule out their presence. In any event, no matter how well the Christian mission may have succeeded, it is clear that Christians everywhere, including in cities, were in the minority.[246]

The spread of Christianity did not encounter any pronounced opposition from the Roman authorities, except in brief and violent crises. To be sure, there were individual martyrs, such as Ignatius of Antioch, whom Trajan sent to Rome to be executed in 115.[247] In general, however, until the middle of the third century we find no general persecution. On the contrary, like other members of the Christian community, bishops were able to lead their lives quite openly. On two occasions, Origen called a council of bishops in Arabia, to combat the errors of Beryllos of Bostra and later those of a Bishop Heracleides (possibly the holder of the same seat). Origen had come to Antioch for the first time in 231 to instruct Iulia Mamaea[248] and, according to Eusebius, he exchanged letters with Philip the

Arab and his wife Otacilia;[249] one long-standing tradition holds that Philip himself was a Christian.[250] Although this seems highly unlikely, the fact remains that the Christian community in Syria seems to have had nothing to fear from the Roman authorities.

The widespread persecution ordered by Decius in 251 was pursued vigorously, and Syria furnished numerous martyrs during that time, including Bishop Babylas of Antioch and Bishop Alexander of Jerusalem. But the persecution did not last, and it did not impede the growth of communities for very long. The *Didascalia of the Apostles,* an original document written in Syriac, describes the organization of these communities in the third century.[251] It depicts the way worshippers positioned themselves for liturgical services, and it outlines the very hierarchical ecclesiastical organization, dominated by a bishop whose authority was monarchical.

The Syrian church seems to have been heavily influenced by the church in Alexandria, particularly on the coast and in the south. Like Christian churches elsewhere, Syria's was riddled with heterodox strains whose errors had to be addressed in council meetings. In addition to the two successive councils that met in Arabia under Origen's direction around 230–240,[252] others met in Antioch between 264–268 to dismiss the city's bishop, Paul of Samosata, who was accused of heresy and of leading a life that did not conform to the demands of his position: he allegedly enriched himself at the expense of the community, led a life of luxury, behaved inappropriately in private life (by regularly having sex with the *subintroductae* or *suneisaktoi,* the virgins who were in his service), and displayed arrogance. The council of 268 concluded in a call for his dismissal, but his ties with Zenobia of Palmyra may have enabled him to remain. It took the intervention of Aurelian in 272–273 to remove him finally from his episcopal seat.[253] Clearly, the Syrian churches experienced all the problems associated with newly emerging institutions and the power struggles inherent in them.

Lives of Christians: Jerusalem, Antioch, Edessa, Dura, and Elsewhere

Jerusalem, the scene of the historic drama that founded the new faith, had lost all its Jewish inhabitants in 70 and again in 135. Had Christians come back to settle there, or had some remained? Probably both. Beginning in the second century Christian pilgrims began coming to the holy city, even though the local Christian community had no special status.[254] The building of a church for Gentiles attests to the appearance of foreign Christians. Moreover, the prohibition preventing Jews from living in Aelia Capitolina after the Bar Kokhba revolt resulted in the transformation of the small

Christian community, which ceased to be Jewish, as Eusebius observes: "after the Jewish bishops the first who was appointed to minister there was Marcus."[255]

Edessa was proud of having been one of the earliest centers of Christianity in Syria.[256] It claimed even to possess letters between Jesus and king Abgar V Ukkama![257] Although this claim is an obvious falsehood (repeated both in Eusebius[258] and in the collection known as the *Doctrine of Addai*),[259] it is clear that Christianity had reached Edessa very early, perhaps owing in some measure to the presence of a strong Jewish community. King Abgar VIII (known as Abgar the Great) may even have been a Christian, if, as Eusebius of Caesarea claims, all the Edessene kings were Christian after Thaddeus preached a sermon in the city,[260] and there was a church in Edessa by 201 at the latest. In any event, this "Athens of the Orient" made an original contribution to the intellectual development of early Christianity.[261] Whereas Greek Antioch was the center of imperial power in the east, Edessa was the capital of Aramaean Christianity. The Syriac Bible *(Peshitta)* was translated there, giving Christian Aramaeans a Bible distinct from that of the Jews, with its Aramaean paraphrases (the targumim). The Acts of Thomas was written in Edessa at the beginning of the third century;[262] it preached a strict asceticism in the tradition of Tatian the Assyrian, who was himself a product of the community in Edessa.[263] Edessene Christianity showed a marked taste for the apocryphal gospels in Syriac, such as the Gospel of Thomas and the Gospel of Philip, which give the illusion of having been written in Jesus's own language, and thus of faithfully reporting his teachings.[264] But Edessa was also the site of the offensive against the Marcionites.[265] The presence of the sect in the city is attested in Bardesanes's *Book of the Laws of the Countries* (probably the work of a student rather than the master himself), as well as in the Odes of Salomon at the beginning of the third century.[266] In this same climate of intellectual emulation and competition, many Manichaean hymns were written; known today in Coptic versions,[267] they are probably Edessene in origin.[268] Into this Christian community where discussions were always percolating, heresies also found their way: that of the Quqites, for example, who took their cosmology from Bardesanes while maintaining close intellectual ties with the Judeo-Christians and the Gnostics.[269] All these factors helped produce a relatively original form of Christianity that was fairly close to its Jewish roots and above all bore the stamp of its Semitic context, whereas the churches of the Syrian coast were closely tied, both intellectually and liturgically, to the practices of Alexandria.[270]

The story of the congregation in Dura-Europos has been the focus of attention ever since its meeting place was identified. Although some scholars have tried to establish a first-century date for the construction of this private home[271] (not necessarily proof that it was used then by Christians), we should probably date the building (which had a peristyle, a surface area of about seventeen meters by twenty meters, and an eastern portico), to the period just after the Roman occupation. It is part of a group of structures with the same orientation, all parts of which date from later than 165. Kraeling leans toward an even later date, around 232.[272] Like the neighboring synagogue, the house was modified and transformed into a gathering place for the community. A baptistery was created in a small corner room on the north side, while the large room to the south was used as a meeting hall. The baptistery was decorated with paintings that were less opulent than those of the neighboring synagogue, but they are among the earliest Christian paintings we have. This House of Christians is not the only evidence of Christian life in Dura: the discovery of a fragment of the *Diatessaron* of Tatian, a second-century Assyrian Christian polemicist, describes an open, cultivated community.[273]

The discovery of a church from the very beginning of the fourth century in Aila, although less well documented, is no less interesting; it is proof of the privileged ties with Egypt enjoyed by the Christians in Aila.[274]

It is difficult to assign a particular profile to Syrian Christianity, because it was still split among quite distinct strains, some very conservative and close to their Jewish roots, and others more innovative. Most remarkable, probably, is the fact that this was a two-headed Christianity: it had a Greek pole in Antioch and a Syrian pole in Edessa, in addition to the strong influence of Alexandria on the Phoenician and Transjordan churches. But it would be a mistake to see Antioch and Edessa as opposites, and in both these centers some Christian apologists showed an intense hostility to Greek culture: Tatian's extremism, arising from the Edessene community, had its counterpart in the hostility expressed by Theophilos and by the *Didascalia of the Apostles* in Antioch.[275]

This examination of religious life would be incomplete without reference to the importance of Manichaeism, beginning in the middle of the third century. Mani, born in 216, advocated a dualist religious system inherited in part from Persian Zoroastrianism (he himself was related to an old Arsacid family). He held that the principle of evil coexists with that of good for all eternity, and that the world is a site of confrontation between the forces of good and evil.[276] His teachings spread widely in Syria in the third century, largely through Addai, a missionary who was very active in the second half of the century.[277] But Mani's influence was probably greater among intellectual Christians—who saw Manichaean Gnosticism as a serious threat and worked hard to refute it—than it was among ordinary believers, who seem not to have been very numerous in the Syrian provinces, with the possible exception of the regions around Antioch and Edessa.

It is much harder to judge the extent to which the growth of Christianity helped transform Syrian society in the second and third centuries. Clearly, Christians were a sizable group, living in a large number of cities; they could not be ignored. Moreover, we have seen that they were actively engaged in intellectual debate in Antioch, Edessa, and Caesarea, and probably in other cities as well. Much more than this we cannot say. On the surface, their presence did not alter the look of the urban landscape at all, as their meeting places were simply private homes. There is little doubt that Christians participated in city governance, as a number of them belonged to milieus that were responsible for civic liturgies. It would be interesting to know how they handled their obligations in civic cults, but of course that question is not limited to Syria. As for their social behavior and customs, they were undoubtedly subject to a stricter morality, but one that was not unique to Christians. Bardesanes, in his *Book of the Laws of the Countries* (607–608), provides an inventory of the customary behaviors of each of the pagan peoples, behaviors to which the Christians among those very peoples put a stop: in Gaul, homosexuality; in Parthia, bigamy; among Jews, circumcision; in Edessa, death without trial for adulterous women at the hands of the men of the family; in Hatra, the stoning of thieves. Bardesanes saw a universal law applying to all people, whatever their traditions. Was this a dream of the future? Recognition of an actual state of affairs? It is hard for us to say.

A TIME OF TRIALS

AROUND the year 224, the Arsacid dynasty of Parthia, which had coexisted with Rome more or less peacefully ever since the beginning of the empire, was replaced by a new dynasty, the Sassanids of Persia. Although the Sassanids probably did not plan from the outset to reconquer the entire Achaemenid Empire, as both Cassius Dio and Herodian claim,[1] they did go to war against Rome immediately, presaging a long period of conflict. An attack launched against Hatra in 229 was unsuccessful.[2] The following year, however, Ardashir headed west: his expedition seems not to have gone beyond Mesopotamia, but his army's success could have quickly threatened northern Syria and Antioch.[3] After an attempt at negotiation failed, Alexander Severus had to fight. He deployed three divisions of his army in the campaign: one was sent from the north into Armenia and Media, and another from the south into the lower Tigris and Euphrates Valley, while the main expeditionary force took a middle route and was supposed to join the other troops inside Persian territory. Despite some difficulties, the northern army managed to defeat Ardashir, cross the Tigris, and penetrate Media, but the division led by the emperor moved more slowly, giving the Persians time to react and to fight the Romans on a number of fronts. Moreover, illness forced Alexander Severus and his army to return to Antioch.[4] The Persian threat continued throughout most of the third century, although the number of confirmed invasions was limited. Nevertheless, Persian raids caused significant damage, even in some regions far from the Euphrates and in areas along the border.

With this menace looming, Syria also had to face problems caused by a series of usurpations. The conflicts caused by the crises of succession that shook the empire periodically did not make it easier to mount an effective response to the Persian attacks. Under these conditions, we find local authorities reestablishing a degree of autonomy, with or without Rome's approval:[5] this was especially true in Palmyra, where Odainathos gained personal standing and considerable power by organizing the resistance against the Persians. However, the same situation could also lead to the usurpation of imperial power: Uranius Antoninus in Emesa (253) was the first to take that step, followed by Vaballathos and Zenobia in Palmyra, although secession was not necessarily their aim. In the meantime, a number of other leaders attempted to seize control of the empire from within Syria, including Macrinus, Quietus, Ballista, and finally Saturninus in Antioch, in 281.

Although it is still difficult to evaluate the precise consequences of these various difficulties, on the eve of Diocletian's reforms the outcome was hardly positive. Northern Syria and the Euphrates Valley had been sacked several times, and cities (Hatra and Dura, for example) had been destroyed. Palmyra was not deserted, but after its capture by Aurelian it ceased to be the great caravan city it had been for three centuries. In the desert, new forces appeared, sometimes at the very edge of the area controlled by Rome: desert lands once controlled by Roman armies, such as the Jawf and northern Hejaz regions, were abandoned and left under the authority of allied tribes whose allegiance appears to have been in name only. The picture was no doubt not entirely bleak, and the country was primarily affected at its margins rather than in the center, but trade routes gradually shifted to the north, along the foot of the Taurus, depriving Syria's traditional centers of commerce of their ancestral role.

EDESSA, HATRA, AND DURA-EUROPOS

The Annexation of Edessa

As we have seen, Edessa had entered into an alliance with Rome even though it found itself surrounded by the new province of Osrhoene. On the eve of his eastward expedition, Caracalla summoned King Abgar to Rome, deposed him (in 212), and annexed Edessa, at the same time elevating it to the status of colony.[6] This Abgar was probably not Abgar VIII the Great, but his successor, King Abgar (IX) Severus. According to Cassius Dio[7] he mistreated his own people, and he ruled for only nineteen months.[8] The heir to the throne, Ma'nu, had to settle for the title *pasgriba* (crown prince); still, if this title was an official one, we may suppose that Rome had not ruled out the possibility of a future restoration. Indeed, there was a dynastic restoration in 239 benefiting Ma'nu's son L. Aelius Aurelius Septimius Abgar (X), who seems to have set up his court in a new capital, the "New Karka d-Sida of King Abgar"—in other words, Batnai of Anthemousia, also called Marcopolis in honor of Gordian III.[9] Thus Gordian returned Osrhoene to the Abgarids, perhaps in order to deal with the Sassanid troops that had appeared the year before, in 238, at the gates of Carrhai.[10] But the restoration was short-lived: before the Roman counteroffensive had even begun (in late 242 and in the spring of 243), Abgar X disappeared, and Edessa was once again a colony, led by two generals under the authority of a resident Roman.[11] The former *polis* was released from the monarchical government it had known for three centuries and given a municipal administration. This did not lead to any decline of the city: as the provincial capital and an important stop on the routes west toward the Persian empire, Edessa enjoyed a period of unsurpassed prosperity, which doubtless had something to do with the flourishing of Syrian culture, in which it played a central role. We should remember that the peak of Bardesanes's production also corresponded to this period of Roman conquest.

The Roman Alliance and the Fall of Hatra

Although Septimius Severus's campaign in 198–199 had been a military failure, it had nevertheless succeeded in bringing Hatra into the Roman alliance. From this point on—or at least from the time of Caracalla's campaign in 217[12]—Hatra was part of the empire, although it kept its autonomous royal government (following Edessa's model), and it was allied with Rome against the Parthians. Evidence of this alliance can be seen on coins minted subsequently in Hatra bearing the symbol SC under an eagle with wings spread, and also in a statue of Sanatruq II carrying a shield portraying Hercules, the protector of the imperial family, beside a young god who can be identified with Brmryn, Hatra's dynastic deity.[13] Such indications leave little doubt about the political alliance.

The alliance does not seem to have had any immediate military consequences, for there is no evidence that Roman troops were in the city during Ardashir's attack in 229.[14] However, three Latin dedications in Hatra indicate that Roman detachments were present in Hatra in 235 and later under Gordian III,[15] right after the first assault by the Sassanid armies. Sir Aurel Stein discovered the presence of many Roman *castella* east of the city, facing in the direction of the Persian enemy. A milestone from the reign of Alexander Severus dating from 231–232, found about five kilometers from Singara, suggests that reinforcements in the frontier zone were built around this time.[16]

The period of actual Roman presence corresponds to the reign of Sanatruq II, the last king of Hatra, attested in October 231 (H. 229) and in 237–238 (H. 36), although his rule may have begun earlier.[17] Sanatruq's son and heir was named for his grandfather, Barsemias or Abdsamya (H. 28, 36, 287). Around 235, a second son, M'n' (H. 779), seems to have been in control of "Arabia of W'l" (H. 79), designating the region of Sumatar Harabesi, southeast of Edessa. The Hatran kings had thus expanded their authority over this region and its local dynasts (slyt), who had been controlled by Edessa in the second and third centuries, but who had been left to their own devices once the Abgarids disappeared.

It is difficult to determine the precise extent of authority of Sanatruq II. The Arab writer 'Adi ibn Zayd, quoted by Tha'libi (1035 C.E.) with reference to the power of the Hatran kings, exclaimed: "Where is the man of Hadr (Hatra), the one who built the citadel and who received tribute from the countries watered by the Tigris and the Khabur?" Are we to understand that he was the sole ruler of the entire area described? That is unlikely, as there were other provincial authorities in Mesopotamia. Still, the presence of a son of Sanatruq as governor of Sumatar shows that the power of the Hatran king could extend far to the west. But it is important not to fix rigid administrative boundaries. Sanatruq II reigned over Hatra and probably over the Arab nomads of the entire region, his son was a delegate to the Arabs of W'l. The Roman authority, for its part, controlled the sedentary northern peoples of Nisibis and Carrhai and those of Dura in the south, as well as trade routes and a number of military posts such as Singara and Rhesaina.

This distribution of power did not imply any weakening of Sanatruq II: in exchange for the Roman alliance, he was put in charge of all Roman Arabs of the Euphrates Valley and Upper Mesopotamia. This reinforced his power and prestige among the desert peoples: Arab legend calls him the builder of Hatra (Hadr); for it is indeed he, the last and most powerful king of Hatra, and not Sanatruq I, the first holder of the royal title, who is identified with the legendary hero Satirun.

The alliance between Hatra and Rome brought about the fall of the city. The first Persian attack, in 229 (?),[18] proves that by that date the Persians saw the city as an ally of Rome. A new Persian expedition to the west begun in 238 resulted in the capture of Nisibis and Carrhai.[19] In 239,[20] the Persians also attacked Dura, which resisted, and it is probably in this context that Edessa regained its king. Hatra in turn was attacked and taken in 240.[21] It was abandoned soon afterward: no dated inscriptions are from later than 240. When Ammianus Marcellinus visited Hatra in 364, he saw only abandoned ruins.[22]

This new Sassanid campaign in Roman Mesopotamia forced the emperor to intervene personally. Gordian III may have been in Antioch by 239,[23] but the war must have started later, for it was not until 242, when all of Mesopotamia had been lost, that the doors of the Temple of Janus in Rome were reopened. The troops, held up in the Balkans by battles against Dacians and Sarmatae, reached Antioch at the end of 242. In the meantime, Ardashir had died (in 241 or 242), and Shapur was the sole king of Persia. The real campaign, begun in the spring of 243, resulted in a string of victories: Carrhai was recaptured; the Persians were defeated at Rhesaina; they evacuated the cities of Nisibis and Singara and, ultimately, all of Mesopotamia. Timesitheus, praetorian prefect and father-in-law of Gordian III (who had ascended to the throne at the age of thirteen and was no more than eighteen years old at this point),[24] was the key figure in the campaign, but he died in battle in 243. Despite this loss, the Roman army prepared to march on Ctesiphon under the command of the new praetorian prefect M. Iulius Philippus, whose brother, C. Iulius Priscus, already held the same office. Using Dura as its rear command post, the Roman army moved up the Euphrates, as far as two hundred kilometers away from its bases. But in early 244, the army was crushed at Mesike, and Emperor Gordian III was killed.[25] M. Iulius Philippus (Philip the Arab) was proclaimed emperor and negotiated a costly peace[26] in order to salvage what he could. When he returned, he erected a cenotaph of Gordian III above Dura, twenty Roman miles from Circesion,[27] and carried Gordian's ashes to Rome.

Despite the success of the Roman campaign and the restoration of the Roman province of Mesopotamia, the fall of Hatra marked an essential step in the Persians' efforts to seize control of Arabian Mesopotamia. With Hatra, one of the guardians of the desert disappeared, facilitating the movements of newly emerging tribes that would eventually lead to a very different organization of the Syro-Mesopotamian desert. Moreover, Gordian's campaign had brought home to Philip, now emperor, the seriousness of the Persian threat in Syria. In naming his brother Priscus *rector Orientis*,[28] Philip put him in charge of all the provinces bordering on the Sassanid Persian territory. Was this exceptional power perceived as intolerable by the Syrian population? Or was Priscus a truly oppressive ruler, perhaps demanding from his people the means to pay for the country's defense? Whatever the case, a usurper named Jotapianus emerged in Syria[29] and was recognized as emperor of Syria and Cappadocia in 248. Completely unknown to us before this coup d'état, Jotapianus may well have been related to the former royal families of the Near East, as his very unusual *cognomen*

PHILIP THE ARAB (M. IULIUS PHILIPPUS):
MARBLE HEAD.

indicates: it recalls *Iotape,* a name widely known in the Commagenian dynasty. He may have been related to the Emesenian family as well.[30] His reign probably did not last beyond the spring of 249;[31] he was eliminated by his own soldiers.[32]

The Campaigns of 252–260 and the Fall of Dura-Europos

Ever since it had joined the empire, around 165, Dura-Europos had benefited greatly from its location as an advance outpost of the empire, facing first the Parthians and then the Persians. When fighting resumed, the city profited from its position on the front lines despite the risks: by 239, it had been attacked, but the Persians had been forced back. The city must have considered any further threat to be remote, for major work on the synagogue was begun during the period between the first Persian attack and the destruction of the city.

Following the costly peace of 244, the Persian front experienced a few years' respite. However, by 252 or early 253 at the latest, the war had resumed.[33] Shapur appears to have taken the initiative, launching a vigorous attack on Syria. In the account he gives of this campaign in his *Res Gestae,* he says simply that "Caesar lied again,"[34] a statement that remains an enigma. Michel Christol has suggested that Trebonianus Gallus may have failed to honor one of the clauses of the peace of 244, probably forfeiting the Roman protectorate over Armenia, and was preparing a wide-scale offensive against the Persians. If true, this would explain the new minting of *antoniniani* in Antioch to pay the army,[35] and also the installation of detachments from Legio II Parthica in Apamaea, as studies published after Michel Christol's work appeared have shown. In reality, Shapur may have simply taken the initiative in the face of Rome's planned offensive.

After the fall of Dura, Persian troops went along the Euphrates as far as Barbalissos, where they wiped out a Roman army. The Persian army separated into three units: one captured and sacked Antioch,[36] then pillaged Seleucia of Pieria, Alexandria near Issos, Cyrrhos, and Nicopolis; a second group marched farther north to Zeugma, Doliche, and Cappadocia; and the third, initially headed toward Hierapolis and Aleppo, veered south to Apamaea,[37] Raphanaea, and Arethusa, before being stopped between Arethusa and Emesa by a local militia led by Uranius Antoninus.[38] An Emesenian related to the ancient dynasty of Sampsigeramus, perhaps the priest of al-Uzza/Aphrodite, and linked to the Severus family,[39] Antoninus proclaimed himself Augustus in the summer of 253 following his victory over Shapur in the fall of 252[40] (his usurpation is attested by coins from the Seleucid year 565, beginning in October 253).[41] In the chaos created by struggles between troops loyal to the various pretenders to imperial power, it may have seemed to Antoninus that proclaiming himself emperor was the best way to mobilize all the Roman forces in Syria around himself against the Persian invader and to give some legitimacy to his action. We do not know what happened next, except that Antoninus disappeared, but we should not conclude that his aim was to dominate the entire empire. As David Stone Potter notes, a ruler who assumed the duties of an emperor might well be led to take on imperial trappings, even if his own political ambitions were limited to his own region.[42]

The Persian threat must have looked very serious in northern Syria, for Trebonianus Gallius had moved the mint from Antioch to Emesa in order to protect it.[43] A number of cities were indeed captured and sacked, even though the Persians did not really intend to occupy the country permanently. The Antioch mint resumed issuing coins by 254. Only one city seemed to have to remain under occupation: Dura-Europos.

Mikhail Ivanovitch Rostovtzeff has argued that the city was taken and occupied briefly first in 253, before being captured and destroyed in 256.[44] Simon James has disputed the hypothesis of an initial capture as pure conjecture, claiming that there is no way to determine whether the city was taken by the Persians in 255 or 256.[45] However, archaeological and epigraphical evidence supports Rostovtzeff's view that the city was taken on two occasions, and this now seems to me to have been confirmed definitively by Frantz Grenet.[46] Thus the first seizure of the city must have occurred, as we have just seen, during 252 rather than in the spring of 253. That occupation must have lasted a few months, because the Persians had time to set up an administration, as attested by graffiti written in Pehlevi (the Sassanid language) in the *dux ripae* palace dating from March or April 253, or possibly even from February 253, if the graffito of February 6 is from the same year and not the following.[47]

A Roman counteroffensive liberated the city, according to evidence from the divorce contract of a Roman soldier in 254. However, during the offensive in 256 directed specifically against Dura,[48] the city was retaken, this time definitively. The siege must have been long and hard,[49] for the city was favorably situated and well defended. Nevertheless, the besieged city had to reinforce its ramparts; earthworks were created along the inside wall, which meant knocking down or filling with dirt everything built along the rampart. This is what partially saved the paintings of the recently completed synagogue there, as well as the nearby baptistery of the House of the Christians. The city's decline was swift and lasting, even though traces of a light Sassanid occupation have been found.[50] The site was presumably no more than a pile of rubble, overrun by deer and gazelles, when Julian passed through in 363.[51] Every trace of the city was lost, and for a long time, on the basis of Strabo's text, it was thought to have been located on the opposite bank, where the city's territory *(chora)* stood. The Roman administration also disappeared from the region: the earliest document in the archives of the Middle Euphrates that can be dated with accuracy is from June 252, and another, necessarily posterior, must have been produced only a short time later, as it concerns the same person.[52]

The incipient state of war that followed the Persian expedition of 252–253 helps explain the defensive works undertaken in certain Syrian cities, even in some located far from the battlefields: Adraha and Bostra had begun reinforcing their ramparts by 259–260.[53] The work continued in Adraha until 274–275 and in Bostra until 282–283,[54] and Apamaea hastily added towers using any available material, including steles from the military cemetery.[55] In addition, it may have been in 259 that troops were transferred from Palestine to Arabia.[56] The fact that Emperor Valerian, who had come to Syria during 254, was still there in 259, when Shapur launched his third great expedition against Roman Syria, may also have been related to the Persian threat. But before turning to that event, we must detour to Palmyra, where one family was gradually emerging as a new power.

PALMYRA

Unlike Hatra and Edessa, Palmyra had been part of the Roman Empire since the beginning of the first century. This probably accounts for the city's great economic prosperity and its remarkable urban and architectural development during the second century. Although it probably had not received its *libertas* from Hadrian, as is frequently claimed because it called itself Hadriane Palmyra, it undoubtedly did become a colony and even a *metrocolonia* under Caracalla.

The Severan period probably marked the high point in Palmyra, but of all the factors that could have impeded its commercial development, it is hard to know which were the most significant. The economic and monetary difficulties that were plaguing the Empire,[57] for instance, may have led to a declining demand for the luxury products that had made the city rich. However, we know of some caravan inscriptions from the third century, and their existence can best be explained by the persistence of a certain level of prosperity in Syria during that period. The recurrence of war affected trade much more seriously: civil war between Niger and Septimius Severus, then the war between the Severi and the Parthians or their allies. Mesopotamia was no longer secure, neither in the Euphrates Valley nor in the desert. The weakening of the successive empires left the trade routes unprotected. Severus's campaigns, and later those of Caracalla and Macrinus, against Edessa and Hatra, followed by a Parthian counteroffensive, all helped make the situation worse. Moreover, the cost of financing these campaigns fell for the most part on the leaders of the eastern cities, the natural clients for products exported from Palmyra. Finally, the defeat of the Arsacids by the Sassanids created additional difficulties. By 226, for example, Ardashir had annexed the Characene region,[58] an act that may have affected trade from Palmyra: the Palmyrene merchants were regular visitors to Spasinou Charax in the second century, but this name disappears from inscriptions in the following century. Still, we cannot conclude from this that the Palmyrenes stopped going there, and as we have seen, the caravan trade from Palmyra continued at least until Aurelian captured the city.

From City to Principality

In an economic climate that may have declined somewhat, the political situation in Palmyra changed. Having long possessed the institutions of an eastern Greek city-state,[59] between 213 and 216 Palmyra received from Caracalla the title *colonia* with *ius italicum* (assimilation to the territory of Italy for legal and fiscal purposes).[60] Its municipal institutions continued to function right up to the ruin of the city. But before the middle of the century, one family acquired such power that to later historians Palmyra resembled a principality more than a city-state. This perspective is mistaken, for Palmyra had not ceased to be a true city, a colony, with the regular magistrates this status required. Moreover, the presence of dominant families was probably not new. The civic life in Palmyra seems to have been marked by a series of prestigious families who succeeded one another in positions of power, probably at the price of ferocious infighting, the details of which are unknown.[61]

As for the family of Odainathos, an inscription discovered in Palmyra has obliged us to reconsider previously held notions about the origins of the Palmyrene dynasty.[62] It was long believed that the founder of the dynasty was a Septimius Odainathos (I), who built the family tomb[63] and whose son Septimius Hairan was exarch of the Palmyrenes in 251. Not until around 257–258 did Odainathos II, Hieran's brother or son (his lineage is never indicated), emerge as leader in Palmyra, with the title *consularis*. The new text indicates that Odainathos II also held the title "Exarch of the Palmyrenes" by April 252, and that the lineage previously thought to belong to Odainathos I—son of Hairan son of Vaballathos son of Nasor—was actually that of Odainathos II. Thus it is now certain that Odainathos, the father of the exarch Septimius Hairan, is none other than the famous Odainathos, and that the exarch Hairan is the Hairan-Herodian-Herod who was Odainathos's eldest son and associated with his father as exarch and as king of kings. This simple solution has the advantage of accounting unproblematically for all the documentation currently available.

This Odainathos was the descendant of a family that acquired Roman citizenship under Septimius Severus, and his father or grandfather was the first to benefit from this, if we assume that Odainathos was born around 220 or a little earlier. This privilege does not seem to have accompanied particular powers in Palmyra; it simply underlines the family's fame. The family's success, however, is probably not unrelated to the appearance of the Emesenian princesses at the head of the empire. We know that in 193 Palmyra officially sided with Pescennius Niger,[64] which could well have provoked Septimius Severus to act in reprisal. However, the latter never moved against the city. There is reason to wonder whether he did not have supporters in Palmyra within a (minority) party of leaders who might have profited from the poor political choice of those in power, and replaced them. The Septimii of the Odainathos family may well have belonged to this group and obtained Roman citizenship in recompense for their loyal services. Alone among all the Palmyrenes, either they did not give up their *gentilicium* in 212 for that of Aurelius—or, if they did so, they managed to take it back shortly afterward, demonstrating their desire to publicize their close ties to Septimius Severus.[65] Their presence among the leadership was henceforth enough to guarantee Palmyra's fidelity to the emperor, eliminating any need on his part to move against the city.[66] We do not know what position the family held at the time of Alexander Severus's visit in 231, but one of the two *strategoi* welcoming the emperor was Iulius Aurelius Zenobios, nicknamed Zabdilas, who seems to have held several important municipal positions and was honored in 242 by the city;[67] it has been suggested, although the claim has not been fully substantiated, that he was Zenobia's father.[68]

We can only conjecture about the ancient origins of the Septimii's privileged status in Palmyra, but they fall within the long-standing Palmyrene tradition in which great families had exercised exceptional authority for a long time.[69] Prior to 251, there is no documentary basis on which to reconstruct the history of the "princes" of Palmyra, and there are a great many gaps in the record even after that time. In October 251 at the latest, Septimius Odainathos and his son Septimius Hairan—called "Herod" in *Historia Augusta* and "Herodian" in several Greek texts from Palmyra (the assumption that the three individuals were one is still controversial)—shared the title *ras Tadmor,* "Exarch of the Palmyrenes." The title is first attested for the son,[70] and then in April 252 for his father,[71] but the chronology is based entirely on random discoveries. We do not know what event occasioned such a promotion. If it occurred in 251, it might reveal an early effort to exploit the confusion following Decius's death in June 251 and achieve semi-independence. The title was ephemeral, however; it does not reappear in any subsequent texts. In contrast, the title "king of kings," taken from the Arsacid tradition, figures among the titles of Odainathos and his son Hairan-Herodian at an uncertain date; the inscription in which it appears states: "To the king of kings, having attained the royal title near the Orontes, crowned by victory over the Persians, Septimius Herodianus, etc. . . ." (the dedication is the work of the two colonial strategoi).[72] The allusion to a victory "near the Orontes" is best understood as referring to the Persian invasion of 252 or the attack of 259–260. We cannot be absolutely sure, but we may suppose that by about 250 Palmyra began to look like a hereditary principality, even though its civic institutions did not change.[73]

Several texts from 257–258 give Odainathos the title *ho lamprotatos hupatikos,* "very illustrious consular,"[74] whereas Hairan was simply called *ho lamprotatos.* Additional undated texts use the same titles and probably belong to those same years.[75] Unlike the title *ras Tadmor* that Odainathos and his son attributed to themselves, the title *consularis*—given to the father alone—could be conferred only by the emperor. This title probably does not imply that Odainathos was granted authority over Syria-Phoenicia; he probably received only the honors attached to the rank of consular.[76] Still, this honor or responsibility, conferred immediately after the fall of Dura, was intended to honor a man and a family who played a leading role in Palmyra and whose loyalty would be crucial to the emperor. Odainathos's ties with the corporations (craft and trade associations), which honored him as *patronus* in 257–258,[77] consolidated his power over the city and were not a departure from the normal operation of a city within the empire.

It was at this point that Shapur launched a third offensive against Roman Syria. The Persian army seems to have moved toward Samosata, then toward Cilicia. Emperor Valerian was taken prisoner while trying to stop the Persians near Edessa in 259 (rather than 260).[78] The *Res Gestae* lists a number of Cilician cities that were pillaged and sacked, and although the rest of Syria suffered little,[79] Antioch itself was taken.[80]

Valerian's capture led to a triple usurpation in the empire. The equestrian Macrinus[81] awarded the imperial title to his two sons, Macrinus the Younger and Quietus,[82] declining power on his own behalf owing to physical incapacity; Odainathos opposed the usurpers and attacked Quietus in Emesa, where the latter was killed by the mob;[83] Macrinus was assassinated in the Balkans. Odainathos appears to have feigned legality, fighting in the name of Valerian's son Gallienus, who had become his father's associate by 253, and who remained as sole emperor after his father's capture. A later source indicates that Odainathos had made offers of alliance to Shapur at an unknown date,[84] perhaps in 252 or 256 around the time of one of the defeats of Dura-Europos, an essential storehouse for Palmyrene commerce. The offers may have come later, however, in relation to the campaign of 260. In any case, the Persian retreat allowed Odainathos to show his loyalty, and he attacked and defeated the Persian troops in the Euphrates Valley.[85] He even pushed on as far as Ctesiphon.[86] It may have been at this time that Odainathos assumed the title "king of kings"—a title used for him in only one posthumous inscription[87]—in which he included his son Hairan-Herodian.[88] Zonaras says that Gallienus conferred the title *dux orientis* on him at this time.[89] There is no need, however, to look for a Roman administrative equivalent of the title "restorer of all the Orient" attributed to him in a posthumous dedication from 271, as this is simply a formulaic title.[90] To Gallienus, Odainathos looked like the defender of Syria against the Persians and the victor over usurpers who were undermining peace and prosperity in the provinces, all in all a loyal defender of the interests of the empire. Nevertheless, relations between Gallienus and Odainathos were not without ambiguity.

Gallienus was too preoccupied in Italy and on the Danube to intervene in the Orient in the years following 260. Odainathos was thus an indispensable auxiliary, and Gallienus must have considered him an ally if it is true, as Zosimus writes, that Gallienus asked Odainathos to defend the Orient against the Persians.[91] Following the Palmyrene's success, Gallienus assumed the title *Persicus Maximus,* in effect claiming for himself the victory of someone he could regard as his general. In exchange, he may have allowed Odainathos to enjoy the usurped titles, which, not being Roman, would not infringe on the emperor's authority. After Odainathos's new victories at Ctesiphon in 262 and again in 267 or 268, Gallienus yielded none of his power, and it is certain that Odainathos never held the title *Augustus*—it was neither conferred by Gallienus[92] nor usurped after Odainathos's victory over Quietus and Ballista.[93] Nor did he ever use the title *dux Romanorum;* we know that Vaballathos bore the title, but many authors have attributed it, without evidence, to his father.[94]

Nevertheless, Odainathos behaved in many respects more like an autonomous dynast than like a subject of the emperor. He did not hesitate to send an embassy to Shapur, who was at war with Rome, in order to protect Palmyra's interests.[95] In taking the title "king of kings" for himself and his son, he was establishing himself as Shapur's rival. Moreover, he adopted a quasi-imperial stance by authorizing the leaders of his entourage to add the gentilicium *Septimius* to their own names[96] and by creating a true court. Just like an imperial princess, Zenobia had a procurator responsible for managing her property.[97] Gallienus probably had no illusions about the significance of these acts, which revealed Odainathos's unmistakable ambition, if not for sovereignty, at least for regional preeminence in Syria.[98] Despite a tradition that afforded numerous precedents (Avidius Cassius between 170–175, and Priscus during the time of Philip the Arab), it is highly unlikely that Gallienus granted Odainathos an *imperium maius* (internal authority) over the entire Orient as *Historia Augusta* states.[99] Gallienus was probably suspicious of what he may have taken to be secessionist tendencies, given Odainathos's power and his behavior.

The authority Odainathos had acquired and the titles he bore did not alter the status of Palmyra, which remained a Roman colony: institutions functioned as usual, with colonial strategoi, an administrator of justice *(dikaiodotes),* and an *agoranomos.*[100] There is thus no legal basis for calling it a principality, and there is no evidence that Palmyra desired to secede. The city was in the same situation as other cities beyond the Euphrates at the end of the Hellenistic era or during the Roman period; traditional municipal institutions coexisted with the exceptional authority of one man or one family. Josephus characterized this form of government as a "tyranny."

Odainathos and Hairan were assassinated in Emesa[101] between August 30, 267, and August 29, 268, under circumstances that remain obscure (none of the known versions can be substantiated).[102] There may have been a plot involving a Roman official, Rufinus, with the help or tacit agreement of Gallienus himself.[103] Soon after the assassinations, an official expedition sent against the Persians was destroyed by the Palmyrenes, who were under no illusion about the true destination of the expeditionary force.[104] Odainathos's death had given Rome an opportunity to take control of an important frontier zone and the opportunity to fill what appeared to be a power vacuum, given that the oldest of Odainathos's surviving sons was barely ten years old. However, the Romans had overlooked the presence of Zenobia, an energetic widow.[105]

The Palmyrene Orient

The rise to power of Zenobia and her son Vaballathos marked not so much a change of policy by the Palmyrene princes as a new decline in relations between Palmyra and Rome. First, because some time seems to have elapsed between Odainathos's death and the proclamation of Vaballathos as imperator.[106] And even after this proclamation, some ambiguity remained. Vaballathos first settled for his father's hereditary titles, *illustrissimus rex regum* and *epanorthotes* (restorer). He had milestones erected in his name, but without the imperial title.[107] However, when Claudius II died in the summer of 270, Vaballathos refused to recognize Quintillus, and he himself then assumed the titles of *consul, dux Romanorum et imperator,* though he stopped short of calling himself Augustus: his Alexandrine coinage bore his name but kept Aurelian's portrait.[108] What Zenobia meant to be taken as an act of conciliation was seen by Aurelian as a veritable usurpation, and Vaballathos was left off of the *Fasti*, the official list of consuls. Meanwhile, Zenobia had launched a very broad offensive that brought almost all of the Roman Near East under her control. At the end of 270, Vaballathos finally took the title *Augustus,* and Zenobia took *Augusta.*[109]

Vaballathos was not the first Arab to claim imperial status. Besides Philip the Arab, a native of the village of Shahba, in the Hauran,[110] Uranius Antoninus's undertaking some fifteen years earlier had foreshadowed almost exactly, if a little less fully, that of the Palmyrene princes. We may wonder whether the same process was not being repeated with Vaballathos: placed de facto at the head of the imperial troops, he usurped the imperial title when it appeared to have fallen into escheat with Quintillus, and then tried to gain acceptance as Aurelian's second in command (there are some Egyptian documents dating from the joint reign of Vaballathos and Aurelian).[111] We cannot rule out the element of personal ambition, but obviously there were political and strategic motives behind the usurpation.

Zenobia clearly intended to assume control of the empire, although her ambitions exceeded her actual accomplishments. She quickly took over the two provinces of Syria-Coele and Syria-Phoenicia,[112] followed by Arabia, where the Palmyrene armies may have met some resistance from the legion in Bostra: an inscription from that city indicates that the sanctuary of the tutelary god of the legion, Jupiter Hammon, was destroyed by the Palmyrenes,[113] and it is possible that Petra was also ravaged at that time.[114] Zenobia next invaded Syria-Palestine, then Egypt (September 270), where—with an army of seventy thousand men, and with the complicity of a strong pro-Palmyrene faction led by Aurelius Timagenes, whom Zosimus called "high priest for life of Alexandria and all Egypt"—she defeated the local army.[115] Palmyrene troops remained in Egypt until May–June 272. In the northwest, there are no archaeological finds to confirm the movement of the Palmyrenes, but Zosimus confirms that they advanced as far as Ancyra (modern Ankara) and that only Aurelian's rise to power curbed their ambition to take the entire region as far as the Straits.[116]

For two years, in any event, Zenobia and Vaballathos played the part of Roman emperors. The venture was too brief for us to know what their long-term political objectives might have been. There is little to suggest that their secession was ethnic in nature, forerunner to an Arab empire that would have opposed Rome and ultimately freed itself from Rome's authority. On the contrary, by adopting Roman imperial titles, Vaballathos and Zenobia were acting in a way consistent with the behavior of every pretender to the empire in Roman political history. Vaballathos's desire to Hellenize his name by changing it to Athenodoros contradicts any charge of ethnic aspirations. Moreover the conquest of Egypt and part of Asia Minor clearly shows that there was no attempt to establish a "Syrian" empire, much less an "Arab" one; instead they sought to seize control of the entire empire, or at least enough of it to force Aurelian to recognize Vaballathos as a partner. Despite some original aspects, notably the adoption of certain titles, Vaballathos's and Zenobia's usurpation was nothing less than an attempt by two audacious people to seize power and lead the empire, not an attempt to create a new independent state in the Near East.

The new Augusti managed to surround themselves with a court that went beyond the Palmyrene elite—additional evidence that theirs was not a "nativist" movement. The rhetorician Longinus of Emesa, who was considered the most able of his time and whose work was viewed as highly instructive,[117] quickly rallied to their camp and wrote an funeral oration for Odainathos that Libanios, a century later, was eager to obtain.[118] Callinicos of Petra, another brilliant mind, dedicated his *History of Alexandria* to Zenobia, calling her "Cleopatra," after her victory in Egypt.[119] She welcomed Manichaean missionaries and may have helped them when they were in Egypt.[120] However, despite numerous stories, there is no evidence of special ties between Zenobia and Bishop Paul of Samosata.[121]

Aurelian, proclaimed emperor in September 270, refused to compromise. He launched his campaign of reconquest in 272. The Palmyrenes were defeated at Tyana,[122] and then again at Immae, near Antioch;[123] the decisive battle took place near Emesa, resulting in a final, crushing defeat for Palmyra.[124] Aurelian's liberal treatment of the cities that had submitted to Zenobia and Vaballathos earned him many allies; from then on, his troops included contingents from every province in Syria. The Palmyrene troops retreated to Palmyra itself, and the city had to build fortifications quickly.[125] It fell in August 272,[126] whereupon Zenobia fled to the east; she was soon caught and taken prisoner.[127] A trial was held in Emesa that ended with the conviction of several of her accomplices, including the rhetorician Longinus.[128] Some months later (we are not sure just when), Septimius Apsaios led an uprising in the city. Apsaios is thought to have tried to urge the prefect of Mesopotamia, Marcellinus, to proclaim himself emperor;[129] when Marcellinus hesitated, the Palmyrenes apparently sought to name Antiochos—a relative of Zenobia—emperor.[130] Aurelian promptly returned and seized the city, which does not appear to have been greatly damaged in this new attack, although the sanctuary of Helios was partially destroyed.[131] To date, archaeologists have found no bed of ash from a major fire that might have been a consequence of the city's defeat.

Palmyra, unlike Hatra, was thus not abandoned. Diocletian moved a legion into the western quarter of the city and had new baths built. In 328, columns from the main road were reused for the façade of a church,[132] and there is evidence of a *logistes* charged with rebuilding the municipal finances. New ramparts surrounded the city, and new churches were probably built by the fifth century at the latest.[133] Some late Christian steles and the presence of a bishop in the early fourth century indicate that not only had the urban complex survived, it had endured as a city of some importance. However, although the local population went on living in the ancient, unchanged environment, the city gradually lost some of its luster as the hub, the capital, of the desert.[134] The main commercial traffic between the Roman Empire and the countries to the east henceforth followed more northern routes, at the foot of the Taurus and the Anti-Taurus.

PHYLARCHS AND NOMAD CHIEFS

When the sedentary states and dynasties that had ruled the Arab nomads of the Syro-Mesopotamian desert disappeared, Rome needed to find new ways of guaranteeing the security of the empire on its borders. It offered opportunities for other tribes or groups of tribes to fill the vacancies left by the collapse of the ancient principalities.

Rome had had direct links with nomadic Arab tribes for a long time. In fact, on the frontier of the province of Arabia, no indigenous state structures had been maintained or installed, apart from a few tribal groupings. At first, Rome ensured the protection of the desert directly, as far away as the distant oases of Jawf[135] and Hegra. However, around the end of the third century, a general withdrawal from the farthest outposts began just as the outermost defensive line around the borders of the sedentary countries was being reinforced. In this new arrangement, allied Arab tribes were brought in to take over from the Roman troops in the desert.

Tribes and Allied Confederations

Two sectors have yielded documentation on the direct relations between Rome and nomad tribes: the eastern Hauran of the so-called Safaites, and the northern Hejaz, where Rome controlled groups called "Thamoudaeans."

In the eastern Hauran, several Greek inscriptions dating from the second half of the second century and from the third century, found in villages of the northern part of Jebel Druze, show that nomads provided some contingents directed by their own chiefs whom Rome recognized as "nomad strategoi," "strategoi of nomad encampments," "ethnarchs," or "phylarchs."[136] Onomastic studies confirm that these were Arabs, and one text specifically confirms that one of the tribes belonged to the group of those mentioned in Safaitic inscriptions: Odainathos, son of Sawadd, is called "phylarch" and "strategos of the Awidh," a tribe clearly attested in the Harra.[137] It is likely, therefore, that in this region far from the routes of the Parthian and later the Persian invasions, Rome entered into privileged alliances with the most powerful tribes so that they would outfit troops, commanded by their own officers, that were intended to control the nomad tribes and their desert routes in conjunction with the Roman garrisons installed along the edge of the steppe.

A similar situation prevailed in the northern Hejaz. Rome was under no threat in this sector throughout the second century: Roman military posts were rare in the steppe region crossed by Trajan's *Via Nova* between Philadelphia, Petra, and Aila, at least until the Severan period. However, garrisons were stationed in distant oases such as Hegra[138] and Dumata[139] and in the centers of nomad gatherings such as the Nabataean sanctuary of Wadi Ramm.[140] The only way to control tribal movements was to negotiate with their chiefs and make them part of the defense of the empire. This was no doubt the case with the Thamoudaeans of Ruwwafa, shown by Michael Macdonald to have actually been part of a military unit integrated into the Roman army.[141]

There may have been similar alliances elsewhere. These were useful so long as the political situation remained stable—in other words, so long as allied tribes were not feeling pressure from more powerful groups attempting to establish themselves on the borders of the empire. However, they could not always prevent incursions of pillagers: in 190–191, Arabs ravaged the Sinai.[142]

The Rise of Tanukh

Reliable Arab traditions confirm that the Arabs allied with Rome were, in turn, Gadhima, the princes of Palmyra, Lakhm, Tanukh, Salih, and Ghassan. The latter two are documented in the fifth and sixth centuries; the first four belong to the third and fourth centuries. Over a long period, the difficulties involved in using and interpreting Arab sources led historians to dismiss or ignore these traditions. Epigraphic and archaeological discoveries now oblige us to take this information into account, and they confirm, at the very least, the order of succession described by Arab authors.[143]

The historical existence of one of these kings has been confirmed by an inscription from Umm al-Jimal referring to the *tropheus,* the foster father or mentor of Gadhima, king of Tanukh.[144] The nomadic Tanukh tribe wandered through the northeastern part of the Arabian Peninsula before settling in Syria, perhaps southwest of Aleppo, in the Chalcidene. We cannot tell from the fragmentary evidence (the funerary stele of a preceptor and a list of sites occupied by the Tanukhids around 630–635) exactly how far Gadhima's power extended. However, there may be archaeological evidence for the battle between the Palmyrenes and Tanukh that is mentioned in traditional Arab sources. The large indigenous settlement of Umm al-Jimal, situated southeast of the later Roman city, appears to have been completely destroyed during the third century. It is tempting to see this as the Palmyrenes' revenge against one of the areas of support, one of the residences even, of their enemy the Tanukhids.[145]

The disappearance of the Banu Odainathos clan of Palmyra left a vacuum in the Syrian desert. With lawlessness mounting, even before Palmyra's fall, there was a clear need for effective policing. The Arabian frontier, which in the second century had remained almost completely free of military installations, saw an active period of construction of fortifications and watchtowers during the reign of the Severi, especially in the northern sector of the Transjordan;[146] at the same time, the cities of Bostra and Adraha were rebuilding their ramparts.[147] These measures were not directed solely against Palmyra, which could not have been considered an enemy before the end of the 260s; they were clearly intended to protect against potential nomad raids, whether by groups inhabiting the Arabian desert seeking to profit from the problems in Syria or—more likely—by tribes in the service of the Persians. Very quickly, in fact, a descendant of the Edessene dynasty, 'Amr ibn 'Adi, had settled in Hira in Lower Mesopotamia, and put himself at the service of the Sassanids.[148]

Gadhima's strength may thus have been used as a bulwark against these threats. Lacking official Roman documentation, we do not know the exact status of the king of Tanukh. He was probably a *foederatus,* allied to Rome by a treaty, like the barbarians from the Rhine-Danube frontier. The title "king" indicates his preeminence over other Arab sheikhs. The structure of the tribal group he led is less clear, but we may surmise that *Tanukh* was the name of the dominant tribe within a larger group called Quda'a, with whom less powerful tribes were affiliated. The Tanukhid galaxy may thus have had branches in widely separated regions. But there is no proof that the Tanukh tribe dominated all the other Arab tribes in the region. Other groups may have benefited from a similar status, in other zones of the Syro-Mesopotamian and Arabian deserts, in the Middle Euphrates as well as in the Hejaz or the Sinai.

In addition, Arabs contributed to the defense of the frontier by furnishing the bulk of the many indigenous units mentioned in the *Notitia Dignitatum.* Some are specifically called Arab: the *Equites Saraceni Thamudeni* and the *cohors secunda Ituraeorum;* but most of the *equite sagittarii indigenae,* the *equites promoti indigenae,* and the *dromedarii* were probably also Arab.

Diocletian's reorganization of frontier defenses had to take into account the new relations with Arab nomads. Roman units had apparently abandoned the most distant bases (Hegra, Dumat al-Jandal), but this did not mean that their sovereignty had been lost. Still, policing of the desert regions was entrusted to Rome's nomad allies. At the same time, defensive fortifications on the edge of the steppe were significantly reinforced: the *strata diocletiana*[149] "linking the Euphrates, Palmyra, Damascus, and the eastern Hauran, the line of forts and encampments that has been found between the oasis of al-Azraq and Aila as well as in the northern Sinai, the transfer of Legio X Fretensis to Aila[150] and the installation of IV Martia in Lejjun (Moab) were all part of this effort to set up a tight defensive network for the nondesert zones of the Syrian provinces, while the steppe and the desert were assigned solely to Arab allies. Similarly, a considerable effort went into opening up an access route to the Jawf region.[151]

The Generalized Royal Authority of Imru' al-Qays

Imru' al-Qays ibn 'Amr, "King of all the Arabs," died in 328. His epitaph was written in Arabic, in a Nabataean script; it presents serious problems of interpretation,[152] not simply because of variant readings, but also because the classical sources have been silent on the events that it reports. Viewed in conjunction with Arab traditions, however, it provides firsthand information of major importance.

Imru' al-Qays was the son of Lakhmid 'Amr ibn 'Adi, the founder of

Hira. At the time of his death, he must have been a Roman official, as his tomb is located in Nemara, in the steppe region bordering the Roman province of Arabia, a site that housed a Roman garrison. Moreover, he claimed to hold his authority from Rome. But he also boasted of governing certain communities held by the Persians. Did he change his allegiance in the course of his reign? This is possible, although the reasons for the shift remain a mystery—conversion to Christianity? disagreement with Shapur II? During the period of relative peace between the Persians and the Romans, Imru' al-Qays may have managed to extend his authority to tribes to the east as well as to the west of the Syro-Mesopotamian desert. In any event, he prided himself on having subjugated tribes living far apart: the two groups of Azdites and the Nizar of northeastern Arabia (he campaigned against the powerful city of Thaj), the Madhhig, defeated at the oasis of Najran southwest of the peninsula, and the Ma'add in the Hejaz. Did he do this on his own behalf, on behalf of the Persians (for example, as part of the expedition of Shapur II against Arabia), or on behalf of the Romans? We can only hypothesize. However, his successes justified the title "King of all the Arabs." Imru' al-Qays was not only the leader of the Lakhm, but also of numerous other tribes, including some sedentary communities, which he put under the authority of his sons.

The power of Imru' al-Qays notwithstanding, there may have been other groups allied with Rome that were not under his authority. As for Tanukh, Arab traditions hold that Gadhima was the maternal uncle of 'Amr ibn 'Adi, great-uncle of Imru' al-Qays. The latter's mother, Mawiyya, and his wife Hind are thought to have been Azdites, members of a clan related to Tanukh that was defeated by Imru' al-Qays. The latter may have had a legitimate claim to Gadhima's legacy. Similarly, it is possible that when he died, other Tanukhids took his place without conflict or interruption. In any case, according to Arab traditions, the death of Imru' al-Qays marked the beginning of Tanukh dominance over the Arab foederati, a dominance that lasted throughout the fourth century, until the Tanukhids were replaced by Salih at the century's end.

The political, social, and economic situation of the Arabs in the Syro-Mesopotamian desert changed dramatically in 337. Agricultural activity became much more important than trade. The old sedentary clans, while they did not disappear, lost their primacy and ceded leadership to newcomers fresh from the peninsula who had no ties to the Greco-Roman or Aramaean culture of their predecessors. Moreover, the policy of protection provided by client states, a legacy of the Julio-Claudian era, gave way to agreements with groups that remained basically nomadic and whose military strength and network of alliances were used to safeguard the borders.

Still, this system was coupled with a considerable reinforcement of fortifications. Rome was thus able to extend its influence into the heart of the peninsula, but it had to rely exclusively on the loyalty of allies—an expensive drawback that required a constant reevaluation of the nomads' strength. Once an allied tribe had lost its influence or suffered a serious setback, making it incapable of playing the role that had justified its advantages, it risked losing its favored status. These advantages (particularly the annona, a tax levied by Rome to be paid in wheat) were considered so desirable that they led to fierce competition and many attempts by tribes that were less well funded to overthrow whichever group was currently on top. This, combined with Sassanid maneuvering, resulted in a perpetual threat of instability.

I have chosen to prolong this history of the desert to include the generalized royal authority of Imru' al-Qays in order to show the extent of the changes that took place on the margins of Syria following the fall of Palmyra and the reorganization of the Syrian provinces. I have done so not because the region seems more important than it once did, but perhaps because historians of the Roman Empire have less often taken it into account; they have tended to focus more often on the classical sources. The power of the great Arab confederations moving between Syria and Mesopotamia and the relationships they maintained with tribes of the Arabian Peninsula played a role in the policies of both Rome and Persia in the Middle East. This new element continued to increase in importance right up to the eve of the Islamic conquest, and it had a lasting influence on the history of Syria.

C O N C L U S I O N

THE capture of Palmyra did not mark the end of an era, either in the empire as a whole or in Syria itself, and I am well aware that, by concluding this work with an event of strictly local significance, I am stopping in the middle of things. I could have gone a little further: I could have included a brief summary of the Persian campaign of Marcus Aurelius Carus and Marcus Aurelius Numerianus. This would have added pages to the book but very little to our understanding of Syria's essential strategic role. I might have continued up to the time when Diocletian reorganized the provinces. Instead, I have chosen to stop in midstream, the better to convey my belief, perhaps, that history does not come with clean breaks, and that real change takes place over long stretches of time. When reforms do occur, either they ratify changes that have been a long time in the making, or else they are not actually felt until many years later. Thus an argument can be made against any date chosen as the conclusion to a historical narrative; the choice will always be an arbitrary one. This work is no exception.

The Macedonians and Greeks found themselves in a world about which they knew virtually nothing, and in order to administer their newly conquered territory they had little choice but to adopt and then adapt existing laws. Nevertheless, within three hundred years they had managed to leave their own distinctive mark throughout Syria, in a variety of ways. As heirs of the Hellenistic kingdoms, the Romans found a land encompassing a great many *poleis* and large pockets of "Greeks," descendants of colonists and Hellenized natives. The process of founding poleis, inaugurated in Syria by Alexander or Antigonos Monophthalmos before the end of the fourth century B.C.E., continued under the Romans without interruption until the beginning of the fourth century C.E. and the founding of Maximianopolis or Constantinople. For almost a thousand years, Syria was marked by the vigor of its cities, or more precisely, its city-states, for while civic institutions underwent many transformations, their decline is scarcely perceptible before the Islamic conquest in 635.

Although the city-state, or *polis,* was an important means of organizing space and power, the model was not followed systematically, and it was not unique. Indeed, the diversity of the systems that Rome established in order to be able to govern such a diverse world is quite striking. We have seen how city-states, sanctuaries, ethnic groups, tribes, and client states as dissimilar as the great kingdoms of Judaea or Nabataea and the smallest tetrarchies of the Syrian mountains were all able to coexist under Rome's rule, in keeping with the Achaeminid and later the Hellenistic traditions of respect for diversity. Syria's Roman leaders were not obsessed with uniformity, and, although ultimately, from Trajan's time on, most of the area was administered as Roman provinces, this reflected the growing conformity in cultural and social customs more than it did a deliberate policy or predetermined goal set by an authority preoccupied with clarity and coherence.

In a way, this lack of administrative uniformity reveals the overall attitude of the authorities in place. They certainly sought to profit from the land they had conquered, relying on recognized communities in the process, but they made no demands not directly related to that objective. Adaptable and flexible, the Romans did not attempt to impose a specific language, cult, or mode of social organization. Even Hadrian's extreme measures against the Jews in 135, like the persecution edict issued by Antiochos IV three hundred years earlier, do not contradict this general rule, because both actions were taken in political retaliation against uprisings that were not well understood. Respect for indigenous cultures, languages, and cults became permanent features, not because authorities found them respectable, but because they had nothing to gain by changing them. Thus there is evidence almost everywhere,[1] even in a region as quickly and thoroughly Hellenized as Phoenicia,[2] that local traditions persisted, even though they are sometimes obscured, as in Phoenicia, by the language or iconography of the Greeks.

For even without cultural proselytizing, or a policy of Hellenization (and still less of Romanization), Hellenism was deeply etched into every aspect of indigenous cultures, and in return Greek culture in Syria took on particular local aspects. The evolution of Hellenistic Judaism seems particularly exemplary. Forged in the revolt against a poorly planned and premature process of modernization, Judaism ultimately borrowed intellectual qualities and habits from the Greeks that rabbis and scribes successfully freed from pagan associations. The fundamental problem was the one faced by any society that finds itself forced to adapt to a culturally attractive environment. The appeal that Greek culture held for almost all indigenous societies is incontrovertible. The Greek language spread to villages, even if it was only used in formal contexts, as on tombs in the Hauran; local leaders sought to found new poleis to their own benefit; "Greek-style" buildings for recreation proliferated, as did "Greek" games. Such examples unmistakably reveal that many people felt a strong attachment to the new culture, and that almost everyone felt attached to its more superficial aspects. And we must not fail to recall how revolutionary it was for Jews as well as Arabs to adopt images of living beings: such images had been completely proscribed for Jews and entirely absent from representations of the deity among Arabs. Synagogue paintings from Dura-Europos have shown how far some Jews had come in this respect, while the coexistence of sacred stones, steles "with eyes," and anthropomorphic statues reveal the stages of another kind of transformation among the Arabs.

These cultures were not mutually exclusive, and so we find one individual depicted in Roman dress with an epitaph written in Palmyrene; Allat could be worshipped in the guise of Phidias's Athena Parthenos; one child in a family could be named Alexander and another Malchos; Semitic cosmogony could be studied in Greek and the teachings of Platonic philosophy analyzed in Aramaic. Still, we should not suppose that the inhabitants of Greco-Roman Syria shared what the Greeks called a *mixobarbaros* culture, at heart barbarian even though cloaked in forms that looked Greek. On the one hand, I am convinced that there were highly diverse communities, families of colonists who clung to the memory of their Greek origins and piously maintained strictly Greek religious traditions and even naming practices. On the other hand, many people, from desert shepherds to peasant farmers in the Euphrates Valley, never learned a word of Greek and continued to worship the gods by their age-old names. Between these two extremes, however, every possible variation is found, and it is impossible to determine to what extent these acculturations were freely chosen or imposed by the pressure of social customs.

I speak of acculturations in the plural, because a two-way process is involved: between and among Greeks, Phoenicians, Aramaeans, Jews, and Arabs. Greeks also borrowed from "indigenous" cultures, even though the spread of the Greek language obscures this phenomenon somewhat. We see it when we look at the cults, where the faithful inevitably mingled and worshipped all the gods among whom they had easily established quite plausible correspondences. But the very notion of "indigenousness" is problematic. After the first generations of colonists, all those whom we call "Greek" ended up looking like "natives," whether they were the children of colonists from other places, born in the country and knowing no other homeland, or whether they came from one of the Hellenized families who quickly became indistinguishable from Greek immigrants. Yet for the latter in particular, their acculturation—no matter how thoroughgoing— never required them to renounce any other tradition. Meleagros of Gadara, Paul of Tarsos, and Iamblichos of Chalcis all proclaimed in no uncertain terms that they belonged to two or even three cultural traditions.

It is more difficult to assess the exchanges among Semitic cultures. The Phoenician and Hebrew languages were unquestionably victims as much of the success of Aramaic as of Greek, but how much influence did Arabs have on the fringes of the settled populations of Syria? The Hauran, Palmyra, the Euphrates Valley, and Edessa were heavily influenced by Arabs, as we can see in cults, proper names, burial customs on occasion, and perhaps certain aspects of the language. But we cannot say much more than this.

Syria had incontestably changed over six centuries. Its urban network was now dense, cultivated lands were extensive, and the borders on the steppe were better controlled; exchanges of every sort had developed throughout the Mediterranean as well as with Mesopotamia and the Arabian Peninsula. At the end of the third century C.E., travelers in the country would have found far more features in common from north to south than their predecessors would have found at the time of Alexander's conquest, if only in terms of the urban landscape or daily social life. However, differences remained, most obviously in language and writing, but also in the gods, and probably in local customs and the rhythms of daily life as well. Nomads from Hejaz, Jewish rabbis from Galilee, Aramaean peasants from the Orontes valley, fishermen from Joppe or Balanaea, craftsmen from Tyre and Antioch, Euphrates herders, foresters from the Limestone Massif, deacons from Edessa—all had borrowed to some extent from Greco-Roman culture, yet all remained distinctively themselves in their infinite diversity. Was it not precisely because the political domination of the Romans, like that of the Macedonians before them, was unaccompanied by any obligation to adopt a foreign culture—although the possibility was always available—that the ancient populations of Syria accepted the weight of occupation so easily and for so long? This is no doubt only part of the explanation, but I remain convinced that it was the subtle, almost inexplicable mix of (fiscal) constraint and (cultural) freedom that enabled this latest "Greek adventure" to enjoy such a long run. For in the history of Syria the Greek presence was not simply a parenthesis: nearly a thousand years of history of the Near East (from 333 B.C.E. to 635 C.E.) bears their stamp, a period longer than the era of the Aramaean kingdoms, more durable than the Ottoman rule. How could this have occurred without the support of a large part of the population? The Macedonian kings and later the Roman emperors unquestionably had the power to elicit such loyalty from communities that were becoming increasingly far-flung; they were able to inspire in anyone who held the slightest position of responsibility a sense of loyalty to Greek culture and Roman authority, and to give others no reason to oppose them. Today one must stroll among the ruins of Palmyra, wander through the remains of Bostra, Apamaea, and Petra, examine the mosaics of Antioch and Philippopolis, and tirelessly crisscross these lands in all their diversity in order to grasp the extent to which the ancient Syrians drew upon differences and the plurality of cultures to create their own complex and infinitely rich civilization. The historian of all this complexity and richness knows in advance that a full accounting is beyond his power. May he be forgiven for having at least tried!

ABBREVIATIONS • NOTES • WORKS CITED • INDEX

ABBREVIATIONS

AAAS	*Annales archéologiques arabes syriennes*
AAE	*Arabian Archaeology and Epigraphy*
AAS	*Annales archéologiques de Syrie*
ABD	David Noel Freedman, ed., *The Anchor Bible Dictionary,* 6 vols. (New York: Doubleday, 1992)
ADAJ	*Annual of the Department of Antiquities of Jordan*
AE	*L'année épigraphique*
AJ	Flavius Josephus, *De antiquitate judaico (Jewish Antiquities)*, trans. Louis H. Feldman, 9 vols. (Loeb Classical Library)
AJA	*American Journal of Archaeology*
AJPh	*American Journal of Philology*
ANRW	*Aufstieg und Niedergang der römischen Welt*
AS	Henri Seyrig, *Antiquités syriennes* (Paris: P. Geuthner, 1934–)
AZ	Maurice Sartre, *D'Alexandre à Zénobie* (Paris: Fayard, 2001)
BASOR	*Bulletin of the American Schools of Oriental Research*
BEO	*Bulletin d'études orientales*
BGU	Ulrich Wilcken et al., eds., *Ägyptische Urkunden aus den Königlichen Museen zu Berlin: Griechische Urkunden* (Berlin: Staatliche Museen, 1903)
BJ	Flavius Josephus, *De bello judaico (The Jewish War)*, trans. Henry St. John Thackeray, 3 vols. (Loeb Classical Library)
BMB	*Bulletin du Musée de Beyrouth*
BSOAS	*Bulletin of the Society for Oriental and African Studies*
BT	*The Babylonian Talmud,* ed. Isidore Epstein, 35 vols. (London: Soncino Press, 1935–1952)
CIL	*Corpus inscriptionum latinarum* (Berlin: G. Reimer / W. de Gruyter, 1893–)

CIS	Académie des inscriptions et belles-lettres, ed., *Corpus inscriptionum semiticarum,* 5 vols. (Paris: e Reipublicae Typographeo, 1881; reprint, Paris: C. Klincksieck, 1972)
CRAI	*Comptes rendus des séances de l'Académie des inscriptions et belles-lettres*
DaM	*Damaszener Mitteilungen*
DTC	Alfred Vacant, Eugène Mangenot, and Émile Amann, eds., *Dictionnaire de théologie catholique* (Paris: Letouzey & Ané, 1925–)
EAEHL	*Encyclopedia of Archaeological Excavations in the Holy Land* (Englewood Cliffs, N.J.: Prentice-Hall, 1975–1978)
EH	Eusebius, *The Ecclesiastical History,* trans. Kirsopp Lake (Loeb Classical Library)
ESI	*Excavations and Surveys in Israel*
FHG	Karl I. Müller, ed. *Fragmenta historicorum graecorum,* 5 vols. (Paris: Firmin-Didot, 1841–1870)
HA	*Historia Augusta,* trans. David Magie (Loeb Classical Library)
HP	Édouard Will, *Histoire politique du monde hellénistique,* 2nd ed., 2 vols. (Nancy: Presses Universitaires de Nancy, 1979–1982)
I.Gerasa	Charles Bradford Welles, "The Inscriptions," in *Gerasa, City of the Decapolis,* ed. Carl Hermann Kraeling (New Haven, Conn.: American Schools of Oriental Research, 1938)
I.Palmyre	Khaled As'ad and Jean-Baptiste Yon, *Inscriptions de Palmyre: Promenades épigraphiques dans la ville antique de Palmyre* (Beirut: Direction générale des antiquités et des musées de la République arabe syrienne, Institut français d'archéologie du Proche-Orient, 2001)
I.Syrie	William Henry Waddington, *Inscriptions grecques et latines de la Syrie* (Paris: Firmin-Didot, 1870)
IEJ	*Israel Exploration Journal*
IGLJ	*Inscriptions grecques et latines de la Syrie,* vol. 21, *Inscriptions grecques et latines de la Jordanie,* 4 vols. (Paris: P. Geuthner, 1986–)
IGLS	*Inscriptions grecques et latines de la Syrie,* 21 vols. (Paris: P. Geuthner, 1929– ; Beirut: Institut français d'archéologie du Proche-Orient, 2005–)
IGR	René Cagnat, Jean Toutain, Georges Lafaye, and Victor Henry, eds., *Inscriptiones graecae ad res romanas pertinentes,* 3 vols. (Paris: E. Leroux, 1906–1927)
ILS	Hermann Dessau, *Inscriptiones latinae selectae.* Berlin: Weidmann, 1892–1916.
INJ	*Israel Numismatic Journal*
Inv.	Jean Cantineau, ed., *Inventaire des inscriptions de Palmyre,* 11 vols. (Beirut: Publications du Musée national syrien de Damas, 1930–)
JJS	*Journal of Jewish Studies*
JRA	*Journal of Roman Archaeology*
JRS	*Journal of Roman Studies*
JSS	*Journal of Semitic Studies*
M.Bible	*Le monde de la Bible*
MEFRA	*Mélanges de l'École française de Rome: Antiquités*
MUSJ	*Mélanges de l'Université Saint-Joseph*
NC	*Numismatic Chronicle*

NH	Pliny, *Natural History,* trans. H. Rackham, 10 vols. (Loeb Classical Library)
OGIS	Wilhelm Dittenberger, ed., *Orientis graeci inscriptiones selectae: Supplementum sylloges inscriptionum graecarum,* 2 vols. (Hildesheim and New York: G. Olms, 1986; 1st ed. 1903–1905)
P.Dura	*Papyrus Dura*
P.Euphr.	*Papyrus de l'Euphrate*
P.Mich.	John Garrett Winter, ed., *Papyri in the University of Michigan Collection* (Ann Arbor: University of Michigan Press, 1936)
P.Oxy	Bernard P. Grenfell and Arthur S. Hunt, eds., *The Oxyrhynchus Papyri* (London: Egypt Exploration Fund, 1898–)
P.Yadin	*Papyrus Yadin*
PAES	Howard Crosby Butler and Enno Littmann, *Syria: Publications of the Princeton University Archaeological Expeditions to Syria in 1904–1905 and 1909* (Leiden: E. J. Brill, 1907–1949)
PAM	*Polish Archaeology in the Mediterranean*
PAT	Delbert R. Hillers and Eleonora Cussini, *Palmyrene Aramaic Texts* (Baltimore: Johns Hopkins University Press, 1994)
PEQ	*Palestine Exploration Quarterly*
RA	*Revue archéologique*
Rbi	*Revue biblique*
RE	August Friedrich von Pauly et al., eds., *Realencyclopädie der classischen Altertumswissenschaft* (Stuttgart: J. B. Metzler, 1894–)
REA	*Revue des études anciennes*
RGDS	*Res gestae divi saporis,* in *Die römisch-persischen Kriege des 3. Jahrhunderts n. Chr.: Nach der Inschrift Sahpuhrs I. an der Ka'be-ye Zartost (SKZ),* by Erich Kettenhofen (Wiesbaden: L. Reichert, 1982)
RIH	Basile Aggoula, "Remarques sur les inscriptions hatréennes" (1981–1987)
RMD	Margaret M. Roxan, *Roman Military Diplomas,* 3 vols. (London: Institute of Archaeology, 1978–1994)
RPC	Andrew Burnett, Michel Amandry, and Pere Paul Ripollès, *Roman Provincial Coinage,* 2 vols. (London and Paris: British Museum Press / Bibliothèque nationale de France, 1992–1999)
SCI	*Scripta classica israelica*
SEG	*Supplementum epigraphicum graecum* (Alphen aan den Rijn: Sijthoff & Noordhoff, 1923–1998)
SHAJ	*Studies in the History and Archaeology of Jordan*
TAPA	*Transactions and Proceedings of the American Philological Association*
TJ	*Le Talmud de Jérusalem,* trans. Moïse Schwab, 11 vols. (Paris: Maisonneuve & Larose, 1871–1890)
ZDPV	*Zeitschrift der deutschen Palästina-Vereins*
ZPE	*Zeitschrift für Papyrologie und Epigraphik*

NOTES

INTRODUCTION

1. These international frontiers remain contested. It goes without saying that the historian of antiquity need not take sides in such a debate.

2. On the history of this false notion, see Maurice Sartre, "La Syrie-Creuse n'existe pas," in *Géographie historique au Proche-Orient: Actes de la table ronde de Valbonne, 16–18 septembre 1985,* ed. Pierre-Louis Gatier, Bruno Helly, and Jean-Paul Rey-Coquais (Paris: Centre national de la recherche scientifique, 1988), pp. 15–40, in which I showed, after Abraham Schalit ("Koile Syria from the Mid-Fourth Century to the Beginning of the Third Century BC," *Scripta Hierosolymitana* 1 [1954]: 64–77), that it was completely useless to insist on searching for a "hollow" (the Beqaa or the Ghab) in order to justify the epithet. This rationalizing approach was developed by Strabo (*The Geography,* trans. Horace Leonard Jones [Loeb Classical Library], 16.2.16) and adopted by Elias Joseph Bikerman, whose authority imposed Strabo's viewpoint: see "La Coelè-Syrie: Notes de géographie historique," *Revue biblique* 54 (1947): 255–256.

3. Félix-Marie Abel, *Histoire de la Palestine depuis la conquête d'Alexandre jusqu'à l'invasion arabe,* vol. 1 (Paris: J. Gabalda, 1952).

4. John D. Grainger, *Hellenistic Phoenicia* (Oxford: Clarendon Press, 1992).

5. Fergus Millar, *The Roman Near East (31 B.C.–A.D. 337)* (Cambridge, Mass.: Harvard University Press, 1993).

6. See the overview of the question offered by Fergus Millar, "The Problem of Hellenistic Syria: The Interaction of Greek and Non-Greek Civilizations from Syria to Central Asia after Alexander," in *Hellenism in the East,* ed. Amélie Kuhrt and Susan Sherwin-White (London: Duckworth, 1987), pp. 110–133. Millar's text constitutes an excellent presentation of the available documentation on the Syrian region as I have defined it above, but it leaves the somewhat discouraging impression that we

possess only a very few pieces of a puzzle that is impossible to reconstruct. To be sure, there is a great deal we do not know. But is it not the job of the historian of antiquity to persevere in trying to reconstruct the past, taking into account each new discovery (and they keep on appearing), even though we know how many elements we lack—and will continue to lack? Otherwise, why not devote ourselves to other tasks?

7. The interested reader may wish to consult the original version of this book: Maurice Sartre, *D'Alexandre à Zénobie* (Paris: Fayard, 2001), pp. 35–433. Only a portion of the information presented on pages 371–433 has been retained.

8. I did so on a single point, that of the history of the Arab tribes, for which I went up to the death of Imru' al-Qays in 328.

I. THE HELLENISTIC LEGACY

1. Édouard Will, *Histoire politique du monde hellénistique,* 2nd ed. (Nancy: Presses Universitaires de Nancy, 1979–1982), vol. 1, pp. 47, 54–55 (hereafter cited as *HP*).

2. Will, *HP* 1, pp. 27–83.

3. Tyre and Sidon remained for a time under the control of Demetrios Poliorcetes, Antigonos's son and successor, but Ptolemy got them back, probably around 288–286. See Maurice Sartre, *D'Alexandre à Zénobie* (Paris: Fayard, 2001), p. 109 (hereafter cited as *AZ*).

4. On the "Syrian" aspects of the Syrian wars (which were not always essential in those wars), see Sartre, *AZ,* pp. 187–201.

5. Han J. W. Drijvers, "Hatra, Palmyra und Edessa: Die Städte der syrisch-mesopotamischen Wüste in politischer, kulturgeschichtlicher und religiongeschichtlicher Beleuchtung," *Aufstieg und Niedergang der römischen Welt* (hereafter cited as *ANRW*) 2.8 (1977): 867. The date of 132 B.C.E. comes from the eighth-century C.E. chronicle attributed to Pseudo-Dionysios of Tell Mahre.

6. It may be objected that the conquerors were not Greeks but Macedonians. However, it is highly unlikely that the inhabitants of the Near East distinguished between them, especially because they all spoke Greek, even though their dialects varied. In addition, there were many Greeks among the mercenaries of Alexander's army.

7. Sartre, *AZ,* pp. 60–63.

8. Pierre Briant, "Des Achéménides aux rois hellénistiques: Continuités et ruptures," *Annali della Scuola Normale Superiore di Pisa* 9 (1979): 1375–1414; Pierre Briant, "Alexandre et l'héritage achéménide: Quelques réflexions et perspectives," in *Alexander the Great: From Macedonia to the Oikoumene, Veria 27–31/5/1998* (Véroia: Nomarchike Autodioikese Emathias, 1999), pp. 209–217.

9. Isocrates, *Panegyricus,* trans. George Norlin (Loeb Classical Library), 50.

10. Pierre Briant, "Colonizzazione ellenistica e popolazioni del Vicino Oriente: Dinamiche sociali e politiche di acculturazione," in *I Greci* II: *Una Storia greca* 3, *Trasformazioni,* ed. Salvatore Settis (Turin: Giulio Einaudi, 1988), pp. 319–333.

11. Victor Tcherikover, *Die hellenistischen Städtgegründungen von Alexander dem Grossen bis auf die Römerzeit* (Leipzig: Deiterich'sche Verlagsbuchhandlung, 1927), suppl. 19; Glanville Downey, *A History of Antioch in Syria: From Seleucus to the Arab Conquest* (Princeton: Princeton University Press, 1961); Getzel M. Cohen,

The Seleucid Colonies: Studies in Founding, Administration, and Organization (Wiesbaden: Steiner, 1978); Rami Arav, *Hellenistic Palestine: Settlement Patterns and City Planning, 337–31 B.C.E.* (Oxford: British Archaeological Reports, 1989); John D. Grainger, *The Cities of Seleukid Syria* (Oxford: Clarendon Press, 1990); Pierre Briant, "Colonisation hellénistique et populations indigènes: La phase d'installation," *Klio: Beiträge zur alten Geschichte* 60 (1978): 57–92.

12. Sartre, *AZ,* pp. 144–150.

13. Ibid., pp. 280–281.

14. Ibid., pp. 294–300.

15. Françoise Briquel-Chatonnet, "Les derniers témoignages sur la langue phénicienne en Orient," *Rivista di Studi Fenici* 19 (1991): 3–21.

16. This complex history cannot be summarized in a few lines; there is a vast scholarly literature on the subject. The best approach may be to list a few works that seem to me to state the problems clearly and suggest the most convincing answers: William D. Davies and Louis Finkelstein, eds., *The Hellenistic Age,* vol. 2 of *The Cambridge History of Judaism* (Cambridge and New York: Cambridge University Press, 1989); Niels Hyldahl, *The History of Early Christianity* (Frankfurt am Main: Peter Lang, 1997); Aryeh Kasher, *Jews, Idumaeans, and Ancient Arabs: Relations of the Jews in Eretz-Israel with the Nations of the Frontier and the Desert during the Hellenistic and Roman Era (332 B.C.E.–70 C.E.)* (Tübingen: J. C. B. Mohr, 1988); idem, *Jews and Hellenistic Cities in Eretz-Israel: Relations of the Jews in Eretz-Israel with the Hellenistic Tribes during the Second Temple Period (332 B.C.E.–70 C.E.)* (Tübingen: J. C. B. Mohr, 1990); Raymond Kuntzmann and Jacques Schlosser, eds., *Études sur le judaïsme hellénistique: Congrès de Strasbourg (1983)* (Paris: Le Cerf, 1984); Christiane Saulnier, *Histoire d'Israel de la conquête d'Alexandre à la destruction du Temple* (Paris: Le Cerf, 1985); Peter Schäfer, *The History of the Jews in Antiquity: The Jews of Palestine from Alexander the Great to the Arab Conquest* (Australia and United States: Harwood Academic, 1995); Emil Schürer, *The History of the Jewish People in the Age of Jesus Christ (75 B.C.–A.D. 135),* rev. and ed. Géza Vermès and Fergus Millar, trans. T. A. Burkhill et al., 3 vols. (Edinburgh: Clark, 1973–1986) (a crucial text); Martin Hengel, *Judaism and Hellenism: Studies in Their Encounter in Palestine during the Early Hellenistic Period,* trans. John Bowden, 2 vols. (Philadelphia: Fortress Press, 1974); Marcel Simon and André Benoît, *Le judaïsme et le christianisme antiques, d'Antiochus Épiphane à Constantin* (Paris: Presses Universitaires de France, 1968; reprinted, with updated bibliography, 1985); Avigdor (Victor) Tcherikover, *Hellenistic Civilization and the Jews* (Philadelphia: Jewish Publication Society of America, 1959); Pierre Vidal-Naquet, "Les Juifs entre l'État et l'apocalypse," in *Rome et la conquête du monde méditerranéen: 264–27 avant J.-C.,* ed. Claude Nicolet, vol. 2 (Paris: Presses Universitaires de France, 1978); Édouard Will and Claude Orrieux, *Joudaïsmos-Hellenismos: Essai sur le judaïsme judéen à l'époque hellénistique* (Nancy: Presses Universitaires de Nancy, 1986). See also Sartre, *AZ,* pp. 303–370.

17. Elias Joseph Bikerman, *The God of the Maccabees: Studies on the Meaning and Origin of the Maccabean Revolt,* trans. Horst R. Moehring (Leiden: E. J. Brill, 1979; originally published 1937); Thomas Fischer, *Seleukiden und Makkabäer: Beiträge zur Seleukidengeschichte und zu den politischen Ereignissen in Judäa während der 1. Hälfte des 2. Jahrhunderts v. Chr.* (Bochum: In Kommission beim Studienverlag Dr. Norbert Brochmeyer, 1980); Klaus Bringmann, *Hellenistische*

Reform und Religionsverfolgung in Judäa: Eine Untersuchung zur jüdisch-hellenistichen-Geschichte (175–163 v. Chr.) (Göttingen: Vandenhoeck & Ruprecht, 1983); Bezalel Bar-Kochva, *Judas Maccabaeus: The Jewish Struggle against the Seleucids* (Cambridge: Cambridge University Press, 1989); Shaye J. D. Cohen, "Religion, Ethnicity and 'Hellenism' in the Emergence of Jewish Identity in Maccabean Palestine," in *Religion and Religious Practice in the Seleucid Kingdom,* ed. Per Bilde, Troels Engberg, Lise Hannestad, and Jan Zahle (Aarhus: Aarhus University Press, 1990), pp. 204–223; Niels Hyldahl, "The Maccabean Rebellion and the Question of 'Hellenization,'" in Bilde et al., *Religion and Religious Practice,* pp. 188–203.

18. This was the term used for Hellenized Jews who supported the reforms of Jason and his rival Menelas.

19. Édouard Will, "Pour une anthropologie coloniale du monde hellénistique," in *The Craft of the Ancient Historian: Essays in Honor of Chester G. Starr,* ed. John W. Eadie and Josiah Ober (Lanham, Md.: University Press of America, 1985), pp. 273–301.

20. Documentation collected and translated, with commentary, by Xavier Durand, *Des Grecs en Palestine au IIIe siècle avant Jésus-Christ: Le dossier syrien des archives de Zénon de Caunos* (Paris: J. Gabalda, 1997).

21. This was notably the case in Egypt and in the lands held by the Ptolemies in Syria, where the rulers adopted a monetary standard different from the Attic standard chosen by Alexander, and instituted a monopoly on the circulation of royal currency. Elsewhere, with few exceptions, all currencies circulated freely.

22. All the sources and all the available information are found in Will, *HP* 2, pp. 365–379, 404–416, 445–459.

23. From a vast and often repetitive bibliography, I am drawing on a certain number of works that can serve as fairly reliable guides (I shall not cite these systematically in the notes). Félix-Marie Abel, *Histoire de la Palestine depuis la conquête d'Alexandre jusqu'à l'invasion arabe,* vol. 1 (Paris: J. Gabalda, 1952), does not go much beyond the level of narrative, faithful to Josephus, and is now by and large outdated. Solomon Zeitlin, *The Rise and Fall of the Judaean State,* 3 vols. (Philadelphia: Jewish Publication Society of America, 1962–1978), is the most thorough (only the first volume deals with the Hasmonaeans). Davies and Finkelstein's *Hellenistic Age* covers much more than the Hasmonaean state, but in that volume there are original points of view on the subject in the article by Jonathan A. Goldstein, "The Hasmonean Revolt and the Hasmonean Dynasty," pp. 292–351. Joseph Sievers (*The Hasmoneans and Their Supporters: From Mattathias to the Death of John Hyrcanus I* [Atlanta: Scholars Press, 1990]) is interested in the political and social milieu, but he also gives an account of the events. Two original collections that combine texts, bibliographies, and synthetic elements are very useful: Lester L. Grabbe, *Judaism from Cyrus to Hadrian,* 2 vols. (Minneapolis: Fortress Press, 1991), and Louis H. Feldman and Meyer Reinhold, *Jewish Life and Thought among Greeks and Romans: Primary Readings* (Minneapolis: Fortress Press, 1996).

24. 1 Macc. 11.67–87. For Ascalon, the situation is unclear: the inhabitants greeted him with pomp and ceremony, and Jonathan seems to have been satisfied with that formal submission. Josephus's more detailed parallel account in *De antiquitate judaico (Jewish Antiquities),* trans. Louis H. Feldman (Loeb Classical Library), 13.91–102 (hereafter cited as *AJ*), is corrupted by the fact that Josephus believes that Apollonios was fighting on behalf of Alexander Balas, whereas Apollonios was ac-

tually the strategist appointed by Demetrios II (or won over to his cause and confirmed in his role).

25. 1 Macc. 11.30; Josephus, *AJ* 13.127–128. We have to conclude that the donation made by Demetrios I (1 Macc. 10.38) went unheeded, because it was renewed by Demetrios II.

26. Josephus, *AJ* 13.255. Yitzhak Magen believes that the destruction must have taken place a little later, around 112–111, at the same time as the destruction of Marisa and the Idumaean cities ("Mount Garizim and the Samaritans," in *Early Christianity in Context: Monuments and Documents,* ed. Frédéric Manns and Eugenio Alliata [Jerusalem: Franciscan Printing Press, 1993], pp. 142–143), but the discovery of coins from Ptolemais dating from 112–111 is fairly weak evidence.

27. Dan Barag, "New Evidence on the Foreign Policy of John Hyrcanus I," *Israel Numismatic Journal* (hereafter cited as *INJ*) 12 (1992–1993): 1–12.

28. Josephus, *AJ* 13.257–258, confirmed by the only extant fragment of Ptolemy, from "The History of King Herod," in *Greek and Latin Authors on Jews and Judaism,* ed. Menahem Stern, vol. 1 (Jerusalem: Israel Academy of Sciences and Humanities, 1974), no. 146; on the meaning of this more or less forced conversion, see Cohen, "Religion, Ethnicity, and 'Hellenism,'" especially pp. 211–218.

29. Josephus, *AJ* 13.275–281; cf. Josephus, *De bello judaico (The Jewish War),* trans. Henry St. John Thackeray (Loeb Classical Library), 1.64–66 (hereafter cited as *BJ*). John Hyrcanos's entire chronology is spelled out in Gérald Finkielsztejn, "More Evidence on John Hyrcanus I's Conquests: Lead Weights and Rhodian Amphora Stamps," *Bulletin of the Anglo-Israel Archaeological Society* 16 (1998): 33–63; Finkielsztejn combines archaeological discoveries with the text of Flavius Josephus.

30. A first embassy was sent by Hyrcanos in the early years of his reign; the exact date is uncertain. The names of the praetors cited in the document transmitted by Josephus (*AJ* 13.260–264) are those of 132, and the demand that the cities taken by Antiochos be evacuated may refer to the reconquest of Antiochos VII. But in "Hasmonean Revolt," p. 327, Goldstein situates the embassy in the second reign of Demetrios II, around 128–127, referring to Menahem Stern, "The Relations between Judea and Rome during the Rule of John Hyrcanus," *Zion* 26 (1961): 12–17 *(non vidi).* See also Thomas Fischer, *Untersuchungen zum Partherkrieg Antiochos' VII im Rahmen der Seleukidengeschichte* (Munich: n. p., 1970), pp. 73ff., and Will, *HP* 2, pp. 450–451.

31. 1 Macc. 15.16–24.

32. The coins attributed to Hyrcanos II, which the best specialists had credited for a long time to the reign of Alexander Jannaeus (see Ya'akov Meshorer, *Ancient Jewish Coinage* [Dix Hills, N.Y.: Amphora Books, 1982]), are now recognized as attributable at least in part to Hyrcanos I. See Dan Barag and Shraga Qedar, "The Beginning of Hasmonean Coinage," *INJ* 4 (1980): 16–19; Uriel Rappaport, "The Emergence of Hasmonean Coinage," *American Jewish Studies Review* 1 (1976): 171–186; idem, "Numismatics," in *Introduction: The Persian Period,* vol. 1 of *The Cambridge History of Judaism,* ed. William David Davies and Louis Finkelstein (Cambridge and New York: Cambridge University Press, 1984), pp. 35–38; and Ya'akov Meshorer's change of heart: "I am now convinced that the coins of . . . (YHW HNN) were struck by John Hyrcanus I" ("Ancient Jewish Coinage: Addendum I," *INJ* 11 [1990–1991]: 106). Another sign of independence: an alliance between the Jews and Athens around 106–105: Josephus, *AJ* 14.148–155.

33. The term *heber* is ambiguous.

34. On Jannaeus's external politics, see Menahem Stern, "Judaea and Her Neighbors in the Days of Alexander Jannaeus," in *The Jerusalem Cathedra,* ed. Lee I. Levine (Jerusalem: Yad Izhak Ben-Zvi / Wayne State University Press, 1981), pp. 22–46.

35. Josephus, *AJ* 13.356.

36. Ibid., 13.359–364.

37. Ibid., 13.375.

38. Will, *HP* 2, p. 450.

39. Josephus, *AJ* 13.392.

40. Ibid., 14.7.

41. For example, Daniel—though he was not a prophet, properly speaking.

42. Goldstein, "Hasmonean Revolt," pp. 325–326, 338.

43. One might think of Hama-Epiphania on the Orontes, but Kasher locates this Hammath in Lebo Hammath in the north of the Beqaa region, near the sources of the Orontes *(Jews, Idumaeans, and Ancient Arabs).*

44. Finkielsztejn, "More Evidence," pp. 38–41.

45. Josephus, *AJ* 13.397.

46. Pliny, *Natural History,* trans. H. Rackham (Loeb Classical Library), 35.58.200 (hereafter cited as *NH*).

47. Josephus, *AJ* 14.75, *BJ* 1.155.

48. Thomas Weber, "Gadarenes in Exile: Two Inscriptions from Greece Reconsidered," *Zeitschrift des deutschen Palästina-Vereins* 112 (1996): 10–17.

49. Uriel Rappaport, "Les Iduméens en Égypte," *Revue de philologie, de littérature et d'histoire anciennes* 43 (1969): 71–82; Dorothy J. Thompson Crawford, "The Idumaeans of Memphis and the Ptolemaic *Politeumata,*" *Atti del XVII Congresso internazionale di papirologia* (Naples: Centro internazionale per lo studio dei papiri ercolanesi, 1984), pp. 1069–1075.

50. According to 1 Macc. 13.43–53, however, Gezer was repopulated after 143.

51. Paul W. Lapp, *Palestinian Ceramic Chronology, 200 B.C.–70 A.D.* (New Haven, Conn.: American Schools of Oriental Research, 1961), p. 230; Moti Aviam, "The Hasmoneans in Galilee," in *Yeme bet Hashmonai* (The Hasmonean Period), ed. David Amit and Hanan Eshel (Jerusalem: Yad Izhak Ben-Zvi Institute, 1995), pp. 257–258 (in Hebrew; *non vidi*).

52. S. S. Weinberg, "Tel Anafa: The Hellenistic Town," *Israel Exploration Journal* 21 (1971): 97. The site was abandoned around 80 B.C.E. and reoccupied on a more modest scale around 40 B.C.E.

53. Friedrich Hiller von Gaertringen, *Inschriften von Priene* (Berlin: G. Reimer, 1906), no. 108.

54. Arthur Ernest Cowley, "Inscriptions from Southern Palestine. Greek: Nabatean: Arabic. II. Semitic," *Palestine Exploration Fund, Annual* 3 (1914–1915): 145–147.

55. Frank M. Cross Jr. hesitates between the third century and the identification with the tyrant Aretas mentioned in 2 Macc. 5.8 ("The Oldest Manuscripts from Qumram," *Journal of Biblical Literature* 74 [1955]: 160, n. 25); Jósef Tadeusz Milik comes down in favor of the third century (cited in Jean Starcky, "Pétra et la Nabatène," in *Dictionnaire de la Bible,* suppl. 7 [Paris: Letouzey & Ané, 1996], col. 904).

56. 2 Macc. 5.8.

57. Javier Teixidor, "Les Nabatéens du Sinaï," in *Le Sinaï durant l'Antiquité et le Moyen-Âge: Proceedings of the Colloquium "Sinai," UNESCO, Sept. 19–21, 1997,* ed. Dominique Valbelle and Charles Bonnet (Paris: Errance, 1998), pp. 83–87.

58. 1 Macc. 5.25.

59. The principal episodes in this battle have been noted above. A systematic study of the Hasmonaean period as a whole, with maps and bibliography, can be found in Kasher, *Jews, Idumaeans, and Ancient Arabs,* pp. 34–125.

60. Académie des inscriptions et belles-lettres, ed., *Corpus inscriptionum semiticarum* (Paris: e Reipublicae Typographeo, 1881; repr., Paris: C. Klincksieck, 1972), vol. 2, no. 349 (hereafter cited as *CIS*); according to scripture, this Aretas must have been Aretas III; as for the date, however, see below.

61. Diodoros, *Diodorus of Sicily,* trans. C. H. Oldfather (Loeb Classical Library), 3.43.4–5 (hereafter cited as Diodoros); there is probably an allusion to the same events in Strabo, *The Geography,* trans. Horace Leonard Jones (Loeb Classical Library), 16.4.8 (hereafter cited as Strabo).

62. Josephus, *AJ* 13.360.

63. Justinus, *Epitome of the Philippic History of Pompeius Trogus,* ed. Robert Develin, trans. J. C. Yardley (Atlanta: Scholars Press, 1994), 39.5.5–6 (hereafter cited as Justinus): he is said to have had seven hundred sons by his concubines!

64. Gustaf Dalman, *Neue Petra-Forschungen und der heilige Felsen von Jerusalem* (Leipzig: J. C. Hinrich, 1912), no. 90; an early date strikes Starcky as quite plausible, on the basis of the handwriting ("Pétra et la Nabatène," col. 906).

65. Josephus, *AJ* 13.375, *BJ* 1.90; see also Maria Giulia Amadasi Guzzo and Eugenia Equini Schneider, *Petra,* trans. Lydia G. Cochrane (Chicago: University of Chicago Press, 2002; originally published 1997), p. 25.

66. Milik (cited in Starcky, "Pétra et la Nabatène," col. 906) believes with good reason that it was indeed Obodas I who took on divine status and became Obodas the god, as is indicated in a passage by Stephanus of Byzantion describing Oboda: "Oboda: Nabataean town where, according to Uranius in the fifth book of his *Arabica,* King Obodas, whom they viewed as a god, is buried" (*Ethnica,* ed. August Meineke [Graz: Akademische Druck und Verlagsanstalt, 1958], s.v. "Oboda"). Milik thinks this was the result of Obodas I's victory over Antiochos XII, which is possible, but Obodas may also have been divinized as the founding hero of the city.

67. Kasher, *Jews, Idumaeans, and Ancient Arabs,* p. 80; see also Avraham Negev, *The Architecture of Oboda: Final Report* (Jerusalem: Institute of Archaeology, Hebrew University of Jerusalem, 1997), p. 1: the site was occupied sporadically in the fourth and third centuries B.C.E.

68. Josephus, *AJ* 13.391, *BJ* 1.100–102. Josephus identifies Cana as the closest village, where the retreating army took refuge.

69. Laïla Nehmé and François Villeneuve seem certain that the king in question was Obodas I (*Pétra: Métropole de l'Arabie antique* [Paris: Le Seuil, 1999], p. 134); following Milik, they associate his divinization with this victory (see above, n. 66).

70. Uranius in Félix Jacoby, *Die Fragmente der griechischen Historiker* (Leiden: E. J. Brill, 1958), vol. 3C, 675 F 25.

71. In any event, Uranius's account is erroneous; but there is no way to know whether the name of the Macedonian king is correct or whether that king died in the battle. If we opt for Antigonos, we gain by learning the name of the Nabataean dynast of 312.

72. Josephus, *AJ* 13.392, *BJ* 1.103.

73. Ibid.

74. A philosopher and friend of Strabo, who cites him as a firsthand witness to Petra in this passage (Strabo, 16.4.21).

75. Javier Teixidor disagrees: he sees this nomenclature as normal in a self-contained tribal world ("Le campement: Ville des Nabatéens," *Semitica* 43–44 [1995]: 114).

76. In 4 B.C.E., in a dedication from Sidon (*CIS*, vol. 2, no. 160); in 37 B.C.E., in Madaba, two strategoi, father and son (ibid., no. 196); in 39 B.C.E., two brothers, strategoi in the Moab region (ibid., no. 195); in Hegra, three strategoi (ibid., nos. 213, 214, 235).

77. In Hegra (ibid., no. 214).

78. In Madaba (ibid., no. 196).

79. The key work on the subject is Ya'akov Meshorer's *Nabataean Coins* (Jerusalem: Institute of Archaeology, Hebrew University of Jerusalem, 1975), with corrections by Alla Kushnir-Stein and Haim Gitler, "Numismatic Evidence from Tel Beer-Sheva and the Beginning of the Nabatean Coinage," *INJ* 12 (1992–1993): 13–20.

80. Meshorer, *Nabataean Coins,* pp. 16–20.

81. This interpretation was proposed by Edward Stanley Gotch Robinson, "Coins from Petra, etc.," *Numismatic Chronicle* (1936): 288–291, and has been widely accepted; coinage of this type has been found nowhere but in the Nabataean kingdom and its immediate environs.

82. Barag and Qedar, "Beginning of Hasmonean Coinage," pp. 16–19; Rappaport, "Numismatics," pp. 35–37.

83. Cf. Crystal-M. Bennett, "Notes and News (Umm el Biyara)," *Palestine Exploration Quarterly* 99 (1966): 123–126; idem, "Fouilles d'Umm el-Biyara: Rapport préliminaire," *Revue biblique* 73 (1966): 372–403; idem, "Des fouilles à Umm el-Biyârah: Les Édomites à Pétra," *Bible et Terre Sainte* 84 (1966): 6–16.

84. Diodoros, 19.94–100.

85. On the urban development at Petra, see Nehmé and Villeneuve, *Pétra,* for a specialized bibliography.

86. See Laïla Nehmé, "Le site dans son milieu naturel," *Le monde de la Bible* 127 (May–June 2000): 30–31.

87. Rolf A. Stucky, "The Nabataean House and the Urbanistic System of the Habitation Quarters in Petra," *Studies in the History and Archaeology of Jordan* (hereafter cited as *SHAJ*) 5 (1995): 193–198.

88. In *The Architecture of Petra* (Oxford: Oxford University Press, 1990), Judith McKenzie establishes the relative chronology of several groups of buildings, but she leaves aside the large number of simple facades; nevertheless, the oldest dated *triclinium* (triclinium 21) goes back to the very beginning of the first century B.C.E. (pp. 33–34); she attributes an early date to the famous Khazneh, sometime during the first century B.C.E. or even earlier (p. 51); see also Judith McKenzie and Angela Phippen, "The Chronology of the Principal Monuments at Petra," *Levant* 19 (1987): 145–165.

89. Alix Barbet, "Les caractéristiques de la peinture murale à Pétra," *SHAJ* 5 (1998): 383–389.

90. In the southern section of the large paved street of the lower city. Peter J. Parr has identified eighteen phases of development, corresponding to three major periods

of the city's history; the first eight phases, which antedated Aretas IV, include only small constructions ("A Sequence of Pottery from Petra," in *Near Eastern Archaeology in the Twentieth Century: Essays in Honor of Nelson Glueck,* ed. James A. Saunders [Garden City, N.Y.: Doubleday, 1970], pp. 348–381).

91. Kasher, *Jews, Idumaeans, and Ancient Arabs,* p. 90. Kasher situates this capture before the seizure of Gaza, following the indication in Josephus (*AJ* 13.357) that Gaza was isolated at the time it was taken by Jannaeus in 100. But this interpretation is somewhat forced.

92. It was included among the cities taken by Jannaeus that Hyrcanos II returned to Aretas III in exchange for the latter's help against Aristobulos: see Josephus, *AJ* 14.18. The observation that the site seems to have been occupied by the Nabataeans without interruption (Kasher, *Jews, Idumaeans, and Ancient Arabs,* p. 98) is not a reason to doubt that the restitution took place at this relatively late date, for Jannaeus's political domination did not prevent the Nabataean population from continuing to live on the site. Kasher once again situates Elusa among the conquests made at the very end of Jannaeus's reign (p. 102).

93. See Avraham Negev, "'Avdat—1989," *Excavations and Surveys in Israel* 12 (1993): 108–109. The identity of the god is given in an inscription from the third century B.C.E. mentioning the reparation of the "House of Aphrodite"; it may be a temple devoted to al-Uzza.

94. See Burton MacDonald, *The Southern Ghors and Northeast 'Arabah Archaeological Survey* (Sheffield: J. R. Collis, Department of Archaeology and Prehistory, University of Sheffield, 1992), pp. 83–95; Rudolf Cohen, "Hellenistic, Roman, and Byzantine Sites in the Negev Hills," in *The New Encyclopedia of Archaeological Excavations in the Holy Land,* ed. Ephraim Stern, vol. 3 (New York: Simon & Schuster, 1993), pp. 1135–1145.

95. Andrew M. Smith II, Michelle Stevens, and Tina M. Niemi have identified fifty-one sites where this association of ceramics is found ("The Southeast Araba Archaeological Survey: A Preliminary Report of the 1994 Season," *Bulletin of the American School of Oriental Research* 305 [1997]: 45–71).

96. On this campaign in Idumaea by Hyrcanos II, see Josephus, *BJ* 1.63. Josephus mentions only the destruction of Adora and Marisa, but he notes that many other cities were taken; cf. the numismatic testimony in Kushnir-Stein and Gitler, "Numismatic Evidence," pp. 13–20.

97. Significant excavations are in progress under the direction of S. Thomas Parker; see Parker, "The Roman 'Aqaba Project: The 1996 Campaign," *Annual of the Department of Antiquities of Jordan* (hereafter cited as *ADAJ*) 42 (1998): 375–394.

98. See Yousef Ghawanmeh, "The Port of Aqaba and Its Role in the Indian Ocean Trade in Ancient and Medieval Times," *ADAJ* 30 (1986): 311–318; Fawzi Zayadine, "Ayla-'Aqaba in the Light of Recent Excavations," *ADAJ* 38 (1994): 485–505.

99. Strabo, 16.2.3.

100. On the borders of Commagene, see David French, "Commagene: Territorial Definitions," in *Studien zum antiken Kleinasien,* in *Asia Minor Studien,* vol. 3 (Bonn: R. Habelt, 1991), pp. 11–19.

101. See Margherita Facella's excellent demonstration in "Basileus Arsames: Sulla storia dinastica di Commagene," *Studi Ellenistici* 12 (2000): 127–158, especially on the identification of Arsames of Commagene with Arsames of Armenia.

102. Strabo, 11.14.15.

103. Diodoros, 31.19a.

104. On the birth and development of the Commagene dynasty, see Richard D. Sullivan, "The Dynasty of Commagene," *ANRW* 2.8 (1977): 732–763, for the period that concerns us here; and Richard D. Sullivan, *Near Eastern Royalty and Rome, 100–30 bc* (Toronto: University of Toronto Press, 1990), pp. 59–62. One can of course speculate about the actual dynastic ties between Ptolemaios and the third-century Commagene kings Samos and Arsames: Ptolemaios might just as well have created a fictitious lineage intended to legitimize his royal authority in the eyes of the indigenous aristocracy attached to the Iranian origins of the dynasty. The very name *Ptolemaios* would argue instead in favor of a Macedonian sent to Commagene as a representative of the Seleucid king, but the onomastic argument is not conclusive.

105. Diodoros, 31.19a.

106. Inscription in Arsameia (now Gerger): Louis Jalabert and René Mouterde, *Inscriptions grecques et latines de la Syrie* (hereafter cited as *IGLS*), vol. 1., *Commagène et Cyrrhestique* (Paris: P. Geuthner, 1929), no. 46, and Wilhelm Dittenberger, ed., *Orientis graeci inscriptiones selectae: Supplementum sylloges inscriptionum graecarum*, 2 vols. (Hildesheim and New York: G. Olms, 1986; 1st ed. 1903–1905), no. 402 (hereafter cited as *OGIS*), corrected by Helmut Waldmann, *Die kommagenischen Kultreformen unter König Mithradates I. Kallinikos und seinem Sohne Antiochos I* (Leiden: E. J. Brill, 1973), p. 141, no. Gf, and Friedrich Karl Dörner, cited in Sullivan, "Dynasty of Commagene," p. 749, n. 58.

107. Seleucos VI, Antiochos XI, Antiochos XII, Philip I, and Demetrios III?

108. See Friedrich Karl Dörner, Theresa Goell, and Wolfram Hoepfner, *Arsameia am Nymphaios* (Berlin: Gebr. Mann, 1963), pl. 48, identified as Mithradate I Kallinikos; but in an inscription published by Jörg Wagner and Georg Petzl ("Eine neue Temenos-Stele des Königs Antiochos I. von Kommagene," *Zeitschrift für Papyrologie und Epigraphik* 20 [1976]: 213), Antiochos I declares that he was the first to wear the *kitaris*, as the Armenian tiara is called.

109. Cf. the royal portraits and the inscriptions from Nemrut Dag that show the dynasty going back to Darius I: *OGIS*, nos. 388, 389, 391–394.

110. Eratosthenes is cited in Strabo, 14.2.29; cf. Franz-Heinrich Weissbach, "Samosata," in August Friedrich von Pauly et al., *Realencyclopädie der classischen Altertumwissenschaft* (Stuttgart: J. B. Metzler, 1894–).

111. In the great inscription at Arsameia, Antiochos I himself declares that Arsameia of Nymphaios was founded by his ancestor Arsames (lines 15–16); for the *complete* text and commentary, see Dörner, Goell, and Hoepfner, *Arsameia am Nymphaios*, p. 40 (text) and pp. 70–72 (commentary on this passage); cf. Facella, "Basileus Arsames."

112. We should doubtless add Arsamosata of Sophene: see Facella, "Basileus Arsames," pp. 135–136.

113. Jalabert and Mouterde, *IGLS*, vol. 1, nos. 1, 2, 5, and so forth.

114. See Will, *HP* 2, p. 407.

115. See Charles Bradford Welles, "The Chronology of Dura Europos," *Eos: Commentarii Societatis philologae polonorum* 48 (1956): 469. The scrupulous examination of the coins found has not brought decisive proof, but it has not led to a better solution, either: see Alfred Raymond Bellinger, *The Excavations at Dura Europos: Final Report*, vol. 6, *The Coins* (New Haven: Yale University Press, 1949), p. 201.

116. See Will, *HP* 2, p. 452.

117. See Édouard Will, "Rome et les Séleucides," *ANRW* 1.1 (1972): 590–632.

118. On the critical micro-Asiatic aspects, see Maurice Sartre, *L'Anatolie hellénistique, de l'Egée au Caucase: 334–31 av. J.-C.* (Paris: A. Colin, 2003), pp. 49–52, 59–64.

119. On this campaign, which did not involve Syria directly, see Will, *HP* 2, pp. 320–325.

120. The episode is related most notably in Polybios, *The Histories,* trans. W. R. Paton (Loeb Classical Library), 29.27 (hereafter cited as Polybios); Livy, *Works,* vol. 13, trans. Alfred C. Schlesinger (Loeb Classical Library), 45.12; Appianus, *The Syrian Wars,* in *Roman History,* trans. Horace White (Loeb Classical Library), 66; Josephus, *AJ* 12.244.

121. Nick Sekunda, *Seleucid and Ptolemaic Reformed Armies,* vol. 1, *The Seleucid Army under Antiochus IV Epiphanes* (Stockport: Montvert, 1994), p. 16.

122. Gualtiero Calboli, ed., *Cornifici Rhetorica ad C. Herennium* (Bologna: Pàtron, 1993), 4.13; this text dates from 91–89 B.C.E., but the expression is found earlier in Polybios.

123. See Israel Shatzman, "The Integration of Judaea into the Roman Empire," *Scripta classica israelica* 18 (1999): 49–84, especially 54–58.

124. 2 Macc. 11.34–37.

125. Polybios, 31.11. Gnaius Octavius and his colleagues were responsible for enforcing the clauses of the peace of Apamaea, which had been ignored: the orders were to destroy the armored warships and hamstring the elephants (31.2).

126. This was the explicit mission of the commissaries sent in 163–162, according to Polybios: "by every means to cripple the royal power" (31.2).

127. See Sartre, *Anatolie,* pp. 222–232.

128. Strabo, 11.14.15, followed by Appian, *Syrian Wars,* 48.

129. The city began minting coins in 76–75: Henri Seyrig, "Sur les ères de quelques villes de Syrie," *Syria* 27 (1950): 18 (= Henri Seyrig, *Antiquités syriennes* [Paris: P. Geuthner, 1934–], vol. 4, art. 42, p. 85 [hereafter cited as *AS*]).

130. See *AS,* vol. 4, pp. 92ff., 105.

131. Frédérique Duyrat, "Arados hellénistique" (Ph.D. diss, Université de Paris IV, 2000), pp. 591–592; forthcoming from Beirut: Bibliothèque archéologique et historique.

132. Justinus, 40.1.4.

133. As the bronzes did not circulate much outside the city's territory, this doubtless proves that the coins were picked up by Tigranes' agents on the periphery of Arados, since the Armenian king never controlled the city itself.

134. On overstruck coins, see Y. T. Nercessian and L. A. Saryan, "Overstruck and Countermarked Coins of the Artaxiad Dynasty of Armenia," *Armenian Numismatic Journal* 22 (June 1996): 21–62 *(non vidi),* cited in Duyrat, *Arados hellénistique,* pp. 586–587; on their significance for Arados, see ibid., pp. 586–592. A catalog of Tigranes' coins can be found in François de Callataÿ, *L'histoire des guerres mithridatiques vue par les monnaies* (Louvain-la-Neuve: Département d'archéologie et d'histoire de l'art, Séminaire numismatique Marcel Hoc, 1997).

135. Jules van Ooteghem, *Lucius Licinius Lucullus* (Brussels: Académie royale de Belgique, 1959), pp. 117–138; Arthur Keaveney, *Lucullus: A Life* (London: Routledge, 1992), pp. 98–128.

2. THE END OF SELEUCID SYRIA AND THE FIRST ROMAN RULE (69–31 B.C.E.)

1. Jean-Marie Dentzer, "L'espace des tribus arabes à l'époque hellénistique et romaine: Nomadisme, sédentarisation, urbanisation," *Comptes rendus des séances de l'Académie des inscriptions et belles-lettres* (1999): 251; Frank Braemer, Jean-Marie Dentzer, Michael Kalos, and Philippe Tondon, "Tours à noyau chemisé de Syrie du Sud," *Syria* 76 (1999): 151–176. These authors hesitate between a cultic interpretation and a defensive use, but they lean rather toward the latter.

2. Josephus, *De antiquitate judaico (Jewish Antiquities)*, trans. Louis H. Feldman (Loeb Classical Library), 14.38–40 (hereafter cited as *AJ*).

3. Cf. Josephus, *AJ* 13.356, and idem, *De bello judaico (The Jewish War)*, trans. Henry St. John Thackeray (Loeb Classical Library) (hereafter cited as *BJ*); see also Pierre-Louis Gatier, "Philadelphie et Gérasa du royaume nabatéen à la province d'Arabie," in *Géographie historique au Proche-Orient: Actes de la table ronde de Valbonne, 16–18 septembre 1985*, ed. Pierre-Louis Gatier, Bruno Helly, and Jean-Paul Rey-Coquais (Paris: Centre national de la recherche scientifique, 1988), pp. 159–170.

4. Strabo, *The Geography*, trans. Horace Leonard Jones (Loeb Classical Library), 16.2.7 (hereafter cited as Strabo).

5. Josephus, *AJ* 13.384.

6. Josephus, *AJ* 13.324: the name may be either Greek or indigenous; in a rare bilingual Greco-Armenian inscription from Tel Dan, the Greek name *Zoilos* is used to transcribe *Silas*.

7. Mentioned in Strabo, 16.2.28.

8. As was the case for Side of Pamphylia, according to Strabo, 14.3.2.

9. Ibid., 16.2.14.

10. Ibid., 16.2.18.

11. It is usually located in Anjar, in the central Beqaa, but Chaker Ghadban locates it in Chadura ("Monuments de Hammara," *Ktema* 10 [1985]: 301, n. 52), while Pierre-Louis Gatier puts it in Majdel ("Phénicie, Liban, Levant: Histoire et géographie historique d'Alexandre à Zénobie," *Annales d'histoire et archéologie, Université Saint-Joseph* 10–11 [1999–2000]: 103–115).

12. The link between the two is established by Strabo, who mentions the Ituraeans both in the Beqaa and in the "two Trachones" south of Damascus (16.2.18–20).

13. Josephus, *AJ* 13.384.

14. Diodoros, *Diodorus of Sicily*, trans. C. H. Oldfather (Loeb Classical Library), 40.1a–1b (hereafter cited as Diodoros).

15. Strabo, 16.2.11.

16. Strabo, 16.2.10.

17. We do not know where these Arabs came from, despite the views expressed earlier by Joshua Benzion Segal, who credited them with a Nabataean origin based on names ending in -*u*: see Joshua Benzion Segal, *Edessa, "The Blessed City"* (Oxford: Clarendon Press, 1970), p. 16. The traditions recorded in the chronicle of Pseudo-Dionysios of Tell Mahre give a certain Orhai b. Hewya—clearly an eponymous name—as ancestor of the dynasty; but Pliny knew the tribe as the Orroei (Pliny, *Natural History*, trans. H. Rackham [Loeb Classical Library], 5.20.85 [hereafter cited as *NH*]). It is much more interesting to note that these Arabs created a prin-

cipality in a Greek city, an important relay station for Seleucid royal power (a coin-making workshop has been found there), and that the dominant language was not Arabic but Edessene (or Syrian) Aramaic.

18. A suggestion by Jean Starcky, in "Stèle d'Élahagabal," *Mélanges de l'Université Saint-Joseph* 49 (1975–1976): 510–511. Starcky believes that the mountain god, who was worshipped by the Emesenes during the imperial era, originated in the same region as the Emeseni tribe, and not in their mountainless Syrian habitat; he notes several deities of the same style in southeastern Anatolia, especially in Commagene, with Jupiter Turmasgadus honored in Dacia by Commagene archers (Hermann Dessau, *Inscriptiones latinae selectae* [Berlin: Weidmann, 1892–1916], no. 9273).

19. Diodoros includes this detail after a discussion of Larissa of the Orontes (33.4a); Josephus calls him Malchos (*AJ* 13.131).

20. Strabo, 16.2.10. Cf. Pierre-Louis Gatier, "Palmyre et Émèse ou Émèse sans Palmyre," in "Palmyra and the Silk Road: International Colloquium, Palmyra, 7–11 April 1992," special issue, *Annales archéologiques arabes syriennes* 42 (1996): 431–436; Gatier suggests that there was a city of some size before the arrival of the Emeseni, who are thought to have taken over the site while adopting (and adapting) the local gods. Until excavations are carried out in the ancient tell, we shall remain ignorant on this point.

21. See Hartel Pohl, *Die römische Politik und der Piraterie im östlichen Mittelmeer vom 3. bis 1. Jh. v. Chr.* (Berlin and New York: W. de Gruyter, 1993).

22. On all this, see Maurice Sartre, *L'Anatolie hellénistique, de l'Egée au Caucase: 334–31 av. J.-C.* (Paris: A. Colin, 2003), pp. 218–219; on piracy in the Mediterranean, Pohl offers an abundant bibliography in *Römische Politik*.

23. On the law on piracy in Cnidos, see Mark Hasall, Michael Crawford, and Joyce Reynolds, "Rome and the Eastern Provinces at the End of the Second Century B.C.: The So-Called 'Piracy Law' and a New Inscription from Cnidos," *Journal of Roman Studies* 64 (1974): 195–220; Jean-Louis Ferrary, "Recherches sur la législation de Saturninus et de Glaucia. I: La *lex de piratis* de Delphes et de Cnide," *Mélanges de l'École française de Rome: Antiquités* 89 (1977): 619–660; G. V. Sumner, "The 'Piracy Law' from Delphi and the Law of the Cnidos Inscription," *Greek, Roman and Byzantine Studies* 19 (1978): 211–225; the text of the law is in Wolfgang Blümel, ed., *Die Inschriften von Knidos* (Bonn: R. Habelt, 1992), no. 31; see also Pohl, *Römische Politik*, and Stefano Framonti, *Hostes communes omnium: La pirateria e la fine della republica romana (145–33 a. C.)* (Ferrara: Università degli studi di Ferrara, 1994).

24. Strabo puts the Arabs' exactions and those allegedly carried out by the Armenians on the same level (16.1.26); however, he is the only ancient author who notes pillaging by the Armenians.

25. On the attempt to specify the location, see Louis Dillemann, *Haute Mésopotamie orientale et pays adjacents* (Paris: P. Geuthner, 1962), pp. 247–272: Dilleman argues for a site in Mygdonia, west of Nisibis; the exact location remains unknown. See Marie-Louise Chaumont, "Quelques notes concernant Tigranocerte," *Revue des études arméniennes*, 21 (1988–1989): 233–249.

26. On all this, see Appianus, *The Syrian Wars*, trans. Horace White, in *Roman History*, vol. 2 (Loeb Classical Library), 48–49 and 69–70; see also Justinus, *Epitome of the Philippic History of Pompeius Trogus*, ed. Robert Develin, trans. J. C. Yardley (Atlanta: Scholars Press, 1994), 40.2.2 (hereafter cited as Justinus).

27. Arthur Keaveney is probably right to emphasize that Lucullus went along with this but did not take the initiative (*Lucullus: A Life* [London: Routledge, 1992], p. 111).

28. On Lucullus's anti-Tigranes policy, see Jules van Ooteghem, *Lucius Licinius Lucullus* (Brussels: Académie royale de Belgique, 1959), pp. 117–138; this remains the fundamental study. See also Édouard Will, *Histoire politique du monde hellénistique*, 2nd ed. (Nancy: Presses Universitaires de Nancy, 1979–1982), vol. 2, pp. 494–498 (hereafter cited as *HP*), and Keaveney, *Lucullus*, pp. 99–112.

29. For the Rhambaeans, see Cassius Dio, *Roman History*, trans. Earnest Cary (Loeb Classical Library), 36.2.5 (hereafter cited as Dio); cf. Strabo, 16.2.10.

30. On Lucullus's political difficulties, see Ooteghem, *Lucullus*, pp. 139–165, and Keaveney, *Lucullus*, pp. 112–128.

31. See Sartre, *Anatolie*, pp. 231–232.

32. See Will, *HP* 2, p. 488.

33. See Francesco Paolo Rizzo, *Le fonti per la storia della conquista pompeiana della Siria, Kôkalos,* suppl. 3 (Palermo: Banco de Sicilia, Fondazione per l'incremento economico culturale e turistica della Sicilia Ignazio Mormino, 1963); Rizzo showed the link between the various authors who deal with Pompey's eastern conquest and the weight of Pompeian propaganda.

34. See Cicero, "The Speech Addressed to His Fellow-Citizens by Marcus Tullius Cicero on the Appointment of Gnaeus Pompeius," trans. H. Grose Hodge, in *Cicero,* vol. 9 (Loeb Classical Library), pp. 14–83. On Pompey in the east, see the classic biography by Jules van Ooteghem, *Pompée le Grand, bâtisseur d'Empire* (Brussels: n. p., 1954); on the struggle against pirates, see ibid., pp. 159–181; see also Henry Arderne Ormerod, *Piracy in the Ancient World* (Liverpool: University Press of Liverpool, 1924; repr., New York, 1987; Baltimore, 1997), and Pohl, *Römische Politik.*

35. Cf. Appianus, *The Mithradatic Wars,* trans. Horace White, in *Appian,* vol. 2 (Loeb Classical Library), 93–96.

36. Ooteghem offers a detailed commentary on the *lex* in *Pompée le Grand,* pp. 183–204.

37. See Sartre, *Anatolie,* p. 232.

38. Ooteghem, *Pompée le Grand,* p. 226–238.

39. Plutarch, "Pompey," in *Plutarch's Lives,* trans. Bernadotte Perrin, vol. 5 (Loeb Classical Library), 39.3 (hereafter cited as *Lives*); Joannes Zonaras, *Epitome historiarum,* ed. Ludwig Dindorf (Leipzig: B. G. Teubner, 1868–1875), 10.5.

40. Josephus, *BJ* 1.129.

41. Diodoros, 40.1a–1b.

42. Ibid.

43. P. Clodius, the envoy of Q. Marcius Rex, seems to have personally fomented an uprising of which he ended up a victim: see Dio, 36.17.3.

44. Appianus, *Syrian Wars,* 49–51; Appianus, *Mithradatic Wars,* 106; Justinus, 40.2.2–5; Porphyry, *Chronica,* in Félix Jacoby, *Die Fragmente der griechischen Historiker* (Leiden: E. J. Brill, 1958), no. 260 F 32 (27); John Malalas, *The Chronicle of John Malalas,* trans. Elizabeth Jeffreys, Michael Jeffreys, Roger Scott, et al. (Melbourne: Australian Association for Byzantine Studies, 1986), pp. 110–112 (5.211–213) (hereafter cited as Malalas). Only this last author asserts that Pompey restored Antiochos and that the latter bequeathed his kingdom to Rome when he died.

45. Plutarch, "Pompey," 39.2.

46. Nothing makes it more obvious that Pompey took Lucullus's decisions to be null and void than the fact that the new era in Antioch, which took the abolition of the Seleucid dynasty as its point of departure, began not in 64–63, at the moment when Pompey moved decisively to annex Syria, but in 66–65, when the defeated Tigranes yielded to Rome. This showed that Pompey held Syria directly from Tigranes, and that the Seleucid restoration ordered by Lucullus did not exist; see Henri Seyrig, "Sur les ères de quelques villes de Syrie," *Syria* 27 (1950): 10–11 (= Henri Seyrig, *Antiquités syriennes* [Paris: P. Geuthner, 1934–], vol. 4, pp. 77–78 [hereafter cited as *AS*]).

47. Appianus, *Syrian Wars*, 49.

48. Justinus, 40.2.3–4.

49. See Josef Dobiáš, "Les premiers rapports des Romains avec les Parthes et l'occupation de la Syrie," *Archiv orientalni* 3 (1931): 244; Marie-Thérèse Liebmann-Frankfort, *La frontière orientale dans la politique extérieure de la République romaine, depuis le traité d'Apamée jusqu'à la fin des conquêtes asiatiques de Pompée (189/8–63)* (Brussels: Palais des Académies, 1969), p. 288; Will, *HP* 2, pp. 508, 511.

50. Józef Wolski, "Les Parthes et la Syrie," *Acta Iranica*, 5 (1977): 395–417; Adrian Nicholas Sherwin-White, *Roman Foreign Policy in the East* (Norman: University of Oklahoma Press, 1984), pp. 213, 225; Pascal Arnaud, "Les guerres parthiques de Gabinius et de Crassus et la politique occidentale des Parthes Arsacides entre 70 et 53 av. J.-C.," *Electrum* 2 (1998): 23.

51. Josephus, *AJ* 13.385–386; Eusebius of Caesarea, *Chronicon*, ed. Alfred Schoene (Berlin: Weidmann, 1875–1876), p. 261; cf. Jerome, *Die Chronik des Hieronymus (Hieronymi Chronicon)*, in *Eusebius Werke*, ed. Rudolf Helm, vol. 7 (Berlin: Akademie-Verlag, 1956), p. 150.

52. As, for example, by Dobiáš in "Premiers rapports," pp. 215–256, especially pp. 244–256; Dobiáš stresses the dangers that piracy and banditry posed to Roman interests. In *Les trafiquants italiens dans l'Orient hellénique* (Paris: E. de Boccard, 1919), Jean Hatzfeld emphasizes the role of the Roman *negotiatores* (pp. 142, 374–375); see also Mikhail Ivanovitch Rostovtzeff, *Social and Economic History of the Hellenistic World*, vol. 2 (Oxford: Clarendon Press, 1941), p. 991.

53. See Philippe Bruneau, "Contribution à l'histoire urbaine de Délos à l'époque hellénique et à l'époque impériale," *Bulletin de Correspondance Hellénique* 92 (1968): 671–691.

54. On the annexation of Syria: in addition to Dobiáš, "Premiers rapports," see Alfred Raymond Bellinger, "The End of Seleucids," *Transactions of the Connecticut Academy of Arts and Sciences* 38 (1948): 51–102; Glanville Downey, "The Occupation of Syria by the Romans," *Transactions and Proceedings of the American Philological Society* (hereafter cited as *TAPA*) 82 (1951): 149–163; and Will, *HP* 2, pp. 508–517.

55. Will's view notwithstanding (*HP* 2, p. 509).

56. If Josephus follows geographical order, Lysias should be somewhere in the Beqaa or Anti-Lebanon region, but Strabo specifies that the citadel in question is located "above a lake near Apamea" (16.2.10); Lysias should therefore be sought in the vicinity of Apamaea.

57. Josephus, *AJ* 14.38–40.

58. Cf. Cicero, *Letters to Atticus,* trans. E. O. Winstedt, in *Cicero,* vol. 22 (Loeb Classical Library), 2.24, 2.16, 2.17, 2.23.

59. Dio, 40.20.

60. Appianus, *Mithradatic Wars,* 114; Strabo, 16.2.3.

61. This is the picture Josephus transmits, but he may be intentionally distorting the image so as to blame Hyrcanos for the disappearance of the national Jewish state; in particular, Josephus must be following Nicolaos of Damascus here. A friend of Herod's, Nicolaos was intent on bringing out Hyrcanos's weakness in order to legitimize the dynastic change in favor of the Herodians and to emphasize the preeminent role of Antipatros, Herod's father: see Daniel R. Schwartz, "Josephus on Hyrcanus II," in *Josephus and the History of the Greco-Roman Period: Essays in Memory of Morton Smith,* ed. Fausto Parente and Joseph Sievers (Leiden: E. J. Brill, 1994), pp. 210–232.

62. Dio, 37.15.2; Josephus, *AJ* 14.30 (mentioning four hundred talents) and *BJ* 1.128 (mentioning three hundred).

63. Josephus, *AJ* 14.33 and *BJ* 1.130. On all this, see Aryeh Kasher, *Jews, Idumaeans, and Ancient Arabs: Relations of the Jews in Eretz-Israel with the Nations of the Frontier and the Desert during the Hellenistic and Roman Era (332 bce–70 ce)* (Tübingen: J. C. B. Mohr, 1988), pp. 111–113. Kasher accepts the traditional localizing of Papyron in the Jordan Valley; there is no particular evidence in favor of this thesis except possibly the name, for papyrus is found only in this valley supplied with water.

64. Josephus, *AJ* 14.46; Pompey's objective can hardly have been anything but booty; cf. Maurice Sartre, "Rome et les Nabatéens à la fin de la République," *Revue des études anciennes* (hereafter cited as *REA*) 81 (1979): 37–53, demonstrating that no diplomatic argument could justify an expedition against Aretas III.

65. Josephus, *AJ* 14.48–73. Josephus left two parallel but rather different accounts of the relations between Pompey and the Jews, one in *BJ* 1.123–154, the other in *AJ* 13.398–14.97. In "Josephus, Pompey and the Jews," *Historia* 48 (1999): 94–118, Jane Bellemore sees the two narratives as diverging sharply enough to support a judgment that the one written first *(BJ)* represents a Jewish viewpoint, probably inspired by the local Jewish sources being used by Josephus at that time, whereas the second represents a Roman viewpoint, derived by Josephus from Nicolaos of Damascus, Strabo, and Livy.

66. These captives were doubtless in large part the original members of the Jewish community in Rome.

67. Josephus points out in overall terms that Pompey attached the cities of Coele Syria (a term that Josephus uses to designate the Decapolis in particular) to Syria, then he gives quite a long list of Palestinian cities without spelling out their status but indicating that they are the ones the Hasmonaeans did not have time to destroy (which is only partly true, for Samaria, Marisa, and Pella had been destroyed) (*BJ* 1.155–156).

68. It is clear that the sanctuary did not belong to Arados at the time privileges were granted by King Antiochos, one of the kings who bore this name at the end of the second or the beginning of the first century: the king never mentions the city-state, but recalls that the village belonged to a certain Demetrios of Tourgona. In contrast, in the decree sent to Augustus by the Aradians, which constitutes lines 32–39 of the inscription (Jean-Paul Rey-Coquais, *Inscriptions grecques et latines de la Syrie,*

vol. 7, *Arados et régions voisines* [Paris: P. Geuthner, 1970], no. 4028), the city-state does seem to control the sanctuary.

69. Pliny, *NH,* 35.58.200; Josephus, *AJ* 15.75, *BJ* 1.155.

70. Plutarch, in "Pompey," 40 (and also in "Cato the Younger," 13 [*Lives,* vol. 8, pp. 235–411]), and Julian, in "Misopogon, or Beard-Hater" (*The Works of the Emperor Julian,* trans. Wilmer Cave Wright, vol. 2 [Loeb Classical Library], 358b–c), report that Cato, arriving in Antioch with a delegation of Romans, was astonished and annoyed that the Antiochenes had prepared an official reception involving magistrates, priests, ephebes, and so on, when instead he had wanted to make a discreet entrance. He was all the more surprised to learn that the whole thing had been prepared because the Antiochenes were expecting Demetrios!

71. Dio, 39.38.6.

72. Demetrios may have been behind the construction of the north theater in Gadara: see Thomas Weber, "Pella Decapolitana: Untersuchungen zur Topographie, Geschichte und bildenden Kunst einer 'Polis Hellenis' in Ostjordanland" (Habilitation diss., Mayence, 1995) *(non vidi),* cited by Weber, "Gadarenes in Exile," p. 14, n. 48; I do not know to what extent this academic treatise by Thomas Weber differs from the book he published with a slightly different subtitle in Wiesbaden in 1993.

73. Alla [Kushnir-]Stein spells out with precision the various eras used in "Studies in Greek and Latin Inscriptions on the Palestinian Coinage under the Principate" (Ph.D. diss., Tel Aviv University, 1990).

74. Josephus, *AJ* 14.39.

75. The sources disagree as to when Pompey learned of Mithradates' death. According to Josephus, it was when Pompey was in the Jordan Valley (*BJ* specifies near Jericho), on his way to Jerusalem; in this view, Pompey let about three months elapse before he set out for the Pontus region—the period of time Josephus gives for the siege of the Temple (*AJ* 14.53, *BJ* 1.138). But according to Plutarch, after settling the Jewish business Pompey resumed his expedition against the Nabataeans and learned of Mithridates' death as he was approaching Petra ("Pompey," 41). Dio sets forth the facts in the reverse order: Pompey led a victorious campaign against Aretas, then turned toward Judaea, and finally left Syria for Pontus (37.15–20). We may note in passing that what is only a plan for Josephus—the expedition against Petra—becomes a quasi reality for Plutarch and a success for Dio! If the siege of Jerusalem took place at the end of the summer, it is unlikely that Pompey would have failed to learn of Mithradates' death before the beginning of the siege, since Mithradates died in spring 63.

76. Josephus, *BJ* 1.127–129.

77. In the biography he devotes to L. Marcius Philippus's father, *Lucius Marcius Philippus et sa famille* (Brussels: Palais des Académies, 1961), pp. 173–183, Jules van Ooteghem brings together various biographical elements concerning the Syrian legate.

78. The latter had been Pompey's legate in the struggle against the pirates; he was responsible for the vicinity of Corsica and the other islands of the Tyrrhenian sea: Appianus, *Mithradatic Wars,* 95.

79. Cicero's powerful brief in favor of recalling a man he detested is in "De provinciis consularibus," trans. R. Gardner, in *Cicero,* vol. 13 (Loeb Classical Library), pp. 523–610; see Eva Matthews Sanford, "The Career of Aulus Gabinius," *TAPA,* 70 (1939): 64–92.

80. Cicero, *Letters to Atticus,* 7.3 (Dec. 9, 50).

81. See the fine study by Michel Amandry, "Le monnayage en bronze de Bibulus, Atratinus et Capito: Une tentative de romanisation en Orient," *Schweizerische Numismatische Rundschau* 65 (1986): 73–85; 66 (1987): 101–112; 69 (1990): 65–96. L. Calpurnius Bibulus was governor of Syria in 32–31 and died in office.

82. Cicero, "De provinciis consularibus," 5.10; Velleius Paterculus, *History of Rome,* trans. Frederick W. Shipley (Loeb Classical Library), 2.37.5 (hereafter cited as Velleius Paterculus).

83. Caesar, *The Civil Wars,* trans. A. G. Peskett (Loeb Classical Library), 3.102.

84. Cicero, "Pro Sestio," trans. R. Gardner, in *Cicero,* vol. 12 (Loeb Classical Library), pp. 23–239, 8.18, 8–9.20, 43.93; "De provinciis consularibus," 4.9 and 5.10–11; "Letters to His Brother Quintus," in *Letters to His Friends,* trans. W. Glynn Williams, in *Cicero,* vol. 28 (Loeb Classical Library), 2.11.2–3 (dated Feb. 13, 54). Dio goes back to this topic (giving the figure of a hundred million deniers: 39.55.5, 39.56.1). On all this, see Maurice Sartre, "Romains et Italiens en Syrie: Contribution à l'histoire de la première province romaine de Syrie," in *The Greek East in the Roman Context: Proceedings of a Colloquium Organised by the Finnish Institute at Athens, May 21 and 22, 1999,* ed. Olli Salomies (Helsinki: Suomen Ateenan-instituutin Säätiö, 2001), pp. 127–140.

85. See Cicero's pitying comments in favor of the publicani, in "De provinciis consularibus," 4–5.

86. Plutarch, "Crassus," in *Lives,* trans. Bernadotte Perrin, vol. 3 (Loeb Classical Library), 17.5, 17.9–10.

87. Cicero, "De domo sua," trans. N. H. Watts, in *Cicero,* vol. 11 (Loeb Classical Library), 23.

88. See Jean Cousin's introduction to *De prouinciis consularibus* in Cicero, *Discours,* vol. 15 (Paris: Belles Lettres, 1962), pp. 168–172; Ernst Badian, *Roman Imperialism in the Late Republic,* 2nd ed. (Oxford: Basil Blackwell, 1968), p. 75.

89. Cicero describes Gabinius as "this new Semiramis" ("De provinciis consularibus," 4.9), "dripping with unguents, with waved hair" ("Pro Sestio," 8.18), and always drunk ("Pro Sestio," 9.20).

90. In "De provinciis consularibus," Cicero alludes to his policy of tax relief (5.10).

91. A seductive but unverifiable hypothesis proposed by Rostovtzeff, *Social and Economic History,* vol. 2, pp. 980–985; cf. Sigfried J. de Laet, who mentions the similar policy carried out in Greece by L. Calpurnius Piso Caesoninus (*Portorium: Étude sur l'organisation douanière chez les Romains, surtout à l'époque du haut-empire* [Bruges: De Tempel, 1949], p. 87).

92. See Weber, *Pella Decapolitana,* p. 14.

93. The epithet appeared only quite late, on coins from the reign of Commodus: see Augustus J. Spijkerman, *The Coins of the Decapolis and Roman Arabia* (Jerusalem: Franciscan Printing Press, 1978), pp. 93–95.

94. See Jean-Baptiste Humbert and Yasser Matar Abu Hassuneh, "Fouilles d'Anthédon (Blakhiyeh)," *Dossiers d'Archéologie* 240 (January–February 1999): 52–53.

95. Thomas Bauzou, "La Gaza romaine (69 B.C.E.–403 C.E.)," in *Gaza méditer-*

ranéenne: Histoire et archéologie en Palestine, ed. Jean-Baptiste Humbert (Paris: Errance, 2000), pp. 47–72, especially p. 48.

96. On all this, and Scaurus's expedition in particular, see Sartre, "Rome et les Nabatéens," pp. 37–53.

97. Cicero, "De provinciis consularibus," 4–5.

98. Ernst Bammel, "The Organisation of Palestine by Gabinius," *Journal of Jewish Studies* 12 (1961): 159–162; Baruch Kanael, "The Partition of Judaea by Gabinius," *Israel Exploration Journal* 7 (1957): 98–106.

99. See Arnaud, "Guerres parthiques."

100. Cicero, "Pro Sestio," 43.93. There is a somewhat similar expression in "De domo sua," 23: "peoples utterly loyal and entirely peaceable."

101. "De domo sua," 60: Gabinius is said to have received from Clodius "Syria, Babylon, and Persia, lands as peaceful as they are opulent, for devastation"; the same point is made in similar terms in ibid., 124.

102. Strabo, 12.3.34.

103. "De domo sua" dates precisely from Sept. 29, 57.

104. On the various possible scenarios (for the ancient texts are irreconcilable, and numismatics is not very explicit), see Arnaud, "Guerres parthiques," pp. 25–27.

105. On this episode, which does not involve Syrian affairs, see Will, *HP* 2, pp. 523–525. Will considers the operation illegal, in particular because Gabinius had already been recalled from his province. The attraction of the ten thousand talents paid by Auletes as the price of his efforts won out over respect for legal formalities.

106. Velleius Paterculus, 2.46.2; Dio, 40.12.1.

107. Ammianus, 2.18. On the sharply contrasting reputation of the Parthians, represented both as fierce warriors thirsting for Roman blood and as effeminate Orientals, see the fundamental article by Dobiáš, "Premiers rapports." Dobiáš clearly demonstrates that the first trait does not appear before the humiliating defeat at Carrhai. However, the Romans had had many occasions to measure themselves against the Parthians and could not have been unaware of the Parthians' military capacities. In reality, the texts mentioned offer very little precise historical information; they stem rather from ideology, as each writer paints the portrait of the Parthians that suits his own aims.

108. Dio, 39.56.1: "[H]e . . . was . . . preparing to make a campaign against the Parthians and their wealth."

109. The idea of such an agreement had been advanced by Liebmann-Frankfort in *Frontière orientale,* pp. 173–175, 240–242, and 276–277. In *A Political History of Parthia* (Chicago: University of Chicago Press, 1938), p. 72, Neilson Carel Debevoise expressed doubt about the agreement, as did Sherwin-White, much more recently, in *Roman Foreign Policy in the East,* p. 221. The information is derived from a passage in Paulus Orosius in which Orodes blames Crassus for having crossed the Euphrates despite the treaty signed by Lucullus and renewed by Pompey (*The Seven Books of History against the Pagans,* trans. Roy J. Deferrari [Washington, D.C.: Catholic University of America Press, 1964], 6.13.2).

110. On all this, see Arnaud, "Guerres parthiques." Cicero, who congratulates himself for not having participated in this "Syrian banditry," indirectly confirms the legitimacy of the Senate's decision, which he could not have opposed: *Letters to Atticus,* 4.13. On Crassus's overall policy in the east, see Bruce A. Marshall, *Crassus:*

A Political Biography (Amsterdam: A. M. Hakkert, 1976), pp. 139–161; Marshall believes that Crassus acted on orders from the Senate. In *Marcus Crassus and the Late Roman Republic* (Columbia and London: University of Missouri Press, 1977), Allan Mason Ward expresses the same opinion (pp. 275–278).

111. Plutarch, "Crassus," 16.2–3; but, as a moralist, he cannot accept such a disastrous outcome in war if the war is not an unjust one—that is, lacking in legitimate motives.

112. Dio, 40.16.3; Plutarch, "Crassus," 18.2.

113. Probably the attack Orodes II launched against Armenia: Arnaud, "Guerres parthiques," pp. 20–30.

114. The looting of the temples in Jerusalem and Hierapolis-Bambyke was probably related to the campaign, although we do not know when it took place: Josephus, *AJ* 14.105–109; Plutarch, "Crassus," 17.5.

115. On the battle, see Plutarch's exhaustive account in "Crassus," 23–31; cf. Debevoise, *Political History of Parthia,* pp. 78–95.

116. Dio, 40.25.5.

117. Cicero, who was on the road to his province of Cilicia, received two messages on Sept. 18, 51, that informed him about the Parthians' crossing of the Euphrates, one from Tarcondimotos of Amanus (specifying that the Parthian camp was at Tyba), the other from Iamblichos of Emesa (Cicero, *Letters to His Friends,* vol. 3, 15.1). Bibulus still had not arrived in his province by that date, although he was in Ephesos in August and Cicero wrote on Sept. 3 that Bibulus had left Ephesos for Syria on Aug. 13 (*Letters to his Friends,* 15.3 [letter incorrectly dated August 28 in Loeb]); in the same letter, he mentions information received from King Antiochos of Commagene indicating that the Parthians had reached the banks of the Euphrates and had begun to cross it.

118. Cassius was still in Antioch with his entire army on Sept. 20, 51, whereas the Parthians were in Cyrrhestica (Cicero, *Letters to Atticus,* 5.18).

119. Dio, 40.28.3.

120. Dio, 40.28.1–30.3.

121. Cicero, *Letters to His Friends,* 2.10.2, Nov. 14, 51: "When I arrived at Amanus . . . , our friend Cassius had already . . . succeeded in driving the enemy back from Antioch." But on Oct. 8 he had written to Appius Claudius that there was no more trace of the Parthians in Syria (*Letters to His Friends,* 3.8.10). However, in mid-October he wrote to Cassius congratulating him (he does not say for what): *Letters to His Friends,* 15.14.2. He gives another summary of the operations in *Letters to Atticus,* 5.20, and *Letters to His Friends,* 15.4; he spells out the defensive measures that he took in the Amanus region, and describes the assault on the free Cilicians of Pindenissos.

122. Cicero points out their presence in Cyrrhestica in February 50 (*Letters to Atticus,* 5.21). But as early as November 51 he anticipates difficulties for the forthcoming military season (*Letters to his Friends,* 2.10).

123. See, among others, Velleius Paterculus, 2.46.4; Dio, 40.28–30; and Justinus, 42.4, 4–5. But this was not Cicero's opinion, for he judged that no decisive victory had been won (*Letters to Atticus,* 5.21).

124. Cicero, *Letters to His Friends,* 15.4.3–4; Cicero, who was his political enemy, presented Bibulus as vain and jealous of his own claims to glory (*Letters to Atticus,* 5.20), an incompetent who piled up losses in the most mediocre battles (against the

mountain people of the Amanus: *Letters to His Friends*, 8.6.4), but also fearful and incapable of leaving Antioch (*Letters to Atticus*, 6.8, 7.2).

125. In a letter dated June 26, 50, Cicero mentioned Syria as "ablaze with war" and declared that he was ready to support Bibulus (*Letters to Atticus*, 6.5). However, in a somewhat later letter, after the threat had been removed, Cicero mentioned that Bibulus was hostile toward him and wished to suffer anything rather than ask for Cicero's help (*Letters to His Friends*, 2.17.6). On July 17 or shortly thereafter he declared that he had no reason not to leave Cilicia, now that there was nothing to fear from the Parthians (*Letters to His Friends*, 2.17.1), but it is true that he was so impatient to get back to Rome that he did not hesitate to play down the risks: he was preparing to leave his province even though his successor had not yet arrived.

126. Malalas, p. 111 (5.212.1–8).

127. On the looting of works of art in Asia Minor, see Maurice Sartre, *L'Anatolie hellénistique, de l'Egée au Caucase: 334–31 av. J.-C.* (Paris: A. Colin, 2003).

128. A statue of Zeus present at Antioch, according to Libanios (who speaks erroneously of Zeus Kasios): see *Antioch as a Centre of Hellenic Culture as Observed by Libanius*, trans. A. F. Norman (Liverpool: Liverpool University Press, 2000), p. 28 (*Oratio* 9.116).

129. See Sherwin-White, *Roman Policy in the East*, pp. 289–297.

130. Cicero, *Letters to Atticus*, 9.1; Caesar, *Civil Wars*, 1.6.

131. Caesar, *Civil Wars*, 3.31–33.

132. Ibid., 3.102–103.

133. Julius Caesar, *The Alexandrian War*, in *Alexandrian, African and Spanish Wars*, trans. A. G. Way (Loeb Classical Library), 1.1, for Malichos I of Nabataea; Josephus, *AJ* 14.8.1, for Antipatros of Judaea, Iamblichos of Emesa, and Ptolemy, son of Sohaimus of Lebanon.

134. Livy, Summary 114, in *Works*, vol. 14, *Summaries, Fragments, and Obsequens*, trans. Alfred C. Schlesinger (Loeb Classical Library); Josephus, *AJ* 14.11.1, *BJ* 1.10.10; Ammianus, 3.77–78.

135. Ammianus, *Civil War*, 3.77–78 and 4.57–63; Dio, 47.26.1–7.

136. Dio, 47.30.1–2.

137. Appianus, *Roman History*, trans. Horace White (Loeb Classical Library), 4.61.

138. Appianus, *Roman History*, 5.1, 5.9; cf. Jean-Paul Rey-Coquais, *Arados et sa pérée aux époques grecque, romaine et byzantine: Recueil des témoignages littéraires anciens, suivi de recherches sur les sites, l'histoire, la civilisation* (Paris: P. Geuthner, 1974), p. 163.

139. Dio, 48.24.3; Jerome in Eusebius, *The Ecclesiastical History*, trans. Kirsopp Lake (Loeb Classical Library), 2.139: one of the envoys, Quintus Curtius Salassus, was even burned alive; cf. August Friedrich von Pauly et al., eds., *Realencyclopädie der classischen Altertumswissenschaft* (Stuttgart: J. B. Metzler, 1894–), s.v. "Curtius" 32.

140. Dio, 48.24.3.

141. Rey-Coquais, *Arados et sa pérée*, p. 163.

142. Dio, 49.22.3.

143. Seyrig, "Sur les ères," pp. 22–23 (= *AS*, vol. 4.42, pp. 88–89); Henri Seyrig, "Questions aradiennes," *Revue numismatique* (1964): 41, 43.

144. Rey-Coquais, *Arados et sa pérée*, p. 164.

145. This Antigonos seems to have succeeded in establishing himself as king in Galilee as early as 42, with the help of Marion of Tyre and Ptolemy of Chalcis; defeated by Herod, he succeeded in regaining power by allying himself with the Parthians.

146. Plutarch, "Antony," in *Lives,* vol. 9, 54.4.

3. FROM AUGUSTUS TO TRAJAN: CREATING A PROVINCE

1. Glen W. Bowersock's *Augustus and the Greek World* (Oxford: Clarendon Press, 1965) remains essential on this point. Among Augustus's friends, the only one native to the new province was his old master Athenodoros of Tarsus, who was probably in his eighties at the time of Actium (Bowersock, *Augustus,* p. 32). But we find no Syrians, properly speaking. The Rhosos inscription is hard to use (see Louis Jalabert and René Mouterde, *Inscriptions grecques et latines de la Syrie* [hereafter cited as *IGLS*], vol. 3.1, *Région de l'Amanus, Antioche* [Paris: P. Geuthner, 1950], no. 718), although we can clearly tell that Seleucos, son of Theodotos, provided important services as a navarch. But whether he was capable of taking Rome's interests in hand is another matter; he remains totally unknown apart from the copy of the Rhosus text.

2. Josephus, *De bello judaico (The Jewish War),* trans. Henry St. John Thackeray (Loeb Classical Library), 1.389 (hereafter cited as *BJ*).

3. Josephus, *De antiquitate judaico (Jewish Antiquities),* trans. Louis H. Feldman (Loeb Classical Library), 15.217 (hereafter cited as *AJ*).

4. Hans Bietenhard, "Die Syrische Dekapolis von Pompeius bis Traian," *Aufstieg und Niedergang der römischen Welt* (hereafter cited as *ANRW*) 2.8 (1977): 220–261; David F. Graf, "Hellenization and the Decapolis," *Aram* 4 (1992): 1–48.

5. Barclay Vincent Head, George Francis Hill, George MacDonald, and Warwick William Wroth, *Historia Numorum: A Manual of Greek Numismatics* (Amsterdam: A. M. Hakkert, 1991), p. 735.

6. Plutarch, "Antony," in *Plutarch's Lives,* trans. Bernadotte Perrin, vol. 9 (Loeb Classical Library), 61.1 (hereafter cited as *Lives*).

7. Cassius Dio, *Roman History,* trans. Earnest Cary (Loeb Classical Library), 51.2.2–3 (hereafter cited as Dio).

8. Cf. Maurice Sartre, *L'Anatolie hellénistique, de l'Egée au Caucase: 334–31 av. J.-C.* (Paris: A. Colin, 2003), pp. 218–219.

9. On the Semitic features of the Cilician cults, see Paolo Desideri, "Cilicia ellenistica," *Quaderni Storici* 76 (1991): 143–164.

10. Fergus Millar, *The Roman Near East (31 B.C.–A.D. 337)* (Cambridge, Mass.: Harvard University Press, 1993), pp. 29–30.

11. Josephus, *AJ* 17.320.

12. Maurizio Ghiretti, "Lo 'status' della Giudea dall'età Augustea all'età Claudia," *Latomus* 44 (1985): 751–766.

13. Benjamin H. Isaac, "The Decapolis in Syria: A Neglected Inscription," *Zeitschrift für Papyrologie und Epigraphik* (hereafter cited as *ZPE*) 44 (1981): 67–74, based on an inscription from Chersonesus of Thrace (Madytos, modern Eceabat) published by Amédée Hauvette-Besnault, "Sur quelques villes anciennes de la Chersonnèse de Thrace," *Bulletin de correspondance hellénique* 4 (1880): 507–509.

14. Hannah M. Cotton, "Some Aspects of the Roman Administration of Judaea/

Syria-Palestine," in *Lokale Autonomie und römische Ordnungsmacht in den kaiserzeitlichen Provinzen vom 1. bis 3. Jahrhundert,* ed. Werner Eck and Elisabeth Müller-Luckner (Munich: R. Oldenbourg, 1999), p. 77.

15. An inscription from Caesarea on the Sea in honor of Pontius Pilate designates him specifically as *praefectus:* see *L'année épigraphique* (hereafter cited as *AE*) (1963): 104; (1964): 39; (1971): 477.

16. On this imprecise notion, see Rudolf Haensch, *Capita provinciarum: Staatthaltersitze und Provinzialverwaltung in der römischen Kaiserzeit* (Mainz: Ph. von Zabern, 1997), pp. 244–258 (and *testimonia,* pp. 563–572) for the first province of Syria.

17. Cf. Fergus Millar, "'Senatorial' Provinces: An Institutionalized Ghost," *Ancient World* 20 (1989): 93–97.

18. To the list established by Bengt E. Thomasson in *Laterculi praesidum,* vol. 2 (Göteborg: Radius, 1984), we must now add Edward Dąbrowa, *The Governors of Roman Syria from Augustus to Septimius Severus* (Bonn: R. Habelt, 1998).

19. On these men, see Dąbrowa's very detailed indications in *Governors,* pp. 22–30.

20. Ibid., pp. 32–33.

21. Josephus, *BJ* 1.541.

22. Taking into account terminological variations, these could be the eparchies attested in the framework of the imperial cult.

23. Cf. William M. Ramsay, "Studies in the Roman Province Galatia," *Journal of Roman Studies* (hereafter cited as *JRS*) 14 (1924): 201–203, no. 40 (= *AE* [1926], no. 82). Ramsay published an inscription from Psidian Antioch in which Lawrence J. F. Keppie recognized a reference to a praefectus of Commagene and not to a praefectus of units stationed in Commagene ("Vexilla veteranorum," *Papers of the British School at Rome* 41 [1973]: 13–14); see also a note by Erich Birley in Hubert Devijver, *Prosopographia militiarum equestrium quae fuerunt ab Augusto ad Gallienum,* vol. 2 [Leuven: Universitaire Pers Leuven, 1977], p. 922). Tacitus points out that Tiberius put Commagene in the hands of Q. Servaeus, *comes Germanici* (companion of Germanicus) (Tacitus, *The Annals,* trans. John Jackson, [Loeb Classical Library], 2.65).

24. Strabo, *The Geography,* trans. Horace Leonard Jones (Loeb Classical Library) 16.2.3 (hereafter cited as Strabo); but it would be forcing the text to assert that the province in question was separate from all others.

25. H. G. Pflaum, *Les carrières procuratoriennes équestres sous le Haut-Empire romain* (Paris: P. Geuthner, 1982), p. 16.

26. Josephus, *BJ* 1.535, 1.542.

27. Josephus designates him under the vague term *epistates* (president, supervisor), as he does Saturninus: Herod's and Syllaios's delegates argue before these two Romans over a debt that Syllaios owes Herod and that has come due (*AJ* 16.280). In *AJ* 16.332 and 16.354, he serves as messenger to Herod and then to Augustus; in 16.369, he pleads in favor of the condemnation of Herod's sons during the trial their father is putting them through.

28. Josephus, *BJ* 2.16. On the riot Sabinus provoked, see Josephus, *BJ* 2.45 and 2.74, *AJ* 16.221 and 16.252.

29. Pflaum, *Carrières,* pp. 13–16, no. 1.

30. Jalabert and Mouterde, *IGLS,* vol. 3.1, no. 837.

31. Pflaum, *Carrières*, Suppl. 21 A.

32. *AE* (1967), no. 525.

33. Louis Jalabert, René Mouterde, and Claude Mondésert, *IGLS*, vol. 5, *Emésène* (Paris: P. Geuthner, 1959), no. 1998; cf. Pflaum, *Carrières*, suppl. 49 and addendum.

34. Keith R. Bradley dates Athenodoros's procuratorship to the final years of Domitian's reign, based on the fact that the exhaustion of the Syrian villagers mentioned in the imperial letter belongs in the context of the difficulties encountered by Pisidia in 92–93 and probably by other eastern Mediterranean provinces ("Claudius Athenodorus," *Historia* [1978]: 336–342).

35. C. Clodius Nigrinus, between 14 and 66 (Jalabert and Mouterde, *IGLS*, vol. 3.1, no. 837), a virtually anonymous individual (we know only part of his name, " . . . inius Secun . . .") around 71 (Wilhelm Dittenberger, ed., *Orientis graeci inscriptiones selectae* [Hildesheim and New York: G. Olms, 1986], vol. 2, no. 586 [hereafter cited as *OGIS*]), and T. Mucius Clemens around 73 (*AE* [1967], no. 525).

36. Hermann Dessau, *Inscriptiones latinae selectae* (Berlin: Weidmann, 1892–1916), no. 2683 (hereafter cited as *ILS*).

37. Jean-Paul Rey-Coquais, "Lucius Iulius Aggrippa et Apamée," *Annales archéologiques arabes syriennes* 23 (1973): 39–84.

38. For example, an inscription from Gerasa names a certain Diogenes, son of Emmeganos, a priest of the four eparchies in Antioch in 119–120: Charles Bradford Welles, "The Inscriptions," in *Gerasa, City of the Decapolis*, ed. Carl Hermann Kraeling (New Haven, Conn.: American Schools of Oriental Research, 1938), p. 399, no. 53 (hereafter cited as *I. Gerasa*) (first published in *Supplementum epigraphicum graecum* [Alphen aan den Rijn: Sijthoff & Noordhoff, 1923–1998], vol. 7 [1934], no. 847 [hereafter cited as *SEG*]).

39. René Cagnat, Jean Toutain, Georges Lafaye, and Victor Henry, eds., *Inscriptiones graecae ad res romanas pertinentes* (hereafter cited as *IGR*), vol. 1 (Paris: E. Leroux, 1911), no. 445, dated from Domitian's reign.

40. On the multiple administrative rearrangements in the Anatolian provinces, see Maurice Sartre, *L'Asie Mineure et l'Anatolie d'Alexandre à Dioclétien* (Paris: A. Colin, 1995).

41. Jean-Paul Rey-Coquais, "Philadelphie de Coelésyrie," *Annual of the Department of Antiquities of Jordan* (hereafter cited as *ADAJ*) 25 (1981): 25–31; Maurice Sartre, "Les manifestations du culte impérial dans les provinces syriennes et en Arabie," in *Rome et ses provinces: Genèse et diffusion d'une image du pouvoir; Hommages à Jean-Charles Balty*, ed. Cécile Evers and Athéna Tsingarida (Brussels: Le Livre Timperman, 2001), pp. 167–186, especially pp. 167–178.

42. *SEG*, vol. 7 (1934), no. 847.

43. See Sartre, *Asie Mineure*, pp. 190–201.

44. If we believe that the Latin *praefectus* is translated in Greek by *eparchos*, the term *eparchy* ought to have a military connotation; however, *eparchia* also translates as "provincia," even though a provincia such as Syria could include several divisions called eparchies: Judaea and the Decapolis on the one hand, the eparchies of the imperial cult on the other. The Greeks have no monopoly on imprecision where administrative vocabulary is concerned!

45. Cf. Haensch, *Capita provinciarum*, pp. 254–258.

46. "Official emissary of Augustus, chief administrator of Syria and Phoenicia for the second time"; *ILS*, no. 918.

47. See Thomasson, *Laterculi praesidum*, col. 309, no. 40, for all the references.

48. Ibid., col. 310, no. 43 (thus Jean-Paul Rey-Coquais, *IGLS*, vol. 6, *Baalbek et Beqa'* [Paris: P. Geuthner, 1967], no. 2775 a and b, restored in part according to Christian Habicht, ed., *Die Inschriften von Pergamon*, vol. 8, fasc. 3, *Die Inschriften des Asklepieions* [Berlin: W. de Gruyter, 1969], no. 21).

49. See the model supplied by the provinces of Asia Minor and Anatolia, in Sartre, *Asie Mineure*, pp. 190–196.

50. *I.Gerasa*, no. 188. According to Welles, M. Aurelius Maron, of Gerasa, fulfilled this function in the first half of the third century—in other words, after his city-state was detached from the eparchy of Phoenicia and reattached to that of Coele Syria. Another phenikarch, a citizen of Gaza, is attested in an inscription from Eleusis: *OGIS*, no. 596. The function also appears in Justinian's codification, "Codex Iustinianus," ed. Paul Krüger, in *Corpus iuris civilis* (Berlin: Weidmann, 1954), vol. 2, 5.27.1 (336 C.E.), and in his "Novellae," ed. Rudolf Schöll and G. Kroll, in *Corpus iuris civilis*, vol. 3, 89.15, p. 444, 18, along with the function of syriarch.

51. The only known syriarch, if I am not mistaken, has a Persian name, Artabanios, and he performed the functions of both the president of the *koinon* and the alytarch in the Antioch games. Malalas presents him as the first syriarch in Commodius's reign, which is probably a misunderstanding on his part (see John Malalas, *The Chronicle of John Malalas*, trans. Elizabeth Jeffreys, Michael Jeffreys, Roger Scott, et al. [Melboune: Australian Association for Byzantine Studies, 1986]). Cf. Glanville Downey, *A History of Antioch in Syria: From Seleucus to the Arab Conquest* (Princeton: Princeton University Press, 1961), p. 232, n. 151.

52. Among others, see René Cagnat et al., *IGR*, vol. 3 (Paris: E. Leroux, 1906), nos. 879, 880, 883, and 912.

53. Downey, *History of Antioch*, p. 209 and notes 36–38; also p. 218.

54. See especially Haensch, *Capita provinciarum*, pp. 255–256.

55. Ibid., pp. 227–237.

56. Maurice Sartre, *IGLS*, vol. 21, *Inscriptions grecques et latines de la Jordanie*, vol. 4, *Pétra et la Nabatène méridionale* (Paris: P. Geuthner, 1993), no. 37. But the title *metropolis* is not reserved for cities that harbor a sanctuary dedicated to the imperial cult; the absence of any *neokoros* (city with one or more imperial temples) in Syria deprives us of precious information about the organization of the provincial imperial cult (see Emmanuelle Collas-Heddeland, "Néocorie" [Ph.D. diss., Paris IV, 1993]). On the organization of the province, especially the choice of capital, see Haensch, *Capita provinciarum*, pp. 238–244. The procurators lived in Gerasa, however.

57. See Ghaleb Amer and Michel Gawlikowski, "Le sanctuaire impérial de Philippopolis," *Damaszener Mitteilungen* 2 (1985): 1–15.

58. A reference to a priest of Rome and of Augustus in Bostra (Maurice Sartre, *IGLS*, vol. 13.1, *Bostra* [Paris: P. Geuthner, 1982], no. 9143) and a reference to former flamines (ibid., nos. 9008 and 9009), do not suffice to prove that a provincial cult existed, for all these people were responsible for the municipal imperial cult alone. Let us note, too, that the *nymphaeum* or monumental shrine found in Philadelphia (which by no means deserves the name *kalybe* [light construction made of twigs or fabric] attributed to it by Warwick Ball in *Rome in the East: The Transformation of an Empire* [London and New York: Routledge, 1999], p. 291; see also the sketch on p. 293) has been shown to be associated with the imperial cult through the pres-

ence of many imperial statues. The work carried out in the mid-1990s by Anne Goguel has unfortunately not been published. Although there is a preliminary report by Mohammad Waheeb and Zuhair Zu'bi ("Recent Excavations at the 'Ammān Nymphaeum: Preliminary Report," *ADAJ* 39 [1995]: 229–240), it does not shed much light on these aspects (I owe thanks to Jean-Marie Dentzer for my own information). A parallel has nevertheless been established in extremis with the sanctuary of Philippopolis (p. 238).

59. Pointed out by Tacitus, *Annals,* 13.38, 13.40, 15.6, 15.26, under Nero, without any localization; nor does Lawrence J. F. Keppie propose any localization in "Legions in the East from Augustus to Trajan," in *The Defence of the Roman and Byzantine East,* ed. Philip Freeman and David L. Kennedy (Oxford: British Archaeological Reports, 1986), pp. 414–415. In "Die Römer an Euphrat und Tigris: Geschichte und Denkmäler des Limes im Orient," in "Die Römer an Euphrat und Tigris," special issue, *Antike Welt* 16 (1985): 26, Jörg Wagner suggests Antioch, as does Millar, *Roman Near East,* p. 34. In this view, Antioch relocated Legio XII Fulminata in Raphanaea in the second century, probably after VI Ferrata had left the Raphanaea camp for Bostra and then Caparcotna.

60. This suggestion was made by Emil Ritterling, "Legio," in *Realencyclopädie der classischen Altertumswissenschaft* (hereafter cited as *RE*), ed. August Friedrich von Pauly et al. (Stuttgart: J. B. Metzler, 1894–), col. 1589.

61. Its presence is attested there under Tiberius (Tacitus, *Annals,* 2.57), but it may have been relocated later in Zeugma.

62. Josephus, *BJ* 7.18.

63. See Jörg Wagner, *Seleukeia am Euphrat, Zeugma* (Wiesbaden: Reichert, 1976), p. 143, and also idem, "Legio IIII Scythica am Euphrat," in *Studien zu den Militärgrenzen Roms,* vol. 2, *Vorträge des 10. Internationalen Limeskongresses in der Germania Inferior,* ed. Dorothea Haupt and Heinz Günter Horn (Cologne and Bonn: R. Habelt, 1977), pp. 517–540. There was a great deal of activity, as evidenced by the presence of numerous stamped tiles; see Guillermo Algaze, Ray Breuninger, and James Knudstad, "The Tigris-Euphrates Archaeological Reconnaissance Project: Final Report of the Birecik and Carchemish Dam Survey Areas," *Anatolica* 20 (1994): 20. Michael A. Speidel, "Legio IIII Scythica, Its Movements and Men," in *The Twin Towns of Zeugma on the Euphrates,* ed. David L. Kennedy (Portsmouth, R.I.: Journal of Roman Archaeology, 1998), pp. 163–203, presents the history of the legion and reprints the related texts; in "Commanders and Officers of Legio IIII Scythica, Its Movements and Men," in *The Twin Towns,* ed. D. L. Kennedy, pp. 205–232, Hubert Devijver offers an in-depth study of the officers of this legion.

64. On the legates of the legions of Syria, see Edward Dąbrowa, "The Commanders of Syrian Legions, 1st–3rd c. A.D.," in *The Roman Army in the East,* ed. David L. Kennedy and David Braund (Ann Arbor, Mich.: Journal of Roman Archaeology, 1996), pp. 277–296 (for III Gallica, VI Ferrata, XII Fulminata, and XVI Flavia Firma); for Legio X Fretensis, see Edward Dąbrowa, *Legio X Fretensis: A Prosopographical Study of Its Officers (I–III A.D.)* (Stuttgart: F. Steiner, 1993).

65. Josephus, *BJ* 7.17.

66. Josephus, *BJ* 7.18.

67. Denis van Berchem, "Une inscription flavienne du Musée d'Antioche," *Museum Helveticum* 40 (1983): 185–196.

68. S. Thomas Parker, "Roman Legionary Fortresses in the East," in *Roman Fortresses and Their Legions: Papers in Honour of George C. Boon,* ed. Richard J.

Brewer (London: Society of Antiquaries of London; Cardiff: National Museums and Galleries of Wales, 2000), pp. 121–138; Parker indicates that the Samosata camp must have been occupied around 72, either by Legio VI Ferrata or by III Gallica, whereas Legio XVI Flavia Firma was posted there only at the beginning of the second century (p. 123).

69. Pliny the Younger, "Panegyricus," in *Letters and Panegyricus,* trans. Betty Radice, vol. 2 (Loeb Classical Library), 14.

70. Josephus, *BJ* 7.244–251; Suetonius, "Domitian," in *Suetonius,* trans. J. C. Rolfe, vol. 2 (Loeb Classical Library), 2.2 (hereafter cited as Suetonius); see Julian Bennett, *Trajan, Optimus Princeps: A Life and Times* (Bloomington and London: Indiana University Press, 1997), p. 18.

71. Michel Reddé, *Mare Nostrum: Les infrastructures, le dispositif et l'histoire de la marine militaire sous l'Empire romain* (Rome: École française de Rome, 1986), pp. 236–241; Denis van Berchem, "Le port de Séleucie de Piérie et la logistique des campagnes parthiques," *Bonner Jahrbücher* 185 (1985): 47–87.

72. See Edward Dąbrowa, "Les troupes auxiliaires de l'armée romaine en Syrie au Ier s. de notre ère," *Dialogues d'histoire ancienne* 5 (1979): 233–254. See also David L. Kennedy, "The Special Command of M. Valerius Lollianus," *Electrum* 1 (1997): 69–81. To the diplomas used by these authors, we must add Peter Weiss, "Neue Militärdiplome," *ZPE* 117 (1997): 229–231, no. 2, and 232–233, no. 3 (damaged) (whence *AE* [1997], nos. 1761–1762).

73. Published by Scarlat Lambrino, "Un nouveau diplôme de l'empereur Claude," *Comptes rendus des séances de l'Académie des inscriptions et belles-lettres* (hereafter cited as *CRAI*) (1930): 137; Lambrino concludes that it has to do with the auxiliaries of Moesia. This view is challenged by Herbert Nesselhauf, who prefers an eastern province (*Corpus inscriptionum latinarum* [hereafter cited as *CIL*], vol. 16, *Diplomata militaria ex constitutionibus imperatorum de civitate et conubio militum veteranorumque expressa,* 2 vols. [Berlin: W. de Gruyter, 1936–1955], p. 3, n. 2); for Walter F. Wagner, it is Syria (*Die Dislokation der römischen Auxiliarformationen in den Provinzen Noricum, Pannonien, Moesien und Dakien von Augustus bis Gallienus* [Berlin: Junker und Dunnhaupt, 1938], p. 40); see also Konrad Kraft, *Zur Rekrutierung der Alen und Kohorten an Rhein und Donau* (Bern: Aedibus A. Francke, 1951), p. 29, n. 7; and Dąbrowa, "Troupes auxiliaires," pp. 233–234.

74. Dąbrowa derives his information from the lists established by Willy Hüttl, *Antoninus Pius,* 2 vols. (Prague: J. G. Calve'sche Universitäts-Buchhandlung, 1933–1936) (*non vidi*). For the inscription from Gradista (Albania), the ancient Byllis, where M. Valerius Lollianus was born, see Kennedy, "Special Command," pp. 69–81; Kennedy rejects a date from the Domitian era for this exceptional command, and proposes the previous era in 132, or perhaps 123.

75. This episode is rather obscure, but it was probably fairly dangerous for the security of the empire: see Tacitus, *The Histories,* trans. Clifford H. Moore, vol. 1 (Loeb Classical Library), 1.2.1; Suetonius, vol. 2, "Nero," 57; Dio, 66.19.3; Joannes Zonaras, *Epitome historiarum,* ed. Ludwig Dindorf (Leipzig: Teubner, 1868–1875), 11.18 (hereafter cited as Zonaras); cf. Paul A. Gallivan, "The False Neros: A Reexamination," *Historia* 22 (1973): 364–365, in which Gallivan shows that there was yet another false Nero in 88.

76. Benjamin H. Isaac, *The Limits of Empire: The Roman Army in the East* (Oxford: Clarendon Press, 1990).

77. J. G. Crow and D. H. French, "New Research on the Euphrates Frontier in

Turkey," in *Roman Frontier Studies 1979,* ed. William S. Hanson and Lawrence J. F. Keppie (Oxford: British Archaeological Reports, 1980); Wagner, *Seleukeia;* Wagner, "Römer."

78. We know very little about the legionnaire camps of the early empire in Syria. Most of these have not been found, and those that have been (Bostra, Caparcotna) have not been excavated, as it were. S. Thomas Parker, "Roman Legionary Fortresses in the East," in *Roman Fortresses and Their Legions,* ed. R. J. Brewer (London: Society of Antiquaries of London; Cardiff: National Museums and Galleries of Wales, 2000), p. 134, notes that Bostra, like Satala of Cappadocia, encompasses about 16.5 hectares, or 20 to 30 percent less than the legionnaires' camps in the west.

79. Isaac, *Limits.*

80. Tacitus, *Annals,* 13.35.

81. Isaac is skeptical (*Limits,* pp. 24–25). In "The Laxity of Syrian Legions" (in Kennedy and Braund, *Roman Army,* pp. 229–276), Everett Wheeler shows that this is for the most part the expression of a common literary trope on the subject of the Orient, a place of *luxuria, indulgentia,* and *licentia.*

82. An old synthesis proposed by Ernest Honigmann in *RE,* s.v. "Syria," sec. 14: "Itinerarien und Römerstrassen," col. 1645, 1647–1650.

83. Peter Thomsen, "Die römischen Meilensteine der Provinzen Syria, Arabia, und Palästina," *Zeitschrift der deutschen Palästina-Vereins* (hereafter cited as *ZDPV*) 40 (1917): 1–103.

84. For example, the royal Parthian route along the Euphrates as depicted by Isidoros of Charax.

85. Antoine Poidebard, *La trace de Rome dans le désert de Syrie* (Paris: P. Geuthner, 1934), pp. 75–76.

86. Louis Jalabert and René Mouterde, *IGLS,* vol. 1, *Commagène et Cyrrhestique* (Paris: P. Geuthner, 1929), no. 38.

87. Poidebard, *Trace de Rome;* René Mouterde and Antoine Poidebard, *Le limes de Chalcis: Organisation de la steppe en haute Syrie romaine; Documents aériens* (Paris: P. Geuthner, 1945).

88. On this road, see Richard George Goodchild, "The Coast Road of Phoenicia and Its Milestones," *Berytus* 9 (1949): 91–127.

89. Erected by C. Ummidius Durmius: Goodchild, "Coast Road," p. 112.

90. See Isaac, *Limits,* p. 110.

91. *AE* (1974), no. 652,

92. *AE* (1933), no. 205.

93. *AE* (1974), no. 653.

94. For the expedition commanded by Antigonos Monophthalmos (the One-Eyed), see Maurice Sartre, *D'Alexandre à Zénobie* (Paris: Fayard, 2001), pp. 52–53.

95. See Glen W. Bowersock, "Perfumes and Power," in *Profumi d'Arabia: Atti del convegno,* ed. Alessandra Avanzini (Rome: L'Erma, 1997), pp. 543–556.

96. Pliny, *Natural History,* trans. H. Rackham (Loeb Classical Library), 12.32.62 (hereafter cited as *NH*); Plutarch, "Alexander," in *Lives,* vol. 7, 25.5, and "Sayings of Kings and Commanders (Regum et imperatorum apophthegmata)," trans. Frank Cole Babbitt, in *Moralia,* vol. 3 (Loeb Classical Library), 179 E–F.

97. Scholars disagree as to whether the campaign began in 26–25 or 25–24; on the reasons for preferring the first date, see Shelagh Jameson, "Chronology of the Campaigns of Aelius Gallus and C. Petronius," *JRS* 58 (1968): 71–84.

98. Hermann von Wissmann, "Die Geschichte des Sabäerreichs und der Feldzug des Aelius Gallus," *ANRW* 2.9.1 (1976): 308–544; according to Christian Marek, the motivation was strategic ("Die Expedition des Aelius Gallus nach Arabien im Jahre 25 v. Chr.," *Chiron* 23 [1993]: 121–156).

99. On the political situation of the southern Arabian kingdoms in the first century B.C.E., see Christian Robin, "Sheba II: Dans les inscriptions sud-arabiques," in *Supplément au Dictionnaire de la Bible,* ed. Jacques Briend and Édouard Cothenet (Paris: Letouzey & Ané, 1996), fasc. 70, cols. 1047–1254; Jean-François Breton, *Arabia Felix from the Time of the Queen of Sheba, Eighth Century B.C. to First Century A.D.,* trans. Albert Lafarge (Notre Dame, Ind.: University of Notre Dame Press, 2000), pp. 159–169.

100. The details are from Strabo (16.4.22–25), who was a friend of Aelius Gallus and thus had his information from a good source.

101. *Res gestae divi saporis,* in Erich Kettenhofen, *Die römisch-persischen Kriege des 3. Jahrhunderts n. Chr.* (Wiesbaden: L. Reichert, 1982), 26.5.

102. Nigel Groom, "The Roman Expedition into South Arabia," *Bulletin of the Society for Arabian Studies* 1 (February 1996): 5–7; Groom is following up on a suggestion made by A. F. L. Beeston.

103. Steven E. Sidebotham offers a welcome opposing view, in "Aelius Gallus and Arabia," *Latomus* 45 (1986): 590–602 (also in *Roman Economic Policy in the Erythra Thalassa, 30 B.C.–A.D. 217,* ed. Steven E. Sidebotham [Leiden: E. J. Brill, 1986], pp. 120–130).

104. Paolo Costa, "A Latin-Greek Inscription from the Jawf of the Yemen," *Proceedings of the Seminar for Arabian Studies* 7 (1977): 69–72, corrected by Christian Marek, "Der römische Inschriftenstein von Baraqi," in *Arabia Felix: Beiträge zur Sprache und Kultur des vorislamischer Arabien; Festschrift Walter W. Müller zum 60. Geburtstag,* ed. Norbert Nebes (Wiesbaden: Harrassowitz, 1994), pp. 178–190.

105. Tacitus, *Annals,* 1.8; cf. Joyce Reynolds, "New Evidence for the Imperial Cult in Julio-Claudian Aphrodisias" *ZPE* 43 (1981): 317–327; idem, "Further Information on Imperial Cult at Aphrodisias," *Studii Clasice* 24 (1986): 109–117; R. R. R. Smith, "Simulacra Gentium: The Ethne from the Sebasteion at Aphrodisias," *JRS* 78 (1988): 50–77, especially 58–59.

106. Lionel Casson, ed., *The Periplus Maris Erythraei: Text, Translation, and Commentary* (Princeton: Princeton University Press, 1989), 23; this annotated edition includes a useful discussion of the debates over the date.

107. The coins are identified by Daniel T. Potts, "Augustus, Aelius Gallus and the Periplus: A Re-Interpretation of the Coinage of San'â Class B," in Nebes, *Arabia Felix,* pp. 212–222; Potts attributes them to a later period; Bowersock proposes an earlier date in "Perfumes and Power," p. 552.

108. We do not know whether there were one, two, three, or even four embassies, or whether one of these was the same one that followed Augustus in his travels: we find Indians with Augustus in 26–25 B.C.E. in Tarragona (Orosius, *The Seven Books of History against the Pagans,* trans. Roy J. Deferrari [Washington, D.C.: Catholic University of America Press, 1964], 6.21.19; Jerome, *Chronicon,* trans. Malcolm Drew Donalson [Lewiston, Me.: Mellen University Press, 1996], 188), in Samos in 20 B.C.E. (Dio, 54.9.8; Strabo, 16.1.4 and 15.1.73), and perhaps in Rome around 11 B.C.E., if we presuppose the presence of an Indian embassy when a tiger was displayed in Rome for the first time (Diodoros, *Diodorus of Sicily,* trans. C. H. Oldfather [Loeb

Classical Library], 2.35–42; Strabo, 15.1.11–12; Pliny, *NH,* 6.21.56–57). On this topic, see Sidebotham, *Roman Economic Policy,* pp. 129–130.

109. Franz Altheim and Ruth Stiehl, *Die Araber in der alten Welt,* vol. 1 (Berlin: W. de Gruyter, 1964–1969), pp. 307–309.

110. P. J. M. Nieskens, "Vers le zérotage définitif des ères préislamiques en Arabie du Sud antique," in *Arabian Studies in Honour of Mahmoud Ghul: Symposium at Yarmuk University, December 8–11, 1984,* ed. Moawiyah M. Ibrahim (Wiesbaden: Harrassowitz, 1989), p. 101.

111. See Michael J. Zwettler, "The 'era of NBT' and 'YMNT': Two Proposals (1)," *Arabian Archaeology and Epigraphy* 7 (1996): 95–107. The inscriptions that refer to this era are from the third century C.E., but various concordances impose a date for the beginning of the era between 49 and 21.

112. On Gaius Caesar's expedition into Arabia, see note 238. A copyist's error led the author of *Periplus,* 26, to assume that Gaius Caesar destroyed Aden during this campaign; see Sidebotham, *Roman Economic Policy,* pp. 130–131.

113. This topic is addressed in all the major studies. See especially Marie-Louise Chaumont, "L'Arménie entre Rome et l'Iran: I. De l'avènement d'Auguste à l'avènement de Dioclétien," *ANRW* 2.9.1 (1976): 71–130; Edward Dąbrowa, *La politique de l'état parthe à l'égard de Rome d'Artaban II à Vologèse I (ca 11–ca 79 de N.E.) et les facteurs qui la conditionnaient* (Cracow: Nakadem Uniwersytet Jagiellonski, 1983).

114. Dio, 55.10.20–21.

115. Velleius Paterculus was an eyewitness (Paterculus, *History of Rome,* trans. Frederick W. Shipley [Loeb Classical Library], 3.101).

116. Dio, 55.10a.6.

117. Tacitus, *Annals,* 2.4.5.

118. Ibid., 2.68.3; Vonones was assassinated after attempting to flee: ibid., 2.68.1; Suetonius, vol. 1, "Tiberius," 46.2.

119. Chaumont, "Arménie," p. 88.

120. Josephus, *AJ* 18.101–102; Suetonius, vol. 1, "Gaius Caligula," 14.3, and "Vitellius," 2.4; Dio, 59.27.2.

121. Tacitus, *Annals,* 12.48.1–2.

122. Ibid., 12.49.3–4.

123. On the causes of these operations, see Chaumont, "Arménie," pp. 97–100.

124. Tacitus, *Annals,* 13.8.2–4; cf. Chaumont, "Arménie," p. 99.

125. Tacitus, *Annals,* 13.35; Dio, 62.19.

126. See Chaumont, "Arménie," pp. 101–116.

127. After Rhandeia, Corbulo sent Legio IV Scythica and Legio XII Fulminata back to Syria and recalled III Gallica and VI Ferrata for his new campaign (Tacitus, *Annals,* 15.26).

128. See Isaac, *Limits,* pp. 60–66 (Lebanon and Trachonitis), pp. 77–85 (Judaea).

129. Henri Seyrig, "L'incorporation de Palmyre à l'empire romain," *Syria* 13 (1932): 266–277.

130. Ernest Will, "Pline l'Ancien et Palmyre: Un problème d'histoire ou d'histoire littéraire?" *Syria* 62 (1985): 263–270. At the same time, Will definitively discredited the image, based on Pliny, of a city whose fortune had come from its position as intermediary between Rome and the Parthians, keeping an equal balance between them; Palmyra is quite simply a city in the Roman Empire.

131. See, for example, Jean Cantineau, ed., *Inventaire des inscriptions de Palmyre,* vol. 9 (Beirut: Publications du Musée national syrien de Damas, 1933), no. 12.

132. *AE* (1933), no. 205.

133. The term *tetrarch* was first used to designate the four parts of Thessaly, but at the end of the Hellenistic period it seems to have been used regularly to designate any section of a larger body that was subject to division, whether or not there were four "commands," in Syria as well as in Galatia. Although the title was less illustrious than that of king, the two titles were ultimately viewed as equivalent (in Hesychius's definition, "tetrarchs = kings"). Cf. Henri Estienne, *Thesaurus graecae linguae* (Paris: A. F. Didot, 1831–1865), s.v. "tetrarches," "tetrarchia."

134. See Hans Buchheim, *Die Orientpolitik des Triumvirn M. Antonius: Ihre Voraussetzungen, Entwicklung und Zusammenhang mit den politischen Ereignissen in Italien* (Heidelberg: C. Winter, 1960); on the system of client princes, see also David Braund, *Rome and the Friendly King: The Character of the Client Kingship* (London: Croom Helm; New York: St. Martin's Press, 1984).

135. Rey-Coquais, "Lucius Iulius Agrippa."

136. Pliny, *NH* 5.19.81–82.

137. Rey-Coquais, "Lucius Iulius Agrippa."

138. Josephus, *BJ* 1.422–428 and *AJ* 19.335–337, 20.211–212.

139. Glen W. Bowersock, "Syria under Vespasian," *JRS* 63 (1973): 123–129; but Gerasa, which Bowersock includes in this operation, is excluded from it by Jacques Seigne in "Jérash romaine et Byzantine: Développement urbain d'une ville provinciale orientale," *Studies in the History and Archaeology of Jordan* (hereafter cited as *SHAJ*) 4 (1992): 331–341; Seigne believes that the renovations came later.

140. Maurice Sartre, *Bostra: Des origines à l'Islam* (Paris: P. Geuthner, 1985), pp. 54–56; but I was probably wrong to imagine that Rabbel had made Bostra his residence. There is no proof that Petra did not remain the customary residence of the Nabataean kings, even if they occasionally spent time in Bostra.

141. Bowersock, *Augustus,* p. 47.

142. Josephus, *AJ* 16.295.

143. The suggestion is Bowersock's (*Roman Arabia* [Cambridge, Mass.: Harvard University Press, 1983], pp. 54–56).

144. M. H. Gracey, "The Armies of the Judaean Client Kings," in Freeman and Kennedy, *Defence,* pp. 311–323; David F. Graf, "The Nabataean Army and the *Cohortes Ulpiae Petraeorum,*" in *The Roman and Byzantine Army in the East* (proceedings of a colloquium held at the Jagiellonian University, Crakow, September 1992), ed. Edward Dąbrowa (Cracow: Drukarnia Uniwersytetu Jagiellonskiego, 1994), pp. 265–311.

145. Josephus, *AJ* 19.338–342; cf. D. R. Schwartz, *Agrippa I: The Last King of Judaea* (Tübingen: J. C. B. Mohr, 1990), pp. 137–140.

146. Josephus, *BJ* 1.535 (tribune) and 1.538 (procurator).

147. Sartre, *IGLS,* vol. 16, *Le Djebel al-Œ Arab* (Beirut: Institut français d'archéologie du Proche-Orient, forthcoming), nos. 175, 197.

148. On the personal motivations of Caligula and Claudius, see especially Edmond Frézouls, "La politique dynastique de Rome en Asie Mineure," *Ktema* 12 (1987): 187.

149. Plutarch, "Pompey," in *Lives,* vol. 5, 38.2.

150. Appianus, *Bellum Civile,* 2.49.202.

151. Caesar, *Bellum Civile*, 3.4–6.

152. The ancient authors held quite divergent opinions: see Josephus, *BJ* 1.321–322 (Samosata captured thanks to Herod); Justinus, 42.4.10; Plutarch, "Antony," 34.2–4 (Antiochos had offered a thousand talents to get Antony to withdraw, but when the latter refused, the defenders fought vigorously and Antony had to settle for three hundred talents); Dio, 49.20–22; Zonaras, 10.26.519 (Antony received neither hostages nor the sum he had requested).

153. Plutarch, "Antony," 61.1–2.

154. Dio, 52.43.1.

155. Dio, 54.9.3.

156. *OGIS*, no. 406.

157. Maachtel J. Mellink, "The Tumulus of Nemrud Dagi and Its Place in the Anatolian Tradition," *Asia Minor Studien* 3 (1991): 7–10; Theresa Goell, H. G. Bachmann, and Donald Hugo Sanders, *Nemrud Dagi: The Hierothesion of Antiochus I of Commagene; Results of the American Excavations Directed by Theresa B. Goell*, 2 vols. (Winona Lake, Ind.: Eisenbrauns, 1996).

158. Friedrich Karl Dörner, Theresa Goell, and Wolfram Heopfner, *Arsameia am Nymphaios: Die Ausgrabungen im Hierothesion des Königs Mithridates Kallinikos 1953–1956* (Berlin: Gebr. Mann Verlag, 1963; repr., *Istanbuler Forschungen* 23); Friedrich Karl Dörner, Wolfram Hoepfner, and Gerhild Hübner, *Arsameia am Nymphaios: Das Hierothesion des Königs Mithridates I. Kallinikos von Kommagene nach Ausgrabungen von 1963 bis 1967* (Berlin and Leipzig: W. de Gruyter, 1983; repr., *Istanbuler Forschungen* 33).

159. On its boundaries, see French, "Commagene," pp. 11–19.

160. Josephus, *AJ* 18.53.

161. Tacitus, *Annals* 2.56.4.

162. Josephus, *AJ* 19.276; Dio, 60.8.1.

163. Maurice Sartre, *L'Orient romain: Provinces et sociétés provinciales en Méditerranée orientale d'Auguste aux Sévères (31 avant J.-C.–235 après J.-C.)* (Paris: Le Seuil, 1991), pp. 38–39, 42.

164. Dio, 50.13.7

165. Ibid., 51.2.2.

166. Ibid., 54.4.2.

167. One needs to be wary of Ball's far-fetched and often unfounded reconstructions (*Rome in the East*, p. 35), and in particular of the connections he establishes between the Emesa dynasty on the one hand and Ptolemy, son of Mennaeos, and Zenodoros, on the other hand; similarly, several of his dates are erroneous. Moreover, Sampsigeramos was the son of Iamblichos II, not of Sohaimus of Chalcis. On all these questions, it is preferable to consult Richard D. Sullivan, "The Dynasty of Emesa," *ANRW* 2.8 (1977): 198–219. See also Henri Seyrig, "Caractères de l'histoire d'Émèse," *Syria* 36 (1959): 184–192 (= *AS*, vol. 6 [Paris, 1966], pp. 64–72); and Carlos Chad, *Les dynastes d'Émèse* (Beirut: Dar el-Machreq, 1972).

168. Jean Cantineau, "Textes palmyréniens provenant de la fouille du temple de Bel," *Syria* 12 (1931): 139–141, no. 18.

169. On the necropolis of Tell Abu Sabun, see Henri Seyrig, "Antiquités de la nécropole d'Émèse," *Syria* 29 (1952): 204–227 (= *AS*, vol. 6, pp. 1–24).

170. Josephus, *AJ* 19.338.

171. Josephus, *AJ* 20.139.

172. Ibid., 20.158. Sohaimos had to manage both his hereditary principality and the small state of East Anatolia: A. A. Barrett, "Sohaemus King of Emese and Sophene," *American Journal of Philology* 98 (1977): 153–159.

173. Rey-Coquais, *IGLS*, vol. 6, no. 2760.

174. But it is completely incorrect to depict the two sun gods as the same, as Ball does (in *Rome in the East*, pp. 37–47), when we know that the Emesan god is the mountain god Elagabalus and Baalbek's is the storm god Hadad.

175. The first civic declarations of Emesa.

176. Josephus, *BJ* 7.226.

177. Epitaph of C. Iulius Sampsigeramos of Emesa, discovered along with the family tomb; see Jalabert, Mouterde, and Mondésert, *IGLS*, vol. 5, no. 2212. Given that the name is common, it is certainly possible to see just an ordinary Emesan here (as Ball does in *Rome in the East*, p. 36), but this means neglecting the fact that we have a Roman citizen whose citizenship goes back to Caesar, Augustus, or Caligula; this could not have been commonplace in Emesa, and it turns out to be the case with all the other client princes.

178. For other members of the family in the second century, see Jalabert, Mouterde, and Mondésert, *IGLS*, vol. 5, nos. 2212–2217, and Rey-Coquais, *IGLS*, vol. 6, no. 2917.

179. Dio, 59.12.2 (on his nomination); Tacitus, *Annals*, 12.23 (on his death); he must not be confused with the one who succeeded his brother Azizus in Emesa in 53 or 54. See Emil Schürer, *The History of the Jewish People in the Age of Jesus Christ (75 B.C.–A.D. 135)*, rev. and ed. Géza Vermès and Fergus Millar, trans. T. A. Burkill et al. (Edinburgh: Clark, 1973–1986), vol. 1, pp. 569–570.

180. Josephus states that his son Noaros is related to Sohaimos, king of Emesa (*BJ* 2.481).

181. Ibid.; cf. Josephus, "The Life," in *The Life and Against Apion*, trans. Henry St. John Thackeray (Loeb Classical Library), p. 52; see also Schürer, *History*, vol. 1, p. 472, n. 7.

182. Josephus, *BJ* 2.481; but after the massacre of a Jewish delegation from Batanaea, he was relieved of his functions.

183. Schürer, *History*, vol. 2, p. 478.

184. Chapter 4, which is devoted to first-century Palestine, deals with the Palestinian states ruled by Herod and his successors.

185. Zenodorus died in 37–36 B.C.E., and his principality was confiscated to Cleopatra's benefit. If we are correctly interpreting Josephus's text (*AJ* 15.344), we are given to understand that the principate of Lysanias became part of the holdings of the Roman state or of the prince and that, deeming it a domain that would be hard to exploit directly, Rome left its exploitation to whoever made the best offer.

186. Josephus simply mentions that the events took place under Varro, who was governor of Syria and charged with implementing this measure (*AJ* 15.345); but elsewhere he situates these events "after the first actiad" (that is, after 27 B.C.E.), while mentioning the same Varro (*BJ* 1.398). This measure should probably not be pushed back much later than 27. On this governor, see Dąbrowa, *Governors*, pp. 17–18; Dąbrowa concludes that the decision was made in the fall of 24.

187. Oddly enough, Zenodorus seems to have sold the Auranitis to some uniden-

tified Arabs (Nabataeans?) for fifty talents, before Augustus officially gave this district to the king of Judaea.

188. We have the date from Josephus (*AJ* 15.354), who specifies that this happened during Augustus's voyage to Syria, when Herod had been ruling for seventeen years.

189. Josephus, *AJ* 15.360; Oulatha designates the region around Lake Houleh (a dry lake today), north of the Sea of Galilee.

190. Schürer, *History*, vol. 1; Sartre, *Orient romain*, pp. 30–32, 41–42.

191. Michael C. A. Macdonald has recognized an echo of Philip's reign in two Safaitic inscriptions: "Herodian Echoes in the Syrian Desert," in "Trade, Contact and the Movement of Peoples in the Eastern Mediterranean: Studies in Honour of J. Basil Hennessy," ed. Stephen Bourke and Jean-Paul Descoeudres, supplement, *Mediterranean Archaeology* (1995): 285–290. The first text, in the region of Burqu', dates from "the year Caesar's son died; and he heard that Philippus had been killed." Caesar's son would be Germanicus, and the allusion to Philip clearly appears as an unfounded rumor. In the second text, the engraving is dated from "the year the inhabitants of the Hawran complained to Caesar about Philippus" or "accused Philippus before Caesar." But this Philip may just as easily be Philip son of Iachimods, grandson of Zamaris, a general and a friend of Agrippa II of whom Josephus speaks (*Life*, 74): the Tyrians accused him of having betrayed the empire. Vespasian, who was still just a general in charge of the repression in Judaea, sent him to Rome to reply to the accusations before Nero.

192. Dio, 60.8.3.

193. One or the other of the Agrippas is mentioned in a Safaitic inscription: Macdonald, "Herodian Echoes," pp. 289–290.

194. Rome may have annexed Chalcis, but it is not impossible that it gave the city to one of Herod of Chalcis's sons: we know that Herod of Chalcis had a son named Aristobulos, who was named king of Armenia Minor by Nero in 54 (Josephus, *BJ* 2.252). As it happens, a certain Aristobulos was king of a Syrian Chalcus under Vespasian (Josephus, *BJ* 7.226). Scholars have pointed to Chalcis of Belos, which is possible, but it is much more probable that the city in question is Chalcis of Lebanon. This Aristobulos was able to reign in both Armenia and Chalcis, as was the case for the princes of Emesa. As for the date, Josephus specifies that these events took place in the thirteenth year of Claudius's reign.

195. Josephus, *BJ* 2.252. The dual system of dating for Agrippa II (see Henri Seyrig, "Les ères d'Agrippa II," *Revue numismatique* [1964]: 55–65) must correspond, for the first era (that of 55), to the awarding of the royal title, and for the second (beginning in 60), to the refounding of the royal capital, Philip's Caesarea, as a Neronias.

196. Not to be confused with Abila of Lysanias in the Damascus region (Suq wadi Barada), or with Abila of the Decapolis (Tell Abil); this one is Tell al-Kuffrein, situated to the west of Amman: see Nelson Glueck, *Explorations in Eastern Palestine*, vol. 4, part 1: *Text* (New Haven, Conn.: American Schools of Oriental Research, 1951), pp. 376–378 (equivalent to Abel ha-Sittim in Num. 33.49).

197. Josephus, *AJ* 20.158–159, *BJ* 2.252; this is Tell ar-Rameh, close to the previous one.

198. While waiting for the definitive publication, see S. Fähndrich and Thomas Weber, "Bemerkungen zum Statuendenkmal aus Sahr al-Ledja, Syrien," *Archäologischer Anzeiger* (2001): 603–612.

199. Sartre, *Orient romain,* pp. 59–65; Maurice Sartre, *Trois études sur l'Arabie romaine et byzantine* (Brussels: Revue d'études latines, 1982); Maurice Sartre, "Villes et villages du Hauran (Syrie) du Ier au IVe siècle," in *Sociétés urbaines, sociétés rurales dans l'Asie Mineure et la Syrie hellénistiques et romaines, Strasbourg, 1985,* ed. Edmond Frézouls (Strasbourg: AECR, 1987), pp. 239–257.

200. We may wonder whether the struggles of the Pompeian legates (Marcius Philippus, Lentulus Marcellinus) against "the Arabs" were not directed against the nomads and brigands who were ravishing the steppes on Syria's borders.

201. Strabo, 16.2.20.

202. Ibid., 16.2.18–20. There is a cave similar to the one Strabo describes in the southern part of the plateau, at 'Ariqah (formerly Aerita); it can easily be visited. In contrast, the mention of huge mountains does not correspond to reality, and Josephus is much more precise when he points out that nothing calls the presence of these caves to the attention of travelers. We should note that Ammianus Marcellinus, in the fourth century, speaks of the Maratocupreni; we can identify the first element in this name as based on the Aramaic *m'arta,* Arab *magharat,* "grotto"; the second element must simply be a derivative from *kapro,* "village," in an ethnic, "villager" form (Ammianus Marcellinus, *The Surviving Books of the History* [Loeb Classical Library], 28.2.11). See Isaac, *Limits,* p. 63 (he does not identify the second element).

203. Josephus, *AJ* 15.342–364.

204. Ibid., 17.23–27; this was probably located in the village of Basir (Maurice Sartre, *IGLS,* vol. 14, *Adraha, le Jawlan oriental et al Batanée* [Beirut: Institut français d'archéologie du Proche-Orient, forthcoming], nos. 586–587), and probably took place in 10 B.C.E. (Isaac, *Limits,* pp. 64–65, 329).

205. Located in Sour al-Lej; see Getzel M. Cohen, "The Hellenistic Military Colony: A Herodian Example," *Transactions and Proceedings of the American Philological Association* 103 (1972): 83–95; Maurice Sartre, "Les *metrokômiai* de Syrie du Sud," *Syria* 76 (1999): 200.

206. Cf. the inscription from Dhunaybeh (formerly Danaba) pointed out in Maurice Sartre, "Communautés villageoises et structures sociales d'après l'épigraphie de la Syrie du Sud," in *L'epigrafia del villaggio,* ed. Alda Calbi, Angela Donati, and Gabriella Poma (Faenza: Fratelli Lega, 1993), pp. 133–135 (= Annie Sartre-Fauriat and Maurice Sartre, *IGLS,* vol. 15, *Le plateau du Trachôn* [Beirut: Institut français d'archéologie du Proche-Orient, forthcoming], no. 228).

207. A lovely inscription from Sour refers to the cavalry-colonizers under the command of Herodes, son of Aumos: *AE* (1895), no. 78; *OGIS,* no. 425; *IGR,* vol. 3, no. 1144 (= Sartre-Fauriat and Sartre, *IGLS,* vol. 15, forthcoming, no. 103); the patronymic is completely typical of the Arab milieus in the Hauran.

208. An inscription of certain Hauranese origin but kept in the National Lebanese Museum in Beirut mentions an officer who was first in Agrippa's service and then in Trajan's: Henri Seyrig, "Deux pièces énigmatiques: 2. Un officier d'Agrippa II," *Syria* 42 (1965): 31–34 (= *AS,* vol. 6, pp. 147–151; see also Sartre, *IGLS,* vol. 16, forthcoming, no. 1484).

209. William Henry Waddington, *Inscriptions grecques et latines de la Syrie* (Paris: Firmin-Didot, 1870), 2329, with commentary (reprinted in *OGIS,* no. 424 = *IGR,* vol. 3, no. 1223). The inscription was found in Sia, near Canatha.

210. Was there an influx of Jewish colonizers during this period? It is impossible to assert that there was; to be sure, Jews were numerous throughout the region, in the

Golan and Batanaea, and several unpublished inscriptions can be added to the monuments that have already been identified, texts and bas-reliefs decorated with seven-branched chandeliers, but because Jews have been identified in the region from the middle of the second century B.C.E. on, we cannot establish a firm link between the Jewish presence and Herodian colonization. In "The Troopers of Zamaris," in *Judaea in Hellenistic and Roman Times,* ed. S. Applebaum (Leiden and New York: E. J. Brill, 1989), pp. 47–65, Shimon Applebaum offers a very thorough study of the group led by Zamaris, but his text is marred by numerous errors of detail and dubious assertions. He tends to connect any Jewish presence in that region of Batanaea to the Herodian military colonization, which is probably going too far.

211. *SEG,* vol. 38 (1988), no. 1647. In "Ères d'Agrippa II," Seyrig established that there were two eras, one beginning in 56, the other in 61; but coins oblige us to shift them both back a year (see the discussion in Andrew Burnett, Michel Amandry, and Pere Pau Ripollès, *Roman Provincial Coinage,* vol. 2 [London: British Museum Press; Paris: Bibliothèque nationale de France, 1998], p. 309). Alla Kushnir-Stein proposes to shift these eras back to 49 and 54, which means that Agrippa II may have died as early as 88–89: see "The Coinage of Agrippa II," *Scripta classica israelica* (hereafter cited as *SCI*) 21 (2002): 123–131. See also Christopher Prestige Jones, "Towards a Chronology of Josephus," *SCI* 21 (2002): 113–121.

212. Seyrig, "Deux pièces énigmatiques."

213. The most recent inscription of Agrippa II in Batanaea dates from 92 ("the year 37, which is the year 32"), in Sanamein (*IGR,* vol. 3, no. 1127); the earlier inscription dates from Domitian's era, in 96 (Maurice Dunand, *Mission archéologique au Djebel Druze: Le Musée de Soueida; Inscriptions et monuments figurés* [Paris: P. Geuthner, 1934], p. 49, no. 75).

214. Marie-Thérèse Frankfort's study, "Le royaume d'Agrippa II et son annexion par Domitien," in *Hommages à Albert Grenier,* ed. Marcel Reynard (Brussels: Latomus, 1962), vol. 2, pp. 659–672, has to be reconsidered in the light of the new chronology: Nikos Kokkinos, *The Herodian Dynasty* (Sheffield, U.K.: Sheffield Academic Press, 1998), pp. 396–400.

215. The date on which the kingdom of Chalcis disappeared is determined by the appearance of currency in that city, inaugurating an era of freedom in 92. Scholars have wondered about the identity of this Chalcis: Chalcis of Lebanon or Chalcis of Belos? The choice of the former does not strike me as open to doubt, for we have never had the slightest indication of an indigenous principate in the vicinity of the second, modern Qinnesrin. The choice of Chalcis of Belos by certain authors goes back in fact to Warwick William Wroth, *A Catalogue of the Greek Coins of Galatia, Cappadocia and Syria* (London: British Museum, 1899), pp. liv–lv, and Head, *Historia Numorum,* p. 785, followed by Arnold H. M. Jones, "The Urbanization of the Ituraean Principality," *JRS* 21 (1931): 267, an essay whose authoritativeness has impressed scholars; see also Schürer's hesitations in *History,* vol. 1, p. 573. We must finally recall that Chalcis of Lebanon was not really localized, despite the repeated affirmations of most scholars, who place it in Anjar, in the Beqaa region; they are probably right about the region, but the site remains to be discovered. See Ernest Will, "Un vieux problème de la topographie de la Beqa' antique: Chalcis du Liban," *ZDPV* 99 (1983): 141–146.

216. Josephus, *AJ* 14.80–81: Aretas paid three hundred talents.

217. For the political history of the Nabataeans, Starcky's "Pétra et la Nabatène"

(in *Dictionnaire de la Bible,* suppl. 7 [Paris: Letouzey & Ané, 1996], col. 904–920) remains indispensable. His work is completed and updated by Schürer, *History,* vol. 1, pp. 574–586; Philip C. Hammond, *The Nabataeans: Their History, Culture and Archaeology* (Göteborg: Äströms Förlag, 1973); Bowersock, *Roman Arabia;* Manfred Lindner, *Petra und das Königreich der Nabatäer: Lebensraum, Geschichte und Kultur eines arabischen Volkes der Antike,* 3rd ed. (Munich and Bad Windsheim: Delp, 1986); and Maria Giulia Amadasi Guzzo and Eugenia Equini Schneider, *Petra,* trans. Lydia G. Cochrane (Chicago: University of Chicago Press, 2002), pp. 29–52.

218. Maurice Sartre, "Rome et les Nabatéens à la fin de la République," *Revue des études anciennes* 81 (1979): 37–53.

219. Zbigniew T. Fiema and Richard N. Jones, "The Nabataean King-List Revised: Further Observations on the Second Nabataean Inscription from Tell esh-Shuqafiya, Egypt," *ADAJ* 34 (1990): 239–248.

220. Avraham Negev, "The Temple of Obodas: Excavations at Oboda in July 1989," *Israel Exploration Journal* 41 (1991): 62–80, especially p. 80.

221. Caesar, "The Alexandrian War," in *Alexandrian, African and Spanish Wars,* trans. A. G. Way (Loeb Classical Library), p. 1.

222. Plutarch, "Antony," 61.

223. Dio, 48.41.5.

224. Josephus, *BJ* 1.364–385; Plutarch, "Antony," 36; Dio, 49.32.15. In reality, Malichos remained in possession of the territory, but he had to pay tribute to Cleopatra, as a sign that the property was actually hers.

225. Josephus, *AJ* 14.370–375, *BJ* 1.274–278.

226. Josephus recounts these battles at great length (*AJ* 15.108–160, *BJ* 1.364–385).

227. Josephus, *AJ* 15.167–175.

228. Académie des inscriptions et belles-lettres, ed., *Corpus inscriptionum semiticarum,* vol. 2 (Paris: e Reipublicae Typographeo, 1881; repr., Paris: C. Klincksieck, 1972), no. 354 (Pétra) (hereafter cited as *CIS*); cf. Klaas Dijkstra, *Life and Loyalty: A Study in the Socio-Religious Culture of Syria and Mesopotamia in the Graeco-Roman Period Based on Epigraphical Evidence* (Leiden: E. J. Brill, 1995), pp. 319–321.

229. At most, it would have been a refounding, because archaeology has uncovered levels from the second century B.C.E.

230. Stephan G. Schmid, "Un roi nabatéen à Délos?," *ADAJ* 43 (1999): 279–298.

231. It is very probably on this occasion that Aretas IV's ambassadors put a bilingual Greek and Latin declaration on the Capitol: Attilio Degrassi, "Le dediche di popoli e re asiatici al popolo romano," *Bullettino della Commissione archeologica comunale di Roma* (1954), pp. 34–37; to be corrected by the new restitution and interpretation by Glen W. Bowersock, "Nabataeans on the Capitoline," *Hyperboreus* 3 (1997): 347–352. We could also recall the reestablishment of the king in 1 C.E., if annexation actually took place in the meantime.

232. Josephus, *AJ* 17.54–57.

233. An Arab phylarch, probably a tribal chief, and a friend of Syllaios were involved in the plot against Herod: ibid., 17.56.

234. Josephus speaks of neither his death nor his condemnation (ibid., 17.54–56), unlike Strabo (16.4.24), but the latter wrongly sees in it the consequence of his "treason" in 26–25 B.C.E.—I doubt that it took nearly twenty years before the "traitor"

was tried. Moreover, scholars have thought they recognized Syllaios's monogram on silver coins bearing the effigy of Obodas III and of Aretas IV (see Ya'akov Meshorer, *Nabataean Coins* [Jerusalem: Institute of Archaeology, Hebrew University of Jerusalem, 1975], pp. 36–40). Finally, in "The Mason's Workshop of Hegra, Its Relation to Petra, and the Tomb of Syllaios," *SHAJ* 3 (1987): 143–150, Andreas Schmidt-Colinet has suggested that a monumental tomb in Hegra, which was never finished and which would have had the same dimensions as the Khazneh in Petra (39 meters high), might well have been the one that Syllaios had started to have built during his lifetime.

235. Bowersock, *Roman Arabia,* p. 51–56.

236. Strabo, 16.4.21.

237. Millar is skeptical: see *Roman Near East,* p. 44, n. 1.

238. Gaius Caesar is thought to have led a campaign in Arabia in 1 C.E., according to a combined reading of Eugen Borman, *CIL,* vol. 11, *Inscriptiones Aemiliae, Etruriae, Umbriae latinae,* 2 vols. (Berlin: G. Reimer, 1888–1926), no. 1421, lines 7–8, and Pliny, *NH* 6.31.141. An unfortunate correction on the part of the copyist of *Periplus Maris Erythraei,* 26, led to the belief that this expedition would have ended in the destruction of Aden. This is by no means the case, and explanations need to be sought elsewhere. We know that the term *Arabia* designates every land occupied by nomads, which leaves open a good number of possibilities. Pliny's mention of the *sinus arabicus* (*NH* 2.67.168) directs us toward the Sinai and thus toward the Nabataean kingdom. Under these conditions, this "expedition" might have consisted simply in crowning Aretas IV officially in Petra, after a few years' delay. All of this remains highly hypothetical. Cf. Sidebotham, *Roman Economic Policy,* pp. 130–135.

239. Many scholars, including Millar, have defended the idea that Damascus was controlled by the Nabataeans at the time when Paul found refuge there, because an ethnarch of the Nabataeans is mentioned (*Roman Near East,* pp. 56–57). Millar judges that this situation lasted from 33–34 to 65–66, a period during which there was indeed a gap in the minting of coins in Damascus. This is not impossible, but the interruption of coin minting is not sufficient proof, for we know that the city-states produced coins only sporadically. Others, such as Michael Baigent and Richard Leigh (*The Dead Sea Scrolls Deception* [New York: Summit Books, 1991], p. 179), prefer to defend the idea that the Damascus of the Acts of the Apostles is another city in the region, but not the current capital of Syria, a claim that strikes me as baseless. As far as the first hypothesis is concerned, we know that the Julio-Claudians did not hesitate to return regions that had been annexed to the Roman Empire to client princes from the region, but I am astonished that no source, not even Josephus, mentions that sumptuous gift to the kings of Petra; moreover, this implies a territorial break in the kingdom, for between the Nabataean Hauran and the Damascus region stood the states of Agrippa I and then Agrippa II. Thus I do not know how to explain the mention of a Nabataean ethnarch in Damascus in the middle or late 30s.

240. Josephus, *AJ* 16.130.275–281.

241. Judith McKenzie, *The Architecture of Petra* (Oxford and New York: Oxford University Press, 1990), p. 51; see also p. 7, where there is a very instructive chart of the different datings proposed according to various criteria by her predecessors, a dating that varies from "no later than Augustus" to "surely not before 106."

242. Martha Sharp Joukowsky, "The Brown University 1998 Excavation at the Petra Great Temple," *ADAJ* 43 (1999): 195–222; on the adjacent paradise, see Leigh-

Ann Bedal, "A Paradeisos in Petra: New Light on the 'Lower Market,'" *ADAJ* 43 (1999): 227–239. I have not seen the overall publication: Martha Sharp Joukowsky, *Petra Great Temple I: Brown University Excavations 1993–1997* (Providence: n.p., 1998). The sacred character of the building is cast in doubt by Zbigniew T. Fiema, "L'urbanisme à Pétra," *Le monde de la Bible* (hereafter cited as *M.Bible*) 127 (May–June 2000): 39, and especially by Glen W. Bowersock, "La surprise du bouleutèrion," *M.Bible* 127, p. 60. It is the whole ensemble that was once called "Thermes," and that Fawzi Zayadine in particular takes to be a palace ("Decorative Stucco at Petra and Other Hellenistic Sites," *SHAJ* 3 [1987], 131–142); this view is shared by Jacques Seigne, in a review of Martha Sharp Joukowsky in *Topoi* 10 (2000): 507–516.

243. This type of arrangement is found several times in Dura-Europus, especially in the first century B.C.E.: see Pierre Leriche, "Matériaux pour une réflexion renouvelée sur les sanctuaries de Doura-Europos," *Topoi* 7 (1997): 889–913. François Villeneuve suggests that it is simply a matter of the *bouleuterion* of the city, well attested in the second century C.E. by the papyri of Nahal Hever ("Pétra revisitée," *M.Bible* 127 [May–June 2000], p. 17).

244. Cf. the list established by Josèf Tadeusz Milik, "Une inscription bilingue nabatéenne et grecque à Pétra," *ADAJ* 21 (1976): 143–152, especially 147–151.

245. *CIS*, vol. 2, nos. 195, 196; Enno Littmann, ed., *Semitic Inscriptions: Safaitic Inscriptions,* vol. 4C of *Syria: Publications of the Princeton University Archaeological Expeditions to Syria in 1904–1905 and 1909* (Leiden: E. J. Brill, 1943), 96; Jean Starcky, "Une inscription nabatéenne provenant du Djof," *Rbi* 64 (1957): 196–217; J. T. Milik, "Nouvelles inscriptions nabatéennes," *Syria* 35 (1958): 243–246, no. 6. Cf. Françoise Briquel-Chatonnet, "La pénétration de la culture du Croissant fertile en Arabie: À propos des inscriptions nabatéennes," in *Présence arabe dans le Croissant fertile avant l'Hégire,* ed. Hélène Lozachmeur (Paris: Éditions Recherche sur les civilisations, 1995), pp. 133–141, especially pp. 135–136.

246. Strabo, 16.4.21. Strabo does not specify what the drink is, but for a Greek it goes without saying that it can only be wine.

247. The construction of the east door and of the *temenos* situated to the east, at least, date from this period: Sartre, *Bostra*, p. 61; Jean-Marie Dentzer, "Les sondages de l'Arc Nabatéen et l'urbanisme de Bosra," *CRAI* (1986): 62–87; idem; "Sondages près de l'Arc Nabatéen de Bosra," *Berytus* 32 (1984): 163–174.

248. See, among others, Jean-Charles Balty, "Architecture et société à Pétra et à Hégra: Chronologie et classes sociales; Sculpteurs et commanditaires," in *Architecture et société: De l'archaïsme grec à la fin de la République romaine* (Rome: École française de Rome; Paris: Centre national de la recherche scientifique, 1983), pp. 303–324; Briquel-Chatonnet, "Pénétration," pp. 133–141, especially pp. 134–135.

249. Bowersock, *Roman Arabia*, pp. 80–84. It seems unlikely to me that the initiative for this annexation came from the Syrian governor Cornelius Palma without explicit instructions from Trajan, as Philip Freeman maintains: "The Annexation of Arabia and Imperial Grand Strategy," in Kennedy and Braund, *Roman Army,* pp. 91–118.

250. Sartre, *Trois études*, pp. 17–35.

251. The existence of a Malichos (III) who took refuge in Hegra is a myth, as was demonstrated long ago; moreover, we know that Rabbel II's heir was called Obodas and not Malichos: Yigael Yadin, "The Nabatean Kingdom, Provincia Arabia, Petra, and En Geddi in the Documents from Nahal Hever," *Ex Oriente Lux* 17 (1963): 230;

cf. the genealogical table of the Nabataean royal family beginning with Aretas IV in Kokkinos, *Herodian Dynasty,* pp. 376–377.

252. Cf. coins showing a camel driver with one knee on the ground, accompanied by the words *Arabia adquisita:* see Harold Mattingly, *Coins of the Roman Empire in the British Museum,* rev. ed., vol. 3, *Nerva to Hadrian* (London: British Museum Publications, 1976), p. 185, no. 877; Harold Mattingly and Edward A. Sydenham, *The Roman Imperial Coinage,* vol. 2, *Vespasian to Hadrian* (London: Spink & Son, 1926), p. 278, nos. 465–468, and p. 287, nos. 610–615.

253. This was the result of a balance of power, not a treaty: in 35, Artaban III demanded that the Parthians be allowed to return to the old frontier dating from the era of the Persians and the Macedonians (Tacitus, *Annals,* 6.31). One might as well speak of the return of all of Asia Minor to Parthian control.

254. With the exception of Commagene, which extended across both banks of the river.

255. Victor Chapot, *La frontière de l'Euphrate de Pompée à la conquête arabe* (Paris: A. Fontemoing, 1907).

4. THE CRISES IN JUDAEA FROM HEROD TO BAR KOKHBA

1. Gedaliah Alon, *Jews, Judaism and the Classical World: Studies in the Jewish History in the Times of the Second Temple and Talmud* (Jerusalem: Magnes Press, Hebrew University, 1977).

2. Doron Mendels, *The Rise and Fall of Jewish Nationalism* (New York: Doubleday, 1992), pp. 209–214.

3. This would explain both Hyrcanos's execution in the spring of 30 (Josephus, *De antiquitate judaico* [*Jewish Antiquities*], trans. Louis H. Feldman [Loeb Classical Library], 15.164 [hereafter cited as *AJ*]) and Mariamme's (in 29), then that of her two sons Aristobulos and Alexander (in 7), and even that of Antipater, Herod's son and the husband of the daughter of Mattathias and Antigonos, the last Hasmonaean ruler, on the very eve of the king's death (*AJ*, 17.82).

4. Mendels, *Rise and Fall,* pp. 209–242.

5. From the very extensive bibliography on Herod, the most useful references include the following: Samuel Sandmel, *Herod: Profile of a Tyrant* (Philadelphia: Lippincott, 1967); Solomon Zeitlin, *The Rise and Fall of the Judaean State* (Philadelphia: Jewish Publication Society of America, 1962–1978), vol. 2, pp. 3–99; Abraham Schalit, *König Herodes: Der Mann und sein Werk* (Berlin: W. de Gruyter, 1969); Michael Grant, *Herod the Great* (New York: American Heritage Press, 1971); Emil Schürer, *The History of the Jewish People in the Age of Jesus Christ (75 B.C.–A.D. 135),* rev. and ed. Géza Vermès and Fergus Millar, trans. T. A. Burkill et al. (Edinburgh: Clark, 1973–1986), vol. 1, pp. 287–329; Menahem Stern, "The Reign of Herod and the Herodian Dynasty," in *The Jewish People in the First Century: Historical, Geographical, Political History, Social, Cultural and Religious Life and Institutions,* ed. Shemuel Safrai and Menahem Stern (Assen: Van Gorcum, 1974), pp. 216–307; Menahem Stern, "The Reign of Herod," in *The World History of the Jewish People,* vol. 7, ed. Michael Avi-Yonah and Zvi Baras (Tel Aviv: Jewish History Publications; London: W. H. Allen, 1975), pp. 71–123, 351–354 (notes), 388 (bibliography). Nikos Kokkinos focuses particularly on the family, in *The Herodian Dynasty: Origins, Role in Society and Eclipse* (Sheffield, U.K.: Sheffield Academic Press, 1998).

6. Books 14 (280–491) and 15–17 of Josephus, *AJ*, relate Herod's reign in great detail. Josephus must surely have profited from information transmitted by Nicolaos of Damascus, Herod's friend and historiographer, whose work is lost.

7. Josephus, *AJ* 15.215–217; Josephus, *De bello judaico (The Jewish War)*, trans. Henry St. John Thackeray (Loeb Classical Library), 1.396–397 (hereafter cited as *BJ*).

8. Josephus, *AJ* 15.292–298, *BJ* 1.403.

9. Building must have begun around 22 B.C.E. (Josephus, *AJ* 15.331–341), for the city was ceremonially dedicated in 10, after twelve years of construction: see ibid., 15.341 (notwithstanding 16.146, which refers to a ten-year period). Cf. Lee I. Levine, *Caesarea under Roman Rule* (Leiden: E. J. Brill, 1975); Joseph Ringel, *Césarée de Palestine: Étude historique et archéologique* (Paris: Ophrys, 1975). For studies of the city after the recent excavations, see Kenneth G. Holum and Robert L. Hohlfelder, eds., *King Herod's Dream: Caesarea on the Sea* (New York: W. W. Norton, 1988); Robert Lindley Vann, ed., *Caesarea Papers: Straton's Tower, Herod's Harbour, and Roman and Byzantine Caesarea* (Ann Arbor, Mich.: Journal of Roman Archaeology, 1992); Avner Raban and Kenneth G. Holum, *Caesarea Maritima: A Retrospective after Two Millennia* (Leiden and New York: E. J. Brill, 1996); Kenneth G. Holum, Avner Raban, and Joseph Patrich, eds., *Caesarea Papers 2: Herod's Temple, the Provincial Governor's Praetorium and Granaries, the Later Harbor* (Portsmouth, R.I.: Journal of Roman Archaeology, 1999).

10. *Sebaste* is the Greek translation of *Augusta*.

11. On the Herodian temple, a veritable "third Temple" when the work done there is taken into account, see T. A. Busink, *Der Tempel von Jerusalem, von Salomo bis Herodes: Eine archäologisch-historische Studie unter Berücksichtigung des west-semitischen Tempelbaus,* vol. 2 (Leiden: E. J. Brill, 1980), especially pp. 1017–1251; for a more concise treatment, see André Parrot, *Le Temple de Jérusalem* (Neuchâtel: Delachaux & Niestlé, 1954).

12. Josephus, *AJ* 15.380: construction began around 20–19.

13. Ibid., 17.41–45.

14. Ibid., 17.149–167; idem, *BJ* 1.640.

15. Josephus, *AJ* 15.268–274. The reference may be to another theater built of wood: see Joseph Patrich, "Herod's Theatre in Jerusalem: A New Proposal," *Israel Exploration Journal* (hereafter cited as *IEJ*) 52 (2002): 231–239.

16. Josephus, *AJ* 16.149.

17. R. R. Chambers, "Greek Athletics and the Jews" (Ph.D. diss., Miami University, Miami, Ohio, 1980): an essential study.

18. Schürer, *History,* vol. 2, pp. 227–236.

19. Josephus, *AJ* 15.41, 15.51–56.

20. Yigael Yadin, *Masada: Herod's Fortress and the Zealots' Last Stand* (London: Weidenfeld & Nicholson, 1966); Hannah M. Cotton and Joseph Geiger, *Masada: The Yigael Yadin Excavations 1963–1965,* vol. 2, *The Latin and Greek Documents* (Jerusalem: Israel Exploration Society, 1989); Gideon Foerster, *Masada: The Yigael Yadin Excavations 1964–1965,* vol. 5, *Art and Architecture* (Jerusalem: Israel Exploration Society, 1995); Mireille Hadas-Lebel, *Massada: Histoire et symbole* (Paris: Albin Michel, 1995).

21. See Ehud Netzer's concise guide, *Herodium: An Archaeological Guide* (Jerusalem: Cana, 1987), and especially idem, *Greater Herodium* (Jerusalem: Institute of Archaeology, Hebrew University of Jerusalem, 1981).

22. On Herod's construction policy, see Duane W. Roller, *The Building Program of Herod the Great* (Berkeley: University of California Press, 1998), and Achim Lichtenberger, *Die Baupolitik Herodes des Grossen* (Wiesbaden: Harrassowitz, 1999), which includes an up-to-date bibliography on every site where Herod intervened. On the palaces, see Ehud Netzer, Dominique Svenson, and Hendrik Svenson-Evers, *Die Paläste der Hasmonäer und Herodes' des Grossen, Sonderhefte der Antiken Welt* (Mainz: Ph. von Zabern, 1999), a work written for a broad audience by one of the finest specialists, with numerous illustrations, architectural plans, and very evocative axionometric restitutions. I have not been able to see Luigi Marino's *Le opere fortificate di Erode il Grande* (Verona: Cierre Edizioni, 1997).

23. Cotton and Geiger, *Masada*, vol. 2, pp. 133–177.

24. Benjamin H. Isaac, "Bandits in Judaea and Arabia," *Harvard Studies in Classical Philology* 88 (1984): 171–203.

25. Josephus, *AJ* 15.365. This may be a result of the famine and the accompanying epidemic in 24–23 B.C.E.; see ibid., 15.299, 15.302, 15.307. On Herod's resources, see Emilio Gabba, "The Finances of King Herod," in *Greece and Rome in Eretz Israel: Collected Essays,* ed. Aryeh Kasher, Gideon Fuks, and Uriel Rappaport (Jerusalem: Yad Izhak ben-Zvi [Israel Exploration Society], 1990), pp. 160–168.

26. Josephus, *AJ* 16.64.

27. Ibid., 15.306.

28. Stewart Perowne's *The Later Herods: The Political Background of the New Testament* (London: Hodder & Stoughton, 1958) is often anecdotal, and Arnold H. M. Jones's *The Herods of Judaea* (Oxford: Clarendon Press, 1967; originally published 1938) appears outdated. See instead Schürer's clarifying account in *History,* vol. 2, pp. 336–357, 442–454, and 471–483, along with several individual monographs mentioned in later notes.

29. See the terms of the debate in Kokkinos, *Herodian Dynasty,* pp. 372–373.

30. He is only the half brother of Antipas and Archelaos; the latter are both sons of Malthake, whereas Philip is the son of a Cleopatra. He must not be confused with Herod Philip, son of Mariamme II, the first husband of Herodias (a sister of Agrippa I) and father of Salome; his widow was married in a scandalous fashion to Antipas, and his daughter Salome married the tetrarch Philip.

31. Josephus, *AJ* 17.317–321.

32. Schürer, *History,* vol. 2, pp. 330–335.

33. On the liquidation of Archelaos's states and Quirinius's census, see Luke, 2:1–5; Josephus, *BJ* 2.111 and 2.117–118; idem, *AJ* 17.339–344, 17.355, 18.1–4, 18.26, and 18.29–32.

34. Josephus, *BJ* 2.111.

35. Josephus, *AJ* 18.2 (see also 17.355); but *BJ* 2.117 may allow us to believe that Judaea became a full-fledged province.

36. Theodor Mommsen, *Corpus inscriptionum latinarum* (hereafter cited as *CIL*), vol. 3, *Inscriptiones Asiae, provinciaeum Europae graecarum, Illyrici latinae,* 4 vols. (Berlin: G. Reimer, 1873–1902), no. 6687 (= Hermann Dessau, *Inscriptiones latinae selectae* [Berlin: Weidmann, 1892–1916], no. 2683 [hereafter cited as *ILS*]): "iussu Quirini censum egi Apamenae civitatis millium homin(um) ciuium CXVII. Idem missu Quirini adversus Ituraeos in Libano monte castellum eorum cepi."

37. His campaign against the Marmarics shortly before 12 B.C.E. is well known, but the Homonadaean war that he had to carry out in Pisidia, as governor of Galatia,

falls into a broad span, between 12 B.C.E., the year he became a consul, and 4 C.E., most probably between 6 and 1 B.C.E.: see Maurice Sartre, *L'Asie Mineure et l'Anatolie d'Alexandre à Dioclétien* (Paris: A. Colin, 1995), p. 169, and Stephen Mitchell, *Anatolia: Land, Men, and Gods in Asia Minor,* vol. 1 (Oxford: Clarendon Press, 1993), pp. 77–78; Mitchell believes that the war must have taken place between 6 B.C.E. and 4 C.E.

38. Luke 1:5. I am not taking into account the fact that Matthew's narrative explicitly places Jesus's birth in Herod's era and indicates that Herod sought to get rid of him (the Massacre of the Innocents), for the story of Jesus's childhood may be only a later addition, based on Luke's mention of the census.

39. The topic is examined quite fully in Schürer, *History,* vol. 1, pp. 399–427; see also Paul Benoît, in *Dictionnaire de la Bible,* suppl. 9 (Paris: Letouzey & Ané, 1979), s.v. "Quirinius (recensement de-)," cols. 693–720. I shall not examine all the statements that have been made on the subject, for many of them are quite fanciful and betray complete ignorance of the way the Roman administration worked. We know, moreover, that the concern for having Jesus born in Bethlehem stems from the Davidic vision of his origins. Recently, in "La date de naissance de Jésus du point de vue romain," *Comptes rendus des séances de l'Académie des inscriptions et belles-lettres* (1995): 799–806, Gilbert Picard has defended Luke's later date; this would necessarily mean making Jesus considerably younger during his active life, because no one contests his death during Pilatus's time—that is, at the latest, 36 C.E.

40. This is a recent hypothesis of Jacques Winandy, "Le recensement dit de Quirinius (Lc 2,2): Une interpolation?" *Revue biblique* (hereafter cited as *Rbi*) (1997): 373–377; Winandy also proposes a somewhat different translation of Luke's text (which does not change very much).

41. Although several months probably elapsed before Augustus intervened, and then several more months before Archelaos took control of his eparchy; he had the time to build or embellish a palace in Jericho, to plant a palm grove in the same neighborhood, and to take on Jews and Samaritans; we have to count two or three months more for his representative in Rome to come find him in Jerusalem, for Archelaos to get there, and for Augustus to prepare his trial. All this cannot have taken place in only a few months.

42. This precise accounting, although not convincing in all respects, is by Étienne Nodet, in *Baptême et résurrection: Le témoignage de Josèphe* (Paris: Le Cerf, 1999), pp. 126–152. One of the major difficulties seems to come from the succession of high priests. In fact, Josephus asserts that Ioazar, son of Boethos, was stripped of his possessions by Archelaos to the benefit of Eleazar and then of Jesus, son of See. Yet the same Ioazar, son of Boethos, appears in another passage as the high priest under Quirinius; at first favorably disposed toward the Romans (he encouraged his fellow citizens to participate in a census), he was later stripped of his possessions by Quirinius because he had been given his power by the people, which presumably means without Rome's authorization; he was replaced by Ananos (Hanan), son of Seth. These contradictions are hard to resolve: see Schürer, *History,* vol. 2, p. 229.

43. Josephus uses the verb *apodidomi,* which ordinarily means "to sell," but which can also mean "to attribute in keeping with what is expected." Let us note that the village of Archelais, founded by Archelaos, was attributed to Salome, his aunt; she bequeathed it a few years later to Julie, Augustus's daughter, at the same time as Iamnia (Josephus, *AJ* 18.31).

44. Edward Dąbrowa, *The Governors of Roman Syria from Augustus to Septimius Severus* (Bonn: R. Habelt, 1998), p. 25.

45. On the possible localization, see Schürer, *History,* vol. 2, p. 355, n. 12.

46. Josephus, *AJ* 17.342–343, *BJ* 2.111–113; Cassius Dio, *Roman History,* trans. Earnest Cary (Loeb Classical Library), 55.27.6 (hereafter cited as Dio); the latter indicates that this took place under the consulate of Aemilius Lepidus and L. Arruntius, consuls in 6 C.E.; however, Dio may owe this information to Josephus.

47. For the essential information, see Schürer, *History,* vol. 1, pp. 336–340.

48. Josephus, *AJ* 18.28.

49. See Maurice Sartre, *Trois études sur l'Arabie romaine et byzantine* (Brussels: Revue d'études latines, 1982), p. 48; on the single inscription at Sia, see Enno Littmann, David Magie, and D. R. Stuart, *Greek and Latin Inscriptions: Southern Syria,* vol. 3A of *Syria: Publications of the Princeton University Archaeological Expeditions to Syria in 1904–1905 and 1909* (Leiden: E. J. Brill, 1921), no. 768.

50. Josephus, *AJ* 18.106–107.

51. This Salome is the daughter of her half brother Herod Antipas and his niece Herodias (the sister of Agrippa I), the one whose second marriage was with her other uncle, Antipas. She is thus both his niece (as the daughter of his half brother) and his grandniece (as the daughter of his niece).

52. Josephus, *AJ* 18.108.

53. See Schürer, *History,* vol. 1, pp. 340–353; Frederick Fyvie Bruce, "Herod Antipas, Tetrarch of Galilee and Peraea," *Annals of Leeds University Oriental Society* 5 (1963–1965): 6–23, and especially Harold W. Hoehner, *Herod Antipas* (Cambridge: Cambridge University Press, 1972); Hoehner paints quite a complete picture of the kingdom and its inhabitants, as well as of the relations between Antipas and John the Baptist.

54. Not Philip the tetrarch, as is indicated only in Mark 6:17, but Herod Philip, the son of Herod the Great and Mariamme II, the daughter of the high priest Simon; this Herodias was herself a niece of Antipas, because she was the daughter of his half brother Aristobolos, whom Herod had had put to death; she was the sister of Agrippa I.

55. Josephus, *AJ* 18.112–115.

56. Philo of Alexandria, *Legatio ad Gaium,* ed. and trans. E. Mary Smallwood, 2nd ed. (Leiden: E. J. Brill, 1970), 38; Philo does not name names, but he points out the intervention of Herod's four sons; see Perowne, *Later Herods,* p. 52.

57. Josephus, *AJ* 18.27; see Hoehner, *Herod Antipas,* pp. 84–87.

58. Josephus points to Iulias (*AJ* 18.27); see Schürer, *History,* vol. 1, p. 342, and Hoehner, *Herod Antipas,* pp. 87–91.

59. In "The Foundation of Tiberias," *IEJ* 1 (1951): 160–169, Michael Avi-Yonah places the foundation in 18; Hoehner prefers to place it in 23 (*Herod Antipas,* pp. 91–100).

60. Josephus, *AJ* 18.237. The last reliable attestation of Lysanias is at the end of the 20s, in Luke 3:1; he may have died around 30, and his tetrarchy may have been temporarily annexed to Syria, as was the case for Philip's between 34 and 37. See Daniel R. Schwartz, *Agrippa I: The Last King of Judaea* (Tübingen: J. C. B. Mohr, 1990), p. 60.

61. Antipas accompanied Vitellius during the negotiations with the Parthians,

in 35, but he took the initiative of sending an exhaustive account to Tiberius even before Vitellius made his official report: Josephus, *AJ* 18.101–105; cf. Hoehner, *Herod Antipas,* pp. 252–253.

62. Josephus sometimes gives Lugdunum (*AJ* 18.252), sometimes Spain (*BJ* 2.183); Lugdunum Convenarum may allow us to reconcile the two traditions.

63. See Zeitlin, *Rise and Fall,* vol. 2, pp. 185–203; Schürer, *History,* vol. 1, pp. 442–454; Schwartz, *Agrippa I.*

64. See the long letter he wrote to Caligula, transmitted by Philo (Philo, *Legatio,* 276–329); on the details and on Agrippa's role, see Schwartz, *Agrippa I,* pp. 77–89.

65. Schwartz, *Agrippa I,* pp. 74–77, 99–106.

66. Josephus, *BJ* 2.218–219 and 5.147–160; it appears that Agrippa's wall remained unfinished at the time of the king's death and covered only the northern sector of the city, protecting the new quarter of Bezetha; see Schwartz, *Agrippa I,* pp. 140–144.

67. Josephus, *AJ* 19.338–343; cf. Schwartz, *Agrippa I,* pp. 137–140.

68. Agrippa seems to have played a role in Claudius's accession to the empire, but this reason strikes Schwartz, who tends to minimize Agrippa's role, as incidental (*Agrippa I,* pp. 91–93).

69. Schwartz supports an early date, probably in October 43 (ibid., pp. 110–111).

70. Ibid., pp. 150–153.

71. Schwartz sees no particular trouble (ibid., p. 153); but cf. Nicole Belayche, "Les figures politiques des Messies en Palestine dans la première moitié du premier siècle de notre ère," in *Politique et religion dans le judaïsme ancien et médiéval,* ed. Daniel Tollet (Paris: Desclée, 1989), pp. 60–61.

72. Tacitus, *The Annals,* trans. John Jackson (Loeb Classical Library), 12.23.1: "Ituraeique et Iudaei defunctis regibus Sohaemo et Agrippa provinciae Syriae additi."

73. Schürer, *History,* vol. 1, pp. 571–573.

74. Josephus, *AJ* 20.15–16 and 20.103.

75. Marie-Thérèse Frankfort, "Le royaume d'Agrippa II et son annexion par Domitien," in *Hommages à Albert Grenier,* ed. Marcel Reynard (Brussels: Latomus, 1962), vol. 2, pp. 659–672, to be corrected according to the indications concerning chronology given above.

76. The widow of her uncle Herod of Chalcis, Berenice went back to live with her brother Agrippa II. To put a stop to rumors of incest (Josephus, *AJ* 20.145, and an allusion in Juvenal, Satire VI, "The Ways of Women," in *Juvenal and Persius,* trans. G. G. Ramsey [Loeb Classical Library], 6.156–160), she married Polemon of Cilicia; but she separated from him quite soon. Once again at her brother's court, she had a liaison with Titus during the war of 66–70, and she almost married him. But in the face of negative Roman public opinion, Titus renounced the marriage.

77. Josephus, *BJ* 2.500–503, 2.523–525.

78. Ibid., 3.444.

79. Ibid., 7.23–24.

80. Gerd Theissen, *Histoire sociale du christianisme primitif: Jésus, Paul, Jean* (Geneva: Labor & Fides, 1996), pp. 72–75; an essential text.

81. Josephus, *The Life,* vol. 1 in *The Life and Against Apion,* trans. Henry St. John Thackeray (Loeb Classical Library), p. 65.

82. Josephus, *AJ* 15.361, *BJ* 1.400.

83. On these privileged relations, see the summary of the seventh Sir Ronald Syme Memorial Lecture, by Stephen Mitchell, in the *Times Literary Supplement* (March 6, 1998): 12–13.

84. Philo, *Legatio*, 276–329.

85. Josephus, *BJ* 2.344–407.

86. Josephus, *AJ* 16.225.

87. Josephus, *AJ* 19.355 (promise of marriage); 20.139 (failure).

88. Maurizio Ghiretti, "Lo 'status' della Giudea dall'età Augustea all'età Claudia," *Latomus* 44 (1985): 751–766.

89. Josephus may have been misled by the vocabulary in use on the eve of the revolt; but the fact that the Judaean administrators were called "prefects" before 41 is definitively attested by the inscription from Caesarea mentioning Pontius Pilatus (*L'année épigraphique* [1963]: 104, followed by a copious bibliography aiming to restore the beginning of the text); see also, finally, with the bibliography, Géza Alföldy, "Pontius Pilatus und das Tiberieum von Caesarea Maritima," *Scripta classica israelica* (hereafter cited as *SCI*) 18 (1999): 85–108; Alföldy makes the Tiberieum the counterpart of the Drusieum (Drusion), protection for the port of Caesarea, and he restores *[nauti]s* to the beginning: "For the sailors, Pontius Pilate, prefect of Judaea, repaired the Tiberieum."

90. Josephus, *BJ* 2.117–118.

91. Tacitus, *Histories,* in *The Histories and the Annals,* trans. Clifford H. Moore (Loeb Classical Library), 5.9; this passage seems to be contradicted by *Annals* 12.23.1, where Tacitus openly evokes the annexation of Syria.

92. See J. Gonzalez Echegaray, "La guarnicion romana de Judea en los tiempos del Nuevo Testamento," *Estudios Biblicos* 36 (1977): 69ff.; Michael p. Speidel, "The Roman Army in Judaea under the Procurators: The Italian and the Augustan Cohort in the Acts of the Apostles," *Ancient Society* 13–14 (1982–1983): 233–240; Benjamin H. Isaac, *The Limits of Empire: The Roman Army in the East* (Oxford and New York: Clarendon Press, 1990), p. 105.

93. See Gerd Theissen, "Jésus et la crise sociale de son temps: Aspects sociohistoriques de la recherche du Jésus historique," in *Jésus de Nazareth: Nouvelles approches d'une énigme,* ed. Daniel Marguerat, Enrico Norelli, and Jean-Michel Poffet (Geneva: Labor & Fides, 1998), p. 147.

94. Lutz Neesen, *Untersuchungen zu den direkten Staasabgaben der römischen Kaiserzeit (27 v. Chr.–284 n. Chr.)* (Bonn: R. Habelt, 1980); Claude Nicolet, *L'inventaire du monde* (Paris: Fayard, 1988).

95. See Mireille Hadas-Lebel, "La fiscalité romaine dans la littérature rabbinique jusqu'à la fin du IIIe siècle apr. J.-C.," *Revue des études juives* 143 (1984): 5–29.

96. Christiane Saulnier, "Les lois romaines sur les Juifs d'après Flavius Josephus," *Rbi* 88 (1981): 161–185.

97. Tessa Rajak, "Was There a Roman Charter for the Jews?" *Journal of Roman Studies* (hereafter cited as *JRS*) 74 (1984): 107–123.

98. See the list in Schürer, *History,* vol. 2, pp. 229–232: between Herod's death and the end of the Jewish War, we know the names of twenty-two high priests.

99. Hugo Mantel, *Studies in the History of the Sanhedrin* (Cambridge, Mass.: Harvard University Press, 1961).

100. See the essential contribution by Theissen, "Jésus et la crise sociale," pp. 125–

155; see also David A. Fiensy, *The Social History of Palestine in the Herodian Period: The Land Is Mine* (Lewiston, N.Y.: E. Mellen Press, 1991).

101. Shimon Applebaum, "Judaea as a Roman Province: The Countryside as a Political and Economic Factor," *Aufstieg und Niedergang der römischen Welt* (hereafter cited as *ANRW*) 2.8 (1977): 355–396.

102. According to Georgius Cedrenus, Antipas had large holdings on the territory of Narbata (*Chronica*, ed. Immanuel Bekker, 2 vols., in *Georgius Cedrenus [et] Ioannis Scylitzae ope* [Bonn: Weber, 1838–1839]).

103. See Shimon Applebaum, "Royal and Imperial Estates in the Sharon and Samaria," in *Judaea in Hellenistic and Roman Times: Historical and Archaeological Essays* (Leiden and New York: E. J. Brill, 1989), pp. 97–110. I am more skeptical about the conclusions drawn from the single place name *Khirbet Bereniki* near Antipatris (p. 108).

104. Josephus, *AJ* 17.289, *BJ* 2.69.

105. Stuart S. Miller, *Studies in the History and Traditions of Sepphoris* (Leiden: E. J. Brill, 1984).

106. Hadas-Lebel, "Fiscalité romaine."

107. Peter A. Brunt, "Josephus on Social Conflicts in Roman Judaea," *Klio: Beiträge zur alten Geschichte* 59 (1977): 149–153.

108. Tacitus, *Annals* 2.42; see Theissen, "Jésus et la crise sociale," p. 151.

109. Martin Hengel and Christoph Markschies, *The "Hellenization" of Judaea in the First Century after Christ* (London: SCM Press; Philadelphia: Trinity Press International, 1989), p. 5. This work has appeared in German translation: "Zum Problem der 'Hellenisierung' Judäas im 1. Jahrhundert nach Christus," *Judaica et Hellenistica: Kleine Schriften* (Tübingen: J. C. B. Mohr, 1996), pp. 1–90 (I am citing the German edition). But Hengel's goal, which he makes clear at the outset, is to define the degree of Hellenization in order to understand the milieu in which Christianity was born.

110. Hengel, *"Hellenization" of Judea*, p. 45.

111. Ibid., p. 57.

112. James L. Kelso and Dimitri C. Baramki, *Excavations at New Testament Jericho and Khirbet en-Nitla* (New Haven, Conn.: American Schools of Oriental Research, 1955), p. 10.

113. Hengel, *"Hellenization" of Judea*, p. 68.

114. Ibid., p. 79.

115. Within the extensive bibliography, the following texts are of particular interest: Louis Finkelstein, *The Pharisees: The Sociological Background of Their Faith*, 3rd ed., 2 vols. (Philadelphia: Jewish Publication Society of America, 1966; originally published 1938); idem, *Pharisaism in the Making: Selected Essays* (New York: Ktav, 1972); Jacob Neusner, *From Politics to Piety: The Emergence of Pharisaic Judaism*, 2nd ed. (New York: Ktav, 1979); Ellis Rivkin, *A Hidden Revolution* (Nashville: Abingdon, 1978); Steve N. Mason, *Flavius Josephus on the Pharisees: A Composition-Critical Study* (Leiden: E. J. Brill, 1991); Anthony J. Saldarini, "Pharisees," in *The Anchor Bible Dictionary*, ed. David Noel Freedman, vol. 5 (New York: Doubleday, 1992), pp. 289–303 (hereafter cited as *ABD*); E. P. Sanders, *Judaism: Practice and Belief, 63 bce–66 ce* (London: SCM Press; Philadelphia: Trinity Press International, 1992), pp. 380–451.

116. Mireille Hadas-Lebel, *Hillel: Un sage au temps de Jésus* (Paris: Albin Michel, 1999).

117. Ibid.

118. The bibliography is vast and still growing. I shall mention here only two titles of special historical interest: André Dupont-Sommer, *Les écrits esséniens découverts près de la Mer morte*, 5th ed., pref. by Marc Philonenko (Paris: Payot, 1996); Ernest-Marie Laperrousaz, *Qoumrân, l'établissement essénien des bords de la Mer morte: Histoire et archéologie du site* (Paris: Picard, 1976); for English translations, see André Dupont-Sommer, *The Essene Writings from Qumran,* trans. Géza Vermès (Gloucester, Mass.: Peter Smith, 1973; originally published 1961).

119. Among the many subjects of debate among scholars regarding the Essenes, the identity of the Qumran sect has a special place. For most specialists, the studious recluses of Qumran belong to Essenism, even if everyone agrees that they represent a particular aspect of the sect; but others prefer not to use the name *Essenes* for the people of Qumran and simply call them "the sect of the Dead Sea." Thus in *Jewish Life and Thought among Greeks and Romans: Primary Readings* (Minneapolis: Fortress Press, 1996), Louis H. Feldman and Meyer Rheinhold devote one section to the Essenes (pp. 244–255) and another to the "Dead Sea Sect" (pp. 255–259). See the account of the fundamental issues by Michael Wise, Martin Abbeg Jr., and Edward Cook, *Les manuscrits de la Mer morte* (Paris: Plon, 2001), pp. 25–46.

120. The "Dead Sea Scrolls" (to which we must add at least the Damascus Document originating from the *guenizah* of the Karaite synagogue of Old Cairo) bring together very different sorts of texts. On the one hand, there are "Essene" texts properly speaking—that is, pertaining to the history or the organization of the sect, or developing their own point of view. In this category, in addition to the Damascus Rule, we find the Temple Scroll, the War Rule, and the Community Rule, or Manual of Discipline. On the other hand, there are fragments (sometimes very extensive) of all the biblical texts except Esther, many apocryphal texts, and commentaries on these. Essential information can be found in several recent publications: Florentino García Martínez, *The Dead Sea Scrolls Translated: The Qumran Texts in English* (Leiden and New York: E. J. Brill, 1994); James H. Charlesworth, ed., *The Dead Sea Scrolls: Hebrew, Aramaic, and Greek Texts with English Translations,* vol. 1, *Rule of the Community and Related Documents* (Tübingen: J. C. B. Mohr; Louisville, Ky.: Westminster / John Knox Press, 1994), and vol. 2, *Damascus Document, War Scroll and Related Documents* (Tübingen: J. C. B. Mohr; Louisville, Ky.: Westminster / John Knox Press, 1995); Géza Vermès, *The Complete Dead Sea Scrolls in English* (New York: Allen Lane / Penguin Press, 1997). For the Essene texts themselves, see André Dupont-Sommer and Marc Philonenko, eds. and trans., *La Bible: Écrits intertestamentaires* (Paris: Gallimard, 1987).

121. Josephus, *BJ* 2.567, 3.11–19.

122. Ibid., 2.152.

123. Philo, *Quod omnis probus liber sit* (Every Good Man Is Free), in *Philo,* vol. 9, trans. F. H. Colson (Loeb Classical Library), 78; a useful French translation of the ancient sources pertaining to the Essenes (Josephus, Philo, and Pliny) is found in Dupont-Sommer and Philonenko, *Écrits esséniens,* pp. 31–49.

124. The fundamental resource is Jean Le Moyne, *Les Sadducéens: Études bibliques* (Paris: J. Gabalda, 1972); see also Hugo Mantel, "The Sadducees and the Pharisees" in *The World History of the Jewish People,* ed. Michael Avi-Yonah and Zvi

Baras, vol. 8 (Jerusalem: Massada; New Brunswick: Rutgers University Press, 1977), pp. 99–123; Anthony J. Saldarini, *Pharisees, Scribes and Sadducees in Palestinian Society: A Sociological Approach* (Wilmington, Del.: M. Glazier, 1988); Gary G. Porton, "Sadducees," *ABD*, vol. 5, pp. 892–895; E. P. Sanders, *Judaism: Practice and Belief, 63 bce–66 ce* (London: SCM Press, 1992), pp. 317–340.

125. Marcel Simon, *Les sectes juives au temps de Jésus* (Paris: Presses Universitaires de France, 1960); Sanders, *Judaism*, pp. 452–457.

126. Josephus, *AJ* 18.23–24. For the Zealots, see William Reuben Farmer, *Maccabees, Zealots, and Josephus: An Inquiry into Jewish Nationalism in the Greco-Roman Period* (New York: Columbia University Press, 1956); Morton Smith, "Zealots and Sicarii: Their Origins and Relations," *Harvard Theological Review* 64 (1971): 1–19; Valentin Nikiprowetzky, "Sicaires et zélotes: Une reconsidération," *Semitica* 23 (1973): 51–63; Menahem Stern, "Sicarii and Zealots," in *The World History of the Jewish People*, vol. 8, ed. Michael Avi-Yonah and Zvi Baras (Jerusalem: Massada; New Brunswick: Rutgers University Press, 1977), pp. 263–301; Richard A. Horsley and John S. Hanson, *Bandits, Prophets and Messiahs: Popular Movements in the Time of Jesus*, 2nd ed. (Harrisburg, Pa.: Trinity Press International, 1999; 1st ed., Minneapolis: Winston Press, 1985); Richard A. Horsley, "The Zealots: Their Origin, Relationships and Importance in the Jewish Revolt," *Novum Testamentum* 2 (1986): 159–192; Martin Hengel, *The Zealots: Investigations into the Jewish Freedom Movement in the Period from Herod I until 70 ad* (Edinburgh: T. & T. Clark, 1989; repr., 1997); Mendels, *Rise and Fall*.

127. Smith, "Zealots and Sicarii"; Nikiprowetzky, "Sicaires et zélotes"; Richard A. Horsley, "The Sicarii: Ancient Jewish 'Terrorists,'" *Journal of Religion* 59 (1979): 435–458.

128. Louis Monloubou and Henri Cazelles, *Apocalypses et théologie de l'espérance* (Paris: Le Cerf, 1977); David Hellholm, ed., *Apocalypticism in the Mediterranean World and the Near East: Proceedings of the International Colloquium on Apocalypticism, Uppsala, August 12–17, 1979* (Tübingen: J. C. B. Mohr, 1983); Ithamar Gruenwald, "Jewish Apocalyptic Literature," *ANRW* 2.19.1 (1979): 89–118.

129. David Syme Russell, *The Method and Message of Jewish Apocalyptic 200 bc–ad 100* (Philadelphia: Westminster Press, 1964).

130. The connection with David is nevertheless much more frequent: see Albert-Louis Descamps, "Le messianisme royal dans le Nouveau Testament," *Recherches bibliques* 1 (1954): 57–84. This is why the Flavians attempted to find all of David's descendants in the aftermath of the first revolt (Eusebius, *The Ecclesiastical History*, trans. Kirsopp Lake [Loeb Classical Library], 3.12 [hereafter cited as *EH*]).

131. Joseph Klausner, *The Messianic Idea in Israel, from Its Beginning to the Completion of the Mishnah* (London: Allen & Unwin, 1956); Ernest-Marie Laperrousaz, *L'attente du Messie en Palestine à la veille et au début de l'ère chrétienne, à la lumière des documents récemment découverts* (Paris: Picard, 1982).

132. See Géza Vermès, *Jesus the Jew: A Historian's Reading of the Gospels* (New York: Macmillan, 1973), pp. 134–140; Schürer, *History*, vol. 2, pp. 547–554. On the special case of the Essenes of Qumran, see Laperrousaz, *Attente du Messie*, p. 96, and Adam Simon Van der Woude, "Le maître de Justice et les deux Messies dans la communauté de Qûmran," *Recherches bibliques* 4 (1959): 121–134.

133. Mathias Delcor, ed., *Qumrân: Sa piété, sa théologie et son milieu* (Paris:

Duculot, 1978); Dupont-Sommer, *Écrits esséniens;* Laperrousaz, *Qoumrân;* Ernest-Marie Laperrousaz, *Les Manuscrits de la Mer morte,* 9th ed. (Paris: Presses Universitaires de France, 1999).

134. Isaac, "Bandits," pp. 66–67, 77–83.

135. As the birthplace of Jesus, first-century Galilee has been the subject of numerous studies (the titles themselves are often quite eloquent on this point): Séan Freyne, *Galilee, from Alexander the Great to Hadrian (323 B.C.E. to 135 C.E.): A Study of Second Temple Judaism* (Wilmington, Del.: M. Glazier; Notre Dame, Ind.: University of Notre Dame Press, 1980); idem, *Galilee, Jesus, and the Gospels: Literary Approaches and Historical Investigations* (Philadelphia: Fortress Press, 1988); Richard A. Batey, *Jesus and the Forgotten City: New Light on Sepphoris and the Urban World of Jesus* (Grand Rapids, Mich.: Baker Book House, 1991); Uriel Rappaport, "How Anti-Roman Was the Galilee?" in *The Galilee in Late Antiquity,* ed. Lee I. Levine (New York and Cambridge, Mass.: Jewish Theological Seminary of America, 1992), pp. 95–102; Séan Freyne, "The Geography, Politics, and Economics of Galilee," in *Studying the Historical Jesus: Evaluations of the State of Current Research,* ed. Bruce Chilton and Craig A. Evans (Leiden and New York: E. J. Brill, 1994); Richard A. Horsley, *Galilee: History, Politics, People* (Valley Forge, Pa.: Trinity Press International, 1995); idem, *Archaeology, History, and Society in Galilee: The Social Context of Jesus and the Rabbis* (Valley Forge, Pa.: Trinity Press International, 1996). These last two works defend an extreme position with respect to the originality of Galilee, based on a sort of spiritual isolation; see the very critical reviews by Joshua Schwartz in *Journal of Jewish Studies* (hereafter cited as *JJS*) 49 (1998): 155–158; Douglas R. Edwards and C. Thomas McCullough, eds., *Archaeology and the Galilee: Texts and Contexts in the Graeco-Roman and Byzantine Periods* (Atlanta: Scholars Press, 1997). But see also Martin Goodman, *The Ruling Class of Judaea: The Origins of the Jewish Revolt against Rome, ad 66–70* (London and New York: Cambridge University Press, 1988).

136. Josephus, *BJ* 2.118.

137. Shimon Applebaum, "The Zealots: The Case for Revaluation," *JRS* 61 (1971): 155–170; idem, *Judaea in Hellenistic and Roman Times* (Leiden: E. J. Brill, 1989); Richard A. Horsley, "Ancient Jewish Banditry and the Revolt against Rome AD 66–70," *Catholic Biblical Quarterly* 43 (1981): 409–432.

138. Farmer, *Maccabees, Zealots and Josephus;* Hengel, *Zealots;* Horsley, "Zealots"; Horsley, *Bandits.*

139. Belayche, "Figures politiques des Messies," pp. 58–74, especially pp. 60–61, on this point.

140. Richard A. Horsley, "Popular Prophetic Movements at the Time of Jesus," *Journal for the Study of the New Testament* 26 (1986): 3–27.

141. Josephus, *AJ* 17.273–277, *BJ* 2.57–59; Tacitus, *Histories,* 5.9.

142. Belayche believes that there were only three, but that the number four derived from an assimilation to the Maccabees, whose memory had been kept alive and who stood as model liberators ("Figures politiques des Messies," p. 62).

143. Josephus, *AJ* 17.278–284, *BJ* 2.60–64: these texts suggest that there was a guerilla war lasting several years.

144. Josephus, *BJ* 2.56.

145. Ibid., 2.55.

146. Philo, *Legatio,* 299–305.

147. The *simpulum* is a small ladle used for making libations, while the *lituus* was

used by diviners. See Ethelbert Stauffer, "Zur Münzprägung und Judenpolitik des Pontius Pilatus," *La Nouvelle Clio* (1949–1950): 495–514; Ya'akov Meshorer, *Jewish Coins of the Second Temple Period* (Tel Aviv: Am Hassefer, 1967), p. 105; idem, *Ancient Jewish Coinage* (Dix Hills, N.Y.: Amphora Books, 1982), p. 180. For a more nuanced discussion, see Jean-Pierre Lémonon, *Pilate et le gouvernement de la Judée: Textes et monuments* (Paris: J. Gabalda, 1981), pp. 110–115; Daniel R. Schwartz, "Pontius Pilate," in *The Anchor Bible Dictionary*, ed. David Noel Freedman, vol. 5 (New York: Doubleday, 1992), pp. 396–401. On the government of Pontius Pilatus, see, in addition to the works listed above, Helen K. Bond, *Pontius Pilate in History and Interpretation* (Cambridge and New York: Cambridge University Press, 1998), which focuses particularly on the image of Pilatus presented by the various sources; Alexander Demandt, *Hände in Unschuld: Pontius Pilatus in der Geschichte* (Cologne: Bölhau, 1999).

148. Joseph Patrich, "A Sadducean Halacha and the Jerusalem Aqueduct," *Jerusalem Cathedra* 2 (1982): 25–39.

149. See P. D. Barnett, "The Jewish Sign Prophets AD 40–70: Their Intentions and Origins," *New Testament Studies* 27 (1981): 679–697; Gérard Rochais, "L'influence de quelques idées-forces de l'apocalyptique sur certains mouvements messianiques et prophétiques populaires juifs du Ier siècle," in Marguerat et al., *Jésus de Nazareth*, pp. 177–208.

150. Matthew 3.1–17 (activity) and 14.1–12 (his death); Mark 6.14–29; Luke 9.7–9; Josephus, *AJ* 18.116–119.

151. There has been a great deal of speculation about the exact date of Jesus's death: it was Friday the 14th (John) or the 15th (the Synoptic Gospels) of the month of Nisan, in the era of Pontius Pilatus, and on the afternoon of that day an astronomical phenomenon occurred that turned the moon blood-red. There was not a solar eclipse, as is generally believed (for an eclipse is always very brief), but a lunar eclipse (a phenomenon that lasts several hours). On the basis of all these elements, the astronomer J.-P. Parisot has established quite convincingly that Friday, April 3, 33, corresponds to all the requirements ("Quand la lune était rouge sang . . . ," *Ciel et Espace* 204 (March–April 1985): 41–44.

152. There is no need to take up the question of the historicity of Jesus—which seems to me settled—here, or even to draw a precise portrait. Some excellent recent studies may be consulted on this question: E. P. Sanders, *The Historical Figure of Jesus* (London: Allen Lane / Penguin Press, 1993); Chilton and Evans, eds., *Studying the Historical Jesus;* Daniel Marguerat, *L'homme qui venait de Nazareth: Ce qu'on peut aujourd'hui savoir de Jésus,* 3rd ed. (Aubonne: Éd. du Moulin, 1995); Daniel Marguerat, Enrico Norelli, and Jean-Michel Poffet, eds., *Jésus de Nazareth: Nouvelles approches d'une énigme* (Geneva: Labor & Fides, 1998); Hugues Cousin, Jean-Pierre Lémonon, and Jean Massonet, *Le monde où vivait Jésus* (Paris: Le Cerf, 1998); Jean-François Baudoz and Michel Fédou, eds., *Vingt ans de publications françaises sur Jésus* (Paris: Desclée, 1998).

153. Josephus, *AJ* 18.85–87.

154. Origen, *Contra Celsum,* ed. and trans. Henry Chadwick (Cambridge: Cambridge University Press, 1953; repr., with revisions and corrections, 1980), 1.57 and 7.11.

155. Richard A. Horsley, *Jesus and the Spiral of Violence: Popular Jewish Resistance in Roman Palestine* (San Francisco: Harper & Row, 1987).

156. Philo offers a lengthy account of these events in *Legatio,* 207–221.

157. Belayche, "Figures politiques des Messies," p. 63.

158. Josephus, *AJ* 20.97–99; Acts 5.36 minimizes the audience (four hundred men), whereas Josephus speaks of a large crowd. This sermon was delivered under the administration of Cuspius Fadus, notwithstanding Origen's claims in *Contra Celsum* 1.57 and 6.11 (Origen places it before the birth of Jesus and before Judas the Galilean).

159. Josephus, *AJ* 10.166, *BJ* 2.258–260, under Felix; *AJ* 20.188, under Festus.

160. Josephus, *AJ* 20.105–111, *BJ* 2.224–227.

161. Josephus, *BJ* 1.253.

162. Horsley, "Sicarii," pp. 435–458.

163. Josephus, *BJ,* 2.261–263.

164. Ibid., 2.273–275.

165. Ibid., 2.277.

166. Josephus, *AJ* 20.169–172, *BJ* 2.266–270, 284; Acts 21.38 depicts him as a leader of *sicarii* training his troops (four thousand men!) in the desert.

167. Josephus, *BJ* 6.283–288.

168. Luke 3.1–20.

169. Samuel George Frederick Brandon, *Jesus and the Zealots: A Study of the Political Factor in Primitive Christianity* (Manchester: Manchester University Press, 1967).

170. On the genre, see John Joseph Collins, *The Apocalyptic Imagination: An Introduction to Jewish Apocalyptic Literature,* 2nd ed. (Grand Rapids, Mich.: Eerdmans, 1998); Bernard McGinn, John Joseph Collins, and Stephen J. Stein, eds., *The Encyclopedia of Apocalypticism,* 3 vols. (New York: Continuum, 1998).

171. Probably an Essene text written shortly after Pompey took Jerusalem: see Schürer, *History,* vol. 3, pp. 192–197; Dupont-Sommer and Philolenko, eds., *La Bible: Écrits intertestamentaires,* p. lxxxiv; Robert R. Hann, "The Community of the Pious: The Social Setting of the Psalms of Solomon," *Studies in Religion / Sciences religieuses* 17 (1988): 169–189.

172. George W. E. Nickelsburg, ed., *Studies on the Testament of Moses: Seminar Papers* (Cambridge, Mass.: Society of Biblical Literature, 1973); Abraham Schalit, *Untersuchungen zur Assumptio Mosis* (Leiden and New York: E. J. Brill, 1989); cf. Schürer, *History,* vol. 3, pp. 278–288; Dupont-Sommer and Philonenko, *La Bible: Écrits intertestamentaires,* pp. lxxxvii, 999–1016; John Joseph Collins, "The Testament of Moses," in *Jewish Writings of the Second Temple Period,* ed. Michael E. Stone (Assen: Van Gorcum; Philadelphia: Fortress Press, 1984), pp. 344–349. The author is aware of Herod's death but not of the deaths of Herod's sons.

173. Here I share the view of André Dupont-Sommer and Marc Philonenko (*La Bible: Écrits intertestamentaires,* p. xciii). Others argue for a much earlier date, in the second century B.C.E., for at least part of the work. This is not impossible, for we know how much this type of literature is adapted over time to meet the needs of the day: see John Joseph Collins, *The Sibylline Oracles of Egyptian Judaism* (Missoula, Mont.: Society of Biblical Literature, 1974), pp. 21–34; idem, "The Sibylline Oracles," in Stone, *Jewish Writings,* pp. 365–371; idem, *Between Athens and Jerusalem: Jewish Identity in the Hellenistic Diaspora* (New York: Crossroad, 1983; 2nd ed., Grand Rapids, Mich.: Eerdmans, 2000), pp. 61–72; cf. Schürer, *History,* vol. 3, pp. 618–654.

174. *Sibylline Oracles,* 3.46–62.

175. Goodman, *Ruling Class.*

176. Josephus, *BJ* 2.293.

177. Ibid., 2.284–292.

178. Ibid., 2.307.

179. Ibid., 2.301–308.

180. Ibid., 2.318–332.

181. Ibid., 2.335–404; sections 358–388 constitute a powerful condemnation of the revolt based on the examination of history and the current state of the empire, which Agrippa depicts in striking fashion.

182. Ibid., 2.408–410.

183. It is important not to confuse the high priest Ananias (son of Nebedaios), who was high priest roughly from 47 to 59, then deposed and later assassinated at the very beginning of the revolt in August (Josephus, *BJ* 2.441), with another Ananos (son of the Ananos who was high priest for three months in 62) who was assassinated, but later on, by the Idumaeans, in the middle of a siege (ibid., 4.316–320). It should be noted that, in Josephus's texts, former high priests keep their titles, which sometimes adds to the confusion. When the revolt began, the high priest in office seems to have been Matthias, son of Theophilos, who was appointed in 65 (Josephus, *AJ* 3.223, *BJ* 6.114).

184. Josephus, *AJ* 20.173–178, 20.183–184.

185. Josephus, *Life,* 44–45.

186. Josephus, *BJ* 2.427–432.

187. Ibid., 2.449–456.

188. Ibid., 2.457: the figure is almost certainly excessive.

189. Ibid., 2.458–460.

190. Ibid., 2.500–501.

191. We cannot determine the exact size of the contingent led by Cestius Gallus, because alae and cohorts could consist of either five hundred or a thousand men, and we do not know how large the contingents based in cities were. Nevertheless, there were thirty thousand men at a minimum. Still, certain details in the Talmuds appear fanciful: I do not believe that Palmyra could have supplied eight thousand archers, as is claimed in *Le Talmud de Jérusalem,* trans. Moïse Schwab (Paris: Maisonneuve & Larose, 1977; originally published 1871–1890), *Toanith* 4.8 and *Midrash Ekha* 2.2 (hereafter cited as *TJ*). For *Midrash Ekha* in English, see *Lamentations,* trans. A. Cohen, in *Midrash Rabbah,* ed. H. Freedman and Maurice Simon, vol. 7 (London and Bournemouth: Soncino Press, 1951).

192. Josephus, *BJ* 2.562.

193. Josephus, *Life,* 30–53.

194. Josephus, *BJ* 3.1–8; Suetonius, "The Deified Vespasian," in *Suetonius,* trans. J. C. Rolfe (Loeb Classical Library), 4; Tacitus, *Histories,* 5.10.

195. Josephus, *BJ* 3.376.

196. Ibid., 2.574: Josephus claims that they were so rich and so ardent that he did not need to give them orders; we may doubt this, because during Cestius Gallus's expedition they enthusiastically opened their doors to the Romans and were then among the very earliest to rally to the Roman cause.

197. Ibid., 2.585–646. Josephus shapes his account in a way that suggests that he had ordered John of Gischala to prepare to defend his city at his own expense; in reality, Josephus had no authority over John and allowed him to act as he wished.

198. Ibid., 2.652–653.

199. The best source remains Josephus, *De bello judaico (The Jewish War)*. Among the works that offer good accounts of the facts, let me recall Félix-Marie Abel, *Histoire de la Palestine depuis la conquête d'Alexandre jusqu'à l'invasion arabe* (Paris: J. Gabalda, 1952), in which the war is presented at the end of vol. 1 (pp. 483–505) and the beginning of vol. 2 (pp. 1–43); David M. Rhoads, *Israel in Revolution, 6–74 C.E.: A Political History Based on the Writings of Josephus* (Philadelphia: Fortress Press, 1976); Jonathan T. Price, *Jerusalem under Siege: The Collapse of the Jewish State, 66–70 C.E.* (Leiden and New York: E. J. Brill, 1992); see also any general history of the Jews in the first century.

200. David Adan-Bayewitz and Moti Aviam, "Jotapata, Josephus and the Siege of 67: Preliminary Report on the 1992–94 Seasons," *Journal of Roman Archaeology* 10 (1997): 131–165.

201. Josephus, *BJ* 3.415–427.

202. A complacent account of the civil war by Josephus, *BJ* 4.121–223.

203. Dio, 65.4–7.

204. The traditional date of 73 is based on Josephus's report that the citadel fell in the fourth year of Vespasian's reign—that is, between July 72 and the end of June 73. The month of Xanthicos falls in Nisan, the month of the Jewish Passover in the spring. But this date has been called into question by the discovery of an inscription reporting on the career of L. Flavius Silva; this led Werner Eck to move ahead to the spring of 74 the date the Masada was taken ("Die Eroberung von Masada und eine neue Inschrift des L. Flavius Silva Nonius Bassus," *Zeitschrift für die neutestamentliche Wissenschaft und die Kunde der alteren Kirche* 60 [1969]: 282–289, and idem, *Senatoren von Vespasian bis Hadrian: Prosopographische Untersuchungen mit Einschluss d. Jahres u. Provinzialfasten d. Statthalter* [Munich: Beck, 1970], pp. 93–111). This conclusion has been adopted by D. B. Campbell ("Dating the Siege of Masada," *Zeitschrift für Papyrologie und Epigraphik* [hereafter cited as ZPE] 73 [1988]: 156–158) and others in his wake. However, Hannah Cotton, even though she too opts for 74, believes that 73 cannot be completely ruled out: see her "The Date of the Fall of Masada: The Evidence of the Masada Papyri," *ZPE* 78 (1989): 157–162. In "The Length of the Siege of Masada," *SCI* 14 (1995): 87–110, Jonathan Roth estimates the siege to have been much shorter—seven weeks?

205. The impressive bibliography on Masada cannot be cited here, even in a reduced form: see Hadas-Lebel, *Massada,* for an overview of the problem.

206. On this intermediate period, see José Ramón Ayaso, *Iudaea capta: La Palestina romana entre las dos guerras judias (70–132 d. C)* (Estella: Editorial Verbo Divino, 1990); Ayaso offers a useful synthesis, in particular on the socioeconomic and ideological aspects.

207. Danny Bar, "Aelia Capitolina and the Location of the Camp of the Tenth Legion," *Palestine Exploration Quarterly* 130 (1998): 8–19.

208. Menahem Mor, "The Roman Army in Eretz-Israel in the Years AD 70–132," in *The Defence of the Roman and Byzantine East,* ed. Philip Freeman and David L. Kennedy (Oxford: British Archaeological Reports, 1986), pp. 575–602.

209. Benjamin H. Isaac, "Judaea after AD 70," *JJS* 35 (1984): 44–50.

210. Shimon Applebaum, *Prolegomena to the Study of the Second Jewish Revolt (A.D. 132–135)* (Oxford: British Archaeological Reports, 1976); Adolf Büchler, *The*

Economic Conditions of Judaea after the Destruction of the Second Temple (London and Oxford: Oxford University Press, 1912).

211. Benjamin H. Isaac and Israel Roll, "Judaea in the Early Years of Hadrian's Reign," *Latomus* 38 (1979): 54–66.

212. Isaac, "Bandits"; idem, *Limits*, pp. 83–85.

213. See Dupont-Sommer and Philonenko, *La Bible: Écrits intertestamentaires,* p. xciv (book 4) and p. xcvi (book 5).

214. Schürer, *History,* vol. 3, pp. 294–306.

215. Pierre Bogaert, *Apocalypse de Baruch* (Paris: Le Cerf, 1969), especially chapters 22–30; Schürer, *History,* vol. 3, pp. 750–756.

216. Miriam Pucci, "Il movimento insurrezionale in Giudea (117–118 a.C.)," *SCI* 4 (1978): 63–76.

217. The first known successor to Lusius Quietus is Q. Tineius Rufus, a consul, attested in 132–133: see Bengt E. Thomasson, *Laterculi praesidum,* vol. 1 (Göteborg: Radius, 1972), col. 325, no. 27; but it is likely that the predecessors of Tineius Rufus were also consuls.

218. Hannah Cotton, "The Legio Sexta Ferrata between 106 and 136," in *Les légions de Rome sous le Haut-Empire: Actes du Congrès de Lyon, septembre 1998,* ed. Yann Le Bohec (Lyon: n. p., 2000), pp. 351–357; Cotton concludes that the date cannot be specified. In 119, VI Ferrata was still in Arabia, and it is likely that III Cyrenaica left Alexandria for Bostra in 127 at the latest.

219. Herbert Nesselhauf, *CIL,* vol. 16, *Diplomata militaria ex constitutionibus imperatorum de civitate et conubio militum veteranorumque expressa,* 2 vols. (Berlin: W. de Gruyter, 1936–1955), no. 87.

220. See Benjamin H. Isaac and Israel Roll, *Roman Roads in Judaea,* vol. 1, *The Legio-Scythopolis Road* (Oxford: British Archaeological Reports, 1982); Moshe Fischer, Benjamin H. Isaac, and Israel Roll, *Roman Roads in Judaea,* vol. 2, *The Jaffa-Jerusalem Road* (Oxford: British Archaeological Reports, 1996); for a more general view, see Isaac, *Limits,* pp. 107–118, especially p. 111.

221. Practically no milestones from Hadrian's time are known in Syria; there is one example on the road from Damascus to Heliopolis. See Peter Thomsen, "Die römischen Meilensteine der Provinzen Syria, Arabia, und Palästina," *Zeitschrift der deutschen Palästina-Vereins* 40 (1917): 1–103, no. 30a 1.

222. His actual name was Bar Kosiba, as proved by a letter written in his own hand that was discovered in a cave in the Judaean desert: see Jósef Tadeusz Milik, "Une lettre de Siméon Bar Kokheba," *Rbi* 60 (1953): 276–294. But custom has imposed the spelling *Kokhba* (or *Kochba, Kokheba,* and so on), and I did not think it useful to go against customs established by the scientific community.

223. "Hadrian," in *Historia Augusta,* trans. David Magie (Loeb Classical Library), vol. 1, 14.2; cf. the excellent account in Peter Schäfer, *Judeophobia: Attitudes toward the Jews in the Ancient World* (Cambridge, Mass.: Harvard University Press, 1997), pp. 103–105.

224. On the causes and consequences of the Bar Kokhba revolt, the following texts are indispensable: Hugo Mantel, "The Causes of the Bar Kokhba Revolt," *Jewish Quarterly Review* 58 (1968): 224–242, 274–296; Applebaum, *Prolegomena;* Glen W. Bowersock, "A Roman Perspective on the Bar Kokhba War," in *Approaches to Ancient Judaism,* ed. William Scott Green, vol. 2 (Missoula, Mont.: Scholars Press,

1980), pp. 135–141; Shimon Applebaum, "Points of View on the Second Jewish Revolt," *SCI* 7 (1983–1984): 77–87; idem, "The Second Jewish Revolt (AD 131–135)," *SCI* 7 (1983–1984): 35–41; Peter Schäfer, "Hadrian's Policy in Judaea and the Bar Kokhba Revolt: A Reassessment," in *A Tribute to G. Vermes: Essays on Jewish and Christian Literature and History,* ed. Philip R. Davies and Richard T. White (Sheffield, U.K.: Journal for the Study of the Old Testament), pp. 282–303. A useful account of the bibliography and of modern attitudes toward the revolt is found in Benjamin H. Isaac and Aharon Oppenheimer, "The Bar Kokhba Revolt: Ideology and Modern Scholarship," *JJS* 36 (1985): 33–60.

225. Benjamin H. Isaac, "Roman Colonies in Judaea: The Foundation of Aelia Capitolina," *Talanta* 12–13 (1980–1981): 31–54.

226. In *Life of Constantine,* ed. and trans. Averil Cameron and Stuart G. Hall (Oxford: Clarendon Press, 1999), 3.26.1, Eusebius defends the idea that the foundation of Aelia was an anti-Christian measure, which obviously precludes him from seeing it as the cause of the Jewish revolt. Sozomen takes a similar position in *Ecclesiasticae historia,* ed. André-Jean Festugière, Guy Sabbah, and Bernard Grillet (Paris: Le Cerf, 1983), 2.1.3; for an English translation, see *The Ecclesiastical History, or Sozomen, Comprising a History of the Church from A.D. 324 to A.D. 440,* trans. Edward Walford (London: Henry G. Bohn, 1855); this interpretation has been followed, not very convincingly, by David Golan, "Hadrian's Decision to Supplant Jerusalem by Aelia Capitolina," *Historia* 35 (1986): 226–239.

227. *TJ, Shabi'ith,* 15 (16).9.

228. In "Hadrian's Policy in Judaea," Schäfer thus defends a more pacific thesis than is supported by the majority of historians; he is concerned with finding the underlying reasons for the unrest.

229. Leo Mildenberg and Patricia Erhart Mottahedeh, *The Coinage of the Bar Kokhba War* (Aarau: Sauerländer, 1984), pp. 78, 85; the authors doubt that the revolts could ever have penetrated into the city. But (limited) discoveries of coins in Jerusalem and to the north of the city call this pessimistic conclusion into question.

230. Ernest-Marie Laperrousaz, "À propos du Maître de Justice et du Temple de Jérusalem: Deux problèmes de nombre," *Revue de Qoumrân* 15 (1991): 267–274 (= *Mémorial Jean Starcky,* I).

231. Louis Finkelstein, *Akiba: Scholar, Saint and Martyr* (New York: Atheneum, 1970).

232. See the bibliography provided by Laperrousaz, "À propos du Maître de Justice," pp. 271–272, nn. 19–25; the most northerly discovery would be in the wadi Daliyyeh, thirty kilometers northeast of Jerusalem.

233. This may be an example of a farm from the Herodian era destroyed at the time of the Bar Kokhba revolt: David Amit, "Khirbet Hilal," *Excavations and Surveys in Israel* 10 (1991): pp. 150–151.

234. Dio, 69.11–15.

235. Menahem Mor, "Two Legions—The Same Fate?" *ZPE* 62 (1986): 267–278.

236. Dio, 69.14.3.

237. On all this, see the essential article by Werner Eck, "The Bar Kokhba Revolt: The Roman Point of View," *JRS* 79 (1999): 76–89.

238. See Werner Eck and Gideon Foerster, "A Triumphal Arch for Hadrian near Tel Shalem in the Beth Shean Valley," *Journal of Roman Archaeology* 12 (1999): 294–313.

239. Caroline Arnould offers a detailed study of these arches (the first is buried under the Damascus gate, the second is still visible in the site known as Ecce Homo) in *Les arcs romains de Jérusalem: Architecture, décor et urbanisme* (Fribourg: Éditions Universitaires Fribourg Suisse; Göttingen: Vandenhoeck & Ruprecht, 1997); but see also Andreas Schmidt-Colinet's review of Ingeborg Kader, *Propylon und Bogentor*, and Caroline Arnould, *Arcs romains*, in *American Journal of Archaeology* 103 (1999): 719–720. On the site of the camp, from which many stamped tiles and bricks have been recovered, see G. J. Wightman, *The Walls of Jerusalem: From the Canaanites to the Mamluks* (Sydney: Mediterranean Archaeology, 1993), pp. 195–196.

240. Ariston of Pella cited in Eusebius, *EH* 4.6.3.

241. Cn. Minicius Faustinus Sex. Iulius Severus is called "imperial legate of Judaea" in one inscription (Mommsen, *CIL*, vol. 3, no. 2830 = *ILS*, no. 1056) and "of Syria-Palestine" in another (*AE* [1904], no. 9).

242. Shimon Applebaum, "The Settlement Pattern of Western Samaria from Hellenistic to Byzantine Times: A Historical Commentary," in *Landscape and Pattern: An Archaeological Survey of Samaria 800 B.C.E.–636 C.E.,* ed. Shimon Dar and Shimon Applebaum, vol. 1 (Oxford: British Archaeological Reports, 1986), pp. 263–265.

5. FROM TRAJAN TO THE SEVERI: CONQUESTS AND REORGANIZATIONS

1. On the false notion of *limes,* see Benjamin H. Isaac, "The Meaning of 'Limes' and 'Limitanei' in Ancient Sources," *Journal of Roman Studies* (hereafter cited as *JRS*) 78 (1988): 125–147.

2. Helmut Halfmann, *Itinera principum: Geschichte und Typologie der Kaiserreisen im Römischen Reich* (Stuttgart: F. Steiner, 1986).

3. A bilingual inscription (here, a translation from the Greek) honoring a benefactor mentions that the costs of oil were taken over during his stay by "Malê, nicknamed Agrippa, son of Iarhai, son of Raai, secretary for the second time during the visit of the god Hadrian, who supplied oil to foreigners and citizens, and met the needs of the army and so on in every respect" (Jean Cantineau, ed., *Inventaire des inscriptions de Palmyre* [Beirut: Publications du Musée national syrien de Damas, 1930–], vol. 1, no. 2 [hereafter cited as *Inv.*] = Delbert R. Hillers and Eleonora Cussini, *Palmyrene Aramaic Texts* [Baltimore: Johns Hopkins University Press, 1994], no. 0305 [hereafter cited as *PAT*] = Khaled As'ad and Jean-Baptiste Yon, *Inscriptions de Palmyre: Promenades épigraphiques dans la ville antique de Palmyre* [Beirut: Direction générale des antiquités et des musées de la République arabe syrienne, Institut français d'archéologie du Proche-Orient, 2001], pp. 46–47, no. 10); on this occasion the city minted some *tesserae* with the image of Empress Sabina. See Dieter Salzmann, "Sabina in Palmyra," in *Festschrift für Nikolaus Himmelmann,* ed. Hans-Ulrich Cain, Hanns Gabelmann, and Dieter Salzmann (Mainz: Ph. von Zabern, 1989), pp. 361–368 and pl. 58.

4. Eight guards from his escort *(equites singulares)* left a dedication there: Charles Bradford Welles, "The Inscriptions," in *Gerasa, City of the Decapolis,* ed. Carl Hermann Kraeling (New Haven, Conn.: American Schools of Oriental Research, 1938), no. 30.

5. Anthony R. Birley, *Hadrian, the Restless Emperor* (London and New York: Routledge, 1997), pp. 226–234.

6. I was wrong to claim, in the first French edition (Sartre, *D'Alexandre à Zénobie* [Paris: Fayard, 2001], p. 610) that Hadrian was the first to grant the title of metropolis to more than one city in a given province, and that Tyre received this designation then thanks to Paul of Tyre. In reality, Tyre was a metropolis from the time of the Flavians; what Paul of Tyre perhaps won for his homeland was that it should remain a metropolis both of the eparchy (district of the imperial cult) of Phoenicia and of the new eparchy of Coele Syria created toward the end of Trajan's reign or at the very beginning of Hadrian's; however, it was stripped of this second function to the benefit of Damascus before the end of Hadrian's reign. On these quite murky questions, see Maurice Sartre, "Les manifestations du culte impérial dans les provinces syriennes et en Arabie," in *Rome et ses provinces: Genèse et diffusion d'une image du pouvoir; Hommages à Jean-Charles Balty,* ed. Cécile Evers and Athéna Tsingarida (Brussels: Le Livre Timperman, 2001), pp. 167–186, especially pp. 171–178.

7. It should also be noted that Sepphoris received the name Diocaesarea on this occasion.

8. Glen W. Bowersock, *Roman Arabia* (Cambridge, Mass.: Harvard University Press, 1983), pp. 76–89; Maurice Sartre, *Bostra: Des origines à l'Islam* (Paris: P. Geuthner, 1985), pp. 61–72. On the possibility of internal problems about which we know nothing, see Zbigniew T. Fiema, "The Roman Annexation of Arabia: A General Perspective," *Ancient World* 15 (1987): 25–35; Philip Freeman, "The Annexation of Arabia and Imperial Grand Strategy," in *The Roman Army in the East,* ed. David L. Kennedy and David Braund (Ann Arbor, Mich.: Journal of Roman Archaeology, 1996), pp. 93–94. On the inscription (very implausible, in my opinion) of the annexation in an overarching design, see John W. Eadie, "Artifacts of Annexation: Trajan's Grand Strategy and Arabia," in *The Craft of the Ancient Historian: Studies in Honor of Chester G. Starr,* ed. John W. Eadie and Josiah Ober (Lanham, Md.: University Press of America, 1985), pp. 407–423.

9. *Prosopographia Imperii Romani saec. I. II. III,* 2nd ed., vol. 1 (Berlin: W. de Gruyter, 1933), C 1411–1412; Edward Dąbrowa, *The Governors of Roman Syria from Augustus to Septimius Severus* (Bonn: R. Habelt, 1998), p. 81.

10. Cassius Dio, *Roman History,* trans. Earnest Cary (Loeb Classical Library), 68.14.5 (hereafter cited as Dio); Ammianus Marcellinus, *The Surviving Books of the History,* trans. John C. Rolfe, vol. 1 (Loeb Classical Library), 14.8.13; Eutropius, *The Breviarium ab urbe condita of Eutropius,* ed. and trans. H. W. Bird (Liverpool: Liverpool University Press, 1993), 8.3.2; Pompeius Festus, *The Breviarium of Festus: A Critical Edition with Historical Commentary,* ed. John W. Eadie (London: Athlone Press, 1967), 14.3.

11. John Garrett Winter, ed., *Papyri in the University of Michigan Collection* (Ann Arbor: University of Michigan Press, 1936), 465–466 (hereafter cited as *P.Mich.*): the soldier Iulius Apollinaris asked the *consularis* (governor) Claudius Severus to take him on as secretary; not needing another secretary, Severus appointed him as his delegate to the *cornicularius* (orderly). Severus's title is not very clear, for Iulius Apollinaris calls him "consularis of the legion" (*P.Mich.* 466, line 32), which does not imply that he actually governs the province with the title of imperial legate *pro praetor.* But we may imagine that Severus initially exercised his authority over the newly conquered territory by virtue of his military command, before the creation of the *provincia* went into effect. Let us note that the title Apollinaris gives him, "consular,"

can only be a courtesy, since Severus did not administer a consul (suffect) until 112; an inscription from Petra reminds us that he was included among the former *questors* (Maurice Sartre, *Inscriptions grecques et latines de la Syrie* [hereafter cited as *IGLS*], vol. 21, *Inscriptions grecques et latines de la Jordanie* [hereafter cited as *IGLJ*], vol. 4, *Pétra et la Nabatène méridionale* [Paris: P. Geuthner, 1993], no. 45), and later among the former tribunes, without having occupied the offices, very probably because he moved quite late from the equestrian to the senatorial order.

12. Cf. J. S. Richardson, "The Administration of Provinces," *Cambridge Ancient History*, 2nd ed., vol. 9 (Cambridge: Cambridge University Press, 1994): 564–571, for an account of the problem at the end of the republican era.

13. Freeman, "Annexation of Arabia," pp. 91–118.

14. Ibid., pp. 97–98, to be read with caution.

15. Julian M. C. Bowsher, "The Nabataean Army," in *The Eastern Frontier of the Roman Empire*, ed. David H. French and C. S. Lightfoot (Oxford: British Archaeological Reports, 1989), pp. 19–30; David F. Graf, "The Nabataean Army and the *Cohortes Ulpiae Petraeorum*," in *The Roman and Byzantine Army in the East*, ed. Edward Dąbrowa (Cracow: Drukarnia Uniwersytetu Jagiellonskiego, 1994), pp. 265–311.

16. Naphtali Lewis, ed., *The Documents from the Bar Kokhba Period in the Cave of Letters*, vol. 1, *Greek Papyri* (Jerusalem: Israel Exploration Society, 1989), pp. 54–56, no. 14.

17. Lewis mentions him in December 127, without there being any question of his presence in Petra or in the region; it is only noted that he organized a census (Lewis, *Documents*, pp. 65–70, no. 16). On his tomb, see Sartre, *IGLJ*, vol. 4, no. 51.

18. Bengt E. Thomasson, *Laterculi praesidum* (Göteborg: Radius, 1972), col. 327, no. 2.

19. Maurice Sartre, "Ti. Iulius Iulianus Alexander, Gouverneur d'Arabie," *Annual of the Department of Antiquities of Jordan* (hereafter cited as *ADAJ*) 21 (1976): 105–108.

20. He was one of Hadrian's favorites: Birley, *Hadrian*, p. 231. I had thought that his name could be restored in one of the hammered-out inscriptions from Gerasa, a hypothesis accepted in large part since then (Maurice Sartre, *Trois études sur l'Arabie romaine et byzantine* [Brussels: Revue d'études latines, 1982], p. 82). However, Werner Eck challenges this deduction in "The Bar Kokhba Revolt: The Roman Point of View," *JRS* 79 (1999): 84, n. 67, and p. 89, and especially in "Vier mysteriöse Rasuren in Inschriften aus Gerasa: Zum 'Schicksal' des Statthalters Haterius Nepos," in Επιγραφαι: *Miscellanea epigrafica in onore di Lidio Gasperini*, ed. Gianfranco Paci (Tivoli and Rome: Tipigraf, 2000), pp. 347–362. Eck observes that Nepos is attested with certainty in Arabia only between November 130 and 134, the date of his consulate suffect, which is already long and casts doubt on his presence in the province during Hadrian's visit in the summer of 130 (the date of the damaged monuments); moreover, at least one inscription from Gerasa has been found in which his name was not assaulted with hammers (Pierre-Louis Gatier, "Gouverneurs et procurateurs à Gérasa," *Syria* 73 [1996]: 48–49), and we know that after being rewarded by Hadrian, Nepos pursued a glorious career. Eck deduces logically from this that the name hammered out in Gerasa was not that of Nepos, and perhaps not even that of a governor of Arabia. The fact remains that a Safaitic inscription published by Sabri Abbadi and Fawzi Zayadine ("Nepos the Governor of the Provincia

Arabia in a Safaitic Inscription?" *Semitica* 46 [1996]: 155–164) treats Nepos as a tyrant, and this has yet to be explained.

21. Thomasson, *Laterculi,* col. 327–328, nos. 3, 5, 6, and 7; for Q. Lollius Mamercianus, see Maria Letizia Lazzarini, "Iscrizioni dal santuario di Artemide 1984–1987," in *Jerash Archaeological Project, 1984–1988 II: Fouilles de Jérash,* ed. Fawzi Zayadine (Paris: P. Geuthner, 1989), p. 42, no. 3 = *Supplementum epigraphicum graecum,* vol. 39 (Alphen aan den Rijn: Sijthoff & Noordhoff, 1989), no. 1648.

22. For the time being, this is attested only in a bilingual Greek-Nabataean inscription: Jósef Tadeusz Milik, "Nouvelles inscriptions nabatéennes," *Syria* 35 (1958): 243–246. Cf. Philip Freeman, "The Era of the Province of Arabia: Problems and Solution?" in *Studies in the History of the Roman Province of Arabia,* ed. Henry Innes Macadam (Oxford: British Archaeological Reports 1986), pp. 38–46: Freeman argues in favor of an initiative taken, not by the Roman authorities (who in fact had other means of dating), but by the residents of Bostra and Petra. I do not believe that the late text *Chronicon Paschale* (ed. and trans. Michael Whitby and Mary Whitby [Liverpool: Liverpool University Press, 1989], 472) can be interpreted in this way; it indicates that the residents of these two cities date their years from the consulates of Candidus and Quadratus, but it is certain that, accustomed to counting according to the years of reign of the Petraean kings, they found themselves without a means of dating. The existence of the era of the province is attested as early as year 3 in Madaba (Pierre-Louis Gatier, *IGLJ,* vol. 2, *Région centrale: Amman, Hesban, Madaba, Main, Dhiban* [Paris: P. Geuthner, 1986], no. 118b), but its use is not universal: the documents from Nahal Hever are always headed by a date referring to a consulate or a reign, and the provincial era comes only in second or third place (Lewis, *Documents,* pp. 27–28). On all this, see Rudolf Haensch, *Capita provinciarum: Staathaltersitze und Provinzialverwaltung in der römischen Kaiserzeit* (Mainz: Ph. von Zabern, 1997), pp. 238–244.

23. See the now-classic article by G. P. Burton, "Proconsuls, Assizes and the Administration of Justice under the Empire," *JRS* 66 (1975): 92–106.

24. *Papyrus Yadin,* in Lewis, *Documents,* no. 23 (November 17, 130) (hereafter cited as *P. Yadin*).

25. See the inventory drawn up by Haensch in *Capita provinciarum,* pp. 562–563: five of the six known procurators of Arabia are known through texts from Gerasa (against one from Petra).

26. Hannah M. Cotton, "Ἡ νεα επαρχεια Ἀραβια: The New Province of Arabia in the Papyri from the Judaean Desert," *Zeitschrift für Papyrologie und Epigraphik* (hereafter cited as *ZPE*) 116 (1997): 204–208.

27. *P. Yadin,* no. 16.

28. Herodian, *History of the Empire from the Time of Marcus Aurelius,* trans. C. R. Whittaker (Loeb Classical Library), 3.1–6 (hereafter cited as Herodian).

29. Antioch was first punished for its active support for Niger; but its importance made it indispensable and its rank of city and provincial capital was soon restored. Fergus Millar contests the very idea that provincial capitals existed (*The Roman Near East [31 B.C.–A.D. 337]* [Cambridge, Mass.: Harvard University Press, 1993], p. 123). This extreme position is absurd to the extent that only the seat of the governor's customary residence and offices is so named, without any implication of special status.

30. Maurice Dunand, "La voie romaine du Ladja," *Mémoires de l'Académie des inscriptions et belles-lettres* (Paris: Imprimerie nationale, 1930): 23.

31. On all this, see Sartre, *Trois études,* pp. 54–64, especially pp. 61–62.

32. Maurice Sartre, *IGLS,* vol. 16, *Le Djebel al-ŒArab* (Beirut: Institut français d'archéologie du Proche-Orient, forthcoming), no. 21; meanwhile, see Maurice Sartre, "Gouverneurs d'Arabie anciens et nouveaux: Textes inédits," in Paci, Επιγραφαι, pp. 982–984.

33. Jörg Wagner, "Provincia Osrhoenae: New Archaeological Finds Illustrating Its Organisation under the Severan Dynasty," in *Armies and Frontiers in Roman and Byzantine Anatolia,* ed. Stephen Mitchell (Oxford: British Archaeological Reports, 1983), pp. 103–129.

34. Here I am adopting the very convincing conclusions of Michel Gawlikowski, "The Last Kings of Edessa," in *Symposium Syriacum 7,* ed. René Lavenant (Rome: Pontificium Institutum Orientale, 1998), pp. 421–428, especially p. 423, which is based on the localization of the markers that delimit the new province of Osrhoene; see Wagner, "Provincia Osrhoene."

35. Dio, 80.16.2.

36. David L. Kennedy, "Ti. Claudius Subatianus Aquila, First Prefect of Mesopotamia," *ZPE* 36 (1979), pp. 255–262; Andreina Magioncalda, "Testimonianze sui prefetti di Mesopotamia (da Settimio Severo a Diocleziano)," *Studia et Documenta Historiae et Iuris* 48 (1982): 161–238.

37. Claire Préaux, "Une source nouvelle sur l'annexion de l'Arabie par Trajan: Les papyrus Michigan 465 et 466," *Mélanges Joseph Hombert* (Brussels: Université Libre de Bruxelles, 1950–1951), pp. 123–139; David L. Kennedy, *"Legio VI Ferrata:* The Annexation and Early Garrison of Arabia," *Harvard Studies in Classical Philology* 84 (1980): 283–309; Pierre-Louis Gatier, "La *Legio III Cyrenaica* et l'Arabie," in *Les légions de Rome sous le Haut-Empire: Actes du congrès de Lyon, 17–19 septembre 1998,* ed. Yann Le Bohec and Catherine Wolff (Lyon: Université Jean-Moulin-Lyon 3, 2000), p. 341.

38. The Bostra camp is located north of the city, up against the ramparts; many stamped tiles found there confirm this site (Raymond Brulet, "Estampilles de la IIIe légion Cyrénaïque à Bostra," *Berytus* 32 [1984]: 175–179). It is currently the object of archaeometric and archaeological research: see Maurice Lenoir, "Bosra (Syrie): Le camp de la légion IIIe Cyrénaïque," *Mélanges de l'École française de Rome: Antiquités* 110 [1998]: 523–528. We should note that, on the basis of the architectural décor, the baths in the camp can be dated to the end of the first century or the beginning of the second, which means that the construction of a camp destined to last was undertaken as soon as the province was annexed.

39. See Benjamin H. Isaac and Israel Roll, "Judaea in the Early Years of Hadrian's Reign," *Latomus* 38 (1979): 54–66; about the site, see Benjamin H. Isaac and Israel Roll, *Roman Roads in Judaea,* vol. 1, *The Legio–Scythopolis Road* (Oxford: British Archaeological Reports, 1982); Tsevikah Tsuk notes that no trace of the camp itself has been found ("The Aqueduct to Legio and the Location of the Camp of the VIth Roman Legion," *Tel Aviv* 15–16 [1988–1989]: 92–97). The site chosen is that of a village populated by Jews and Samaritans, near a crossroads where roads going from Scythopolis or Sepphoris to Caesarea and from Ptolemais to Samaria and Neapolis intersect; it is located not far from Gaba, where Herod had installed mercenaries; see Benjamin H. Isaac, *The Limits of Empire: The Roman Army in the East* (Oxford and New York: Clarendon Press, 1990), pp. 432–433.

40. Ptolemy, *Geographia,* ed. C. F. A. Nobbe (Hildesheim: G. Olms, 1966), 5.14.8; Wilhelm Henzen, *Corpus inscriptionum latinarum* (hereafter cited as *CIL*), vol. 6,

Inscriptiones urbis Romae latinae (Berlin: G. Reimer, 1876), nos. 1408, 1409. See Michael Alexander Speidel, *"Legio IV Scythica,"* in *Les légions de Rome sous le Haut-Empire,* ed. Yann Le Bohec (Lyon: n. p., 2000), pp. 327–337.

41. Dio, 55.24.4.

42. Emil Ritterling, "Legio," in *Realencyclopädie der classischen Altertumswissenschaft* (hereafter cited as *RE*), ed. August Friedrich von Pauly et al. (Stuttgart: J. B. Metzler, 1894–), col. 1435.

43. See David L. Kennedy, "The Garrisoning of Mesopotamia in the Late Antonine and Early Severan Period," *Antichthon* (1987): pp. 57–66. Kennedy believes that the three Parthica legions could have been created right after the expedition of 195 (p. 59). He argues against situating III Parthica at Rhesaina, deeming it improbable that a city the size of Nisibis would not harbor a legion; the only argument in favor of Rhesaina is supplied by the coins bearing a *vexillum* and the inscription *l[egio] III P[arthica],* which speaks more in favor of the colonial status of the city than for its role as a garrison: colonial coins with *vexilla* have been found in Aelia Capitolina, Ptolemais, and Neapolis, among other sites.

44. Unless an error has been made, a single military diploma dating from September 28, 157 (Herbert Nesselhauf, *CIL,* vol. 16, *Diplomata militaria ex constitutionibus imperatorum de civitate et conubio militum veteranorumque expressa,* 2 vols. [Berlin: W. de Gruyter, 1936–1955], no. 106) can surely be attributed to the Syrian army; a second (ibid., no. 103) may come from either the Syrian or the Syro-Palestinian army (see Margarat M. Roxan, *Roman Military Diplomas 1985–1993* [London: Institute of Archaeology, 1994], pp. 245–246, n. 43 [hereafter cited as *RMD* 3]). But we must also add the lists of units commanded, under Hadrian's reign (?), by M. Valerius Lollianus: David L. Kennedy, "The Special Command of M. Valerius Lollianus," *Electrum* 1 (1997): 69–81. A very fragmentary diploma of 157 or early 158 belonged to a veteran of the Ala VII Phrygum, stationed in Syria-Palestine, but it does not supply any information about the auxiliaries of that province: *L'année épigraphique* (hereafter cited as *AE*) (1997), no. 1768.

45. Mikhail Ivanovitch Rostovtzeff et al., eds., *The Excavations at Dura-Europos: Final Report,* vol. 5, *Parchments and Papyri* (New Haven: Yale University Press, 1955), pp. 24–25.

46. Kennedy, "Garrisoning of Mesopotamia," pp. 62–63.

47. Welles et al., *Excavations,* vol. 5, pp. 26–46.

48. David L. Kennedy, "Cohors XX Palmyrenorum: An Alternative Explanation of the Numeral," *ZPE* 53 (1983): 214–216; idem, *"Cohors XX Palmyrenorum* at Dura," in Dąbrowa, *Roman and Byzantine Army,* pp. 89–98. It is true that this high figure is somewhat surprising, since we know of no other cohort of Palmyrenes; the figure thus cannot be explained as a point of reference with respect to other units with the same name.

49. On the palace of the *dux ripae,* see Welles et al., *Excavations,* vol. 9, p. 3.

50. The house known as "The House of the Roman Scribes," along the rampart, occupied by the army: see Mikhail Ivanovitch Rostovtzeff, "The Residents of the House," in *The Excavations at Dura-Europos,* vol. 6, *Preliminary Report of Sixth Season of Work, October 1932–March 1933,* ed. Mikhail Ivanovitch Rostovtzeff (New Haven: Yale University Press, 1936), pp. 299–304.

51. Lucinda Dirven, *The Palmyrenes of Dura Europos: A Study of Religious Interaction in Roman Syria* (Boston: E. J. Brill, 1999), pp. 190–191.

52. Mikhail Ivanovitch Rostovtzeff, Frank E. Brown, and Charles Bradford Welles, eds., *The Excavations at Dura-Europos,* vols. 7–8, *Preliminary Report of the Seventh and Eighth Seasons of Work, 1933–1934 and 1934–1935* (New Haven: Yale University Press, 1939), p. 63.

53. On the archives, whose most famous holding is the cultural calendar of the garrison, the *Feriale Duranum,* see Welles et al., *Excavations,* vol. 5.

54. Henri Seyrig, "Postes romains sur la route de Médine," *Syria* 22 (1941): 218–223 (= Henri Seyrig, *Antiquités syriennes* [Paris: P. Geuthner, 1934–], vol. 3, pp. 162–167 [hereafter cited as *AS*]); Sartre, *Trois études,* pp. 29–35; Julian M. C. Bowsher, "The Frontier Post of Medain Saleh," in *The Defence of the Roman and Byzantine East: Proceedings of a Colloquium Held at the University of Sheffield in April 1986,* ed. Philip Freeman and David L. Kennedy (Oxford: British Archaeological Reports, 1986), pp. 23–29.

55. See the graffiti in Sartre, *IGLS,* vol. 16, forthcoming, nos. 1385–1414.

56. A camp established at the latest under Lucius Verus and Marcus Aurelius, repaired under Valerian: William Henry Waddington, *Inscriptions grecques et latines de la Syrie* (Paris: Firmin-Didot, 1870), 2562d–e (hereafter cited as *I.Syrie*).

57. Glen W. Bowersock, "Nabataeans and Romans in the Wadi Sirhan," in *Pre-Islamic Arabia,* ed. Abdelgadir Mahmoud Abdalla, Sami Saqqar, and Richard T. Mortel (Riyadh: King Saud University Press, 1984), pp. 133–136.

58. Michael P. Speidel, "The Roman Army in Arabia," *Aufstieg und Niedergang der römischen Welt* (hereafter cited as *ANRW*) 2.8 (1977): 687–730.

59. In chronological order, the diplomas are the following: *RMD* 3, 160 (136–137); Nesselhauf, *CIL,* vol. 16, no. 87 (Nov. 22, 139) and no. 103 (ca. 134–146, but this one may belong to Syria); *RMD* 3, 173 (Mar. 7, 160); Margaret M. Roxan, *Roman Military Diplomas 1954–1977* (London: Institute of Archaeology, 1978), 60 (ca. 154–161), and no. 69 (Nov. 24–27, 186) (hereafter cited as *RMD* 1).

60. Henri Seyrig, "Le cimetière des marins à Séleucie de Piérie," in *Mélanges syriens offerts à M. René Dussaud* (Paris: P. Geuthner, 1939), pp. 451–459.

61. Victor Chapot has provided the most complete account of Seleucia, in "Séleucie de Piérie," *Mémoires de la Société nationale des antiquaires de France* 66 (1906): 149–226; cf. Victor Tourneur, "Les villes amirales de l'Orient gréco-romain," *Revue belge de numismatique* 69 (1913): 407–424 (on the title *navarchis* borne by certain cities on coins); Peter Thomsen, "Die römische Flotte im Palästina-Syrien," *Beiträge zur biblischen Landes und Altertumskunde* 68 (1951): 73–89; Gian Carlo Susini, "La classis syriaca e le flotte provinciali," *Corso di Cultura sull'Arte Ravennate e Bizantina* (1976): 327–329; Dieter Kienast, *Untersuchungen zu den Kriegsflotten der römischen Kaiserzeit* (Bonn: R. Habelt, 1966); Michel Reddé, *Mare Nostrum: Les infrastructures, le dispositif et l'histoire de la marine militaire sous l'Empire romain* (Rome: École française de Rome, 1986), pp. 236–241. On the development of the port, see Denis van Berchem, "Le port de Séleucie de Piérie et l'infrastructure logistique des guerres parthiques," *Bonner Jahrbücher* 185 (1985): 47–87.

62. Vittorio Galliazzo, *I ponti romani,* vol. 1 (Treviso: Canova, 1994), nos. 813–815: one bridge with three arches over the Afrin at Azaz, over the Sabun Suyu.

63. On all these bridges, see the references in ibid., vol. 2 (catalogue). The bridges of Antioch (no. 853) stem from the municipal administration. The one in Bezabde (no. 806), known as the "Alexander Bridge," has impressive vestiges still standing on

the Syrian side of the Tigris, at the border with Turkey; it may go back to the Trajan era (116–117), but it was so often rebuilt in later years that the ancient parts cannot be identified.

64. Theodor Mommsen, *CIL*, vol. 3, *Inscriptiones Asiae, provinciaeum Europae graecarum, Illyrici latinae*, 4 vols. (Berlin: G. Reimer, 1873–1902), nos. 199–201.

65. For the Bostra–Philadelphia sector, see Thomas Bauzou, "Le secteur nord de la *via nova* en Arabie, de Bostra à Philadelphia," in *Fouilles de Khirbet es-Samra*, ed. Jean-Baptiste Humbert and Alain Desreumaux (Turnhout: Brepols, 1998), pp. 101–255; this is an exhaustive study with a historical component; for the southern part, see David F. Graf, "The *Via Nova Traiana* in Arabia Petraea," in *The Roman and Byzantine Near East: Some Recent Archaeological Research*, ed. John H. Humphrey (Ann Arbor, Mich.: Journal of Roman Archaeology, 1995), 241–268; Graf studies the road to the south of Petra, where he has discovered milestones with painted texts; see also Burton MacDonald, "The Route of the Via Nova Traiana Immediately South of Wadi al-Hasa," *Palestine Exploration Quarterly* (1996): 11–15 (correcting map VIII in Millar, *Roman Near East*).

66. *P.Mich.* 466; but these may be stones cut for various construction projects.

67. Andrew M. Smith II, Michelle Stevens, and Tina M. Niemi, "The Southeast Araba Archaeological Survey: A Preliminary Report of the 1994 Season," *Bulletin of the American Schools of Oriental Research* 305 (1997): 45–71, especially p. 62 (five milestones).

68. This thesis is developed in particular by S. Thomas Parker, "The Nature of Rome's Arabian Frontier," in *Roman Frontier Studies 1989: Proceedings of the 15th International Congress of Roman Frontier Studies*, ed. Valerie A. Maxfield and Michael J. Dobson (Exeter: University of Exeter Press, 1991): 498–504.

69. Michael C. A. Macdonald, "Nomads and the Hawran in the Late Hellenistic and Roman Periods: A Reassessment of the Epigraphic Evidence," *Syria* 70 (1993): 323–336.

70. David F. Graf, "The *Via Militaris* in Arabia," *Dumbarton Oak Papers* 51 (1997): 271–281. On the provision of meat for the troops, see Michael Richard Toplyn, "Meat for Mars: Livestock, Limitanei and Pastoral Provisioning for the Roman Army on the Arabian Frontier, A.D. 284–551" (Ph.D. diss., Harvard University, 1994). Toplyn shows that, during the later period, goats and sheep were raised by the soldiers themselves, or at least near the camps.

71. Isaac, *Limits of Empire*, p. 111.

72. See Thomas Bauzou, "Les routes romaines de Syrie," in *Archéologie et histoire de la Syrie*, ed. Jean-Marie Dentzer and Winfried Orthmann, vol. 2 (Saarbrucken: Saarbrücker Druckerei und Verlag, 1989), pp. 205–221; for southern Syria and northern Arabia, see Thomas Bauzou, "Les voies de communication dans le Hauran à l'époque romaine," in *Hauran: Recherches archéologiques sur la Syrie du sud à l'époque hellénistique et romaine*, ed. Jean-Marie Dentzer, vol. 1 (Paris: P. Geuthner, 1985), pp. 137–165.

73. Dunand, "Voie romaine," p. 539; on this governor, who served from 157 to 162, see Thomasson, *Laterculi*, col. 312, no. 57.

74. Bowersock, *Roman Arabia*, pp. 164–186, especially pp. 177–178. The Peutinger Table is a medieval (thirteenth-century) copy of an ancient map that may have been produced shortly after the middle of the fourth century. It was discovered in Worms (Germany) at the end of the fifteenth century by Konrad Celtes, and be-

queathed by him to a municipal scribe in Augsburg named Peutinger; scholars have continued refer to the map as Peutinger's. The map does not aim to give a realistic picture of the Roman world. It describes itineraries; stopping places are marked and the distances between them are indicated.

75. Dunand, "Voie romaine," pp. 521–557; Bauzou, "Routes romaines," pp. 208–209, 217.

76. *I.Syrie*, no. 2524 = Annie Sartre-Fauriat and Maurice Sartre, *IGLS*, vol. 15, *Le plateau du Trachôn* (Beirut: Institut français d'archéologie du Proche-Orient, forthcoming), no. 13, between 183 and 187; we know the content of the villagers' complaint only through the governor's reply, which the residents had engraved in plain sight in the village.

77. *AE* (1933), no. 205.

78. Mommsen, *CIL*, vol. 3, no. 203.

79. David L. Kennedy, *Archaeological Explorations on the Roman Frontier in the North-Eastern Jordan: The Roman and Byzantine Military Installations and Road Network on the Ground and from the Air* (Oxford: British Archaeological Reports, 1982), pp. 171–175.

80. On the *Strata Diocletiana*, see René Mouterde, "La strata Diocletiana et ses bornes milliaires," *Mélanges de l'Université Saint-Joseph* 15 (1930): 221–233; Bauzou, "Routes romaines," pp. 211–213; on the exploration undertaken between Palmyra and Dmeir (Thelsea), see Thomas Bauzou, "Épigraphie et toponymie: Le cas de la Palmyrène du Sud-Ouest," *Syria* 70 (1993): 27–50, where Bauzou notes that the word *strata* appears only rarely, a little to the north and a little to the south of Palmyra.

81. Anne-Michèle Rasson-Seigne and Jacques Seigne, "Notes préliminaires à l'étude de la voie romaine Gérasa/Philadelphia," *ADAJ* 39 (1995): 193–210: the oldest milestones go back to 112.

82. David L. Kennedy, "Roman Roads and Routes in North-East Jordan," *Levant* 29 (1997): 71–93.

83. Michele Piccirillo, "La strada romana Esbus–Livias," *Liber Annuus* 46 (1996): 285–300.

84. Richard George Goodchild, "The Coast Road of Phoenicia and Its Milestones," *Berytus* 9 (1949): 91–127; Bauzou, "Routes romaines," p. 208. In 216–217, the roadway along the nahr al-Kelb was reconstructed; the nahr al-Kelb is a narrow passageway between the mountains and the sea just north of Berytus.

85. Jean-Paul Rey-Coquais, *IGLS*, vol. 6, *Baalbek et Beqa'* (Paris: P. Geuthner, 1967), no. 2958.

86. *AE* (1927), no. 161; cf. David Oates, *Studies in the Ancient History of Northern Iraq* (London: Oxford University Press, 1968), pp. 71–72.

87. Antoine Poidebard, *La trace de Rome dans le désert de Syrie: Le limes de Trajan à la conquête arabe; Recherches aériennes (1925–1932)* (Paris: P. Geuthner, 1934), pp. 165–167.

88. Peter Thomsen, "Die römischen Meilensteine der Provinzen Syria, Arabia, und Palästina," *Zeitschrift der deutschen Palästina-Vereins* 40 (1917): nos. 34–35.

89. Isaac, *Limits of Empire*, especially pp. 101–160.

90. Ibid.; René Mouterde and Antoine Poidebard, *Le limes de Chalcis: Organisation de la steppe en haute Syrie romaine; Documents aériens* (Paris: P. Geuthner, 1945).

91. David L. Kennedy and Derrick Riley, *Rome's Desert Frontier: From the Air* (Austin: University of Texas Press, 1990).

92. On this notion, see Isaac, "The Meaning of '*limes*' and '*limitanei*,'"; see also Jean-Michel Carrié and Aline Rousselle, *L'empire romain en mutation: Des Sévères à Constantin, 192–337* (Paris: Le Seuil, 1999), pp. 616–621.

93. Poidebard, *Trace de Rome;* Mouterde and Poidebard, *Limes de Chalcis.* On Poidebard's methods, see the excellent study prepared for an exhibition in Poidebard's memory under the direction of Lévon Nordiguian and Jean-François Salles, *Aux origines de l'archéologie aérienne: A. Poidebard (1878–1955)* (Beirut: Presses de l'Université Saint-Joseph, 2000), especially the contributions by Thomas Bauzou, Corinne Castel, and Pierre-Louis Gatier. All things considered, perhaps what is of principal interest today is preserving aerial coverage of Syria before the postwar urban development of the region, which retains the traces of ancient and medieval land divisions much better than could be done today. The text cited here offers a superb sample of photographs taken at Poidebard's initiative (Poidebard prepared the work, but he did not take any vertical shots; all his photos were taken at an angle).

94. Victor Chapot, *La frontière de l'Euphrate de Pompée à la conquête arabe* (Paris: A. Fontemoing, 1907).

95. David and Joan Oates, "Aspects of Hellenistic and Roman Settlement in the Khabur Basin," in *Resurrecting the Past: A Joint Tribute to Adnan Bounni,* ed. Paolo Matthiae, Maurits van Loon, and Harvey Weiss (Istanbul and Leiden: Nederlands Historisch-Archaeologisch Instituut te Istanbul and Nederlands instituut voor het Nabije Oosten, 1990), pp. 227–248.

96. S. Thomas Parker, *Romans and Saracens: A History of the Arabian Frontier* (Philadelphia: American Schools of Oriental Research, 1986).

97. S. Thomas Parker, "The Typology of Roman and Byzantine Forts and Fortresses in Jordan," *Studies in the History and Archaeology of Jordan* (hereafter cited as *SHAJ*) 5 (1995): 251–260.

98. Smith II, Stevens, and Niemi, "Southeast Araba Archaeological Survey," pp. 45–71, especially pp. 56–64, 67.

99. K. W. Russell, in an oral communication cited by Zbigniew T. Fiema, "Military Architecture and the Defense 'System' of Roman-Byzantine Southern Jordan: A Critical Reappraisal of Current Interpretations," *SHAJ* 5 (1995): 264.

100. See Maurice Sartre, "Une garnison romaine aux marges de l'Arabie romaine: Mothana," *Syria* (forthcoming).

101. Seyrig, "Postes romains"; Sartre, *Trois études,* pp. 29–34.

102. Fiema, "Military Architecture."

103. Isaac, *Limits of Empire.*

104. Marie-Louise Chaumont offers a clear and convenient summary in "L'Arménie entre Rome et l'Iran: I. De l'avènement d'Auguste à l'avènement de Dioclétien," *ANRW* 2.9.1 (1976): 130–194.

105. The date of December 13, 115, is generally accepted; this is a purely arbitrary reconstruction by John Malalas. A much more probable date is January 115, for we know that one of the consuls serving in 115, M. Pedo Vergilianus, died on this occasion; he was replaced early in the year by a consul suffect, whereas his colleague remained in place for some time. See Birley, *Hadrian,* p. 71 and p. 324, n. 13.

106. Suidas, *Suidae Lexicon,* ed. Ada Adler, vol. 3 (Stuttgart: Teubner, 1967

[1933]), s.v. "ωνητη," p. 611; cf. Han J. W. Drijvers, "Hatra, Palmyra und Edessa: Die Städte der syrisch-mesopotamischen Wüste in politischer, kulturgeschichtlicher und religiongeschichtlicher Beleuchtung," *ANRW* 2.8 (1977): 872; Birley, *Hadrian*, p. 68.

107. Dio, 68.31; if excerpt 75.9.6, which mentions a certain Vologases, son of Sanatruq, is correctly placed here (immediately preceding 68.31), it implies that there was a peace agreement between Trajan and Hatra, for the name *Sanatruq* appears to be characteristic of this city. But Dio does not speak of a king of Hatra, and the first one who is mentioned, Sanatruq I, is not attested before 177–178: Drijvers, "Hatra, Palmyra und Edessa," p. 820.

108. It was on this occasion that Legio III Cyrenaica put up a triumphal arch a mile to the west of the Palmyra Gate in Dura; its foundations and fragments of the dedication have been discovered. See S. Gould, "The Triumphal Arch," in *Excavations at Dura-Europos*, vol. 4, *Preliminary Report of Fourth Season of Work, October 1930–March 1931*, ed. Paul V. C. Baur, Mikhail Ivanovitch Rostovtzeff, and Alfred Raymond Bellinger (New Haven: Yale University Press, 1933), pp. 56–65.

109. André Maricq thinks that this province must have encompassed Parthian Babylonia ("La province d'"Assyrie' créée par Trajan: À propos de la guerre parthique de Trajan," *Syria* 36 [1959]: 254–263); but Millar believes that it never existed, and he observes that no source mentions it before the fourth century (*Roman Near East*, p. 101); had it existed, it would have been located instead in Adiabene, for Dio establishes an equivalence between the names *Assyria* and *Adiabene* (68.26.4).

110. Dio, 68.30.3: this is Parthamaspates.

111. André Maricq, "Classica et Orientalia," *Syria* 42 (1965): 103–111.

112. Dio, 68.30.2.

113. The list of Edessene royalty transmitted in the *Chronicle* of Pseudo Denis of Tell Mahre (*Chronicon anonymum Pseudo Dionysianum vulgo dictum*, ed. Jean-Baptiste Chabot [Louvain: L. Durbecq, 1953]) indicates a two-year interregnum (116–118) during which the Romans governed Edessa, then a period of joint reign by Ialud/Yalur and Parthamaspates, for three years and ten months, which brings us to late 121 or early 122; see also "Hadrian," in *Historia Augusta*, trans. David Magie, vol. 1 (Loeb Classical Library), 5.4; Drijvers, "Hatra, Palmyra und Edessa," pp. 874–875; Birley, *Hadrian*, pp. 153–154; but Han J. W. Drijvers and John F. Healey note only an interregnum from 116 to 118 reestablishing the dynasty through Hadrian (*The Old Syriac Inscriptions of Edessa and Osrhoene: Texts, Translations and Commentary* [Leiden and Boston: E. J. Brill, 1999], p. 36). On all these problems of chronology, I agree with Gawlikowski, "Last Kings of Edessa."

114. Sheldon Arthur Nodelman, "A Preliminary History of Characene," *Berytus* 13 (1960): 83–121; on this episode, see pp. 109–110.

115. This Mithridates is in place as early as 131, for he is the same person as Meherdatos, king of Mesene, for whom a Palmyrene, Yahrai, son of Nebuzabad, carried out a mission in Bahrein (he was the satrap of the island known as Thiluana): *Inv.*, vol. 10, no. 38; Henri Seyrig, "Inscriptions grecques de l'agora de Palmyre," *Syria* 22 (1941): 253–255 (= *AS*, vol. 3, pp. 197–199).

116. All the information comes from a bilingual Greek-Parthian inscription engraved on the thigh of a statuette of Heracles that was probably pillaged during the operations and reconsecrated by Vologases IV in Seleucia on the Tigris in 150–151 or 151–152 (it depends on which Seleucid era the writer used, that of Antioch or that of Babylonia): Fabrizio A. Pennachietti, "L'iscrizione bilingue greco-partica dell'Eracle

di Seleucia," *Mesopotamia* 22 (1987): 169–185; Daniel T. Potts, "Arabia and the Kingdom of Characene," in *Araby the Blest: Studies in Arabian Archaeology*, ed. Daniel T. Potts (Copenhagen: Carsten Niebuhr Institute of Ancient Near Eastern Studies, 1988), pp. 137–167; and Glen W. Bowersock, "La Mésène (Maishân) antonine," in *L'Arabie préislamique et son environnement historique et culturel: Actes du colloque de Strasbourg, 24–27 juin 1987*, ed. Toufic Fahd (Leiden: E. J. Brill, 1989), pp. 159–168. An in-depth commentary on all aspects of the question, replacing the previous commentaries, is provided by Paul Bernard, "Vicissitudes au gré de l'histoire d'une statue d'Héraclès entre Séleucie du Tigre et la Mésène," *Journal des Savants* (1990): 3–67. Nodelman had already noted the replacement of Athambelos around 117, in relation to Trajan's arrival ("Preliminary History," p. 111).

117. Dio, 71.2.1.

118. Ibid., 71.2.1–2.

119. Joshua Benzion Segal, *Edessa, "The Blessed City"* (Oxford: Clarendon Press, 1970), p. 19.

120. Inscription from 6 C.E.: Drijvers and Healey, *Old Syriac Inscriptions*, pp. 140–144, no. As 55; the owner of the tomb, Zarbiyan, son of Abgaros, governor of Birtha, was at the same time the tutor of Ma'nu, son of Ma'nu. The most recent editors dismiss for want of proof the idea that this Ma'nu may be Ma'nu IV, who came to power in 7 C.E. This prudence is well advised, but despite the absence of any reference to the royal family, it is curious that a local governor as important as the one who guarded the border all along the Euphrates would have thought it useful to his glory to add that he was the tutor of an individual who did not belong to a social category still higher than his own. For this reason, I believe that we must not rule out the possibility that Ma'nu was indeed the future Ma'nu IV, and that Zarbiyan was related to him in some way.

121. Many dedications to the god Sin of Harran made at Sumatar under the reign of Tiridates: Han J. W. Drijvers, *Cults and Beliefs at Edessa* (Leiden: E. J. Brill, 1980): 122–145.

122. Dio, 71.2.3–4.

123. Pierre Leriche and Mahmoud al-A'sad, "Doura-Europos: Bilan des recherches récentes," *Comptes rendus des séances de l'Académie des inscriptions et belles-lettres* (1994): 411; the city resisted the assailants, however.

124. Segal, *Edessa*.

125. Dio, 69.3.5. On Avidius Cassius, see Maria Laura Astarita, *Avidio Cassio* (Rome: Ed. di storia e letteratura, 1983); Sir Ronald Syme, "Avidius Cassius: His Rank, Age and Quality," *Bonner Historia-Augusta Colloquium 1984/1985* (Bonn: R. Habelt, 1987), pp. 207–222 (= *Roman Papers*, vol. 5 [Oxford: Oxford University Press, 1988], pp. 687–701); Millar, *Roman Near East*, pp. 115–118.

126. See Astarita, *Avidio Cassio*, pp. 18–23.

127. Dio, 72.3.1.

128. Philostrates, "The Lives of the Sophists," in *Philostratus and Eunapius: The Lives of the Sophists*, trans. Wilmer Cave Wright (Loeb Classical Library), 2.1.563. Let us note that Dio and Philostrates use the same term, whose noun form *epitropos* corresponds to the Latin *procurator*.

129. Cf. the list established by David Stone Potter, "Rome and Palmyra: Odaenathus' Titulature and the Use of the *Imperium maius*," *ZPE* 113 (1996): 277–278.

130. See Astarita, *Avidio Cassio*, p. 78–89.

131. H. 79, 223, 277. The inscriptions from Hatra, numbered continuously from the beginning of their publication, have been collected from H. 1 to H. 341 by Francesco Vattioni, *Le Iscrizioni di Hatra* (Naples: Istituto orientale di Napoli, 1981) (= *Annali dell'Istituto orientale di Napoli*, suppl. 28). Next, H. 343–344 were published by Jaber Khalil Ibrahim, "Kitabat al-hadr" (Two Legal Texts from Hatra), *Sumer* 38 (1982): 120–125 (cf. Joshua Benzion Segal, "Aramaic Legal Texts from Hatra," *Journal of Jewish Studies* [hereafter cited as *JJS*] [1982]: 109–115), and H. 345–387 by Hazim al-Najafi, "The Inscriptions of Hatra," *Sumer* 39 (1983): 175–199; cf. Basile Aggoula, "Remarques sur les inscriptions hatréennes [hereafter cited as RIH] (VI)," *Syria* 58 (1981): 363–378; "RIH (VII)," *Aula Orientalis* 1 (1983): 31–38; "*RIH* (VIII)," *Syria* 60 (1983): 101–105; "RIH IX," *Syria* 60 (1983): 251–257; "RIH (XI)," *Syria* 64 (1987): 91–106; "RIH (XII)," *Syria* 63 (1986): 353–374. See also Basile Aggoula, *Inscriptions et graffites araméens d'Assour* (Naples: Istituto orientale de Napoli, 1985) (= *Annali dell'Istituto orientale di Napoli*, suppl. 43), and more recently, idem, *Inventaire des inscriptions hatréennes* (Paris: P. Geuthner, 1991).

132. H. 195.

133. H. 198 (Nyhr'); H. 139, 198 (Nsryhb); H. 139 (grandson).

134. Herodian, 3.9.2–7.

135. Dio, 76.10.11.

136. *Feriale Duranum*, 1.14–16.

137. Ibid., 76.11.12.

138. Zeev Rabin, "Dio, Herodian and Severus' Second Parthian War," *Chiron* 5 (1975): 419–441. On the siege operations, see Michael p. Speidel, "European-Syrian Elite Troops at Dura-Europos and Hatra," in *Roman Army Studies*, ed. Michael p. Speidel, vol. 1 (Amsterdam: J. C. Gieben, 1984), pp. 301–309; D. B. Campbell, "What Happened at Hatra? The Problem of the Severan Siege Operations," in Freeman and Kennedy, *Defence*, pp. 51–58; David L. Kennedy, "'European' Soldiers and the Severan Siege of Hatra," in Freeman and Kennedy, *Defence*, pp. 397–409.

139. Joël Le Gall and Marcel Le Glay, *L'Empire romain* (Paris: Presses Universitaires de France, 1987), pp. 593–594.

140. Drijvers, "Hatra, Palmyra und Edessa," pp. 799–906.

6. CIVIC LIFE AND URBAN DEVELOPMENT DURING THE EARLY EMPIRE

1. One could obviously debate figures that no one can establish with even rough precision; we have to take into account the fact that a very large number of small cities in Greece proper flourished during the archaic and classical eras and disappeared over time, absorbed by more powerful neighbors. A precise calculation at a given moment would thus have to take into account both creations and disappearances.

2. See Maurice Sartre and Alain Tranoy, *La Méditerranée antique, 4e siècle av. J.-C.–3e siècle ap. J.-C.* (Paris: A. Colin, 1990), pp. 160–187; Maurice Sartre, *L'Orient romain: Provinces et sociétés provinciales en Méditerranée orientale d'Auguste aux Sévères (31 avant J.-C.–235 après J.-C)* (Paris: Le Seuil, 1991), pp. 121–198.

3. Arnold H. M. Jones, *The Greek City, from Alexander to Justinian* (Oxford: Clarendon Press, 1941).

4. Pliny, *Natural History*, trans. H. Rackham (Loeb Classical Library) 5.19.81–82 (hereafter cited as *NH*).

5. For the details, see Maurice Sartre, *D'Alexandre à Zénobie* (Paris: Fayard, 2001), pp. 144–145.

6. Sartre, *Orient romain*, pp. 195–196.

7. I have mentioned Caesarea-Eitha in the Hauran on several occasions, on the basis of an inscription copied and published by William Henry Waddington, *Inscriptions grecques et latines de la Syrie* (Paris: Firmin-Didot, 1870), no. 2115 (herafter cited as *I.Syrie*) (= Maurice Sartre, *Inscriptions grecques et latines de la Syrie* [hereafter cited as *IGLS*], vol. 16, *Le Djebel al-CEArab* [Paris: Institut français d'archéologie du Proche-Orient, forthcoming], no. 597). A new unpublished copy of this text leads me to question this interpretation and to remove this Caesarea from the list of cities without any doubt; in fact, the inhabitants of Eitha simply built a Kaisareion.

8. Josephus, *De antiquitate judaico (Jewish Antiquities)*, trans. Louis H. Feldman (Loeb Classical Library), 16.5.2 (the Kapharsaba plain) (hereafter cited as *AJ*); Eusebius, *Chronicon*, ed. Albert Schoene (Berlin: Weidmann, 1875–1876), 142: "Herod renamed Parsanaba Antipatris in honor of his father Antipatros"; cf. Peter Thomsen, *Loca sancta: Verzeichnis der im 1. bis 6. Jahrhundert n. Chr. erwähnten Ortschaften Palästinas, mit besonderer Berücksichtigung der Lokalisierung der biblischen Stätten* (Halle: S. R. Haupt, 1907), p. 22; Félix-Marie Abel, *Géographie de la Palestine*, vol. 2 (Paris: Librairie Lecoffre / J. Gabalda, 1933–1938), pp. 245–246; Emil Schürer, *The History of the Jewish People in the Age of Jesus Christ (175 B.C.– A.D. 135)*, rev. and ed. Géza Vermès and Fergus Millar, trans. T. A. Burkill et al. (Edinburgh: Clark, 1973–1986), vol. 3, pp. 167–168. This is indeed a city, because it minted coins; see the bibliography in Arye Kindler and Alla Stein, *A Bibliography of the City Coinage of Palestine, from the 2nd Century B.C. to the 3rd Century A.D.* (Oxford: British Archaeological Reports, 1987), pp. 41–42.

9. To earlier studies of the foundation and urban development of Caesarea by Lee I. Levine (*Caesarea under Roman Rule* [Leiden: E. J. Brill, 1975]) and Joseph Ringel (*Césarée de Palestine: Étude historique et archéologique* [Paris: Ophrys 1975]), we must now add publications reporting on the digs of the 1980s and 1990s: Kenneth G. Holum, Robert L. Hohlfelder, Robert J. Bull, and Avner Raban, *King Herod's Dream: Caesarea on the Sea* (New York and London: W. W. Norton, 1988), a book for the general public with good illustrations; Robert Lindley Vann, ed., *Caesarea Papers: Straton's Tower, Herod's Harbour, and Roman and Byzantine Caesarea* (Ann Arbor: University of Michigan Press, 1992); Avner Raban and Kenneth G. Holum, *Caesarea Maritima: A Retrospective after Two Millennia* (Leiden and New York: E. J. Brill, 1996), an essential work giving excellent syntheses on various aspects of the city (sanctuary ports, decoration, but also religious life); Kenneth G. Holum, Avner Raban, and Joseph Patrich, eds., *Caesarea Papers 2: Herod's Temple, the Provincial Governor's Praetorium and Granaries, the Later Harbor, a Gold Coin Hoard, and Other Studies* (Portsmouth, R.I.: Journal of Roman Archaeology, 1999).

10. Alla Kushnir-Stein, "The Predecessor of Caesarea: On the Identification of Demetrias in South Phoenicia," in *The Roman and Byzantine Near East: Some Recent Archaeological Research*, ed. John H. Humphrey (Ann Arbor, Mich.: Journal of Roman Archaeology, 1995), 9–14.

11. Josephus, *De bello judaico (The Jewish War)*, trans. Henry St. John Thackeray (Loeb Classical Library), 1.156 (hereafter cited as *BJ*); Josephus, *AJ* 14.76.

12. Josephus, *BJ* 1.396, *AJ* 15.217.

13. Josephus, *BJ* 1.408–415, *AJ* 15.331–341.

14. There is a fine identification of a bronze in Henri Seyrig, "La Tychè de Césarée de Palestine," *Syria* 49 (1972): 112–115 (= Henri Seyrig, *Antiquités syriennes* [Paris: P. Geuthner, 1934–], 100 [hereafter cited as *AS*]), and of a marble statue in Rivka Gersht, "The Tyche of Caesarea Maritima," *Palestine Exploration Quarterly* (hereafter cited as *PEQ*) 116 (1984): 110–114. See also Robert Wenning, "Die Stadtgöttin von Caesarea Maritima," *Boreas* 9 (1986): 113–129; Rivka Gersht, "Representations of Deities and the Cults of Caesarea," in Raban and Holum, *Caesarea Maritima*, pp. 307–309. This Tyche appears before a temple on the "Caesarea Cup": Ernest Will, "La coupe de Césarée de Palestine au Musée du Louvre," *Monuments Piot* 65 (1983): 1–24; this monument from the second or third quarter of the fourth century includes a very faithful reproduction of the marble statue mentioned above.

15. See the dedications published by Silva Lake: "Greco-Roman Inscriptions," in *Samaria-Sebaste*, vol. 3, *The Objects from Samaria*, ed. John Winter Crowfoot (London: Palestine Exploration Fund, 1957), p. 36, no. 9; p. 37, nos. 12, 14; p. 41, no. 48 (Kore); p. 37, no. 13 (Isis and Serapis).

16. Pliny, *NH* 5.15.71; Josephus, *BJ* 2.168; cf. Thomsen, *Loca sancta*, p. 111; Schürer, *History*, vol. 2, pp. 178–183; Harold W. Hoehner, *Herod Antipas* (Cambridge: Cambridge University Press, 1972), pp. 91–100.

17. Josephus, *BJ* 2.168; the name was given in honor of Livia. The site, identified as Beth Haram, Betharamatha, or Betharamphtha (*AJ* 17.10.6, 18.2.1, 20.8.4), contained a royal residence burned down by Simon, one of the self-proclaimed "kings" after Herod's death (*BJ* 2.59); it is now known as Tell ar-Rame. See Thomsen, *Loca sancta*, p. 83; Abel, *Géographie*, vol. 2, p. 158; Schürer, *History*, vol. 2, pp. 176–178; Hoehner, *Herod Antipas*, pp. 87–89.

18. Josephus, *BJ* 2.168; he specifies that it is located in "lower Gaulanitis." This site, dedicated to Iulia, daughter of Augustus, was the former Bethsaida (*AJ* 18.2.1, 18.4.6) and is now known as al-Tell. See Thomsen, *Loca sancta*, p. 41; Abel, *Géographie*, vol. 2, p. 158; Schürer, *History*, vol. 2, pp. 171–172.

19. Josephus, *BJ* 2.168.

20. Josephus, *AJ* 20.211. The palace of Agrippa II may have been found there: see John F. Wilson and Vassilios Tzaferis, "Banias Dig Reveals King's Palace (But Which King?)," *Biblical Archaeology Review* 24, no. 1 (1998): 54–61, 85; Farah Mébarki, "Banyas: Le palais d'Agrippa II?" *Le monde de la Bible* (hereafter cited as *M.Bible*) 124 (January–February 2000): 66.

21. On this city, about which we still know too little for the Hellenistic and Roman periods, see Josephus, *BJ* 7.97; Pliny mentions it as a tetrarchy (*NH* 5.16.74). Cf. Arnold H. M. Jones, "The Urbanization of the Ituraean Principality," *Journal of Roman Studies* (hereafter cited as *JRS*) 21 (1931): 267; Henri Seyrig, "Une monnaie de Césarée du Liban," *AS*, vol. 6, pp. 11–16.

22. In Bostra, there is a reference to a *proedros* (president) of the civic *boule* (council) as early as 115–120: Maurice Sartre, *IGLS*, vol. 13.1, *Bostra* (Paris: P. Geuthner, 1982), nos. 9054–9055; in Petra, there are several references to papyri of Nahal Hever in the 120s: Naphtali Lewis, ed., *The Documents from the Bar Kokhba Period in the Cave of Letters*, vol. 1, *Greek Papyri* (Jerusalem: Israel Exploration Society, 1989), no. 12, in the first part of 124.

23. See E. E. Hölscher, "Medeba," in *Realencyclopädie der classischen Altertumswissenschaft* (hereafter cited as *RE*), ed. August Wilhelm von Pauly et al.

(Stuttgart: J. B. Metzler, 1894–); Abel, *Géographie*, vol. 2, pp. 381–382. The city is mentioned in only one inscription: Pierre-Louis Gatier, *IGLS*, vol. 21, *Inscriptions grecques et latines de la Jordanie* (hereafter cited as *IGLJ*), vol. 2, *Région centrale: Amman, Hesban, Madaba, Main, Dhiban* (Paris: P. Geuthner, 1986), no. 117, probably dating from the second century. Cf. the coins in Augustus J. Spijkerman, *The Coins of the Decapolis and Provincia Arabia*, ed. Michele Piccirillo (Jerusalem: Franciscan Printing Press, 1978), pp. 180–185, and Mayer Rosenberger, *The Coinage of Eastern Palestine and Legionary Countermarks, Bar-Kochba Overstrucks* (Jerusalem: Rosenberger, 1978), pp. 56–58: the first mintings date from the time of Septimius Severus.

24. See Thomsen, *Loca sancta*, p. 25, s.v. "Areopolis"; Spijkerman, *Coins of the Decapolis*, pp. 262–275; and Rosenberger, *Coinage of Eastern Palestine*, pp. 74–78 (under the Severi). The name *Areopolis* appears on the coinage of Elagabalus: see Rosenberger, *Coinage of Eastern Palestine*, pp. 77–78, and Spijkerman, *Coins of the Decapolis*, p. 275.

25. Spijkerman, *Coins of the Decapolis*, pp. 108–115, and Rosenberger, *Coinage of Eastern Palestine*, p. 22: a single minting under Elagabalus.

26. Abel, *Géographie*, vol. 2, pp. 348–349; Werner K. Vyhmeister, "The History of Heshbon from Literary Sources," *Andrews University Seminaries Studies* 6 (1968): 158–177; Schürer, *History*, vol. 2, pp. 165–166; Spijkerman, *Coins of the Decapolis*, pp. 122–125; and Rosenberger, *Coinage of Eastern Palestine*, p. 35: a single minting under Elagabalus. See also the reports on the American digs: L. T. Geraty and L. G. Running, eds., *Historical Foundations: Studies of Literary References to Hesban and Vicinity* (Berrien Springs, Mich.: Andrews University Press, 1989); L. A. Mitchell, *Hellenistic and Roman Strata: A Study of the Stratigraphy of Tell Hesban from 2nd Century B.C. to 4th Century A.D.* (Berrien Springs, Mich.: Andrews University Press, 1992); S. Douglas Waterhouse, *The Necropolis of Hesban: A Typology of Tombs* (Berrien Springs. Mich.: Andrews University Press, 1998). There are two additional volumes on the environment, and one volume on the archaeological exploration of the region: Robert D. Ibach, *Archaeological Survey of the Hesban Region: Catalogue of Sites and Characterizations of Periods* (Berrien Springs, Mich.: Andrews University Press, 1987).

27. Spijkerman, *Coins of the Decapolis*, pp. 58–65, and Rosenberger, *Coinage of Eastern Palestine*, pp. 5–6. The coinage appeared as early as the reign of Marcus Aurelius (or even that of Antoninus Pius, according to Spijkerman [p. 60, no. 1]), but we do not know how much earlier the city itself was founded.

28. The name *Soada* is attested for the last time in 149 (see *I.Syrie*, 2307 = René Cagnat, Jean Toutain, Georges Lafaye, and Victor Henry, eds., *Inscriptiones graecae ad res romanas pertinentes*, vol. 3 [Paris: E. Leroux, 1906], no. 1275 [hereafter cited as *IGR*] = Σαρτρε, in Sartre, *IGLS*, vol. 16, forthcoming, no. 321), and the reference to the city of Dionysias is certain in 185–186 (*I.Syrie*, no. 2309 = Sartre, *IGLS*, vol. 16, forthcoming, no. 333). Thus the promotion took place between these two dates, although we cannot be more precise. The mention of the city in an inscription from Suweida referring to the water supply brought from Raha (*I.Syrie*, no. 2308 = Sartre, *IGLS*, vol. 16, forthcoming, no. 332) in 182–183 does not allow us to determine whether the city in question is already Dionysias (as Henry Innes Macadam believes: *Studies in the History of the Roman Province of Arabia* [Oxford: British Archaeological Reports, 1986], p. 72) or whether the reference is instead to Canatha.

29. The operation was probably planned, if not immediately carried out, when Philip came through the region on his way back from the Euphrates Valley in 244, on his way to Rome, according to Michael Peachin, "Philip's Program: From Mesopotamia to Rome in AD 244," *Historia* 40 (1991): 331–342; cf. Georgius Cedrenus, *Chronica,* in *Georgius Cedrenus [et] Ioannis Scylitzae ope,* ed. Immanuel Bekker, 2 vols. (Bonn: Weber, 1838–1839), p. 451.

30. Josephus, *BJ* 4.449; cf. Thomsen, *Loca sancta,* p. 93.

31. Pliny, *NH* 5.14.69.

32. Spijkerman, *Coins of the Decapolis,* pp. 96–107, and Rosenberger, *Coinage of Eastern Palestine,* pp. 19–22; the date of founding has been deduced from the era in use on the coins minted starting in 165–166 C.E.; the coins representing Macrinus (who reigned from April 11, 217, to June 8, 218) are dated from the year 120 of the local era; this authorizes us to place the beginning of the local era between the middle of 96 and the very beginning of 99. On the site and its history, see Cherie J. Lenzen and Ernst Axel Knauf, "Beit Ras / Capitolias: A Preliminary Evaluation of the Archaeological and Textual Evidence," *Syria* 64 (1987): 21–46.

33. Schürer, *History,* vol. 2, pp. 172–176; Christa Möller and Götz Schmitt, *Siedlungen Palästinas nach Flavius Josephus* (Wiesbaden: Reichert, 1976), pp. 172–173; Yoram Tsafrir, Leah Di Segni, and Judith Green, *Tabula Imperii Romani: Iudaea-Palaestina. Eretz Israel in the Hellenistic, Roman and Byzantine Periods: Maps and Gazetteer* (Jerusalem: Israel Academy of Sciences and Humanities, 1994), s.v. "Sepphoris."

34. Josephus, *AJ* 14.19, *BJ* 1.170.

35. Josephus, *AJ* 14.414–415.

36. Josephus, *AJ* 17.271, 289; *BJ* 2.56, 68.

37. Josephus, *AJ* 18.27; cf. Hoehner, *Herod Antipas,* pp. 89–91.

38. Cf. Eric M. Meyers, "Aspects of Roman Sepphoris," in *Early Christianity in Context: Monuments and Documents,* ed. Frédéric Manns and Eugenio Alliata (Jerusalem: Franciscan Printing Press, 1993), pp. 29–36. The name *Diocaesarea* appears on a milestone from 130 on the road between Ptolemais and Tiberias, thus supplying a *terminus ante quem:* Eric M. Meyers, Ehud Netzer, and Carol L. Meyers, *Sepphoris* (Winona Lake: Eisenbrauns, 1992), pp. 12–13.

39. Lucia Septimia Seuera Eleutheropolis on coins and in *Corpus inscriptionum latinarum* (hereafter cited as *CIL*), vol. 3, *Inscriptiones Asiae, provinciaeum Europae graecarum, Illyrici latinae,* ed. Theodor Mommsen (Berlin: G. Reimer, 1873–1902), no. 14155, at the site of Bet Guvrin, formerly Betogabris; see Tsafrir et al., *Tabula,* s.v. "Eleutheropolis."

40. Pliny, *NH* 5.14.70; cf. Abel, *Géographie,* vol. 2, p. 370; Tsafrir et al., *Tabula,* s.v. "Lod," "Lydda."

41. Louis-Hugues Vincent and Félix-Marie Abel, *Emmaüs: Sa basilique et son histoire* (Paris: E. Leroux, 1932); Abel, *Géographie,* vol. 2, p. 314; *contra:* Sextus Iulius Africanus, *Les "Cestes" de Julius Africanus,* ed. and trans. Jean-René Vieillefond (Florence: Sansoni antiquariato; Paris: Librairie M. Didier, 1970), pp. 19–20, and Tsafrir et al., *Tabula,* s.v. "Emmaus."

42. Mentioned in *Papyrus de l'Euphrate* (hereafter cited as *P.Euphr.*), in Denis Feissel, Jean Gascou, and Javier Teixidor, "Documents d'archives romains inédits du Moyen Euphrate (IIIe s. après J.-C.)," *Journal des Savants* (1997): 6–7. On the multiple names of the site *(Charax Sidou, Haykla Karka, Anthemusia, Batnai)* and their

relationships, see Tommaso Gnoli, "I papiri dell'Eufrate: Studio di geografia storica," *Mediterraneo Antico* 2 (1999): 341–344.

43. *P.Euphr.*, in Feissel and Gascou, "Documents" (1997), 3–4; cf. Denis Feissel and Jean Gascou, "Documents d'archives romains inédits du Moyen Euphrate (IIIe siècle après J.-C.)," *Comptes rendus des séances de l'Académie des inscriptions et belles-lettres* (hereafter cited as *CRAI*) (1989): 535–561; Denis Feissel and Jean Gascou, "Documents d'archives romains inédits du Moyen-Euphrate (IIIe s. apr. J.-C.)," *Journal des Savants* (1995): 65–119. On the difficulty of choosing among the four sites known as Appadana, see Gnoli, "I papiri dell'Eufrate," pp. 350–354; Gnoli comes out against the Appadana near Dura in favor either of Ptolemy's Appadana in the Khabur valley (Ptolemy, *Geographia*, ed. C. F. A. Nobbe [Hildesheim: G. Olds, 1966], 5.17.7) or the Appadana-Basileia near Zalabiyyeh (which he prefers). In this text he announces a future publication in which he will argue in favor of a somewhat earlier date for this foundation, around 244–248; the publication in question is probably *Roma, Edessa e Palmira nel III sec. d. C. Problemi istituzionali: Uno studio sui papyri dell'Eufrate* (Pisa: Istituti editoriali e poligrafici internazionali, 2000), in which the author reaffirms his opposition to an identification with the Appadana near Dura and leans toward Appadana-Basileia (p. 63).

44. Colonia Augusta Iulia Felix Berytus: Pliny, *NH* 5.17.78; see René Mouterde, "Regards sur Beyrouth," *Mélanges de l'Université Saint-Joseph* (hereafter cited as *MUSJ*) 40 (1964): 163–166; Jean Lauffray, "Beyrouth Archéologie et histoire, époques gréco-romaines: I. Période hellénistique et Haut-Empire romain," *Aufstieg und Niedergang der römischen Welt* (hereafter cited as *ANRW*) 2.8 (1977): 144–145; Jean-Paul Rey-Coquais, "Syrie romaine, de Pompée à Dioclétien," *JRS* 68 (1978): 51; all these authors accept the early date. We cannot go back further because the last minting of coins from the city of Berytos dates from 28–27 B.C.E. Strabo (*The Geography*, trans. Horace Leonard Jones [Loeb Classical Library], 16.2.19 [hereafter cited as Strabo]) seems to indicate a later date, in 15 B.C.E., while others have tended to see only a reinforcement of the colony by Marcus Agrippa at that point: Jean-Michel Roddaz, *Marcus Agrippa* (Rome: École française de Rome; Paris: E. de Boccard, 1984), pp. 432–433. In favor of the later date, see Peter A. Brunt, *Italian Manpower* (Oxford: Oxford University Press, 1971), p. 601; Fergus Millar, *The Roman Near East (31 B.C.–A.D. 337)* (Cambridge, Mass.: Harvard University Press, 1993), pp. 36, 279. Benjamin H. Isaac adopts an intermediate viewpoint (*The Limits of Empire: The Roman Army in the East* [Oxford and New York: Clarendon Press, 1990], p. 318, n. 32): he hypothesizes that veterans were installed there between 30 and 27 (Mommsen, *CIL*, vol. 3, no. 14165), but that the colony as such was only founded in 14 B.C.E. See also Schürer, *History*, vol. 1, p. 323, n. 150. The earliest coins minted mention p. Quinctilius Varus, governor from 6 to 4 B.C.E.: Andrew Burnett, Michel Amandry, and Pere Paul Ripollès, *Roman Provincial Coinage* (hereafter cited as *RPC*), vol. 1, *Julio-Claudian Period* (London: British Museum Press; Paris: Bibliothèque nationale de France: 1992), pp. 648–649. On Berytos, see Fergus Millar, "The Roman *Coloniae* of the Near East: A Study of Cultural Relations," in *Roman Eastern Policy and Other Studies in Roman History*, ed. Heikki Solin and Mika Kajava (Helsinki: Finnish Society of Sciences and Letters, 1990), pp. 10–23.

45. The date when Heliopolis became an autonomous colony is still subject to debate: see Roddaz, *Marcus Agrippa*, p. 433; Jean-Paul Rey-Coquais, *IGLS*, vol. 6, *Baalbek et Beqa'* (Paris: P. Geuthner, 1967), p. 34, n. 9, and idem, "Syrie romaine,"

p. 52. I think we can be certain that this was not during the reign of the Severi, even if the new colony sought to stress the fact that it had existed under Augustus by calling itself colonia Iulia Augusta Felix Heliopolis. This was a way of reminding people that the colonial population of Heliopolis could boast of a very long history at a time when many cities in Syria, Arabia, and Mesopotamia were obtaining the status of colony in their turn. In Heliopolis, independence was new, but not colonial status. On all this see Millar, "Roman *Coloniae*," pp. 19–20, 32–34, and Maurice Sartre, "Les colonies romaines dans le monde grec: Essai de synthèse," *Electrum* 5 (2001): 111–152.

46. Colonia Claudia Stabilis Germanica Felix Ptolemais: Pliny, *NH* 5.17.75; cf. Schürer, *History*, vol. 2, p. 125; Shimon Applebaum, "The Roman Colony of Ptolemaïs-'Ake and Its Territory," in *Judaea in Hellenistic and Roman Times: Historical and Archaeological Essays*, ed. Shimon Applebaum (Leiden and New York: E. J. Brill, 1989), pp. 70–96. The epithet *Germanica* may refer to Germanicus's eastern voyage, since the term appears on the city's precolonial coinage (Isaac, *Limits*, p. 322). The last precolonial minting dates from 51–52 (Leo Kadman, *The Coins of Akko-Ptolemais* [Tel-Aviv: Schocken, 1961], nn. 86–90, and especially the excellent study of the coinage by Henri Seyrig, "Le monnayage de Ptolemaïs en Phénicie," *Revue numismatique* [1962]: 25–50; see also *RPC*, vol. 1, pp. 658–659), and Claudius died in 54: thus the foundation of the colony has to date from the very end of the reign: a milestone from 56 makes reference to the construction of a road from Antioch *ad nouam coloniam Ptolemaida*: Richard George Goodchild, "The Coast Road of Phoenicia and Its Milestones," *Berytus* 9 (1949): 91–123, especially p. 120. Cf. Isaac, *Limits*, pp. 322–323; Isaac, *Roman Near East*, pp. 92–93; Millar, "Roman *Coloniae*," pp. 24–26.

47. Millar, "Roman *Coloniae*," pp. 24–26. See also an important study by Nicole Belayche, *Iudaea-Palaestina: The Pagan Cults in Roman Palestine (Second to Fourth Century)* (Tübingen: Mohr Siebeck, 2001), pp. 108–170.

48. Millar, "Roman *Coloniae*," pp. 28–30.

49. *Jerusalem Talmud, Sifré Dt*, 32, 17, 118: "Jerusalem and Samaria kept the whole world supplied with idols"; cited by Nicole Belayche, "Les cultes païens dans la *Palaestina romana*" (Ph.D. diss., Université de Paris IV, 1999), p. 126; cf. Ysé Tardan-Masquelier, ed., *Sifre: A Tannaitic Commentary on the Book of Deuteronomy*, trans. Reuven Hammer (New Haven: Yale University Press, 1986).

50. Cf. Leir Y. Rahmani, "More Lead Coffins from Israel," *Israel Exploration Journal* 37 (1987): 144.

51. Shimon Applebaum points out the well-to-do houses of Jerusalem with mosaics, without going into more detail, in "The Roman Villa in Judaea: A Problem," in *Judaea in Hellenistic and Roman Times*, ed. Shimon Applebaum (Leiden: E. J. Brill, 1989), p. 128; to compare Jerusalem with Apamaea, see Janine Balty, "Mosaïque de Gê et des saisons à Apamée," *Syria* 50 (1973): 311–347.

52. Ulpian, *Digesta*, 50.15.1, in *Corpus iuris civilis*, ed. Paul Krüger et al. (Berlin: Weidmann, 1928), vol. 1.

53. Millar, "Roman *Coloniae*," pp. 26–28.

54. See Pascal Arnaud, "Doura-Europos, microcosme grec ou rouage de l'administration arsacide? Modes de maîtrise du territoire et intégration des notables locaux dans la pratique administrative des rois arsacides," *Syria* 63 (1986): 135–155.

55. On this recent discovery, see Pierre Leriche, "Salle à gradins du temple

d'Artémis à Doura-Europos," *Topoi* 9 (1999): 725–726, and especially idem, "Une nouvelle inscription dans la salle à gradins du temple d'Artémis à Doura-Europos," *CRAI* (1999): 1309–1346.

56. On all this, see Leriche, "Salle à gradins," pp. 719–739.

57. In Bostra, the tribes called Romana (P. J. Parsons, ed. and trans., *The Oxyrhynchus Papyri*, vol. 42 [London: Egypt Exploration Society, 1974], 3054), and Athena (Pierre-Louis Gatier, "Inscriptions grecques des carrières de Hallabat," *Studies in the History and Archaeology of Jordan* [hereafter cited as *SHAJ*] 5 [1995]: 400); in Dionysias, the tribes called Bitaienoi (*I.Syrie*, no. 2309 = Sartre, *IGLS*, vol. 16, forthcoming, no. 333) and Somaithenoi (*I.Syrie*, no. 2308 = Sartre, *IGLS*, vol. 16, forthcoming, no. 332); in Gerasa, twelve tribes whose names are engraved on the steps of the north theater (in "The Jerash North Theatre: Architecture and Archaeology," in *Jerash Archaeological Project, 1981–1983*, ed. Fawzi Zayadine [Amman: Department of Antiquities, 1986], p. 229, V. A. Clark, Julian M. C. Bowsher, and J. D. Stewart mention only nine, but in "Civic Organization within the Decapolis," *Aram* 4 [1992]: 273, Julian M. C. Bowsher points out that twelve different names are in fact engraved); in Palmyra, four civic tribes whose identity remains in part disputed (Maurice Sartre, "Palmyre, cité grecque," in "Palmyra and the Silk Road: International Colloquium, Palmyra, 7–11 April 1992," special issue, *Annales archéologiques arabes syriennes* [hereafter cited as *AAAS*] 42 [1996]: 396). In Seleucia-Pieria, the Laodikis tribe is mentioned in 186 B.C.E. (Louis Jalabert and René Mouterde, *IGLS*, vol. 3.2, *Antioche (suite): Antiochene* [Paris: P. Geuthner, 1953], no. 1183), though we do not know whether it survived into the imperial epoch; in Edessa, there is a reference to an archonte of the Twelfth Tribe, in the contract published by Alfred Raymond Bellinger and Charles Bradford Welles, "A Contract of Sale from Edessa in Osrhoene," *Yale Classical Studies* 5 (1935): 95–153 (dated May 19, 243—that is, from the time when Edessa was a colony); in Neapolis, names of tribes are engraved on the seats of the theater, as in the north theater of Gerasa: Yitzhak Magen, "The Roman Theatre at Shechem," in *Sefer Ze'ev Vilnay* (Ze'ev Vilnay's Jubilee Volume), ed. Eli Schiller, vol. 1 (Jerusalem: Hotsa'at sefarim Ari'el, 1984), p. 275; in Dura, the Zebeina tribe may have been a civic rather than a Bedouin tribe.

58. Cf. the situation in Philadelphia-Amman: Gatier, *IGLJ*, vol. 2, pp. 51–54, no. 29 (where the reference to a gymnasiarch is certain but the rest remains open to question); in Arados (Jean-Paul Rey-Coquais, *IGLS*, vol. 7, *Arados et régions voisines* [Paris: P. Geuthner, 1970], no. 4001); in Gerasa (Charles Bradford Welles, "The Inscriptions," in *Gerasa: City of the Decapolis,* ed. Carl Hermann Kraeling [New Haven, Conn.: American Schools of Oriental Research, 1938], nos. 3–4 [hereafter cited as *I.Gerasa*], and several unpublished texts); in Byblos (Maurice Dunand, *Fouilles de Byblos, 2, 1933–1938* [Paris: P. Geuthner, 1954], p. 60, no. 7041).

59. See Sartre, "Palmyre, cité grecque." As Françoise Briquel-Chatonnet observes, it was only in the realm of religious institutions that Aramaic vocabulary predominated ("Palmyre, une cité pour les nomades," *Semitica* 43–44 [1995]: pp. 123–134). Javier Teixidor mistakes the import of the article cited at the beginning of this note ("Antiquités sémitiques," *Annuaire du Collège de France 1997–1998* [1998]: 713); I have never believed or asserted that Palmyra was, generally speaking, "a Greek city on the same basis as the cities of Asia Minor"; I have only sought to show that, as far as municipal institutions—and only those institutions—are concerned, Palmyra for

the most part had the typical structure of a Greek city-state of its day. In this I am not prejudging either the way those institutions actually functioned or the weight of the leading families (which was also founding in Asia Minor, moreover), and still less, of course, the obvious durability of Semitic traditions in religious and cultural life, among other areas.

60. Cassius Dio, *Roman History,* trans. Earnest Cary (Loeb Classical Library), 54.7.6 (hereafter cited as Dio).

61. Jacques Seigne, "À l'ombre de Zeus et d'Artémis: Gérasa de la Décapole," *Aram* 4 (1992): 185–195; idem, "Jérash romaine et byzantine: Développement urbain d'une ville provinciale orientale," *SHAJ* 4 (1992): 331–341. On this reorganization of the space around sanctuaries, see also idem, "Sanctuaires urbains: Acteurs ou témoins de l'urbanisation? Les exemples de Gérasa et de Palmyre," *Topoi* 9 (1999): 833–848, especially pp. 834–837.

62. Jean-Baptiste Yon, *Les notables de Palmyre* (Beirut: Institut français d'archéologie du Proche-Orient, 2002), pp. 84–85.

63. On the transformations of the Nabu temple, see Adnan Bounni, "Le sanctuaire de Nabu à Palmyre" (Ph.D. diss., Université de Paris I, 1986); see also idem, "Le sanctuaire de Nabu à Palmyre," in *Contribution française à l'archéologie syrienne,* ed. Alice Naccache (Beirut and Damascus: Institut français d'archéologie du Proche-Orient, 1989), pp. 167–170; idem, "Le sanctuaire de Nabu à Palmyre," in *Petra and the Caravan Cities,* ed. Fawzi Zayadine (Amman: Department of Antiquities, 1990), pp. 157–167; Adnan Bounni, Jacques Seigne, and Nassib Saliby, *Le sanctuaire de Nabu à Palmyre* (Paris: P. Geuthner, 1992) (plates only); Seigne, "Sanctuaires urbains," especially pp. 838–842.

64. For Palmyra, see Yon, *Notables de Palmyre;* for the Hauran, see Annie Sartre-Fauriat, "Les élites de la Syrie intérieure et leur image à l'époque romaine," in *Les élites et leurs facettes, Colloque de Clermont-Ferrand, 24–26 novembre 2000,* ed. Mireille Cébeillac-Gervasoni (Rome: École française de Rome, 2003; Clermont-Ferrand: Presses Universitaires Blaise Pascal, 2003), pp. 517–538.

65. Herodian, *History of the Empire from the Time of Marcus Aurelius,* trans. C. R. Whittaker (Loeb Classical Library), 3.3.3 (hereafter cited as Herodian).

66. Ibid., 3.3.5.

67. An inscription in the Louvre, AO 4924, commemorates Antipatros, "the best of men," who defended "his fatherland with his blood and with his whole soul at the time of the war with the Moors." This may be understood to mean that Sidon had chosen the same side as Tyre, whereas one would have expected instead, in Herodian's enumeration, that the antinomic couple Tyre and Sidon would be opposed. In reality, we observe in the imperial era that the real rivalry opposed Tyre to Berytos, which confirms the relative decline of Tyre in the hierarchy of Phoenician cities.

68. The theater in Canatha: *IGR,* vol. 3, no. 1235 = Sartre, *IGLS,* vol. 16, forthcoming, no. 198.

69. In Palmyra, during the visit of Hadrian's army, it was Malê, nicknamed Agrippa, who paid all the expenses: Jean Cantineau, ed., *Inventaire des inscriptions de Palmyre* (Beirut: Publications du Musée national syrien de Damas, 1930–1933), vol. 1, pp. 10–12, no. 2 (hereafter cited as *Inv.*) = Delbert R. Hillers and Eleonora Cussini, *Palmyrene Aramaic Texts* (Baltimore: Johns Hopkins University Press, 1994), no. 0305 (hereafter cited as *PAT*).

70. In Gerasa: *I.Gerasa*, no. 4.

71. Thus L. Iulius Agrippa offered Apamaea the land to rebuild the baths and donated the sculpture groups that adorned them: Jean-Paul Rey-Coquais, "Lucius Iulius Agrippa et Apamée," *AAAS* 23 (1973): 39–84. For gifts of statues in Gerasa, see *I.Gerasa*, nos. 6, 53.

72. Accurately noted by Léopold Migeotte, "Les finances publiques des cités grecques: Bilan et perspectives de recherche," *Topoi* 5 (1995): 7–32, especially p. 24, where he is right to characterize my analysis in *Orient romain*, pp. 134–138, as excessively pessimistic.

73. L. Burbuleius Optatus Ligarianus held the title *logistes Syriae*: Theodor Mommsen, *CIL*, vol. 10, *Inscriptiones Bruttiorum, Lucaniae, Campaniae, Sicilae, Sardiniae latinae*, 2 vols. (Berlin: G. Reimer, 1883), no. 6006 (= Hermann Dessau, *Inscriptiones latinae selectae* [Berlin: Weidmann, 1892–1916], no. 1066 [hereafter cited as *ILS*]), although we cannot assert that his mission had to do with municipal finances; he may have had an assistant of the equestrian rank, M. Claudius Restitutus, whose mission to the cities was quite explicit: Gustav Wilmanns, *CIL*, vol. 8, *Inscriptiones Africae latinae*, 7 vols. (Berlin: G. Reimer, 1881–1959), no. 7039 (= *ILS*, no. 1437) (it has been dated to Hadrian's reign by Michael Grierson Jarrett, "An Album of the Equestrians from North Africa in the Emperor's Services," *Epigraphische Studien* 9 [1972]: 170, but Hans-Georg Pflaum places his career instead under Antoninus Pius; see *Les carrières procuratoriennes équestres sous le Haut-Empire romain*, vol. 1 [Paris: P. Geuthner, 1982], pp. 379–385, no. 158). Similarly, p. Pactumeius Clemens was explicitly designated as *legatus diui Hadriani ad rationas ciuitatium Syriae putandas* (Wilmanns, *CIL*, vol. 8, no. 7059 = *ILS*, no. 1067).

74. Ti. Claudius Proculus Cornelianus: *L'année épigraphique* (hereafter cited as *AE*) (1956), no. 123; but nothing proves that he was responsible for the accounts of Syrian cities, for his title remains vague: *procurator prouinciae Syriae ad rationes putandas*.

75. Ti. Antonius Claudius Alfenus Arignotus: *IGR*, vol. 4, no. 1213 (= *ILS*, no. 8853).

76. Eric Guerber and Maurice Sartre, "Un *logistès* à Canatha (Syrie)," *Zeitschrift für Papyrologie und Epigraphik* (hereafter cited as *ZPE*) 120 (1998): 93–98.

77. Fulvius Titianus: *Inv.*, vol. 10, no. 34, which Seyrig locates in the first half of the second century; the only certainty is that he antedated the creation of the colony of Palmyra.

78. For the Aramaic text, see *CIS*, no. 3913 = *PAT*, no. 0259; for the Greek text, see Wilhelm Dittenberger, *Orientis graeci inscriptiones selectae* (Hildesheim and New York: G. Olms, 1986; first published 1903–1905), no. 629, and *IGR*, vol. 3, no. 1056. Cf. Javier Teixidor, *Un port romain du désert: Palmyre et son commerce d'Auguste à Caracalla* (Paris: A. Maisonneuve, 1984); John F. Matthews, "The Tax Law of Palmyra," *JRS* 74 (1984): 157–180; Michel Gawlikowski and Khaled As'ad, "Le péage à Palmyre en 11 après J.-C.," *Semitica* 41–42 (1993): 163–172.

79. We have indirect proof of this through a decree by the *boule* of Palmyra (*Inv.*, vol. 10, no. 114 = *PAT*, no. 1414) in honor of Iarhibol, son of Lishamsh, an important individual who led an embassy to Elymais and was the object of laudatory letters from at least two governors of Syria, Bruttius Praesens and Iulius Minor, and probably from their predecessor, Gn. Minicius Faustinus: because this took place between the death of Gn. Minicius in Syrie in 136 and the date of the decree of Palmyra in

April 138, the Lishamsh embassies must have something to do with the negotiation of the Tariff, promulgated on April 18, 137; see Teixidor, *Port romain*, pp. 58–59.

80. Léopold Migeotte, *L'emprunt public dans les cités grecques* (Quebec: Éditions du Sphinx; Paris: Les Belles Lettres, 1984); idem, *Les souscriptions publiques dans les cités grecques* (Geneva: Droz; Quebec: Éditions du Sphinx, 1992).

81. Financed by the treasury of the gods: *Supplementum epigraphicum graecum* (Alphen aan den Rijn: Sijthoff & Noordhoff, 1923–1998), vol. 2, no. 830, and vol. 39, no. 1579 (hereafter cited as *SEG*); by private individuals: ibid., vol. 7 (1934), nos. 127, 230.

82. Cf. Jacques Seigne, "Recherches sur le sanctuaire de Zeus à Jerash (Oct. 1982–Dec. 83)," in Zayadine, *Jerash Archaeological Project, 1981–1983*, pp. 29–106.

83. Strabo, 16.2.5.

84. Paul Bernard, "Une légende de fondation hellénistique: Apamée sur l'Oronte d'après les *Cynégétiques* du Pseudo-Oppien," *Topoi* 5 (1995): 353–382.

85. Strabo, 16.2.28.

86. Damascios, *The Philosophical History* (= *Vita Isidori*), ed. and trans. Polymnia Athanassiadi (Athens: Apamea Cultural Association, 1999), p. 301, 134B; cf. Maurice Sartre, *Bostra: Des origines à l'Islam* (Paris: P. Geuthner, 1985), pp. 48–49.

87. Stephanus of Byzantium, "Damascos," in *Ethnica*, ed. August Meineke (Graz: Akademische Druck und Verlagsanstalt, 1958). On these foundation legends and the construction of a civic identity, see Maurice Sartre, "La construction de l'identité civique des villes de la Syrie hellénistique et impériale," in *Idéologies et valeurs civiques dans le monde romain: Hommage à Claude Lepelley; Actes d'un colloque tenu à Paris les 25 et 26 septembre 2001*, ed. Hervé Inglebert (Paris: Picard, 2002), pp. 93–105.

88. See, most recently, Olivier Curty, *Les parentés légendaires entre cités grecques* (Geneva: Droz, 1995). It is nevertheless quite remarkable that Syrian cities are practically absent from this epigraphic catalogue of relationships among peoples, with the exception of Tyre, which boasted of a kinship with Delphi. But Curty limits his investigation to epigraphic texts, which reflect only a part of the reality; to the extent that there is essentially no such thing as an epigraphy of Hellenistic Syria, it is unsurprising that this was lacking from his repertory. But it is improbable that the Syrians were not involved, like the others, in the process of establishing kinships; we know that the Jews maintained close relations with their Spartiate "relatives."

89. Maurice Sartre, "Les progrès de la citoyenneté romaine en Arabie," *SHAJ* 4 (1992): 327–329; idem, "Les progrès de la citoyenneté romaine dans les provinces romaines de Syrie et d'Arabie sous le Haut-Empire," in *Roman Onomastics in the Greek East, Social and Political Aspects: Proceedings of the International Colloquium on Roman Onomastics, Athens, 7–9 September 1993*, ed. A. D. Rizakis (Athens: Research Centre for Greek and Roman Antiquity / National Hellenic Research Foundation, 1996), pp. 239–250.

90. Louis Jalabert and René Mouterde, *IGLS*, vol. 3.1, *Région de l'Amanus, Antioche* (Paris: P. Geuthner, 1950), no. 718; this very important text has given rise to a considerable bibliography: Pierre Roussel, "Un Syrien au service de Rome et d'Octave," *Syria* 15 (1934): 33–74, pl. IX–X and fig. 1; Vincenzo Arangio Ruiz, "Epigrafia giuridica greca e romana," *Studia et Documenta Historiae et Juris* 2 (1936): 497–515; ibid., "Epigrafia giuridica greca e romana II," *Studia et Documenta Historiae et Juris* 5 (1939): 552; Fernand De Visscher, "La condition juridique des

nouveaux citoyens romains," *CRAI* (1938): 24–39; Margarita Garducci, *Rendiconti: Atti della Pontificio Academia Romana di Archeologia* (Vatican City: Tipografia Poliglotta Vaticana, 1938), pp. 5ff.; Mario Attilio Levi, "La grande iscrizione di Ottaviano trovata a Roso," *Rivista di filologia e d'istruzione classica* (1938): 125–128; Ernst Schönbauer, "Die Inschrift von Rhosos und die Constitutio Andetoniniana," *Archiv für Papyrusforschung* 13 (1939): 177–209; idem, "Diokletian in einem verzweifelten Abwehrkampfe? Studien zur Rechtsentwicklung in der römischen Kaiserzeit," *Zeitschrift der Savigny-Stiftung für Rechtsgeschichte, Romanistische Abteilung* 62 (1942): 267–340; Fernand De Visscher, *Les édits d'Auguste découverts à Cyrène* (Louvain: Bibliothèque de l'Université, 1940), pp. 108–118; Salvatore Riccobono et al., eds., *Fontes iuris romani anteiustiniani*, 2nd ed., vol. 1 (Florence: G. Barbèra, 1941), p. 308, no. 55; Mikhail Ivanovitch Rostovtzeff, *Social and Economic History of the Hellenistic World*, vol. 2 (Oxford: Clarendon Press, 1941), pp. 1012, 1570, 1581; James H. Oliver, "Notes on Documents of the Roman East," section 1, "On the Great Inscription of Octavian Found at Rhosos," *American Journal of Archaeology* (hereafter cited as *AJA*) 45 (1941): 537; G. I. Luzzato, *Epigrafia giuridica greca e romana* (Milan: Giuffré, 1942), pp. 285–321; Fernand De Visscher, "Le statut juridique des nouveaux citoyens romains et l'inscription de Rhosos," *Antiquité classique* 13 (1944): 11–35, and 14 (1946): 29–59; Henri Seyrig, "Sur les ères de quelques villes de Syrie," *Syria* 27 (1950): 34 (on the date of document 1: December 35); Jeanne Robert and Louis Robert, "Bulletin épigraphique," *Revue des études grecques* (1951), 39 (= Jeanne Robert and Louis Robert, *Bulletin épigraphique*, vol. 2, *1940–1951* [Paris: Les Belles Lettres, 1982]).

91. Maurice Sartre, "Romains et Italiens en Syrie: Contribution à l'histoire de la première province romaine de Syrie," in *The Greek East in the Roman Context: Proceedings of a Colloquium Organised by the Finnish Institute at Athens, May 21–22, 1999*, ed. Olli Salomies (Vammala: Foundation of the Finnish Institute at Athens, 2001): 127–140.

92. Jean-Charles Balty, *Guide d'Apamée* (Brussels: Centre belge de recherches archéologiques à Apamée de Syrie, 1981); idem, "Apamea in Syria in the Second and Third Centuries AD," *JRS* 78 (1988): 91–104.

93. Gérard Degeorge, *Palmyre, métropole du désert* (Paris: Librairie Séguier [Archimbaud], 1987).

94. Iain Browning, *Jerash and the Decapolis* (London: Chatto & Windus, 1982).

95. Sartre, *Bostra*.

96. John Malalas, *The Chronicle of John Malalas*, trans. Elizabeth Jeffreys, Michael Jeffreys, Roger Scott, et al. (Melbourne: Australian Association for Byzantine Studies, 1986), p. 114 (9.216) (hereafter cited as Malalas); see Jean-Charles Balty, *Curia ordinis: Recherches d'architecture et d'urbanisme antiques sur les curies provinciales du monde romain* (Brussels: Académie royale de Belgique, 1990), pp. 281–285.

97. Ibid.; reconstructed by Marcus Agrippa (222), then by Tiberius (234).

98. Ibid., 216–217; cf. Glanville Downey, *A History of Antioch in Syria: From Seleucus to the Arab Conquest* (Princeton: Princeton University Press, 1961), pp. 154–156.

99. Malalas, pp. 117–118 (9.222); cf. Downey, *History of Antioch*, pp. 170–172.

100. Malalas, pp. 123–125 (10.232–234); cf. Downey, *History of Antioch*, pp. 174–184.

101. Malalas, p. 129 (10.243); cf. Downey, *History of Antioch*, p. 191.

102. Malalas, p. 138 (10.261); cf. Downey, *History of Antioch,* pp. 206–207.

103. Malalas, p. 139 (10.–263); cf. Downey, *History of Antioch,* pp. 207–208.

104. Malalas, pp. 145–146 (11.275–276); cf. Downey, *History of Antioch,* pp. 213–218.

105. Malalas, p. 147 (11.278); cf. Downey, *History of Antioch,* pp. 221–223.

106. Malalas, pp. 149–150 (11.282); cf. Downey, *History of Antioch,* p. 229.

107. Malalas, p. 141 (12.283); cf. Downey, *History of Antioch,* p. 233.

108. Malalas, p. 156 (12.294); cf. Downey, *History of Antioch,* pp. 242–243 (Septimius Severus); Malalas, p. 165 (12.302); cf. Downey, *History of Antioch,* p. 270.

109. Josephus, *BJ* 1.422.

110. Josephus, *AJ* 19.335–337, 20.211–212.

111. Rey-Coquais, "Lucius Iulius Agrippa."

112. *I.Gerasa,* no. 56–57 (north gate), no. 58 (Hadrian's arch).

113. Catherine Saliou, "Du portique à la rue à portiques: Les rues à colonnades de Palmyre dans le cadre de l'urbanisme romain impérial; originalité et conformisme," in "Palmyra and the Silk Road," special issue, *AAAS* 42 (1996): 322.

114. Annie Sartre-Fauriat, "Les notables et leur rôle dans l'urbanisme du Hauran à l'époque romaine," in *Construction, reproduction et représentation des patriciats urbains, de l'Antiquité au XXe siècle,* ed. Claude Petitfrère (Tours: Université François-Rabelais, Centre d'histoire de la ville moderne et contemporaine, 1999), pp. 223–240.

115. For Antipatris and Samaria, see Shimon Applebaum, "Economic Life in Palestine," in *The Jewish People in the First Century,* ed. Shemuel Safrai et Menaham Stern (Assen and Amsterdam: Van Gorcum, 1976), p. 667; a detailed inventory still needs to be undertaken for the countryside, taking into account all the dated inscriptions, but, according to the *IGLS* volumes in preparation, it is clear that improvements and offerings seem no less numerous than before, although the buildings often go back to the time of the Antonii.

116. Andreas Schmidt-Colinet and Khaled al-Asád, "Zur Urbanistik des hellenistischen Palmyra: Ein Vorbericht," *Damaszener Mitteilungen* (hereafter cited as *DaM*) 12 (2000): 61–93. On the use of old aerial photographs and what can be learned from them, especially regarding the importance of the south bank of the wadi, see Jean-Marie Dentzer and René Saupin, "L'espace urbain à Palmyre: Remarques sur des photographies aériennes anciennes," in "Palmyra and the Silk Road," special issue, *AAAS* 42 (1996): 297–318.

117. *Inv.,* vol. 9, no. 6 (which gives a restored date corresponding to 19 C.E.); see Michel Gawlikowski, *Le temple palmyrénien* (Warsaw: Éditions scientifiques de Pologne, 1973), pp. 53–66.

118. The dating does not rely so much on the inscriptions on the consoles, which may have been added long after the consoles were set up, as on the manner in which the columns were cut. Andreas Schmidt-Colinet, who has studied the quarries situated to the northeast of the city, has shown that the shafts of the columns were extracted first; the grain of the stone was placed horizontally, which avoided infiltrations of water and ensured the solidity of the column; later, probably to meet increased demand, columns were cut in a single piece in which the grain was placed vertically; this is a faster process, but the quality is lower. Thanks to the coexistence of these two types of columns in the temple of Baalshamin, the shift from one way of cutting to another can be placed around 130 C.E.; this does not exclude the use of the

earlier method later on, for clients ready to spend the money; see Andreas Schmidt-Colinet, "Considérations sur les carrières de Palmyre en Syrie," in *Pierre éternelle: Du Nil au Rhin, carrières et préfabrication,* ed. Marc Waelkens (Brussels: Crédit communal, 1990), pp. 87–92 (sommaire); Schmidt-Colinet, ed., *Palmyra: Kulturbegegnung in Grenzbereich* (Mainz: Ph. von Zabern, 1995), pp. 74–76. For the final phase, see the note by Michel Gawlikowski in Marek Baranski, "The Great Colonnade of Palmyra Reconsidered," *Aram* 7 (1995): 45–46.

119. Michel Gawlikowski, "Le premier temple d'Allat," in *Resurrecting the Past: A Joint Tribute to Adnan Bounni,* ed. Paolo Matthiae, Matthiae Nanning van Loon, and Harvey Weiss (Istanbul: Nederlands historisch-archaeologisch instituut te Istanbul; Leiden: Nederlands instituut voor het nabije oosten, 1990), pp. 101–108.

120. Kevin Butcher and Richard Thorpe, "A Note on Excavations in Central Beirut 1994–96," *Journal of Roman Archaeology* (hereafter cited as *JRA*) 10 (1997): pp. 291–306, concerning the BEY 006 site (the old souk quarter).

121. Dominic Perring, "Excavations in the Souks of Beirut," *Berytus* 43 (1997–1998): 9–34, especially p. 26–27; the site in question is BEY 045.

122. Perring, "Excavations," pp. 27–29.

123. Personal communication from Mikaël Kalos, to whom I am very grateful.

124. Catherine Abadie-Reynal, Rifat Ergeç, et al., "Zeugma-Moyenne vallée de l'Euphrate: Rapport préliminaire de la campagne de fouilles de 1997," *Anatolia antiqua* 6 (1998): p. 392.

125. Michel Gawlikowski, "A Residential Area by the South Decumanus," in Zayadine, *Jerash Archaeological Project, 1981–1983,* pp. 107–136, especially p. 109.

126. Roberto Parapetti, "Public Building Design and Techniques in Roman Imperial Times: Achievements in Gerasa," *SHAJ* 5 (1995): 177–181.

127. Seigne, "Recherches," p. 55.

128. The essential part consists of the vestiges of the enclosure dated with care to around the middle of the first century B.C.E.: T. W. Hillard, "A Mid-1st c. B.C. Date for the Walls of Straton's Tower?" in Vann, *Caesarea Papers,* pp. 42–48; the city probably was seriously damaged by the earthquake that shook all of Judaea in 31–30: Duane W. Roller, "Straton's Tower: Some Additional Thoughts," in Vann, *Caesarea Papers,* pp. 24–25; contra: Avner Raban, "In Search of Straton's Tower," in Vann, *Caesarea Papers,* p. 22.

129. Thus the vestiges of a temple of Isis from the third century B.C.E. have been found under the Kore temple, built during the Herodian refoundation: see Eleazar L. Sukenik, "The Temple of the Kore," in *Samaria-Sebaste,* vol. 1, *The Buildings at Samaria,* ed. John Winter Crowfoot, Kathleen M. Kenyon, and Eleazar L. Sukenik (London: Palestine Exploration Fund, 1942), pp. 62–67.

130. Josephus, *BJ* 1.403.

131. For Bostra, see Sartre, *Bostra,* pp. 96–97; for Rhesaina, see Isaac, *Limits,* pp. 324, 360; but it is not certain that the city harbored a standing legion, because the latter may have been at Nisibis instead.

132. Michael Whitby and Mary Whitby, eds. and trans., *Chronicon Paschale* (Liverpool: Liverpool University Press, 1989), 119. Scythopolis was also divided into seven quarters: *SEG,* vol. 8, no. 44.

133. Virgilio C. Corbo, *Il Santo Sepolcro di Gerusalemme: Aspetti archeologici dalle origini al periodo crociato,* vol. 2 (Jerusalem: Franciscan Printing Press, 1981–

1982), pl. 68; Dan Bahat and Chaim T. Rubinstein, *The Illustrated Atlas of Jerusalem*, trans. Shlomo Ketko (New York: Simon & Schuster, 1990).

134. On all this, see Belayche's fine study, *Iudaea-Palaestina*, pp. 131–169; for a short version, see idem, *"Dimenticare . . . Gerusalemme:* Les paganismes à Aelia Capitolina du IIe au IVe siècle de notre ère," *Revue des études juives* 158 (1999): 287–348.

135. Cf. the detailed map supplied by Avraham Negev, *The Architecture of Mampsis: Final Report*, vol. 1, *The Middle and Late Nabatean Periods* (Jerusalem: Institute of Archaeology, Hebrew University of Jerusalem, 1988), pp. 28–29.

136. This corresponds to only two-fifths of the old Jerusalem: Magen Broshi, "The Population of Western Palestine in the Roman-Byzantine Period," *Bulletin of the American Schools of Oriental Research* (hereafter cited as *BASOR*) 236 (1979): 1–10. See also Pierre-Louis Gatier, "Villages du Proche-Orient protobyzantin," in *Land Use and Settlement Patterns,* ed. Geoffrey R. D. King and Averil Cameron, vol. 2 of *The Byzantine and Early Islamic Near East,* ed. Averil Cameron, Lawrence I. Conrad, and Geoffrey R. D. King (Princeton: Darwin Press, 1995), pp. 24–25.

137. These figures are from Negev, *Architecture of Mampsis,* vol. 1, p. 2, n. 10.

138. Jean-Charles Balty, "Apamée (1986): Nouvelles données sur l'armée romaine d'Orient et les raids sassanides du milieu du IIIe siècle," *CRAI* (1987): 213–242.

139. Josephus, *BJ* 1.422; we know that during the same period brigandage had not disappeared, because Aemilius Secundus recalls that he was called upon to combat Ituraean bandits during his career (Theodor Mommsen, Otto Hirschfeld, and Alfred von Domaszewski, *CIL,* vol. 3S, *Inscriptionum orientis et Illyrici latinarum supplementum,* 2 vols. [Berlin: G. Reimer, 1902], no. 6687).

140. G. J. Wightman, *The Walls of Jerusalem: From the Canaanites to the Mamluks* (Sydney: Mediterranean Archaeology 1993), pp. 199–200; Benjamin H. Isaac mentions its reinforcement during the fourth century ("The Eastern Frontier," in *Cambridge Ancient History,* vol. 13, *The Late Empire* [Cambridge: Cambridge University Press, 1998], p. 452).

141. Jean Sauvaget, "Le plan antique de Damas," *Syria* 26 (1949): 331–338.

142. The wall of Herod Antipas enclosed only the northern part of the city, and it was extended to the south to enclose the Hamath suburb only in the third century: see Daniel Sperber, *The City in Roman Palestine* (Oxford: Oxford University Press, 1998), pp. 118–119. The monumental gate from the early wall has probably been discovered: Gideon Foerster, "Tiberias," in *Encyclopedia of Archaeological Excavations in the Holy Land* (hereafter cited as *EAEHL*), ed. Michael Avi-Yonah, vol. 4 (Englewood Cliffs, N.J.: Prentice-Hall, 1978), pp. 1173–1175.

143. Michel Gawlikowski, "Les défenses de Palmyre," *Syria* 51 (1974): 231–242.

144. Lee I. Levine, *Roman Caesarea: An Archaeological-Topographical Study* (Jerusalem: Hebrew University, 1975), p. 7.

145. Jacques Seigne, "Recherches sur le sanctuaire de Zeus à Jérash (oct. 1982–déc. 83)," in Zayadine, *Jerash Archaeological Project, 1982–1983,* p. 55.

146. Ernest Will, "Les villes de la Syrie à l'époque hellénistique et romaine," in *Archéologie et histoire de la Syrie,* ed. Jean-Marie Dentzer and Winfried Orthmann, vol. 2 (Saarbrücken: Saarbrücker Druckerei und Verlag, 1989), pp. 241–242.

147. Josephus, *BJ* 1.425: "And that broad street in Syrian Antioch, once shunned on account of the mud—was it not he who paved its twenty furlongs with polished

marble, and, as a protection from the rain, adorned it with a colonnade of equal length?"

148. Jean Lassus and Richard Stillwell, *Les portiques d'Antioche*, vol. 5, *Antioch-on-the-Orontes* (Princeton: Princeton University Press, 1972); Bernadette Cabouret, "Sous les portiques d'Antioche," *Syria* 76 (1999): 127–150.

149. Janine Balty and Jean-Charles Balty, "Apamée de Syrie, archéologie et histoire: I. Des origines à la tétrarchie," *ANRW* 2.8 (1977): 127; Jean-Charles Balty, *Guide d'Apamée,* pp. 64–69.

150. Saliou emphasizes the extent to which colonnade-lined streets were also the place where urban structures were displayed, especially in Palmyra, where the tribes had well-defined sectors in which to display their honorific decrees ("Du portique à la rue à portiques," pp. 319–330).

151. Malalas, p. 125 (10.235), "eastern gate"; see Downey, *Antioch,* p. 181; cf. the description of a tetrapylon in Antioch by Libanios, in *Antioch as a Centre of Hellenic Culture as Observed by Libanius,* trans. A. F. Norman (Liverpool: Liverpool University Press, 2000), p. 48 (*Oratio* 11.204–205).

152. Malalas attributes the construction of a tetrapylon to Augustus (p. 118 [9.223]), but the one that has survived does not seem to go back that far, notwithstanding the views expressed in Ingeborg Kader, *Propylon und Bogentor: Untersuchungen zum Tetrapylon von Latakia und anderer frühkaiserzeitlichen Bogenmonumenten im Nahen Osten* (Mainz: Ph. von Zabern, 1996; repr., *Damaszener Forschungen* 7). According to Kader, this gate was the monumental entry to some sanctuary devoted to the cult of the rulers, first kings and then emperors; this is not impossible, but the claim is not easy to prove. The dating also appears too early; a second-century date would be more plausible, especially because Kader's approach requires moving back the date of other Syrian arches, in Damascus, Gadara, Tiberias, Tyre, and Bostra.

153. Caroline Arnould offers a detailed study of the arches in Jerusalem-Aelia Capitolina: *Les arcs romains de Jérusalem: Architecture, décor et urbanisme* (Fribourg: Éditions Universitaires Fribourg Suisse; Göttingen: Vandenhoeck & Ruprecht, 1997); in his review of Arnould's book, Andreas Schmidt-Colinet is critical but does not challenge either the dating or the function attributed to the arches: he sees the Ecce Homo arch as marking the entrance to the legionnaires' camp, and the Damascus gate as marking the northern boundary of the colony (review *Propylon und Bogentor,* by Kader, and *Arcs romains,* by Arnould, in *American Journal of Archaeology* 103 [1999]: 719–720).

154. Vestiges of two arches have been found, one about five hundred meters from the west gate, the other closer to the east gate (it has been restored): Sauvaget, "Plan antique de Damas," pp. 327–328.

155. This observation has already been made by Ernest Will, "Villes de la Syrie," p. 242.

156. For Jerusalem, see Caroline Arnould, "La porte de Damas (porte romaine) à Jérusalem: Quelques questions d'urbanisme," *Revue biblique* (hereafter cited as *Rbi*) 106 (1999): 101–111. Arnould observes that the Roman gate is out of line in relation to the main road; this even appears on the representation of the city on the map of Madaba.

157. Crowfoot et al., *Buildings;* there were about six hundred columns in the colonnade (Nahman Avigad, "Samaria," in *EAEHL* p. 1048).

158. Butcher and Thorpe, "Note on excavations," pp. 305–306.

159. This is the term used in "The Sibylline Oracles," 13.64–68 (in English translation by John Joseph Collins in *The Old Testament Pseudepigrapha*, ed. James H. Charlesworth, vol. 1 [New York: Doubleday, 1983], pp. 317–472) to describe the splendor of Bostra and Philippopolis.

160. See the many texts cited in Sperber, *City in Roman Palestine*, pp. 9–57.

161. See Jean-Marie Dentzer, "Le développement urbain en Syrie à l'époque hellénistique et romaine: Modèles 'occidentaux et orientaux,'" *Bulletin d'études orientales* 52 (2000): 161.

162. Félix-Marie Abel, *Histoire de la Palestine depuis la conquête d'Alexandre jusqu'à l'invasion arabe*, vol. 2 (Paris: J. Gabalda, 1952), p. 115. For this whole paragraph I have benefited from the invaluable help of a DEA mémoire by Valérie Mottu, "La romanisation du paysage urbain dans les provinces de Syrie, Palestine et Arabie sous le Haut-Empire romain" (Mémoire de Diplôme d'études avancées, Université de Tours, 1997).

163. Amos Kloner, "Bet Guvrin, Amphitheater," *Excavations and Surveys in Israel* (hereafter cited as *ESI*) 12 (1993): 87–88, and Amos Kloner and Alain Hübsch, "The Roman Amphitheater of Bet Guvrin: A Preliminary Report on the 1992, 1993 and 1994 Seasons," *Atiqot* 30 (1996): 85–106, especially p. 96 for the dates.

164. Ryad al-Mougdad, Pierre-Marie Blanc, and Jean-Marie Dentzer, "Un amphithéâtre à Bostra?" *Syria* 67 (1990): 201–204.

165. Jean-Claude Golvin, *L'amphithéâtre romain: Essai sur la theorisation de la forme et de ses fonctions* (Paris: E. de Boccard, 1988), pp. 139, 155. Built by and for the soldiers in 216: *AE* (1937), no. 239.

166. Gideon Foerster and Yoram Tsafrir, "The Beth Shean Project," *ESI* 6 (1987–1988): 36–43.

167. Antoni A. Ostrasz, "The Hippodrome of Gerasa: A Report on Excavations and Research 1982–1987," *Syria* 66 (1989): 51–77; idem, "The Hippodrome of Gerasa: A Case of the Dichotomy of Art and Building Technology," *SHAJ* 5 (1995): 183–192.

168. Josephus, *BJ* 1.415. The site of the amphitheater to the northwest of the city, outside the walls, is perfectly visible in aerial photos: Holum and Hohlfelder, eds., *King Herod's Dream*, pp. 85–86; the dimensions of the *cavea*, sixty meters by ninety-five meters, are larger than those of the Coliseum.

169. Josephus, *BJ* 2.491–492.

170. Josephus, *AJ* 15.267–268; Orosius, *The Seven Books of History against the Pagans*, trans. Roy J. Deferrari (Washington, D.C.: Catholic University of America Press, 1964), 7.30.5.

171. Downey observes that the amphitheater at Antioch, built in Caesar's day, is not much later than the oldest amphitheaters in Italy (*Antioch*, p. 156).

172. Malalas, p. 118 (9.223).

173. Yorum Tsafrir and Gideon Foerster, "The Hebrew University Excavations at Beth Shean 1980–1994," *Qadmoniot* 107–108 (1995): 93–116 (in Hebrew).

174. Ephraim Stern, ed., *The New Encyclopedia of Archaeological Excavations in the Holy Land* (Jerusalem: Israel Exploration Society / Carta; New York: Simon & Schuster, 1993), vol. 4, pp. 1357–1358.

175. This is the building Josephus calls an amphitheater: *AJ* 17.194–196, *BJ* 1.33, 8.

176. Jean Rougé, ed., *Expositio totius mundi et gentium: Introduction, texte cri-

tique, traduction, notes et commentaire (Paris: Le Cerf, 1966), 32; this may be a circus that Josephus calls an amphitheater: Josephus, *BJ* 1.414–415, *AJ* 15.341 and 16.137. Cf. John H. Humphrey, *Roman Circuses: Arenas for Chariot Racing* (London: B. T. Batsford, 1986), pp. 477–491, for the one on the Haifa road; the second one was identified in the early 1990s.

177. Ostrasz, "Hippodrome of Gerasa: A Report"; idem, "Hippodrome of Gerasa: A Case." This is probably the smallest one in the entire Roman world, but the building's purpose is solidly attested by the altar dedications made by race winners.

178. It is perfectly visible on the aerial photos, to the south of the city, outside the walls.

179. Malalas, pp. 156–157 (12.294), attributes the construction to Septimius Severus; *Expositio*, 32; cf. Humphrey, *Roman Circuses*, p. 492.

180. *Expositio*, 32; it was identified in the wadi ab-Jamil.

181. Ute Wagner-Lux and K. J. H. Vriezen, "Vorläufiger Bericht über die Ausgräbungen in Gadara in Jordanien im Jahre 1990," *Zeitschrift der deutschen Palästina-Vereins* (hereafter cited as *ZDPV*) 98 (1982): 158–162; Humphrey, *Roman Circuses*, pp. 504–505.

182. *Expositio*, 32; cf. Humphrey, *Roman Circuses*, pp. 461–477; it is 480 meters long by 92 meters wide.

183. In addition to the "harem" baths, which have been known for a long time, recent digs have revealed three sets of baths at the center of the Roman city and three others on the periphery: Renata Ortali-Tarazi, "Beyrouth: À la lumière des principales découvertes récentes," in *Liban, l'autre rive*, ed. Institut du monde arabe (Paris: Flammarion, 1998), p. 193.

184. These have not yet given rise to publications, but the discoveries have been pointed out in Jean-Marie Dentzer, "Bosra," in *The Oxford Encyclopedia of Archaeology in the Near East*, ed. Eric M. Meyers, vol. 1 (Oxford and New York: Oxford University Press, 1997); the description and the attributions made by Warwich Ball in *Rome in the East: The Transformation of an Empire* (London and New York: Routledge, 1999), pp. 198–204, are false.

185. See Sperber, *City in Roman Palestine*, pp. 58–72, with numerous references to the Talmudic texts.

186. Poseidonius, cited by Athenaeus, *The Deipnosophists*, trans. Charles Burton Gulick (Loeb Classical Library), vol. 2, 5.210f, and vol. 5, 12.527e; he is actually repeating an old *topos* already developed by Aristophanes in "The Clouds" (in *Aristophanes*, trans. Benjamin Bickley Rogers [Loeb Classical Library], 990–991).

187. For Apamaea, see Jean-Charles Balty, "Problèmes de l'eau à Apamée de Syrie," in *L'homme et l'eau en Méditerranée et au Proche-Orient*, vol. 4, *L'eau dans l'agriculture*, ed. Françoise Métral, Jean Métral, and Pierre Louis (Lyon: Groupement d'intérêt scientifique, Maison de l'Orient, 1987), pp. 9–23. For Beirut, see Yasmine Makaroun and Levon Nordiguian, "Les Qanater Zubaydé et l'alimentation en eau de Beyrouth et de ses environs à l'époque romaine," *Bulletin d'archéologie et d'antiquité libanaise* 2 (1997): 262–289.

188. Annie Sartre-Fauriat, "Le nymphée et les adductions d'eau de Soada-Dionysias de Syrie au IIe siècle apr. J.-C.," *Ktema* 17 (1992 [published in 1996]): 133–151.

189. Direct observation by the author: the aqueduct has been preserved over at least a kilometer, near the villages of Kteibeh and Khirbet Ghazaleh, and it is oriented

northeast–southeast. It is not very high, but the canal is very well preserved in spots. The English traveler William-John Bankes saw it over a much longer distance, but we do not know with any precision either where the water went (probably Adraha) or where it came from (perhaps the Dille region, where there are many swamps). To date there is no study of this monument: see Annie Sartre-Fauriat, *Les voyages de William-John Bankes dans le Hauran* (Bordeaux: Ausonius; Beirut: Institut français d'archéologie du Proche-Orient, 2004).

190. Suzanne Kerner, Hamke Krebs, and Dietmar Michaelis, "Water Management in Northern Jordan: The Example of Gadara Umm Qays," *SHAJ* 6 (1997): 265–270.

191. W. Harold Mare, "The Technology of the Hydrological System at Abila of the Decapolis," *SHAJ* 5 (1995): 727–736.

192. Carl Hermann Kraeling, *Gerasa, City of the Decapolis* (New Haven, Conn.: American Schools of Oriental Research, 1938), pp. 21–22.

193. This is the old "kalybe": see Sartre, *Bostra*, p. 93; it has been pointed out as a monumental fountain by Jean-Marie Dentzer in "Bosra." The clearing undertaken by the Department of Antiquities in 1994 made this embellishment apparent; however, no publication about the monument has been produced. Immediately across from it there is another, smaller nymphea, which has been studied summarily by Souleiman Mougdad and Christophe Makowski, "Nymphée de Bosra et ses abords," *AAAS* 33 (1983): 35–46.

194. Jean Lauffray, "Une fouille au pied de l'acropole de Byblos," *Bulletin du Musée de Beyrouth* 4 (1940): 7–36; Maurice Dunand, *Byblos: Son histoire, ses ruines, ses légendes,* 3rd ed. (Beirut: Khayats; Paris: Librairie Adrien-Maisonneuve, 1973; originally published 1968), pp. 72–73.

195. On the nymphea, see J.-C. Balty, *Guide d'Apamée,* p. 76; on the public latrine, see Andreas Schmidt-Colinet, "Die sogenannte 'maison à atrium,'" in *Apamée de Syrie: Bilan des recherches archéologiques 1973–1979,* ed. Janine Balty (Brussels: Centre belge de recherches archéologiques à Apamée de Syrie, 1984), pp. 141–150.

196. Gustaf Dalman, *Petra und seine Felsheiligtümer* (Leipzig: J. C. Hinrich, 1908), pp. 199–200; Iain Browning, *Petra,* 3rd ed. (London: Chatto & Windus, 1989 [1977]), p. 140.

197. Nothing remains of these monuments, and at least the one in the north must have been carried off by flooding from the wadi: Walter Bachman, Carl Watzinger, and Theodor Wiegand, *Petra* (Berlin and Leipzig: Vereinigung Wissenschaftlicher Verleger, 1921), pp. 34–36 and fig. 27–28; cf. Judith McKenzie, *The Architecture of Petra* (Oxford and New York: Oxford University Press, 1990), p. 132; in Palmyra, its existence can be deduced only from a reference to a gymnasiarch (Dalman, *Petra,* X, 102).

198. Jean Lassus, "Sur les maisons d'Antioche," in J. Balty, *Apamée de Syrie,* p. 368.

199. Personal communication from Pierre-Marie Blanc, to whom I am extremely grateful.

200. Souleiman Mougdad, "Note préliminaire sur le cryptoportique de Bosra, Syrie," in *Les cryptoportiques dans l'architecture romaine,* ed. Colloques internationaux du Centre national de la recherche scientifique (Rome: École française de Rome, 1973), pp. 411–412.

201. Jean-Charles Balty, "Surprise hellénistique à Apamée," *M.Bible* 103 (March 1997): 55.

202. See Manuel Martín-Bueno, "Notes préliminaires sur le Macellum de

Gérasa," in *Jerash Archaeological Project 1984–1988,* ed. Fawzi Zayadine (Paris: P. Geuthner, 1989) = *Syria* 66 (1989): 177–199; Alexandra Uscatescu and Martin Martín-Bueno, "The *Macellum* of Gerasa (Jerash, Jordan): From a Marketplace to an Industrial Area," *BASOR* 307 (1997): 67–88; Teresa Marot, *Las monedas del Macellum de Gerasa (Yara, Jordania): Aproximación a la circulación monetaria en la provincia de Arabia* (Madrid: Museo Casa de la Moneda, 1998).

203. Jean Lauffray, "Beyrouth, ce qui n'a pas été dit," *Archeologia* 317 (November 1995): 4–11; Anne-Charlotte Lefèvre, "Beyrouth: L'archéologie par le vide," *Archeologia* 318 (December 1995): 4–9.

204. Ephraim Stern and Ilan Sharon, "Tel Dor—1992–1993," *ESI* 14 (1995): 65.

205. Crowfoot et al., *Buildings,* pp. 129–130.

206. Malalas, p. 114 (9.216); the basilica was built under Caesar.

207. Dunand, *Fouilles de Byblos,* pp. 49–51, dating from the Flavian period.

208. J.-C. Balty, *Curia ordinis,* p. 396.

209. Nahman Avigad and Benjamin Mazar, "Beth She'arim," in *EAEHL.*

210. It appears most notably on the map provided by Gideon Foerster, "Tiberias," in *EAEHL,* p. 1172, on the edge of Lake Tiberias.

211. Foerster and Tsafrir, "Beth Shean Project," pp. 31–32.

212. J.-C. Balty, *Curia ordinis,* p. 396.

213. W. Harold Mare, "Abila: A Thriving Greco-Roman City of the Decapolis," *Aram* 4 (1992): 62–66.

214. A group of buildings heavily remodeled in the fourth century: see Ghaleb Amer, Jean-Luc Biscop, Jacqueline Dentzer[-Feydy], and Jean-Pierre Sodini, "L'ensemble basilical de Qanawât (Syrie du Sud)," *Syria* 59 (1982): 257–318.

215. Butcher and Thorpe, "Note on Excavations," p. 304.

216. Identified in Louis Jalabert and René Mouterde, *IGLS,* vol. 4, *Laodicée, Apamène: Chronologie des inscriptions datées des tomes I–IV* (Paris: P. Geuthner, 1955), 1317; cf. Jean-Charles Balty, "Apamée, 1969–1971," in *Apamée de Syrie: Bilan des recherches archéologiques, 1969–1971; Actes du colloque tenu à Bruxelles les 15, 17 et 18 avril 1972,* ed. Janine Balty and Jean-Charles Balty (Brussels: Centre belge de recherches archéologiques à Apamée de Syrie, 1972), pp. 24–25; idem, *Guide d'Apamée,* pp. 69–75.

217. A team led by Klaus Stefan Freyberger is conducting a dig here. While the identification of the sanctuary of Zeus Megistos has never been a problem, the other sanctuary has long been attributed to Helios on the basis of a bad reading: it is actually the sanctuary of a god of Rabbos—that is, Theandrios: see Robert Donceel and Maurice Sartre, "Théandrios, dieu de Canatha," *Electrum* 1 (1997): 21–34.

218. Martin Jessop Price and Bluma Trell, *Coins and Their Cities: Architecture on the Ancient Coins of Greece, Rome, and Palestine* (London: Vecchi, 1977), figs. 43 and 413, in the era of Philip the Arab.

219. Temple of Zeus: Spijkerman, *Coins of the Decapolis,* nos. 31, 35–36, and so on.

220. Temple of Apollo: Spijkerman, *Coins of the Decapolis,* nos. 8, 14, 15, 18.

221. I am summarizing here a study by Edmond Frézouls that remains pertinent: "Aspects de l'histoire architecturale du théâtre romain," *ANRW* 2.12.1 (1982): 409–420 (for the Near East); see also idem, "Les édifices de spectacles en Syrie," in Dentzer and Orthmann, *Archéologie et histoire,* vol. 2, pp. 385–406. Since this publication, the theaters of Adraha and Dionysias have been discovered but not described in print. There is a regional study by Arthur Segal, *Theatres in Roman Palestine and*

Provincia Arabia (Leiden: E. J. Brill, 1995), which supplies a useful corpus, with maps and photographs, but the analyses remain quite general.

222. This is the case for Gerasa (where there are even three theaters, if we add the one in Birketein, north of the city) and for Gadara (see Robert L. J. J. Guinée and Niede F. Mulder, "Gadara: The Terrace, Theatre and *Cardo* Quarter in the Roman Period. Architectural Design Integrated in the Landscape: The Design of the West Theatre," *SHAJ* 6 [1997]: 317–322), and finally for Petra.

223. Jean Pouilloux, "Deux inscriptions au théâtre sud de Gérasa," *Liber annuus* 27 (1977): 246–254; idem, "Une troisième dédicace au théâtre de Gérasa," *Liber annuus* 29 (1979): 276–278.

224. This date is proposed for the one in Bostra by Klaus Stefan Freyberger, "Eine Beobachtungen zur städtebaulichen Entwicklung des römischen Bosra," *DaM* 4 (1989): 45–60.

225. Map and detailed plan in Helge Finsen, *Le levé du théâtre romain à Bosra, Syrie* (Copenhagen: Munksgaard, 1972).

226. I am thinking especially of the small temples at Sfire, perched at an altitude of more than two thousand meters, but many other examples could be found: see George Taylor, *The Roman Temples of Lebanon* (Beirut: Dar al-Machreq, 1967), p. 118.

227. Marianne Sawicki, "Spatial Management of Gender and Labor in Graeco-Roman Galilee," in *Archaeology and the Galilee: Texts and Contexts in the Graeco-Roman and Byzantine Periods,* ed. Douglas R. Edwards and C. Thomas McCullough (Atlanta: Scholars Press, 1997), pp. 7–28; but James F. Strange shows that at least at the beginning of this period, manifestations of Judaism remained largely confined to the private sphere ("First Century Galilee from Archaeology and from the Texts," in Edwards and McCullough, *Archaeology and the Galilee,* pp. 39–47).

228. Syrian cities were not exempt from fire or earthquakes. We know that Antioch burned under Tiberius in 23–24 (Malalas, p. 125 [10.235.15–236.1]); as for earthquakes, that of 115 was a disaster for Antioch as for Apamaea, and no doubt for all of northwestern Syria. On earthquakes, see K. W. Russell, "The Earthquake Chronology of Palestine and Northwest Arabia," *BASOR* 260 (1985): 37–59.

229. Pierre Gros, "Modèle urbain et gaspillage des ressources dans les programmes édilitaires des villes de Bithynie au début du IIe siècle ap. J.-C.," in *L'origine des richesses dépensées dans la ville antique: Actes du colloque organisé à Aix-en-Provence les 11 et 12 mai 1984,* ed. Philippe Leveau (Aix-en-Provence: Université de Provence, 1985), pp. 69–85.

230. Although one must still be cautious on this point.

231. For Palestine see Moshe Fischer, *Marble Studies: Roman Palestine and the Marble Trade* (Konstanz: Universitätsverlag Konstanz, 1998); for Syria proper, there is no overall study, but one can find scattered remarks in McKenzie, *Architecture of Petra,* and Hazel Dodge, "Palmyra and the Roman Marble Trade: The Evidence from the Baths of Diocletian," *Levant* 20 (1988): 215–230.

232. Fischer, *Marble Studies,* pp. 257–258.

233. Ibid., pp. 263–265.

234. Klaus Stefan Freyberger, "Zur Datierung des Theaters in Bosra," *DaM* 3 (1988): 20–21.

235. McKenzie, *Architecture of Petra,* pp. 38–39; a marble-cutters shop near the temple known as "the winged lions," pp. 138–140.

236. Dodge, "Palmyra and the Roman Marble Trade."

237. Patrizio Pensabene, "Marmi d'importazione, pietre locali e committenza nelle decorazione archittetonica di età severiana in alcuni centri delle province *Syria e Palaestina e Arabia,*" in *Miscellanea in onore di Maria Floriani Squarciapino* (Rome: L'Erma, 1998), pp. 275–422 (= *Archeologia classica,* 49, 1997).

238. A very thorough inventory of the discoveries of architectural marble in Syria is found in Pensabene, "Marmi d'importazione."

239. For a first approach, through the examples of Palmyra, Apamaea, and Dura, see Jean-Charles Balty, "La maison urbaine en Syrie," in Dentzer and Orthmann, *Archéologie et histoire,* vol. 2, pp. 407–422, with numerous maps and illustrations.

240. Doro Levi, *Antioch Mosaic Pavements* (Princeton: Princeton University Press, 1947), p. 1; but many of these discoveries come from small olive groves located on the periphery of the city, and local growers were not prepared to sell their trees to allow archaeologists to unearth an entire set of buildings: see Lassus, "Sur les maisons d'Antioche," p. 361.

241. Two synthetic studies: Richard Stillwell, "Houses of Antioch," *Dumbarton Oak Papers* 15 (1961): 44–57; Lassus, "Sur les maisons d'Antioche," pp. 361–372.

242. Levi, *Antioch Mosaic Pavements* p. 36.

243. Ibid., p. 40.

244. Ibid., pp. 45–46.

245. Ibid., p. 25.

246. Ibid., p. 66.

247. Ibid., pp. 68–91.

248. Ibid., p. 91.

249. Ibid., p. 117.

250. For example, the House of Dionysos Triumphant; ibid., p. 92.

251. Ibid., p. 67; Levi gives a map showing at least four houses embedded one within another, of which two (the House of Menander and the House with Red Pavement) have been almost completely excavated.

252. Ibid., pp. 15–16: the house, from the Augustan period, was destroyed in an earthquake during Caligula's reign and rebuilt between that date and 115; it was later abandoned.

253. Ibid., p. 29.

254. Ibid., p. 34.

255. Ibid., p. 141.

256. Ibid., pp. 57–59: it takes its name from the allegorical representation of Cilicia and Mesopotamia, framed by four rivers of which the Tigris and the Pyramos remain; the two others must have been the Euphrates and the Cydnos.

257. Ibid., p. 105.

258. Ibid., p. 156.

259. Ibid., p. 142.

260. Ibid., p. 167.

261. See Albert Gabriel, "Recherches archéologiques à Palmyre," *Syria* 7 (1926): 84–87.

262. Edmond Frézouls, "À propos de l'architecture domestique à Palmyre," *Ktema* 1 (1976): 29–52.

263. Henri Stern attributes the mosaics in the two houses to the period 245–273 (*Les mosaïques des maisons d'Achille et de Cassiopée à Palmyre* [Paris: P. Geuthner, 1977], p. 42).

264. Michel Gawlikowski, "Palmyre, mission polonaise 1990," *Syria* 70 (1993): 561–563, and idem, "Palmyre, mission polonaise 1991," *Syria* 70 (1993): 563–567.

265. Jean-Charles Balty, "Notes sur l'habitat romain, byzantin et arabe d'Apamée: Rapport de synthèse," in *Apamée de Syrie: Bilan des recherches archéologiques 1973–1979*, p. 482.

266. Frézouls, "À propos de l'architecture domestique," p. 37.

267. Ibid., pp. 47–49.

268. This was the object of the colloquium whose proceedings are recorded in J. Balty, *Apamée de Syrie*.

269. François Baratte, "La Maison des Chapiteaux à Consoles," in ibid., p. 120.

270. See the synthesis by J.-C. Balty, "Notes sur l'habitat," pp. 471–501.

271. Janine Balty, "La Maison aux Consoles," in J. Balty, *Apamée de Syrie*, p. 19.

272. Baratte, "La Maison des Chapiteaux à Consoles," p. 108.

273. Claudine Donnay-Rocmans and Guy Donnay, "La Maison du Cerf," in J. Balty, *Apamée de Syrie*, p. 158.

274. J. Balty, "Maison aux Consoles," p. 28; Jean-Robert Gisler and Madeleine Huwiler, "La Maison aux Pilastres," in J. Balty, *Apamée de Syrie*, p. 93.

275. J. Balty, "Maison aux Consoles," p. 30.

276. J.-C. Balty, *Guide d'Apamée*, p. 63.

277. Georges Raepsaet and Marie-Thérèse Raepsaet-Charlier, "La Maison aux Colonnes Trilobées," in J. Balty, *Apamée de Syrie*, p. 191, but the date is uncertain.

278. Donnay-Rocmans and Donnay, "Maison du Cerf," p. 162.

279. Rolf A. Stucky, "The Nabataean House and the Urbanistic System of the Habitation Quarters in Petra," *SHAJ* 5 (1995): 197.

280. Laïla Nehmé, "L'habitat rupestre dans le bassin de Pétra à l'époque nabatéenne," *SHAJ* 6 (1997): 281–288.

281. Strabo, 16.4.26.

282. Nabil I. Khairy, *The 1981 Petra Excavations*, Abhandlungen des deutschen Palästinavereins 13 (Wiesbaden: Harrassowitz, 1990); John p. Zeitler, "A Private Building from the First Century B.C. in Petra," *Aram* 2 (1990): 385–420, in the eastern sector of the lower city, at the foot of the grave with an urn.

283. Bernhard Kolb, "Les maisons patriciennes d'az-Zantûr," *M.Bible* 127 (May–June 2000): 42–43.

284. Cf. Fawzi Zayadine, "Decorative Stucco at Petra and Other Hellenistic Sites," *SHAJ* 3 (1987): 131–142; Laïla Nehmé and François Villeneuve, *Pétra: Métropole de l'Arabie antique* (Paris: Le Seuil, 1999), pp. 62–71.

285. Estelle Villeneuve, "Des archéologues à Pétra," *M.Bible* 127 (May–June 2000): 57–58.

286. Catherine Abadie-Reynal, Rifat Ergeç, et al., "Mission de Zeugma-Moyenne vallée de l'Euphrate" *Anatolia antiqua* 5 (1997): 362; idem, "Zeugma-Moyenne," pp. 379–381, 392–395.

287. Philippopolis developed late because it was only founded in 244–245; it was rapidly covered not only by public buildings (baths, theater, sanctuary of the imperial cult, ramparts), but also by private homes decorated with superb mosaics: Janine Balty dates them for the most part between the middle of the third century and the period of the tetrarchy (*Mosaïques antiques du Proche-Orient: Chronologie, iconographie, interprétation* [Paris: Les Belles Lettres, 1995], pp. 141–148).

288. George Andrew Reisner, Clarence Stanley Fisher, and David Gordon Lyon,

eds., *Harvard Excavations at Samaria, 1908–1910*, vol. 1 (Cambridge, Mass.: Harvard University Press, 1924), p. 181, fig. 97.

289. Ann Perkins, *The Art of Dura-Europos* (Oxford: Clarendon Press, 1973), pp. 21–23.

290. For example, house XII, perhaps an exceptional one, in Negev, *Architecture of Mampsis*, vol. 1, pp. 111–162, 147–162, for the frescos from the end of the second century and the beginning of the third.

291. Ibid., pp. 133–141, for the stables.

292. On rural houses in the Hauran, which quite possibly were also found in cities, see François Villeneuve, "Recherches sur les villages antiques du Haurâne (Ier siècle avant J.-C.–VIe siècle après J.-C.): Le peuplement, les maisons rurales" (Ph.D. diss., Université de Paris I, 1983); parts of this material can be found in idem, "L'économie rurale et la vie des campagnes dans le Hauran antique (Ier s. av. J.-C.–VIème s. ap. J.-C.)," in *Hauran I: Recherches archéologiques sur la Syrie du Sud à l'époque hellénistique et romaine*, ed. Jean-Marie Dentzer (Paris: P. Geuthner, 1985), pp. 63–136.

293. To date no urban houses have been excavated, either in Bostra or in Canatha, but many village houses are still quite visible. The procedure that consisted in covering the walls with a paste of mud and straw is attested in some of the late buildings like the cathedral of Bostra (where remains of frescos exist), and the practice was followed until cement invaded the villages some thirty years ago.

294. For paintings in the House of the Scribes in Dura, see H. F. Pearson, "The House of the Roman Scribes: Architecture and History," in *The Excavations at Dura-Europos, conducted by Yale University and the French Academy of Inscriptions and Letters: Preliminary Report of Sixth Season of Work, October 1932–March 1933*, ed. Mikhail Ivanovitch Rostovtzeff (New Haven: Yale University Press, 1936), pp. 265–275; Mikhail Ivanovitch Rostovtzeff, "Interior Decoration," in Rostovtzeff, *Excavations at Dura-Europos*, pp. 275–279. This private home was requisitioned by Roman officers: idem, "The Residents of the House," in Rostovtzeff, *Excavations at Dura-Europos*, pp. 299–304. Anny Allara by and large validates the earlier work in "Les maisons de Doura-Europos: Les données du terrain," *Syria* 65 (1988): 323–342.

295. A summary of the principal theories on this subject is found in Michael Jeffrey Fuller, "Abila of the Decapolis: A Roman-Byzantine City in Transjordan" (Ph.D. diss., Washington University, St. Louis, 1987); Fuller shows that, depending on the theory adopted, Abila's population varies, in the Roman period, from 331 to 7,900 inhabitants (p. 246).

296. Inscription by Q. Aemilius Secundus, Mommsen, *CIL*, vol. 3S, no. 6687; Balty and Balty, "Apamée de Syrie I," pp. 117–120.

297. This is a maximum for Jean Durliat, *De la ville antique à la ville byzantine: Le problème des subsistances* (Rome: École française de Rome, 1990), pp. 350–381.

298. See Jean-Pierre Callu, "Antioche la Grande, la cohérence des chiffres," *Mélanges de l'École française de Rome: Antiquités* 109 (1997): 127–169, and Ernest Will, "Antioche sur l'Oronte, métropole de l'Asie," *Syria* 74 (1997): 99–113; idem, "Antioche, la métropole de l'Asie," in *Mégapoles méditerranéennes*, ed. Claude Nicolet, Robert Ilbert, and Jean-Charles Depaule (Paris and Rome: École française de Rome, 2000), pp. 482–491.

299. Dora P. Crouch, "A Note on the Population and Area of Palmyra," *MUSJ* 47 (1972): 241–250.

300. Ernest Will, "La population de Doura-Europos: Une évaluation," *Syria* 65 (1988): 315–321.

301. Henner von Hesberg "The Significance of the Cities in the Kingdom of Herod," in *Judaea and the Greco-Roman World in the Time of Herod in the Light of Archaeological Evidence,* ed. Klaus Fittschen and Gideon Foerster (Göttingen: Vandenhoeck & Ruprecht, 1996), pp. 9–25.

302. See Sartre, *Orient romain,* pp. 190–198, especially p. 198.

303. Jean-Charles Balty, "Grande colonnade et quartiers nord d'Apamée à la fin de l'époque héllenistique," *CRAI* (1994): 90, and idem, "Claudia Apamea: Données nouvelles sur la topographie et l'histoire d'Apamée," *CRAI* (2000): 459–481. We should note that the city inaugurated a new era in the same period; see Seyrig, "Sur les ères," *AS,* vol. 4, p. 87).

304. *Aurelia Esbous:* Spijkerman, *Coins of the Decapolis,* pp. 124–125, nos. 1–2 and 4–5; all the coins date from the reign of Elagabalus.

305. Sartre, "Palmyre, cité grecque," p. 393, with the arguments.

306. Sartre, *IGLS,* vol. 13.1, no. 9063.

307. Zbigniew T. Fiema, "La découverte des papyrus byzantins de Pétra," *CRAI* (1997): 736.

308. Maurice Sartre, *IGLJ,* vol. 4, *Pétra et la Nabatène méridionale* (Paris: P. Geuthner, 1993), no. 37.

309. See the list in Arye Kindler, "The Status of Cities in the Syro-Palestinian Area as Reflected by Their Coins," *Israel Numismatic Journal* (hereafter cited as *INJ*) 6–7 (1982–1983): 84–85.

310. Millar, "Roman *Coloniae.*"

311. Pliny, *NH* 5.18.79.

312. Kindler, "Status of Cities," p. 81.

313. For the coinages of Sidon and Tyre, see Brooks Emmons Levy, "The Autonomous Silver of Sidon, 107/6 B.C.–43/44 C.E.," in *XII. Internationaler Numismatischer Kongress Berlin 1997, Akten-Proceedings-Actes,* vol. 1, ed. Bernd Kluge and Bernhard Weisser (Berlin: Staatliche Museen zu Berlin / Gebr. Mann Verlag, 2000). This makes Dio enigmatic where he says that Augustus made Sidon and Tyre "slaves" because they were ravaged by factional struggles (Dio, 54.7.6); perhaps it was a matter of a temporary deprivation of freedom that left no trace in the coinage, for cities did not produce coins on a continuous basis.

314. Kent J. Rigsby, *Asylia: Territorial Inviolability in the Hellenistic World* (Berkeley: University of California Press, 1996).

315. Tacitus, *The Annals,* trans. John Jackson (Loeb Classical Library), 3.60–63, 4.14.

316. Rigsby, *Asylia,* p. 29.

317. Ibid., n. 95; but on p. 535, Rigsby does not mention a grant. Capitolias, founded in 97 or 98 C.E., was able to acquire the titles and privileges of a nearby city.

318. *Papyrus Dura* (hereafter cited as *P.Dura*), in Charles Bradford Welles, Robert O. Fink, and James Frank Gilliam, *The Excavations at Dura-Europos: Final Report,* part 1, *The Parchments and Papyri,* ed. Ann Perkins (New Haven: Yale University Press, 1959), 32, 4–5.

319. Rigsby, *Asylia,* 515–517.

320. Kindler, "Status of Cities," pp. 79–87.

321. Ibid.

322. See Victor Tourneur, "Les villes amirales de l'Orient gréco-romain," *Revue belge de numismatique* 69 (1913): 407–424; Jean-Paul Rey-Coquais, "Laodicée sur mer et l'armée romaine à partir de quelques inscriptions," in *The Roman and Byzantine Army in the East,* ed. Edward Dąbrowa (Cracow: Drukarnia Uniwersytetu Jagiellonskiego, 1994), pp. 149–163, especially pp. 153–154.

323. In this sense, see Glen W. Bowersock, "Hadrian and Metropolis," in *Bonner Historia-Augusta-Colloquium 1982–1983: Beiträge,* ed. Jean Béranger and Johannes Straub (Bonn: R. Habelt, 1985), pp. 75–88.

324. Sartre, *IGLJ,* vol. 4, no. 37.

325. Ruprecht Ziegler, "Laodicea, Antiochia und Sidon in der Politik der Severer," *Chiron* 8 (1978): 493–514.

326. See George Francis Hill, *Catalogue of the Greek Coins of Arabia, Mesopotamia and Persia* (London: British Museum, 1922), p. 83.

327. For Edessa, even before Elagabalus's death, see ibid., p. 103.

328. Ibid., p. 119.

329. See Kindler, "Status of Cities," pp. 79–87; certain dates need to be corrected.

330. Paul Veyne offers a judicious explanation in his preface to *Palmyre, métropole caravanière,* by Gérard Degeorge (Paris: Imprimerie nationale, 2001), p. 24.

331. Millar, "Roman *Coloniae*"; Sartre, "Colonies romaines."

332. Edward Dąbrowa, "Les légions romaines au Proche-Orient: L'apport de la numismatique," *Electrum* 5 (2001): 73–85.

333. Millar, "Roman *Coloniae,*" p. 32.

334. Ulpian, *Digesta,* 50.15.1, in *Corpus iuris civilis,* 17th ed., ed. Theodor Mommsen, vol. 1 (repr., Berlin: Weidmann, 1988), (revised by Paul Krüger, who is very forthcoming when he is talking about his own homeland); cf. Millar, "Roman *Coloniae,*" pp. 34–35.

335. Millar, "Roman *Coloniae,*" p. 33.

336. Ibid., p. 38.

337. Dio is not clear (75.3.2 [second occurrence]; 36.6.2), but one of the documents from the Middle Euphrates mentions the *Septimia kolonia metropolis Nisibis* (*P.Euphr.,* in Feissel and Gascou, "Documents" [1997], 8.15).

338. Millar, "Roman *Coloniae,*" p. 39.

339. *P.Dura,* 32.

340. Ibid., p. 55. The date *ante quem* would be supplied by a dedication for Iulia Domna: see Paul V. C. Baur and Mikhail Ivanovitch Rostovtzeff, eds., *The Excavations at Dura-Europos: Preliminary Report of 1st–9th Seasons of Work,* vol. 3 (New Haven: Yale University Press, 1932), p. 51, no. 149.

341. Ulpian, *Digesta,* 50.15.1; Millar, "Roman *Coloniae,*" p. 41.

342. Paul, *Digesta,* in *Corpus iuris civilis,* 17th ed., ed. Theodor Mommsen, rev. Paul Krüger, vol. 1 (repr., Berlin: Weidmann, 1988), 50.15.8.5; cf. Millar, "Roman *Coloniae,*" pp. 41–42.

343. Ulpian, *Digesta,* 50.15.1.5; Millar, "Roman *Coloniae,*" pp. 42–46; Sartre, "Palmyre, cité grecque," p. 394.

344. Feissel and Gascou, "Documents" (1995), 28; cf. Millar, "Roman *Coloniae,*" pp. 46–50.

345. Millar, "Roman *Coloniae,*" pp. 50–51.

346. Ibid., p. 51.

347. Ibid., pp. 51–52.

348. Sartre, *Bostra*, pp. 76–77; Millar, "Roman *Coloniae*," p. 52.

349. Millar, "Roman *Coloniae*," p. 53.

350. Ibid.

351. Ibid., pp. 53–55.

352. Isaac, *Roman Near East*, p. 111; no coinage is attested there, perhaps because Scythopolis was promoted to colonial status after the disappearance of civic coinage in the Orient; but around 308–311 a dedication to Galerius was erected by the *strategoi* of the colony: see Rosa Last, Avshalom Laniado, and Pinchas Porath, "A Dedication to Galerius from Scythopolis: A Revised Reading," *ZPE* 98 (1993): 229–237 (*AE* [1993], no. 1618).

353. Cf. Millar, "Roman *Coloniae*," pp. 55–56.

354. A sale of slaves described by Ulrich Wilcken, "Papyruskunde über einen Sclavenkauf aus dem Jahre 359 n. Chr.," *Hermes* 19 (1884): 417–431: *kolonia Askalon he piste kai eleuthera;* although the name of the city has been restored, the first three letters, which are unmistakable, are enough for the identification. It is troubling, nevertheless, that no document from the city attests this title.

355. *I.Syrie*, 1904; cf. Carol A. M. Glucker, *The City of Gaza in the Roman and Byzantine Periods* (Oxford: British Archaeological Reports, 1987), p. 148, no. 42.1. The date is uncertain; I note that the eponymous magistrate does not bear the *tria nomina*.

356. *SEG*, vol. 30, no. 1687, and vol. 32, no. 1501; cf. Jean Bingen, cited in Jacques Noret, "La Société belge d'études Byzantines," *Byzantion* 54 (1984): 369–370.

357. It is indeed necessary to eliminate Emil Hübner, *CIL*, vol. 2, *Inscriptiones Hispaniae latinae*, 2 vols. (Berlin: G. Reimer, 1869–1892), no. 181, which has long been invoked in favor of a colony in Gadara, for the text has to be interpreted in an entirely different way: *AE* (1991), no. 1575.

358. *The Babylonian Talmud*, ed. Isidore Epstein, 35 vols. (London: Soncino Press, 1935–1952), *Avodah Zara* 10a (hereafter cited as *BT*). Millar implicitly challenges the testimony as belated, and uses it only to show the prestige attached to colonial status until much later (the fifth century C.E.), that of the writing of the Babylonian Talmud ("Roman *Coloniae*," p. 10).

359. A reading by Ya'akov Meshorer: see "Tiberias, from the Foundation to the Arab Conquest," in Yizhar Hirschfeld, *Idan*, 11 (Jerusalem, 1988), p. 96 (in Hebrew), cited by Millar, "Roman *Coloniae*," p. 10, n. 10.

360. In *Judaea in Hellenistic and Roman Times*, p. 150, n. 51, Applebaum refers to an article (in Hebrew) by Simha Asaf, in *Tarbiz* (1948): 28.

361. For Petra, cf. Sartre, *IGLJ*, vol. 4, nos. 24 and 48. For Palmyra, *IGR*, vol. 3, no. 1045.

362. For Emesa and Antioch, the title appears only on coins, but in an ambiguous way, because the juxtaposition *METROCOL* could be developed as *metro[polis] kol[onia]* and also as *metrokol[onia]*. However, I think the second solution is preferable, for *metropolis* is regularly abbreviated as *mht* and not *mhtro*. For the coins of Antioch and Emesa, see Barclay Vincent Head, *Catalogue of the Greek Coins in the British Museum: Galatia, Cappadocia, Syria* (London: British Museum, 1895), pp. 215, 240. For the cities that minted coins with Latin legends, the title never appears, and the indications *col[onia]* and *met[ropolis]* are generally separated by the name of the city itself.

363. Fiema, "Découverte des papyrus byzantins," p. 736.

364. "La petition de Bostra (*P.Bostra* 1; 29 mai 260)," published by Jean Gascou as an appendix to "Unités administratives locales et fonctionnaires romains: Les données des nouveaux papyrus du Moyen Euphrate et d'Arabie," in *Lokale Autonomie und römische Ordnungsmacht in den kaiserzeitlichen Provinzen vom 1. bis 3. Jahrhundert,* ed. Werner Eck and Elisabeth Müller-Luckner (Munich: R. Oldenbourg, 1999), pp. 71–73.

365. Sartre, "Construction de l'identité civique des villes."

366. See Christian Augé, "Sur des types monétaires de Canatha," in *Travaux de numismatique grecque offerts à Georges Le Rider,* ed. Michel Amandry and Silvia Mani Hurter (London: Spink, 1999), pp. 25–35.

367. See Spijkerman, *Coins of the Decapolis,* pp. 164–165, no. 31, under Caracalla; mention of Alexandros Makedon alone, pp. 166–167, nos. 34–35, under Elagabalus. Cf. Henri Seyrig, "Alexandre le Grand, fondateur de Gérasa," *Syria* 42 (1965): 25–28.

368. Spijkerman, *Coins of the Decapolis,* p. 158. The oldest attestation is found in an inscription from Pergamon dating perhaps from 102; in any case, it is from Trajan's reign and probably anterior to the creation of the province of Arabia: see *Die Inschriften von Pergamon,* vol. 8, fasc. 2, *Römische Zeit,* ed. Max Fränkel (Berlin: W. Spemann, 1895), no. 437. In Gerasa itself, the name is attested under Trajan on an inscription on the north gate (*I.Gerasa,* nos. 56–57, from 115) and on the large agonistic inscription dating from 105–114 (*I.Gerasa,* no. 192).

369. Sartre, *Orient romain,* pp. 195–196, 337, rightly corrected by Pierre-Louis Gatier, "À propos de la culture grecque à Gérasa," in *Arabia Antiqua: Hellenistic Centers around Arabia,* ed. Antonio Invernizzi and Jean-François Salles (Rome: Istituto italiano per il Medio ed Estremo Oriente, 1993), p. 18.

370. Sartre, "Progrès de la citoyenneté romaine."

371. Glen W. Bowersock, "Roman Senators from the Near East," *Epigraphia e ordine senatorio: Atti* (Rome: Ed. di storia e letteratura, 1982), pp. 651–668.

372. Although there probably was a gymnasium in Petra: Bachman et al., *Petra,* pp. 65–68; in Palmyra, the existence of a gymnasium can only be deduced from the mention of a gymnasiarch: *Inv.,* vol. 10, no. 102.

373. Jean-Pierre Callu, "Antioche la Grande," p. 132.

374. Josephus presents the large Jewish community at the moment of the war of 70 (*BJ* 7.43–62); he claims that the Jews of Antioch had the right to live in the city on equal footing with the Greeks (7.44), which is more doubtful; the assertion is probably based on the fact that the Jews of Antioch were called "Antiochenes," which does not imply any civic rights. The Antiochenes asked Titus to expel the Jews from the city in 70, but he refused: *BJ* 7.103–111. Cf. Carl Hermann Kraeling, "The Jewish Community at Antioch," *Journal of Biblical Literature* 51 (1932): 130–160.

375. Acts 11.26.

376. On Ignatius of Antioch, the second bishop of the city and one of the first theoreticians of episcopal power, see Charles Munier, "Où en est la question d'Ignace d'Antioche? Bilan d'un siècle de recherches 1870–1988," *ANRW* 2.27.1 (1993): 359–484.

377. In "Une panégyrie antiochienne: Le Maïouma," *Actes du Colloque sur Antioche, Lyon, 4–6 octobre 2001,* forthcoming in *Topoi,* Nicole Belayche established decisively the meaning and timing of the festival; most authors place the celebration

of the maiouma in May, following Malalas's etymology (p. 151 [12.285]). For an October celebration, see Pierre Chuvin, *Chronique des derniers païens: La disparition du paganisme dans l'Empire romain, du règne de Constantin à celui de Justinien* (Paris: Fayard, 1991), p. 274.

378. Julian, "Misopogon, or Beard-Hater," in *The Works of the Emperor Julian*, trans. Wilmer Cave Wright, vol. 2 (Loeb Classical Library), 355d: "you give yourselves up to pleasure throughout the whole year."

379. Cf. Emmanuel Soler, *Le sacré et le salut à Antioche au IVe siècle ap. J.-C.: Pratiques festives et comportements religieux dans le processus de christianisation de la cité* (Ph.D. diss, Rouen, 1999; Beirut: Institut français du Proche Orient, forthcoming). Although the work deals with the fourth century, it offers a good deal of information on pagan or Jewish festivals that existed before the period under consideration.

380. Lassus, *Antioch-on-the-Orontes*, vol. 5, p. 61.

381. Herodian, 6.4.3; he took advantage of this to go as far as Palmyra (*Inv.*, vol. 3, no. 22).

382. *Res gestae divi saporis*, 10–19, in *Die römisch-persischen Kriege des 3. Jahrhunderts n. Chr.: Nach der Inschrift Sahpuhrs I. an der Ka'be-ye Zartost (SKZ)*, by Erich Kettenhofen (Wiesbaden: L. Reichert, 1982); Zosimus, *New History: A Translation with Commentary*, trans. and ed. Ronald T. Ridley (Canberra: Australian Association for Byzantine Studies, 1982), 1.27.2.

383. Malalas evokes the treachery of a certain Mariades or Mareades, a former city magistrate who delivered the city to Shapur (pp. 156–162 [12.295–296]), but the date he gives, the 314th year of Antioch, would correspond to 265–266, which does not correlate. Other allusions may refer just as well to the events of 252 as to those of 260: see Libanios, *Antioch as a Centre of Hellenic Culture*, p. 38 (Oratio 11.158); idem, *Selected Works with an English Translation*, trans. A. F. Norman, vol. 1, *The Julianic Orations* (Loeb Classical Library), p. 157 (Oratio 15.16); ibid., pp. 519–521 (Oratio 24.38); idem, *Libanii Opera*, ed. Richard Foerster, vol. 4 (Hildesheim: G. Olms, 1963), pp. 312–313. (Oratio 60.2–3); Ammianus Marcellinus, *The Surviving Books of the History*, trans. John C. Rolfe, vol. 2 (Loeb Classical Library), 20.11.11, 23.5.3.

384. We know that the Seleucids were forbidden to possess any by the peace of Apamaea in 188.

385. The site seems in fact to have been deliberately leveled; the debris was used to fill in the irregularities of the terrain. This explains why we have no vestiges in place of monuments anterior to 115, or virtually none.

386. Balty and Balty, "Apamée de Syrie I," pp. 125–126.

387. J.-C. Balty, "Note sur l'habitat romain," p. 492: 1,336 square meters for the peristyle of the house with console capitals, as opposed to 1,245 for the forum of Tipasa, 1,292 in Sbeitla, 1,390 in Cuicul, and 1,400 in Thuburbo Maius!

388. J.-C. Balty, "Apamée (1986)."

389. Balty and Balty, "Apamée de Syrie I," pp. 133–134.

390. J. Balty, *Mosaïques antiques*, especially pp. 43–46, 299–305.

391. We do not know the poet's real name, but his work has been preserved under the name of Oppianus of Cilicia, the author of *Halieutica;* hence the designation Pseudo-Oppianus. Cf. Rudolf Keydell, "Oppianus," in *RE*.

392. Cf. Fergus Millar, "Dura-Europos under Parthian Rule," in *Das Partherreich*

und seine Zeugnisse: The Arsacid Empire, Sources and Documentation, ed. Josef Wiesehöfer (Stuttgart: F. Steiner, 1998), pp. 473–492.

393. The crucial article remains the one by Charles Bradford Welles, "The Population of Roman Dura," in *Studies in Roman Economic and Social History in Honour of Allan Chester Johnson,* ed. Paul Robinson Coleman-Norton (Princeton: Princeton University Press, 1951), pp. 251–274.

394. Lucinda Dirven, *The Palmyrenes of Dura-Europos: A Study of Religious Interaction in Roman Syria* (Boston: E. J. Brill, 1999), p. 6.

395. Mikhail Ivanovitch Rostovtzeff, Frank E. Brown, and Charles Bradford Welles, eds., *The Excavations at Dura-Europos Conducted by Yale University and the French Academy of Inscriptions and Letters,* vols. 7–8, *Preliminary Report of the Seventh and Eighth Seasons of Work, 1933–1934 and 1934–1935* (New Haven: Yale University Press, 1939) pp. 319–320, inscription no. 916 = Dirven, *Palmyrenes of Dura-Europos,* p. 199, no. 1.

396. Alfred Raymond Bellinger, *The Excavations at Dura-Europos: Final Report,* vol. 6, *The Coins* (New Haven: Yale University Press, 1949), pp. 196–198, 203.

397. Ann Perkins, *The Excavations at Dura-Europos: Final Report,* vol. 4, part 5, *The Glass* (New Haven: Yale University Press, 1963), p. 149.

398. G. D. Kirkpatrick, "Dura-Europos: The Parchments and Papyri," *Greek, Roman and Byzantine Studies* 5 (1964): 215–225.

399. At the beginning of the word we recognize the root 'zz, "power," then *anath,* but we do not know whether this is the toponym of the Middle Euphrates or the Babylonian divinity of the same name (but it may be both at once): the ending remains unexplained.

400. Robert O. Fink, Allan S. Hoey, and Walter F. Snyder, "The *Feriale Duranum,*" *Yale Classical Studies* 7 (1940): 1–222 (*P.Dura* 54); cf. Duncan Fishwick, "Dated Inscriptions and the *Feriale Duranum,*" *Syria* 65 (1988): 349–361.

401. Cf. Perkins, *Art of Dura-Europos,* pp. 36–52.

402. Carl Hermann Kraeling, *The Excavations at Dura Europos: Final Report,* vol. 8, part 2, *The Christian Building* (New Haven: Yale University Press, 1967).

403. Dirven, *Palmyrenes of Dura-Europos,* pp. 190–195.

404. Edward Dąbrowa, "La garnison romaine à Doura-Europos: Influence du camp sur la vie de la ville et ses conséquences," *Prace Historyczne* 70 (1981): 61–75.

405. Pierre Leriche, "Une nouvelle inscription dans la salle à gradins du temple d'Artémis à Doura-Europos," *CRAI* (1999): 1309–1346.

406. Charles Bradford Welles, Robert O. Fink, and James Frank Gilliam, *The Excavations at Dura Europos: Final Report,* vol. 5, *The Parchments and Papyri* (New Haven: Yale University Press, 1959), p. 271.

407. Bellinger, *Excavations, Final Report,* vol. 6, p. 209 and n. 48.

408. Welles et al., *Excavations, Final Report,* vol. 5, pp. 142–149, no. 28.

409. Charles Bradford Welles, "The House of Nebuchelus," in Baur and Rostovtzeff, *Excavations at Dura-Europos,* vol. 4, pp. 79–145; idem, "La maison des archives à Doura-Europos," *CRAI* (1931): 162–188; Kai Ruffing, "Die Geschäfte des Aurelius Nebuchelos," *Laverna* 11 (2000): 71–105.

410. Hans-Georg Pflaum, "La fortification de la ville d'Adraha d'Arabie (259–260 à 274–275) d'après des inscriptions récemment découvertes," *Syria* 29 (1952): 307–330; for Bostra, see Sartre, *IGLS,* vol. 13.1, nos. 9105, 9106, 9108, 9109.

411. The hypothesis cannot be proved, given the current state of the documenta-

tion, but I note the construction of an arch dating from the same period at Tyre, which was also promoted to colony status.

412. I was probably wrong in *Bostra* (pp. 156–158) to yield to the influence of Charles Clermont-Ganneau and to date the organization of these contests back to the reign of Caracalla; they were not known before Philip's era.

413. Christian Wallmer has just drawn attention to a text from Hermopolis that had escaped my attention and that mentions this contest in 267 or 268 ("Der olympische Agon von Bostra," *ZPE* 129 [2000]: 97–107). He shows quite convincingly that the contest had to have been authorized by Valerian or by Gallienus to recompense the city for the efforts it had put forward on the defense front during those crucial years. This corresponds to the moment when new troops were transferred from Palestine to Arabia (Enno Littmann, David Magie, and D. R. Stuart, *Greek and Latin Inscriptions: Southern Syria,* vol. 3A of *Syria: Publications of the Princeton University Archaeological Expeditions to Syria in 1904–1905 and 1909* [Leiden: E. J. Brill, 1921], no. 10, reproduced in translation by Michael H. Dodgeon and Samuel N. C. Lieu, *The Roman Eastern Frontier and the Persian Wars (ad 226–363): A Documentary History* [London and New York: Routledge, 1991], p. 56).

414. Sartre, *Bostra*, pp. 158–159.

415. Jean Scherer, ed., *Entretien d'Origène avec Héraclide* (Paris: Le Cerf, 1960).

416. Pliny, *NH* 5.17.76.

417. Rivka Gersht and Ze'ev Pearl, "Decoration and Marble Sources of Sarcophagi from Caesarea," in Vann, *Caesarea Papers*, pp. 223–243.

418. See Rivka Gersht, "Representations of Deities and the Cults of Caesarea," in *Caesarea Maritima: A Retrospective after Two Millennia,* ed. Avner Raban and Kenneth G. Holum (Leiden: E. J. Brill, 1996), pp. 305–324; Gersht highlights the diversity of cultures and representations.

419. Edgar Krentz, "Caesarea and Early Christianity," in Vann, *Caesarea Papers*, pp. 261–267.

420. Lewis M. Hopfe, "Caesarea Palaestinae as a Religious Center," *ANRW* 2.18.4 (1990): 2394, but one may wonder whether the reference is not to Caesarea of Galilee—that is, Panias.

421. Saul Lieberman, *Greek in Jewish Palestine: Studies in the Life and Manners of Jewish Palestine in the II–IV Centuries* C.E., 2nd ed. (New York: Jewish Theological Seminary of America, 1965), pp. 21–23.

422. Lieberman, *Greek in Jewish Palestine.* In the preface (unpaginated), Lieberman refers to his own earlier works (in Hebrew).

423. David L. Kennedy offers an extremely precise presentation in "The Identity of Roman Gerasa: An Archaeological Approach," *Mediterranean Archaeology* 11 (1998): 39–69.

424. Seyrig, "Alexandre le Grand"; cf. a statue of Perdiccas built in the first century C.E.; see *I.Gerasa*, no. 137.

425. A weight that Welles dated from the year 73 of the Gerasene era—that is, 10–11 C.E. (*I.Gerasa*, no. 251)—but that Seyrig read as 170, or 107–108 C.E. according to the local era; Seyrig was calculating according to the Seleucid era, which gave 143–142 B.C.E. (Henri Seyrig, *Notes on Syrian Coins* [New York: American Numismatic Society, 1950], p. 33, n. 45).

426. Josephus, *AJ* 13.393 and 13.398, *BJ* 1.104.

427. Pierre-Louis Gatier, "La présence arabe à Gérasa et en Décapole," in

Présence arabe dans le Croissant fertile avant l'Hégire, ed. Hélène Lozachmeur (Paris: Éditions Recherche sur les civilisations, 1995), p. 115.

428. Josephus, *AJ* 14.356, *BJ* 1.87.

429. See Gatier, "À propos de la culture grecque," pp. 20–25.

430. We know that the territory of Bostra came as close as eleven kilometers to the east of Gerasa: Pierre-Louis Gatier, cited in Denis Feissel, "Bulletin épigraphique," *Revue des études grecques* (1997), 663; Jacques Seigne has pointed out marks that could indicate the boundaries of the city's territory six kilometers to the east ("Les limites orientale et méridionale du territoire de Gerasa," *Syria* 74 [1997]: 121–138 [with an appendix by Maurice Sartre, pp. 139–140]).

431. Pierre-Louis Gatier, "Philadelphie et Gérasa du royaume nabatéen à la province d'Arabie," in *Géographie historique du Proche-Orient: Actes de la table ronde de Valbonne, 17–18 septembre 1985,* ed. Pierre-Louis Gatier, Bruno Helly, and Jean-Paul Rey-Coquais (Paris: Centre national de la recherche scientifique, 1988), pp. 159–170.

432. The first one was published in *I.Gerasa,* no. 2; the other two are unpublished, but they are mentioned in Gatier, "Présence arabe," p. 115.

433. *I.Gerasa,* no. 10.

434. Six texts mention this arabic god: *I.Gerasa,* no. 19–22; Roland de Vaux, "Une nouvelle inscription au dieu arabique," *Annual of the Department of Antiquities of Jordan* (hereafter cited as *ADAJ*) 1 (1951): 23–24; Pierre-Louis Gatier, "Inscriptions religieuses de Gérasa," *ADAJ* 26 (1982): 272–274. On the relationship of identity with Paqeidas, see Louis-Hugues Vincent, "Le dieu saint Paqeidas à Gérasa," *Rbi* 49 (1940): 98–129, using *I.Gerasa,* no. 17, as his basis; *contra,* see René Dussaud, "Le saint dieu Paqeidas," *Syria* 22 (1941): 295–297.

435. On the presence of the Nabataeans in Decapolis, see the inventory drawn up by Robert Wenning, "Die Dekapolis und die Nabatäer," *ZDPV* 110 (1994): 1–35.

436. Josephus, *BJ* 2.480: they even supplied an escort for those who wanted to leave the country.

437. Maurice Sartre, "Ti. Iulius Iulianus Alexander, Gouverneur d'Arabie," *ADAJ* 21 (1976): 105–108.

438. On all this, see David L. Kennedy, "The Identity of Roman Gerasa: An Archaeological Approach," *Mediterranean Archaeology* 11 (1998): 39–69, especially 56–64, with the requisite archaeological bibliography.

7. RURAL LIFE IN THE EARLY EMPIRE

1. Josephus, *De antiquitate judaico (Jewish Antiquities),* trans. Louis H. Feldman (Loeb Classical Library), 17.355 and 18.26 (hereafter cited as *AJ*).

2. Jean-François Breton, ed., *Inscriptions grecques et latines de la Syrie* (hereafter cited as *IGLS*), vol. 8.3, *Les inscriptions forestières d' Hadrien dans le Mont Liban* (Paris: P. Geuthner, 1980; original eds. Louis Jalabert and René Mouterde).

3. The constitution of an imperial domain encompassing not a certain land area but rather part of what the land produces is not unprecedented: Anne-Marie Rouanet-Liesenfelt, in "Les plantes médicinales de Crète à l'époque romaine," *Cretan Studies* 3 (1992): 173–190 (especially pp. 184–189), has shown that the abundant medicinal plants that could be collected in Crete also constituted a type of imperial domain, over which operated the emperor's *botanikoi andres* (these men were responsible for collecting medicinal plants that were the exclusive property of the

emperor); this was also the case for oil from Tithorea in Phokis: see Pausanias, *Description of Greece*, trans. W. H. S. Jones and H. A. Ormerod, vol. 4 (Loeb Classical Library), 10.32.19.

4. In an inscription from Ephesos describing the *cursus* (career) of T. Flavius Pergamus, an imperial freedman of one of the Flavians: see *L'année épigraphique* (hereafter cited as *AE*) (1982), no. 877, with a detailed commentary.

5. He is mentioned on a rectangular lead *tessera* from Syria (Péretié collection), but we have no further information: see M. Baudouin and Edmond Pottier, "Collection de Monsieur Péretié: Inscriptions," *Bulletin de correspondance hellénique* 3 (1879): 270, no. 42.

6. This Emmaus is probably not the small town southwest of Jerusalem that later became a Nicopolis, but rather Ammaus-Motaza or Hamotza, near Jerusalem: see Gedaliah Alon, *The Jews in Their Land in the Talmudic Age (70–640 ce)*, trans. Gershon Levi (Cambridge, Mass., and London: Harvard University Press, 1989), p. 59, n. 15.

7. Josephus, *De bello judaico (The Jewish War)*, trans. Henry St. John Thackeray (Loeb Classical Library), 7.216–217 (hereafter cited as *BJ*).

8. Benjamin H. Isaac, "Judaea after AD 70," *Journal of Jewish Studies* 35 (1984): 44–50; Ze'ev Safrai, *The Economy of Roman Palestine* (London and New York: Routledge, 1994), p. 324; Alon, *Jews in their Land*, pp. 59–64.

9. Ysé Tardan-Masquelier, ed., *Sifre: A Tannaitic Commentary on the Book of Deuteronomy*, trans. Reuven Hammer, vol. 10 (New Haven: Yale University Press, 1986), p. 272, nos. 41, 85, p. 272, cited by Gedaliah Alon, "The Hasmoneans—Logistics, Taxation and the Constitution," in *Judaea in Hellenistic and Roman Times: Historical and Archaeological Essays*, ed. Shimon Applebaum (Leiden and New York: E. J. Brill, 1989), pp. 15–16. On the antecedents, see Shimon Applebaum, "The Settlement Pattern of Western Samaria from Hellenistic to Byzantine Times: A Historical Commentary," in *Landscape and Pattern: An Archaeological Survey of Samaria*, ed. Shimon Dar and Shimon Applebaum, vol. 1 (Oxford: British Archaeological Reports, 1986, pp. 259–260.

10. Safrai, *Economy of Roman Palestine*, p. 325.

11. See Shimon Applebaum, "Royal and Imperial Estates in the Sharon and Samaria," in Applebaum, *Judaea in Hellenistic and Roman Times*, pp. 97–110, especially pp. 102–103.

12. Jean-Paul Rey-Coquais, "Une inscription du Liban-Nord," *Mélanges de l'Université Saint-Joseph* (hereafter cited as *MUSJ*) 47, 1972, pp. 96–97; idem, "Syrie romaine, de Pompée à Dioclétien," *Journal of Roman Studies* (hereafter cited as *JRS*) 68 (1978): 44–73.

13. Jean-Paul Rey-Coquais also rightly observed that dating by the year of an emperor's reign was practiced in Syria only on the territory of the imperial domains; the same system was used in the ancient Herodian states of southern Syria, where the Arabian era does not appear until the third century or even later. Rey-Coquais's conclusions have been adopted with supplementary—but untenable—arguments by Shimon Applebaum, "The Troopers of Zamaris," in Applebaum, *Judaea in Hellenistic and Roman Times*, p. 50 (the only viable argument is the mention of an *epitropos* in Sanamein; all the rest is speculation).

14. See Maurice Sartre, "Les *metrokômiai* de Syrie du Sud," *Syria* 76 (1999): 197–222.

15. George of Cyprus, *Georgii Cyprii Descriptio orbis romani*, ed. Heinrich

Gelzer (Leipzig: B. G. Teubner, 1890) (hereafter cited as George of Cyprus). In *Géographie de la Palestine,* vol. 2 (Paris: Librairie Lecoffre, 1933–1938), pp. 184, 443, Félix-Marie Abel identifies the village of Deir es-Salt, in the Nuqrah, as the center of this domain. The name surely preserves the memory of a *saltus,* but I am not sure that the saltus of Batanaea extended that far. In any case, the village was within the Herodian realm.

16. Maurice Sartre, *IGLS,* vol. 14, *Adraha, le Jawlan oriental et la Batanée* (Beirut: Institut français d'archéologie du Proche-Orient, forthcoming), no. 565.

17. Sartre, *"Metrokômiai."* In support of my demonstration, I should have cited a passage from Josephus that I had missed. After Jerusalem was taken, Vespasian gave the order "to farm out all Jewish territory. For he founded no city there, reserving the country as his private property" (*BJ* 7.216–217); for Josephus, it is clear that the existence of a city was incompatible with the presence of an imperial domain.

18. *Le Talmud de Jérusalem,* trans. Moïse Schwab (Paris: Maisonneuve & Larose, 1977; originally published 1871–1890), *Shebiith* 6.1 (hereafter cited as *TJ*).

19. George of Cyprus, 1041.

20. Josephus, *AJ* 17.147 (without details); but in *AJ* 18.31, Josephus specifies that Salome bequeathed her territory to Livia Iamnia; it included Phasaelis and Archelais, where there were vast palm groves of very high quality.

21. Josephus, *AJ* 18.31.

22. Pliny, *Natural History,* trans. H. Rackham (Loeb Classical Library), 12.54 (hereafter cited as *NH*); Pliny points out that during the war the Jews sought to destroy the balsa plantations completely: "The Jews vented their wrath upon this plant as they also did upon their own lives, but the Romans protected it against them, and there have been pitched battles in defence of a shrub. It is now cultivated by the treasury authorities, and was never before more plentiful."

23. *Papyrus Yadin,* 16 (hereafter cited as *P. Yadin*), in *The Documents from the Bar Kokhba Period in the Cave of Letters,* vol. 1, *Greek Papyri,* ed. Naphtali Lewis (Jerusalem: Israel Exploration Society, 1989), p. 68: the *"moschantic* estate of our lord Caesar," whose name evokes calf-raising; see Hannah M. Cotton and Jonas C. Greenfield, "Babatha's Property and the Law of Succession in the Babatha Archive," *Zeitschrift für Papyrologie und Epigraphik* (hereafter cited as *ZPE*) 104 (1994): 211–218.

24. *P. Yadin* 11, in Lewis, *Documents,* p. 44; Naphtali Lewis, Ranon Katzoff, and Jonas C. Greenfield, "Papyrus Yadin 18," *Israel Exploration Journal* (hereafter cited as *IEJ*) 37 (1987): 229–250; on the Babatha archives, see also Glen W. Bowersock's inventory, "The Babatha Papyri, Masada and Rome," *Journal of Roman Archaeology* (hereafter cited as *JRA*) 4 (1991): 336–344, and Martin Goodman's inventory in his review of Lewis, *Documents,* and *Aramaic and Nabatean Signatures and Subscriptions,* ed. Yigael Yadin and Jonas C. Greenfield, *JRS* 81 (1991): 169–175. On the "imperial" village of En Geddi, see Safrai, *Economy of Roman Palestine,* p. 326. Safrai does not view the village as an imperial domain, properly speaking, but his description (p. 335) corresponds quite well to that of an imperial domain, where free tenants work lands that are the emperor's personal property.

25. Benjamin H. Isaac, "The Babatha Archive: A Review Article," *IEJ* 42 (1992): 70–71.

26. *P. Yadin* 2 (line 4), and 3 (line 5): Yigael Yadin, "The Expedition to the Judean Desert, 1960–1961: Expedition D—The Cave of Letters," *IEJ* 12 (1962): 240–241;

idem., "The Nabataean Kingdom, Provincia Arabia, Petra, and En Geddi in the Documents from Nahal Hever," *Ex Oriente Lux* 17 (1963): 231.

27. Hannah M. Cotton, "Land Tenure in the Documents from the Nabataean Kingdom and the Roman Province of Arabia," *ZPE* 119 (1997): 255–265.

28. See note 23 above.

29. *Papyrus de l'Euphrate* (hereafter cited as *P.Euphr.*), lines 4–5, in Denis Feissel and Jean Gascou, "Documents d'archives romains inédits du Moyen-Euphrate (IIIe s. apr. J.-C.)," *Journal des Savants* (1995): 71.

30. Rey-Coquais, "Inscription du Liban-Nord," especially pp. 101–104.

31. Theodoretos, Bishop of Cyrrhos, *Correspondance,* ed. and trans. Yvan Azéma (Paris: Le Cerf, 1982–), 42. I note that Cyrrhos has supplied the only inscription from northern Syria in which there may be a reference to a *metrokome:* see Sartre, "*Metrokômiai,*" p. 203.

32. When the provincial boundaries were modified, beginning under Diocletian, the former Syria-Palestine was split in two (First Palestine and Second Palestine), while the southern part of the former Arabia, first attached to Syria-Palestine, became Third Palestine. Because these transformations took place beyond the chronological limits I have adopted, I can only mention them in passing here.

33. George of Cyprus, 1056–1057; it is pointed out without an epithet, right after Elusa, by Hierocles, in *Synekdèmos d'Hiérocles et l'opuscule géographique de Georges de Chypre,* ed. Ernest Honigmann (Brussels: Éditions de l'Institut de philologie et d'histoire orientales et slaves, 1939), 721.11; we have no way to localize this saltus in Arabia Petraea rather than in Idumenaea, despite Abel's claim in *Géographie,* vol. 2, p. 443, that it was located near Shaubak, north of Petra—a claim made solely on the basis of a similarity in meaning with Khirbet al-Meqdes. On the relation between metrokomia and saltus, see Sartre, "*Metrokômiai,*" especially pp. 219–222, and above. Even if, for the time being, epigraphic mentions of metrokomiai have been found only in the Hauran, there is clearly no reason for Rome not to have adopted this type of organization in other regions of the Syrian provinces.

34. George of Cyprus, 1027; it was also mentioned by Theodoretos, bishop of Cyrrhos, in "II Paralipomena," 14.13 (in *Patrologiae cursus completus: Series graeca,* ed. Jacques-Paul Migne et al. [Paris: Garnier Frères, 1857–1905], vol. 80, cols. 527–858); Abel has situated it in Gerara, the seat of a bishopric (*Géographie,* vol. 2, p. 443); its bishop is mentioned in *AE* (1996), no. 1566; cf. Yoram Tsafrir, Leah Di Segni, and Judith Green, *Tabula Imperii Romani: Iudaea-Palaestina. Eretz Israel in the Hellenistic, Roman and Byzantine Periods: Maps and Gazetteer* (Jerusalem: Israel Academy of Sciences and Humanities, 1994), pp. 132–133, 220. George of Cyprus refers (1026) to a Salton Konstantianike, which necessarily refers to a later period than the one that concerns us: see Tsafrir et al., *Tabula,* p. 220. On other imperial domains attested late in northern Syria, see Georges Tchalenko, *Villages antiques de la Syrie du Nord: Le massif Bélus à l'époque romaine* (Paris: P. Geuthner, 1953–1958), vol. 1, p. 393.

35. George of Cyprus, 981: *Gouasi tois Salton.*

36. George of Cyprus, 994: *Salton Gonaitikon.* We can juxtapose this reference to that of Stephanus of Byzantium, "Gouna," in *Ethnica,* ed. August Meineke (Graz: Akademische Druck und Verlagsanstalt, 1958): "establishment of Syria on fertile soil rich in fruits, hence its name, because of the seed (*gonimon*); the ethnic name is

Gounaites." The specification that the land is deep and fertile is not a casual observation. It appears again in Justinian, "Codex Iustinianus," in *Corpus iuris civilis*, vol. 2 (Berlin: Weidmann, 1954), 11.69.2: "possessiones Gonatici saltus . . . ," in a constitution from Zeno to Sebastianus, prefect of the court. Let us note that in Louis Jalabert and René Mouterde, *IGLS*, vol. 4, *Laodicée, Apamène: Chronologie des inscriptions dates des tomes I–IV* (Paris: P. Geuthner, 1955), a text addressed to a procurator comes from the Emesa region (no. 1998).

37. George of Cyprus, 1016–1019: Regeon Apathous, Iericho, Libias, Gadara. We should note that to the northwest of Philadelphia there is a village called Salt, which is the former Gadora (Abel, *Géographie,* vol. 2, p. 167). We may wonder whether the Gadara mentioned by George of Cyprus should not rather be Gadora; we know that the confusion between *a* and *o* is frequent in Syria (cf. Canatha-Canotha); but if we decide not to correct George of Cyprus, we observe that Salt is located not far from Livias.

38. George of Cyprus, 990 and 993: *klima Iabroudon, klima Magloudon.*

39. Ibid., 996; cf. Martin Hartmann, "Beiträge zur Kenntniss der Syrischen Steppe," *Zeitschrift des deutschen Palästina-Vereins* (hereafter cited as *ZDPV*) 22 (1899): 159.

40. Dorothy J. Crawford, "Imperial Estates," in *Studies in Roman Property,* ed. M. I. Finley (Cambridge: Cambridge University Press, 1976).

41. Safrai, *Economy of Roman Palestine,* p. 324; Safrai observes that, as far as we know, almost no veterans settled in Judaea, Samaria, or Galilee.

42. Jean-Paul Rey-Coquais, *IGLS,* vol. 7, *Arados et régions voisines* (Paris: P. Geuthner, 1970), no. 4028.

43. In *Villages antiques,* p. 398, Tchalenko offers Khirbet Sheikh Barakat and Kafr Nabu as examples, perhaps also Baqir and Brad. The only example of which we can be certain is the village near the sanctuary of Zeus Baitokaike; the texts state explicitly that it belonged to the god: Rey-Coquais, *IGLS,* vol. 7, no. 4028.

44. George Tate, *Les campagnes de la Syrie du Nord du IIe au VIIe siècle: Un exemple d'expansion démographique et économique à la fin de l'antiquité* (Paris: P. Geuthner, 1992), pp. 287–289; Pierre-Louis Gatier does not believe, either, that the villages were controlled by the temples ("Villages et sanctuaires en Antiochène autour de Qalaat Kalota," *Topoi* 7 [1997]: 751–775, especially p. 768).

45. We may doubt that this treasury consisted only of the offerings of the faithful; a "treasury of the god" is mentioned in the Hauran. See Maurice Sartre, "Communautés villageoises et structures sociales d'après l'épigraphie de la Syrie du Sud," in *L'Epigrafia del villagio,* ed. Alda Calbi, Angela Donati, Giancarlo Susini, and Gabriella Poma (Faenza: Fratelli Lego, 1993), p. 127 (with the references). In Palestine, it is doubtful that this situation was unknown in the urban centers whose dominant population was pagan, yet Safrai, in *Economy of Roman Palestine,* does not even raise the issue.

46. Thomas Weber, "Karawanengötter in der Dekapolis," *Damaszener Mitteilungen* 8 (1995): 210, n. 29, and pl. 29 b = Annie Sartre-Fauriat and Maurice Sartre, *IGLS,* vol. 15, *Le plateau du Trachôn* (Beirut: Institut français d'archéologie du Proche-Orient, forthcoming), no. 40, at Sahr du Lej.

47. Maurice Dunand, *Mission archéologique au Djebel Druze: Le Musée de Soueida* (Paris: P. Geuthner, 1934), pp. 73–74, no. 158 = Maurice Sartre, *IGLS,* vol. 16, *Le Djebel al-Œ̓Arab* (Paris: Institut français d'archéologie du Proche-Orient, forthcoming). no. 279.

48. Michel Dodinet, Jacques Leblanc, Jean-Pierre Vallat, and François Villeneuve, "Le paysage antique en Syrie: L'exemple de Damas," *Syria* 67 (1990): 339–355.

49. Ibid., pp. 339–347.

50. W. J. van Liere, "*Ager centuriatus* of the Roman Colonia of Emesa (Homs)," *Annales archéologiques de Syrie* (hereafter cited as *AAS*) 8–9 (1958–1959): 55–58, corrected by Dodinet et al., "Paysage antique," p. 348.

51. Maurice Sartre, *L'Asie Mineure et l'Anatolie d'Alexandre à Dioclétien* (Paris: A. Colin, 1995), pp. 211–212.

52. Jacques Leblanc and Grégoire Poccardi, "Étude de la permanence de tracés urbains et ruraux antiques à Antioche sur l'Oronte," *Syria* 76 (1999): 91–110.

53. Michel Dodinet, Jacques Leblanc, and Jean-Pierre Vallat, "Étude morphologique de paysages antiques de Syrie," in *Structures rurales et sociétés antiques,* ed. Panagiotis N. Doukellis and Lina G. Mendoni (Paris: Les Belles Lettres, 1994), pp. 425–427; the square network, seven hundred meters on a side, extended from nahr al-Kandil in the north to nahr Snuber in the south.

54. See Jacques Leblanc and Jean-Pierre Vallat, "L'organisation de l'espace antique dans la zone de Suweïda et de Qanawat (Syrie du Sud)," in *La dynamique des paysages protohistoriques, antiques, médiévaux et modernes: Actes des XVIIe Rencontres internationales d'archéologie et d'histoire d'Antibes, 19–21 octobre 1996,* ed. Joëlle Burnouf, Jean-Paul Bravard, and Gérard Chouquer (Sophia Antipolis: Association pour la publication et la diffusion des connaissances archéologiques, 1997), pp. 35–67.

55. Dodinet et al., "Étude morphologique," pp. 427–442. Another Roman land division has been identified in the northern sector, organized along the axes of the Roman camp. By contrast, the zones located to the west and southwest of the city have retained a cadastre on the Hellenistic model of 99 by 149 meters.

56. François Villeneuve, "L'économie rurale et la vie des campagnes dans le Hauran antique (Ier siècle av. J.-C.–VIIe siècle ap. J.-C): Une approche," in *Hauran: Recherches archéologiques sur la Syrie du sud à l'époque hellénistique et romaine,* ed. Jean-Marie Dentzer, vol. 1 (Paris: P. Geuthner, 1985), p. 137; David L. Kennedy, "Aerial Photography: Ancient Settlements in Syria," *Popular Archaeology* (September 1985): 42–44.

57. David L. Kennedy, Henry Innes MacAdam, and Derrick n. Riley, "Preliminary Report on the Southern Hauran Survey, 1985," *Annual of the Department of Antiquities of Jordan* (hereafter cited as *ADAJ*) 30 (1986): 151–153; David L. Kennedy cited in Bert de Vries and Pierre Bikai, "Archaeology in Jordan," *American Journal of Archaeology* 97 (1993): 495–496.

58. David L. Kennedy and Derrick Riley, *Rome's Desert Frontier: From the Air* (Austin: University of Texas Press, 1990), pp. 205–207.

59. Tchalenko, *Villages antiques;* Tate, *Campagnes.*

60. Jean-Marie Dentzer and François Villeneuve, "Les villages de la Syrie romaine dans une tradition d'urbanisme oriental," in *De l'Indus aux Balkans: Recueil Jean Deshayes,* ed. Jean-Louis Huot, Marguerite Yon, and Yves Calvet (Paris: Recherche sur les civilisations, 1985), pp. 213–248; Dentzer, *Hauran,* vol. 1.

61. Tate, *Campagnes,* pp. 290–295.

62. Ibid., p. 294.

63. However, see the reservations expressed by Panagiotis N. Doukellis, in *Libanios et la terre: Discours et idéologie politique* (Paris: Institut français d'archéologie du Proche-Orient, 1995), p. 98.

64. Tate, *Campagnes*, pp. 297–298.

65. Ibid., pp. 298–299.

66. See Gatier, "Villages et sanctuaires en Antiochène," pp. 761–762.

67. Noted by Jean-Marie Dentzer in *The Oxford Encyclopedia of Archaeology in the Near East*, ed. Eric M. Meyers (Oxford and New York: Oxford University Press, 1997), vol. 1, s.v. "Bosra," p. 352.

68. See Leblanc and Vallat, "Organisation de l'espace antique."

69. Sartre, "Communautés villageoises," pp. 118–119.

70. Annie Sartre-Fauriat, "Architecture funéraire de la Syrie," in *Archéologie et histoire de la Syrie*, ed. Jean-Marie Dentzer and Winfried Orthmann, vol. 2 (Sarrebrück: Saarbrücker Druckerei und Verlag, 1989), pp. 423–446, and especially Annie Sartre-Fauriat, *Des tombeaux et des morts*, vol. 2 (Beirut: Institut français d'archéologie du Proche-Orient, 2001), pp. 103–112.

71. Dentzer and Villeneuve, "Villages de la Syrie romaine," pp. 213–248.

72. Villeneuve, "Economie rurale"; see also idem, "Recherches sur les villages antiques du Haurâne, Ier s. av. J.-C.–VIIe s. ap. J.-C.: Le peuplement, les maisons rurales" (Ph.D. diss, Université de Paris I, 1983).

73. See Safrai, *Economy of Roman Palestine;* Safrai's work is based both on the Talmuds and on numerous archaeological publications; see also Adolf Büchler, *The Economic Conditions of Judaea after the Destruction of the Second Temple* (London and Oxford: Oxford University Press, 1912); Arye Ben-David, *Talmudische Ökonomie: Die Wirtschaft des jüdisches Palästina zur Zeit des Mischna und der Talmud* (Hildesheim and New York: G. Olms, 1974); A'haron Oppenheimer, *The 'Am ha-Aretz: A Study in the Social History of the Jewish People in the Hellenistic-Roman Period* (Leiden: E. J. Brill, 1977); Shimon Applebaum, "Economic Life in Palestine," in *The Jewish People in the First Century*, ed. Shemuel Safrai and Menahem Stern, vol. 2 (Assen: Van Gorcum, 1976), pp. 631–700, especially pp. 646–664, regarding agriculture. In contrast, one can scarcely rely on Daniel Sperber, *Roman Palestine 200–400: The Land; Crisis and Change in Agrarian Society as Reflected in Rabbinic Sources* (Ramat Gan: Bar Ilan University, 1978), for Sperber takes only rabbinic sources into account, and he starts with a preconceived notion of an agrarian crisis in the third century; despite the considerable interest of the Talmuds for a reconstitution of the Palestinian economy in the second, third, and fourth centuries, rabbinic sources give only a partial vision, insofar as their discussions always deal with situations involving Jews, whereas in entire sectors of Roman Palestine there were no longer any Jews, or practically none. Moreover, many of the situations described in the Talmuds are scholastic exercises, or belong to other periods, when it is not a matter of contrasting the "good old days" with the harsh realities of daily life.

74. There are allusions to large landowners in Luke 16.1–8, 17.7, 19.19; Mark 12.1–11; and Matthew 20.1–15.

75. *Midrash Lamentations, Rabba I*, cited by Shimon Applebaum in Safrai and Stern, eds., *Jewish People*, vol. 2, p. 659 (see also *Midrash Rabbah*, ed. H. Freedman and Maurice Simon, vol. 7, *Lamentations*, trans. A. Cohen [London and Bournemouth: Soncino Press, 1951]).

76. Applebaum, "Economic Life," p. 657.

77. Josephus, *The Life*, trans. Henry St. John Thackeray (Loeb Classical Library), 11.54. A correction to Batanaea has been suggested, as the place where they settled in Syria: see the documentation in Applebaum, "Troopers," p. 53. It could be the village

of al-Ahmadiyeh, about fifteen kilometers from Lake Houleh, where two ancient synagogues have been found; in Hebrew, Ecbatane is called Ahmata.

78. Sartre, "Communautés villageoises," pp. 133–135 = Sartre-Fauriat and Sartre, *IGLS*, vol. 15, forthcoming, no. 228. I note that the unusual wording of the Danaba inscription, "The Greeks (who live) in Danaba," has an exact counterpart in Josephus, *Life*, 11.54: "The Babylonian Jews [who live] in Ecbatana."

79. Michael Avi-Yonah, "Newly Discovered Latin and Greek Inscriptions," *Quarterly of the Department of Antiquities of Palestine* 12 (1946): 85, no. 2 = *AE* (1948), no. 142; this opinion has already been sketched out by Shimon Applebaum in *Judaea in Hellenistic and Roman Times*, p. 71.

80. Justus Meyer, "A Centurial Stone from Shavei Tziyyon," *Scripta classica israelica* 7 (1983–1984): 119.

81. The phenomenon has been thoroughly studied at Patras and Corinth: see Maurice Sartre, "Les colonies romaines dans le monde grec: Essai de synthèse," *Electrum* 5 (2001): 111–152, especially pp. 132–134 and the bibliography.

82. *TJ, Yebamot* 8.8d.

83. See, for example, Matthew 20.3–7.

84. On all this, see Alon, *Jews in Their Land*, pp. 157–160. The term *'ikkar* seems less precise in legal terms; it must have been used to designate workers close to the owner, but their legal status is not specified.

85. Javier Teixidor, "Un document syriaque de fermage de 242 apr. J.-C.," *Semitica* 41–42 (1991–1992): 195–208.

86. See the presentation by Paul Sanlaville, "Milieu naturel et irrigation en Syrie," in *Techniques et pratiques hydro-agricoles traditionnelles en domaine irrigué: Approche multidisciplinaire des modes de culture avant la motorisation en Syrie; Actes du Colloque de Damas 27 juin–1er juillet 1987*, ed. Bernard Geyer (Paris: P. Geuthner, 1990), pp. 3–21, with good maps indicating rainfall.

87. See Frank Braemer's observations in "Formes d'irrigation dans le Hawran (Syrie du Sud)," in Geyer, *Techniques et pratiques hydro-agricoles*, pp. 453–474, especially p. 465. Geyer believes that it is almost impossible to go back before the nineteenth century, except for a very few occasions in the sixteen century when tax documents are available, but he acknowledged that certain arrangements may be much older. See also Yves Calvet and Bernard Geyer, *Barrages antiques de Syrie* (Lyon: Maison de l'Orient, 1992).

88. Maurice Sartre, *Bostra: Des origines à l'Islam* (Paris: P. Geuthner, 1982), p. 96.

89. In "The Origins and Design of Nabataean Water-Supply Systems," *Studies in the History and Archaeology of Jordan* 5 (1995): 714, John Peter Oleson estimates its output at 500 cubic meters per day, in comparison with the 187,600 cubic meters of Rome's *aqua Marcia*.

90. Braemer, "Formes d'irrigation."

91. Dar and Applebaum, *Landscape and Pattern*, vol. 1, pp. 200–202.

92. On the technology, see John Peter Oleson, *Greek and Roman Mechanical Water-Lifting Devices: The History of a Technology* (Toronto: University of Toronto Press, 1984). Oleson's book is complemented by a collection of texts: John William Humphrey, John Peter Oleson, and Andrew N. Sherwood, *Greek and Roman Technology: A Sourcebook* (London and New York: Routledge, 1998).

93. In *Channels and a Royal Estate from the Hellenistic Period in the Western Plains of Jericho* (Brunswick: Leichweiss-Institut für Wasserbau der Technischen

Universität Braunschweig, 1984), no. 82, Ehud Netzer offers a very thorough study of the water system in Jericho: most of the work was completed during the Hasmonaean period, between 130 and 100 C.E.

94. See Iwao Kobori, "Les *qanât* en Syrie," in Geyer, *Techniques et pratiques hydro-agricoles,* pp. 321–328.

95. Michael Even-Ari, Leslie Shanan, and Naphtali Tadmor, *The Negev: The Challenge of a Desert,* 2nd ed. (Cambridge, Mass.: Harvard University Press, 1982).

96. According to Uranius, in Félix Jacoby, *Die Fragmente der griechischen Historiker* (Leiden: E. J. Brill, 1958), vol. 3C, fragment 2.

97. Oleson, "Origin and Design."

98. This situation was observed in 1999, when there was virtually no precipitation during the entire winter of 1998–1999; in the spring of 1999, entire regions were left essentially uncultivated, as in the Hauran, where the land was not even plowed except where it was possible to irrigate.

99. *The Babylonian Talmud,* ed. Isodore Epstein (London: Soncino, 1935–1952), *Bava Mezia,* 107a.

100. Jean-Pierre Rey-Coquais, "Lucius Iulius Agrippa et Apamée," *Annales archéologiques arabes syriennes* 23 (1973): 39–84.

101. Safrai, *Economy of Roman Palestine,* p. 108.

102. This is particularly the case in Samaria, in a region where speculative crops are highly developed. See Dar and Applebaum, *Landscape and Pattern,* vol. 1, p. 247, concerning the Qarawat Bene Hassan sector; on cereal crops in Samaria, see ibid., pp. 191–198.

103. Safrai, *Economy of Roman Palestine,* pp. 112–113.

104. There is an allusion in *The Tosefta,* ed. and trans. Jacob Neusner (New York: Ktav, 1977–1986), Division 1, *Zeraim* (The Order of Agriculture), *Makhshirin,* 3.4.

105. Safrai, *Economy of Roman Palestine,* p. 114.

106. Sperber, *Roman Palestine,* pp. 11–44; the whole book, relying exclusively on rabbinic texts, strikes me as open to question; it is based on an a priori assumption drawn from Arthur H. M. Jones, who is cited on the very first page—namely, that the Roman Empire underwent an agrarian crisis during the third century. One cannot maintain, as Sperber does (pp. 48–49), that Palestine was subjected to direct military engagements in the third century, or that it suffered the consequences of its "proximity" to the Romano-Persian battlefield; this is to see the events through the wrong end of a telescope.

107. See Annie Sartre-Fauriat, "Les notables et leur rôle dans l'urbanisme du Hauran à l'époque romaine," in *Construction, représentation, et représentation des patriciats urbains,* ed. Claude Petitfrère (Tours: Université François-Rabelais, Centre d'histoire de la ville moderne et contemporaine, 1999), pp. 223–240.

108. Josephus, *AJ* 15.299–316.

109. Josephus, *AJ* 15.311: Herod supplied the inhabitants of Syria with seed.

110. Josephus, *AJ* 20.51: she also arranged to have an entire boatload of figs purchased in Cyprus.

111. It is probable that the oases in Arabia bought at least part of their cereal supplies in Syria; this is attested for Medina and Mecca at the end of the sixth century.

112. Safrai, *Economy of Roman Palestine,* pp. 117–118.

113. Pliny mentions the olives of the Syrian Decapolis: while "extremely small,"

"not larger than a caper," they "nevertheless have an attractive flesh" (*NH* 15.4); but it is unreasonable to conclude that they were imported to Rome, as Safrai does (*Economy of Roman Palestine*, pp. 121–122).

114. François Villeneuve, "The Pottery of the Oil-Factory at Khirbet edh-Dharih (2nd Century A.D.): A Contribution to the Study of the Material Culture of the Nabataeans," *Aram* 2 (1990): 367–384.

115. Tchalenko, *Villages antiques*, vol. 1, pp. 40–42.

116. Josephus gives different figures in *BJ* 2.591–592 (he bought several amphorae for a Tyrian coin worth four Attic drachms and sold the half-amphora for the same price) and in *Life* 74–76 (he bought eighty measures for four drachms and sold two measures for one drachm). The purchase of oil from Gischala by Jews from Laodicea in Syria is also mentioned in Tardan-Masquelier, *Sifre*, 33.24. However, the prohibition appears neither very old nor unanimously respected; moreover, it was abolished by rabbi Juda I: see Martin Goodman, "Kosher Olive Oil in Antiquity," in *A Tribute to Geza Vermes: Essays on Jewish and Christian Literature and History*, ed. Philip R. Davies and R. T. White (Sheffield, U.K.: Sheffield Academic Press, 1990), pp. 227–245.

117. Safrai, *Roman Palestine*, pp. 118–126.

118. *Leges saeculares* 121, in Salvatore Riccobono et al., eds., *Fontes iuris romani anteiustinianni*, 2nd ed., vol. 2 (Florence: G. Barbèra, 1941), p. 795.

119. Safrai, *Roman Palestine*, p. 131.

120. Dar and Applebaum, *Landscape and Pattern*, vol. 1, p. 247; on wine in general in this region, see pp. 147–164.

121. Alon, *Jews in Their Land*, p. 164.

122. In a small valley in the Anti-Lebanon, northwest of Damascus, modern Halbun, which has kept the old name; see René Dussaud, *Topographie de la Syrie antique et médiévale* (Paris: P. Geuthner, 1927), pp. 285–286. Dussaud notes that there had already been vineyards there for a long time: in Ezechiel 28.18, there is a reference to wine from Chalybon sent from Damascus to Tyre. Strabo points out that the Achaeminid kings drank wine from Chalybon in Syria (*The Geography*, trans. Horace Leonard Jones [Loeb Classical Library], 15.3.22). Ptolemy, in the mid-second century, gives the name *Chalybonitides* to a whole region of central Syria that encompasses Chalybon itself. Thus the Greek name may have replaced a local place name with the same meaning.

123. *Der Midrash Kohelet*, ed. J. Fürst and O. Straschun, trans. August Wünschel (Hildesheim: G. Olms, 1993), 9.9.

124. See the report on the excavations in Jacqueline Dentzer[-Feydy], Jean-Marie Dentzer, and Pierre-Marie Blanc, eds., *Hauran II: Les installations de Si' 8; Du sanctuaire à l'établissement viticole* (Beirut: Institut français d'archéologie du Proche-Orient, 2003).

125. Dan Urman, *The Golan: A Profile of a Region during the Roman and Byzantine Periods* (Oxford: British Archaeological Reports, 1985), p. 162.

126. Sartre, *Bostra*, p. 129; Patricia Crone points out the purchase of Syrian wine, without indicating its precise origin (*Meccan Trade and the Rise of Islam* [Oxford: Blackwell, 1987], p. 105). But Meccans frequented Bostra in particular (pp. 118–119).

127. Tchalenko, *Villages antiques*, pp. 73–74.

128. For the Hauran, see Villeneuve's preliminary publication, "Économie rurale"; for the Golan, see Urman, *Golan,* pp. 148–155, with photos of stables of the Hauranese type.

129. See Villeneuve, *Recherches.*

130. Claudine Dauphin, "Encore des Judéo-chrétiens au Golan?" in *Early Christianity in Context,* ed. Frédéric Manns and Eugenio Alliata (Jerusalem: Franciscan Printing Press, 1993), pp. 76–77.

131. Safrai, *Roman Palestine,* pp. 136–138.

132. But Pliny seems to find them of little interest except for medicinal purposes (*NH* 13.10).

133. Ibid., 13.10.

134. Strabo, 16.2.29; Pliny, *NH* 19.32.105.

135. Applebaum, "Economic Life in Palestine," p. 650.

136. This was probably the case for *comacum* (Pliny, *NH* 12.63.135), and probably also for Syrian nard (ibid., 12.26.45).

137. Ibid., 12.54.111–123.

138. Ibid., 12.55.124. Styrax is also mentioned in the Price Edict: see Marta Giacchero, *Edictum Diocletiani et Collegarum de pretiis rerum venalium* (Genoa: Istituto di Storia Antica e scienze ausiliarie, 1974), 34.12.

139. Pliny, *NH* 12.37.73–74.

140. Ibid., 12.46.100–102.

141. Ibid., 12.48.104.

142. Ibid., 12.51.109.

143. Ibid., 12.56.126.

144. Ibid., 13.13.

145. Ibid., 12.57.127.

146. Ibid., 12.59.129.

147. Ibid., 12.62.134.

148. Giacchero, *Edictum Diocletiani,* 34.14.

149. Mordechai Gichon, *En Boqeq: Ausgrabungen in einer Oase am Toten Meer; Geographie und Geschichte der Oase; Das spätrömische-byzantinische Kastell* (Mainz: Ph. von Zabern, 1993), chap. 2.

150. Safrai, *Economy of Roman Palestine,* p. 211; cf. the toponym Papyron or Calamon, at the mouth of the Jordan, where Aristobulos II defeated his brother Hyrcanos II and the Nabataeans.

151. See Shimon Applebaum, "The Roman Villa in Judaea: A Problem," in idem, *Judaea in Hellenistic and Roman Times,* pp. 124–131. The word *villa* seems to be used without distinction for any country house that was slightly more elaborate than a simple farmhouse.

152. Ibid., p. 125.

153. Shimon Dar, *ha-Tifroset ha-yishuvit shel ma'arav ha-Shomron bi-yeme ha-Bayit ha-sheni, ha-mishnah veha-Talmud, veha-tekufah ha-Bizantit* (The Settlement Pattern of Western Samaria in the Periods of the Second Temple, Mishnah, the Talmud and the Byzantine Period) (Tel Aviv: ha-Hevah la-haganat ha-teva', 1982), pp. 21–25 (in Hebrew), cited by Applebaum, "Roman Villa," p. 126, n. 13.

154. Zeev Yeivin and Gershon Edelstein, "Excavation at Tirat Yehuda," *Atiqot* 6 (1970): 56–69 (in Hebrew; *non vidi*).

155. Yizhar Hirschfeld and R. Birger-Calderon, "Early Roman and Byzantine Estates near Caesarea," *IEJ* 41 (1991): 81–111.

156. Yitzhak Magen, "Kalandia: A Vineyard Farm and Winery of the Second Temple Times," *Qadmoniot* 17 (1987): 61–71 (in Hebrew).

157. Applebaum, "Roman Villa," p. 127.

158. Ibid., p. 129.

159. Cf. the Samaritan village Samaritain of Qedunim: Yitzhak Magen, "Qedumin: A Samaritan Site of the Roman-Byzantine Period," in Manns and Alliata, *Early Christianity in Context*, pp. 167–179.

160. Yohanon Aharoni, *Excavations at Ramat Rahel, Season 1959–1960* (Rome: Università degli studi, Centro di studi semitici, 1962); idem, *Excavations at Ramat Rahel, Season 1961–1962* (Rome: Università degli studi, Centro di studi semitici, 1964); cf. Hans-Peter Kuhnen, *Palästina in griechisch-römischer Zeit* (Munich: C. H. Beck'she Verlagsbuchhandlung, 1990), pp. 170–172.

161. Gershon Edelstein, "What's a Roman Villa Doing outside Jerusalem?" *Biblical Archaeology Review* 16, no. 6 (1990): 32–42.

162. Louis-Hugues Vincent, "Une villa gréco-romaine à Beit Djebrin," *Revue biblique* (hereafter cited as *Rbi*) 31 (1922): 259–281.

163. Félix-Marie Abel, "Une villa romaine à Djifna," *Rbi* 32 (1923): 111–114.

164. Dar, *Landscape and Pattern*, vol. 1, pp. 24–26.

165. Jean-Pierre Sodini and Georges Tate, "Maisons d'époque romaine et byzantine (IIe–VIe siècles) du Massif Calcaire de Syrie du Nord: Étude typologique," in *Apamée de Syrie: Bilan des recherches archéologiques 1973–1979*, ed. Janine Balty (Brussels: Centre belge de recherches archéologiques à Apamée de Syrie, 1984): 377–429.

166. Tchalenko, *Villages antiques*, vol. 1, p. 10; Tchalenko actually refers to two models, but there appears to be hardly any difference between them.

167. Safrai, *Roman Palestine*, p. 87.

168. Tchalenko, *Villages antiques*, pp. 309–311.

169. See Safrai's inventories in *Roman Palestine*, pp. 86–96. Safrai makes little few distinctions by period; however, isolated farmhouses were particularly common in the Byzantine era.

170. Shimon Dar, "Qalat Bustra: A Temple and Farmhouse from the Roman Period in the Mount Hermon," *Eretz Israel* 23 (1992): 302–308 (in Hebrew) and p. 156* (in English).

171. Tchalenko, *Villages antiques*, vol. 1, p. 194.

172. On all this, see Villeneuve's essential work in *Recherches,* and his more succinct presentation in "Économie rurale." Dentzer also offers an approach to the subject in *Hauran*, vol. 1, pp. 64–136; for the Golan, there are some examples in Urman, *Golan*, pp. 148–155.

173. Listed in Sartre-Fauriat, "Notables," especially pp. 224–231.

174. Thus the evocative title of Bert de Vries's volume, *Umm el-Jimal: A Frontier Town and Its Landscape in Northern Jordan* (Portsmouth, R.I.: Journal of Roman Archaeology, 1998).

175. Dentzer and Villeneuve, "Villages de la Syrie romaine."

176. Tchalenko, *Villages antiques*, vol. 2, pl. 59; a village from the pagan era at least in part; see vol. 1, p. 189.

177. Ibid., vol. 2, pl. 60; a village from the second century, or even the first; see vol. 1, p. 195.

178. Safrai, *Roman Palestine*, p. 66 (with an erroneous reference: see Yeivin and Edelstein, "Excavation at Tirat Yehuda").

179. See De Vries, *Umm el Jimal.*

180. S. Thomas Parker, "The Defenses of the Roman and Byzantine Town," in de Vries, *Umm el-Jimal*, p. 145.

181. S. Thomas Parker, *Romans and Saracens: A History of the Arabian Frontier* (Philadelphia: American Schools of Oriental Research, 1986), pp. 30–32 (Qasr al-Hallabat), pp. 16–17 (Qasr al-Aseikhin).

182. Safrai, *Roman Palestine*, pp. 65–67.

183. Tchalenko, *Villages antiques*, vol. 1, p. 193.

184. Ibid., p. 194.

185. Dar, *Landscape and Pattern*, vol. 1, p. 47, and vol. 2, fig. 35.

186. George McLean Harper Jr., "Village Administration in the Roman Province of Syria," *Yale Classical Studies* 1 (1928): 105–168; Henry Innes Macadam, "Epigraphy and Village Life in Southern Syria during the Roman and Early Byzantine Periods," *Berytus* 31 (1983): 103–115; idem, "Some Aspects of Land Tenure and Social Development in the Roman Near East: Arabia, Phoenicia and Syria," in *Land Tenure and Social Transformation in the Middle East,* ed. Tarif Khalidi (Beirut: American University of Beirut, 1984), p. 45–62; Maurice Sartre, "Villes et villages du Hauran (Syrie) du Ier au IVe siècle," in *Sociétés urbaines, sociétés rurales dans l'Asie Mineure et la Syrie hellénistiques et romaines,* ed. Edmond Frézouls (Strasbourg: AECR, 1987), pp. 239–257. It should be noted that the title of Harper's article is quite misleading, implying that it deals with all of Syria whereas all the author's documentation comes from the Hauran.

187. See a brief inventory in Sartre, "Communautés villageoises"; there is a more complete listing in Steven Menno Moors, *De Decapolis: Steden en dorpen in de romeinse provincies Syria en Arabia* ('s-Gravenhage: S. M. Moors, 1992), but Moors does not do much to draw out the historical consequences.

188. Marc Griesheimer, cited in Feissel and Gascou, "Documents" (1995), p. 113: "the centurion assigned to the territories."

189. Feissel and Gascou, "Documents" (1995), p. 87 (*P.Euphr.*, 2, line 12: "the centurion assigned to the territory"); p. 108 (*P.Euphr.*, 5, lines 1–2: "the centurion responsible for maintaining order in Sphoracene").

190. Jean Gascou, "La pétition de Bostra (*P.Bostra* 1; 29 mai 260)," in *Lokale Autonomie und römische Ordnungsmacht in den kaiserzeitlichen Provinzen vom 1. bis 3. Jahrhundert,* ed. Werner Eck and Elisabeth Müller-Luckner (Munich: R. Oldenbourg, 1999). In Rabbathmoba, it was a cavalry prefect who certified the declarations made to the tax authorities by Babatha: *P.Yadin* 16.

191. For the time being, I am counting as Bostra's territory the lands that correspond to the jurisdiction of the bishop of Bostra in later periods; on this point, see Maurice Sartre, "Bostra," in *Reallexicon für Antike und Christentum* (Stuttgart: A. Hiersemann, 2002), cols. 98–149.

192. Jean Gascou, "Unités administratives locales et fonctionnaires romains: Les données des nouveaux papyrus du Moyen Euphrate et d'Arabie," in Eck and Müller-Luckner, *Lokale Autonomie,* p. 69; this is the Aianitis on Bostra's territory (Gascou, "La pétition de Bostra," pp. 71–73), the Zoarene on Petra's (*P.Yadin* 16, 37).

193. See Hannah Cotton, "Some Aspects of the Roman Administration of Judaea / Syria-Palestine," in Eck and Müller-Luckner, *Lokale Autonomie*, pp. 84–89.

194. Ibid., p. 90–91; Cotton cites Gascou, *Papyrus Bostra 1*, in the same volume.

195. Maurice Sartre, *L'Orient romain: Provinces et sociétés provinciales en Méditerranée orientale d'Auguste aux Sévères (31 avant J.-C.–235 après J.-C.* (Paris: Le Seuil, 1991), pp. 330–331, and idem, "L'Orient sémitique," in *Rome et l'intégration de l'Empire*, ed. Claude Lepelley, vol. 2 (Paris: Presses Universitaires de France, 1998), p. 404.

196. Sartre, "*Métrokômiai.*"

197. Cf. Jean-Paul Rey-Coquais, *IGLS*, vol. 6, *Baalbek et Beqa'* (Paris: P. Geuthner, 1967), no. 2986, completed in *Supplementum epigraphicum graecum*, vol. 37 (Alphen aan den Rijn: Sijthoff & Noordhoff, 1923–1998), no. 1445.

198. Wilhelm Dittenberger, *Orientis graeci inscriptiones selectae*, 2 vols. (Hildesheim and New York: G. Olms, 1903–1905), no. 611.

199. René Cagnat, Jean Toutain, Georges Lafaye, and Victor Henry, *Inscriptiones graecae ad res romanas pertinentes*, vol. 3 (Paris: E. Leroux, 1906), no. 1074 (hereafter cited as *IGR*), and William Henry Waddington, *Inscriptions grecques et latines de la Syrie* (Paris: Firmin-Didot, 1870), no. 2556 (hereafter cited as *I.Syrie*).

200. A village *strategos* in Ma'aret Betar, in the Jebel Riha: Jalabert and Mouterde, *IGLS*, vol. 4, no. 1533, highly doubtful.

201. A few of these sanctuaries still exist today; others have disappeared but are known through travelers' sketches: see, provisionally, Norman N. Lewis, Annie Sartre-Fauriat, and Maurice Sartre, "William-John Bankes: Travaux en Syrie d'un voyageur oublié," *Syria* 73 (1996): 57–95, while awaiting full publication of the Hauranese part by Annie Sartre-Fauriat, *Les voyages de William-John Bankes dans le Hauran* (Bordeaux: Ausonius; Beirut: Institut français du Proche-Orient, 2004); see also Gaiter, "Villages et sanctuaries."

202. Gatier, "Villages et sanctuaires"; Olivier Callot and Pierre-Louis Gatier, "Le réseau des sanctuaires en Syrie du Nord," *Topoi* 9 (1999): 665–688.

203. Martin Goodman, *State and Society in Roman Palestine A.D. 132–212* (Totowa, N.J.: Rowman and Allanheld, 1993), p. 121.

204. Ibid., pp. 124–125; Goodman sets up an explicit parallel that is not justified on all points (for example, what he says about the *metrokomiai*) but that has been verified for the most part.

205. *IGR*, vol. 3, no. 1155 = Sartre-Fauriat and Sartre, *IGLS*, vol. 15, forthcoming, no. 191.

206. See Goodman's description in *State and Society*.

207. Sartre, *Asie Mineure*, pp. 213–216.

208. Feissel and Gascou, "Documents" (1995), p. 106.

209. *P.Euphr.* 3–4, in Feissel and Gascou, "Documents" (1995), p. 106.

210. *Lucia Septimia Seuera Eleutheropolis* on coins and in Herbert Nesselhauf, *Corpus inscriptionum latinarum*, vol. 3 (Berlin: G. Reimer / W. de Gruyter, 1893–), no. 14155; the indigenous agglomeration of Bet Guvrin, formerly Betogabris, acquired city status and the name Eleutheropolis in 199–200 according to the era in use. See Tsafrir et al., *Tabula*, s.v. "Eleutheropolis."

211. Strabo, 16.1.27.

212. Benjamin H. Isaac, "Bandits in Judaea and Arabia," *Harvard Studies in Classical Philology* 88 (1984): 171–203; idem, *The Limits of Empire: The Roman Army in*

the East (Oxford and New York: Clarendon Press, 1990), pp. 60–62 (Lebanon), 62–66 (Arabia), 66–67 and 77–89 (Judaea).

213. David F. Graf, "Rome and the Saracens: Reassessing the Nomadic Menace," in *L'Arabie préislamique et son environnement historique et culturel: Actes du colloque de Strasbourg, 24–27 juin 1987,* ed. Toufic Fahd (Leiden: E. J. Brill, 1989), pp. 341–400; S. Thomas Parker, "Peasants, Pastoralists and *Pax Romana:* A Different View," *Bulletin of the American Schools of Oriental Research* (hereafter cited as *BASOR*) 265 (1987): 35–51.

214. E. B. Banning, "Peasants, Pastoralists and *Pax Romana:* Mutualism in the Southern Highlands of Jordan," *BASOR* 261 (1986): 25–50; idem, "De Bello Paceque: A Reply to Parker," *BASOR* 265 (1987): 52–54; Isaac, *Limits of Empire,* pp. 68–77; Michael C. A. Macdonald, "Nomads and the Hawran in the Late Hellenistic and Roman Periods: A Reassessment of the Epigraphic Evidence," *Syria* 70 (1993): 323–336.

215. Some groups may have gone fairly far toward the southwest, for Safaitic graffiti from the Jawf have been published: S. A. al-Theeb, "New Safaitic Inscriptions from the North of Saudi Arabia," *Arabian Archaeology and Epigraphy* (hereafter cited as *AAE*) 7 (1996): 32–37. On the Safa as such, a small volcanic sector southwest of Damascus with an area of about fifty-five by twenty-five kilometers, see Frank Braemer and Michael C. A. Macdonald, "al-Safa," in *Encyclopédie de l'Islam,* ed. C. E. Bosworth, E. van Donzel, W. P. Heinrichs, et al., 2nd ed. (Leiden: E. J. Brill, 1995), p. 781.

216. On this site, the center of a cult of the god Sin of Harran, linked to Edessa, see Han J. W. Drijvers, *Cults and Beliefs at Edessa* (Leiden: E. J. Brill, 1980). It goes without saying that we know nothing about the precise ethnic origin of these populations, which the ancient sources designate only as "Arabic" because they are nomadic; still, their group leaders call themselves *salita d-'Arab,* "chiefs of the Arabs."

217. We know of at least twenty or thirty of these: see Gerald L. Harding, "The Safaitic Tribes," *Al-Abhath* 22 (1969): 3–25. To these we need to add several more recent discoveries: see Macdonald, "Nomads and the Hawran," pp. 352–368. Macdonald adopts a hypercritical attitude that strikes me as excessive insofar as it concerns the possibility of identifying certain tribes known in Greek with their counterparts attested in Safaitic; I have no doubt but that the Aouidenoi of the Greek inscriptions are the same as the Uawidh of the texts from the desert.

218. The fundamental study remains Macdonald's "Nomads and the Hawran," which includes an inventory of sources and the prior biography. His devastating critique of all previous literature is based on several good arguments, but it goes too far at times.

219. Macdonald, "Nomads and the Hawran," pp. 306–310.

220. Ibid., p. 385, n. 487.

221. Macdonald contests this (ibid., pp. 315–316), given that no Safaitic inscriptions have been found in the so-called summering zones. This is partly true (although there are some inscriptions in Rushayde), but the reasons for writing that existed in the desert were not necessarily present during summer pasturing (see below on the "Safaites'" taste for writing).

222. Maurice Sartre, "Transhumance, économie et société de montagne en Syrie du Sud," Colloque de Pau 1990, in *La Montagne dans l'Antiquité,* ed. Georges Fabre

(Pau: Publications de l'Université de Pau, 1992), pp. 39–54. This text could be corrected on a number of points; it includes an excessive critique of Macdonald's "Nomads and the Hawran," pp. 346–352.

223. Bert de Vries shows that these are carefully written texts, not graffiti left by passing Bedouins ("Towards a History of Umm el-Jimal in Late Antiquity," in de Vries, *Umm el-Jimal*, p. 236).

224. On camels, see Hilde Gauthier-Pilters and Anne Innes Dagg, *The Camel: Its Evolution, Ecology, Behavior, and Relationship to Man* (Chicago: University of Chicago Press, 1981). The Romans had only a rough idea of this animal; they did not make much of a distinction between camels and dromedaries: *cameli quos appellant dromadas* (Livy, *Works*, vol. 11, trans. Evan T. Sage [Loeb Classical Library], 38.40.10). On coins of the Trajan era, the engraver represented a camel with two humps (today known as the Bactrian camel); some have read this as a political program, a sign of the ambition to conquer the Parthian Empire. See Kevin Butcher, "Bactrian Camels in Roman Arabia," *Berytus* 42 (1995–1996): 113–116; Butcher showed (based on an analysis of the metals) that these coins were struck in Rome and sent to Arabia. For the image of the camel, the coins' designers were simply inspired by what they had been able to see in the west (Vindonissa, Vienne [now Vienna], Soissons), where it was known that some two-humped camels existed, without worrying about whether the animal differed from the Arabian camel (or, more precisely, the Arabian dromedary).

225. These fertile depressions must not be confused with the sterile *qi'an* (sing. *qa'*) where water sometimes stagnates: see Braemer and Macdonald, "al-Safa," p. 757.

226. Macdonald, "Nomads and the Hawran," p. 318.

227. Maurice Sartre, *Trois études sur l'Arabie romaine et byzantine* (Brussels: Revue d'études latines, 1982), pp. 122–124; Macdonald, "Nomads and the Hawran," p. 368–377.

228. Most of the inscriptions can be found in *I.Syrie*, nos. 2264–2285 = Sartre, *IGLS*, vol. 16, forthcoming, nos. 1385–1414 (along with those of Littmann and Dussaud).

229. Michael C. A. Macdonald, "Herodian Echoes in the Syrian Desert," in *Trade, Contact and the Movement of Peoples in the Eastern Mediterranean: Studies in Honour of J. Basil Hennesssy*, ed. John Basil Hennessy, Stephen Bourke, and Jean-Paul Descoeudres (Sydney: Mediterranean Archaeology, 1995), pp. 285–290 (quotes from pp. 286, 288, 289).

230. Macdonald, "Nomads and the Hawran," p. 353; the toponym is unknown.

231. V. A. Clark, "The Desert Survey," in *The Roman Frontier in Central Jordan*, ed. S. Thomas Parker (Oxford: British Archaeological Reports, 1987), pp. 107–163.

232. Macdonald, "Nomads and the Hawran," pp. 382–388.

233. Beyond the historical allusions mentioned above, there are a small number of references to Rome: Macdonald, "Nomads and the Hawran," pp. 331–332; an allusion to a "year in which the Persians fought the Romans at Bostra": Academie des inscriptions et belles-lettres, *Corpus inscriptionum semiticarum* (Paris: e Reipublicae Typographeo, 1881), vol. 5, no. 4448; to conflicts with Haterius Nepos: Sabri Abbadi and Fawzi Zayadine, "Nepos the Governor of the Provincia Arabia in a Safaitic Inscription?" *Semitica* 46 (1996): 155–164.

234. David F. Graf sees them clearly in the empire ("Rome and the Saracens: Reas-

sessing the Nomadic Menace," in Fahd, *L'Arabie préislamique*); contra: Macdonald, "Nomads and the Hawran," p. 346. In reality, the Romans probably viewed them as subjects of the empire (thus the titles conferred on some of their leaders), but they themselves must have been by and large quite indifferent to what happened there.

235. Raphaël Savignac, "Le sanctuaire d'Allat à Iram," *Rbi* 42 (1933): 405–422; Raphaël Savignac and George Horsfield, "Chronique: Le Temple de Ramm," *Rbi* 44 (1935): 245–278; Sartre, *Trois études*, p. 129; Laurent Tholbecq, "The Nabataeo-Roman Site of Wadi Ramm *(Iram)*: A New Appraisal," *ADAJ* 42 (1998): 241–254. Tholbecq located the site of a large dwelling where the local authority—whoever it was—may well have lived.

236. Joëlle Beaucamp, "Rawwafa," *Dictionnaire de la Bible*, suppl. 9 (Paris: Letouzey & Ané, 1979), fasc. 53, cols. 1467–1475; Sartre, *Trois études*, p. 130.

237. A first publication by Jósef Tadeusz Milik, "Inscriptions grecques et nabatéennes de Rawwafah," is in Peter J. Parr, G. L. Harding, and J. E. Dayton, "Preliminary Survey in N. W. Arabia, 1968," *Bulletin of the Institute of Archaeology* 10 (1971): 54–58. Cf. Glen W. Bowersock, "The Greek-Nabataean Bilingual Inscription at Ruwwafa, Saudi Arabia," in *Le Monde Grec: Hommages à Claire Préaux*, ed. Jean Bingen and Guy Cambier (Brussels: Éditions de l'Université de Bruxelles, 1975), pp. 513–522; Bowersock offers a classic explanation that is found in most authors and that I myself have used up to now. In "Quelques réflexions sur les Saracènes, l'inscription de Rawwafa et l'armée romaine," in *Présence arabe dans le Croissant fertile avant l'Hégire*, ed. Hélène Lozachmeur (Paris: Recherche sur les civilisations, 1995), pp. 93–101, Michael C. A. Macdonald proposes a new interpretation that I find particularly interesting. Returning to the problem of the etymology of the term *Saracen*, and challenging in particular the etymology given by David F. Graf and M. P. O'Connor in "The Origin of the Term *Saracen* and the Rawwafa Inscriptions," *Byzantine Studies / Études Byzantines* 4 (1977): 52–66, he comes to the conclusion that the word, translated into Greek as *ethnos*, simply designates a military unit, as I had suggested in connection with the inscription *I.Syrie*, no. 2203, in *Trois études*, p. 124. The end of the text is difficult to interpret, but it seems to rule out the hypothesis of an intertribal war. In any case, Macdonald's hypothesis has the advantage of offering a convincing explanation for the presence of this sanctuary of the imperial cult in a very remote region of the province, where it would be quite surprising to find members of an indigenous tribe creating such a sanctuary. It is an entirely different matter if the builders are members of a military unit. We should note that the presence of the Equites Saraceni Thamudeni is attested two centuries later (Otto Seeck, ed., *Notitia dignitatum* [Berlin: Weidmann, 1876], *Oriens* 28.17), and also that of the Equites Thamudeni Illyriciani (idem, 34.22). David F. Graf has returned to the question in *"Foederati* on the Northern and Eastern Frontiers: A Comparative Analysis," *Studia Danubiana*, vol. 1, *The Roman Frontier at the Lower Danube, 4th–6th Centuries: The Second International Symposium* (Bucharest: S. C. Vavila Edinf, 1998), pp. 17–31; he maintains his own position on the etymology and develops the idea that the Thamudeans of Ruwwafa were a local militia comparable to those that existed elsewhere in the empire, rather than a well-constituted unit like a *numerus*. It becomes a matter of playing with words. On the etymology of *Saracen*, see also M. P. O'Connor, "The Etymology of *Saracen* in Aramaic and Pre-Islamic Contexts," in *The Defence of the Roman and Byzantine East: Proceedings of a Colloquium Held at the University of Sheffield in April, 1986*, ed. Philip Freeman and Da-

vid L. Kennedy (Oxford: British Archaeology Reports, 1986), pp. 603–632; see also Irfan Shahid, "Saracens," in *Encyclopédie de l'Islam*, 2nd ed.

238. Cf. two "Thamudean" inscriptions in Gerasa: E. A. Knauf, "Zwei thamudenische Inschriften aus der Gegend von Geras," *ZDPV* 97 (1981): 188–192.

239. See Fawzi Zayadine and Saba Farès-Drappeau, "Two North-Arabian Inscriptions from the Temple of Lat at Wadi Iram," *ADAJ* 42 (1998): 255–258. A recent dig has significantly altered our understanding of the sanctuary itself; see Tholbecq, "Nabataeo-Roman Site of Wadi Ramm."

240. Albert van den Branden has collected the documentation, in *Histoire de Thamoud* (Beirut: al-Jami ah al-Lubnaniyah, 1960), but his conclusions need to be thoroughly revised; for a recent study of the linguistic aspects, see Michael C. A. Macdonald, "Reflections on the Linguistic Map of Pre-Islamic Arabia," *AAE* 11 (2000): 28–79. The history of this tribe, or these groups of tribes, still remains to be written.

241. See, for example, the hundreds of inscriptions noted by Antonin Jaussen and Raphaël Savignac in *Mission en Arabie*, vol. 2 (Paris: E. Leroux, 1914), pp. 187–235, on the road between Ma'an and Hegra, between Hegra and Tayma, and so on. But we know from the example of the Nabataean inscriptions in Egypt that these texts can generally be attributed to caravan drivers.

242. Sartre, *Trois études*, p. 129.

243. Dennine Dudley and M. Barbara Reeves, "The Wadi Ramm Recovery Project: Preliminary Report of the 1996 Season," *Echos du monde classique / Classical Views* 41, no. 16 (1956): 81–106.

244. Jean-Marie Dentzer, "L'espace des tribus arabes à l'époque hellénistique et romaine: Nomadisme, sédentarisation, urbanisation," *Comptes rendus des séances de l'Académie des inscriptions et belles-lettres* (1999): 231–242.

245. Pliny, *NH* 12.33.

246. Besides an image that has been known for a long time at the Deir site, a large relief depicting four dromedaries led by their drivers was discovered during a recent cleaning of the procession of the Siq.

247. See René Dussaud, *Les Arabes en Syrie avant l'Islam* (Paris: E. Leroux, 1907), published in a revised version as *La pénétration des Arabes en Syrie avant l'Islam* (Paris: P. Geuthner, 1955).

248. See Daniel Schlumberger, Harald Ingholt, and Jean Starcky, *La Palmyrène du Nord-Ouest* (Paris: P. Geuthner, 1951).

249. Pointed out by Henri Seyrig, "Trois bas-reliefs religieux de type palmyrénien," *Syria* 13 (1932): 269–260; described by Jean Cantineau in "Tadmorea," *Syria* 14 (1933): 178–180.

250. See Jean Cantineau, ed., *Inventaire des inscriptions de Palmyre* (Beirut: Publications du Musée national syrien de Damas, 1930), vol. 3, no. 28 (the merchants avoided an expense of three hundred gold deniers) (hereafter cited as *Inv.*); ibid., vol. 10, no. 44 (the tribes honored Ogelos, "who helped them against the nomads by means of his numerous commandments *[strategia]*, who always provided security for the merchants and caravan drivers when he was leading caravans, and who spent large sums from his personal fortune to this end"); Christiane Dunant, *Le sanctuaire de Baalshamin à Palmyre*, vol. 3, *Les inscriptions* (Rome: n. p., 1971), pp. 56–59, no. 45, although money is not mentioned.

251. See Françoise Briquel-Chatonnet, "Les Arabes en Arabie du Nord et au

Proche-Orient avant l'Hégire," in "L'Arabie de Karib'îl à Mahomet: Nouvelles données sur l'histoire des Arabes grâce aux inscriptions," special issue, *Revue du monde musulman et de la Méditerranée* 61 (1991–1993): 37–43, especially pp. 42–43.

252. Pliny, *NH* 5.20.

253. Ibid., 5.21.

254. Ibid., 5.21.

255. Strabo, 16.1.27.

8. THE URBAN ECONOMY IN ROMAN SYRIA

1. Maurice Sartre, *D'Alexandre à Zénobie* (Paris: Fayard, 2001), pp. 231–240.

2. See Javier Teixidor, *Un port romain du désert: Palmyre et son commerce d'Auguste à Caracalla* (Paris: A. Maisonneuve, 1984), with its evocative title.

3. Shimon Applebaum, cited in Shemuel Safrai and Menahem Stern, *The Jewish People in the First Century: Historical Geography, Political History, Social, Cultural and Religious Life and Institutions,* vol. 2 (Assen: Van Gorcum, 1976), p. 676.

4. See Strabo, *The Geography,* trans. Horace Leonard Jones (Loeb Classical Library), 16.2.23 (hereafter cited as Strabo); M. Annaeus Lucan, *The Civil War,* trans. J. D. Duff (Loeb Classical Library), 3.217 (hereafter cited as Lucan); Pliny, *Natural History,* trans. H. Rackham (Loeb Classical Library), 5.17.76, 9.60–64 (hereafter cited as *NH*); Martial, *Epigrams,* trans. D. R. Shackleton Bailey (Loeb Classical Library), 2.29; Clement of Alexandria, *Christ the Educator,* ed. Joseph Deferrari, trans. Simon P. Wood (New York: Fathers of the Church, 1954), book 2, 10.115.1.

5. Procopios, *The Anecdota or Secret History,* vol. 6 of *Procopius,* trans. H. B. Dewing (Loeb Classical Library), 25.14–15.

6. In Cos, the *pachypara otus* was used; on silk in Gischala, see Ze'ev Safrai, *The Economy of Roman Palestine* (London and New York: Routledge, 1994), p. 162.

7. Lucan, 10.141.

8. Josephus, *De bello judaico (The Jewish War),* trans. Henry St. John Thackeray (Loeb Classical Library), 5.331 (hereafter cited as *BJ*). Josephus alludes to a wool merchants' quarter and to a clothing market in Jerusalem, but we cannot be sure that the items sold were locally produced; see Clement, *Christ the Educator,* book 2, 10.115.2.

9. *Byssos* (flax) from Elide was considered just as good as that of the Hebrews, even though it was not as yellow (Pausanias, *Description of Greece,* trans. W. H. S. Jones and H. Ormerod, vol. 2 [Loeb Classical Library], 5.5.2).

10. I am using the edition published by Marta Giacchero, *Edictum Diocletiani et collegarum de pretiis verum venalium* (Genoa: Istituto di Storia Antica e scienze ausiliarie, 1974); for flax products from Scythopolis, see 26, *passim.*

11. "Damascene" cloth is mentioned in the Price Edict (ibid., 26.244).

12. Safrai, *Economy,* p. 156.

13. Ibid., p. 158.

14. Ibid., pp. 158–161.

15. Charles Bradford Welles, "The Inscriptions," in *Gerasa, City of the Decapolis,* ed. Carl Hermann Kraeling (New Haven, Conn.: American Schools of Oriental Research, 1938), no. 190 (hereafter cited as *I.Gerasa*): "the sacred corporation *(techne)* of linen weavers *(linuphoi)*."

16. Moshe Schwabe, "Tiberias Revealed through Inscriptions," in *All the Land of Naphtali*, ed. Haim Zeev Hirschberg (Jerusalem: ha-Hevrah la-hakirat Erets-Yisra'el ve-'atikoteha, 1967), p. 181 (in Hebrew; *non vidi*).

17. *Supplementum epigraphicum graecum* (Alphen ann den Rijn: Sijthoff & Noordhof, 1960), vol. 17, no. 776 (third and fourth centuries) (hereafter cited as *SEG*).

18. Dio Chrysostom comes to the defense of the *linourgoi* (linenworkers) of Tarsos, who were a powerful force in the city even though they were kept at a distance from civic activities (*Dio Chrysostom*, trans. J. W. Cohoon, vol. 5 [Loeb Classical Library], 34.15–23).

19. Gedaliah Alon, *The Jews in Their Land in the Talmudic Age, 70–640 ce*, trans. Gershon Levi (Cambridge, Mass., and London: Harvard University Press, 1989), p. 170.

20. Safrai, *Economy*, pp. 192–196.

21. In "The Deified Claudius," in *Historia Augusta*, trans. David Magie, vol. 3 (Loeb Classical Library), handkerchiefs from Sarepta are mentioned (17.7), but in the context of a gift from Gallienus to Claudius; we may thus assume that these are very expensive handkerchiefs, dyed royal purple, and that Sarepta is where they were dyed, not woven.

22. Jean Rougé, ed., *Expositio totius mundi et gentium: Introduction, texte critique, traduction, notes et commentaire* (Paris: Le Cerf, 1966), 31.

23. *SEG*, vol. 8 (1937), no. 138a.

24. Safrai, *Economy*, p. 211.

25. Annemarie Stauffer, "Kleider, Kissen, bunte Tücher: Einheimische Textilproduktion und weltweiter Handel," in *Palmyra: Kulturbegegnung in Grenzbereich*, ed. Andreas Schmidt-Colinet (Mainz: Ph. von Zabern, 1995), pp. 57–71; Lothar von Falkenhausen, "Die Seiden mit chinesischen Inscriften," in *Die Textilien aus Palmyra: Neue und alte Funde*, ed. Andreas Schmidt-Colinet, Annemarie Stauffer, and Khaled al-As'ad (Mainz: Ph. von Zabern, 2000), p. 60, dated from the second half of the first century c.e.

26. Schmidt-Colinet makes this striking connection in *Palmyra*, pp. 46–50.

27. Stauffer, "Kleider, Kissen, bunte Tücher," p. 71; Schmidt-Colinet et al., *Textilien aus Palmyra*, pp. 145–146, no. 240.

28. Pointed out by Louis Robert, "Contribution à la topographe de villes de l'Asie Mineure méridionale," in *Comptes rendus des séances de l'Académie des inscriptions et belles-lettres* (1951): 255–256; published in full detail by Denis Feissel, "Deux listes de quartiers d'Antioche astreints au creusement d'un canal (73–74 après J.-C.)," *Syria* 62 (1985): 77–103 (whence *SEG*, vol. 35 [1985], no. 1483; *L'année épigraphique* [hereafter cited as *AE*] [1986], no. 694).

29. Pierre-Louis Gatier, "Nouvelles inscriptions de Gérasa," *Syria* 62 (1985): 308–310, no. 2 (= *SEG*, vol. 35 [1985], no. 1572): "the embers of the great Artemisian association *(systema)* of fullers."

30. *SEG*, vol. 8 (1937), no. 143, dating from the third or fourth century.

31. Louis Jalabert, René Mouterde, and Claude Mondésert, *Inscriptions grecques et latines de la Syrie* (hereafter cited as *IGLS*), vol. 5, *Emésène* (Paris: P. Geuthner, 1959), no. 2114, in 272–273 c.e.; the reconstitution of the inscription remains questionable.

32. Moshe Schwabe and Baruch Lifshitz, *Beth She'arim,* vol. 2, *The Greek Inscriptions* (New Brunswick: Rutgers University Press, 1974), no. 188 (= *SEG,* vol. 17, no. 777).

33. Maurice Sartre, *IGLS,* vol. 13.1, *Bostra* (Paris: P. Geuthner, 1982), nos. 9158–9160.

34. Henri Seyrig, "Les fils du roi Odainat," *Annales archéologiques de Syrie* (hereafter cited as *AAS*) 13 (1963): 161–162, 166–168.

35. Palmyra Tariff Law, in Teixidor, *Port romain,* lines 17–18, 21–26, and 29–31.

36. Ibid., lines 56 and 122 (for camel skins).

37. Giacchero, *Edictum* 8.1.5.

38. Cassius Dio (*Roman History,* trans. Earnest Carey [Loeb Classical Library] [hereafter cited as Dio]) relates that the Jews deliberately manufactured weapons of poor quality so that the orders would be rejected and the manufacturers could keep the weapons for themselves in the expectation of a new rebellion (69.12).

39. S. Thomas Parker, "The Roman 'Aqaba Project: The 1994 Campaign," *Annual of the Department of Antiquities of Jordan* (hereafter cited as *ADAJ*) 40 (1996): 253; idem, "The Roman 'Aqaba Project: The 1996 Campaign," *ADAJ* 42 (1998): 389.

40. See the catalog of an exhibition presented by Benno Rothenberg, *Timna, Tal des biblischen Kupfers: Ausgrabungen in Timna-Tal (Israel) 1964–1972 durch die Arabah-Expedition* (Bochum: Bergbau Museum, 1973). The exhibit focuses on mining in the pharaonic era, but it also mentions. Roman exploitation of the mines, and provides some illustrations (plates 64–69). See also idem, "Timna," in *The New Encyclopedia of Archaeological Excavations in the Holy Land,* ed. Ephraim Stern (Jerusalem: Israel Exploration Society / Carta; New York: Simon & Schuster, 1993); Andreas Hauptmann and Gerd Weisgerber, "Archaeometallurgical and Mining-Archaeological Investigations in the Area of Feinan, Wadi 'Arabah (Jordan)," *ADAJ* 31 (1987): 419–431; idem, "Periods of Ore Exploration and Metal Production in the Area of Feinan, Wadi 'Arabah, Jordan," *Studies in the History and Archaeology of Jordan* (hereafter cited as *SHAJ*) 4 (1992): 61–66.

41. René Mouterde, "Sarcophages de plomb trouvés en Syrie," *Syria* 10 (1929): 238–251; Maurice Chéhab, "Sarcophages en plomb du Musée National Libanais," *Syria* 15 (1934): 337–350 and *Syria* 16 (1935): 51–72; A.-M. Bertin, "Les sarcophages en plomb syriens du musée du Louvre," *Revue archéologique* (1974): 43–82.

42. E. Marianne Stern offers a very useful introduction and numerous illustrations in *Roman Mould-Blown Glass: The First through Sixth Centuries* (Rome: L'Erma / Toledo Museum of Art, 1995); on the famous signatures, especially that of Ennion of Sidon, see pp. 69–72. There are also fine illustrations in M. J. Klein, *Römische Glaskunst und Wandmalerei* (Mainz: Ph. von Zabern, 1999), although this text does not devote much space to chronology or places of origin.

43. *Vitrum iudaicum* is mentioned in the Price Edict: see Giacchero, *Edictum,* 16.1, 16.2, and 16.4.

44. Sartre, *D'Alexandre à Zénobie,* p. 255.

45. See Odile Dussart, *Le verre en Jordanie et en Syrie du Sud* (Beirut: Institut français d'archéologie du Proche-Orient, 1998), pp. 2, 190.

46. Strabo, 16.2.25; see also Pliny, *NH* 5.76, 36.190, and 36.193; Josephus, *BJ* 2.189–191; and Tacitus, *The Histories,* trans. Clifford H. Moore (Loeb Classical Library), 5.7.

47. Safrai, *Economy,* p. 203.

48. For the elements of the problem and a basic bibliography, see Maurice Sartre, *L'Asie Mineure et l'Anatolie d'Alexandre à Dioclétien* (Paris: A. Colin, 1995), pp. 297–298; for further information, see Catherine Abadie-Reynal, "Courants commerciaux et échanges dans le bassin égéen entre la fin du IIe s. av. J.-C. et le VIe s. apr. J.-C." (Mémoire d'habilitation, Université de Paris I, 1999), pp. 65–67. Most specialists have abandoned the hypotheses that have been formulated as to a production of this Eastern Sigillata A in Tarsos, Oboda of the Negev, or Cyprus. The conclusions presented by Jan Gunneweg, Isadore Perlman, and Joseph Yellin in *The Provenence, Typology and Chronology of Eastern Terra Sigillata* (Jerusalem: Institute of Archaeology, Hebrew University of Jerusalem, 1983) have been reexamined by J. Michael Elam, Michael D. Glascock, and Kathleen Warner Slane, "A Re-Examination of the Provenance of Eastern Sigillata A," in *Proceedings of the 26th International Archaeometry Symposium,* ed. R. M. Farquhar, R. G. V. Hancock, and L. A. Pavlish (Toronto: Archaeometry Laboratory, Dept. of Physics, University of Toronto, 1988), pp. 179–183, and by Kathleen Warner Slane, J. Michael Elam, Michael D. Glascock, and Hector Neff, "Compositional Analysis of Eastern Sigillata A and Related Wares from Tel Anafa (Israel)," *Journal of Archaeological Science* 21 (1994): 51–64. Let us recall in passing the ingenious suggestion of Avraham Negev (*The Late Hellenistic and Early Roman Pottery of Nabatean Oboda* [Jerusalem: Institute of Archaeology, Hebrew University of Jerusalem, 1986], p. xix), who accepted the conclusions drawn by Jan Gunneweg on the basis of physical and chemical analyses as to the Cypriot origin of sigillata A but also believes that Oboda must have been an important center of production nonetheless, thanks to the importation of Cypriot clays used as ballast in boats that came to take on products of Nabataean trade in Gaza and ports in southern Palestine.

49. Marcus Rautman, "Neutron Activation Analysis of Cypriot and Related Ceramics at the University of Missouri," in *Hellenistic and Roman Pottery in the Eastern Mediterranean: Advances in Scientific Studies; Acts of the II Nieborów Pottery Workshop,* ed. Henryk Meyza and Jolanta Mlynarczyk (Warsaw: Research Center for Mediterranean Archaeology, Polish Academy of Sciences, 1995), pp. 331–349; but the analyses were made on the basis of the discoveries at Tel Anafa alone, which may distort the conclusions. According to Gerwulf Schneider ("Roman Red and Black Slipped Pottery from NE-Syria and Jordan: First Results of Chemical Analysis," in Meyza and Mlynarczyk, *Hellenistic and Roman Pottery,* pp. 415–422), the workshops were situated a little north of Antioch, given the petrographic analysis of the clays, but they may have extended from Laodicea to Tarsos.

50. At Tel Anafa, a fairly small site, twenty-three thousand sherds have been found: see Kathleen Warner Slane, "The Fine Wares," in *Tel Anafa II,* part 1: *The Hellenistic and Roman Pottery,* ed. Sharon C. Herbert (Ann Arbor: Kelsey Museum of the University of Michigan, 1997), p. 265 (*Journal of Roman Archaeology* [hereafter cited as *JRA*], suppl. 10). At Panaya Ematoussa, southeast of Cyprus, sigillata A represent 60 percent of the sigillata, as opposed to 30 percent for Cypriot sigillata: see John Lund, "Trade Patterns in the Levant from ca. 100 BC to AD 200—as Reflected by the Distribution of Ceramic Fine Wares in Cyprus," *Münstersche Beiträge zur antiken Handelsgeschichte* 18 (1999): 6–7; at Akamas, on the other hand, Cypriot sigillata constitute 85 percent of the finds, as opposed to 12 percent for Eastern Sigillata A: ibid., p. 7.

51. Frank Braemer, "Une fabrique (locale?) de céramique fine à Jérash au tournant

de l'ère," in *Jerash Archaeological Project 1984–1988 II: Fouilles de Jérash,* ed. Fawzi Zayadine, vol. 2 (Paris: P. Geuthner, 1989), pp. 153–167.

52. Abadie-Reynal, "Courants commerciaux," p. 33.

53. Karl Schmitt-Korte, "Nabataean Pottery: A Typical and Chronological Framework," in *Studies in the History of Arabia,* vol. 2, *Pre-Islamic Arabia* (Riyadh: Jami'at al-Malik Sa'ud, 1984), pp. 7–40; idem, "Die bemalte nabatäische Keramik: Verbreitung, Typologie und Chronologie," in ibid., pp. 174–197; and idem, "Die Entwicklung des Granatapfel-Motivs in der nabatäischen Keramik," in *Petra und das Königreich der Nabatäer: Lebensraum, Geschichte und Kultur eines arabischen Volkes der Antike,* ed. Manfred Lindner, 3rd ed. (Munich: Delp, 1986), pp. 198–203; Avraham Negev, *The Nabatean Potter's Workshop at Oboda* (Bonn: R. Habelt, 1974).

54. Stephan G. Schmid, "Die Feinkeramik der Nabatäer im Spiegel ihrer kulturhistorischen Kontakte," in *Hellenistische und kaiserzeitliche Keramik des östilichen Mittelmeergebietes,* ed. Marlene Herfort-Koch, Ursula Mandel, and Ulrich Schädler (Frankfurt am Main: Arbeitskreis Frankfurt und die Antike, Archäologisches Institut der Johann Wolfgang Goethe-Universität, 1996), pp. 127–145. Schmid proposes a three-phase classification beginning at the end of the second century B.C.E. and ending at the beginning of the second century C.E., in which we witness a massive destruction of the workshops; however, fine Nabataean ceramics are found up to the fourth century (p. 129). Plates 26 and 27 give a good illustration of the evolution of the forms (which are more and more streamlined over time) and the ornamentation.

55. See Crystal-M. Bennett, "The Nabataeans in Petra," *Archaeology* 15 (1962): 239; Peter J. Parr, "A Sequence of Pottery from Petra," in *Near Eastern Archaeology in the Twentieth Century: Essays in Honor of Nelson Glueck,* ed. James A. Sanders (Garden City, N.Y.: Doubleday, 1970), pp. 348–381; Negev, *Nabatean Potter's Workshop;* Avraham Negev and Renée Sivan, "The Pottery of the Nabatean Necropolis at Mampsis," *Rei Cretariae Romanae Fautorum: Acta* 17–18 (1977): 109–131; Negev, *Late Hellenistic and Early Roman Pottery,* pp. xvii–xviii; Nabil I. Khairy, "The Painted Nabataean Pottery from the 1981 Petra Excavations," *Levant* 19 (1987): 167–181; Joseph Patrich, *The Formation of Nabatean Art: Prohibition of a Graven Image among the Nabateans* (Jerusalem: Magnes Press; Leiden: E. J. Brill, 1990), pp. 124–130.

56. On the potters' kilns in Petra, both in the center of the city and at its entrance at Wadi Musa, see Fawzi Zayadine, "The Pottery Kilns at Petra," in *Pottery and Potters: Past and Present,* ed. Denyse Homès-Frédéricq and H. J. Franken (Tübingen: Attempto, 1986), pp. 185–189; Khairieh 'Amr and Ahmed al-Momani, "The Discovery of Two Additional Pottery Kilns at az-Zurraba/Wadi Musa," *ADAJ* 43 (1999): 175–194 (kilns from the mid-second century C.E.).

57. Negev, *Nabatean Potter's Workshop;* idem, *Late Hellenistic and Early Roman Pottery,* p. xvii.

58. Isadore Perlman, Jan Gunneweg, and Joseph Yellin, "Pseudo-Nabataean Ware and Pottery of Jerusalem," *Bulletin of the American Schools of Oriental Research* 262 (1986): 77–82.

59. Howard Comfort, "Imported Western Terra Sigillata," in *Antioch-on-the-Orontes,* vol. 4, part 1: *Ceramics and Islamic Coins,* ed. Frederick Oswin Waagé

(Princeton: Department of Art and Archaeology of Princeton University, 1948), pp. 61–77.

60. Michel Vanderhoeven, *Les terres sigillées, 1966–1972* (Brussels: Centre belge de recherches archéologiques à Apamée de Syrie, 1989), pp. 111–113 (La Graufesenque) and p. 43 (Asia Minor).

61. Safrai, *Economy*, p. 208.

62. For Palestine, see Fanny Vitto, "Potters and Pottery Manufacture in Roman Palestine," *Bulletin of the Institute of Archaeology* 23 (1986): 47–64. Yvonne Gerber brings to light a Nabataean production of everyday pottery at Petra, in "Die Entwicklung der lokalen nabatäischen Grosskeramik aus Petra/Jordanien," in Herfort-Koch et al., *Hellenistische und kaiserzeitliche Keramik,* pp. 147–151; see also Yvonne Gerber, "The Nabataean Coarse Ware Pottery: A Sequence from the End of the Second Century BC to the Beginning of the Second Century AD," *SHAJ* 6 (1997): 407–411.

63. Stanislao Loffreda, *Cafarnao,* vol. 2, *La Ceramica* (Jerusalem: Franciscan Printing Press, 1974), p. 237.

64. *The Tosefta,* trans. Jacob Neusner, 6 vols. (New York: Ktav, 1977–1986), *Bava Mezi'a* 6.3.

65. David Adan-Bayewitz, *Common Pottery in Roman Galilee: A Study of Local Trade* (Ramat-Gan: Bar Ilan University Press, 1993), pp. 23–41.

66. Ibid., pp. 33–35.

67. Ibid., pp. 219–220.

68. Ibid., pp. 235–239.

69. Grzegorz Majcherek, "Gazan Amphorae: Typology Reconsidered," in Meyza and Mlynarczyk, *Hellenistic and Roman Pottery,* pp. 163–178.

70. Paul Reynolds, "Pottery Production and Economic Exchange in Second Century Beirut," *Berytus* 43 (1997–1998): 35–110, especially pp. 59–61.

71. See Séverine Lemaître, "Les importations d'amphores orientales dans la vallée du Rhône de l'époque d'Auguste à la fin du IIIe siècle apr. J.-C." (Ph.D. diss., Université de Lyon II, 1999).

72. Reynolds, "Pottery Production," p. 40 (Laodicea rather than Ras Bassit), pp. 41–42 (Palestine), p. 43 (Tyre).

73. Yitzhak Magen, "Jerusalem as a Center of the Stone Vessel Industry during the Second Temple Period," in *Ancient Jerusalem Revealed,* ed. Hillel Geva (Jerusalem: Israel Exploration Society, 1994), pp. 244–256.

74. For the Roman era in the Orient, see Onno M. van Nijf, *The Civic World of Professional Associations in the Roman East* (Amsterdam: J. C. Gieben, 1997); however, van Nijf neglects virtually all the Syrian documentation, except that which involves the fuller's earth in Antioch and inscriptions on the seats of the theater in Bostra.

75. Sartre, *IGLS,* vol. 13.1, nos. 9158–9160.

76. More specifically, makers of goatskin rafts are mentioned: see Seyrig, "Fils du roi Odainat," pp. 161–162, 166–168.

77. Ibid.

78. Sartre, *IGLS,* vol. 13.1, nos. 9161–9163.

79. Jean Cantineau, ed., *Inventaire des inscriptions de Palmyre,* vol. 3 (Beirut: Publications du Musée National Syrien de Damas), no. 17 (hereafter cited as *Inv*).

80. Sartre, *IGLS*, vol. 13.1, no. 9156.

81. Jean-Paul Rey-Coquais, *IGLS*, vol. 6, *Baalbek et Beqa'* (Paris: P. Geuthner, 1967), no. 2801.

82. Charles Clermont-Ganneau, *Études d'archéologie orientale*, vol. 1 (Paris: F. Vieweg, 1880), pp. 100–104: an inscription from 47 C.E. mentions the archonte of their brotherhood.

83. *SEG*, vol. 18 (1962), no. 599.

84. *I.Gerasa*, no. 190.

85. Ibid., no. 79.

86. *SEG*, vol. 35 (1985), no. 1572.

87. *I.Gerasa*, nos. 80–81; Welles sees them as notaries rather than merchants trading in the agora.

88. Christiane Dunant, *Le sanctuaire de Baalshamin à Palmyre*, vol. 3, *Les inscriptions* (Rome: n. p., 1971), pp. 66–67—at least if this is the way to interpret "to symposion ton ouannon."

89. Ibid., pp. 66–67: "hoi konetai."

90. Taha Batayneh, Wajih Karasneh, and Thomas Weber, "Two New Inscriptions from Umm Qeis," *ADAJ* 38 (1994): 379 (*SEG*, vol. 44 [1994], no. 1354): "syntechnia oikodomon."

91. See Feissel's dossier, "Deux listes," and van Nijf's commentary in *Civic World*, pp. 89–91.

92. Only in the second half of the fourth century: Libanios is the patron of his city's bakers: see Peter Robert Lamont Brown, *Power and Persuasion in Late Antiquity: Towards a Christian Empire* (Madison: University of Wisconsin Press, 1992), pp. 79–80.

93. *SEG*, vol. 7 (1937), no. 829.

94. See Annie Sartre-Fauriat, *Des tombeaux et des morts*, vol. 2 (Beirut: Institut français d'archéologie du Proche-Orient, 2001), pp. 86–88, 162; see also Marie-Christine Hellmann, "Les signatures d'architectes en langue grecque: Essai de mise au point," *Zeitschrift für Papyrologie und Epigraphik* (hereafter cited as *ZPE*) 104 (1994): 151–178.

95. Maurice Sartre, *IGLS*, vol. 16, *Le Djebel al-Œ Arab* (Beirut: Institut français d'archéologie du Proche-Orient, forthcoming), no. 1050, at Tahuleh.

96. This has already been pointed out by Andreas Schmidt-Colinet, "Nabatäische Felsarchitektur: Bemerkungen zum gegenwärtigen Forschungsstand," *Bonner Jahrbücher* 180 (1980): 189–230, and by Jean-Charles Balty, "Architecture et société à Pétra et à Hégra: Chronologie et classes sociales; Sculpteurs et commanditaires," in *Architecture et société de l'archaïsme grec à la fin de la République romaine* (Rome: École française de Rome; Paris: Centre national de la recherche scientifique, 1983), pp. 303–324, especially pp. 309–315. This study has been resumed and completed by Andreas Schmidt-Colinet, "A Nabataean Family of Sculptors at Hegra," *Berytus* 31 (1983): 95–102; Schmidt-Colinet shows that sixteen monumental tombs in the city can be attributed to five sculptors from the same family; they were probably born in Petra or at least worked there, which also explains the stylistic similarities.

97. Balty, "Architecture et société," pp. 305–306, 321.

98. See Kevin Butcher, "Coinage and Currency in Syria and Palestine to the Reign of Gallienus," in *Coin Finds and Coin Use in the Roman World*, ed. Cathy E. King and David G. Wigg (Berlin: Gebr. Mann Verlag, 1996), pp. 101–112.

99. Gold mines may have been located in the Wadi Afal, southwest of Aila: see Ahmed Kisnawski, Prentiss S. de Jesus, and Baseem Rihani, "Preliminary Report on the Mining Survey, North-West Hijaz, 1982," *Al-Atlal* 7 (1983): 81.

100. The publication of *Coinage in Roman Syria: Northern Syria 64 bc–ad 253*, an overview by Kevin Butcher, has been announced, but the work was unavailable while I was writing these pages (it is probably drawn from his "Coinage in Roman Syria 64 bc–ad 253" (Ph.D. diss., University College, London, 1991). The only systematic presentation available, quite dated now, is that of Waldemar Wruck, *Die syrische Provinzialprägung von Augustus bis Klaudius* (Stuttgart and Druck: W. Kohhammer, 1931); this study has to be corrected by the pages Kenneth W. Harl devotes to Syria in *Coinage in the Roman Economy 300 bc to ad 700* (Baltimore: Johns Hopkins University Press, 1996).

101. The striking of gold and silver is explicitly mentioned in Tacitus, *Histories*, 2.82.

102. See Michel Amandry, "La politique monétaire des Flaviens en Syrie de 69 à 73," in *Les monnayages syriens: Quel apport pour l'histoire du Proche-Orient hellénistique et romain? Actes de la table ronde de Damas, 10–12 novembre 1999*, ed. Christian Augé and Frédérique Duyrat (Beirut: Institut français d'archéologie du Proche-Orient, 2002), pp. 141–143: Amandry estimates the minting as equivalent to fifty million at a minimum, forty-seven million of which were in the form of *aurei*.

103. William E. Metcalf, "The End of Antioch's Silver Coinage," in Augé and Duyrat, *Monnayages syriens*, pp. 175–180.

104. Harl, *Coinage*, pp. 103–106.

105. Tyrian denarii are heavier and richer in fine metal than those of Antioch, so that the legal equivalent established between them amounted to a devaluation of the Tyrian tetradrachm by at least 13 percent: Harl, *Coinage*, p. 104.

106. In addition to the minting of aurei and denarii mentioned above, Amandry estimates the Flavian issues between 69 and 73 at 6.5 million tetradrachms ("Politique monétaire des Flaviens," p. 141).

107. On the reduction in weight of municipal bronzes and other coins in Syria, see Jean-Pierre Callu, *La politique monétaire des empereurs romains de 238 à 311* (Paris: E. de Boccard, 1969), pp. 104–108. But the metal content varies more: see Giles F. Carter, "Chemical Composition of Copper-Based Roman Coins: VIII. Bronze Coins Minted in Antioch," *Israel Numismatic Journal* (hereafter cited as *INJ*) 6–7 (1982–1983): 22–38. Carter has brought to light the beginning of a devaluation as early as the Domitian era through an increase in the proportion of lead in the alloy.

108. Andrew Burnett, "Syrian Coinage and Romanisation from Pompey to Domitian," in Augé and Duyrat, *Monnayages syriens*, pp. 115–122.

109. See Dorothy B. Waagé, *Antioch-on-the-Orontes*, vol. 4, part 2: *Greek, Roman, Byzantine and Crusaders' Coins* (Princeton: Department of Art and Archaeology of Princeton University, 1952), p. 39.

110. Burnett, "Syrian Coinage."

111. Dan Barag, "The Palestinian 'Judaea Capta' Coins of Vespasian and Titus and the Era on the Coins of Agrippa II Minted under the Flavians," *Numismatic Chronicle* (hereafter cited as *NC*) (1978): 14–23; Andrew Burnett, Michel Amandry, and Ian Carradice, *Roman Provincial Coinage*, vol. 2, *The Flavians* (London: British Museum Press; Paris: Bibliothèque nationale de France, 1999), pp. 317–318 (hereafter

cited as *RPC* 2), which limits the issue to Vespasian's reign. In contrast, the coins that are considered provincial by Arye Kindler ("The Coin Issues of the Roman Administration in the Provincia Judaea during the Reign of Domitian," *Bulletin Museum Ha'aretz* 10 [1968]: 6–16) and by Ian Carradice ("Coinage in Judaea in the Flavian Period, A.D. 70–96," *INJ* 6–7 [1982–1983]: 14–21) probably belong to the civic coinage in Caesarea, without any mention of ethnicity: *RPC* 2, p. 315.

112. Callu, *Politique monétaire,* pp. 163–164.

113. William E. Metcalf, "The Tell Kalak Hoard and Trajan's Arabian Mint," *American Numismatic Society: Museum Notes* 20 (1975): 39–108.

114. Kevin Butcher, "Two Notes on Syrian Silver of the Third Century AD: Drachms of Caracalla from Petra," *NC* (1989): 169–171.

115. Henri Seyrig, "Les inscriptions de Bostra," *Syria* 22 (1941): 47–48 (= idem, *Antiquités syriennes* [Paris: P. Geuthner, 1934–]), vol. 3, pp. 140–141 [hereafter cited as *AS*]); Arye Kindler, "Two Coins of the Third Legion Cyrenaica Struck under Antoninus Pius," *Israel Exploration Journal* (hereafter cited as *IEJ*) 25 (1975): 144–147; idem, *The Coinage of Bostra* (Warminster: Aris & Phillips, 1983), pp. 92–95.

116. For example, a coin with Zeus-Ammon, the tutelary god of III Cyrenaica, under Commodus: Kindler, *Coinage of Bostra,* p. 110, no. 17.

117. Thus twenty-one Nabataean coinages have been found in digs at Antioch (Waagé, *Antioch-on-the-Orontes,* vol. 4, part 2, nos. 940–945); an isolated coinage in Kourion in Cyprus (Ya'akov Meshorer, *Nabataean Coins* [Jerusalem: Institute of Archaeology, Hebrew University of Jerusalem, 1975], p. 41, no. 118), others in Dura-Europos and Susa, and even one in Avenches, in Switzerland: see Robert Wenning, *Die Nabatäer-Denkmäler und Geschichte* (Freiburg: Universitätsverlag; Göttingen: Vandenhoeck & Ruprecht, 1987), p. 22.

118. Glen W. Bowersock, *Roman Arabia* (Cambridge, Mass.: Harvard University Press, 1983), pp. 54–56.

119. The basic work remains Meshorer, *Nabataean Coins.*

120. Ya'akov Meshorer, *Ancient Jewish Coinage,* vol. 2 (Dix Hills, N.Y.: Amphora Books, 1982); Andrew Burnett, Michel Amandry, and Pere Pau Ripollès, *Roman Provincial Coinage,* vol. 1, *Julio-Claudian Period,* 2nd ed. (London: British Museum Press; Paris: Bibliothèque nationale de France, 1998), pp. 678–685 (hereafter cited as *RPC* 1).

121. The most common denomination was the prutah, a tiny coin worth an eighth of an as.

122. *RPC* 1, p. 663.

123. Meshorer, *Ancient Jewish Coinage,* vol. 2, pp. 51–64 (workshops in Jerusalem and Caesarea); Andrew Burnett, "The Coinage of King Agrippa I of Judaea and a New Coin of King Herod of Chalcis," in *Mélanges de numismatique offerts à Pierre Bastien,* ed. Hélène Huvelin, Michel Christol, and Georges Gautier (Wetteren: Éditions NR, 1987), pp. 25–38.

124. See Meshorer, *Ancient Jewish Coinage,* vol. 2; Burnett, "Syrian Coinage."

125. Meshorer, *Ancient Jewish Coinage,* vol. 2, pp. 7–8.

126. Dio, 54.7.6.

127. See *RPC* 1, p. 656, which notes that the end of minting in Tyre was inscribed within a general politics of reorganization of the Syrian workshops, but without putting forward any more proof than Meshorer offers in support of his hypothesis.

128. *RPC* 1, pp. 662–663: an issue under Lysanias in 40–36, next under Zenodoros

in 32–31 (with a portrait of Augustus), then in 27–26 (with his own portrait); in the interval, an issue under Cleopatra, who had received the tetrarchy directly from Antony.

129. There is no good study of the coinage of Commagene; we must still refer to Warwick William Wroth, *A Catalog of the Greek Coins in the British Museum: Galatia, Cappadocia and Syria* (London: British Museum, 1899), pp. 96 and 104; there may have been some bronzes of king Samos.

130. See the masterful study by Leo Mildenberg and Patricia Erhart Mottahedeh, *The Coinage of the Bar Kokhba War* (Aarau: Sauerländer, 1984).

131. See the brief sketch in Maurice Sartre, *L'Orient romain: Provinces et sociétés provincials en Méditerranée orientale d'Auguste aux Sévères (31 avant J.-C.–235 après J.-C.)* (Paris: Le Seuil, 1991), pp. 91–103.

132. T. B. Jones, "A Numismatic Riddle: The So-Called Greek Imperial," *Proceedings of the American Philosophical Society* 107 (1963): 308–347.

133. *RPC* 1 (with suppl. 1); *RPC* 2.

134. Some useful collections are available for Palestine and Arabia (especially those of Augustus J. Spijkerman, *The Coins of the Decapolis and Roman Arabia,* ed. Michele Piccirillo [Jerusalem: Franciscan Printing Press, 1978], and Mayer Rosenberger, *The Coinage of Eastern Palestine and Legionary Countermarks, Bar-Kochba Overstrucks* [Jerusalem: Rosenberger, 1978], but there are no equivalents for the rest of Syria. Still, for the first century we now have an exceptional instrument in the two volumes of *Roman Provincial Coinage.* For a categorized bibliography for Palestine, see Arye Kindler and Alla Stein, *A Bibliography of the City Coinage of Palestine, from the 2nd Century B.C. to the 3rd Century A.D.* (Oxford: British Archaeological Reports, 1987). For Antioch, we await the publication of Arthur Houghton's corpus, which will parallel Georges Le Rider's *Antioche de Syrie sous les Séleucides* (Paris: Institut de France, 2000). On one particular point, see Kevin Butcher, "The Colonial Coinage of Antioch-on-the-Orontes, AD 218–253," *NC* 148 (1988): 63–76.

135. For the coinages of Sidon and Tyre, see Brooks Emmons Levy, "The Autonomous Silver of Sidon, 107/6 B.C.–43/44 C.E.," in *XII. Internationaler Numismatischer Kongress Berlin 1997: Akten-Proceedings-Actes,* ed. Bernd Kluge and Bernhard Weisser (Berlin: Staatliche Museen zu Berlin / Gebr. Mann Verlag, 2000), p. 614, n. 159. On the "Tyrian" silver of Jerusalem, see above.

136. Alfred Raymond Bellinger, *The Syrian Tetradrachms of Caracalla and Macrinus* (New York: American Numismatic Society, 1940); Bellinger observes that the issues did not even bear the names of the workshops, but only the names and titles of the emperors.

137. See Burnett, "Syrian Coinage."

138. Fergus Millar, *The Roman Near East (31 B.C.–A.D. 377)* (Cambridge, Mass.: Harvard University Press, 1993), p. 527.

139. *RPC* 1, pp. 668–669; *RPC* 2, p. 296.

140. *RPC* 1, pp. 663–665; *RPC* 2, p. 296, emphasizing that Damascus issued no coinages under the Flavians.

141. *RPC* 1, pp. 666–667; *RPC* 2, pp. 296–297.

142. Haim Gitler, "Numismatic Evidence on the Visit of Marcus Aurelius to the East," *INJ* 11 (1990–1991): 36–51: workshops that had issued nothing since the years 159–165, or even earlier, began to mint coins between 175 and 178: Antioch-Hippos, Ascalon, Bostra, Gadara, Scythopolis, and Pella.

143. In *The Coinage of Aelia Capitolina* (Tel Aviv: Schocken, 1956), Leo Kadman notes that there was only a single interruption in the workshop's production of coins, a fourteen-year period between Alexander Severus and the advent of Trajan Decius (p. 25). Minting ceased under Decius and Trebonianus Gallus.

144. On intercity rivalries, see above. On issues and circulation of coins in the Transjordan, see Christian Augé, "La place des monnaies de Décapole et d'Arabie dans la numismatique du Proche-Orient à l'époque romaine," in Augé and Duyrat, *Monnayages syriens*, pp. 153–166.

145. C. M. Kraay, "Notes on the Early Imperial Tetradrachms of Syria," *Revue numismatique* (1966): 58–68.

146. Callu, *Politique*, pp. 21–23.

147. A suggestion made by William E. Metcalf, in "The Antioch Hoard of Antoniniani and the Eastern Coinage of Trebonianus Gallus and Volusian," in *American Numismatic Society: Museum Notes* 22 (1977): 71–77.

148. Augé, "Place des monnaies,"

149. Ibid.

150. Cécile Morrisson, "Les monnaies," section D in Jean-Pierre Sodini, Georges Tate, Bernard Bavant, Swantje Bavant Bavant, Jean-Luc Biscop, and Dominique Orssaud, "Déhès, campagnes I–III (1976–1978), recherches sur l'habitat rural," *Syria* 67 (1980): 267–273; in contrast, four Hellenistic coinages have been found there.

151. Two *publicani*, made freedmen by Roman citizens as early as 56–57, in an inscription published by Michel Gawlikowski, "Deux publicains et leur tombeau," *Syria* 75 (1998): 145–151: Chrysanthos, a tax collector buried in Palmyra in 58 (Académie des inscriptions et belles-lettres, *Corpus inscriptionum semiticarum* [Paris: e Reipublicae Typographeo, 1881], vol. 2, no. 4235 [hereafter cited as *CIS*] = *Inv.*, vol. 8, no. 57); M. Aemilius Marcianus Asclepiades, a *decurion* (municipal counselor) in Antioch, collector of the *quart* tax, in 161 (*AE* [1947], no. 179 = *Inv.*, vol. 10, no. 29); L. Antonius Callistratos, *manceps quartae mercaturae* (recipient of a 25 percent tax on transactions), and Galenus, an *actor* (agent of an agricultural society), in 176 (*AE* [1947], no. 180 = *Inv.*, vol. 10, no. 113).

152. Sigfried J. de Laet, *Portorium: Étude sur l'organisation douanière chez les Romains, surtout à l'époque du haut-empire* (Bruges: De Tempel, 1949), pp. 336–337, based on *SEG*, vol. 7 (1937), nos. 570, 537, 591, 623, 593.

153. Philostrates, *The Life of Apollonius of Tyana*, trans. F. C. Conybeare (Loeb Classical Library), 1.20; on the road to Ctesiphon, Apollonios is asked to declare the goods he is transporting, as well as the accompanying slaves; this gives rise to an amusing quid pro quo, because the customs officer thinks that the virtues Apollonios obligingly lists are names of slaves.

154. De Laet, *Portorium*, pp. 340–341.

155. After a great deal of argument, it seems that we are going to have to retain a date for this *Periplus* as being a little after the middle of the first century C.E.

156. Lionel Casson, ed., *The Periplus Maris Erythraei: Text, Translation, and Commentary* (Princeton: Princeton University Press, 1989), 19.

157. See the bibliography in Manfred G. Raschke, "New Studies in Roman Commerce with the East," *Aufstieg und Niedergang der römischen Welt* (hereafter cited as *ANRW*) 2.9.1 (1978): 982.

158. See, for example, Bowersock, *Roman Arabia*, p. 70; Casson in his edition of the *Periplus*, p. 145; and Sartre, *Orient romain*, p. 63.

159. That of centurion, attested on a tomb at Hegra (*CIS,* vol. 2, part 1, no. 217 = John F. Healey, *The Nabataean Tomb Inscriptions of Mada'in Salih* [Oxford: Oxford University Press, 1993], p. 206, no. H 31).

160. Steven E. Sidebotham, *Roman Economic Policy in the Erythra Thalassa, 30 B.C.–A.D. 217* (Leiden: E. J. Brill, 1986), pp. 106–107, and also idem, "Roman Interests in the Red Sea and Indian Ocean," in *The Indian Ocean in Antiquity,* ed. Julian Reade (London: Kegan Paul, 1996), p. 293.

161. Gary K. Young, "The Customs-Officer at the Nabataean Port of Leuke Kome (*Periplus Maris Erythraei* 19)," *ZPE* 119 (1997): 266–268.

162. Pliny, *NH* 12.32. Similarly, I see no reason why luxury goods such as myrhh and incense would not have been taxed: Young claims that the Romans did not view them as luxuries ("Customs-Officer," p. 268). On the one hand, this is untrue (see Glen W. Bowersock, "Perfumes and Power," in *Profumi di Arabia: Atti del convegno,* ed. Alessandra Avanzini [Rome: L'Erma, 1997], pp. 543–556); on the other hand, nothing allows us to say that only luxury goods were taxed at 25 percent. Similarly, Young seems to believe that the tax was paid at Antioch for products coming from Mesopotamia (p. 268); he fails to take into account the Roman customs at Palmyra.

163. The Aramaean text is found in *CIS,* vol. 2, no. 3913 (= Dilbert R. Hillers and Eleonora Cussini, *Palmyrene Aramaic Texts* [Baltimore: Johns Hopkins University Press, 1994, no. O259 [hereafter cited as *PAT*]); for the Greek text, see Wilhelm Dittenberger, *Orientis graeci inscriptiones selectae: Supplementum sylloges inscriptionum graecarum,* 2 vols. (Hildesheim and New York: G. Olms, 1986; originally published 1903–1905), no. 629 (hereafter cited as *OGIS*), and René Cagnat, Jean Toutain, Georges Lafaye, and Victor Henry, eds., *Inscriptiones graecae ad res romanas pertinentes,* vol. 3 (Paris: E. Leroux, 1906), no. 1056; there is a French translation based on the Palmyrene text in Teixidor, *Port romain,* with a detailed commentary. It is dated April 18, 137, but it incorporates a number of earlier rulings.

164. Safrai, *Economy,* p. 289.

165. In "The Exiled God of Sarepta," *Berytus* 9 (1949): 45–49, Charles Cutler Torrey pointed out that *OGIS* (no. 594) mentioned the sending of the sacred god of Sarepta, a little north of Tyre, to the Tyrians of Pozzuoli, on May 29, 79 C.E., under the control of a magistrate charged with sacred matters, an *elim.* A second inscription from Syria (now at Yale) in honor of the same god may have been erected at the moment of departure for Pozzuoli. A third mention of the sacred god of Sarepta has been found at the site itself: James B. Pritchard, "The Roman Port at Sarafand (Sarepta): Preliminary Report on the Seasons of 1969 and 1970," *Bulletin du Musée de Beyrouth* 24 (1971): 54–56. The city, which had probably been independent in the distant past, was a possession of the Tyrians starting in the seventh century, after having been a Sidonian holding: James B. Pritchard, *Recovering Sarepta, a Phoenician City* (Princeton: Princeton University Press, 1978), pp. 42–43. On the identity of the sacred god of Sarepta, who might be Melqart, see Corinne Bonnet, *Melqart: Cultes et mythes de l'Héracles tryien en Méditerranée* (Leuven: Peeters, 1988), pp. 121–122.

166. See the very thorough work by Heikki Solin, "Juden und Syrer im westlichen Teil der römischen Welt: Eine ethnisch-demographische Studie mit besonderer Berücksichtigung der sprachlichen Zustände," *ANRW* 2.29.2 (1983): 587–789 and 1222–1249 (indexes).

167. The sanctuary of the Syrian gods on the Janiculum, which existed as early as

the first century, was reconstructed in 176 by an M. Antonius Gaionas whose *cognomen* is characteristic of northern Syria: see Paul Gauckler, *Le sanctuaire syrien du Janicule* (Paris: Picard, 1912); Filippo Coarelli, *Guide archéologique de Rome* (Paris: Hachette, 1994), p. 246. The ending *-as* was common in names derived from the Aramaean. See Eugenia Equini Schneider, "Il santuario di Bel e della divinita di Palmira: Communità e tradizione religiose dei Palmireni a Roma," *Dialoghi di archeologia* 5 (1987): 69–85; Claudio Moccheggiani Carpano, *L'area del "Santuario siriaco del Gianicolo": Problemi archeologici e storico-religiosi* (Rome: Quasar, 1992).

168. See Antoine Poidebard, *Un grand port disparu: Tyr; Recherches aériennes et sous-marines* (Paris: P. Geuthner, 1939).

169. Strabo, 16.2.23.

170. Arrian, *The Anabasis of Alexander*, ed. and trans. E. J. Chinnock (London: Hodder & Stoughton, 1884), in particular chap. 24.

171. Achilles Tatius, *Leucippe and Clitophon*, trans. Tim Whitmarsh (Oxford and New York: Oxford University Press, 2001), 1.1, p. 3.

172. Antoine Poidebard and Jean Lauffray, *Sidon: Aménagements antiques du ports de Saïda* (Beirut: Ministère des Travaux Publics, 1951).

173. Ibid. Sand began seeping in around 3000 B.C.E.: see Christophe Morange et al., "Étude paléoenvironnementale du port antique de Sidon: Premiers résultats du programme CEDRE," *Méditerranée* 94 (2000): 91–100.

174. Ernest Renan, *Mission de Phénicie* (Paris: Imprimerie impériale, 1864), plates 67, 1 and 2.

175. Honor Frost, "The Offshore Island Harbour at Sidon and Other Phoenician Sites in the Light of New Dating Evidence," *International Journal of Nautical Archaeology* 2 (1973): 75–94.

176. On the variations in the sea level in Lebanon, see Paul Sanlaville, "Les variations holocènes du niveau de la mer au Liban," *Revue de géographie de Lyon* 45 (1970), especially pp. 280–287.

177. John Peter Oleson, *The Harbours of Caesarea Maritima*, vol. 2, *The Finds and the Ship* (Oxford: British Archaeological Reports, 1994), pp. 153–161; several chapters are devoted to the topic in *Caesarea Maritima: A Retrospective after Two Millennia*, ed. Avner Raban and Kenneth G. Holum (Leiden: E. J. Brill 1996), pp. 3–49, 359–377.

178. Poidebard, in Poidebard and Lauffray, *Sidon*, pp. 32–33.

179. Raphaël Savignac, "Une visite à l'île de Rouad," *Revue biblique* (hereafter cited as *Rbi*) (1916): 565; Poidebard, in Poidebard and Lauffray, *Sidon*, pp. 34–35; Honor Frost, "Rouad, ses récifs et mouillages: Prospection sous-marine," *Annales archéologiques arabes syriennes* (hereafter cited as *AAAS*) 14 (1964): 67–74; idem, "The Arwad Plans 1964: A Photogrammetric Survey of Marine Installations," *AAAS* 16.1 (1966): 13–28.

180. Poidebard points out that the northern port in Tyre today is narrower than the medieval port located on the same site.

181. Karl Lehmann-Hartleben, *Die antiken Hafenanlagen des Mittelmeeres: Beiträge zur Geschichte des Städtebaues im Altertum* (Leipzig: Dieterich, 1923) (*Klio*, vol. 14); Poidebard, in Poidebard and Lauffray, *Sidon*, pp. 31–32.

182. Denis Van Berchem, "Le port de Séleucie de Piérie et la logistique des campagnes parthiques," *Bonner Jahrbücher* 185 (1985): 47–87.

183. Pritchard, *Recovering Sarepta*, pp. 49–70.

184. Louis Jalabert and René Mouterde, *IGLS,* vol. 3.1, *Région de l'Amanus, Antioche* (Paris: P. Geuthner, 1950), no. 6696. I was not able to consult Honor Frost and Christophe Morange, "Proposition de localisation des ports antiques de Byblos (Liban)," *Méditerranée* 94 (2000): 101–104.

185. See the abundant documentation studied by Daniel Sperber, *The City in Roman Palestine* (Oxford: Oxford University Press, 1998), pp. 9–47.

186. See Safrai, *Economy,* pp. 254–256. For descriptions, see Shimon Applebaum, "Mamre," in *Encyclopedia of Archaeological Excavations in the Holy Land* (hereafter cited as *EAEHL*), ed. Michael Avi-Yonah, vol. 3 (Englewood Cliffs, N.J.: Prentice-Hall, 1977), pp. 776–778; Yitzhad Magen, "Mamre" in *The New Encyclopedia of Archaeological Excavations in the Holy Land,* ed. Ephraim Stern (Jerusalem: Israel Exploration Society / Carta; New York: Simon & Schuster, 1998); it was located near an important pagan sanctuary and served as a slave market after the revolt of 132–135.

187. Adan-Bayewitz, *Common Pottery,* pp. 231–233.

188. David Adan-Bayewitz and Isadore Perlman, "The Local Trade of Sepphoris in the Roman Period," *IEJ* 40 (1990): 151–172.

189. Reynolds, "Pottery Production," pp. 40–43, 52–53.

190. Parker, "Roman 'Aqaba Project: 1994," p. 252.

191. John Lund, "A Fresh Look at the Roman and Late Roman Fine Wares from the Danish Excavations at Hama, Syria," in Meyza and Mlynarczyk, *Hellenistic and Roman Pottery,* pp. 136–137.

192. Reynolds, "Pottery Production," p. 38.

193. Francesca Sogliani, "La Ceramica," *Felix Ravenna* 137–138 (1989): 130–131, 133.

194. Eastern Sigillata A pottery was also dominant in Tel Anafa between 125 and 80 C.E.: see Herbert, *Tel Anafa II,* part 1, pp. 263–264; at that point, it constituted 90 percent of the fine ceramics; the proportion fell to around 54 to 70 percent in the reoccupation period during the first half of the second century C.E., but the population of soldiers and foreign veterans that had settled there had different needs and were more inclined to import ceramics from Italy and Asia.

195. Parker, "Roman 'Aqaba Project: 1994," p. 252.

196. See, for example, 2 Chron. 17.11.

197. *I.Gerasa,* nos. 3 and 4.

198. Harl, *Coinage,* p. 103.

199. Ibid., p. 104.

200. The coinages from the workshop in Rome that we have from Trajan's day are clearly connected to the campaign of the Roman armies in 115–116.

201. On all this, see Alfred Raymond Bellinger, *The Excavations at Dura-Europos: Final Report,* vol. 6, *The Coins* (New Haven: Yale University Press, 1949), pp. 196–207.

202. Waagé, *Antioch-on-the-Orontes,* vol. 4, part 2, pp. 57, 63.

203. Bellinger, *Excavations,* vol. 6, p. 205.

204. See Lemaître, "Importations," a fundamental work. The oil and fat transported in this way to Palmyra are explicitly mentioned in the Palmyra Tariff Law, 18, 22, 23, 26, and so on, but the products could also be preserved in alabasters (perfumed oil).

205. Ibid., pp. 347, 355.

206. Lund, "Trade Patterns."

207. John Lund, "The Distribution of Cypriot Sigillata as Evidence of Sea-Trade Involving Cyprus," in *Res Maritimae: Cyprus and the Eastern Mediterranean from Prehistory to Late Antiquity,* ed. Stuart Swiny, Robert L. Hohlfelder, and Helena Wylde Swiny (Atlanta: Scholars Press, 1997), pp. 201–215.

208. Karl Michael Zelle, "Terra Sigillata-Import nach Assos," in Herfort-Koch et al., *Hellenistische und kaiserzeitliche Keramik,* p. 19.

209. Catherine Abadie-Reynal, "La céramique romaine de Porsuk," *XI Kazi Sonuçlari Toplantisi* 1 (1990): 221–228.

210. Abadie-Reynal, "Courants commerciaux," pp. 65–66.

211. Hannah Cotton and Joseph Geiger, *Masada: The Yigael Yadin Excavations 1963–1965,* vol. 2, *The Latin and Greek Documents* (Jerusalem: Israel Exploration Society, Hebrew University of Jerusalem, 1989), pp. 140–177.

212. Jacqueline Studer, "Roman Fish Sauce in Petra, Jordan," in *Fish Exploitation in the Past: Proceedings of the 7th Meeting of the ICAZ Fish Remains Working Group,* ed. Wim Van Neer (Tervuren: Koninklijk Museum voor Midden-Africa, 1994), pp. 191–196.

213. Parker, "Roman 'Aqaba Project: 1994," p. 252.

214. Zvi Ma'oz, "Temple of Pan, 1991–1992," *Excavations and Surveys in Israel* 12 (1993): 2–7.

215. Reynolds, "Pottery Production," pp. 43–44.

216. Ibid., p. 54.

217. Ibid., pp. 46–57.

218. Ibid., p. 54.

219. Guntram Koch, "The Import of Attic Sarcophagi in the Near East," in Ο Ελληνισμοσ στην Ανατολη (Athens: EPKED, 1991), p. 69.

220. Ibid., pp. 69–70.

221. Guntram Koch, "Der Import kaiserzeitlicher Sarkophage in den römischen Provinzen Syria, Palaestina und Arabia," *Bonner Jahrbücher* 189 (1989): 161–211; idem, "Import of Attic Sarcophagi"; idem, "Ein attischer Schiffkampf-Sarkophag aus Arethousa in Damaskus," *Damaszener Mitteilungen* (hereafter cited as *DaM*) 9 (1996): 197–207.

222. Pascale Linant de Bellefonds, *Sarcophages attiques de la nécropole de Tyr* (Paris: Éditions Recherche sur les civilisations, 1985).

223. Mordechai Aviam and Edna J. Stern, "Burial in Clay Sarcophagi in Galilee during the Roman Period," *Atiqot* 33 (1997): 151–162 (in Hebrew; summary in English, p. 19*).

224. Loffreda, *Cafarnao,* vol. 2, p. 237.

225. Lund, "Fresh Look," p. 137.

226. Vanderhoeven, *Terres sigillées,* pp. 39–40.

227. Abadie-Reynal, "Courants commerciaux," pp. 33, 49.

228. Lund, "Fresh Look," p. 139.

229. Abadie-Reynal, "Courants commerciaux," p. 36.

230. Lund, "Fresh Look," pp. 145–146.

231. Abadie-Reynal, "Courants commerciaux," p. 52.

232. Hermann von Wissmann, "Die Geschichte des Sabäerreichs und der Feldzug des Aelius Gallus," *ANRW* 2.9.2 (1978): 308–544.

233. Yves Janvier, "Rome et l'Orient lointain: Le problème des Sères; Réexamen d'une question de géographie antique," *Ktema* 9 (1984 [1988]): 261–303.

234. Sidebotham, *Roman Economic Policy;* Nigel Groom, *Frankincense and Myrrh: A Study of the Arabian Incense Trade* (London and New York: Longman, 1981); Alessandra Avanzini, ed., *Profumi d'Arabia: Atti del convegno* (Rome: L'Erma, 1997); Kai Ruffing, "Wege in den Osten," in *Stuttgarter Kolloquium zur historischen Geographie des Altertums, 7, 1999: Zu Wasser und zu Land; Werkehrswege in der antiken Welt,* ed. Eckart Olshausen and Holger Sonnabend (Stuttgart: Franz Steiner Verlag, 2002), pp. 360–378.

235. De Laet, *Portorium.*

236. Paul Veyne, "Rome et le problème de la fuite de l'or," *Annales: Économies, sociétés, civilisations* (1979): 211–244. Pliny's figures have been challenged, probably wrongly, for, as Claude Nicolet astutely observes in *L'inventaire du monde* (Paris: Fayard, 1988), p. 135, the Roman administration was good at bookkeeping and probably knew in detail the amount of customs duties levied in the various *portus.*

237. Manfred G. Raschke, "The Role of Oriental Commerce in the Economies of the Cities of the Eastern Mediterranean in the Roman Period," in *The Archaeology of Trade in the East Mediterranean: A Symposium,* ed. Eric Meyers and William West (Tallahassee, Fla.: Archaeological News, 1979), pp. 68–77.

238. Strabo, 16.4.23–24.

239. Laila Nehmé and François Villeneuve, *Pétra: Métropole de l'Arabie antique* (Paris: Le Seuil, 1999), pp. 28–34.

240. Fawzi Zayadine, "L'espace urbain du grand Pétra: Les routes et les stations caravanières," *ADAJ* 36 (1992): 217–239; Leo Mildenberg, "Petra on the Frankincense Road?" *Transeuphratène* 10 (1995): 69–72, and idem, "Petra on the Frankincense Road?—Again," *Aram* 8 (1996): 55–65.

241. See Zbigniew T. Fiema, "Nabataean and Palmyrene Commerce—The Mechanics of Intensification," in "Palmyra and the Silk Road: International Colloquium, Palmyra, 7–11 April 1992," special issue, *AAAS* 42 (1996): 189–195, especially p. 191, citing D. J. Johnson, "Nabataean Trade: Intensification and Culture Change" (Ph.D. diss., University of Utah, 1987), p. 53 (*non vidi*); Johnson points out that plants whose sugars, resins, and other essences are necessary for these transformations are present around Petra.

242. Jean-Marie Dentzer, Frank Braemer, Jacqueline Dentzer[-Feydy], and François Villeneuve, "Six campagnes de fouilles à Si': Développement et culture en Syrie méridionale," *DaM* 2 (1985): 69.

243. Clermont-Ganneau, *Études,* vol. 1, p. 47; on all this, see Fawzi Zayadine, "Palmyre, Pétra, la mer Érythrée et les routes de la soie," in "Palmyra and the Silk Road: International Colloquium, Palmyra, 7–11 April 1992," special issue, *AAAS* 42 (1996): 167–173.

244. Enno Littmann and David Meredith, "Nabataean Inscriptions from Egypt," *Bulletin of the Society for Oriental and African Studies* 15 (1953): 1–28, and 16 (1954): 211–246. In contrast, graffiti from the same region seem closely related to Sinaitic inscriptions, and they cannot be dated: Françoise Briquel-Chatonnet and Laila Nehmé, "Graffiti nabatéens d'al-Muwayh et de Bir al-Hammamat (Égypte)," *Semitica* 47 (1997): 81–88.

245. Zbigniew T. Fiema and Richard N. Jones, "The Nabataean King-List Re-

vised: Further Observations on the Second Nabataean Inscription from Tell esh-Shuqafiya, Egypt," *ADAJ* 34 (1990): 239–248.

246. Michael C. A. Macdonald, "A Dated Nabataean Inscription from Southern Arabia," in *Arabia Felix: Beiträge zur Sprache und Kultur des vorislamischen Arabian; Festschrift Walter W. Müller zum 60. Geburtstag,* ed. Norbert Nebes (Wiesbaden: Harrassowitz, 1994), pp. 132–141.

247. Abdul Raman al-Ansary, *Qaryat al Faw: A Portrait of Pre-Islamic Civilisation in Saudi Arabia* (Riyadh: University of Riyadh; New York: St. Martin's Press, 1982), pp. 28, 63–64.

248. Daniel T. Potts, "Nabataean Finds from Thaj and Qatif," *Arabian Archaeology and Epigraphy* (hereafter cited as *AAE*) 2 (1991): 138–144. In contrast, there are no Nabataean ceramics at Failaka-Ikaros, in Kuwait, notwithstanding the claims of Lise Hannestad, *Ikaros* (Aarhus: Jutland Archaeological Society Publications, 1983): see the review by Jean-François Salles in *Syria* 64 (1987): 163–164.

249. Garth Bawden, Christopher Edens, and Robert Miller, "Preliminary Archaeological Investigations at Tayma," *Al-Atlal* 4 (1980): 90 (ceramics); Alasdair Livingstone, Bachir Spaie, Mohommed Ibrahim, Mohammed Kamal, and Selim Taimani, "Taima: Recent Soundings and New Inscribed Material," *Al-Atlal* 7 (1983): 102–114.

250. Macdonald, "Dated Nabataean Inscription."

251. Konrad Weidemann, *Könige aus dem Yemen: Zwei spätantike Bronzestatuen* (Mainz: Das Museum, 1983).

252. See Ernest Will, "De la Syrie au Yémen: Problèmes des relations dans le domaine de l'art," in *L'Arabie préislamique et son environnement historique et culturel: Actes du colloque de Strasbourg, 24–27 juin 1987,* ed. Toufic Fahd (Leiden: E. J. Brill, 1989), pp. 271–279.

253. Al-Ansary, *Qaryat al Faw,* pp. 104–117, 130–139; cf. Glen W. Bowersock, *Hellenism in Late Antiquity: Thomas Spencer Jerome Lectures* (Ann Arbor: University of Michigan Press, 1990), pp. 74–76; Françoise Briquel-Chatonnet, "La pénétration de la culture du Croissant fertile en Arabie: À propos des inscriptions nabatéennes," in *Présence arabe dans le Croissant fertile avant l'Hégire,* ed. Hélène Lozachmeur (Paris: Éditions Recherche sur les civilisations, 1995), pp. 140–141.

254. Jean Starcky and Michel Gawlikowski, *Palmyre* (Paris: J. Maisonneuve, 1985); Ernest Will, *Les Palmyréniens: La Venise des sables = Ier siècle avant–IIIème siècle après J.-C.* (Paris: A. Colin, 1992). There is an overabundant bibliography on trade; apart from the chapters devoted to the topic in general works on the city, see in particular Ernest Will, "Marchands et chefs de caravanes à Palmyre," *Syria* 34 (1957): 262–271; Raphaela Drexhage, "Der Handel Palmyras in römischer Zeit," *Münstersche Beiträge zur antiken Handelgeschichte* 1 (1982):17–34; John F. Matthews, "The Tax Law of Palmyra," *Journal of Roman Studies* (hereafter cited as JRS) 74 (1984): 157–180; Michel Gawlikowski, "Le commerce de Palmyre sur terre et sur eau," in *L'Arabie et ses mers bordières,* ed. Jean-François Salles (Lyon: Maison de l'Orient, 1988), pp. 163–172; idem, "Palmyra and Its Caravan Trade," in "Palmyra and the Silk Road: International Colloquium, Palmyra, 7–11 April 1992," special issue, *AAAS* 42 (1996): 139–145 (with a list of inscriptions relating to caravans) (the same article is found under the title "Palmyra as a Trading Center," *Iraq* 56 [1994]: 27–33); Edmond Frézouls, "Palmyre et les conditions politiques du développement de son activité commerciale," *Iraq* 56 (1994): 147–155.

255. Ernest Will, "Pline l'Ancien et Palmyre: Un problème d'histoire ou d'histoire littéraire?" *Syria* 62 (1985): 263–270.

256. Daniel Schlumberger, Harald Ingholt, and Jean Starcky, *La Palmyrène du Nord-Ouest* (Paris: P. Geuthner, 1951).

257. André Maricq, "Vologésias, l'emporium de Ctésiphon," *Syria* 36 (1959): 264–276; there is disagreement over its localization.

258. A Palmyrene, Iarhai, satrap of Thilouos (Bahrein), on behalf of the king of Mesene: *Inv.*, vol. 10, no. 38; Khaled As'ad and Jean-Baptiste Yon, *Inscriptions de Palmyre: Promenades épigraphiques dans la ville antique de Palmyre* (Beirut: Direction générale des antiquités et des musées de la Répubeliue arabe syrienne, Institut français d'archéologie du Proche-Orient, 2001), p. 60, no. 15; Iarhai may have had nothing to do with his compatriots' trading practices.

259. See Ernie Haerinck, "Quelques monuments funéraires de l'île de Kharg dans le Golfe Persique," *Iranica antiqua* 11 (1975): 134–167; Henri Seyrig, "Inscription relative au commerce maritime de Palmyre," in *Mélanges Franz Cumont* (Brussels: Secrétariat de l'Institut, 1936), pp. 397–402. In "Palmyre et les routes de la soie" ("Palmyra and the Silk Road: International Colloquium, Palmyra, 7–11 April 1992," special issue, *AAAS* 42 [1996]: 125–130), Ernest Will notes that the Palmyrenes seemed to avoid the major Parthian capitals after the first century, and that we have no evidence that they crossed Iran, whereas they readily took the maritime route in the Persian Gulf, as if they were seeking to go around the Parthian Empire. For a mention of the boat that came back from Scythia, see *Inv.*, vol. 10, no. 96. The tombs of Kharq have parallels throughout the entire Syro-Mesopotamian region and not only in Palmyra, as Eugenia Equini Schneider emphasizes in *Septimia Zenobia Sebaste* (Rome: L'Erma, 1993), pp. 101–102, n. 2, whereas in "Sur l'île de Kharg, dans le Golfe persique" (*Dossiers d'archéologie* 243 [May 1999], pp. 74–80), M.-J. Steve suggests a Nabataean origin. On a Palmyrene graffito in South Arabia, see Alexander V. Sedov, "New Archaeological and Epigraphical Material from Qana (South Arabia)," *AAE* 3 (1993): 110–137.

260. The tomb of Marona, dating from the middle of the third century.

261. *Inv.*, vol. 10, no. 96 = *PAT,* no. 1403.

262. The Palmyrene steles discovered in the oasis of Merv, the former Alexandria of Margiane, attest not to the presence of Palmyrenes, but to that of a high Russian official who owned a fine collection: see Mikhail Evgen'evitch Masson, "Two Palmyrene Stelae of the Merv Oasis," *East and West* 17 (1967): 239–247; Paul Bernard, "Un nouveau livre sur les Parthes," *Studia Iranica* 8 (1979): 135–139.

263. David F. Graf, "The Roman East from the Chinese Perspective," in "Palmyra and the Silk Road: International Colloquium, Palmyra, 7–11 April 1992," special issue, *AAAS* 42 (1996): 199–216; Graf shows the extent of the uncertainties about identification.

264. Will, "Marchands et chefs de caravanes," pp. 262–271; idem, *Palmyréniens;* Matthews, "Tax Law"; Teixidor, *Port romain.*

265. Michal Gawlikowski, "Les comptes d'un homme d'affaires dans une tour funéraire à Palmyre," *Semitica* 36 (1986): 87–99.

266. Jean-Marie Dentzer, "Khans ou casernes à Palmyre? À propos de structures visibles sur des photographies aériennes anciennes," *Syria* 71 (1994): 45–112.

267. See the early article by Albert Gabriel, "Recherches archéologiques à

Palmyre," *Syria* 7 (1926): 71–92, especially pp. 74–78, on the ramparts. See also Armin von Gerkan, "Die Stadtmauern von Palmyra," *Berytus* 2 (1935): 25–33; Dora p. Crouch, "The Ramparts of Palmyra," *Studia Palmirenskie* 6–7 (1975): 6–41; Michel Gawlikowski, "Les défenses de Palmyre," *Syria* 51 (1974): 231–242.

268. Michal Gawlikowski and Khaled As'ad, "Le péage à Palmyre en 11 après J.-C.," *Semitica* 41–42 (1993): 163–172.

269. In "Palmyra and Its Caravan Trade," Gawlikowski lists the thirty-four inscriptions known to date.

270. Gawlikowski, "Comptes d'un homme d'affaires," pp. 87–99.

271. Mikhail I. Rostovtzeff popularized the notion of "caravan cities," which probably applies only to Palmyra (*Caravan Cities* [Oxford: Clarendon Press, 1932]); see Fergus Millar, "Caravan Cities: The Roman Near East and Long Distance Trade by Land," in *Modus Operandi: Essays in Honour of Geoffrey Rickman*, ed. M. Austin, J. Harries, and C. Smith (London: Institute of Classical Studies, 1998), pp. 119–137.

272. In the classification by David Philip Spencer Peacock and D. F. Williams in *Amphorae and the Roman Economy: An Introductory Guide* (New York: Longman, 1986).

273. Parker, "Roman 'Aqaba Project: 1996," p. 379.

274. Ibid.

275. Casson, ed., *Periplus.* On the term *Erythrean Sea,* which designates the Indian Ocean and its annexes, the Red Sea and the Persian Gulf, see Jean-François Salles, "*Fines Indiae,* ardh el-Hind: Recherches sur le devenir de la mer Érythrée," in *The Roman and Byzantine Army in the East: Proceedings of a colloqium* [sic] *held at the Jagiellonian University, Kraków in September 1992, ed.* Edward Dąbrowa (Cracow: Drukarnia Uniwersytetu Jagiellonskiego, 1994), pp. 165–187.

276. On the legend according to which a certain Hippalos discovered this phenomenon, see Santo Mazzarino, "Sul nome del vento *hipalus* ('ippalo') in Plinio," *Helikon* 22–27 (1982–1987): vii–xiv. Mazzarino shows that it is inappropriate to correct Pliny's text (*NH* 6.26.100) in order to find a man's name in *hippalum* or *hypilum,* when it only involves the Latin transcription of the name of a wind from the sea, *huphalos* in Greek. See also Federico de Romanis, "Hypalos: Distanze e venti tra Arabia e India nella scienza ellenistica," *Topoi* 7 (1997): 671–692, especially pp. 682–692, on winds: the term *hypalos* actually designates the monsoon from the southwest.

277. The arrival in the port of Hippuros (now Kudiramalai) of a freedman employed by Annius Plocamus, during Claudius's reign, was a matter of chance and does not imply a regular flow of direct exchanges. Nevertheless, an embassy from Sri Lanka arrived in Rome shortly afterward (Pliny, *NH* 6.24.84). But we have no description of the island between Ptolemy's in the mid-second century and that of Cosmas Indicopleustes in the sixth; see D. P. M. Weerakkody, *Taprobanê: Ancient Sri Lanka as Known to Greeks and Romans* (Turnhout: Brepols, 1997), which brings together, in the original and in translation, all the Greek and Latin sources on the island the ancient authors called Taprobane, a Greek transcription of the Sanskrit *Tamraparni* or the Pali *Tambapanni.* However, we find Paleisimoundou in *Periplus* 61, whereas Pliny gives this only as the name of the island's capital (*NH* 6.24.85–86).

278. See Annie Sartre-Fauriat, "Les notables et leur rôle dans l'urbanisme du Hauran à l'époque romaine," in *Construction, reproduction et représentation des patriciats urbains, de l'Antiquité au XXe siècle,* ed. Claude Petitfrère (Tours:

Université François-Rabelais, Centre d'histoire de la ville moderne et contemporaine, 1999), p. 224, n. 5.

279. Avraham Negev, *The Architecture of Mampsis: Final Report,* vol. 2, *The Late Roman and Byzantine Periods* (Jerusalem: Institute of Archaeology, Hebrew University of Jerusalem, 1988), p. 1.

280. For Adraha, see Hans-Georg Pflaum, "La fortification de la ville d'Adraha d'Arabie (259–260 à 274–275) d'après des inscriptions récemment découvertes," *Syria* 29 (1952): 307–330; for Bostra, see Sartre, *IGLS,* vol. 13.1, nos. 9105, 9106, 9108, 9109, and idem, *Bostra,* p. 89.

281. Claudine Dauphin, "Encore des Judéo-chrétiens au Golan?" in *Early Christianity in Context,* ed. Frédéric Manns and Eugenio Alliata (Jerusalem: Franciscan Press, 1993), pp. 76–77.

9. HELLENIZATION AND INDIGENOUS CULTURES

1. See the excellent analysis by Nicole Belayche, to whom I owe a great deal: "La perception de l'Orient dans le monde romain impérial" (Mémoire d'habilitation, Université de Paris IV, 2000), vol. 2, pp. 29–52, and especially pp. 43ff.

2. Livy, *Works,* vol. 11, trans. Evan T. Sage (Loeb Classical Library), 38.17.11: "The Macedonians, who hold Alexandria in Eygpt, who hold Seleucia and Babylonia and other colonies scattered throughout the world, have degenerated into Syrians, Parthians, Egyptians." Livy attributes these words to T. Manlius Vulso: addressing his troops before they confront the Galatians (189 B.C.E.), he seeks to show that owing to their contact with the east, the Galatians are not at all like the savage Gauls the Romans had known before. The polemical character of the remarks takes nothing away from the widely held Roman view of Syria as a place that turned its conquerors into barbarians.

3. C. E. V. Nixon and Barbara Saylor Rodgers, eds., *In Praise of Later Roman Emperors: The Panegyrici Latini; Introduction, Translation, and Historical Commentary with the Latin Text of R. A. B. Mynors* (Berkeley: University of California Press, 1994), p. 330, 12.24.1.

4. Juvenal, Satire III, "Quid Romae Faciam?" in *Juvenal and Persius,* trans. G. G. Ramsay (Loeb Classical Library).

5. On the Syrians in the West, see Heikki Solin, "Juden und Syrer im westlichen Teil der römischen Welt: Eine ethnisch-demographische Studie mit besonderer Berücksichtigung der sprachlichen Zustände," *Aufstieg und Niedergang der römischen Welt* (hereafter cited as *ANRW*) 2.29.2 (1983): 587–789.

6. This was his usual dress, according to Cassius Dio, *Roman History,* trans. Earnest Cary (Loeb Classical Library), 80.11.2.

7. Herodian, *History of the Empire from the Time of Marcus Aurelius,* trans. C. R. Whittaker (Loeb Classical Library), 5.5.3–5; see Glen W. Bowersock, "Herodian and Elagabalus," *Yale Classical Studies* 24 (1975): 229–236.

8. "Antoninus Elagabalus," in *Historia Augusta,* trans. David Magie, vol. 2 (Loeb Classical Library), 7.3.

9. On the linguistic situation of the Near Eastern provinces under the empire, see Rüdiger Schmitt, "Die Ostgrenze von Armenien über Mesopotamien, Syrien bis Arabien," in *Die Sprachen im römischen Reich der Kaiserzeit: Kolloquium vom 8. bis 10. April 1974,* ed. Günter Neumann and Jürgen Untermann (Cologne and Bonn:

R. Habelt, 1980), pp. 194–214 (with an abundant bibliography); on Palestine, see Haiim B. Rosen, "Die Sprachsituation im römischen Palästina," in Neumann and Untermann, *Die Sprachen,* pp. 215–239.

10. Joseph Geiger, "How Much Latin in Greek Palestine?" in *Aspects of Latin: Papers from the VIIth International Colloquium on Latin Linguistics, Jerusalem, April 1993,* ed. Hannah Rosén (Innsbruck: Institut für Sprachwissenschaft der Universität Innsbruck, 1996), pp. 39–57.

11. For Bostra, see Maurice Sartre, *Inscriptions grecques et latines de la Syrie* (hereafter cited as *IGLS*), vol. 13.1, *Bostra* (Paris: P. Geuthner, 1982), part 1, nos. 9170–9205; for Apamaea, see Jean-Charles Balty and Wilfried van Rengen, *Apamée de Syrie, quartiers d'hiver de la IIe légion Parthique: Monuments funéraires de la nécropole militaire* (Brussels: VUB Press, 1993); for Seleucia, see Henri Seyrig, "Le cimetière des marins à Séleucie de Piérie," in *Mélanges syriens offerts à M. René Dussaud* (Paris: P. Geuthner, 1939), pp. 451–459.

12. On the Dmeir text, see Pierre Roussel and Fernand de Visscher, "Les inscriptions du temple de Dmeir," *Syria* 23 (1942–1943): 173–194; there are substantial bibliographies in James H. Oliver, "Minutes of a Trial Conducted by Caracalla at Antioch in A.D. 216," in *Mélanges helléniques offerts à Georges Daux* (Paris: E. de Boccard, 1974), pp. 289–294, and in Bruno Rochette, *Le latin dans le monde grec: Recherches sur la diffusion de la langue et des lettres latines* (Brussels: Latomus, 1997), p. 114.

13. Rochette, *Latin,* pp. 167–174.

14. See Maurice Sartre, "Les colonies romaines dans le monde grec: Essai de synthèse," *Electrum* 5 (2001) 111–152.

15. Thomas Weber, *Syrisch-römische Sarkophagbeschläge: Orientalische Bronzewerkstätten in römischer Zeit* (Mainz: Ph. von Zabern, 1989); Annie Sartre-Fauriat, *Des tombeaux et des morts* (Beirut: Institut français d'archéologie du Proche-Orient, 2001), vol. 1, pp. 222–225; vol. 2, pp. 208–210.

16. For some examples, see, for Amman, Hans Wiegartz, "Zu Problemen einer Chronologie der attischen Sarkophage," *Archäologischer Anzeiger* (1977): 387, pl. 63; for Gadara, Guntram Koch, "Ein attischer Meleagersarkophag aus Arethousa in Syrien," *Damaszener Mitteilungen* (hereafter cited as *DaM*) 1 (1983): 147, n. 89; for Bostra, Sartre-Fauriat, *Tombeaux,* vol. 1, pp. 222–225.

17. Guntram Koch, "Der Import kaiserzeitlicher Sarkophage in den römischen Provinzen Syria, Palaestina und Arabia," *Bonner Jahrbücher* 189 (1989): 161–211; idem, "The Import of Attic Sarcophagi in the Near East," in Ο Ελληνισμοσ στην Ανατολη (Athens: EPKED, 1991), pp. 67–80; idem, "Ein attischer Schiffkampf-Sarkophag aus Arethousa in Damaskus," *DaM* 9 (1996): 197–207; Pascale Linant de Bellefonds, *Sarcophages attiques de la nécropole de Tyr* (Paris: Éditions Recherche sur les civilisations, 1985).

18. Guntram Koch, *Die mythologischen Sarkophage,* vol. 6, *Meleager* (Berlin: Gebr. Mann Verlag, 1975), nos. 168, 200. Both date from the first half or the middle of the third century.

19. In "La mosaïque antique au Proche-Orient: I. Des origines à la Tétrarchie," *ANRW* 2.12.2 (1981): 347–429, Janine Balty gives a very complete picture to date; see also Janine Balty and Jean-Charles Balty, *Mosaïques antiques de Syrie* (Brussels: Musées royaux d'art et d'histoire, 1977), and Janine Balty, *Mosaïques antiques du Proche-Orient: Chronologie, iconographie, interprétation* (Paris: Les Belles Lettres, 1995).

20. Except at Arsameia in Commagène: J. Balty, "Mosaïque antique," pp. 355–356.

21. Ibid., p. 426.

22. Henri Stern, *Les mosaïques des maisons d'Achille et de Cassiopée à Palmyre* (Paris: P. Geuthner, 1997), p. 42.

23. On the cultural significance of the mosaics, see, for example, Marie-Henriette Quet, "La mosaïque dite d'*Aiôn* de Shahba-Philippopolis: Philippe l'Arabe et la conception hellène de l'ordre du monde, en Arabie, à l'aube du christianisme," *Cahiers Glotz* 10 (1999): 269–330; idem, "Atemporalité du mythe et temps de l'image: Les mosaïques romaines figurant une *dextrarum iunctio* de 'noces' légendaires grecques," in *Constructions du temps dans le monde grec antique,* ed. Catherine Darbo-Peschanski (Paris: Centre national de la recherche scientifique, 2000), pp. 169–218 (where she examines two works from Philippopolis, representing the marriage of Thetis and Peleus and that of Pelops and Hippodamia).

24. Just because the city was founded by Philip the Arab does not mean that all the constructions found there have to be attributed to his reign: the city prospered later, and new houses must have been added. Arguments to this effect are already presented by J. Balty, in "Mosaïque antique," p. 397; on the basis of stylistic criteria, she estimates that the mosaics of Philippopolis can be dated from the middle of the third century to the Constantine era.

25. Han J. W. Drijvers, *Cults and Beliefs at Edessa* (Leiden: E. J. Brill, 1980), pp. 189–192. On the mosaics depicting Orpheus, see the collection of essays by Ilona Julia Jesnick, *The Image of Orpheus in Roman Mosaic: An Exploration of the Figure of Orpheus in Graeco-Roman Art and Culture with Special Reference to Its Expression in the Medium of Mosaic in Late Antiquity* (Oxford: Archaeopress, 1997). Let us note that the mosaics in Edessa are reserved for funerary use: see J. Balty, "Mosaïque antique," p. 387.

26. Drijvers, *Cults and Beliefs,* pp. 191–192; another mosaic from the same city, dating from 235–236, bears the image of Phoenix and refers to the same hopes (ibid., p. 189).

27. See Eric M. Meyers, Ehud Netzer, and Carol L. Meyers, "Artistry on Stone: The Mosaics of Ancient Sepphoris," *Biblical Archaeologist* 50 (1987): 223–231; Carol L. Meyers, Eric M. Meyers, Ehud Netzer, and Zeev Weiss, "The Dionysos Mosaic," in *Sepphoris in Galilee: Crosscurrents of Culture,* ed. Rebecca Martin Nagy, Carol L. Meyers, Eric M. Meyers, and Zeev Weiss, eds. (Raleigh: North Carolina Museum of Art, 1996), pp. 111–115. For the Orpheus mosaic, see Zeev Weiss and Ehud Netzer, "Hellenistic and Roman Sepphoris: The Archaeological Evidence," in Nagy et al., *Sepphoris in Galilee,* p. 35.

28. Josephus, *De bello judaico (The Jewish War),* trans. Henry St. John Thackeray (Loeb Classical Library), 5.210 (hereafter cited as *BJ*).

29. On the traditions related to the god of wine, see Morton Smith, "On the Wine God in Palestine (Gen. 18, Jn. 2, and Achilles Tatius)" in *Salo Wittmayer Baron Jubilee Volume on the Occasion of his Eightieth Birthday,* ed. Saul Lieberman and Arthur Hyman, vol. 2 (Jerusalem: American Academy for Jewish Research, 1975), pp. 815–829.

30. In "Les caractéristiques de la peinture murale à Pétra," *Studies in the History and Archaeology of Jordan* (hereafter cited as *SHAJ*) 5 (1995): 383–389, Alix Barbet shows that the oldest examples of painting in Petra go back to the end of the first cen-

tury B.C.E. at the latest, in the "baths" located to the south of the main street (in reality a palace, according to Fawzi Zayadine, "Decorative Stucco at Petra and Other Hellenistic Sites," *SHAJ* 3 [1987]: 139).

31. Alix Barbet, Pierre-Louis Gatier, and Norman n. Lewis, "Un tombeau peint inscrit de Sidon," *Syria* 74 (1997): 141–156.

32. Alix Barbet and Claude Vibert-Guigue, *Les peintures des nécropoles romaines d'Abila et du Nord de la Jordanie,* 2 vols. (Beirut: Institut français d'archéologie du Proche-Orient, 1988–1994).

33. Fawzi Zayadine, "Une tombe peinte de Beit Ras (Capitolias)," in *Studia Hierosolymitana in onore del p. Bellarmino Bagatti,* ed. Emmanuele Testa, Ignazio Mancini, and Michele Picirillo, vol. 1 (Jerusalem: Franciscan Printing Press, 1976), pp. 285–294; Ute Wagner-Lux, "Ein bemaltes Grab im Sôm, Jordanien," in *The Archaeology of Jordan and Other Studies, Presented to Siegfried H. Horn,* ed. L. T. Geraty and L. G. Herr (Berrien Springs, Mich.: Andrews University Press, 1986), pp. 287–300; C. C. MacCown, "A Painted Tomb at Marwa," *Quarterly of the Department of Antiquities of Palestine* 9 (1942): 1–30; Farah S. Ma'ayeh, "Recent Archaeological Discoveries in Jordan," *Annual of the Department of Antiquities of Jordan* 4–5 (1960): 115–116; idem, "Jérash," contribution to "Chronique archéologique," in *Revue biblique* 67 (1960): 228–229 (Gerasa).

34. Barbet and Vibert-Guigue, *Peintures des nécropoles,* vol. 1, pp. 278–279.

35. Zayadine, "Tombe peinte"; Barbet and Vibert-Guigue, *Peintures des nécropoles,* vol. 1, pp. 237–238.

36. Maurice Dunand, "Tombe peinte dans la campagne de Tyr," *Bulletin du Musée de Beyrouth* (hereafter cited as *BMB*) 18 (1965): 5–49 (with an additional note by Jean-Paul Rey-Coquais, pp. 49–51).

37. Carl Hermann Kraeling, "Color Photographs of the Painting in the Tomb of the Three Brothers at Palmyra," *Annales archéologiques de Syrie* 11–12 (1961–1962): 13–18.

38. Fernand Chapouthier, "Les peintures murales d'un hypogée funéraire près de Massyaf," *Syria* 31 (1954): 172–211.

39. Robert du Mesnil du Buisson, *Les peintures de la synagogue de Doura-Europos, 245–256 apr. J.-C.* (Rome: Pontifico istituto biblico, 1939).

40. Carl Hermann Kraeling, *The Excavations at Dura-Europos: Final Report,* vol. 8, part 2, *The Christian Building* (New Haven: Yale University Press, 1967), pp. 45–88.

41. Bernhard Kolb, "Les maisons patriciennes d'az-Zantûr," *Le monde de la Bible* 127 (May–June 2000): 42–43.

42. Fawzi Zayadine, "Die Ausgrabungen des Qasr el Bint," in *Petra: Neue Ausgrabungen und Entdeckungen,* ed. Manfred Lindner (Munich: Delp, 1986), p. 248 and ill. 49. Other traces of painted walls have been found in the thermal baths located to the south of the monumental arch: see Fawzi Zayadine, "Ein Turmgrab in Bab es-Siq," in Lindner, *Petra,* p. 217, ill. 5.

43. See Silvia Rozenberg, "The Wall Paintings of the Herodian Palace at Jericho," in *Judaea and the Greco-Roman World in the Time of Herod in the Light of Archaeological Evidence,* ed. Klaus Fittschen and Gideon Foerster (Göttingen: Vandenhoeck & Ruprecht, 1996), pp. 121–138; Rozenberg does not rule out the presence of Italian artists. See also Klaus Fittschen, "Wall Decorations in Herod's Kingdom: Their Rela-

tionship with Wall Decorations in Greece and Italy," in Fittschen and Foerster, *Judaea and the Greco-Roman World*, pp. 139–161.

44. Cf. Maurice Dunand, *Mission archéologique au Djebel Druze: Le Musée de Soueida* (Paris: P. Geuthner, 1934), pp. 11–13 (the judgment of Paris) and pp. 13–14 (Athena and Aphrodite). I completely disagree with Vassilios Christides, "The Beginning of Graeco-Nabataean Syncretism: Two Stone Lintels from Sweydah in Nabatene, 'The Judgment of Paris' and 'Athena and Aphrodite with the Lion,'" *Graeco-Arabica* 6 (1995): 272–300, because nothing justifies bringing the Nabataeans into this: Soueida was located outside their kingdom, on territory belonging to the Greek city of Canatha.

45. Kamal Chéhadeh and Marc Griesheimer, "Les reliefs funéraires du tombeau du prêtre Raspsônès (Babulin, Syrie du Nord)," *Syria* 75 (1998): 171–192.

46. For one example among others, see Khaled al-As'ad and Andreas Schmidt-Colinet, "Kulturbegegnung im Grenzbereich," in *Palmyra: Kulturbegegnung in Grenzbereich,* ed. Andreas Schmidt-Colinet (Mainz: Ph. von Zabern, 1995), pp. 36–37.

47. Jean-Charles Balty, "Palmyre entre Orient et Occident: Acculturation et résistances," in "Palmyra and the Silk Road: International Colloquium, Palmyra, 7–11 April 1992," special issue, *Annales archéologiques arabes syriennes* 42 (1996): 437–441.

48. Sartre-Fauriat, *Tombeaux*, vol. 1, pp. 247–295; vol. 2, pp. 203–208.

49. Hannah M. Cotton, "The Archive of Salome Komaïse, Daughter of Levi: Another Archive from the 'Cave of Letters,'" *Zeitschrift für Papyrologie und Epigraphik* (hereafter cited as *ZPE*) 105 (1995): 206.

50. Louis Jalabert and René Mouterde, *IGLS*, vol. 4, *Laodicée, Apamène: Chronologie des inscriptions datées des tomes I–IV* (Paris: P. Geuthner, 1955), no. 1265.

51. For Bostra, the *Dousaria Actia* are attested by coinages from the era of Philip the Arab; for Adraha, the only indication pointing to a contest seems very tenuous to me: the regular consecrations of panegyriarchs from Adraha who went to Petra to announce the festival (see Maurice Sartre, *IGLS*, vol. 21, *Inscriptions grecques et latines de la Jordanie* [hereafter cited as *IGLJ*], vol. 4, *Pétra et la Nabatène méridionale* [Paris: P. Geuthner, 1993], nos. 9–16); but was there a context, or a festival without a contest?

52. Scholia on a manuscript by Iamblichos transmitted by Photius (*Bibliothèque,* ed. and trans. René Henry, vol. 2 [Paris: Les Belles Lettres, 1959], codex 94): see Fergus Millar, "Paul of Samosata, Zenobia and Aurelian: The Church, Local Culture and Political Allegiance in 3rd Century Syria," *Journal of Roman Studies* (hereafter cited as *JRS*) 61 (1971): 6.

53. See Maurice Sartre, *D'Alexandre à Zénobie* (Paris: Fayard, 2001), pp. 294–299.

54. Eugene Vanderpool, "An Athenian Monument to Theodorus of Gadara," *American Journal of Philology* (hereafter cited as *AJPh*) 80 (1959): 366–369.

55. Ada Adler, ed., *Suidae Lexicon*, vol. 1 (Leipzig: B. J. Teubner, 1928–1938), s.v. "Apsines," 443 I; Caspar Hammer, *Rhetores graeci ex recognitione Leonardi Spengel*, vol. 1 (Leipzig: B. G. Teubner, 1894), p. 217.

56. Not to be confused with his homonym, a Stoic from the Hellenistic period (Sartre, *D'Alexandre à Zénobie,* p. 296): see H. B. Gottschalk, "Aristotelian Philoso-

phy in the Roman World from the Time of Cicero to the End of the Second Century AD," *ANRW* 2.36.2 (1987): 1079–1174.

57. Galen, *De praenotione ad Posthumum liber,* in *Klaudiou Galenou hapanta = Clavdii Galeni Opera omnia,* ed. Karl Gottlob Kühn (Leipzig: Knobloch, 1821–1833) vol. 14, p. 627; see Gottschalk, "Aristotelian Philosophy," p. 1152.

58. See Jürgen Hammerstaedt, "Der Kyniker Oenomaus von Gadara," *ANRW* 2.36.4 (1990): 2834–2865; Marie-Odile Goulet-Cazé, "Le cynisme ancien à l'époque impériale," *ANRW* 2.36.4 (1990): 2802–2803; Marie-Odile Goulet-Cazé and Richard Goulet, eds., *Le cynisme ancien et ses prolongements* (Paris: Presses Universitaires de France, 1993), pp. 399–418.

59. M. F. Smith, "An Epicurean Priest from Apamea in Syria," *ZPE* 112 (1996): 120–130.

60. Andrew Smith, "Porphyrian Studies since 1913," *ANRW* 2.36.2 (1978): 717–773; Luc Deitz, "Bibliographie du platonisme impérial antérieur à Plotin, 1926–1986," *ANRW* 2.36.1 (1990): 24–182; cf. Jean Sirinelli, *Les enfants d'Alexandre: La littérature et la pensée grecques (331 av. J.-C.–519 ap. J.-C.)* (Paris: Fayard, 1993), p. 335, and especially pp. 393–396.

61. See Giuseppe Martano, *Numenio d'Apamea: Un precursore del neo-platonismo* (Naples: Armanni, 1960); Michael Frede, "Numenius," *ANRW* 2.36.2 (1987): 1034–1075. For fragments from his work, see Numenius of Apamaea, *Fragments,* ed. Édouard des Places (Paris: Les Belles Lettres, 1973).

62. Luc Brisson, "Amélius: Sa vie, son oeuvre, sa doctrine, son style," *ANRW* 2.36.2 (1987): 793–860.

63. Adler, ed., *Suidae Lexicon,* vol. 4, s.v. "Philostratos": see Karl Gerth, "Zweite Sophistik," in *Realencyclopädie der classischen Altertumswissenschaft* (hereafter cited as *RE*), ed. August Friedrich von Pauly et al. (Stuttgart: J. B. Metzler, 1894–), suppl. 8 (1956), col. 752.

64. See the very detailed two-part study by Luc Brisson and Michel Patillon, "Longinus Platonicus Philosophus et Philologus: I. Longinus Philosophus," *ANRW* 2.36.7 (1994): 5214–5299, and idem, "Longinus Platonicus Philosophus et Philologus: II. Longinus Philologus," *ANRW* 2.34.4 (1998): 3023–3108, with translations of the fragments.

65. Joseph Bidez, *Vie de Porphyre: Le philosophe neo-platonicien* (Leipzig: B. G. Teubner, 1913); Heinrich Dörrie, ed., *Porphyre: Huit exposés suivis de discussions* (Geneva: Fondation Hardt, 1966); bibliography in Smith, "Porphyrian Studies," pp. 717–773. In English, see *Plotinus,* trans. A. H. Armstrong (Cambridge, Mass.: Harvard University Press, 1989–), and *Porphyry's Against the Christians: The Literary Remains,* ed. and trans. R. Joseph Hoffmann (Amherst, N.Y.: Prometheus Books, 1994).

66. Only Bent Dalsgaard Larsen presents him as originally from Chalcis of Lebanon: "Jamblique de Chalcis, exegete et philosophe" (Ph.D. diss., Universitetsforlaget, Aarhus, 1972).

67. John Dillon, "Iamblichus of Chalcis (c. 240–325 A.D.)," *ANRW* 2.36.2 (1987): 862–909; H. J. Blumenthal and E. G. Clark, eds., *The Divine Iamblichus: Philosopher and Man of Gods* (London: Bristol Classical Press, 1993).

68. Stern, *Les mosaïques.*

69. J. Balty brings clearly to light a program inspired by Neoplatonism in Julian's era (*Mosaïques antiques du Proche-Orient*); cf. Marie-Henriette Quet, "Naissance

d'image: La mosaïque des Thérapénides d'Apamée de Syrie, représentation figurée des connaissances encycliques, 'servantes' de la philosophie hellène," *Cahiers du Centre Glotz* 4 (1993): 129–187.

70. Pliny the Younger, *Letters and Panegyricus,* trans. Betty Radice, vol. 1 (Loeb Classical Library), 2.3; Philostrates, "The Lives of the Sophists," in *Philostratus and Eunapius,* trans. Wilmer Cave Wright (Loeb Classical Library), 1.20.513.

71. Wilhelm Schmid, "Genethlios," in *RE,* cols. 1134–1135; Gerth, "Zweite Sophistik," in *RE,* col. 752.

72. Felix Jacoby, "Kallinikos 1," in *RE,* cols. 1649–1650.

73. Philostrates, *Lives of the Sophists,* 2.10; cf. Gerth, "Zweite Sophistik," col. 753; Sirinelli, *Enfants d'Alexandre,* p. 310.

74. Philostrates, *The Life of Apollonius of Tyana,* trans. F. C. Conybeare (Loeb Classical Library), 1.7.

75. On all this, see Gerth, "Zweite Sophistik," col. 741–770.

76. Specialists disagree strongly about the date of Heliodorus of Emesa, between the second and the fifth centuries: in *The Cambridge History of Classical Literature,* vol. 1, *Greek Literature,* ed. P. E. Easterling and Bernard M. W. Knox (Cambridge: Cambridge University Press, 1985), he is placed around 220–230 (p. 696); Bryan P. Reardon discusses the question in *Courants littéraires grecs des IIe et IIIe siècles apr. J.-C.* (Paris: Les Belles Lettres, 1971), p. 334, n. 57; Pierre Chuvin argues in favor of the second half of the fourth century in *Chronique des derniers païens: La disparition du paganisme dans l'Empire romain, du règne de Constantin à celui de Justinien* (Paris: Fayard, 1990), p. 321; Simon Swain prefers the third century, in *Hellenism and Empire: Language, Classicism and Power in the Greek World ad 50–250* (Oxford: Clarendon Press, 1996), pp. 423–424; in his French translation, *Romans grecs et latins* (Paris: Gallimard, 1958), pp. 521–789, Pierre Grimal comes out in favor of the second third of the third century (p. 518).

77. There is a vast bibliography on Lucian: see, first, the already dated biography by Jacques Schwartz, *Biographie de Lucien de Samosate* (Brussels: Latomus, 1965); see also Alain Billault, ed., *Lucien de Samosate: Actes du colloque international de Lyon* (Lyon: Centre d'études romaines et gallo-romaines, 1994); Swain, *Hellenism and Empire,* pp. 298–329; finally, see Jacques Bompaire's republished 1958 thesis, *Lucien écrivain: Imitation et création* (Paris: Les Belles Lettres; Turin: Nino Aragno, 2000). Some twenty works, collected in two volumes, are available in the Collection des Universités de France (Lucian, *Oeuvres,* ed. Jacques Bompaire, 2 vols. [Paris: Les Belles Lettres, 1993–1998]).

78. Ernest Honigmann, "Marinos," in *RE,* vol. 14 (1930), cols. 1767–1796, and K. G. Photinos, "Marinos von Tyros," in *RE,* suppl. 12 (1970), cols. 791–838.

79. Germaine Aujac, *Claude Ptolémée, astronome, astrologue, géographe: Connaissance et représentation du monde habité* (Paris: Comité des travaux historiques et scientifiques, 1993), pp. 112–127; Ptolemy, *Tetrabiblos,* ed. and trans. F. E. Robbins (Loeb Classical Library).

80. Nicomachos of Gerasa, *Introduction to Arithmetic,* trans. Martin Luther D'Ooge (London: Macmillan, 1972 [1926]), with a comprehensive biography (pp. 71–78) and an inventory of the works (pp. 79–87); see also Flora R. Levin, *The Harmonics of Nicomachus and the Pythagorean Tradition* (University Park, Pa.: American Philological Association, 1975); William Coffman McDermott, "Plotina Augusta and Nicomachus of Gerasa," *Historia* 26 (1977): 192–203; Nicomachos of

Gerasa, *Introduction arithmétique,* ed. and trans. Janine Bertier (Paris: Vrin, 1978). The few biographical elements we have place him between Tiberius and Antonin the Pious, probably closer to the latter than to the former.

81. Dorotheos of Sidon, "Dorothei Sidonii Carmen astrologicum (= Penta-teuchos)," in *Die Fragmente des Dorotheos von Sidon,* ed. David Edwin Pingree (Leipzig: B. G. Teubner, 1976).

82. See Vettius Valens of Antioch, *Anthologies: Book I,* ed. Joëlle-Frédérique Bara (Leiden: E. J. Brill, 1989), with an introduction to the work; the date is controversial (some have tried to place him in the fourth century), but a date under the Antonini, and even under Hadrian, is most probable. For the complete works, see *Vettii Valentis Antiocheni anthologiarum libri novem,* ed. David Edwin Pingree (Leipzig: B. G. Teubner, 1986).

83. Heinrich Gelzer, *Julius Africanus und die byzantinische Chronographie* (Leipzig: J. C. Hinrichs, 1898).

84. *Les "Cestes" de Julius Africanus,* ed. and trans. Jean René Vieillefond (Florence: Sansoni antiquariato; Paris: Librairie M. Didier, 1970); Francis C. R. Thee, *Julius Africanus and the Early Christian View of Magic* (Tübingen: J. C. B. Mohr, 1984); Tiziana Rampoldi, "I 'kestoi' di Giulio Africano e l'imperatore Severo Alessandro," *ANRW* 2.34.3 (1997): 2451–2470. The author's origin is called into question by Vieillefond, who considers that others have read too much meaning into the reference to "our former fatherland Aelia Capitolina of Palestine" (*"Cestes,"* p. 17); similarly, he rejects any notion that the author settled in Emmaus, concluding that he could have been of service to the embassy that had come to demand the status of city only because he was then in Rome, close to the seat of power (he set up a library for Alexander Severus): see ibid., pp. 19–21.

85. Ben Zion Wacholder, *Nicolaus of Damascus* (Berkeley: University of California Press, 1962).

86. The scope of the bibliography devoted to Josephus can be assessed in the monumental work by Louis H. Feldman, *Josephus and Modern Scholarship (1937–1980)* (Berlin and New York: W. de Gruyter, 1984), offering 1,055 pages of bibliography, with commentary, covering a little less than half a century. Since Feldman, the inflation has not diminished: see idem, *Josephus: A Supplementary Bibliography* (New York: Garland, 1986), 696 pages. For a historian's view, see Mireille Hadas-Lebel, *Flavius Josèphe, le Juif de Rome* (Paris: Fayard, 1989).

87. See Tessa Rajak, "Justus of Tiberias," *Classical Quarterly* 23 (1973): 344–368; and Alberto Barzano, "Giusto di Tiberiade," *ANRW* 2.20.1 (1987): 337–358, offering perhaps too positive a judgment on the work.

88. See Felix Jacoby, *Die Fragmente der griechischen Historiker,* vol. 2 (Leiden: E. J. Brill, 1958), no. 90.

89. See the fundamental text by Pierre Vidal-Naquet, "Du bon usage de la trahison," an introduction to the translation of *La Guerre des Juifs* (The Jewish Wars) by Pierre Savinel (Paris: Éditions de Minuit, 1977), pp. 9–115.

90. All that remains comes either from Josephus (who may well distort the content) or from the summary by Photius (*Bibliothèque,* vol. 1, pp. 18–19, codex 33), who could still read the complete text, *Chronique des rois juifs disposée en forme de tableau généalogique.* Probably under the influence of Josephus's autobiography, *The Life* (in *The Life and Against Apion,* trans. Henry St. John Thackeray [Loeb Classical Library], pp. 1–159), in particular, Photius passed a harsh judgment on

Justus's version, which covered history from Moses to the death of Agrippa II. Josephus accuses Justus of lacking access to the field notes made by Vespasian and Titus, and of compounding the errors. See also Marie-Thérèse Frankfort, "Sur la date de l'Autobiographie de Flavius Josèphe et les oeuvres de Juste de Tibériade," *Revue belge de philologie et d'histoire* 39 (1961): 52–58.

91. See Philo of Byblos, *The Phoenician History of Philo of Byblos,* ed. Albert I. Baumgarten (Leiden: E. J. Brill, 1981); Philo of Byblos, *The Phoenician History: Introduction, Critical Text, Translation, Notes,* ed. and trans. Harold W. Attridge and Robert A. Oden Jr. (Washington, D.C.: Catholic Biblical Association of America, 1981); see also Lucio Troiani, *L'opera storiografica di Filone di Byblos* (Pisa: Goliardica, 1974); R. A. Oden, "Philo of Byblos and Hellenistic Historiography," *Palestine Exploration Quarterly* 110 (1978): 115–126; Jürgen Ebach, *Weltentstehung und Kulturentwicklung bei Philo von Byblos* (Stuttgart and Berlin: Kohlhammer, 1979); Lucio Troiani, "Contributuo alla problematica dei rapporti tra storiografia greca e storiografia vicino-orientale," *Athenaeum* 61 (1983): 427–428; Edward Lipinski, "The Phoenician History of Philo of Byblos," *Bibliotheca orientalis* 40 (1983): 304–310; Sergio Ribichini, *Poenus Advena: Gli dei fenici e l'interpretazione classica* (Rome: Consiglio nazionale delle ricerche, 1985); idem, "Questions de mythologie phénicienne d'après Philon de Byblos," in *Religio Phoenicia,* ed. Corinne Bonnet, Edward Lipinski, and Patrick Marchetti (Namur: Société des etudes classiques, 1986); Jordi Cors i Meya, *A Concordance of the Phoenician History of Philo of Byblos* (Sabadell and Barcelona: Editorial AUSA, 1995) = *Aula orientalis,* suppl. 10, with *corrigenda* in idem, "A Concordance to the Phoenician History of Philo of Byblos: Errata corrige," *Aula orientalis* 13 (1995): 264–266.

92. Baumgarten, *Phoenician History,* p. 31, n. 2.

93. Anthony. R. Birley, *Hadrian, the Restless Emperor* (London and New York: Routledge, 1997), p. 227.

94. Gerth, "Zweite Sophistik," cols. 756, 763.

95. See Gustave Bardy, "Justin," in *Dictionnaire de théologie catholique,* ed. Alfred Vacant, Eugène Mangenot, and Émile Amann (Paris: Letouzey & Ané, 1925–) (hereafter cited as *DTC*). However, Bardy's text is dated; see Oskar Skarsaune, "Justin der Märtyrer," in *Theologische Realenzyklopädie,* ed. Gerhard Müller, vol. 17 (Berlin and New York: W. de Gruyter, 1988).

96. We have no way of knowing whether he is from Roman Syria or Assyria.

97. See Sirinelli, *Enfants d'Alexandre,* pp. 351–355.

98. Ibid., pp. 355–356. For the text itself with an English translation, see Theophilos of Antioch, *Ad Autolycum,* ed. and trans. Robert M. Grant (Oxford: Clarendon Press, 1970).

99. See the now-dated presentations by P. Godet in *Le Dictionnaire de Théologie Catholique,* vol. 2 (Paris: Letouzey & Ané, 1925–), s.v. "Bérylle," cols. 799–800, and by Gustave Bardy, in Alfred Baudrillart, Albert de Meyer, and Étienne Van Cauwenbergh, *Dictionnaire d'histoire et de géographie ecclésiastiques* (Paris: Letouzey & Ané, 1935), vol. 8, s.v. "Beryllus, évêque de Bostra."

100. Eusebius, *The Ecclesiastical History,* trans. Kirsopp Lake (Loeb Classical Library), 7.30.7–8.

101. Gustave Bardy, *Paul de Samosate: Étude historique,* 2nd ed. (Louvain: Spicilegium Sacrum Lovaniense, 1929); Henri de Riedmatten, *Les actes du procès de Paul de Samosate: Étude sur la christologie du 3e au 4e siècle* (Fribourg: Éditions St-

Paul, 1952). (For additional fragments of the record of the trial, see José Declerck, "Deux nouveaux fragments attribués à Paul de Samosate," *Byzantion* 54 (1984): 116–140; Marcel Richard, "Malchion et Paul de Samosate: Le témoignage d'Eusèbe de Césarée," *Ephemerides theologicae lovanienses* 35 (1959): 325–329. In "Paul of Samosate," Fergus Millar showed that Paul was not accused of combining the functions of bishop with those of procurator ducenarius, but of behaving like a ducenarius (p. 13), and that Paul's ties to Zenobia (explained by their common tendency to "Judaize," pp. 12–13) are largely a matter of legend.

102. Gustave Bardy, *Saint Lucien d'Antioche et son école* (Paris: Beauchesne, 1936).

103. It also appears in Herbert Murusillo, *The Acts of the Pagan Martyrs: Acta Alexandrinorum* (Oxford: Clarendon Press, 1954).

104. Ulpian's glory was such that his city had an inscription engraved in his honor long after his death: see Maurice Chéhab, "Inscription en l'honneur d'Ulpien," *BMB* 33 (1983): 125–129. Chéhab proposes to date the engraving from the time of Gordian III for paleographic reasons; having examined the inscription myself on site (it is preserved within the excavation of the old city, on the island), I myself believe it is significantly later. On Ulpian's career and the date of his death, see Joseph Modrzejewski and Tadeusz Zawadzki, "La date de la mort d'Ulpien et la préfecture du prétoire au début du règne d'Alexandre Sévère," *Revue historique du droit français et étranger* (1967): 565–611, showing that the date of 228 for Ulpian's assassination by M. Aurelius Epagathos, a date accepted by most scholars, must be pushed back to the summer of 223.

105. Paul Collinet, *Histoire de l'École de droit de Beyrouth* (Paris: Sirey, 1923).

106. Jean-Paul Rey-Coquais, "Du sanctuaire de Pan à la 'guirlande' de Méléagre: Cultes et cultures dans la Syrie hellénistique," in *Aspetti e Problemi dell'Ellenismo: Atti del Convegno di studi, Pisa 6–7 novembre 1992*, ed. Biagio Virgilio (Pisa: Giardini, 1994), pp. 47–90; P.-L. Gatier, "À propos de la culture grecque à Gérasa," in Antonio Invernizzi and Jean-François Salles, *Arabia Antiqua: Hellenistic Centres around Arabia* (Rome: Istituto italiano per il Medio ed Estremo Oriente, 1993), pp. 15–35.

107. See especially Michel Tardieu, *Les paysages reliques, routes et haltes syriennes d'Isidore à Simplicius* (Louvain and Paris: Peeters, 1990).

108. John Chrysostom, Homily 19, "Ad populum Antiochenum," section 1, in *Patrologiae cursus completus: Series graeca,* ed. Jacques-Paul Migne et al. (Paris: Garnier Frères, 1859; repr., Turnhout: Brepols, 1996), vol. 49, col. 188.

109. Eusebius, "The Martyrs of Palestine," in *The Ecclesiastical History and The Martyrs of Palestine,* trans. Hugh Jackson Lawlor and John Ernest Leonard Oulton (London: Society for Promoting Christian Knowledge, 1927), p. 332, on the martyr Procopius, executed in 202; but information about his functions appears only in the longer Syriac version.

110. Jean-Paul Rey-Coquais, "Onomastique et histoire de la Syrie gréco-romaine," in *Actes du Congrès international d'épigraphie grecque et latine, Constantsa, 9–15 septembre 1977,* ed. D. M. Pippidi (Bucharest: Editura Academiei; Paris: Les Belles Lettres, 1979), pp. 171–183.

111. Françoise Briquel-Chatonnet observes that in novels, the Phoenicians all have Greek names during the imperial era and have often had a Greek-style education, even though they are represented as carrying out commercial activities in con-

formity with the traditional image of the Phoenician, combined with all the usual clichés (piracy, luxury, sensuality, licentiousness, and cruel religious ceremonies): see "L'image des Phéniciens dans les romans grecs," in *Le monde du roman grec: Actes du colloque international tenu à l'École normale supérieure, Paris 17–19 décembre 1987*, ed. Marie-Françoise Baslez, Philippe Hoffmann, and Monique Trédé-Boulmer (Paris: Presses de l'École normale supérieure, 1992), pp. 189–197.

112. Françoise Briquel-Chatonnet, "Les derniers témoignages sur la langue phénicienne en Orient," *Rivista dei Studi Fenici* 19 (1991): 3–21, especially pp. 16–19.

113. On all this, see Briquel-Chatonnet's definitive study, "Derniers témoignages," in which the author refuses to support either the extreme position adopted by Mark Lidzbarski, who believed that Phoenician was virtually a dead language as early as the beginning of the second century B.C.E. (see *Kanaanäische Inschriften* [Giessen: A. Töpelmann, 1907], p. 40), or the view espoused by Schmitt ("Ostgrenze," pp. 200–201) and Fergus Millar ("The Phoenician Cities: A Case Study of Hellenisation," *Proceedings of the Cambridge Philological Society* 209 [1983]: 55–71), who argue that it was still widely used in the Roman era. Let us recall that the last dated Phoenician inscription is a bilingual one (Greco-Phoenician) from Arados, in 25–24 B.C.E. (Jean-Paul Rey-Coquais, *IGLS*, vol. 7, *Arados et régions voisines* [Paris: P. Geuthner, 1970], no. 4001), and that the indirect evidence of spoken usage weighs in favor of the use of Aramaic rather than Phoenician, even if some people may have retained a memory of the latter. Contrary to what John D. Grainger seems to think (*Hellenistic Phoenicia* [Oxford: Clarendon Press, 1991], p. 191), Phoenician is not an Aramaic dialect, and we have no evidence that a Phoenician speaker could understand Aramaic: see Françoise Briquel-Chatonnet, "Les Phéniciens en leur contexte historique," in *I Fenici: Ieri, oggi, domani* (Rome: Grupo editoriale internazionale, 1995), p. 63.

114. Gatier, "À propos de la culture grecque à Gérasa," pp. 15–35.

115. Cf. Pierre-Louis Gatier, "La présence arabe à Gérasa et en Décapole," in *Présence arabe dans le Croissant fertile avant l'Hégire*, ed. Hélène Lozachmeur (Paris: Éditions Recherche sur les civilisations, 1995), pp. 109–118, especially pp. 115–116. Semitic names appear in particular among high-placed figures such as gymnasiarchs and priests of the imperial cult, as well as among the ambassadors sent to Pergamonsart: see Max Fränkel, ed., *Die Inschriften von Pergamon*, vol. 8, fasc. 2, *Römische Zeit* (Berlin: W. Spemann, 1895), no. 437.

116. Maurice Sartre, *Bostra: Des origines à l'Islam* (Paris: P. Geuthner, 1985).

117. See Maurice Sartre, "Le peuplement et le développement du Hauran antique à la lumière des inscriptions grecques et latines," in *Hauran: Recherches archéologiques sur la Syrie du sud à l'époque hellénistique et romaine*, ed. Jean-Marie Dentzer, vol. 1 (Paris: P. Geuthner, 1985), pp. 189–204.

118. Although Aramaic remained the spoken language of the majority, we have few written attestations for it before late antiquity; still, some proto-Syriac inscriptions attest to the maintenance of a written Aramaic culture: on the recent discovery in Apamaea on the Euphrates of an epitaph in Edessenian Aramaic dated from 191 C.E., see Alain Desreumaux and Jean-Baptiste Yon, "La nécropole: Une tombe à inscriptions syriaques," *Anatolia antiqua* 6 (1998): 405–406 (section D in Catherine Abadie-Reynal and Rifat Ergeç, "Zeugma-Moyenne Vallée de l'Euphrate: Rapport préliminaire de la campagne de fouilles de 1997"). This is the westernmost find; the others come from Sumatar Harabesi (see Joshua Benzion Segal, "Some Syriac In-

scriptions of the 2nd–3rd Century A.D.," *Bulletin of the Society for Oriental and African Studies* [hereafter cited as *BSOAS*] 16 [1954]: 19–20, 24–28), Birecik, Serrin, and Urfa (Edessa). See Han J. W. Drijvers and John F. Healey, *The Old Syriac Inscriptions of Edessa and Osrhoene: Texts, Translations and Commentary* (Leiden and Boston: E. J. Brill, 1999).

119. Text and translation by William Cureton, *Spicilegium Syriacum, Containing Remains of Bardesan, Meliton, Ambrose, and Mara Bar Serapion* (London: F. and J. Rivington, 1855; repr., Lexington, Ky.: American Theological Library Association, 1965), pp. 70–76; see also Rubens Duval, *La littérature syriaque*, 2nd ed. (Paris: V. Lecoffre, 1900), pp. 248–250, and Anton Baumstark, *Geschichte der syrischen Literatur* (Bonn: A. Marcus and E. Weber, 1922), p. 10.

120. Ramsay MacMullen, "Provincial Languages in the Roman Empire," in *Changes in the Roman Empire: Essays in the Ordinary,* ed. Ramsay MacMullen (Princeton: Princeton University Press, 1990), pp. 33–35 (originally published in *American Journal of Philology* 67 [1966]); Han J. W. Drijvers, *Bardaisan of Edessa* (Assen: Van Gorcum, 1966); Javier Teixidor, *Bardesane d'Édesse: La première philosophie syriaque* (Paris: Le Cerf, 1992). His name, Bar Daisan, means "son of the Daisan," Daisan being the name of the river that flows through Edessa.

121. Han J. W. Drijvers, *The Book of the Laws of the Countries: Dialogue on the Fate of Bardaisan of Edessa* (Assen: Van Gorcum, 1965).

122. Han J. W. Drijvers, "Facts and Problems in Early Syriac-Speaking Christianity," *Second Century* 2 (1982): 174 (reprinted in Han J. W. Drijvers, *East of Antioch: Studies in Early Syriac Christianity* [London: Variorum Reprints, 1984], essay 6).

123. Han J. W. Drijvers, "Greek and Aramaic in Palmyrene Inscriptions," in *Studia Aramaica,* ed. J. M. Geller, Jonas C. Greenfield, and M. P. Weitzmann (Oxford: Oxford University Press, 1995), pp. 31–42 (= *Journal of Semitic Studies* [hereafter cited as *JSS*], suppl. 4).

124. The title of an article by Riccardo Contini, "Il Hawran preislamico: Ipotesi di storia linguistica" (*Felix Ravenna* [1987]: 25–79) is intriguing, but the article itself is quite disappointing, for it uses a now-obsolete linguistic classification and does no more than establish a repertory of language use without drawing any real historical conclusions.

125. Hans P. Roschinski, "Sprachen, Schriften und Inschriften in Nordwestarabien," *Bonner Jahrbücher* 180 (1980): 155–188. However, some scholars challenge the idea that Arab writing has a Nabataean origin, preferring to attribute a Syriac origin instead; like Arabic and unlike Nabataean, Syriac is written above an ideal line: see Teixidor, *Bardesane d'Édesse,* p. 22; for a more fully developed argument, see Françoise Briquel-Chatonnet, "De l'araméen à l'arabe: Quelques réflexions sur la genèse de l'écriture arabe," in *Scribes et manuscrits du Moyen-Orient,* ed. François Déroche and Francis Richard (Paris: Bibliothèque nationale de France, 1997), pp. 136–149.

126. There are inscriptions in Arabic (texts from Qaryat al-Faw, in central Arabia), but they are written in a form deriving from pre-Christian southern Arabian alphabets: Alfred Felix L. Beeston, "Nemara and Faw," *BSOAS* 42 (1979): 1–6; Christian Robin, "Les plus anciens monuments de la langue arabe," in "L'Arabie antique de Karaib'îl à Mahomet," ed. Christian Robin, special issue, *Revue du monde musulman et de la Méditerranée* 61 (1991): 113–116. For the Avdat inscription, see Avraham Negev, "Obodas the God," *Israel Exploration Journal* 36 (1986): 56–60, dating the entry between 88 and 125, but this early dating is not necessary; the date

can be shifted to the third century, because the temple was rebuilt in 268; see Javier Teixidor, "Une inscription araméenne provenant de l'Émirat de Sharjah (Émirats Arabes Unis)," *Comptes rendus des séances de l'Académie des inscriptions et belles-lettres* (1992): 703, n. 20; on the Arabic character of the text, see James A. Bellamy, "Arabic Verses from the First/Second Century: The inscription of 'En 'Avdat," *JSS* 35 (1990): 73–79. For the inscription from Hegra, see John F. Healey and G. Rex Smith, "Jaussen-Savignac 17: The Earliest Dated Arabic Document (A.D. 267)," *Al-Atlal* 12 (1989): 77–84. On the connection between Nabataean writing and Arabic writing, see John F. Healey, "The Nabataean Contribution to the Development of the Arabic Script," *Aram* 2 (1990): 93–98.

127. Fergus Millar, "Empire, Community and Culture in the Roman Near East: Greeks, Syrians, Jews and Arabs," *JJS* 38 (1987): 143–164.

128. Sartre-Fauriat, *Tombeaux,* especially volume 2, which brings together very extensive documentation on culture, beliefs, and social behavior in the light of funerary architecture and practices.

129. On the survival of Hellenism in these two regions, see Tardieu, *Les paysages reliques,* and, for the Near East more generally, Glen W. Bowersock, *Hellenism in Late Antiquity: Thomas Spencer Jerome Lectures* (Ann Arbor: University of Michigan Press, 1990).

10. PAGANS, JEWS, AND CHRISTIANS IN ROMAN SYRIA IN THE SECOND AND THIRD CENTURIES

1. For example, the cult of the god-mountain Elagabalos of Emesa, who became a Heliogabalos: Julian, citing Iamblichos, associates the gods Azizos and Monimos with the sun in Edessa ("Hymn to King Helios Dedicated to Sallust," in *The Works of the Emperor Julian,* trans. Wilmer Cave Wright [Loeb Classical Library], vol. 1, 150c–d and 154a [hereafter cited as *Works*]); he was rightly corrected concerning Emesa (Henri Seyrig, "Inscriptions diverses," *Syria* 27 [1950]: 237–238 = Henri Seyrig, *Antiquités syriennes* [Paris: P. Geuthner, 1934–], vol. 4, 45, pp. 132–133 [hereafter cited as *AS*]); Henri Seyrig, "Le culte du Soleil en Syrie à l'époque romaine," *Syria* 48 (1971): 337–373.

2. Henri Seyrig, "Monuments syriens du culte de Némésis," *Syria* 13 (1932): 50–64 (= *AS,* vol. 1, pp. 11–26); idem, "Inscriptions diverses," pp. 242–247 (= *AS,* vol. 4, 42, pp. 137–142). Here Nemesis is not a goddess of vengeance, but instead the image of cosmic destiny.

3. By titling the chapter he devotes to Syrian paganism "Synkretismus zwischen griechisch-römischen und orientalischen Gottheiten" (Syncretism between Greco-Roman and Oriental Gods), (in *Religionsgeschichte Syriens,* ed. Peter W. Haider, Manfred Hutter, and Siegfried Kreuzer [Stuttgart: Kohlhammer, 1996], pp. 145–241), Peter W. Haider gives a distorted view, although in the end he offers a relatively complete account of religious life in Hellenistic and Roman Syria, without limiting himself to its syncretic aspects alone. However, the author is not conversant with the recent bibliography, especially in the realm of archaeology, so he is overly reliant on outdated publications; this is particularly evident with respect to his discussion of the Hauran, in which there are numerous errors.

4. Javier Teixidor, "Cultes tribaux et religion civique à Palmyre," *Revue d'histoire des religions* (1980): 277–287.

5. Maurice Sartre, *L'Orient romain: Provinces et sociétés provinciales en*

Méditerranée orientale d'Auguste aux Sévères (31 avant J.-C–235 après J.-C.) (Paris: Le Seuil, 1991), pp. 459–500. On Adonis, see Henri Seyrig, "La résurrection d'Adonis et le texte de Lucien," *Syria* 49 (1972): 97–100; Ernest Will, "Le rituel des Adonies," *Syria* 52 (1975): 93–105; Brigitte Soyez, *Byblos et la fête des Adonies* (Leiden: E. J. Brill, 1977).

6. Jean-Paul Rey-Coquais, "Note sur deux sanctuaires de la Syrie romaine," *Topoi* 7 (1997): 931–934.

7. Youssef Hajjar, *La triade d'Héliopolis-Baalbeck* (Leiden: E. J. Brill, 1977); idem, "Baalbek, grand centre religieux sous l'Empire," *Aufstieg und Niedergang der römischen Welt* (hereafter cited as *ANRW*) 2.18.4 (1990): 2458–2508.

8. See Gerard Mussies, "Marnas God of Gaza," *ANRW* 2.18.4 (1990): 2412–2457.

9. See Dominique Tarrier, "Baalshamin dans le monde nabatéen: À propos de découvertes récentes," *Aram* 2 (1990): 197–203.

10. There is a good example of double names at Niha in the Beqaa, where the goddess was venerated in Latin as *dea Syria Nihathena* and in Greek as *thea Atargateis* (Jean-Paul Rey-Coquais, *Inscriptions grecques et latines de la Syrie* (hereafter cited as *IGLS*), vol. 6, *Baalbek et Beqa'* [Paris: P. Geuthner, 1967], nos. 2929, 2936). At Qal'at Faqra, in the Lebanese mountains behind Byblos, she was known as "the goddess Atargatis of the Arabs," presumably a reference to the Ituraeans of the region: see Jean-Paul Rey-Coquais, "Qalaat Faqra: Un monument du culte impérial dans la montagne libanaise," *Topoi* 9 (1999): 638–640. The treatise attributed to Lucian of Samosata, *On the Syrian Goddess* (ed. and trans. Jane L. Lightfoot [Oxford: Oxford University Press, 2003]), is probably not by him: see Marie-Françoise Baslez, "L'auteur du *De Dea Syria* et les réalités religieuses de Hiérapolis," in *Lucien de Samosate,* ed. Alain Billault and André Buisson (Lyon: Centre d'études romaines et gallo-romaines, 1994), pp. 171–176; Baslez shows the heterogeneous character of this compilation, very unlike the writings of the highly cultivated Lucian (see also Per Bilde, "Atargatis/Dea Syria: Hellenization of Her Cult in the Hellenistic-Roman Period?" in *Religion and Religious Practice in the Seleucid Kingdom,* ed. Per Bilde, Troels Engberg, Lise Hannestad, and Jan Zahle [Aarhus: Aarhus University Press, 1990], pp. 162–166).

11. See Per Bilde's excellent article, "Atargatis/Dea Syria," with all the available bibliography.

12. Charles Clermont-Ganneau, "Une nouvelle dédicace à Baal Marcod," *Recueil d'archéologie orientale* 1 (1888): 94–97; Sébastien Ronzevalle, "Inscription bilingue de Deir el-Qala'a dans le Liban, près de Béryte," *Revue archéologique* (hereafter cited as *RA*) 2 (1903): 29–49; Charles Clermont-Ganneau, "Une nouvelle dédicace à Baal Marcod," *RA* 2 (1903): 225–229; Robert du Mesnil du Buisson and René Mouterde, "Inscriptions grecques de Beyrouth: III. Dédicace à Baalmarqod et à Poséidon," *Mélanges de l'Université Saint-Joseph* (hereafter cited as *MUSJ*) 7 (1914–1921): 387–390. A major epigraphic dossier was presented by Jean-Paul Rey-Coquais at a colloquium in Beirut in April 1999 (Colloque de Beyrouth sur les santuaires au Proche-Orient) and published in abridged form as "Deir el Qalaa," *Topoi* 9 (1999): 607–628.

13. See Jean Starcky, "Stèle d'Élahagabal," *MUSJ* 49 (1975–1976): 503–520; on the rites celebrated by the high priest of Emesa, see Herodian, *History of the Empire from the Time of Marcus Aurelius,* trans. C. R. Whittaker (Loeb Classical Library), 5.3.4–8.

14. Jupiter Turmasgadus was honored in Dacia by Commagene archers (Hermann

Dessau, *Inscriptiones latinae selectae* [Berlin: Weidmann, 1892–1916], no. 9273 [hereafter cited as *ILS*]), Mithra-Turmasgades in the *Dolichenum* of Dura-Europos (James Frank Gilliam, "The Dolicheneum: The Inscriptions" and "The Dolicheneum: Interpretation," in *Excavations at Dura-Europos: Preliminary Report of the Ninth Season of Work*, vol. 9, part 3, *The Palace of the Dux Ripae and the Dolicheneum*, ed. Mikhail Ivanovitch Rostovtzeff, Alfred Raymond Bellinger, Frank E. Brown, and Charles Bradford Welles [New Haven: Yale University Press, 1952], pp. 114–117 and 130–134). He was also honored in an inscription at Caesarea: see Baruch Lifshitz, "Inscriptions latines de Césarée en Palestine," *Latomus* 21 (1962): 149, no. 1; cf. James Frank Gilliam, "Jupiter Turmasgades," in *Actes du IXe Congrès international d'études sur les frontières romaines (1972)* (Bucharest and Cologne: Edituru Academiei, 1974), pp. 311–313; Émile Puech, "Note d'épigraphie palestinienne: Le dieu Turmasgada à Césarée Maritime," *Revue biblique* (hereafter cited as *Rbi*) 89 (1982): 210–221; this could be the name of Nemrud Dagh, in Commagène.

15. Olivier Callot and Jean Marcillet-Jaubert, "Hauts-lieux de Syrie du Nord," in *Temples et sanctuaires*, ed. Georges Roux (Lyon: Groupement d'intérêt scientifique, Maison de l'Orient, 1984), pp. 185–202.

16. Cf. *L'année épigraphique* (hereafter cited as *AE*) (1978), no. 718.

17. Tacitus, *The Histories*, trans. Clifford H. Moore (Loeb Classical Library), 2.78.5–6; Michael Avi-Yonah, "Mount Carmel and the God of Baalbek," *Israel Exploration Journal* (hereafter cited as *IEJ*) 2 (1952): 118–119: Zeus Heliopolitan Carmel, where Heliopolitan is probably a recent addition, for the baal at Carmel is much older; see Nicole Belayche, *Iudaea-Palaestina: The Pagan Cults in Roman Palestine (Second to Fourth Century)* (Tübingen: Mohr Siebeck, 2001), p. 188. Cf. *Le Talmud de Jérusalem*, trans. Moïse Schwab, vol. 11 (Paris: Maisonneuve & Larose, 1889), p. 214 (hereafter cited as *TJ*): "The Canaanites left no mountain, no hillside, without adoring an idol there."

18. Pierre-Louis Gatier, *IGLS*, vol. 21, *Inscriptions grecques et latines de la Jordanie* (hereafter cited as *IGLJ*), vol. 2, *Région centrale: Amman, Hesban, Madaba, Main, Dhiban* (Paris: P. Geuthner, 1986), no. 154.

19. Rey-Coquais, "Qalaat Faqra," pp. 632–638.

20. Jean Starcky, "Pétra et la Nabatène," in *Dictionnaire de la Bible*, suppl. 7 (Paris: Letouzey & Ané, 1996), cols. 886–1017; Michel Gawlikowski, "Les dieux des Nabatéens," *ANRW* 2.18.4 (1990): 2659–2677.

21. Paul Naster, "Le culte du dieu nabatéen Dousarès reflété par les monnaies d'époque impériale," *Actes du IXe congrès international de numismatique, Berne, 1979* (Louvain-la-Neuve: Association internationale des numismates professionnels, 1982), pp. 399–408.

22. Dominique Sourdel, *Les cultes du Hauran à l'époque gréco-romaine* (Paris: P. Geuthner, 1952).

23. Sourdel, *Cultes*, pp. 81–83; Lycurgos appears clearly in Dionysian mythology as the adversary of Dionysos, since he is the god who drinks no wine; but in the Hauran, he is also conflated with another deity: see Pierre Chuvin, *Mythologie et géographie dionysiaques: Recherches sur l'oeuvre de Nonnos de Panopolis* (Clermont-Ferrand: Adosa, 1991), pp. 264–270; we can fairly safely identify this god with Shai al-Qawm, who is characterized in Semitic inscriptions as a "god who never drinks wine"; see Ernst Axel Knauf, "Dushara and Shai' al-Qaum," *Aram* 2 (1990): 175–183, with numerous references to Palmyra and the Hauran.

24. Robert Donceel and Maurice Sartre, "Théandrios, dieu de Canatha," *Electrum*

1 (1997): 21–34; a new dedication confirms that the peripheral temple at Canatha was indeed dedicated to him and that he is indeed designated the "god of Rabbos": see Yannis Augier and Maurice Sartre, "Le dieu de Rabbos, maître du 'Temple périptère' de Canatha," *Damaszener Mitteilungen* (hereafter cited as *DaM*) 13 (2002): 125–130.

25. Marc Griesheimer alludes to a forthcoming dossier on this subject in "Le sanctuaire de Schnaan (Gebel Zawiye, Syrie du Nord)," *Topoi* 9 (1999): 703, 705; I thank the author for allowing me to cite this very valuable work.

26. Javier Teixidor, *The Pantheon of Palmyra* (Leiden: E. J. Brill, 1979); Michel Gawlikowski, "Les dieux de Palmyre," *ANRW* 2.18.4 (1990): 2605–2658.

27. Han J. W. Drijvers, *Cults and Beliefs at Edessa* (Leiden: E. J. Brill, 1980), pp. 122–145; idem, "Syriac Culture in Late Antiquity: Hellenism and Local Traditions," *Mediterraneo antico* 1 (1998): 100.

28. Drijvers, *Cults and Beliefs* (an indispensable work).

29. Cf. Janine Balty, "Le sanctuaire oraculaire de Zeus Bêlos à Apamée," *Topoi* 7 (1997): 791–799; the sanctuary had an excellent reputation well beyond the Apamene—it was consulted seven times by Septimius Severus (Cassius Dio, *Roman History* [Loeb Classical Library], 79.8.5 [hereafter cited as Dio]), then by Macrinus (Dio, 79.40.4). This is probably the only Apamaean sanctuary of which any vestiges remain (J. Balty, "Sanctuaire," p. 796). According to the ancient texts, in particular an inscription from Vaison (Georg Kaibel, ed., *Inscriptiones graecae* [Berlin: G. Reimer, 1890] 14.2482 = René Cagnat, Jean Toutain, Georges Lafaye, and Victor Henry, eds., *Inscriptiones graecae ad res romanas pertinentes*, vol. 1 [Paris: Leroux, 1911], no. 4 = Otto Hirschfeld, *Corpus inscriptionum latinarum* [hereafter cited as *CIL*], vol. 12, *Inscriptiones galliae narbonensis latinae* [Berlin: G. Reimer, 1888], no. 1277), it is the one that directs Fortune.

30. See Rey-Coquais, "Note sur deux sanctuaires," pp. 935–936. Cf. Youssef Hajjar, "Dieux et cultes non héliopolitains de la Béqa', de l'Hermon et de l'Abilène à l'époque romaine," *ANRW* 2.18.4 (1990): 2509–2604.

31. Pierre Merlat, *Répertoire des inscriptions et monuments figurés du culte de Jupiter Dolichenus* (Paris: P. Geuthner, 1951); idem, *Jupiter Dolichenus: Essai d'interprétation et de synthèse* (Paris: Presses Universitaires de France, 1960); Monica Hörig, "Jupiter Dolichenus," *ANRW* 2.17.4 (1984): 2136–2179; Horig's inventory shows the dearth of traces of the Dolichenian cult in Syria, outside of Dura and the Beqaa.

32. Suetonius, "The Deified Vespasian," in *Suetonius*, trans. J. C. Rolfe (Loeb Classical Library), vol. 1, 5.6.

33. To my knowledge, the only mention we have of Zeus of Nikephorion is in "Hadrian," in *Historia Augusta*, trans. David Magie (Loeb Classical Library), vol. 1, 2.9: he is said to have predicted Hadrian's empire.

34. Jodi Magness, "Some Observations on the Roman Temple at Kedesh," *IEJ* 40 (1990): 173–181: the sanctuary is dedicated to Zeus-Baalshamin and Apollo, and it was active during the second and third centuries C.E.

35. Youssef Hajjar, "Divinités oraculaires et rites divinatoires en Syrie et en Phénicie à l'époque gréco-romaine," *ANRW* 2.18.4 (1990): 2236–2320.

36. Rey-Coquais, *IGLS*, vol. 6, no. 2928; see also no. 2929.

37. Maurice Sartre, *D'Alexandre à Zénobie* (Paris: Fayard, 1992), p. 286.

38. *AE* (1955), no. 85.

39. *CIL*, vol. 3, nos. 6674–6675; *AE* (1900), no. 141; Louis Jalabert, "Inscriptions grecques et latines de la Syrie," *Mélanges de la Faculté orientale de Beyrouth* 1 (1906): 185.

40. *CIL*, vol. 3, no. 6680.

41. For Venus, see *AE* (1924), no. 137; for Mercury, *AE* (1924), no. 138, and *AE* (1958), no. 167.

42. *AE* (1940), no. 171. Other inscriptions in honor of the Genius of the colony are found in Theodor Mommsen, *CIL*, vol. 3, *Inscriptiones Asiae, proinviaeum Europae graecarum, Illyrici latinae*, 2 vols. (Berlin: G. Reimer, 1883), nos. 153, 6671; *AE* (1926), no. 57; *AE* (1950), no. 233.

43. Belayche, *Iudaea-Palaestina*, pp. 142–149.

44. Ibid., pp. 157–160.

45. Rey-Coquais, "Note sur deux sanctuaires," p. 935.

46. John Winter Crowfoot, G. M. Crowfoot, and Kathleen M. Kenyon, *The Objects from Samaria* (London: Palestine Exploration Fund, 1957), p. 37, no. 13.

47. Peter J. Parr, "Recent Discoveries at Petra," *Palestine Exploration Quarterly* 89 (1957): 6–7; Fawzi Zayadine, "Ein Turmgrab in Bab es-Siq," in *Petra: Neue Ausgrabungen und Entdeckungen*, ed. Manfred Lindner (Munich: Delp, 1986), p. 215, ill. 1.

48. Augustus J. Spijkerman, *The Coins of the Decapolis and Roman Arabia* (Jerusalem: Franciscan Printing Press, 1978), pp. 74–75, no. 25.

49. John Peter Oleson, Erik de Bruijn, and M. Barbara Reeves, "Field Reports: Humayma," *ACOR Newsletter* [American Center of Oriental Research] 12.1 (Summer 2000): 3; the (Greek) inscription was found with a dedication to Zeus Ammon, the tutelary god of III Cyrenaica, which suggests that Serapis was also venerated there by soldiers.

50. Belayche, *Iudaea-Palaestina*, p. 157.

51. Ibid., pp. 160–167.

52. Charles Bradford Welles, "The Inscriptions," in *Gerasa, City of the Decapolis*, ed. Carl Hermann Kraeling (New Haven, Conn.: American Schools of Oriental Research, 1938), no. 15 (hereafter cited as *I.Gerasa*).

53. Pierre Roussel, "Décret des péliganes de Laodicée-sur-mer," *Syria* 23 (1942–1943): 21–32 = Louis Jalabert and René Mouterde, *IGLS*, vol. 4, *Laodicée, Apamène: Chronologie des inscriptions datées des tomes I–IV* (Paris: P. Geuthner, 1955), no. 1261.

54. Jósef Tadeusz Milik and Jean Starcky, "Inscriptions récemment découvertes à Pétra," *Annual of the Department of Antiquities of Jordan* (hereafter cited as *ADAJ*) 20 (1975): 125–126.

55. Fawzi Zayadine, "Die Felsarchitektur Petra," in *Petra und das Königsreich der Nabatäer*, ed. Manfred Lindner, 3rd ed. (Munich: Delp, 1989), p. 244; idem, "L'iconographie d'Isis à Pétra," *Mélanges de l'École française de Rome: Antiquités* (hereafter cited as *MEFRA*) 103 (1991): 283–306.

56. Peter J. Parr, "A Nabataean Sanctuary near Petra: A Preliminary Notice," *ADAJ* 6–7 (1962): 21–23.

57. Maurice Sartre, *IGLJ*, vol. 4, *Pétra et la Nabatène méridionale* (Paris: P. Geuthner, 1993), no. 18, but I am quite skeptical about the restitution: see Marie-Jeanne Roche, "Le culte d'Isis et l'influence égyptienne à Pétra," *Syria* 64: 217–222; Fawzi Zayadine, "L'iconographie d'Isis à Pétra," *MEFRA* 103 (1991): 283–306; Alicia

I. Meza, "The Egyptian Statuette in Petra and the Isis Cult Connection," *ADAJ* 40 (1996): 167–176.

58. William Henry Waddington, *Inscriptions grecques et latines de la Syrie* (Paris: Firmin-Didot, 1870), 2526 (hereafter cited as *I.Syrie*).

59. Jósef Tadeusz Milik, "Une bilingue araméo-grecque de 105–104 av. J.-C.," in *Hauran II: Les installations de Si' 8 ; Du sanctuaire à l'établissement viticole*, ed. Jacqueline Dentzer[-Feydy], Jean-Marie Dentzer, and Pierre-Marie Blanc (Beirut: Institut français d'archéologie du Proche-Orient, 2003), pp. 269–275; the inscription bears the date 204. If the date refers to the Seleucid era, as Milik believes, it corresponds to 107–106. Canatha used a Pompeian era starting in 64 or 63; here, the Aramaic writing seems to indicate an earlier date, according to Milik. For the Greek, we have no point of comparison, for this is believed to be the only Hauranese inscription anterior to the Christian era.

60. There is an old inventory of the monuments in Maarten Jozef Vermaseren, *Corpus Inscriptionum et monumentorum religionis mithriacae*, vol. 1 (The Hague: M. Nijhoff, 1956), pp. 57–77. A disappointing account is offered by Lewis M. Hopfe, "Mithraism in Syria," *ANRW* 2.18.4 (1990): 2214–2235; see "Actes de la Table Ronde 'Mithra en Syrie,' Lyon, 18 novembre 2000," *Topoi* 11 (2001): 35–281.

61. Robert J. Bull, "The Mithraeum at Caesarea Maritima," *Études Mithriaques: Actes du 2e Congrès international [d'études mithriaques], Téhéran, du 1er au 8 septembre 1975* (Leiden: E. J. Brill, 1978), pp. 75–89; Lewis M. Hopfe and Gary Lease, "The Caesarea Mithraeum: A Preliminary Report," *Biblical Archaeologist* 38 (1975): 1–10; we find precise dating in Jeffrey A. Blakely, *Caesarea Maritima, The Pottery and Dating of Vault 1: Horreum, Mithraeum and Later Uses* (Lewiston, N.Y.: Edwin Mellen Press, 1987); see also Kenneth G. Holum and Robert L. Hohlfelder, eds., *King Herod's Dream: Caesarea on the Sea* (New York: W. W. Norton, 1988), pp. 148–153.

62. The date of the *mithraeum* at Sidon, long placed toward the end of the second century, has been shifted to the end of the fourth century by Ernest Will, "La date du Mithréum de Sidon," *Syria* 27 (1950): 262–269. The sculptures raise some problems of dating, however: see François Baratte, "Le mithraeum de Sidon: Certitudes et questions," *Topoi* 11 (2001): 205–227.

63. Maurice Dunand, "Le Temple d'Echmoun à Sidon: Essai de chronologie," *Bulletin du Musée de Beyrouth* 26 (1973): pl. 13.1 (including a very readable photo of the stele dedicated to Eschmoun by the priest Theodotos).

64. Franz Cumont, "The Dura Mithraeum," in *Mithraic Studies,* ed. E. D. Francis, vol. 2 (Manchester, U.K.: Mithraic Studies, 1975), pp. 151–214. Nothing remains on the site, and the monument has been entirely reinstalled in the Yale University Museum in New Haven, Connecticut.

65. Mikhail Ivanovitch Rostovtzeff, Frank E. Brown, and Charles Bradford Welles, *The Excavations at Dura-Europos, Conducted by Yale University and the French Academy of Inscriptions and Letters,* vols. 7–8, *Preliminary Report of the Seventh and Eighth Seasons of Work, 1933–1934 and 1934–1935* (New Haven: Yale University Press, 1939), pp. 62–134; Cumont, "Dura Mithraeum."

66. On the cult of Mithra in Sia, see Howard Crosby Butler, *Syria: Publications of the Princeton University Archaeological Expeditions to Syria, 1904–1905 and 1909* (hereafter cited as *PAES*), vol. 2A, *Architecture* (Leiden: E. J. Brill, 1919), p. 398; on the reliefs, see Vermaseren, *Corpus,* p. 76, nos. 88–89, and especially Ernest Will,

"Nouveaux monuments sacrés de la Syrie romaine," *Syria* 29 (1952): 67–73; for the sanctuary, my information comes from a contribution by Jean-Marie Dentzer during the roundtable "Mithra en Syrie" held in Lyon (France) on November 18, 2000.

67. Mikaël Kalos, "Un sanctuaire de Mithra inédit en Syrie du sud," *Topoï* 11 (2001): 229–277; for a provisional presentation, see idem, "Un nouveau culte à Mithra," *Le monde de la Bible* 139 (November–December 2001): 58.

68. Michel Gawlikowski, "Hawarti, Preliminary Report," in "Reports 1998," *Polish Archaeology in the Mediterranean* (hereafter cited as *PAM*) 10 (1999): 197–204; idem, "Hawarte, Excavations, 1999," *PAM* 11 (1999), 261–271; idem, "Hawarte, Third Interim Report on the Work in the Mithraeum," *PAM* 12 (2000): 309–314; idem, "Hawarte: Excavation and Restoration Work in 2001," *PAM* 13 (2001): 271–278; idem, "Le mithraeum de Haouarte," *Topoï* 11 (2001): 183–193.

69. Vermaseren, *Corpus*, p. 72, no. 71.

70. Pointed out by Rifat Ergeç, Anke Schutte-Maischatz, and Engelbert Winter, in "Doliche, 17," *Arastima Sonuçlari Topantlisi* (2000), pp. 185–194; Engelbert Winter, "Mithraism and Christianity in Late Antiquity," in *Ethnicity and Culture in Late Antiquity*, ed. Stephen Mitchell and Geoffrey Greatrex (London: Duckworth; Swansea: Classical Press of Wales, 2000), pp. 173–182. Although the last known configuration is a late one, it is probable that the *mithraea* are older.

71. To this inventory of well-attested cults we must add a head of Mithra in the Aleppo museum that may come from the coastal region (Laodicea-Balanaea): see Ernest Will, "Nouveaux monuments"; an inscription from Sahin, near Tartous, in honor of Mithra: Vermaseren, *Corpus*, p. 72, no. 72; a fragment of a Mithraic relief pointed out in the *Annuaire de la Société royale d'archéologie de Bruxelles* 49 (1956–1957): 12–13, cited by Manfred Clauss in *Cultores Mithrae* (Stuttgart: F. Steiner, 1992), p. 238 (a relief that I have never seen).

72. Phaina of Trachon housed many soldiers, but not Sha'arah; Apamaea, but not Huarte.

73. Zvi Ma'oz, "Temple of Pan, 1991–1992," *Excavations and Surveys in Israel* (hereafter cited as *ESI*) 12 (1993): 2–7.

74. For a later state of the tradition, see Arrian, *The Anabasis of Alexander*, ed. and trans. E. J. Chinnock (London: Hodder & Stoughton, 1884), 2.14.1–6. Other examples: Adonis-Osiris: Lucian, *De Dea Syria*, 6–8; Cybele, Rhea, and Atargatis: Lucian, ibid., 15.

75. Sourdel, *Cultes*, p. 44, with references.

76. *AE* (1976), no. 687.

77. Sourdel, *Cultes*, pp. 21–22.

78. Despite an often-repeated erroneous tradition that sees Dushara in the features of Dionysus, an assimilation based on a gloss of Hesychius and a reference in Damascios, *The Philosophical History* (= *Vita Isidori*), ed. and trans. Polymnia Athanassiadi (Athens: Apamea Cultural Association, 1999), p. 305, 136A. This preconceived idea invalidates the conclusions of V. Tam Tinh Tran, "Remarques sur l'iconographie de Dousarès," in *Petra and the Caravan Cities*, ed. Fawzi Zayadine (Amman: Department of Antiquities, 1990), pp. 107–114; Tran rejects the identification of certain statues of Dushara on the pretext that they present no Dionysian symbols. In contrast, there are also correspondences between Dushara/Dousares, Ares, and Arsu: Glen W. Bowersock, "The Cult and Representation of Dusares in Roman Arabia," in Zayadine, *Petra*, pp. 31–33. Certain other examples of assimilation be-

tween Dionysus and Dushara are baseless: Knauf, "Dushara and Shai' al-Qaum"; Margaret B. Lyttleton and Thomas F. C. Blagg, "Sculpture from the Temenos of Qasr el-Bint," *Aram* 2 (1990): 267–286, especially p. 280, pl. 1.

79. Contrary to long-held views, Zeus Safatenos may well not be the Ruda of the Safaites (Maurice Sartre, *IGLS*, vol. 13.1, *Bostra* [Paris: P. Geuthner, 1982], no. 9001), for we cannot easily dismiss the reservations of Michael C. A. Macdonald ("North Arabian Epigraphic Notes—I," *AAE* 3 [1992]: 25–27), who prefers to see Zeus Safatenos just as an ordinary local village god; we have virtually no examples of a local god of a region, especially none as obscure as this one.

80. The equivalence is ensured by the inscription from Cordova: Franz Cumont, "Une dédicace à des dieux syriens trouvée à Cordoue," *Syria* 5 (1924): 342–345.

81. Glen W. Bowersock, "The Arabian God Ares," in *Tria corda: Scritti in onore di Arnaldo Momigliano,* ed. Emilio Gabba (Como: New Press, 1983), pp. 43–47.

82. Fawzi Zayadine, "L'iconographie d'al-Uzza-Aphrodite," in *Mythologies gréco-romaines, mythologies périphériques,* ed. Lily Kahil and Christian Augé (Paris: Centre national de la recherche scientifique, 1981), pp. 113–118.

83. Fawzi Zayadine, "The God(ess) Aktab-Kutbay and his (her) iconography," in Zayadine, *Petra,* pp. 37–51.

84. See Maurice Sartre, "Du fait divers à l'histoire des mentalités: À propos de quelques noyés et de trois petits cochons," *Syria* 70 (1993): 51–67. This interpretation has been challenged by Corinne Bonnet, in "De l'histoire des mentalités à l'histoire des religions: À propos de Leucothéa et de trois petits cochons," *Studi epigraphici e linguistici sul Vicino Oriente antico* 14 (1997): 91–104; Bonnet recognizes an initiatory rite in the episode without there necessarily being the death of a man. But the identity between Leucothea and Atargatis is not in question: to the examples provided, we may now add a very fragmentary inscription from Tel Jezreel where little but the name of the goddess can be read: see Pinhas Porath, "A Fragmentary Greek Inscription from Tel Jezreel," *Tel Aviv* 24 (1997): 167–168, the sole attestation of this cult in Palestine.

85. Michal Gawlikowski, "Le Temple d'Allat à Palmyre," *RA* 1977, pp. 253–274.

86. Pascale Linant de Bellefonds, "Les divinités 'bédouines' du désert syrien et leur iconographie," in Zayadine, *Petra,* pp. 169–183.

87. On these divine figures, who include Artemis of Ephesos as well as Zeus of Panamara, see Robert Fleischer, *Artemis von Ephesos und verwandte Kultstatuen aus Anatolien und Syrien* (Leiden: E. J. Brill, 1973), pp. 326–369; for Jupiter of Heliopolis, see Hajjar, *Triade.* A torso of the Artemis of Ephesis type was recently discovered in Gadara: see Peter Cornelius Bol, "Das Sogenannnte Nymphäum," *Archäologischer Anzeiger* (1990): 204.

88. Fleischer, *Artemis,* pl. 157–159, and p. 337 for the bibliography to date.

89. He appears on the rare coinage of this little-known city: see Christian Augé, "Sur le monnayage de Dion de Coelé-Syrie," in *Géographie historique au Proche-Orient,* ed. Pierre-Louis Gatier, Bruno Helly, and Jean-Paul Rey-Coquais (Paris: Centre national de la recherche scientifique, 1988), pp. 325–341, especially p. 339, fig. 2 i.

90. Fleischer, *Artemis,* pp. 377–384. Apollo of Hierapolis, who is thought to be identified with Nabu, is found on a relief from Hatra (see Henri Seyrig, "Bas-relief des dieux de Hiérapolis," *Syria* 49 [1972]: 107–108), in which the costume is rather that of a Roman soldier; however, we find him framed by wild animals, with a feminine figure kneeling in the foreground.

91. For instance, the god represented in the votive hand of Niha, in the Louvre: see Fleischer, *Artemis*, pp. 369–377 and pl. 164; Hajjar, *Triade*, pp. 596–597 and pl. 49, 136.

92. Henri Seyrig, "Les dieux armés et les Arabes en Syrie," *Syria* 47 (1970): 77–112.

93. Joseph Patrich, *The Formation of Nabatean Art: Prohibition of a Graven Image among the Nabateans* (Jerusalem: Magnes Press; Leiden: E. J. Brill, 1990), pp. 82–86.

94. Ibid., pp. 50–113.

95. See Sartre, *IGLJ*, vol. 4, nos. 9–19.

96. Spijkerman, *Coins*, pp. 60–65, nos. 2, 3, 4, 12, 17.

97. Ibid., pp. 77–79, nos. 38, 42.

98. Ibid., p. 111, no. 5.

99. Ibid., pp. 184–185, nos. 8, 12.

100. Philip C. Hammond, "Ein nabatäisches Weiherrelief aus Petra," *Bonner Jahrbücher* 180 (1980): 265–269. The sanctuary itself was dedicated to Allat, according to Philip C. Hammond, "The Goddess of the Temple of the 'Winged Lions' at Petra (Jordan)," in Zayadine, *Petra*, pp. 115–130. This identification has been vigorously challenged by Zayadine, who holds out for al-Uzza, assimilated to Isis ("God[ess] Aktab-Kutbay," p. 127).

101. Sartre, *IGLJ*, vol. 4, no. 10.

102. A goddess for Philip C. Hammond, "The Medallion and Block Relief at Petra," *Bulletin of the American Schools of Oriental Research* 192 (1968): 16–21; Dionysus for Fawzi Zayadine, "Un ouvrage sur les Nabatéens," *RA* 70 (1975): 336–337.

103. See Nelson Glueck, *Deities and Dolphins: The Story of the Nabataeans* (New York: Farrar, Straus and Giroux, 1965).

104. Bowersock, "Cult."

105. See Ernest Will, "À propos de quelques monuments sacrés de la Syrie et de l'Arabie romaines," in Zayadine, *Petra*, pp. 197–205; Will establishes the Phoenician origin of these monuments, which are spread out as far away as Hatra.

106. Klaus Stefan Freyberger, "Zur Funktion der Hamana im Kontext lokaler Heiligtumer in Syrien und Palästina," *DaM* 9 (1996): 143–161.

107. On the *naiskoi* of the Hauran, see Pascal Arnaud, "Naiskoi monolithes du Hauran," in *Hauran: Recherches archéologiques sur la Syrie du sud à l'époque hellénistique et romaine*, ed. Jean-Marie Dentzer, vol. 1 (Paris: P. Geuthner, 1985), pp. 373–386. On their meaning, see Jean-Marie Dentzer, "Naiskoi du Hauran et qubbah arabe," in Zayadine, *Petra*, pp. 207–219; Dentzer's article seems definitive to me, settling the question of the enigmatic *kalybe,* a term that has been applied indiscriminately to completely unrelated structures, or even to structures that have clearly been identified as nymphaea (as in Bostra). The three clearly identifiable *kalybai* are the one at Umm az-Zeitun (designated as such by an inscription), and those at Shaqqa and Hayat, which offer obvious structural resemblances with the first; the imperial sanctuary at Philippopolis, identified by Ghaleb Amer and Michel Gawlikowski, "Le sanctuaire impérial de Philippopolis," (*DaM* 2 [1985]: 1–15), is visibly inspired by the same model: a wide vaulted central niche of the *iwan* type flanked by two rooms with cupolas.

108. *Maioumas* is well known as a place name, the best-known representative of which is the port at Gaza; scholars have occasionally deduced from this that the fes-

tival honored Zeus Marnas of Gaza, but this is unreasonable, since no festival by that name has been attested in Gaza or in Maioumas of Gaza. The name derives from the Semitic word for water, *mai*. See the definitive study of the maioumas of Antioch and elsewhere by Nicole Belayche in "Une panégyrie antiochienne: Le Maïouma," in "Actes du Colloque sur Antioche, Lyon, 4–6 octobre 2001," forthcoming in *Topoi*.

109. However, see Soyez, *Byblos*, and especially Belayche, *Iudaea-Palaestina*, pp. 249–255; idem, "Panégyrie antiochienne"; and Emmanuel Soler, "Le sacré et le salut à Antioche au Ive siècle ap. J.-C.: Pratiques festives et comportements religieux dans le processus de christianisation de la cité" (Ph.D. diss., Rouen, 1999; Beirut: Institut français d'archéologie du Proche-Orient, forthcoming).

110. The close relationship between the Temple in Jerusalem and the "pagan" temples of the Near East has been stressed many times, and there is no need to return to it here; see the masterful publication by T. A. Busink, *Der Tempel von Jerusalem von Salomo bis Herodes: Eine archäologisch-historische Studie unter Berücksichtigung des westsemitischen Tempelbaus*, vol. 2 (Leiden: E. J. Brill, 1980), especially pp. 1252–1358, for the sanctuaries of Nabataea and Syria.

111. Theodor Wiegand, *Baalbek: Ergebnisse der Ausgrabungen und Untersuchungen in den Jahren 1898 bis 1905* (Berlin and Leipzig: W. de Gruyter, 1921–1925); Friedrich Ragette, *Baalbek* (London: Chatto & Windus, 1980); and see the excellent, richly illustrated presentation by Margaret von Ess and Thomas Weber, *Baalbek: Im Bann römischer Monumentalarchitektur* (Mainz: Ph. Von Zabern, 1999).

112. Henri Seyrig, Robert Amy, and Ernest Will, *Le Temple de Bêl à Palmyre* (Paris: P. Geuthner, 1968–1975).

113. See George Francis Hill, *Catalogue of the Greek Coins of Phoenicia* (Bologna: A. Forni, 1980), pp. 102–103, nos. 37–38 (coins from Macrinus's era).

114. Butler, *PAES*, vol. 2A, p. 373; Butler's reconstructions need to be reviewed, but this does not call into question the presence of courtyards.

115. Glueck, *Deities and Dolphins*.

116. See Daniel M. Krencker and Willy Zschietzschmann, *Römische Tempel in Syrien* (Berlin: W. de Gruyter, 1938), for the most recent study; cf. an illustrated article by A. I. Steinsapir, "The Sanctuary Dedicated to Holy Heavenly Zeus Baetocaece," *Near Eastern Archaeology* 62 (September 1999): 182–194.

117. Krencker and Zschietzschmann, *Römische Tempel;* George Taylor, *The Roman Temples of Lebanon* (Beirut: Dar al-Mashreq, 1967), for example at Ni (p. 37), Qsarnaba (p. 43), and Dayr al-Asha'ir (p. 86).

118. Butler, *PAES*, vol. 2A.

119. Robert Amy, "Temples à escaliers," *Syria* 27 (1950): 82–186.

120. Seyrig et al., *Temple de Bel*.

121. On the meaning of the word, see Xavier Loriot, "Deux inscriptions métrôaques de Cordoue," *Bulletin de la Société nationale des antiquaires de France* (1992): 352–353.

122. See Ernest Will, "Les salles de banquet de Palmyre et d'autres lieux," *Topoi* 7 (1997): 873–887.

123. See Adnan Bounni, Jacques Seigne, and Nassib Saliby, *Le sanctuaire de Nabu à Palmyre* (Paris: P. Geuthner, 1992) (only the plates have been published).

124. Michel Gawlikowski, "Réflexions sur la chronologie du sanctuaire d'Allat à

Palmyre," *DaM* 1 (1983): 59–67; idem, "Du Hamana au naos: Le temple palmyrénien hellénisé," *Topoi* 7 (1997): 837–849; on the function of the Hamana, see Klaus Stefan Freyberger, "La fonction du Hamana et les sanctuaires des cultes indigènes en Syrie et en Palestine," *Topoi* 7 (1997): 851–871.

125. Michel Gawlikowski and Michal Pietrzykowski, "Les sculptures du temple de Baalshamin à Palmyre," *Syria* 56 (1980): 421–452.

126. Paul Collart and Jacques Vicari, *Le sanctuaire de Baalshamin à Palmyre,* vols. 1–2, *Topographie et architecture* (Rome: Institut Suisse de Rome, 1969).

127. The publications of Diana Kirkbride, in "Le temple nabatéen de Ramm, son évolution architecturale," *Rbi* 67 (1960): 65–92, need to be corrected by Laurent Tholbecq's recent observations concerning the successive transformations of this sanctuary: see Laurent Tholbecq, "The Nabataeo-Roman Site of Wadi Ramm (*Iram*): A New Appraisal," *ADAJ* 42 (1998): 241–254.

128. See Philip C. Hammond, "Die Ausgrabung des Löwen-Greifen-Tempels in Petra (1973–1983)," in *Petra: Neue Ausgrabungen und Entdeckungen,* ed. Manfred Lindner (Munich: Delp, 1986), pp. 16–30; idem, *The Temple of the Winged Lions, Petra, Jordan, 1973–1990* (Fountain Hills, Ariz.: Petra Publications, 1996).

129. See Eliezer D. Oren, "Excavations at Qasrawet in North-Western Sinai: Preliminary Report," *IEJ* 32 (1982): 206–207.

130. Tholbecq, "Nabataeo-Roman Site," pp. 250–251.

131. The basic publication is Krencker and Zschietzschmann, *Römische Tempel;* there is a good illustration, for the Lebanese part, by Taylor, *Roman Temples;* on a recent excavation in the temple of Chhim, in the back country near Sidon, see Lévon Nordiguian, "Le temple de Marjiyyat (Chhîm) à la faveur de nouvelles fouilles," *Topoi* 7 (1997): 945–964.

132. See Olivier Callot and Jean Marcillet-Jaubert, "Hauts-lieux de Syrie du Nord," in *Temples et sanctuaires,* ed. Georges Roux (Lyon: Groupement d'intérêt scientifique, Maison de l'Orient, 1984), pp. 185–202; the drawings have been reprinted in Olivier Callot, "La christianisation des sanctuaires romains de la Syrie du Nord," *Topoi* (1997): 745–750. More generally, see Michel Gawlikowski, "Les temples dans la Syrie hellénistique et romaine," in *Archéologie et histoire de la Syrie,* ed. Jean-Marie Dentzer and Winfried Orthman, vol. 2 (Sarrebrück: Saarbrücker Druckerei und Verlag, 1989), pp. 323–346.

133. Rüdiger Gogräfe, "The Temple of Seriane-Esriye," in "Palmyra and the Silk Road: International Colloquium, Palmyra, 7–11 April 1992," special issue, *Annales archéologiques arabes syriennes* 42 (1996): 179–186; idem, "Der Tempel von Isriye: Zwischen nahöstlicher Kulttradition une römischer Architektur," *Topoi* 7 (1997): 801–836.

134. Margaret B. Lyttleton, *Baroque Architecture in Classical Antiquity* (Ithaca, N.Y.: Cornell University Press, 1974).

135. In particular, see coinages minted under Philip the tetrarch: Andrew Burnett, Michel Amandry, and Pere Pau Ripollès, eds., *Roman Provincial Coinage,* vol. 1, *Julio-Claudian Period* (London: British Museum Press; Paris: Bibliothèque nationale de France, 1998), p. 681, nos. 4944–4946.

136. Zvi Ma'oz, "Temple of Pan."

137. Raphaël Savignac, "Le sanctuaire d'Allat à Iram," *Rbi* 42 (1933): 405–422; Raphaël Savignac and George Horsfield, "Chronique: Le Temple de Ramm," *Rbi* 44 (1935): 245–278.

138. Jean Starcky, "Pétra et la Nabatène," *Dictionnaire de la Bible* (Paris: Letouzey & Ané, 1996), suppl. 7, cols. 1006–1007; on the variety of forms of sanctuary in Nabataea, see Laurent Tholbecq, "Les sanctuaires des Nabatéens: État de la question à la lumière des recherches archéologiques récentes," *Topoi* 7 (1997): 1069–1095.

139. See Fawzi Zayadine, "Les sanctuaires nabatéens," in *La Jordanie de l'âge de la pierre à l'époque byzantine: Rencontres de l'École du Louvre*, ed. Geneviève Dolfus (Paris: La Documentation française, 1987), pp. 93–108; Laïla Nehmé, "L'espace cultuel à Pétra à l'époque nabatéenne," *Topoi* (1997): 1023–1067; Tholbecq, "Les sanctuaires des Nabatéens."

140. In "Le temple nabatéen de Khirbet Tannur: À propos d'un livre récent," *Rbi* 75 (1968): 206–235, Jean Starcky includes an important critique (concerning chronology) of Nelson Glueck, *Deities and Dolphins*; see also Marie-Jeanne Roche, "Khirbet et-Tannûr et les contacts entre Édomites et Nabatéens: Une nouvelle approche," *Transeuphratène* 18 (1999): 59–69.

141. Spijkerman, *Coins*, p. 87, no. 66, and p. 89, no. 72; cf. Maurice Sartre, *Bostra: Des origines à l'Islam* (Paris: P. Geuthner, 1985), p. 93.

142. Nehmé, "Espace cultuel," pp. 1023–1067.

143. See Callot and Marcillet-Jaubert, "Hauts-lieux."

144. For a coin of Antoninus Pius, see Ya'akov Meshorer, *City-Coins of Eretz-Israel and the Decapolis in the Roman Period* (Jerusalem: Israel Museum, 1985), p. 48, no. 126; and see the reconstitution by Yitzhak Magen, "Mount Garizim and the Samaritans," in *Early Christianity in Context: Monuments and Documents*, ed. Frédéric Manns and Eugenio Alliata (Jerusalem: Franciscan Printing Press, 1993), pp. 91–147, especially pp. 123–124.

145. See Susan B. Downey, *Mesopotamian Religious Architecture: Alexander through the Parthians* (Princeton: Princeton University Press, 1988); Pierre Leriche, "Matériaux pour une réflexion renouvelée sur les sanctuaires de Doura-Europos," *Topoi* 7 (1997): 889–913.

146. See, for example, that of the sanctuary at Azzanathkona: Pascal Arnaud, "Les salles W9 et W10 du temple d'Azzanathkôna à Doura-Europos: Développement historique et topographie familiale d'une 'salle aux gradins,'" in *Doura-Europos: Études IV, 1991–1993*, ed. Pierre Leriche and Mathilde Gélin, vol. 4 (Beirut: Institut français d'archéologie du Proche-Orient, 1997), pp. 117–144.

147. For example, the recently identified "north temple": see Leriche, "Matériaux," pp. 896–897.

148. Ibid., p. 904.

149. Javier Teixidor, "L'Hellénisme et les Barbares," *Le temps de la réflexion* 2 (1981): 257–294.

150. Philippe Escolan, *Monachisme et Église: Le monachisme syrien du IVe au VIIe siècle, un monachisme charismatique* (Paris: Beauchesne, 1999).

151. Drijvers, *Cults and Beliefs*, pp. 189–192. The Orpheus mosaic dates from 227–228, the Phoenix mosaic from 235–236.

152. It has seemed astonishing that the texts so often mention synagogues and yet we have archaeological evidence of so few, at least before the fourth century. The explanation may well be that for a long time nothing distinguished a synagogue from a private house; it was only later, not before the third century at the earliest, that certain details (such as the decor) made synagogues identifiable as such: cf. Stuart S.

Miller, "On the Number of Synagogues in the Cities of Eretz Israel," *Journal of Jewish Studies* 49 (1998): 51–66.

153. Steve N. Mason, *Josephus on the Pharisees* (Leiden: E. J. Brill, 1990); Marcel Pelletier, *Les Pharisiens: Histoire d'un parti méconnu* (Paris: Le Cerf, 1990).

154. Jacob Neusner, *A Life of Rabban Yohanan ben Zakkai, ca. 1–80 CE* (Leiden: E. J. Brill, 1962; 2nd ed., 1970); a revised edition has been published as *First Century Judaism in Crisis: Yohanan ben Zakkai and the Renaissance of Torah* (New York: Ktav, 1975).

155. Jacob Neusner, "The Formation of Rabbinic Judaism: Yavneh (Jamnia) from A.D. 70 to 100," *ANRW* 2.19.2 (1979): 3–42.

156. On this original and very influential social group, see Lee I. Levine, *The Rabbinic Class of Roman Palestine in Late Antiquity* (Jerusalem: Yad Izhak Ben-Zvi; New York: Jewish Theological Seminary of America, 1989); Levine's study begins in the third century.

157. He is thought to have rented imperial domains on the Golan in order to collect the tax revenues: see *TJ, Shebi'ith,* 6.1.

158. Shemuel Safrai, "The Holy Congregation in Jerusalem," *Scripta hierosolymitana* 23 (1972): 62–78; Gedaliah Alon, *The Jews in Their Land in the Talmudic Age (70–640 ce)* (Cambridge, Mass., and London: Harvard University Press, 1898), pp. 695–696.

159. For example, Rabbi Jose b. Eliakim speaks in the name of "the holy kehilla in Jerusalem": *TJ, Berakhoth,* 9b.

160. Alon, *Jews in Their Land,* p. 696.

161. Benjamin H. Isaac, "Jews, Christian and Others in Palestine: The Evidence from Eusebius," in *Jews in a Graeco-Roman World,* ed. Martin Goodman (Oxford and New York: Clarendon Press, 1998), pp. 65–74.

162. *TJ, Avodah Zarah,* 4 (5), 3.

163. See Eric M. Meyers, "Aspects of Roman Sepphoris," in Manns and Alliata, *Early Christianity,* pp. 31–32.

164. See ibid., p. 34.

165. See Moshe Dothan, *Hammath Tiberias: Early Synagogues and the Hellenistic and Roman Remains* (Jerusalem: Israel Exploration Society, 1983), pp. 15–26.

166. Levine, *Rabbinic Class,* p. 25.

167. Ephrat Hadas-Rubin, "The Halachic Status of Bostra, Metropolis Arabiae," *Tsinan* (1995): 375–391.

168. Barat Hauran is not identified. Adolf Neubauer mentions Mount Hauran as the whole of the "Hauran in Peraea" (*Géographie du Talmud* [Paris: Michel Lévy Frères, 1868; repr., Hildesheim: G. Olms, 1967], p. 43).

169. *TJ, Shebi'ith,* 6.36c; see Ephrat Hadas-Rubin, "The Nawa-Der'a Road," *Scripta classica israelica* (hereafter cited as *SCI*) 14 (1995): 138–142.

170. I would be inclined to see the word as a toponym based on the Greek *paradeisos,* designating a large domain in the Achaeminid tradition.

171. To date, a fairly large number of vestiges of the Jewish community have been found, most notably lintels with seven-branched candelabra.

172. *TJ, Shebi'ith,* 6.1, especially p. 379, which has it extending as far as Trachon, thus confirming the previous observation.

173. Josephus, *De bello judaico (The Jewish War),* trans. Henry St. John Thackeray (Loeb Classical Library), 7.43 (hereafter cited as *BJ*).

174. In *The Golan: A Profile of a Region during the Roman and Byzantine Periods* (Oxford: British Archaeological Reports, 1985), Dan Urman seems to me to suffer from powerful a priori positions concerning the identification of the synagogues; more interesting is Robert C. Gregg and Dan Urman, *Jews, Pagans and Christians in the Golan Heights: Greek and Other Inscriptions of the Roman and Byzantine Eras* (Atlanta: Scholars Press, 1996), where the focus is not limited exclusively to the western Golan, the part currently occupied by Israel.

175. Neubauer, *Géographie*, pp. 245–246; rabbis from Neve (Nawa): Isidore Epstein, ed., *The Babylonian Talmud* (hereafter cited as *BT*), 35 vols. (London: Soncino Press, 1935–1952), *Shabbath,* 30a; *Midrash Rabbah,* ed. H. Freedman and Maurice Simon, vol. 4, *Leviticus,* trans. J. Israelstam and Judah J. Slotki (London and Bournemouth: Soncino Press, 1951), "Midrash Rabha Vayikra"; *BT, Avodah Zarah,* 36.

176. Jean-Baptiste Frey, *Corpus inscriptionum iudaicarum,* vol. 2 (Vatican City: Pontifico istituto di archeologia cristiana, 1952), 861; see also an unpublished inscription mentioning a Dositheos known as Makabaios: Maurice Sartre, *IGLS,* vol. 14, *Adraha, le Jawlan oriental, et la Batanée* (Beirut: Institut français d'archéologie du Proche-Orient, forthcoming), no. 273.

177. Lintels with seven-branched candelabra, undatable.

178. Sartre, *IGLS,* vol. 14, forthcoming, no. 408.

179. *Supplementum epigraphicum graecum* (Alphen aan den Rijn: Sijthoff & Noordhoff, 1934), vol. 7, no. 987 = Annie Fauriat-Sartre and Maurice Sartre, *IGLS,* vol. 15, *Le plateau du Trachôn* (Beirut: Institut français d'archéologie du Proche-Orient, forthcoming), no. 440.

180. 1 Macc. 5.17 and 5.24–54.

181. *TJ, Mo'ed Katan,* 3.1, and *Kila'yim,* 9.1 (Rabbi Yona), cited in Neubauer, *Géographie,* p. 255.

182. For example, a Jewish silversmith in 'Ayn Musa, near Kafr, on the Jebel Druze: Maurice Sartre, *IGLS,* vol. 16, *Le Djebel al-Œ̄Arab* (Beirut: Institut français d'archéologie du Proche-Orient, forthcoming), no. 387; Jews perhaps at Busan in the Jebel Druze in 341–342 (ibid., no. 893). Seven-branched candelabra have also been found in a few villages (such as Sahwet Balatah, a little south of Soueida), but they cannot be dated with precision.

183. A Jew from Phaina buried in Beth Shearim: Moshe Schwabe and Baruch Lifshitz, *Beth She'arim,* vol. 2, *The Greek Inscriptions* (New Brunswick: Rutgers University Press, 1974), p. 151, no. 178.

184. Libanios, *Selected Works with an English Translation,* trans. A. F. Norman, vol. 1, *The Julianic Orations* (Loeb Classical Library), pp. 513–515 (*Oratio* 47.13–16): Libanios notes that Jewish tenant farmers have been working on his lands for four generations (p. 513).

185. Schwabe and Lifshitz, *Beth She'arim,* vol. 2, pp. 125–127, nos. 138–140.

186. Josephus, *De antiquitate judaico (Jewish Antiquities),* trans. Louis H. Feldman (Loeb Classical Library), 12.119 (hereafter cited as *AJ*); Josephus, "Against Apion," in *The Life and Against Apion,* trans. Henry St. John Thackeray (Loeb Classical Library), 2.38–39.

187. Josephus, *AJ* 12.119.

188. Josephus, *AJ* 12.119–124.

189. 1 Macc. 12.41–51; Josephus, *AJ* 13.135–142.

190. Antioch is called Aspamia in the Talmuds (Neubauer, *Géographie*, p. 304). There is a reference to a Jewish community, including a certain Ariston, who had been the first to bring the first fruits of the harvest to Jerusalem: see Avner Tomaschoff, ed., *Mishnah: A New Translation with Commentary*, trans. Pinhas Kehati (Jerusalem: Eliner Library, 1994), *Mishnah Hallah*, 4.11.

191. Jalabert and Mouterde, *IGLS*, vol. 4, nos. 1319–1337; Baruch Lifshitz, *Donateurs et fondateurs dans les synagogues juives: Répertoire des dédicaces grecques relatives à la construction et à la réfection des synagogues* (Paris: J. Gabalda, 1967), pp. 39–46.

192. Schwabe and Lifshitz, *Beth She'arim*, vol. 2, nos. 147, 199.

193. Ibid., nos. 172, 221.

194. Ibid., nos. 148, 164.

195. Ibid., nos. 136–137.

196. Ibid., nos. 92, 100.

197. Ibid., no. 141.

198. Named Asia, the equivalent of Ezion Geber, the biblical name of the place: ibid., nos. 119, 121.

199. Tal Ilan, "New Ossuary Inscriptions from Jerusalem," *SCI* 11 (1991–1992): 149–159.

200. Gideon Avni, Zvi Greenhut, and Tal Ilan, "Three New Burial Caves of the Second Temple Period in Haceldama (Kidron Valley)," *Qadmoniot* 99–100 (1992): 104 (in Hebrew); cf. Raqui Milman Baron, "A Survey of Inscriptions Found in Israel and Published in 1992–1993," *SCI* 13 (1994): 143–144.

201. Michel Gawlikowski and Khaled As'ad, "Inscriptions de Palmyre nouvelles et revisitées," *Studia Palmyrenskie* 10 (1997): 33–34, no. 20.

202. Josephus, *BJ* 3.10; Philo of Alexandria, *Legatio ad Gaium*, 2nd ed., ed. and trans. E. Mary Smallwood (Leiden: E. J. Brill, 1970), 205.

203. Josephus, "Against Apion," 1.70.

204. Josephus, *BJ* 7.361–363.

205. Philo, *Legatio*, 200–205.

206. Josephus, *BJ* 7.46–53, *AJ* 12.120.

207. Josephus, *BJ* 2.559–561; in 7.368, the figure goes up to eighteen thousand.

208. Ibid., 7.362.

209. Ibid., 2.477–478.

210. Ibid., 2.560.

211. Ibid., 7.45.

212. Acts 6.5.

213. Acts 10.1–2.

214. Josephus, *BJ* 2.480.

215. Ibid., 2.479.

216. Han J. W. Drijvers, "Syrian Christianity and Judaism," in *The Jews among Pagans and Christians in the Roman Empire*, ed. Judith Lieu, John North, and Tessa Rajak (London: Routledge, 1992), p. 138.

217. Carl Hermann Kraeling, *The Excavations at Dura-Europos: Final Report*, vol. 8, part 1: *The Synagogue* (New Haven: Yale University Press, 1956); Joseph Gutmann, *The Dura-Europos Synagogue: A Re-evaluation (1932–1972)* (Chambersburg, Pa.: American Academy of Religion, 1973).

218. Alfred Raymond Bellinger, *The Excavations at Dura-Europos: Final Report*,

vol. 6, *The Coins* (New Haven: Yale University Press, 1949), p. 199; but one cannot relate the coins from the reign of John Hyrcanos to the expedition of Antiochos VII into Iran in 127 (with the participation of a Jewish contingent led by Hyrcanos himself), for Hasmonaean coinage was probably not minted before the 110s.

219. Kraeling, *Excavations: The Synagogue,* p. 327.

220. See ibid., pp. 263–268, no. 1 (the dedicatory inscription of the synagogue).

221. John Joseph Collins, ed. and trans., "The Sibylline Oracles," in *The Old Testament Pseudepigraphia,* ed. James H. Charlesworth (New York: Doubleday, 1983), 4.28–29; on the author and his milieu, see André Caquot and Marc Philonenko, "Introduction générale," in *La Bible: Écrits intertestamentaires,* by André Dupont-Sommer and Marc Philonenko (Paris: Gallimard, 1987), pp. xciv–xcv. The work dates from the aftermath of the destruction of the Temple, in the 80s, but the opinion it expresses is not new; it converges with ideas already expressed in "Règle de la Communauté," trans. André Dupont-Sommer, in *Écrits intertestamentaires,* 9.3–5.

222. We can be sure of very little except the disappearance of the members of the Qumran sect, whose establishment was destroyed in 68; but some Essene masters no doubt survived elsewhere—for instance, the author of the fourth Sibylline Oracle, who lived in Syria or in Asia Minor. Their influence appears inconsequential, in any event.

223. Levine, *Rabbinic Class,* pp. 30–32; for example, they lifted the prohibitions on sculpted decors, which were omnipresent in the Greek cities of the Near East, and even the Jews adopted Greek decorative motifs, such the eagle and Heracles' knot.

224. However, there exists an entire Haggadic literature that is not part of Talmudic literature, in particular many apocrypha and pseudepigraphs.

225. The title *rabbi,* "my master," awarded to all teachers and learned men, replaced the term *sofer,* which formerly designated the scribes. But in the Mishna, four teachers merit the higher title *rabban,* "our master": Gamaliel the Elder, Yohanan ben Zakkai, Gamaliel II, and Simeon bar Gamaliel II.

226. Éric Smilévitch, *Leçons des Pères du Monde: Pirqé Avot et Avot de Rabbi Nathan, Versions A et B* (Lagrasse: Verdier, 1983), p. 9.

227. Neusner, *Rabban Yohanan ben Zakkai;* idem, *"Formation of Rabbinic Judaism."*

228. Kraeling, *Excavations: The Synagogue;* Erwin R. Goodenough, *Jewish Symbols in the Graeco-Roman Period,* vols. 9–11: *Symbolism in the Dura Synagogue* (New York: Pantheon Books, 1964); Gutmann, *Dura-Europos Synagogue.* For Neusner's work on the Jews of Mesopotamia, see especially *A History of the Jews in Babylonia,* vol. 1, *The Parthian Period* (Leiden: E. J. Brill, 1965), and vol. 2, *The Early Sasanian Period* (Leiden: E. J. Brill, 1966).

229. To examine all the issues related to the origins of Christianity would be to go well beyond the scope of this book. My inquiry here is limited to the spread of Christian communities throughout the Near Eastern provinces, the establishment of community structures, and the problems raised by the partial Christianization of the population.

230. See the quite remarkable example of the funerary epigraphy of wealthy landowners in the Hauran: Annie Sartre-Fauriat, "Culture et société dans le Hauran (Syrie du Sud) d'après les épigrammes funéraires (IIIe–IVe siècles apr. J.-C.)," *Syria* 75 (1998): 213–224.

231. I shall list only some important recent publications in French: Étienne

Trocmé, *L'enfance du christianisme* (Paris: Éditions Noêsis, 1997); François Vouga, *Les premiers pas du christianisme: Les écrits, les acteurs, les débats* (Geneva: Labor & Fides, 1997); Étienne Nodet and Justin Taylor, *Essai sur les origines du christianisme: Une secte éclatée* (Paris: Le Cerf, 1998), and Jean-Marie Mayeur et al., eds., *Histoire du christianisme, des origines à nos jours,* vol. 1 (Paris: Desclée, 2000).

232. Acts 9.29.

233. On the very early church and the difficulty of differentiating it from Judaism, see Daniel Marguerat, "Juifs et chrétiens: La séparation," in Mayeur et al., *Histoire du christianisme,* vol. 1, pp. 189–224.

234. Eusebius, *The Ecclesiastical History,* trans. Kirsopp Lake (Loeb Classical Library), 3.5.3 (hereafter cited as *EH*).

235. Marcel Simon, *Recherches d'histoire judéo-chrétienne* (Paris and The Hague: Mouton, 1962); Daniel Marguerat, ed., *Le déchirement: Juifs et chrétiens au premier siècle* (Geneva: Labor & Fides, 1996); Simon C. Mimouni, *Le judéo-christianisme ancien: Essais historiques* (Paris: Le Cerf, 1998).

236. Epiphanius of Salamis, *The Panarion of Epiphanius of Salamis, Book I,* trans. Frank Williams (Leiden and New York: E. J. Brill, 1987), 29, pp. 112–119, and see commentary by Aline Pourkier, *L'hérésiologie chez Épiphane de Salamine* (Paris: Beauchesne 1992), pp. 415–475. The Nazoraeans are considered orthodox by Mimouni, *Judéo-christianisme ancien,* pp. 82–86; cf. M. C. de Boer, "L'Évangile de Jean et le christianisme juif (nazoréen)," in Marguerat, *Déchirement,* pp. 184–200; Simon C. Mimouni, "Les Nazoréens: Recherche étymologique et historique," *Rbi* 105 (1998): 208–262. The difficulty has to do with the fact that it is hard to make the connection between the Nazoraeans attested in the first century (that is, the church of Jerusalem) and the Nazoraeans of the fourth century, whom a writer such as Epiphanius cannot help but consider heretics. But the connection is unquestionable, according to Mimouni and most specialists.

237. Epiphanius, *Panarion,* 30; see Mimouni, *Judéo-christianisme ancien,* pp. 87–89 and 257–286, with the relevant bibliography.

238. Epiphanius, *Panarion,* 19; 53; 30.3.1–6; 30.17.4–8; see Mimouni, *Judéo-christianisme ancien,* pp. 287–316, with the bibliography. The Elcesaites were widespread in Mesopotamia in particular, but they were also found in Syria, because the Elcesaite missionary to Rome at the beginning of the third century was a certain Alcibiades of Apamaea. Epiphanes' observations are translated in Luigi Cirillo, "Livre de la Révélation d'Elkasaï," in *Écrits apocryphes chrétiens,* ed. François Bovon, Pierre Géoltrain, and Sever J. Voicu (Paris: Gallimard, 1997), pp. 852–864.

239. Claudine Dauphin, "Encore des Judéo-chrétiens au Golan?" in Manns and Alliata, *Early Christianity,* pp. 69–84, especially pp. 77–79.

240. Wayne A. Meeks and Robert L. Wilken, *Jews and Christians in Antioch in the First Four Centuries of the Common Era* (Missoula, Mont.: Scholars Press, 1978).

241. See the overview of the present state of knowledge by Pierre Maraval, "La diversité de l'Orient chrétien," in Mayeur et al., *Histoire du christianisme,* vol. 1, pp. 500–517.

242. Without taking literally the story of the exchange of letters between Jesus and Abgar V, we can be certain that Christians, including Marcionites, were numerous as early as the second century; the Anonymous Chronicle of the sixth century (see note 243) mentions the destruction of a church in the catastrophic flood of 201.

243. An indication supplied by the Anonymous Chronicle drafted by the archi-

vist in Edessa at the end of the sixth century; cf. Javier Teixidor, *Bardesane d'Édesse: La première philosophie syriaque* (Paris: Le Cerf, 1992), p. 49. Eusebius mentions parishes in Osroene during a synod in 198, without speaking of a bishop, which seems to support the anonymous chronicler (*EH* 5.23.3–4); let us note that this chronicler, a city archivist, had access to the best sources and that it is thus difficult to contradict his testimony without powerful arguments. But the Chronicle of Michael the Syrian explains in an account of Bardesanes's upbringing that the young man was drawn to Christianity as he passed by a church in Edessa where the bishop Hystasp was explaining the Holy Scriptures: see *Chronique de Michel le Syrien, patriarche jacobite d'Antioche (1166–1199)*, ed. Jean-Baptiste Chabot (Paris, 1899; repr., Brussels: Culture et civilisation, 1963), vol. 1, pp. 183–184.

244. Charles Piétri, "La géographie nouvelle: A. L'Orient," in Mayeur et al., *Histoire du Christianisme*, vol. 2 (1995), p. 91, citing Athanasius of Alexandria, *Epistola de synodis*, 43, and Hilary of Poitiers, *De Synodis*, 86.

245. Eusebius of Caesarea, *The Onomasticon: Palestine in the Fourth Century A.D.*, trans. G. S. P. Freeman-Grenville, ed. Joan E. Taylor (Jerusalem: Carta, 2003), 26, 108, 112.

246. We obviously have no statistical records, but in a letter to the people of Bostra in 363, the emperor Julian acknowledged that there were at that time as many pagans as Christians in his city: Julian, *Works*, vol. 3, letter 41, p. 133.

247. Anthony R. Birley, *Hadrian, the Restless Emperor* (London and New York: Routledge, 1997), p. 71. Cf. Cyril Charles Richardson, *The Christianity of Ignatius of Antioch* (New York: Columbia University Press, 1935); Virginia Corwin, *St. Ignatius and Christianity in Antioch* (New Haven: Yale University Press, 1960); Peter Meinhold, *Studien zu Ignatius von Antiochien* (Wiesbaden: F. Steiner, 1979).

248. Eusebius, *EH* 6.21.3–4.

249. Ibid., 6.36.3.

250. Orosius, *The Seven Books of History against the Pagans* (= *Adversus Paganos*), trans. Roy Deferrari (Washington, D.C.: Catholic University of America Press, 1964), 7.20; Henri Crouzel, "Le christianisme de Philippe l'Arabe," *Gregorianum* (1956): pp. 545–550; H. A. Pohlsander, "Philip the Arab and Christianity," *Historia* 29 (1980): 463–473.

251. François Nicolas Nau, ed. and trans., *La Didascalie des douze apôtres* (Paris: p. Lethielleux, 1912); see Victor Saxer, "La mission: L'organisation de l'Église au IIIe siècle," in Mayeur, *Histoire du christianisme*, vol. 2, pp. 51–52, 60–62.

252. The first was intended to bring Beryllos of Bostra, accused of monarchism, back to the right path; the second was directed against anonymous bishops accused of professing the mortality of the soul: Eusebius, *EH* 6.20.2; 6.33.1–3.

253. Eusebius, *EH* 7.30.18–19; cf. Piétri, "Géographie nouvelle," pp. 86–89.

254. See Pierre Maraval, *Lieux saints et pélerinages d'Orient: Histoire et géographie des origines à la conquête arabe; histoire et géographie des origines à la conquête arabe* (Paris: Le Cerf, 1985), pp. 25–27.

255. Eusebius, *EH* 4.6.4.

256. Joshua Benzion Segal, "When Did Christianity Come to Edessa?" in *Middle East Studies and Libraries: A Felicitation Volume for Professor J. D. Pearson*, ed. B. C. Bloomfield (London: Mansell, 1980), pp. 179–191.

257. Eusebius, *EH* 1.13, 2.1.6–7; Abgar V Ukkama reigned from 4 B.C.E. to 7 C.E.,

then again from 13 to 50 C.E. See Alain Desreumaux, *Histoire du roi Abgar et de Jésus* (Turnhout: Brepols, 1993).

258. Eusebius, *EH* 1.13.

259. For an account of the beginning of Christianization in Edessa, see George Philipps, ed., *The Doctrine of Addai the Apostle* (London: Trübner, 1876).

260. Eusebius, *EH*, 2.1.7, but the formulation is obscure.

261. Han J. W. Drijvers, "The School of Edessa: Greek Learning and Local Culture," in *Centers of Learning: Learning and Location in Pre-Modern Europe and the Near East*, ed. Jan Willem Drijvers and Alasdair A. Macdonald (Leiden: E. J. Brill, 1995), pp. 49–59.

262. A. F. Klijn, *The Acts of Thomas* (Leiden: E. J. Brill, 1962); Han J. W. Drijvers, "The Acts of Thomas," in *New Testament Apocrypha*, ed. Wilhelm Schneemelcher, vol. 1 (Cambridge: J. Clarke; Louisville, Ky.: Westminster / John Knox Press, 1991), pp. 492–500; Drijvers, "Syrian Christianity and Judaism," p. 132.

263. Tatian of Assyria, *Oratio ad Graecos and Fragments*, ed. and trans. Molly Whittaker (Oxford and New York: Clarendon Press, 1982). Tatian advocates complete sexual abstinence. The Encratist tendency, very widespread among Syrian monks, appears only later: see Arthur Vööbus, *A History of Asceticism in the Syrian Orient: A Contribution to the History of the East* (Louvain: Secrétariat du Corpus scriptorium Christianorum orientalium, 1958–1988); Escolan, *Monachisme et Église*.

264. Drijvers, "Syrian Christianity," p. 139.

265. Marcion's disciples positioned themselves in one sense at the opposite pole from the Judeo-Christian tradition, since they rejected any connection between the Old and New Testaments, going so far as to distinguish between the Hebrew God and the Christian God. See Eugène de Faye, *Gnostiques et gnosticisme: Étude critique des documents du gnosticisme chrétien aux IIe et IIIe siècles* (Paris: P. Geuthner, 1925), pp. 143–188.

266. Han J. W. Drijvers, "Marcionism in Syria," *Second Century* 6 (1987–1988): 153–172; cf. idem, "Die Odes Salomos und die Polemik mit den Markioniten in syrischen Christentum," in *East of Antioch* (London: Variorum Reprints, 1984), essay 7.

267. Charles Robert Cecil Allberry, *A Manichean Psalm-Book* (Stuttgart: W. Kohlhammer, 1938).

268. Han J. W. Drijvers, "Odes of Salomon and Psalms of Mani: Christians and Manicheans in the Third Century," in *Studies in Gnosticism and Hellenistic Religions: Presented to Gilles Quispel on the Occasion of His 65th Birthday*, ed. Roelof van den Broek and M. J. Vermaseren (Leiden: E. J. Brill, 1981), pp. 117–130 (republished as *East of Antioch*, section 10).

269. Han J. W. Drijvers, "Quq and the Quqites: An Unknown Sect in Edessa in the Second Century AD," *Numen* 14 (1967): 104–129.

270. Robert Murray, "The Characteristics of the Earliest Syriac Christianity," in *East of Byzantium: Syria and Armenia in the Formative Period*, ed. Nina G. Garsoïan, Thomas F. Mathews, and Robert W. Thomson (Washington, D.C.: Dumbarton Oaks, 1982), pp. 3–16.

271. See Carl Hermann Kraeling, *The Excavations at Dura Europos: Final Report*, vol. 8, part 2, *The Christian Building* (New Haven: Yale University Press, 1967), with a comprehensive bibliography to date.

272. Ibid., p. 38.

273. Carl Hermann Kraeling, *A Greek Fragment of Tatian's Diatessaron from Dura* (London: Christophers, 1935).

274. S. Thomas Parker, "The Roman 'Aqaba Project: The 1996 Campaign," *ADAJ* 42 (1998): 381–383.

275. Bernard Pouderon, ed., *Foi chrétienne et culture classique*, trans. M. Bourlet et al. (Paris: Migne, 1998), pp. 39–40; idem, "Les chrétiens et la culture antique: A. Les premiers chrétiens et la culture grecque," in Mayeur et al., *Histoire du christianisme*, vol. 1, pp. 827–828, 840–841.

276. For an essential document found in the Manichaean Codex of Cologne, see Ron Cameron and Arthur J. Dewey, *The Cologne Mani Codex (P. Colon. Inv. Nr. 4780): Concerning the Origin of His Body* (Missoula, Mont.: Scholars Press, 1979); Ludwig Koenen and Cornelia Römer, *Der Kölner Mani-Codex: Über das Werden seines Leibes* (Opladen: Westdeutscher Verlag, 1988). On the doctrine, see Henri-Charles Puech, *Le Manichéisme, son fondateur, sa doctrine* (Paris: Civilisations du Sud / SAEP, 1949); François Decret, *Mani et la tradition manichéenne* (Paris: Le Seuil, 1974); Michel Tardieu, *Le manichéisme* (Paris: Presses Universitaires de France, 1981); idem, "Mani et le Manichéisme," in *Encyclopédie des Religions,* ed. Frédéric Lenoir, Ysé Tardan-Masquelier, Michel Meslin, and Jean-Pierre Rosa, 2nd ed. (Paris: Bayard, 2000), pp. 225–230.

277. *The Teaching of Addai,* trans. George Howard (Chico, Calif.: Scholars Press, 1981); Samuel N. C. Lieu, *Manichaeism in the Later Roman Empire and Medieval China: A Historical Survey* (Manchester, U.K., and Dover, N.H.: Manchester University Press, 1985; 2nd ed., rev. and exp., Tübingen: J. C. B. Mohr, 1992).

II. A TIME OF TRIALS

1. Cassius Dio, *Roman History* (Loeb Classical Library), 80.4.1 (hereafter cited as Dio); Herodian, *History of the Empire from the Time of Marcus Aurelius,* trans. C. R. Whittaker (Loeb Classical Library), 6.2.2 (hereafter cited as Herodian); Erich Kettenhofen, "Die Einforderung des Achämenidenerbes durch Ardashir: Eine Interpretatio Romana," *Orientalia lovaniensia periodica* 15 (1984): 177–190.

2. Dio, 80.3.2.

3. Herodian clearly establishes that Ardashir (= Artaxerxes) invaded Mesopotamia and threatened Syria (6.2.1), but a little later on he recounts the pillaging of all the Roman provinces (6.2.5). Joannes Zonaras mentions Cappadocia (*Epitome historiarum,* ed. Ludwig Dindorf [Leipzig: B. G. Teubner, 1868–1875], 12.15 [p. 572], 12.22 [p. 573] [hereafter cited as Zonaras]), but associates it with the siege of Nisibis—that is, of a Mesopotamian city. See Engelbert Winter, *Die Sasanidish-römischen Friedensverträge des 3. Jahrhunderts n. Chr.: Ein Beitrag zum verstandnis der aussenpolitischen Beziehungen zwischen den beiden Grossmachten* (Frankfurt am Main: Peter Lang, 1988), along with Erich Kettenhofen's review of Winter's book in *Bibliotheca orientalis* (January–March 1990), cols. 163–178; see also idem, *Die römische-persischen Kriege des 3. Jahrhunderts n. Chr. nach der Inschrift Sahpuhrs I. an der Ka'be-ye Zartost (SKZ)* (Wiesbaden: L. Reichert, 1982).

4. Herodian, 6.5–6.

5. The sources of information about Roman-Persian relations have been usefully collected in an English translation by Michael H. Dodgeon and Samuel N. C.

Lieu, *The Roman Eastern Frontier and the Persian Wars, AD 226–363* (London and New York: Routledge, 1991).

6. The latest publication of an Aramaean parchment from Dura, *P1*, in Han J. W. Drijvers and John F. Healey, *The Old Syriac Inscriptions of Edessa and Osrhoene: Texts, Translations and Commentary* (Leiden and Boston: E. J. Brill, 1999), p. 240, dates from year 6 of Gordian III, from the consulate of Annius Arrianus and Cervonius Papus, from year 554 of the Seleucids and from "year 31 of the liberation of Antoniana Edessa the Glorious, Colony, Metropolis," that is, 243 C.E., which shifts the annexation of the city back to 213.

7. Dio, 78.12.

8. See Drijvers and Healey, *Old Syriac Inscriptions*, p. 39.

9. See Javier Teixidor, "Deux documents syriaques du IIIe siècle après J.-C. provenant du Moyen-Euphrate," *Comptes rendus des séances de l'Académie des inscriptions et belles-lettres* (hereafter cited as *CRAI*) (1990): 144–166. Batnai is called "Saroug" in Syriac, and also "Saruç."

10. Javier Teixidor, "Les derniers rois d'Édesse d'après deux nouveaux documents syriaques," *Zeitschrift für Papyrologie und Epigraphik* (hereafter cited as *ZPE*) 76: (1989): 219–222; idem, "Deux documents syriaques," pp. 144–166; Steven Ross, "The Last King of Edessa: New Evidence from the Middle Euphrates," *ZPE* 97 (1993): 187–206. Michel Gawlikowski ("The Last Kings of Edessa," in *Symposium Syriacum 1996 VII*, ed. René Lavenant [Rome: Pontificium Institutum Orientale, 1998], pp. 421–428) believes that it is Septimius Abgar who is represented on the Barsimya funerary mosaic in Edessa, and not Abgar VIII, as Han J. W. Drijvers argues in "A Tomb for the Life of a King: Recently Discovered Edessene Mosaic with a Portrait of King Abgar the Great," *Le Museon* 95 (1982): 167–189. This identification has already been challenged by Joshua Benzion Segal, "A Note on a Mosaic from Edessa," *Syria* 60 (1983): 107–110; in fact, the invocation "for the life of Abgar, my lord and benefactor," without any mention of a royal title, is best understood if Barsimya, an Edessan leader close to the dynasty, is awaiting the reestablishment of a potential heir who is not certain to become king. This would date the mosaic quite precisely to the few months that separated the death of the crown prince Man'u from the restoration of his son in 239.

11. Teixidor, "Derniers rois d'Édesse," pp. 219–222; idem, "Deux documents syriaques." Xavier Loriot offers a different chronology and a more thorough examination of the sources in "Les premières années de la grande crise du IIIe siècle: De l'avènement de Maximin le Thrace (235) à la mort de Gordien III (244)," *Aufstieg und Niedergang der römischen Welt* (hereafter cited as *ANRW*) 2.2 (1975): 768, nn. 822 and 823; Loriot could not have been aware of the two parchments from the Euphrates on which the chronology proposed here is based. On the dossier of papyri and parchments from the Euphrates, see Denis Feissel and Jean Gascou, "Documents d'archives romains inédits du Moyen Euphrate (IIIe s. apr. J.-C.)," *CRAI* (1989): 535–561; idem, "Documents d'archives romains inédits du Moyen Euphrate (IIIe s. apr. J.-C.)," *Journal des Savants* (1995): 65–119.

12. But Caracalla was assassinated on April 8, 217, which hardly left him to time to undertake a campaign; on the chronology, see André Maricq, "Classica et orientalia: 3. La chronologie des dernières années de Caracalla," *Syria* 34 (1957): 297–302, though Maricq's chronology needs to be corrected regarding the relations between Caracalla and Edessa.

13. Fuad Safar, "Inscriptions from Hatra," *Sumer* 17 (1961): 10 (Arabic section).

14. Dio merely points out that Ardashir sought to make the city one of his bases against the Romans (80.3.2). The city seems to have resisted the siege on its own.

15. *L'année épigraphique* (hereafter cited as *AE*) (1958), nos. 238–240.

16. André Maricq, "Classica et orientalia: 2. Les dernières années de Hatra: l'alliance romaine," *Syria* 34 (1957): 294.

17. His father was still king after the siege of Septimius Severus, in 200–201: see Roberta Venco Ricciardi, "Preliminary Report on the 1987 Excavation at Hatra," *Mesopotamia* 23 (1988): 31.

18. The date is not certain, but we know that the assault by Sassanid armies took place shortly after Ardashir took power—that is, around 227–229.

19. "Maximus and Balbinus," in *Historia Augusta* (hereafter cited as *HA*), trans. David Magie (Loeb Classical Library), vol. 1, 13.5 (identifying Pupienus, Maximinus, and the Persians, called Parthians); the text points out that Pupienus was charged with leading a campaign in the east. George Synkellos places the event under Maximinus's reign: *The Chronography of George Synkellos: A Byzantine Chronicle of Universal History from the Creation,* ed. and trans. William Adler and Paul Tuffin (Oxford: Oxford University Press), p. 522. See Loriot, "Premières années," p. 657.

20. Charles Bradford Welles, "The Epitaph of Julius Terentius," *Harvard Theological Review* 34 (1941): 96–102 (= *Supplementum epigraphicum graecum* [Alphen aan den Rijn: Sijthoff & Noordhoff, 1923–1998], vol. 7, 743b): graffiti by the merchant Aurelius Nebuchelos, dated April 239, indicating that "in the year 550, in the month of Xanthicos, the Persians came down on us," and thus supplying a precise date; as was logical, Dura was attacked at the very beginning of the military season.

21. A passage from the *Codex Manichaicus Coloniensis* 18, 1–16 (Ludwig Koenen and Cornelia Römer, eds., *Der Kölner Mani-Kodex: Abbildungen und diplomatischer Text* [Bonn: Habelt, 1985], fragment 18, 1–16, pp. 10–12); see the English translation by Ron Cameron and Arthur J. Dewey, *The Cologne Mani Codex (P. Colon inv. Nr. 4780): Concerning the Origin of His Body* (Missoula, Mont.: Scholars Press, 1979), and the German translation by Ludwig Koenen and Cornelia Römer, *Der Kölner Mani-Kodex: Über das Werden seines Leibes* (Opladen: Westdeutscher Verlag, 1988), which establishes that Shapur was crowned king on April 17 or 18, 240, the year in which Hatra fell.

22. Ammianus Marcellinus, *The Surviving Books of the History,* trans. John C. Rolfe (Loeb Classical Library), vol. 2, 25.8.5 (hereafter cited as Ammianus).

23. Xavier Loriot, "Itinera Gordiani Augusti: I. Un voyage de Gordien III à Antioche en 239 après J.-C.," *Bulletin de la Société française de numismatique* 26 (1971): 18–21, relying on the mention of an imperial constitution of April 1, 239, promulgated in Antioch. Loriot's thesis is vigorously contested by Helmut Halfmann, *Itinera principum: Geschichte und Typologie der Kaiserreisen im Romischen Reich* (Stuttgart: F. Steiner, 1986), p. 234 (Halfmann thinks that Gordian was in Rome in January 239: see Wilhelm Henzen, *Corpus inscriptionum latinarum,* vol. 6, *Inscriptiones urbis Romae latinae* [Berlin: G. Reimer, 1876], no. 37165), but it is supported by Axel Jürging, "Die erste Emission Gordians III," *Jahrbuch für Numismatik und Geldgeschichte* 45 (1995): 95–128 (especially pp. 121–127).

24. Herodian, 8.8.8.

25. The battle of Mesike: *Res gestae divi saporis,* lines 6–10, trans. André Maricq, in "Classica et orientalia: 5. Res gestae divi saporis," *Syria* 35 (1958): 306–308; there is

an allusion to it in an inscription from Barm-e Delak (Persis): Philippe Gignoux, "D'Abnun à Mahan: Étude de deux inscriptions sassanides," *Studia Iranica* 20 (1991): 9–22; Probs O. Skjaervø, "L'inscription d'Abnun et l'imparfait en Moyen-Perse," *Studia Iranica* 21 (1992): 153–160. A tradition hostile to Philip the Arab holds him responsible for the emperor's death, but it has little credibility; see David Macdonald, "The Death of Gordian III: Another Tradition," *Historia* 30 (1981): 502–508; David Stone Potter, *Prophecy and History in the Crisis of the Roman Empire: A Historical Commentary on the Thirteenth Sibylline Oracle* (Oxford and New York: Clarendon Press, 1990), pp. 204–212. It appears from the *Res gestae divi saporis* (in *Die römisch-persischen Kriege des 3. Jahrhunderts n. Chr.: Nach der Inschrift Sahpuhrs I. an der Ka'be-ye Zartost [SKZ],* by Erich Kettenhofen [Wiesbaden: L. Reichert, 1982] [hereafter cited as *RGDS*]) that Gordian III was killed on the battlefield, but Ammianus Marcellinus places his death at Zitha between Circesion and Dura (23.5.17); cf. Potter, *Prophecy and History,* pp. 201–212. On the traditions taken together, see Michael H. Dodgeon and Samuel N. C. Lieu, *The Roman Eastern Frontier and the Persian Wars (ad 226–363): A Documentary History* (London and New York: Routledge, 1991) pp. 35–45; see also Loriot, "Premières années," pp. 770–774.

26. Maricq, "Classica et orientalia: 5," 308, lines 9–10: he committed himself to paying a high ransom, five hundred thousand deniers in gold; on his real importance, see Kevin Butcher, "Imagined Emperors: Personalities and Failure in the Third Century," *Journal of Roman Archaeology* 9 (1996): 520–522. The Greek sources speak of this shameful peace without specifying that it resulted from a ransom (*The Ecclesiastical History of Evagrius Scholasticus,* ed. and trans. Michael Whitby [Liverpool: Liverpool University Press, 2000], 5.7; Zosimus, *New History: A Translation with Commentary,* ed. and trans. Ronald T. Ridley [Canberra: Australian Association for Byzantine Studies], 3.32.4 [hereafter cited as Zosimus]; Zonaras, 12.19, p. 583, 1–5). In "The Sibylline Oracles," ed. and trans. John Joseph Collins (in *The Old Testament Pseudepigrapha,* ed. James A. Charlesworth [New York: Doubleday]) (hereafter cited as "Sibylline Oracles"), its fragility is stressed (13.28–34).

27. The site was obviously not in Persia, contrary to the assertion in "The Three Gordians," *HA,* vol. 2, 34.2; cf. Eutropius, *The Breviarium ab urbe condita of Eutropius,* ed. and trans. H. W. Bird (Liverpool: Liverpool University Press, 1993), 9.2.3; Sextus Pompeius Festus, *The Breviarum of Festus: A Critical Edition with Historical Commentary,* ed. J. W. Eadie (London: Athlone Press, 1967), 22; Zosimus, 3.14.2. Ammianus Marcellinus saw it still standing in 363 (Ammianus, vol. 2, 23.5.7).

28. Dedication by L. Trebonius Sossianus in Philippopolis (Hermann Dessau, *Inscriptiones latinae selectae* [Berlin: Weidmann, 1892–1916], no. 9005 [hereafter cited as *ILS*] = Annie Fauriat-Sartre and Maurice Sartre, *Inscriptions grecques et latines de la Syrie* [hereafter cited as *IGLS*], vol. 15, *Le plateau du Trachôn* [Beirut: Institut français d'archéologie du Proche-Orient, forthcoming], no. 429), confirmed by the indication in Zosimus (1.20.2) that Iulius Priscus was responsible for administering all the eastern provinces.

29. Zosimus, 1.20.2 and 1.22.2; Aurelius Victor, *Liber de Caesaribus,* ed. and trans. H. W. Bird (Liverpool: Liverpool University Press, 1994), 29; Academiae litterarum borussicae, ed., *Prosopographia Imperii Romani, saec. I. II. III.,* 2nd ed., vol. 1 (Berlin: W. de Gruyter, 1933), no. 49; Potter, *Prophecy and History,* pp. 248–249. The reality of his usurpation is confirmed by some coinages: see Roger F. Bland, "The Coinage of Jotapian," in *Essays in Honour of Robert Carson and Kenneth Jenkins,*

ed. Martin Price, Andrew Burnett, and Roger F. Bland (London: Spink, 1993), pp. 191–206.

30. François Chausson "Théoclia, soeur de Sévère Alexandre," *Mélanges de l'École française de Rome: Antiquités* 109 (1997): 683–690; Aurelius Victor notes that Jotapianus claimed to be a descendant of Alexander (*Liber de Caesaribus,* 29), presumably referring to Alexander Severus rather than Alexander the Great; this would confirm his connection with Emesa.

31. See Bland, "Coinage," pp. 191–206.

32. Aurelius Victor, *Liber de Caesaribus,* 29, 2.

33. In a long-standing debate, historians and archaeologists continue to disagree over the dates for the fall of Dura and the capture of Antioch. The discoveries at Apamaea have allowed Jean-Charles Balty to move the date of Shapur's campaign back to the spring and summer of 252, and that of the Roman campaign to the following spring at the latest ("Apamée [1986]: Nouvelles données sur l'armée romaine d'Orient et les raids sassanides du milieu du IIIe siècle," *CRAI* [1987], pp. 213–241, especially pp. 229–239); Fergus Millar agrees with this chronology (*The Roman Near East [31 B.C.–A.D. 337]* [Cambridge, Mass.: Harvard University Press, 1993], p. 159). This view is in harmony, moreover, with the only dates supplied by ancient authors: see *Chronicle of 724* (in "Chronica minora II," ed. E. W. Brooks, trans. J.-B. Chabot, in *Corpus scriptorium christianorum orientalium,* ed. Addaï Scher [Paris: Imprimerie nationale, 1904; repr., Louvain: Secrétariat du Corpus scriptorum christianorum orientalium, 1960], vol. 3, part 3, 563 Seleucid, or 251–252; French translation by J.-B. Chabot in vol. 4, part 4) and Zosimus, 1.27.2; Zosimus is less precise, but he places the Sassanid and Gothic raids before Aemilianus's usurpation in June–July 253. Moreover, the oldest Pehlevi graffiti in Dura, positively dated, are from March–April 253 (that is, from a time when the campaign would have scarcely begun); it is thus better to imagine that the city fell the year before. On Shapur's campaign, see Kettenhofen, *Römisch-persischen Kriege,* pp. 38–96.

34. *Res gestae divi saporis,* in Maricq, "Classica et orientalia: 5," 1.10.

35. Michel Christol, "À propos de la politique extérieure de Trébonien Galle," *Revue numismatique* (1980): 63–84.

36. This was perhaps the moment when Antioch was turned over to the Persians by Mariades: "The Thirty Pretenders," in *HA,* vol. 3, 2.2 (Cyriades); John Malalas, *The Chronicle of John Malalas,* trans. Elizabeth Jeffreys, Michael Jeffreys, Roger Scott, et al. (Melbourne: Australian Association for Byzantine Studies, 1986), pp. 156–162 (12.295–296) (hereafter cited as Malalas); Continuator Dionis (Dio's anonymous successor), in *Fragmenta historicorum graecorum,* ed. Karl I. Müller (Paris: Firmin-Didot, 1851), vol. 4, p. 193, frag. 1 (hereafter cited as *FHG*).

37. A collection of epitaphs from Tower 15 in Apamaea is directly related to these operations: see J.-C. Balty, "Apamée (1986): Nouvelles données sur l'armée romaine d'Orient et les raides sassanides du milieu du IIIe siècle," *Comtes rendus des séances de l'Académie des inscriptions et belles-lettres* (1987): 229–231.

38. "Sibylline Oracles," 13.150–154, calling him "sent from the sun" (151); Domninus, cited by Malalas (pp. 162–163 [12.297]), calls him Sampsigeramos, a traditional name in the family. On this usurper of the royal purple, see Hans Roland Baldus, *Uranius Antoninus: Münzprägung und Geschichte* (Bonn: R. Habelt, 1971), reviewed by James D. Breckenridge in the *American Journal of Anthropology* 79 (1975): 395–396; J.-C. Balty, "Apamée (1986)"; Hans Roland Baldus, "Uranius

Antoninus of Emesa, a Roman Emperor from Palmyra's Neighbouring-City and His Coinage," in "Palmyra and the Silk Road: International Colloquium, Palmyra, 7–11 April 1992," special issue, *Annales archéologiques arabes syriennes* (hereafter cited as *AAAS*) 42 (1996): 371–377.

39. Millar deems the connection between Malalas's Sampsigeramus and Uranius Antoninus "pure speculation," along with Antoninus's ties to the family of Iulia Domna and to the ancient Emesenian dynasty (*Roman Near East*, p. 161); but see Chausson, "Théoclia," pp. 681–683.

40. Perhaps this victory should be considered in relation to the inscriptions found in Louise Jalabert and René Mouterde, *IGLS*, vol. 4, *Laodicée, Apamène: Chronologie des inscriptions datées des tomes I–IV* (Paris: P. Geuthner, 1955), nos. 1799ff.; however, J.-C. Balty has offered strong arguments for a Persian invasion as early as 252 ("Apamée [1986]," p. 237).

41. Baldus, "Uranius Antoninus of Emesa," especially p. 374.

42. David Stone Potter, "Rome and Palmyra: Odaenathus' Titulature and the Use of the *Imperium Maius*," ZPE 113 (1996): 271–285, especially pp. 282 and 284.

43. Mikhail Ivanovitch Rostovtzeff, "Res gestae divi saporis and Dura," *Berytus* 8 (1943): 61–64.

44. Ibid., pp. 7–66. This position has been supported by Baldus (*Uranius Antoninus*, pp. 229–269) and Kettenhofen (*Römisch-persischen Kriege*, pp. 38–96). Contrary voices in favor of 256 include Ernest Honigmann and André Maricq, *Recherches sur les Res gestae divi saporis* (Brussels: Palais des Académies, 1953), pp. 131–142; Glanville Downey, *A History of Antioch in Syria: From Seleucus to the Arab Conquest* (Princeton: Princeton University Press, 1961), pp. 255–258, 587–595; Thomas Pekáry, "Bemerkungen zur Chronologie des Jahrzehnts 250–260 n. Chr.," *Historia* 11 (1962): 123–128; Wolfgang Felix, *Antike literarische Quellen zur Aussenpolitik des Sasanidenstaates: I. 224–309* (Vienna: Verlag der Österreichischen Akademie der Wissenschaften, 1985), pp. 56–58, nos. 57–58; David Macdonald denies that the city was taken by anyone in 252 or 253, and argues in favor of a single capture in 256 or 257 ("Dating the Fall of Dura-Europos," *Historia* 35 [1986]: 45–68).

45. Simon James, "Dura-Europos and the Chronology of Syria in the 250s AD," *Chiron* 15 (1985): 111–124. The coinages of Antioch that were thought to be dated to 255 or 256 have been pushed back to 254; in contrast, not a single coin dating from 257 has been found.

46. Franz Grenet, "Les Sassanides à Doura-Europos (253 ap. J.-C.): Réexamen du matériel épigraphique iranien du site," in *Géographie historique au Proche-Orient*, ed. Pierre-Louis Gatier, Bruno Helly, and Jean-Paul Rey-Coquais (Paris: Centre national de la recherche scientifique, 1988), pp. 133–158.

47. See especially the documents in Pehlevi and Parthian mentioned by Grenet in "Sassanides," pp. 134–137; the graffiti of Parthian scribes in the synagogue date from the years 14 and 15 of the reign of Shapur I—that is, 253 (p. 141).

48. There is no reference to this Persian attack in *Res gestae*, where Shapur nonetheless complacently presents his successes against the Romans; but he mentions nothing between the 252 campaign and that of 260. I do not understand on what grounds Richard Stoneman gives 256 as the date of a powerful offensive by Shapur that would have led him all the way to the sea and would have had him capturing Antioch thanks to Mariades (Richard Stoneman, *Palmyra and Its Empire: Zenobia's*

Revolt against Rome [Ann Arbor: University of Michigan Press, 1992], pp. 102–103); Stoneman seems unaware of Kettenhofen's fundamental work, *Römische-persischen Kriege*, and seems to blindly follow Drijvers's chronology.

49. Remains of siege machinery have been found in front of the western Palmyra gate: see Pierre Leriche and Mahmoud al-A'sad, "Doura-Europos: Bilan des recherches récentes," *CRAI* (1994): 415–416.

50. Ibid., pp. 418–419.

51. Ammianus, 23.5.7, 24.1.6; but Patrice Brun has rightly pointed out to me that this can stem from a literary *topos;* still, I do not believe that for now the archaeologists have picked up the slightest trace of a later occupation of the site, apart from temporary Bedouin encampments.

52. *Papyrus de l'Euphrate,* in Denis Feissel, Jean Gascou, and Javier Teixidor, "Documents d'archives romains inédits du Moyen Euphrate (IIIe s. après J.-C.)," *Journal des Savants* (1997), no. 9 (in 252) and nos. 3–4; cf. Millar, *Roman Near East,* p. 163.

53. Adraha: Hans-Georg Pflaum, "La fortification de la ville d'Adraha d'Arabie (259–260 à 274–275) d'après des inscriptions récemment découvertes," *Syria* 29 (1952): 307; Bostra: Maurice Sartre, *IGLS,* vol. 13.1, *Bostra* (Paris: P. Geuthner, 1982), no. 9106.

54. Sartre, *IGLS,* vol. 13.1, no. 9109.

55. J.-C. Balty, "Apamée (1986)."

56. Enno Littmann, David Magie, and D. R. Stuart, *Greek and Latin Inscriptions: Southern Syria,* vol. 3A of *Syria: Publications of the Princeton University Archaeological Expeditions to Syria in 1904–1905 and 1909* (hereafter cited as *PAES*) (Leiden: E. J. Brill, 1921), no. 10.

57. Or, more precisely, certain provinces within the empire.

58. The region had already been annexed by the Parthians in 151, and Ardashir thus only seized it from his Arsacid adversaries.

59. Maurice Sartre, "Palmyre, cité grecque," in "Palmyra and the Silk Road," special issue, *AAAS* 42 (1996): 385–405; Paul Veyne contests the claim that the city-state organization was as recent as the Roman era, and believes that Palmyra must have imitated its neighbors as early as the Hellenistic period (preface to *Palmyre, métropole caravanière,* by Gérard Degeorge [Paris: Imprimerie nationale, 2001], p. 21).

60. Ulpian, *Digesta,* 50.15.1, in *Corpus iuris civilis,* ed. Paul Krüger, Theodor Mommsen, Rudolf Schöll, and Wilhelm Kroll, (Berlin: Weidmann, 1928).

61. See the crucial work by Jean-Baptiste Yon, *Les notables de Palmyre* (Beirut: Institut français d'archéologie du Proche-Orient), especially pp. 97–113.

62. Michel Gawlikowski, "Les princes de Palmyre," *Syria* 62 (1985): 251–261.

63. Jean Cantineau, *Inventaire des inscriptions de Palmyre* (Beirut: Publications du Musée national syrien de Damas, 1930–1933), 8.55 (hereafter cited as *Inv.*).

64. An inscription in his honor was engraved on the propylaea of the Temple of Bel in August 193 (*Inv.,* vol. 9, no. 26), but only the hammering inflicted on the emperor's name allows us to think that the name in question was indeed Pescennius Niger.

65. Everywhere else only the new citizens adopted the *gentilicium* Aurelius at the time of the edict of 212 granting citizenship to all residents of the empire, but in Palmyra even the residents who were already citizens gave up their former names to adopt the new gentilicium.

66. A factional struggle had divided the city at the time of the Roman civil war: see Harald Ingholt, "Deux inscriptions bilingues de Palmyre," *Syria* 13 (1932): 278–289.

67. Académie des inscriptions et belles-lettres, *Corpus inscriptionum semiticarum* (Paris: e Reipublicae Typographeo, 1881; repr., Paris: C. Klincksieck, 1972), vol. 2, no. 3932 (hereafter cited as *CIS*) = *Inv.*, vol. 3, no. 22 = Delbert R. Hillers and Eleonora Cussini, *Palmyrene Aramaic Texts* (Baltimore: Johns Hopkins University Press, 1994), no. 0278 (hereafter cited as *PAT*) = Khaled As'ad and Jean-Baptiste Yon, *Inscriptions de Palmyre: Promenades épigraphiques dans la ville antique de Palmyre* (Beirut: Direction générale des antiquités et des musées de la République arabe syrienne, Institut français d'archéologie du Proche-Orient, 2001), pp. 66–67, no. 18 (hereafter cited as *I.Palmyre*).

68. Millar, *Roman Near East*, p. 149.

69. See Yon, *Notables de Palmyre;* the same phenomenon can be observed in Dura, where a single family held the function of *strategos epistrate.*

70. *Inv.*, vol. 3, no. 6 = *PAT*, no. 0290.

71. Gawlikowski, "Princes de Palmyre," p. 257, no. 13.

72. Ibid., p. 255; it is engraved under a niche in the monumental arch and concerns Herodian alone. A tessera also attributes the title of king to Hairan-Herodian: see Henri Seyrig, "Note sur Hérodien, prince de Palmyre," *Syria* 18 (1937): 1–4.

73. Veyne, preface to Degeorge, *Palmyre*, p. 26.

74. *Inv.*, vol. 3, no. 17 (April 258), and vol. 12, no. 37 (257/8); Henri Seyrig, "Les fils du roi Odainat," *Annales archéologiques de Syrie* (hereafter cited as *AAS*) 13 (1963): 161 (dedication of the leatherworkers) (257.8); Christiane Dunant, *Le sanctuaire de Baalshamin à Palmyre*, vol. 3, *Les inscriptions* (Rome: n.p., 1971), p. 66, no. 52.

75. Seyrig, "Fils du roi Odainat," p. 161 (dedication of Worod).

76. See Gawlikowski, "Princes de Palmyre," p. 261, for an opposing view. Millar thinks that he must have held an official position, perhaps that of legate of Syria-Phoenicia (*Roman Near East*, p. 165).

77. Inscriptions by tanners and leatherworkers in honor of Hairan: see Seyrig, "Fils du roi Odainat," pp. 161–163 (but there could have been a parallel dedication in honor of Odainathos): for inscriptions by silversmiths and jewelers in honor of Odainathos, see *CIS*, vol. 2, no. 3945 = *Inv.*, vol. 3, no. 17 = *PAT*, no. 0291.

78. Georges Lopuszanski, *La date de la capture de Valérien et la chronologie des empereurs gaulois* (Brussels: Institut d'études polonaises en Belgique, 1951).

79. The bishop Demetrianus, who was succeeded by Paul of Samosata, must have died around this time, but nothing proves that he was taken captive by the Persians, as the "Histoire nestorienne" claims (see *Chronique de Seert*, ed. and trans. Addaï Scher [Paris: Firmin-Didot, 1907; repr., Turnhout: Brepols, 1971], vol. 4, fasc. 3, p. 221, no. 17), whereas Eusebius of Caesarea specifies that Demetrianus died in Antioch (*The Ecclesiastical History*, trans. Kirsopp Lake [Loeb Classical Library], 7.27).

80. Millar, *Roman Near East*, pp. 166–167.

81. Continuator Dionis (*FHG*, vol. 4, p. 193, frag. 3) makes him a "count of holy benefactions and prefect of the *Annona*"; the first title is anachronistic, but it is plausible that the individual indeed had a high financial position under Valerian.

82. Zonaras, 12.24.

83. Petrus Patricius, in *FHG*, vol. 4, p. 185; Zonaras, 12.24; see Annie Sartre-Fauriat, "Palmyre de la mort de Commode à Nicée (192–325 apr. J.-C.)," in *L'Empire*

romain de la mort de Commode à Nicée (192–325 ap. J.-C.), ed. Yann Le Bohec (Paris: Éditions du Temps, 1997), pp. 264–267. According to "Thirty Pretenders," *HA*, 18.1, Ballista (who had played a major role in the expulsion of the Persians from Cilicia) was the prefect of the praetorium under Quietus and was besieged along with Quietus in Emesa; spared by Odainathos, he then proclaimed himself emperor and was killed on his own lands at Daphne; but the text points out that historians disagree about the reality of his usurpation. Zonaras depicts Ballista as the master of cavalry under Quietus (whom he calls Quintus) and says that he was killed at the hand of Odainathos himself at Emesa (12.24).

84. Petrus Patricius, in *FHG*, vol. 4, frag. 10.

85. Zonaras, pp. 141–142, 12.23; George Synkellos, *Chronography*, p. 466, 23, to p. 467, 7; according to these authors, this is how Odainathos won the title "strategos of the Orient."

86. An allusion in a late Jewish letter attributes the destruction of Nehardea, in Mesopotamia, to Odainathos: see Sherira ben Hanina, *Iggeret Rav Sherira Ge'on*, ed. Binyamin Menasheh Levin (Jerusalem: Makor, 1971 or 1972) (in Hebrew), p. 82 (cited in Dodgeon and Lieu, *Roman Eastern Frontier*, p. 70); the text is thought to have been written in 987. On his expedition against Ctesiphon, see Festus, *Breviarium*, 23.13–18; Eutropius, *Breviarum*, 9.10; Jerome, in *Eusebius Werke*, vol. 7, *Die Chronik des Hieronymus (Hieronymi Chronicon)*, ed. Rudolf Helm (Berlin: Akademie-Verlag, 1956), p. 221, 10–12; "The Two Gallieni," *HA*, vol. 3, 10.6. 10.12; "Thirty Pretenders," *HA*, 15.4; Orosius, *The Seven Books of History against the Pagans* (= *Adversus Paganos*), trans. Roy Deferrari (Washington, D.C.: Catholic University of America Press, 1964), 7.22; Zosimus, 1.39.2.

87. *Inv.*, vol. 3, no. 19 = *PAT*, no. 0292 = *I.Palmyre*, p. 68, no. 19.

88. *Inv.*, vol. 3, no. 3. This inscription is fragmentary, but it does seem to attribute the title "king of kings" to Septimius Herodian and to relate the granting of the title to a victory over the Persians. Daniel Schlumberger presents an improved text in "L'inscription d'Hérodien," *Bulletin d'études orientales* (hereafter cited as *BEO*) 9 (1942–1943): 35–38. See also Gawlikowski, "Princes de Palmyre," p. 255, and Potter, "Rome and Palmyra," pp. 273–274.

89. Zonaras, pp. 141–143, 12.23.

90. See Simon Swain, "Greek into Palmyrene: Odaenathus as 'Corrector Totius Orientis'?" *ZPE* 99 (1993): 157–164. After examining numerous bilingual inscriptions, Swain concludes that the title *epanorthotes*, Palmyrene "PNRT_," does not translate the title *corrector*, but that it does convey an idea of power.

91. Zosimus, 1.39.1.

92. "Two Gallieni," *HA*, 12.4.

93. "Thirty Pretenders," *HA*, 15.5.

94. For example, Ernest Will, *Les Palmyréniens: La Venise des sables* = *1er siècle avant–IIIème siècle après J.-C.* (Paris: A. Colin, 1992), p. 179. Michel Christol retains the two Odainathoses and seems to view the Palmyrene princes as foreign sovereigns, forgetting that Palmyra had belonged to the empire for two and a half centuries (*L'Empire romain du IIIe siècle, histoire politique: de 192, mort de Commode, à 325, concile de Nicée* [Paris: Errance, 1997], p. 148).

95. Petrus Patricius, frag. 10.

96. This is the case most notably for Septimius Worod, honored in several dedications in Odainathos's lifetime: see *PAT*, nos. 0284–0289, between 262 and 267; I be-

lieve this is the same individual who was still only an Aurelius Worod in 258: *PAT,* nos. 0283. We should note that Zenobia also bears the gentilicium *Septimia,* which is not logical if her father is the Iulius Aurelius Zenobius of *Inv.* vol. 3, no. 22 = *PAT,* no. 0278, unless the latter, like other leading figures in the city, had adopted the gentilicium *Septimius* between 258 and 262. Cf. also the generals Septimius Zabdas and Septimius Zabbaios, in 271 (*PAT,* no. 0293).

97. For the text, see Schlumberger, "Inscription," pp. 35–50; Gawlikowski, "Princes de Palmyre," p. 255; Potter, "Rome and Palmyra," pp. 273–274.

98. See Potter, "Rome and Palmyra."

99. "Two Gallieni," *HA,* 10.1.

100. *Inv.,* vol. 3, no. 10 = *PAT,* no. 0285; *Inv.,* vol. 3, no. 7 = *PAT,* no. 0288.

101. Zosimus, 1.39.2.

102. See the texts collected by Dodgeon and Lieu in *Roman Eastern Frontier,* pp. 80–82. Most traditions make them victims of family infighting.

103. Gawlikowski, "Princes de Palmyre," p. 259.

104. "Two Gallieni," *HA,* 13.4–5; this expedition, not attested elsewhere, remains doubtful.

105. In *Septimia Zenobia Sebaste* (Rome: L'Erma, 1993), Eugenia Equini Schneider has provided what I consider the best biography of Zenobia, who has too often been the victim of a romanticized or ideological history. There are many legends about her presumed origins (for example, her kinship with Cleopatra), but she was obviously the daughter of a wealthy Palmyrene family; her father may have been the Zenobios known as Zabdilas, strategos of the colony during Severus Alexander's visit, whose name is preserved in an inscription from 242–243 (*Inv.,* vol. 3, no. 22 = *PAT,* no. 0278): cf. Javier Teixidor, "Antiquités sémitiques," *Annuaire du Collège de France 1997–1998* (1998): 719. The chief argument in favor of this thesis is that the statue dedicated to Zenobios stands across from that of Zenobia; the argument is extremely weak, and seems to me to carry little weight in the face of the text of the milestone (*CIS,* vol. 2, no. 3971), where Zenobia is named, in the Palmyrene version, Septimia Bethzabbai, daughter of Antiochus.

106. Christol, *Empire romain,* p. 156.

107. A bilingual milestone found west of Palmyra gives an unambiguous text: the Palmyrene version gives Wahballath the titles *mlk mlk' w'pnrt' dy mdnh' klh* ("king of kings, restorer of all the Orient"), and the Greek, which is fragmentary, calls him "king" *(basileus),* whereas Zenobia is described as "illustrious queen, mother of the king" (*CIS,* vol. 2, no. 3971 = *PAT,* no. 0317).

108. Reginald Stuart Poole, *Catalogue of Greek Coins of Alexandria and the Nomes* (London: Trustees of the British Museum, 1892).

109. It is remarkable that on the milestones in the name of Vaballathos, the latter does not always bear on his head the title *Imperator Caesar,* nor that of *Augustus:* see Thomas Bauzou, "Deux milliaires inédits de Vaballath en Jordanie du Nord," in Philip Freeman and David L. Kennedy, eds., *The Defence of the Roman and Byzantine East* (Oxford: British Archaeological Reports, 1986), pp. 1–8; cf., however, *AE* (1904), no. 60 (*ILS,* no. 8924); cf. also the formulas for dating papyri in Egypt: Bernard P. Grenfell and Arthur S. Hunt, eds., *The Oxyrhynchus Papyri* (London: Egypt Exploration Fund, 1898–), 1264, lines 20–27 (hereafter cited as *P.Oxy*); Ulrich Wilcken et al., eds., *Ägyptische Urkunden aus den Königlichen Museen zu Berlin: Griechische Urkunden* (Berlin: Staatliche Museen, 1903), no. 946 (hereafter cited

as *BGU*); in March 272, Vaballathos was in the fifth year of his reign, which means that he retroactively shifted his accession to the throne to the very aftermath of Odainathos's assassination.

110. Nothing allows us to assert that Philip was the son of an indigenous chief and was thus an Arab in the ethnic sense; his gentilicium indicates citizenship of long standing, probably antedating the creation of the province of Arabia. I would not be surprised if he belonged to a family from elsewhere (on the Levantine side, or even from the west) that had settled in this region at the time of its annexation or shortly thereafter. On the fine portrait of the emperor found in Shahba, see J.-Ch. Balty, "Un portrait de Shahba-*Philippopolis* et l'iconographie de Philippe l'Arabe," in *Resurrecting the Past: A Joint Tribute to Adnan Bounn,* ed. Paolo Matthiae, Matthiae Nannong van Loon, and Harvey Weiss (Istanbul: Nederlands historisch-archaeologisch instituut te Istanbul; Leiden: Nederlands instituut voor het nabije oosten, 1990), pp. 5–15; on the praise addressed to an anonymous emperor who is probably Philip the Arab, see Louis J. Swift, "The Anonymous Encomium of Philip the Arab," *Greek, Roman and Byzantine Studies* 7 (1966): 268–289, and the French translation in Laurent Pernot, ed., *Éloges grecs de Rome* (Paris: Les Belles Lettres, 1997), pp. 139–161.

111. *P. Oxy.* 1264; *BGU* 946.

112. *Antoniniani* in the name of Vaballathos alone were issued by the workshop in Antioch: see Henri Seyrig, "Vhabalathus Augustus," *Mélanges offerts à Kazimierz Michalowski* (Warsaw: Panstwowe wydawnictwo naukowe, 1966), p. 659. In addition, the sources indicate that Paul of Samosata, the bishop of Antioch dismissed by a local council in 268, succeeded in maintaining his position thanks to the presence of Palmyrenes in the city.

113. Sartre, *IGLS*, vol. 13.1, no. 9107. The only literary reference to the invasion is in Malalas, p. 163 (12.299.3–10).

114. In the *temenos* of the Qasr al-Bint, traces of brutal destruction in the second half of the third century have been discovered: see Jacqueline Dentzer and François Renel, "Qasr al-Bint," *Le monde de la Bible* (May 2000): 61.

115. Zosimus, 1.44.1–2; see also George Synkellos, *Chronography,* p. 721, 4–9; "The Deified Claudius," *HA,* vol. 3, 11.1–2; "Probus," *HA,* vol. 3, 9.5. Cf. Jacques Schwartz, "Les Palmyréniens en Égypte," *Bulletin de la Société archéologique d'Alexandrie* 40 (1953): 3–21.

116. Zosimus, 1.50.1.

117. Ibid., 1.56.2–3.

118. Libanios, *Libanii Opera,* ed. Richard Förster and Eberhard Richsteig (Hildesheim: G. Olms, 1963–1985), vol. 11, p. 195.

119. Arthur Stein, "Kallinikos von Petrai," *Hermes* 58 (1923): 448.

120. Michel Tardieu, "L'arrivée des manichéens à al-Hira," in *La Syrie de Byzance à l'Islam, VIIe–VIIIe siècles: Actes du colloque international Lyon-Maison de l'Orient méditerranéen, Paris-Institut du monde arabe, 11–14 septembre 1990,* ed. Pierre Canivet and Jean-Paul Rey-Coquais (Damascus: Institut français de Damas, 1995), pp. 15–24; I. M. F. Gardner and Samuel N. C. Lieu, "From Narmouthis to Kellis: Manichaean Documents from Roman Egypt," *Journal of Roman Studies* (hereafter cited as *JRS*) 86 (1996): 153–154.

121. See Fergus Millar, "Paul of Samosata, Zenobia and Aurelian: The Church, Local Culture and Political Allegiance in Third-Century Syria," *JRS* 61 (1971): 1–17;

for the contrary position, see Teixidor, "Antiquités sémitiques," pp. 730–731. Teixidor seems to me to give too much credit to traditions of which the oldest, that of Athanasios of Alexandria, is posterior to Zenobia's era by more than a century.

122. Continuator Dionis, 10.4 (*FHG*, vol. 4, p. 197).

123. Festus, *Breviarium*, 24.1–6; Eutropius (who does not designate Immae), *Breviarium*, 9.13.2; Jerome, *Chronik*, p. 222, 15–22 (year 273); Zosimus, 1.50.2–1.54.2. Immae is a strategic site where the decisive confrontation between Macrinus and Elagabal had already taken place in 218, where the passage of Bab al-Hawa comes out in the plain of Antioch, on the Aleppo road: see Glanville Downey, "Aurelian's Victory over Zenobia at Immae, A.D. 272," *Transactions and Proceedings of the American Philological Society* 81 (1950): 57–68; idem, *History of Antioch*, p. 249 and n. 77. "The Deified Aurelian," *HA*, vol. 3, 25.1, refers to "a brief engagement" at Daphne and locates the decisive battle at Emesa; see Sartre-Fauriat, "Palmyre," p. 271. The engagement at Daphne is thought to have brought the Roman troops into conflict with a Palmyrene unit charged with protecting the queen's flight (Zosimus, 1.52.1–2).

124. Zosimus, 1.52–53.

125. Contrary to the indications provided in "The Deified Aurelian," *HA*, 26.1 and 28.1, there cannot have been a siege at Palmyra, because there were no ramparts; see Michel Gawlikowski, "Les défenses de Palmyre," *Syria* 51 (1974): 231–242; at the very most, the Palmyrenes tried to protect the western approach to the city, but the vestiges discovered may just as well have come from the attackers' camp as from that of the defenders: see Michel Gawlikowski, "Palmyre, mission polonaise 1991," *Syria* 70 (1993): 564–566, for an argument in favor of a Palmyrene unit lying in wait for Aurelian's army.

126. Michel Gawlikowski, "Inscriptions de Palmyre," *Syria* 48 (1971): 407–426, especially p. 420 (= *Inv.*, vol. 9, no. 28); the negotiations were conducted by a member of the Palmyrene curia, Septimius Haddudan, who also appears in an inscription made after the fall of the city (ibid.).

127. We do not know what happened to Vaballathos, but Zenobia was taken to Rome to appear in Aurelian's triumphal procession. An abundant literature has been devoted to her fate after the fall of Palmyra, based on ancient sources that differ among themselves; see Equini Schneider, *Septimia Zenobia Sebaste*, pp. 53–60.

128. Zosimus, 1.56.2–3.

129. Ibid., 1.60; an inscription on the great colonnade honors an Apsaios at an unknown date: *Inv.*, vol. 3, no. 18.

130. Zosimus, 1.60; let us recall that Zenobia's father called himself Antiochos; "The Deified Aurelian," *HA*, 31.1–10, calls him Achilleus.

131. This has been attributed by Ernest Will to Legio III Cyrenaica ("Le sac de Palmyre," in *Mélanges d'archéologie et d'histoire offerts à André Piganiol*, ed. Raymond Chevallier [Paris: SEVPEN, 1966], pp. 1409–1416); in Will's view, the Romans avenged themselves in this way for the destruction of the sanctuary of Jupiter Hammon in Bostra in 270. See also Ernest Will, *Palmyréniens*, pp. 191–197; Eugen Cizek, *L'empereur Aurélien et son temps* (Paris: Les Belles Lettres, 1994), pp. 76–80 and 101–117, relying perhaps too confidently on the anonymous author of *Historia Augusta*; Han J. W. Drijvers, "Hatra, Palmyra und Edessa: Die Städte der syrisch-mesopotamischen Wüste in politischer, kulturgeschichtlicher und religiongeschichtlicher Beleuchtung," *ANRW* 2.8 (1977): 799–906; Maurice Sartre, "Arabs

and the Desert Peoples," *Cambridge Ancient History,* vol. 12, 2nd ed. (Cambridge: Cambridge University Press, forthcoming).

132. Gawlikowski, "Palmyre, mission polonaise 1990," p. 561.

133. Michel Gawlikowski has already excavated three churches, which attests to the fact that the urban complex was not abandoned.

134. See the second-century stuccos that had fallen on the ground at the beginning of the ninth century during the looting of certain roofs. See also S. P. Kowalski, "Late Roman Palmyra in Literature and Epigraphy," *Studia Palmyrenskie* 10 (1997): 39–62.

135. See Glen W. Bowersock, "Nabataeans and Romans in the Wadi Sirhan," in *Pre-Islamic Arabia,* ed. Abdelgadir Mahmoud Abdalla, Sami Saqqar, and Richard T. Mortel (Riyadh: Jami'at al-Malik Sa'ud, 1984), pp. 133–136.

136. Maurice Sartre, *Trois études sur l'Arabie romaine et byzantine* (Brussels: Revue d'études latines, 1982), pp. 122–128; see also Michael C. A. Macdonald, "Nomads and the Hawran in the Late Hellenistic and Roman Periods: A Reassessment of the Epigraphic Evidence," *Syria* 70 (1993): 368–377.

137. Gerald L. Harding, "The Arab Tribes," *Al-Abhath* 22 (1969): pp. 3–25.

138. See the early study by Antonin Jaussen and Raphaël Savignac, *Mission en Arabie,* vol. 2 (Paris: E. Leroux, 1914), pp. 644–649; Henri Seyrig, "Postes romains sur la route de Médine," *Syria* 22 (1941): 218–223; Sartre, *Trois études,* pp. 30–35.

139. David L. Kennedy, *Archaeological Explorations on the Roman Frontier in the North-Eastern Jordan* (Oxford: British Archaeological Reports, 1982), p. 190, no. 39; there is a photograph in Glen W. Bowersock, *Roman Arabia* (Cambridge, Mass.: Harvard University Press, 1983), pl. 14 (for the epitaph of Flavius Dionysius); Michael P. Speidel, "The Roman Road to Dumata (Jawf in Saudi Arabia) and the Frontier Strategy of *Praetensione Coligare,*" *Historia* 36 (1987): 214. The name is known to Stephanus of Byzantion: see *Ethnica,* ed. August Meineke (Graz: Akademische Druck und Verlagsanstalt, 1958), s.v. "Doumatha: city of Arabia; the citizen, Doumathênos." We have no archaeological traces of a Roman outpost, beyond a dedication erected to the god Zeus Hammon and the god Salmos, for the long life of the emperors (two unidentified emperors from the third century), by Flavius Dionysius, a centurion from Legio III Cyrenaica. It may have been a matter of a simple remote patrol unit without a fixed post.

140. Sartre, *Trois études,* pp. 22–25.

141. Macdonald, "Nomads and the Hawran."

142. *CIS,* vol. 2, no. 964; cf. Sartre, *Trois études,* p. 127.

143. Werner Caskel, *Gamharat an-Nasab, das genealogische Werk des Hisam Ibn Muhammad al-Kalbi* (Leiden: E. J. Brill, 1966); Irfan Shahid, *Byzantium and the Arabs in the Fourth Century* (Washington, D.C.: Dumbarton Oaks Research Library and Collection, 1984), pp. 349–417.

144. Enno Littman, *Semitic Inscriptions: Nabataean Inscriptions,* vol. 4A of *PAES* (Leiden: E. J. Brill, 1914), no. 41.

145. Bert de Vries, "Umm El-Jimal in the First Three Centuries AD," in Freeman and Kennedy, *Defence of the Roman and Byzantine East,* pp. 237–238.

146. S. Thomas Parker, *Romans and Saracens: A History of the Arabian Frontier* (Philadelphia: American Schools of Oriental Research, 1986), pp. 130–131.

147. Pflaum, "Fortification"; Sartre, *IGLS,* vol. 13.1, nos. 9105–9106 and 9108–9109.

148. Sartre, "Lakhmids," in *Late Antiquity: A Guide to the Postclassical World,* ed.

Glen W. Bowersock, Peter Brown, and Oleg Grabar (Cambridge, Mass.: Harvard University Press, 1999), pp. 536–537.

149. See, finally, Thomas Bauzou, "Épigraphie et toponymie: Le cas de la Palmyrène du sud-ouest," *Syria* 70 (1993): 27–50. The passageway may be much older than the improvements made in the third century: in "Frühkaiserzeitliche Befestigungen an der Strata Diocletiana," *Damaszener Mitteilungen* 9 (1996): 163–180, Michaela Konrad has noted traces indicating occupation from the end of the Hellenistic period and the beginning of the early empire on several sites along the northern part of the itinerary, at Resafa and at Quseir as-Saila, in particular a coinage depicting Aretas IV and others from the Augusto-Tiberian era.

150. Aila remained a prosperous city, open to the outside world: as early as the third century, African red-slip sigillata are definitely present: see S. Thomas Parker, "Human Settlement at the Northern Head of the Gulf of al-'Aqaba: Evidence of Site Migration," *Studies in the History and Archaeology of Jordan* 6 (1997): 189–193.

151. Similarly, an inscription whose interpretation and dating have been contested refers to a road that led toward the Jawf from Bostra and Qasr al-Azraq. This road has received a great deal of careful attention; see, in particular, Speidel, "Roman Road to Dumata," *Historia* 36 (1987); Thomas Bauzou, "La *praetensio* de Bostra à Dumata (el-Jowf)," *Syria* 73 (1996): 23–35. In "À propos de l'inscription d'el-Azraq (province d'Arabie)," *Cahiers du Centre Gustave Glotz* 10 (1999): 375–377, Michel Christol has suggested that this text belongs to the Aurelian era rather than to that of the tetrarchy; see also Michel Christol and Maurice Lenoir, "Qasr el-Azraq et la reconquête de l'Orient par Aurélien," *Syria* 78 (2001): 163–178.

152. See Alfred Felix L. Beeston, "Nemara and Faw," *Bulletin of the Society for Oriental and African Studies* 42 (1979): 1–6, for the linguistic aspects; on the historical interpretations, there is an impressive bibliography whose conclusions of course vary depending on what is read; among recent interpretations (with a current bibliography), see Manfred Kropp, "Grande re degli Arabi e vassalo de nessuno: Mar'al-Qays ibn 'Amr e l'iscrizione ad En-Nemara," *Quaderni di Studi Arabi* 9 (1991): 3–28; Christian Robin, "Autres Objets d'Arabie," in *L'Arabie avant l'Islam au Musée du Louvre*, ed. Yves Calvet and Christian Robin (Paris: Éditions de la Réunion des musées nationaux, 1997), pp. 265–269; Michael J. Zwettler, "Imra'alqays, son of 'Amr: king of . . .???" in *Literary Heritage of Classical Islam: Arabic and Islamic Studies in Honor of James A. Bellam*, ed. Mustansir Mir and Jarl E. Fossum (Princeton, N.J.: Darwin Press, 1993), pp. 3–37.

CONCLUSION

1. Fergus Millar, "Empire, Community and Culture in the Roman Near East: Greeks, Syrians, Jews and Arabs," *Journal of Jewish Studies* 38 (1987): 143–164.

2. Fergus Millar, "The Phoenician Cities: A Case Study of Hellenisation," *Proceedings of the Cambridge Philological Society* 209 (1983): 55–71.

WORKS CITED

Abadie-Reynal, Catherine. "La céramique romaine de Porsuk." *XI Kazi Sonuçlari Toplantisi* 1 (1990): 221–228.

———. "Courants commerciaux et échanges dans le bassin égéen entre la fin du IIe s. av. J.-C. et le VIe s. apr. J.-C." Mémoire d'habilitation, Université de Paris I, 1999.

Abadie-Reynal, Catherine, Rifat Ergeç, et al. "Mission de Zeugma-Moyenne vallée de l'Euphrate." *Anatolia antiqua* 5 (1997): 349–370.

———. "Zeugma-Moyenne vallée de l'Euphrate: Rapport préliminaire de la campagne de fouilles de 1997." *Anatolia antiqua* 6 (1998): 376–406.

Abbadi, Sabri, and Fawzi Zayadine. "Nepos the Governor of the Provincia Arabia in a Safaitic Inscription?" *Semitica* 46 (1996): 155–164.

Abel, Félix-Marie. *Géographie de la Palestine*. 2 vols. Paris: Libraire Lecoffre / J. Gabalda, 1933–1938.

———. *Histoire de la Palestine depuis la conquête d'Alexandre jusqu'à l'invasion arabe*. 2 vols. Paris: J. Gabalda, 1952.

———. "Une villa romaine à Djifna." *Revue biblique* 32 (1923): 111–114.

Académie des inscriptions et belles-lettres, ed. *Corpus inscriptionum semiticarum*. 5 vols. Paris: e Reipublicae Typographeo, 1881. Reprint, Paris: C. Klincksieck, 1972.

Achilles Tatius. *Leucippe and Clitophon*, trans. Tim Whitmarsh. Oxford and New York: Oxford University Press, 2000.

"Actes de la Table Ronde 'Mithra en Syrie,' Lyon, 18 novembre 2000." *Topoi* 11 (2001): 35–281.

Adan-Bayewitz, David. *Common Pottery in Roman Galilee: A Study of Local Trade*. Ramat-Gan: Bar Ilan University Press, 1993.

Adan-Bayewitz, David, and Moti Aviam. "Jotapata, Josephus and the Siege of 67:

Preliminary Report on the 1992–94 Seasons." *Journal of Roman Archaeology* 10 (1997): 131–165.

Adan-Bayewitz, David, and Isadore Perlman. "The Local Trade of Sepphoris in the Roman Period." *Israel Exploration Journal* 40 (1990): 151–172.

Adler, Ada, ed. *Suidae Lexicon*. 4 vols. Leipzig: B. G. Teubner, 1928–1938.

Africanus, Sextus Iulius. *Les "Cestes" de Julius Africanus*, ed. and trans. Jean-René Vieillefond. Florence: Sansoni antiquariato; Paris: Librairie M. Didier, 1970.

Aggoula, Basile. *Inscriptions et graffites araméens d'Assour*. Naples: Istituto Orientale di Napoli, 1985.

———. *Inventaire des inscriptions hatréennes*. Paris: P. Geuthner, 1991.

———. "Remarques sur les inscriptions hatréennes (VI)." *Syria* 58 (1981): 363–378.

———. "Remarques sur les inscriptions hatréennes (VII)." *Aula Orientalis* 1 (1983): 31–38.

———. "Remarques sur les inscriptions hatréennes (VIII)." *Syria* 60 (1983): 101–105.

———. "Remarques sur les inscriptions hatréennes (IX)." *Syria* 60 (1983): 251–257.

———. "Remarques sur les inscriptions hatréennes (XII)." *Syria* 63 (1986): 353–374.

———. "Remarques sur les inscriptions hatréennes (XI)." *Syria* 64 (1987): 91–106.

Aharoni, Yohanon. *Excavations at Ramat Rahel, Season 1959–1960*. Rome: Università degli studi, Centro di studi semitici, 1962.

———. *Excavations at Ramet Rahel, Season 1961–1962*. Rome: Università degli studi, Centro di studi semitici, 1964.

Alföldy, Géza. "Pontius Pilatus und das Tiberieum von Caesarea Maritima." *Scripta classica israelica* 18 (1999): 85–108.

Algaze, Guillermo, Ray Breuninger, and James Knudstad. "The Tigris-Euphrates Archaeological Reconnaissance Project: Final Report of the Birecik and Carchemish Dam Survey Areas." *Anatolica* 20 (1994): 1–96.

Allara, Anny. "Les maisons de Doura-Europos: Les données du terrain." *Syria* 65 (1988): 323–342.

Allberry, Charles Robert Cecil. *A Manichean Psalm-Book*. Stuttgart: W. Kohlhammer, 1938.

Alon, Gedaliah. *The Jews in Their Land in the Talmudic Age (70–640 ce)*, trans. Gershon Levi. Cambridge, Mass., and London: Harvard University Press, 1989.

———. *Jews, Judaism and the Classical World: Studies in Jewish History in the Times of the Second Temple and Talmud*. Jerusalem: Magnes Press (Hebrew University), 1977.

Altheim, Franz, and Ruth Stiehl. *Die Araber in der alten Welt*. 6 vols. Berlin: W. de Gruyter, 1964–1969.

Amadasi Guzzo, Maria Giulia, and Eugenia Equini Schneider. *Petra*, trans. Lydia G. Cochrane. Chicago: University of Chicago Press, 2002.

Amandry, Michel. "Le monnayage en bronze de Bibulus, Atratinus et Capito: Une tentative de romanisation en Orient." *Schweizerische Numismatische Rundschau* 65 (1986): 73–85.

———. "Le monnayage en bronze de Bibulus, Atratinus et Capito: Une tentative de romanisation en Orient." *Schweizerische Numismatische Rundschau* 66 (1987): 101–112.

———. "Le monnayage en bronze de Bibulus, Atratinus et Capito: Une tentative de romanisation en Orient." *Schweizerische Numismatische Rundschau* 69 (1990): 65–96.

————. "La politique monétaire des Flaviens en Syrie de 69 à 73." In *Les monnayages syriens: Quel apport pour l'histoire du Proche-Orient hellénistique et romain? Actes de la table ronde de Damas, 10–12 novembre 1999*, ed. Christian Augé and Frédérique Duyrat, 141–143. Beirut: Institut français d'archéologie du Proche-Orient, 2002.

Amer, Ghaleb, Jean-Luc Biscop, Jacqueline Dentzer[-Feydy], and Jean-Pierre Sodini. "L'ensemble basilical de Qanawât (Syrie du Sud)." *Syria* 59 (1982): 257–318.

Amer, Ghaleb, and Michel Gawlikowski. "Le sanctuaire impérial de Philippopolis." *Damaszener Mitteilunger* 2 (1985): 1–15.

Amit, David. "Khirbet Hilal." *Excavations and Surveys in Israel* 10 (1991): 150–151.

Ammianus Marcellinus. *The Surviving Books of the History*, trans. John C. Rolfe. 2 vols. Loeb Classical Library.

'Amr, Khairieh, and Ahmed Al-Momani. "The Discovery of Two Additional Pottery Kilns at az-Zurraba / Wadi Musa." *Annual of the Department of Antiquities of Jordan* 43 (1999): 175–194.

Amy, Robert. "Temples à escaliers." *Syria* 27 (1950): 82–186.

Ansary (al-), Abdul Rahman. *Qaryat al-Faw: A Portrait of Pre-Islamic Civilization in Saudi Arabia*. Riyadh: University of Riyadh; New York: St. Martin's Press, 1982.

"Antoninus Elagabalus." In *Historia Augusta*, trans. David Magie, vol. 2, 104–177. Loeb Classical Library.

Appianus. *The Civil Wars*. In *Roman History*, trans. Horace White, vols. 3–4. Loeb Classical Library.

————. *The Mithradatic Wars*. In *Roman History*, trans. Horace White, vol. 2, 237–447. Loeb Classical Library.

————. *Roman History*, trans. Horace White. 4 vols. Loeb Classical Library.

————. "The Syrian Wars." In *Roman History*, trans. Horace White, vol. 2, 103–237. Loeb Classical Library.

Applebaum, Shimon. "Economic Life in Palestine." In *The Jewish People in the First Century: Historical Geography, Political History, Social, Cultural and Religious Life and Institutions*, ed. Shemuel Safrai and Menahem Stern, vol. 2, 631–700. Assen: Van Gorcum, 1976.

————. "The Hasmoneans: Logistics, Taxation and the Constitution." In *Judaea in Hellenistic and Roman Times: Historical and Archaeological Essays*, ed. Shimon Applebaum, 9–29. Leiden and New York: E. J. Brill, 1989.

————. "Judaea as a Roman Province: The Countryside as a Political and Economic Factor." *Aufstieg und Niedergang der römischen Welt* 2.8 (1977): 355–396.

————. *Judaea in Hellenistic and Roman Times: Historical and Archaeological Essays*. Leiden and New York: E. J. Brill, 1989.

————. "Mamre." In *Encyclopedia of Archaeological Excavations in the Holy Land*, ed. Michael Avi-Yonah, vol. 4, 776–778. Englewood Cliffs, N.J.: Prentice-Hall, 1977.

————. "Points of View on the Second Jewish Revolt." *Scripta classica israelica* 7 (1983–1984): 77–87.

————. *Prolegomena to the Study of the Second Jewish Revolt (A.D. 132–135)*. Oxford: British Archaeological Reports, 1976.

————. "The Roman Colony of Ptolemaïs-'Ake and Its Territory." In *Judaea in Hel-*

lenistic and Roman Times: Historical and Archaeological Essays, ed. Shimon Applebaum, 70–96. Leiden and New York: E. J. Brill, 1989.

———. "The Roman Villa in Judaea: A Problem." In Judaea in Hellenistic Times, ed. Shimon Applebaum, 124–131. Leiden: E. J. Brill, 1989.

———. "Royal and Imperial Estates in the Sharon and Samaria." In Judaea in Hellenistic and Roman Times: Historical and Archaeological Essays, ed. Shimon Applebaum, 97–110. Leiden and New York: E. J. Brill, 1989.

———. "The Second Jewish Revolt (AD 131–135)." Palestine Exploration Quarterly 116 (1984): 35–41.

———. "The Settlement Pattern of Western Samaria from Hellenistic to Byzantine Times: A Historical Commentary." In Landscape and Pattern: An Archaeological Survey of Samaria 800 B.C.E.–636 C.E., ed. Shimon Dar and Shimon Applebaum, vol. 1, 255–269. Oxford: British Archaeological Reports, 1986.

———. "The Troopers of Zamaris." In Judaea in Hellenistic and Roman Times: Historical and Archaeological Essays, ed. Shimon Applebaum, 47–65. Leiden and New York: E. J. Brill, 1989.

———. "The Zealots: The Case for Revaluation." Journal of Roman Studies 61 (1971): 155–170.

Arangio Ruiz, Vincenzo. "Epigrafia giuridica greca e romana." Studia et Documenta Historiae et Iuris 2 (1936): 429–520.

———. "Epigrafia giuridica greca e romana (II)." Studia et Documenta Historiae et Iuris 5 (1939): 521–633.

Arav, Rami. Hellenistic Palestine: Settlement Patterns and City Planning, 337–31 B.C.E. Oxford: British Archaeological Reports, 1989.

Architecture et société: De l'archaïsme grec à la fin de la République romaine; Actes du Colloque international organisé par le Centre national de la recherche scientifique et l'École française de Rome (Rome, 2–4 décembre 1980). Rome: École française de Rome; Paris: Centre national de la recherche scientifique, 1983.

Aristophanes. "The Clouds." In Aristophanes, trans. Benjamin Bickley Rogers, 261–401. Loeb Classical Library.

Arnaud, Pascal. "Doura-Europos, microcosme grec ou rouage de l'administration arsacide? Modes de maîtrise du territoire et intégration des notables locaux dans la pratique administrative des rois arsacides." Syria 63 (1986): 135–155.

———. "Les guerres parthiques de Gabinius et de Crassus et la politique occidentale des Parthes Arsacides entre 70 et 53 av. J.-C." Electrum 2 (1998): 13–34.

———. "Naiskoi monolithes du Hauran." In Hauran: Recherches archéologiques sur la Syrie du sud à l'époque hellénistique et romaine, ed. Jean-Marie Dentzer, vol. 1, 373–386. Paris: P. Geuthner, 1985.

———. "Les salles W9 et W10 du temple d'Azzanathkôna à Doura-Europos: Développement historique et topographie familiale d'une 'salle aux gradins.'" In Doura-Europos: Études IV, 1991–1993, ed. Pierre Leriche and Mathilde Gélin, 117–144. Beirut: Institut français d'archéologie du Proche-Orient, 1997.

Arnould, Caroline. Les arcs romains de Jérusalem: Architecture, décor et urbanisme. Fribourg: Éditions Universitaires Fribourg Suisse; Göttingen: Vandenhoeck & Ruprecht, 1997.

———. "La porte de Damas (porte romaine) à Jérusalem: Quelques questions d'urbanisme." Revue biblique 106 (1999): 101–111.

Arrian. *The Anabasis of Alexander*, ed. and trans. E. J. Chinnock. London: Hodder & Stoughton, 1884.

As'ad (al-), Khaled, and Andreas Schmidt-Colinet. "Kulturbegegnung im Grenzbereich." In *Palmyra: Kulturbegegnung in Grenzbereich*, ed. Andreas Schmidt-Colinet, 28–53. Mainz: Ph. von Zabern, 1995.

As'ad (al-), Khaled, and Jean-Baptiste Yon. *Inscriptions de Palmyre: Promenades épigraphiqes dans la ville antique de Palmyre*. Beirut: Direction générale des antiquités et des musées de la République arabe syrienne, Institut français d'archéologie du Proche-Orient, 2001.

Asaf, Simha. In *Tarbiz: Riv'on le-mada'e ha-yahadut* (1948).

Astarita, Maria Laura. *Avidio Cassio*. Rome: Ed. di storia e letteratura, 1983.

Athenaeus. *The Deipnosophists*, trans. Charles Burton Gulick. 7 vols. Loeb Classical Library.

Augé, Christian. "La place des monnaies de Décapole et d'Arabie dans la numismatique du Proche-Orient à l'époque romaine." In *Les monnayages syriens: Quel apport pour l'histoire du Proche-Orient hellénistique et romain? Actes de la table ronde de Damas, 10–12 novembre 1999*, ed. Christian Augé and Frédérique Duyrat, 153–166. Beirut: Institut français d'archéologie du Proche-Orient, 2002.

———. "Sur des types monétaires de Canatha." In *Travaux de numismatique grecque offerts à Georges Le Rider*, ed. Michel Amandry and Silvia Mani Hurter, 25–35. London: Spink, 1999.

———. "Sur le monnayage de Dion de Coelé-Syrie." In *Géographie historique au Proche-Orient*, ed. Pierre-Louis Gatier, Bruno Helly, and Jean-Paul Rey-Coquais, 325–341. Paris: Centre national de la recherche scientifique, 1988.

Augier, Yannis, and Maurice Sartre. "Le dieu de Rabbos, maître du 'Temple périptère' de Canatha." *Damaszener Mitteilungen* 13 (2002): 125–130.

Aujac, Germaine. *Claude Ptolémée, astronome, astrologue, géographe: Connaissance et représentation du monde habité*. Paris: Comité des travaux historiques et scientifiques, 1993.

Aurelius Victor, Sextus. *Liber de Caesaribus*, ed. and trans. H. W. Bird. Liverpool: Liverpool University Press, 1994.

Avanzini, Alessandra, ed. *Profumi d'Arabia: Atti del convegno, Saggi di storia antica; 11*. Rome: L'Erma, 1997.

Aviam, Mordechai, and Edna J. Stern. "Burial in Clay Sarcophagi in Galilee during the Roman Period." *Atigot* 33 (1997): 19*, 151–162.

Aviam, Moti. "The Hasmoneans in Galilee." In *Yeme bet Hashmonai* (The Hasmonean Period), ed. David Amit and Hanan Eshel, 257–258. Jerusalem: Yad Izhak Ben-Zvi Institute, 1995.

Avigad, Nahman. "Samaria." In *Encyclopedia of Archaeological Excavations in the Holy Land*. London: Oxford University Press, 1975–1978.

Avigad, Nahman, and Benjamin Mazar. "Beth She'arim." In *Encyclopedia of Archaeological Excavations in the Holy Land*. Englewood Cliffs, N.J.: Prentice-Hall, 1975–1978.

Avi-Yonah, Michael. "The Foundation of Tiberias." *Israel Exploration Journal* 1 (1951): 160–169.

———. "Mount Carmel and the God of Baalbek." *Israel Exploration Journal* 2 (1952): 118–124.

———. "Newly Discovered Latin and Greek Inscriptions." *Quarterly of the Department of Antiquities of Palestine* 12 (1946): 84–102.

———, ed. *Encyclopedia of Archaeological Excavations in the Holy Land.* 4 vols. Englewood Cliffs, N.J.: Prentice-Hall, 1975–1978.

Avni, Gideon, Zvi Greenhut, and Tal Ilan. "Three New Burial Caves of the Second Temple Period in Haceldama (Kidron Valley)." *Qadmoniot* 99–100 (1992): 100–110.

Ayaso, José Ramón. *Iudaea capta: La Palestina romana entre las dos guerras judías (70–132 d. C.).* Estella: Editorial Verbo Divino, 1990.

Bachman, Walter, Carl Watzinger, and Theodor Wiegand. *Petra.* Berlin and Leipzig: Vereinigung Wissenschaftlicher Verleger, 1921.

Badian, Ernst. *Roman Imperialism in the Late Republic.* 2nd ed. Ithaca, N.Y.: Cornell University Press, 1968. Reprint, 1971.

Bahat, Dan, and Chaim T. Rubinstein. *The Illustrated Atlas of Jerusalem,* trans. Shlomo Ketko. New York: Simon & Schuster, 1990.

Baigent, Michael, and Richard Leigh. *The Dead Sea Scrolls Deception.* New York: Summit Books, 1991.

Baldus, Hans Roland. *Uranius Antoninus, Münzprägung und Geschichte.* Bonn: R. Habelt, 1971.

———. "Uranius Antoninus of Emesa, a Roman Emperor from Palmyra's Neighbouring-City and His Coinage." In "Palmyra and the Silk Road: International Colloquium, Palmyra, 7–11 April 1992." Special issue, *Annales archéologiques arabes syriennes* 42 (1996): 371–377.

Ball, Warwick. *Rome in the East: The Transformation of an Empire.* London and New York: Routledge, 1999.

Balty, Janine. "La Maison aux Consoles." In *Apamée de Syrie: Bilan des recherches archéologiques 1973–1979; Actes du colloque tenu à Bruxelles les 29, 30 et 31 mai 1980,* ed. Janine Balty, 19–38. Brussels: Centre belge de recherches archéologiques à Apamée de Syrie, 1984.

———. "La mosaïque antique au Proche-Orient: I. Des origines à la Tétrarchie." *Aufstieg und Niedergang der römischen Welt* 2.12.2 (1981): 347–429.

———. "Mosaïque de Gê et des saisons à Apamée." *Syria* 50 (1973): 311–347.

———. *Mosaïques antiques du Proche-Orient: Chronologie, iconographie, interprétation.* Paris: Les Belles Lettres, 1995.

———. "Le sanctuaire oraculaire de Zeus Bêlos à Apamée." *Topoi* 7 (1997): 791–799.

———, ed. *Apamée de Syrie: Bilan des recherches archéologiques 1973–1979; Actes du colloque tenu à Bruxelles les 29, 30 et 31 mai 1980.* Brussels: Centre belge de recherches archéologiques à Apamée de Syrie, 1984.

Balty, Janine, and Jean-Charles Balty. "Apamée de Syrie, archéologie et histoire: I. Des origines à la Tétrarchie." *Aufstieg und Niedergang der römischen Welt* 2.8 (1977): 103–134.

———. *Mosaïques antiques de Syrie.* Brussels: Musées royaux d'art et d'histoire, 1977.

Balty, Jean-Charles. "Apamea in Syria in the Second and Third Centuries AD." *Journal of Roman Studies* 78 (1988): 91–104.

———. "Apamée, 1969–1971." In *Apamée de Syrie: Bilan des recherches archéologiques, 1969–1971; Actes du colloque tenu à Bruxelles les 15, 17 et 18 avril 1972*, ed. Janine Balty and Jean-Charles Balty, 15–31. Brussels: Centre belge de recherches archéologiques à Apamée de Syrie, 1972.

———. "Apamée (1986): Nouvelles données sur l'armée romaine d'Orient et les raids sassanides du milieu du IIIe siècle." *Comptes rendus des séances de l'Académie des inscriptions et belles-lettres* (1987): 213–242.

———. "Architecture et société à Pétra et à Hégra: Chronologie et classes sociales; Sculpteurs et commanditaires." In *Architecture et société: De l'archaïsme grec à la fin de la République romaine*, 303–324. Rome: École française de Rome; Paris: Centre national de la recherche scientifique, 1983.

———. "Claudia Apamea: Données nouvelles sur la topographie et l'histoire d'Apamée." *Comptes rendus des séances de l'Académie des inscriptions et belles-lettres* (2000): 459–481.

———. "Curia ordinis: Recherches d'architecture et d'urbanisme antiques sur les curies provinciales du monde romain." Brussels: Académie royale de Belgique, 1990.

———. "Grande colonnade et quartiers nord d'Apamée à la fin de l'époque héllenistique." *Comptes rendus des séances de l'Académie des inscriptions et belles-lettres* (1994): 77–101.

———. *Guide d'Apamée*. Brussels: Centre belge de recherches archéologiques à Apamée de Syrie, 1981.

———. "La maison urbaine en Syrie." In *Archéologie et histoire de la Syrie*, ed. Jean-Marie Dentzer and Winfried Orthmann, 407–422. Saarbrücken: Saarbrücker Druckerei und Verlag, 1989.

———. "Notes sur l'habitat romain, byzantin et arabe d'Apamée: Rapport de synthèse." In *Apamée de Syrie: Bilan des recherches archéologiques 1973–1979*, ed. Janine Balty, 471–501. Brussels: Centre belge de recherches archéologiques à Apamée de Syri, 1984.

———. "Palmyre entre Orient et Occident: Acculturation et résistances." In "Palmyra and the Silk Road: International Colloquium, Palmyra, 7–11 April 1992." Special issue, *Annales archéologiques arabes syriennes* 42 (1996): 437–441.

———. "Un portrait de Shahba-Philippopolis et l'iconographie de Philippe l'Arabe." In *Resurrecting the Past: A Joint Tribute to Adnan Bounni*, ed. Paolo Matthiae, Matthiae Nannong van Loon, and Harvey Weiss, 5–15. Istanbul: Nederlands historisch-archaeologisch instituut te Istanbul; Leiden: Nederlands instituut voor het nabije oosten, 1990.

———. "Problèmes de l'eau à Apamée de Syrie." In *L'homme et l'eau en Méditerranée et au Proche-Orient*, vol. 4, *L'eau dans l'agriculture*, ed. Françoise Métral, Jean Métral and Pierre Louis, 9–23. Lyon: Groupement d'intérêt scientifique, Maison de l'Orient, 1987.

———. "Surprise hellénistique à Apamée." *Le monde de la Bible* (March 1997): 55.

———, ed. *Apamée de Syrie: Bilan des recherches archéologiques 1973–1979, aspects de l'architecture domestique d'Apamée; Actes du colloque tenu à Bruxelles les 29, 30 et 31 mai 1980*. Brussels: Centre belge de recherches archéologiques à Apamée de Syrie, 1984.

Balty, Jean-Charles, and Wilfried van Regen. *Apamée de Syrie, quartiers d'hiver de la IIe légion parthique: Monuments funéraires de la nécropole militaire*. Brussels: VUB Press, 1993.

Bammel, Ernst. "The Organisation of Palestine by Gabinius." *Journal of Jewish Studies* 12 (1961): 159–162.

Banning, E. B. "De Bello Paceque: A Reply to Parker." *Bulletin of the American Schools of Oriental Research* 265 (1987): 52–54.

———. "Peasants, Pastoralists and Pax Romana: Mutualism in the Southern Highlands of Jordan." *Bulletin of the American Schools of Oriental Research* 261 (1986): 25–50.

Bar, Danny. "Aelia Capitolina and the Location of the Camp of the Tenth Legion." *Palestine Exploration Quarterly* 130 (1998): 8–19.

Barag, Dan. "New Evidence on the Foreign Policy of John Hyrcanus I." *Israel Numismatic Journal* 12 (1992–1993): 1–12.

———. "The Palestinian 'Judaea Capta' Coins of Vespasian and Titus and the Era on the Coins of Agrippa II Minted under the Flavians." *Numismatic Chronicle* (1978): 14–73.

Barag, Dan, and Shraga Qedar. "The Beginning of Hasmonean Coinage." *Israel Numismatic Journal* 4 (1980): 8–21.

Baranski, Marek. "The Great Colonnade of Palmyra Reconsidered." *Aram* 7 (1995): 37–46.

Baratte, François. "La Maison des Chapiteaux à Consoles." In *Apamée de Syrie: Bilan des recherches archéologiques 1973–1979; Actes du colloque tenu à Bruxelles les 29, 30 et 31 mai 1980*, ed. Janine Balty, 101–140. Brussels: Centre belge de recherches archéologiques à Apamée de Syrie, 1984.

———. "Le mithraeum de Sidon: Certitudes et questions." *Topoi* 11 (2001): 205–227.

Barbet, Alix. "Les caractéristiques de la peinture murale à Pétra." *Studies in the History and Archaeology of Jordan* 5 (1995): 383–389.

Barbet, Alix, Pierre-Louis Gatier, and Norman N. Lewis. "Un tombeau peint inscrit de Sidon." *Syria* 74 (1997): 141–156.

Barbet, Alix, and Claude Vibert-Guigue. *Les peintures des nécropoles romaines d'Abila et du Nord de la Jordanie*. 2 vols. Beirut: Institut français d'archéologie du Proche-Orient, 1988–1994.

Bardy, Gustave. "Beryllus, évêque de Bostra." In *Dictionnaire d'histoire et de géographie ecclésiastiques*, ed. Alfred Baudrillart, Albert de Meyer, and Étienne Van Cauwenbergh. Paris: Letouzey & Ané, 1935.

———. "Justin." In *Dictionnaire de théologie catholique*, ed. Alfred Vacant, Eugène Mangenot, and Émile Amann. Paris: Letouzey & Ané, 1925–.

———. *Paul de Samosate: Étude historique*. 2nd ed. Louvain: Spicilegium Sacrum Lovaniense, 1929.

———. *Saint Lucien d'Antioche et son école*. Paris: Beauchesne, 1936.

Bar-Kochva, Bezalel. *Judas Maccabaeus: The Jewish Struggle against the Seleucids*. Cambridge: Cambridge University Press, 1989.

Barnett, P. D. "The Jewish Sign Prophets AD 40–70: Their Intentions and Origins." *New Testament Studies* 27 (1981): 679–697.

Baron, Raqui Milman. "A Survey of Inscriptions Found in Israel and Published in 1992–1993." *Scripta classica israelica* 13 (1994): 142–161.

Barrett, A. A. "Sohaemus King of Emese and Sophene." *American Journal of Philology* 98 (1977): 153–159.

Barzano, Alberto. "Giusto di Tiberiade." *Aufstieg und Niedergang der römischen Welt* 2.20.1 (1987): 337–358.

Baslez, Marie-Françoise. "L'auteur du De Dea Syria et les réalités religieuses de Hiérapolis." In *Lucien de Samosate,* ed. Alain Billault and André Buisson, 171–176. Lyon: Centre d'études romaines et gallo-romaines, 1994.

Batayneh, Taha, Wajih Karasneh, and Thomas Weber. "Two New Inscriptions from Umm Qeis." *Annual of the Department of Antiquities of Jordan* 38 (1994): 379–384.

Batey, Richard A. *Jesus and the Forgotten City: New Light on Sepphoris and the Urban World of Jesus.* Grand Rapids, Mich.: Baker Book House, 1991.

Baudouin, M., and Edmond Pottier. "Collection de Monsieur Péretié: Inscriptions." *Bulletin de correspondance hellénique* 3 (1879): 257–271.

Baudoz, Jean-François, and Michel Fédou, eds. *Vingt ans de publications françaises sur Jésus.* Paris: Desclée, 1998.

Baumstark, Anton. *Geschichte der syrischen Literatur.* Bonn: A. Marcus and E. Weber, 1922.

Baur, Paul V. C., and Michael Ivanovitch Rostovtzeff, eds. *The Excavations at Dura-Europos: Preliminary Report of 1st–9th Seasons of Work.* 9 vols. New Haven: Yale University Press, 1929–1952.

Bauzou, Thomas. "Deux milliaires inédits de Vaballath en Jordanie du Nord." In *The Defence of the Roman and Byzantine East,* ed. Philip Freeman and David L. Kennedy, 1–8. Oxford: British Archaeological Reports, 1986.

———. "Épigraphie et toponymie: Le cas de la Palmyrène du sud-ouest." *Syria* 70 (1993): 27–50.

———. "La Gaza romaine (69 B.C.E.–403 C.E.)." In *Gaza méditerranéenne: Histoire et archéologie en Palestine,* ed. Jean-Baptiste Humbert, 47–72. Paris: Errance, 2000.

———. "La *praetensio* de Bostra à Dumata (el-Jowf)." *Syria* 73 (1996): 23–35.

———. "Les routes romaines de Syrie." In *Archéologie et histoire de la Syrie,* ed. Jean-Marie Dentzer and Winfried Orthmann, vol. 2, 205–221. Saarbrücken: Saarbrücker Druckerei und Verlag, 1989.

———. "Le secteur nord de la *via nova* en Arabie, de Bostra à Philadelphia." In *Fouilles de Khirbet es-Samra,* ed. Jean-Baptiste Humbert and Alain Desreumaux, 101–255. Turnhout: Brepols, 1998.

———. "Les voies de communication dans le Hauran à l'époque romaine." In *Hauran: Recherches archéologiques sur la Syrie du sud à l'époque hellénistique et romaine,* ed. Jean-Marie Dentzer, vol. 2, 137–165. Paris: P. Geuthner, 1985.

Bawden, Garth, Christopher Edens, and Robert Miller. "Preliminary Archaeological Investigations at Tayma." *Al-Atlal* 4 (1980): 69–106.

Beaucamp, Joëlle. "Rawwafa." In *Dictionnaire de la Bible.* Paris: Letouzey & Ané, 1979.

Bedal, Leigh-Ann. "A Paradeisos in Petra: New Light on the Lower Market." *Annual of the Department of Antiquities of Jordan* 43 (1999): 227–239.

Beeston, Alfred Felix L. "Nemara and Faw." *Bulletin of the Society for Oriental and African Studies* 42 (1979): 1–6.

Belayche, Nicole. "Les cultes païens dans la *Palaestina romana.*" Ph.D. diss., Université de Paris IV, 1999.

———. "*Dimenticare . . . Gerusalemme:* Les paganismes à *Aelia Capitolina* du IIe au IVe siècle de notre ère." *Revue des études juives* 158 (1999): 287–348.

———. "Les figures politiques des Messies en Palestine dans la première moitié du premier siècle de notre ère." In *Politique et religion dans le judaïsme ancien et médiéval,* ed. Daniel Tollet, 60–61. Paris: Desclée, 1898.

———. *Iudaea-Palestina: The Pagan Cults in Roman Palestine (Second to Fourth Century).* Tübingen: Mohr Siebeck, 2001.

———. "Une panégyrie antiochienne: Le Maïouma." In "Actes du colloque sur Antioche, Lyon, 4–6 octobre 2001." Special issue, *Topoi,* forthcoming.

———. "La perception de l'Orient dans le monde romain impérial." Mémoire d'habilitation, Université de Paris IV, 2000.

Bellamy, James A. "Arabic Verses from the First/Second Century: The Inscription of 'En 'Avdat." *Journal of Semitic Studies* 35 (1990): 3–79.

Bellemore, Jane. "Josephus, Pompey and the Jews." *Historia* 48 (1999): 94–118.

Bellinger, Alfred Raymond. "The End of Seleucids." *Transactions of the Connecticut Academy of Arts and Sciences* 38 (1948): 51–102.

———. *The Excavations at Dura Europos: Final Report.* Vol. 6, *The Coins.* New Haven: Yale University Press, 1949.

———. *The Syrian Tetradrachms of Caracalla and Macrinus.* New York: American Numismatic Society, 1940.

Bellinger, Alfred Raymond, and Charles Bradford Welles. "A Contract of Sale from Edessa in Osrhoene." *Yale Classical Studies* 5 (1936): 95–153.

Ben-David, Arye. *Talmudische Ökonomie: Die Wirtschaft des jüdisches Palästina zur Zeit des Mischna und der Talmud.* Hildesheim and New York: G. Olms, 1974.

ben Hanina, Sherira. *Iggeret Rav Sherira Ge'on,* ed. Binyamin Menasheh Lewin. Jerusalem: Makor, 1971 or 1972.

Bennett, Crystal-M. "Des fouilles à Umm el-Biyârah: Les Édomites à Pétra." *Bible et Terre Sainte* 84 (1966): 6–16.

———. "Fouilles à Umm el-Biyara: Rapport préliminaire." *Revue biblique* 73 (1966): 372–403.

———. "The Nabataeans in Petra." *Archaeology* 15 (1962): 233–243.

———. "Notes and News (Umm el Biyara)." *Palestine Exploration Quarterly* 99 (1966): 123–126.

Bennett, Julian. *Trajan, Optimus Princeps: A Life and Times.* Bloomington and London: Indiana University Press, 1997.

Benoît, Paul. "Quirinius." In *Dictionnaire de la Bible,* suppl. 9. Paris: Letouzey & Ané, 1979.

Berchem, Denis van. "Une inscription flavienne du Musée d'Antioche." *Museum Helveticum* 40 (1983): 185–196.

———. "Le port de Séleucie de Piérie et l'infrastructure logistique des guerres parthiques." *Bonner Jahrbücher* 185 (1985): 47–87.

Berchem, Max van. *Die muslimischen inschriften von Pergamon.* Berlin: Verlag der Königlichen akademie der wissenschaften in kommission bei Georg Reimer, 1912.

Bernard, Paul. "Une légende de fondation hellénistique: Apamée sur l'Oronte d'après les *Cynégétiques* du Pseudo-Oppien." *Topoi* 5 (1995): 353–382.

———. "Un nouveau livre sur les Parthes." *Studia Iranica* 8 (1979): 119–139.

———. "Vicissitudes au gré de l'histoire d'une statue d'Héraclès entre Séleucie du Tigre et la Mésène." *Journal des Savants* (1990): 3–67.

Bertin, A.-M. "Les sarcophages en plomb syriens du musée du Louvre." *Revue archéologique* (1974): 43–82.

Bidez, Joseph. *Vie de Porphyre: Le philosophe neo-platonicien.* Leipzig: B. G. Teubner, 1913.

Bietenhard, Hans. "Die Syrische Dekapolis von Pompeius bis Traian." *Aufstieg und Niedergang der römischen Welt* 2.8 (1977): 220–261.

Bikerman, Elias Joseph. "La Coelè-Syrie: Notes de géographie historique." *Revue biblique* 54 (1947): 255–256.

———. *The God of the Maccabees: Studies on the Meaning and Origin of the Maccabean Revolt,* trans. Horst R. Moehring. Leiden: E. J. Brill, 1979.

Bilde, Per. "Atargatis/Dea Syria: Hellenization of Her Cult in the Hellenistic-Roman Period?" In *Religion and Religious Practice in the Seleucid Kingdom,* ed. Per Bilde, Troels Engberg, Lise Hannestad, and Jan Zahle, 162–166. Aarhus: Aarhus University Press, 1990.

Billault, Alain. *Lucien de Samosate: Actes du colloque international de Lyon.* Lyon: Centre d'études romaines et gallo-romaines, 1994.

Birley, Anthony R. *Hadrian, the Restless Emperor.* London and New York: Routledge, 1997.

Birley, Erich. Note in *Prosopographia militiarum equestrium,* ed. Hubert Devijver, 922. Leuven: Universitaire Pers Leuven, 1977.

Blakely, Jeffrey A. *Caesarea Maritima, The Pottery and Dating of Vault 1: Horreum, Mithraeum, and Later Uses.* Lewiston, N.Y.: Edwin Mellen Press, 1987.

Bland, Roger F. "The Coinage of Jotapian." In *Essays in Honour of Robert Carson and Kenneth Jenkins,* ed. Martin Price, Andrew Burnet, and Roger F. Bland, 191–206. London: Spink, 1993.

Blümel, Wolfgang, ed. *Die Inschriften von Knidos.* Bonn: R. Habelt, 1992.

Blumenthal, H. J., and E. G. Clark. *The Divine Iamblichus: Philosopher and Man of Gods.* London: Bristol Classical Press, 1993.

Boer, M. C. de. "L'Évangile de Jean et le christianisme juif (nazoréen)." In *Le déchirement: Juifs et chrétiens au premier siècle,* ed. Simon C. Mimouni, 184–200. Geneva: Labor & Fides, 1996.

Bogaert, Pierre. *Apocalypse de Baruch.* Paris: Le Cerf, 1969.

Bol, Peter Cornelius. "Das Sogenannte Nymphäum." *Archaeologischer Anzeiger* (1990): 199–204.

Bompaire, Jacques. *Lucien écrivain: Imitation et création.* Paris: Les Belles Lettres; Turin: Nino Aragno, 2000.

Bond, Helen K. *Pontius Pilate in History and Interpretation.* Cambridge and New York: Cambridge University Press, 1998.

Bonnet, Corinne. "De l'histoire des mentalités à l'histoire des religions: À propos de Leucothéa et de trois petits cochons." *Studi epigraphici e linguistici sul Vicino Oriente antico* 14 (1997): 91–104.

———. *Melqart: Cultes et mythes de l'Héracles tryien en Méditerranée.* Leuven: Peeters, 1988.

Borman, Eugen. *Corpus inscriptionum latinarum.* Vol. 11, *Inscriptiones Aemiliae, Etruriae, Umbriae latinae.* 2 vols. Berlin: G. Reimer, 1888–1926.

Bounni, Adnan. "Le sanctuaire de Nabu à Palmyre." Ph.D. diss., Université de Paris I, 1986.

———. "Le sanctuaire de Nabu à Palmyre." In *Contribution française à l'archéologie syrienne,* ed. Alice Naccache, 167–170. Beirut and Damascus: Institut français d'archéologie du Proche-Orient, 1989.

————. "Le sanctuaire de Nabu à Palmyre." In *Petra and the Caravan Cities*, ed. Fawzi Zayadine, 157–167. Amman: Department of Antiquities, 1990.

Bounni, Adnan, Jacques Seigne, and Nassib Saliby. *Le sanctuaire de Nabu à Palmyre*. Paris: P. Geuthner, 1992.

Bourke, Stephen, and Jean-Paul Descoeudres. *Trade, Contact, and the Movement of Peoples in the Eastern Mediterranean: Studies in Honour of J. Basil Hennessy*. Sydney: Mediterranean Archaeology, 1995.

Bowersock, Glen W. "The Arabian God Ares." In *Tria corda: Scritti in onore di Arnaldo Momigliano*, ed. Emilio Gabba, 43–47. Como: New Press, 1983.

————. *Augustus and the Greek World*. Oxford: Clarendon Press, 1965.

————. "The Babatha Papyri, Masada and Rome." *Journal of Roman Archaeology* 4 (1991): 336–344.

————. "The Cult and Representation of Dusares in Roman Arabia." In *Petra and the Caravan Cities*, ed. Fawzi Zayadine, 31–36. Amman: Department of Antiquities, 1990.

————. "The Greek-Nabataean Bilingual Inscription at Ruwwafa, Saudi Arabia." In *Le Monde Grec: Hommages à Claire Préaux*, ed. Jean Bingen and Guy Cambier, 513–522. Brussels: Éditions de l'Université de Bruxelles, 1975.

————. "Hadrian and Metropolis." In *Bonner Historia-Augusta-Colloquium 1982–1983, Beiträge*, ed. Jean Béranger and Johannes Straub, 75–88. Bonn: R. Habelt, 1985.

————. *Hellenism in Late Antiquity: Thomas Spencer Jerome Lectures*. Ann Arbor: University of Michigan Press, 1990.

————. "Herodian and Elagabalus." *Yale Classical Studies* 24 (1975): 229–236.

————. "La Mésène (Maishân) antonine." In *L'Arabie préislamique et son environnement historique et culturel: Actes du colloque de Strasbourg, 24–27 juin 1987*, ed. Toufic Fahd, 159–168. Leiden: E. J. Brill, 1989.

————. "Nabataeans and Romans in the Wadi Sirhan." In *Pre-Islamic Arabia*, ed. Abdelgadir Mahmoud Abdalla, Sami Saqqar, and Richard T. Mortel, 133–136. Riyadh: King Saud University Press, 1984.

————. "Nabataeans on the Capitoline." *Hyperboreus* 3 (1997): 347–352.

————. "Perfumes and Power." In *Profumi d'Arabia: Atti del convegno*, ed. Alessandra Avanzini, 543–556. Rome: L'Erma, 1997.

————. *Roman Arabia*. Cambridge, Mass.: Harvard University Press, 1983.

————. "A Roman Perspective on the Bar Kokhba War." In *Approaches to Ancient Judaism*, ed. William Scott Green, vol. 2, 135–141. Missoula, Mont.: Scholars Press, 1980.

————. "Roman Senators from the Near East." In *Epigraphia e ordine senatori: Atti*, 651–668. Rome: Ed. di storia e letteratura, 1982.

————. "La surprise du bouleutèrion." *Le monde de la Bible* 127 (2000): 60.

————. "Syria under Vespasian." *Journal of Roman Studies* 63 (1973): 123–129.

Bowsher, Julian M. C. "Civic Organization within the Decapolis." *Aram* 4 (1992): 265–281.

————. "The Frontier Post of Medain Saleh." In *The Defence of the Roman and Byzantine East: Proceedings of a Colloquium Held at the University of Sheffield in April 1986*, ed. Philip Freeman and David L. Kennedy, 23–29. Oxford: British Archaeological Reports, 1986.

———. "The Nabataean Army." In *The Eastern Frontier of the Roman Army*, ed. David French and C. S. Lightfoot, 19–30. Oxford: British Archaeological Reports, 1989.

Bradley, Keith R. "Claudius Athenodorus." *Historia* (1978): 336–342.

Braemer, Frank. "Une fabrique (locale?) de céramique fine à Jérash au tournant de l'ère." In *Jerash Archaeological Project 1984–1988*, ed. Fawzi Zayadine, 153–167. Paris: P. Geuthner, 1989.

———. "Formes d'irrigation dans le Hawran (Syrie du Sud)." In *Techniques et pratiques hydro-agricoles traditionnelles et domaine irrigué*, ed. Bernard Geyer, 453–474. Paris: P. Geuthner, 1990.

Braemer, Frank, Jean-Marie Dentzer, Michael Kalos, and Philippe Tondon. "Tours à noyau chemisé de Syrie du Sud." *Syria* 76 (1999): 151–176.

Braemer, Frank, and Michael C. A. Macdonald. "Al-Safa." In *Encyclopédie de l'Islam*, ed. C. E. Bosworth, E. van Donzel, W. P. Heinrichs, et al. 2nd ed. Leiden: E. J. Brill, 1995.

Branden, Albert van den. *Histoire de Thamoud*. Beirut: al-Jami ah al-Lubnaniyah, 1960.

Brandon, Samuel George Frederick. *Jesus and the Zealots: A Study of the Political Factor in Primitive Christianity*. Manchester: Manchester University Press, 1967.

Braund, David. *Rome and the Friendly King: The Character of the Client Kingship*. London: Croom Helm; New York: St. Martin's Press, 1984.

Breckenridge, James D. Review of *Uranius Antoninus: Münzprägung und Geschichte*, by Hans Roland Baldus. *American Journal of Archaeology* 79 (1975): 395–396.

Breton, Jean-François. *Arabia Felix from the Time of the Queen of Sheba, Eighth Century* B.C. *to First Century* A.D., trans. Albert Lafarge. Notre Dame, Ind.: University of Notre Dame Press, 2000.

———. *Inscriptions grecques et latines de la Syrie*. Vol. 8.3, *Les inscriptions forestières d'Hadrien dans le Mont Liban*. Paris: P. Geuthner, 1980.

Brewer, Richard J., and George C. Boon. *Roman Fortresses and Their Legions: Papers in Honour of George C. Boon*. London: Society of Antiquaries of London; Cardiff: National Museums and Galleries of Wales, 2000.

Briant, Pierre. "Des Achéménides aux rois hellénistiques: Continuités et ruptures." *Annali della Scuola Normale Superiore di Pisa* 9 (1979): 1375–1414.

———. "Alexandre et l'héritage achéménide: Quelques réflexions et perspectives." In *Alexander the Great: From Macedonia to the Oikoumene, Veria 27–31/5/ 1998*, 209–217. Véroia: Nomarchiake Autodioikese Emathias, 1999.

———. "Colonizzazione ellenistica e popolazioni del Vicino Oriente: Dinamiche sociali e politiche di acculturazione." In *I Greci II: Una Storia greca 3, Trasformazioni*, ed. Salvatore Settis, 319–333. Turin: Giulio Einaudi, 1988.

———. "Colonisation hellénistique et populations indigènes: La phase d'installation." *Klio: Beiträge zur alten Geschichte* 60 (1978): 57–92.

Bringmann, Klaus. *Hellenistische Reform und Religionsverfolgung in Judäa: Eine Untersuchung zur jüdisch-hellenistichen-Geschichte (175–163 v. Chr.)*. Göttingen: Vandenhoeck & Ruprecht, 1983.

Briquel-Chatonnet, Françoise. "Les Arabes en Arabie du Nord et au Proche-Orient avant l'Hégire." In "L'Arabie de Karib'îl à Mahomet: Nouvelles données sur l'histoire des Arabes grâce aux inscriptions." Special issue, *Revue du monde musulman et de la Méditerranée* 62 (1991): 37–43.

———. "De l'araméen à l'arabe: Quelques réflexions sur la genèse de l'écriture arabe." In *Scribes et manuscrits du Moyen-Orient,* ed. François Déroche and Francis Richard, 136–149. Paris: Bibliothèque nationale de France, 1997.

———. "Les derniers témoignages sur la langue phénicienne en Orient." *Rivista di Studi Fenici* 19 (1991): 3–21.

———. "L'image des Phéniciens dans les romans grecs." In *Le monde du roman grec: Actes du colloque international tenu à l'École normale supérieure, Paris 17–19 décembre 1987,* ed. Marie-Françoise Baslez, Philippe Hoffmann and Monique Trédé-Boulmer, 189–197. Paris: Presses de l'École normale supérieure, 1992.

———. "Palmyre, une cité pour les nomades." *Semitica* 43–44 (1995): 123–134.

———. "La pénétration de la culture du Croissant fertile en Arabie: À propos des inscriptions nabatéennes." In *Présence arabe dans le Croissant fertile avant l'Hégire,* ed. Hélène Lozachmeur, 133–141. Paris: Éditions Recherche sur les civilisations, 1995.

———. "Les Phéniciens en leur contexte historique." In *I Fenici: Ieri, oggi, domani,* 55–64. Rome: Grupo editoriale internazionale, 1995.

Briquel-Chatonnet, Françoise, and Laila Nehmé. "Graffiti nabatéens d'al-Muwayh et de Bir al-Hammamat (Égypte)." *Semitics* 47 (1997): 81–88.

Brisson, Luc. "Amélius: Sa vie, son oeuvre, sa doctrine, son style." *Aufstieg und Niedergang der römischen Welt* 2.36.2 (1987): 793–860.

Brisson, Luc, and Michel Patillon. "Longinus Platonicus Philosophus et Philologus: I. Longinus Philosophus." *Aufstieg und Niedergang der römischen Welt* 2.36.7 (1994): 5214–5299.

———. "Longinus Platonicus Philosophus et Philologus: II. Longinus Philologus." *Aufstieg und Niedergang der römischen Welt* 2.34.4 (1998): 3023–3108.

Broshi, Magen. "The Population of Western Palestine in the Roman-Byzantine Period." *Bulletin of the American Schools of Oriental Research* 236 (1979): 1–10.

Brown, Peter Robert Lamont. *Power and Persuasion in Late Antiquity: Towards a Christian Empire.* Madison: University of Wisconsin Press, 1992.

Browning, Iain. *Jerash and the Decapolis.* London: Chatto & Windus, 1982.

———. *Petra.* 3rd ed. London: Chatto & Windus, 1989.

Bruce, Frederick Fyvie. "Herod Antipas, Tetrarch of Galilee and Perea." *Annals of Leeds University Oriental Society* 5 (1963–1965): 6–23.

Brulet, Raymond. "Estampilles de la IIIe légion Cyrénaïque à Bostra." *Berytus* 32 (1984): 175–179.

Bruneau, Philippe. "Contribution à l'histoire urbaine de Délos à l'époque hellénistique et à l'époque impériale." *Bulletin de correspondance hellénique* 92 (1968): 633–709.

Brunt, Peter A. *Italian Manpower.* Oxford: Oxford University Press, 1971.

———. "Josephus on Social Conflicts in Roman Judaea." *Klio: Beiträge zur alten Geschichte* 59 (1977): 149–153.

Buchheim, Hans. *Die Orientpolitik des Triumvirn M. Antonius: Ihre Voraussetzungen, Entwicklung und Zusammenhang mit den politischen Ereignissen in Italien.* Heidelberg: C. Winter, 1960.

Büchler, Adolf. *The Economic Conditions of Judaea after the Destruction of the Second Temple.* London and Oxford: Oxford University Press, 1912.

Bull, Robert J. "The Mithraeum at Caesarea Maritima." In *Études mithriaques: Actes du 2e Congrès international [d'études mithriaques], Téhéran, du 1er au 8 septembre 1975,* 75–89. Leiden: E. J. Brill, 1978.

Burnett, Andrew. "The Coinage of King Agrippa I of Judaea and a New Coin of King Herod of Chalcis." In *Mélanges de numismatique offerts à Pierre Bastien,* ed. Hélène Huvelin, Michel Christol, and Georges Gautier, 25–38. Wetteren: Éditions NR, 1987.

————. "Syrian Coinage and Romanisation from Pompey to Domitian." In *Les monnayages syriens: Quel apport pour l'histoire du Proche-Orient hellénistique et romain? Actes de la table ronde de Damas, 10–12 novembre 1999,* ed. Christian Augé and Frédérique Duyrat, 115–122. Beirut: Institut français d'archéologie du Proche-Orient, 2002.

Burnett, Andrew, Michel Amandry, and Pere Paul Ripollès. *Roman Provincial Coinage.* 2 vols. London: British Museum Press; Paris: Bibliothèque nationale de France, 1992–1999.

Burton, G. P. "Proconsuls, Assizes and the Administration of Justice under the Empire." *Journal of Roman Studies* 66 (1975): 92–106.

Busink, T. A. *Der Tempel von Jerusalem, von Salomo bis Herodes: Eine archäologisch-historische Studie unter Berücksichtigung des westsemitischen Tempelbaus.* 2 vols. Leiden: E. J. Brill, 1970–1980.

Butcher, Kevin. "Bactrian Camels in Roman Arabia." *Berytus* 42 (1995–1996): 113–116.

————. "Coinage and Currency in Syria and Palestine to the Reign of Gallienus." In *Coin Finds and Coin Use in the Roman World,* ed. Cathy E. King and David G. Wigg, 101–112. Berlin: Gebr. Mann Verlag, 1996.

————. "Coinage in Roman Syria 64 BC–AD 253." Ph.D. diss., University College, London, 1991.

————. "The Colonial Coinage of Antioch-on-the-Orontes, AD 218–253." *Numismatic Chronicle* 148 (1988): 63–76.

————. "Imagined Emperors: Personalities and Failure in the Third Century." *Journal of Roman Archaeology* 9 (1996): 515–527.

————. "Two Notes on Syrian Silver of the Third Century AD: Drachms of Caracalla from Petra." *Numismatic Chronicle* (1989): 169–171.

Butcher, Kevin, and Richard Thorpe. "A Note on Excavations in Central Beirut 1994–1996." *Journal of Roman Archaeology* 10 (1997): 291–306.

Butler, Howard Crosby. *Syria: Publications of the Princeton University Archaeological Expeditions to Syria in 1904–1905 and 1909.* Vol. 2A, *Architecture.* Leiden: E. J. Brill, 1919.

Cabouret, Bernadette. "Sous les portiques d'Antioche." *Syria* 76 (1999): 127–150.

Caesar, Julius. "The Alexandrian War." In *Alexandrian, African and Spanish Wars,* trans. A. G. Way, 1–135. Loeb Classical Library.

————. *The Civil Wars (De bello civili),* trans. A. G. Peskett. Loeb Classical Library.

Cagnat, René, Jean Toutain, Georges Lafaye, and Victor Henry, eds. *Inscriptiones graecae ad res romanas pertinentes.* 3 vols. Paris: E. Leroux, 1906–1927.

Calbi, Alda, Angela Donati, and Gabriella Poma, eds. *L'Epigrafia del villaggio.* Faenza: Fratelli Lega, 1993.

Calboli, Gualtiero, ed. *Cornifici Rhetorica ad C. Herennium.* Bologna: Pàtron, 1993.

Callataÿ, François de. *L'histoire des guerres mithridatiques vue par les monnaies.* Louvain-la-Neuve: Département d'archéologie et d'histoire de l'art, Séminaire numismatique Marcel Hoc, 1997.

Callot, Olivier. "La christianisation des sanctuaires romains de la Syrie du Nord." *Topoi* 7 (1997): 735–750.

Callot, Olivier, and Pierre-Louis Gatier. "Le réseau des sanctuaires en Syrie du Nord." *Topoi* 9 (1999): 665–688.

Callot, Olivier, and Jean Marcillet-Jaubert. "Hauts-lieux de Syrie du Nord." In *Temples et sanctuaires,* ed. Georges Roux, 185–202. Lyon: Groupement d'intérêt scientifique, Maison de l'Orient, 1984.

Callu, Jean-Pierre. "Antioche la Grande, la cohérence des chiffres." *Mélanges de l'École française de Rome: Antiquités* 109 (1997): 127–169.

———. *La politique monétaire des empereurs romains de 238 à 311.* Paris: E. de Boccard, 1969.

Calvet, Yves, and Bernard Geyer. *Barrages antiques de Syrie.* Lyon: Maison de l'Orient, 1992.

Cameron, Ron, and Arthur J. Dewey, eds. *The Cologne Mani Codex (P. Colon. Inv. Nr. 4780): Concerning the Origin of His Body.* Missoula, Mont.: Scholars Press, 1979.

Campbell, D. B. "Dating the Siege of Masada." *Zeitschrift für Papyrologie und Epigraphik* 73 (1988): 156–158.

———. "What Happened at Hatra? The Problem of the Severan Siege Operations." In *The Defence of the Roman and Byzantine East: Proceedings of a Colloquium Held at the University of Sheffield in April 1986,* ed. Philip Freeman and David L. Kennedy, 51–58. Oxford: British Archaeological Reports, 1986.

Cantineau, Jean. "Tadmorea." *Syria* 14 (1933): 169–202.

———. "Textes palmyréniens provenant de la fouille du temple de Bel." *Syria* 12 (1931): 116–141.

———, ed. *Inventaire des inscriptions de Palmyre.* 11 vols. Beirut: Publications du Musée national syrien de Damas, 1930–.

Caquot, André, and Marc Philonenko. "Introduction générale." In *La Bible: Écrits intertestamentaires,* ed. André Dupont-Sommer and Marc Philonenko, xv–cxlvi. Paris: Gallimard, 1987.

Carradice, Ian. "Coinage in Judaea in the Flavian Period, A.D. 70–96." *Israel Numismatic Journal* 6–7 (1982–1983): 14–21.

Carrié, Jean-Michel, and Aline Rousselle. *L'empire romain en mutation: Des Sévères à Constantin, 192–337.* Paris: Le Seuil, 1999.

Carter, Giles F. "Chemical Composition of Copper-Based Roman Coins: VIII. Bronze Coins Minted in Antioch." *Israel Numismatic Journal* 6–7 (1982–1983): 22–38.

Caskel, Werner, and Gert Strenziok. *Gamharat an-Nasab: Das genealogische Werk des Hisam Ibn Muhammad al-Kalbi.* Leiden: E. J. Brill, 1966.

Cassius Dio. *Roman History,* trans. Earnest Cary. Loeb Classical Library.

Casson, Lionel, ed. *The Periplus Maris Erythraei: Text, Translation, and Commentary.* Princeton: Princeton University Press, 1989.

Chad, Carlos. *Les dynastes d'Émèse.* Beirut: Dar el-Machreq, 1972.

Chambers, R. R. "Greek Athletics and the Jews." Ph.D. diss., Miami University, Miami, Ohio, 1980.

Chapot, Victor. *La frontière de l'Euphrate de Pompée à la conquête arabe.* Paris: A. Fontemoing, 1907.

———. "Séleucie de Piérie." *Mémoires de la Société nationale des antiquaires de France* 66 (1906): 149–226.

Chapouthier, Fernand. "Les peintures murales d'un hypogée funéraire près de Massyaf." *Syria* 31 (1954): 172–211.

Charlesworth, James H., ed. *The Dead Sea Scrolls: Hebrew, Aramaic, and Greek Texts with English Translations.* Tübingen: J. C. B. Mohr; Louisville, Ky.: Westminster / John Knox Press, 1994.

Chaumont, Marie-Louise. "L'Arménie entre Rome et l'Iran: I. De l'avènement d'Auguste à l'avènement de Dioclétien." *Aufstieg und Niedergang der römischen Welt* 2.9.1 (1976): 71–194.

———. "Quelques notes concernant Tigranocerte." *Revue des études arméniennes* 21 (1988–89): 233–249.

Chausson, François. "Théoclia, soeur de Sévère Alexandre." *Mélanges de l'École française de Rome: Antiquités* 109 (1997): 659–690.

Chéhab, Maurice. "Inscription en l'honneur d'Ulpien." *Bulletin du Musée de Beyrouth* 33 (1983): 125–129.

———. "Sarcophages en plomb du Musée National Libanais." *Syria* 15 (1934): 337–350.

———. "Sarcophages en plomb du Musée National Libanais." 16 (1935): 51–72.

Chéhadeh, Kamal, and Marc Griesheimer. "Les reliefs funéraires du tombeau du prêtre Raspsônès (Babylon, Syrie du Nord)." *Syria* 75 (1998): 171–192.

Chilton, Bruce, and Craig A. Evans, eds. *Studying the Historical Jesus: Evaluations of the State of Current Research.* Leiden and New York: E. J. Brill, 1994.

Christides, Vassilios. "The Beginning of Graeco-Nabataean Syncretism: Two Stone Lintels from Sweydah in Nabatene, 'The Judgment of Paris' and 'Athena and Aphrodite with the Lion.'" *Graeco-Arabica* 6 (1995): 272–300.

Christol, Michel. "À propos de l'inscription d'el-Azraq (province d'Arabie)." *Cahiers du Centre Gustave Glotz* 10 (1999): 373–377.

———. "À propos de la politique extérieure de Trébonien Galle." *Revue numismatique* (1980): 63–84.

———. *L'Empire romain du IIIe siècle, histoire politique: De 192, mort de Commode, à 325, concile de Nicée.* Paris: Errance, 1997.

Christol, Michel, and Maurice Lenoir. "Qasr el-Azraq et la reconquête de l'Orient par Aurélien." *Syria* 78 (2001): 163–178.

Chronicle of 724. In "Chronica minora II," ed. E. W. Brooks, trans. J.-B. Chabot, in *Corpus scriptorium christianorum orientalium,* ed. Addaï Scher. Paris: Imprimerie nationale, 1904. Reprint, Louvain: Secrétariat du Corpus scriptorum christianorum orientalium, 1960.

Chronicon Paschale, ed. and trans. Michael Whitby and Mary Whitby. Liverpool: Liverpool University Press, 1989.

Chronique de Seert, ed. and trans. Addaï Scher. Paris: Firmin-Didot, 1907. Reprint, Turnhout: Brepols, 1971.

Chrysostom, John. "Ad populum Antiochenum." In *Patrologiae cursus completus:*

Series graeca, ed. Jacques-Paul Migne et al., vol. 49. Paris: Garnier Frères, 1859. Reprint, Turnhout: Brepols, 1996).

Chuvin, Pierre. *Chronique des derniers païens: La disparition du paganisme dans l'Empire romain, du règne de Constantin à celui de Justinien.* Paris: Fayard, 1991.

————. *Mythologie et géographie dionysiaques: Recherches sur l'oeuvre de Nonnos de Panopolis.* Clermont-Ferrand: Adosa, 1991.

Cicero, Marcus Tullius. "De domo sua," trans. N. H. Watts. In *Cicero,* vol. 11, 132–311. Loeb Classical Library.

————. "De provinciis consularibus," trans. R. Gardner. In *Cicero,* vol. 13, 523–610. Loeb Classical Library.

————. *Letters to Atticus,* trans. E. O. Winstedt. Vol. 22 of *Cicero.* Loeb Classical Library.

————. "Letters to His Brother Quintus," trans. W. Glynn Williams et al. In *Cicero,* vol. 28, 383–611. Loeb Classical Library.

————. *Letters to His Friends,* trans. D. R. Shackleton Bailey. Vols. 25–28 of *Cicero.* Loeb Classical Library.

————. "Pro Sestio," trans. R. Gardner. In *Cicero,* vol. 12, 36–239. Loeb Classical Library.

————. "The Speech Addressed to His Fellow-Citizens by Marcus Tullius Cicero on the Appointment of Gnaeus Pompeius," trans. H. Grose Hodge. In *Cicero,* vol. 9, 14–83. Loeb Classical Library.

Cirillo, Luigi. "Livre de la Révélation d'Elkasaï." In *Écrits apocryphes chrétiens,* ed. François Bovon, Pierre Géoltrain and Sever J. Voicu, 824–864. Paris: Gallimard, 1997.

Cizek, Eugen. *L'empereur Aurélien et son temps.* Paris: Les Belles Lettres, 1994.

Clark, V. A. "The Desert Survey." In *The Roman Frontier in Central Jordan,* ed. S. Thomas Parker, 107–163. Oxford: British Archaeological Reports, 1987.

Clark, V. A., Julian M. C. Bowsher, and J. D. Stewart. "The Jerash North Theatre: Architecture and Archaeology." In *Jerash Archaeological Project 1981–1983,* ed. Fawzi Zayadine, ed. Fawzi Zayadine, 205–302. Amman: Department of Antiquities, 1986.

Clauss, Manfred. *Cultores Mithrae.* Stuttgart: F. Steiner, 1992.

Clement of Alexandria. *Christ the Educator,* ed. Joseph Deferrari, trans. Simon P. Wood. New York: Fathers of the Church, 1954.

Clermont-Ganneau, Charles. *Études d'archéologie orientale.* Vol. 1. Paris: F. Vieweg, 1880.

————. "Une nouvelle dédicace à Baal Marcod." *Recueil d'archéologie orientale* 1 (1888): 94–97.

————. "Une nouvelle dédicace à Baal Marcod." *Revue archéologique* 2 (1903): 225–229.

Coarelli, Filippo. *Guide archéologique de Rome.* Paris: Hachette, 1994.

Cohen, Getzel M. "The Hellenistic Military Colony: A Herodian Example." *Transactions and Proceedings of the American Philological Association* 103 (1972): 83–95.

————. *The Seleucid Colonies: Studies in Founding, Administration and Organization.* Wiesbaden: Steiner, 1978.

Cohen, Rudolf. "Hellenistic, Roman, and Byzantine Sites in the Negev Hills." In

The New Encyclopedia of Archaeological Excavations in the Holy Land, ed. Ephraim Stern, 1135–1145. Jerusalem: Israel Exploration Society and Carta; New York: Simon & Schuster, 1993.

Cohen, Shaye J. D. "Religion, Ethnicity and 'Hellenism' in the Emergence of Jewish Identity in Maccabean Palestine." In *Religion and Religious Practice in the Seleucid Kingdom,* ed. Per Bilde, Troels Engberg, Lise Hannestad, and Jan Zahle, 204–223. Aarhus: Aarhus University Press, 1990.

Collart, Paul, and Jacques Vicari. *Le sanctuaire de Baalshamin à Palmyre.* 1–2: *Topographie et architecture.* Rome: Institut Suisse de Rome, 1969.

Collas-Heddeland, Emmanuelle. "Néocorie." Ph.D. diss., Université de Paris IV, 1993.

Collinet, Paul. *Histoire de l'École de droit de Beyrouth.* Paris: Sirey, 1925.

Collins, John Joseph. *The Apocalyptic Imagination: An Introduction to Jewish Apocalyptic Literature.* 2nd ed. Grand Rapids, Mich.: Eerdmans, 1998.

———. *Between Athens and Jerusalem: Jewish Identity in the Hellenistic Diaspora.* New York: Crossroad, 1983.

———. "The Sibylline Oracles." In *Jewish Writings of the Second Temple Period,* ed. Michael E. Stone, 365–371. Assen: Van Gorcum; Philadelphia: Fortress Press, 1984.

———. "The Sibylline Oracles." In *The Old Testament Pseudepigrapha,* ed. James A. Charlesworth, 317–472. New York: Doubleday, 1983.

———. *The Sybilline Oracles of Egyptian Judaism.* Missoula, Mont.: Society of Biblical Literature, 1974.

———. "The Testament of Moses." In *Jewish Writings of the Second Temple Period,* ed. Michael E. Stone, 344–349. Assen: Van Gorcum, 1984.

Comfort, Howard. "Imported Western Terra Sigillata." In *Antioch-on-the-Orontes.* Vol. 4, part 1, *Ceramics and Islamic Coins,* ed. Frederick Oswin Waagé, 61–77. Princeton: Department of Art and Archaeology of Princeton University, 1948.

Contini, Riccardo. "Il Hawran preislamico: Ipotesi di storia linguistica." *Felix Ravenna* (1987): 25–79.

Continuator Dionis. "Fragments." In *Fragmenta historicorum graecorum,* ed. Karl I. Müller. Paris: Firmin-Didot, 1841–1870.

Corbo, Virgilio C. *Il Santo Sepolcro di Gerusalemme: Aspetti archeologici dalle origini al periodo crociato.* Jerusalem: Franciscan Printing Press, 1981–1982.

Cors i Meya, Jordi. *A Concordance of the Phoenician History of Philo of Byblos.* Sabadell and Barcelona: Editorial AUSA, 1995.

———. "A Concordance to the Phoenician History of Philo of Byblos: Errata corrige." *Aula orientalis* 13 (1995): 264–266.

Corwin, Virginia. *St. Ignatius and Christianity in Antioch.* New Haven: Yale University Press, 1960.

Costa, Paolo. "A Latin-Greek Inscription from the Jawf of the Yemen." *Proceedings of the Seminar for Arabian Studies* 7 (1977): 69–72.

Cotton, Hannah M. "The Archive of Salome Komaïse, Daughter of Levi: Another Archive from the 'Cave of Letters.'" *Zeitschrift für Papyrologie und Epigraphik* 105 (1995): 171–208.

———. "The Date of the Fall of Masada: The Evidence of the Masada Papyri." *Zeitschrift für Papyrologie und Epigraphik* 78 (1989): 157–162.

———. "Ἡ νέα ἐπαρχεία Ἀραβία: The New Province of Arabia in the Papyri from the Judaean Desert." *Zeitschrift für Papyrologie und Epigraphik* 116 (1997): 204–208.

———. "Land Tenure in the Documents from the Nabataean Kingdom and the Roman Province of Arabia." *Zeitschrift für Papyrologie und Epigraphik* 119 (1997): 255–265.

———. "The Legio Sexta Ferrata between 106 and 136." In *Les légions de Rome sous le Haut-Empire: Actes du Congrès de Lyon, septembre 1998,* ed. Yann Le Bohec, 351–357. Lyon: n. p., 2000.

———. "Some Aspects of the Roman Administration of Judaea/Syria-Palestine." In *Lokale Autonomie und römische Ordnungsmacht in den kaiserzeitlichen Provinzen vom 1. bis 3. Jahrhundert,* ed. Werner Eck and Elisabeth Müller-Luckner, 75–91. Munich: R. Oldenbourg, 1999.

Cotton, Hannah M., and Joseph Geiger. *Masada: The Yigael Yadin Excavations 1963–1965.* Vol. 2, *The Latin and Greek Documents.* Jerusalem: Israel Exploration Society, 1989.

Cotton, Hannah M., and Jonas C. Greenfield. "Babatha's Property and the Law of Succession in the Babatha Archive." *Zeitschrift für Papyrologie und Epigraphik* 104 (1994): 211–218.

Cousin, Hugues, Jean-Pierre Lémonon, and Jean Massonnet. *Le monde où vivait Jésus.* Paris: Le Cerf, 1998.

Cousin, Jean. "Introduction to *De prouinciis consularibus.*" In *Cicero, Discours,* 168–172. Paris: Les Belles Lettres, 1962.

Cowley, Arthur Ernest. "Inscriptions from Southern Palestine. Greek: Nabatean: Arabic. II. Semitic." *Palestine Exploration Fund, Annual* 3 (1914–1915): 145–147.

Crawford, Dorothy J. "The Idumaeans of Memphis and the Ptolemaic *Politeumata.*" In *Atti del XVII Congresso internazionale di papirologia,* 1069–1075. Naples: Centro internazionale per lo studio del papiri ercolanesi, 1984.

———. "Imperial Estates." In *Studies in Roman Property,* ed. M. I. Finlay, 35–70. Cambridge: Cambridge University Press, 1976.

Crone, Patricia. *Meccan Trade and the Rise of Islam.* Oxford: Blackwell, 1987.

Cross, Frank M., Jr. "The Oldest Manuscripts from Qumram." *Journal of Biblical Literature* 74 (1955): 147–172.

Crouch, Dora P. "A Note on the Population and Area of Palmyra." *Mélanges de l'Université Saint-Joseph* 47 (1972): 241–250.

———. "The Ramparts of Palmyra." *Studia Palmirenskie* 6–7 (1975): 6–41.

Crouzel, Henri. "Le christianisme de Philippe l'Arabe." *Gregorianum* (1956): 545–550.

Crow, J. G., and D. H. French. "New Research on the Euphrates Frontier in Turkey." In *Roman Frontier Studies,* ed. William S. Hanson and Lawrence J. F. Keppie, 903–909. Oxford: British Archaeological Reports, 1980.

Crowfoot, John Winter, G. M. Crowfoot, and Kathleen M. Kenyon. *The Objects from Samaria.* London: Palestine Exploration Fund, 1957.

Crowfoot, John Winter, Kathleen M. Kenyon, and Eleazar L. Sukenik. *The Buildings at Samaria.* London: Palestine Exploration Fund, 1942.

Cumont, Franz. "Une dédicace à des dieux syriens trouvée à Cordoue." *Syria* 5 (1924): 342–345.

———. "The Dura Mithraeum." In *Mithriac Studies,* ed. E. D. Francis, 151–214. Manchester: Mithraic Studies, 1975.

Cureton, William, ed. *Spicilegium Syriacum, Containing Remains of Bardesan, Meliton, Ambrose, and Mara Bar Serapion.* London: F. and J. Rivington, 1855.

Curty, Olivier. *Les parentés légendaires entre cités grecques.* Geneva: Droz, 1995.

Dąbrowa, Edward. "The Commanders of Syrian Legions, 1st–3rd c. A.D." In *The Roman Army in the East,* ed. David L. Kennedy and David Braund, 277–296. Ann Arbor, Mich.: Journal of Roman Archaeology, 1996.

———. "La garnison romaine à Doura-Europos: Influence du camp sur la vie de la ville et ses conséquences." *Prace Historyczne* 70 (1981): 61–75.

———. *The Governors of Roman Syria from Augustus to Septimius Severus.* Bonn: R. Habelt, 1998.

———. *Legio X Fretensis: A Prosopographical Study of Its Officers (I–III c. A.D.).* Stuttgart: F. Steiner, 1993.

———. "Les légions romaines au Proche-Orient: L'apport de la numismatique." *Electrum* (2001): 73–85.

———. *La politique de l'état parthe à l'égard de Rome d'Artaban II à Vologèse I (ca 11–ca 79 de N.E.) et les facteurs qui la conditionnaient.* Cracow: Nakadem Uniwersytetu Jagiellonskiego, 1983.

———. "Les troupes auxiliaires de l'armée romaine en Syrie au Ier s. de notre ère." *Dialogues d'histoire ancienne* 5 (1979): 233–254.

———, ed. *The Roman and Byzantine Army in the East: Proceedings of a Colloqium* [sic] *held at the Jagiellonian University, Kraków in September 1992.* Cracow: Drukarnia Uniwersytetu Jagiellonskiego, 1994.

Dalman, Gustaf. *Neue Petra-Forschungen und der heilige Felsen von Jerusalem.* Leipzig: J. C. Hinrich, 1912.

———. *Petra und seine Felsheiligtümer.* Leipzig: J. C. Hinrich, 1908.

Damascios. *The Philosophical History (= Vita Isidori),* ed. and trans. Polymnia Athanassiadi. Athens: Apamea Cultural Association, 1999.

Dar, Shimon. *ha-Tifroset ha-yishuvit shel ma'arav ha-Shomron bi-yeme ha-Bayit ha-sheni, ha-mishnah veha-Talmud, veha-tekufah ha-Bizantit* (The Settlement Pattern of Western Samaria in the Periods of the Second Temple, Mishnah, the Talmud and the Byzantine Period). Tel Aviv: ha-Hevah la-haganat ha-teva', 1982.

———. "Qalat Bustra: A Temple and Farmhouse from the Roman Period in the Mount Hermon." *Eretz Israel* 23 (1992): 156*, 302–308.

Dar, Shimon, and Shimon Applebaum. *Landscape and Pattern: An Archaeological Survey of Samaria 800 B.C.E.–636 C.E.* 2 vols. Oxford: British Archaeological Reports, 1986.

Dauphin, Claudine. "Encore des Judéo-chrétiens au Golan?" In *Early Christianity in Context,* ed. Frédéric Manns and Eugenio Alliata, 69–84. Jerusalem: Franciscan Printing Press, 1993.

Davies, Philip R., and Richard T. White. *A Tribute to Geza Vermes: Essays on Jewish and Christian Literature and History, Journal for the Study of the Old Testament.* Supplement series no. 100. Sheffield: JSOT Press, 1990.

Davies, William David, and Louis Finkelstein, eds. *Introduction: The Persian Period.* Vol. 1 of *The Cambridge History of Judaism.* Cambridge and New York: Cambridge University Press, 1984.

—, eds. *The Hellenistic Age.* Vol. 2 of *The Cambridge History of Judaism.* Cambridge and New York: Cambridge University Press, 1989.

Debevoise, Neilson Carel. *A Political History of Parthia.* Chicago: University of Chicago Press, 1938.

Declerck, José H. "Deux nouveaux fragments attribués à Paul de Samosate." *Byzantion* 54 (1984): 116–140.

Decret, François. *Mani et la tradition manichéenne.* Paris: Le Seuil, 1974.

Degeorge, Gérard. *Palmyre, métropole caravanière.* Paris: Imprimerie nationale, 2001.

—. *Palmyre, métropole du désert.* Paris: Librairie Séguier (Archimbaud), 1987.

Degrassi, Attilio. "Le dediche di popoli e re asiatici al popolo romano." *Bullettino della Commissione archeologica comunale di Roma* (1954): 34–37.

"The Deified Aurelian." In *Historia Augusta,* trans. David Magie, vol. 3, 192–293. Loeb Classical Library.

"The Deified Claudius." In *Historia Augusta,* trans. David Magie, vol. 3, 152–191. Loeb Classical Library.

Deitz, Luc. "Bibliographie du platonisme impérial antérieur à Plotin, 1926–1986." *Aufstieg und Niedergang der römischen Welt* 2.36.1 (1990): 124–182.

Delcor, Mathias, ed. *Qumrân: Sa piété, sa théologie et son milieu.* Paris: Duculot, 1978.

Demandt, Alexander. *Hände in Unschuld: Pontius Pilatus in der Geschichte.* Cologne: Bölhau, 1999.

Denis of Tell Mahre (Pseudo). *Chronicon anonymum Pseudo Dionysianum vulgo dictum,* ed. Jean-Baptiste Chabot. Louvain: L. Durbecq, 1953.

Dentzer, Jacqueline, and François Renel. "Qasr al-Bint." *Le monde de la Bible* (May 2000): 61.

Dentzer[-Feydy], Jacqueline, Jean-Marie Dentzer, and Pierre-Marie Blanc. *Hauran II: Les installations de Si' 8; Du sanctuaire à l'établissement viticole.* Beirut: Institut français d'archéologie du Proche-Orient, 2003.

Dentzer, Jean-Marie. "Bosra." In *The Oxford Encyclopedia of Archaeology of the Near East,* ed. Eric M. Meyers, vol. 1. Oxford and New York: Oxford University Press, 1997.

—. "Le développement urbain en Syrie à l'époque hellénistique et romaine: Modèles 'occidentaux et orientaux.'" *Bulletin d'études orientales* 52 (2000): 159–163.

—. "L'espace des tribus arabes à l'époque hellénistique et romaine: Nomadisme, sédentarisation, urbanisation." *Comptes rendus des séances de l'Académie des inscriptions et belles-lettres* (1999): 231–261.

—. "Khans ou casernes à Palmyre? À propos de structures visibles sur des photographies aériennes anciennes." *Syria* 71 (1994): 45–112.

—. "Naiskoi du Hauran et qubbah arabe." In *Petra and the Caravan Cities,* ed. Fawzi Zayadine, 207–219. Amman: Department of Antiquities, 1990.

—. "Les sondages de l'Arc Nabatéen et l'urbanisme de Bosra." *Comptes rendus des séances de l'Académie des inscriptions et belles-lettres* (1986): 62–87.

—. "Sondages près de l'Arc Nabatéen de Bosra." *Berytus* 32 (1984): 163–174.

—, ed. *Hauran: Recherches archéologiques sur la Syrie du sud à l'époque hellénistique et romaine.* 2 vols. Paris: P. Geuthner, 1985–1986.

Dentzer, Jean-Marie, Frank Braemer, Jacqueline Dentzer[-Feydy], and François

Villeneuve. "Six campagnes de fouilles à Si': Développement et culture indigène en Syrie méridionale." *Damaszener Mitteilungen* 2 (1985): 65–83.

Dentzer, Jean-Marie, and René Saupin. "L'espace urbain à Palmyre: Remarques sur des photographies aériennes anciennes." In "Palmyra and the Silk Road: International Colloquium, Palmyra, 7–11 April 1992." Special issue, *Annales archéologiques arabes syriennes* 42 (1996): 297–318.

Dentzer, Jean-Marie, and François Villeneuve. "Les villages de la Syrie romaine dans une tradition d'urbanisme oriental." In *De l'Indus aux Balkans: Recueil Jean Deshayes,* ed. Jean-Louis Huot, Marguerite Yon, and Yves Calvet, 213–248. Paris: Recherche sur les civilisations, 1985.

Descamps, Albert-Louis. "Le messianisme royal dans le Nouveau Testament." *Recherches bibliques* 1 (1954): 57–84.

Desideri, Paolo. "Cilicia ellenistica." *Quaderni Storici* 76 (1991): 143–164.

Desreumaux, Alain. *Histoire du roi Abgar et de Jésus.* Turnhout: Brepols, 1993.

Desreumaux, Alain, and Jean-Baptiste Yon. "La nécropole: Une tombe à inscriptions syriaques." *Anatolia antiqua* 6 (1998): 403–406.

Dessau, Hermann. *Inscriptiones latinae selectae.* Berlin: Weidmann, 1892–1916.

Deveboise, Neilson Carel. *A Political History of Parthia.* Chicago: University of Chicago Press, 1938.

Devijver, Hubert. "Commanders and Officers of Legio IIII Sythica, Its Movements and Men." In *The Twin Towns of Zeugma on the Euphrates: Rescue Work and Historical Studies,* ed. David L. Kennedy, 205–232. Portsmouth, R.I.: Journal of Roman Archaeology, 1998.

———. *Prosopographia militiarum equestrium quae fuerunt ab Augusto ad Gallienum.* 5 vols. Leuven: Universitaire Pers Leuven, 1976–1993.

Dijkstra, Klaas. *Life and Loyalty: A Study in the Socio-Religious Culture of Syria and Mesopotamia in the Graeco-Roman Period Based on Epigraphical Evidence.* Leiden and New York: E. J. Brill, 1995.

Dillemann, Louis. *Haute Mésopotamie orientale et pays adjacents.* Paris: P. Geuthner, 1962.

Dillon, John. "Iamblichus of Chalcis (c. 240–325 A.D.)." *Aufstieg und Niedergang der römischen Welt* 2.36.2 (1987): 862–909.

Dio Chrysostom. *Dio Chrysostom,* trans. J. W. Cohoon. 5 vols. Loeb Classical Library.

Diodoros. *Diodorus of Sicily,* trans. C. H. Oldfather. Loeb Classical Library.

Dirven, Lucinda. *The Palmyrenes of Dura Europos: A Study of Religious Interaction in Roman Syria.* Boston: E. J. Brill, 1999.

Dittenberger, Wilhelm, ed. *Orientis graeci inscriptiones selectae: Supplementum sylloges inscriptionum graecarum.* 2 vols. Hildesheim and New York: G. Olms, 1986.

Dobiáš, Josef. "Les premiers rapports des Romains avec les Parthes et l'occupation de la Syrie." *Archiv orientalni* 3 (1931): 215–256.

Dodge, Hazel. "Palmyra and the Roman Marble Trade: The Evidence from the Baths of Diocletian." *Levant* 20 (1988): 215–230.

Dodgeon, Michael H., and Samuel N. C. Lieu. *The Roman Eastern Frontier and the Persian Wars (AD 226–363): A Documentary History.* London and New York: Routledge, 1991.

Dodinet, Michel, Jacques Leblanc, and Jean-Pierre Vallat. "Étude morphologique de paysages antiques de Syrie." In *Structures rurales et sociétés antiques,* ed. Panagiotis N. Doukellis and Lina G. Mendoni, 425–442. Paris: Les Belles Lettres, 1994.

Dodinet, Michel, Jacques Leblanc, Jean-Pierre Vallat, and François Villeneuve. "Le paysage antique en Syrie: L'exemple de Damas." *Syria* 67 (1990): 339–355.

Donceel, Robert, and Maurice Sartre. "Théandrios, dieu de Canatha." *Electrum* 1 (1997): 21–34.

Donnay-Rocmans, Claudine, and Guy Donnay. "La Maison du Cerf." In *Apamée de Syrie: Bilan des recherches archéologiques 1973–1979,* ed. Janine Balty, 155–169. Brussels: Centre belge de recherches archéologiques à Apamée de Syrie, 1984.

Dörner, Friedrich Karl, Theresa Goell, and Wolfram Hoepfner. *Arsameia am Nymphaios: Die Ausgrabungen im Hierothesion des Königs Mithridates Kallinikos 1953–1956.* Berlin: Gebr. Mann Verlag, 1963. Reprint, *Istanbuler Forschungen* 23.

Dörner, Friedrich Karl, Wolfram Hoepfner, and Gerhild Hübner. *Arsameia am Nymphaios: Das Hierothesion des Königs Mithridates I. Kallinikos von Kommagene nach Ausgrabungen von 1963 bis 1967.* Berlin and Leipzig: W. de Gruyter, 1983. Reprint, *Istanbuler Forschungen* 33.

Dorotheos of Sidon. "Dorothei Sidonii Carmen astrologicum (= Pentateuchos)." In *Die Fragmente des Dorotheos von Sidon,* ed. David Edwin Pingree. Leipzig: B. G. Teubner, 1976.

Dörrie, Heinrich, ed. *Porphyre: Huit exposés suivis de discussions.* Geneva: Fondation Hardt, 1955.

Dothan, Moshe. *Hammath Tiberias: Early Synagogues and the Hellenistic and Roman Remains.* Jerusalem: Israel Exploration Society, 1983.

Doukellis, Panagiotis N. *Libanios et la terre: Discours et idéologie politique.* Paris: Institut français d'archéologie du Proche-Orient, 1995.

Downey, Glanville. *Antioch in the Age of Theodosius the Great.* Norman: University of Oklahoma Press, 1962.

———. "Aurelian's Victory over Zenobia at Immae, A.D. 272." *Transactions and Proceedings of the American Philological Society* 81 (1950): 57–68.

———. *A History of Antioch in Syria: From Seleucus to the Arab Conquest.* Princeton: Princeton University Press, 1961.

———. "The Occupation of Syria by the Romans." *Transactions and Proceedings of the American Philological Association* 82 (1951): 149–163.

Downey, Susan B. *Mesopotamian Religious Architecture: Alexander through the Parthians.* Princeton: Princeton University Press, 1988.

Drexhage, Raphaela. "Der Handel Palmyras in römischer Zeit." *Münstersche Beiträge zur antiken Handelgeschicte* 1 (1982): 17–34.

Drijvers, Han J. W. "The Acts of Thomas." In *New Testament Apocrypha,* ed. Wilhelm Schneemelcher, 492–500. Cambridge: J. Clarke; Louisville, Ky.: Westminster / John Knox Press, 1991.

———. *Bardaisan of Edessa.* Assen: Van Gorcum, 1966.

———. *The Book of the Laws of the Countries: Dialogue on the Fate of Bardaisan of Edessa.* Assen: Van Gorcum, 1965.

———. *Cults and Beliefs at Edessa.* Leiden: E. J. Brill, 1980.

———. *East of Antioch: Studies in Early Syriac Christianity.* London: Variorum Reprints, 1984.

———. "Facts and Problems in Early Syriac-Speaking Christianity." *Second Century* 2 (1982): 157–175.

———. "Greek and Aramaic in Palmyrene Inscriptions." In *Studia Aramaica*, ed. J. M. Geller, Jonas C. Greenfield and M. P. Weitzmann, 31–42. Oxford: Oxford University Press, 1995.

———. "Hatra, Palmyra und Edessa: Die Städte der syrisch-mesopotamischen Wüste in politischer, kulturgeschichtlicher und religiongeschichtlicher Beleuchtung." *Aufstieg und Niedergang der römischen Welt* 2.8 (1977): 799–906.

———. "Marcionism in Syria." *Second Century* 6 (1987–1988): 153–172.

———. "Odes of Salomon and Psalms of Mani: Christians and Manicheans in the Third Century." In *Studies in Gnosticism and Hellenistic Religions: Presented to Gilles Quispel on the Occasion of His 65th Birthday,* ed. Roelof van den Broek and M. J. Vermaseren, 117–130. Leiden: E. J. Brill, 1981.

———. "Die Odes Salomos und die Polemik mit den Markioniten in syrischen Christentum." In *East of Antioch*, 39–55. London: Variorum Reprints, 1984.

———. "Quq and the Quqites: An Unknown Sect in Edessa in the Second Century AD." *Numen* 14 (1967): 104–129.

———. "The School of Edessa: Greek Learning and Local Culture." In *Centers of Learning: Learning and Location in Pre-Modern Europe and the Near East,* ed. Jan Willem Drijvers and Alasdair A. Macdonald, 49–59. Leiden: E. J. Brill, 1995.

———. "Syriac Culture in Late Antiquity: Hellenism and Local Traditions." *Mediterraneo antico* 1 (1998): 95–113.

———. "Syrian Christianity and Judaism." In *The Jews among Pagans and Christians in the Roman Empire,* ed. Judith Lieu, John North, and Tessa Rajak, 124–146. London: Routledge, 1992.

———. "A Tomb for the Life of a King: Recently Discovered Edessene Mosaic with a Portrait of King Abgar the Great." *Le Museon* 95 (1982): 167–189.

Drijvers, Han J. W., and John F. Healey. *The Old Syriac Inscriptions of Edessa and Osrhoene: Texts, Translations and Commentary.* Leiden and Boston: E. J. Brill, 1999.

Dudley, Dennine, and M. Barbara Reeves. "The Wadi Ramm Recovery Project: Preliminary Report of the 1996 Season." *Echos du monde classique / Classical Views* 41, no. 16 (1956): 81–106.

du Mesnil du Buisson, Robert. "Inscriptions grecques de Beyrouth: III. Dédicace à Baalmarqod et à Poseïdon." *Mélanges de l'Université Saint-Joseph* (1914–1921): 387–390.

———. *Les peintures de la synagogue de Doura-Europos, 245–256 apr. J.-C.* Rome: Pontifico istituto biblico, 1939.

Dunand, Maurice. *Byblos: Son histoire, ses ruines, ses légendes.* 3rd ed. Beirut: Khayats; Paris: Librairie Adrien-Maisonneuve, 1973.

———. *Fouilles de Byblos 2, 1933–1938.* Paris: P. Geuthner, 1954.

———. *Mission archéologique au Djebel Druze: Le Musée de Soueida; Inscriptions et monuments figurés.* Paris: P. Geuthner, 1934.

———. "Le Temple d'Echmoun à Sidon: Essai de chronologie." *Bulletin du Musée de Beyrouth* 26 (1973): 7–25.

———. "Tombe peinte dans la campagne de Tyr." *Bulletin du Musée de Beyrouth* 18 (1965): 5–49.

———. "La voie romaine du Ladja." In *Mémoires de l'Académie des inscriptions et belles-lettres*, 1–37. Paris: Imprimerie nationale, 1930.

Dunant, Christiane. *Le sanctuaire de Baalshamin à Palmyre*. Vol. 3, *Les inscriptions*. Rome: n. p., 1971.

Dupont-Sommer, André. *Les écrits esséniens découverts près de la Mer morte*. 5th ed., revised and expanded, pref. Marc Philonenko. Paris: Payot, 1996.

———. *The Essene Writings from Qumran*, trans. Géza Vermès. Gloucester, Mass.: Peter Smith, 1973.

Dupont-Sommer, André, and Marc Philonenko, eds. and trans. *La Bible: Écrits intertestamentaires*. Paris: Gallimard, 1987.

Durand, Xavier. *Des Grecs en Palestine au IIIe siècle avant Jésus-Christ: Le dossier syrien des archives de Zénon de Caunos*. Paris: J. Gabalda, 1997.

Durliat, Jean. *De la ville antique à la ville byzantine: Le problème des subsistances*. Rome: École française de Rome, 1990.

Dussart, Odile. *Le verre en Jordanie et en Syrie du Sud*. Beirut: Institut français d'archéologie du Proche-Orient, 1998.

Dussaud, René. *Les Arabes en Syrie avant l'Islam*. Paris: E. Leroux, 1907.

———. *La pénétration des Arabes en Syrie avant l'Islam*. Paris: P. Geuthner, 1955. 2nd ed., rev., of *Les Arabes en Syrie avant l'Islam*.

———. "Le saint dieu Paqeidas." *Syria* 22 (1941): 295–297.

———. *Topographie de la Syrie antique et médiévale*. Paris: P. Geuthner, 1927.

Duval, Rubens. *La littérature syriaque*. 2nd ed. Paris: V. Lecoffre, 1900.

Duyrat, Frédérique. "Arados hellénistique." Ph.D. diss., Université de Paris IV, 2000.

Eadie, John W. "Artifacts of Annexation: Trajan's Grand Strategy and Arabia." In *The Craft of the Ancient Historian: Studies in Honor of Chester G. Starr*, ed. John W. Eadie and Josiah Ober, 407–423. Lanham, Md.: University Press of America, 1985.

Easterling, P. E., and Bernard M. W. Knox, eds. *Greek Literature*. Vol. 1 of *The Cambridge History of Classical Literature*. Cambridge: Cambridge University Press, 1985.

Ebach, Jürgen. *Weltentstehung und Kulturentwicklung bei Philo von Byblos*. Stuttgart and Berlin: Kohlhammer, 1979.

Eck, Werner. "The Bar Kokhba Revolt: The Roman Point of View." *Journal of Roman Studies* 79 (1999): 76–89.

———. "Die Eroberung von Masada und eine neue Inschrift des L. Flavius Silva Nonius Bassus." *Zeitschrift für die neutestamentliche Wissenschaft und die Kunde der alteren Kirche* 60 (1969): 282–289.

———. *Senatoren von Vespasian bis Hadrian: Prosopographische Untersuchungen mit Einschluss d. Jahres u. Provinzialfasten d. Statthalter*. Munich: Beck, 1970.

———. "Vier mysteriöse Rasuren in Inschriften aus Gerasa: Zum 'Schicksal' des Statthalters Haterius Nepos." In Ἐπιγραφαί: *Miscellanea epigrafica in onore di Lidio Gasperini*, ed. Gianfranco Paci, 347–362. Tivoli and Rome: Tipigraf, 2000.

Eck, Werner, and Gideon Foerster. "A Triumphal Arch for Hadrian near Tel Shalem in the Beth Shean Valley." *Journal of Roman Archaeology* 12 (1999): 294–313.

Eck, Werner, and Elisabeth Müller-Luckner. *Lokale Autonomie und römische Ordnungsmacht in den kaiserzeitlichen Provinzen vom 1. bis 3. Jahrhundert*. Munich: R. Oldenbourg, 1999.

Edelstein, Gershon. "What's a Roman Villa Doing outside Jerusalem?" *Biblical Archaeology Review* 16, no. 6 (1990): 32–42.

Edwards, Douglas R., and C. Thomas McCollough, eds. *Archaeology and the Galilee: Texts and Contexts in the Graeco-Roman and Byzantine Periods.* Atlanta: Scholars Press, 1997.

Elam, J. Michael, Michael D. Glascock, and Kathleen Warner Slane. "A Re-Examination of the Provenance of Eastern Sigillata A." In *Proceedings of the 26th International Archaeometry Symposium,* ed. R. M. Farquhar, R. G. V. Hancock, and L. A. Pavlish, 179–183. Toronto: Archaeometry Laboratory, Dept. of Physics, University of Toronto, 1988.

Epiphanius. *The Panarion of Epiphanius of Salamis, Book I,* trans. Frank Williams. 3 vols. Leiden: E. J. Brill, 1987.

Epstein, Isidore, ed. *The Babylonian Talmud.* 35 vols. London: Soncino Press, 1935–1952.

Equini Schneider, Eugenia. "Il santuario di Bel e della divinita di Palmira: Communità e tradizione religiose dei Palmireni a Roma." *Dialoghi di archeologia* 5 (1992): 69–85.

———. *Septimia Zenobia Sebaste.* Rome: L'Erma, 1993.

Ergeç, Rifat, Anke Schutte-Maischatz, and Engelbert Winter. "Doliche, 17." *Arastima Sonuçlari Topantlisi* (2000): 185–194.

Escolan, Philippe. *Monachisme et Église: Le monachisme syrien du IVe au VIIe siècle, un monachisme charismatique.* Paris: Beauchesne, 1999.

Estienne, Henri. *Thesaurus graecae linguae.* Paris: A. F. Didot, 1831–1865.

Eusebius. *Chronicon,* ed. Albert Schoene. Berlin: Weidmann, 1875–1876.

———. *The Ecclesiastical History,* trans. Kirsopp Lake. Loeb Classical Library.

———. *Life of Constantine,* ed. and trans. Averil Cameron and Stuart G. Hall. Oxford: Clarendon Press, 1999.

———. "The Martyrs of Palestine." In *The Ecclesiastical History and The Martyrs of Palestine,* trans. Hugh Lawlor Jackson and John Ernest Leonard. London: Society for Promoting Christian Knowledge, 1927.

———. *The Onomasticon: Palestine in the Fourth Century* A.D., ed. Joan E. Taylor, trans. G. S. P. Freeman-Grenville. Jerusalem: Carta, 2003.

Eutropius. *The Breviarum ab urbe condita of Eutropius,* ed. and trans. H. W. Bird. Liverpool: Liverpool University Press, 1993.

Evagrius Scholasticus. *The Ecclesiastical History of Evagrius Scholasticus,* ed. and trans. Michael Whitby. Liverpool: Liverpool University Press, 2000.

Even-Ari, Michael, Leslie Shanan, and Naphtali Tadmre. *The Negev: The Challenge of a Desert.* 2nd ed. Cambridge, Mass.: Harvard University Press, 1982.

Evers, Cécile, and Athéna Tsingarida, eds. *Rome et ses provinces: Genèse et diffusion d'une image du pouvoir; Hommages à Jean-Charles Balty.* Brussels: Le Livre Timperman, 2001.

Facella, Margherita. "Basileus Arsames: Sulla storia dinastica di Commagene." *Studi Ellenistici* 12 (2000): 127–158.

Fähndrich, S., and Thomas Weber, "Bemerkungen zum Statuendenkmal aus Sahr al-Ledja, Syrien," *Archäologischer Anzeiger* (2001): 603–612.

Falkenhausen, Lothar von. "Die Seiden mit chinesischen Inschriften." In *Die Textilien aus Palmyra: Neue und alte Funde,* ed. Andreas Schmidt-Colinet, Annemarie Stauffer, and Khaled al-As'ad, 58–81. Mainz: Ph. von Zabern, 2000.

Farmer, William Reuben. *Maccabees, Zealots, and Josephus: An Inquiry into Jewish Nationalism in the Greco-Roman Period.* New York: Columbia University Press, 1956.

Faye, Eugène de. *Gnostiques et gnosticisme: Étude critique des documents du gnosticisme chrétien aux IIe et IIIe siècles.* Paris: P. Geuthner, 1925.

Feissel, Denis. "Bulletin épigraphique." *Revue des études grecques* 110 (1997).

———. "Deux listes de quartiers d'Antioche astreints au creusement d'un canal (73–74 après J.-C.)." *Syria* 62 (1985): 77–103.

Feissel, Denis, and Jean Gascou. "Documents d'archives romains inédits du Moyen Euphrate (IIIe siècle apr. J.-C.)." *Comptes rendus des séances de l'Académie des inscriptions et belles-lettres* (1989): 535–561.

———. "Documents d'archives romains inédits du Moyen-Euphrate (IIIe s. apr. J.-C.)." *Journal des Savants* (1995): 65–119.

Feissel, Denis, Jean Gascou, and Javier Teixidor. "Documents d'archives romains inédits du Moyen Euphrate (IIIe s. après J.-C.)." *Journal des Savants* (1997): 3–57.

Feldman, Louis H. *Josephus and Modern Scholarship (1937–1980).* Berlin and New York: W. de Gruyter, 1984.

———. *Josephus: A Supplementary Bibliography.* New York: Garland, 1986.

Feldman, Louis H., and Meyer Reinhold. *Jewish Life and Thought among Greeks and Romans: Primary Readings.* Minneapolis: Fortress Press, 1996.

Felix, Wolfgang. *Antike literarische Quellen zur Aussenpolitik des Sasanidenstaates: I. 224–309.* Vienna: Verlag der Österreichischen Akademie der Wissenschaften, 1985.

Ferrary, Jean-Louis. "Recherches sur la législation de Saturninus et de Glaucia: I. La *lex de piratis* de Delphes et de Cnide." *Mélanges de l'École française de Rome: Antiquités* 89 (1977): 619–660.

Festus, Sextus Pompeius. *The Breviarium of Festus: A Critical Edition with Historical Commentary,* ed. John W. Eadie. London: Athlone Press, 1967.

Fiema, Zbigniew T. "La découverte des papyrus byzantins de Pétra." *Comptes rendus des séances de l'Académie des inscriptions et belles-lettres* (1997): 733–738.

———. "Military Architecture and the Defense 'System' of Roman-Byzantine Southern Jordan: A Critical Reappraisal of Current Interpretations." *Studies in the History and Archaeology of Jordan* 5 (1995): 261–269.

———. "Nabataean and Palmyrene Commerce: The Mechanics of Intensification." In "Palmyra and the Silk Road: International Colloquium, Palmyra, 7–11 April 1992." Special issue, *Annales archéologiques arabes syriennes* 42 (1996): 189–195.

———. "The Roman Annexation of Arabia: A General Perspective." *Ancient World* 15 (1987): 25–35.

———. "L'urbanisme à Pétra." *Le monde de la Bible* 127 (May–June 2000): 37–41.

Fiema, Zbigniew T., and Richard N. Jones. "The Nabataean King-List Revised: Further Observations on the Second Nabataean Inscription from Tell esh-Shuqafiya, Egypt." *Annual of the Department of Antiquities of Jordan* 34 (1990): 239–248.

Fiensy, David A. *The Social History of Palestine in the Herodian Period: The Land Is Mine.* Vol. 20, *Studies in the Bible and Early Christianity.* Lewiston, N.Y.: E. Mellen Press, 1991.

Fink, Robert O., Allan S. Hoey, and Walter F. Snyder. "The *Feriale Duranum.*" *Yale Classical Studies* 7 (1940): 1–222.

Finkelstein, Louis. *Akiba: Scholar, Saint and Martyr.* New York: Atheneum, 1963.

———. *Pharisaism in the Making: Selected Essays.* New York: Ktav, 1972.

———. *The Pharisees: The Sociological Background of their Faith.* 3rd ed. Philadelphia: Jewish Publication Society of America, 1966.

Finkielsztejn, Gérald. "More Evidence on John Hyrcanus I's Conquests: Lead Weights and Rhodian Amphora Stamps." *Bulletin of the Anglo-Israel Archaeological Society* 16 (1998): 33–63.

Finsen, Helge. *Le levé du théâtre romain à Bosra, Syrie.* Copenhagen: Munksgaard, 1972.

Fischer, Moshe. *Marble Studies: Roman Palestine and the Marble Trade.* Konstanz: Universitätsverlag Konstanz, 1998.

Fischer, Moshe, Benjamin H. Isaac, and Israel Roll. *Roman Roads in Judaea.* Vol. 2, *The Jaffa–Jerusalem Road.* Oxford: British Archaeological Reports, 1996.

Fischer, Thomas. *Seleukiden und Makkabäer: Beiträge zur Seleukidengeschichte und zu den politischen Ereignissen in Judäa während der 1. Hälfte des 2. Jahrhunderts v. Chr.* Bochum: In Kommission beim Studienverlag Dr. Norbert Brochmeyer, 1980.

———. *Untersuchungen zum Partherkrieg Antiochos' VII im Rahmen der Seleukidengeschichte.* Munich: n. p., 1970.

Fishwick, Duncan. "Dated Inscriptions and the Feriale Duranum." *Syria* 65 (1988): 349–361.

Fittschen, Klaus. "Wall Decorations in Herod's Kingdom: Their Relationship with Wall Decorations in Greece and Italy." In *Judaea and the Greco-Roman World in the Time of Herod in the Light of Archaeological Evidence,* ed. Klaus Fittschen and Gideon Foerster, 139–161. Göttingen: Vandenhoeck & Ruprecht, 1996.

Fleischer, Robert. *Artemis von Ephesos und verwandte Kultstatuen aus Anatolien und Syrien.* Leiden: E. J. Brill, 1973.

Foerster, Gideon. *Masada: The Yigael Yadin Excavations 1964–1965.* Vol. 5, *Art and Architecture.* Jerusalem: Israel Exploration Society, 1955.

———. "Tiberias." In *Encyclopedia of Archaeological Excavations in the Holy Land,* ed. Michael Avi-Yonah, vol. 4, 1171–1177. Englewood Cliffs, N.J.: Prentice-Hall, 1978.

Foerster, Gideon, and Yoram Tsafrir. "The Beth Shean Project." *Excavations and Surveys in Israel* 6 (1987–1988): 36–43.

Framonti, Stefano. *Hostes communes omnium: La pirateria e la fine della republica romana (145–33 a. C.).* Ferrara: Università degli studi di Ferrara, 1994.

Fränkel, Max, ed. *Die Inschriften von Pergamon.* Vol. 8, fasc. 2, *Römische Zeit.* Berlin: W. Spemann, 1895.

Frankfort, Marie-Thérèse. "Le royaume d'Agrippa II et son annexion par Domitien." In *Hommages à Albert Grenier,* ed. Marcel Reynard, vol. 2, 659–672. Brussels: Latomus, 1962.

———. "Sur la date de l'Autobiographie de Flavius Josèphe et les oeuvres de Juste de Tibériade." *Revue belge de philologie et d'histoire* 39 (1961): 52–58.

Frede, Michael. "Numenius." *Aufstieg und Niedergang der römischen Welt* 2.36.2 (1987): 1034–1075.

Freedman, David Noel, ed. *The Anchor Bible Dictionary.* 6 vols. New York: Doubleday, 1992.

Freedman, H., and Maurice Simon, eds. *Midrash Rabbah.* Vol. 4, *Leviticus,* trans. J. Israelstam and Judah J. Slotki. London and Bournemouth: Soncino Press, 1951.

———. *Midrash Rabbah.* Vol. 7, *Lamentations,* trans. A. Cohen. London and Bournemouth: Soncino Press, 1951.

Freeman, Philip. "The Annexation of Arabia and Imperial Grand Strategy." In *The Roman Army in the East,* ed. David L. Kennedy and David Braund, 91–118. Ann Arbor, Mich.: Journal of Roman Archaeology, 1996.

———. "The Era of the Province of Arabia: Problems and Solution?" In *Studies in the History of the Roman Province of Arabia,* ed. Henry Innes Macadam, 38–46. Oxford: British Archaeological Reports, 1986.

Freeman, Philip, and David L. Kennedy. *The Defence of the Roman and Byzantine East: Proceedings of a Colloquium Held at the University of Sheffield in April 1986.* Oxford: British Archaeological Reports, 1986.

French, David. "Commagene: Territorial Definitions." In *Asia Minor Studien,* vol. 3, *Studien zum antiken Kleinasien,* 11–19. Bonn: R. Habelt, 1991.

Frey, Jean-Baptiste. *Corpus inscriptionum iudaicarum.* Vatican City: Pontifico istituto di archeologia cristiana, 1952.

Freyberger, Klaus Stefan. "Eine Beobachtungen zur städtebaulichen Entwicklung des römischen Bosra." *Damaszener Mitteilungen* 4 (1989): 45–60.

———. "La fonction du Hamana et les sanctuaires des cultes indigènes en Syrie et en Palestine." *Topoi* 7 (1997): 851–871.

———. "Zur Datierung des Theaters in Bosra." *Damaszener Mitteilungen* 3 (1988): 17–26.

———. "Zur Funktion der Hamana im Kontext lokaler Heiligtumer in Syrien und Palästina." *Damaszener Mitteilungen* 9 (1996): 142–163.

Freyne, Séan. *Galilee, from Alexander the Great to Hadrian, 323 B.C.E. to 135 C.E.: A Study of Second Temple Judaism.* Wilmington, Del.: M. Glazier; Notre Dame, Ind.: University of Notre Dame Press, 1980.

———. *Galilee, Jesus, and the Gospels: Literary Approaches and Historical Investigations.* Philadelphia: Fortress Press, 1988.

———. "The Geography, Politics, and Economics of Galilee." In *Studying the Historical Jesus: Evaluations of the State of Current Research,* ed. Bruce Chilton and Craig A. Evans, 75–121. Leiden: E. J. Brill, 1994.

Frézouls, Edmond. "À propos de l'architecture domestique à Palmyre." *Ktema* 1 (1976): 29–52.

———. "Aspects de l'histoire architecturale du théâtre romain." *Aufstieg und Niedergang der römischen Welt* 2.12.2 (1982): 343–441.

———. "Les édifices de spectacles en Syrie." In *Archéologie et histoire de la Syrie,* ed. Jean-Marie Dentzer and Winfried Orthmann, 38–406. Saarbrücken: Saarbrücker Druckerei und Verlag, 1989.

———. "Palmyre et les conditions politiques du développement de son activité commerciale." *Iraq* 56 (1994): 147–155.

———. "La politique dynastique de Rome en Asie Mineur." *Ktema* 12 (1987).

———. *Sociétés urbaines, sociétés rurales dans l'Asie Mineure et la Syrie hellénistiques et romaines.* Strasbourg: Association pour l' étude de la civilisation romaine, 1987.

Frost, Honor. "The Arwad Plans 1964: A Photogrammetric Survey of Marine Installations." *Annales archéologiques arabes syriennes* 16, no. 1 (1966): 13–28.

———. "The Offshore Island Harbour at Sidon and Other Phoenician Sites in the Light of New Dating Evidence." *International Journal of Nautical Archaeology* 2 (1973): 75–94.

———. "Rouad, ses récifs et mouillages: Prospection sous-marine." *Annales archéologiques arabes syriennes* 14 (1964): 67–74.

Frost, Honor, and Christophe Morange. "Proposition de localisation des ports antiques de Byblos (Liban)." *Méditerranée* 94 (2000): 101–104.

Fuller, Michael Jeffrey. "Abila of the Decapolis: A Roman-Byzantine City in Transjordan." Ph.D. diss., Washington University, St. Louis, 1987.

Fürst, J., and O. Straschun, eds. *Der Midrash Kohelet.* Vol. 1, *Biblioteca rabbinica.* Hildesheim: G. Olms.

Gabba, Emilio. "The Finances of King Herod." In *Greece and Rome in Eretz Israel: Collected Essays,* ed. Aryeh Kasher, Gideon Fuks, and Uriel Rappaport, 160–168. Jerusalem: Yad Izhak ben-Zvi (Israel Exploration Society), 1990.

Gabriel, Albert. "Recherches archéologiques à Palmyre." *Syria* 7 (1926): 71–92.

Galen. "De praenotione ad Posthumum liber." In *Klaudiou Galenou hapanta = Clavdii Galeni Opera omnia,* ed. Karl Gottlob Kühn. Leipzig: Knobloch, 1821–1833.

Galliazzo, Vittorio. *I ponti romani.* Treviso: Canova, 1994.

Gallivan, Paul A. "The False Neros: A Re-examination." *Historia* 22 (1973): 364–365.

García Martínez, Florentino. *The Dead Sea Scrolls Translated: The Qumran Texts in English.* Leiden and New York: E. J. Brill, 1994.

Gardner, I. M. F., and Samuel N. C. Lieu. "From Narmouthis to Kellis: Manichaean Documents from Roman Egypt." *Journal of Roman Studies* 86 (1996): 149–169.

Garducci, Margarita. *Rendiconti: Atti della Pontificio Academia Romana di Archeologia.* Vatican City: Tipografia Poliglotta Vaticana, 1938.

Gascou, Jean. "La pétition de Bostra (P.Bostra 1; 29 mai 260)." In *Lokale Autonomie und römische Ordnungsmacht in den kaiserzeitlichen Provinzen vom 1. bis 3. Jahrhundert,* ed. Werner Eck and Elisabeth Müller-Luckner, 71–73. Munich: R. Oldenbourg, 1999.

———. "Unités administratives locales et fonctionnaires romains: Les données des nouveaux papyrus du Moyen Euphrate et d'Arabie." In *Lokale Autonomie und römische Ordnungsmacht in den kaiserzeitlichen Provinzen vom 1. bis 3. Jahrhundert,* ed. Werner Eck and Elisabeth Müller-Luckner, 61–70. Munich: R. Oldenbourg, 1999.

Gatier, Pierre-Louis. "À propos de la culture grecque à Gérasa." In *Arabia Antiqua: Hellenistic Centers around Arabia,* ed. Antonio Invernizzi and Jean-François Salles, 15–35. Rome: Istituto italiano per il Medio ed Estremo Oriente, 1993.

———. "Gouverneurs et procurateurs à Gérasa." *Syria* 73 (1996): 47–56.

———. "Inscriptions grecques des carrières de Hallabat." *Studies in the History and Archaeology of Jordan* 5 (1995): 399–402.

———. *Inscriptions grecques et latines de la Syrie.* Vol. 21, *Inscriptions grecques et latines de la Jordanie.* Vol. 2, *Région centrale: Amman, Hesban, Madaba, Main, Dhiban.* Paris: P. Geuthner, 1986.

———. "Inscriptions religieuses de Gérasa." *Annual of the Department of Antiquities of Jordan* 26 (1982): 269–275.

———. "*La Legio III Cyrenaica* et l'Arabie." In *Les légions de Rome sous le Haut-Empire, actes du congrès de Lyon, 17–19 septembre 1998,* ed. Yann Le Bohec and Catherine Wolff, 341–349. Lyon: Université Jean-Moulin-Lyon 3, 2000.

———. "Nouvelles inscriptions de Gérasa." *Syria* 62 (1985): 297–312.

———. "Palmyre et Émèse ou Émèse sans Palmyre." In "Palmyra and the Silk Road: International Colloquium, Palmyra, 7–11 April 1992." Special issue, *Annales archéologiques arabes syriennes* 42 (1996): 431–436.

———. "Phénicie, Liban, Levant: Histoire et géographie historique d'Alexandre à Zénobie." *Annales d'histoire et archéologie, Université Saint-Joseph* 10–11 (1999–2000).

———. "Philadelphie et Gérasa du royaume nabatéen à la province d'Arabie." In *Géographie historique du Proche-Orient: Actes de la table ronde de Valbonne, 17–18 septembre 1985,* ed. Pierre-Louis Gatier, Bruno Helly, and Jean-Paul Rey-Coquais, 159–170. Paris: Centre national de la recherche scientifique, 1988.

———. "La présence arabe à Gérasa et en Décapole." In *Présence arabe dans le Croissant fertile avant l'Hégire,* ed. Hélène Lozachmeur, 109–118. Paris: Éditions Recherche sur les civilisations, 1995.

———. "Villages du Proche-Orient protobyzantin." In *Land Use and Settlement Patterns,* ed. Geoffrey R. D. King and Averil Cameron, 17–48. Princeton, N.J.: Darwin Press, 1995.

———. "Villages et sanctuaires en Antiochène autour de Qalaat Kalota." *Topoi* 7 (1997): 751–775.

Gatier, Pierre-Louis, Bruno Helly, and Jean-Paul Rey-Coquais, eds. *Géographie historique au Proche-Orient: Actes de la table ronde de Valbonne, 16–18 septembre 1985.* Paris: Centre national de la recherche scientifique, 1988.

Gauckler, Paul. *Le sanctuaire syrien du Janicule.* Paris: Picard, 1912.

Gauthier-Pilters, Hilde, and Anne Innis Dagg. *The Camel: Its Evolution, Ecology, Behavior, and Relationship to Man.* Chicago: University of Chicago Press, 1981.

Gawlikowski, Michel. "Le commerce de Palmyre sur terre et sur eau." In *L'Arabie et ses mers bordières,* ed. Jean-François Salles, 163–172. Lyon: Maison de l'Orient, 1988.

———. "Les comptes d'un homme d'affaires dans une tour funéraire à Palmyre." *Semitica* 36 (1986): 87–99.

———. "Les défenses de Palmyre." *Syria* 51 (1974): 231–242.

———. "Deux publicains et leur tombeau." *Syria* 75 (1998): 145–151.

———. "Les dieux de Palmyre." *Aufstieg und Niedergang der römischen Welt* 2.18.4 (1990): 2605–2658.

———. "Les dieux des Nabatéens." *Aufstieg und Niedergang der römischen Welt* 2.18.4 (1990): 2659–2677.

———. "Du Hamana au naos: Le temple palmyrénien hellénisé." *Topoi* 7 (1997): 837–849.

———. "Havarte: Excavations, 1999." *Polish Archaeology in the Mediterranean* 11 (1999): 261–271.

———. "Hawarte: Excavation and Restoration Work in 2001." *Polish Archaeology in the Mediterranean* 13 (2001): 271–278.

———. "Hawarti: Preliminary Report." In "Reports 1998," *Polish Archaeology in the Mediterranean* 10 (1999): 197–204.

————. "Hawarte: Third Interim Report on the Work in the Mithraeum." *Polish Archaeology in the Mediterranean* 12 (2000): 309–314.

————. "Inscriptions de Palmyre." *Syria* 48 (1971): 407–426.

————. "The Last Kings of Edessa." In *Symposium Syriacum VII,* ed. René Lavenant, 421–428. Rome: Pontificium Institutum Orientale, 1998.

————. "Le mithraeum de Haouarte." *Topoi* 11 (2001): 183–193.

————. "Palmyra and Its Caravan Trade." In "Palmyra and the Silk Road: International Colloquium, Palmyra, 7–11 April 1992." Special issue, *Annales archéologiques arabes syriennes* 42 (1996): 139–145.

————. "Palmyra as a Trading Center." *Iraq* 56 (1994): 27–33.

————. "Palmyre, mission polonaise 1990." *Syria* 70 (1993): 561–563.

————. "Palmyre, mission polonaise 1991." *Syria* 70 (1993): 563–567.

————. "Le premier temple d'Allat." In *Resurrecting the Past: A Joint Tribute to Adnan Bounni,* ed. Paolo Matthiae, Matthiae Nannong van Loon, and Harvey Weiss, 101–108. Istanbul: Nederlands historisch-archaeologisch instituut te Istanbul; Leiden: Nederlands instituut voor het nabije oosten, 1990.

————. "Les princes de Palmyre." *Syria* 62 (1985): 251–261.

————. "Réflexions sur la chronologie du sanctuaire d'Allat à Palmyre." *Damaszener Mitteilungen* 1 (1983): 59–67.

————. "A Residential Area by the South Decumanus." In *Jerash Archaeological Project 1981–1983,* ed. Fawzi Zayadine, 107–136. Amman: Department of Antiquities, 1986.

————. "Le Temple d'Allat à Palmyre." *Revue archéologique* (1977): 253–274.

————. *Le temple palmyrénien.* Warsaw: Éditions scientifiques de Pologne, 1973.

————. "Les temples dans la Syrie hellénistique et romaine." In *Archéologie et histoire de la Syrie,* ed. Jean-Marie Dentzer and Winfried Orthmann, 323–346. Saarbrücken: Saarbrücker Druckerei und Verlag, 1989.

Gawlikowski, Michel, and Khaled As'ad. "Inscriptions de Palmyre nouvelles et revisitées." *Studia Palmyrenskie* 10 (1997): 33–34.

————. "Le péage à Palmyre en 11 après J.-C." *Semitica* 41–42 (1993): 163–172.

Gawlikowski, Michel, and Michal Pietrzykowski. "Les sculptures du temple de Baalshamin à Palmyre." *Syria* 56 (1980): 421–452.

Geiger, Joseph. "How Much Latin in Greek Palestine?" In *Aspects of Latin: Papers from the 7th International Colloquium on Latin Linguistics, Jerusalem, April 1993,* ed. Hannah Rosén, 39–57. Innsbruck: Institut für Sprachwissenschaft der Universität Innsbruck, 1996.

Gelzer, Heinrich. *Julius Africanus und die byzantinische Chronographie.* Leipzig: J. C. Hinrichs, 1898.

George of Cyprus. *Georgii Cyprii Descriptio orbis romani,* ed. Heinrich Gelzer. Leipzig: B. G. Teubner, 1890.

George Synkellos. *The Chronography of George Synkellos: A Byzantine Chronicle of Universal History from the Creation,* ed. and trans. William Adler and Paul Tuffin. Oxford: Oxford University Press, 2002.

Georgius Cedrenus. *Chronica,* ed. Immanuel Bekker. In *Georgius Cedrenus [et] Ioannis Scylitzae ope.* 2 vols. Bonn: Weber, 1838–1839.

Geraty, L. T., and L. G. Running, eds. *Historical Foundations: Studies of Literary References to Hesban and Vicinity.* Berrien Springs, Mich.: Andrews University Press, 1989.

Gerber, Yvonne. "Die Entwicklung der lokalen nabatäischen Grosskeramik aus Petra/Jordanien." In *Hellenistische und kaiserzeitliche Keramik des östilichen Mittelmeergebietes,* ed. Marlene Herfort-Koch, Ursula Mandel, and Ulrich Schädler, 147–151. Frankfurt am Main: Arbeitskreis Frankfurt und die Antike, Archäologisches Institut der Johann Wolfgang Goethe-Universität, 1996.

———. "The Nabataean Coarse Ware Pottery: A Sequence from the End of the Second Century BC to the Beginning of the Second Century AD." *Studies in the History and Archaeology of Jordan* 6 (1997): 407–441.

Gerkan, Armin von. "Die Stadtmauern von Palmyra." *Berytus* 2 (1935): 25–33.

Gersht, Rivka. "Representations of Deities and the Cults of Caesarea." In *Caesarea Maritima: A Retrospective after Two Millennia,* ed. Avner Raban and Kenneth G. Holum, 305–324. Leiden: E. J. Brill, 1996.

———. "The Tyche of Caesarea Maritima." *Palestine Exploration Quarterly* 116 (1984): 110–114.

Gersht, Rivka, and Ze'ev Pearl. "Decoration and Marble Sources of Sarcophagi from Caesarea." In *Caesarea Papers,* ed. Robert Lindley Vann, 222–243. Ann Arbor: University of Michigan Press, 1992.

Gerth, Karl. "Zweite Sophistik." In *Realencyclopädie der classischen Altertumswissenschaft,* ed. August Friedrich von Pauly et al. Stuttgart: J. B. Metzler, 1956.

Geyer, Bernard, ed. *Techniques et pratiques hydro-agricoles traditionnelles et domaine irrigué.* Paris: P. Geuthner, 1990.

Ghadban, Chaker. "Monuments de Hammara." *Ktema* 10 (1985): 287–309.

Ghawanmeh, Yousef. "The Port of Aqaba and Its Role in the Indian Ocean Trade in Ancient and Medieval Times." *Annual of the Department of Antiquities of Jordan* 30 (1986): 311–318.

Ghiretti, Maurizio. "Lo 'status' della Giudea dall'età Augustea all'età Claudia." *Latomus* 44 (1985): 751–766.

Giacchero, Marta. *Edictum Diocletiani et Collegarum de pretiis rerum venalium.* Genoa: Istituto di Storia Antica e scienze ausiliarie, 1974.

Gichon, Mordechai. *En Boqeq: Ausgrabungen in einer Oase am Toten Meer; Geographie und Geschichte der Oase; Das spätrömische-byzantinische Kastell.* Mainz: Ph. von Zabern, 1993.

Gignoux, Philippe. "D'Abnun à Mahan: Étude de deux inscriptions sassanides." *Studia Iranica* 20 (1991): 9–22.

Gilliam, James Frank. "The Dolicheneum: Interpretation." In *The Excavations at Dura Europos: Preliminary Report of the Ninth Season of Work.* Vol. 9, part 3, *The Palace of the Dux Ripae and the Dolicheneum,* ed. Mikhail Ivanovitch Rostovtzeff, Alfred Raymond Bellinger, Frank E. Brown, and Charles Bradford Welles, 130–134. New Haven: Yale University Press, 1952.

———. "The Dolicheneum: The Inscriptions." In *The Excavations at Dura-Europos: Preliminary Report of the Ninth Season of Work.* Vol. 9, part 3, *The Palace of the Dux Ripae and the Dolicheneum,* ed. Mikhail Ivanovitch Rostovtzeff, Alfred Raymond Bellinger, Frank E. Brown, and Charles Bradford Welles, 107–124. New Haven: Yale University Press, 1952.

———. "Jupiter Turmasgades." In *Actes du IXe Congrès international d'études sur les frontières romaines (1972),* ed. D. M. Pippidi, 311–313. Bucharest and Cologne: Edituru Academiei, 1974.

Gisler, Jean-Robert, and Madeleine Huwiler. "La Maison aux Pilastres." In *Apamée de Syrie: Bilan des recherches archéologiques 1973–1979*, ed. Janine Balty, 79–94. Brussels: Centre belge de recherches archéologiques à Apamée de Syrie, 1984.

Gitler, Haim. "Numismatic Evidence on the Visit of Marcus Aurelius to the East." *Israel Numismatic Journal* 11 (1990–1991): 36–51.

Glucker, Carol A. M. *The City of Gaza in the Roman and Byzantine Periods*. Oxford: British Archaeological Reports, 1987.

Glueck, Nelson. *Deities and Dolphins: The Story of the Nabataeans*. New York: Farrar, Straus and Giroux, 1965.

———. *Explorations in Eastern Palestine*. Vol. 4, part 1, *Text*. New Haven, Conn.: American Schools of Oriental Research, 1951.

Gnoli, Tommaso. "I papiri dell'Eufrate: Studio di geografia storica." *Mediterraneo Antico* 2 (1999): 321–358.

———. *Roma, Edessa e Palmira nel III sec. d. C. Problemi istituzionali: Uno studio sui papyri dell'Eufrate*. Pisa: Istituti editoriali e poligrafici internazionali, 2000.

Godet, P. "Bérylle." In *Dictionnaire de théologie catholique*, ed. Alfred Vacant, Eugène Mangenot, and Émile Amann, cols. 799–800. Paris: Letouzey & Ané, 1925–.

Goell, Theresa, H. G. Bachmann, and Donald Hugo Sanders. *Nemrud Dagi: The Hierothesion of Antiochus I of Commagene; Results of the American Excavations Directed by Theresa B. Goell*. Winona Lake, Ind.: Eisenbrauns, 1996.

Gogräfe, Rüdiger. "Der Tempel von Isriye: Zwischen nahöstlicher Kulttradition une römischer Architektur." *Topoi* 7 (1997).

———. "The Temple of Seriane-Esriye." In "Palmyra and the Silk Road: International Colloquium, Palmyra, 7–11 April 1992." Special issue, *Annales archéologiques arabes syriennes* 42 (1996): 179–196.

Golan, David. "Hadrian's Decision to Supplant Jerusalem by Aelia Capitolina." *Historia* 35 (1986): 226–239.

Goldstein, Jonathan A. "The Hasmonean Revolt and the Hasmonean Dynasty." In *The Cambridge History of Judaism*, vol. 2, *The Hellenistic Age*, ed. William D. Davies and Louis Finkelstein, 292–351. Cambridge: Cambridge University Press, 1989.

Golvin, Jean-Claude. *L'amphithéâtre romain: Essai sur la théorisation de la forme et de ses fonctions*. Paris: E. de Boccard, 1988.

Gonzalez Echegaray, J. "La guarnicion romana de Judea en los tiempos del Nuevo Testamento." *Estudios Biblicos* 36 (1977): 57–84.

Goodchild, Richard George. "The Coast Road of Phoenicia and Its Milestones." *Berytus* 9 (1949): 91–127.

Goodenough, Erwin Ramsdell. *Jewish Symbols in the Graeco-Roman Period*. Vols. 9–11, *Symbolism in the Dura Synagogue*. New York: Pantheon Books, 1964.

Goodman, Martin. "Kosher Olive Oil in Antiquity." In *A Tribute to Geza Vermes: Essays on Jewish and Christian Literature and History*, ed. Philip R. Davies and Richard T. White, 227–245. Sheffield, U.K.: Sheffield Academic Press, 1990.

———. Review of *The Documents from the Bar Kokhba Period in the Cave of Letters*, vol. 1, *Greek Papyri*, ed. Naphtali Lewis, and *Aramaic and Nabatean Signatures and Subscriptions*, ed. Yigael Yadin and Jonas C. Greenfield. *Journal of Roman Studies* 81 (1991): 169–175.

————. *The Ruling Class of Judaea: The Origins of the Jewish Revolt against Rome, A.D. 66–70.* London and New York: Cambridge University Press, 1988.

————. *State and Society in Roman Palestine A.D. 132–212.* Totowa, N.J.: Rowman & Allanheld, 1993.

Gottschalk, H. B. "Aristotelian Philosophy in the Roman World from the Time of Cicero to the End of the Second Century AD." *Aufstieg und Niedergang der römischen Welt* 2.36.2 (1987): 1079–1174.

Gould, S. "The Triumphal Arch." In *The Excavations at Dura Europos,* vol. 4, *Preliminary Report of Fourth Season of Work, October 1930–March 1931,* ed. Paul V. C. Baur, Mikhail Ivanovitch Rostovtzeff, and Alfred Raymond Bellinger, 56–65. New Haven: Yale University Press, 1933.

Goulet-Caze, Marie-Odile. "Le cynisme ancien à l'époque impériale." *Aufstieg und Niedergang der römischen Welt* 2.36.4 (1990): 2802–2803.

Goulet-Cazé, Marie-Odile, and Richard Goulet, eds. *Le cynisme ancien et ses prolongements.* Paris: Presses Universitaires de France, 1993.

Grabbe, Lester L. *Judaism from Cyrus to Hadrian.* 2 vols. Minneapolis: Fortress Press, 1991.

Gracey, M. H. "The Armies of the Judaean Client Kings." In *The Defence of the Roman and Byzantine East,* ed. Philip Freeman and David L. Kennedy, 311–323. Oxford: British Archaeological Reports, 1986.

Graf, David F. "Foederati on the Northern and Eastern Frontiers: A Comparative Analysis." In *Studia Danubiana,* vol. 1, *The Roman Frontier at the Lower Danube, 4th–6th Centuries: The Second International Symposium,* 17–31. Bucharest: S. C. Vavila Edinf, 1998.

————. "Hellenization and the Decapolis." *Aram* 4 (1992): 1–48.

————. "The Nabataean Army and the *Cohortes Ulpiae Petraeorum.*" In *The Roman and Byzantine Army in the East,* ed. Edward Dąbrowa, 265–311. Cracow: Drukarnia Uniwersytetu Jagiellonskiego, 1994.

————. "The Roman East from the Chinese Perspective." In "Palmyra and the Silk Road: International Colloquium, Palmyra, 7–11 April 1992." Special issue, *Annales archéologiques arabes syriennes* 42 (1996): 199–216.

————. "Rome and the Saracens: Reassessing the Nomadic Menace." In *L'Arabie préislamique et son environnement historique et culturel: Actes du colloque de Strasbourg, 24–27 juin 1987,* ed. Toufic Fahd, 341–400. Leiden: E. J. Brill, 1989.

————. "The *Via Militaris* in Arabia." *Dumbarton Oak Papers* 51 (1997): 271–281.

————. "The Via Nova Traiana in Arabia Petraea." In *The Roman and Byzantine Near East: Some Recent Archaeological Research,* ed. John H. Humphrey, 241–268. Ann Arbor, Mich.: Journal of Roman Archaeology, 1995.

Graf, David F., and Michael Patrick O'Connor. "The Origin of the Term *Saracen* and the Rawwafa Inscriptions." *Byzantine Studies / Études Byzantines* 4 (1977): 52–66.

Grainger, John D. *The Cities of Seleukid Syria.* Oxford: Clarendon Press, 1990.

————. *Hellenistic Phoenicia.* Oxford: Clarendon Press, 1991.

Grant, Michael. *Herod the Great.* New York: American Heritage Press, 1971.

Green, William Scott, ed. *Approaches to Ancient Judaism.* 2 vols. Missoula, Mont.: Scholars Press, 1978–1989.

Gregg, Robert C., and Dan Urman. *Jews, Pagans and Christians in the Golan*

Heights: Greek and Other Inscriptions of the Roman and Byzantine Eras. Atlanta: Scholars Press, 1996.

Grenet, Franz. "Les Sassanides à Doura-Europos (253 ap. J.-C.): Réexamen du matériel épigraphique iranien du site." In *Géographie historique du Proche-Orient,* ed. Pierre-Louis Gatier, Bruno Helly, and Jean-Paul Rey-Coquais, 133–158. Paris: Centre national de la recherche scientifique, 1988.

Grenfell, Bernard P., and Arthur S. Hunt, eds. *The Oxyrhynchus Papyri.* London: Egypt Exploration Society, 1898–.

Griesheimer, Marc. "Le sanctuaire de Schnaan (Gebel Zawiye, Syrie du Nord)." *Topoi* 9 (1999): 689–717.

Grimal, Pierre, ed. *Romans grecs et latins.* Paris: Gallimard, 1958.

Groom, Nigel. *Frankincense and Myrrh: A Study of the Arabian Incense Trade.* London and New York: Longman, 1981.

———. "The Roman Expedition into South Arabia." *Bulletin of the Society for Arabian Studies* 1 (February 1996): 5–7, 23.

Gros, Pierre. "Modèle urbain et gaspillage des ressources dans les programmes édilitaires des villes de Bithynie au début du IIe siècle ap. J.-C." In *L'origine des richesses dépensées dans la ville antique: Actes du colloque organisé à Aix-en-Provence les 11 et 12 mai 1984,* ed. Philippe Leveau, 69–85. Aix-en-Provence: Université de Provence, 1985.

Gruenwald, Ithamar. "Jewish Apocalyptic Literature." *Aufstieg und Niedergang der römischen Welt* 2.19.1 (1979): 89–118.

Guerber, Eric, and Maurice Sartre. "Un *logistès* à Canatha (Syrie)." *Zeitschrift für Papyrologie und Epigraphik* 120 (1998): 93–98.

Guinée, Robert L. J. J., and Niede F. Mulder. "Gadara: The Terrace, Theatre and Cardo Quarter in the Roman Period. Architectural Design Integrated in the Landscape: The Design of the West Theatre." *Studies in the History and Archaeology of Jordan* 6 (1997): 317–322.

Gunneweg, Jan, Isadore Perlman, and Joseph Yellin. *The Provenence, Typology and Chronology of Eastern Terra Sigillata.* Jerusalem: Institute of Archaeology, Hebrew University of Jerusalem, 1983.

Gutmann, Joseph. "The Dura-Europos Synagogue: A Re-evaluation." Chambersburg, Pa.: American Academy of Religion, 1973.

Habicht, Christian, ed. *Die Inschriften von Pergamon.* Vol. 8, fasc. 3, *Die Inschriften des Asklepieions.* Berlin: W. de Gruyter, 1969.

Hadas-Lebel, Mireille. "La fiscalité romaine dans la littérature rabbinique jusqu'à la fin du IIIe siècle apr. J.-C." *Revue des études juives* 143 (1984): 5–29.

———. *Flavius Josèphe: Le Juif de Rome.* Paris: Fayard, 1989.

———. *Hillel: Un sage au temps de Jésus.* Paris: Albin Michel, 1999.

———. *Massada: Histoire et symbole.* Paris: Albin Michel, 1995.

Hadas-Rubin, Ephrat. "The Halachic Status of Bostra, Metropolis Arabiae." *Tsinan* (1995): 375–391.

———. "The Nawa-Der'a Road." *Scripta classica israelica* 14 (1995): 138–142.

"Hadrian." In *Historia Augusta,* trans. David Magie, vol. 1, 3–81. Loeb Classical Library.

Haensch, Rudolf. *Capita provinciarum: Staatthaltersitze und Provinzialverwaltung in der römischen Kaiserzeit.* Mainz: Ph. von Zabern, 1997.

Haerinck, Ernie. "Quelques monuments funéraires de l'île de Kharg dans le Golfe Persique." *Iranica antiqua* 11 (1975): 134–167.

Haider, Peter W. "Synkretismus zwischen griechisch-römischen und orientalischen Gottheiten." In *Religionsgeschichte Syriens,* ed. Peter W. Haider, Manfred Hutter, and Siegfried Kreuzer. Stuttgart: Kohlhammer, 1996.

Hajjar, Youssef. "Baalbek, grand centre religieux sous l'Empire." *Aufstieg und Niedergang der römischen Welt* 2.18.4 (1990): 2458–2508.

———. "Dieux et cultes non héliopolitains de la Béqa', de l'Hermon et de l'Abilène à l'époque romaine." *Aufstieg und Niedergang der römischen Welt* 2.18.4 (1990): 2509–2604.

———. "Divinités oraculaires et rites divinatoires en Syrie et en Phénicie à l'époque gréco-romaine." *Aufstieg und Niedergang der römischen Welt* 2.18.4 (1990): 2236–2320.

———. *La triade d'Héliopolis-Baalbeck.* Leiden: E. J. Brill, 1977.

Halfmann, Helmut. *Itinera principum: Geschichte und Typologie der Kaiserreisen im Romischen Reich.* Stuttgart: F. Steiner, 1986.

Hammer, Caspar. *Rhetores graeci ex recognitione Leonardi Spengel.* 3 vols. Leipzig: B. G. Teubner, 1894.

Hammerstaedt, Jürgen. "Der Kyniker Oenomaus von Gadara." *Aufstieg und Niedergang der römischen Welt* 2.36.4 (1990): 2834–2865.

Hammond, Philip C. "Die Ausgrabung des Löwen-Greifen-Tempels in Petra (1973–1983)." In *Petra: Neue Ausgrabungen und Entdeckungen,* ed. Manfred Lindner, 16–30. Munich: Delp, 1986.

———. "The Goddess of the Temple of the 'Winged Lions' at Petra (Jordan)." In *Petra and the Caravan Cities,* ed. Fawzi Zayadine, 115–130. Amman: Department of Antiquities, 1990.

———. "The Medallion and Block Relief at Petra." *Bulletin of the American Schools of Oriental Research* 192 (1968): 16–21.

———. "Ein nabatäisches Weiherrelief aus Petra." *Bonner Jahrbücher* 180 (1980): 265–269.

———. *The Nabataeans: Their History, Culture and Archaeology.* Göteborg: Äströms Förlag, 1973.

———. "The Temple of the Winged Lions, Petra, Jordan, 1873–1990." Fountain Hills, Ariz.: Petra Publications, 1996.

Hann, Robert R. "The Community of the Pious: The Social Setting of the Psalms of Solomon." *Studies in Religion / Sciences religieuses* 17 (1988): 169–189.

Hannestad, Lise. *Ikaros.* Aarhus: Jutland Archaeological Society Publications, 1983.

Hanson, William S., and Lawrence J. F. Keppie. *Roman Frontier Studies 1979: Papers Presented to the 12th International Congress of Roman Frontier Studies.* Oxford: British Archaeological Reports, 1980.

Harding, Gerald L. "The Arab Tribes." *Al-Abhath* 22 (1969): 3–25.

———. "The Safaitic Tribes." *Al-Abhath* 22 (1969): 3–25.

Harl, Kenneth W. *Coinage in the Roman Economy 300 bc to ad 700.* Baltimore: Johns Hopkins University Press, 1996.

Harper, George McLean, Jr. "Village Administration in the Roman Province of Syria." *Yale Classical Studies* 1 (1928): 105–168.

Hartmann, Martin. "Beiträge zur Kenntniss der Syrischen Steppe." *Zeitschrift des deutschen Palästina-Vereins* 22 (1899): 153–177.

Hasall, Mark, Michael Crawford, and Joyce Reynolds. "Rome and the Eastern Provinces at the End of the Second Century B.C.: The So-Called 'Piracy Law' and a New Inscription from Cnidos." *Journal of Roman Studies* 64 (1974): 195–220.

Hatzfeld, Jean. *Les trafiquants italiens dans l'Orient hellénique.* Paris: E. de Boccard, 1919.

Hauptmann, Andreas, and Gerd Weisgerber. "Archaeometallurgical and Mining-Archaeological Investigations in the Area of Feinan, Wadi 'Arabah (Jordan)." *Annual of the Department of Antiquities of Jordan* 31 (1987): 419–431.

———. "Periods of Ore Exploration and Metal Production in the Area of Feinan, Wadi 'Arabah, Jordan." *Studies in the History and Archaeology of Jordan* 4 (1992): 61–66.

Hauvette-Besnault, Amédée. "Sur quelques villes anciennes de la Chersonnèse de Thrace." *Bulletin de correspondance hellénique* 4 (1980): 507–509.

Head, Barclay Vincent. *Catalogue of the Greek Coins in the British Museum: Galatia, Cappadocia, Syria.* London: British Museum, 1895.

Head, Barclay Vincent, George Francis Hill, George MacDonald, and Warwick William Wroth. *Historia Numorum: A Manual of Greek Numismatics.* New ed., augmented. Amsterdam: A. M. Hakkert, 1991.

Healey, John F. "The Nabataean Contribution to the Development of the Arabic Script." *Aram* 2 (1990): 93–98.

———, ed. *The Nabataean Tomb Inscriptions of Mada'in Salih.* Oxford: Oxford University Press, 1993.

Healey, John F., and G. Rex Smith. "Jaussen-Savignac 17: The Earliest Dated Arabic Document (A.D. 267)." *Al-Atlal* 12 (1989): 77–84.

Hellholm, David. *Apocalypticism in the Mediterranean World and the Near East: Proceedings of the International Colloquium on Apocalypticism, Uppsala, August 12–17, 1979.* Tübingen: J. C. B. Mohr, 1983.

Hellmann, Marie-Christine. "Les signatures d'architectes en langue grecque: Essai de mise au point." *Zeitschrift für Papyrologie und Epigraphik* 104 (1994): 151–178.

Hengel, Martin. *Judaism and Hellenism: Studies in Their Encounter in Palestine during the Early Hellenistic Period,* trans. John Bowden. 2 vols. Philadelphia: Fortress Press, 1974.

———. *The Zealots: Investigations into the Jewish Freedom Movement in the Period from Herod I until 70 A.D.* Edinburgh: T. & T. Clark, 1989. Reprint, 1997.

———. "Zum Problem der 'Hellenisierung' Judäas im 1. Jahrhundert nach Christus." In *Judaica et Hellenistica: Kleine Schriften,* 1–90. Tübingen: J. C. B. Mohr, 1996.

Hengel, Martin, and Christoph Markschies. *The "Hellenization" of Judaea in the First Century after Christ.* London: SCM Press; Philadelphia: Trinity Press International, 1989.

Henzen, Wilhelm. *Corpus inscriptionum latinarum.* Vol. 6, *Inscriptiones urbis Romae latinae.* Berlin: G. Reimer, 1876–.

Herbert, Sharon C., ed. *Tel Anafa II: The Hellenistic and Roman Pottery.* Ann Arbor: Kelsey Museum of the University of Michigan, 1997.

Herodian. *History of the Empire from the Time of Marcus Aurelius,* trans. C. R. Whittaker. 2 vols. Loeb Classical Library.

Hesberg, Henner von. "The Significance of the Cities in the Kingdom of Herod." In *Judaea and the Greco-Roman World in the Time of Herod in the Light of*

Archaeological Evidence, ed. Klaus Fittschen and Gideon Foerster, 9–25. Göttingen: Vandenhoeck & Ruprecht, 1996.

Hierocles. *Synekdèmos d'Hiérocles et l'opuscule géographique de Georges de Chypre,* ed. Ernest Honigmann. Brussels: Editions de l'Institut de philologie et d'histoire orientales et slaves, 1939.

Hill, George Francis. *Catalogue of the Greek Coins of Arabia, Mesopotamia and Persia.* London: British Museum, 1922.

———. *Catalogue of the Greek Coins of Phoenicia.* Bologna: A. Forni, 1980.

Hillard, T. W. "A Mid-1st c. B.C. Date for the Walls of Straton's Tower?" In *Caesarea Papers,* ed. Robert Lindley Vann, 42–48. Ann Arbor: University of Michigan Press, 1992.

Hiller von Gaertringen, Friedrich. *Inschriften von Priene.* Berlin: G. Reimer, 1906.

Hillers, Delbert R., and Eleonora Cussini. *Palmyrene Aramaic Texts.* Baltimore: Johns Hopkins University Press, 1994.

Hirschfeld, Otto. *Corpus inscriptionum latinarum.* Vol. 12, *Inscriptiones Galliae narbonensis latinae.* Berlin: G. Reimer, 1888.

Hirschfeld, Yizhar, and R. Birger-Calderon. "Early Roman and Byzantine Estates near Caesarea." *Israel Exploration Journal* 41 (1991): 81–111.

Historia Augusta. trans. David Magie. 3 vols. Loeb Classical Library.

Hoehner, Harold W. *Herod Antipas.* Cambridge: Cambridge University Press, 1972.

Hölscher, E. E. "Medeba." In *Realencyclopädie der classischen Altertumwissenschaft,* ed. August Wilhelm von Pauly et al. Stuttgart: J. B. Metzler, 1894–.

Holum, Kenneth G., and Robert L. Hohlfelder, eds. *King Herod's Dream: Caesarea on the Sea.* New York: W. W. Norton, 1988.

Holum, Kenneth G., Avner Raban, and Joseph Patrich, eds. *Caesarea Papers 2: Herod's Temple, the Provincial Governor's Praetorium and Granaries, the Later Harbor, a Gold Coin Hoard, and Other Studies.* Portsmouth, R.I.: Journal of Roman Archaeology, 1999.

Honigmann, Ernest. "Marinos." In *Realencyclopädie der classischen Altertumswissenschaft,* ed. August Friedrich von Pauly et al. Stuttgart: J. B. Metzler, 1930.

———. "Syria." In *Realencyclopädie der classischen Altertumswissenschaft,* ed. August Friedrich von Pauly et al. Stuttgart: J. B. Metzler, 1894–.

Honigmann, Ernest, and André Maricq. *Recherches sur les Res gestae divi saporis.* Brussels: Palais des Académies, 1953.

Hopfe, Lewis M. "Caesarea Palaestinae as a Religious Center." *Aufstieg und Niedergang der römischen Welt* 2.18.4 (1990): 2380–2411.

———. "Mithraism in Syria." *Aufstieg und Niedergang der römischen Welt* 2.18.4 (1990): 2214–2235.

Hopfe, Lewis M., and Gary Lease. "The Caesarea Mithraeum: A Preliminary Report." *Biblical Archaeologist* 38 (1975): 1–10.

Hörig, Monica. "Jupiter Dolichenus." *Aufstieg und Niedergang der römischen Welt* 2.17.4 (1984): 2136–2179.

Horsley, Richard A. "Ancient Jewish Banditry and the Revolt against Rome AD 66–70." *Catholic Biblical Quarterly* 43 (1981): 409–432.

———. *Archaeology, History, and Society in Galilee: The Social Context of Jesus and the Rabbis.* Valley Forge, Pa.: Trinity Press International, 1996.

————. *Galilee: History, Politics, People.* Valley Forge, Pa.: Trinity Press International, 1995.

————. *Jesus and the Spiral of Violence: Popular Jewish Resistance in Roman Palestine.* San Francisco: Harper & Row, 1987.

————. "Popular Prophetic Movements at the Time of Jesus." *Journal for the Study of the New Testament* 26 (1986): 3–27.

————. "The Sicarii: Ancient Jewish 'Terrorists.'" *Journal of Religion* 59 (1979): 435–458.

————. "The Zealots: Their Origin, Relationships and Importance in the Jewish Revolt." *Novum Testamentum* 2 (1986): 159–192.

Horsley, Richard A., and John S. Hanson. *Bandits, Prophets, and Messiahs: Popular Movements in the Time of Jesus.* 2nd ed. Harrisburg, Pa.: Trinity Press International, 1999.

Howard, George, ed. *The Teaching of Addai.* Chico, Calif.: Scholars Press, 1981.

Hübner, Emil. *Corpus inscriptionum latinarum.* Vol. 2, *Inscriptiones Hispaniae latinae.* 2 vols. Berlin: G. Reimer, 1869–1892.

Humbert, Jean-Baptiste, and Yasser Matar Abu Hassuneh. "Fouilles d'Anthédon (Blakhiyeh)." *Dossiers d'archéologie* 240 (January–February 1999): 52–53.

Humphrey, John H. *Roman Circuses: Arenas for Chariot Racing.* London: B. T. Batsford, 1986.

Humphrey, John William, John Peter Oleson, and Andrew N. Sherwood. *Greek and Roman Technology: A Sourcebook.* London and New York: Routledge, 1998.

Hüttl, Willy. *Antoninus Pius.* 2 vols. Prague: J. G. Calve'sche Universitäts-Buchhandlung, 1933–1936.

Hyldahl, Niels. *The History of Early Christianity.* Frankfurt am Main: Peter Lang, 1997.

————. "The Maccabean Rebellion and the Question of 'Hellenization.'" In *Religion and Religious Practice in the Seleucid Kingdom,* ed. Per Bilde, Troels Engberg, Lise Hannestad, and Jan Zahle, 188–203. Aarhus: Aarhus University Press, 1990.

Ibach, Robert D. *Archaeological Survey of the Hesban Region: Catalogue of Sites and Characterizations of Periods.* Berrien Springs, Mich.: Andrews University Press, 1987.

Ibrahim, Moawiyah M. *Arabian Studies in Honour of Mahmoud Ghul: Symposium at Yarmouk University, December 8–11, 1984.* Wiesbaden: Harrassowitz, 1989.

Ilan, Tal. "New Ossuary Inscriptions from Jerusalem." *Scripta classica israelica* 11 (1991–1992): 149–159.

Ingholt, Harald. "Deux inscriptions bilingues de Palmyre." *Syria* 13 (1932): 278–292.

Isaac, Benjamin H. "The Babatha Archive: A Review Article." *Israel Exploration Journal* 42 (1992): 62–73.

————. "Bandits in Judaea and Arabia." *Harvard Studies in Classical Philology* 88 (1984): 171–203.

————. "The Decapolis in Syria: A Neglected Inscription." *Zeitschrift für Papyrologie und Epigraphik* 44 (1981): 67–74.

————. "The Eastern Frontier." In *Cambridge Ancient History,* vol. 13, *The Late Empire,* 437–460. Cambridge: Cambridge University Press, 1998.

————. "Jews, Christians and Others in Palestine: The Evidence from Eusebius." In

Jews in a Graeco-Roman World, ed. Martin Goodman, 65–74. Oxford and New York: Clarendon Press, 1998.

———. "Judaea after AD 70." *Journal of Jewish Studies* 35 (1984): 44–50.

———. *The Limits of Empire: The Roman Army in the East.* Oxford and New York: Clarendon Press, 1990. Rev. ed., 1992.

———. "The Meaning of 'Limes' and 'Limitanei' in Ancient Sources." *Journal of Roman Studies* 78 (1988): 125–147.

———. "Roman Colonies in Judaea: The Foundation of Aelia Capitolina." *Talanta* 12–13 (1980–1981): 31–54.

Isaac, Benjamin H., and Aharon Oppenheimer. "The Bar Kokhba Revolt: Ideology and Modern Scholarship." *Journal of Jewish Studies* 36 (1985): 33–60.

Isaac, Benjamin H., and Israel Roll. "Judaea in the Early Years of Hadrian's Reign." *Latomus* 38 (1979): 54–66.

———. *Roman Roads in Judaea.* Vol. 1, *The Legio-Scythopolis Road.* Oxford: British Archaeological Reports, 1982.

Isocrates. "Panegyricus." In *Isocrates,* trans. George Norlin, 116–243. Loeb Classical Library.

Jacoby, Felix. *Die Fragmente der griechischen Historiker.* 3 vols. Leiden: E. J. Brill, 1950–1963.

———. "Kallinikos 1." In *Realencyclopädie der classischen Altertumswissenschaft,* ed. August Friedrich von Pauly et al. Stuttgart: J. B. Metzler, 1894–.

Jalabert, Louis. "Inscriptions grecques et latines de la Syrie." *Mélanges de la Faculté Orientale de Beyrouth* 1 (1906): 132–188.

Jalabert, Louis, and René Mouterde. *Inscriptions grecques et latines de la Syrie.* Vol. 1, *Commagène et Cyrrhestique.* Paris: P. Geuthner, 1929.

———. *Inscriptions grecques et latines de la Syrie.* Vol. 3.1, *Région de l'Amanus, Antioch.* Paris: P. Geuthner, 1950.

———. *Inscriptions grecques et latines de la Syrie.* Vol. 3.2, *Antioch (suite): Antiochene.* Paris: P. Geuthner, 1953.

———. *Inscriptions grecques et latines de la Syrie.* Vol. 4, *Laodicée, Apamène: Chronologie des inscriptions datées des tomes I–IV.* Paris: P. Geuthner, 1955.

Jalabert, Louis, René Mouterde, and Claude Mondésert. *Inscriptions grecques et latines de la Syrie.* Vol. 5, *Emésène.* Paris: P. Geuthner, 1959.

James, Simon. "Dura-Europos and the Chronology of Syria in the 250s AD." *Chiron* 15 (1985): 111–124.

Jameson, Shelagh. "Chronology of the Campaigns of Aelius Gallus and C. Petronius." *Journal of Roman Studies* 58 (1968): 71–84.

Janvier, Yves. "Rome et l'Orient lointain: Le problème des Sères; Réexamen d'une question de géographie antique." *Ktema* 9 (1984 [1988]): 261–303.

Jarrett, Michael Grierson. "An Album of the Equestrians from North Africa in the Emperor's Services." *Epigraphische Studien* 9 (1972).

Jaussen, Antonin, and Raphaël Savignac. *Mission en Arabie.* Vol. 2. Paris: E. Leroux, 1914.

Jerome. *Chronicon,* trans. Malcolm Drew Donalson. Lewiston, Me.: Mellen University Press, 1996.

———. *Die Chronik des Hieronymus (Hieronymi Chronicon),* ed. Rudolf Helm. Vol. 7, *Eusebius Werke.* Berlin: Akademie-Verlag, 1956.

Jesnick, Ilona Julia. *The Image of Orpheus in Roman Mosaic: An Exploration of* the Figure of Orpheus in Graeco-Roman Art and Culture with Special Reference to Its Expression in the Medium of Mosaic in Late Antiquity. Oxford: Archaeopress, 1997.

Johnson, D. J. "Nabataean Trade: Intensification and Culture Change." Ph.D. diss., University of Utah, 1987.

Jones, Arnold H. M. The Greek City, from Alexander to Justinian. Oxford: Clarendon Press, 1941.

———. The Herods of Judaea. Oxford: Clarendon Press, 1967.

———. "The Urbanization of the Ituraean Principality." Journal of Roman Studies 21 (1931): 265–275.

Jones, Christopher Prestige. "Towards a Chronology of Josephus." Scripta classica israelica 21 (2002): 113–121.

Jones, T. B. "A Numismatic Riddle: The So-Called Greek Imperial." Proceedings of the American Philosophical Society 107 (1963): 308–347.

Josephus, Flavius. De antiquitate judaico (Jewish Antiquities), trans. Louis H. Feldman. 9 vols. Loeb Classical Library.

———. De bello judaico (The Jewish War), trans. Henry St. John Thackeray. 3 vols. Loeb Classical Library.

———. The Life and Against Apion, trans. Henry St. John Thackeray. Loeb Classical Library.

Joukowsky, Martha Sharp. "The Brown University 1998 Excavation at the Petra Great Temple." Annual of the Department of Antiquities of Jordan 43 (1999): 195–222.

———. Petra Great Temple I: Brown University Excavations 1993–1997. Providence: n.p., 1998.

Julian. "Hymn to King Helios Dedicated to Sallust." In The Works of the Emperor Julian, trans. Wilmer Cave Wright, vol. 1, 352–435. Loeb Classical Library.

———. "Misopogon, or Beard-Hater." In The Works of the Emperor Julian, trans. Wilmer Cave Wright, vol. 2, 417–511. Loeb Classical Library.

———. The Works of the Emperor Julian, trans. Wilmer Cave Wright. Loeb Classical Library.

Jürging, Axel. "Die erste Emission Gordians III." Jahrbuch für Numismatik und Geldgeschichte 45 (1995): 95–128.

Justinian. "Codex Iustinianus," ed. Paul Krüger. In Corpus iuris civilis. Berlin: Weidmann, 1954.

———. "Novellae," ed. Rudolf Schöll and G. Kroll. In Corpus iuris civilis. Berlin: Weidmann, 1954.

Justinus. Epitome of the Philippic History of Pompeius Trogus, ed. Robert Develin, trans. J. C. Yardley. Atlanta: Scholars Press, 1994.

Juvenal. "Quid Romae Faciam?" In Juvenal and Persius, trans. G. G. Ramsay, 31–57. Loeb Classical Library.

———. "The Ways of Women." In Juvenal and Persius, trans. G. G. Ramsay, 83–137. Loeb Classical Library.

Kader, Ingeborg. Propylon und Bogentor: Untersuchungen zum Tetrapylon von Latakia und anderer frühkaiserzeitlichen Bogenmonumenten im Nahen Osten. Mainz: Ph. von Zabern, 1996. Reprint, Damaszener Forschungen 7.

Kadman, Leo. The Coinage of Aelila Capitolina. Tel Aviv: Schocken, 1956.

———. The Coins of Akko-Ptolemais. Tel-Aviv: Schocken, 1961.

Kaibel, Georg, ed. *Inscriptiones graecae.* Vol. 14. Berlin: G. Reimer, 1890.

Kalos, Mikaël. "Un nouveau culte à Mithra." *Le monde de la Bible* 139 (November–December 2001): 58.

———. "Un sanctuaire de Mithra inédit en Syrie du Sud." *Topoi* 11 (2001): 229–277.

Kanael, Baruch. "The Partition of Judaea by Gabinius." *Israel Exploration Journal* 7 (1957): 98–106.

Kasher, Aryeh. *Jews and Hellenistic Cities in Eretz-Israel: Relations of the Jews in Eretz-Israel with the Hellenistic Tribes during the Second Temple Period (332 B.C.E.–70 C.E.).* Tübingen: J. C. B. Mohr, 1990.

———. *Jews, Idumaeans, and Ancient Arabs: Relations of the Jews in Eretz-Israel with the Nations of the Frontier and the Desert during the Hellenistic and Roman Era (332 bce–70 ce).* Tübingen: J. C. B. Mohr, 1988.

Kasher, Aryeh, Gideon Fuks, and Uriel Rappaport. *Greece and Rome in Eretz Israel: Collected Essays.* Jerusalem: Yad Izhak ben-Zvi (Israel Exploration Society), 1990.

Keaveney, Arthur. *Lucullus: A Life.* London: Routledge, 1992.

Kelso, James L., and Dimitri C. Baramki. *Excavations at New Testament Jericho and Khirbet en-Nitla.* New Haven, Conn.: American Schools of Oriental Research, 1955.

Kennedy, David L. "Aerial Photography: Ancient Settlements in Syria." *Popular Archaeology* (September 1985): 42–44.

———. *Archaeological Explorations on the Roman Frontier in the North-Eastern Jordan: The Roman and Byzantine Military Installations and Road Network on the Ground and from the Air.* Oxford: British Archaeological Reports, 1982.

———. "Archaeology in Jordan." *American Journal of Archaeology* 97 (1993): [496].

———. "Cohors XX Palmyrenorum: An Alternative Explanation of the Numeral." *Zeitschrift für Papyrologie und Epigraphik* 53 (1983): 214–216.

———. "Cohors XX Palmyrenorum at Dura." In *The Roman and Byzantine Army in the East: Proceedings of a Colloqium* [sic] *Held at the Jagiellonian University, Kraków in September 1992,* ed. Edward Dąbrowa, 89–98. Cracow: Drukarnia Uniwersytetu Jagiellonskiego, 1994.

———. "'European' Soldiers and the Severan Siege of Hatra." In *The Defence of the Roman and Byzantine East: Proceedings of a Colloquium Held at the University of Sheffield in April 1986,* ed. Philip Freeman and David L. Kennedy, 397–409. Oxford: British Archaeological Reports, 1986.

———. "The Garrisoning of Mesopotamia in the Late Antonine and Early Severan Period." *Antichthon* (1987): 57–66.

———. "The Identity of Roman Gerasa: An Archaeological Approach." *Mediterranean Archaeology* 11 (1998): 39–69.

———. "*Legio VI Ferrata:* The Annexation and Early Garrison of Arabia." *Harvard Studies in Classical Philology* 84 (1980): 283–309.

———. "Roman Roads and Routes in North-East Jordan." *Levant* 29 (1997): 71–93.

———. "The Special Command of M. Valerius Lollianus." *Electrum* 1 (1997): 69–81.

———. "Ti. Claudius Subatianus Aquila, First Prefect of Mesopotamia." *Zeitschrift für Papyrologie und Epigraphik* 36 (1979): 255–262.

———. *The Twin Towns of Zeugma on the Euphrates: Rescue Work and Historical Studies.* Portsmouth, R.I.: Journal of Roman Archaeology, 1998.

Kennedy, David L., and David Braund, eds. *The Roman Army in the East.* Ann Arbor, Mich.: Journal of Roman Archaeology, 1996.

Kennedy, David L., Henry Innes MacAdam, and D. N. Riley. "Preliminary Report on the Southern Hauran Survey, 1985." *Annual of the Department of Antiquities of Jordan* 30 (1986): 145–153.

Kennedy, David L., and Derrick Riley. *Rome's Desert Frontier: From the Air.* Austin: University of Texas Press, 1990.

Keppie, Lawrence J. F. "Legions in the East from Augustus to Trajan." In *The Defence of the Roman and Byzantine East,* ed. Philip Freeman and David L. Kennedy, 411–429. Oxford: British Archaeological Reports, 1986.

———. "Vexilla veteranorum." *Papers of the British School at Rome* 41 (1973): 13–14.

Kerner, Suzanne, Hamke Krebs, and Dietmar Michaelis. "Water Management in Northern Jordan: The Example of Gadara Umm Qays." *Studies in the History and Archaeology of Jordan* 6 (1997): 265–270.

Kettenhofen, Erich. "Die Einforderung des Achämenidenerbes durch Ardashir: Eine Interpretatio Romana." *Orientalia lovaniensia periodica* 15 (1984): 177–190.

———. Review of *Die sasanidisch-römischen Friedensverträge des 3. Jahrhunderts n. Chr.,* by Engelbert Winter. *Bibliotheca orientalis* 47 (January–March 1990): cols. 163–178.

———. *Die römische-persischen Kriege des 3. Jahrhunderts n. Chr.: Nach der Inschrift Sahpuhrs I. an der Ka'be-ye Zartost (SKZ).* Wiesbaden: L. Reichert, 1982.

Keydell, Rudolf. "Oppianus." In *Realencyclopädie der classischen Altertumswissenschaft,* ed. August Friedrich von Pauly et al. Stuttgart: J. B. Metzler, 1894–.

Khairy, Nabil I. *The 1981 Petra Excavations.* Abhandlungen des deutschen Palästinavereins 13. Wiesbaden: Harrassowitz, 1990.

———. "The Painted Nabataean Pottery from the 1981 Petra Excavations." *Levant* 19 (1987): 167–181.

Khalil Ibrahim, Jaber. "Kitabat al-hadr"" [Two Legal Texts from Hatra]. *Sumer* 38 (1982): 120–125.

Kienast, Dieter. *Untersuchungen zu den Kriegsflotten der römischen Kaiserzeit.* Bonn: R. Habelt, 1966.

Kindler, Arye. *The Coinage of Bostra.* Warminster: Aris & Phillips, 1983.

———. "The Coin Issues of the Roman Administration in the Provincia Judaea during the Reign of Domitian." *Bulletin Museum Ha'aretz* 10 (1968): 6–16.

———. "The Status of Cities in the Syro-Palestinian Area as Reflected by Their Coins." *Israel Numismatic Journal* 6–7 (1982–1983): 79–87.

———. "Two Coins of the Third Legion Cyrenaica Struck under Antoninus Pius." *Israel Exploration Journal* 25 (1975): 144–147.

Kindler, Arye, and Alla Stein. *A Bibliography of the City Coinage of Palestine, from the 2nd Century B.C. to the 3rd Century A.D.* Oxford: British Archaeological Reports, 1987.

Kirkbride, Diana. "Le temple nabatéen de Ramm: Son évolution architecturale." *Revue biblique* 67 (1960): 65–92.

Kirkpatrick, G. D. "Dura-Europos: The Parchments and Papyri." *Greek, Roman and Byzantine Studies* 5 (1964): 215–225.

Kisnawski, Ahmed, Prentiss S. de Jesus, and Baseem Rihani. "Preliminary Report on the Mining Survey, North-West Hijaz, 1982." *Al-Atlal* 7 (1983): 76–83.

Klausner, Joseph. *The Messianic Idea in Israel, from Its Beginning to the Completion of the Mishnah.* London: Allen & Unwin, 1956.

Klein, M. J. *Römische Glaskunst und Wandmalerei.* Mainz: Ph. von Zabern, 1999.

Klijn, A. F., ed. *The Acts of Thomas.* Leiden: E. J. Brill, 1962.

Kloner, Amos. "Bet Guvrin, Amphitheater." *Excavations and Surveys in Israel* 12 (1993): 87–88.

Kloner, Amos, and Alain Hübsch. "The Roman Amphitheater of Bet Guvrin: A Preliminary Report on the 1992, 1993 and 1994 Seasons." *Atiqot* 30 (1996): 85–106.

Knauf, Ernst Axel. "Dushara and Shai' al-Qaum." *Aram* 2 (1990): 175–183.

———. "Zwei thamudenische Inschriften aus der Gegend von Geras." *Zeitschrift der deutschen Palästina-Vereins* 97 (1981): 188–192.

Kobori, Iwao. "Les qanât en Syrie." In *Techniques et pratiques hydro-agricoles traditionnelles en domaine irrigué: Approche pluridisciplinaire des modes de culture avant la motorisation en Syrie; Actes du Colloque de Damas 27 juin–ler juillet 1987,* ed. Bernard Geyer, 321–328. Paris: P. Geuthner, 1990.

Koch, Guntram. "Ein attischer Meleagersarkophag aus Arethousa in Syrien." *Damaszener Mitteilungen* 1 (1983): 137–148.

———. "Ein attischer Schiffkampf-Sarkophag aus Arethousa in Damaskus." *Damaszener Mitteilungen* 9 (1996): 197–207.

———. "Der Import kaiserzeitlicher Sarkophage in den römischen Provinzen Syria, Palaestina und Arabia." *Bonner Jahrbücher* 189 (1989): 161–211.

———. "The Import of Attic Sarcophagi in the Near East." In O Ἑλληνισμὸς στὴν Ἀνατολή, 67–80. Athens: EPKED, 1991.

———. *Die mythologischen Sarkophage.* Vol. 6, *Meleager.* Berlin: Gebr. Mann Verlag, 1975.

Koenen, Ludwig, and Cornelia Römer, eds. *Der Kölner Mani-Kodex: Abbildungen und diplomatischer Text* (Codex Manichaicus Coloniensis). Bonn: R. Habelt, 1985.

———. *Der Kölner Mani-Codex: Über das Werden seines Leibes.* Opladen: Westdeutscher Verlag, 1988.

Kokkinos, Nikos. *The Herodian Dynasty: Origins, Role in Society and Eclipse.* Sheffield, U.K.: Sheffield Academic Press, 1998.

Kolb, Bernhard. "Les maisons patriciennes d'az-Zantûr." *Le monde de la Bible* 127 (May–June 2000): 42–43.

Konrad, Michaela. "Frühkaiserzeitliche Befestigungen an der Strata Diocletiana." *Damaszener Mitteilungen* 9 (1996): 163–180.

Kowalski, S. P. "Late Roman Palmyra in Literature and Epigraphy." *Studia Palmyrenskie* 10 (1997).

Kraay, C. M. "Notes on the Early Imperial Tetradrachms of Syria." *Revue numismatique* (1966): 58–68.

Kraeling, Carl Hermann. "Color Photographs of the Painting in the Tomb of the Three Brothers at Palmyra." *Annales archéologiques de Syrie* 11–12 (1961–1962): 13–18.

———. *The Excavations at Dura-Europos: Final Report.* Vol. 8, part 1, *The Synagogue.* New Haven: Yale University Press, 1956.

———. *The Excavations at Dura-Europos: Final Report.* Vol. 8, part 2, *The Christian Building.* New Haven: Yale University Press, 1967.

———. *A Greek Fragment of Tatian's Diatessaron from Dura.* London: Christophers, 1935.

———. "The Jewish Community at Antioch." *Journal of Biblical Literature* 51 (1932): 130–160.

———, ed. *Gerasa, City of the Decapolis.* New Haven, Conn.: American Schools of Oriental Research, 1938.

Kraft, Konrad. *Zur Rekrutierung der Alen und Kohorten an Rhein und Donau.* Bern: Aedibus A. Francke, 1951.

Krencker, Daniel M., and Willy Zschietzschmann. *Römische Tempel in Syrien.* Berlin: W. de Gruyter, 1938.

Krentz, Edgar. "Caesarea and Early Christianity." In *Caesarea Papers,* ed. Robert Lindley Vann, 261–267. Ann Arbor: University of Michigan Press, 1992.

Kropp, Manfred. "Grande re degli Arabi e vassalo de nessuno: Mar'al-Qays ibn 'Amr e l'iscrizione ad En-Nemara." *Quaderni di Studi Arabi* 9 (1991): 3–28.

Krüger, Paul, Theodor Mommsen, Rudolf Schöll, and Wilhelm Kroll, eds. *Corpus iuris civilis.* 3 vols. Berlin: Weidmann, 1928.

Kuhnen, Hans-Peter. *Palästina in griechisch-römischer Zeit.* Munich: C. H. Beck'she Verlagsbuchhandlung, 1990.

Kuntzmann, Raymond, and Jacques Schlosser, eds. *Études sur le judaïsme hellénistique: Congrès de Strasbourg (1983).* Paris: Le Cerf, 1984.

Kushnir-Stein, Alla. "The Coinage of Agrippa II." *Scripta classica israelica* 21 (2002): 123–131.

———. "The Predecessor of Caesarea: On the Identification of Demetrias in South Phoenicia." In *The Roman and Byzantine Near East: Some Recent Archaeological Research,* ed. John H. Humphrey, 9–14. Ann Arbor, Mich.: Journal of Roman Archaeology, 1995.

[Kushnir-]Stein, Alla. "Studies in Greek and Latin Inscriptions on the Palestinian Coinage under the Principate." Ph.D. diss., Tel Aviv University, 1990.

Kushnir-Stein, Alla, and Haim Gitler. "Numismatic Evidence from Tel Beer-Sheva and the Beginning of the Nabatean Coinage." *Israel Numismatic Journal* 12 (1992–1993): 13–20.

Laet, Sigfried J. de. *Portorium: Étude sur l'organisation douanière chez les Romains, surtout à l'époque du haut-empire.* Brugge: De Tempel, 1949.

Lake, Silva. "Greco-Roman Inscriptions." In *Samaria-Sebaste,* vol. 3, *The Objects from Samaria,* ed. John Winter Crowfoot, 35–42. London: Palestine Exploration Fund, 1957.

Lambrino, Scarlat. "Un nouveau diplôme de l'empereur Claude." *Comptes rendus des séances de l'Académie des inscriptions et belles-lettres* (1930): 131–137.

Laperrousaz, Ernest-Marie. "À propos du Maître de Justice et du Temple de Jérusalem: Deux problèmes de nombre." *Revue de Qoumrân* 15 (1991): 267–274.

———. *L'attente du Messie en Palestine à la veille et au début de l'ère chrétienne, à la lumière des documents récemment découverts.* Paris: Picard, 1982.

———. *Les manuscrits de la Mer morte.* 9th ed. Paris: Presses Universitaires de France, coll. Que Sais-Je? 1999.

————. *Qoumrân, l'établissement essénien des bords de la Mer morte: Histoire et archéologie du site.* Paris: Picard, 1976.

Lapp, Paul W. *Palestinian Ceramic Chronology, 200 B.C.–70 A.D.* New Haven, Conn.: American Schools of Oriental Research, 1961.

Larsen, Bent Dalsgaard. "Jamblique de Chalcis, exégète et philosophe." Ph.D. diss., Universitetsforlaget i Aarhus, 1972.

Lassus, Jean. "Sur les maisons d'Antioche." In *Apamée de Syrie: Bilan des recherches archéologiques 1973–1979,* ed. Jeanine Balty, 361–372. Brussels: Centre belge de recherches archéologiques à Apamée de Syrie, 1984.

Lassus, Jean, and Richard Stillwell. *Les portiques d'Antioche.* Vol. 5, *Antioch-on-the-Orontes.* Princeton: Princeton University Press, 1972.

Last, Rosa, Avshalom Lanadio, and Pinchas Porath. "A Dedication to Galerius from Scythopolis: A Revised Reading." *Zeitschrift für Papyrologie und Epigraphik* 98 (1993): 229–237.

Lauffray, Jean. "Beyrouth archéologie et histoire, époques gréco-romaines: I. Période hellénistique et Haut-Empire romain." *Aufstieg und Niedergang der römischen Welt* 2.8 (1977): 135–163.

————. "Beyrouth, ce qui n'a pas été dit." *Archeologia* 317 (November 1995): 4–11.

————. "Une fouille au pied de l'acropole de Byblos." *Bulletin du Musée de Beyrouth* 4 (1940): 7–36.

Lazzarini, Maria Letizia. "Iscrizioni dal santuario di Artemide 1984–1987." In *Jerash Archaeological Project 1984–1988 II: Fouilles de Jérash,* ed. Fawzi Zayadine, 41–49. Paris: P. Geuthner, 1989.

Leblanc, Jacques, and Grégoire Poccardi. "Étude de la permanence de tracés urbains et ruraux antiques à Antioche sur l'Oronte." *Syria* 76 (1999): 91–126.

Leblanc, Jacques, and Jean-Pierre Vallat. "L'organisation de l'espace antique dans la zone de Suweïda et de Qanawat (Syrie du Sud)." In *La dynamique des paysages protohistoriques, antiques, médiévaux et moderne: Actes des XVIIe Rencontres internationales d'archéologie et d'histoire d'Antibes, 19–21 octobre 1996,* ed. Joëlle Burnouf, Jean-Paul Bravard, and Gérard Chouquer, 35–67. Sophia Antipolis: Association pour la publication et la diffusion des connaissances archéologiques, 1997.

Le Bohec, Yann. *Les légions de Rome sous le haut-empire: Actes du congrès de Lyon (17–19 septembre 1998).* 2 vols. Lyon: n. p., 2000.

Lefèvre, A.-Ch. "Beyrouth: L'archéologie par le vide." *Archeologia* 318 (December 1995): 4–9.

Le Gall, Joël, and Marcel Le Glay. *L'empire romain.* Paris: Presses Universitaires de France, 1987.

Lehmann-Hartleben, Karl. *Die antiken Hafenanlagen des Mittelmeeres: Beiträge zur Geschichte des Städtebaues im Altertum.* Leipzig: Dieterich, 1923.

Lemaître, Séverine. "Les importations d'amphores orientales dans la vallée du Rhône de l'époque d'Auguste à la fin du IIIe siècle apr. J.-C." Ph.D. diss., Université de Lyon II, 1999.

Lémonon, Jean-Pierre. *Pilate et le gouvernement de la Judée: Textes et monuments.* Paris: J. Gabalda, 1981.

Le Moyne, Jean. *Les Sadducéens: Etudes bibliques.* Paris: J. Gabalda, 1972.

Lenoir, Maurice. "Bosra (Syrie): Le camp de la légion IIIe Cyrénaïque." *Mélanges de l'École française de Rome: Antiquités* 110 (1998): 523–528.

Lenzen, Cherie J., and Ernst Axel Knauf. "Beit Ras / Capitolias: A Preliminary Evaluation of the Archaeological and Textual Evidence." *Syria* 64 (1987): 21–46.

Leriche, Pierre. "Matériaux pour une réflexion renouvelée sur les sanctuaires de Doura-Europos." *Topoi* 7 (1997): 889–913.

———. "Une nouvelle inscription dans la salle à gradins du temple d'Artémis à Doura-Europos." *Comptes rendus des séances de l'Académie des inscriptions et belles-lettres* (1999): 1309–1346.

———. "Salle à gradins du temple d'Artémis à Doura-Europos." *Topoi* 9 (1999): 719–739.

Leriche, Pierre, and A'sad al Mahmoud. "Doura-Europos: Bilan des recherches récentes." *Comptes rendus des séances de l'Académie des inscriptions et belles-lettres* (1994): 395–420.

Le Rider, Georges. *Antioche de Syrie sous les Séleucides.* Paris: Institut de France, 2000.

Levi, Doro. *Antioch Mosaic Pavements.* Princeton: Princeton University Press, 1947.

Levi, Mario Attilio. "La grande iscrizione di Ottaviano trovata a Roso." *Rivista di filologia e d'istruzione classica* (1938): 113–128.

Levin, Flora R. *The Harmonics of Nicomachus and the Pythagorean Tradition.* University Park, Pa.: American Philological Association, 1975.

Levine, Lee I. *Caesarea under Roman Rule.* Leiden: E. J. Brill, 1975.

———. *The Galilee in Late Antiquity.* New York and Cambridge, Mass.: Jewish Theological Seminary of America, distributed by Harvard University, 1992.

———. *The Rabbinic Class of Roman Palestine in Late Antiquity.* Jerusalem: Yad Izhak Ben-Zvi; New York: Jewish Theological Seminary of America, 1989.

———. *Roman Caesarea: An Archaeological-Topographical Study.* Jerusalem: Hebrew University, 1975.

Levy, Brooks Emmons. "The Autonomous Silver of Sidon, 107/6 B.C.–43/44 C.E." In *XII. Internationaler Numismatischer Kongress Berlin 1997: Akten-Proceedings-Actes,* ed. Bernd Kluge and Bernhard Weisser, 324–332. Berlin: Staatliche Museen zu Berlin / Gebr. Mann Verlag, 2000.

Lewis, Naphtali, ed. *The Documents from the Bar Kokhba Period in the Cave of Letters.* Vol. 1, *Greek Papyri.* Jerusalem: Israel Exploration Society, 1989.

Lewis, Naphtali, Ranon Katzoff, and Jonas C. Greenfield. "Papyrus Yadin 18." *Israel Exploration Journal* 37 (1987): 229–250.

Lewis, Norman N., Annie Sartre-Fauriat, and Maurice Sartre. "William-John Bankes: Travaux en Syrie d'un voyageur oublié." *Syria* 73 (1996): 57–95.

Libanios. *Antioch as a Centre of Hellenic Culture as Observed by Libanius,* trans. A. F. Norman. Liverpool: Liverpool University Press, 2000.

———. *The Julianic Orations.* In *Selected Works with an English Translation,* trans. A. F. Norman, vol. 1. Loeb Classical Library.

———. *Libanii opera,* ed. Richard Foerster and Eberhard Richsteig. 12 vols. Hildesheim: G. Olms, 1963–1985.

———. *Selected Works with an English Translation,* trans. A. F. Norman. Loeb Classical Library, 1969.

Lichtenberger, Achim. *Die Baupolitik Herodes des Grossen.* Wiesbaden: Harrassowitz, 1999.

Lidzbarski, Mark. *Kanaanäische Inscriften.* Giessen: A. Töpelmann, 1907.

Lieberman, Saul. *Greek in Jewish Palestine: Studies in the Life and Manners of Jewish*

Palestine in the II–IV Centuries C.E. 2nd ed. New York: Jewish Theological Seminary of America, 1965.

Liebmann-Frankfort, Marie-Thérèse. *La frontière orientale dans la politique extérieure de la République romaine, depuis le traité d'Apamée jusqu'à la fin des conquêtes asiatiques de Pompée (189/188–63).* Brussels: Palais des Académies, 1969.

Liere, W. J. van. "Ager centuriatus of the Roman Colonia of Emesa (Homs)." *Annales archéologiques de Syrie* 8–9 (1958–1959): 55–58.

Lieu, Samuel N. C. *Manichaeism in the Later Roman Empire and Medieval China: A Historical Survey.* Manchester, U.K., and Dover, N.H.: Manchester University Press, 1985. 2nd ed., rev. and augmented, Tübingen: J. C. B. Mohr, 1992.

Lifshitz, Baruch. *Donateurs et fondateurs dans les synagogues juives: Répertoire des dédicaces grecques relatives à la construction et à la réfection des synagogues.* Paris: J. Gabalda, 1967.

———. "Inscriptions latines de Césarée en Palestine." *Latomus* 21 (1962): 149–150.

Linant de Bellefonds, Pascale. "Les divinités 'bédouines' du désert syrien et leur iconographie." In *Petra and the Caravan Cities,* ed. Fawzi Zayadine, 169–183. Amman: Department of Antiquities, 1990.

———. *Sarcophages attiques de la nécropole de Tyr.* Paris: Éditions Recherche sur les civilisations, 1985.

Lindner, Manfred. *Petra und das Königreich der Nabatäer: Lebensraum, Geschichte und Kultur eines arabischen Volkes der Antike.* 3rd ed. Munich and Bad Windsheim: Delp, 1986.

Lipinski, Edward. "The Phoenician History of Philo of Byblos." *Bibliotheca orientalis* 40 (1983): 304–310.

Littmann, Enno. *Syria: Publications of the Princeton University Archaeological Expeditions to Syria in 1904–1905 and 1909.* Vol. 4A, *Semitic Inscriptions: Nabataean Inscriptions.* Leiden: E. J. Brill, 1914.

———. *Syria: Publications of the Princeton University Archaeological Expeditions to Syria in 1904–1905 and 1909.* Vol. 4C, *Semitic Inscriptions: Safaitic Inscriptions.* Leiden: E. J. Brill, 1943.

Littmann, Enno, David Magie, and D. R. Stuart. *Syria: Publications of the Princeton University Archaeological Expeditions to Syria in 1904–1905 and 1909.* Vol. 3A, *Greek and Latin Inscriptions: Southern Syria.* Leiden: E. J. Brill, 1921.

Littmann, Enno, and David Meredith. "Nabataean Inscriptions from Egypt." *Bulletin of the Society for Oriental and African Studies* 15 (1953): 1–28.

———. "Nabataean Inscriptions from Egypt." *Bulletin of the Society for Oriental and African Studies* 16 (1954): 211–246.

Livingstone, Alasdair, Bachir Spaie, Mohammed Ibrahim, Mohammed Kamal, and Selim Taimani. "Taima: Recent Soundings and New Inscribed Material." *Al-Atlal* 7 (1983): 102–114.

Livy. "Summaries." In *Works,* vol. 14, *Summaries, Fragments, and Obsequens,* trans. Alfred C. Schlesinger, 1–169. Loeb Classical Library.

———. *Works.* 14 vols. Loeb Classical Library.

Loffreda, Stanislao. *Cafarnao.* Vol. 2, *La Ceramica.* Jerusalem: Franciscan Printing Press, 1974.

Lopuszanski, Georges. *La date de la capture de Valérien et la chronologie des empereurs gaulois.* Brussels: Institut d'études polonaises en Belgique, 1951.

Loriot, Xavier. "Deux inscriptions métrôaques de Cordoue." *Bulletin de la Société nationale des antiquaires de France* (1992): 352–353.

———. "Itinera Gordiani Augusti: I. Un voyage de Gordien III à Antioche en 239 après J.-C." *Bulletin de la Société française de numismatique* 26 (1971): 18–21.

———. "Les premières années de la grande crise du IIIe siècle: De l'avènement de Maximin le Thrace (235) à la mort de Gordien III (244)." *Aufstieg und Niedergang der römischen Welt* 2.2 (1975): 657–787.

Lozachmeur, Hélène, ed. *Présence arabe dans le Croissant fertile avant l'Hégire: Actes de la Table ronde internationale organisée par l'Unité de recherche associée 1062 du CNRS, Études sémitiques au Collège de France, le 13 novembre 1993.* Paris: Éditions Recherche sur les civilisations, 1995.

Lucan, M. Annaeus. *The Civil War,* trans. J. D. Duff. Loeb Classical Library.

Lucian. *Oeuvres,* ed. Jacques Bompaire. 2 vols. Paris: Les Belles Lettres, 1993–1998.

———. *On the Syrian Goddess,* ed. and trans. Jane L. Lightfoot. Oxford: Oxford University Press, 2003.

Lund, John. "The Distribution of Cypriot Sigillata as Evidence of Sea-Trade Involving Cyprus." In *Res Maritimae: Cyprus and the Eastern Mediterranean from Prehistory to Late Antiquity,* ed. Stuart Swiny, Robert L. Hohlfelder, and Helena Wylde Swiny, 201–215. Atlanta: Scholars Press, 1997.

———. "A Fresh Look at the Roman and Late Roman Fine Wares from the Danish Excavations at Hama, Syria." In *Hellenistic and Roman Pottery in the Eastern Mediterranean: Advances in Scientific Studies; Acts of the II Nieborów Pottery Workshop,* ed. Henryk Meyza and Jolanta Mlynarczyk, 135–161. Warsaw: Research Center for Mediterranean Archaeology, Polish Academy of Sciences, 1995.

———. "Trade Patterns in the Levant from ca. 100 BC to AD 200—as Reflected by the Distribution of Ceramic Fine Wares in Cyprus." *Münstersche Beiträge zur antiken Handelsgeschichte* 18 (1999): 1–22.

Luzzato, G. I. *Epigrafia giuridica greca e romana.* Milan: Giuffré, 1942.

Lyttleton, Margaret B. *Baroque Architecture in Classical Antiquity.* Ithaca, N.Y.: Cornell University Press, 1974.

Lyttleton, Margaret B., and Thomas F. C. Blagg. "Sculpture from the Temenos of Qasr el-Bint." *Aram* 2 (1990): 267–286.

Ma'ayeh, Farah S. "Jérash." Contribution to "Chronique archéologique." *Revue biblique* 67 (1960): 228–229.

———. "Recent Archaeological Discoveries in Jordan." *Annual of the Department of Antiquities of Jordan* 4–5 (1960): 114–116.

Macadam, Henry Innes. "Epigraphy and Village Life in Southern Syria during the Roman and Early Byzantine Periods." *Berytus* 31 (1983): 103–115.

———. "Some Aspects of Land Tenure and Social Development in the Roman Near East: Arabia, Phoenicia and Syria." In *Land Tenure and Social Transformation in the Middle East,* ed. Tarif Khalidi, 45–62. Beirut: American University of Beirut, 1984.

———. "Studies in the History of the Roman Province of Arabia." Oxford: British Archaeological Reports, 1986.

MacCown, C. C. "A Painted Tomb at Marwa." *Quarterly of the Department of Antiquities of Palestine* 9 (1942): 1–30.

MacDonald, Burton. "The Route of the Via Nova Traiana Immediately South of Wadi al-Hasa." *Palestine Exploration Quarterly* (1996): 11–15.

———. *The Southern Ghors and Northeast 'Arabah Archaeological Survey.* Sheffield: J. R. Collis, Department of Archaeology and Prehistory, University of Sheffield, 1992.

Macdonald, David. "Dating the Fall of Dura-Europos." *Historia* 35 (1986): 45–68.

———. "The Death of Gordian III: Another Tradition." *Historia* 30 (1981): 502–508.

Macdonald, Michael C. A. "A Dated Nabataean Inscription from Southern Arabia." In *Arabia Felix: Beiträge zur Sprache und Kultur des vorislamischen Arabian; Festschrift Walter W. Müller zum 60. Geburtstag,* ed. Norbert Nebes, 132–141. Wiesbaden: Harrassowitz, 1994.

———. "Herodian Echoes in the Syrian Desert." In "Trade, Contact and the Movement of Peoples in the Eastern Mediterranean: Studies in Honour of J. Basil Hennessy," ed. Stephen Bourke and Jean-Paul Descoeudres. Supplement, *Mediterranean Archaeology* (1995): 285–290.

———. "Nomads and the Hawran in the Late Hellenistic and Roman Periods: A Reassessment of the Epigraphic Evidence." *Syria* 70 (1993): 303–403.

———. "North Arabian Epigraphic Notes: I." *Arabian Archaeology and Epigraphy* 3 (1992): 23–43.

———. "Reflections on the Linguistic Map of Pre-Islamic Arabia." *Arabian Archaeology and Epigraphy* 11 (2000): 28–79.

———. "Quelques réflexions sur les Saracènes, l'inscription de Rawwafa et l'armée romaine." In *Présence arabe dans le Croissant fertile avant l'Hégire,* ed. Hélène Lozachmeur, 93–101. Paris: Recherche sur les civilisations, 1995.

MacMullen, Ramsay. "Provincial Languages in the Roman Empire." In *Changes in the Roman Empire: Essays in the Ordinary,* ed. Ramsay MacMullen, 32–40. Princeton: Princeton University Press, 1990. Reprint, *American Journal of Philology* 67 (1960): 1–17.

Magen, Yitzhak. "Jerusalem as a Center of the Stone Vessel Industry during the Second Temple Period." In *Ancient Jerusalem Revealed,* ed. Hillel Geva, 244–256. Jerusalem: Israel Exploration Society, 1994.

———. "Kalandia: A Vineyard Farm and Winery of the Second Temple Times." *Qadmoniot* 17 (1987): 61–71.

———. "Mamre." In *The New Encyclopedia of Archaeological Excavations in the Holy Land,* ed. Ephraim Stern. Jerusalem: Israel Exploration Society / Carta; New York: Simon & Schuster, 1998.

———. "Mount Garizim and the Samaritans." In *Early Christianity in Context: Monuments and Documents,* ed. Frédéric Manns and Eugenio Alliata, 91–147. Jerusalem: Franciscan Printing Press, 1993.

———. "Qedumin: A Samaritan Site of the Roman-Byzantine Period." In *Early Christianity in Context,* ed. Frédéric Manns and Eugenia Alliata, 167–179. Jerusalem: Franciscan Printing Press, 1993.

———. "The Roman Theatre at Shechem." In *Sefer Ze'ev Vilnay* [Zev Vilnay's Jubilee Volume], ed. Eli Schiller, 260–277. Jerusalem: Hotsa'at sefarim Ari'el, 1984.

Magioncalda, Andreina. "Testimonianze sui prefetti di Mesopotamia (da Settimio Severo a Diocleziano)." *Studia et Documenta Historiae et Iuris* 48 (1982): 161–238.

Magness, Jodi. "Some Observations on the Roman Temple at Kedesh." *Israel Exploration Journal* 40 (1990): 173–181.

Majcherek, Grzegorz. "Gazan Amphorae: Typology Reconsidered." In *Hellenistic and Roman Pottery in the Eastern Mediterranean: Advances in Scientific Studies; Acts of the II Nieborów Pottery Workshop,* ed. Henryk Meyza and Jolanta Mlynarczyk, 163–178. Warsaw: Research Center for Mediterranean Archaeology, Polish Academy of Sciences, 1995.

Makaroun, Yasmine, and Lévon Nordiguian. "Les Qanater Zubaydé et l'alimentation en eau de Beyrouth et de ses environs à l'époque romaine." *Bulletin d'archéologie et d'antiquité libanaise* (1997): 262–289.

Malalas, John. *The Chronicle of John Malalas,* trans. Elizabeth Jeffreys, Michael Jeffreys, Roger Scott, et al. Melbourne: Australian Association for Byzantine Studies, 1986.

Manns, Frédéric, and Eugenio Alliata, eds. *Early Christianity in Context: Monuments and Documents.* Jerusalem: Franciscan Printing Press, 1993.

Mantel, Hugo. "The Causes of the Bar Kokhba Revolt." *Jewish Quarterly Review* 58 (1968): 224–242, 274–296.

———. "The Sadducees and the Pharisees." In *The World History of the Jewish People,* ed. Michael Avi-Yonah and Zvi Baras, 92–123. Jerusalem: Massada; New Brunswick: Rutgers University Press, 1977.

———. *Studies in the History of the Sanhedrin.* Cambridge, Mass.: Harvard University Press, 1961.

Ma'oz, Zvi. "Temple of Pan, 1991–1992." *Excavations and Surveys in Israel* 12 (1993): 2–7.

Maraval, Pierre. "La diversité de l'Orient chrétien." In *Histoire du christianisme, des origines à nos jours,* ed. Jean-Marie Mayeur, Charles Piétri, Luce Piétri, André Vauchez, and Marc Venard, vol. 1, 509–529. Paris: Desclée, 2000.

———. *Lieux saints et pélerinages d'Orient: Histoire et géographie des origines à la conquête arabe.* Paris: Le Cerf, 1985.

Mare, W. Harold. "Abila: A Thriving Greco-Roman City of the Decapolis." *Aram* 4 (1992): 57–77.

———. "The Technology of the Hydrological System at Abila of the Decapolis." *Studies in the History and Archaeology of Jordan* 5 (1995): 727–736.

Marek, Christian. "Die Expedition des Aelius Gallus nach Arabien im Jahre 25 v. Chr." *Chiron* 23 (1993): 121–156.

———. "Der römische Inschriftenstein von Baraqi." In *Arabia Felix: Beiträge zur Sprache und Kultur des vorislamischer Arabien; Festschrift Walter W. Müller zum 60. Geburtstag,* ed. Norbert Nebes, 178–190. Wiesbaden: Harrassowitz, 1994.

Marguerat, Daniel. *L'homme qui venait de Nazareth: Ce qu'on peut aujourd'hui savoir de Jésus.* 3rd ed. Aubonne: Éd. du Moulin, 1995.

———. "Juifs et chrétiens: La séparation." In *Histoire du christianisme, des origines à nos jours,* ed. Jean-Marie Mayeur, Charles Piétri, Luce Piétri, André Vauchez, and Marc Venard, vol. 1, 189–224. Paris: Desclée, 2000.

———, ed. *Le déchirement: Juifs et chrétiens au premier siècle.* Geneva: Labor & Fides, 1996.

Marguerat, Daniel, Enrico Norelli, and Jean-Michel Poffet, eds. *Jésus de Nazareth: Nouvelles approches d'une énigme.* Geneva: Labor & Fides, 1998.

Maricq, André. "Classica et orientalia." *Syria* 42 (1965): 103–111.

———. "Classica et orientalia: 2. Les dernières années de Hatra: L'alliance romaine." *Syria* 34 (1957): 288–296.

———. "Classica et orientalia: 3. La chronologie des dernières années de Caracalla." *Syria* 34 (1957): 297–302.

———. "Classica et orientalia: 5. Res gestae divi saporis." *Syria* 35 (1958): 295–360.

———. "La province d'"Assyrie' créée par Trajan: À propos de la guerre parthique de Trajan." *Syria* 36 (1959): 254–263.

———. "Vologésias, l'emporium de Ctésiphon." *Syria* 36 (1958): 264–276.

Marino, Luigi. *Le opere fortificate di Erode il Grande.* Verona: Cierre Edizioni, 1997.

Marot, Teresa. *Las monedas del Macellum de Gerasa (Yara, Jordania): Aproximación a la circulación monetaria en la provincia de Arabia.* Madrid: Museo Casa de la Moneda, 1998.

Marshall, Bruce A. *Crassus: A Political Biography.* Amsterdam: A. M. Hakkert, 1976.

Martano, Giuseppe. *Numenio d'Apamea: Un precursore del neo-platonismo.* Naples: Armanni, 1960.

Martial. *Epigrams,* trans. D. R. Shackleton Bailey. 3 vols. Loeb Classical Library.

Martín-Bueno, Manuel. "Notes préliminaires sur le Macellum de Gérasa." *Syria* 66 (1989): 177–199.

Mason, Steve N. *Josephus on the Pharisees.* Leiden: E. J. Brill, 1990.

Masson, Mikhail Evgen'evitch. "Two Palmyrene Stelae of the Merv Oasis." *East and West* 17 (1967): 239–247.

Matthews, John F. "The Tax Law of Palmyra." *Journal of Roman Studies* 74 (1984): 157–180.

Mattingly, Harold. *Coins of the Roman Empire in the British Museum.* Rev. ed. Vol. 3, *Nerva to Hadrian.* London: British Museum Publications, 1976.

Mattingly, Harold, and Edward A. Sydenham. *The Roman Imperial Coinage.* Vol. 2, *Vespasian to Hadrian.* London: Spink & Son, 1926.

"Maximus and Balbinus." In *Historia Augusta,* trans. David Magie, vol. 1, 448–485. Loeb Classical Library.

Mayeur, Jean-Marie, Charles Piétri, Luce Piétri, André Vauchez, and Marc Venard, eds. *Histoire du christianisme, des origines à nos jours.* 14 vols. Paris: Desclée, 1990–2000.

Mazzarino, Santo. "Sul nome del vento hipalus ('ippalo') in Plinio." *Helikon* 22–27 (1982–1987): vii-xiv.

McDermott, William Coffman. "Plotina Augusta and Nicomachus of Gerasa." *Historia* 26 (1977): 192–203.

McGinn, Bernard, John Joseph Collins, and Stephen J. Stein, eds. *The Encyclopedia of Apocalypticism.* New York: Continuum, 1998.

McKenzie, Judith. *The Architecture of Petra.* Oxford and New York: Oxford University Press, 1990.

McKenzie, Judith, and Angela Phippen. "The Chronology of the Principal Monuments at Petra." *Levant* 19 (1987): 145–165.

Mébarki, Farah. "Banyas: Le palais d'Agrippa II?" *Le monde de la Bible* 124 (January–February 2000): 66.

Meeks, Wayne A., and Robert L. Wilken. *Jews and Christians in Antioch in the First Four Centuries of the Common Era.* Missoula, Mont.: Scholars Press, 1978.

Meinhold, Peter. *Studien zu Ignatius von Antiochien.* Wiesbaden: F. Steiner, 1979.

Mellink, Maachtel J. "The Tumulus of Nemrud Dagi and Its Place in the Anatolian Tradition." *Asia Minor Studien* 3 (1991): 7–10.

Mendels, Doron. *The Rise and Fall of Jewish Nationalism.* New York: Doubleday, 1992.

Merlat, Pierre. *Jupiter Dolichenus: Essai d'interprétation et de synthèse.* Paris: Presses Universitaires de France, 1960.

———. *Répertoire des inscriptions et monuments figurés du culte de Jupiter Dolichenus.* Paris: P. Geuthner, 1951.

Meshorer, Ya'akov. *Ancient Jewish Coinage.* Dix Hills, N.Y.: Amphora Books, 1982.

———. "Ancient Jewish Coinage: Addendum I." *Israel Numismatic Journal* 11 (1990–1991): 104–132.

———. *City-Coins of Eretz-Israel and the Decapolis in the Roman Period.* Jerusalem: Israel Museum, 1985.

———. *Jewish Coins of the Second Temple Period.* Tel Aviv: Am Hassefer, 1967.

———. *Nabataean Coins.* Jerusalem: Institute of Archaeology, Hebrew University of Jerusalem, 1975.

———. *Tiberias, from the Foundation to the Arab Conquest.* Jerusalem, 1986.

Metcalf, William E. "The Antioch Hoard of Antoniniani and the Eastern Coinage of Trebonianus Gallus and Volusian." *American Numismatic Society: Museum Notes* 22 (1977).

———. "The End of Antioch's Silver Coinage." In *Les monnayages syriens: Quel apport poour l'histoire du Proche-Orient hellénistique et romain? Actes de la table ronde de Damas, 10–12 novembre 1999,* ed. Christian Augé and Frédérique Duyrat, 175–180. Beirut: Institut français d'archéologie du Proche-Orient, 2002.

———. "The Tell Kalak Hoard and Trajan's Arabian Mint." *American Numismatic Society: Museum Notes* 20 (1975): 39–108.

Meyer, Justus. "A Centurial Stone from Shavei Tziyyon." *Scripta classica israelica* 7 (1983–1984): 119–128.

Meyers, Carol L., Eric M. Meyers, Ehud Netzer, and Zeev Weiss. "The Dionysos Mosaic." In *Sepphoris in Galilee: Crosscurrents of Culture,* ed. Rebecca Martin Nagy, Carol L. Meyers, Eric M. Meyers, and Zeev Weiss, 111–115. Raleigh: North Carolina Museum of Art, 1996.

Meyers, Eric M. "Aspects of Roman Sepphoris." In *Early Christianity in Context: Monuments and Documents,* ed. Frédéric Manns and Eugenio Alliata, 29–36. Jerusalem: Franciscan Printing Press, 1993.

———, ed. *The Oxford Encyclopedia of Archaeology in the Near East.* New York and Oxford: Oxford University Press, 1997.

Meyers, Eric M., Ehud Netzer, and Carol L. Meyers. "Artistry on Stone: The Mosaics of Ancient Sepphoris." *Biblical Archaeologist* 50 (1987): 223–231.

———. *Sepphoris.* Winona Lake, Ind.: Eisenbrauns, 1992.

Meza, Alicia I. "The Egyptian Statuette in Petra and the Isis Cult Connection." *Annual of the Department of Antiquities of Jordan* 40 (1996): 167–176.

Michael the Syrian. *Chronique de Michel le Syrien, patriarche jacobite d'Antioche (1166–1199),* ed. Jean-Baptiste Chabot. 4 vols. Brussels: Culture et civilisation, 1963.

Migeotte, Léopold. *L'emprunt public dans les cités grecques.* Quebec: Éditions du Sphinx; Paris: Les Belles Lettres, 1984.

———. "Les finances publiques des cités grecques: Bilan et perspectives de recherche." *Topoi* 5 (1995): 7–32.

———. *Les souscriptions publiques dans les cités grecques.* Geneva: Droz; Quebec: Éditions du Sphinx, 1992.

Migne, Jacques-Paul, et al. *Patrologiae cursus completus: Series graeca.* 161 vols. Paris: Garnier Frères, 1857–1905.

Mildenberg, Leo. "Petra on the Frankincense Road?" *Transeuphratène* 10 (1995): 69–72.

———. "Petra on the Frankincense Road?—Again." *Aram* 8 (1996): 55–65.

Mildenberg, Leo, and Patricia Erhart Mottahedeh. *The Coinage of the Bar Kokhba War.* Aarau: Sauerländer, 1984.

Milik, Jósef Tadeusz. "Une bilingue araméo-grecque de 105/104 av. J.-C." In *Hauran II: Les installations de si 8 du sanctuaire à l'établissement viticole,* ed. Jacqueline Dentzer[-Feydy], Jean-Marie Dentzer, and Pierre-Marie Blanc, 269–275. Beirut: Institut français d'archéologie du Proche-Orient, 2003.

———. "Une inscription bilingue nabatéenne et grecque à Pétra." *Annual of the Department of Antiquities of Jordan* 21 (1976): 143–152.

———. "Inscriptions grecques et nabatéennes de Rawwafa." *Bulletin of the Institute of Archaeology,* no. 10 (1972): 54–58.

———. "Une lettre de Siméon Bar Kokheba." *Revue biblique* 60 (1953): 276–294.

———. "Nouvelles inscriptions nabatéennes." *Syria* 35 (1958): 227–251.

Milik, Jósef Tadeusz, and Jean Starcky. "Inscriptions récemment découvertes à Pétra." *Annual of the Department of Antiquities of Jordan* 20 (1975): 111–130.

Millar, Fergus. "Caravan Cities: The Roman Near East and Long Distance Trade by Land." In *Modus Operandi: Essays in Honour of Geoffrey Rickman,* ed. M. Austin, J. Harries, and C. Smith. London: Institute of Classical Studies, 1998.

———. "Dura-Europos under Parthian Rule." In *Das Partherreich und seine Zeugnisse: The Arsacid Empire, Sources and Documentation,* ed. Josef Wiesehöfer, 473–492. Stuttgart: F. Steiner, 1998.

———. "Empire, Community and Culture in the Roman Near East: Greeks, Syrians, Jews and Arabs." *Journal of Jewish Studies* 38 (1987): 143–164.

———. "Paul of Samosata, Zenobia and Aurelian: The Church, Local Culture and Political Allegiance in 3rd Century Syria." *Journal of Roman Studies* 61 (1971): 1–17.

———. "The Phoenician Cities: A Case Study of Hellenisation." *Proceedings of the Cambridge Philological Society* 209 (1983): 55–71.

———. "The Problem of Hellenistic Syria: The Interaction of Greek and Non-Greek Civilizations from Syria to Central Asia after Alexander." In *Hellenism in the East,* ed. Amélie Kuhrt and Susan Sherwin-White, 110–133. London: Duckworth, 1987.

———. "The Roman *Coloniae* of the Near East: A Study of Cultural Relations." In *Roman Eastern Policy and Other Studies in Roman History,* ed. Heikki Solin and Mika Kajava, 10–23. Helsinki: Finnish Society of Sciences and Letters, 1990.

———. *The Roman Near East (31 B.C.–A.D. 337).* Cambridge, Mass.: Harvard University Press, 1993.

———. "'Senatorial' Provinces: An Institutionalized Ghost." *Ancient World* 20 (1989): 93–97.

Miller, Stuart S. "On the Number of Synagogues in the Cities of Eretz Israel." *Journal of Jewish Studies* (1998): 51–66.

———. *Studies in the History and Traditions of Sepphoris.* Leiden: E. J. Brill, 1984.

Mimouni, Simon C. *Le judéo-christianisme ancien: Essais historiques.* Paris: Le Cerf, 1998.

———. "Les Nazoréens: Recherche étymologique et historique." *Revue biblique* 105 (1998): 205–262.

Mitchell, L. A. *Hellenistic and Roman Strata: A Study of the Stratigraphy of Tell Hesban from 2nd Century B.C. to 4th Century A.D.* Berrien Springs, Mich.: Andrews University Press, 1992.

Mitchell, Stephen. *Anatolia: Land, Men, and Gods in Asia Minor.* 2 vols. Oxford and New York: Clarendon Press, 1993.

———. "Summary, Seventh Sir Ronald Syme Memorial Lecture." *Times Literary Supplement* (1998): 12–13.

Moccheggiani Carpano, Claudio. *L'area del "Santuario siriaco del Gianicolo": Problemi archeologici e storico-religiosi.* Rome: Quasar, 1992.

Modrzejewski, Joseph, and Tadeusz Zawadzki. "La date de la mort d'Ulpien et la préfecture du prétoire au début du règne d'Alexandre Sévère." *Revue historique du droit français et étranger* (1967): 565–611.

Möller, Christa, and Götz Schmitt. *Siedlungen Palästinas nach Flavius Josephus.* Wiesbaden: Reichert, 1976.

Mommsen, Theodor. *Corpus inscriptionum latinarum.* Vol. 3, *Inscriptiones Asiae, provinciaeum Europae graecarum, Illyrici latinae.* 4 vols. Berlin: G. Reimer, 1873–1902.

———. *Corpus inscriptionum latinarum.* Vol. 10, *Inscriptiones Bruttiorum, Lucaniae, Campaniae, Sicilae, Sardiniae latinae.* 2 vols. Berlin: G. Reimer, 1883.

Mommsen, Theodor, Otto Hirschfeld, and Alfred von Domaszewski. *Corpus inscriptionum latinarum.* Vol. 3S, *Inscriptionum orientis et illyrici latinarum supplementum.* 2 vols. Berlin: G. Reimer, 1902.

Monloubou, Louis, and Henri Cazelles. *Apocalypses et théologie de l'espérance.* Paris: Le Cerf, 1977.

Moors, Steven Menno. *De Decapolis: Steden en dorpen in de romeinse provincies Syria en Arabia.* 's-Gravenhage: S. M. Moors, 1992.

Mor, Menahem. "The Roman Army in Eretz-Israel in the Years AD 70–132." In *The Defence of the Roman and Byzantine East,* ed. Philip Freeman and David L. Kennedy, 562–575. Oxford: British Archaeological Reports, 1986.

———. "Two Legions—The Same Fate?" *Zeitschrift für Papyrologie und Epigraphik* 62 (1986): 267–278.

Morange, Christophe, et al. "Étude paléoenvironnementale du port antique de Sidon: Premiers résultats du programme CEDRE." *Méditerranée* 94 (2000): 91–100.

Morrisson, Cécile. "Les monnaies." *Syria* 67 (1980): 267–287.

Mottu, Valérie. "La romanisation du paysage urbain dans les provinces de Syrie, Palestine et Arabie sous le Haut-Empire romain." Mémoire de DEA, Université de Tours, 1997.

Mougdad (al-), Ryad, Pierre-Marie Blanc, and Jean-Marie Dentzer. "Un amphithéâtre à Bostra?" *Syria* 67 (1990): 201–204.

Mougdad, Souleiman. "Note préliminaire sur le cryptoportique de Bosra, Syrie." In *Les cryptoportiques dans l'architecture romaine,* ed. Colloques internationaux du Centre national de la recherche scientifique, 411–412. Rome: École française de Rome, 1973.

Mougdad, Souleiman, and Christophe Makowski. "Nymphée de Bosra et ses abords." *Annales archéologiques arabes syriennes* 33 (1983): 35–46.

Mouterde, René. "Regards sur Beyrouth." *Mélanges de l'Université Saint-Joseph* 40 (1964): 163–166.

———. "Sarcophages de plomb trouvés en Syrie." *Syria* 10 (1929): 238–251.

———. "La strata Diocletiana et ses bornes milliaires." *Mélanges de l'Université Saint-Joseph* 15 (1930): 221–233.

Mouterde, René, and Antoine Poidebard. *Le limes de Chalcis: Organisation de la steppe en haute Syrie romaine; Documents aériens.* Paris: P. Geuthner, 1945.

Müller, Karl I., ed. *Fragmenta historicorum graecorum.* 5 vols. Paris: Firmin-Didot, 1841–1870.

Munier, Charles. "Où en est la question d'Ignace d'Antioche? Bilan d'un siècle de recherches 1870–1988." *Aufstieg und Niedergang der römischen Welt* 2.27.1 (1993): 359–484.

Murray, Robert. "The Characteristics of the Earliest Syriac Christianity." In *East of Byzantium: Syria and Armenia in the Formative Period,* ed. Nina G. Garsoïan, Thomas F. Mathews, and Robert W. Thomson, 3–16. Washington, D.C.: Dumbarton Oaks, 1982.

Murusillo, Herbert. *The Acts of the Pagan Martyrs: Acta Alexandrinorum.* Oxford: Clarendon Press, 1954.

Mussies, Gerard. "Marnas God of Gaza." *Aufstieg und Niedergang der römischen Welt* 2.18.4 (1990): 2412–2457.

Najafi (al-), Hazim. "The Inscriptions of Hatra." *Sumer* 39 (1983): 175–199.

Naster, Paul. "Le culte du dieu nabatéen Dousarès reflété par les monnaies d'époque impériale." In *Actes du IXe congrès international de numismatique, Berne, 1979,* 399–408. Louvain-la-Neuve: Association internationale des numismates professionnels, 1982.

Nau, François Nicolas, ed. *La Didascalie des douze apôtres.* Paris: P. Lethielleux, 1912.

Nebes, Norbert. *Arabia Felix: Beiträge zur Sprache und Kultur des vorislamischen Arabien; Festschrift Walter W. Müller zum 60. Geburtstag.* Wiesbaden: Harrassowitz, 1994.

Neesen, Lutz. *Untersuchungen zu den direkten Staatsabgaben der römischen Kaiserzeit (27 v. Chr.–284 n. Chr.).* Bonn: R. Habelt, 1980.

Negev, Avraham. *The Architecture of Mampsis: Final Report.* Vol. 1, *The Middle and Late Nabatean Periods.* Jerusalem: Institute of Archaeology, Hebrew University of Jerusalem, 1988.

———. *The Architecture of Mampsis: Final Report.* Vol. 2. *The Late Roman and Byzantine Periods.* Jerusalem: Institute of Archaeology, Hebrew University of Jerusalem, 1988.

———. *The Architecture of Oboda: Final Report.* Jerusalem: Institute of Archaeology, Hebrew University of Jerusalem, 1997.

———. "'Avdat—1989." *Excavations and Surveys in Israel* 12 (1993): 108–109.

———. "The Late Hellenistic and Early Roman Pottery of Nabatean Oboda." Jerusalem: Institute of Archaeology, Hebrew University of Jerusalem, 1986.

———. *The Nabatean Potter's Workshop at Oboda.* Bonn: R. Habelt, 1974.

———. "Obodas the God." *Israel Exploration Journal* 36 (1986): 56–60.

———. "The Temple of Obodas: Excavations at Oboda in July 1989." *Israel Exploration Journal* 41 (1991): 62–80.

Negev, Avraham, and Renée Sivan. "The Pottery of the Nabatean Necropolis at Mampsis." *Rei Cretariae Romanae fautorum* 17–18 (1977): 109–131.

Nehmé, Laïla. "L'espace cultuel à Pétra à l'époque nabatéenne." *Topoi* 7 (1997): 1023–1067.

———. "L'habitat rupestre dans le bassin de Pétra à l'époque nabatéenne." *Studies in the History and Archaeology of Jordan* 6 (1997): 281–288.

———. "Le site dans son milieu naturel." *Le monde de la Bible* 127 (2000): 30–31.

Nehmé, Laïla, and François Villeneuve. *Pétra: Métropole de l'Arabie antique.* Paris: Le Seuil, 1999.

Nercessian, Y. T., and L. A. Saryan. "Overstruck and Countermarked Coins of the Artaxiad Dynasty of Armenia." *Armenian Numismatic Journal* 22 (199): 21–62.

Nesselhauf, Herbert. *Corpus inscriptionum latinarum.* Vol. 16, *Diplomata militaria ex constitutionibus imperatorum de civitate et conubio militum veteranorumque expressa.* 2 vols. Berlin: W. de Gruyter, 1936–1955.

Netanyahu, Benzion, and Ephraim Avigdor Speiser. *The World History of the Jewish People.* Tel Aviv: Jewish History Publications; New Brunswick: Rutgers University Press, 1964.

Netzer, Ehud. *Channels and a Royal Estate from the Hellenistic Period in the Western Plains of Jericho.* Brunswick: Leichweiss-Institut für Wasserbau der Technischen Universität Braunschweig, 1984.

———. *Greater Herodium.* Jerusalem: Institute of Archaeology, Hebrew University of Jerusalem, 1981.

———. *Herodium: An Archaeological Guide.* Jerusalem: Cana, 1987.

Netzer, Ehud, Dominique Svenson, and Hendrik Svenson-Evers. *Die Paläste der Hasmonäer und Herodes' des Grossen, Sonderhefte der Antiken Welt.* Mainz: Ph. von Zabern, 1999.

Neubauer, Adolf. *Géographie du Talmud.* Paris: Michel Levy Frères, 1868. Reprint, Hildesheim: G. Olms, 1967.

Neusner, Jacob. *First Century Judaism in Crisis: Yohanan ben Zakkai and the Renaissance of Torah.* New York: Ktav, 1975.

———. "The Formation of Rabbinic Judaism: Yavneh (Jamnia) from A.D. 70 to 100." *Aufstieg und Niedergang der römischen Welt* 2.19.2 (1979): 3–42.

———. *From Politics to Piety: The Emergence of Pharisaic Judaism.* 2nd ed. New York: Ktav, 1979.

———. *A History of the Jews in Babylonia.* Vol. 1, *The Parthian Period.* Leiden: E. J. Brill, 1965.

———. *A History of the Jews in Babylonia.* Vol. 2, *The Early Sasanian Period.* Leiden: E. J. Brill, 1966.

———. *A Life of Rabban Yohanan ben Zakkai, ca. 1–80 ce.* Leiden: E. J. Brill, 1962. Reprint, 1970.

Nickelsburg, George W. E. *Studies on the Testament of Moses: Seminar Papers.* Cambridge, Mass.: Society of Biblical Literature, 1973.

Nicolet, Claude. *L'inventaire du monde.* Paris: Fayard, 1988.

Nicomachos of Gerasa. *Introduction arithmétique,* ed. and trans. Janine Bertier. Paris: Vrin, 1978.

———. *Introduction to Arithmetic,* trans. Martin Luther D'Ooge. London: Macmillan, 1972.

Nieskens, P. J. M. "Vers le zérotage définitif des ères préislamiques en Arabie du Sud antique." In *Arabian Studies in Honour of Mahmoud Ghul: Symposium at Yarmuk University, December 8–11, 1984,* ed. Moawiyah M. Ibrahim, 97–103. Wiesbaden: Harrassowitz, 1989.

Nijf, Onno M. van. *The Civic World of Professional Associations in the Roman East.* Amsterdam: J. C. Gieben, 1997.

Nikiprowetzky, Valentin. "Sicaires et zélotes: Une reconsidération." *Semitica* 23 (1973): 51–63.

Nixon, C. E. V., and Barbara Saylor Rodgers, eds. *In Praise of Later Roman Emperors: The Panegyrici Latini; Introduction, Translation, and Historical Commentary with the Latin Text of R. A. B. Mynors.* Berkeley: University of California Press, 1994.

Nodelman, Sheldon Arthur. "A Preliminary History of Characene." *Berytus* 13 (1960): 83–121.

Nodet, Étienne. *Baptême et résurrection: Le témoignage de Josèphe.* Paris: Le Cerf, 1999.

Nodet, Étienne, and Justin Taylor. *Essai sur les origines du christianisme.* Paris: Le Cerf, 1998.

Nordiguian, Lévon. "Le temple de Marjiyyat (Chhîm) à la faveur de nouvelles fouilles." *Topoi* 7 (1997): 945–964.

Nordiguian, Lévon, and Jean-François Salles, eds. *Aux origines de l'archéologie aérienne: A. Poidebard (1878–1955).* Beirut: Presses de l'Université Saint-Joseph, 2000.

Noret, Jacques. "La Société belge d'études Byzantines." *Byzantion* 54 (1984): 367–370.

Numenius of Apamaea. *Fragments,* ed. Édouard des Places. Paris: Les Belles Lettres, 1973.

Oates, David. *Studies in the Ancient History of Northern Iraq.* London: Oxford University Press, 1968.

Oates, David, and Joan Oates. "Aspects of Hellenistic and Roman Settlement in the Khabur Basin." In *Resurrecting the Past: A Joint Tribute to Adnan Bounni,* ed. Paolo Matthiae, Maurits van Loon, and Harvey Weiss, 227–248. Istanbul: Nederlands Historisch-Archaeologisch Instituut te Istanbul; Leiden: Nederlands instituut voor het Nabije Oosten, 1990.

O'Connor, Michael Patrick. "The Etymology of Saracen in Aramaic and Pre-Islamic Contexts." In *The Defence of the Roman and Byzantine East: Proceedings of a Colloquium Held at the University of Sheffield in April, 1986,* ed. Philip Freeman and David L. Kennedy, 603–632. Oxford: British Archaeology Reports, 1986.

Oden, Robert A., Jr. "Philo of Byblos and Hellenistic Historiography." *Palestine Exploration Quarterly* 110 (1978): 115–126.

Oleson, John Peter. *Greek and Roman Mechanical Water-Lifting Devices: The History of a Technology.* Toronto: University of Toronto Press, 1984.

———. *The Harbours of Caesarea Maritima.* Vol. 2, *The Finds and the Ship.* Oxford: British Archaeological Reports, 1994.

———. "The Origins and Design of Nabataean Water-Supply Systems." *Studies in the History and Archaeology of Jordan* 5 (1995): 707–719.

Oleson, John Peter, Erik de Bruijn, and M. Barbara Reeves. "Field Reports: Humayma." *ACOR Newsletter* [American Center of Oriental Research] 12, no. 1 (2000): 3.

Oliver, James H. "Minutes of a Trial Conducted by Caracalla at Antioch in A.D. 216." In *Mélanges helléniques offerts à Georges Daux,* 289–294. Paris: E. de Boccard, 1974.

———. "Notes on Documents of the Roman East." Section 1, "On the Great Inscription of Octavian Found at Rhosos." *American Journal of Archaeology* 45 (1941): 537–543.

Ooteghem, Jules van. *Lucius Licinius Lucullus.* Brussels: Académie royale de Belgique, 1959.

———. *Lucius Marcius Philippus et sa famille.* Brussels: Palais des Académies, 1961.

———. *Pompée le Grand, bâtisseur d'Empire.* Brussels: n. p., 1954.

Oppenheimer, A'haron. *The 'Am ha-Aretz: A Study in the Social History of the Jewish People in the Hellenistic-Roman Period.* Leiden: E. J. Brill, 1977.

Oren, Eliezer D. "Excavations at Qasrawet in North-Western Sinai: Preliminary Report." *Israel Exploration Journal* 32 (1982): 203–211.

Origen. *Contra Celsum,* ed. and trans. Henry Chadwick. Cambridge: Cambridge University Press, 1953. Reprint, with revisions and corrections, 1980.

Ormerod, Henry Arderne. *Piracy in the Ancient World.* Liverpool, U.K.: University Press of Liverpool, 1924. Reprint, New York, 1987.

Orosius, Paulus. *The Seven Books of History against the Pagans,* trans. Roy J. Deferrari. Washington, D.C.: Catholic University of America Press, 1964.

Ortali-Tarazi, Renata. "Beyrouth: À la lumière des découvertes récentes." In *Liban, l'autre rive,* ed. Institut du monde arabe, 192–193. Paris: Flammarion, 1998.

Ostrasz, Antoni A. "The Hippodrome of Gerasa: A Case of the Dichotomy of Art and Building Technology." *Studies in the History and Archaeology of Jordan* 5 (1995): 183–192.

———. "The Hippodrome of Gerasa: A Report on Excavations and Research 1982–1987." *Syria* 66 (1989): 51–77.

Papyrus Yadin. In *The Documents from the Bar Kokhba Period in the Cave of Letters,* vol. 1, *Greek Papyri,* ed. Naphtali Lewis. Jerusalem: Israel Exploration Society, 1989.

Parapetti, Roberto. "Public Building Design and Techniques in Roman Imperial Times: Achievements in Gerasa." *Studies in the History and Archaeology of Jordan* 5 (1995): 177–181.

Parisot, J.-P. "Quand la lune était rouge sang . . ." *Ciel et Espace* 204 (March–April 1985): 41–44.

Parker, S. Thomas. "The Defenses of the Roman and Byzantine Town." In *Umm el-Jimal: A Frontier Town and Its Landscape in Northern Jordan,* ed. Bert de Vries, 143–147. Portsmouth, R.I.: Journal of Roman Archaeology, 1998.

———. "Human Settlement at the Northern Head of the Gulf of al-'Aqaba: Evidence of Site Migration." *Studies in the History and Archaeology of Jordan* (1997): 189–193.

———. "The Nature of Rome's Arabian Frontier." In *Roman Frontier Studies 1989: Proceedings of the 15th International Congress of Roman Frontier Studies,* ed. Valerie A. Maxfield and Michael J. Dobson, 498–504. Exeter: University of Exeter Press, 1991.

———. "Peasants, Pastoralists and Pax Romana: A Different View." *Bulletin of the American Schools of Oriental Research* 265 (1987): 35–51.

———. "The Roman 'Aqaba Project: The 1994 Campaign." *Annual of the Department of Antiquities of Jordan* 40 (1996): 231–257.

———. "The Roman 'Aqaba Project: The 1996 Campaign." *Annual of the Department of Antiquities of Jordan* 42 (1998): 375–394.

———. "Roman Legionary Fortresses in the East." In *Roman Fortresses and Their Legions: Papers in Honour of George C. Boon,* ed. Richard J. Brewer, 121–138. London: Society of Antiquaries of London; Cardiff: National Museums and Galleries of Wales, 2000.

———. *Romans and Saracens: A History of the Arabian Frontier.* Philadelphia: American Schools of Oriental Research, 1986.

———. "The Typology of Roman and Byzantine Forts and Fortresses in Jordan." *Studies in the History and Archaeology of Jordan* 5 (1995): 251–260.

Parr, Peter J. "A Nabataean Sanctuary near Petra: A Preliminary Notice." *Annual of the Department of Antiquities of Jordan* 6–7 (1962): 21–23.

———. "Recent Discoveries at Petra." *Palestine Exploration Quarterly* 89 (1957): 5–16.

———. "A Sequence of Pottery from Petra." In *Near Eastern Archaeology in the Twentieth Century: Essays in Honor of Nelson Glueck,* ed. James A. Sanders, 348–381. Garden City, N.Y.: Doubleday, 1970.

Parr, Peter J., G. L. Harding, and J. E. Dayton. "Preliminary Survey in N. W. Arabia, 1968." *Bulletin of the Institute of Archaeology* 10 (1971): 23–61.

Parrot, André. *Le temple de Jérusalem.* Neuchâtel: Delachaux & Niestlé, 1954. 2nd ed., 1962.

Parsons, P. J., ed. *The Oxyrynchus Papyri.* Vol. 42. London: Egypt Exploration Society, 1974.

Paterculus, Velleius. *History of Rome,* trans. Frederick W. Shipley. Loeb Classical Library.

Patrich, Joseph. *The Formation of Nabatean Art: Prohibition of a Graven Image among the Nabateans.* Jerusalem: Magnes Press; Leiden: E. J. Brill, 1990.

———. "Herod's Theatre in Jerusalem: A New Proposal." *Israel Exploration Journal* 52 (2002): 231–239.

———. "A Sadducean Halacha and the Jerusalem Aqueduct." *Jerusalem Cathedra* 2 (1982): 25–39.

Paul. "Digesta." In *Corpus iuris civilis,* ed. Theodor Mommsen and Paul Krüger. 17th ed. Berlin: Weidmann, 1988.

Pauly, August Friedrich von, et al., eds. *Realencyclopädie der classischen Altertumswissenschaft.* Stuttgart: J. B. Metzler, 1894–.

Pausanias. *Description of Greece,* trans. W. H. S. Jones and H. A. Ormerod. 5 vols. Loeb Classical Library.

Peachin, Michael. "Philip's Program: From Mesopotamia to Rome in AD 244." *Historia* 40 (1991): 331–342.

Peacock, David, Philip Spencer, and D. F. Williams. *Amphorae and the Roman Economy: An Introductory Guide.* New York: Longman, 1986.

Pearson, H. F. "The House of the Roman Scribes: Architecture and History." In *The Excavations at Dura-Europos, Conducted by Yale University and the French Academy of Inscriptions and Letters: Preliminary Report of Sixth Season of Work, October 1932–March 1933,* ed. Mikhail Ivanovitch Rostovtzeff, 265–275. New Haven: Yale University Press, 1936.

Pekáry, Thomas. "Bemerkungen zur Chronologie des Jahrzehnts 250–260 n. Chr." *Historia* 11 (1962): 123–128.

Pelletier, Marcel. *Les Pharisiens: Histoire d'un parti méconnu.* Paris: Le Cerf, 1990.

Pennachietti, Fabrizio A. "L'iscrizione bilingue greco-partica dell'Eracle di Seleucia." *Mesopotamia* 22 (1987): 169–185.

Pensabene, Patrizio. "Marmi d'importazione, pietre locali e committenza nelle decorazione archittetonica di età severiana in alcuni centri delle province Syria e Palaestina e Arabia." In *Miscellanea in onore di Maria Floriani Squarciapino,* 275–422. Rome: L'Erma, 1998.

Perkins, Ann. *The Art of Dura-Europos.* Oxford: Clarendon Press, 1973.

———. *The Excavations at Dura Europos: Final Report.* Vol. 4, part 5, *The Glass.* New Haven: Yale University Press, 1963.

Perlman, Isadore, Jan Gunneweg, and Joseph Yellin. "Pseudo-Nabataean Ware and Pottery of Jerusalem." *Bulletin of the American Schools of Oriental Research* 262 (1986): 77–82.

Pernot, Laurent, ed. *Éloges grecs de Rome.* Paris: Les Belles Lettres, 1997.

Perowne, Stewart. *The Later Herods: The Political Background of the New Testament.* London: Hodder & Stoughton, 1958.

Perring, Dominic. "Excavations in the Souks of Beirut." *Berytus* 43 (1997–1998): 9–34.

Petrus Patricius. "Fragments." In *Fragmenta historicorum graecorum,* ed. Karl I. Müller, vol. 4, 181–191. Paris: Firmin-Didot, 1851.

Pflaum, Hans-Georg. *Les carrières procuratoriennes équestres sous le Haut-Empire romain.* Paris: P. Geuthner, 1982.

———. "La fortification de la ville d'Adraha d'Arabie (259–260 à 274–275) d'après des inscriptions récemment découvertes." *Syria* 29 (1952): 307–330.

Philipps, George, ed. *The Doctrine of Addai the Apostle.* London: Trübner, 1876.

Philo of Alexandria. *Legatio ad Gaium,* ed. and trans. Mary Smallwood. 2nd ed. Leiden: E. J. Brill, 1970.

———. *Quod omnis probus liber sit* [Every Good Man Is Free]. In *Philo,* vol. 9, trans. F. H. Colson, 1–101. Loeb Classical Library.

Philo of Byblos. *The Phoenician History: Introduction, Critical Text, Translation, Notes,* ed. and trans. Harold W. Attridge and Robert A. Oden Jr. Washington, D.C.: Catholic Biblical Association of America, 1981.

———. *The Phoenician History of Philo of Byblos,* ed. Albert I. Baumgarten. Leiden: E. J. Brill, 1981.

Philostrates. *The Life of Apollonius of Tyana,* trans. F. C. Conybeare. 2 vols. Loeb Classical Library.

———. "The Lives of the Sophists." In *Philostratus and Eunapius: The Lives of the Sophists,* trans. Wilmer Cave Wright. Loeb Classical Library.

Photinos, K. G. "Marinos von Tyros." In *Realencyclopädie der classischen Altertumswissenschaft,* ed. August Friedrich von Pauly et al. Stuttgart: J. B. Metzler, 1970.

Photius. *Bibliothèque,* ed. and trans. René Henry. 9 vols. Paris: Les Belles Lettres, 1959.

Picard, Gilbert. "La date de naissance de Jésus du point de vue romain." *Comptes rendus des séances de l'Académie des inscriptions et belles-lettres* (1995): 799–806.

Piccirillo, Michele. "La strada romana Esbus-Livias." *Liber annuus* 46 (1996): 285–300.

Piétri, Charles. "La géographie nouvelle: A. L'Orient." In *Histoire du christianisme, des origines à nos jours,* ed. Jean-Marie Mayeur, Charles Piétri, Luce Piétri, André Vauchez, and Marc Venard, vol. 2, 77–125. Paris: Desclée, 1995.

Pliny. *Natural History,* trans. H. Rackham. 10 vols. Loeb Classical Library.

Pliny the Younger. *Letters and Panegyricus,* trans. Betty Radice. 2 vols. Loeb Classical Library.

Plutarch. "Alexander." In *Plutarch's Lives,* trans. Bernadotte Perrin, vol. 7, 223–439. Loeb Classical Library.

———. "Antony." In *Plutarch's Lives,* trans. Bernadotte Perrin, vol. 9, 137–333. Loeb Classical Library.

———. "Cato the Younger." In *Plutarch's Lives,* trans. Bernadotte Perrin, vol. 8, 235–411. Loeb Classical Library.

———. "Crassus." In *Plutarch's Lives,* trans. Bernadotte Perrin, vol. 3, 313–423. Loeb Classical Library.

———. *Plutarch's Lives,* trans. Bernadotte Perrin. 11 vols. Loeb Classical Library.

———. "Pompey." In *Plutarch's Lives,* trans. Bernadotte Perrin, vol. 5, 115–325. Loeb Classical Library.

———. "Sayings of Kings and Commanders (Regum et imperatorum apophthegmata)," trans. Frank Cole Babbitt. In Plutarch, *Moralia,* vol. 3, 1–153. Loeb Classical Library.

Pohl, Hartel. *Die römische Politik und der Piraterie im östlichen Mittelmeer vom 3. bis 1. Jh. v. Chr.* Berlin and New York: W. de Gruyter, 1993.

Pohlsander, H. A. "Philip the Arab and Christianity." *Historia* 29 (1980): 463–473.

Poidebard, Antoine. *Un grand port disparu: Tyr; Recherches aériennes et sous-marines.* Paris: P. Geuthner, 939.

———. *La trace de Rome dans le désert de Syrie: Le limes de Trajan à la conquête arabe; Recherches aériennes (1925–1932).* Paris: P. Geuthner, 1934.

Poidebard, Antoine, and Jean Lauffray. *Sidon: Aménagements antiques du ports de Saïda.* Beirut: Ministère des Travaux Publics, 1951.

Polybios. *The Histories,* trans. W. R. Paton. Loeb Classical Library.

Poole, Reginald Stuart. *Catalogue of Greek Coins of Alexandria and the Nomes.* London: Trustees of the British Museum, 1892.

Porath, Pinhas. "A Fragmentary Greek Inscription from Tel Jezreel." *Tel Aviv* 24 (1997): 167–168.

Porphyry. "Chronica." In *Die Fragmente der griechischen Historiker,* ed. Félix Jacoby. Leiden: E. J. Brill, 1958.

———. *Plotinus,* trans. A. H. Armstrong. Loeb Classical Library, 1989–.

————. *Against the Christians: The Literary Remains,* ed. and trans. R. Joseph Hoffmann. Amherst, N.Y.: Prometheus Books, 1994.

Porton, Gary G. "Sadducees." In *The Anchor Bible Dictionary,* ed. David Noel Freedman, 892–895. New York: Doubleday, 1992.

Potter, David Stone. *Prophecy and History in the Crisis of the Roman Empire: A Historical Commentary on the Thirteenth Sibylline Oracle.* Oxford and New York: Clarendon Press, 1990.

————. "Rome and Palmyra: Odaenathus' Titulature and the Use of the *Imperium Maius.*" *Zeitschrift für Papyrologie und Epigraphik* 113 (1996): 271–285.

Potts, Daniel T. "Arabia and the Kingdom of Characene." In *Araby the Blest: Studies in Arabian Archaeology,* ed. Daniel T. Potts, 137–167. Copenhagen: Carsten Niebuhr Institute of Ancient Near Eastern Studies, 1988.

————. "Augustus, Aelius Gallus and the Periplus: A Re-Interpretation of the Coinage of San'â Class B." In *Arabia Felix: Beiträge zur Sprache und Kultur des vorislamischen Arabian; Festschrift Walter W. Müller zum 60. Geburtstag,* ed. Norbert Nebes, 212–222. Wiesbaden: Harrassowitz, 1994.

————. "Nabataean Finds from Thaj and Qatif." *Arabian Archaeology and Epigraphy* 2 (1991): 138–144.

Pouderon, Bernard. "Les chrétiens et la culture antique: A. Les premiers chrétiens et la culture grecque." In *Histoire du christianisme, des origines à nos jours,* ed. Jean-Marie Mayeur, Charles Piétri, Luce Piétri, André Vauchez, and Marc Venard, vol. 1, 817–880. Paris: Desclée, 2000.

————, ed. *Foi chrétienne et culture classique,* trans. M. Bourlet et al. Paris: Migne, 1998.

Pouilloux, Jean. "Deux inscriptions au théâtre sud de Gérasa." *Liber annuus* 27 (1977): 246–254.

————. "Une troisième dédicace au théâtre de Gérasa." *Liber annuus* 29 (1979): 276–278.

Pourkier, Aline. *L'hérésiologie chez Épiphane de Salamine.* Paris: Beauchesne, 1992.

Préaux, Claire. "Une source nouvelle sur l'annexion de l'Arabie par Trajan: Les papyrus Michigan 465 et 466." In *Mélanges Joseph Hombert,* 123–139. Brussels: Université Libre de Bruxelles, 1950–1951.

Price, Jonathan T. *Jerusalem under Siege: The Collapse of the Jewish State, 66–70 C.E.* Leiden and New York: E. J. Brill, 1992.

Price, Martin Jessop, and Bluma Trell. *Coins and Their Cities: Architecture on the Ancient Coins of Greece, Rome, and Palestine.* London: Vecchi, 1977.

Pritchard, James B. *Recovering Sarepta, a Phoenician City.* Princeton: Princeton University Press, 1978.

————. "The Roman Port at Sarafand (Sarepta): Preliminary Report on the Seasons of 1969 and 1970." *Bulletin du Musée de Beyrouth* 24 (1971): 39–56.

"Probus." In *Historia Augusta,* trans. David Magie, vol. 3, 334–385. Loeb Classical Library.

Procopios. *The Anecdota or Secret History,* trans. H. B. Dewing. Vols. 6–7 of *Procopius.* Loeb Classical Library.

Propospographia Imperii Romani saec. I.II.III . . . Berlin: W. de Gruyter, 1933–.

Ptolemy. *Geographia,* ed. C. F. A. Nobbe. Hildesheim: G. Olds, 1966.

————. *Tetrabiblos,* trans. F. E. Robbins. Loeb Classical Library.

Pucci, Miriam. "Il movimento insurrezionale in Giudea (117–118 a.C.)." *Scripta classica israelica* 4 (1978): 63–76.

Puech, Émile. "Note d'épigraphie palestinienne: Le dieu Turmasgada à Césarée Maritime." *Revue biblique* 89 (1982): 210–221.

Puech, Henri-Charles. "Le Manichéisme, son fondateur, sa doctrine." Paris: Civilisations du Sud / SAEP, 1949.

Quet, Marie-Henriette. "Atemporalité du mythe et temps de l'image: Les mosaïques romaines figurant une dextrarum iunctio de 'noces' légendaires grecques." In *Constructions du temps dans le monde grec antique,* ed. Catherine Darbo-Peschanski, 169–218. Paris: Centre national de la recherche scientifique, 2000.

———. "La mosaïque dite d'Aiôn de Shahba-Philippopolis, Philippe l'Arabe et la conception hellène de l'ordre du monde, en Arabie, à l'aube du christianisme." *Cahiers Glotz* 10 (1999): 266.

———. "Naissance d'image: La mosaïque des Thérapénides d'Apamée de Syrie, représentation figurée des connaissances encycliques, 'servantes' de la philosophie hellène." *Cahiers du Centre Glotz* 4 (1993): 129–187.

Raban, Avner. "In Search of Straton's Tower." In *Caesarea Papers,* ed. Robert Lindley Vann, 7–22. Ann Arbor: University of Michigan Press, 1992.

Raban, Avner, and Kenneth G. Holum. *Caesarea Maritima: A Retrospective after Two Millenia.* Leiden and New York: E. J. Brill, 1996.

Rabin, Zeev. "Dio, Herodian and Severus' Second Parthian War." *Chiron* 5 (1975): 419–441.

Raepsaet, Georges, and Marie-Thérèse Raepsaet-Charlier. "La Maison aux Colonnes Trilobées." In *Apamée de Syrie: Bilan des recherches archéologiques 1973–1979,* ed. Janine Balty, 181–193. Brussels: Centre belge de recherches archéologiques à Apamée de Syrie, 1984.

Ragette, Friedrich. *Baalbek.* London: Chatto & Windus, 1980.

Rahmani, Leir Y. "More Lead Coffins from Israel." *Israel Exploration Journal* 37 (1987): 123–146.

Rajak, Tessa. "Justus of Tiberias." *Classical Quarterly* 23 (1973): 344–368.

———. "Was There a Roman Charter for the Jews?" *Journal of Roman Studies* 74 (1984): 107–123.

Rampoldi, Tiziana. "I 'kestoi' di Giulio Africano e l'imperatore Severo Alessandro." *Aufstieg und Niedergang der römischen Welt* 2.34.3 (1997): 2451–2470.

Ramsay, William M. "Studies in the Roman Province Galatia." *Journal of Roman Studies* 14 (1924): 201–203.

Rappaport, Uriel. "The Emergence of Hasmonean Coinage." *American Jewish Studies Review* 1 (1976): 171–186.

———. "How Anti-Roman was the Galilee?" In *The Galilee in Late Antiquity,* ed. Lee I. Levine, 95–102. New York and Cambridge, Mass.: Jewish Theological Seminary of America, 1992.

———. "Les Iduméens en Égypte." *Revue de philologie, de littérature et d'histoire anciennes* 43 (1969): 71–82.

———. "Numismatics." In *The Cambridge History of Judaism,* vol. 1, *The Persian Period,* 25–59. Cambridge: Cambridge University Press, 1984.

Raschke, Manfred G. "New Studies in Roman Commerce with the East." *Aufstieg und Niedergang der römischen Welt* 2.9.2 (1978): 604–1361.

———. "The Role of Oriental Commerce in the Economies of the Cities of the Eastern Mediterranean in the Roman Period." In *The Archaeology of Trade in the East Mediterranean: A Symposium,* ed. Eric Meyers and William West, 68–77. Tallahassee, Fla.: Archaeological News, 1979.

Rasson-Seigne, Anne-Michèle, and Jacques Seigne. "Notes préliminaires à l'étude de la voie romaine Gérasa/Philadelphia." *Annual of the Department of Antiquities of Jordan* 39 (1995): 193–210.

Rautman, Marcus. "Neutron Activation Analysis of Cypriot and Related Ceramics at the University of Missouri." In *Hellenistic and Roman Pottery in the Eastern Mediterranean: Advances in Scientific Studies; Acts of the II Nieborów Pottery Workshop,* ed. Henryk Meyza and Jolanta Mlynarczyk, 331–349. Warsaw: Research Center for Mediterranean Archaeology, Polish Academy of Sciences, 1995.

Reardon, Bryan P. *Courants littéraires grecs des IIe et IIIe siècles apr. J.-C.* Paris: Les Belles Lettres, 1971.

Reddé, Michel. *Mare Nostrum: Les infrastructures, le dispositif et l'histoire de la marine militaire sous l'Empire romain.* Rome: École française de Rome, 1986.

"Règle de la communauté." In *La Bible: Écrits intertestamentaires,* ed. André Dupont-Sommer and Marc Philonenko, 3–52. Paris: Gallimard, 1987.

Reisner, George Andrew, Clarence Stanley Fisher, and David Gordon Lyon, eds. *Harvard Excavations at Samaria, 1908–1910.* Vol. 1. Cambridge, Mass.: Harvard University Press, 1924.

Renan, Ernest. *Mission de Phénicie.* Paris: Imprimerie impériale, 1846.

Rey-Coquais, Jean-Paul. *Arados et sa pérée aux époques grecque, romaine et byzantine: Recueil des témoignages littéraires anciens, suivi de recherches sur les sites, l'histoire, la civilisation.* Paris: P. Geuthner, 1974.

———. "Deir el Qalaa." *Topoi* 9 (1999): 607–628.

———. "Du sanctuaire de Pan à la 'guirlande' de Méléagre: Cultes et cultures dans la Syrie hellénistique." In *Aspetti e Problemi dell'Ellenismo: Atti del Convegno di studi, Pisa 6–7 novembre 1992,* ed. Biagio Virgilio, 47–90. Pisa: Giardini, 1994.

———. "Une inscription du Liban-Nord." *Mélanges de l'Université Saint-Joseph* 47 (1972): 87–105.

———. *Inscriptions grecques et latines de la Syrie.* Vol. 6, *Baalbek et Beqa'.* Paris: P. Geuthner, 1967.

———. *Inscriptions grecques et latines de la Syrie.* Vol. 7, *Arados et régions voisines.* Paris: P. Geuthner, 1970.

———. "Laodicée sur mer et l'armée romaine à partir de quelques inscriptions." In *The Roman and Byzantine Army in the East,* ed. Edward Dąbrowa, 149–163. Cracow: Drukarnia Uniwersytetu Jagiellonskiego, 1994.

———. "Lucius Iulius Agrippa et Apamée." *Annales archéologiques arabes syriennes* 23 (1973): 39–84.

———. Note in Maurice Dunand, "Tombe peinte dans la campagne de Tyr." *Bulletin du Musée de Beyrouth* 18 (1965): 49–51.

———. "Note sur deux sanctuaires de la Syrie romaine." *Topoi* 7 (1997): 929–944.

———. "Onomastique et histoire de la Syrie gréco-romaine." In *Actes du VIIe Congrès international d'épigraphie grecque et latine, Constantsa, 9–15 septembre 1977,* ed. D. M. Pippidi, 171–183. Bucharest: Editura Academiei; Paris: Les Belles Lettres, 1979.

————. "Philadelphie de Coelésyrie." *Annual of the Department of Antiquities of Jordan* 25 (1981): 25–31.

————. "Qalaat Faqra: Un monument du culte impérial dans la montagne libanaise." *Topoi* 9 (1999): 629–664.

————. "Syrie romaine, de Pompée à Dioclétien." *Journal of Roman Studies* 68 (1978): 44–73.

————. "Les villes amirales de l'Orient gréco-romain." In *The Roman and Byzantine Army in the East,* ed. Edward Dąbrowa, 149–163. Cracow: Drukarnia Uniwersytetu Jagiellonskiego, 1994.

Reynolds, Joyce. "Further Information on Imperial Cult at Aphrodisias." *Studii Clasice* 24 (1986): 109–117.

————. "New Evidence for the Imperial Cult in Julio-Claudian Aphrodisias." *Zeitschrift für Papyrologie und Epigraphik* 43 (1981): 317–327.

Reynolds, Paul. "Pottery Production and Economic Exchange in Second Century Beirut." *Berytus* 43 (1997–1998): 35–110.

Rhoads, David M. *Israel in Revolution, 6–74 C.E.: A Political History Based on the Writings of Josephus.* Philadelphia: Fortress Press, 1976.

Ribichini, Sergio. *Poenus Advena: Gli dei fenici e l'interpretazione classica.* Rome: Consiglio nazionale delle ricerche, 1985.

————. "Questions de mythologie phénicienne d'après Philon de Byblos." In *Religio Phoenicia,* ed. Corinne Bonnet, Edward Lipinski, and Patrick Marchetti, 41–52. Namur: Société des études classiques, 1986.

Riccobono, Salvatore, et al., eds. *Fontes iuris romani anteiustiniani.* 2nd ed. Florence: G. Barbèra, 1941.

Richard, Marcel. "Malchion et Paul de Samosate: Le témoignage d'Eusèbe de Césarée." *Ephemerides theologicae lovanienses* 35 (1959): 325–338.

Richardson, Cyril Charles. *The Christianity of Ignatius of Antioch.* New York: Columbia University Press, 1935.

Richardson, J. S. "The Administration of Provinces." In *Cambridge Ancient History,* vol. 9, 564–571. Cambridge: Cambridge University Press, 1994.

Riedmatten, Henri de. *Les actes du procès de Paul de Samosate: Étude sur la christologie du 3e au 4e siècle.* Fribourg: Éditions St-Paul, 1952.

Rigsby, Kent J. *Asylia: Territorial Inviolability in the Hellenistic World.* Berkeley: University of California Press, 1996.

Ringel, Joseph. *Césarée de Palestine: Étude historique et archéologique.* Paris: Ophrys, 1975.

Ritterling, Emil. "Legio." In *Realencyclopädie der classischen Altertumswissenschaft,* ed. August Friedrich von Pauly et al. Stuttgart: J. B. Metzler, 1894–.

Rivkin, Ellis. *A Hidden Revolution.* Nashville: Abingdon, 1978.

Rizzo, Francesco Paolo. *Le fonti per la storia della conquista pompeiana della Siria.* Palermo: Banco de Sicilia, Fondazione per l'incremento economico culturale e turistica della Sicilia Ignazio Mormino, 1963.

Robert, Jeanne, and Louis Robert. "Bulletin épigraphique." *Revue des études grecques* (1951). Reprinted in *Bulletin épigraphique 2 (1940–1951).* Paris: Les Belles Lettres, 1972.

Robert, Louis. "Contribution à la topographie de villes de l'Asie Mineure méridionale." *Comptes rendus des séances de l'Académie des inscriptions et belles-lettres* (1951): 254–259.

Robin, Christian. "Autres Objets d'Arabie." In *Arabie heureuse, Arabie déserte: Les antiquités arabiques du Musée du Louvre,* ed. Christian Robin and Yves Calvet, 265–269. Paris: Éditions de la Réunion des musées nationaux, 1997.

———. "Les plus anciens monuments de la langue arabe." In "L'Arabie antique de Karaib'îl à Mahomet," ed. Christian Robin. Special issue, *Revue du monde musulman et de la Méditerranée* 61 (1991): 13–116.

———. "Sheba II: Dans les inscriptions sud-arabiques." In *Supplément au Dictionnaire de la Bible,* ed. Jacques Briend and Édouard Cothenet, cols. 1047–1245. Paris: Letouzey & Ané, 1996.

Robinson, Edward Stanley Gotch. "Coins from Petra, etc." *Numismatic Chronicle* (1936): 288–291.

Rochais, Gérard. "L'influence de quelques idées-forces de l'apocalyptique sur certains mouvements messianiques et prophétiques populaires juifs du Ier siècle." In *Jésus de Nazareth: Nouvelles approches d'une énigme,* ed. Daniel Marguerat, Enrico Norelli, and Jean-Michel Poffet, 177–208. Geneva: Labor & Fides, 1998.

Roche, Marie-Jeanne. "Le culte d'Isis et l'influence égyptienne à Pétra." *Syria* 64 (1987): 217–222.

———. "Khirbet et-Tannûr et les contacts entre Édomites et Nabatéens: Une nouvelle approche." *Transeuphratène* 18 (1999): 59–69.

Rochette, Bruno. *Le latin dans le monde grec: Recherches sur la diffusion de la langue et des lettres latines.* Brussels: Latomus, 1997.

Roddaz, Jean-Michel. *Marcus Agrippa.* Rome: École française de Rome; Paris: E. de Boccard, 1984.

Roller, Duane W. *The Building Program of Herod the Great.* Berkeley: University of California Press, 1998.

———. "Straton's Tower: Some Additional Thoughts." In *Caesarea Papers,* ed. Robert Lindley Vann, 23–25. Ann Arbor: University of Michigan Press, 1992.

Romanis, Federico de. "Hypalos: Distanze e venti tra Arabia e India nella scienza ellenistica." *Topoi* 7 (1997): 671–692.

Ronzevalle, Sébastien. "Inscription bilingue de Deir el-Qala'a dans le Liban, près de Béryte." *Revue archéologique* 2 (1930): 29–49.

Roschinski, Hans P. "Sprachen, Schriften und Inschriften in Nordwestarabien." *Bonner Jahrbücher* 180 (1980): 155–188.

Rosen, Haiim B. "Die Sprachsituation im römischen Palästina." In *Die Sprachen im römischen Reich der Kaiserzeit: Kolloquium vom 8. bis 10. April 1974,* ed. Günter Neumann and Jürgen Untermann, 215–239. Bonn: R. Habelt, 1980.

Rosenberger, Mayer. *The Coinage of Eastern Palestine and Legionary Countermarks, Bar-Kochba Overstrucks.* Jerusalem: Rosenberger, 1978.

Ross, Steven. "The Last King of Edessa: New Evidence from the Middle Euphrates." *Zeitschrift für Papyrologie und Epigraphik* 97 (1993): 187–206.

Rostovtzeff, Mikhail Ivanovitch. *Caravan Cities.* Oxford: Clarendon Press, 1932.

———. "Interior Decoration." In *The Excavations at Dura-Europos, Conducted by Yale University and the French Academy of Inscriptions and Letters: Preliminary Report of Sixth Season of Work, October 1932–March 1933,* ed. Mikhail Ivanovitch Rostovtzeff, 275–279. New Haven: Yale University Press, 1936.

———. "Res Gestae Divi Saporis and Dura." *Berytus* 8 (1943): 7–66.

———. "The Residents of the House." In *The Excavations at Dura-Europos, Con-*

ducted by Yale University and the French Academy of Inscriptions and Letters: Preliminary Report of Sixth Season of Work, October 1932–March 1933, ed. Mikhail Ivanovitch Rostovtzeff, 299–304. New Haven: Yale University Press, 1936.

———. *Social and Economic History of the Hellenistic World.* 3 vols. Oxford: Clarendon Press, 1941.

Rostovtzeff, Mikhail Ivanovitch, et al., eds. *The Excavations at Dura-Europos: Final Report.* Vol. 5, *Parchments and Papyri.* New Haven: Yale University Press, 1955.

Rostovtzeff, Mikhail Ivanovitch, Frank E. Brown, and Charles Bradford Welles, eds. *The Excavations at Dura-Europos, Conducted by Yale University and the French Academy of Inscriptions and Letters.* Vols. 7–8, *Preliminary Report of the Seventh and Eighth Seasons of Work, 1933–1934 and 1934–1935.* New Haven: Yale University Press, 1939.

Roth, Jonathan. "The Length of the Siege of Masada." *Scripta classica israelica* 14 (1995): 87–110.

Rothenberg, Benno. "Timna." In *The New Encyclopedia of Archaeological Excavations in the Holy Land,* ed. Ephraim Stern. Jerusalem: Israel Exploration Society / Carta; New York: Simon & Schuster, 1983.

———. *Timna, Tal des biblischen Kupfers: Ausgrabungen in Timna-Tal (Israel) 1964–1972 durch die Arabah-Expedition.* Bochum: Bergbau Museum, 1973.

Rouanet-Liesenfelt, Anne-Marie. "Les plantes médicinales de Crète à l'époque romaine." *Cretan Studies* 3 (1992): 173–190.

Rougé, Jean, ed. *Expositio totius mundi et gentium: Introduction, texte critique, traduction, notes et commentaire.* Paris: Le Cerf, 1966.

Roussel, Pierre. "Décret des péliganes de Laodicée-sur-mer." *Syria* 23 (1942–1943): 21–32.

———. "Un Syrien au service de Rome et d'Octave." *Syria* 15 (1934): 33–74.

Roussel, Pierre, and Fernand de Visscher. "Les inscriptions du temple de Dmeir." *Syria* 23 (1942–1943): 173–200.

Roxan, Margaret M. *Roman Military Diplomas 1954–1977.* London: Institute of Archaeology, 1978.

———. *Roman Military Diplomas 1978–1984.* London: Institute of Archaeology, 1985.

———. *Roman Military Diplomas 1985–1993.* London: Institute of Archaeology, 1994.

Rozenberg, Silvia. "The Wall Paintings of the Herodian Palace at Jericho." In *Judaea and the Greco-Roman World in the Time of Herod in the Light of Archaeological Evidence,* ed. Klaus Fittschen and Gideon Foerster, 121–138. Göttingen: Vandenhoeck & Ruprecht, 1996.

Ruffing, Kai. "Die Geschäfte des Aurelius Nebuchelos." *Laverna* 11 (2000): 71–105.

———. "Wege in den Osten." In *Stuttgarter Kolloquium zur historischen Geographie des Altertums, 7, 1999: Zu Wasser und zu Land—Werkehrswege in der antiken Welt,* ed. Eckart Olshausen and Holger Sonnabend, 360–378. Stuttgart: Franz Steiner Verlag, 2002.

Russell, David Syme. *The Method and Message of Jewish Apocalyptic 200 bc–ad 100.* Philadelphia: Westminster Press, 1964.

Russell, K. W. "The Earthquake Chronology of Palestine and Northwest Arabia." *Bulletin of the American Schools of Oriental Research* 260 (1985): 37–59.

Safar, Fuad. "Inscriptions from Hatra." *Sumer* 17 (1961): 9–42 (Arabic section).

Safrai, Shemuel. "The Holy Congregation in Jerusalem." *Scripta hiereosolymitana* 23 (1972): 62–78.

Safrai, Shemuel, and Menahem Stern. *The Jewish People in the First Century: Historical Geography, Political History, Social, Cultural and Religious Life and Institutions.* 2 vols. Assen: Van Gorcum, 1974–1976.

Safrai, Ze'ev. *The Economy of Roman Palestine.* London and New York: Routledge, 1994.

Saldarini, Anthony J. "Pharisees." In *The Anchor Bible Dictionary,* ed. David Noel Freedman, 289–303. New York: Doubleday, 1992.

———. *Pharisees, Scribes and Sadducees in Palestinian Society: A Sociological Approach.* Wilmington, Del.: M. Glazier, 1988.

Saliou, Catherine. "Du portique à la rue à portiques: Les rues à colonnades de Palmyre dans le cadre de l'urbanisme romain impérial, originalité et conformisme." In "Palmyra and the Silk Road: International Colloquium, Palmyra, 7–11 April 1992." Special issue, *Annales archéologiques arabes syriennes* 42 (1996): 319–330.

Salles, Jean-François. "Fines Indiae, ardh el-Hind: Recherches sur le devenir de la mer Érythrée." In *The Roman and Byzantine Army in the East: Proceedings of a colloqium* [sic] *held at the Jagiellonian University, Kraków in September 1992,* ed. Edward Dąbrowa, 165–187. Cracow: Drukarnia Uniwersytetu Jagiellonskiego, 1994.

———. Review of *Ikaros,* by Lise Hannestad. *Syria* 64 (1987): 162–165.

Salzmann, Dieter. "Sabina in Palmyra." In *Festschrift für Nicolaus Himmelmann,* ed. Hans-Ulrich Cain, Hanns Gabelmann, and Dieter Salzmann, 361–368. Mainz: Ph. von Zabern, 1989.

Sanders, E. P. *The Historical Figure of Jesus.* London: Allen Lane / Penguin Press, 1993.

———. *Judaism: Practice and Belief, 63 bce–66 ce.* London: SCM Press; Philadelphia: Trinity Press International, 1992.

Sandmel, Samuel. *Herod: Profile of a Tyrant.* Philadelphia: Lippincott, 1967.

Sanford, Eva Matthews. "The Career of Aulus Gabinius." *Transactions and Proceedings of the American Philological Association* 70 (1939): 64–92.

Sanlaville, Paul. "Milieu naturel et irrigation en Syrie." In *Techniques et pratiques hydro-agricoles traditionnelles et domaine irrigué: Approche multidisciplinaire des modes de culture avant la motorisation en Syrie,* ed. Bernard Geyer, 3–21. Paris: P. Geuthner, 1990.

———. "Les variations holocènes du niveau de la mer au Liban." *Revue de géographie de Lyon* 45 (1970): 279–304.

Sartre, Maurice. *D'Alexandre à Zénobie.* Paris: Fayard, 2001.

———. *L'Anatolie hellénistique, de l'Egée au Caucase: 334–31 av. J.-C.* Paris: A. Colin, 2003.

———. "Arabs and the Desert Peoples." In *Cambridge Ancient History,* 2nd ed., vol. 12. Cambridge: Cambridge University Press, forthcoming.

———. *L'Asie Mineure et l'Anatolie d'Alexandre à Dioclétien.* Paris: A. Colin, 1995.

———. "Bostra." In *Reallexicon für Antike und Christentum,* cols. 98–149. Stuttgart: A. Hiersemann, 2002.

———. *Bostra: Des origines à l'Islam.* Paris: P. Geuthner, 1985.

———. "Les colonies romaines dans le monde grec: Essai de synthèse." *Electrum.* 5 (2001): 111–152.

———. "Communautés villageoises et structures sociales d'après l'épigraphie de la Syrie du Sud." In *L'Epigrafia del villagio,* ed. Alda Calbi, Angela Donati, Giancarlo Susini, and Gabriella Poma, 117–135. Faenza: Fratelli Lega, 1993.

———. "La construction de l'identité civique des villes de la Syrie hellénistique et romaine." In *Idéologies et valeurs civiques dans le monde romain: Hommage à Claude Lepelley; Actes d'un colloque tenu à Paris les 25 et 26 septembre 2001,* ed. Hervé Inglebert, 93–105. Paris: Picard, 2002.

———. "Du fait divers à l'histoire des mentalités: À propos de quelques noyés et de trois petits cochons." *Syria* 70 (1993): 51–67.

———. "Une garnison romaine aux marges de l'Arabie romaine: Mothana." *Syria.* Forthcoming.

———. "Gouverneurs d'Arabie anciens et nouveaux: Textes inédits." In Επιγραπηαι: *Miscellanea epigrafica in onore di Lidio Gasperini,* ed. Gianfranco Paci, 971–990. Tivoli: Tipigraf, 2000.

———. *Inscriptions grecques et latines de la Syrie.* Vol. 13.1, *Bostra.* Paris: P. Geuthner, 1982.

———. *Inscriptions grecques et latines de la Syrie.* Vol. 13.2, *Bostra (Supplément) et la plaine de la Nuqra.* Beirut: Institut français d'archéologie du Proche-Orient, forthcoming.

———. *Inscriptions grecques et latines de la Syrie.* Vol. 14, *Adraha, le Jawlan oriental et la Batanée.* Beirut: Institut français d'archéologie du Proche-Orient, forthcoming.

———. *Inscriptions grecques et latines de la Syrie.* Vol. 16.2, *Le Djebel al-ŒArab: La montagne et le désert.* Beirut: Institut français d'archéologie du Proche-Orient, forthcoming.

———. *Inscriptions grecques et latines de la Syrie.* Vol. 21, *Inscriptions grecques et latines de la Jordanie.* Vol. 4, *Pétra et la Nabatène méridionale.* Paris: P. Geuthner, 1993.

———. "Lakhmids." In *Late Antiquity: A Guide to the Postclassical World,* ed. Glen W. Bowersock, Peter Brown, and Oleg Grabar, 536–537. Cambridge, Mass.: Harvard University Press, 1999.

———. "Les manifestations du culte impérial dans les provinces syriennes et en Arabie." In *Rome et ses provinces: Genèse et diffusion d'une image du pouvoir; Hommages à Jean-Charles Balty,* ed. Athéna Tsingarida and Cécile Evers, 167–186. Brussels: Le Livre Timperman, 2001.

———. "Les metrokômiai de Syrie du Sud." *Syria* 76 (1999): 197–222.

———. *L'Orient romain: Provinces et sociétés provinciales en Méditerranée orientale d'Auguste aux Sévères (31 avant J.-C.–235 après J.-C.).* Paris: Le Seuil, 1991.

———. "L'Orient sémitique." In *Rome et l'intégration de l'Empire,* ed. Claude Lepelley, 385–433. Paris: Presses Universitaires de France, 1998.

———. "Palmyre, cité grecque." In "Palmyra and the Silk Road: International Colloquium, Palmyra, 7–11 April 1992." Special issue, *Annales archéologiques arabes syriennes* 42 (1996): 385–405.

———. "Le peuplement et le développement du Hauran antique à la lumière des inscriptions grecques et latines." In *Hauran: Recherches archéologiques sur la Syrie du sud à l'époque hellénistique et romaine,* ed. Jean-Marie Dentzer, 189–204. Paris: P. Geuthner, 1985.

———. "Les progrès de la citoyenneté romaine dans les provinces romaines de Syrie et d'Arabie sous le Haut-Empire." In *Roman Onomastics in the Greek East, Social and Political Aspects: Proceedings of the International Colloquium on Roman Onomastics, Athens, 7–9 September 1993*, ed. A. D. Rizakis, 327–329. Athens: Research Centre for Greek and Roman Antiquity / National Hellenic Research Foundation, 1996.

———. "Les progrès de la citoyenneté romaine en Arabie." *Studies in the History and Archaeology of Jordan* 4 (1992): 327–329.

———. "Romains et Italiens en Syrie: Contribution à l'histoire de la première province romaine de Syrie." In *The Greek East in the Roman Context: Proceedings of a Colloquium Organised by the Finnish Institute at Athens, May 21–22, 1999*, ed. Olli Salomies, 127–140. Vammala: Foundation of the Finnish Institute at Athens, 2001.

———. "Rome et les Nabatéens à la fin de la République." *Revue des études anciennes* 81 (1979): 37–53.

———. "La Syrie-Creuse n'existe pas." In *Géographie historique au Proche-Orient: Actes de la table ronde de Valbonne, 16–18 septembre 1985*, ed. Pierre-Louis Gatier, Bruno Helly, and Jean-Paul Coquais, 15–40. Paris: Centre national de la recherche scientifique, 1988.

———. "Ti. Iulius Iulianus Alexander, Gouverneur d'Arabie." *Annual of the Department of Antiquities of Jordan* 21 (1976): 105–108.

———. "Transhumance, économie et société de montagne en Syrie du Sud." In *La montagne dans l'Antiquité*, ed. Georges Fabre, 39–54. Pau: Publications de l'Université de Pau, 1992.

———. *Trois études sur l'Arabie romaine et byzantine*. Brussels: Revue d'études latines, 1982.

———. "Villes et villages du Hauran (Syrie) du Ier au IVe siècle." In *Sociétés urbaines, sociétés rurales dans l'Asie Mineure et la Syrie hellénistiques et romaines (Strasbourg, 1985)*, ed. Edmond Frézouls, 239–257. Strasbourg: Association pour l' étude de la civilisation romaine, 1987.

Sartre, Maurice, with Robert Donceel and Mikaël Kalos. *Inscriptions grecques et latines de la Syrie*. Vol. 16.1, *Le Djebel al-ŒArab: Le Nord-Ouest*. Beirut: Institut français d'archéologie du Proche-Orient, forthcoming.

Sartre, Maurice, and Alain Tranoy. *La Méditerranée antique, 4e siècle av. J.-C. = 3e siècle ap. J.-C.* Paris: A. Colin, 1990.

Sartre-Fauriat, Annie. "Architecture funéraire de la Syrie." In *Archéologie et histoire de la Syrie*, ed. Jean-Marie Dentzer and Winfried Orthmann, 423–446. Saarbrücken: Saarbrücker Druckerei und Verlag, 1989.

———. "Culture et société dans le Hauran (Syrie du Sud) d'après les épigrammes funéraires (IIIe–IVe siècles apr. J.-C.)." *Syria* 75 (1998): 213–224.

———. "Les élites de la Syrie intérieure et leur image à l'époque romaine." In *Les élites et leurs facettes: Colloque de Clermont-Ferrand, 24–26 novembre 2000*, ed. Mireille Cébeillac-Gervasoni, 517–538. Rome: École française de Rome; Clermont-Ferrand: Presses Universitaires Blaise-Pascal, 2003.

———. "Les notables et leur rôle dans l'urbanisme du Hauran à l'époque romaine." In *Construction, représentation, et représentation des patriciats urbains, de l'Antiquité au XXe siècle*, ed. Claude Petitfrère, 223–240. Tours: Université François-Rabelais, Centre d'histoire de la ville moderne et contemporaine, 1999.

———. "Le nymphée et les adductions d'eau de Soada-Dionysias de Syrie au IIe siècle apr. J.-C." *Ktema* 17 (1992): 133–151.

———. "Palmyre de la mort de Commode à Nicée (192–325 apr. J.-C.)." In *L'Empire romain de la mort de Commode à Nicée (192–325 apr. J.-C.)*, ed. Yann Le Bohec, 251–278. Paris: Éditions du Temps, 1997.

———. *Des tombeaux et des morts.* Vol. 2. Beirut: Institut français d'archéologie du Proche-Orient, 2001.

———. *Les voyages de William-John Bankes dans le Hauran.* Bordeaux: Ausonius; Beirut: Institut français du Proche-Orient, 2004.

Sartre-Fauriat, Annie, and Maurice Sartre. *Inscriptions grecques et latines de la Syrie.* Vol. 15, *Le plateau du Trachôn.* Beirut: Institut français d'archéologie du Proche-Orient, forthcoming.

Saulnier, Christiane. *Histoire d'Israël de la conquête d'Alexandre à la destruction du Temple.* Paris: Le Cerf, 1985.

———. "Les lois romaines sur les Juifs d'après Flavius Josephus." *Revue biblique* 88 (1981): 161–185.

Sauvaget, Jean. "Le plan antique de Damas." *Syria* 26 (1949): 314–358.

Savignac, Raphaël. "Le sanctuaire d'Allat à Iram." *Revue biblique* 42 (1933): 405–422.

———. "Une visite à l'île de Rouad." *Revue biblique* 25 (1916): 565–592.

Savignac, Raphaël, and George Horsfield. "Chronique: Le Temple de Ramm." *Revue biblique* 44 (1935): 245–278.

Sawicki, Marianne. "Spatial Management of Gender and Labor in Graeco-Roman Galilee." In *Archaeology and the Galilee: Texts and Contexts in the Graeco-Roman and Byzantine Periods,* ed. Douglas R. Edwards and C. Thomas McCullough, 7–28. Atlanta: Scholars Press, 1997.

Saxer, Victor. "La mission: L'organisation de l'Église au IIIe siècle." In *Histoire du Christianisme, des origines à nos jours,* ed. Jean-Marie Mayeur, Charles Piétri, Luce Piétri, André Vauchez, and Marc Venard, vol. 2, 41–75. Paris: Desclée, 1995.

Schäfer, Peter. "Hadrian's Policy in Judaea and the Bar Kokhba Revolt: A Reassessment." In *A Tribute to G. Vermes: Essays on Jewish and Christian Literature and History,* ed. Philip R. Davies and Richard T. White, 282–303. Sheffield, U.K.: Journal for the Study of the Old Testament, 1990.

———. *The History of the Jews in Antiquity: The Jews of Palestine from Alexander the Great to the Arab Conquest.* Australia and the United States: Harwood Academic, 1995.

———. *Judeophobia: Attitudes toward the Jews in the Ancient World.* Cambridge, Mass.: Harvard University Press, 1997.

Schalit, Abraham. "Koile Syria from the Mid-Fourth Century to the Beginning of the Third Century BC." *Scripta Hierosolymitana* 1 (1954): 64–77.

———. *Könige Herodes: Der Mann und sein Werk.* Berlin: W. de Gruyter, 1969.

———. *Untersuchungen zur Assumptio Mosis.* Leiden and New York: E. J. Brill, 1989.

Scherer, Jean, ed. *Entretien d'Origène avec Héraclide.* Paris: Le Cerf, 1960.

Schlumberger, Daniel. "L'inscription d'Hérodien." *Bulletin d'études orientales* 9 (1942–1943): 35–50.

Schlumberger, Daniel, Harald Ingholt, and Jean Starcky. *La Palmyrène du Nord-Ouest*. Paris: P. Geuthner, 1951.

Schmid, Stephan G. "Die Feinkeramik der Nabatäer im Spiegel ihrer kulturhistorischen Kontakte." In *Hellenistische und kaiserzeitliche Keramik des östlichen Mittelmeergebietes: Lebensraum, Geschichte und Kultur eines arabischen Volkes der Antike*, ed. Marlene Herfort-Koch, Ursula Mandel, and Ulrich Schädler, 127–145. Frankfurt am Main: Arbeitskreis Frankfurt und die Antike, Archäologisches Institut der Johann Wolfgang Goethe-Universität, 1996.

———. "Un roi nabatéen à Délos?" *Annual of the Department of Antiquities of Jordan* 43 (1999): 279–298.

Schmid, Wilhelm. "Genethlios 2." In *Realencyclopädie der classischen Altertumswissenschaft*, ed. August Friedrich von Pauly et al. Stuttgart: J. B. Metzler, 1894–.

Schmidt-Colinet, Andreas. "Considérations sur les carrières de Palmyre en Syrie." In *Pierre éternelle: Du Nil au Rhin, carrières et préfabrication*, ed. Marc Waelkens, 87–92. Brussels: Crédit communal, 1990.

———. "The Mason's Workshop of Hegra, Its Relation to Petra, and the Tomb of Syllaios." *Studies in History and Archaeology of Jordan* 3 (1987): 143–150.

———. "A Nabataean Family of Sculptors at Hegra." *Berytus* 31 (1983): 95–102.

———. "Nabatäische Felsarchitektur: Bemerkungen zum gegenwärtigen Forschungsstand." *Bonner Jahrbücher* 180 (1980): 189–230.

———. Review of *Propylon und Bogentor*, by Ingeborg Kader, and *Les arcs romains de Jérusalem*, by Caroline Arnould. *American Journal of Archaeology* 103 (1999): 719–720.

———. "Die sogennante 'maison à atrium.'" In *Apamée de Syrie: Bilan des recherches archéologiques 1973–1979*, ed. Janine Balty, 141–150. Brussels: Centre belge de recherches archéologiques à Apamée de Syrie, 1984.

———, ed. *Palmyra: Kulturbegegnung in Grenzbereich*. Mainz: Ph. von Zabern, 1995.

Schmidt-Colinet, Andreas, and Khaled al-As'ad. "Zur Urbanistik des hellenistichen Palmyra: Ein Vorbericht." *Damaszener Mitteilungen* 12 (2000): 61–93.

Schmitt, Rüdiger. "Die Ostgrenze von Armenien über Mesopotamien, Syrien bis Arabien." In *Die Sprachen im römischen Reich der Kaiserzeit: Kolloquium vom 8. bis 10. April 1974*, ed. Günter Neumann and Jürgen Untermann, 187–214. Cologne and Bonn: R. Habelt, 1980.

Schmitt-Korte, Karl. "Die bemalte nabatäische Keramik: Verbreitung, Typologie und Chronologie." In *Pre-Islamic Arabia*, 174–197. Riyadh: Jami'at al-Malik Sa'ud, 1984.

———. "Die Entwicklung des Granatapfel-Motivs in der nabatäischen Keramik." In *Petra und das Königreich der Nabatäer: Lebensraum, Geschichte und Kultur eines arabischen Volkes der Antike*, ed. Manfred Lindner, 198–203. Munich: Delp, 1986.

———. "Nabataean Pottery: A Typical and Chronological Framework." In *Studies in the History of Arabia*, vol. 2, *Pre-Islamic Arabia*. Riyadh: Jami'at al-Malik Sa'ud, 1984.

Schneider, Eugenia Equini. *Septimia Zenobia Sebaste*. Rome: L'Erma, 1993.

Schneider, Gerwulf. "Roman Red and Black Slipped Pottery from NE-Syria and Jordan: First Results of Chemical Analysis." In *Hellenistic and Roman Pottery in the Eastern Mediterranean: Advances in Scientific Studies; Acts of the II Nieborów Pottery Workshop,* ed. Henryk Meyza and Jolanta Mlynarczyk, 415–422. Warsaw: Research Center for Mediterranean Archaeology, Polish Academy of Sciences, 1995.

Schönbauer, Ernst. "Diokletian in einem verzweifelten Abwehrkampfe? Studien zur Rechtsentwicklung in der römischen Kaiserzeit." *Zeitschrift der Savigny-Stiftung für Rechtsgeschichte, Romanistiche Abteilung* 62 (1942): 267–346.

———. "Die Inscrift von Rhosos und die Constitutio Antoniniana." *Archiv für Papyrusforschung* 13 (1939): 177–209.

Schürer, Emil. *The History of the Jewish People in the Age of Jesus Christ (175 B.C.–A.D. 135),* revised and edited by Géza Vermès and Fergus Millar, trans. T. A. Burkill et al. 3 vols. Edinburgh: Clark, 1973–1986.

Schwabe, Moshe. "Tiberias Revealed through Inscriptions." In *All the Land of Naphtali,* ed. Haim Zeev Hirschberg, 180–191. Jerusalem: ha-Hevrah la-hakirat Erets-Yisra'el ve-'atikoteha, 1967.

Schwabe, Moshe, and Baruch Lifshitz. *Beth She'arim.* Vol. 2, *The Greek Inscriptions.* New Brunswick: Rutgers University Press, 1974.

Schwartz, Daniel R. *Agrippa I: The Last King of Judaea.* Tübingen: J. C. B. Mohr, 1990.

———. "Josephus on Hyrcanus II." In *Josephus and the History of the Greco-Roman Period: Essays in Memory of Morton Smith,* ed. Fausto Parente and Joseph Sievers, 210–232. Leiden: E. J. Brill, 1994.

———. "Pontius Pilate." In *The Anchor Bible Dictionary,* ed. David Noel Freedman, 396–401. New York: Doubleday, 1992.

Schwartz, Jacques. *Biographie de Lucien de Samosate.* Brussels: Latomus, 1965.

———. "Les Palmyréniens en Égypte." *Bulletin de la Société archéologique d'Alexandrie* 40 (1953): 3–21.

Schwartz, Joshua. Review of *Galilee: History, Politics, People* (1995) and *Archaeology, History, and Society in Galilee* (1996), by Richard A. Horsley. *Journal of Jewish Studies* 49 (1998): 155–158.

Sedov, Alexander V. "New Archaeological and Epigraphical Material from Qana (South Arabia)." *Arabian Archaeology and Epigraphy* 3 (1993): 110–137.

Seeck, Otto, ed. *Notitia dignitatum.* Berlin: Weidmann, 1876.

Segal, Arthur. *Theatres in Roman Palestine and Provincia Arabia.* Leiden: E. J. Brill, 1995.

Segal, Joshua Benzion. "Aramaic Legal Texts from Hatra." *Journal of Jewish Studies* (1992): 109–115.

———. *Edessa, "The Blessed City."* Oxford: Clarendon Press, 1970. Reprint, Piscataway, N.J.: Gorgias Press, 1971.

———. "A Note on a Mosaic from Edessa." *Syria* 60 (1983): 107–110.

———. "Some Syriac Inscriptions of the 2nd–3rd Century A.D." *Bulletin of the Society for Oriental and African Studies* 16 (1954): 24–28.

———. "When Did Christianity Come to Edessa?" In *Middle East Studies and Libraries: A Felicitation Volume for Professor J. D. Pearson,* ed. B. C. Bloomfield, 179–191. London: Mansell, 1980.

Seigne, Jacques. "À l'ombre de Zeus et d'Artémis: Gérasa de la Décapole." *Aram* 4 (1992): 185–195.

———. "Jérash romaine et byzantine: Développement urbain d'une ville provinciale orientale." *Studies in the History and Archaeology of Jordan* 4 (1992): 331–341.

———. "Les limites orientale et méridionale du territoire de Gerasa." *Syria* 74 (1997): 121–138.

———. "Recherches sur le sanctuaire de Zeus à Jerash (oct. 1982–déc. 83)." In *Jerash Archaeological Project, 1981–1983*, ed. Fawzi Zayadine, 29–106. Amman: Department of Antiquities, 1986.

———. Review of *Petra Great Temple*, vol. 1, *Brown University Excavations 1993–1997*, by Martha Sharp Joukowsky. *Topoi* 10 (2000): 507–516.

———. "Sanctuaires urbains: Acteurs ou témoins de l'urbanisation? Les exemples de Gérasa et de Palmyre." *Topoi* 9 (1999): 833–848.

Sekunda, Nick. *Seleucid and Ptolemaic Reformed Armies: The Seleucid Army under Antiochus IV Epiphanes*. 2 vols. Stockport: Montvert, 1994.

Seyrig, Henri. "Alexandre le Grand, fondateur de Gérasa." *Syria* 42 (1965): 25–28.

———. "Antiquités de la nécropole d'Émèse." *Syria* 29 (1952): 204–227.

———. *Antiquités syriennes*. Paris: P. Geuthner, 1934–.

———. "Bas-relief des dieux de Hiérapolis." *Syria* 49 (1972): 104–108.

———. "Caractères de l'histoire d'Émèse." *Syria* 36 (1959): 148–192.

———. "Le cimetière des marins à Séleucie de Piérie." In *Mélanges syriens offerts à M. René Dussaud*, 451–459. Paris: P. Geuthner, 1939.

———. "Le culte du Soleil en Syrie à l'époque romaine." *Syria* 48 (1971): 337–373.

———. "Deux pièces énigmatiques." *Syria* 42 (1965): 28–34.

———. "Deux pièces énigmatiques: 2. Un officier d'Agrippa II." *Syria* 42 (1965): 31–35.

———. "Les dieux armés et les Arabes en Syrie." *Syria* 47 (1970): 77–112.

———. "Les ères d'Agrippa II." *Revue numismatique* (1964): 55–65.

———. "Les fils du roi Odainat." *Annales archéologiques de Syrie* 13 (1963): 159–172.

———. "L'incorporation de Palmyre à l'empire romain." *Syria* 13 (1932): 266–277.

———. "Inscription relative au commerce maritime de Palmyre." In *Mélanges Franz Cumont*, 397–402. Brussels: Secrétariat de l'Institut, 1936.

———. "Les inscriptions de Bostra." *Syria* 22 (1941): 44–48.

———. "Inscriptions diverses." *Syria* 27 (1950): 236–250.

———. "Inscriptions grecques de l'agora de Palmyre." *Syria* 22 (1941): 223–270.

———. "Une monnaie de Césarée du Liban." In *Antiquités syriennes*, 11–16. Paris: P. Geuthner, 1966.

———. "Le monnayage de Ptolemaïs en Phénicie." *Revue numismatique* (1962): 25–50.

———. "Monuments syriens du culte de Némésis." *Syria* 13 (1932): 50–64.

———. *Notes on Syrian Coins*. Numismatic Notes and Monographs 119. New York: American Numismatic Society, 1950.

———. "Note sur Hérodien, prince de Palmyre." *Syria* 18 (1937): 1–4.

———. "Postes romains sur la route de Médine." *Syria* 22 (1941): 218–223.

———. "Questions aradiennes." *Revue numismatique* (1964): 9–50.

———. "La résurrection d'Adonis et le texte de Lucien." *Syria* 49 (1972): 97–100.

————. "Sur les ères de quelques villes de Syrie." *Syria* 27 (1950): 5–56.

————. "Trois bas-reliefs religieux de type palmyrénien." *Syria* 13 (1932): 258–266.

————. "La Tychè de Césarée de Palestine." *Syria* 49 (1972): 112–115.

————. "Vhabalathus Augustus." In *Mélanges offerts à Kazimierz Michalowski*, ed. Marie-Louise Bernhard, 659–662. Warsaw: Panstwowe wydawnictwo naukowe, 1966.

Seyrig, Henri, Robert Amy, and Ernest Will. *Le Temple de Bêl à Palmyre*. Paris: P. Geuthner, 1968–1975.

Shahid, Irfan. *Byzantium and the Arabs in the Fourth Century*. Washington, D.C.: Dumbarton Oaks Research Library and Collection, 1984.

————. "Saracens." In *Encyclopédie de l'Islam*, ed. C. E. Bosworth, E. van Donzel, and W. P. Heinrichs. Leiden: E. J. Brill, 1995.

Shatzman, Israel. "The Integration of Judaea into the Roman Empire." *Scripta classica israelica* 18 (1999): 49–84.

Sherwin-White, Adrian Nicholas. *Roman Foreign Policy in the East*. Norman: University of Oklahoma Press, 1984.

Sidebotham, Steven E. "Aelius Gallus and Arabia." *Latomus* 45 (1986): 590–602.

————. *Roman Economic Policy in the Erythra Thalassa, 30 B.C.–A.D. 217*. Leiden: E. J. Brill, 1986.

————. "Roman Interests in the Red Sea and Indian Ocean." In *The Indian Ocean in Antiquity*, ed. Julian Reade, 287–308. London: Kegan Paul, 1996.

Sievers, Joseph. *The Hasmoneans and Their Supporters: From Mattathias to the Death of John Hyrcanus I*. Atlanta: Scholars Press, 1990.

Simon, Marcel. *Recherches d'histoire judéo-chrétienne*. Paris and The Hague: Mouton, 1962.

————. *Les sectes juives au temps de Jésus*. Paris: Presses Universitaires de France, 1960.

Simon, Marcel, and André Benoît. *Le judaïsme et le christianisme antiques, d'Antiochus Épiphane à Constantin*. Paris: Presses Universitaires de France, 1968. Reprint, 1985.

Sirinelli, Jean. *Les enfants d'Alexandre: La littérature et la pensée grecques (331 av. J.-C.–519 ap. J.-C.)*. Paris: Fayard, 1933.

Skarsaune, Oskar. "Justin der Märtyrer." In *Theologische Realenzyklopëdie*, ed. Gerhard Müller, 471–478. Berlin and New York: W. de Gruyter, 1988.

Skjaervø, Probs O. "L'inscription d'Abnun et l'imparfait en Moyen-Perse." *Studia Iranica* 21 (1992): 153–160.

Slane, Kathleen Warner. "The Fine Wares." In *Tel Anafa II*, part 1, *The Hellenistic and Roman Pottery*, ed. Sharon C. Herbert, 247–393. Ann Arbor: Kelsey Museum of the University of Michigan, 1997.

Slane, Kathleen Warner, J. Michael Elam, Michael D. Glascock, and Hector Neff. "Compositional Analysis of Eastern Sigillata A and Related Wares from Tel Anafa (Israel)." *Journal of Archaeological Science* 21 (1984): 51–64.

Smilévitch, Éric, ed. *Leçons des pères du Monde: Pirgé Avot et Avot de Rabbi Nathan, Versions A et B*. Lagrasse: Verdier, 1983.

Smith, Andrew. "Porphyrian Studies since 1913." *Aufstieg und Niedergang der römischen Welt* 2.36.2 (1987): 717–773.

Smith, Andrew M., II, Michelle Stevens, and Tina M. Niemi. "The Southeast Araba

Archaeological Survey: A Preliminary Report of the 1994 Season." *Bulletin of the American Schools of Oriental Research* 305 (1997): 45–71.

Smith, M. F. "An Epicurean Priest from Apamea in Syria." *Zeitschrift für Papyrologie und Epigraphik* 112 (1996): 120–130.

Smith, Morton. "On the Wine God in Palestine (Gen. 18, Jn. 2, and Achilles Tatius)." In *Salo Wittmayer Baron Jubilee Volume on the Occasion of his Eightieth Birthday,* ed. Saul Lieberman and Arthur Hyman, vol. 2, 815–829. Jerusalem: American Academy for Jewish Research, 1975.

———. "Zealots and Sicarii: Their Origins and Relations." *Harvard Theological Review* 64 (1971): 1–19.

Smith, R. R. R. "Simulacra Gentium: The Ethne from the Sebasteion at Aphrodisias." *Journal of Roman Studies* 78: 50–77.

Sodini, Jean-Pierre, and Georges Tate. "Maisons d'époque romaine et byzantine (IIe–VIe siècles) du Massif Calcaire de Syrie du Nord: Étude typologique." In *Apamée de Syrie: Bilan des recherches archéologiques 1973–1979,* ed. Janine Balty, 377–429. Brussels: Centre belge de recherches archéologiques à Apamée de Syrie, 1984.

Sogliani, Francesca. "La Ceramica." *Felix Ravenna* 137–138 (1989): 125–169.

Soler, Emmanuel. "Le sacré et le salut à Antioche au IVe siècle ap. J.-C.: Pratiques festives et comportements religieux dans le processus de christianisation de la cité." Ph.D. diss., Rouen, 1999. Beirut: Institut français d'archéologie du Proche-Orient, forthcoming.

Solin, Heikki. "Juden und Syrer im westlichen Teil der römischen Welt: Eine ethnisch-demographische Studie mit besonderer Berücksichtigung der sprachlichen Zustände." *Aufstieg und Niedergang der römischen Welt* 2.29.2 (1983): 587–789, 1222–1249 (indices).

Sourdel, Dominique. *Les cultes du Hauran à l'époque gréco-romaine.* Paris: P. Geuthner, 1952.

Soyez, Brigitte. *Byblos et la fête des Adonies.* Leiden: E. J. Brill, 1977.

Sozomen. *Ecclesiasticae historia,* ed. André-Jean Festugière, Guy Sabbah, and Bernard Grillet. Paris: Le Cerf, 1983.

———. *The Ecclesiatical History, or Sozomen, Comprising a History of the Church from A.D. 324 to A.D. 440,* trans. Edward Walford. London: Henry G. Bohn, 1855.

Speidel, Michael Alexander. "Legio IIII Scythica, Its Movements and Men." In *The Twin Towns of Zeugma on the Euphrates,* ed. David L. Kennedy, 163–203. Portsmouth, R.I.: Journal of Roman Archaeology, 1998.

———. "*Legio IV Scythica.*" In *Les légions de Rome sous le Haut-Empire,* ed. Yann Le Bohec, 327–337. Lyon: n. p., 2000.

Speidel, Michael P. "European-Syrian Elite Troops at Dura-Europos and Hatra." In *Roman Army Studies,* ed. Michael P. Speidel, 301–309. Amsterdam: J. C. Gieben, 1984.

———. "The Roman Army in Arabia." *Aufstieg und Niedergang der römischen Welt* 2.8 (1977): 687–730.

———. "The Roman Army in Judaea under the Procurators: The Italian and the Augustan Cohort in the Acts of the Apostles." *Ancient Society* 13–14 (1982–1983): 233–240.

———. "The Roman Road to Dumata (Jawf in Saudi Arabia) and the Frontier Strategy of *Praetensione Coligare.*" *Historia* 36 (1987): 213–221.

Sperber, Daniel. *The City in Roman Palestine.* Oxford: Oxford University Press, 1998.

———. *Roman Palestine 200–400: The Land; Crisis and Change in Agrarian Society as Reflected in Rabbinic Sources.* Ramat Gan: Bar Ilan University, 1978.

Spijkerman, Augustus J. *The Coins of the Decapolis and Provincia Arabia,* ed. Michele Piccirillo. Jerusalem: Franciscan Printing Press, 1978.

Starcky, Jean. "Une inscription nabatéenne provenant du Djof." *Revue biblique* 64 (1957): 196–217.

———. "Pétra et la Nabatène." In *Dictionnaire de la Bible,* suppl. 7. Paris: Letouzey & Ané, 1996.

———. "Stèle d'Élahagabal." *Mélanges de l'Université Saint-Joseph* 49 (1975–1976): 501–520.

———. "Le temple nabatéen de Khirbet Tannur: À propos d'un livre récent." *Revue biblique* 75 (1968): 206–235.

Starcky, Jean, and Michel Gawlikowski. *Palmyre.* Paris: J. Maisonneuve, 1985.

Stauffer, Annemarie. "Kleider, Kissen, bunte Tücher: Einheimische Textilproduktion und weltweiter Handel." In *Palmyra: Kulturbegegnung in Grenzbereich,* ed. Andreas Schmidt-Colinet, 57–71. Mainz: Ph. von Zabern, 1995.

Stauffer, Ethelbert. "Zur Münzprägung und Judenpolitik des Pontius Pilatus." *La Nouvelle Clio* (1949–1950): 495–514.

Stein, Arthur. "Kallinikos von Petrai." *Hermes* 58 (1923): 448–456.

Steinsapir, A. I. "The Sanctuary Dedicated to Holy Heavenly Zeus Baetocaece." *Near Eastern Archaeology* 62 (1999): 182–194.

Stephanus of Byzantium. *Ethnica,* ed. August Meineke. Graz: Akademische Druck und Verlagsanstalt, 1958.

Stern, E. Marianne. *Roman Mould-Blown Glass: The First through Sixth Centuries.* Rome: L'Erma / Toledo Museum of Art, 1995.

Stern, Ephraim, ed. *The New Encyclopedia of Archaeological Excavations in the Holy Land.* 4 vols. Jerusalem: Israel Exploration Society / Carta; New York: Simon & Schuster, 1993.

Stern, Ephraim, and Ilan Sharon. "Tel Dor—1992–1993." *Excavations and Surveys in Israel* 14 (1995): 61–71.

Stern, Henri. *Les mosaïques des maisons d'Achille et de Cassiopée à Palmyre.* Paris: P. Geuthner, 1977.

Stern, Menahem, ed. *Greek and Latin Authors on Jews and Judaism.* 3 vols. Jerusalem: Israel Academy of Sciences and Humanities, 1974–1984.

———. "Judaea and Her Neighbors in the Days of Alexander Jannaeus." In *The Jerusalem Cathedra,* ed. Lee I. Levine, 22–46. Jerusalem: Yad Izhak Ben-Zvi Institute / Wayne State University Press, 1981.

———. "The Reign of Herod." In *The World History of the Jewish People,* ed. Michael Avi-Yonah and Zvi Baras, vol. 7, 71–123. Tel Aviv: Jewish History Publications; London: W. H. Allen, 1975.

———. "The Reign of Herod and the Herodian Dynasty." In *The Jewish People in the First Century: Historical, Geographical, Political History, Social, Cultural and Religious Life and Institutions,* ed. Shemuel Safrai and Menahem Stern, 216–307. Assen: Van Gorcum, 1974.

―――. "The Relations between Judea and Rome during the Rule of John Hyrcanus." *Zion* 26 (1961): 12–17.

―――. "Sicarii and Zealots." In *The World History of the Jewish People,* ed. Michael Avi-Yonah and Zvi Baras, vol. 8, 263–301. Jerusalem: Massada; New Brunswick: Rutgers University Press, 1977.

Steve, M.-J. "Sur l'île de Kharg, dans le Golfe persique." *Dossiers d'archéologie* 243 (May 1998): 74–80.

Stillwell, Richard. "Houses of Antioch." *Dumbarton Oak Papers* 15 (1961): 44–57.

Stone, Michael E. *Jewish Writings in the Second Temple Period.* Vol. 3, *The Literature of the Jewish People in the Period of the Second Temple and the Talmud.* Assen: Van Gorcum; Philadelphia: Fortress Press, 1984–.

Stoneman, Richard. *Palmyra and Its Empire: Zenobia's Revolt against Rome.* Ann Arbor: University of Michigan Press, 1992.

Strabo. *The Geography.* Trans. Horace Leonard Jones. 10 vols. Loeb Classical Library.

Strange, James F. "First Century Galilee from Archaeology and from the Texts." In *Archaeology and the Galilee: Texts and Contexts in the Graeco-Roman and Byzantine Periods,* ed. Douglas R. Edwards and C. Thomas McCullough, 39–47. Atlanta: Scholars Press, 1997.

Stucky, Rolf A. "The Nabataean House and the Urbanistic System of the Habitation Quarters in Petra." *Studies in the History and Archaeology of Jordan* 5 (1995): 193–198.

Studer, Jacqueline. "Roman Fish Sauce in Petra, Jordan." In *Fish Exploitation in the Past: Proceedings of the 7th Meeting of the ICAZ Fish Remains Working Group,* ed. Wim Van Neer, 191–196. Tervuren: Koninklijk Museum voor Midden-Africa, 1994.

Suetonius. "The Deified Vespasian." In *Suetonius,* trans. J. C. Rolfe, vol. 2, 279–321. Loeb Classical Library.

―――. "Domitian." In *Suetonius,* trans. J. C. Rolfe, vol. 2, 338–385. Loeb Classical Library.

―――. "Gaius Caligula." In *Suetonius,* trans. J. C. Rolfe, vol. 1, 403–497. Loeb Classical Library.

―――. "Nero." In *Suetonius,* trans. J. C. Rolfe, vol. 2, 85–187. Loeb Classical Library.

―――. *Suetonius,* trans. J. C. Rolfe. 2 vols. Loeb Classical Library.

―――. "Tiberius." In *Suetonius,* trans. J. C. Rolfe, vol. 1, 289–401. Loeb Classical Library.

―――. "Vitellius." In *Suetonius,* trans. J. C. Rolfe, vol. 2, 246–277. Loeb Classical Library.

Suidas. *Suidae Lexicon,* ed. Ada Adler. Vol. 3. Stuttgart: Teubner, 1967.

Sukenik, Eleazar L. "The Temple of the Kore." In *Samaria-Sebaste,* vol. 1, *The Buildings at Samaria,* ed. John Winter Crowfoot, Kathleen M. Kenyon, and Eleazar L. Sukenik, 62–67. London: Palestine Exploration Fund, 1942.

Sullivan, Richard D. "The Dynasty of Commagene." *Aufstieg und Niedergang der römischen Welt* 2.8 (1977): 732–798.

―――. "The Dynasty of Emesa." *Aufstieg und Niedergang der römischen Welt* 2.8 (1977): 198–219.

———. *Near Eastern Royalty and Rome, 100–30 BC.* Toronto: University of Toronto Press, 1990.

Sumner, G. V. "The 'Piracy Law' from Delphi and the Law of the Cnidos Inscription." *Greek, Roman and Byzantine Studies* 19 (1978): 211–225.

Supplementum epigraphicum graecum. Alphen aan den Rijn: Sijthoff & Noordhoff, 1923–1998.

Susini, Gian Carlo. "La classis syriaca e le flotte provinciali." *Corso di Cultura sull'Arte Ravennate e Bizantina* (1976): 327–329.

Swain, Simon. "Greek into Palmyrene: Odaenathus as 'Corrector Totius Orientis'?" *Zeitschrift für Papyrologie und Epigraphik* 99 (1993): 157–164.

———. *Hellenism and Empire: Language, Classicism and Power in the Greek World ad 50–250.* Oxford: Clarendon Press, 1996.

Swift, Louis J. "The Anonymous Encomium of Philip the Arab." *Greek, Roman and Byzantine Studies* 7 (1966): 268–289.

Syme, Sir Ronald. "Avidius Cassius: His Rank, Age and Quality." In *Bonner Historia-Augusta Colloquium 1984/1985*, 207–222. Bonn: R. Habelt, 1987.

Tacitus. *The Annals,* trans. John Jackson. Loeb Classical Library.

———. *The Histories,* trans. Clifford H. Moore. 3 vols. Loeb Classical Library.

Le Talmud de Jérusalem. Trans. Moïse Schwab. 11 vols. Paris: Maisonneuve & Larose, 1871–1890.

Tardan-Masquelier, Ysé, ed. *Sifre: A Tannaitic Commentary on the Book of Deuteronomy,* trans. Reuven Hammer. New Haven: Yale University Press, 1986.

Tardieu, Michel. "L'arrivée des manichéens à al-Hira." In *La Syrie de Byzance à l'Islam, VIIe–VIIIe siècles: Actes du colloque international Lyon-Maison de l'Orient méditerranéen, Paris-Institut du monde arabe, 11–14 septembre 1990,* ed. Pierre Canivet and Jean-Paul Rey-Coquais, 15–24. Damascus: Institut français de Damas, 1995.

———. "Mani et le Manichéisme." In *Encyclopédie des Religions,* ed. Frédéric Lenoir, Ysé Tardan-Masquelier, Michel Meslin, and Jean-Pierre Rosa, 225–230. Paris: Bayard, 2000.

———. *Le Manichéisme.* Paris: Presses Universitaires de France, 1981.

———. *Les paysages reliques, routes et haltes syriennes d'Isidore à Simplicius.* Louvain and Paris: Peeters, 1990.

Tarrier, Dominique. "Baalshamin dans le monde nabatéen: À propos de découvertes récentes." *Aram* 2 (1990): 197–203.

Tate, Georges. *Les campagnes de la Syrie du Nord du IIe au VIIe siècle: Un exemple d'expansion démographique et économique à la fin de l'antiquité.* Paris: P. Geuthner, 1992.

Tatian of Assyria. "Discours aux Grecs." In *Foi chrétienne et culture classique,* ed. Bernard Pouderon, 39–102. Paris: Migne, 1998.

———. *Oratio ad Graecos and Fragments,* ed. Molly Whittaker. Oxford and New York: Clarendon Press, 1982.

Taylor, George. *The Roman Temples of Lebanon.* Beirut: Dar al-Machreq, 1967.

Tchalenko, Georges. *Villages antiques de la Syrie du Nord: Le massif Bélus à l'époque romaine.* 3 vols. Paris: P. Geuthner, 1953–1958.

Tcherikover, Avigdor (Victor). *Hellenistic Civilization and the Jews.* Philadelphia: Jewish Publication Society of America, 1959.

————. *Die hellenistischen Städtgegründungen von Alexander dem Grossen bis auf die Römerzeit.* Leipzig: Deiterich'sche Verlagsbuchhandlung, 1927.

Teixidor, Javier. "Antiquités sémitiques." *Annuaire du Collège de France, 1997–1998* (1998): 713–736.

————. *Bardesane d'Édesse: La première philosophie syriaque.* Paris: Le Cerf, 1992.

————. "Le campement: Ville des Nabatéens." *Semitica* 43–44 (1995): 111–121.

————. "Cultes tribaux et religion civique à Palmyre." *Revue d'histoire des religions* (1980): 277–287.

————. "Les derniers rois d'Édesse d'après deux nouveaux documents syriaques." *Zeitschrift für Papyrologie und Epigraphik* 76 (1989): 219–222.

————. "Deux documents syriaques du IIIe siècle après J.-C. provenant du Moyen-Euphrate." *Comptes rendus des séances de l'Académie des inscriptions et belles-lettres* (1990): 144–166.

————. "Un document syriaque de fermage de 242 apr. J.-C." *Semitica* 41–42 (1991–1992): 195–208.

————. "L'Hellénisme et les Barbares." *Le temps de la réflexion* 2 (1981): 257–294.

————. "Une inscription araméenne provenant de l'Émirat de Sharjah (Émirats Arabes Unis)." *Comptes rendus des séances de l'Académie des inscriptions et belles-lettres* (1992): 695–707.

————. "Les Nabatéens du Sinaï." In *Le Sinaï durant l'Antiquité et le Moyen-Âge: Proceedings of the Colloquium "Sinai," UNESCO, Sept. 19–21, 1997,* ed. Dominique Valbelle and Charles Bonnet, 83–87. Paris: Errance, 1998.

————. *The Pantheon of Palmyra.* Leiden: E. J. Brill, 1979.

————. *Un port romain du désert: Palmyre et son commerce d'Auguste à Caracalla.* Paris: A. Maisonneuve, 1984.

Thee, Francis C. R. *Julius Africanus and the Early Christian View of Magic.* Tübingen: J. B. C. Mohr, 1984.

Theeb (al-), S. A. "New Safaitic Inscriptions from the North of Saudi Arabia." *Arabian Archaeology and Epigraphy* 7 (1996): 32–37.

Theissen, Gerd. *Histoire sociale du christianisme primitif: Jésus, Paul, Jean.* Geneva: Labor & Fides, 1996.

————. "Jésus et la crise sociale de son temps: Aspects socio-historiques de la recherche du Jésus historique." In *Jésus de Nazareth: Nouvelles approches d'une énigme,* ed. Daniel Marguerat, Enrico Norelli, and Jean-Michel Poffet, 125–155. Geneva: Labor & Fides, 1998.

Theodoretos, Bishop of Cyrrhos. *Correspondance,* ed. and Yvan Azéma. Paris: Le Cerf, 1982–.

————. "II Paralipomena." In *Patrologiae cursus completus: Series graeca,* ed. Jacques-Paul Migne et al. Paris: Garnier Frères, 1857–1905.

Theophilos of Antioch. *Ad Autolycum,* ed. and trans. Robert M. Grant. Oxford: Clarendon Press, 1970.

"The Thirty Pretenders." In *Historia Augusta,* trans. David Magie, vol. 3, 64–151. Loeb Classical Library.

Tholbecq, Laurent. "The Nabataeo-Roman Site of Wadi Ramm (Iram): A New Appraisal." *Annual of the Department of Antiquities of Jordan* 42 (1998): 241–254.

————. "Les sanctuaires des Nabatéens: État de la question à la lumière de recherches archéologiques récentes." *Topoi* 7 (1997): 1069–1095.

Thomasson, Bengt E. *Laterculi praesidum.* 3 vols. Göteborg: Radius, 1972–1990.

Thomsen, Peter. *Loca sancta: Verzeichnis der im 1. bis 6. Jahrhundert n. Chr. erwähnten Ortschaften Palästinas, mit besonderer Berücksichtigung der Lokalisierung der biblischen Stätten.* Halle: S. R. Haupt, 1907.

———. "Die römische Flotte im Palästina-Syrien." *Beiträge zur biblischen Landes und Altertumskunde* 68 (1951): 73–89.

———. "Die römischen Meilensteine der Provinzen Syria, Arabia, und Palästina." *Zeitschrift der deutschen Palästina-Vereins* 40 (1917): 1–103.

"The Three Gordians." In *Historia Augusta,* trans. David Magie, vol. 2, 380–447. Loeb Classical Library.

Tollet, Daniel, and Centre d'études juives de Paris-Sorbonne. *Politique et religion dans le judaïsme ancien et médiéval: Interventions au colloque des 8 et 9 décembre 1987.* Paris: Desclée, 1989.

Tomaschoff, Avner, ed. *Mishnah: A New Translation with Commentary.* Jerusalem: Eliner Library, 1994.

Toplyn, Michael Richard. "Meat for Mars: Livestock, Limitanei, and Pastoral Provisioning for the Roman Army on the Arabian Frontier, A.D. 284–551." Ph.D. diss., Harvard University, 1994.

Torrey, Charles Cutler. "The Exiled God of Sarepta." *Berytus* 9 (1949): 45–49.

The Tosefta, ed. and trans. Jacob Neusner. New York: Ktav, 1977–1986.

Tourneur, Victor. "Les villes amirales de l'Orient gréco-romain." *Revue belge de numismatique* 69 (1913): 407–424.

Tran, V. Tam Tinh. "Remarques sur l'iconographie de Dousarès." In *Petra and the Caravan Cities,* ed. Fawzi Zayadine, 107–114. Amman: Department of Antiquities, 1990.

Trocmé, Étienne. *L'enfance du christianisme.* Paris: Éditions Noêsis, 1997.

Troiani, Lucio. "Contributuo alla problematica dei rapporti tra storiografia greca e storiografia vicino-orientale." *Athenaeum* 61 (1983): 427–428.

———. *L'opera storiografica di Filone di Byblos.* Pisa: Goliardica, 1974.

Tsafrir, Yoram, and Gideon Foerster. "The Hebrew University Excavations at Beth Shean 1980–1994." *Qadmoniot* 107–108 (1995): 93–116.

Tsafrir, Yoram, Leah Di Segni, and Judith Green. *Tabula Imperii Romani: Iudaea-Palaestina. Eretz Israel in the Hellenistic, Roman and Byzantine Periods: Maps and Gazetteer.* Jerusalem: Israel Academy of Sciences and Humanities, 1994.

Tsuk, Tsevikah. "The Aqueduct to Legio and the Location of the Camp of the VIth Roman Legion." *Tel Aviv* 15–16 (1988–1989): 92–97.

"The Two Gallieni." In *Historia Augusta,* trans. David Magie, vol. 3, 2–63. Loeb Classical Library.

Ulpian. "Digesta." In *Corpus iuris civilis,* ed. Theodor Mommsen and Paul Krüger. 17th ed. Berlin: Weidmann, 1988.

Urman, Dan. *The Golan: A Profile of a Region during the Roman and Byzantine Periods.* Oxford: British Archaeological Reports, 1985.

Uscatescu, Alexandra, and Manuel Martín-Bueno. "The Macellum of Gerasa (Jerash, Jordan): From a Marketplace to an Industrial Area." *Bulletin of the American Schools of Oriental Research* 307 (1997): 67–88.

Vanderhoeven, Michel. *Les terres sigillées, 1966–1972.* Brussels: Centre belge de recherches archéologiques à Apamée de Syrie, 1989.

Vanderpool, Eugene. "An Athenian Monument to Theodorus of Gadara." *American Journal of Philology* 80 (1959): 366–369.

Vann, Robert Lindley. *Caesarea Papers: Straton's Tower, Herod's Harbour, and Roman and Byzantine Caesarea.* Ann Arbor: University of Michigan Press, 1992.

Vattioni, Francesco. *Le Iscrizioni di Hatra, Annali dell'Istituto Orientale di Napoli.* Naples: Istitutito orientale di Napoli, 1981.

Vaux, Roland de. "Une nouvelle inscription au dieu arabique." *Annual of the Department of Antiquities of Jordan* 1 (1951): 23–24.

Venco Ricciardi, Roberta. "Preliminary Report on the 1987 Excavation at Hatra." *Mesopotamia* 23 (1988): 31–42.

Vermaseren, Maarten Jozef. *Corpus inscriptionum et monumentorum religionis mithriacae.* 2 vols. The Hague: M. Nijhoff, 1956–1960.

Vermès, Géza. *The Complete Dead Sea Scrolls in English.* New York: Allen Lane / Penguin Press, 1997.

———. *Jesus the Jew: A Historian's Reading of the Gospels.* New York: Macmillan, 1973.

Vettius Valens. *Anthologies: Book I,* ed. Joëlle-Frédérique Bara. Leiden: E. J. Brill, 1989.

———. *Vettii Valentis Antiocheni anthologiarum libri novem,* ed. David Edwin Pingree. Leipzig: B. G. Teubner, 1986.

Veyne, Paul. Preface to *Palmyre, métropole caravanière,* by Gérard Degeorge, 8–57. Paris: Imprimerie nationale, 2001.

———. "Rome et le problème de la fuite de l'or." *Annales: Économies, sociétés, civilisations* (1979): 211–244.

Vidal-Naquet, Pierre. "Du bon usage de la trahison." Introduction to *Flavius Josephus: La Guerre des Juifs,* trans. Pierre Savinel, 9–115. Paris: Éditions de Minuit, 1977.

———. "Les Juifs entre l'État et l'apocalypse." In *Rome et la conquête du monde méditerranéen: 264–27 avant J.-C.,* ed. Claude Nicolet, 846–882. Paris: Presses Universitaires de France, 1978.

Villeneuve, Estelle. "Des archéologues à Pétra." *Le monde de la Bible* 127 (May–June 2000): 56–58.

Villeneuve, François. "L'économie rurale et la vie des campagnes dans le Hauran antique (Ier siècle av. J.-C.–VIIe siècle ap. J.-C.): Une approche." In *Hauran,* ed. Jean-Marie Dentzer, 64–136. Paris: P. Geuthner, 1985.

———. "Pétra revisitée." *Le monde de la Bible* 127 (May–June 2000): 16–17.

———. "The Pottery of the Oil-Factory at Khirbet edh-Dharih (2nd Century A.D.): A Contribution to the Study of the Material Culture of the Nabataeans." *Aram* 2 (1990): 367–384.

———. "Recherches sur les villages antiques du Haurâne, Ier s. av. J.-C.–VIIe s. ap. J.-C.: Le peuplement, les maisons rurales." Ph.D. diss., Université de Paris I, 1983.

Vincent, Louis-Hugues. "Le dieu saint Paqeidas à Gérasa." *Revue biblique* 49 (1940): 98–129.

———. "Une villa gréco-romaine à Beit Djebrin." *Revue biblique* 31 (1922): 259–281.

Vincent, Louis-Hugues, and Félix-Marie Abel. *Emmaüs: Sa basilique et son histoire.* Paris: E. Leroux, 1932.

Visscher, Fernand De. "La condition juridique des nouveaux citoyens romains." *Comptes rendus des séances de l'Académie des inscriptions et belles-lettres* (1938): 24–39.

———. *Les édits d'Auguste découverts à Cyrène.* Louvain: Bibliothèque de l'Université, 1940.

———. "Le statut juridique des nouveaux citoyens romains et l'inscription de Rhosos." *Antiquité classique* 13 (1944): 11–35.

———. "Le statut juridique des nouveaux citoyens romains et l'inscription de Rhosos." *Antiquité classique* 14 (1946): 29–59.

Vitto, Fanny. "Potters and Pottery Manufacture in Roman Palestine." *Bulletin of the Institute of Classical Archeaology* 23 (1986): 47–64.

von Ess, Margaret, and Thomas Weber. *Baalbek: Im Bann römischer Monumentalarchitektur.* Mainz: Ph. von Zabern, 1999.

von Wissmann, Hermann. "Die Geschichte des Sabäerreichs und der Feldzug des Aelius Gallus." *Aufstieg und Niedergang der römischen Welt* 2.9.1 (1976): 308–544.

Vööbus, Arthur. *A History of Asceticism in the Syrian Orient: A Contribution to the History of the East.* Louvain: Secrétariat du Corpus scriptorum Christianorum orientalium, 1958–1988.

Vouga, François. *Les premiers pas du christianisme: Les écrits, les acteurs, les débats.* Geneva: Labor & Fides, 1997.

Vries, Bert de. "Towards a History of Umm el-Jimal in Late Antiquity." In *Umm el-Jimal: A Frontier Town and Its Landscape in Northern Jordan,* ed. Bert De Vries, 229–241. Portsmouth, R.I.: Journal of Roman Archaeology, 1998.

———. "Umm El-Jimal in the First Three Centuries AD." In *The Defence of the Roman and Byzantine East,* ed. Philip Freeman and David L. Kennedy, 227–241. Oxford: British Archaeological Reports, 1986.

———, ed. *Umm el-Jimal: A Frontier Town and Its Landscape in Northern Jordan.* Vol. 1. *Fieldwork 1972–1981.* Portsmouth, R.I.: Journal of Roman Archaeology, 1998.

Vries, Bert de, and Pierre Bikai. "Archaeology in Jordan." *American Journal of Archaeology* 97 (1993): 457–520.

Vyhmeister, Werner K. "The History of Heshbon from Literary Sources." *Andrews University Seminary Studies* 6 (1968): 158–177.

Waagé, Dorothy B. *Antioch on-the-Orontes.* Vol. 4, part 2, *Greek, Roman, Byzantine and Crusaders' Coins.* Princeton: Department of Art and Archaeology of Princeton University, 1952.

Wacholder, Ben Zion. *Nicolaus of Damascus.* Berkeley: University of California Press, 1962.

Waddington, William Henry. *Inscriptions grecques et latines de la Syrie.* Paris: Firmin-Didot, 1870.

Wagner, Jörg. "Legio IIII Scythica am Euphrat." In *Studien zu den Militärgrenzen Roms,* vol. 2, *Vorträge des 10. Internationalen Limeskongresses in der Germania Inferior,* ed. Dorothea Haupt and Heinz Günter Horn, 517–540. Cologne and Bonn: R. Habelt, 1977.

———. "Provincia Osrhoenae: New Archaeological Finds Illustrating Its Organisation under the Severan Dynasty." In *Armies and Frontiers in Roman and*

Byzantine Anatolia, ed. Stephen Mitchell, 103–129. Oxford: British Archaeological Reports, 1983.

———. "Die Römer an Euphrat." In "Commagene." Special issue, *Antike Welt* 6 (1975): 66–82.

———. "Die Römer an Euphrat und Tigris: Geschichte und Denkmäler des Limes im Orient." In "Die Römer an Euphrat und Tigris." Special issue, *Antike Welt* 16 (1985), 3–75.

———. *Seleukeia am Euphrat, Zeugma.* Wiesbaden: Reichert, 1976.

Wagner, Jörg, and Georg Petzl. "Eine neue Temenos-Stele des Königs Antiochos I. von Kommagene." *Zeitschrift für Papyrologie und Epigraphik* 20 (1976): 201–224.

Wagner, Walter F. *Die Dislokation der römischen Auxiliarformationen in den Provinzen Noricum, Pannonien, Moesien und Dakien von Augustus bis Gallienus.* Berlin: Junker und Dunnhaupt, 1938.

Wagner-Lux, Ute. "Ein bemaltes Grab im Sôm, Jordanien." In *The Archaeology of Jordan and Other Studies, Presented to Siegfried H. Horn,* ed. L. T. Geraty and L. G. Herr, 287–300. Berrien Springs, Mich.: Andrews University Press, 1986.

Wagner-Lux, Ute, and K. J. H. Vriezen. "Vorläufiger Bericht über die Ausgräbungen in Gadara in Jordanien im Jahre 1990." *Zeitschrift der deutschen Palästina-Vereins* 98 (1982): 158–162.

Waheeb, Mohammad, and Zuhair Zu'bi. "Recent Excavations at the 'Amman Nymphaeum: Preliminary Report." *Annual of the Department of Antiquities of Jordan* 39 (1995): 229–240.

Waldmann, Helmut. *Die kommagenischen Kultreformen unter König Mithradates I. Kallinikos und seinem Sohne Antiochos I.* Leiden: E. J. Brill, 1973.

Wallmer, Christian. "Der olympische Agon von Bostra." *Zeitschrift für Papyrologie und Epigraphik* 129 (2000): 97–107.

Ward, Allan Mason. *Marcus Crassus and the Late Roman Republic.* Columbia and London: University of Missouri Press, 1977.

Waterhouse, S. Douglas. *The Necropolis of Hesban: A Typology of Tombs.* Berrien Springs, Mich.: Andrews University Press, 1998.

Weber, Thomas. "Gadarenes in Exile: Two Inscriptions from Greece Reconsidered." *Zeitschrift der deutschen Palästina-Vereins* 112 (1996): 10–17.

———. "Karawanengötter in der Dekapolis." *Damaszener Mitteilungen* 8 (1995): 203–211.

———. "Pella Decapolitana: Untersuchungen zur Topographie, Geschichte und bildenden Kunst einer 'Polis Hellenis' in Ostjordanland." Habilitation diss., Mainz, 1995.

———. *Syrisch-römische Sarkophagbeschläge: Orientalische Bronzewerkstätten in römischer Zeit.* Mainz: Ph. von Zabern, 2001.

Weerakkody, D. P. M. *Taprobanê: Ancient Sri Lanka as Known to Greeks and Romans.* Turnhout: Brepols, 1997.

Weidemann, Konrad. *Könige aus dem Yemen: Zwei spätantike Bronzestatuen.* Mainz: Das Museum, 1983.

Weinberg, S. S. "Tel Anafa: The Hellenistic Town." *Israel Exploration Journal* 21 (1971): 86–109.

Weiss, Peter. "Neue Militärdiplome." *Zeitschrift für Papyrologie und Epigraphik* 117 (1997): 227–268.

Weiss, Zeev, and Ehud Netzer. "Hellenistic and Roman Sepphoris: The Archaeological Evidence." In *Sepphoris in Galilee: Crosscurrents of Culture*, ed. Rebecca Martin Nagy, Carol L. Meyers, Eric M. Meyers, and Zeev Weiss, 29–37. Raleigh: North Carolina Museum of Art, 1996.

Weissbach, Franz-Heinrich. "Samosata." In *Realencyclopädie der classischen Altertumswissenschaft,* ed. August Friedrich von Pauly et al. Stuttgart: J. B. Metzler, 1894–.

Welles, Charles Bradford. "The Chronology of Dura-Europos." *Eos: Commentarii Societatis philologae polonorum* 48 (469): 467–474.

———. "The Epitaph of Julius Terentius." *Harvard Theological Review* 34 (1941): 79–102.

———. "The House of Nebuchelus." In *The Excavations at Dura-Europos: Preliminary Report,* ed. Paul V. C. Baur and Michael Ivanovitch Rostovtzeff, vol. 4, 79–145. New Haven: Yale University Press.

———. "The Inscriptions." In *Gerasa, City of the Decapolis,* ed. Carl Hermann Kraeling. New Haven, Conn.: American Schools of Oriental Research, 1938.

———. "La maison des archives à Doura-Europos." *Comptes rendus des séances de l'Académie des inscriptions et belles-lettres* (1931): 162–188.

———. "The Population of Roman Dura." In *Studies in Roman Economic and Social History in Honour of Allan Chester Johnson,* ed. Paul Robinson Coleman-Norton, 251–274. Princeton: Princeton University Press, 1951.

Welles, Charles Bradford, Robert O. Fink, and James Frank Gilliam. *The Excavations at Dura-Europos: Final Report.* Vol. 5, part 1, *The Parchments and Papyri,* ed. Ann Perkins. New Haven: Yale University Press, 1959.

Wenning, Robert. "Die Dekapolis und die Nabatäer." *Zeitschrift der deutschen Palästina-Vereins* 110 (1994): 1–35.

———. *Die Nabatäer-Denkmäler und Geschichte.* Freiburg: Universitätsverlag; Göttingen: Vandenhoeck & Ruprecht, 1987.

———. "Die Stadtgöttin von Caesarea Maritima." *Boreas* 9 (1986): 113–129.

Wheeler, Everett. "The Laxity of Syrian Legions." In *The Roman Army in the East,* ed. David L. Kennedy and David Braund, 229–276. Ann Arbor, Mich.: Journal of Roman Archaeology, 1996.

Whitby, Michael, and Mary Whitby, eds. *Chronicon Paschale.* Liverpool: Liverpool University Press, 1989.

Wiegand, Theodor. *Baalbek: Ergebnisse der Ausgrabungen und Untersuchungen in den Jahren 1898 bis 1905.* Berlin and Leipzig: W. de Gruyter, 1921–1925.

Wiegartz, Hans. "Zu Problemen einer Chronologie der attischen Sarkophage." *Archäologischer Anzeiger* (1977): 383–388.

Wightman, G. J. *The Walls of Jerusalem: From the Canaanites to the Mamluks.* Sydney: Mediterranean Archaeology, 1993.

Wilcken, Ulrich. "Papyruskunde über einen Sclavenkauf aus dem Jahre 359 n. Chr." *Hermes* 19 (1884): 417–431.

Wilcken, Ulrich, et al., eds. *Ägyptische Urkunden aus den Königlichen Museen zu Berlin: Griechische Urkunden.* Berlin: Staatliche Museen, 1903.

Will, Édouard. *Histoire politique du monde hellénistique.* 2nd ed. 2 vols. Nancy: Presses Universitaires de Nancy, 1979–1982.

———. "Pour une anthropologie coloniale du monde hellénistique." In *The Craft of the Ancient Historian: Essays in Honor of Chester G. Starr,* ed. John W. Eadie and Josiah Ober, 273–301. Lanham, Md.: University Press of America, 1985.

———. "Rome et les Séleucides." *Aufstieg und Niedergang der römischen Welt* 1.1 (1972): 590–632.

Will, Édouard, and Claude Orrieux. *Joudaïsmos-Hellenismos: Essai sur le judaïsme judéen à l'époque hellénistique.* Nancy: Presses Universitaires de Nancy, 1986.

Will, Ernest. "Antioche, la métropole de l'Asie." In *Mégapoles méditerranéennes,* ed. Claude Nicolet, Robert Ilbert, and Jean-Charles Depaule, 99–113. Paris and Rome: École française de Rome, 2000.

———. "Antioche sur l'Oronte, métropole de l'Asie." *Syria* 74 (1997): 99–113.

———. "À propos de quelques monuments sacrés de la Syrie et de l'Arabie romaines." In *Petra and the Caravan Cities,* ed. Fawzi Zayadine, 197–205. Amman: Department of Antiquities, 1990.

———. "La coupe de Césarée de Palestine au Musée du Louvre." *Monuments Piot* 65 (1983): 1–24.

———. "La date du Mithréum de Sidon." *Syria* 27 (1950): 261–269.

———. "De la Syrie au Yémen: Problèmes des relations dans le domaine de l'art." In *L'Arabie préislamique et son environnement historique et culturel: Actes du colloque de Strasbourg, 24–27 juin 1987,* ed. Toufic Fahd, 271–279. Leiden: E. J. Brill, 1989.

———. "Marchands et chefs de caravanes à Palmyre." *Syria* 34 (1957): 262–277.

———. "Nouveaux monuments sacrés de la Syrie romaine." *Syria* 29 (1952): 60–73.

———. "Palmyre et les routes de la soie." In "Palmyra and the Silk Road: International Colloquium, Palmyra, 7–11 April 1992." Special issue, *Annales archéologiques arabes syriennes* 42 (1996): 125–130.

———. *Les Palmyréniens: La Venise des sables = Ier siècle avant–IIIème siècle après J.-C.* Paris: A. Colin, 1992.

———. "Pline l'Ancien et Palmyre: Un problème d'histoire ou d'histoire littéraire?" *Syria* 62 (1985): 263–270.

———. "La population de Doura-Europos: Une évaluation." *Syria* 65 (1988): 315–321.

———. "Le rituel des Adonies." *Syria* 52 (1975): 93–105.

———. "Le sac de Palmyre." In *Mélanges d'archéologie et d'histoire offerts à André Piganiol,* ed. Raymond Chevallier, 1409–1416. Paris: SEVPEN, 1966.

———. "Les salles de banquet de Palmyre et d'autres lieux." *Topoi* 7 (1997): 873–887.

———. "Un vieux problème de la topographie de la Beqa' antique: Chalcis du Liban." *Zeitschrift der deutschen Palästina-Vereins* 99 (1983): 141–146.

———. "Les villes de la Syrie à l'époque hellénistique et romaine." In *Archéologie et histoire de la Syrie,* ed. Jean-Marie Dentzer and Winfried Orthmann, vol. 2, 223–250. Saarbrücken: Saarbrücker Druckerei und Verlag, 1989.

Wilmanns, Gustav. *Corpus inscriptionum latinarum.* Vol. 8, *Inscriptiones Africae latinae.* 7 vols. Berlin: G. Reimer, 1881–1959.

Wilson, J. F., and Vassilios Tzaferis. "Banias Dig Reveals King's Palace (But Which King?)." *Biblical Archaeology Review* 24, no. 1 (1998): 54–61, 85.

Winandy, Jacques. "Le recensement dit de Quirinius (Lc 2,2): Une interpolation?" *Revue biblique* (1997): 373–377.

Winter, Engelbert. "Mithraism and Christianity in Late Antiquity." In *Ethnicity and*

Culture in Late Antiquity, ed. Stephen Mitchell and Geoffrey Greatrex, 173–182. London: Duckworth; Swansea: Classical Press of Wales, 2000.

———. *Die Sasanidish-römischen Friedensverträge des 3. Jahrhunderts n. Chr.: Ein Beitrag zum verstandnis der aussenpolitischen Beziehungen zwischen den beiden Grossmachten.* Frankfurt am Main: Peter Lang, 1988.

Winter, John Garrett, ed. *Papyri in the University of Michigan Collection.* Ann Arbor: University of Michigan Press, 1936.

Wise, Michael, Martin Abbeg Jr., and Edward Cook. *Les manuscrits de la Mer morte.* Paris: Plon, 2001.

Wolski, Józef. "Les Parthes et la Syrie." *Acta Iranica* 5 (1977): 395–417.

Woude, Adam Simon Van der. "Le maître de Justice et les deux Messies dans la communauté de Qûmran." *Recherches bibliques* 4 (1959): 121–134.

Wroth, Warwick William. *A Catalogue of the Greek Coins in the British Museum: Galatia, Cappadocia and Syria.* London: British Museum, 1899.

Wruck, Waldemar. *Die syrische Provinzialprägung von Augustus bis Klaudius.* Stuttgart and Druck: W. Kohlhammer, 1931.

XII Panegyrici Latini, ed. Dominicus Lassandro. Turin: Paravia, 1992.

Yadin, Yigael. "The Expedition to the Judean Desert, 1960–1961: Expedition D—The Cave of Letters." *Israel Exploration Journal* 12 (1962): 227–257.

———. *Masada: Herod's Fortress and the Zealots' Last Stand.* London: Weidenfeld & Nicholson, 1966.

———. *Masada: The Yigael Yadin Excavations 1963–1965: Final Reports.* Jerusalem: Israel Exploration Society, Hebrew University of Jerusalem, 1989.

———. "The Nabataean Kingdom, Provincia Arabia, Petra, and En Geddi in the Documents from Nahal Hever." *Ex Oriente Lux* 17 (1963): 227–241.

Yeivin, Zeev, and Gershon Edelstein. "Excavation at Tirat Yehuda." *Atiqot* 6 (1970): 56–69.

Yon, Jean-Baptiste. *Les notables de Palmyre.* Beirut: Institut français d'archéologie du Proche-Orient, 2002.

Young, Gary K. "The Customs-Officer at the Nabataean Port of Leuke Kome (*Periplus Maris Erythraei* 19)." *Zeitschrift für Papyrologie und Epigraphik* 119 (1997): 266–268.

Zayadine, Fawzi. "Die Ausgrabungen des Qasr el Bint." In *Petra: Neue Ausgrabungen und Entdeckungen,* ed. Manfred Lindner, 237–248. Munich: Delp, 1986.

———. "Ayla-'Aqaba in the Light of Recent Excavations." *Annual of the Department of Antiquities of Jordan* 38 (1994): 485–505.

———. "Decorative Stucco at Petra and Other Hellenistic Sites." *Studies in the History and Archaeology of Jordan* 3 (1987): 131–142.

———. "L'espace urbain du grand Pétra: Les routes et les stations caravanières." *Annual of the Department of Antiquities of Jordan* 36 (1992): 217–239.

———. "Die Felsarchitektur Petra." In *Petra und das Königsreich der Nabatäer,* ed. Manfred Lindner, 39–69. Munich: Delp, 1989.

———. "The God(ess) Aktab-Kutbay and his (her) iconography." In *Petra and the Caravan Cities,* ed. Fawzi Zayadine, 37–51. Amman: Department of Antiquities, 1990.

———. "L'iconographie d'al-Uzza-Aphrodite." In *Mythologies gréco-romaines, my-*

thologies périphériques, ed. Lily Kahil and Christian Augé, 113–118. Paris: Centre national de la recherche scientifique, 1981.

———. "L'iconographie d'Isis à Pétra." *Mélanges de l'École française de Rome: Antiquités* 103 (1991): 283–306.

———. "Un ouvrage sur les Nabatéens." *Revue archéologique* 70 (1975): 333–338.

———. "Palmyre, Pétra, la mer Érythrée et les routes de la soie." In "Palmyra and the Silk Road: International Colloquium, Palmyra, 7–11 April 1992." Special issue, *Annales archéologiques arabes syriennes* 42 (1996): 167–173.

———. "The Pottery Kilns at Petra." In *Pottery and Potters: Past and Present,* ed. Denyse Homès-Frédéricq and H. J. Franken, 185–189. Tübingen: Attempto, 1986.

———. "Les sanctuaires nabatéens." In *La Jordanie de l'âge de la pierre à l'époque byzantine: Rencontres de l'École du Louvre,* ed. Geneviève Dolfus, 93–108. Paris: La Documentation française, 1987.

———. "Une tombe peinte de Beit Ras (Capitolias)." In *Studia Hierosolymitana in onore del P. Bellarmino Bagatti,* ed. Emmanuele Testa, Ignazio Mancini and Michele Picirillo, 285–294. Jerusalem: Franciscan Printing Press, 1976.

———. "Ein Turmgrab in Bab es-Siq." In *Petra: Neue Ausgrabungen und Entdeckungen,* ed. Manfred Lindner, 217–221. Munich: Delp, 1986.

———, ed. *Petra and the Caravan Cities.* Amman: Department of Antiquities, 1990.

Zayadine, Fawzi, and Saba Farès-Drappeau. "Two North-Arabian Inscriptions from the Temple of Lat at Wadi Iram." *Annual of the Department of Antiquities of Jordan* 42 (1998): 255–258.

Zeitler, John P. "A Private Building from the First Century B.C. in Petra." *Aram* 2 (1990): 385–420.

Zeitlin, Solomon. *The Rise and Fall of the Judaean State.* 3 vols. Philadelphia: Jewish Publication Society of America, 1962–1978.

Zelle, Karl Michael. "Terra Sigillata-Import nach Assos." In *Hellenistische und kaiserzeitliche Keramik des östilichen Mittelmeergebietes,* ed. Marlene Herfort-Koch, Ursula Mandel, and Ulrich Schädler, 19–21. Frankfurt am Main: Arbeitskreis Frankfurt und die Antike, Archäologisches Institut der Johann Wolfgang Goethe-Universität, 1996.

Ziegler, Ruprecht. "Laodicea, Antiochia und Sidon in der Politik der Severer." *Chiron* 8 (1978): 493–514.

Zonaras, Joannes. *Epitome historiarum,* ed. Ludwig Dindorf. Leipzig: B. G. Teubner, 1868–1875.

Zosimus. *New History: A Translation with Commentary,* ed. and trans. Ronald T. Ridley. Canberra: Australian Association for Byzantine Studies, 1982.

Zwettler, Michael J. "The 'Era of NBT' and 'YMNT': Two Proposals (1)." *Arabian Archaeology and Epigraphy* 7 (1996): 95–107.

———. "Imra'alqays, son of 'Amr: King of . . .???" In *Literary Heritage of Classical Islam: Arabic and Islamic Studies in Honor of James A. Bellamy,* ed. Mustansir Mir and Jarl E. Fossum, 3–37. Princeton, N.J.: Darwin Press, 1993.

INDEX

Bathyra, 79
Batnai, 147
Bedouins, 64, 147, 307–308
Beersheba, 12, 16, 18, 22
Beida, 21
Belayche, Nicole, 114
Beqaa, region of, 33, 43
Berenice, 22
Berenice, sister of Agrippa II, 101, 118, 121
Bernard, Paul, 146
Beroea (Aleppo), 32, 33, 63, 152, 338, 348
Beryllos of Bostra, Bishop, 288
Berytos, 33, 102; amphora production in, 248; architecture of, 165–166, 171; Christianity in, 338; and customs tax, 257; and governor's visits, 60; Jews in, 324; and land tenure, 216; law school in, 289–290; metal-work in, 244; plan of, 165–166, 170; and roads, 64; textiles in, 243; and trade, 265, 266; and Tyre, 199; water for, 218
Betharamphtha (Betharamatha), 98
Bethel, 16
Bethsaida, 97
Bethshan, 16
Bethzur, 16
Bibulus, 49, 50
Birtha, 147
Bithynia, 35, 42
Bithynia-Pontus, 36, 58, 59
Boethos, 92
Boethos of Sidon, 285
Bostra, 87; architecture of, 163, 171, 172, 175, 290; Christianity in, 338; and coinage, 251, 255; dwellings in, 182; fortifications of, 360; and imperial cult, 60; institutions of, 154; Jews in, 323, 324; metalwork in, 244; and military fortifications, 272; and Persian invasion, 350; plan of, 170, 197–198; popu-lation of, 182, 198; profile of, 197–199; reli-gion in, 317; and roads, 140, 141; size of, 167; status of, 184; villages around, 215; water for, 218; and Zenobia, 356
Bowersock, Glen, 67, 83, 252, 309
Braemer, Frank, 218
Brutus, 51, 52
Burj Baqirha, 317
Butler, Howard C., 304
Byblos, 8, 29, 33, 243, 255, 260, 300, 312, 324

Cadastres, 212, 214
Caecilius Bassus, Quintus, 51
Caesar, Gaius, 68, 83
Caesar, Gaius Julius, 44, 48, 50–51
Caesarea: architecture in, 175; Christianity in,
336, 337, 338; and coinage, 251; and Herod the Great, 92, 93; and Jewish War, 121–122; and Jews, 116, 325; municipal cult in, 60; profile of, 201–202; and roads, 65; and ru-ral dwellings, 225
Caesarea-Arca, 210
Caesarea of Lebanon, 77
Caesarea on the Sea (Strato's Tower): and ar-chitecture, 171, 204; and coinage, 250; as colony, 156; construction of, 91, 153–154; and customs tax, 257; plan of, 166; port at, 259–260; textiles in, 243. See also Strato's Tower
Caesarea-Philippi, 97, 101, 154
Caesennius Paetus, Lucius, 69, 77
Caligula, 23, 73, 75, 98–99, 103, 115, 163–164, 254
Callinicos of Petra, 286; History of Alexan-dria, 357
Calpurnius Bibulus, M., 44, 45
Calpurnius Piso, Gn., 57, 68
Calpurnius Piso Pontifex, L., 56, 96
Campania, 15
Cana, battle of, 13, 18
Canatha, 46, 81, 152, 154, 161, 167, 182, 187, 209, 218, 256
Cape Sarpedon, 34
Capharnaum, 247
Capito, 45
Cappadocia, 23, 28, 61, 63, 348
Caracalla, 149, 251, 254, 321, 344, 350, 351
Carmel, Mount, 13, 244, 250
Carrhai, 49, 147, 263, 346, 347
Cassius, 49
Cassius, Gaius, 51
Cassius Dio, 130, 149, 253, 344
Cassius Longinus, G., 44
Census, 58, 94–96, 104
Ceramics, 22, 240, 244–248, 261–262, 265, 266, 270, 272
Cestius Gallus, 61, 101, 120, 122, 124
Chabinas River, 64
Chalcis, 63, 76, 78, 79
Chalcis of Belos, 65, 152
Chalcis of Lebanon, 28, 33, 71
Chapot, Victor, 143
Charachmoba, 154
China, 10, 243, 269, 270
Chosroes, 146
Christianity: and Agrippa I, 100; in Antioch, 190; beginnings of, 335–342; in Bostra, 199; in Caesarea, 201–202; in Dura, 195, 336, 340–341, 350; emergence of, 88; growth of, 298–299; and Jerusalem, 155;

language of, 293; literature of, 288–289; and paganism, 298

Christol, Michel, 348

Cicero, 45, 47, 50, 56

Cilicia, 28, 34, 38, 42, 53, 55, 58, 59, 87, 245

Cilicia Campestris, 36, 55–56

Cilicia Pedias, 75

Cilicia Tracheia, 34, 70, 75

City/cities, 171; beautification of, 72; building in, 164–183; Christianity in, 342; as colonies, 185–186; development of, 151–156; dwellings in, 177–180, 198; finances of, 160–161; foundation stories of, 161–162; fountains of, 172–173; freedom for, 184; and Hellenistic culture, 8; under Herod Antipas, 97–98; imperial favors to, 160; institutions of, 154, 156–162, 193; markets of, 173–174; as metropolis, 185; planning of, 159; population of, 182–183; rivalry of, 159–160, 183; Roman administration of, 153; status of, 183–188; urban decor of, 168–169; and villages, 232–233; walls of, 168

City-state(s): consolidation of, 53; foundation of, 8; as governmental structure, 365; influence of, 71; leaders of, 43; names of, 46; Pompey's restoration of, 42–43, 46; and Roman administration, 42–43

Classis Syriaca, 61, 139. *See also* Military

Claudius: and Agrippa I, 78, 99–100, 102; and Agrippa II, 79; and client states, 73; and coinage, 253; and colonies, 155; and Commagene, 75; and military, 61; and Palmyra, 69

Claudius Athenodorus, 58

Claudius II, 356

Claudius Ptolemy, 287

Claudius Severus, C., 133, 134, 135, 140

Cleopatra Selene, 28

Cleopatra VII, 47, 52, 53, 54, 56, 81, 82, 287

Client states, 3, 31, 32, 70–87, 132; alliance of, 73; and Antony, 52, 54, 55; and Augustus, 54, 65, 72–73; cities founded in, 153; and citizenship, 162; and city-states, 42; coinage of, 249; consolidation of, 53; expectations of, 79; independence of, 73; indirect rule by, 71–72, 73; integration of, 73; and land tenure, 207; under Pompey, 43; and urban landscape, 164

Clodius, 45

Clodius Priscus, G., 58

Clothing/dress, 282

Coele Syria, 53, 58, 59, 338

Coinage: and Aelius Gallus, 67; of Arab emirs, 33; of Aretas IV, 83; of client states, 249; and Commagene kingdom, 23, 24; Greek example in, 7; Hasmonaean, 13, 20, 325; and Hatra, 345; imperial, 249–251, 264; language on, 254, 276–277, 293; municipal production of, 184, 187, 249; and Nabataea, 18, 20, 87; and Obodas II, 81; and Persian invasion, 349; Roman organization of, 44–45; royal and tetrarchic, 251–254; Seleucid, 45; and Tigranes, 29, 45; and trade, 263–264; of Tyre, 199–200. *See also* Monetary system

Colony/colonies: Caesarea as, 201; Caesarea on the Sea (Strato's Tower) as, 156; cities as, 185–186; Dura as, 195–197; establishment of, 155; Greek, 7, 10; and Hasmonaean state, 14; Judaean military, 79–80; and land tenure, 215–216; Macedonian, 10

Commagene, 6, 11; annexation of, 59, 75, 76; and Augustus, 74–75; campaign of Caesennius Paetus against, 77; as client state, 70, 73, 74–76; and coinage, 251; emergence as kingdom, 23–25; and eparchies, 58; and Euphrates River, 74, 76; and land tenure, 210; legions at, 61; and Parthian Empire, 24, 26, 52, 74, 75; and Pompey, 25, 40, 74, 81; prefect of, 57, 75; Rome's confiscation of, 73; royal tombs of, 75; strategic importance of, 74, 75; and Syria-Coele, 135

Commodus, 137, 141, 160, 250

Conventus system, 59, 60

Coponius, 94, 96

Cornelius, 201, 336

Cornelius, P., 66

Cornelius Dolabella, Gnaeus, 51

Cornelius Lentulus Marcellinus, Gnaeus, 44

Cornelius Palma Frontonianus, Aulus, 133

Cos, 15

Cotton, Hannah M., 56, 210

Cotyx IX, 76

Crassus, 48–49

Crete, 34

Crete-Cyrenaica, 59

Creticus Silanus, 68

Crouch, Dora P., 182

Ctesiphon, 147, 149

Cult: foreign, 303–306; imperial, 58, 59, 60, 108, 299; indigenous, 299–303; Jewish sacrificial, 327–328; municipal, 60, 299. *See also* Pagan/paganism; Religion; Sanctuaries/temples

Customs tax, 45, 256–258, 270. *See also* Taxation

Cyprus, 26

Cyrrhestica, 52

Cyrrhos, 62, 152, 348

Damascus: and agriculture, 223; and Aretas III, 46; and banditry, 79; Christianity in, 336, 337; development of, 152, 153; finances of, 161; foundation story of, 161; and governor's visits, 60; and Hasmonaean state, 14; and Hellenistic culture, 8; Jews in, 324, 325; land tenure in, 213; metalwork in, 244; and military dispositions, 62; and Nabataea, 11, 18, 19, 22, 83; plan of, 170; Pompey at, 40; Pompey's legates in, 37–38; ransom of, 33; and roads, 65, 141; and rural life, 206; and Syria, 55; and Tigranes, 28; and water, 218

Danaba, 79

Dardanos, peace of, 35

Darius III Codomanos, 5

David, King, 15, 89

Dead Sea, 14, 22

Decapolis: and Coele Syria, 58; and Hasmonaean state, 15; and Jewish War, 122; and Nabataean state, 22; prefect of, 56, 57; and Syria, 55; urban development in, 153

Decidius Saxa, 51

Decius, 339

Delos, 39

Demetrias-by-the-Sea, 153

Demetrios (ex-slave), 43

Demetrios I, 153

Demetrios II, 11, 12, 15, 27

Demetrios III, 33

Dentzer, Jean-Marie, 309

Der'a (Adraha), 154

Dexandros of Apamaea, 70, 74

Diaspora, 319, 332

Didascalia of the Apostles, 339, 341

Diocletian, 260, 344, 358, 361

Diodotos Tryphon, 34

Dion, 14, 15, 41, 42, 59, 81

Dionysios, 141

Dionysios, son of Heraklion, 32

Dobiáš, Josef, 39

Doliche, 56, 348

Domitian, 58, 64, 164

Domitius Corbulo, Gnaeus, 68–69

Dor, 15, 16

Dora, 32, 42, 55

Dorotheos of Sidon, *Pentateuch,* 287

Dothan, 16

Drijvers, Han J. W., 294, 325

Drusilla, 76, 101, 103

Ducenarii, 57

Dumata, 359

Dura (Dura-Europos): and architecture, 171; art in, 280, *280, 282,* 350; Christianity in, 195, 336, 340–341, 350; construction in, 271; and customs tax, 256, 257; development of, 156; dwellings in, 181, *181,* 182; freedom of, 184–185; frontier at, 147; and Hellenistic culture, 8; House of Christians in, 336, 350; Jews in, 195, 325–326, 332, 333–335, 366; and military, 137, 138; and Parthian Empire, 26, 31; and Persian invasion, 346, 347, 348, 349–350; plan of, 167, 168; population of, 182; profile of, 194–197; religion in, 317–318; synagogue paintings in, *326,* 333–335; and trade, 263, 264, 267

Dwellings, 156, 177–180, 181, 182, 198, 213, 223, 225–227, 280

Dye, 241–242, 261

Eastern Sigillata A, 22, 245, 246, 262, 272

Economy: after Alexander's conquest, 10; and agriculture, 222; and annexation of Syria, 39–40; and Caesarea, 201; of Dura, 196–197; and Palmyra, 351; of Tyre, 199–200; village, 229, 232. *See also* Finances; Trade/commerce

Edessa: annexation of, 149, 344–345; Arab control of, 6, 33; Christianity in, 337, 338, 340, 341; as client state, 148, 150; coinage in, 263; Jews in, 332; kingdom of, 146–147; and Osrhoene, 136; and trade, 270

Edom, 15, 140, 143

Edom plateau, 219

Education, 276, 289, 290. *See also* Intellectual life

Egypt, 47, 48, 50, 51, 86, 90, 271

Elagabalus, 251, 255

Eleazar bar Simon, 124

Eleazar bar Yair, 126

Eleazar ben Ananias, 118, 120, 122

Elusa, 16, 18, 21

Emesa, 344; and Antony, 52; and Augustus, 55; and Caesar, 50; as client state, 70; and coinage, 254; dynasty of, 33–34, 76; integration into Rome, 76–77; and land tenure, 210, 213; and Persian invasion, 349; and roads, 65; Sampsigeramos's power over, 43; and sea, 76

Eparchies, 58

Epicureanism, 285
Epiphanaea, 152, 153
Epiphanius of Salamis, 337
Eratosthenes, 24
Esbous, 14
Essenes, 110–111, 116, 321, 327, 328
Estates, imperial, 207–211
Euphrates River, 23, 65, 74, 76, 87, 143, 238–239, 257
Euphrates River valley, 218, 317–318
Eusebius of Caesarea, 129, 202, 289, 322, 337, 338, 340
Ezechias the Galilean, 113

Feissel, Denis, 197
Felix, 117, 120
Festivals, 190–191, 310
Festus, 115, 117
Fiema, Zbigniew T., 145
Finances, 45–46, 57, 73, 103–104, 134, 160–161. See also Economy; Taxation; Trade/commerce
Finkielsztejn, Gérald, 15
Flavians, 56, 59, 61, 69
Flavius Silva, 126
Flax, 242–243
Florentinus, 135
Florus, 120, 121
Fronton of Emesa, 285
Frost, Honor, 259

Gabala, 52, 260
Gabinius, Aulus, 44, 45–46, 47–48, 50
Gadara, 13, 15, 41, 42, 43, 55, 56, 59, 90, 94, 152, 171, 285
Gadhima, 360–361, 362
Galaad, 13, 17
Galilee, 78, 79; architecture in, 174–175; and ceramics, 247; and coinage, 252; glassmaking in, 244; and Hasmonaean state, 15, 41; Herod the Great in, 50; and Jewish War, 120; Jews in, 174–175, 321, 322, 324; pottery in, 261; rural dwellings of, 227; textiles in, 242, 243; trade in, 261, 262, 263; unrest in, 113
Gallienus, 354, 355
Gamala, 14, 101
Gamaliel II, 320
Gascou, Jean, 197
Gatier, Pierre-Louis, 231
Gaza, 6, 12, 152; and Alexander Jannaeus, 18; annexation of, 56, 94; and customs tax, 257; and Hasmonaean state, 13, 15, 16; and Hellenistic culture, 8; and Herod the Great,

90; independence of, 42; and Nabataean state, 17, 18, 19; in province of Syria, 42; rebuilding of, 46; and trade, 262, 267
Genethlios of Petra, 286
George of Cyprus, 209–210
Gerasa: architecture of, 163, 164, 171, 171, 175, 204; and ceramics, 245; Christianity in, 338; crime in, 32; and dye, 241; finances of, 161; founding of, 152; fullers in, 243; and Hasmonaean state, 15; and imperial cult, 59; independence of, 42; Jews in, 324; plan of, 159, 166, 167–168, 170, 203; profile of, 202–204; in province of Syria, 41; and roads, 65
Germanicus, 57, 68, 69
Gessius Florus, 115, 116, 118
Gezer, 16
Glaphyra, 96
Glass/glassmaking, 22, 244–245, 261, 262, 265, 271
Gods/pantheons, 299–310. See also Pagan/paganism; Religion
Golan, 13, 17, 18, 22, 56, 223, 231, 247, 323, 324
Goldstein, J. A., 15
Goodenough, Edwin, 334
Gordian III, 250, 345, 347
Gospel of Luke, 94, 95, 96, 97, 115
Gospel of Matthew, 95, 97
Gospel of Philip, 340
Gospel of Thomas, 340
Grainger, John D., 2
Grains, 207, 213, 220, 221, 264. See also Agriculture
Granucometai, tetrarchies of, 71
Grapes, 10, 207, 220, 222–223, 262. See also Agriculture; Wine
Greek language, 8, 86, 108, 158, 188, 195, 275, 276–277, 291, 295, 301, 306, 366, 367
Greeks, 6–7, 364; borrowing by, 366–367; and Jews, 121; and religion, 300, 301, 302, 303, 306; in Syria, 43. See also Hellenism
Gregory Thaumaturgus, 289
Grenet, Frantz, 349
Gros, Pierre, 175

Hadramaout, 66
Hadrian: and Arabia, 134, 135; and Bar Kokhba revolt, 128–129; and Coele Syria, 59; and coinage, 250, 255; construction by, 129, 133; and eparchies, 58; and Jerusalem, 129, 365; and Judaea, 128; and military, 61; and Palmyra, 350; and roads, 65, 140; and Sepphoris, 322; visits to Syria by, 132–133

Intellectual life, 190, 194, 199, 200, 201, 284–291, 297, 342
Ipsos, battle of, 6
Iran, 26
Isaac, Benjamin H., 62, 128, 145
Isaeus the Syrian, 286
Ituraea, 14, 15, 28, 78, 233
Ituraean Arabs, 33
Ituraean dynasty, 43
Iulias, 154
Iulias (Betharamphtha), 98
Iulias (Bethsaida), 97
Iulius Africanus: *Cesti,* 287; *Chronology,* 287
Iulius Agrippa, L., 71
Iulius Alexander, Tiberius, 134
Iulius Aurelius Zenobios, 352
Iulius Caesar, Sextus, 51
Iulius Paelignus, 68
Iulius Philippus, M. *See* Philip the Arab
Iulius Priscus, C., 347

James, brother of Jesus, 337–338
Jason (High Priest), 9, 18
Jawf, 358
Jebel Druze, 234
Jebel Harun, 21
Jebel Sheikh Barakat, 316, 317
Jebel Srir, 316, 317
Jerusalem, *119*; and architecture, 171; art in, 280; and Bar Kokhba revolt, 130; besieged by Antiochos VII, 12; and Caesar, 50; and Christianity, 298, 336–337, 339–340; and coinage, 252, 253, 254; development of, 166–167; and diaspora Jews, 332; garrison in, 61, 127; and Hadrian, 129; and Hasmonaeans, 12, 40, 41; and Hellenistic culture, 8, 9; and Jewish War, 118, 120, 121, 123–125; Jews in, 325, 339–340; metalwork in, 244; municipal cult in, 60; as pagan, 321; plan of, 170; Pompey in, 41; rabbis in, 321; and rural dwellings, 225; stone vessels of, 248; textiles in, 243. *See also* Aelia Capitolina
Jesus, 94, 97, 109, 112, 114–115, 298, 336, 340
Jesus, son of Sappha, 122
Jewish War, 66-70, 117–126; and Agrippa II, 101; and Caesarea, 201; causes of, 120–121; and Christianity, 336, 337; and imperial estates, 208; and land tenure, 211, 217; and military dispositions, 61, 62; and Ouaros, 77
Jews: in Antioch, 190; and art, 278–279; and assimilation, 107–108; in Bostra, 199; and Caesarea, 201; and Christianity, 337; and cities, 155; of Diaspora, 319–335; disdain for Rome by, 43; documentation about, 88;

in Dura, 195, 366; in Gerasa, 203; and Greeks, 121; and Hellenistic culture, 9, 10; and Herod the Great, 90; and metalwork, 244; and pagans, 323, 325, 332; and Pompey, 40–42, 46; rural dwellings of, 225–226; villages of, 232. *See also* Judaism
John Chrysostom, 291
John Hyrcanos, 12, 13, 15
John of Gischala, 123, 124, 125
John the Baptist, 97, 114, 116
John the Essene, 122
Jonathan, 12, 13, 18
Jones, T. B., 254
Joppa, 12, 13, 15, 18, 32, 42, 90, 161, 257
Jordan River, 14
Joseph ben Gurion, 122
Josephus, Flavius, 287; and agriculture, 220–221; on Agrippa I, 98; on Aineas, 82; on Archelaos (son of Herod), 95, 96; on banditry, 79; on Commagene, 75; and Hasmonaean state, 14; on Herodians, 94; on Herod the Great, 102; and Jewish War, 117, 122, 123; on Judaea, 56; on Judaean unrest, 113, 115–116, 117; on Judaism, 109, 110, 111; and military, 61; and Nabataeans, 18; on Philip, 97; on Volumnius, 57, 73; work of, 288
Jotapianus, 347–348
Juba of Mauretania, 96
Judaea: administration of, 80, 103–106; agriculture in, 80, 106, 107, 127, 321; and Agrippa I, 100; annexation of, 56, 80, 95, 96, 100; and Antony, 52; and Archelaos (son of Herod), 94; attacked by Aretas III, 13; autonomy from Seleucids, 11; and Caesar, 50; and Cleopatra VII, 53; client state of, 70; eparchia of, 94; fall of, 7; fiscal policy in, 103–104; and Gabinius, 47, 48; garrison in, 128; Hasmonaean, 12, 14, 41; and Hellenism, 107–109; under Herodians, 89–103; imperial procurators in, 57–58; independence of, 89; Jews in, 321, 322; land tenure in, 106–107, 127; legion in, 61; military in, 138–139; nationalism of, 100; organization of, 89; prefect of, 56, 57; as province, 60, 100, 127, 132; rebellion in, 105, 110–111, 113–117; religious groups in, 109–113; and roads, 64, 65, 128, 141; Roman aid to, 73; Roman organization of, 44; rural dwellings of, 225–226, 227; social crisis in, 106–107; status of, 298; as Syria-Palestine, 131; taxation in, 103–104, 107, 114, 118, 127; territory of, 77–80, 89, 90; textiles in, 242; transformation of, 89; unrest in, 88, 128; villages in, 229. *See also* Palestine

Judaea-Syria Palestine, 59

Juda I, Rabbi, 186, 209, 320, 321, 322, 329, 330

Judaism, 97; and Aelia Capitolina, 131; and Agrippa I, 100; and Agrippa II, 101; and Bar Kokhba revolt, 128–129; circumcision in, 128, 129, 320; Day of Yahweh in, 112; groups in, 109–113; and Haggada, 329, 331; and Halakha, 329, 331, 333; and Hellenism, 365–366; and Herod, 90, 91–92, 103; and Herod Antipas, 98; and Herodians, 101–103; High Priest in, 10, 14, 91, 92, 105–106, 319; and Jewish unrest, 116–117; and Jewish War, 121, 128; marriage in, 96; Midrash in, 331; and Mishna, 320, 322, 329–330, 331, 333; nasi in, 319, 320, 321; and paganism, 298; and Pharisees, 90–91, 98, 105, 106, 109–110, 111, 117–118, 319–320, 328; privilege of, 104–105; and Promised Land, 15; rabbis in, 91–92, 130, 155–156, 321, 326–335; resurrection of dead in, 10; sacrifice in, 327–328; and synagogue, 88, 319, 322, *326*, 328, 333–335, 366; Talmuds in, 202, 215, 217, 258–260, 261, 320, 329, 330–331, 333; transformation of, 88. *See also* Jews

Judaization, 15–16

Judas Maccabaeus, 6, 13, 17

Judas of Archelaus, 73

Judas the Galilean, 98, 113–114

Julio-Claudians, 58, 67

Jupiter Capitolinus, 127, 129

Justin Martyr, 288

Justus of Tiberias, 287

Kalos, Mikaël, 304

Kapharsaba, 13

Karib'il, 67

Kelso, J. L., 109

Kennedy, David L., 137, 142

Khazneh Fira'un, *84, 85*

Kilikarch, 59

Kraeling, Carl Hermann, 334

Kypros (fortress), 93

Labienus, Quintus, 52

Labor, 213, 215, 216–217. *See also* Agriculture; Artisans

Lachish, 16

Lake Genesareth, 154

Lakhmid 'Amr ibn 'Adi, 361–362

Land tenure, 10, 106–107, 127, 207–217, 226–227, 321. *See* Agriculture

Language: and abstraction, 328; and civic institutions, 158; and coinage, 254, 276–277, 293; and culture, 8, 9, 188, 366, 367; and Dura, 195; and identity, 275–277; and indigenous cultures, 291–295; and law, 289, 290; and Nabataea, 86; and religion, 195, 301, 306; success of, 367. *See also specific languages*

Laodicea: and architecture, 171; as capital, 135; and ceramics, 245; and coinage, 250, 251; and dye, 241; and Hellenistic culture, 8; land tenure in, 213; legion at, 60; and military dispositions, 62; port at, 260; size of, 167; textiles in, 243; and Tigranes, 28, 29

Laodicea on the Sea, 152, 223

Laodice Thea Philadelphia, 24

Latin language, 188, 195, 275–276

Lauffray, Jean, 170, 259

Law, 200, 276, 289–290; Jewish, 104, 105, 106, 109–110, 121, 319, 320, 329, 331, 333

Leatherwork, 243–244

Lebanon, 6, 28, 70, 78, 210, 312, 313, 315–316

Lebanon, Mount, 43

Legio I Parthica, 136, 137

Legio II Parthica, 348

Legio II Traiana, 137

Legio II Traiana Fortis, 128

Legio III Cyrenaica, 87, 137

Legio III Gallica, 60, 68, 137, 147

Legio III Parthica, 136, 137

Legio IV Ferrata, 87

Legio IV Martia, 361

Legio IV Scythica, 60–61, 69, 137

Legio V Macedonica, 131

Legio VI Ferrata, 60, 68, 128, 137

Legio X Fretensis, 60, 61, 65, 68, 127, 131, 137, 361

Legio XII Fulminata, 60, 61, 69, 122

Legio XVI Flavia Firma, 61, 137

Legio XXII Deioteriana, 130

Leja, 141

Lemaître, Séverine, 264, 265

Leriche, Pierre, 318

Lex Gabinia, 35, 37

Lex Manilia, 37

Licinius Crassus, Marcus, 44

Limestone Massif, 206, 213–214, 218, 219, 223, 227, 229, 262, 367

Literature, 284–291. *See also* Intellectual life

Livias, 98

Livias-Iulias, 79, 154

Loffreda, Stanislao, 247

Lollius, Lucius, 37, 40

Longinus of Emesa, 285, 286, 357, 358

315, 316; and roads, 65, 141, 142, 159, 165; sculpture of, *283, 284, 301, 306, 307*; status of, 184; and Tanukh, 360; and trade, 70, 76, 86–87, 147, 269, 270, 271, 272, 350–351; and water, 219

Panias, 78, 92, 97, 152, 316

Papinian of Emesa, 289

Parker, S. Thomas, 144, 270

Parthian Empire, 15, 25–26, 61, 343; and Antiochos IV, 75; aspirations of, 31; and Augustus, 55, 75; and Commagene, 24, 26, 52, 74, 75; Crassus's attack on, 48–49; and Dura, 31; Euphrates River as border with, 65; expeditions against, 63, 145–147, 148, 149–150; and Gabinius, 47–48; and Gaius Caesar, 68; and Herod the Great, 52, 89, 90; invasion by, 44, 52, 53, 74; Jews in, 332, 333; and military dispositions, 62, 63; and Nabataea, 81; and Palmyra, 70; and Pompey, 39, 43; and Seleucids, 11, 26, 27; threat from, 46; and Trigranes, 28

Paul of Samosata, 289, 290, 338, 339

Pausanius, 129

Peasants, 32, 213, 216, 240

Pella, 14, 15, 41, 42, 46, 59, 65, 152, 161, 298, 337

Pensabene, Patrizio, 175, 176

Peraea, 16, 77, 79

Pergamon, kingdom of, 34

Periplus Maris Erythraei, 67

Perseus, 26

Persian empire, 343, 345, 346, 347, 348, 353–354, 355, 362

Pescennius Niger, 148, 149, 199, 250, 351, 352

Petra: and agriculture, 218; architecture of, 86, 175; art in, 280, *289, 309*; and ceramics, 245; characteristics of, 20–21; and Cleopatra, 54; and coinage, 251, 252; dwellings of, 179–180, 280; and imperial cult, 60; institutions of, 154; Khazneh Fira'un, *84, 85*; as metrocolonia, 187; as metropolis, 60; Obodas I in, 18; and Pompey, 41; religion in, 316; and roads, 140; Scaurus's expedition against, 46–47; status of, 184; and trade, 86–87, 267–268; villages around, 229; water for, 218. *See also* Nabataea

Phanni ben Samuel, 124

Pharisees, 90–91, 98, 105, 106, 109–110, 111, 117–118, 319–320, 328

Pharnaces, 50

Pharsallus, 50

Phasael, 50

Phenikarch, 59

Philadelphia, 17, 32, 59, 152, 153

Philip (Herod's son), 56, 78, 94, 97, 98, 99, 154, 253

Philip I, 44

Philip II, 32, 33, 38

Philippi, battle of, 51

Philippopolis, 167, 218, 277

Philip the Arab, 60, 132, 185, 232, 335, 347, *348, 356*

Philodemos, 15

Philo of Alexandria, 327

Philo of Byblos, *Phoinikika,* 288

Philosophy, 285–286, 297. *See also* Intellectual life

Philostratus of Athens, 286

Philoteria, 153

Phoenicia, 52; under Alexander the Great, 5; city-states in, 42; and Cleopatra VII, 53; and dye, 241–242; eparchy of, 58; glassmaking in, 244; and Hasmonaeans, 16; and imperial cult, 59; and military dispositions, 63; ports of, 10; religion in, 299, 305–306; and Syria, 55; and textiles, 242; and trade, 6–7, 10; urban development in, 152; villages of, 232

Phoenician language, 9, 292, 293, 367

Phraates III, 48

Phraates IV, 68

Phraates V, 68

Piracy, 29, 32–33, 34–35, 37, 39

Piraeus, 7

Plato, 286

Platonism, 285

Pliny the Elder, 16, 71, 239

Pliny the Younger, 61, 257

Plotinus, 285, 286

Plutarch, 38, 45, 48

Poidebard, Antoine, 64, 143, 259

Polemon of Cilicia, 101

Pompeius Trogus, 38–39

Pompey, 87; and annexation of Syria, 3, 38–40; and Antioch, 38, 49; and Antiochos I, 74; and Artetas III, 19; and banditry, 37, 39, 40; and Caesar, 50; and client states, 43, 70; and Commagene, 25, 40, 74, 81; and Crassus, 48; at Damascus, 40; defeat at Pharsallus, 50; and Demetrios, 43; era of, 43; and Hasmonaean territories, 14, 41, 42; in Jerusalem, 41; and Jews, 40–42, 46; legates of, 37–38, 41, 44–50; and Meleagros of Gadara, 16; and Mithradates VI Eupator, 37; and Nabataea, 22, 46, 65; pacification by, 47; and Parthian Empire, 39, 43; and Petra, 41; and piracy, 35; and Scaurus, 46; and Seleucids, 31, 38; and Syria, 37–44; and urban development, 153

Ummidius Quadratus, 68
Uranius, *Arabica,* 19
Uranius Antoninus, 344, 349, 356

Vaballathos, 344, 356, 357
Valerian, 350, 353, 354
Valerius Gratus, 105
Valerius Lollianus, M., 61
Ventidius, 74, 81
Ventidius Bassus, Publius, 52
Verus, Lucius, 97, 137, 140, 141, 146, 147, 156
Vespasian, 69, 125; and Agrippa II, 101; and
   Chabinas River bridge, 64; cities founded
   by, 154; and client states, 73; and coinage,
   250; and eparchies, 58; and Jewish War,
   122, 123–124; and land tenure, 208, 211;
   leniency of, 127; and Seleucian port, 260
Veterans. *See* Military
Vettius Valens, *Anthologies,* 287
Village(s), 213, 215, 219–220, 224–233
Vitellius, 68, 97, 98, 124, 125
Volumnius, 57, 73
Volusius Saturninus, Lucius, 57
Vonones, 68

Wadi al-Hasa, 140
Wadi 'Arabah, 22
Wadi Mujib, 140

Wadi Ramm, 316, 359
Wadi Sabra, 21
Wadi Sleysel, 21
Wadi Wala, 140
Wajh, al-, 66
Water, 172, 217–220. *See also* Agriculture
Will, Ernest, 182, 269
Wine, 22, 106, 200, 207, 222, 223, 248, 264,
   265. *See also* Grapes

Yohanan ben Zakkai, Rabbi, 201, 319, 328
Yon, Jean-Baptiste, 159
Yose ben Hanina, Rabbi, 202
Young, Gary K., 257

Zamaris, son of, 79
Zealots, 111, 114, 118, 124–125, 127, 128, 131
Zeno archive, 10
Zenobia, 339, 344, 355, 356–357, 358
Zeno Cotylas, 32
Zenodoros, 78, 83, 90, 253
Zenodotia, 49
Zeugma, 56, 61, 62, 245, 257, 266, 267, 348.
   See also Seleucia on Euphrates (Zeugma)
Zoilos, 32
Zonaras, 354
Zosimus, 354, 356, 357